Sixth Edition Textbook Questionnaire
Temple University, Economics 1101/1102

1) Why did you take Economics 1101/1102? (Check all that apply)

   ☐ I have a personal interest in the subject.
   ☐ I am considering a major in economics.
   ☐ The course is required for my major. My major is _____.
   ☐ I am using this to fulfill a social science requirement needed to graduate.

2) Did you purchase a book for this course?   Yes   No

   ☐ I bought a new book.
   ☐ I bought a used book.
   ☐ I bought access to the e-book online.
   ☐ N/A. I did not buy a book for this course.

3) Where did you buy your textbook? Give the name of the store, e-commerce site, etc.

4) If your text was available in a format that was full-color, 3-hole punch, and loose leaf – and was priced lower than the regular bound book – would you be likely to buy that instead? [Note that if you choose the loose-leaf version, you'd be saving up front but you may not be able to sell it back after the course.]

   ☐ I would be more likely to buy the lower-priced, loose-leaf, 3-hole punched version.
   ☐ I would be more likely to buy the bound book.

5) The following questions ask you about how you use the textbook for this course.

   a) Did you read the book before or after your professor covered the topic in class? (Circle one)
      Before   After

   b) How often did you refer the textbook during the course? (Check only one

      ☐ I referred to the book 3-5 times per week throughout the semes
      ☐ I referred to the book only once each week.
      ☐ I waited to open the book until I was studying for the first big e
      ☐ N/A – I never referred to the book during the semester.

   c) When you opened the book, how did you use the chapter material? (Check only one.)

      ☐ I read the chapter, from start to finish.
      ☐ I did not read the full chapter. I only read sections of the chapter that I did not fully understand from the lecture.
      ☐ N/A. I did not refer to the book during the semester.

d) Consider how you answered parts (5a) through (5c). Was this textbook effectively designed for the way that you use the book during this course? Why or why not?

6) Complete the following table by indicating how helpful you found each of these chapter resources. (<u>Check one box in each row</u>.)

	Extremely helpful when trying to master the material.	Somewhat helpful when trying to master the material.	I read this feature, but it didn't really help me master the material.	N/A I did not read or refer to this feature.
Figures and tables, along with their captions				
News and policy boxed examples				
End of chapter summary and key terms				
Reading Between the Lines				
Interviews with famous economists				
Study Guide				
Other: _____				

7) How would you describe the writing style for this text?

8) How useful did you find the graphs in the book? Were they clear and easy to follow? Are there ways in which they could be improved?

9) Did the text help you to understand the concepts you needed to know for this course? Explain your answer, highlighting specific aspects of the book that you found particularly helpful or that could be improved in future editions.

10) MyEconLab is an online tutorial and homework system that comes automatically with a new copy of the textbook. **Please answer questions (a) through (e) <u>regardless</u> of whether you used MyEconLab for this course.**

a) Did you log into the MyEconLab site during the semester? Why or why not?

b) If you did not log in, how did you work practice problems to prepare for your exams? (Which problems did you work? How did you practice?)

c) Regardless of whether you used MyEconLab: For each chapter, MyEconLab has a practice test and at the end of the test, the program generates a personalized Study Plan that tells you which specific topics you've mastered, and which sections of the book you need to review.

□ I used MyEconLab's Study Plan feature when studying for this course.
□ I did not use MyEconLab's Study Plan feature because I did not know this was available.
□ I knew about MyEconLab's Study Plan feature, but I chose not to use it.
□ I did not log into MyEconLab, but I think this sounds like a useful feature.
□ I did not log into MyEconLab, and I do not think this sounds like a useful feature.

d) For every chapter in the book, MyEconLab offers two practice tests and then additional Study Plan practice problems. The practice problems give you automated feedback and includes Draw-Graph questions.

□ I used MyEconLab for additional practice when studying for this course.
□ I did not use MyEconLab for additional practice because I did not know it was available.
□ I knew about MyEconLab's additional practice, but I chose not to use it.

e) Regardless of whether you used MyEconLab: Do you think it would be helpful to study for this course using additional practice and draw-graph problems? Why or why not?

f) <u>If you used MyEconLab</u> when studying for this course, would you recommend the program to a friend who is taking this course next semester? Why or why not?

11) Do you have any other comments or suggestions for the text and/or MyEconLab?

Thank you for filling out this questionnaire. Your feedback helps us to develop the books and software for future editions.

MICROECONOMICS

Practice, Engage, and Assess

- **Enhanced eText**—Students actively read and learn, and with more engagement than ever before, through embedded and auto-graded practice, real-time data-graph updates, animations, author videos, and more.

- **Practice**—Algorithmically generated homework and study plan exercises with instant feedback ensure varied and productive practice, helping students improve their understanding and prepare for quizzes and tests. Draw-graph exercises encourage students to practice the language of economics.

- **Learning Resources**—Personalized learning aids such as Help Me Solve This problem walkthroughs, Teach Me explanations of the underlying concept, and figure Animations provide on-demand help when students need it most.

- **Adaptive Study Plan**—Monitors each student's progress and offers a continuously personalized study plan based on his or her own homework, quiz, and test results. Includes unlimited practice exercises and the opportunity to prove mastery through quizzes based on recommended learning objectives.

- **Dynamic Study Modules**—With a focus on key topics, these modules work by continuously assessing student performance and activity in real time and, using data and analytics, provide personalized content to reinforce concepts that target each student's particular strengths and weaknesses.

- **Digital Interactives**—Focused on a single core topic and organized in progressive levels, each interactive immerses students in an assignable and auto-graded activity. Digital Interactives are also engaging lecture tools for traditional, online, and hybrid courses, many incorporating real-time data, data displays, and analysis tools for rich classroom discussions.

with MyEconLab®

- **Learning Catalytics**—Generates classroom discussion, guides lectures, and promotes peer-to-peer learning with real-time analytics. Students can use any device to interact in the classroom, engage with content, and even draw and share graphs.

- **Current News Exercises**—Every week, current microeconomic and macroeconomic news stories, with accompanying exercises, are posted to MyEconLab. Assignable and auto-graded, these multi-part exercises ask students to recognize and apply economic concepts to real-world events.

- **Experiments**—Flexible, easy-to-assign, auto-graded, and available in Single and Multiplayer versions, Experiments in MyEconLab make learning fun and engaging.

- **Reporting Dashboard**—View, analyze, and report learning outcomes clearly and easily. Available via the Gradebook and fully mobile-ready, the Reporting Dashboard presents student performance data at the class, section, and program levels in an accessible, visual manner.

- **LMS Integration**—Link from any LMS platform to access assignments, rosters, and resources, and synchronize MyLab grades with your LMS gradebook. For students, new direct, single sign-on provides access to all the personalized learning MyLab resources that make studying more efficient and effective.

- **Mobile Ready**—Students and instructors can access multimedia resources and complete assessments right at their fingertips, on any mobile device.

PEARSON

Microeconomics

Sixth Custom Edition for Temple University

Taken from:
Microeconomics, Twelfth Edition
by Michael Parkin

Solutions Manual for Microeconomics, Twelfth Edition
by Mark Rush

Microeconomics, Fifth Edition
by R. Glenn Hubbard and Anthony Patrick O'Brien

Instructor's Manual for Microeconomics, Fifth Edition
by Edward Scahill

Cover Art: Courtesy of Temple University

Taken from:

Microeconomics, Twelfth Edition
by Michael Parkin
Copyright © 2016, 2014, 2012 by Pearson Education, Inc.
New York, New York 10013

Solutions Manual for Microeconomics, Twelfth Edition
by Mark Rush
Copyright © 2015 by Pearson Education, Inc.

Microeconomics, Fifth Edition
by R. Glenn Hubbard and Anthony Patrick O'Brien
Copyright © 2015, 2013, 2010 by Pearson Education, Inc.

Instructor's Manual for Microeconomics, Fifth Edition
by Edward Scahill
Copyright © 2015, 2013, 2010 by Pearson Education, Inc.

Pearson Learning Solutions, 330 Hudson Street, New York, New York 10013
A Pearson Education Company
www.pearsoned.com

Printed in the United States of America

3 4 5 6 7 8 9 10 V092 18 17 16 15

000200010271976738

SK

ISBN 10: 1-323-14653-9
ISBN 13: 978-1-323-14653-8

TO ROBIN

Michael Parkin is Professor Emeritus in the Department of Economics at the University of Western Ontario, Canada. Professor Parkin has held faculty appointments at Brown University, the University of Manchester, the University of Essex, and Bond University. He is a past president of the Canadian Economics Association and has served on the editorial boards of the *American Economic Review* and the *Journal of Monetary Economics* and as managing editor of the *Canadian Journal of Economics*. Professor Parkin's research on macroeconomics, monetary economics, and international economics has resulted in over 160 publications in journals and edited volumes, including the *American Economic Review,* the *Journal of Political Economy,* the *Review of Economic Studies*, the *Journal of Monetary Economics,* and the *Journal of Money, Credit and Banking*. He became most visible to the public with his work on inflation that discredited the use of wage and price controls. Michael Parkin also spearheaded the movement toward European monetary union. Professor Parkin is an experienced and dedicated teacher of introductory economics.

Taken from: *Microeconomics*, Fifth Edition, by R. Glenn Hubbard and Anthony Patrick O'Brien

Taken from: *Instructor's Solutions Manual for Microeconomics*, Twelfth Edition, by Michael Parkin

Taken from: *Instructor's Manual for Microeconomics*, Fifth Edition, by Edward Scahill

Flexibility

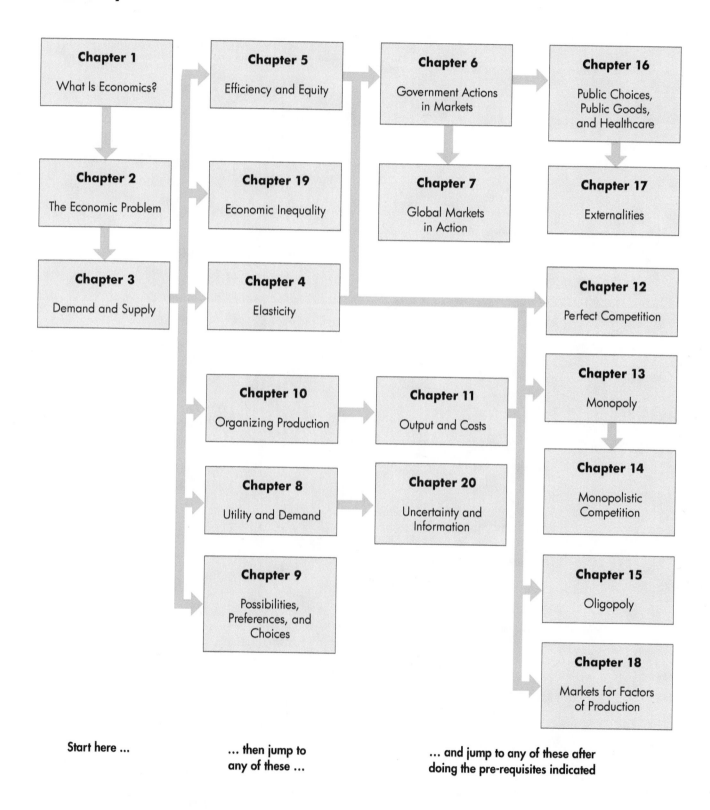

| Chapter 1 | Chapter 5 | Chapter 6 | Chapter 16 |
| What Is Economics? | Efficiency and Equity | Government Actions in Markets | Public Choices, Public Goods, and Healthcare |

| Chapter 2 | Chapter 19 | Chapter 7 | Chapter 17 |
| The Economic Problem | Economic Inequality | Global Markets in Action | Externalities |

| Chapter 3 | Chapter 4 | | Chapter 12 |
| Demand and Supply | Elasticity | | Perfect Competition |

| | | | Chapter 13 |
| | | | Monopoly |

| | Chapter 10 | Chapter 11 | |
| | Organizing Production | Output and Costs | |

| | Chapter 8 | Chapter 20 | Chapter 14 |
| | Utility and Demand | Uncertainty and Information | Monopolistic Competition |

| | Chapter 9 | | Chapter 15 |
| | Possibilities, Preferences, and Choices | | Oligopoly |

| | | | Chapter 18 |
| | | | Markets for Factors of Production |

Start here ...   ... then jump to any of these ...   ... and jump to any of these after doing the pre-requisites indicated

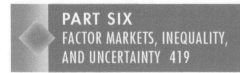

Taken from: *Microeconomics*, Fifth Edition, by R. Glenn Hubbard
and Anthony Patrick O'Brien

Taken from: *Instructor's Solutions Manual for Microeconomics*,
Twelfth Edition, by Michael Parkin

Taken from: *Instructor's Manual for Microeconomics*, Fifth Edition,
by Edward Scahill

The future is always uncertain. But at some times, and now is one such time, the range of possible near-future events is unusually large. Political tensions in the Middle East and Eastern Europe are one source of this uncertainty. But economic policy is another source. There is uncertainty about the way in which international trade policy will evolve as bilateral deals reshape the competitive landscape. There is uncertainty about exchange rate policy as currency fluctuations bring changes in international relative prices. There is extraordinary uncertainty about monetary policy with the Fed having quadrupled the quantity of bank reserves and continuing to delay the return of interest rates to levels considered normal. And there is uncertainty about fiscal policy as an ongoing federal budget deficit interacts with an aging population and rising healthcare costs to create a national debt time bomb.

In the years since the subprime mortgage crisis of August 2007 moved economics from the business report to the front page, a justified fall in confidence has gripped producers, consumers, financial institutions, and governments.

Even the idea that the market is an efficient allocation mechanism has come into question. Many thoughtful people worry about rising income inequality, and some political leaders called for the end of capitalism and the dawn of a new economic order in which tighter regulation reins in unfettered greed.

Rarely do teachers of economics have such a rich feast on which to draw. And rarely are the principles of economics more surely needed to provide the solid foundation on which to think about economic events and navigate the turbulence of economic life.

Although thinking like an economist can bring a clearer perspective to and deeper understanding of today's events, students don't find the economic way of thinking easy or natural. *Microeconomics* seeks to put clarity and understanding in the grasp of the student with a careful and vivid exploration of the tension between self-interest and the social interest, the role and power of incentives—of opportunity cost and marginal benefit—and demonstrating the possibility that markets supplemented by other mechanisms might allocate resources efficiently.

Parkin students begin to think about issues the way real economists do and learn how to explore difficult policy problems and make more informed decisions in their own economic lives.

The Twelfth Edition Revision

Thoroughly updated, intuitive rather than technical, grounded in data and empirical evidence, extensively illustrated with well-chosen examples and photographs, enlivened with applications that focus on issues at play in today's world, focused on learning-by-doing, and seamlessly integrated with MyEconLab: These are the hallmarks of this twelfth edition of *Microeconomics*.

This revision builds on the foundation of the previous edition and retains a thorough and careful presentation of the principles of economics, an emphasis on real-world examples and applications, the development of critical thinking skills, diagrams renowned for pedagogy and clarity, and path-breaking technology.

Highpoints of the Text Revision

This revision has many detailed changes and responses to reviewers, but its highpoints are a new feature and two content changes.

The new feature is a full-page end-of-chapter **worked problem**. As part of the chapter review, the student has an opportunity to work a multi-part problem that covers the core content of the chapter and consists of questions, solutions, and key figures. This new feature increases the incentive for the student to learn-by-doing and actively, rather than passively, review the chapter.

The two main content changes are in the coverage of

- Healthcare
- Externalities

Healthcare A reorganized and renamed Chapter 16, Public Choices, Public Goods, and Healthcare, opens with a new discussion of public choices and the political marketplace and the reasons why healthcare features so prominently in public choices. It presents a revealing pie chart of the allocation of government expenditures, one third of which is on healthcare programs. A new major section on the economics of healthcare describes the healthcare markets, the reasons why they fail, the alternative public choice solutions, the efficiency and equity issues they raise, and the U.S. and international experience. An *At Issue* box looks at Obamacare and one of its critics.

Externalities A reorganized Chapter 17 brings together all the material on externalities (both negative and positive). A major section on negative externalities describes and analyzes the problem of carbon emission and climate change and includes an account of the prisoners' dilemma that arises in coping with global externalities. The chapter includes an *Economics in the News* on the idea of lowering carbon emissions by generating more electricity from gas and less from coal and an *At Issue* on the carbon debate.

Many other chapters have been thoroughly reworked to achieve even greater clarity and to place greater emphasis on applications to current issues. And every chapter now contains a new opening vignette linked directly to an *Economics in the News*, an end-of-chapter problem, and online practice.

All the end-of-chapter *Economics in the News* articles have been updated, and the analysis of the news and the linked problems and applications have been appropriately revised.

Enhanced Pearson eText and New Interactive Features

MyEconLab with Enhanced eText combines digital resources that illuminate content with accessible self-assessment tools to provide students with a comprehensive learning experience—all in one place.

The Enhanced eText's digital resources include animations of figures that bring learning to life, interactive graph drawing exercises, problem solving tools, and news applications.

The results of all the activities in the Enhanced eText feed into the MyEconLab Adaptive Study Plan, which provides an exceptional adaptive learning experience uniquely tailored to the learning challenges of each individual student.

This powerful digital resource enables students to actively use the concepts they're reading about and, through learning-by-doing, achieve deeper understanding of the key economic principles.

◆ Features to Enhance Teaching and Learning

The changes that I have described are adjustments to an already powerful teaching and learning package. Here, I briefly review the features retained from the previous edition.

Economics in the News

This Parkin hallmark helps students think like economists by connecting chapter tools and concepts to the world around them. In this new edition, *Economics in the News* comes in two formats. One format, as in the previous edition, presents a brief newsclip supplemented by data where needed, and then poses some questions and walks through the answers.

The other format of *Economics in the News* is a rebranding of what I called *Reading Between the Lines* in all the earlier editions. This feature, which appears at the end of every chapter (except the first), shows students how to apply the tools they have learned by analyzing an article from a newspaper or news Web site. The news article connects with the questions first raised in the chapter opener, and the analysis is reinforced with a related end-of-chapter problem.

At Issue

Eleven *At Issue* boxes, three of which are new, engage the student in debate and controversy. An *At Issue* box introduces an issue and then presents two opposing views. It leaves the matter unsettled so that the student and instructor can continue the argument in class and reach their own conclusions.

Economics in Action Boxes

This feature uses boxes within the chapter to provide data and information that links models to real-world economic activity. Some of the issues covered in these boxes include the best affordable choice of recorded music, movies and DVDs; the cost of selling a pair of shoes; how Apple doesn't make the iPhone; opposing trends in air pollution and carbon concentration; structural unemployment in Michigan; how loanable funds fuel a home price bubble; and the size of the fiscal stimulus multipliers.

Chapter Openers

Each chapter opens with a student-friendly vignette that raises questions to motivate the student and focus the chapter. This chapter-opening story is woven into the main body of the chapter and is explored in the *Economics in the News* feature that ends each chapter.

Key Terms

Highlighted terms simplify the student's task of learning the vocabulary of economics. Each highlighted term appears in an end-of-chapter list with its page number, in an end-of-book glossary with its page number, boldfaced in the index, and in MyEconLab in the interactive glossary and the Flash Cards.

Diagrams That Show the Action

Through the past eleven editions, this book has set the standard of clarity in its diagrams; the twelfth edition continues to uphold this tradition. My goal is to show "where the economic action is." The diagrams in this book continue to generate an enormously positive response, which confirms my view that graphical analysis is the most powerful tool available for teaching and learning economics at the principles level.

Because many students find graphs hard to work with, I have developed the entire art program with the study and review needs of the student in mind.

The diagrams feature

- Original curves consistently shown in blue
- Shifted curves, equilibrium points, and other important features highlighted in red
- Color-blended arrows to suggest movement
- Graphs paired with data tables
- Diagrams labeled with boxed notes
- Extended captions that make each diagram and its caption a self-contained object for study and review

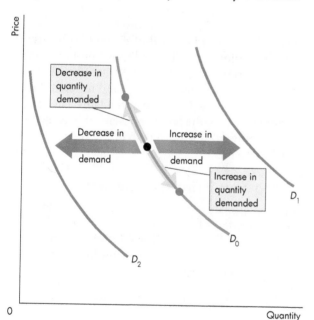

In-Text Review Quizzes

A review quiz at the end of each major section enables students to determine whether a topic needs further study before moving on. This feature includes a reference to the appropriate MyEconLab study plan and a new **Key Terms Quiz** to help students further test their understanding.

End-of-Chapter Study Material

Each chapter closes with a concise summary organized by major topics, a list of key terms with page references, a worked problem, and problems and applications. These learning tools provide students with a summary for review and exam preparation.

Interviews with Economists

Each part closes with an overview of the chapters and a teaser of an interview with a leading economist whose work correlates to what the student is learning. These interviews explore the education and research of these prominent economists and their advice for those who want to continue the study of economics. This edition has new interviews with Esther Duflo (MIT) and Raj Chetty (Harvard). The 65 past and present interviews I have conducted are available in full in MyEconLab.

◆ For the Instructor

This book enables you to focus on the economic way of thinking and choose your own course structure in your principles course.

Focus on the Economic Way of Thinking

As an instructor, you know how hard it is to encourage a student to think like an economist. But that is your goal. Consistent with this goal, the text focuses on and repeatedly uses the central ideas: choice; tradeoff; opportunity cost; the margin; incentives; the gains from voluntary exchange; the forces of demand, supply, and equilibrium; the pursuit of economic rent; the tension between self-interest and the social interest; and the scope and limitations of government actions.

Flexible Structure

You have preferences for how you want to teach your course, and I've organized this book to enable you to choose your teaching path. The chart on p. xi illustrates the book's flexibility. By following the arrows through the charts you can select the path that best fits your preference for course structure. Whether you want to teach a traditional course that blends theory and policy, or one that takes a fast-track through either theory or policy issues, *Microeconomics* gives you the choice.

Instructor's Supplemental Resources

The supplements for instructors are

- Test Item Files
- PowerPoint Resources
- Instructor's Manual
- Solutions Manual

Test Item Files Three separate Test Item Files with nearly 7,000 questions, provide multiple-choice, true/false, numerical, fill-in-the-blank, short-answer, and essay questions. Mark Rush reviewed and edited all the questions to ensure their clarity and consistency.

New questions were written by Svitlana Maksymenko of the University of Pittsburgh and James K. Self of the University of Indiana, Bloomington.

Questions follow the style and format of the end-of-chapter text problems. End-of-part tests contain integrative questions that cover all the chapters in the part. News-based application questions are available for each chapter of the text.

Fully networkable and available for Windows® and Macintosh®, TestGen's graphical interface enables instructors to view the Test Item Files; edit and add questions; transfer questions to tests; and print different forms of tests. Tests can be formatted as in any word-processing document with varying fonts, styles, margins, headers, and footers. Search and sort features let the instructor quickly locate questions and arrange them in a preferred order. QuizMaster, working with your school's computer network, automatically grades exams, stores the results, and allows the instructor to view or print a variety of reports.

BlackBoard- and WebCT-ready conversions of the TestGen Test Item Files are available for download from www.pearsonhighered.com/irc.

PowerPoint Resources A set of full-color Microsoft® PowerPoint Presentations, created by Robin Bade, are available. Each chapter contains

- Lecture notes with all the textbook figures animated, tables from the textbook, and speaking notes from the Instructor's Manuals
- Large-scale versions of all the figures and tables in the textbook, animated for instructors to incorporate into their own slide shows
- A student version of the lecture notes with animated textbook figures

The presentations can be used electronically in the classroom or printed to create transparency masters.

Instructor's Manual The Instructor's Manual integrates the teaching and learning resources and serve as a guide to all the supplements. Written by Laura A. Wolff of Southern Illinois University Edwardsville, the Instructor's Manual is available electronically from MyEconLab or the Instructor's Resource Center.

Each chapter contains an overview, a list of what's new in the twelfth edition, and ready-to-use lecture notes, which enable a new user of Parkin to walk into a classroom and deliver a polished lecture.

Solutions Manual A comprehensive Solutions Manual provides instructors with solutions to the Review Quizzes and the end-of-chapter Problems and Applications as well as additional problems and the solutions to these problems. Written by Mark Rush of the University of Florida and reviewed for accuracy by Jeannie Gillmore of the University of Western Ontario, the Solutions Manual is available electronically from MyEconLab or the Instructor Resource Center.

Getting Your Instructor's Resources

Instructor's Resource Center Instructors can download supplements from a secure, instructor-only source via the Pearson Higher Education Instructor Resource Center Web page, which is found at (www.pearsonhighered.com/irc).

MyEconLab

MyEconLab has been designed and refined with a single purpose in mind: to create those moments of understanding that transform the difficult into the clear and obvious. With comprehensive homework, quiz, test, activity, and tutorial options, instructors can manage all their assessment in one program.

- All of the Review Quiz questions and end-of-chapter Problems and Applications were recreated as assignable auto-graded exercises with targeted feedback and related "Help-me-solve-this" tools by Robin Bade, Jeannie Gillmore of the University of Western Ontario, and Sharmistha Nag of Fairleigh Dickinson University, and were reviewed for accuracy by Trevor Collier of the University of Dayton.

- All of the Review Quiz questions and end-of chapter Problems and Applications are assignable and automatically graded in MyEconLab.

- All of the Review Quiz questions and end-of-chapter Study Plan Problems and Applications are available for students to work in the Adaptive Study Plan.

- All the end-of-chapter Additional Problems and Applications are not available to students in MyEconLab unless assigned by the instructor.

- Many of the problems and applications are algorithmic, draw-graph, and numerical exercises.

- All *Economics in the News* and Test Item questions are available for instructors to assign as test, quiz, or homework.

- Custom Exercise Builder enables instructors to create their own problems for assignment.

- Gradebook records each student's performance and time spent on the Tests and Study Plan and generates reports by student or by chapter.

Features of the Enhanced eText

The features of the enhanced eText are

- Embedded MyEconLab study plan and assessment
- Figure animations
- Interactive graph-drawing exercises
- More *Economics in the News*
- Worked problems
- Key terms quizzes

Embedded MyEconLab Study Plan and Assessment Every Review Quiz question and Study Plan Problem and Application in the enhanced eText can be worked by the student directly from the eText page on which it occurs and receive instant targeted feedback. These exercises are auto-graded and feed into MyEconLab's Adaptive Study Plan, where students receive recommendations based upon their performance. Study Plan links provide opportunities for more practice with exercises similar to those in the eText and give targeted feedback to guide the student in answering the exercises.

Figure Animations Every textbook figure can be worked through using a step-by-step animation, with audio, to help students learn the intuition behind reading and interpreting graphs. These animations may be used for review, or as an instructional aid in the classroom.

Interactive Graph-Drawing Exercises For each major figure, a graph-drawing exercise accompanies the step-by-step animation. The student builds and interprets the key diagrams and develops understanding by working a multiple-choice question about the figure. Each Draw Graph exercise is auto-graded and feeds into MyEconLab's Adaptive Study Plan.

More Economics in the News Each in-text *Economics in the News* is reinforced through an extended application of the same analysis. More *Economics in the News* problems are auto-graded and feed into MyEconLab's Adaptive Study Plan.

Worked Problems Each chapter concludes with a Worked Problem that consists of questions, solutions, and a key figure. These problems can be worked in the enhanced eText directly from the Worked Problem page. As the student works through each problem, feedback and just-in-time learning aids help the student develop proficiency with the concept.

Key Terms Quizzes Key Terms Quiz links provide opportunities for students to check their knowledge of the definitions and uses of the key terms.

Other MyEconLab Features

Adaptive Learning Study Plan Adaptive Learning Study Plan is powered by a sophisticated learning engine that tailors assessment material to the unique needs of each student. The Adaptive Learning Study Plan monitors the student's performance on homework, quizzes, and tests and continuously makes recommendations based on that performance.

If a student is struggling with a concept such as supply and demand, or having trouble calculating a price elasticity of demand, the Adaptive Learning Study Plan provides customized remediation activities— a pathway based on personal proficiencies, the number of attempts, or the difficulty of the questions—to get the student back on track. Students will also receive recommendations for additional practice in the form of rich multi-media learning aids such as videos, an interactive eText, Help Me Solve This tutorials, and graphing tools.

The Adaptive Learning Study Plan can extrapolate a student's future trouble spots and provide learning material and practice to avoid pitfalls. In addition, students who are showing a high degree of success with the assessment material are offered a chance to work on future topics based on the professor's course coverage preferences. This personalized and adaptive feedback and support ensures that your students are optimizing their current and future course work and mastering the concepts, rather than just memorizing and guessing answers.

Dynamic Study Modules The Dynamic Study Modules in MyEconLab engage the student in learning activities, continuously monitor and assess performance in real time, and by analyzing the data, personalize content to reinforce concepts that target each student's strengths and weaknesses. Instructors well-know that not every student learns the same way and at the same rate. And now, thanks to the advances in adaptive learning technology embedded in the Dynamic Study Modules, it is no longer necessary to teach as if they do.

Dynamic Study Modules can be set as homework and the results received right in the gradebook. And,

because your students are always on the go, Dynamic Study Modules can be accessed from any computer, tablet, or smartphone.

Economics in the News *Economics in the News* is a turn-key solution to bringing daily news into the classroom. Updated daily during the academic year, we upload a relevant article and provide questions that may be assigned for homework or for classroom discussion.

Current News Each week during the academic year, we upload multi-part microeconomic exercises, with links to relevant articles, into the MyEconLab assignment manager. These enable instructors to bring current issues and events into the course with easy-to-assign and auto-graded exercises.

Experiments in MyEconLab Experiments are a fun and engaging way to promote active learning and mastery of major economic concepts. Pearson's Experiments program is flexible and easy for instructors to assign and students to use.

- Available experiments cover a competitive market, price floors, price ceilings, taxes, price controls, public goods, and a lemons market.
- Single-player experiments, available to assign, allow your students to play against virtual players from anywhere at any time as long as they have an Internet connection.
- Multi-player experiments allow you to assign and manage a real-time experiment with your class.
- Experiments can be assigned in MyEconLab as homework integrated with pre-questions and post-questions.
- Experiments are auto-graded using algorithms that objectively evaluate a student's economic gain and performance during the experiment.

Digital Interactives Digital Interactives immerse the student in an activity that leads to the discovery of a fundamental economic idea or principle. Digital Interactives are designed for use in traditional, online, and hybrid courses, and many incorporate real-time data, as well as data display and analysis tools. A Digital Interactive can be presented in class as a visually stimulating, engaging lecture tool, and can be assigned with assessment questions for grading.

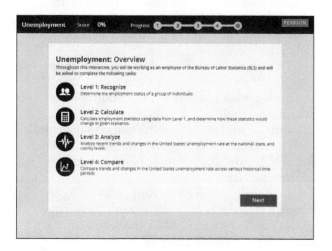

Learning Catalytics MyLab & Mastering with eText now provides Learning Catalytics, a web-based system for managing the interactive classroom that uses students' smartphones, tablets, or laptops to support the peer-instruction teaching method. Instructors can pose a variety of open-ended questions that help students develop critical thinking skills. Real-time monitoring of responses provides data on what students are struggling with and enables instructors to adjust their strategy and try other ways of engaging the students during class. Instructors can also manage student interactions and automatically group students for discussion and teamwork.

AACSB and Learning Outcomes All end-of-chapter and Test Item File questions are tagged in two ways: to AACSB standards and to discipline-specific Learning Outcomes. These two separate tagging systems allow professors to build assessments around desired departmental and course outcomes and track results in MyEconLab's gradebook.

Office Hours Students and instructors can consult the authors using the "Office Hours" links in MyEconLab. The link for students is in Chapter Resources and for Instructors it is in Instructor Resources/Instructor Tools.

Reporting Dashboard View, analyze, and report learning outcomes clearly and easily, and get the information you need to keep your students on track throughout the course, with the new Reporting Dashboard. Available via the Gradebook and fully mobile-ready, the Reporting Dashboard presents student performance data at the class, section, and program levels in an accessible, visual manner.

Acknowledgments

I thank my current and former colleagues and friends at the University of Western Ontario who have taught me so much. They are Jim Davies, Jeremy Greenwood, Ig Horstmann, Peter Howitt, Greg Huffman, David Laidler, Phil Reny, Chris Robinson, John Whalley, and Ron Wonnacott. I also thank Doug McTaggart and Christopher Findlay, co-authors of the Australian edition, and Melanie Powell and Kent Matthews, co-authors of the European edition. Suggestions arising from their adaptations of earlier editions have been helpful to me in preparing this edition.

I thank Rebecca Stein for her thoughtful suggestions and constructive criticism that brought the extensive revision to my treatment of healthcare, public goods, and externalities; Yoram Bauman for careful and helpful reviews of my new coverage of environmental externalities; and Sameh Ajlouni of Yarmouk University for spotting an embarrassing error.

I thank the several thousand students whom I have been privileged to teach. The instant response that comes from the look of puzzlement or enlightenment has taught me how to teach economics.

It is a special joy to thank the many outstanding editors, media specialists, and others at Pearson who contributed to the concerted publishing effort that brought this edition to completion. Denise Clinton, Digital Editor, has played a major role in the evolution of this text since its third edition, and her insights and ideas can still be found in this new edition. Donna Battista, Vice President, Business Publishing, is hugely inspiring and has provided overall direction to the project.

As ever, Adrienne D'Ambrosio, Executive Acquisitions Editor for Economics and my sponsoring editor, played a major role in shaping this revision and the many outstanding supplements that accompany it. Adrienne brings intelligence and insight to her work and is the unchallengeable pre-eminent economics editor. Sarah Dumouchelle, Project Manager, oversaw the production and design process, coordinated the photo research program, and worked with rights and permissions advisors. Andra Skaalrud, Supplements Project Manager, managed our immense supplements program. Nancy Freihofer, Program Manager, provided a steady hand throughout the revision process and helped develop the cover.

Digital Content Team Lead Noel Lotz managed a complex and thorough reviewing process for the content of MyEconLab; and Melissa Honig, Digital Studio Project Manager, ensured that all our media assets were correctly assembled.

Lori DeShazo, Executive Field Marketing Manager, and Alison Haskins, Senior Product Marketing Manager, provided inspired marketing strategy and direction. Jonathan Boylan designed the cover and package and yet again surpassed the challenge of ensuring that we meet the highest design standards.

Catherine Baum provided a careful, consistent, and intelligent copy edit and accuracy check. And Heather Johnson with the other members of an outstanding editorial and production team at Integra-Chicago kept the project on track on an impossibly tight schedule.

I thank all of these wonderful people. It has been inspiring to work with them and to share in creating what I believe is a truly outstanding educational tool.

I thank our talented twelfth edition supplements authors and contributors—Svitlana Maksymenko, Jim Self, Laurie Wolff, Jeannie Gillmore, and Sharmistha Nag.

I especially thank Mark Rush, who yet again played a crucial role in creating another edition of this text and package. Mark has been a constant source of good advice and good humor.

I thank the many exceptional reviewers who have shared their insights through the various editions of this book. Their contribution has been invaluable.

I thank the people who work directly with me. Jeannie Gillmore provided outstanding research assistance on many topics, including the *Economics in the News* news articles. Richard Parkin created the electronic art files and offered many ideas that improved the figures in this book. Robin Bade managed an ever-growing and ever more complex MyEconLab database. And Sharmistha Nag has helped me to create *Economics in the News* and Draw Graph exercises.

As with the previous editions, this one owes an enormous debt to Robin Bade. I dedicate this book to her and again thank her for her work. I could not have written this book without the tireless and selfless help she has given me. My thanks to her are unbounded.

Classroom experience will test the value of this book. I would appreciate hearing from instructors and students about how I can continue to improve it in future editions.

Michael Parkin
London, Ontario, Canada
michael.parkin@uwo.ca

Reviewers

Eric Abrams, Hawaii Pacific University

Christopher Adams, Federal Trade Commission

John T. Addison, University of South Carolina

Tajudeen Adenekan, Bronx Community College

Syed Ahmed, Cameron University

Frank Albritton, Seminole Community College

Milton Alderfer, Miami-Dade Community College

William Aldridge, Shelton State Community College

Donald L. Alexander, Western Michigan University

Terence Alexander, Iowa State University

Stuart Allen, University of North Carolina, Greensboro

Sam Allgood, University of Nebraska, Lincoln

Neil Alper, Northeastern University

Alan Anderson, Fordham University

Lisa R. Anderson, College of William and Mary

Jeff Ankrom, Wittenberg University

Fatma Antar, Manchester Community Technical College

Kofi Apraku, University of North Carolina, Asheville

John Atkins, University of West Florida

Moshen Bahmani-Oskooee, University of Wisconsin, Milwaukee

Donald Balch, University of South Carolina

Mehmet Balcilar, Wayne State University

Paul Ballantyne, University of Colorado

Sue Bartlett, University of South Florida

Jose Juan Bautista, Xavier University of Louisiana

Klaus Becker, Texas Tech University

Valerie R. Bencivenga, University of Texas, Austin

Ben Bernanke, Chairman of Federal Reserve

Radha Bhattacharya, California State University, Fullerton

Margot Biery, Tarrant County College, South

John Bittorowitz, Ball State University

David Black, University of Toledo

Kelly Blanchard, Purdue University

S. Brock Blomberg, Claremont McKenna College

William T. Bogart, Case Western Reserve University

Giacomo Bonanno, University of California, Davis

Tan Khay Boon, Nanyard Technological University

Sunne Brandmeyer, University of South Florida

Audie Brewton, Northeastern Illinois University

Baird Brock, Central Missouri State University

Byron Brown, Michigan State University

Imam Bulbul, University of Miami

Jeffrey Buser, Columbus State Community College

Alison Butler, Florida International University

Colleen Callahan, American University

Tania Carbiener, Southern Methodist University

Kevin Carey, American University

Scott Carrell, University of California at Davis

Kathleen A. Carroll, University of Maryland, Baltimore County

Michael Carter, University of Massachusetts, Lowell

Edward Castronova, California State University, Fullerton

Francis Chan, Fullerton College

Ming Chang, Dartmouth College

Subir Chakrabarti, Indiana University-Purdue University

Joni Charles, Texas State University

Adhip Chaudhuri, Georgetown University

Gopal Chengalath, Texas Tech University

Daniel Christiansen, Albion College

Kenneth Christianson, Binghamton University

John J. Clark, Community College of Allegheny County, Allegheny Campus

Cindy Clement, University of Maryland

Meredith Clement, Dartmouth College

Michael B. Cohn, U. S. Merchant Marine Academy

Robert Collinge, University of Texas, San Antonio

Carol Condon, Kean University

Doug Conway, Mesa Community College

Larry Cook, University of Toledo

Bobby Corcoran, retired, Middle Tennessee State University

Kevin Cotter, Wayne State University

James Peery Cover, University of Alabama, Tuscaloosa

Erik Craft, University of Richmond

Eleanor D. Craig, University of Delaware

Jim Craven, Clark College

Jeremy Cripps, American University of Kuwait

Elizabeth Crowell, University of Michigan, Dearborn

Stephen Cullenberg, University of California, Riverside

David Culp, Slippery Rock University

Norman V. Cure, Macomb Community College

Dan Dabney, University of Texas, Austin

Andrew Dane, Angelo State University

James D'Angelo, University of Cincinnati

Joseph Daniels, Marquette University

Gregory DeFreitas, Hofstra University

David Denslow, University of Florida

Shatakshee Dhongde, Rochester Institute of Technology

Mark Dickie, University of Central Florida

James Dietz, California State University, Fullerton

Carol Dole, State University of West Georgia

Ronald Dorf, Inver Hills Community College

John Dorsey, University of Maryland, College Park

Eric Drabkin, Hawaii Pacific University

Amrik Singh Dua, Mt. San Antonio College

Thomas Duchesneau, University of Maine, Orono

Lucia Dunn, Ohio State University

Donald Dutkowsky, Syracuse University

John Edgren, Eastern Michigan University

David J. Eger, Alpena Community College

Harold W. Elder, University of Alabama

Harry Ellis, Jr., University of North Texas

Ibrahim Elsaify, Goldey-Beacom College

Kenneth G. Elzinga, University of Virginia

Patrick Emerson, Oregon State University

Tisha Emerson, Baylor University

Monica Escaleras, Florida Atlantic University

Antonina Espiritu, Hawaii Pacific University

Gwen Eudey, University of Pennsylvania

Barry Falk, Iowa State University

M. Fazeli, Hofstra University

Philip Fincher, Louisiana Tech University

F. Firoozi, University of Texas, San Antonio

Nancy Folbre, University of Massachusetts, Amherst

Kenneth Fong, Temasek Polytechnic (Singapore)

Steven Francis, Holy Cross College

David Franck, University of North Carolina, Charlotte

Mark Frank, Sam Houston State University

Roger Frantz, San Diego State University

Mark Frascatore, Clarkson University

Alwyn Fraser, Atlantic Union College

Connel Fullenkamp, Duke University

Marc Fusaro, East Carolina University

James Gale, Michigan Technological University

Susan Gale, New York University

Roy Gardner, Indiana University

Eugene Gentzel, Pensacola Junior College

Kirk Gifford, Brigham Young University-Idaho

Scott Gilbert, Southern Illinois University, Carbondale

Andrew Gill, California State University, Fullerton

Robert Giller, Virginia Polytechnic Institute and State
    University

Robert Gillette, University of Kentucky

James N. Giordano, Villanova University

Maria Giuili, Diablo College

Susan Glanz, St. John's University

Robert Gordon, San Diego State University

Richard Gosselin, Houston Community College

John Graham, Rutgers University

John Griffen, Worcester Polytechnic Institute

Wayne Grove, Syracuse University

Robert Guell, Indiana State University

William Gunther, University of Southern Mississippi

Jamie Haag, Pacific University, Oregon

Gail Heyne Hafer, Lindenwood University

Rik W. Hafer, Southern Illinois University, Edwardsville

Daniel Hagen, Western Washington University

David R. Hakes, University of Northern Iowa

Craig Hakkio, Federal Reserve Bank, Kansas City

Bridget Gleeson Hanna, Rochester Institute of Technology

Ann Hansen, Westminster College

Seid Hassan, Murray State University

Jonathan Haughton, Suffolk University

Randall Haydon, Wichita State University

Denise Hazlett, Whitman College

Julia Heath, University of Memphis

Jac Heckelman, Wake Forest University

Jolien A. Helsel, Kent State University

James Henderson, Baylor University

Doug Herman, Georgetown University

Jill Boylston Herndon, University of Florida

Gus Herring, Brookhaven College

John Herrmann, Rutgers University

John M. Hill, Delgado Community College

Jonathan Hill, Florida International University

Lewis Hill, Texas Tech University

Steve Hoagland, University of Akron

Tom Hoerger, Fellow, Research Triangle Institute

Calvin Hoerneman, Delta College

George Hoffer, Virginia Commonwealth University

Dennis L. Hoffman, Arizona State University

Paul Hohenberg, Rensselaer Polytechnic Institute

Jim H. Holcomb, University of Texas, El Paso

Robert Holland, Purdue University

Harry Holzer, Georgetown University

Linda Hooks, Washington and Lee University

Gary Hoover, University of Alabama

Jim Horner, Cameron University

Djehane Hosni, University of Central Florida

Harold Hotelling, Jr., Lawrence Technical University

Calvin Hoy, County College of Morris

Ing-Wei Huang, Assumption University, Thailand

Julie Hunsaker, Wayne State University

Beth Ingram, University of Iowa

Jayvanth Ishwaran, Stephen F. Austin State University

Michael Jacobs, Lehman College

S. Hussain Ali Jafri, Tarleton State University

Dennis Jansen, Texas A&M University

Andrea Jao, University of Pennsylvania

Barbara John, University of Dayton

Barry Jones, Binghamton University

Garrett Jones, Southern Florida University

Frederick Jungman, Northwestern Oklahoma State University

Paul Junk, University of Minnesota, Duluth

Leo Kahane, California State University, Hayward

Veronica Kalich, Baldwin-Wallace College

John Kane, State University of New York, Oswego

Eungmin Kang, St. Cloud State University

Arthur Kartman, San Diego State University

Theresa Kauffman, Chattahoochee Technical College

Gurmit Kaur, Universiti Teknologi (Malaysia)

Louise Keely, University of Wisconsin, Madison

Manfred W. Keil, Claremont McKenna College

Elizabeth Sawyer Kelly, University of Wisconsin, Madison

Rose Kilburn, Modesto Junior College

Amanda King, Georgia Southern University

John King, Georgia Southern University

Robert Kirk, Indiana University-Purdue University,
    Indianapolis

Norman Kleinberg, City University of New York, Baruch College

Robert Kleinhenz, California State University, Fullerton

John Krantz, University of Utah

Joseph Kreitzer, University of St. Thomas

Patricia Kuzyk, Washington State University

David Lages, Southwest Missouri State University

W. J. Lane, University of New Orleans

Leonard Lardaro, University of Rhode Island

Kathryn Larson, Elon College

Luther D. Lawson, University of North Carolina, Wilmington

Elroy M. Leach, Chicago State University

Jim Lee, Texas A & M, Corpus Christi

Sang Lee, Southeastern Louisiana University

Robert Lemke, Florida International University

Mary Lesser, Iona College

Philip K. Letting, Harrisburg Area Community College

Jay Levin, Wayne State University

Arik Levinson, University of Wisconsin, Madison

Tony Lima, California State University, Hayward

William Lord, University of Maryland, Baltimore County

Nancy Lutz, Virginia Polytechnic Institute and State University

Brian Lynch, Lakeland Community College

Murugappa Madhavan, San Diego State University

K. T. Magnusson, Salt Lake Community College

Mark Maier, Glendale Community College

Svitlana Maksymenko, University of Pittsburgh

Jean Mangan, Staffordshire University Business School

Denton Marks, University of Wisconsin, Whitewater

Michael Marlow, California Polytechnic State University

Akbar Marvasti, University of Houston

Wolfgang Mayer, University of Cincinnati

John McArthur, Wofford College

Katherine McClain, University of Georgia

Amy McCormick, Mary Baldwin College

Russ McCullough, Iowa State University

Catherine McDevitt, Central Michigan University

Gerald McDougall, Wichita State University

Stephen McGary, Brigham Young University-Idaho

Richard D. McGrath, Armstrong Atlantic State University

Richard McIntyre, University of Rhode Island

John McLeod, Georgia Institute of Technology

Mark McLeod, Virginia Polytechnic Institute and State University

B. Starr McMullen, Oregon State University

Sandra McPherson, Millersville University

Mary Ruth McRae, Appalachian State University

Kimberly Merritt, Cameron University

Charles Meyer, Iowa State University

Peter Mieszkowski, Rice University

John Mijares, University of North Carolina, Asheville

Richard A. Miller, Wesleyan University

Judith W. Mills, Southern Connecticut State University

Glen Mitchell, Nassau Community College

Jeannette C. Mitchell, Rochester Institute of Technology

Bagher Modjtahedi, University of California, Davis

Michael A. Mogavero, University of Notre Dame

Khan Mohabbat, Northern Illinois University

Shahruz Mohtadi, Suffolk University

Barbara Moore, University of Central Florida

W. Douglas Morgan, University of California, Santa Barbara

William Morgan, University of Wyoming

James Morley, Washington University in St. Louis

William Mosher, Clark University

Joanne Moss, San Francisco State University

Nivedita Mukherji, Oakland University

Francis Mummery, Fullerton College

Edward Murphy, Southwest Texas State University

Kevin J. Murphy, Oakland University

Kathryn Nantz, Fairfield University

William S. Neilson, Texas A&M University

Paul Nelson, University of Louisiana, Monroe

Bart C. Nemmers, University of Nebraska, Lincoln

Alexandra Nica, University of Iowa

Melinda Nish, Orange Coast College

Anthony O'Brien, Lehigh University

Norman Obst, Michigan State University

Constantin Ogloblin, Georgia Southern University

Neal Olitsky, University of Massachusetts, Dartmouth

Mary Olson, Tulane University

Terry Olson, Truman State University

James B. O'Neill, University of Delaware

Farley Ordovensky, University of the Pacific

Z. Edward O'Relley, North Dakota State University

Donald Oswald, California State University, Bakersfield

Jan Palmer, Ohio University

Michael Palumbo, Chief, Federal Reserve Board

Chris Papageorgiou, Louisiana State University

G. Hossein Parandvash, Western Oregon State College

Randall Parker, East Carolina University

Robert Parks, Washington University

David Pate, St. John Fisher College

James E. Payne, Illinois State University

Donald Pearson, Eastern Michigan University

Steven Peterson, University of Idaho

Mary Anne Pettit, Southern Illinois University, Edwardsville

William A. Phillips, University of Southern Maine

Dennis Placone, Clemson University

Charles Plot, California Institute of Technology, Pasadena

Mannie Poen, Houston Community College

Kathleen Possai, Wayne State University

Ulrika Praski-Stahlgren, University College in Gavle-Sandviken, Sweden

Edward Price, Oklahoma State University

Rula Qalyoubi, University of Wisconsin, Eau Claire

K. A. Quartey, Talladega College

Herman Quirmbach, Iowa State University

Jeffrey R. Racine, University of South Florida

Ramkishen Rajan, George Mason University

Peter Rangazas, Indiana University-Purdue University, Indianapolis

Vaman Rao, Western Illinois University

Laura Razzolini, University of Mississippi

Rob Rebelein, University of Cincinnati

J. David Reed, Bowling Green State University

Robert H. Renshaw, Northern Illinois University

Javier Reyes, University of Arkansas

Jeff Reynolds, Northern Illinois University

Rupert Rhodd, Florida Atlantic University

W. Gregory Rhodus, Bentley College

Jennifer Rice, Indiana University, Bloomington

John Robertson, Paducah Community College

Malcolm Robinson, University of North Carolina, Greensboro

Richard Roehl, University of Michigan, Dearborn

Carol Rogers, Georgetown University

William Rogers, University of Northern Colorado

Thomas Romans, State University of New York, Buffalo

David R. Ross, Bryn Mawr College

Thomas Ross, Baldwin Wallace College

Robert J. Rossana, Wayne State University

Jeffrey Rous, University of North Texas

Rochelle Ruffer, Youngstown State University

John Ruggiero, University of Daytona

Mark Rush, University of Florida

Allen R. Sanderson, University of Chicago

Gary Santoni, Ball State University

Jeffrey Sarbaum, University of North Carolina at Chapel Hill

John Saussy, Harrisburg Area Community College

Don Schlagenhauf, Florida State University

David Schlow, Pennsylvania State University

Paul Schmitt, St. Clair County Community College

Jeremy Schwartz, Hampden-Sydney College

Martin Sefton, University of Nottingham

James K. Self, Indiana University

Esther-Mirjam Sent, University of Notre Dame

Rod Shadbegian, University of Massachusetts, Dartmouth

Neil Sheflin, Rutgers University

Gerald Shilling, Eastfield College

Dorothy R. Siden, Salem State College

Mark Siegler, California State University at Sacramento

Scott Simkins, North Carolina Agricultural and Technical State University

Jacek Siry, University of Georgia

Chuck Skoro, Boise State University

Phil Smith, DeKalb College

William Doyle Smith, University of Texas, El Paso

Sarah Stafford, College of William and Mary

Rebecca Stein, University of Pennsylvania

Frank Steindl, Oklahoma State University

Jeffrey Stewart, New York University

Rayna Stocheva, University of Miami

Allan Stone, Southwest Missouri State University

Courtenay Stone, Ball State University

Paul Storer, Western Washington University

Richard W. Stratton, University of Akron

Mark Strazicich, Ohio State University, Newark

Michael Stroup, Stephen F. Austin State University

Robert Stuart, Rutgers University

Della Lee Sue, Marist College

Abdulhamid Sukar, Cameron University

Terry Sutton, Southeast Missouri State University

Gilbert Suzawa, University of Rhode Island

David Swaine, Andrews University

Jason Taylor, Central Michigan University

Mark Thoma, University of Oregon

Janet Thomas, Bentley College

Kiril Tochkov, SUNY at Binghamton

Kay Unger, University of Montana

Anthony Uremovic, Joliet Junior College

David Vaughn, City University, Washington

Don Waldman, Colgate University

Francis Wambalaba, Portland State University

Sasiwimon Warunsiri, University of Colorado at Boulder

Rob Wassmer, California State University, Sacramento

Paul A. Weinstein, University of Maryland, College Park

Lee Weissert, St. Vincent College

Robert Whaples, Wake Forest University

David Wharton, Washington College

Mark Wheeler, Western Michigan University

Charles H. Whiteman, University of Iowa

Sandra Williamson, University of Pittsburgh

Brenda Wilson, Brookhaven Community College

Larry Wimmer, Brigham Young University

Mark Witte, Northwestern University

Willard E. Witte, Indiana University

Mark Wohar, University of Nebraska, Omaha

Laura Wolff, Southern Illinois University, Edwardsville

Cheonsik Woo, Vice President, Korea Development Institute

Douglas Wooley, Radford University

Arthur G. Woolf, University of Vermont

John T. Young, Riverside Community College

Michael Youngblood, Rock Valley College

Peter Zaleski, Villanova University

Jason Zimmerman, South Dakota State University

David Zucker, Martha Stewart Living Omnimedia

Supplements Authors

Luke Armstrong, Lee College
Sue Bartlett, University of South Florida
Kelly Blanchard, Purdue University
James Cobbe, Florida State University
Carol Dole, Jacksonville University
Karen Gebhardt, Colorado State University
John Graham, Rutgers University
Jill Herndon, University of Florida
Gary Hoover, University of Alabama
Patricia Kuzyk, Washington State University
Sang Lee, Southeastern Louisiana University
Svitlana Maksymenko, University of Pittsburgh
Robert Martel, University of Connecticut
Katherine McClain, University of Georgia

Russ McCullough, Iowa State University
Barbara Moore, University of Central Florida
James Morley, Washington University in St. Louis
William Mosher, Clark University
Alexandra Nica, University of Iowa
Constantin Ogloblin, Georgia Southern University
Edward Price, Oklahoma State University
Mark Rush, University of Florida
James K. Self, University of Indiana, Bloomington
Rebecca Stein, University of Pennsylvania
Michael Stroup, Stephen F. Austin State University
Della Lee Sue, Marist College
Nora Underwood, University of Central Florida
Laura A. Wolff, Southern Illinois University, Edwardsville

Taken from: *Microeconomics*, Twelfth Edition, by Michael Parkin

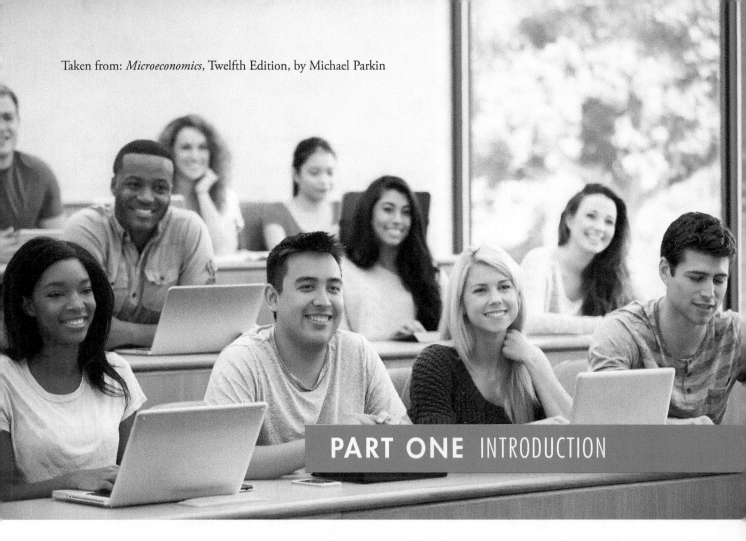

PART ONE INTRODUCTION

1 WHAT IS ECONOMICS?

After studying this chapter, you will be able to:

◆ Define economics and distinguish between microeconomics and macroeconomics

◆ Explain the two big questions of economics

◆ Explain the key ideas that define the economic way of thinking

◆ Explain how economists go about their work as social scientists and policy advisers

Is economics about money: How people make it and spend it? Is it about business, government, and jobs? Is it about why some people and some nations are rich and others poor? Economics is about all these things. But its core is the study of *choices* and their *consequences*.

Your life will be shaped by the choices that you make and the challenges that you face. To face those challenges and seize the opportunities they present, you must understand the powerful forces at play. The economics that you're about to learn will become your most reliable guide. This chapter gets you started by describing the questions that economists try to answer and looking at how economists think as they search for the answers.

Definition of Economics

A fundamental fact dominates our lives: We want more than we can get. Our inability to get everything we want is called **scarcity**. Scarcity is universal. It confronts all living things. Even parrots face scarcity!

Not only do I want a cracker—we all want a cracker!

© The New Yorker Collection 1985
Frank Modell from cartoonbank.com. All Rights Reserved.

Think about the things that *you* want and the scarcity that *you* face. You want to go to a good school, college, or university. You want to live in a well-equipped, spacious, and comfortable home. You want the latest smartphone and the fastest Internet connection for your laptop or iPad. You want some sports and recreational gear—perhaps some new running shoes, or a new bike. You want much more time than is available to go to class, do your homework, play sports and games, read novels, go to the movies, listen to music, travel, and hang out with your friends. And you want to live a long and healthy life.

What you can afford to buy is limited by your income and by the prices you must pay. And your time is limited by the fact that your day has 24 hours.

You want some other things that only governments provide. You want to live in a safe neighborhood in a peaceful and secure world, and enjoy the benefits of clean air, lakes, rivers, and oceans.

What governments can afford is limited by the taxes they collect. Taxes lower people's incomes and compete with the other things they want to buy.

What *everyone* can get—what *society* can get—is limited by the productive resources available. These resources are the gifts of nature, human labor and ingenuity, and all the previously produced tools and equipment.

Because we can't get everything we want, we must make *choices*. You can't afford *both* a laptop *and* an iPhone, so you must *choose* which one to buy. You can't spend tonight *both* studying for your next test *and* going to the movies, so again, you must *choose* which one to do. Governments can't spend a tax dollar on *both* national defense *and* environmental protection, so they must *choose* how to spend that dollar.

Your choices must somehow be made consistent with the choices of *others*. If you choose to buy a laptop, someone else must choose to sell it. Incentives reconcile choices. An **incentive** is a reward that encourages an action or a penalty that discourages one. Prices act as incentives. If the price of a laptop is too high, more will be offered for sale than people want to buy. And if the price is too low, fewer will be offered for sale than people want to buy. But there is a price at which choices to buy and sell are consistent.

> **Economics** is the social science that studies the *choices* that individuals, businesses, governments, and entire societies make as they cope with *scarcity* and the *incentives* that influence and reconcile those choices.

The subject has two parts:

- Microeconomics
- Macroeconomics

Microeconomics is the study of the choices that individuals and businesses make, the way these choices interact in markets, and the influence of governments. Some examples of microeconomic questions are: Why are people downloading more movies? How would a tax on e-commerce affect eBay?

Macroeconomics is the study of the performance of the national economy and the global economy. Some examples of macroeconomic questions are: Why does the U.S. unemployment rate fluctuate? Can the Federal Reserve make the unemployment rate fall by keeping interest rates low?

REVIEW QUIZ

1 List some examples of the scarcity that you face.
2 Find examples of scarcity in today's headlines.
3 Find an example of the distinction between microeconomics and macroeconomics in today's headlines.

Work these questions in Study Plan 1.1 and get instant feedback. Do a Key Terms Quiz.   MyEconLab

Two Big Economic Questions

Two big questions summarize the scope of economics:

- How do choices end up determining *what, how,* and *for whom* goods and services are produced?
- Do choices made in the pursuit of *self-interest* also promote the *social interest*?

What, How, and For Whom?

Goods and services are the objects that people value and produce to satisfy wants. *Goods* are physical objects such as cellphones and automobiles. *Services* are tasks performed for people such as cellphone service and auto-repair service.

What? *What* we produce varies across countries and changes over time. In the United States today, agriculture accounts for 1 percent of total production, manufactured goods for 20 percent, and services (retail and wholesale trade, healthcare, and education are the biggest ones) for 79 percent. In contrast, in China today, agriculture accounts for 10 percent of total production, manufactured goods for 45 percent, and services for 45 percent.

Figure 1.1 shows these numbers and also the percentages for Brazil, which fall between those for the United States and China.

What determines these patterns of production? How do choices end up determining the quantities of cellphones, automobiles, cellphone service, auto-repair service, and the millions of other items that are produced in the United States and around the world?

How? *How* we produce is described by the technologies and resources that we use. The resources used to produce goods and services are called **factors of production**, which are grouped into four categories:

- Land
- Labor
- Capital
- Entrepreneurship

Land The "gifts of nature" that we use to produce goods and services are called **land**. In economics, *land* is what in everyday language we call *natural resources*. It includes land in the everyday sense

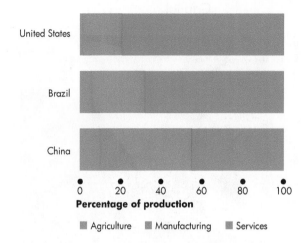

FIGURE 1.1   What Three Countries Produce

Percentage of production

■ Agriculture   ■ Manufacturing   ■ Services

Agriculture and manufacturing are small percentages of production in rich countries such as the United States and large percentages of production in poorer countries such as China. Most of what is produced in the United States is services.

Source of data: CIA Factbook 2014, Central Intelligence Agency.

MyEconLab Animation

together with minerals, oil, gas, coal, water, air, forests, and fish.

Our land surface and water resources are renewable and some of our mineral resources can be recycled. But the resources that we use to create energy are nonrenewable—they can be used only once.

Labor The work time and work effort that people devote to producing goods and services is called **labor**. Labor includes the physical and mental efforts of all the people who work on farms and construction sites and in factories, shops, and offices.

The *quality* of labor depends on **human capital**, which is the knowledge and skill that people obtain from education, on-the-job training, and work experience. You are building your own human capital right now as you work on your economics course, and your human capital will continue to grow as you gain work experience.

Human capital expands over time. Today, 88 percent of the adult population of the United States have completed high school and 32 percent have a college or university degree. Figure 1.2 shows these measures of human capital in the United States and its growth over the past 110 years.

FIGURE 1.2   A Measure of Human Capital

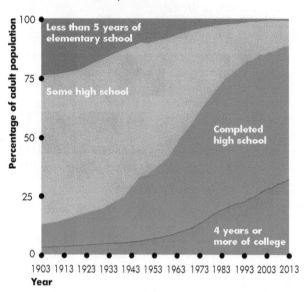

In 2013, 32 percent of the population aged 25 and older had 4 years or more of college, up from 2 percent in 1903. A further 56 percent had completed high school, up from 10 percent in 1903.

Source of data: U.S. Census Bureau, 2014.

—————— MyEconLab Animation ——————

Capital The tools, instruments, machines, buildings, and other constructions that businesses use to produce goods and services are called **capital**.

In everyday language, we talk about money, stocks, and bonds as being "capital." These items are *financial capital*. Financial capital plays an important role in enabling businesses to borrow the funds that they use to buy physical capital. But financial capital is not used to produce goods and services and it is not a factor of production.

Entrepreneurship The human resource that organizes labor, land, and capital is called **entrepreneurship**. Entrepreneurs are the drivers of economic progress. They develop new ideas about what and how to produce, make business decisions, and bear the risks that arise from these decisions.

What determines how the factors of production are used to produce each good and service?

For Whom? *Who* consumes the goods and services that are produced depends on the incomes that people earn. People with large incomes can buy a wide range of goods and services. People with small incomes have fewer options and can afford a smaller range of goods and services.

People earn their incomes by selling the services of the factors of production they own:

- Land earns **rent**.
- Labor earns **wages**.
- Capital earns **interest**.
- Entrepreneurship earns **profit**.

Which factor of production earns the most income? The answer is labor. In 2011, wages were 68 percent of total income and the incomes from land, capital, and entrepreneurship totaled 32 percent. These shares remain remarkably constant over time.

Knowing how income is shared among the factors of production doesn't tell us how it is shared among individuals. And the distribution of income among individuals is extremely unequal. You know of some people who earn very large incomes: Dwayne "The Rock" Johnson (Hercules) earned $46 million in 2013; and Clayton Kershaw has a $215 million 7-year deal with the LA Dodgers.

You know of even more people who earn very small incomes. Servers at McDonald's average around $7.25 an hour; checkout clerks, cleaners, and textile and leather workers all earn less than $10 an hour.

You probably know about other persistent differences in incomes. Men, on average, earn more than women; whites earn more than minorities; college graduates earn more than high-school graduates.

We can get a good sense of who consumes the goods and services produced by looking at the percentages of total income earned by different groups of people. The 20 percent of people with the lowest incomes earn about 5 percent of total income, while the richest 20 percent earn close to 50 percent of total income. So on average, people in the richest 20 percent earn more than 10 times the incomes of those in the poorest 20 percent. There is even huge inequality within the richest 20 percent and the top 1 percent earns almost 15 percent of total income.

Why is the distribution of income so unequal?

Economics provides some answers to all these questions about *what, how*, and *for whom* goods and services are produced and much of the rest of this book will help you to understand those answers.

We're now going to look at the second big question of economics: Do choices made in the pursuit of self-interest also promote the social interest?

Do Choices Made in the Pursuit of Self-Interest also Promote the Social Interest?

Every day, you and 320 million other Americans, along with 7.2 billion people in the rest of the world, make economic choices that result in *what, how*, and *for whom* goods and services are produced. These choices are made by people who are pursuing their self-interest.

Self-Interest You make a choice in your **self-interest** if you think that choice is the best one available for you. All the choices that people make about how to use their time and other resources are made in the pursuit of self-interest. When you allocate your time or your budget, you do what makes the most sense to you. You might think about how your choices affect other people and take into account how you feel about that, but it is how *you* feel that influences your choice. You order a home-delivery pizza because you're hungry, not because the delivery person needs a job. And when the pizza delivery person shows up at your door, he's not doing you a favor. He's pursuing *his* self-interest and hoping for a tip and another call next week.

The big question is: Is it possible that all the choices that each one of us makes in the pursuit of self-interest could end up achieving an outcome that is best for everyone?

Social Interest An outcome is in the **social interest** if it is best for society as a whole. It is easy to see how you decide what is in *your* self-interest. But how do we decide if something is in the social interest? To help you answer this question, imagine a scene like that in *Economics in the News* on the next page.

Ted, an entrepreneur, creates a new business. He hires a thousand workers and pays them $20 an hour, $1 an hour more than they earned in their old jobs. Ted's business is extremely profitable and his own earnings increase by $1 million per week.

You can see that Ted's decision to create the business is in his self-interest—he gains $1 million a week. You can also see that for Ted's employees, their decisions to work for Ted are in their self-interest—they gain $1 an hour (say $40 a week). And the decisions of Ted's customers must be in their self-interest, otherwise they wouldn't buy from him. But is this outcome in the social interest?

The economist's answer is "Yes." It is in the social interest because it makes everyone better off. There are no losers.

Efficiency and the Social Interest Economists use the everyday word "efficient" to describe a situation that can't be improved upon. Resource use is **efficient** if it is *not* possible to make someone better off without making someone else worse off. If it *is* possible to make someone better off without making anyone worse off, society can be made better off and the situation is not efficient.

In the Ted story everyone is better off, so it improves efficiency and the outcome is in the social interest. But notice that it would also have been efficient if the workers and customers had gained nothing and Ted had gained even more than $1 million a week. But would that efficient outcome be in the social interest?

Many people have trouble seeing the outcome in which Ted is the only winner as being in the social interest. They say that the social interest requires Ted to share some of his gain either with his workers in higher wages or with his customers in lower prices, or with both groups.

Fair Shares and the Social Interest The idea that the social interest requires "fair shares" is a deeply held one. Think about what you regard as a fair share. To help you, imagine the following game.

I put $100 on the table and tell someone you don't know and who doesn't know you to *propose* a share of the money between the two of you. If you *accept* the proposed share, you each get the agreed upon shares. If you don't accept the proposed share, you both get nothing.

It would be efficient—you would both be better off—if the proposer offered to take $99 and leave you with $1 and you accepted that offer.

But would you accept the $1? If you are like most people, the idea that the other person gets 99 times as much as you is just too much to stomach. "No way," you say and the $100 disappears. That outcome is inefficient. You have both given up something.

When the game I've just described is played in a classroom experiment, about half of the players reject offers of below $30.

So fair shares matter. But what is *fair*? There isn't a crisp definition of fairness to match that of efficiency. Reasonable people have a variety of views about it. Almost everyone agrees that too much inequality is unfair. But how much is too much? And inequality of what: income, wealth, or the *opportunity* to work, earn an income, and accumulate wealth?

You will examine efficiency again in Chapter 2 and efficiency and fairness in Chapter 5.

Questions about the social interest are hard ones to answer and they generate discussion, debate, and disagreement. Four issues in today's world put some flesh on these questions. The issues are:

- Globalization
- Information-age monopolies
- Climate change
- Financial instability

Globalization The term *globalization* means the expansion of international trade, borrowing and lending, and investment.

When Nike produces sports shoes, people in Malaysia get work; and when China Airlines buys new airplanes, Americans who work at Boeing in Seattle build them. While globalization brings expanded production and job opportunities for some workers, it destroys many American jobs. Workers across the manufacturing industries must learn new skills, take service jobs, which are often lower-paid, or retire earlier than previously planned.

Globalization is in the self-interest of those consumers who buy low-cost goods and services produced in other countries; and it is in the self-interest of the multinational firms that produce in low-cost regions and sell in high-price regions. But is globalization in the self-interest of the low-wage worker in Malaysia who sews your new running shoes and the displaced shoemaker in Atlanta? Is it in the social interest?

ECONOMICS IN THE NEWS

The Invisible Hand

From Brewer to Bio-Tech Entrepreneur

Kiran Mazumdar-Shaw trained to become a master brewer and learned about enzymes, the stuff from which bio-pharmaceuticals are made. Discovering it was impossible for a woman in India to become a master brewer, the 25-year-old Kiran decided to create a bio-pharmaceutical business.

Kiran's firm, Biocom, employed uneducated workers who loved their jobs and the living conditions made possible by their high wages. But when a labor union entered the scene and unionized the workers, a furious Kiran fired the workers, automated their jobs, and hired a smaller number of educated workers. Biocom continued to grow and today, Kiran's wealth exceeds $1 billion.

Kiran has become wealthy by developing and producing bio-pharmaceuticals that improve people's lives. But Kiran is sharing her wealth in creative ways. She has opened a cancer treatment center to help thousands of patients who are too poor to pay and created a health insurance scheme.

Source: Ariel Levy, "Drug Test,"
The New Yorker, January 2, 2012

THE QUESTIONS

- Whose decisions in the story were taken in self-interest?
- Whose decisions turned out to be in the social interest?
- Did any of the decisions harm the social interest?

THE ANSWERS

- All the decisions—Kiran's, the workers', the union's, and the firm's customers'—are taken in the pursuit of self-interest.
- Kiran's decisions serve the social interest: She creates jobs that benefit her workers and products that benefit her customers. And her charitable work brings yet further social benefits.
- The labor union's decision might have harmed the social interest because it destroyed the jobs of uneducated workers.

Kiran Mazumdar-Shaw, founder and CEO of Biocom

Information-Age Monopolies The technological change of the past forty years has been called the *Information Revolution*. Bill Gates, a co-founder of Microsoft, held a privileged position in this revolution. For many years, Windows was the only available operating system for the PC. The PC and Mac competed, but the PC had a huge market share.

An absence of competition gave Microsoft the power to sell Windows at prices far above the cost of production. With lower prices, many more people would have been able to afford and buy a computer.

The information revolution has clearly served your self-interest: It has provided your cellphone, laptop, loads of handy applications, and the Internet. It has also served the self-interest of Bill Gates who has seen his wealth soar.

But did the information revolution best serve the social interest? Did Microsoft produce the best possible Windows operating system and sell it at a price that was in the social interest? Or was the quality too low and the price too high?

Climate Change Burning fossil fuels to generate electricity and to power airplanes, automobiles, and trucks pours a staggering 28 billion tons—4 tons per person—of carbon dioxide into the atmosphere each year. These carbon emissions, two thirds of which comes from the United States, China, the European Union, Russia, and India, bring global warming and climate change.

Every day, when you make self-interested choices to use electricity and gasoline, you leave your carbon footprint. You can lessen this footprint by walking, riding a bike, taking a cold shower, or planting a tree.

But can each one of us be relied upon to make decisions that affect the Earth's carbon-dioxide concentration in the social interest? Must governments change the incentives we face so that our self-interested choices are also in the social interest? How can governments change incentives? How can we

encourage the use of wind and solar power to replace the burning of fossil fuels that brings climate change?

Financial Instability In 2008, banks were in trouble. They had made loans that borrowers couldn't repay and they were holding securities the values of which had crashed.

Banks' choices to take deposits and make loans are made in self-interest, but does this lending and borrowing serve the social interest? Do banks lend too much in the pursuit of profit?

When banks got into trouble in 2008, the Federal Reserve (the Fed) bailed them out with big loans backed by taxpayer dollars. Did the Fed's bailout of troubled banks serve the social interest? Or might the Fed's rescue action encourage banks to repeat their dangerous lending in the future?

We've looked at four topics and asked many questions that illustrate the potential conflict between the pursuit of self-interest and the social interest. We've asked questions but not answered them because we've not yet explained the economic principles needed to do so. We will answer these questions in future chapters.

◆ REVIEW QUIZ

1 Describe the broad facts about *what, how,* and *for whom* goods and services are produced.
2 Use headlines from the recent news to illustrate the potential for conflict between self-interest and the social interest.

Work these questions in Study Plan 1.2 and get instant feedback. Do a Key Terms Quiz. **MyEconLab**

AT **ISSUE**

The Protest Against Market Capitalism

Market capitalism is an economic system in which individuals own land and capital and are free to buy and sell land, capital, and goods and services in markets. Markets for goods and services, along with markets for land and capital, coordinate billions of self-interested choices, which determine what, how, and for whom goods and services are produced. A few people earn enormous incomes, many times the average income. There is no supreme planner guiding the use of scarce resources and the outcome is unintended and unforeseeable.

Centrally planned socialism is an economic system in which the government owns all the land and capital, directs workers to jobs, and decides what, how, and for whom to produce. The Soviet Union, several Eastern European countries, and China have used this system in the past but have now abandoned it. Only Cuba and North Korea use this system today. A few bureaucrats in positions of great power receive huge incomes, many times that of an average person.

Our economy today is a **mixed economy**, which is market capitalism with government regulation.

The **Protest**

The protest against market capitalism takes many forms. Historically, **Karl Marx** and other communist and socialist thinkers wanted to replace it with *socialism* and *central planning*. Today, thousands of people who feel let down by the economic system want less market capitalism and more government regulation. The **Occupy Wall Street** movement, with its focus on the large incomes of the top 1 percent, is a visible example of today's protest. Protesters say:

- Big corporations (especially big banks) have too much power and influence on governments.
- Democratically elected governments can do a better job of allocating resources and distributing income than uncoordinated markets.
- More regulation in the social interest is needed—to serve "human need, not corporate greed."
- In a market, for every winner, there is a loser.
- Big corporations are the winners. Workers and unemployed people are the losers.

The **Economist's Response**

Economists agree that market capitalism isn't perfect. But they argue that it is the best system available and while some government intervention and regulation can help, government attempts to serve the social interest often end up harming it.

Adam Smith (see p. 53), who gave the first systematic account of how market capitalism works, says:

- The self-interest of big corporations is *maximum profit*.
- But an *invisible hand* leads production decisions made in pursuit of self-interest to *unintentionally* promote the social interest.
- Politicians are ill-equipped to regulate corporations or to intervene in markets, and those who think they can improve on the market outcome are most likely wrong.
- In a market, buyers get what they want for less than they would be willing to pay and sellers earn a profit. Both buyers and sellers gain. A market transaction is a "win-win" event.

An Occupy Wall Street protester

"It is not from the benevolence of the butcher, the brewer, or the baker that we expect our dinner, but from their regard to their own interest."
The Wealth of Nations,
1776

Adam Smith

◢ The Economic Way of Thinking

The questions that economics tries to answer tell us about the *scope of economics,* but they don't tell us how economists *think* and go about seeking answers to these questions. You're now going to see how economists go about their work.

We're going to look at six key ideas that define the *economic way of thinking.* These ideas are

- A choice is a *tradeoff.*
- People make *rational choices* by comparing *benefits* and *costs.*
- *Benefit* is what you gain from something.
- *Cost* is what you *must give up* to get something.
- Most choices are "*how-much*" choices made at the *margin.*
- Choices respond to *incentives.*

A Choice Is a Tradeoff

Because we face scarcity, we must make choices. And when we make a choice, we select from the available alternatives. For example, you can spend Saturday night studying for your next economics test or having fun with your friends, but you can't do both of these activities at the same time. You must choose how much time to devote to each. Whatever choice you make, you could have chosen something else.

You can think about your choices as tradeoffs. A **tradeoff** is an exchange—giving up one thing to get something else. When you choose how to spend your Saturday night, you face a tradeoff between studying and hanging out with your friends.

Making a Rational Choice

Economists view the choices that people make as rational. A **rational choice** is one that compares costs and benefits and achieves the greatest benefit over cost for the person making the choice.

Only the wants of the person making a choice are relevant to determine its rationality. For example, you might like your coffee black and strong but your friend prefers his milky and sweet. So it is rational for you to choose espresso and for your friend to choose cappuccino.

The idea of rational choice provides an answer to the first question: *What* goods and services will be produced and in what quantities? The answer is those that people rationally choose to buy!

But how do people choose rationally? Why do more people choose an iPad rather than a Microsoft Surface? Why has the U.S. government chosen to build an interstate highway system and not an interstate high-speed railroad system? The answers turn on comparing benefits and costs.

Benefit: What You Gain

The **benefit** of something is the gain or pleasure that it brings and is determined by **preferences**—by what a person likes and dislikes and the intensity of those feelings. If you get a huge kick out of "League of Legends," that video game brings you a large benefit. If you have little interest in listening to Yo-Yo Ma playing a Vivaldi cello concerto, that activity brings you a small benefit.

Some benefits are large and easy to identify, such as the benefit that you get from being in school. A big piece of that benefit is the goods and services that you will be able to enjoy with the boost to your earning power when you graduate. Some benefits are small, such as the benefit you get from a slice of pizza.

Economists measure benefit as the most that a person is *willing to give up* to get something. You are willing to give up a lot to be in school. But you would give up only an iTunes download for a slice of pizza.

Cost: What You *Must* Give Up

The **opportunity cost** of something is the highest-valued alternative that must be given up to get it.

To make the idea of opportunity cost concrete, think about *your* opportunity cost of being in school. It has two components: the things you can't afford to buy and the things you can't do with your time.

Start with the things you can't afford to buy. You've spent all your income on tuition, residence fees, books, and a laptop. If you weren't in school, you would have spent this money on tickets to ball games and movies and all the other things that you enjoy. But that's only the start of your opportunity cost. You've also given up the opportunity to get a job. Suppose that the best job you could get if you weren't in school is working at Citibank as a teller earning $25,000 a year. Another part of your opportunity cost of being in school is all the things that you could buy with the extra $25,000 you would have.

As you well know, being a student eats up many hours in class time, doing homework assignments, preparing for tests, and so on. To do all these school activities, you must give up many hours of what would otherwise be leisure time spent with your friends.

So the opportunity cost of being in school is all the good things that you can't afford and don't have the spare time to enjoy. You might want to put a dollar value on that cost or you might just list all the items that make up the opportunity cost.

The examples of opportunity cost that we've just considered are all-or-nothing costs—you're either in school or not in school. Most situations are not like this one. They involve choosing *how much* of an activity to do.

How Much? Choosing at the Margin

You can allocate the next hour between studying and chatting online with your friends, but the choice is not all or nothing. You must decide how many minutes to allocate to each activity. To make this decision, you compare the benefit of a little bit more study time with its cost—you make your choice at the **margin**.

The benefit that arises from an increase in an activity is called **marginal benefit**. For example, your marginal benefit from one more night of study before a test is the boost it gives to your grade. Your marginal benefit doesn't include the grade you're already achieving without that extra night of work.

The *opportunity cost* of an *increase* in an activity is called **marginal cost**. For you, the marginal cost of studying one more night is the cost of not spending that night on your favorite leisure activity.

To make your decisions, you compare marginal benefit and marginal cost. If the marginal benefit from an extra night of study exceeds its marginal cost, you study the extra night. If the marginal cost exceeds the marginal benefit, you don't study the extra night.

Choices Respond to Incentives

Economists take human nature as given and view people as acting in their self-interest. All people—you, other consumers, producers, politicians, and public servants—pursue their self-interest.

Self-interested actions are not necessarily *selfish* actions. You might decide to use your resources in ways that bring pleasure to others as well as to yourself. But a self-interested act gets the most benefit for *you* based on *your* view about benefit.

The central idea of economics is that we can predict the self-interested choices that people make by looking at the *incentives* they face. People undertake those activities for which marginal benefit exceeds marginal cost; and they reject options for which marginal cost exceeds marginal benefit.

For example, your economics instructor gives you a problem set and tells you these problems will be on the next test. Your marginal benefit from working these problems is large, so you diligently work them. In contrast, your math instructor gives you a problem set on a topic that she says will never be on a test. You get little marginal benefit from working these problems, so you decide to skip most of them.

Economists see incentives as the key to reconciling self-interest and social interest. When our choices are *not* in the social interest, it is because of the incentives we face. One of the challenges for economists is to figure out the incentives that result in self-interested choices being in the social interest.

Economists emphasize the crucial role that institutions play in influencing the incentives that people face as they pursue their self-interest. Laws that protect private property and markets that enable voluntary exchange are the fundamental institutions. You will learn as you progress with your study of economics that where these institutions exist, self-interest can indeed promote the social interest.

▶ REVIEW QUIZ

1 Explain the idea of a tradeoff and think of three tradeoffs that you have made today.
2 Explain what economists mean by rational choice and think of three choices that you've made today that are rational.
3 Explain why opportunity cost is the best forgone alternative and provide examples of some opportunity costs that you have faced today.
4 Explain what it means to choose at the margin and illustrate with three choices at the margin that you have made today.
5 Explain why choices respond to incentives and think of three incentives to which you have responded today.

Work these questions in Study Plan 1.3 and get instant feedback. Do a Key Terms Quiz.   MyEconLab

▶ Economics as Social Science and Policy Tool

Economics is both a social science and a toolkit for advising on policy decisions.

Economist as Social Scientist

As social scientists, economists seek to discover how the economic world works. In pursuit of this goal, like all scientists, economists distinguish between positive and normative statements.

Positive Statements A *positive* statement is about what *is*. It says what is currently believed about the way the world operates. A positive statement might be right or wrong, but we can test it by checking it against the facts. "Our planet is warming because of the amount of coal that we're burning" is a positive statement. We can test whether it is right or wrong.

A central task of economists is to test positive statements about how the economic world works and to weed out those that are wrong. Economics first got off the ground in the late 1700s, so it is a young science compared with, for example, physics, and much remains to be discovered.

Normative Statements A *normative* statement is about what *ought to be*. It depends on values and cannot be tested. Policy goals are normative statements. For example, "We ought to cut our use of coal by 50 percent" is a normative policy statement. You may agree or disagree with it, but you can't test it. It doesn't assert a fact that can be checked.

Unscrambling Cause and Effect Economists are particularly interested in positive statements about cause and effect. Are computers getting cheaper because people are buying them in greater quantities? Or are people buying computers in greater quantities because they are getting cheaper? Or is some third factor causing both the price of a computer to fall and the quantity of computers bought to increase?

To answer such questions, economists create and test economic models. An **economic model** is a description of some aspect of the economic world that includes only those features that are needed for the purpose at hand. For example, an economic model of a cellphone network might include features such as the prices of calls, the number of cellphone users, and the volume of calls. But the model would ignore cellphone colors and ringtones.

A model is tested by comparing its predictions with the facts. But testing an economic model is difficult because we observe the outcomes of the simultaneous change of many factors. To cope with this problem, economists look for natural experiments (situations in the ordinary course of economic life in which the one factor of interest is different and other things are equal or similar); conduct statistical investigations to find correlations; and perform economic experiments by putting people in decision-making situations and varying the influence of one factor at a time to discover how they respond.

Economist as Policy Adviser

Economics is useful. It is a toolkit for advising governments and businesses and for making personal decisions. Some of the most famous economists work partly as policy advisers.

Carmen M. Reinhart at the John F. Kennedy School of Government, Harvard University, has written widely on policy issues arising from government debt and international capital markets.

Maurice Obstfeld of the University of California, Berkeley, and Betsey Stevenson of the University of Michigan are on leave from their academic jobs and serving as economic adviser to President Barack Obama and members of the President's Council of Economic Advisers.

All the policy questions on which economists provide advice involve a blend of the positive and the normative. Economics can't help with the normative part—the policy goal. But it can help to clarify the goal. And for a given goal, economics provides the tools for evaluating alternative solutions—comparing marginal benefits and marginal costs and finding the solution that makes the best use of the available resources.

▶ REVIEW QUIZ

1 Distinguish between a positive statement and a normative statement and provide examples.
2 What is a model? Can you think of a model that you might use in your everyday life?
3 How do economists try to disentangle cause and effect?
4 How is economics used as a policy tool?

Work these questions in Study Plan 1.4 and get instant feedback. Do a Key Terms Quiz.   MyEconLab

◆ ECONOMICS IN THE NEWS

The Internet for Everyone

Mark Zuckerberg's Big Idea: The "Next 5 Billion"
Facebook founder Mark Zuckerberg wants to make it so that anyone, anywhere, can get online. To achieve this goal, he has created internet.org, "a global partnership between technology leaders, nonprofits, local communities, and experts who are working together to bring the Internet to the two thirds of the world's population that doesn't have it."

Sources: *CNN Money*, August 21, 2013 and internet.org

THE DATA

- The figure shows that almost 80 percent of Americans and Canadians have Internet access compared to only 16 percent of Africans and 28 percent of Asians.

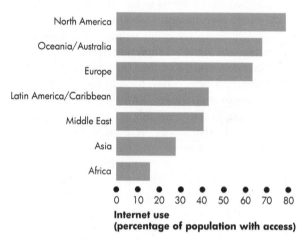

Internet Access by Region

- Of the 5 billion people who Mark Zuckerberg wants to have Internet access, 1 billion live in Africa and 2.8 billion live in Asia.
- To figure out what it would take for everyone to have Internet access, we must make an assumption about how many people share resources.
- If four people shared, it would cost about $285 billion for computers and $115 billion a year for Internet access for everyone to get online.
- Satisfying Mark Zuckerberg's want would cost the equivalent of 400 years of Facebook's 2012 profit, or 1,600 Boeing 787 Dreamliners, or 90 aircraft carriers, or 87 billion Big Macs.

THE QUESTIONS

- What is the fundamental economic problem and how does this news clip illustrate it?
- What are some of the things that might be forgone for more people to get online?
- Why don't more people make the tradeoffs needed to get online?
- Why might it be in Mark Zuckerberg's self-interest to get everyone online?
- Why might it not be in the social interest for everyone to get online?

In Africa, 4 in 5 people lack Internet access.

THE ANSWERS

- The fundamental economic problem is scarcity—the fact that wants exceed the resources available to satisfy them. The news clip illustrates scarcity because Mark Zuckerberg's want for everyone to get online *exceeds* the resources available to satisfy it.
- Some of the scarce resources that are used to produce airplanes, war ships, and Big Macs could be reallocated and used to produce more computers and Internet service.
- People don't make the tradeoffs needed to get online because for them, the marginal cost of doing so would exceed the marginal benefit.
- It might be in Mark Zuckerberg's self-interest to get everyone online because that would increase the number of Facebook users and increase the firm's advertising revenues.
- It would not be in the social interest to get everyone online if the marginal cost of an Internet connection exceeded its marginal benefit.

SUMMARY

Key Points

Definition of Economics (p. 2)

- All economic questions arise from scarcity—from the fact that wants exceed the resources available to satisfy them.
- Economics is the social science that studies the choices that people make as they cope with scarcity.
- The subject divides into microeconomics and macroeconomics.

Working Problem 1 will give you a better understanding of the definition of economics.

Two Big Economic Questions (pp. 3–8)

- Two big questions summarize the scope of economics:

  1. How do choices end up determining *what, how,* and *for whom* goods and services are produced?
  2. When do choices made in the pursuit of *self-interest* also promote the *social interest*?

Working Problems 2 and 3 will give you a better understanding of the two big questions of economics.

The Economic Way of Thinking (pp. 9–10)

- Every choice is a tradeoff—exchanging more of something for less of something else.
- People make rational choices by comparing benefit and cost.
- Cost—*opportunity cost*—is what you must give up to get something.
- Most choices are "how much" choices made at the *margin* by comparing marginal benefit and marginal cost.
- Choices respond to incentives.

Working Problems 4 and 5 will give you a better understanding of the economic way of thinking.

Economics as Social Science and Policy Tool (p. 11)

- Economists distinguish between positive statements—what is—and normative statements—what ought to be.
- To explain the economic world, economists create and test economic models.
- Economics is a toolkit used to provide advice on government, business, and personal economic decisions.

Working Problem 6 will give you a better understanding of economics as social science and policy tool.

Key Terms

MyEconLab Key Terms Quiz

Benefit, 9
Capital, 4
Economic model, 11
Economics, 2
Efficient, 5
Entrepreneurship, 4
Factors of production, 3
Goods and services, 3
Human capital, 3
Incentive, 2

Interest, 4
Labor, 3
Land, 3
Macroeconomics, 2
Margin, 10
Marginal benefit, 10
Marginal cost, 10
Microeconomics, 2
Opportunity cost, 9
Preferences, 9

Profit, 4
Rational choice, 9
Rent, 4
Scarcity, 2
Self-interest, 5
Social interest, 5
Tradeoff, 9
Wages, 4

STUDY PLAN PROBLEMS AND APPLICATIONS

MyEconLab   You can work Problems 1 to 6 in Chapter 1 Study Plan and get instant feedback.

Definition of Economics (Study Plan 1.1)

1. Apple Inc. decides to make iTunes freely available in unlimited quantities.
   a. Does Apple's decision change the incentives that people face?
   b. Is Apple's decision an example of a microeconomic or a macroeconomic issue?

Two Big Economic Questions (Study Plan 1.2)

2. Which of the following pairs does not match?
   a. Labor and wages
   b. Land and rent
   c. Entrepreneurship and profit
   d. Capital and profit

3. Explain how the following news headlines concern self-interest and the social interest.
   a. Starbucks Expands in China
   b. McDonald's Moves into Gourmet Coffee
   c. Food Must Be Labeled with Nutrition Data

The Economic Way of Thinking (Study Plan 1.3)

4. The night before an economics test, you decide to go to the movies instead of staying home and working your MyEconLab Study Plan. You get 50 percent on your test compared with the 70 percent that you normally score.
   a. Did you face a tradeoff?
   b. What was the opportunity cost of your evening at the movies?

5. **Cost of Sochi Winter Olympics**
   The Russian government spent $6.7 billion on Olympic facilities and $16.7 billion upgrading Sochi area infrastructure. Sponsors spent $27.6 billion on hotels and facilities hoping to turn Sochi into a year-round tourist magnet.
   Source: *The Washington Post*, February 11, 2014
   Was the opportunity cost of the Sochi Olympics $6.7, $23.4, or $51 billion? Explain your answer.

Economics as Social Science and Policy Tool
(Study Plan 1.4)

6. Which of the following statements is positive, which is normative, and which can be tested?
   a. The United States should cut its imports.
   b. China is the largest trading partner of the United States.
   c. If the price of antiretroviral drugs increases, HIV/AIDS sufferers will decrease their consumption of the drugs.

ADDITIONAL PROBLEMS AND APPLICATIONS

MyEconLab   You can work these problems in MyEconLab if assigned by your instructor.

Definition of Economics

7. **Rapper Offers Free Tickets for Concert**
   Eminem will hit the road with Rihanna offering an awesome deal—buy one and get one free!
   Source: *Mstars News*, February 24, 2014
   When Eminem gave away tickets, what was free and what was scarce? Explain your answer.

Two Big Economic Questions

8. How does the creation of a successful movie influence *what, how*, and *for whom* goods and services are produced?

9. How does a successful movie illustrate self-interested choices that are also in the social interest?

The Economic Way of Thinking

10. Before starring in *Iron Man*, Robert Downey Jr. had appeared in 45 movies that grossed an average of $5 million on the opening weekend. In contrast, *Iron Man* grossed $102 million.
    a. How will the success of *Iron Man* influence the opportunity cost of hiring Robert Downey Jr.?
    b. How have the incentives for a movie producer to hire Robert Downey Jr. changed?

11. What might be an incentive for you to take a class in summer school? List some of the benefits and costs involved in your decision. Would your choice be rational?

Economics as Social Science and Policy Tool

12. Look at today's *Wall Street Journal*. What is the leading economic news story? With which of the big economic questions does it deal and what tradeoffs does it discuss or imply?

13. Provide two microeconomic statements and two macroeconomic statements. Classify your statements as positive or normative, and explain your classifications.

APPENDIX

Graphs in Economics

After studying this appendix, you will be able to:

◆ Make and interpret a scatter diagram
◆ Identify linear and nonlinear relationships and relationships that have a maximum and a minimum
◆ Define and calculate the slope of a line
◆ Graph relationships among more than two variables

Graphing Data

A graph represents a quantity as a distance on a line. In Fig. A1.1, a distance on the horizontal line represents temperature, measured in degrees Fahrenheit. A movement from left to right shows an increase in temperature. The point 0 represents zero degrees Fahrenheit. To the right of 0, the temperature is positive. To the left of 0, the temperature is negative (as indicated by the minus sign). A distance on the vertical line represents height, measured in thousands of feet. The point 0 represents sea level. Points above 0 represent feet above sea level. Points below 0 represent feet below sea level (indicated by a minus sign).

In Fig. A1.1, the two scale lines are perpendicular to each other and are called *axes*. The vertical line is the *y*-axis, and the horizontal line is the *x*-axis. Each axis has a zero point, which is shared by the two axes and called the *origin*.

To make a two-variable graph, we need two pieces of information: the value of the variable *x* and the value of the variable *y*. For example, off the coast of Alaska, the temperature is 32 degrees—the value of *x*. A fishing boat is located at 0 feet above sea level—the value of *y*. These two bits of information appear as point *A* in Fig. A1.1. A climber at the top of Mount McKinley on a cold day is 20,320 feet above sea level in a zero-degree gale. These two pieces of information appear as point *B*. On a warmer day, a climber might be at the peak of Mt. McKinley when the temperature is 32 degrees, at point *C*.

We can draw two lines, called *coordinates*, from point *C*. One, called the *x*-coordinate, runs from *C* to the vertical axis. This line is called "the *x*-coordinate"

FIGURE A1.1   Making a Graph

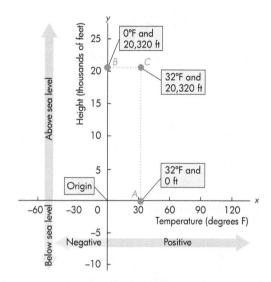

Graphs have axes that measure quantities as distances. Here, the horizontal axis (*x*-axis) measures temperature, and the vertical axis (*y*-axis) measures height. Point *A* represents a fishing boat at sea level (0 on the *y*-axis) on a day when the temperature is 32°F. Point *B* represents a climber at the top of Mt. McKinley, 20,320 feet above sea level at a temperature of 0°F. Point *C* represents a climber at the top of Mt. McKinley, 20,320 feet above sea level at a temperature of 32°F.

MyEconLab Animation

because its length is the same as the value marked off on the *x*-axis. The other, called the *y*-coordinate, runs from *C* to the horizontal axis. This line is called "the *y*-coordinate" because its length is the same as the value marked off on the *y*-axis.

We describe a point on a graph by the values of its *x*-coordinate and its *y*-coordinate. For example, at point *C, x* is 32 degrees and *y* is 20,320 feet.

A graph like that in Fig. A1.1 can be made using any quantitative data on two variables. The graph can show just a few points, like Fig. A1.1, or many points. Before we look at graphs with many points, let's reinforce what you've just learned by looking at two graphs made with economic data.

Economists measure variables that describe *what, how,* and *for whom* goods and services are produced. These variables are quantities produced and prices. Figure A1.2 shows two examples of economic graphs.

FIGURE A1.2   Two Graphs of Economic Data

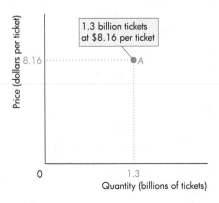

(a) Movie tickets: quantity and price

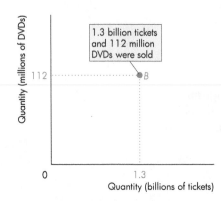

(b) Movies: tickets and DVDs

The graph in part (a) tells us that in 2013, 1.3 billion movie tickets were sold at an average price of $8.16 per ticket.

The graph in part (b) tells us that in 2013, 1.3 billion movie tickets and 112 million DVDs were sold.

Figure A1.2(a) is a graph about movies in 2013. The *x*-axis measures the quantity of movie tickets sold and the *y*-axis measures the average price of a ticket. Point *A* tells us what the quantity and price were. You can "read" this graph as telling you that in 2013, 1.3 billion movie tickets were sold at an average ticket price of $8.16.

Figure A1.2(b) is a graph about movie-going and DVD buying. The *x*-axis measures the quantity of movie tickets sold in 2013 and the *y*-axis measures the quantity of DVDs sold in the same year. Point *B* tells us what these quantities were. You can "read" this graph as telling you that in 2013, 1.3 billion movie tickets and 112 million DVDs were sold.

The three graphs that you've just seen tell you how to make a graph and how to read a data point on a graph, but they don't improve on the raw data. Graphs become interesting and revealing when they contain a number of data points because then you can visualize the data.

Economists create graphs based on the principles in Figs. A1.1 and A1.2 to reveal, describe, and visualize the relationships among variables. We're now going to look at some examples. These graphs are called scatter diagrams.

Scatter Diagrams

A **scatter diagram** is a graph that plots the value of one variable against the value of another variable for a number of different values of each variable. Such a graph reveals whether a relationship exists between two variables and describes their relationship.

The table in Fig. A1.3 shows some data on two variables: the number of tickets sold at the box office and the number of DVDs sold for nine of the most popular movies in 2013.

What is the relationship between these two variables? Does a big box office success generate a large volume of DVD sales? Or does a box office success mean that fewer DVDs are sold?

We can answer these questions by making a scatter diagram. We do so by graphing the data in the table. In the graph in Fig. A1.3, each point shows the number of box office tickets sold (the *x* variable) and the number of DVDs sold (the *y* variable) of one of the movies. There are nine movies, so there are nine points "scattered" within the graph.

The point labeled *A* tells us that *Monsters University* sold 33 million tickets at the box office and 2.3 million DVDs. The points in the graph don't form a distinct pattern. They suggest that large box office sales do not directly bring large DVD sales. If you want to predict a movie's DVD sales in a given year with any confidence, you need to know more than the number of tickets sold at the box office in that year.

Figure A1.4 shows two scatter diagrams of economic variables. Part (a) shows the relationship between income and expenditure, on average, from 2001 to 2013. Each point represents income and expenditure in a given year. For example, point *A* shows that in 2006, income was $38,000 and expenditure was $31,000. This graph shows that as income increases, so does expenditure, and the relationship is a close one.

FIGURE A1.3 A Scatter Diagram

Movie	Tickets	DVDs
	(millions)	
Iron Man 3	50	1.1
The Hunger Games: Catching Fire	49	1.3
Despicable Me 2	45	1.8
Man of Steel	36	1.2
Frozen	34	0
Monsters University	33	2.3
Gravity	31	0
Fast and Furious 6	29	0
Oz the Great and Powerful	29	1.4

The table lists the number of tickets sold at the box office and the number of DVDs sold for nine popular movies.

The scatter diagram reveals the relationship between these two variables. Each point shows the values of the variables for a specific movie. For example, point A shows the point for *Monsters University*, which sold 33 million tickets and 2.3 million DVDs.

The pattern formed by the points shows no tendency for large box office sales to bring greater DVD sales. You cannot predict how many DVDs of a movie will sell in a given year just by knowing its box office sales in that year.

—— MyEconLab Animation ——

Figure A1.4(b) shows a scatter diagram of U.S. inflation and unemployment from 2001 through 2013. Here, the points show no relationship between the two variables. For example, when unemployment was high, the inflation rate was high in 2009 and low in 2010.

You can see that a scatter diagram conveys a wealth of information, and it does so in much less space than we have used to describe only some of its features. But you do have to "read" the graph to obtain all this information.

FIGURE A1.4 Two Economic Scatter Diagrams

(a) Income and expenditure

(b) Unemployment and inflation

The scatter diagram in part (a) shows the relationship between income and expenditure from 2001 to 2013. Point A shows that in 2006, income was $38,000 on the x-axis and expenditure was $31,000 on the y-axis. This graph shows that as income rises, so does expenditure and the relationship is a close one.

The scatter diagram in part (b) shows a weak relationship between unemployment and inflation in the United States during most of the years.

—— MyEconLab Animation ——

Breaks in the Axes The graph in Fig. A1.4(a) has breaks in its axes, as shown by the small gaps. The breaks indicate that there are jumps from the origin, 0, to the first values recorded.

The breaks are used because the lowest value of income is $30,000 and the lowest value of expenditure exceeds $25,000. If we made this graph with no breaks in its axes, there would be a lot of empty space, the points would be crowded into the top right corner, and it would be difficult to see whether a relationship exists between these two variables. By breaking the axes, we are able to bring the relationship into view.

Putting a break in one or both axes is like using a zoom lens to bring the relationship into the center of the graph and magnify it so that the relationship fills the graph.

Misleading Graphs Breaks can be used to highlight a relationship, but they can also be used to mislead—to make a graph that lies. The most common way of making a graph lie is to put a break in the axis and either to stretch or compress the scale. For example, suppose that in Fig. A1.4(a), we remove the break on the *y*-axis and expenditure ran from zero to $40,000 while the *x*-axis was unchanged. The graph would now create the impression that despite a huge increase in income, expenditure had barely changed.

To avoid being misled, it is a good idea to get into the habit of always looking closely at the values and the labels on the axes of a graph before you start to interpret it.

Correlation and Causation A scatter diagram that shows a clear relationship between two variables, such as Fig. A1.4(a), tells us that the two variables have a high correlation. When a high correlation is present, we can predict the value of one variable from the value of the other variable. But correlation does not imply causation.

Sometimes a high correlation does arise from a causal relationship. It is likely that rising income causes rising expenditure (Fig. A1.4a). But a high correlation can mean that two variables have a common cause. For example, ice cream sales and pool drownings are correlated not because one causes the other, but because both are caused by hot weather.

You've now seen how we can use graphs in economics to show economic data and to reveal relationships. Next, we'll learn how economists use graphs to construct and display economic models.

Graphs Used in Economic Models

The graphs used in economics are not always designed to show real-world data. Often they are used to show general relationships among the variables in an economic model.

An *economic model* is a stripped-down, simplified description of an economy or of a component of an economy such as a business or a household. It consists of statements about economic behavior that can be expressed as equations or as curves in a graph. Economists use models to explore the effects of different policies or other influences on the economy in ways that are similar to the use of model airplanes in wind tunnels and models of the climate.

You will encounter many different kinds of graphs in economic models, but there are some repeating patterns. Once you've learned to recognize these patterns, you will instantly understand the meaning of a graph. Here, we'll look at the different types of curves that are used in economic models, and we'll see some everyday examples of each type of curve. The patterns to look for in graphs are the four cases in which

- Variables move in the same direction.
- Variables move in opposite directions.
- Variables have a maximum or a minimum.
- Variables are unrelated.

Let's look at these four cases.

Variables That Move in the Same Direction

Figure A1.5 shows graphs of the relationships between two variables that move up and down together. A relationship between two variables that move in the same direction is called a **positive relationship** or a **direct relationship**. A line that slopes upward shows such a relationship.

Figure A1.5 shows three types of relationships: one that has a straight line and two that have curved lines. All the lines in these three graphs are called curves. Any line on a graph—no matter whether it is straight or curved—is called a *curve*.

A relationship shown by a straight line is called a **linear relationship**. Figure A1.5(a) shows a linear relationship between the number of miles traveled in

FIGURE A1.5   Positive (Direct) Relationships

(a) Positive linear relationship

(b) Positive, becoming steeper

(c) Positive, becoming less steep

Each part shows a positive (direct) relationship between two variables. That is, as the value of the variable measured on the x-axis increases, so does the value of the variable measured on the y-axis. Part (a) shows a linear positive relationship—as the two variables increase together, we move along a straight line.

Part (b) shows a positive relationship such that as the two variables increase together, we move along a curve that becomes steeper.

Part (c) shows a positive relationship such that as the two variables increase together, we move along a curve that becomes flatter.

MyEconLab Animation

5 hours and speed. For example, point A shows that you will travel 200 miles in 5 hours if your speed is 40 miles an hour. If you double your speed to 80 miles an hour, you will travel 400 miles in 5 hours.

Figure A1.5(b) shows the relationship between distance sprinted and recovery time (the time it takes the heart rate to return to its normal resting rate). This relationship is an upward-sloping one that starts out quite flat but then becomes steeper as we move along the curve away from the origin. The reason this curve becomes steeper is that the additional recovery time needed from sprinting an additional 100 yards increases. It takes less than 5 minutes to recover from sprinting 100 yards but more than 10 minutes to recover from 200 yards.

Figure A1.5(c) shows the relationship between the number of problems worked by a student and the amount of study time. This relationship is an upward-sloping one that starts out quite steep and becomes flatter as we move along the curve away from the origin. Study time becomes less productive as the student spends more hours studying and becomes more tired.

Variables That Move in Opposite Directions

Figure A1.6 shows relationships between things that move in opposite directions. A relationship between variables that move in opposite directions is called a **negative relationship** or an **inverse relationship**.

Figure A1.6(a) shows the relationship between the hours spent playing squash and the hours spent playing tennis when the total time available is 5 hours. One extra hour spent playing tennis means one hour less spent playing squash and vice versa. This relationship is negative and linear.

Figure A1.6(b) shows the relationship between the cost per mile traveled and the length of a journey. The longer the journey, the lower is the cost per mile. But as the journey length increases, even though the cost per mile decreases, the fall in the cost per mile is smaller the longer the journey. This feature of the relationship is shown by the fact that the curve slopes downward, starting out steep at a short journey length and then becoming flatter as the journey length increases. This relationship arises because some of the costs are fixed, such as auto insurance, and the fixed costs are spread over a longer journey.

FIGURE A1.6   Negative (Inverse) Relationships

(a) Negative linear relationship   **(b) Negative, becoming less steep**   **(c) Negative, becoming steeper**

Each part shows a negative (inverse) relationship between two variables. Part (a) shows a linear negative relationship. The total time spent playing tennis and squash is 5 hours. As the time spent playing tennis increases, the time spent playing squash decreases, and we move along a straight line.

Part (b) shows a negative relationship such that as the journey length increases, the travel cost decreases as we move along a curve that becomes less steep.

Part (c) shows a negative relationship such that as leisure time increases, the number of problems worked decreases as we move along a curve that becomes steeper.

MyEconLab Animation

Figure A1.6(c) shows the relationship between the amount of leisure time and the number of problems worked by a student. Increasing leisure time produces an increasingly large reduction in the number of problems worked. This relationship is a negative one that starts out with a gentle slope at a small number of leisure hours and becomes steeper as the number of leisure hours increases. This relationship is a different view of the idea shown in Fig. A1.5(c).

Variables That Have a Maximum or a Minimum

Many relationships in economic models have a maximum or a minimum. For example, firms try to make the maximum possible profit and to produce at the lowest possible cost. Figure A1.7 shows relationships that have a maximum or a minimum.

Figure A1.7(a) shows the relationship between rainfall and wheat yield. When there is no rainfall, wheat will not grow, so the yield is zero. As the rainfall increases up to 10 days a month, the wheat yield increases. With 10 rainy days each month, the wheat yield reaches its maximum at 40 bushels an acre (point *A*). Rain in excess of 10 days a month starts to lower the yield of wheat. If every day is rainy, the wheat suffers from a lack of sunshine and the yield decreases to zero. This relationship is one that starts out sloping upward, reaches a maximum, and then slopes downward.

Figure A1.7(b) shows the reverse case—a relationship that begins sloping downward, falls to a minimum, and then slopes upward. Most economic costs are like this relationship. An example is the relationship between the cost per mile and the speed of the car. At low speeds, the car is creeping in a traffic snarl-up. The number of miles per gallon is low, so the cost per mile is high. At high speeds, the car is traveling faster than its efficient speed, using a large quantity of gasoline, and again the number of miles per gallon is low and the cost per mile is high. At a speed of 55 miles an hour, the cost per mile is at its minimum (point *B*). This relationship is one that starts out sloping downward, reaches a minimum, and then slopes upward.

FIGURE A1.7   Maximum and Minimum Points

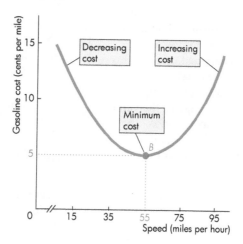

(a) Relationship with a maximum

(b) Relationship with a minimum

Part (a) shows a relationship that has a maximum point, *A*. The curve slopes upward as it rises to its maximum point, is flat at its maximum, and then slopes downward.

Part (b) shows a relationship with a minimum point, *B*. The curve slopes downward as it falls to its minimum, is flat at its minimum, and then slopes upward.

MyEconLab Animation

Variables That Are Unrelated

There are many situations in which no matter what happens to the value of one variable, the other variable remains constant. Sometimes we want to show the independence between two variables in a graph, and Fig. A1.8 shows two ways of achieving this.

In describing the graphs in Fig. A1.5 through Fig. A1.7, we have talked about curves that slope upward or slope downward, and curves that become less steep or steeper. Let's spend a little time discussing exactly what we mean by *slope* and how we measure the slope of a curve.

FIGURE A1.8   Variables That Are Unrelated

(a) Unrelated: *y* constant

(b) Unrelated: *x* constant

This figure shows how we can graph two variables that are unrelated. In part (a), a student's grade in economics is plotted at 75 percent on the *y*-axis regardless of the price of bananas on the *x*-axis. The curve is horizontal.

In part (b), the output of the vineyards of France on the *x*-axis does not vary with the rainfall in California on the *y*-axis. The curve is vertical.

MyEconLab Animation

The Slope of a Relationship

We can measure the influence of one variable on another by the slope of the relationship. The **slope** of a relationship is the change in the value of the variable measured on the *y*-axis divided by the change in the value of the variable measured on the *x*-axis. We use the Greek letter Δ (*delta*) to represent "change in." Thus Δ*y* means the change in the value of the variable measured on the *y*-axis, and Δ*x* means the change in the value of the variable measured on the *x*-axis. Therefore the slope of the relationship is

$$\text{Slope} = \frac{\Delta y}{\Delta x}.$$

If a large change in the variable measured on the *y*-axis (Δ*y*) is associated with a small change in the variable measured on the *x*-axis (Δ*x*), the slope is large and the curve is steep. If a small change in the variable measured on the *y*-axis (Δ*y*) is associated with a large change in the variable measured on the *x*-axis (Δ*x*), the slope is small and the curve is flat.

We can make the idea of slope clearer by doing some calculations.

The Slope of a Straight Line

The slope of a straight line is the same regardless of where on the line you calculate it. The slope of a straight line is constant. Let's calculate the slope of the positive relationship in Fig. A1.9. In part (a),

---

FIGURE A1.9   The Slope of a Straight Line

(a) Positive slope

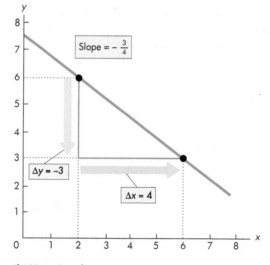

(b) Negative slope

To calculate the slope of a straight line, we divide the change in the value of the variable measured on the *y*-axis (Δ*y*) by the change in the value of the variable measured on the *x*-axis (Δ*x*) as we move along the line.

Part (a) shows the calculation of a positive slope. When *x* increases from 2 to 6, Δ*x* equals 4. That change in *x* brings about an increase in *y* from 3 to 6, so Δ*y* equals 3. The slope (Δ*y*/Δ*x*) equals 3/4.

Part (b) shows the calculation of a negative slope. When *x* increases from 2 to 6, Δ*x* equals 4. That increase in *x* brings about a decrease in *y* from 6 to 3, so Δ*y* equals –3. The slope (Δ*y*/Δ*x*) equals –3/4.

when x increases from 2 to 6, y increases from 3 to 6. The change in x is +4—that is, Δx is 4. The change in y is +3—that is, Δy is 3. The slope of that line is

$$\frac{\Delta y}{\Delta x} = \frac{3}{4}.$$

In part (b), when x increases from 2 to 6, y decreases from 6 to 3. The change in y is *minus 3*—that is, Δy is -3. The change in x is *plus 4*—that is, Δx is 4. The slope of the curve is

$$\frac{\Delta y}{\Delta x} = \frac{-3}{4}.$$

Notice that the two slopes have the same magnitude (3/4), but the slope of the line in part (a) is positive (+3/+4 = 3/4) while that in part (b) is negative ($-3/+4 = -3/4$). The slope of a positive relationship is positive; the slope of a negative relationship is negative.

The Slope of a Curved Line

The slope of a curved line is trickier. The slope of a curved line is not constant, so the slope depends on where on the curved line we calculate it. There are two ways to calculate the slope of a curved line: You can calculate the slope at a point, or you can calculate the slope across an arc of the curve. Let's look at the two alternatives.

Slope at a Point To calculate the slope at a point on a curve, you need to construct a straight line that has the same slope as the curve at the point in question. Figure A1.10 shows how this is done. Suppose you want to calculate the slope of the curve at point A. Place a ruler on the graph so that the ruler touches point A and no other point on the curve, then draw a straight line along the edge of the ruler. The straight red line is this line, and it is the tangent to the curve at point A. If the ruler touches the curve only at point A, then the slope of the curve at point A must be the same as the slope of the edge of the ruler. If the curve and the ruler do not have the same slope, the line along the edge of the ruler will cut the curve instead of just touching it.

Now that you have found a straight line with the same slope as the curve at point A, you can calculate the slope of the curve at point A by calculating the slope of the straight line. Along the straight line, as x

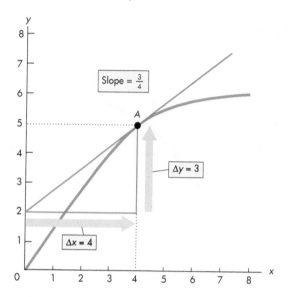

FIGURE A1.10 Slope at a Point

Slope = $\frac{3}{4}$

$\Delta y = 3$

$\Delta x = 4$

To calculate the slope of the curve at point A, draw the red line that just touches the curve at A—the tangent. The slope of this straight line is calculated by dividing the change in y by the change in x along the red line. When x increases from 0 to 4, Δx equals 4. That change in x is associated with an increase in y from 2 to 5, so Δy equals 3. The slope of the red line is 3/4, so the slope of the curve at point A is 3/4.

MyEconLab Animation

increases from 0 to 4 (Δx is 4) y increases from 2 to 5 (Δy is 3). Therefore the slope of the straight line is

$$\frac{\Delta y}{\Delta x} = \frac{3}{4}.$$

So the slope of the curve at point A is 3/4.

Slope Across an Arc An arc of a curve is a piece of a curve. Figure A1.11 shows the same curve as in Fig. A1.10, but instead of calculating the slope at point A, we are now going to calculate the slope across the arc from point B to point C. You can see that the slope of the curve at point B is greater than at point C. When we calculate the slope across an arc, we are calculating the average slope between two points. As we move along the arc from B to C, x increases from 3 to 5 and y increases from 4.0 to 5.5. The change in x is 2 (Δx is 2), and the change in y is 1.5 (Δy is 1.5).

FIGURE A1.11   Slope Across an Arc

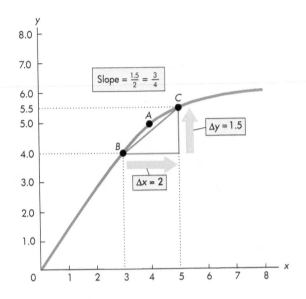

To calculate the average slope of the curve along the arc *BC*, draw a straight line from point *B* to point *C*. The slope of the line *BC* is calculated by dividing the change in *y* by the change in *x*. In moving from *B* to *C*, the increase in *x* is 2 (Δ*x* equals 2) and the change in *y* is 1.5 (Δ*y* equals 1.5). The slope of the line *BC* is 1.5 divided by 2, or 3/4. So the slope of the curve across the arc *BC* is 3/4.

MyEconLab Animation

Therefore the slope is

$$\frac{\Delta y}{\Delta x} = \frac{1.5}{2} = \frac{3}{4}.$$

So the slope of the curve across the arc *BC* is 3/4.

This calculation gives us the slope of the curve between points *B* and *C*. The actual slope calculated is the slope of the straight line from *B* to *C*. This slope approximates the average slope of the curve along the arc *BC*. In this particular example, the slope across the arc *BC* is identical to the slope of the curve at point *A*, but the calculation of the slope of a curve does not always work out so neatly. You might have fun constructing some more examples and a few counterexamples.

You now know how to make and interpret a graph. So far, we've limited our attention to graphs of two variables. We're now going to learn how to graph more than two variables.

Graphing Relationships Among More Than Two Variables

We have seen that we can graph the relationship between two variables as a point formed by the *x*- and *y*-coordinates in a two-dimensional graph. You might be thinking that although a two-dimensional graph is informative, most of the things in which you are likely to be interested involve relationships among many variables, not just two. For example, the amount of ice cream consumed depends on the price of ice cream and the temperature. If ice cream is expensive and the temperature is low, people eat much less ice cream than when ice cream is inexpensive and the temperature is high. For any given price of ice cream, the quantity consumed varies with the temperature; and for any given temperature, the quantity of ice cream consumed varies with its price.

Figure A1.12 shows a relationship among three variables. The table shows the number of gallons of ice cream consumed each day at two different temperatures and at a number of different prices of ice cream. How can we graph these numbers?

To graph a relationship that involves more than two variables, we use the *ceteris paribus* assumption.

Ceteris Paribus

Ceteris paribus (often shortened to *cet par*) means "if all other relevant things remain the same." To isolate the relationship of interest in a laboratory experiment, a scientist holds everything constant except for the variable whose effect is being studied. Economists use the same method to graph a relationship that has more than two variables.

Figure A1.12 shows an example. There, you can see what happens to the quantity of ice cream consumed when the price of ice cream varies but the temperature is held constant.

The curve labeled 70°F shows the relationship between ice cream consumption and the price of ice cream if the temperature remains at 70°F. The numbers used to plot that curve are those in the first two columns of the table. For example, if the temperature is 70°F, 10 gallons are consumed when the price is $2.75 a scoop and 18 gallons are consumed when the price is $2.25 a scoop.

The curve labeled 90°F shows the relationship between ice cream consumption and the price of ice cream if the temperature remains at 90°F. The

FIGURE A1.12   Graphing a Relationship Among Three Variables

Price (dollars per scoop)	Ice cream consumption (gallons per day)	
	70°F	90°F
2.00	25	50
2.25	18	36
2.50	13	26
2.75	**10**	**20**
3.00	7	14
3.25	5	10
3.50	3	6

Ice cream consumption depends on its price and the temperature. The table tells us how many gallons of ice cream are consumed each day at different prices and two different temperatures. For example, if the price is $2.75 a scoop and the temperature is 70°F, 10 gallons of ice cream are consumed.

To graph a relationship among three variables, the value of one variable is held constant. The graph shows the relationship between price and consumption when temperature is held constant. One curve holds temperature at 70°F and the other holds it at 90°F.

A change in the price of ice cream brings a movement along one of the curves—along the blue curve at 70°F and along the red curve at 90°F.

When the temperature *rises* from 70°F to 90°F, the curve that shows the relationship between consumption and price *shifts* rightward from the blue curve to the red curve.

MyEconLab Animation

numbers used to plot that curve are those in the first and third columns of the table. For example, if the temperature is 90°F, 20 gallons are consumed when the price is $2.75 a scoop and 36 gallons are consumed when the price is $2.25 a scoop.

When the price of ice cream changes but the temperature is constant, you can think of what happens in the graph as a movement along one of the curves. At 70°F there is a movement along the blue curve and at 90°F there is a movement along the red curve.

When Other Things Change

The temperature is held constant along each of the curves in Fig. A1.12, but in reality the temperature changes. When that event occurs, you can think of what happens in the graph as a shift of the curve. When the temperature rises from 70°F to 90°F, the curve that shows the relationship between ice cream consumption and the price of ice cream shifts rightward from the blue curve to the red curve.

You will encounter these ideas of movements along and shifts of curves at many points in your study of economics. Think carefully about what you've just learned and make up some examples (with assumed numbers) about other relationships.

With what you have learned about graphs, you can move forward with your study of economics. There are no graphs in this book that are more complicated than those that have been explained in this appendix.

MATHEMATICAL NOTE

Equations of Straight Lines

If a straight line in a graph describes the relationship between two variables, we call it a linear relationship. Figure 1 shows the *linear relationship* between a person's expenditure and income. This person spends $100 a week (by borrowing or spending previous savings) when income is zero. Out of each dollar earned, this person spends 50 cents (and saves 50 cents).

All linear relationships are described by the same general equation. We call the quantity that is measured on the horizontal axis (or x-axis) *x,* and we call the quantity that is measured on the vertical axis (or y-axis) *y*. In the case of Fig. 1, *x* is income and *y* is expenditure.

A Linear Equation

The equation that describes a straight-line relationship between *x* and *y* is

$$y = a + bx.$$

In this equation, *a* and *b* are fixed numbers and they are called *constants*. The values of *x* and *y* vary, so these numbers are called *variables*. Because the equation describes a straight line, the equation is called a *linear equation*.

The equation tells us that when the value of *x* is zero, the value of *y* is *a*. We call the constant *a* the *y*-axis intercept. The reason is that on the graph the straight line hits the *y*-axis at a value equal to *a*. Figure 1 illustrates the *y*-axis intercept.

For positive values of *x*, the value of *y* exceeds *a*. The constant *b* tells us by how much *y* increases above *a* as *x* increases. The constant *b* is the slope of the line.

Slope of Line

As we explain in the chapter, the *slope* of a relationship is the change in the value of *y* divided by the change in the value of *x*. We use the Greek letter Δ (delta) to represent "change in." So Δy means the change in the value of the variable measured on the *y*-axis, and Δx means the change in the value of the variable measured on the *x*-axis. Therefore the slope of the relationship is

$$\text{Slope} = \frac{\Delta y}{\Delta x}.$$

To see why the slope is *b*, suppose that initially the value of *x* is x_1, or $200 in Fig. 2. The corresponding value of *y* is y_1, also $200 in Fig. 2. The equation of the line tells us that

$$y_1 = a + bx_1. \tag{1}$$

Now the value of *x* increases by Δx to $x_1 + \Delta x$ (or $400 in Fig. 2). And the value of *y* increases by Δy to $y_1 + \Delta y$ (or $300 in Fig. 2).

The equation of the line now tells us that

$$y_1 + \Delta y = a + b(x_1 + \Delta x). \tag{2}$$

Figure 1 Linear Relationship

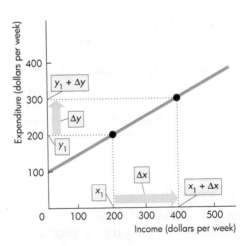

Figure 2 Calculating Slope

To calculate the slope of the line, subtract equation (1) from equation (2) to obtain

$$\Delta y = b\Delta x \qquad (3)$$

and now divide equation (3) by Δx to obtain

$$\Delta y / \Delta x = b.$$

So the slope of the line is b.

Position of Line

The y-axis intercept determines the position of the line on the graph. Figure 3 illustrates the relationship between the y-axis intercept and the position of the line. In this graph, the y-axis measures saving and the x-axis measures income.

When the y-axis intercept, a, is positive, the line hits the y-axis at a positive value of y—as the blue line does. Its y-axis intercept is 100. When the y-axis intercept, a, is zero, the line hits the y-axis at the origin—as the purple line does. Its y-axis intercept is 0. When the y-axis intercept, a, is negative, the line hits the y-axis at a negative value of y—as the red line does. Its y-axis intercept is −100.

As the equations of the three lines show, the value of the y-axis intercept does not influence the slope of the line. All three lines have a slope equal to 0.5.

Positive Relationships

Figure 1 shows a positive relationship—the two variables x and y move in the same direction. All positive relationships have a slope that is positive. In the equation of the line, the constant b is positive. In this example, the y-axis intercept, a, is 100. The slope b equals $\Delta y / \Delta x$, which in Fig. 2 is 100/200 or 0.5. The equation of the line is

$$y = 100 + 0.5x.$$

Negative Relationships

Figure 4 shows a negative relationship—the two variables x and y move in the opposite direction. All negative relationships have a slope that is negative. In the equation of the line, the constant b is negative. In the example in Fig. 4, the y-axis intercept, a, is 30. The slope, b, equals $\Delta y / \Delta x$, which is −20/2 or −10. The equation of the line is

$$y = 30 + (-10)x$$

or

$$y = 30 - 10x.$$

Example

A straight line has a y-axis intercept of 50 and a slope of 2. What is the equation of this line? The equation of a straight line is

$$y = a + bx$$

where a is the y-axis intercept and b is the slope. So the equation is

$$y = 50 + 2x.$$

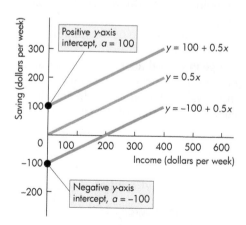

Figure 3 The y-Axis Intercept

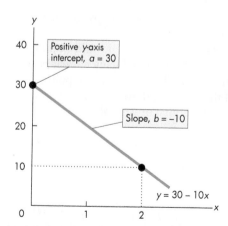

Figure 4 Negative Relationship

◆ REVIEW QUIZ

1 Explain how we "read" the three graphs in Figs. A1.1 and A1.2.
2 Explain what scatter diagrams show and why we use them.
3 Explain how we "read" the three scatter diagrams in Figs. A1.3 and A1.4.
4 Draw a graph to show the relationship between two variables that move in the same direction.
5 Draw a graph to show the relationship between two variables that move in opposite directions.
6 Draw a graph of two variables whose relationship shows (i) a maximum and (ii) a minimum.
7 Which of the relationships in Questions 4 and 5 is a positive relationship and which is a negative relationship?
8 What are the two ways of calculating the slope of a curved line?
9 How do we graph a relationship among more than two variables?
10 Explain what change will bring a *movement along* a curve.
11 Explain what change will bring a *shift* of a curve.

Work these questions in Study Plan 1A and get instant feedback.   MyEconLab

◆ SUMMARY

Key Points

Graphing Data (pp. 15–18)

- A graph is made by plotting the values of two variables x and y at a point that corresponds to their values measured along the x-axis and the y-axis.
- A scatter diagram is a graph that plots the values of two variables for a number of different values of each.
- A scatter diagram shows the relationship between the two variables. It shows whether they are positively related, negatively related, or unrelated.

Graphs Used in Economic Models (pp. 18–21)

- Graphs are used to show relationships among variables in economic models.
- Relationships can be positive (an upward-sloping curve), negative (a downward-sloping curve), positive and then negative (have a maximum point), negative and then positive (have a minimum point), or unrelated (a horizontal or vertical curve).

The Slope of a Relationship (pp. 22–24)

- The slope of a relationship is calculated as the change in the value of the variable measured on the y-axis divided by the change in the value of the variable measured on the x-axis—that is, $\Delta y/\Delta x$.
- A straight line has a constant slope.
- A curved line has a varying slope. To calculate the slope of a curved line, we calculate the slope at a point or across an arc.

Graphing Relationships Among More Than Two Variables (pp. 24–25)

- To graph a relationship among more than two variables, we hold constant the values of all the variables except two.
- We then plot the value of one of the variables against the value of another.
- A *cet par* change in the value of a variable on an axis of a graph brings a movement along the curve.
- A change in the value of a variable held constant along the curve brings a shift of the curve.

Key Terms

MyEconLab Key Terms Quiz

Ceteris paribus, 24
Direct relationship, 18
Inverse relationship, 19

Linear relationship, 18
Negative relationship, 19
Positive relationship, 18

Scatter diagram, 16
Slope, 22

STUDY PLAN PROBLEMS AND APPLICATIONS

MyEconLab   You can work Problems 1 to 11 in Chapter 1A Study Plan and get instant feedback.

Use the following spreadsheet to work Problems 1 to 3. The spreadsheet provides data on the U.S. economy: Column A is the year, column B is the inflation rate, column C is the interest rate, column D is the growth rate, and column E is the unemployment rate.

	A	B	C	D	E
1	2003	1.6	1.0	2.8	6.0
2	2004	2.3	1.4	3.8	5.5
3	2005	2.7	3.2	3.4	5.1
4	2006	3.4	4.9	2.7	4.6
5	2007	3.2	4.5	1.8	4.6
6	2008	2.9	1.4	−0.3	5.8
7	2009	3.8	0.2	−2.8	9.3
8	2010	−0.3	0.1	2.5	9.6
9	2011	1.6	0.1	1.8	8.9
10	2012	3.1	0.1	2.8	8.1
11	2013	2.1	0.1	1.9	7.4

1. Draw a scatter diagram of the inflation rate and the interest rate. Describe the relationship.

2. Draw a scatter diagram of the growth rate and the unemployment rate. Describe the relationship.

3. Draw a scatter diagram of the interest rate and the unemployment rate. Describe the relationship.

Use the following news clip to work Problems 4 to 6.

LEGO Tops the Box Office

Movie	Theaters (number)	Revenue (dollars per theater)
The LEGO Movie	3,775	$16,551
About Last Night	2,253	$12,356
RoboCop	3,372	$7,432
The Monuments Men	3,083	$5,811

Source: boxofficemojo.com,
Data for weekend of February 14–17, 2014

4. Draw a graph of the relationship between the revenue per theater on the *y*-axis and the number of theaters on the *x*-axis. Describe the relationship.

5. Calculate the slope of the relationship in Problem 4 between 3,775 and 2,253 theaters.

6. Calculate the slope of the relationship in Problem 4 between 2,253 and 3,372 theaters.

7. Calculate the slope of the following relationship.

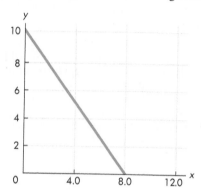

Use the following relationship to work Problems 8 and 9.

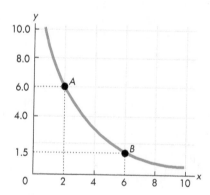

8. Calculate the slope of the relationship at point *A* and at point *B*.

9. Calculate the slope across the arc *AB*.

Use the following table to work Problems 10 and 11. The table gives the price of a balloon ride, the temperature, and the number of rides a day.

Price (dollars per ride)	Balloon rides (number per day)		
	50°F	70°F	90°F
5	32	40	50
10	27	32	40
15	18	27	32

10. Draw a graph to show the relationship between the price and the number of rides when the temperature is 70°F. Describe this relationship.

11. What happens in the graph in Problem 10 if the temperature rises to 90°F?

◆ ADDITIONAL PROBLEMS AND APPLICATIONS

MyEconLab   You can work these problems in MyEconLab if assigned by your instructor.

Use the following spreadsheet to work Problems 12 to 14. The spreadsheet provides data on oil and gasoline: Column A is the year, column B is the price of oil (dollars per barrel), column C is the price of gasoline (cents per gallon), column D is U.S. oil production, and column E is the U.S. quantity of gasoline refined (both in millions of barrels per day).

	A	B	C	D	E
1	2003	31	160	5.7	8.9
2	2004	42	190	5.4	9.1
3	2005	57	231	5.2	9.2
4	2006	66	262	5.1	9.3
5	2007	72	284	5.1	9.3
6	2008	100	330	5.0	9.0
7	2009	62	241	5.4	9.0
8	2010	79	284	5.5	9.0
9	2011	95	354	5.7	9.1
10	2012	94	364	6.5	9.0
11	2013	98	353	7.5	9.1

12. Draw a scatter diagram of the price of oil and the quantity of U.S. oil produced. Describe the relationship.
13. Draw a scatter diagram of the price of gasoline and the quantity of gasoline refined. Describe the relationship.
14. Draw a scatter diagram of the quantity of U.S. oil produced and the quantity of gasoline refined. Describe the relationship.

Use the following data to work Problems 15 to 17. Draw a graph that shows the relationship between the two variables x and y:

x	0	1	2	3	4	5
y	25	24	22	18	12	0

15. a. Is the relationship positive or negative?
    b. Does the slope of the relationship become steeper or flatter as the value of x increases?
    c. Think of some economic relationships that might be similar to this one.
16. Calculate the slope of the relationship between x and y when x equals 3.
17. Calculate the slope of the relationship across the arc as x increases from 4 to 5.
18. Calculate the slope of the curve in the figure in the next column at point A.

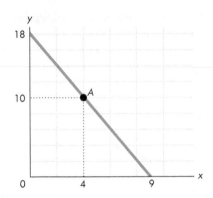

Use the following relationship to work Problems 19 and 20.

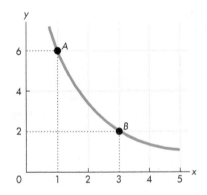

19. Calculate the slope at point A and at point B.
20. Calculate the slope across the arc AB.

Use the following table to work Problems 21 to 23. The table gives information about umbrellas: price, the number purchased, and rainfall in inches.

Price (dollars per umbrella)	Umbrellas (number purchased per day)		
	0 inches	1 inch	2 inches
20	4	7	8
30	2	4	7
40	1	2	4

21. Draw a graph to show the relationship between the price and the number of umbrellas purchased, holding the amount of rainfall constant at 1 inch. Describe this relationship.
22. What happens in the graph in Problem 21 if the price rises and rainfall is constant?
23. What happens in the graph in Problem 21 if the rainfall increases from 1 inch to 2 inches?

2 THE ECONOMIC PROBLEM

After studying this chapter, you will be able to:

◆ Define the production possibilities frontier and use it to calculate opportunity cost

◆ Distinguish between production possibilities and preferences and describe an efficient allocation of resources

◆ Explain how current production choices expand future production possibilities

◆ Explain how specialization and trade expand production possibilities

◆ Describe the economic institutions that coordinate decisions

Hydraulic fracturing, or "fracking," is expanding U.S. oil and gas production and cutting our imports. Should we produce more oil and gas? How do we know when we are using our energy and other resources efficiently?

In this chapter, you study an economic model that answers questions about the efficiency of production and trade.

At the end of the chapter, in *Economics in the News*, we'll apply what you learn to understand how fracking is expanding our production possibilities but why we are still better off importing rather than producing some of our oil and gas.

Production Possibilities and Opportunity Cost

Every working day, in mines, factories, shops, and offices and on farms and construction sites across the United States, 142 million people produce a vast variety of goods and services valued at $60 billion. But the quantities of goods and services that we can produce are limited by our available resources and by technology. And if we want to increase our production of one good, we must decrease our production of something else—we face a tradeoff. You are now going to study the limits to production.

The **production possibilities frontier** (*PPF*) is the boundary between those combinations of goods and services that can be produced and those that cannot. To illustrate the *PPF*, we look at a *model economy* in which the quantities produced of only two goods change, while the quantities produced of all the other goods and services remain the same.

Let's look at the production possibilities frontier for cola and pizza, which represent *any* pair of goods or services.

Production Possibilities Frontier

The *production possibilities frontier* for cola and pizza shows the limits to the production of these two goods, given the total resources and technology available to produce them. Figure 2.1 shows this production possibilities frontier. The table lists combinations of the quantities of pizza and cola that can be produced in a month and the figure graphs these combinations. The *x*-axis shows the quantity of pizzas produced, and the *y*-axis shows the quantity of cola produced.

The *PPF* illustrates *scarcity* because the points outside the frontier are *unattainable*. These points describe wants that can't be satisfied.

We can produce at any point *inside* the *PPF* or *on* the *PPF*. These points are *attainable*. For example, we can produce 4 million pizzas and 5 million cans of cola. Figure 2.1 shows this combination as point *E* on the graph and as possibility *E* in the table.

Moving along the *PPF* from point *E* to point *D* (possibility *D* in the table) we produce more cola and less pizza: 9 million cans of cola and 3 million pizzas. Or moving in the opposite direction from point *E* to point *F* (possibility *F* in the table), we produce more pizza and less cola: 5 million pizzas and no cola.

FIGURE 2.1   Production Possibilities Frontier

Possibility	Pizzas (millions)		Cola (millions of cans)
A	0	and	15
B	1	and	14
C	2	and	12
D	3	and	9
E	4	and	5
F	5	and	0

The table lists six production possibilities for cola and pizzas. Row *A* tells us that if we produce no pizzas, the maximum quantity of cola we can produce is 15 million cans. Points *A*, *B*, *C*, *D*, *E*, and *F* in the figure represent the rows of the table. The curve passing through these points is the production possibilities frontier (*PPF*).

The *PPF* separates the attainable from the unattainable. Production is possible at any point *inside* the orange area or *on* the frontier. Points outside the frontier are unattainable. Points inside the frontier, such as point *Z*, are inefficient because resources are wasted or misallocated. At such points, it is possible to use the available resources to produce more of either or both goods.

MyEconLab Animation and Draw Graph

Production Efficiency

We achieve **production efficiency** if we produce goods and services at the lowest possible cost. This outcome occurs at all the points *on* the *PPF*. At points *inside* the *PPF*, production is inefficient because we are giving up more than necessary of one good to produce a given quantity of the other good.

For example, at point *Z* in Fig. 2.1, we produce 3 million pizzas and 5 million cans of cola, but we have enough resources to produce 3 million pizzas and 9 million cans of cola. Our pizzas cost more cola than necessary. We can get them for a lower cost. Only when we produce *on* the *PPF* do we incur the lowest possible cost of production.

Production inside the *PPF* is *inefficient* because resources are either *unused* or *misallocated* or both.

Resources are *unused* when they are idle but could be working. For example, we might leave some of the factories idle or some workers unemployed.

Resources are *misallocated* when they are assigned to tasks for which they are not the best match. For example, we might assign skilled pizza chefs to work in a cola factory and skilled cola workers to cook pizza in a pizzeria. We could get more pizzas *and* more cola if we reassigned these workers to the tasks that more closely match their skills.

Tradeoff Along the *PPF*

A choice *along* the *PPF* involves a *tradeoff*. Tradeoffs like that between cola and pizza arise in every imaginable real-world situation in which a choice must be made. At any given time, we have a fixed amount of labor, land, capital, and entrepreneurship and a given state of technology. We can employ these resources and technology to produce goods and services, but we are limited in what we can produce.

When doctors want to spend more on AIDS and cancer research, they face a tradeoff: more medical research for less of some other things. When Congress wants to spend more on education and healthcare, it faces a tradeoff: more education and healthcare for less national defense or homeland security. When an environmental group argues for less logging, it is suggesting a tradeoff: greater conservation of endangered wildlife for less paper. When you want a higher grade on your next test, you face a tradeoff: spend more time studying and less leisure or sleep time.

All the tradeoffs you've just considered involve a cost—an opportunity cost.

Opportunity Cost

The **opportunity cost** of an action is the highest-valued alternative forgone. The *PPF* makes this idea precise and enables us to calculate opportunity cost. Along the *PPF*, there are only two goods, so there is only one alternative forgone: some quantity of the other good. To produce more pizzas we must produce less cola. The opportunity cost of producing an additional pizza is the cola we *must* forgo. Similarly, the opportunity cost of producing an additional can of cola is the quantity of pizza we must forgo.

In Fig. 2.1, if we move from point *C* to point *D*, we produce an additional 1 million pizzas but 3 million fewer cans of cola. The additional 1 million pizzas *cost* 3 million cans of cola. Or 1 pizza costs 3 cans of cola. Similarly, if we move from *D* to *C*, we produce an additional 3 million cans of cola but 1 million fewer pizzas. The additional 3 million cans of cola *cost* 1 million pizzas. Or 1 can of cola costs 1/3 of a pizza.

Opportunity Cost Is a Ratio

Opportunity cost is a ratio. It is the decrease in the quantity produced of one good divided by the increase in the quantity produced of another good as we move along the production possibilities frontier.

Because opportunity cost is a ratio, the opportunity cost of producing an additional can of cola is equal to the *inverse* of the opportunity cost of producing an additional pizza. Check this proposition by returning to the calculations we've just done. In the move from *C* to *D*, the opportunity cost of a pizza is 3 cans of cola. And in the move from *D* to *C*, the opportunity cost of a can of cola is 1/3 of a pizza. So the opportunity cost of pizza is the inverse of the opportunity cost of cola.

Increasing Opportunity Cost

The opportunity cost of a pizza increases as the quantity of pizzas produced increases. The outward-bowed shape of the *PPF* reflects increasing opportunity cost. When we produce a large quantity of cola and a small quantity of pizza—between points *A* and *B* in Fig. 2.1—the frontier has a gentle slope. An increase in the quantity of pizzas costs a small decrease in the quantity of cola—the opportunity cost of a pizza is a small quantity of cola.

When we produce a large quantity of pizzas and a small quantity of cola—between points *E* and *F* in Fig. 2.1—the frontier is steep. A given increase in the quantity of pizzas *costs* a large decrease in the quantity of cola, so the opportunity cost of a pizza is a large quantity of cola.

◆ ECONOMICS IN THE NEWS

The Opportunity Cost of Cocoa

World's Sweet Tooth Heats Up Cocoa

Chocolate consumption is soaring as people in developing countries are getting wealthier. Cocoa farmers are ramping up production to keep the chocolate flowing, but the price of cocoa keeps rising.

Source: *The Wall Street Journal*, February 13, 2014

THE QUESTIONS

- How does the *PPF* illustrate (1) the limits to cocoa production; (2) the tradeoff we must make to increase cocoa production; and (3) the effect of increased chocolate consumption on the cost of producing cocoa?

THE ANSWERS

- The figure shows the global *PPF* for cocoa and other goods and services. Point *A* on the *PPF* tells us that if 4 million tons of cocoa are produced, a maximum of 96 units of other goods and services can be produced.

- The movement along the *PPF* from *A* to *B* illustrates the tradeoff we must make to increase chocolate and cocoa production.

- The slope of the *PPF* measures the opportunity cost of cocoa. If cocoa production increases from zero to 4 million tons, the production of other goods and services decreases from 100 units to 96 units. The opportunity cost of 1 ton of cocoa is 1 unit of other goods and services.

- But if cocoa production increases from 4 million tons to 8 million tons, the production of other goods and services decreases from 96 units to 80 units. The opportunity cost of 1 ton of cocoa is now 4 units of other goods and services.

- As resources are moved into producing cocoa, labor, land, and capital less suited to the task of cocoa production are used and the cost of the additional cocoa produced increases.

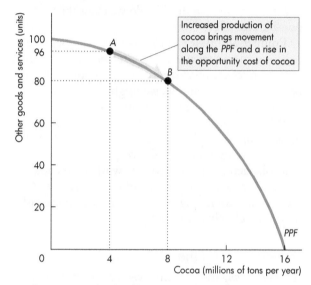

PPF for Cocoa and Other Goods and Services

MyEconLab More Economics in the News

The *PPF* is bowed outward because resources are not all equally productive in all activities. People with many years of experience working for PepsiCo are good at producing cola but not very good at making pizzas. So if we move some of these people from PepsiCo to Domino's, we get a small increase in the quantity of pizzas but a large decrease in the quantity of cola.

Similarly, people who have spent years working at Domino's are good at producing pizzas, but they have no idea how to produce cola. So if we move some of these people from Domino's to PepsiCo, we get a small increase in the quantity of cola but a large decrease in the quantity of pizzas. The more of either good we try to produce, the less productive are the additional resources we use to produce that good and the larger is the opportunity cost of a unit of that good.

How do we choose among the points on the *PPF*? How do we know which point is the best?

◆ REVIEW QUIZ

1 How does the production possibilities frontier illustrate scarcity?
2 How does the production possibilities frontier illustrate production efficiency?
3 How does the production possibilities frontier show that every choice involves a tradeoff?
4 How does the production possibilities frontier illustrate opportunity cost?
5 Why is opportunity cost a ratio?
6 Why does the *PPF* bow outward and what does that imply about the relationship between opportunity cost and the quantity produced?

Work these questions in Study Plan 2.1 and get instant feedback. Do a Key Terms Quiz.   MyEconLab

Using Resources Efficiently

We achieve *production efficiency* at every point on the *PPF*, but which of these points is best? The answer is the point on the *PPF* at which goods and services are produced in the quantities that provide the greatest possible benefit. When goods and services are produced at the lowest possible cost and in the quantities that provide the greatest possible benefit, we have achieved **allocative efficiency**.

The questions that we raised when we reviewed the four big issues in Chapter 1 are questions about allocative efficiency. To answer such questions, we must measure and compare costs and benefits.

The *PPF* and Marginal Cost

The **marginal cost** of a good is the opportunity cost of producing one more unit of it. We calculate marginal cost from the slope of the *PPF*. As the quantity of pizzas produced increases, the *PPF* gets steeper and the marginal cost of a pizza increases. Figure 2.2 illustrates the calculation of the marginal cost of a pizza.

Begin by finding the opportunity cost of pizza in blocks of 1 million pizzas. The cost of the first million pizzas is 1 million cans of cola; the cost of the second million pizzas is 2 million cans of cola; the cost of the third million pizzas is 3 million cans of cola, and so on. The bars in part (a) illustrate these calculations.

The bars in part (b) show the cost of an average pizza in each of the 1 million pizza blocks. Focus on the third million pizzas—the move from *C* to *D* in part (a). Over this range, because 1 million pizzas cost 3 million cans of cola, one of these pizzas, on average, costs 3 cans of cola—the height of the bar in part (b).

Next, find the opportunity cost of each additional pizza—the marginal cost of a pizza. The marginal cost of a pizza increases as the quantity of pizzas produced increases. The marginal cost at point *C* is less than it is at point *D*. On average over the range from *C* to *D*, the marginal cost of a pizza is 3 cans of cola. But it exactly equals 3 cans of cola only in the middle of the range between *C* and *D*.

The red dot in part (b) indicates that the marginal cost of a pizza is 3 cans of cola when 2.5 million pizzas are produced. Each black dot in part (b) is interpreted in the same way. The red curve that passes through these dots, labeled *MC*, is the marginal cost curve. It shows the marginal cost of a pizza at each quantity of pizzas as we move along the *PPF*.

FIGURE 2.2 The *PPF* and Marginal Cost

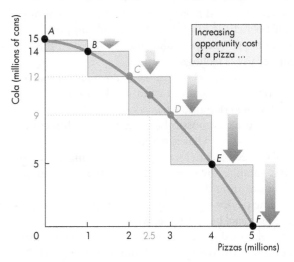

(a) PPF and opportunity cost

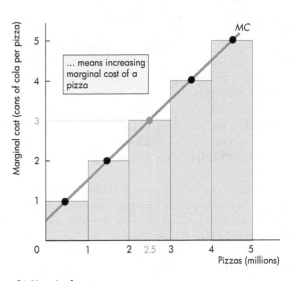

(b) Marginal cost

Marginal cost is calculated from the slope of the *PPF*. As the quantity of pizzas produced increases, the *PPF* gets steeper and the marginal cost of a pizza increases. The bars in part (a) show the opportunity cost of pizza in blocks of 1 million pizzas. The bars in part (b) show the cost of an average pizza in each of these 1 million blocks. The red curve, *MC*, shows the marginal cost of a pizza at each point along the *PPF*. This curve passes through the center of each of the bars in part (b).

MyEconLab Animation

Preferences and Marginal Benefit

The **marginal benefit** from a good or service is the benefit received from consuming one more unit of it. This benefit is subjective. It depends on people's **preferences**—people's likes and dislikes and the intensity of those feelings.

Marginal benefit and *preferences* stand in sharp contrast to *marginal cost* and *production possibilities.* Preferences describe what people like and want and the production possibilities describe the limits or constraints on what is feasible.

We need a concrete way of illustrating preferences that parallels the way we illustrate the limits to production using the *PPF.*

The device that we use to illustrate preferences is the **marginal benefit curve**, which is a curve that shows the relationship between the marginal benefit from a good and the quantity consumed of that good. Note that the *marginal benefit curve* is *unrelated* to the *PPF* and cannot be derived from it.

We measure the marginal benefit from a good or service by the most that people are *willing to pay* for an additional unit of it. The idea is that you are willing to pay less for a good than it is worth to you but you are not willing to pay more: The most you are willing to pay for something is its marginal benefit.

It is a general principle that the more we have of any good or service, the smaller is its marginal benefit and the less we are willing to pay for an additional unit of it. This tendency is so widespread and strong that we call it a principle—the *principle of decreasing marginal benefit.*

The basic reason why marginal benefit decreases is that we like variety. The more we consume of any one good or service, the more we tire of it and would prefer to switch to something else.

Think about your willingness to pay for a pizza. If pizza is hard to come by and you can buy only a few slices a year, you might be willing to pay a high price to get an additional slice. But if pizza is all you've eaten for the past few days, you are willing to pay almost nothing for another slice.

You've learned to think about cost as opportunity cost, not as a dollar cost. You can think about marginal benefit and willingness to pay in the same way. The marginal benefit, measured by what you are willing to pay for something, is the quantity of other goods and services that you are willing to forgo. Let's continue with the example of cola and pizza and illustrate preferences this way.

FIGURE 2.3   Preferences and the Marginal Benefit Curve

Possibility	Pizzas (millions)	Willingness to pay (cans of cola per pizza)
A	0.5	5
B	1.5	4
C	2.5	3
D	3.5	2
E	4.5	1

The smaller the quantity of pizzas available, the more cola people are willing to give up for an additional pizza. With 0.5 million pizzas available, people are willing to pay 5 cans of cola per pizza. But with 4.5 million pizzas, people are willing to pay only 1 can of cola per pizza. Willingness to pay measures marginal benefit. A universal feature of people's preferences is that marginal benefit decreases.

MyEconLab Animation

Figure 2.3 illustrates preferences as the willingness to pay for pizza in terms of cola. In row *A,* with 0.5 million pizzas available, people are willing to pay 5 cans of cola per pizza. As the quantity of pizzas increases, the amount that people are willing to pay for a pizza falls. With 4.5 million pizzas available, people are willing to pay only 1 can of cola per pizza.

Let's now use the concepts of marginal cost and marginal benefit to describe allocative efficiency.

FIGURE 2.4   Efficient Use of Resources

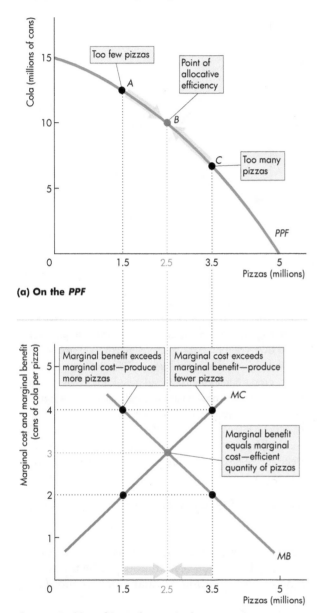

(a) On the PPF

(b) Marginal benefit equals marginal cost

The greater the quantity of pizzas produced, the smaller is the marginal benefit (*MB*) from pizza—the less cola people are willing to give up to get an additional pizza. But the greater the quantity of pizzas produced, the greater is the marginal cost (*MC*) of a pizza—the more cola people must give up to get an additional pizza. When marginal benefit equals marginal cost, resources are being used efficiently.

MyEconLab Animation

Allocative Efficiency

At *any* point on the *PPF*, we cannot produce more of one good without giving up some other good. At the *best* point on the *PPF*, we cannot produce more of one good without giving up some other good that provides greater benefit. We are producing at the point of allocative efficiency—the point on the *PPF* that we prefer above all other points.

Suppose in Fig. 2.4, we produce 1.5 million pizzas. In part (b), the marginal cost of a pizza is 2 cans of cola, and the marginal benefit from a pizza is 4 cans of cola. Because someone values an additional pizza more highly than it costs to produce, we can get more value from our resources by moving some of them out of producing cola and into producing pizza.

Now suppose we produce 3.5 million pizzas. The marginal cost of a pizza is now 4 cans of cola, but the marginal benefit from a pizza is only 2 cans of cola. Because the additional pizza costs more to produce than anyone thinks it is worth, we can get more value from our resources by moving some of them away from producing pizza and into producing cola.

Suppose we produce 2.5 million pizzas. Marginal cost and marginal benefit are now equal at 3 cans of cola. This allocation of resources between pizzas and cola is efficient. If more pizzas are produced, the forgone cola is worth more than the additional pizzas. If fewer pizzas are produced, the forgone pizzas are worth more than the additional cola.

◆ REVIEW QUIZ

1   What is marginal cost? How is it measured?

2   What is marginal benefit? How is it measured?

3   How does the marginal benefit from a good change as the quantity produced of that good increases?

4   What is allocative efficiency and how does it relate to the production possibilities frontier?

5   What conditions must be satisfied if resources are used efficiently?

Work these questions in Study Plan 2.2 and get instant feedback. Do a Key Terms Quiz.   *MyEconLab*

You now understand the limits to production and the conditions under which resources are used efficiently. Your next task is to study the expansion of production possibilities.

⬛▶ Economic Growth

During the past 30 years, production per person in the United States has doubled. The expansion of production possibilities is called **economic growth**. Economic growth increases our *standard of living*, but it doesn't overcome scarcity and avoid opportunity cost. To make our economy grow, we face a tradeoff—the faster we make production grow, the greater is the opportunity cost of economic growth.

The Cost of Economic Growth

Economic growth comes from technological change and capital accumulation. **Technological change** is the development of new goods and of better ways of producing goods and services. **Capital accumulation** is the growth of capital resources, including *human capital*.

Technological change and capital accumulation have vastly expanded our production possibilities. We can produce automobiles that provide us with more transportation than was available when we had only horses and carriages. We can produce satellites that provide global communications on a much larger scale than that available with the earlier cable technology. But if we use our resources to develop new technologies and produce capital, we must decrease our production of consumption goods and services. New technologies and new capital have an opportunity cost. Let's look at this opportunity cost.

Instead of studying the *PPF* of pizzas and cola, we'll hold the quantity of cola produced constant and examine the *PPF* for pizzas and pizza ovens. Figure 2.5 shows this *PPF* as the blue curve PPF_0. If we devote no resources to producing pizza ovens, we produce at point *A*. If we produce 3 million pizzas, we can produce 6 pizza ovens at point *B*. If we produce no pizza, we can produce 10 ovens at point *C*.

The amount by which our production possibilities expand depends on the resources we devote to technological change and capital accumulation. If we devote no resources to this activity (point *A*), our *PPF* remains the blue curve PPF_0 in Fig. 2.5. If we cut the current pizza production and produce 6 ovens (point *B*), then in the future, we'll have more capital and our *PPF* will rotate outward to the position shown by the red curve PPF_1. The fewer resources we use for producing pizza and the more resources we use for producing ovens, the greater is the expansion of our future production possibilities.

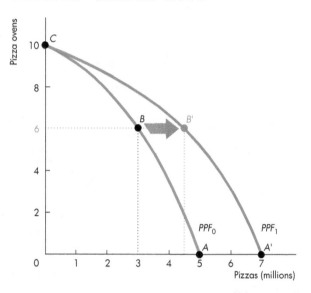

FIGURE 2.5   Economic Growth

PPF_0 shows the limits to the production of pizzas and pizza ovens, with the production of all other goods and services remaining the same. If we devote no resources to producing pizza ovens and produce 5 million pizzas, our production possibilities will remain the same at PPF_0. But if we decrease pizza production to 3 million and produce 6 ovens, at point *B*, our production possibilities expand. After one period, the *PPF* rotates outward to PPF_1 and we can produce at point *B'*, a point outside the original PPF_0. We can rotate the *PPF* outward, but we cannot avoid opportunity cost. The opportunity cost of producing more pizzas in the future is fewer pizzas today.

_____ MyEconLab Animation and Draw Graph _____

Economic growth brings enormous benefits in the form of increased consumption in the future, but economic growth is not free and it doesn't abolish scarcity.

In Fig. 2.5, to make economic growth happen we must use some resources to produce new ovens, which leaves fewer resources to produce pizzas. To move to *B'* in the future, we must move from *A* to *B* today. The opportunity cost of more pizzas in the future is fewer pizzas today. Also, on the new *PPF*, we still face a tradeoff and opportunity cost.

The ideas about economic growth that we have explored in the setting of the pizza industry also apply to nations. Hong Kong and the United States provide a striking case study.

ECONOMICS IN ACTION

Hong Kong Catching Up to the United States

In 1963, the production possibilities per person in the United States were more than four times those in Hong Kong (see the figure). The United States devotes one fifth of its resources to accumulating capital, and in 1963, the United States was at point *A* on its *PPF*. Hong Kong devotes one third of its resources to accumulating capital, and in 1963, Hong Kong was at point *A* on its *PPF*.

Since 1963, both economies have experienced economic growth, but because Hong Kong devotes a bigger fraction of its resources to accumulating capital, its production possibilities have expanded more quickly.

By 2013, production possibilities per person in Hong Kong equaled those in the United States. If Hong Kong continues to devote more resources to accumulating capital than the United States does (at point *B* on its 2013 *PPF*), Hong Kong will continue to grow more rapidly. But if Hong Kong decreases its capital accumulation (moving to point *D* on its 2013 *PPF*), then its rate of economic growth will slow.

Hong Kong is typical of the fast-growing Asian economies, which include Taiwan, Thailand, South Korea, China, and India. Production possibilities

Economic Growth in the United States and Hong Kong

expand in these countries by between 5 percent and almost 10 percent a year.

If such high economic growth rates are maintained, these other Asian countries will continue to close the gap between themselves and the United States, as Hong Kong is doing.

A Nation's Economic Growth

The experiences of the United States and Hong Kong make a striking example of the effects of our choices about consumption and capital accumulation on the rate of economic growth.

If an economy devotes all its factors of production to producing consumption goods and services and none to advancing technology and accumulating capital, its production possibilities in the future will be the same as they are today.

To expand production possibilities in the future, a nation or an economy must devote fewer resources to producing current consumption goods and services and some resources to accumulating capital and developing new technologies. As production possibilities expand, consumption in the future can increase. The decrease in today's consumption is the opportunity cost of tomorrow's increase in consumption.

Work these questions in Study Plan 2.3 and get instant feedback. Do a Key Terms Quiz.   MyEconLab

◆ REVIEW QUIZ

1 What generates economic growth?
2 How does economic growth influence the production possibilities frontier?
3 What is the opportunity cost of economic growth?
4 Explain why Hong Kong has experienced faster economic growth than the United States.
5 Does economic growth overcome scarcity?

Next, we're going to study another way in which we expand our production possibilities—the amazing fact that *both* buyers and sellers gain from specialization and trade.

Gains from Trade

People can produce for themselves all the goods and services that they consume, or they can produce one good or a few goods and trade with others. Producing only one good or a few goods is called *specialization*. We are going to learn how people gain by specializing in the production of the good in which they have a *comparative advantage* and trading with others.

Comparative Advantage and Absolute Advantage

A person has a **comparative advantage** in an activity if that person can perform the activity at a lower opportunity cost than anyone else. Differences in opportunity costs arise from differences in individual abilities and from differences in the characteristics of other resources.

No one excels at everything. One person is an outstanding pitcher but a poor catcher; another person is a brilliant lawyer but a poor teacher. In almost all human endeavors, what one person does easily, someone else finds difficult. The same applies to land and capital. One plot of land is fertile but has no mineral deposits; another plot of land has outstanding views but is infertile. One machine has great precision but is difficult to operate; another is fast but often breaks down.

Although no one excels at everything, some people excel and can outperform others in a large number of activities—perhaps even in all activities. A person who is more productive than others has an **absolute advantage**.

Absolute advantage involves comparing productivities—production per hour—whereas comparative advantage involves comparing opportunity costs.

A person who has an absolute advantage does not have a *comparative* advantage in every activity. John Grisham is a better lawyer and a better author of fast-paced thrillers than most people. He has an absolute advantage in these two activities. But compared to others, he is a better writer than lawyer, so his *comparative* advantage is in writing.

Because ability and resources vary from one person to another, people have different opportunity costs of producing various goods. These differences in opportunity cost are the source of comparative advantage.

Let's explore the idea of comparative advantage by looking at two smoothie bars: one operated by Liz and the other operated by Joe.

Joe's Smoothie Bar Joe produces smoothies and salads in a small, low-tech bar. He has only one blender, and it's a slow, old machine that keeps stopping. Even if Joe uses all his resources to produce smoothies, he can produce only 6 an hour—see Table 2.1. But Joe is good at making salads, and if he uses all his resources in this activity, he can produce 30 salads an hour.

Joe's ability to make smoothies and salads is the same regardless of how he splits an hour between the two tasks. He can make a salad in 2 minutes or a smoothie in 10 minutes. For each additional smoothie Joe produces, he must decrease his production of salads by 5. And for each additional salad he produces, he must decrease his production of smoothies by 1/5 of a smoothie. So

> Joe's opportunity cost of producing 1 smoothie is 5 salads,

and

> Joe's opportunity cost of producing 1 salad is 1/5 of a smoothie.

Joe's customers buy smoothies and salads in equal quantities. So Joe spends 50 minutes of each hour making smoothies and 10 minutes of each hour making salads. With this division of his time, Joe produces 5 smoothies and 5 salads an hour.

Figure 2.6(a) illustrates the production possibilities at Joe's smoothie bar—Joe's *PPF*.

Joe's *PPF* is linear (not outward bowed) because his ability to produce salads and smoothies is the same no matter how he divides his time between the two activities. Joe's opportunity cost of a smoothie is constant—it is the same at all quantities of smoothies produced.

TABLE 2.1   Joe's Production Possibilities

Item	Minutes to produce 1	Quantity per hour
Smoothies	10	6
Salads	2	30

Liz's Smoothie Bar Liz also produces smoothies and salads but in a high-tech bar that is much more productive than Joe's. Liz can turn out either a smoothie or a salad every 2 minutes—see Table 2.2.

If Liz spends all her time making smoothies, she can produce 30 an hour. And if she spends all her time making salads, she can also produce 30 an hour.

Liz's ability to make smoothies and salads, like Joe's, is the same regardless of how she divides her time between the two tasks. She can make a salad in 2 minutes or a smoothie in 2 minutes. For each additional smoothie Liz produces, she must decrease her production of salads by 1. And for each additional salad she produces, she must decrease her production of smoothies by 1. So

> Liz's opportunity cost of producing 1 smoothie is 1 salad,

and

> Liz's opportunity cost of producing 1 salad is 1 smoothie.

TABLE 2.2   Liz's Production Possibilities

Item	Minutes to produce 1	Quantity per hour
Smoothies	2	30
Salads	2	30

Liz's customers buy smoothies and salads in equal quantities, so she splits her time equally between the two items and produces 15 smoothies and 15 salads an hour.

Figure 2.6(b) illustrates the production possibilities at Liz's smoothie bar—Liz's *PPF*.

Like Joe's, Liz's *PPF* is linear because her ability to produce salads and smoothies is the same no matter how she divides her time between the two activities. Liz's opportunity cost of a smoothie is 1 salad at all quantities of smoothies produced.

FIGURE 2.6   The Production Possibilities Frontiers

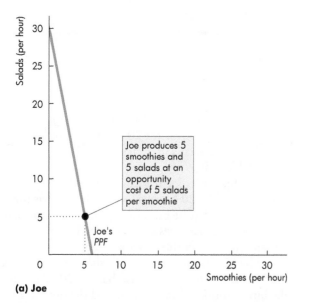

(a) Joe

Joe can produce 30 salads per hour, 1 every two minutes, if he produces no smoothies. Or, he can produce 6 smoothies per hour, 1 every 10 minutes, if he produces no salads. Joe's customers buy equal quantities of salads and smoothies, so Joe produces 5 of each. His opportunity cost of a smoothie is 5 salads.

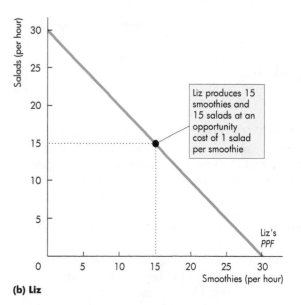

(b) Liz

Liz can produce 30 salads or 30 smoothies per hour, 1 of either item every two minutes. Liz's customers buy equal quantities of salads and smoothies, so she produces 15 of each. Liz's opportunity cost of a smoothie is 1 salad.

—— MyEconLab Animation ——

Joe's Comparative Advantage In which of the two activities does Joe have a comparative advantage? To answer this question, first recall the definition of comparative advantage. A person has a comparative advantage when that person's opportunity cost of producing a good is lower than another person's opportunity cost of producing that same good.

Joe's opportunity cost of producing a salad is only 1/5 of a smoothie, while Liz's opportunity cost of producing a salad is 1 smoothie. So Joe has a comparative advantage in producing salads.

Liz's Comparative Advantage If Joe has a comparative advantage in producing salads, Liz must have a comparative advantage in producing smoothies. Check the numbers. For Joe, a smoothie costs 5 salads, and for Liz, a smoothie costs only 1 salad. So Liz has a comparative advantage in making smoothies.

Achieving the Gains from Trade

Liz and Joe run into each other one evening in a singles bar. After a few minutes of getting acquainted, Liz tells Joe about her amazing smoothie business. Her only problem, she tells Joe, is that she would like to produce more because potential customers leave when her lines get too long.

Joe doesn't want to risk spoiling a blooming relationship by telling Liz about his own struggling business, but he takes the risk. Joe explains to Liz that he spends 50 minutes of every hour making 5 smoothies and 10 minutes making 5 salads. Liz's eyes pop. "Have I got a deal for you!" she exclaims.

Liz's Proposal Here's the deal that Liz sketches on a paper napkin. Joe stops making smoothies and allocates all his time to producing salads; Liz stops making salads and allocates all her time to producing smoothies. That is, they both specialize in producing the good in which they have a comparative advantage. Together they produce 30 smoothies and 30 salads—see Table 2.3(b).

They then trade. Liz suggests trading at a price of 2 salads per smoothie. For her, that is a good deal because she can produce a smoothie at a cost of 1 salad and sell it to Joe for 2 salads. It is also a good deal for Joe because he can produce a salad at a cost of 1/5 of a smoothie and sell it to Liz for 1/2 a smoothie.

Liz explains that any price above 1 salad per smoothie is good for her and any price below 5 salads per smoothie is good for Joe, so a price of 2 salads per smoothie lets them both gain, as she now describes.

TABLE 2.3   Liz and Joe Gain from Trade

(a) Before trade	Liz	Joe
Smoothies	15	5
Salads	15	5

(b) Specialization	Liz	Joe
Smoothies	30	0
Salads	0	30

(c) Trade	Liz	Joe
Smoothies	sell 10	buy 10
Salads	buy 20	sell 20

(d) After trade	Liz	Joe
Smoothies	20	10
Salads	20	10

(e) Gains from trade	Liz	Joe
Smoothies	+5	+5
Salads	+5	+5

At the proposed price, Liz offers to sell Joe 10 smoothies in exchange for 20 salads. Equivalently, Joe sells Liz 20 salads in exchange for 10 smoothies. —see Table 2.3(c).

After this trade, Joe has 10 salads—the 30 he produces minus the 20 he sells to Liz. He also has the 10 smoothies that he buys from Liz. So Joe now has increased the quantities of smoothies and salads that he can sell to his customers—see Table 2.3(d).

Liz has 20 smoothies—the 30 she produces minus the 10 she sells to Joe. She also has the 20 salads that she buys from Joe. Liz has increased the quantities of smoothies and salads that she can sell to her customers—see Table 2.3(d). Both Liz and Joe gain 5 smoothies and 5 salads an hour—see Table 2.3(e).

Illustrating Liz's Idea To illustrate her idea, Liz grabs a fresh napkin and draws the graphs in Fig. 2.7. First, she sketches Joe's *PPF* in part (a) and shows the point at which he is producing before they meet.

FIGURE 2.7   The Gains from Trade

(a) Joe

(b) Liz

Initially, Joe produces at point *A* on his *PPF* in part (a), and Liz produces at point *A* on her *PPF* in part (b). Joe's opportunity cost of producing a salad is less than Liz's, so Joe has a comparative advantage in producing salads. Liz's opportunity cost of producing a smoothie is less than Joe's, so Liz has a comparative advantage in producing smoothies.

If Joe specializes in making salads, he produces 30 salads and no smoothies at point *B* on his *PPF*. If Liz specializes in

making smoothies, she produces 30 smoothies and no salads at point *B* on her *PPF*. They exchange salads for smoothies along the red "Trade line." Liz buys salads from Joe for less than her opportunity cost of producing them. Joe buys smoothies from Liz for less than his opportunity cost of producing them. Each goes to point *C*—a point outside his or her *PPF*. With specialization and trade, Joe and Liz gain 5 smoothies and 5 salads each with no extra resources.

MyEconLab Animation and Draw Graph

Recall that he is producing 5 smoothies and 5 salads an hour at point *A*.

She then sketches her own *PPF* in part (b), and marks the point *A* at which she is producing 15 smoothies and 15 salads an hour.

She then shows what happens when they each specialize in producing the good in which they have a comparative advantage. Joe specializes in producing salads and produces 30 salads and no smoothies at point *B* on his *PPF*.

Liz specializes in producing smoothies and produces 30 smoothies and no salads at point *B* on her *PPF*.

They then trade smoothies and salads at a price of 2 salads per smoothie or 1/2 a smoothie per salad. The red "Trade line" that Liz draws on each part of the figure illustrates the tradeoff that each faces at the proposed price.

Liz now shows Joe the amazing outcome of her idea. After specializing and trading, Joe gets 10 smoothies and 10 salads at point *C*—a gain of 5 smoothies and 5 salads. He moves to a point *outside*

his *PPF*. And Liz gets 20 smoothies and 20 salads at point *C*—also a gain of 5 smoothies and 5 salads—and moves to a point *outside* her *PPF*.

Despite Liz being more productive than Joe, both gain from specializing at producing the good in which they have a comparative advantage and trading.

◆ REVIEW QUIZ

1 What gives a person a comparative advantage?
2 Distinguish between comparative advantage and absolute advantage.
3 Why do people specialize and trade?
4 What are the gains from specialization and trade?
5 What is the source of the gains from trade?

Work these questions in Study Plan 2.4 and get instant feedback. Do a Key Terms Quiz.   MyEconLab

◆ Economic Coordination

For 7 billion people to specialize and produce millions of different goods and services, individual choices must somehow be coordinated. Two competing coordination systems have been used: central economic planning and markets (see *At Issue*, p. 8).

Central economic planning works badly because economic planners don't know people's production possibilities and preferences, so production ends up *inside* the *PPF* and the wrong things are produced.

Decentralized coordination works best but to do so it needs four complementary social institutions. They are

- Firms
- Markets
- Property rights
- Money

Firms

A **firm** is an economic unit that hires factors of production and organizes them to produce and sell goods and services.

Firms coordinate a huge amount of economic activity. For example, Wal-Mart buys or rents large buildings, equips them with storage shelves and checkout lanes, and hires labor. Wal-Mart directs the labor and decides what goods to buy and sell.

But Sam Walton would not have become one of the wealthiest people in the world if Wal-Mart produced everything that it sells. He became rich by specializing in providing retail services and buying from other firms that specialize in producing goods (just as Liz and Joe did). This trade needs markets.

Markets

In ordinary speech, the word *market* means a place where people buy and sell goods such as fish, meat, fruits, and vegetables.

In economics, a **market** is any arrangement that enables buyers and sellers to get information and to do business with each other. An example is the world oil market, which is not a place but a network of producers, consumers, wholesalers, and brokers who buy and sell oil. In the world oil market, decision makers make deals by using the Internet. Enterprising individuals and firms, each pursuing their own self-interest, have profited by making markets—by standing ready to buy or sell items in which they specialize. But markets can work only when property rights exist.

Property Rights

The social arrangements that govern the ownership, use, and disposal of anything that people value are called **property rights**. *Real property* includes land and buildings—the things we call property in ordinary speech—and durable goods such as plant and equipment. *Financial property* includes stocks and bonds and money in the bank. *Intellectual property* is the intangible product of creative effort. This type of property includes books, music, computer programs, and inventions of all kinds and is protected by copyrights and patents.

Where property rights are enforced, people have the incentive to specialize and produce the goods and services in which they have a comparative advantage. Where people can steal the production of others, resources are devoted not to production but to protecting possessions.

Money

Money is any commodity or token that is generally acceptable as a means of payment. Liz and Joe don't need money. They can exchange salads and smoothies. In principle, trade in markets can exchange any item for any other item. But you can perhaps imagine how complicated life would be if we exchanged goods for other goods. The "invention" of money makes trading in markets much more efficient.

Circular Flows Through Markets

Trading in markets for goods and services and factors of production creates a circular flow of expenditures and incomes. Figure 2.8 shows the circular flows. Households specialize and choose the quantities of labor, land, capital, and entrepreneurial services to sell or rent to firms. Firms choose the quantities of factors of production to hire. These (red) flows go through the *factor markets*. Households choose the quantities of goods and services to buy, and firms choose the quantities to produce. These (red) flows go through the *goods markets*. Households receive incomes and make expenditures on goods and services (the green flows).

How do markets coordinate all these decisions?

FIGURE 2.8   Circular Flows in the Market Economy

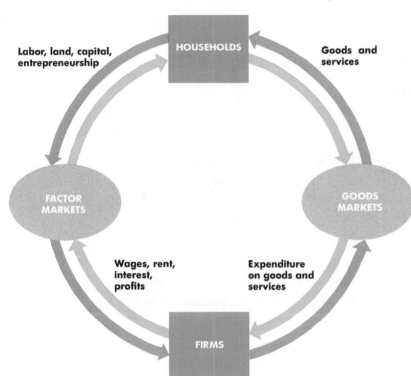

Households and firms make economic choices and markets coordinate these choices.

Households choose the quantities of labor, land, capital, and entrepreneurial services to sell or rent to firms in exchange for wages, rent, interest, and profits. Households also choose how to spend their incomes on the various types of goods and services available.

Firms choose the quantities of factors of production to hire and the quantities of goods and services to produce.

Goods markets and factor markets coordinate these choices of households and firms.

The counterclockwise red flows are real flows—the flow of factors of production from households to firms and the flow of goods and services from firms to households.

The clockwise green flows are the payments for the red flows. They are the flow of incomes from firms to households and the flow of expenditure on goods and services from households to firms.

MyEconLab Animation

Coordinating Decisions

Markets coordinate decisions through price adjustments. Suppose that some people who want to buy hamburgers are not able to do so. To make buying and selling plans the same, either more hamburgers must be offered for sale or buyers must scale down their appetites (or both). A rise in the price of a hamburger produces this outcome. It encourages producers to offer more hamburgers for sale and encourages some people to change their lunch plans. When the price is right, buying plans and selling plans match.

Alternatively, suppose that more hamburgers are available than people want to buy. In this case, more hamburgers must be bought or fewer hamburgers must be offered for sale (or both). A fall in the price of a hamburger achieves this outcome. It encourages people to buy more hamburgers and it encourages firms to produce a smaller quantity of hamburgers.

◆ REVIEW QUIZ

1   Why are social institutions such as firms, markets, property rights, and money necessary?
2   What are the main functions of markets?
3   What are the flows in the market economy that go from firms to households and the flows from households to firms?

Work these questions in Study Plan 2.5 and get instant feedback. Do a Key Terms Quiz.   MyEconLab

◆ You have now begun to see how economists approach economic questions. You can see all around you the lessons you've learned in this chapter. *Economics in the News* on pp. 46–47 provides an opportunity to apply the *PPF* model to deepen your understanding of why, despite advances in "fracking" technology, we still rely on imports for our energy.

Expanding Production Possibilities

Fracking Is Turning the United States into a Bigger Oil Producer Than Saudi Arabia

The Independent
March 11, 2014

Hector Gallegos sits in the cab of his pick-up enjoying a few hours of calm. A day earlier, workers finished carting off the huge rig that had drilled three new wells beneath this small patch of south Texas farmland and he's now getting ready to prime them for production. He reckons that about three weeks from now each will be producing 1,000 to 2,000 barrels a day. "That's money!" he exclaims with a broad smile.

It's also power, and not in the combustion sense. Thanks to the success of engineers like Mr. Gallegos in pushing the frontiers of hydraulic fracturing, or "fracking," to access reserves of oil trapped in shale formations, notably here in Texas and North Dakota, America is poised to displace Saudi Arabia as the world's top producer. …

So rapid has been the change in its energy fortunes that even some experts, as well as policymakers in Washington, are struggling to keep up. Nor are we just talking oil. So much natural gas is being released by the shale also that for now outlandish quantities of it are simply being burned off into the atmosphere.

Even predicting future oil output isn't the precise science you'd expect. "We keep raising our forecasts, and we keep underestimating production," Lejla Alic, an analyst with the International Energy Agency, noted recently. Last year U.S. production reached 7.4 million barrels a day, an increase over 2012 of 15.3 percent. A jump that large hasn't been seen since 1951. This year the United States should produce 8.3 million barrels a day. …

MyEconLab More Economics in the News

ESSENCE OF THE STORY

- Hydraulic fracturing, or "fracking," is tapping oil and gas reserves trapped in shale formations in Texas, North Dakota, and other areas.

- U.S. oil production in 2013 was 15.3 percent higher than in 2012 at 7.4 million barrels a day.

- U.S. oil production will increase again in 2014 and reach 8.3 million barrels a day.

- Fracking will enable the United States to displace Saudi Arabia as the world's top oil producer.

ECONOMIC ANALYSIS

- The table shows some data on U.S. production and imports in 2000 and 2013.

U.S. production and imports	2000	2013
Oil and gas (million barrels per day)	16	21
Other goods and services (units per day)	34	42
Oil and gas imports (million barrels per day)	13	8

- The news story provides data on oil production and the table adds together the production of oil and natural gas, both of which come from shale formations.

- "Fracking" has increased the production of oil and gas from 16 million barrels per day in 2000 to 21 million barrels per day in 2013, an increase of 31 percent.

- The consumption of oil and gas has remained at 29 million barrels per day, so the increase in production has decreased the imports of oil and gas from 13 million barrels per day in 2000 to 8 million barrels per day in 2013.

- "Fracking" is not the only advance in technology and productivity. Other advances in technology and investment include such items as cellphone networks, Internet services, and industrial robots.

- These advances in technology and investment in capital have increased the production of other goods and services from 34 units in 2000 to 42 units in 2013, an increase of 24 percent. (Think of these "units" as giant shopping carts of goods and services each one of which costs $1 billion in the prices of 2013.)

- We can use the data in the table to make a graph of the U.S. *PPF*, with other goods and services (on the y-axis), and oil and gas (on the x-axis). Figure 1 shows the *PPF* for 2000 and for 2013 and marks the points on the *PPFs* at which the U.S. economy produced.

- Figure 2 also shows the *PPF* for 2013 and explains why we still import some oil and gas.

- We could easily produce the 29 million barrels per day that we consume. But to increase production from 21 million barrels per day to 29 million barrels, we would incur a higher opportunity cost of energy.

- Recall that the slope of the *PPF* measures opportunity cost. So the slope of the *PPF* at point A, the production point in 2013, measures the opportunity cost of producing oil and gas in 2013.

- If our production of oil and gas is efficient, we produce only the quantity at which the opportunity cost equals the cost of buying it from other countries.

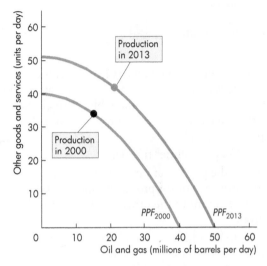

Figure 1 *PPF* for Oil and Gas and Other Goods and Services: 2000 and 2013

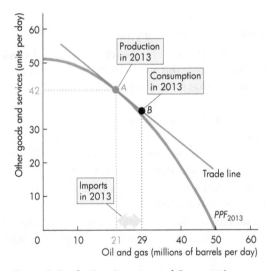

Figure 2 Production, Imports, and Consumption of Oil and Gas in 2013

- The red "Trade line" in Fig. 2 shows our import possibilities. By importing 8 million barrels per day, we can consume 29 million barrels at point B outside our *PPF*.

- The opportunity cost of producing more oil and gas in the United States is greater than the opportunity cost of importing it, so it is efficient to limit our production and import some energy.

- With further expansion of "fracking," we might eventually stop importing oil and gas and even start to export it.

SUMMARY

Key Points

Production Possibilities and Opportunity Cost (pp. 32–34)

- The production possibilities frontier is the boundary between production levels that are attainable and those that are not attainable when all the available resources are used to their limits.
- Production efficiency occurs at points on the production possibilities frontier.
- Along the production possibilities frontier, the opportunity cost of producing more of one good is the amount of the other good that must be given up.
- The opportunity cost of all goods increases as the production of the good increases.

Working Problems 1 to 3 will give you a better understanding of production possibilities and opportunity cost.

Using Resources Efficiently (pp. 35–37)

- Allocative efficiency occurs when goods and services are produced at the least possible cost and in the quantities that bring the greatest possible benefit.
- The marginal cost of a good is the opportunity cost of producing one more unit of it.
- The marginal benefit from a good is the benefit received from consuming one more unit of it and is measured by the willingness to pay for it.
- The marginal benefit of a good decreases as the amount of the good available increases.
- Resources are used efficiently when the marginal cost of each good is equal to its marginal benefit.

Working Problems 4 to 6 will give you a better understanding of the efficient use of resources.

Economic Growth (pp. 38–39)

- Economic growth, which is the expansion of production possibilities, results from capital accumulation and technological change.
- The opportunity cost of economic growth is forgone current consumption.
- The benefit of economic growth is increased future consumption.

Working Problem 7 will give you a better understanding of economic growth.

Gains from Trade (pp. 40–43)

- A person has a comparative advantage in producing a good if that person can produce the good at a lower opportunity cost than everyone else.
- People gain by specializing in the activity in which they have a comparative advantage and trading with others.

Working Problems 8 and 9 will give you a better understanding of the gains from trade.

Economic Coordination (pp. 44–45)

- Firms coordinate a large amount of economic activity, but there is a limit to the efficient size of a firm.
- Markets coordinate the economic choices of people and firms.
- Markets can work efficiently only when property rights exist.
- Money makes trading in markets more efficient.

Working Problem 10 will give you a better understanding of economic coordination.

Key Terms

MyEconLab Key Terms Quiz

Absolute advantage, 40
Allocative efficiency, 35
Capital accumulation, 38
Comparative advantage, 40
Economic growth, 38
Firm, 44

Marginal benefit, 36
Marginal benefit curve, 36
Marginal cost, 35
Market, 44
Money, 44
Opportunity cost, 33

Preferences, 36
Production efficiency, 33
Production possibilities frontier, 32
Property rights, 44
Technological change, 38

◆ WORKED PROBLEM

MyEconLab   You can work this problem in Chapter 2 Study Plan.

Leisure Island has 50 hours of labor a day that it can use to produce entertainment and good food. The table shows the maximum quantity of each good that it can produce with different quantities of labor.

Labor (hours)	Entertainment (shows per week)		Good food (meals per week)
0	0	or	0
10	2	or	5
20	4	or	9
30	6	or	12
40	8	or	14
50	10	or	15

Questions

1. Can Leisure Island produce 4 shows and 14 meals a week?

2. If Leisure Island produces 4 shows and 9 meals a week, is production efficient?

3. If Leisure Island produces 8 shows and 5 meals a week, does it face a tradeoff?

4. Suppose that Leisure Island produces 4 shows and 12 meals a week. Calculate the opportunity cost of producing 2 extra shows a week.

Solutions

1. To produce 4 shows it would use 20 hours and to produce 14 meals it would use 40 hours, so to produce 4 shows and 14 meals a week, Leisure Island would use 60 hours of labor. Leisure Island has only 50 hours of labor available, so it cannot produce 4 shows and 14 meals a week.

Key Point: Production is *unattainable* if it uses more resources than are available.

2. When Leisure Island produces 4 shows it uses 20 hours of labor and when it produces 9 meals it uses 20 hours. In total, it uses 40 hours, which is *less than* the 50 hours of labor available. So Leisure Island's production is not efficient.

Key Point: Production is *efficient* only if the economy uses all its resources.

3. When Leisure Island produces 8 shows and 5 meals, it uses 50 hours of labor. Leisure Island is using all its resources, so to produce more of either good, it would face a tradeoff.

Key Point: An economy faces a *tradeoff* only when it uses all the available resources.

4. When Leisure Island produces 4 shows and 12 meals a week, it uses 50 hours of labor. To produce 2 more shows a week, Leisure Island faces a tradeoff and incurs an opportunity cost.

To produce 2 extra shows a week, Leisure Island moves 10 hours of labor from good food production, which decreases the quantity of meals from 12 to 9 a week—a decrease of 3 meals. That is, to get 2 extra shows a week, Leisure Island *must give up* 3 meals a week. The opportunity cost of the 2 extra shows is 3 meals a week.

Key Point: When an economy is using all its resources and it decides to increase production of one good, it incurs an opportunity cost equal to the quantity of the good that it *must* forgo.

Key Figure

Each row of the following table sets out the combination of shows and meals that Leisure Island can produce in a week when it uses 50 hours of labor.

	Entertainment (shows per week)		Good food (meals per week)
A	0	and	15
B	2	and	14
C	4	and	12
D	6	and	9
E	8	and	5
F	10	and	0

Points *A* through *F* plot these combinations in the rows. The blue curve shows Leisure Island's *PPF*. Point *X* (4 shows and 14 meals in Question 1) is unattainable; Point *Y* (4 shows and 9 meals in Question 2) is inefficient. Point *E* (8 shows and 5 meals in Question 3) is on the *PPF*. The arrow illustrates the tradeoff and the calculation of the opportunity cost of 2 extra shows a week.

MyEconLab Interactive Animation

STUDY PLAN PROBLEMS AND APPLICATIONS

MyEconLab   You can work Problems 1 to 10 in Chapter 2 Study Plan and get instant feedback.

Production Possibilities and Opportunity Cost

(Study Plan 2.1)

Use the following data to work Problems 1 to 3.

Brazil produces ethanol from sugar, and the land used to grow sugar can be used to grow food crops. The table sets out Brazil's production possibilities for ethanol and food crops:

Ethanol (barrels per day)		Food crops (tons per day)
70	and	0
64	and	1
54	and	2
40	and	3
22	and	4
0	and	5

1. a. Draw a graph of Brazil's *PPF* and explain how your graph illustrates scarcity.

   b. If Brazil produces 40 barrels of ethanol a day, how much food must it produce to achieve production efficiency?

   c. Why does Brazil face a tradeoff on its *PPF*?

2. a. If Brazil increases ethanol production from 40 barrels per day to 54 barrels a day, what is the opportunity cost of the additional ethanol?

   b. If Brazil increases food production from 2 tons per day to 3 tons per day, what is the opportunity cost of the additional food?

   c. What is the relationship between your answers to parts (a) and (b)?

3. Does Brazil face an increasing opportunity cost of ethanol? What feature of Brazil's *PPF* illustrates increasing opportunity cost?

Using Resources Efficiently (Study Plan 2.2)

Use the table above to work Problems 4 and 5.

4. Define marginal cost and calculate Brazil's marginal cost of producing a ton of food when the quantity produced is 2.5 tons per day.

5. Define marginal benefit. Explain how it is measured and why the data in the table does not enable you to calculate Brazil's marginal benefit from food.

6. Distinguish between *production efficiency* and *allocative efficiency*. Explain why many production possibilities achieve production efficiency but only one achieves allocative efficiency.

Economic Growth (Study Plan 2.3)

7. A farm grows wheat and produces pork. The marginal cost of producing each of these products increases as more of it is produced.

   a. Make a graph that illustrates the farm's *PPF*.

   b. The farm adopts a new technology that allows it to use fewer resources to fatten pigs. On your graph sketch the impact of the new technology on the farm's *PPF*.

   c. With the farm using the new technology described in part (b), has the opportunity cost of producing a ton of wheat increased, decreased, or remained the same? Explain and illustrate your answer.

   d. Is the farm more efficient with the new technology than it was with the old one? Why?

Gains from Trade (Study Plan 2.4)

8. In an hour, Sue can produce 40 caps or 4 jackets and Tessa can produce 80 caps or 4 jackets.

   a. Calculate Sue's opportunity cost of producing a cap.

   b. Calculate Tessa's opportunity cost of producing a cap.

   c. Who has a comparative advantage in producing caps?

   d. If Sue and Tessa specialize in producing the good in which they have a comparative advantage, and they trade 1 jacket for 15 caps, who gains from the specialization and trade?

9. Suppose that Tessa buys a new machine that enables her to make 20 jackets an hour. (She can still make only 80 caps per hour.)

   a. Who now has a comparative advantage in producing jackets?

   b. Can Sue and Tessa still gain from trade?

   c. Would Sue and Tessa still be willing to trade 1 jacket for 15 caps? Explain your answer.

Economic Coordination (Study Plan 2.5)

10. For 50 years, Cuba has had a centrally planned economy in which the government makes the big decisions on how resources will be allocated.

   a. Why would you expect Cuba's production possibilities (per person) to be smaller than those of the United States?

   b. What are the social institutions that Cuba might lack that help the United States to achieve allocative efficiency?

ADDITIONAL PROBLEMS AND APPLICATIONS

MyEconLab   You can work these problems in MyEconLab if assigned by your instructor.

Production Possibilities and Opportunity Cost

Use the following table to work Problems 11 and 12.
Suppose that Yucatan's production possibilities are

Food (pounds per month)		Sunscreen (gallons per month)
300	and	0
200	and	50
100	and	100
0	and	150

11. a. Draw a graph of Yucatan's *PPF* and explain how your graph illustrates a tradeoff.

   b. If Yucatan produces 150 pounds of food per month, how much sunscreen must it produce if it achieves production efficiency?

   c. What is Yucatan's opportunity cost of producing (i) 1 pound of food and (ii) 1 gallon of sunscreen?

   d. What is the relationship between your answers to part (c)?

12. What feature of a *PPF* illustrates increasing opportunity cost? Explain why Yucatan's opportunity cost does or does not increase.

Using Resources Efficiently

13. In problem 11, what is the marginal cost of 1 pound of food in Yucatan when the quantity produced is 150 pounds per day? What is special about the marginal cost of food in Yucatan?

14. The table describes the preferences in Yucatan.

Sunscreen (gallons per month)	Willingness to pay (pounds of food per gallon)
25	3
75	2
125	1

   a. What is the marginal benefit from sunscreen and how is it measured?

   b. Use the table in Problem 11. What does Yucatan produce to achieve allocative efficiency?

15. **U.K. Music Stores Squeezed off Main Street**

   Music retailing is changing: Sony Music and Amazon are selling online, discount stores are selling at low prices, and Main Street music retailers are all struggling.

   Source: *The Economist,* January 20, 2007

   a. Draw the *PPF* curves for Main Street music retailers and online music retailers before and after the Internet became available.

   b. Draw the marginal cost and marginal benefit curves for Main Street music retailers and online music retailers before and after the Internet became available.

   c. Explain how changes in production possibilities, preferences or both have changed the way in which recorded music is retailed.

Use the following news clip to work Problems 16 and 17.

Malaria Eradication Back on the Table

In response to the Gates Malaria Forum in October 2007, countries are debating the pros and cons of eradication. Dr. Arata Kochi of the World Health Organization believes that with enough money malaria cases could be cut by 90 percent but it would be very expensive to eliminate the remaining 10 percent of cases, so countries should not strive to eradicate malaria.

   Source: *The New York Times*, March 4, 2008

16. Is Dr. Kochi talking about *production efficiency* or *allocative efficiency* or both?

17. Make a graph with the percentage of malaria cases eliminated on the *x*-axis and the marginal cost and marginal benefit of driving down malaria cases on the *y*-axis. On your graph:

   (i) Draw a marginal cost curve and marginal benefit curve that are consistent with Dr. Kochi's opinion.

   (ii) Identify the quantity of malaria eradicated that achieves allocative efficiency.

Economic Growth

18. Capital accumulation and technological change bring economic growth: Production that was unattainable yesterday becomes attainable today; production that is unattainable today will become attainable tomorrow. Why doesn't economic growth bring an end to scarcity one day?

19. **Toyota Plans to Build a Better Company**

   In 2014, Toyota will produce 3 million cars per year and use the balance of its resources to upgrade its workers' skills and create new technology. In three years' time, Toyota plans to produce better cars and be more productive.

   Source: *Financial Post*, April 7, 2014

   a. What is the opportunuity cost of upgrading its workers' skills and creating new technology?

b. Sketch Toyota's *PPF* and mark its production point in 2014. Now show on your graph Toyota's *PPF* in 2018.

Gains from Trade

Use the following data to work Problems 20 and 21. Kim can produce 40 pies or 400 cakes an hour. Liam can produce 100 pies or 200 cakes an hour.

20. a. Calculate Kim's opportunity cost of a pie and Liam's opportunity cost of a pie.
    b. If each spends 30 minutes of each hour producing pies and 30 minutes producing cakes, how many pies and cakes does each produce?
    c. Who has a comparative advantage in producing (i) pies and (ii) cakes?

21. a. Draw a graph of Kim's *PPF* and Liam's *PPF* and show the point at which each produces when they spend 30 minutes of each hour producing pies and 30 minutes producing cakes.
    b. On your graph, show what Kim produces and what Liam produces when they specialize.
    c. When they specialize and trade, what are the total gains from trade?
    d. If Kim and Liam share the total gains equally, what trade takes place between them?

22. Tony and Patty produce skis and snowboards. The tables show their production possibilities. Tony produces 5 snowboards and 40 skis a week; Patty produces 10 snowboards and 5 skis a week.

Tony's Production Possibilities

Snowboards (units per week)		Skis (units per week)
25	and	0
20	and	10
15	and	20
10	and	30
5	and	40
0	and	50

Patty's Production Possibilities

Snowboards (units per week)		Skis (units per week)
20	and	0
10	and	5
0	and	10

a. Who has a comparative advantage in producing (i) snowboards and (ii) skis?
b. If Tony and Patty specialize and trade 1 snowboard for 1 ski, what are the gains from trade?

Economic Coordination

23. Indicate on a graph of the circular flows in the market economy, the real and money flows in which the following items belong:
    a. You buy an iPad from the Apple Store.
    b. Apple Inc. pays the designers of the iPad.
    c. Apple Inc. decides to expand and rents an adjacent building.
    d. You buy a new e-book from Amazon.
    e. Apple Inc. hires a student as an intern during the summer.

Economics in the News

24. After you have studied *Economics in the News* on pp. 46–47, answer the following questions.
    a. How has "fracking" changed the U.S. production possibilities?
    b. How have advances in technologies for producing other goods and services changed the U.S. production possibilities?
    c. If "fracking" had been the only technological advance, how would the *PPF* have changed?
    d. If "fracking" had been the only technological advance, how would the opportunity cost of producing oil and gas have changed? Would it have been lower or higher than it actually was?

25. **Lots of Little Screens**

    Inexpensive broadband access has created a generation of television producers for whom the Internet is their native medium. As they redirect the focus from TV to computers, cellphones, and iPods, the video market is developing into an open digital network.

    Source: *The New York Times*, December 2, 2007

    a. How has inexpensive broadband changed the production possibilities of video entertainment and other goods and services?
    b. Sketch a *PPF* for video entertainment and other goods and services before broadband.
    c. Show how the arrival of inexpensive broadband has changed the *PPF*.
    d. Sketch a marginal benefit curve for video entertainment.
    e. Show how the new generation of TV producers for whom the Internet is their native medium might have changed the marginal benefit from video entertainment.
    f. Explain how the efficient quantity of video entertainment has changed.

Your Economic Revolution

Three periods in human history stand out as ones of economic revolution. The first, the *Agricultural Revolution,* occurred 10,000 years ago. In what is today Iraq, people learned to domesticate animals and plant crops. People stopped roaming in search of food and settled in villages, towns, and cities where they specialized in the activities in which they had a comparative advantage and developed markets in which to exchange their products. Wealth increased enormously.

Economics was born during the *Industrial Revolution,* which began in England during the 1760s. For the first time, people began to apply science and create new technologies for the manufacture of textiles and iron, to create steam engines, and to boost the output of farms.

You are studying economics at a time that future historians will call the *Information Revolution.* Over the entire world, people are embracing new information technologies and prospering on an unprecedented scale.

During all three economic revolutions, many have prospered but others have been left behind. It is the range of human progress that poses the greatest question for economics and the one that Adam Smith addressed in the first work of economic science: What causes the differences in wealth among nations?

Many people had written about economics before **Adam Smith***, but he made economics a science. Born in 1723 in Kirkcaldy, a small fishing town near Edinburgh, Scotland, Smith was the only child of the town's customs officer. Lured from his professorship (he was a full professor at 28) by a wealthy Scottish duke who gave him a pension of £300 a year—ten times the average income at that time—Smith devoted ten years to writing his masterpiece:* An Inquiry into the Nature and Causes of the **Wealth of Nations***, published in 1776.*

Why, Adam Smith asked, are some nations wealthy while others are poor? He was pondering these questions at the height of the Industrial Revolution, and he answered by emphasizing the power of the division of labor and free markets in raising labor productivity.

To illustrate his argument, Adam Smith described two pin factories. In the first, one person, using the hand tools available in the 1770s, could make 20 pins a day. In the other, by using those same hand tools but breaking the process into a number of individually small operations in which people specialize—by the division of labor—ten people could make a staggering 48,000 pins a day. One draws

> Every individual who intends only his own gain is led by an invisible hand to promote an end (the public good) which was no part of his intention.
>
> **ADAM SMITH**
> *The Wealth of Nations*

out the wire, another straightens it, a third cuts it, a fourth points it, a fifth grinds it. Three specialists make the head, and a fourth attaches it. Finally, the pin is polished and packaged.

But a large market is needed to support the division of labor: One factory employing ten workers would need to sell more than 15 million pins a year to stay in business!

ESTHER DUFLO is the Abdul Latif Jameel Professor of Poverty Alleviation and Development Economics at the Massachusetts Institute of Technology. Among her many honors are the 2010 John Bates Clark Medal for the best economist under 40 and the Financial Times and Goldman Sachs Business Book of the Year Award in 2011 for her book (with Abhijit Banerjee) *Poor Economics: A Radical Rethinking of the Way to Fight Global Poverty.* Professor Duflo's research seeks to advance our understanding of the economic choices of the extremely poor by conducting massive real-world experiments.

Professor Duflo was an undergraduate student of history and economics at École Normale Supérieure and completed a master's degree at DELTA in Paris before moving to the United States. She earned her PhD in Economics at MIT in 1999.

Michael Parkin talked with her about her work, which advances our understanding of the economic choices and condition of the very poor.

Professor Duflo, what's the story about how you became an economist and in particular the architect of experiments designed to understand the economic choices of the very poor?

When I was a kid, I was exposed to many stories and images of poor children: through my mother's engagement as a doctor in a small NGO dealing with child victims of war and through books and stories about children living all around the world. I remember asking myself how I could justify my luck of being born where I was. I had a very exaggerated idea of what it was to be poor, but this idea caused sufficient discomfort that I knew I had to do something about it, if I could. Quite by accident, I discovered that economics was the way in which I could actually be useful: While spending a year in Russia teaching French and studying History, I realized that academic economists have the ability to intervene in the world while keeping enough sanity to analyze it. I thought this would be ideal for me and I have never regreted it. I have the best job in the world.

> ... imagine living on under a dollar a day after your rent is paid in Seattle or Denver. Not easy!

The very poor who you study are people who live on $1 a day or $2 a day. ... Is $1 a day a true measure that includes everything these poor people consume?

For defining the poverty line, we don't include the cost of housing. The poor also get free goods, sometimes of bad quality (education, healthcare) and the value of those is also not included. Other than that, yes, it is everything.

Moreover, you have to realize this is everything, taking into account the fact that life is much cheaper in many poor countries because salaries are lower, so anything that is made and consumed locally (e.g. a haircut) is cheaper.

For example, in India, the purchasing power of a dollar (in terms of the real goods you can buy) is about 3 times what it is in the United States. So the poverty line we use for India is 33 cents per day, not a dollar.

All told, you really have to imagine living on under a dollar a day after your rent is paid in Seattle or Denver. Not easy!

*Read the full interview with Esther Duflo in MyEconLab.

3 DEMAND AND SUPPLY

After studying this chapter, you will be able to:

◆ Describe a competitive market and think about a price as an opportunity cost

◆ Explain the influences on demand

◆ Explain the influences on supply

◆ Explain how demand and supply determine prices and quantities bought and sold

◆ Use the demand and supply model to make predictions about changes in prices and quantities

A disease that kills banana trees is jumping continents and left unchecked will bring a big drop in banana production. What will happen to the price of bananas if the disease isn't contained? The demand and supply model answers this question.

This model that you're about to study is the main tool of economics. It explains how prices are determined and how they guide the use of resources to influence *What*, *How*, and *For Whom* goods and services are produced.

Economics in the News at the end of the chapter answers the question about the price of bananas.

◆ Markets and Prices

When you need a new pair of running shoes, want a bagel and a latte, plan to upgrade your cellphone, or need to fly home for Thanksgiving, you must find a place where people sell those items or offer those services. The place in which you find them is a *market*. You learned in Chapter 2 (p. 44) that a market is any arrangement that enables buyers and sellers to get information and to do business with each other.

A market has two sides: buyers and sellers. There are markets for *goods* such as apples and hiking boots, for *services* such as haircuts and tennis lessons, for *factors of production* such as computer programmers and earthmovers, and for other manufactured *inputs* such as memory chips and auto parts. There are also markets for money such as Japanese yen and for financial securities such as Yahoo! stock. Only our imagination limits what can be traded in markets.

Some markets are physical places where buyers and sellers meet and where an auctioneer or a broker helps to determine the prices. Examples of this type of market are the New York Stock Exchange and the wholesale fish, meat, and produce markets.

Some markets are groups of people spread around the world who never meet and know little about each other but are connected through the Internet or by telephone and fax. Examples are the e-commerce markets and the currency markets.

But most markets are unorganized collections of buyers and sellers. You do most of your trading in this type of market. An example is the market for basketball shoes. The buyers in this $3-billion-a-year market are the 45 million Americans who play basketball (or who want to make a fashion statement). The sellers are the tens of thousands of retail sports equipment and footwear stores. Each buyer can visit several different stores, and each seller knows that the buyer has a choice of stores.

Markets vary in the intensity of competition that buyers and sellers face. In this chapter, we're going to study a **competitive market**—a market that has many buyers and many sellers, so no single buyer or seller can influence the price.

Producers offer items for sale only if the price is high enough to cover their opportunity cost. And consumers respond to changing opportunity cost by seeking cheaper alternatives to expensive items.

We are going to study how people respond to *prices* and the forces that determine prices. But to pursue these tasks, we need to understand the relationship between a price and an opportunity cost.

In everyday life, the *price* of an object is the number of dollars that must be given up in exchange for it. Economists refer to this price as the **money price**.

The *opportunity cost* of an action is the highest-valued alternative forgone. If, when you buy a cup of coffee, the highest-valued thing you forgo is some gum, then the opportunity cost of the coffee is the *quantity* of gum forgone. We can calculate the quantity of gum forgone from the money prices of the coffee and the gum.

If the money price of coffee is $1 a cup and the money price of gum is 50¢ a pack, then the opportunity cost of one cup of coffee is two packs of gum. To calculate this opportunity cost, we divide the price of a cup of coffee by the price of a pack of gum and find the *ratio* of one price to the other. The ratio of one price to another is called a **relative price**, and a *relative price is an opportunity cost.*

We can express the relative price of coffee in terms of gum or any other good. The normal way of expressing a relative price is in terms of a "basket" of all goods and services. To calculate this relative price, we divide the money price of a good by the money price of a "basket" of all goods (called a *price index*). The resulting relative price tells us the opportunity cost of the good in terms of how much of the "basket" we must give up to buy it.

The demand and supply model that we are about to study determines *relative prices,* and the word "price" means *relative* price. When we predict that a price will fall, we do not mean that its *money* price will fall—although it might. We mean that its *relative* price will fall. That is, its price will fall *relative* to the average price of other goods and services.

◆ REVIEW QUIZ

1 What is the distinction between a money price and a relative price?
2 Explain why a relative price is an opportunity cost.
3 Think of examples of goods whose relative price has risen or fallen by a large amount.

Work these questions in Study Plan 3.1 and get instant feedback. Do a Key Terms Quiz.   MyEconLab

Let's begin our study of demand and supply, starting with demand.

◆ Demand

If you demand something, then you

1. Want it.
2. Can afford it.
3. Plan to buy it.

Wants are the unlimited desires or wishes that people have for goods and services. How many times have you thought that you would like something "if only you could afford it" or "if it weren't so expensive"? Scarcity guarantees that many—perhaps most—of our wants will never be satisfied. Demand reflects a decision about which wants to satisfy.

The **quantity demanded** of a good or service is the amount that consumers plan to buy during a given time period at a particular price. The quantity demanded is not necessarily the same as the quantity actually bought. Sometimes the quantity demanded exceeds the amount of goods available, so the quantity bought is less than the quantity demanded.

The quantity demanded is measured as an amount per unit of time. For example, suppose that you buy one cup of coffee a day. The quantity of coffee that you demand can be expressed as 1 cup per day, 7 cups per week, or 365 cups per year.

Many factors influence buying plans, and one of them is the price. We look first at the relationship between the quantity demanded of a good and its price. To study this relationship, we keep all other influences on buying plans the same and we ask: How, other things remaining the same, does the quantity demanded of a good change as its price changes?

The law of demand provides the answer.

The Law of Demand

The **law of demand** states:

> Other things remaining the same, the higher the price of a good, the smaller is the quantity demanded; and the lower the price of a good, the greater is the quantity demanded.

Why does a higher price reduce the quantity demanded? For two reasons:

- Substitution effect
- Income effect

Substitution Effect When the price of a good rises, other things remaining the same, its *relative* price— its opportunity cost—rises. Although each good is unique, it has *substitutes*—other goods that can be used in its place. As the opportunity cost of a good rises, the incentive to economize on its use and switch to a substitute becomes stronger.

Income Effect When a price rises, other things remaining the same, the price rises *relative* to income. Faced with a higher price and an unchanged income, people cannot afford to buy all the things they previously bought. They must decrease the quantities demanded of at least some goods and services. Normally, the good whose price has increased will be one of the goods that people buy less of.

To see the substitution effect and the income effect at work, think about the effects of a change in the price of an energy bar. Several different goods are substitutes for an energy bar. For example, an energy drink could be consumed instead of an energy bar.

Suppose that an energy bar initially sells for $3 and then its price falls to $1.50. People now substitute energy bars for energy drinks—the substitution effect. And with a budget that now has some slack from the lower price of an energy bar, people buy even more energy bars—the income effect. The quantity of energy bars demanded increases for these two reasons.

Now suppose that an energy bar initially sells for $3 and then the price doubles to $6. People now buy fewer energy bars and more energy drinks—the substitution effect. And faced with a tighter budget, people buy even fewer energy bars—the income effect. The quantity of energy bars demanded decreases for these two reasons.

Demand Curve and Demand Schedule

You are now about to study one of the two most used curves in economics: the demand curve. You are also going to encounter one of the most critical distinctions: the distinction between *demand* and *quantity demanded*.

The term **demand** refers to the entire relationship between the price of a good and the quantity demanded of that good. Demand is illustrated by the demand curve and the demand schedule. The term *quantity demanded* refers to a point on a demand curve—the quantity demanded at a particular price.

Figure 3.1 shows the demand curve for energy bars. A **demand curve** shows the relationship between the quantity demanded of a good and its price when all other influences on consumers' planned purchases remain the same.

The table in Fig. 3.1 is the demand schedule for energy bars. A *demand schedule* lists the quantities demanded at each price when all the other influences on consumers' planned purchases remain the same. For example, if the price of a bar is 50¢, the quantity demanded is 22 million a week. If the price is $2.50, the quantity demanded is 5 million a week. The other rows of the table show the quantities demanded at prices of $1.00, $1.50, and $2.00.

We graph the demand schedule as a demand curve with the quantity demanded on the *x*-axis and the price on the *y*-axis. The points on the demand curve labeled *A* through *E* correspond to the rows of the demand schedule. For example, point *A* on the graph shows a quantity demanded of 22 million energy bars a week at a price of 50¢ a bar.

Willingness and Ability to Pay   Another way of looking at the demand curve is as a willingness-and-ability-to-pay curve. The willingness and ability to pay is a measure of *marginal benefit*.

If a small quantity is available, the highest price that someone is willing and able to pay for one more unit is high. But as the quantity available increases, the marginal benefit of each additional unit falls and the highest price that someone is willing and able to pay also falls along the demand curve.

In Fig. 3.1, if only 5 million energy bars are available each week, the highest price that someone is willing to pay for the 5 millionth bar is $2.50. But if 22 million energy bars are available each week, someone is willing to pay 50¢ for the last bar bought.

A Change in Demand

When any factor that influences buying plans changes, other than the price of the good, there is a **change in demand**. Figure 3.2 illustrates an increase in demand. When demand increases, the demand curve shifts rightward and the quantity demanded at each price is greater. For example, at $2.50 a bar, the quantity demanded on the original (blue) demand curve is 5 million energy bars a week. On the new (red) demand curve, at $2.50 a bar, the quantity demanded is 15 million bars a week. Look closely at the numbers in the table and check that the quantity demanded at each price is greater.

FIGURE 3.1   The Demand Curve

	Price (dollars per bar)	Quantity demanded (millions of bars per week)
A	0.50	22
B	1.00	15
C	1.50	10
D	2.00	7
E	2.50	5

The table shows a demand schedule for energy bars. At a price of 50¢ a bar, 22 million bars a week are demanded; at a price of $1.50 a bar, 10 million bars a week are demanded. The demand curve shows the relationship between quantity demanded and price, other things remaining the same. The demand curve slopes downward: As the price falls, the quantity demanded increases.

The demand curve can be read in two ways. For a given price, the demand curve tells us the quantity that people plan to buy. For example, at a price of $1.50 a bar, people plan to buy 10 million bars a week. For a given quantity, the demand curve tells us the maximum price that consumers are willing and able to pay for the last bar available. For example, the maximum price that consumers will pay for the 15 millionth bar is $1.00.

MyEconLab Animation

FIGURE 3.2   An Increase in Demand

Original demand schedule Original income		New demand schedule New higher income		
	Price (dollars per bar)	Quantity demanded (millions of bars per week)		Price (dollars per bar)	Quantity demanded (millions of bars per week)

	Price (dollars per bar)	Quantity demanded (millions of bars per week)		Price (dollars per bar)	Quantity demanded (millions of bars per week)
A	0.50	22	A'	0.50	32
B	1.00	15	B'	1.00	25
C	1.50	10	C'	1.50	20
D	2.00	7	D'	2.00	17
E	2.50	5	E'	2.50	15

A change in any influence on buying plans other than the price of the good itself results in a new demand schedule and a shift of the demand curve. A change in income changes the demand for energy bars. At a price of $1.50 a bar, 10 million bars a week are demanded at the original income (row C of the table) and 20 million bars a week are demanded at the new higher income (row C'). A rise in income increases the demand for energy bars. The demand curve shifts *rightward*, as shown by the shift arrow and the resulting red curve.

MyEconLab Animation

Six main factors bring changes in demand. They are changes in

- The prices of related goods
- Expected future prices
- Income
- Expected future income and credit
- Population
- Preferences

Prices of Related Goods The quantity of energy bars that consumers plan to buy depends in part on the prices of substitutes for energy bars. A **substitute** is a good that can be used in place of another good. For example, a bus ride is a substitute for a train ride; a hamburger is a substitute for a hot dog; and an energy drink is a substitute for an energy bar. If the price of a substitute for an energy bar rises, people buy less of the substitute and more energy bars. For example, if the price of an energy drink rises, people buy fewer energy drinks and more energy bars. The demand for energy bars increases.

The quantity of energy bars that people plan to buy also depends on the prices of complements with energy bars. A **complement** is a good that is used in conjunction with another good. Hamburgers and fries are complements, and so are energy bars and exercise. If the price of an hour at the gym falls, people buy more gym time *and more* energy bars.

Expected Future Prices If the expected future price of a good rises and if the good can be stored, the opportunity cost of obtaining the good for future use is lower today than it will be in the future when people expect the price to be higher. So people retime their purchases—they substitute over time. They buy more of the good now before its price is expected to rise (and less afterward), so the demand for the good today increases.

For example, suppose that a Florida frost damages the season's orange crop. You expect the price of orange juice to rise, so you fill your freezer with enough frozen juice to get you through the next six months. Your current demand for frozen orange juice has increased, and your future demand has decreased.

Similarly, if the expected future price of a good falls, the opportunity cost of buying the good today is high relative to what it is expected to be in the future. So again, people retime their purchases. They buy less of the good now before its price is expected to fall, so the demand for the good decreases today and increases in the future.

Computer prices are constantly falling, and this fact poses a dilemma. Will you buy a new computer now, in time for the start of the school year, or will you wait until the price has fallen some more? Because people expect computer prices to keep falling, the current demand for computers is less (and the future demand is greater) than it otherwise would be.

Income Consumers' income influences demand. When income increases, consumers buy more of most goods; and when income decreases, consumers buy less of most goods. Although an increase in income leads to an increase in the demand for *most* goods, it does not lead to an increase in the demand for *all* goods. A **normal good** is one for which demand increases as income increases. An **inferior good** is one for which demand decreases as income increases. As incomes increase, the demand for air travel (a normal good) increases and the demand for long-distance bus trips (an inferior good) decreases.

Expected Future Income and Credit When expected future income increases or credit becomes easier to get, demand for a good might increase now. For example, a salesperson gets the news that she will receive a big bonus at the end of the year, so she goes into debt and buys a new car right now, rather than waiting until she receives the bonus.

Population Demand also depends on the size and the age structure of the population. The larger the population, the greater is the demand for all goods and services; the smaller the population, the smaller is the demand for all goods and services.

For example, the demand for parking spaces, running shoes, movies, or just about anything that you can imagine is much greater in New York City (population 8.3 million) than it is in Boise, Idaho (population 212,000).

Also, the larger the proportion of the population in a given age group, the greater is the demand for the goods and services used by that age group.

For example, during the 1990s, a decrease in the college-age population decreased the demand for college places. During those same years, the number of Americans aged 85 years and over increased by more than 1 million. As a result, the demand for nursing home services increased.

TABLE 3.1   The Demand for Energy Bars

The Law of Demand

The quantity of energy bars demanded

Decreases if:	Increases if:
▪ The price of an energy bar rises	▪ The price of an energy bar falls

Changes in Demand

The demand for energy bars

Decreases if:	Increases if:
▪ The price of a substitute falls	▪ The price of a substitute rises
▪ The price of a complement rises	▪ The price of a complement falls
▪ The expected future price of an energy bar falls	▪ The expected future price of an energy bar rises
▪ Income falls*	▪ Income rises*
▪ Expected future income falls or credit becomes harder to get*	▪ Expected future income rises or credit becomes easier to get*
▪ The population decreases	▪ The population increases

*An energy bar is a normal good.

Preferences Demand depends on preferences. *Preferences* determine the value that people place on each good and service. Preferences depend on such things as the weather, information, and fashion. For example, greater health and fitness awareness has shifted preferences in favor of energy bars, so the demand for energy bars has increased.

Table 3.1 summarizes the influences on demand and the direction of those influences.

A Change in the Quantity Demanded Versus a Change in Demand

Changes in the influences on buying plans bring either a change in the quantity demanded or a change in demand. Equivalently, they bring either a movement along the demand curve or a shift of the demand curve. The distinction between a change in the quantity demanded and a change in demand is the same as that between a movement along the demand curve and a shift of the demand curve.

A point on the demand curve shows the quantity demanded at a given price, so a movement along the demand curve shows a **change in the quantity demanded**. The entire demand curve shows demand, so a shift of the demand curve shows a *change in demand*. Figure 3.3 illustrates these distinctions.

Movement Along the Demand Curve If the price of the good changes but no other influence on buying plans changes, we illustrate the effect as a movement along the demand curve.

A fall in the price of a good increases the quantity demanded of it. In Fig. 3.3, we illustrate the effect of a fall in price as a movement down along the demand curve D_0.

A rise in the price of a good decreases the quantity demanded of it. In Fig. 3.3, we illustrate the effect of a rise in price as a movement up along the demand curve D_0.

A Shift of the Demand Curve If the price of a good remains constant but some other influence on buying plans changes, there is a change in demand for that good. We illustrate a change in demand as a shift of the demand curve. For example, if more people work out at the gym, consumers buy more energy bars regardless of the price of a bar. That is what a rightward shift of the demand curve shows—more energy bars are demanded at each price.

In Fig. 3.3, there is a *change in demand* and the demand curve shifts when any influence on buying plans changes, other than the price of the good. Demand *increases* and the demand curve *shifts rightward* (to the red demand curve D_1) if the price of a substitute rises, the price of a complement falls, the expected future price of the good rises, income increases (for a normal good), expected future income or credit increases, or the population increases. Demand *decreases* and the demand curve *shifts leftward* (to the red demand curve D_2) if the price of a substitute falls, the price of a complement rises, the expected future price of the good falls, income decreases (for a normal good), expected future income or credit decreases, or the population decreases. (For an inferior good, the effects of changes in income are in the opposite direction to those described above.)

FIGURE 3.3 A Change in the Quantity Demanded Versus a Change in Demand

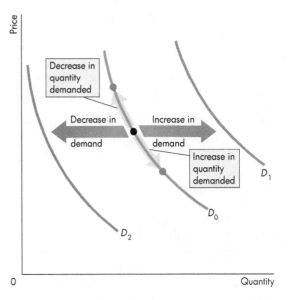

When the price of the good changes, there is a movement along the demand curve and *a change in the quantity demanded*, shown by the blue arrows on demand curve D_0. When any other influence on buying plans changes, there is a shift of the demand curve and a *change in demand*. An increase in demand shifts the demand curve rightward (from D_0 to D_1). A decrease in demand shifts the demand curve leftward (from D_0 to D_2).

MyEconLab Animation and Draw Graph

◆ REVIEW QUIZ

1 Define the quantity demanded of a good or service.
2 What is the law of demand and how do we illustrate it?
3 What does the demand curve tell us about the price that consumers are willing to pay?
4 List all the influences on buying plans that change demand, and for each influence, say whether it increases or decreases demand.
5 Why does demand not change when the price of a good changes with no change in the other influences on buying plans?

Work these questions in Study Plan 3.2 and get instant feedback. Do a Key Terms Quiz.   **MyEconLab**

▶ Supply

If a firm supplies a good or service, the firm

1. Has the resources and technology to produce it.
2. Can profit from producing it.
3. Plans to produce it and sell it.

A supply is more than just having the *resources* and the *technology* to produce something. *Resources and technology* are the constraints that limit what is possible.

Many useful things can be produced, but they are not produced unless it is profitable to do so. Supply reflects a decision about which technologically feasible items to produce.

The **quantity supplied** of a good or service is the amount that producers plan to sell during a given time period at a particular price. The quantity supplied is not necessarily the same amount as the quantity actually sold. Sometimes the quantity supplied is greater than the quantity demanded, so the quantity sold is less than the quantity supplied.

Like the quantity demanded, the quantity supplied is measured as an amount per unit of time. For example, suppose that GM produces 1,000 cars a day. The quantity of cars supplied by GM can be expressed as 1,000 a day, 7,000 a week, or 365,000 a year. Without the time dimension, we cannot tell whether a particular quantity is large or small.

Many factors influence selling plans, and again one of them is the price of the good. We look first at the relationship between the quantity supplied of a good and its price. Just as we did when we studied demand, to isolate the relationship between the quantity supplied of a good and its price, we keep all other influences on selling plans the same and ask: How does the quantity supplied of a good change as its price changes when other things remain the same?

The law of supply provides the answer.

The Law of Supply

The **law of supply** states:

> Other things remaining the same, the higher the price of a good, the greater is the quantity supplied; and the lower the price of a good, the smaller is the quantity supplied.

Why does a higher price increase the quantity supplied? It is because *marginal cost increases*. As the quantity produced of any good increases, the marginal cost of producing the good increases. (See Chapter 2, p. 35 to review marginal cost.)

It is never worth producing a good if the price received for the good does not at least cover the marginal cost of producing it. When the price of a good rises, other things remaining the same, producers are willing to incur a higher marginal cost, so they increase production. The higher price brings forth an increase in the quantity supplied.

Let's now illustrate the law of supply with a supply curve and a supply schedule.

Supply Curve and Supply Schedule

You are now going to study the second of the two most used curves in economics: the supply curve. You're also going to learn about the critical distinction between *supply* and *quantity supplied*.

The term **supply** refers to the entire relationship between the price of a good and the quantity supplied of it. Supply is illustrated by the supply curve and the supply schedule. The term *quantity supplied* refers to a point on a supply curve—the quantity supplied at a particular price.

Figure 3.4 shows the supply curve of energy bars. A **supply curve** shows the relationship between the quantity supplied of a good and its price when all other influences on producers' planned sales remain the same. The supply curve is a graph of a supply schedule.

The table in Fig. 3.4 sets out the supply schedule for energy bars. A *supply schedule* lists the quantities supplied at each price when all the other influences on producers' planned sales remain the same. For example, if the price of an energy bar is 50¢, the quantity supplied is zero—in row *A* of the table. If the price of an energy bar is $1.00, the quantity supplied is 6 million energy bars a week—in row *B*. The other rows of the table show the quantities supplied at prices of $1.50, $2.00, and $2.50.

To make a supply curve, we graph the quantity supplied on the *x*-axis and the price on the *y*-axis. The points on the supply curve labeled *A* through *E* correspond to the rows of the supply schedule. For example, point *A* on the graph shows a quantity supplied of zero at a price of 50¢ an energy bar. Point *E* shows a quantity supplied of 15 million bars at $2.50 an energy bar.

FIGURE 3.4   The Supply Curve

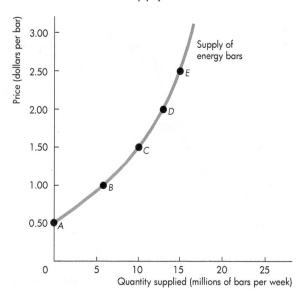

	Price (dollars per bar)	Quantity supplied (millions of bars per week)
A	0.50	0
B	1.00	6
C	1.50	10
D	2.00	13
E	2.50	15

The table shows the supply schedule of energy bars. For example, at a price of $1.00, 6 million bars a week are supplied; at a price of $2.50, 15 million bars a week are supplied. The supply curve shows the relationship between the quantity supplied and the price, other things remaining the same. The supply curve slopes upward: As the price of a good increases, the quantity supplied increases.

A supply curve can be read in two ways. For a given price, the supply curve tells us the quantity that producers plan to sell at that price. For example, at a price of $1.50 a bar, producers are planning to sell 10 million bars a week. For a given quantity, the supply curve tells us the minimum price at which producers are willing to sell one more bar. For example, if 15 million bars are produced each week, the lowest price at which a producer is willing to sell the 15 millionth bar is $2.50.

MyEconLab Animation

Minimum Supply Price The supply curve can be interpreted as a minimum-supply-price curve—a curve that shows the lowest price at which someone is willing to sell. This lowest price is the *marginal cost.*

If a small quantity is produced, the lowest price at which someone is willing to sell one more unit is low. But as the quantity produced increases, the marginal cost of each additional unit rises, so the lowest price at which someone is willing to sell an additional unit rises along the supply curve.

In Fig. 3.4, if 15 million bars are produced each week, the lowest price at which someone is willing to sell the 15 millionth bar is $2.50. But if 10 million bars are produced each week, someone is willing to accept $1.50 for the last bar produced.

A Change in Supply

When any factor that influences selling plans other than the price of the good changes, there is a **change in supply**. Six main factors bring changes in supply. They are changes in

- The prices of factors of production
- The prices of related goods produced
- Expected future prices
- The number of suppliers
- Technology
- The state of nature

Prices of Factors of Production The prices of the factors of production used to produce a good influence its supply. To see this influence, think about the supply curve as a minimum-supply-price curve. If the price of a factor of production rises, the lowest price that a producer is willing to accept for that good rises, so supply decreases. For example, during 2008, as the price of jet fuel increased, the supply of air travel decreased. Similarly, a rise in the minimum wage decreases the supply of hamburgers.

Prices of Related Goods Produced The prices of related goods that firms produce influence supply. For example, if the price of an energy drink rises, firms switch production from bars to drinks. The supply of energy bars decreases. Energy bars and energy drinks are *substitutes in production*—goods that can be produced by using the same resources. If the price of beef rises, the supply of cowhide increases. Beef and cowhide are *complements in production*—goods that must be produced together.

Expected Future Prices If the expected future price of a good rises, the return from selling the good in the future increases and is higher than it is today. So supply decreases today and increases in the future.

The Number of Suppliers The larger the number of firms that produce a good, the greater is the supply of the good. As new firms enter an industry, the supply in that industry increases. As firms leave an industry, the supply in that industry decreases.

Technology The term "technology" is used broadly to mean the way that factors of production are used to produce a good. A technology change occurs when a new method is discovered that lowers the cost of producing a good. For example, new methods used in the factories that produce computer chips have lowered the cost and increased the supply of chips.

The State of Nature The state of nature includes all the natural forces that influence production. It includes the state of the weather and, more broadly, the natural environment. Good weather can increase the supply of many agricultural products and bad weather can decrease their supply. Extreme natural events such as earthquakes, tornadoes, and hurricanes can also influence supply.

Figure 3.5 illustrates an increase in supply. When supply increases, the supply curve shifts rightward and the quantity supplied at each price is larger. For example, at $1.00 per bar, on the original (blue) supply curve, the quantity supplied is 6 million bars a week. On the new (red) supply curve, the quantity supplied is 15 million bars a week. Look closely at the numbers in the table in Fig. 3.5 and check that the quantity supplied is larger at each price.

Table 3.2 summarizes the influences on supply and the directions of those influences.

A Change in the Quantity Supplied Versus a Change in Supply

Changes in the influences on selling plans bring either a change in the quantity supplied or a change in supply. Equivalently, they bring either a movement along the supply curve or a shift of the supply curve.

A point on the supply curve shows the quantity supplied at a given price. A movement along the supply curve shows a **change in the quantity supplied**. The entire supply curve shows supply. A shift of the supply curve shows a *change in supply*.

FIGURE 3.5   An Increase in Supply

Original supply schedule Old technology			New supply schedule New technology		
	Price (dollars per bar)	Quantity supplied (millions of bars per week)		Price (dollars per bar)	Quantity supplied (millions of bars per week)
A	0.50	0	A'	0.50	7
B	1.00	6	B'	1.00	15
C	1.50	10	C'	1.50	20
D	2.00	13	D'	2.00	25
E	2.50	15	E'	2.50	27

A change in any influence on selling plans other than the price of the good itself results in a new supply schedule and a shift of the supply curve. For example, a new, cost-saving technology for producing energy bars changes the supply of energy bars. At a price of $1.50 a bar, 10 million bars a week are supplied when producers use the old technology (row C of the table) and 20 million energy bars a week are supplied when producers use the new technology (row C'). An advance in technology *increases* the supply of energy bars. The supply curve shifts *rightward*, as shown by the shift arrow and the resulting red curve.

———— MyEconLab Animation ————

Figure 3.6 illustrates and summarizes these distinctions. If the price of the good changes and other things remain the same, there is a *change in the quantity supplied* of that good. If the price of the good falls, the quantity supplied decreases and there is a movement down along the supply curve S_0. If the price of the good rises, the quantity supplied increases and there is a movement up along the supply curve S_0. When any other influence on selling plans changes, the supply curve shifts and there is a *change in supply*. If supply increases, the supply curve shifts rightward to S_1. If supply decreases, the supply curve shifts leftward to S_2.

FIGURE 3.6   A Change in the Quantity Supplied Versus a Change in Supply

When the price of the good changes, there is a movement along the supply curve and a *change in the quantity supplied*, shown by the blue arrows on supply curve S_0. When any other influence on selling plans changes, there is a shift of the supply curve and a *change in supply*. An increase in supply shifts the supply curve rightward (from S_0 to S_1), and a decrease in supply shifts the supply curve leftward (from S_0 to S_2).

MyEconLab Animation and Draw Graph

TABLE 3.2   The Supply of Energy Bars

The Law of Supply

The quantity of energy bars supplied

Decreases if:	Increases if:
■ The price of an energy bar falls	■ The price of an energy bar rises

Changes in Supply

The supply of energy bars

Decreases if:	Increases if:
■ The price of a factor of production used to produce energy bars rises	■ The price of a factor of production used to produce energy bars falls
■ The price of a substitute in production rises	■ The price of a substitute in production falls
■ The price of a complement in production falls	■ The price of a complement in production rises
■ The expected future price of an energy bar rises	■ The expected future price of an energy bar falls
■ The number of suppliers of bars decreases	■ The number of suppliers of bars increases
■ A technology change decreases energy bar production	■ A technology change increases energy bar production
■ A natural event decreases energy bar production	■ A natural event increases energy bar production

◆ REVIEW QUIZ

1 Define the quantity supplied of a good or service.
2 What is the law of supply and how do we illustrate it?
3 What does the supply curve tell us about the producer's minimum supply price?
4 List all the influences on selling plans, and for each influence, say whether it changes supply.
5 What happens to the quantity of cellphones supplied and the supply of cellphones if the price of a cellphone falls?

Work these questions in Study Plan 3.3 and get instant feedback. Do a Key Terms Quiz.   *MyEconLab*

Now we're going to combine demand and supply and see how prices and quantities are determined.

Market Equilibrium

We have seen that when the price of a good rises, the quantity demanded *decreases* and the quantity supplied *increases*. We are now going to see how the price adjusts to coordinate buying plans and selling plans and achieve an equilibrium in the market.

An *equilibrium* is a situation in which opposing forces balance each other. Equilibrium in a market occurs when the price balances buying plans and selling plans. The **equilibrium price** is the price at which the quantity demanded equals the quantity supplied. The **equilibrium quantity** is the quantity bought and sold at the equilibrium price. A market moves toward its equilibrium because

- Price regulates buying and selling plans.
- Price adjusts when plans don't match.

Price as a Regulator

The price of a good regulates the quantities demanded and supplied. If the price is too high, the quantity supplied exceeds the quantity demanded. If the price is too low, the quantity demanded exceeds the quantity supplied. There is one price at which the quantity demanded equals the quantity supplied. Let's work out what that price is.

Figure 3.7 shows the market for energy bars. The table shows the demand schedule (from Fig. 3.1) and the supply schedule (from Fig. 3.4). If the price is 50¢ a bar, the quantity demanded is 22 million bars a week but no bars are supplied. There is a shortage of 22 million bars a week. The final column of the table shows this shortage. At a price of $1.00 a bar, there is still a shortage but only of 9 million bars a week.

If the price is $2.50 a bar, the quantity supplied is 15 million bars a week but the quantity demanded is only 5 million. There is a surplus of 10 million bars a week.

The one price at which there is neither a shortage nor a surplus is $1.50 a bar. At that price, the quantity demanded equals the quantity supplied: 10 million bars a week. The equilibrium price is $1.50 a bar, and the equilibrium quantity is 10 million bars a week.

Figure 3.7 shows that the demand curve and the supply curve intersect at the equilibrium price of $1.50 a bar. At each price *above* $1.50 a bar, there is a surplus of bars. For example, at $2.00 a bar, the surplus is 6

FIGURE 3.7   Equilibrium

Price (dollars per bar)	Quantity demanded	Quantity supplied	Shortage (−) or surplus (+)
	(millions of bars per week)		
0.50	22	0	−22
1.00	15	6	−9
1.50	10	10	0
2.00	7	13	+6
2.50	5	15	+10

The table lists the quantity demanded and the quantity supplied as well as the shortage or surplus of bars at each price. If the price is $1.00 a bar, 15 million bars a week are demanded and 6 million bars are supplied. There is a shortage of 9 million bars a week, and the price rises.

If the price is $2.00 a bar, 7 million bars a week are demanded and 13 million bars are supplied. There is a surplus of 6 million bars a week, and the price falls.

If the price is $1.50 a bar, 10 million bars a week are demanded and 10 million bars are supplied. There is neither a shortage nor a surplus, and the price does not change. The price at which the quantity demanded equals the quantity supplied is the equilibrium price, and 10 million bars a week is the equilibrium quantity.

—————— **MyEconLab** Animation and Draw Graph ——————

million bars a week, as shown by the blue arrow. At each price *below* $1.50 a bar, there is a shortage of bars. For example, at $1.00 a bar, the shortage is 9 million bars a week, as shown by the red arrow.

Price Adjustments

You've seen that if the price is below equilibrium, there is a shortage; and if the price is above equilibrium, there is a surplus. But can we count on the price to change and eliminate a shortage or a surplus? We can, because such price changes are beneficial to both buyers and sellers. Let's see why the price changes when there is a shortage or a surplus.

A Shortage Forces the Price Up Suppose the price of an energy bar is $1. Consumers plan to buy 15 million bars a week, and producers plan to sell 6 million bars a week. Consumers can't force producers to sell more than they plan, so the quantity that is actually offered for sale is 6 million bars a week. In this situation, powerful forces operate to increase the price and move it toward the equilibrium price. Some producers, noticing lines of unsatisfied consumers, raise the price. Some producers increase their output. As producers push the price up, the price rises toward its equilibrium. The rising price reduces the shortage because it decreases the quantity demanded and increases the quantity supplied. When the price has increased to the point at which there is no longer a shortage, the forces moving the price stop operating and the price comes to rest at its equilibrium.

A Surplus Forces the Price Down Suppose the price of a bar is $2. Producers plan to sell 13 million bars a week, and consumers plan to buy 7 million bars a week. Producers cannot force consumers to buy more than they plan, so the quantity that is actually bought is 7 million bars a week. In this situation, powerful forces operate to lower the price and move it toward the equilibrium price. Some producers, unable to sell the quantities of energy bars they planned to sell, cut their prices. In addition, some producers scale back production. As producers cut the price, the price falls toward its equilibrium. The falling price decreases the surplus because it increases the quantity demanded and decreases the quantity supplied. When the price has fallen to the point at which there is no longer a surplus, the forces moving the price stop operating and the price comes to rest at its equilibrium.

The Best Deal Available for Buyers and Sellers When the price is below equilibrium, it is forced upward. Why don't buyers resist the increase and refuse to buy at the higher price? The answer is because they value the good more highly than its current price and they can't satisfy their demand at the current price. In some markets—for example, the markets that operate on eBay—the buyers might even be the ones who force the price up by offering to pay a higher price.

When the price is above equilibrium, it is bid downward. Why don't sellers resist this decrease and refuse to sell at the lower price? The answer is because their minimum supply price is below the current price and they cannot sell all they would like to at the current price. Sellers willingly lower the price to gain market share.

At the price at which the quantity demanded and the quantity supplied are equal, neither buyers nor sellers can do business at a better price. Buyers pay the highest price they are willing to pay for the last unit bought, and sellers receive the lowest price at which they are willing to supply the last unit sold.

When people freely make offers to buy and sell and when demanders try to buy at the lowest possible price and suppliers try to sell at the highest possible price, the price at which trade takes place is the equilibrium price—the price at which the quantity demanded equals the quantity supplied. The price coordinates the plans of buyers and sellers, and no one has an incentive to change it.

◆ REVIEW QUIZ

1 What is the equilibrium price of a good or service?
2 Over what range of prices does a shortage arise? What happens to the price when there is a shortage?
3 Over what range of prices does a surplus arise? What happens to the price when there is a surplus?
4 Why is the price at which the quantity demanded equals the quantity supplied the equilibrium price?
5 Why is the equilibrium price the best deal available for both buyers and sellers?

Work these questions in Study Plan 3.4 and get instant feedback. Do a Key Terms Quiz.   MyEconLab

Predicting Changes in Price and Quantity

The demand and supply model that we have just studied provides us with a powerful way of analyzing influences on prices and the quantities bought and sold. According to the model, a change in price stems from a change in demand, a change in supply, or a change in both demand and supply. Let's look first at the effects of a change in demand.

An Increase in Demand

If more people join health clubs, the demand for energy bars increases. The table in Fig. 3.8 shows the original and new demand schedules for energy bars as well as the supply schedule of energy bars.

The increase in demand creates a shortage at the original price, and to eliminate the shortage the price must rise.

Figure 3.8 shows what happens. The figure shows the original demand for and supply of energy bars. The original equilibrium price is $1.50 an energy bar, and the equilibrium quantity is 10 million energy bars a week. When demand increases, the demand curve shifts rightward. The equilibrium price rises to $2.50 an energy bar, and the quantity supplied increases to 15 million energy bars a week, as highlighted in the figure. There is an *increase in the quantity supplied* but *no change in supply*—a movement along, but no shift of, the supply curve.

A Decrease in Demand

We can reverse this change in demand. Start at a price of $2.50 a bar with 15 million energy bars a week being bought and sold, and then work out what happens if demand decreases to its original level. Such a decrease in demand might arise if people switch to energy drinks (a substitute for energy bars). The decrease in demand shifts the demand curve leftward. The equilibrium price falls to $1.50 a bar, the quantity supplied decreases, and the equilibrium quantity decreases to 10 million bars a week.

We can now make our first two predictions:

1. When demand increases, the price rises and the quantity increases.
2. When demand decreases, the price falls and the quantity decreases.

FIGURE 3.8   The Effects of a Change in Demand

Price (dollars per bar)	Quantity demanded (millions of bars per week)		Quantity supplied (millions of bars per week)
	Original	New	
0.50	22	32	0
1.00	15	25	6
1.50	**10**	20	**10**
2.00	7	17	13
2.50	5	15	15

Initially, the demand for energy bars is the blue demand curve. The equilibrium price is $1.50 a bar, and the equilibrium quantity is 10 million bars a week. When more health-conscious people do more exercise, the demand for energy bars increases and the demand curve shifts rightward to become the red curve.

At $1.50 a bar, there is now a shortage of 10 million bars a week. The price of a bar rises to a new equilibrium of $2.50. As the price rises to $2.50, the quantity supplied increases—shown by the blue arrow on the supply curve—to the new equilibrium quantity of 15 million bars a week. Following an increase in demand, the quantity supplied increases but supply does not change—the supply curve does not shift.

MyEconLab Animation and Draw Graph

ECONOMICS IN THE NEWS

The Market for College Education

Obama Decries Rising Cost of College Education

President Obama told colleges, "You can't assume that you'll just jack up tuition every single year. ... In the coming decade, 60 percent of new jobs will require more than a high school diploma ... Higher education is not a luxury. It's an economic imperative that every family in America should be able to afford."

Source: *The Associated Press*, January 27, 2012

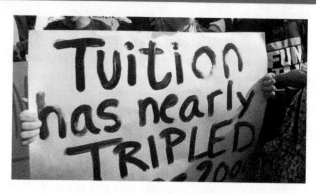

THE DATA

The scatter diagram provides data on college enrollments and tuition from 1994 through 2013.

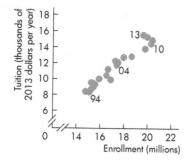

THE QUESTIONS

- What does the scatter diagram tell us?
- Why has college tuition increased? Is it because demand increased or supply increased?

THE ANSWERS

- The scatter diagram tells us that in most years through 2010, both tuition and enrollments increased. Since 2010, tuition has increased and enrollments have decreased.
- An increase in demand brings a rise in the price (tuition) and an increase in the quantity (enrollments).
- Because both the price and quantity increased through 2010, the demand for college education increased during those years.
- A decrease in supply brings a rise in price and a decrease in the quantity.
- Because the price increased and the quantity decreased after 2010, the supply of college education decreased during those recent years.
- The figure shows the market for college education.

- The supply curve of college education, S, slopes upward because the principle of increasing opportunity cost applies to college education just as it does to other goods and services.
- In 1994, the demand for college education was D_{1994}. The equilibrium tuition was $8,000 and 15 million students were enrolled in college.
- Between 1994 and 2010:
  1) Income per person increased
  2) Population increased, and
  3) More new jobs required higher education.
- These (and possibly other) factors increased the demand for a college education. The demand curve shifted rightward to D_{2010}. Equilibrium tuition increased to $15,000 and the quantity supplied increased to 20 million students.

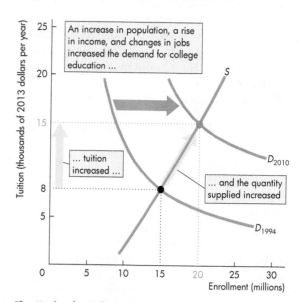

The Market for College Education

An Increase in Supply

When Nestlé (the producer of PowerBar) and other energy bar producers switch to a new cost-saving technology, the supply of energy bars increases. Figure 3.9 shows the new supply schedule (the same one that was shown in Fig. 3.5). What are the new equilibrium price and quantity? The price falls to $1.00 a bar, and the quantity increases to 15 million bars a week. You can see why by looking at the quantities demanded and supplied at the old price of $1.50 a bar. The new quantity supplied at that price is 20 million bars a week, and there is a surplus. The price falls. Only when the price is $1.00 a bar does the quantity supplied equal the quantity demanded.

Figure 3.9 illustrates the effect of an increase in supply. It shows the demand curve for energy bars and the original and new supply curves. The initial equilibrium price is $1.50 a bar, and the equilibrium quantity is 10 million bars a week. When supply increases, the supply curve shifts rightward. The equilibrium price falls to $1.00 a bar, and the quantity demanded increases to 15 million bars a week, highlighted in the figure. There is an *increase in the quantity demanded* but *no change in demand*—a movement along, but no shift of, the demand curve.

A Decrease in Supply

Start out at a price of $1.00 a bar with 15 million bars a week being bought and sold. Then suppose that the cost of labor or raw materials rises and the supply of energy bars decreases. The decrease in supply shifts the supply curve leftward. The equilibrium price rises to $1.50 a bar, the quantity demanded decreases, and the equilibrium quantity decreases to 10 million bars a week.

We can now make two more predictions:

1. When supply increases, the price falls and the quantity increases.
2. When supply decreases, the price rises and the quantity decreases.

You've now seen what happens to the price and the quantity when either demand or supply changes while the other one remains unchanged. In real markets, both demand and supply can change together. When this happens, to predict the changes in price and quantity, we must combine the effects that you've just seen. That is your final task in this chapter.

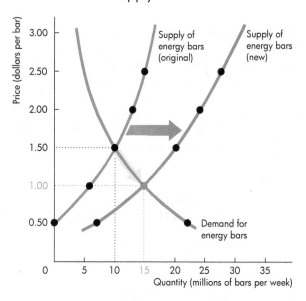

FIGURE 3.9   The Effects of a Change in Supply

Price (dollars per bar)	Quantity demanded (millions of bars per week)	Quantity supplied (millions of bars per week)	
		Original	New
0.50	22	0	7
1.00	15	6	15
1.50	10	10	20
2.00	7	13	25
2.50	5	15	27

Initially, the supply of energy bars is shown by the blue supply curve. The equilibrium price is $1.50 a bar, and the equilibrium quantity is 10 million bars a week. When the new cost-saving technology is adopted, the supply of energy bars increases and the supply curve shifts rightward to become the red curve.

At $1.50 a bar, there is now a surplus of 10 million bars a week. The price of an energy bar falls to a new equilibrium of $1.00 a bar. As the price falls to $1.00, the quantity demanded increases—shown by the blue arrow on the demand curve—to the new equilibrium quantity of 15 million bars a week. Following an increase in supply, the quantity demanded increases but demand does not change—the demand curve does not shift.

_____ **MyEconLab** Animation and Draw Graph _____

ECONOMICS IN THE NEWS

The Market for Coffee

Coffee Price Slides

With plentiful crops in Brazil and a recovery in Colombian production, the price of arabica beans has fallen.

Source: *The Financial Times*, October 24, 2013

THE DATA

	Quantity (millions of tons per year)	Price (dollars per pound)
2013	134	6.00
2014	145	5.00

THE QUESTIONS

- What does the data table tell us?
- Why did the price of coffee decrease? Is it because demand changed or because supply changed, and in which direction?

THE ANSWERS

- The data table tells us that during 2014, the quantity of coffee produced increased and the price of coffee fell.
- An increase in demand brings an increase in the quantity and a rise in the price.
- An increase in supply brings an increase in the quantity and a fall in the price.
- Because the quantity of coffee increased and the average price fell, there must have been an increase in the supply of coffee.
- The supply of coffee increases if the crop yields increase or if producers increase their plantings.
- The news clip says the Brazilian crop was plentiful and that the Colombian production recovered. These increases in production brought an increase in the supply of coffee.
- The figure illustrates the market for coffee in 2013 and 2014. The demand curve D shows the demand for coffee.
- In 2013, the supply curve was S_{13}, the average price was $6.00 per pound and the quantity of coffee traded was 134 million tons.
- In 2014, the increased coffee production in Brazil and Colombia increased the supply of coffee to S_{14}.

- The price fell to $5.00 per pound and the quantity traded increased to 145 million tons.
- The lower price brought an increase in the quantity of coffee demanded, which is shown by the movement along the demand curve.

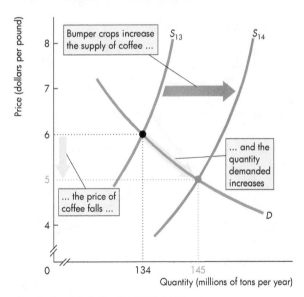

The Market for Coffee in 2013–2014

Changes in Both Demand and Supply

You now know how a change in demand or a change in supply changes the equilibrium price and quantity. But sometimes, events occur that change both demand and supply. When both demand and supply change, we find the resulting change in the equilibrium price and equilibrium quantity by combining the separate cases you've just studied.

Four cases need to be considered. Both demand and supply might increase or decrease, and demand or supply might increase and the other decrease.

Both Demand and Supply Change in the Same Direction When demand and supply change in the same direction, the equilibrium quantity changes in that same direction, but to predict whether the price rises or falls, we need to know the magnitudes of the changes in demand and supply.

If demand increases by more than supply increases, the price rises. But if supply increases by more than demand increases, the price falls.

Figure 3.10(a) shows the case when both demand and supply increase and by the same amount. The

equilibrium quantity increases. But because the increase in demand equals the increase in supply, neither a shortage nor a surplus arises so the price doesn't change. A bigger increase in demand would have created a shortage and a rise in the price; a bigger increase in supply would have created a surplus and a fall in the price.

Figure 3.10(b) shows the case when both demand and supply decrease by the same amount. Here the equilibrium quantity decreases and again the price might either rise or fall.

Both Demand and Supply Change in Opposite Directions When demand and supply change in opposite directions, we can predict how the price changes, but we need to know the magnitudes of the changes in demand and supply to say whether the equilibrium quantity increases or decreases.

If demand changes by more than supply, the equilibrium quantity changes in the same direction as the change in demand. But if supply changes by more than demand, the equilibrium quantity changes in the same direction as the change in supply.

FIGURE 3.10   The Effects of Changes in Both Demand and Supply in the Same Direction

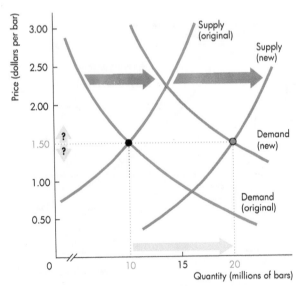

(a) Increase in both demand and supply

An increase in demand shifts the demand curve rightward to become the red new demand curve and an increase in supply shifts the supply curve rightward to become the red new supply curve. The price might rise or fall, but the quantity increases.

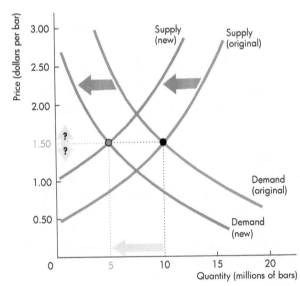

(b) Decrease in both demand and supply

A decrease in demand shifts the demand curve leftward to become the red new demand curve and a decrease in supply shifts the supply curve leftward to become the red new supply curve. The price might rise or fall, but the quantity decreases.

FIGURE 3.11   The Effects of Changes in Both Demand and Supply in Opposite Directions

(a) Decrease in demand; increase in supply

A decrease in demand shifts the demand curve leftward to become the red new demand curve and an increase in supply shifts the supply curve rightward to become the red new supply curve. The price falls, but the quantity might increase or decrease.

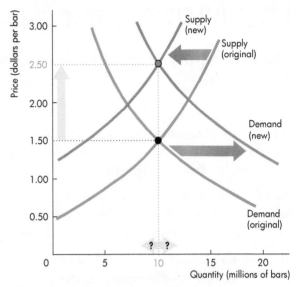

(b) Increase in demand; decrease in supply

An increase in demand shifts the demand curve rightward to become the red new demand curve and a decrease in supply shifts the supply curve leftward to become the red new supply curve. The price rises, but the quantity might increase or decrease.

MyEconLab Animation

Figure 3.11(a) illustrates what happens when demand decreases and supply increases by the same amount. At the initial price, there is a surplus, so the price falls. A decrease in demand decreases the quantity and an increase in supply increases the quantity, so when these changes occur together, we can't say what happens to the quantity unless we know the magnitudes of the changes.

Figure 3.11(b) illustrates what happens when demand increases and supply decreases by the same amount. In this case, at the initial price, there is a shortage, so the price rises. An increase in demand increases the quantity and a decrease in supply decreases the quantity, so again, when these changes occur together, we can't say what happens to the quantity unless we know the magnitudes of the changes in demand and supply.

For all the cases in Fig. 3.10 and Fig. 3.11 where you "can't say" what happens to the price or the quantity, draw some examples that go in each direction.

◆ REVIEW QUIZ

What is the effect on the price and quantity of MP3 players (such as the iPod) if

1 The price of a PC falls or the price of an MP3 download rises? (Draw the diagrams!)

2 More firms produce MP3 players or electronics workers' wages rise? (Draw the diagrams!)

3 Any two of the events in questions 1 and 2 occur together? (Draw the diagrams!)

Work these questions in Study Plan 3.5 and get instant feedback.   MyEconLab

◆ To complete your study of demand and supply, take a look at *Economics in the News* on pp. 74–75, which explains what would happen to the price of bananas if a disease that kill plants were to jump continents to Central America. Try to get into the habit of using the demand and supply model to understand the changes in prices in your everyday life.

Demand and Supply: The Market for Bananas

Banana Supply Seen at Risk as Disease Spreads

Bloomberg News
April 9, 2014

A disease damaging banana crops in Southeast Asia has spread to the Middle East and Africa, posing risks to world supply and trade totaling $8.9 billion, according to the United Nations' Food and Agriculture Organization.

The TR4 strain of Panama disease, a soil-born fungus that attacks plant roots, is deadly for the Cavendish banana that makes up about 95 percent of supplies to importers, including North America and Europe, Fazil Dusunceli, an agriculture officer at the FAO, said. ...

While the disease hasn't reached top Latin America exporters such as Ecuador, Costa Rica, or Colombia, TR4 was discovered in Jordan and Mozambique, indicating it moved beyond Asia, he said.

"The export market is dominated by the Cavendish, and it is unfortunately susceptible to this particular race of the disease," Dusunceli said. "This is serious for the medium term, but at the same time we should avoid panicking too."

Global exports reached a record value in 2011 and totaled 18.7 million metric tons, making bananas the world's most widely-traded fruit, according to the most recent FAO data. The United States is the top importer, followed by Belgium, the data show. Belgium's Port of Antwerp is the world's largest banana port, it says.

U.S. consumer prices for bananas were 59.9 cents a pound in February, 2.2 percent higher than an almost three-year low reached in October at 58.6 cents a pound, according to data from the Bureau of Labor Statistics. The export price of bananas from Ecuador, the world's biggest shipper, and Central America for U.S. destinations was $966.85 a ton in March, the highest in 18 months, according to the International Monetary Fund. ...

Whitney McFerron, "Banana Supply Seen by UN's FAO at Risk as Disease Spreads," Bloomberg News, April 4, 2014. Copyright © by Jessica Stremmel. Used by permission of Jessica Stremmel.

ESSENCE OF THE STORY

- The U.S. consumer price of bananas was 59.9 cents a pound in February 2014.

- About 95 percent of bananas traded are a variety called Cavendish.

- Cavendish banana plants can be destroyed by the TR4 strain of Panama disease.

- TR4 hasn't reached Latin America but it has jumped from Asia to the Middle East and Africa.

- Fazil Dusunceli of the United Nations' Food and Agriculture Organization says "This is serious for the medium term, but at the same time we should avoid panicking too."

MyEconLab More Economics in the News

ECONOMIC ANALYSIS

- In the market for bananas, a decrease in world production would decrease supply.

- A decrease in the supply of bananas would raise their price, decrease the equilibrium quantity, and decrease the quantity of bananas demanded.

- We can see the likely price increase by looking at previous events in the banana market.

- Figure 1 shows the price of bananas since 2004. You can see that there was a big temporary jump in the price in 2008.

- That jump in price was *not* caused by a decrease in banana production because as Fig. 2 shows, banana production has increased every year since 2004 except for 2012.

- What happened in 2008? The answer is a spike in the price of oil.

- Transporting bananas from plantations in Central and South America to your neighborhood grocery store uses a lot of fuel. So when the cost of fuel increased in 2008, the cost of delivering bananas increased, and the U.S. consumer price of bananas increased.

- A decrease in supply caused by the TR4 disease would have a similar effect on the banana market to what happened in 2008.

- Figure 3 illustrates this effect. The supply of bananas decreases from S_N (normal) to S_D (disease), the price rises, the equilibrium quantity decreases, and the quantity of bananas demanded decreases.

Figure 1 The Price of Bananas: 2004–2014

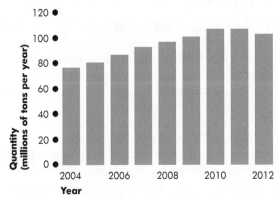

Figure 2 Banana Production: 2004–2012

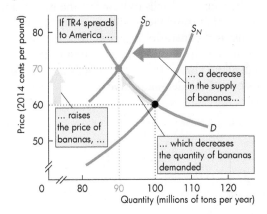

Figure 3 The Market for Bananas

MATHEMATICAL NOTE

Demand, Supply, and Equilibrium

Demand Curve

The law of demand says that as the price of a good or service falls, the quantity demanded of that good or service increases. We can illustrate the law of demand by drawing a graph of the demand curve or writing down an equation. When the demand curve is a straight line, the following equation describes it:

$$P = a - bQ_D,$$

where P is the price and Q_D is the quantity demanded. The a and b are positive constants.

The demand equation tells us three things:

1. The price at which no one is willing to buy the good (Q_D is zero). That is, if the price is a, then the quantity demanded is zero. You can see the price a in Fig. 1. It is the price at which the demand curve hits the y-axis—what we call the demand curve's "y-intercept."
2. As the price falls, the quantity demanded increases. If Q_D is a positive number, then the price P must be less than a. As Q_D gets larger, the price P becomes smaller. That is, as the quantity increases, the maximum price that buyers are willing to pay for the last unit of the good falls.
3. The constant b tells us how fast the maximum price that someone is willing to pay for the good falls as the quantity increases. That is, the constant b tells us about the steepness of the demand curve. The equation tells us that the slope of the demand curve is $-b$.

Supply Curve

The law of supply says that as the price of a good or service rises, the quantity supplied of that good or service increases. We can illustrate the law of supply by drawing a graph of the supply curve or writing down an equation. When the supply curve is a straight line, the following equation describes it:

$$P = c + dQ_S,$$

where P is the price and Q_S is the quantity supplied. The c and d are positive constants.

The supply equation tells us three things:

1. The price at which sellers are not willing to supply the good (Q_S is zero). That is, if the price is c, then no one is willing to sell the good. You can see the price c in Fig. 2. It is the price at which the supply curve hits the y-axis—what we call the supply curve's "y-intercept."
2. As the price rises, the quantity supplied increases. If Q_S is a positive number, then the price P must be greater than c. As Q_S increases, the price P becomes larger. That is, as the quantity increases, the minimum price that sellers are willing to accept for the last unit rises.
3. The constant d tells us how fast the minimum price at which someone is willing to sell the good rises as the quantity increases. That is, the constant d tells us about the steepness of the supply curve. The equation tells us that the slope of the supply curve is d.

Figure 1 Demand Curve

Figure 2 Supply Curve

Market Equilibrium

Demand and supply determine market equilibrium. Figure 3 shows the equilibrium price (P^*) and equilibrium quantity (Q^*) at the intersection of the demand curve and the supply curve.

We can use the equations to find the equilibrium price and equilibrium quantity. The price of a good adjusts until the quantity demanded Q_D equals the quantity supplied Q_S. So at the equilibrium price (P^*) and equilibrium quantity (Q^*),

$$Q_D = Q_S = Q^*.$$

To find the equilibrium price and equilibrium quantity, substitute Q^* for Q_D in the demand equation and Q^* for Q_S in the supply equation. Then the price is the equilibrium price (P^*), which gives

$$P^* = a - bQ^*$$
$$P^* = c + dQ^*.$$

Notice that

$$a - bQ^* = c + dQ^*.$$

Now solve for Q^*:

$$a - c = bQ^* + dQ^*$$
$$a - c = (b + d)Q^*$$
$$Q^* = \frac{a - c}{b + d}.$$

To find the equilibrium price P^*, substitute for Q^* in either the demand equation or the supply equation.

Using the demand equation, we have

$$P^* = a - b\left(\frac{a - c}{b + d}\right)$$
$$P^* = \frac{a(b + d) - b(a - c)}{b + d}$$
$$P^* = \frac{ad + bc}{b + d}.$$

Alternatively, using the supply equation, we have

$$P^* = c + d\left(\frac{a - c}{b + d}\right)$$
$$P^* = \frac{c(b + d) + d(a - c)}{b + d}$$
$$P^* = \frac{ad + bc}{b + d}.$$

An Example

The demand for ice-cream cones is

$$P = 800 - 2Q_D.$$

The supply of ice-cream cones is

$$P = 200 + 1Q_S.$$

The price of a cone is expressed in cents, and the quantities are expressed in cones per day.

To find the equilibrium price (P^*) and equilibrium quantity (Q^*), substitute Q^* for Q_D and Q_S and P^* for P. That is,

$$P^* = 800 - 2Q^*$$
$$P^* = 200 + 1Q^*$$

Now solve for Q^*:

$$800 - 2Q^* = 200 + 1Q^*$$
$$600 = 3Q^*$$
$$Q^* = 200.$$

And

$$P^* = 800 - 2(200)$$
$$= 400.$$

The equilibrium price is $4 a cone, and the equilibrium quantity is 200 cones per day.

Figure 3 Market Equilibrium

SUMMARY

Key Points

Markets and Prices (p. 56)

- A competitive market is one that has so many buyers and sellers that no single buyer or seller can influence the price.
- Opportunity cost is a relative price.
- Demand and supply determine relative prices.

Working Problem 1 will give you a better understanding of markets and prices.

Demand (pp. 57–61)

- Demand is the relationship between the quantity demanded of a good and its price when all other influences on buying plans remain the same.
- The higher the price of a good, other things remaining the same, the smaller is the quantity demanded—the law of demand.
- Demand depends on the prices of related goods (substitutes and complements), expected future prices, income, expected future income and credit, the population, and preferences.

Working Problems 2 to 4 will give you a better understanding of demand.

Supply (pp. 62–65)

- Supply is the relationship between the quantity supplied of a good and its price when all other influences on selling plans remain the same.
- The higher the price of a good, other things remaining the same, the greater is the quantity supplied—the law of supply.

- Supply depends on the prices of factors of production used to produce a good, the prices of related goods produced, expected future prices, the number of suppliers, technology, and the state of nature.

Working Problems 5 and 6 will give you a better understanding of supply.

Market Equilibrium (pp. 66–67)

- At the equilibrium price, the quantity demanded equals the quantity supplied.
- At any price above the equilibrium price, there is a surplus and the price falls.
- At any price below the equilibrium price, there is a shortage and the price rises.

Working Problem 7 will give you a better understanding of market equilibrium.

Predicting Changes in Price and Quantity (pp. 68–73)

- An increase in demand brings a rise in the price and an increase in the quantity supplied. A decrease in demand brings a fall in the price and a decrease in the quantity supplied.
- An increase in supply brings a fall in the price and an increase in the quantity demanded. A decrease in supply brings a rise in the price and a decrease in the quantity demanded.
- An increase in demand and an increase in supply bring an increased quantity but an uncertain price change. An increase in demand and a decrease in supply bring a higher price but an uncertain change in quantity.

Working Problems 8 to 10 will give you a better understanding of predicting changes in price and quantity.

Key Terms

MyEconLab Key Terms Quiz

Change in demand, 58
Change in supply, 63
Change in the quantity
    demanded, 61
Change in the quantity supplied, 64
Competitive market, 56
Complement, 59
Demand, 57

Demand curve, 58
Equilibrium price, 66
Equilibrium quantity, 66
Inferior good, 60
Law of demand, 57
Law of supply, 62
Money price, 56
Normal good, 60

Quantity demanded, 57
Quantity supplied, 62
Relative price, 56
Substitute, 59
Supply, 62
Supply curve, 62

WORKED PROBLEM

MyEconLab   You can work this problem in Chapter 3 Study Plan.

The table sets out the demand and supply schedules for roses on a normal weekend.

Price (dollars per rose)	Quantity demanded	Quantity supplied
	(roses per week)	
6.00	150	60
7.00	100	100
8.00	70	130
9.00	50	150

Questions

1. If the price of a rose is $6, describe the situation in the rose market. Explain how the price adjusts.

2. If the price of a rose is $9, describe the situation in the rose market. Explain how the price adjusts.

3. What is the market equilibrium?

4. Rose sellers know that Mother's Day is next weekend and they expect the price to be higher, so they withhold 60 roses from the market this weekend. What is the price this weekend?

5. On Mother's Day, demand increases by 160 roses. What is the price of a rose on Mother's Day?

Solutions

1. At $6 a rose, the quantity demanded is 150 and the quantity supplied is 60. The quantity demanded exceeds the quantity supplied and there is a *shortage* of 90 roses. With people lining up and a shortage, the price rises above $6 a rose.

Key Point: When a shortage exists, the price rises.

2. At $9 a rose, the quantity demanded is 50 and the quantity supplied is 150. The quantity supplied exceeds the quantity demanded and there is a *surplus* of 100 roses. With slow sales of roses and a surplus, the price falls to below $9 a rose.

Key Point: When a surplus exists, the price falls.

3. Market equilibrium occurs at the price at which the quantity demanded *equals* the quantity supplied. That price is $7 a rose. The market equilibrium is a price is $7 a rose and 100 roses a week. Point *A* on the figure.

Key Point: At market equilibrium, there is no shortage or surplus.

4. Sellers expect a higher price next weekend, so they decrease the quantity supplied this weekend by 60 roses at each price. Create the new table:

Price (dollars per rose)	Quantity demanded	Quantity supplied
	(roses per week)	
6.00	150	0
7.00	**100**	**40**
8.00	70	70
9.00	50	90

At $7 a rose, there is a shortage of 60 roses, so the price rises to $8 a rose, where the quantity demanded equals the quantity supplied. (Point *B*)

Key Point: When supply decreases, the price rises.

5. Demand increases by 160 roses. Sellers plan to increase the normal supply by the 60 roses withheld last weekend. Create the new table:

Price (dollars per rose)	Quantity demanded	Quantity supplied
	(roses per week)	
6.00	310	120
7.00	**260**	**160**
8.00	230	190
9.00	210	210

At $7 a rose, there is a shortage of 100 roses, so the price rises until, at $9 a rose, the quantity demanded equals the quantity supplied. The price on Mother's Day is $9 a rose. (Point *C*)

Key Point: When demand increases by more than supply, the price rises.

Key Figure

MyEconLab Interactive Animation

STUDY PLAN PROBLEMS AND APPLICATIONS

MyEconLab   You can work Problems 1 to 10 in Chapter 3 Study Plan and get instant feedback.

Markets and Prices (Study Plan 3.1)

1. In April 2014, the money price of a carton of milk was $2.01 and the money price of a gallon of gasoline was $3.63. Calculate the relative price of a gallon of gasoline in terms of milk.

Demand (Study Plan 3.2)

2. The price of food increased during the past year.
   a. Explain why the law of demand applies to food just as it does to other goods and services.
   b. Explain how the substitution effect influences food purchases when the price of food rises and other things remain the same.
   c. Explain how the income effect influences food purchases and provide some examples of the income effect.

3. Which of the following goods are likely substitutes and which are likely complements? (You may use an item more than once):

   coal, oil, natural gas, wheat, corn, pasta, pizza, sausage, skateboard, roller blades, video game, laptop, iPad, cellphone, text message, email

4. As the average income in China continues to increase, explain how the following will change:
   a. The demand for beef
   b. The demand for rice

Supply (Study Plan 3.3)

5. In 2013, the price of corn fell and some corn farmers will switch from growing corn in 2014 to growing soybeans.
   a. Does this fact illustrate the law of demand or the law of supply? Explain your answer.
   b. Why would a corn farmer grow soybeans?

6. Dairies make low-fat milk from full-cream milk, and in the process they produce cream, which is made into ice cream. The following events occur one at a time:
   (i)   The wage rate of dairy workers rises.
   (ii) The price of cream rises.
   (iii) The price of low-fat milk rises.
   (iv) With a drought forecasted, dairies raise their expected price of low-fat milk next year.
   (v)   New technology lowers the cost of producing ice cream.

   Explain the effect of each event on the supply of low-fat milk.

Market Equilibrium (Study Plan 3.4)

7. The demand and supply schedules for gum are

Price (cents per pack)	Quantity demanded	Quantity supplied
	(millions of packs a week)	
20	180	60
40	140	100
60	100	140
80	60	180

   a. Suppose that the price of gum is 70¢ a pack. Describe the situation in the gum market and explain how the price adjusts.
   b. Suppose that the price of gum is 30¢ a pack. Describe the situation in the gum market and explain how the price adjusts.

Predicting Changes in Price and Quantity (Study Plan 3.5)

8. The following events occur one at a time:
   (i)   The price of crude oil rises.
   (ii) The price of a car rises.
   (iii) All speed limits on highways are abolished.
   (iv) Robots cut car production costs.

   Explain the effect of each of these events on the market for gasoline.

9. In Problem 7, a fire destroys some factories that produce gum and the quantity of gum supplied decreases by 40 million packs a week at each price.
   a. Explain what happens in the market for gum and draw a graph to illustrate the changes.
   b. At the same time as the fire, the teenage population increases and the quantity of gum demanded increases by 40 million packs a week at each price. What is the new market equilibrium? Show the changes on your graph.

10. **Frigid Florida Winter is Bad News for Tomato Lovers**

    An unusually cold January in Florida destroyed entire fields of tomatoes. Florida's growers are shipping only a quarter of their usual 5 million pounds a week. The price has risen from $6.50 for a 25-pound box a year ago to $30 now.

    Source: *USA Today*, March 3, 2010

    a. Make a graph to illustrate the market for tomatoes before the unusually cold January and show how the events in the news clip influence the market for tomatoes.
    b. Why is the news "bad for tomato lovers"?

ADDITIONAL PROBLEMS AND APPLICATIONS

MyEconLab   You can work these problems in MyEconLab if assigned by your instructor.

Markets and Prices

11. What features of the world market for crude oil make it a competitive market?

12. The money price of a textbook is $90 and the money price of the Wii game *Super Mario Galaxy* is $45.
    a. What is the opportunity cost of a textbook in terms of the Wii game?
    b. What is the relative price of the Wii game in terms of textbooks?

Demand

13. The price of gasoline has increased during the past year.
    a. Explain why the law of demand applies to gasoline just as it does to all other goods and services.
    b. Explain how the substitution effect influences gasoline purchases and provide some examples of substitutions that people might make when the price of gasoline rises and other things remain the same.
    c. Explain how the income effect influences gasoline purchases and provide some examples of the income effects that might occur when the price of gasoline rises and other things remain the same.

14. Think about the demand for the three game consoles: Xbox One, PlayStation 4, and Wii U. Explain the effect of each of the following events on the demand for Xbox One games and the quantity of Xbox One games demanded, other things remaining the same. The events are
    a. The price of an Xbox One falls.
    b. The prices of a PlayStation 4 and a Wii U fall.
    c. The number of people writing and producing Xbox One games increases.
    d. Consumers' incomes increase.
    e. Programmers who write code for Xbox One games become more costly to hire.
    f. The expected future price of an Xbox One game falls.
    g. A new game console that is a close substitute for Xbox One comes onto the market.

Supply

15. Classify the following pairs of goods and services as substitutes in production, complements in production, or neither.
    a. Bottled water and health club memberships
    b. French fries and baked potatoes
    c. Leather boots and leather shoes
    d. Hybrids and SUVs
    e. Diet coke and regular coke

16. When a timber mill makes logs from trees it also produces sawdust, which is used to make plywood.
    a. Explain how a rise in the price of sawdust influences the supply of logs.
    b. Explain how a rise in the price of sawdust influences the supply of plywood.

17. **New Maple Syrup Sap Method**
    With the new way to tap maple trees, farmers could produce 10 times as much maple syrup per acre.

    Source: cbc.ca, February 5, 2014

    Will the new method change the supply of maple syrup or the quantity supplied of maple syrup, other things remaining the same? Explain.

Market Equilibrium

Use the following figure to work Problems 18 and 19.

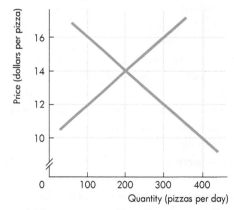

18. a. Label the curves. Which curve shows the willingness to pay for a pizza?
    b. If the price of a pizza is $16, is there a shortage or a surplus and does the price rise or fall?

c. Sellers want to receive the highest possible price, so why would they be willing to accept less than $16 a pizza?

19. a. If the price of a pizza is $12, is there a shortage or a surplus and does the price rise or fall?

b. Buyers want to pay the lowest possible price, so why would they be willing to pay more than $12 for a pizza?

20. The demand and supply schedules for potato chips are

Price (cents per bag)	Quantity demanded	Quantity supplied
	(millions of bags per week)	
50	160	130
60	150	140
70	140	150
80	130	160
90	120	170
100	110	180

a. Draw a graph of the potato chip market and mark in the equilibrium price and quantity.

b. If the price is 60¢ a bag, is there a shortage or a surplus, and how does the price adjust?

Predicting Changes in Price and Quantity

21. In Problem 20, a new dip increases the quantity of potato chips that people want to buy by 30 million bags per week at each price.

a. Does the demand for chips change? Does the supply of chips change? Describe the change.

b. How do the equilibrium price and equilibrium quantity of chips change?

22. In Problem 20, if a virus destroys potato crops and the quantity of potato chips produced decreases by 40 million bags a week at each price, how does the supply of chips change?

23. If the virus in Problem 22 hits just as the new dip in Problem 28 comes onto the market, how do the equilibrium price and equilibrium quantity of chips change?

24. **Strawberry Prices Drop as Late Harvest Hits Market**

Shoppers bought strawberries in March for $1.25 a pound rather than the $3.49 a pound they paid last year. With the price so low, some growers plowed over their strawberry plants to make way for spring melons; others froze their harvests and sold them to juice and jam makers.

Source: *USA Today*, April 5, 2010

a. Explain how the market for strawberries would have changed if growers had not plowed in their

plants but offered locals "you pick for free."

b. Describe the changes in demand and supply in the market for strawberry jam.

25. **"Popcorn Movie" Experience Gets Pricier**

Cinemas are raising the price of popcorn.

Demand for field corn, which is used for animal feed, corn syrup, and ethanol, has increased and its price has exploded. That's caused some farmers to shift from growing popcorn to easier-to-grow field corn.

Source: *USA Today*, May 24, 2008

Explain and illustrate graphically the events described in the news clip in the market for

a. Popcorn

b. Movie tickets

26. **Watch Out for Rising Dry-Cleaning Bills**

In the past year, the price of dry-cleaning solvent doubled. More than 4,000 dry cleaners across the United States disappeared as budget-conscious consumers cut back. This year the price of hangers used by dry cleaners is expected to double.

Source: CNN Money, June 4, 2012

a. Explain the effect of rising solvent prices on the market for dry cleaning.

b. Explain the effect of consumers becoming more budget conscious along with the rising price of solvent on the price of dry cleaning.

c. If the price of hangers does rise this year, do you expect additional dry cleaners to disappear? Explain why or why not.

Economics in the News

27. After you have studied *Economics in the News* on pp. 74–75, answer the following questions.

a. What would happen to the price of bananas if TR4 spread to Central America?

b. What are some of the substitutes for bananas and what would happen to demand, supply, price, and quantity in the markets for these items if TR4 were to come to America?

c. What are some of the complements of bananas and what would happen to demand, supply, price, and quantity in the markets for these items if TR4 were to come to America?

d. When the price of bananas increased in 2008, did it rise by as much as the rise in the price of oil? Why or why not?

e. Why would the expectation of the future arrival of TR4 in the Americas have little or no effect on today's price of bananas?

4 ELASTICITY

After studying this chapter, you will be able to:

◆ Define, calculate, and explain the factors that influence the price elasticity of demand

◆ Define, calculate, and explain the factors that influence the income elasticity of demand and the cross elasticity of demand

◆ Define, calculate, and explain the factors that influence the elasticity of supply

In 2013, coffee production soared and the price tumbled. Despite the increased production, coffee producers saw their revenue fall. How does the quantity of coffee produced influence the price of coffee and the revenue of coffee producers?

To answer this and similar questions, we use the neat tool that you study in this chapter: elasticity.

At the end of the chapter, in *Economics in the News*, we use the concept of elasticity to answer the question about the market for coffee. But we begin by explaining elasticity in another familiar setting: the market for pizza.

Price Elasticity of Demand

You know that when supply decreases, the equilibrium price rises and the equilibrium quantity decreases. But does the price rise by a large amount and the quantity decrease by a little? Or does the price barely rise and the quantity decrease by a large amount?

The answer depends on the responsiveness of the quantity demanded of a good to a change in its price. If the quantity demanded is not very responsive to a change in the price, the price rises a lot and the equilibrium quantity doesn't change much. If the quantity demanded *is* very responsive to a change in the price, the price barely rises and the equilibrium quantity changes a lot.

You might think about the responsiveness of the quantity demanded of a good to a change in its price in terms of the slope of the demand curve. If the demand curve is steep, the quantity demanded of the good isn't very responsive to a change in the price. If the demand curve is almost flat, the quantity demanded *is* very responsive to a change in the price.

But the slope of a demand curve depends on the units in which we measure the price and the quantity—we can make the curve steep or almost flat just by changing the units in which we measure the price and the quantity. Also we often want to compare the demand for different goods and services and quantities of these goods are measured in unrelated units. For example, a pizza producer might want to compare the demand for pizza with the demand for soft drinks. Which quantity demanded is more responsive to a price change? This question can't be answered by comparing the slopes of two demand curves. The units of measurement of pizza and soft drinks are unrelated. But the question *can* be answered with a measure of responsiveness that is *independent* of units of measurement. Elasticity is such a measure.

The **price elasticity of demand** is a units-free measure of the responsiveness of the quantity demanded of a good to a change in its price when all other influences on buying plans remain the same.

Calculating Price Elasticity of Demand

We calculate the *price elasticity of demand* by using the formula:

$$\text{Price elasticity of demand} = \frac{\text{Percentage change in quantity damanded}}{\text{Percentage change in price}}.$$

To calculate the price elasticity of demand for pizza, we need to know the quantity demanded of pizza at two different prices, when all other influences on buying plans remain the same.

Figure 4.1 zooms in on a section of the demand curve for pizza and shows how the quantity demanded responds to a small change in price. Initially, the price is $20.50 a pizza and 9 pizzas an hour are demanded—the original point. The price then falls to $19.50 a pizza, and the quantity demanded increases to 11 pizzas an hour—the new point. When the price falls by $1 a pizza, the quantity demanded increases by 2 pizzas an hour.

To calculate the price elasticity of demand, we express the change in price as a percentage of the *average price* and the change in the quantity demanded as a percentage of the *average quantity*. By using the average price and average quantity, we calculate the elasticity at a point on the demand curve midway between the original point and the new point.

The original price is $20.50 and the new price is $19.50, so the price change is $1 and the average price is $20 a pizza. Call the percentage change in the price $\%\Delta P$, then

$$\%\Delta P = \Delta P/P_{ave} \times 100 = (\$1/\$20) \times 100 = 5\%.$$

The original quantity demanded is 9 pizzas and the new quantity demanded is 11 pizzas, so the quantity change is 2 pizzas and the average quantity demanded is 10 pizzas. Call the percentage change in the quantity demanded $\%\Delta Q$, then

$$\%\Delta Q = \Delta Q/Q_{ave} \times 100 = (2/10) \times 100 = 20\%.$$

The price elasticity of demand equals the percentage change in the quantity demanded (20 percent) divided by the percentage change in price (5 percent) and is 4. That is,

$$\begin{aligned} \text{Price elasticity of demand} &= \frac{\%\Delta Q}{\%\Delta P} \\ &= \frac{20\%}{5\%} = 4. \end{aligned}$$

Average Price and Quantity Notice that we use the *average* price and *average* quantity. We do this because it gives the most precise measurement of elasticity—at the *midpoint* between the original price and the new price. If the price falls from $20.50 to $19.50, the $1 price change is 4.9 percent of $20.50. The change in quantity of 2 pizzas is 22.2 percent of 9 pizzas, the original quantity. So if we use these

FIGURE 4.1   Calculating the Elasticity of Demand

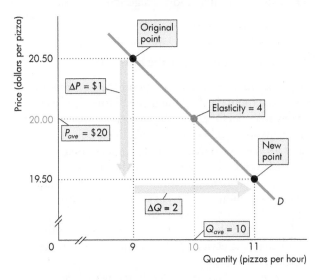

The elasticity of demand is calculated by using the formula:*

$$\text{Price elasticity of demand} = \frac{\text{Percentage change in quantity demanded}}{\text{Percentage change in price}}$$

$$= \frac{\%\Delta Q}{\%\Delta P}$$

$$= \frac{\Delta Q/Q_{ave}}{\Delta P/P_{ave}}$$

$$= \frac{2/10}{1/20} = 4.$$

This calculation measures the elasticity at an average price of $20 a pizza and an average quantity of 10 pizzas an hour.

* In the formula, the Greek letter delta (Δ) stands for "change in" and %Δ stands for "percentage change in."

MyEconLab Animation and Draw Graph

numbers, the price elasticity of demand is 22.2 divided by 4.9, which equals 4.5. But if the price rises from $19.50 to $20.50, the $1 price change is 5.1 percent of $19.50. The change in quantity of 2 pizzas is 18.2 percent of 11 pizzas, the original quantity. So if we use these numbers, the price elasticity of demand is 18.2 divided by 5.1, which equals 3.6.

By using percentages of the *average* price and *average* quantity, we get the *same value* for the elasticity regardless of whether the price falls from $20.50 to $19.50 or rises from $19.50 to $20.50.

Percentages and Proportions   Elasticity is the ratio of two percentage changes, so when we divide one percentage change by another, the 100s cancel. A percentage change is a *proportionate* change multiplied by 100. The proportionate change in price is $\Delta P/P_{ave}$, and the proportionate change in quantity demanded is $\Delta Q/Q_{ave}$. So if we divide $\Delta Q/Q_{ave}$ by $\Delta P/P_{ave}$ we get the same answer as we get by using percentage changes.

A Units-Free Measure   Now that you've calculated a price elasticity of demand, you can see why it is a *units-free measure*. Elasticity is a units-free measure because the percentage change in each variable is independent of the units in which the variable is measured. The ratio of the two percentages is a number without units.

Minus Sign and Elasticity   When the price of a good *rises*, the quantity demanded *decreases*. Because a *positive* change in price brings a *negative* change in the quantity demanded, the price elasticity of demand is a negative number. But it is the magnitude, or *absolute value*, of the price elasticity of demand that tells us how responsive the quantity demanded is. So to compare price elasticities of demand, we use the *magnitude* of the elasticity and ignore the minus sign.

Inelastic and Elastic Demand

If the quantity demanded remains constant when the price changes, then the price elasticity of demand is zero and the good is said to have a **perfectly inelastic demand**. One good that has a very low price elasticity of demand (perhaps zero over some price range) is insulin. Insulin is of such importance to some diabetics that if the price rises or falls, they do not change the quantity they buy.

If the percentage change in the quantity demanded equals the percentage change in the price, then the price elasticity equals 1 and the good is said to have a **unit elastic demand.**

Between perfectly inelastic demand and unit elastic demand is a general case in which *the percentage change in the quantity demanded is less than the percentage change in the price*. In this case, the price elasticity of demand is between zero and 1 and the good is said to have an **inelastic demand**. Food and shelter are examples of goods with inelastic demand.

If the quantity demanded changes by an infinitely large percentage in response to a tiny price change, then the price elasticity of demand is infinity and the good is said to have a **perfectly elastic demand**. An example of a good that has a very high elasticity of demand (almost infinite) is a soft drink from two campus machines located side by side. If the two machines offer the same soft drinks for the same price, some people buy from one machine and some from the other. But if one machine's price is higher than the other's, by even a small amount, no one buys from the machine with the higher price. Drinks from the two machines are perfect substitutes. The demand for a good that has a perfect substitute is perfectly elastic.

Between unit elastic demand and perfectly elastic demand is another general case in which *the percentage change in the quantity demanded exceeds the percentage change in price*. In this case, the price elasticity of demand is greater than 1 and the good is said to have an **elastic demand**. Automobiles and furniture are examples of goods that have elastic demand.

Figure 4.2 shows three demand curves that cover the entire range of possible elasticities of demand that you've just reviewed. In Fig. 4.2(a), the quantity demanded is constant regardless of the price, so this demand is perfectly inelastic. In Fig. 4.2(b), the percentage change in the quantity demanded equals the percentage change in price, so this demand is unit elastic. In Fig. 4.2(c), the price is constant regardless of the quantity demanded, so this figure illustrates a perfectly elastic demand.

You now know the distinction between elastic and inelastic demand. But what determines whether the demand for a good is elastic or inelastic?

The Factors that Influence the Elasticity of Demand

The elasticity of demand for a good depends on

- The closeness of substitutes
- The proportion of income spent on the good
- The time elapsed since the price change

Closeness of Substitutes The closer the substitutes for a good, the more elastic is the demand for it. Oil as fuel or raw material for chemicals has no close substitutes so the demand for oil is inelastic. Plastics are close substitutes for metals, so the demand for metals is elastic.

The degree of substitutability depends on how narrowly (or broadly) we define a good. For example, a smartphone has no close substitutes, but an Apple iPhone is a close substitute for a Samsung Galaxy. So the elasticity of demand for smartphones is lower than the elasticity of demand for an iPhone or a Galaxy.

In everyday language we call goods such as food and shelter *necessities* and goods such as exotic vacations *luxuries*. A necessity has poor substitutes, so it generally has an inelastic demand. A luxury usually has many substitutes, one of which is not buying it. So a luxury generally has an elastic demand.

Proportion of Income Spent on the Good Other things remaining the same, the greater the proportion of income spent on a good, the more elastic (or less inelastic) is the demand for it.

FIGURE 4.2   Inelastic and Elastic Demand

(a) Perfectly inelastic demand   **(b) Unit elastic demand**   **(c) Perfectly elastic demand**

Each demand illustrated here has a constant elasticity. The demand curve in part (a) illustrates the demand for a good that has a zero elasticity of demand. The demand curve in part (b) illustrates the demand for a good with a unit elasticity of demand. And the demand curve in part (c) illustrates the demand for a good with an infinite elasticity of demand.

Think about your own elasticity of demand for chewing gum and housing. If the price of gum rises, you consume almost as much as before. Your demand for gum is inelastic. If apartment rents rise, you look for someone to share with. Your demand for housing is not as inelastic as your demand for gum. Why the difference? Housing takes a big chunk of your budget, and gum takes little. You barely notice the higher price of gum, while the higher rent puts your budget under severe strain.

Time Elapsed Since Price Change The longer the time that has elapsed since a price change, the more elastic is demand. When the price of oil increased by 400 percent during the 1970s, people barely changed the quantity of oil and gasoline they bought. But gradually, as more efficient auto and airplane engines were developed, the quantity bought decreased. The demand for oil became more elastic as more time elapsed following the huge price hike.

Elasticity Along a Linear Demand Curve

Elasticity of demand is not the same as slope. And a good way to see this fact is by studying a demand curve that has a constant slope but a varying elasticity.

The demand curve in Fig. 4.3 is linear, which means that it has a constant slope. Along this demand curve, a $5 rise in the price brings a decrease of 10 pizzas an hour.

But the price elasticity of demand is not constant along this demand curve. To see why, let's calculate some elasticities.

At the midpoint of the demand curve, the price is $12.50 and the quantity is 25 pizzas per hour. If the price rises from $10 to $15 a pizza, the quantity demanded decreases from 30 to 20 pizzas an hour and the average price and average quantity are at the midpoint of the demand curve. So

$$\text{Price elasticity of demand} = \frac{10/25}{5/12.50}$$
$$= 1.$$

That is, at the midpoint of a linear demand curve, the price elasticity of demand is 1.

At prices *above* the midpoint, the price elasticity of demand is greater than 1: Demand is elastic. To see that demand is elastic, let's calculate the elasticity when the price rises from $15 to $25 a pizza. You can see that quantity demanded decreases from 20 to zero pizzas an hour. The average price is $20 a pizza, and

FIGURE 4.3   Elasticity Along a Linear Demand Curve

On a linear demand curve, demand is unit elastic at the midpoint (elasticity is 1), elastic above the midpoint, and inelastic below the midpoint.

―――――― MyEconLab Animation and Draw Graph ――――――

the average quantity is 10 pizzas. Putting these numbers into the elasticity formula:

$$\text{Price elasticity of demand} = \frac{\Delta Q/Q_{ave}}{\Delta P/P_{ave}}$$
$$= \frac{20/10}{10/20}$$
$$= 4.$$

That is, the price elasticity of demand at an average price of $20 a pizza is 4.

At prices *below* the midpoint, the price elasticity of demand is less than 1: Demand is inelastic. For example, if the price rises from zero to $10 a pizza, the quantity demanded decreases from 50 to 30 pizzas an hour. The average price is now $5 and the average quantity is 40 pizzas an hour. So

$$\text{Price elasticity of demand} = \frac{20/40}{10/5}$$
$$= 1/4.$$

That is, the price elasticity of demand at an average price of $5 a pizza is 1/4.

Total Revenue and Elasticity

The **total revenue** from the sale of a good equals the price of the good multiplied by the quantity sold. When a price changes, total revenue also changes. But a cut in the price does not always decrease total revenue. The change in total revenue depends on the elasticity of demand in the following way:

- If demand is elastic, a 1 percent price cut increases the quantity sold by more than 1 percent and total revenue increase s.
- If demand is inelastic, a 1 percent price cut increases the quantity sold by less than 1 percent and total revenue decreases.
- If demand is unit elastic, a 1 percent price cut increases the quantity sold by 1 percent and total revenue does not change.

In Fig. 4.4(a), over the price range $25 to $12.50 a pizza, demand is elastic. At a price of $12.50 a pizza, demand is unit elastic. Over the price range from $12.50 a pizza to zero, demand is inelastic.

Figure 4.4(b) shows total revenue. At a price of $25, the quantity sold is zero, so total revenue is zero. At a price of zero, the quantity demanded is 50 pizzas an hour and total revenue is again zero. A price cut in the elastic range brings an increase in total revenue—the percentage increase in the quantity demanded is greater than the percentage decrease in price. A price cut in the inelastic range brings a decrease in total revenue—the percentage increase in the quantity demanded is less than the percentage decrease in price. At unit elasticity, total revenue is at a maximum.

Figure 4.4 shows how we can use this relationship between elasticity and total revenue to estimate elasticity using the total revenue test. The **total revenue test** is a method of estimating the price elasticity of demand by observing the change in total revenue that results from a change in the price, when all other influences on the quantity sold remain the same.

- If a price cut increases total revenue, demand is elastic.
- If a price cut decreases total revenue, demand is inelastic.
- If a price cut leaves total revenue unchanged, demand is unit elastic.

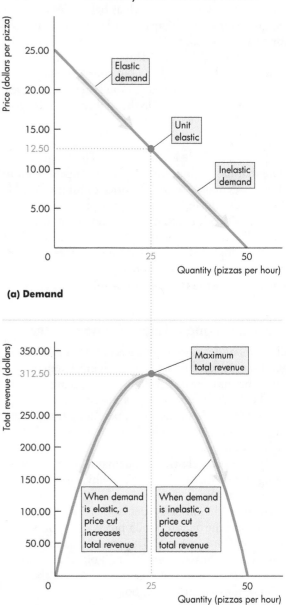

FIGURE 4.4   Elasticity and Total Revenue

(a) Demand

(b) Total revenue

When demand is elastic, in the price range from $25 to $12.50, a decrease in price (part a) brings an increase in total revenue (part b). When demand is inelastic, in the price range from $12.50 to zero, a decrease in price (part a) brings a decrease in total revenue (part b). When demand is unit elastic, at a price of $12.50 (part a), total revenue is at a maximum (part b).

MyEconLab Animation

ECONOMICS IN ACTION
Elastic and Inelastic Demand

The real-world price elasticities of demand in the table range from 1.52 for metals, the item with the most elastic demand in the table, to 0.05 for oil, the item with the most inelastic demand in the table. The demand for food is also inelastic.

Oil and food, which have poor substitutes and inelastic demand, might be classified as necessities. Furniture and motor vehicles, which have good substitutes and elastic demand, might be classified as luxuries.

Price Elasticities of Demand

Good or Service	Elasticity
Elastic Demand	
Metals	1.52
Electrical engineering products	1.39
Mechanical engineering products	1.30
Furniture	1.26
Motor vehicles	1.14
Instrument engineering products	1.10
Transportation services	1.03
Inelastic Demand	
Gas, electricity, and water	0.92
Chemicals	0.89
Clothing	0.64
Banking and insurance services	0.56
Housing services	0.55
Agricultural and fish products	0.42
Books, magazines, and newspapers	0.34
Food	0.12
Cigarettes	0.11
Soft drinks	0.05
Oil	0.05

Sources of data: Ahsan Mansur and John Whalley, "Numerical Specification of Applied General Equilibrium Models: Estimation, Calibration, and Data," in *Applied General Equilibrium Analysis,* eds. Herbert E. Scarf and John B. Shoven (New York: Cambridge University Press, 1984), 109, Henri Theil, Ching-Fan Chung, and James L. Seale, Jr., *Advances in Econometrics, Supplement I,* 1989, *International Evidence on Consumption Patterns* (Greenwich, Conn.: JAI Press Inc., 1989), and Emilio Pagoulatos and Robert Sorensen, "What Determines the Elasticity of Industry Demand," *International Journal of Industrial Organization,* 1986, and Geoffrey Heal, Columbia University, Web site.

Price Elasticities of Demand for Food

The price elasticity of demand for food in the United States is estimated to be 0.12. This elasticity is an average over all types of food. The demand for most food items is inelastic, but there is a wide range of elasticities as the figure below shows for a range of fruits, vegetables, and meats.

The demand for grapes and the demand for beef are elastic. The demand for oranges is unit elastic. These food items, especially grapes and beef, have many good substitutes. Florida winter tomatoes have closer substitutes than tomatoes in general, so the demand for the Florida winter variety is more elastic (less inelastic) than the demand for tomatoes.

Carrots and cabbage, on which we spend a very small proportion of income, have an almost zero elastic demand.

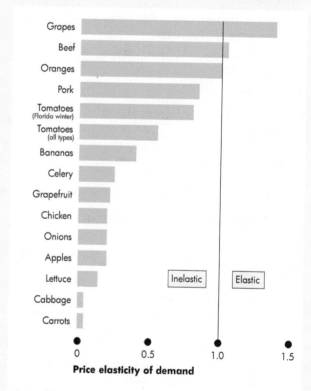

Price Elasticities of Demand for Food

Sources of data: Kuo S. Huang, *U.S. demand for food: A complete system of price and income effects* U.S. Dept. of Agriculture, Economic Research Service, Washington, DC, 1985; J. Scott Shonkwiler and Robert D. Emerson, "Imports and the Supply of Winter Tomatoes: An Application of Rational Expectations," *American Journal of Agricultural Economics,* Vol. 64, No. 4 (Nov., 1982), pp. 634–641; and Kuo S. Huang, "A Further Look at Flexibilities and Elasticities," *American Journal of Agricultural Economics,* Vol. 76, No. 2 (May, 1994), pp. 313–317.

ECONOMICS IN THE NEWS

The Elasticity of Demand for Peanut Butter

Peanut Butter Prices to Rise 30 to 40 Percent

Scott Karns, president and CEO of Karns Foods, said "People are still going to need it for their family. It's still an extremely economical item." Patty Nolan, who is on a fixed income, said "I love peanut butter so I'm using a little less so I don't go through it."

Source: *The Patriot-News*, November 2, 2011

THE DATA

	Quantity (millions of tons per year)	Price (dollars per pound)
2011	350	2.00
2012	300	2.80

THE QUESTIONS

- Does the news clip imply that the demand for peanut butter is elastic or inelastic?
- If the data are two points on the demand curve for peanut butter, what is the price elasticity of demand?

THE ANSWERS

- The two remarks in the news clip suggest that the quantity of peanut butter demanded will decrease when the price rises, but not by much. The demand for peanut butter is inelastic.

- The data table says the price of peanut butter increased by $0.80 with an average price of $2.40, so the price increased by 33.3 percent. The quantity demanded decreased by 50 million tons with an average quantity of 325 million tons, so the quantity demanded decreased by 15.4 percent. The price elasticity of demand equals 15.4 percent divided by 33.3 percent, which is 0.46.

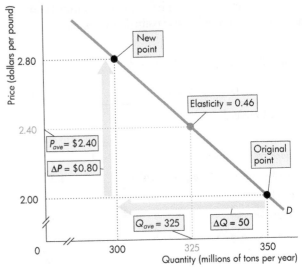

Calculating the Price Elasticity of Demand for Peanut Butter

MyEconLab More Economics in the News

Your Expenditure and Your Elasticity

When the price of a good changes, the change in your expenditure on the good depends on *your* elasticity of demand.

- If your demand for the good is elastic, a 1 percent price cut increases the quantity you buy by more than 1 percent and your expenditure on the item increases.
- If your demand for the good is inelastic, a 1 percent price cut increases the quantity you buy by less than 1 percent and your expenditure on the item decreases.
- If your demand for the good is unit elastic, a 1 percent price cut increases the quantity you buy by 1 percent and your expenditure on the item does not change.

So if you spend more on an item when its price falls, your demand for that item is elastic; if you spend the same amount, your demand is unit elastic; and if you spend less, your demand is inelastic.

REVIEW QUIZ

1. Why do we need a units-free measure of the responsiveness of the quantity demanded of a good or service to a change in its price?
2. Define the price elasticity of demand and show how it is calculated.
3. What makes the demand for some goods elastic and the demand for other goods inelastic?
4. Why is the demand for a luxury generally more elastic (or less inelastic) than the demand for a necessity?
5. What is the total revenue test?

Work these questions in Study Plan 4.1 and get instant feedback. Do a Key Terms Quiz.   MyEconLab

You've now completed your study of the *price* elasticity of demand. Two other elasticity concepts tell us about the effects of other influences on demand. Let's look at these other elasticities of demand.

More Elasticities of Demand

Suppose the economy is expanding and people are enjoying rising incomes. You know that a change in income changes demand. So this increased prosperity brings an increase in the demand for most types of goods and services. By how much will a rise in income increase the demand for pizza? This question is answered by the income elasticity of demand.

Income Elasticity of Demand

The **income elasticity of demand** is a measure of the responsiveness of the demand for a good or service to a change in income, other things remaining the same. It tells us by how much a demand curve shifts at a given price.

The income elasticity of demand is calculated by using the formula:

$$\text{Income elasticity of demand} = \frac{\text{Percentage change in quantity demanded}}{\text{Percentage change in income}}.$$

Income elasticities of demand can be positive or negative and they fall into three interesting ranges:

- Positive and greater than 1 (*normal* good, income elastic)
- Positive and less than 1 (*normal* good, income inelastic)
- Negative (*inferior* good)

Income Elastic Demand Suppose that the price of pizza is constant and 9 pizzas an hour are bought. Then incomes rise from $975 to $1,025 a week. No other influence on buying plans changes and the quantity of pizzas sold increases to 11 an hour.

The change in the quantity demanded is +2 pizzas. The average quantity is 10 pizzas, so the quantity demanded increases by 20 percent. The change in income is +$50 and the average income is $1,000, so incomes increase by 5 percent. The income elasticity of demand for pizza is

$$\frac{20\%}{5\%} = 4.$$

The demand for pizza is income elastic. The percentage increase in the quantity of pizza demanded exceeds the percentage increase in income.

ECONOMICS IN ACTION

Necessities and Luxuries

The demand for a necessity such as food or clothing is income inelastic, while the demand for a luxury such as airline and foreign travel is income elastic. But what is a necessity and what is a luxury depends on the level of income. For people with a low income, food and clothing can be luxuries. So the level of income has a big effect on income elasticities of demand.

The figure shows this effect on the income elasticity of demand for food in 10 countries. In countries with low incomes, such as Tanzania and India, the income elasticity of demand for food is high. In countries with high incomes, such as Canada, the income elasticity of demand for food is low. That is, as income increases, the income elasticity of demand for food decreases. Low-income consumers spend a larger percentage of any increase in income on food than do high-income consumers.

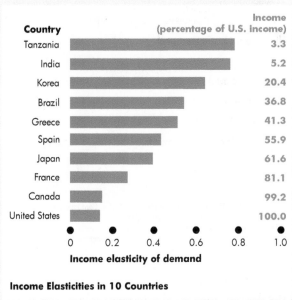

Income Elasticities in 10 Countries

Income Inelastic Demand If the income elasticity of demand is positive but less than 1, demand is income inelastic. The percentage increase in the quantity demanded is positive but less than the percentage increase in income.

Whether demand is income elastic or income inelastic has an important implication for the percentage of income spent on a good. If the demand for a good is *income elastic,* the percentage of income spent on that good *increases* as income increases. And

ECONOMICS IN ACTION

Income Elastic and Inelastic Demand

The table shows some real-world income elasticites of demand and confirms that a necessity such as food or clothing is income inelastic, while the demand for a luxury such as airline travel is income elastic.

Some Real-World Income Elasticities of Demand

Income Elastic Demand

Airline travel	5.82
Movies	3.41
Foreign travel	3.08
Electricity	1.94
Restaurant meals	1.61
Local buses and trains	1.38
Haircuts	1.36
Automobiles	1.07

Income Inelastic Demand

Tobacco	0.86
Alcoholic drinks	0.62
Furniture	0.53
Clothing	0.51
Newspapers and magazines	0.38
Telephone	0.32
Food	0.14

Sources of data: H.S. Houthakker and Lester D. Taylor, *Consumer Demand in the United States* (Cambridge, Mass.: Harvard University Press, 1970), and Henri Theil, Ching-Fan Chung, and James L. Seale, Jr., *Advances in Econometrics, Supplement 1, 1989, International Evidence on Consumption Patterns* (Greenwich, Conn.: JAI Press, Inc., 1989).

if the demand for a good is *income inelastic,* the percentage of income spent on that good *decreases* as income increases.

Inferior Goods If the income elasticity of demand is negative, the good is an *inferior* good. The quantity demanded of an inferior good and the amount spent on it *decrease* when income increases. Goods in this category include small motorcycles, potatoes, and rice. Low-income consumers buy these goods and spend a large percentage of their incomes on them.

Cross Elasticity of Demand

The burger shop next to your pizzeria has just raised its price of a burger. You know that pizzas and burgers are substitutes. You also know that when the price of a substitute for pizza *rises*, the demand for pizza *increases*. But how big is the influence of the price of a burger on the demand for pizza?

You know, too, that pizza and soft drinks are complements. And you know that if the price of a complement of pizza *rises*, the demand for pizza *decreases*. So you wonder, by how much will a rise in the price of a soft drink decrease the demand for your pizza?

To answer this question, you need to know about the cross elasticity of demand for pizza. Let's examine this elasticity measure.

We measure the influence of a change in the price of a substitute or complement by using the concept of the cross elasticity of demand. The **cross elasticity of demand** is a measure of the responsiveness of the demand for a good to a change in the price of a substitute or complement, other things remaining the same.

We calculate the *cross elasticity of demand* by using the formula:

$$\text{Cross elasticity of demand} = \frac{\text{Percentage change in quantity demanded}}{\text{Percentage change in price of a substitute or complement}}.$$

The cross elasticity of demand can be positive or negative. If the cross elasticity of demand is *positive*, demand and the price of the other good change in the *same* direction, so the two goods are *substitutes*. If the cross elasticity of demand is *negative*, demand and the price of the other good change in *opposite* directions, so the two goods are *complements*.

Substitutes Suppose that the price of pizza is constant and people buy 9 pizzas an hour. Then the price of a burger rises from $1.50 to $2.50. No other influence on buying plans changes and the quantity of pizzas bought increases to 11 an hour.

The change in the quantity demanded at the current price is +2 pizzas—the new quantity, 11 pizzas, minus the original quantity, 9 pizzas. The average quantity is 10 pizzas. So the quantity of pizzas demanded increases by 20 percent. That is,

$$\Delta Q/Q_{ave} \times 100 = (+2/10) \times 100 = +20\%.$$

The change in the price of a burger, a substitute for pizza, is +$1—the new price, $2.50, minus the original price, $1.50. The average price is $2 a burger. So the price of a burger rises by 50 percent. That is,

$$\Delta P/P_{ave} \times 100 = (+\$1/\$2) \times 100 = +50\%.$$

So the cross elasticity of demand for pizza with respect to the price of a burger is

$$\frac{+20\%}{+50\%} = 0.4.$$

Figure 4.5 illustrates the cross elasticity of demand. Because pizza and burgers are substitutes, when the price of a burger rises, the demand for pizza increases. The demand curve for pizza shifts rightward from D_0 to D_1. Because a *rise* in the price of a burger brings an *increase* in the demand for pizza, the cross elasticity of demand for pizza with respect to the price of a burger is *positive*. Both the price and the quantity change in the same direction.

Complements   Now suppose that the price of pizza is constant and 11 pizzas an hour are bought. Then the price of a soft drink rises from $1.50 to $2.50. No other influence on buying plans changes and the quantity of pizzas bought falls to 9 an hour.

FIGURE 4.5   Cross Elasticity of Demand

A burger is a *substitute* for pizza. When the price of a burger rises, the demand for pizza increases and the demand curve for pizza shifts rightward from D_0 to D_1. The cross elasticity of demand is *positive*.

A soft drink is a *complement* of pizza. When the price of a soft drink rises, the demand for pizza decreases and the demand curve for pizza shifts leftward from D_0 to D_2. The cross elasticity of demand is *negative*.

MyEconLab   Animation and Draw Graph

ECONOMICS IN THE NEWS

More Peanut Butter Demand Elasticities

Peanut Butter Related Markets
Professor Timothy Mathews teaches economics at Kennesaw State University, Georgia, the nation's number one peanut-producing state. The data table below shows his guesses about some demand elasticities for peanut butter.

Source: Timothy Mathews

THE DATA

Income elasticity	-0.31
Cross elasticity peanut butter and grape jelly	-0.27
Cross elasticity peanut butter and American cheese	+0.18

THE QUESTIONS

■ What do the data provided tell us about the demand for peanut butter? Is it a normal good?

■ Is grape jelly a substitute for or a complement of peanut butter? Is American cheese a substitute for or a complement of peanut butter?

THE ANSWERS

■ The income elasticity of demand for peanut butter is *negative*, which means that peanut butter is an *inferior good*. People buy less peanut butter as income rises.

■ The cross elasticity of demand of peanut butter with respect to the price of grape jelly is *negative*, which means that peanut butter and grape jelly are *complements*.

■ The cross elasticity of demand of peanut butter with respect to the price of American cheese is *positive*, which means that peanut butter and American cheese are *substitutes*.

MyEconLab   More Economics in the News

The change in the quantity demanded is the opposite of what we've just calculated: The quantity of pizzas demanded decreases by 20 percent (−20%).

The change in the price of a soft drink, a rise of $1 from $1.50 to $2.50, is the same as the change in the price of a burger that we've just calculated. That is, the price rises by 50 percent (+50%).

So the cross elasticity of demand for pizza with respect to the price of a soft drink is

$$\frac{-20\%}{+50\%} = -0.4.$$

Because pizza and soft drinks are complements, when the price of a soft drink rises, the demand for pizza decreases.

In Fig. 4.5, when the price of soft drinks rises the demand curve for pizza shifts leftward from D_0 to D_2. Because a *rise* in the price of a soft drink brings a *decrease* in the demand for pizza, the cross elasticity of demand for pizza with respect to the price of a soft drink is *negative*. The price and quantity change in *opposite* directions.

The magnitude of the cross elasticity of demand determines how far the demand curve shifts. The larger the cross elasticity (absolute value), the greater is the change in demand and the larger is the shift in the demand curve.

If two items are close substitutes, such as two brands of spring water, the cross elasticity is large. If two items are close complements, such as movies and popcorn, the cross elasticity is large.

If two items are somewhat unrelated to each other, such as newspapers and orange juice, the cross elasticity is small—perhaps even zero.

◆ REVIEW QUIZ

1 What does the income elasticity of demand measure?
2 What does the sign (positive/negative) of the income elasticity tell us about a good?
3 What does the cross elasticity of demand measure?
4 What does the sign (positive/negative) of the cross elasticity of demand tell us about the relationship between two goods?

Work these questions in Study Plan 4.2 and get instant feedback. Do a Key Terms Quiz.   MyEconLab

Elasticity of Supply

You know that when demand increases, the equilibrium price rises and the equilibrium quantity increases. But does the price rise by a large amount and the quantity increase by a little? Or does the price barely rise and the quantity increase by a large amount?

The answer depends on the responsiveness of the quantity supplied to a change in the price. If the quantity supplied is not very responsive to price, then an increase in demand brings a large rise in the price and a small increase in the equilibrium quantity. If the quantity supplied is highly responsive to price, then an increase in demand brings a small rise in the price and a large increase in the equilibrium quantity.

The problems that arise from using the slope of the supply curve to indicate responsiveness are the same as those we considered when discussing the responsiveness of the quantity demanded, so we use a units-free measure—the elasticity of supply.

Calculating the Elasticity of Supply

The **elasticity of supply** measures the responsiveness of the quantity supplied to a change in the price of a good when all other influences on selling plans remain the same. It is calculated by using the formula:

$$\text{Elasticity of supply} = \frac{\text{Percentage change in quantity supplied}}{\text{Percentage change in price}}.$$

We use the same method that you learned when you studied the elasticity of demand. (Refer back to p. 84 to check this method.)

Elastic and Inelastic Supply If the elasticity of supply is greater than 1, we say that supply is elastic; and if the elasticity of supply is less than 1, we say that supply is inelastic.

Suppose that when the price rises from $20 to $21, the quantity supplied increases from 10 to 20 pizzas per hour. The price rise is $1 and the average price is $20.50, so the price rises by 4.9 percent of the average price. The quantity increases from 10 to 20 pizzas an hour, so the increase is 10 pizzas, the average quantity is 15 pizzas, and the quantity increases by 67 percent. The elasticity of supply is equal to 67 percent divided by 4.9 percent, which equals 13.67. Because the elasticity of supply exceeds 1 (in this case by a lot), supply is elastic.

In contrast, suppose that when the price rises from $20 to $30, the quantity of pizza supplied increases from 10 to 13 per hour. The price rise is $10 and the average price is $25, so the price rises by 40 percent of the average price. The quantity increases from 10 to 13 pizzas an hour, so the increase is 3 pizzas, the average quantity is 11.5 pizzas an hour, and the quantity increases by 26 percent. The elasticity of supply is equal to 26 percent divided by 40 percent, which equals 0.65. Now, because the elasticity of supply is less than 1, supply is inelastic.

Figure 4.6 shows the range of elasticities of supply. If the quantity supplied is fixed regardless of the price, the supply curve is vertical and the elasticity of supply is zero. Supply is perfectly inelastic. This case is shown in Fig. 4.6(a). A special intermediate case occurs when the percentage change in price equals the percentage change in quantity. Supply is then unit elastic. This case is shown in Fig. 4.6(b). No matter how steep the supply curve is, if it is linear and passes through the origin, supply is unit elastic. If there is a price at which sellers are willing to offer any quantity for sale, the supply curve is horizontal and the elasticity of supply is infinite. Supply is perfectly elastic. This case is shown in Fig. 4.6(c).

The Factors That Influence the Elasticity of Supply

The elasticity of supply of a good depends on

- Resource substitution possibilities
- Time frame for the supply decision

Resource Substitution Possibilities Some goods and services can be produced only by using unique or rare productive resources. These items have a low, perhaps even a zero, elasticity of supply. Other goods and services can be produced by using commonly available resources that could be allocated to a wide variety of alternative tasks. Such items have a high elasticity of supply.

A van Gogh painting is an example of a good with a vertical supply curve and a zero elasticity of supply. At the other extreme, wheat can be grown on land that is almost equally good for growing corn, so it is just as easy to grow wheat as corn. The opportunity cost of wheat in terms of forgone corn is almost constant. As a result, the supply curve of wheat is almost horizontal and its elasticity of supply is very large. Similarly, when a good is produced in many different countries (for example, sugar and beef), the supply of the good is highly elastic.

The supply of most goods and services lies between these two extremes. The quantity produced

---

FIGURE 4.6   Inelastic and Elastic Supply

(a) Perfectly inelastic supply

(b) Unit elastic supply

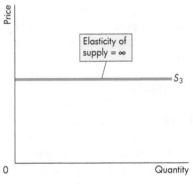

(c) Perfectly elastic supply

Each supply illustrated here has a constant elasticity. The supply curve in part (a) illustrates the supply of a good that has a zero elasticity of supply. Each supply curve in part (b) illustrates the supply of a good with a unit elasticity of supply. All linear supply curves that pass through the origin illustrate supplies that are unit elastic. The supply curve in part (c) illustrates the supply of a good with an infinite elasticity of supply.

can be increased but only by incurring a higher cost. If a higher price is offered, the quantity supplied increases. Such goods and services have an elasticity of supply between zero and infinity.

Time Frame for the Supply Decision To study the influence of the amount of time elapsed since a price change, we distinguish three time frames of supply:

- Momentary supply
- Short-run supply
- Long-run supply

Momentary Supply When the price of a good changes, the immediate response of the quantity supplied is determined by the *momentary supply* of that good.

Some goods, such as fruits and vegetables, have a perfectly inelastic momentary supply—a vertical supply curve. The quantities supplied depend on crop-planting decisions made earlier. In the case of oranges, for example, planting decisions have to be made many years in advance of the crop being available. Momentary supply is perfectly inelastic because, on a given day, no matter what the price of oranges, producers cannot change their output. They have picked, packed, and shipped their crop to market, and the quantity available for that day is fixed.

In contrast, some goods have a perfectly elastic momentary supply. Long-distance phone calls are an example. When many people simultaneously make a call, there is a big surge in the demand for telephone cables, computer switching, and satellite time. The quantity supplied increases, but the price remains constant. Long-distance carriers monitor fluctuations in demand and reroute calls to ensure that the quantity supplied equals the quantity demanded without changing the price.

Short-Run Supply The response of the quantity supplied to a price change when only *some* of the possible adjustments to production can be made is determined by *short-run supply*. Most goods have an inelastic short-run supply. To increase output in the short run, firms must work their labor force overtime and perhaps hire additional workers. To decrease their output in the short run, firms either lay off workers or reduce their hours of work. With the passage of time, firms can make more adjustments, perhaps training additional workers or buying additional tools and other equipment.

For the orange grower, if the price of oranges falls, some pickers can be laid off and oranges left on the trees to rot. Or if the price of oranges rises, the grower can use more fertilizer and improved irrigation to increase the yield of the existing trees.

But an orange grower can't change the number of trees producing oranges in the short run.

Long-Run Supply The response of the quantity supplied to a price change after *all* the technologically possible ways of adjusting supply have been exploited is determined by *long-run supply*. For most goods and services, long-run supply is elastic and perhaps perfectly elastic.

For the orange grower, the long run is the time it takes new tree plantings to grow to full maturity—about 15 years. In some cases, the long-run adjustment occurs only after a completely new production plant has been built and workers have been trained to operate it—typically a process that might take several years.

REVIEW QUIZ

1 Why do we need a units-free measure of the responsiveness of the quantity supplied of a good or service to a change in its price?
2 Define the elasticity of supply and show how it is calculated.
3 What are the main influences on the elasticity of supply that make the supply of some goods elastic and the supply of other goods inelastic?
4 Provide examples of goods or services whose elasticities of supply are (a) zero, (b) greater than zero but less than infinity, and (c) infinity.
5 How does the time frame over which a supply decision is made influence the elasticity of supply? Explain your answer.

Work these questions in Study Plan 4.3 and get instant feedback. Do a Key Terms Quiz.   MyEconLab

◆ You have now learned about the elasticities of demand and supply. Table 4.1 summarizes all the elasticities that you've met in this chapter. In the next chapter, we study the efficiency of competitive markets. But first study *Economics in the News* on pp. 98–99, which puts the elasticity of demand to work and looks at the market for coffee.

TABLE 4.1   A Compact Glossary of Elasticities

Price Elasticities of Demand

A relationship is described as	When its magnitude is	Which means that
Perfectly elastic	Infinity	The smallest possible increase in price causes an infinitely large decrease in the quantity demanded*
Elastic	Less than infinity but greater than 1	The percentage decrease in the quantity demanded exceeds the percentage increase in price
Unit elastic	1	The percentage decrease in the quantity demanded equals the percentage increase in price
Inelastic	Less than 1 but greater than zero	The percentage decrease in the quantity demanded is less than the percentage increase in price
Perfectly inelastic	Zero	The quantity demanded is the same at all prices

Cross Elasticities of Demand

A relationship is described as	When its value is	Which means that
Close substitutes	Large	The smallest possible increase in the price of one good causes an infinitely large increase in the quantity demanded* of the other good
Substitutes	Positive	If the price of one good increases, the quantity demanded of the other good also increases
Unrelated goods	Zero	If the price of one good increases, the quantity demanded of the other good remains the same
Complements	Negative	If the price of one good increases, the quantity demanded of the other good decreases

Income Elasticities of Demand

A relationship is described as	When its value is	Which means that
Income elastic (normal good)	Greater than 1	The percentage increase in the quantity demanded is greater than the percentage increase in income*
Income inelastic (normal good)	Less than 1 but greater than zero	The percentage increase in the quantity demanded is greater than zero but less than the percentage increase in income
Negative (inferior good)	Less than zero	When income increases, quantity demanded decreases

Elasticities of Supply

A relationship is described as	When its magnitude is	Which means that
Perfectly elastic	Infinity	The smallest possible increase in price causes an infinitely large increase in the quantity supplied*
Elastic	Less than infinity but greater than 1	The percentage increase in the quantity supplied exceeds the percentage increase in the price
Unit elastic	1	The percentage increase in the quantity supplied equals the percentage increase in the price
Inelastic	Greater than zero but less than 1	The percentage increase in the quantity supplied is less than the percentage increase in the price
Perfectly inelastic	Zero	The quantity supplied is the same at all prices

*In each description, the directions of change may be reversed. For example, in the case of a perfectly elastic demand, the smallest possible *decrease* in price causes an infinitely large *increase* in the quantity demanded.

The Elasticity of Demand for Coffee

Drop in Global Coffee Prices Shrinks Farmers' Revenue

Daily Monitor
November 6, 2013

Global coffee prices have continued on a downward trend, casting a gloomy picture on ... farmers' income.

Latest records from the International Coffee Organization (ICO) show the drop has continued even as the new coffee calendar begins.

By close of October, ICO [average price] dropped to 100.38 cents, down from the 111.82 cents per pound in September. ...

In an interview with the *Daily Monitor*, Mr. David Barry, the managing director of Kyagalanyi Coffee Ltd., Uganda's leading coffee exporting company, said: "We may not know what's ahead of us but trends show a further fall in prices and everyone has to brave this."

The drop in price has been attributed to increased production, with the biggest producers being Brazil and Vietnam. ... [Their] combined production reached 90 million bags, with the latter posting 60 million bags and the former 30 million.

Crop year 2012/13 has now closed in all exporting countries and according to available information, total production is estimated at 145.2 million bags. This is 12.8 million bags more than 2011/12, representing a 9.6 percent increase. ...

MyEconLab More Economics in the News

ESSENCE OF THE STORY

- Global coffee prices fell from 111.82 cents per pound in September 2013 to 100.38 cents per pound in November 2013.

- The fall in price was the result of increased production.

- Output in Brazil, the world's largest producer, was 60 million bags, and in Vietnam, the second-largest producer, it was 30 million bags.

- For the crop year 2012/13, total production was estimated at 145.2 million bags.

- Production in 2012/13 was 12.8 million bags more than 2011/12, a 9.6 percent increase.

ECONOMIC ANALYSIS

- The table below summarizes data provided by the International Coffee Organization, which supplements and updates some of the information in this news article.

Summary of Coffee Data

Year	Quantity produced (millions of bags)	Price (U.S. cents per pound)
2012	134	135
2013	145	100

- Figure 1 provides yet more data and shows that after falling through 2013, the price of coffee climbed steeply in 2014.

- The price of coffee fluctuates because the supply of coffee fluctuates. And the price fluctuates by much more than the quantity of coffee produced because the demand for coffee is inelastic.

- The news headline provides the first clue that demand is inelastic: When the price falls, revenue shrinks. This information enables us to use the *total revenue test*, "If a price cut decreases total revenue, then demand is inelastic."

- We can estimate the price elasticity of demand for coffee, assuming that demand didn't change, by using the events in the market in 2012 and 2013.

- Figure 2 illustrates the global market for coffee in these two years. The demand curve for coffee is D and in 2012, the supply curve of coffee was S_{12}. The equilibrium price was 135 cents per pound, and the equilibrium quantity was 134 million bags.

- In 2013, supply increased to S_{13}, the price fell to 100 cents per pound, and the quantity increased to 145 million bags.

- Figure 3 focuses on the demand curve and summarizes the elasticity calculation. The price fell by 35 cents, which is 30 percent of the average price of 117 cents. The quantity demanded increased by 11 million bags, which is 7.9 percent of the average quantity.

- The price elasticity of demand is 7.9 percent/30 percent, which equals 0.26. A 1 percent fall in price brings a 0.26 percent increase in the quantity demanded. And a 1 percent increase in the quantity brings a fall in price equal to 1/0.26, or almost 4 percent.

- When demand is inelastic, a small percentage change in the supply brings a large percentage change in the price.

Figure 1 The Coffee-Price Roller Coaster

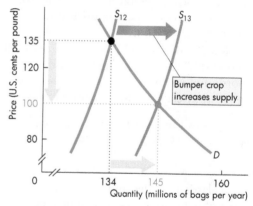

Figure 2 The Market for Coffee: 2012 and 2013

Figure 3 The Price Elasticity of Demand for Coffee

SUMMARY

Key Points

Price Elasticity of Demand (pp. 84–90)

- Elasticity is a measure of the responsiveness of the quantity demanded of a good to a change in its price, other things remaining the same.
- Price elasticity of demand equals the percentage change in the quantity demanded divided by the percentage change in the price.
- The larger the magnitude of the price elasticity of demand, the greater is the responsiveness of the quantity demanded to a given price change.
- If demand is elastic, a cut in price leads to an increase in total revenue. If demand is unit elastic, a cut in price leaves total revenue unchanged. And if demand is inelastic, a cut in price leads to a decrease in total revenue.
- Price elasticity of demand depends on how easily one good serves as a substitute for another, the proportion of income spent on the good, and the length of time elapsed since the price change.

Working Problems 1 to 5 will give you a better understanding of the price elasticity of demand.

More Elasticities of Demand (pp. 91–94)

- Income elasticity of demand measures the responsiveness of demand to a change in income, other things remaining the same. For a normal good, the income elasticity of demand is positive. For an inferior good, the income elasticity of demand is negative.
- When the income elasticity of demand is greater than 1 (income elastic), the percentage of income spent on the good increases as income increases.
- When the income elasticity of demand is less than 1 (income inelastic or inferior), the percentage of income spent on the good decreases as income increases.
- Cross elasticity of demand measures the responsiveness of the demand for one good to a change in the price of a substitute or a complement, other things remaining the same.
- The cross elasticity of demand with respect to the price of a substitute is positive. The cross elasticity of demand with respect to the price of a complement is negative.

Working Problems 6 to 8 will give you a better understanding of cross and income elasticities of demand.

Elasticity of Supply (pp. 94–96)

- Elasticity of supply measures the responsiveness of the quantity supplied of a good to a change in its price, other things remaining the same.
- The elasticity of supply is usually positive and ranges between zero (vertical supply curve) and infinity (horizontal supply curve).
- Supply decisions have three time frames: momentary, short run, and long run.
- Momentary supply refers to the response of the quantity supplied to a price change at the instant that the price changes.
- Short-run supply refers to the response of the quantity supplied to a price change after some of the technologically feasible adjustments in production have been made.
- Long-run supply refers to the response of the quantity supplied to a price change when all the technologically feasible adjustments in production have been made.

Working Problem 9 will give you a better understanding of the elasticity of supply.

Key Terms

MyEconLab Key Terms Quiz

Cross elasticity of demand, 92
Elastic demand, 86
Elasticity of supply, 94
Income elasticity of demand, 91

Inelastic demand, 85
Perfectly elastic demand, 85
Perfectly inelastic demand, 85
Price elasticity of demand, 84

Total revenue, 88
Total revenue test, 88
Unit elastic demand, 85

◆ WORKED PROBLEM

MyEconLab   You can work this problem in Chapter 4 Study Plan.

A rise in the price of a smoothie from $2 to $3 results in a fall in the quantity of smoothies demanded from 220 million to 180 million a day and at today's price of a muffin, $1.50, the quantity of muffins demanded increases from 80 million to 100 million a day.

Questions

1. Calculate the percentage change in the price of a smoothie and the percentage change in the quantity demanded of smoothies.
2. Calculate the price elasticity of demand for smoothies.
3. Is the demand for smoothies elastic or inelastic?
4. Calculate the cross elasticity of demand for muffins with respect to the price of a smoothie.

Solutions

1. The price of a smoothie rises by $1 and the quantity demanded falls by 40 million a day.

   To calculate the percentage changes in the price and quantity demanded, use the average price and average quantity. The figure illustrates the calculations.

   The average price of a smoothie is $2.50, so the percentage change in the price was ($1/$2.50) × 100, or 40 percent.

   The average quantity of smoothies is 200 million, so the percentage change in the quantity demanded was (40 million/200 million) × 100, or 20 percent.

Key Point: When working with elasticity, the percentage change in the price and quantity is the percentage of the average price and average quantity.

2. The price elasticity of demand is the ratio of the percentage change in the quantity to the percentage change in price.

   To calculate the price elasticity of demand for smoothies, divide the percentage change in quantity by the percentage change in the price. The ratio of two percentage changes has no units.

Key Point: The price elasticity calculated is the price elasticity of demand at the price midway between the original and the new prices. That is, it calculates the elasticity at the average price.

3. The price elasticity of demand for smoothies is *less than* 1, so the demand is inelastic.

Key Point: When the percentage change in the quantity demanded is *less than* the percentage change in the price, demand is inelastic and the price elasticity of demand is less than 1.

4. To calculate the cross elasticity of demand for muffins with respect to the price of a smoothie, divide the percentage change in quantity of muffins demanded by the percentage change in the price of a smoothie.

   When the price of a smoothie rises by 40 percent, the quantity of muffins demanded increases from 80 million to 100 million, a change of 20 million.

   The average quantity of muffins is 90 million, so the percentage change in the quantity of muffins is (20 million/90 million) × 100, which equals 22.2 percent.

   The cross elasticity of the demand for muffins with respect to the price of a smoothie equals 22.2 percent/40 percent, which equals 0.55.

   The cross elasticity of demand for muffins with respect to the price of a smoothie is *positive*, which means that muffins and smoothies are substitutes—just as you thought!

Key Point: The cross elasticity of demand is positive for substitutes and negative for complements.

Key Figure

MyEconLab Interactive Animation

◆ STUDY PLAN PROBLEMS AND APPLICATIONS

MyEconLab You can work Problems 1 to 9 in Chapter 4 Study Plan and get instant feedback.

Price Elasticity of Demand (Study Plan 4.1)

1. Rain spoils the strawberry crop, the price rises from $4 to $6 a box, and the quantity demanded decreases from 1,000 to 600 boxes a week.
   a. Calculate the price elasticity of demand over this price range.
   b. Describe the demand for strawberries.

2. If the quantity of dental services demanded increases by 10 percent when the price of dental services falls by 10 percent, is the demand for dental services inelastic, elastic, or unit elastic?

3. The demand schedule for hotel rooms is

Price (dollars per room per night)	Quantity demanded (millions of rooms per night)
200	100
250	80
400	50
500	40
800	25

   a. What happens to total revenue when the price falls from $400 to $250 a room per night and from $250 to $200 a room per night?
   b. Is the demand for hotel rooms elastic, inelastic, or unit elastic?

4. The figure shows the demand for pens.

   Calculate the elasticity of demand when the price rises from $4 to $6 a pen. Over what price range is the demand for pens elastic?

5. In 2003, when music downloading first took off, Universal Music slashed the average price of a CD from $21 to $15. The company expected the price cut to boost the quantity of CDs sold by 30

percent, other things remaining the same.
   a. What was Universal Music's estimate of the price elasticity of demand for CDs?
   b. If you were making the pricing decision at Universal Music, what would be your pricing decision? Explain your decision.

More Elasticities of Demand (Study Plan 4.2)

6. When Judy's income increased from $130 to $170 a week, she increased her demand for concert tickets by 15 percent and decreased her demand for bus rides by 10 percent. Calculate Judy's income elasticity of demand for (a) concert tickets and (b) bus rides.

7. If a 12 percent rise in the price of orange juice decreases the quantity of orange juice demanded by 22 percent and increases the quantity of apple juice demanded by 14 percent, calculate the
   a. Price elasticity of demand for orange juice.
   b. Cross elasticity of demand for apple juice with respect to the price of orange juice.

8. If a rise in the price of sushi from 98¢ to $1.02 a piece decreases the quantity of soy sauce demanded from 101 units to 99 units an hour and decreases the quantity of sushi demanded by 1 percent an hour, calculate the:
   a. Price elasticity of demand for sushi.
   b. Cross elasticity of demand for soy sauce with respect to the price of sushi.

Elasticity of Supply (Study Plan 4.3)

9. The table sets out the supply schedule of jeans.

Price (dollars per pair)	Quantity supplied (millions of pairs per year)
120	24
125	28
130	32
135	36

   a. Calculate the elasticity of supply when the price rises from $125 to $135 a pair.
   b. Calculate the elasticity of supply when the average price is $125 a pair.
   c. Is the supply of jeans elastic, inelastic, or unit elastic?

ADDITIONAL PROBLEMS AND APPLICATIONS

MyEconLab   You can work these problems in MyEconLab if assigned by your instructor.

Price Elasticity of Demand

10. With higher fuel costs, airlines raised their average fare from 75¢ to $1.25 per passenger mile and the number of passenger miles decreased from 2.5 million a day to 1.5 million a day.

    a. What is the price elasticity of demand for air travel over this price range?

    b. Describe the demand for air travel.

11. The figure shows the demand for DVD rentals.

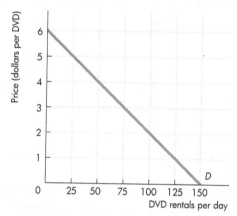

    a. Calculate the elasticity of demand when the price of a DVD rental rises from $3 to $5.

    b. At what price is the elasticity of demand for DVD rentals equal to 1?

Use the following table to work Problems 12 to 14. The demand schedule for computer chips is

Price (dollars per chip)	Quantity demanded (millions of chips per year)
200	50
250	45
300	40
350	35
400	30

12. a. What happens to total revenue if the price falls from $400 to $350 a chip and from $350 to $300 a chip?

    b. At what price is total revenue at a maximum?

13. At an average price of $350, is the demand for chips elastic, inelastic, or unit elastic? Use the total revenue test to answer this question.

14. At $250 a chip, is the demand for chips elastic or inelastic? Use the total revenue test to answer this question.

15. Your price elasticity of demand for bananas is 4. If the price of bananas rises by 5 percent, what is

    a. The percentage change in the quantity of bananas you buy?

    b. The change in your expenditure on bananas?

16. **As Gasoline Prices Soar, Americans Slowly Adapt**

    As gas prices rose in March 2008, Americans drove 11 billion fewer miles than in March 2007. Realizing that prices were not going down, Americans adapted to higher energy costs. Americans spent 3.7 percent of their disposable income on transportation fuels. How much we spend on gasoline depends on the choices we make: what car we drive, where we live, how much time we spend driving, and where we choose to go. For many people, higher energy costs mean fewer restaurant meals, deferred weekend outings with the kids, less air travel, and more time closer to home.

    Source: *International Herald Tribune*, May 23, 2008

    a. List and explain the elasticities of demand that are implicitly referred to in the news clip.

    b. Why, according to the news clip, is the demand for gasoline inelastic?

More Elasticities of Demand

Use this information to work Problems 17 and 18.
Economy Forces Many to Shorten Holiday Plans
This year Americans are taking fewer exotic holidays by air and instead are visiting local scenic places by car. The global financial crisis has encouraged many Americans to cut their holiday budgets.

Source: *USA Today*, May 22, 2009

17. Given the prices of the two holidays, is the income elasticity of demand for exotic holidays positive or negative? Are exotic holidays a normal good or an inferior good? Are local holidays a normal good or an inferior good?

18. Are exotic holidays and local holidays substitutes? Explain your answer.

19. When Alex's income was $3,000, he bought 4 bagels and 12 donuts a month. Now his income is $5,000 and he buys 8 bagels and 6 donuts a month. Calculate Alex's income elasticity of demand for (a) bagels and (b) donuts.

20. **Walmart's Recession-Time Pet Project**

During the recession, Walmart moved its pet food and supplies to the front with its other fast-growing business, baby products. Retail experts point out that kids and pets tend to be fairly recession-resistant businesses—even in a recession, dogs will be fed and kids will get their toys.

Source: *CNN*, May 13, 2008

a. What does this news clip imply about the income elasticity of demand for pet food and baby products?

b. Would the income elasticity of demand be greater or less than 1? Explain.

21. If a 5 percent fall in the price of chocolate sauce increases the quantity demanded of chocolate sauce by 10 percent and increases the quantity of ice cream demanded by 15 percent, calculate the

a. Price elasticity of demand for chocolate sauce.

b. Cross elasticity of demand for ice cream with respect to the price of chocolate sauce.

22. **To Love, Honor, and Save Money**

In a survey of caterers and event planners, nearly half of them said that they were seeing declines in wedding spending in response to the economic slowdown; 12% even reported wedding cancellations because of financial concerns.

Source: *Time*, June 2, 2008

a. Based upon this news clip, are wedding events a normal good or an inferior good? Explain.

b. Are wedding events more a necessity or a luxury? Would the income elasticity of demand be greater than 1, less than 1, or equal to 1? Explain.

Elasticity of Supply

23. The table sets out the supply schedule of long-distance phone calls.

Price (cents per minute)	Quantity supplied (millions of minutes per day)
10	200
20	400
30	600
40	800

Calculate the elasticity of supply when

a. The price falls from 40¢ to 30¢ a minute.

b. The average price is 20¢ a minute.

24. **Weak Coal Prices Hit China's Third-Largest Coal Miner**

The chairman of Yanzhou Coal Mining reported that the recession had decreased the demand for coal, with its sales falling by 11.9 percent to 7.92 million tons from 8.99 million tons a year earlier, despite a 10.6 percent cut in the price.

Source: *Dow Jones*, April 27, 2009

Calculate the price elasticity of supply of coal. Is the supply of coal elastic or inelastic?

Economics in the News

25. After you have studied *Economics in the News* on pp. 98–99, answer the following questions.

a. Looking at Fig. 1 on p. 99, explain what must have happened in 2014 to the supply of coffee.

b. Given the information in Fig. 1 and the estimated elasticity of demand for coffee, by what percentage did the quantity of coffee change in 2014 and in which direction?

c. The news article says that farmers' revenue shrank as the price of coffee fell. Explain why this fact tells us that the demand for coffee is inelastic.

d. How does the total revenue test work for a rise in the price? What do you predict happened to total revenue in 2014? Why?

e. Coffee isn't just coffee. It comes in different varieties, the main two being Arabica and Robusta. Would you expect the elasticity of demand for Arabica to be the same as the elasticity of demand for coffee? Explain why or why not.

26. **Comcast Deal Won't Lead to Netflix Price Hike**

Under the deal, Netflix will buy Internet service from Comcast, rather than connect directly for free with some smaller ISPs like Cablevision as it does now.

Source: *CNN*, April 24, 2014

a. How will Netflix's decision to buy more expensive Internet service influence Netflix's supply of online movie viewing?

b. Given your answer to part (a), explain why Netflix says it will not hike its price.

c. What can you say about the price elasticity of demand for Netflix online movie viewing?

5 EFFICIENCY AND EQUITY

After studying this chapter, you will be able to:

◆ Describe the alternative methods of allocating scarce resources

◆ Explain the connection between demand and marginal benefit and define consumer surplus; and explain the connection between supply and marginal cost and define producer surplus

◆ Explain the conditions under which markets are efficient and inefficient

◆ Explain the main ideas about fairness and evaluate claims that markets result in unfair outcomes

Every day, millions of people make self-interested choices to drive to work rather than take the bus or train. The outcome of these choices is gridlock and a lot of lost time. Are we using our highways and our time efficiently?

One way of eliminating traffic jams is to make people pay for road use—to make all the highways toll-roads. Rich people can easily pay a toll, but poor people can't afford to pay. Would tolls be fair?

We'll answer these questions about highway use in *Economics in the News* at the end of the chapter. But first, we examine the efficiency and fairness of alternative ways of allocating scarce resources.

◆ Resource Allocation Methods

If resources were abundant, and not scarce, we would not need to allocate them among alternative uses. But resources *are* scarce: They must be allocated somehow. Our goal is to discover how resources might be allocated efficiently and fairly. So what are the alternative methods of allocating scarce resources?

Eight alternative methods that might be used are

- Market price
- Command
- Majority rule
- Contest
- First-come, first-served
- Lottery
- Personal characteristics
- Force

Let's briefly examine each method.

Market Price

When a market price allocates a scarce resource, the people who are willing and able to pay that price get the resource. Two kinds of people decide not to pay the market price: those who can afford to pay but choose not to buy and those who are too poor and simply can't afford to buy.

For many goods and services, distinguishing between those who choose not to buy and those who can't afford to buy doesn't matter. But for a few items, it does matter. For example, poor people can't afford to pay school fees and doctors' fees. Because poor people can't afford items that most people consider to be essential, these items are usually allocated by one of the other methods.

Command

A **command system** allocates resources by the order (command) of someone in authority. In the U.S. economy, the command system is used extensively inside firms and government departments. For example, if you have a job, most likely someone tells you what to do. Your labor is allocated to specific tasks by a command.

A command system works well in organizations in which the lines of authority and responsibility are clear and it is easy to monitor the activities being per-

formed. But a command system works badly when the range of activities to be monitored is large and when it is easy for people to fool those in authority. North Korea uses a command system and it works so badly that it even fails to deliver an adequate supply of food.

Majority Rule

Majority rule allocates resources in the way that a majority of voters choose. Societies use majority rule to elect representative governments that make some of the biggest decisions. For example, majority rule decides the tax rates that end up allocating scarce resources between private use and public use. And majority rule decides how tax dollars are allocated among competing uses such as education and healthcare.

Majority rule works well when the decisions being made affect large numbers of people and self-interest must be suppressed to use resources most effectively.

Contest

A contest allocates resources to a winner (or a group of winners). Sporting events use this method. Serena Williams competes with other tennis professionals, and the winner gets the biggest payoff. But contests are more general than those in a sports arena, though we don't normally call them contests. For example, Bill Gates won a contest to provide the world's personal computer operating system.

Contests do a good job when the efforts of the "players" are hard to monitor and reward directly. When a manager offers everyone in the company the opportunity to win a big prize, people are motivated to work hard and try to become the winner. Only a few people end up with a big prize, but many people work harder in the process of trying to win. The total output produced by the workers is much greater than it would be without the contest.

First-Come, First-Served

A first-come, first-served method allocates resources to those who are first in line. Many casual restaurants won't accept reservations. They use first-come, first-served to allocate their scarce tables. Highway space is allocated in this way too: The first to arrive at the on-ramp gets the road space. If too many vehicles enter the highway, the speed slows and people wait in line for some space to become available.

First-come, first-served works best when, as in the above examples, a scarce resource can serve just one user at a time in a sequence. By serving the user who arrives first, this method minimizes the time spent waiting for the resource to become free.

Lottery

Lotteries allocate resources to those who pick the winning number, draw the lucky cards, or come up lucky on some other gaming system. State lotteries and casinos reallocate millions of dollars' worth of goods and services every year.

But lotteries are more widespread than jackpots and roulette wheels in casinos. They are used to allocate landing slots to airlines at some airports and places in the New York and Boston marathons, and have been used to allocate fishing rights and the electromagnetic spectrum used by cellphones.

Lotteries work best when there is no effective way to distinguish among potential users of a scarce resource.

Personal Characteristics

When resources are allocated on the basis of personal characteristics, people with the "right" characteristics get the resources. Some of the resources that matter most to you are allocated in this way. For example, you will choose a marriage partner on the basis of personal characteristics. But this method can also be used in unacceptable ways. Allocating the best jobs to white, Anglo-Saxon males and discriminating against visible minorities and women is an example.

Force

Force plays a crucial role, for both good and ill, in allocating scarce resources. Let's start with the ill.

War, the use of military force by one nation against another, has played an enormous role historically in allocating resources. The economic supremacy of European settlers in the Americas and Australia owes much to the use of this method.

Theft, the taking of the property of others without their consent, also plays a large role. Both large-scale organized crime and small-scale petty crime collectively allocate billions of dollars worth of resources annually.

But force plays a crucial positive role in allocating resources. It provides the state with an effective method of transferring wealth from the rich to the poor, and it provides the legal framework in which voluntary exchange in markets takes place.

A legal system is the foundation on which our market economy functions. Without courts to enforce contracts, it would not be possible to do business. But the courts could not enforce contracts without the ability to apply force if necessary. The state provides the ultimate force that enables the courts to do their work.

More broadly, the force of the state is essential to uphold the principle of the rule of law. This principle is the bedrock of civilized economic (and social and political) life. With the rule of law upheld, people can go about their daily economic lives with the assurance that their property will be protected—that they can sue for violations against their property (and be sued if they violate the property of others).

Free from the burden of protecting their property and confident in the knowledge that those with whom they trade will honor their agreements, people can get on with focusing on the activity in which they have a comparative advantage and trading for mutual gain.

◆ REVIEW QUIZ

1   Why do we need methods of allocating scarce resources?
2   Describe the alternative methods of allocating scarce resources.
3   Provide an example of each allocation method that illustrates when it works well.
4   Provide an example of each allocation method that illustrates when it works badly.

Work these questions in Study Plan 5.1 and get instant feedback. Do a Key Terms Quiz.   MyEconLab

In the next sections, we're going to see how a market can achieve an efficient use of resources, examine the obstacles to efficiency, and see how sometimes an alternative method might improve on the market. After looking at efficiency, we'll turn our attention to the more difficult issue of fairness.

Benefit, Cost, and Surplus

Resources are allocated efficiently and in the *social interest* when they are used in the ways that people value most highly. You saw in Chapter 2 that this outcome occurs when the quantities produced are at the point on the *PPF* at which marginal benefit equals marginal cost (see pp. 35–37). We're now going to see whether competitive markets produce the efficient quantities.

We begin on the demand side of a market.

Demand, Willingness to Pay, and Value

In everyday life, we talk about "getting value for money." When we use this expression, we are distinguishing between *value* and *price*. Value is what we get, and price is what we pay.

The value of one more unit of a good or service is its marginal benefit. We measure marginal benefit by the maximum price that is willingly paid for another unit of the good or service. But willingness to pay determines demand. *A demand curve is a marginal benefit curve.*

In Fig. 5.1(a), Lisa is willing to pay $1 for the 30th slice of pizza and $1 is her marginal benefit from that slice. In Fig. 5.1(b), Nick is willing to pay $1 for the 10th slice of pizza and $1 is his marginal benefit from that slice. But at what quantity is the market willing to pay $1 for the marginal slice? The answer is provided by the *market demand curve*.

Individual Demand and Market Demand

The relationship between the price of a good and the quantity demanded by one person is called *individual demand*. And the relationship between the price of a good and the quantity demanded by all buyers is called *market demand*.

> The market demand curve is the horizontal sum of the individual demand curves and is formed by adding the quantities demanded by all the individuals at each price.

Figure 5.1(c) illustrates the market demand for pizza if Lisa and Nick are the only people in the market. Lisa's demand curve in part (a) and Nick's demand curve in part (b) sum horizontally to the market demand curve in part (c).

FIGURE 5.1   Individual Demand, Market Demand, and Marginal Social Benefit

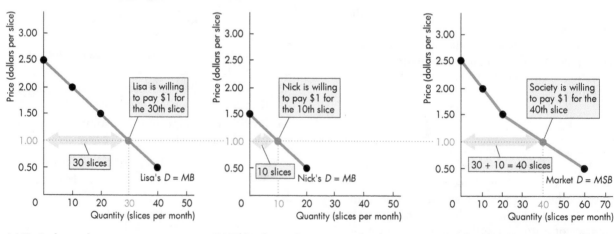

(a) Lisa's demand   **(b) Nick's demand**   **(c) Market demand**

At a price of $1 a slice, the quantity demanded by Lisa is 30 slices and the quantity demanded by Nick is 10 slices, so the quantity demanded by the market is 40 slices. Lisa's demand

curve in part (a) and Nick's demand curve in part (b) sum horizontally to the market demand curve in part (c). The market demand curve is the marginal social benefit (*MSB*) curve.

At a price of $1 a slice, Lisa demands 30 slices and Nick demands 10 slices, so the market quantity demanded at $1 a slice is 40 slices.

For Lisa and Nick, their demand curves are their marginal benefit curves. For society, the market demand curve is the marginal benefit curve. We call the marginal benefit to the entire society *marginal social benefit*. So the market demand curve is also the *marginal social benefit (MSB) curve*.

Consumer Surplus

We don't always have to pay as much as we are willing to pay. We get a bargain. When people buy something for less than it is worth to them, they receive a consumer surplus. **Consumer surplus** is the excess of the benefit received from a good over the amount paid for it. We can calculate consumer surplus as the marginal benefit (or value) of a good minus its price, summed over the quantity bought.

Figure 5.2(a) shows Lisa's consumer surplus from pizza when the price is $1 a slice. At this price, she buys 30 slices a month because the 30th slice is worth exactly $1 to her. But Lisa is willing to pay $2 for the 10th slice, so her marginal benefit from this slice is

$1 more than she pays for it—she receives a surplus of $1 on the 10th slice.

Lisa's consumer surplus is the sum of the surpluses on *all of the slices she buys*. This sum is the area of the green triangle—the area below the demand curve and above the market price line. The area of this triangle is equal to its base (30 slices) multiplied by its height ($1.50) divided by 2, which is $22.50. The area of the blue rectangle in Fig. 5.2(a) shows what Lisa pays for 30 slices of pizza.

Figure 5.2(b) shows Nick's consumer surplus, and part (c) shows the consumer surplus for the market. The consumer surplus for the market is the sum of the consumer surpluses of Lisa and Nick.

All goods and services have decreasing marginal benefit, so people receive more benefit from their consumption than the amount they pay.

Supply and Marginal Cost

Your next task is to see how market supply reflects marginal cost. The connection between supply and cost closely parallels the related ideas about demand and benefit that you've just studied. Firms are in business to make a profit. To do so, they must sell

FIGURE 5.2 Demand and Consumer Surplus

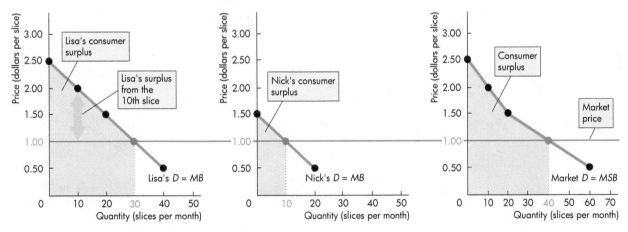

(a) Lisa's consumer surplus **(b) Nick's consumer surplus** **(c) Market consumer surplus**

Lisa is willing to pay $2 for her 10th slice of pizza in part (a). At a market price of $1 a slice, Lisa receives a surplus of $1 on the 10th slice. The green triangle shows her consumer surplus on the 30 slices she buys at $1 a slice. The

green triangle in part (b) shows Nick's consumer surplus on the 10 slices that he buys at $1 a slice. The green area in part (c) shows the consumer surplus for the market. The blue rectangles show the amounts spent on pizza.

their output for a price that exceeds the cost of production. Let's investigate the relationship between cost and price.

Supply, Cost, and Minimum Supply-Price

Firms make a profit when they receive more from the sale of a good or service than the cost of producing it. Just as consumers distinguish between value and price, so producers distinguish between *cost* and *price*. Cost is what a firm gives up when it produces a good or service and price is what a firm receives when it sells the good or service.

The cost of producing one more unit of a good or service is its marginal cost. Marginal cost is the minimum price that producers must receive to induce them to offer one more unit of a good or service for sale. But the minimum supply-price determines supply. *A supply curve is a marginal cost curve.*

In Fig. 5.3(a), Maria is willing to produce the 100th pizza for $15, her marginal cost of that pizza. In Fig. 5.3(b), Max is willing to produce the 50th pizza for $15, his marginal cost.

What quantity is this market willing to produce for $15 a pizza? The answer is provided by the *market supply curve*.

Individual Supply and Market Supply

The relationship between the price of a good and the quantity supplied by one producer is called *individual supply*. And the relationship between the price of a good and the quantity supplied by all producers is called *market supply*.

> The market supply curve is the horizontal sum of the individual supply curves and is formed by adding the quantities supplied by all the producers at each price.

Figure 5.3(c) illustrates the market supply of pizzas if Maria and Max are the only producers. Maria's supply curve in part (a) and Max's supply curve in part (b) sum horizontally to the market supply curve in part (c).

At a price of $15 a pizza, Maria supplies 100 pizzas and Max supplies 50 pizzas, so the quantity supplied by the market at $15 a pizza is 150 pizzas.

For Maria and Max, their supply curves are their marginal cost curves. For society, the market supply curve is its marginal cost curve. We call the society's marginal cost *marginal social cost*. So the market supply curve is also the *marginal social cost (MSC) curve*.

FIGURE 5.3   Individual Supply, Market Supply, and Marginal Social Cost

(a) Maria's supply   **(b) Max's supply**   **(c) Market supply**

At a price of $15 a pizza, the quantity supplied by Maria is 100 pizzas and the quantity supplied by Max is 50 pizzas, so the quantity supplied by the market is 150 pizzas. Maria's

supply curve in part (a) and Max's supply curve in part (b) sum horizontally to the market supply curve in part (c). The market supply curve is the marginal social cost (MSC) curve.

Producer Surplus

When price exceeds marginal cost, the firm receives a producer surplus. **Producer surplus** is the excess of the amount received from the sale of a good or service over the cost of producing it. We calculate producer surplus as the price received minus the marginal cost (or minimum supply-price), summed over the quantity sold.

Figure 5.4(a) shows Maria's producer surplus from pizza when the price is $15 a pizza. At this price, she sells 100 pizzas a month because the 100th pizza costs her $15 to produce. But Maria is willing to produce the 50th pizza for her marginal cost, which is $10, so she receives a surplus of $5 on this pizza.

Maria's producer surplus is the sum of the surpluses on the pizzas she sells. This sum is the area of the blue triangle—the area below the market price and above the supply curve. The area of this triangle is equal to its base (100) multiplied by its height ($10) divided by 2, which is $500.

The red area below the supply curve in Fig. 5.4(a) shows what it costs Maria to produce 100 pizzas.

The area of the blue triangle in Fig. 5.4(b) shows Max's producer surplus and the blue area in Fig. 5.4(c) shows the producer surplus for the market.

The producer surplus for the market is the sum of the producer surpluses of Maria and Max.

1. What is the relationship between the marginal benefit, value, and demand?
2. What is the relationship between individual demand and market demand?
3. What is consumer surplus? How is it measured?
4. What is the relationship between the marginal cost, minimum supply-price, and supply?
5. What is the relationship between individual supply and market supply?
6. What is producer surplus? How is it measured?

Work these questions in Study Plan 5.2 and get instant feedback. Do a Key Terms Quiz.   MyEconLab

Consumer surplus and producer surplus can be used to measure the efficiency of a market. Let's see how we can use these concepts to study the efficiency of a competitive market.

FIGURE 5.4   Supply and Producer Surplus

(a) Maria's producer surplus   **(b) Max's producer surplus**   **(c) Market producer surplus**

Maria is willing to produce the 50th pizza for $10 in part (a). At a market price of $15 a pizza, Maria gets a surplus of $5 on the 50th pizza. The blue triangle shows her producer surplus on the 100 pizzas she sells at $15 each.

The blue triangle in part (b) shows Max's producer surplus on the 50 pizzas that he sells at $15 each. The blue area in part (c) shows producer surplus for the market. The red areas show the cost of producing the pizzas sold.

MyEconLab Animation and Draw Graph

▶ Is the Competitive Market Efficient?

Figure 5.5(a) shows the market for pizza. The market forces that you studied in Chapter 3 (pp. 66–67) pull the pizza market to its equilibrium price of $15 a pizza and equilibrium quantity of 10,000 pizzas a day. Buyers enjoy a consumer surplus (green area) and sellers enjoy a producer surplus (blue area), but is this competitive equilibrium efficient?

Efficiency of Competitive Equilibrium

You've seen that the market demand curve for a good or service tells us the marginal social benefit from it. You've also seen that the market supply curve of a good or service tells us the marginal social cost of producing it.

Equilibrium in a competitive market occurs when the quantity demanded equals the quantity supplied at the intersection of the demand curve and the supply curve. At this intersection point, marginal social benefit on the demand curve equals marginal social cost on the supply curve. This equality is the condition for allocative efficiency. So in equilibrium, a competitive market achieves allocative efficiency.

Figure 5.5 illustrates the efficiency of competitive equilibrium. The demand curve and the supply curve intersect in part (a) and marginal social benefit equals marginal social cost in part (b).

If production is less than 10,000 pizzas a day, the marginal pizza is valued more highly than it costs to produce. If production exceeds 10,000 pizzas a day, the marginal pizza costs more to produce than the value that consumers place on it. Only when 10,000 pizzas a day are produced is the marginal pizza worth exactly what it costs.

The competitive market pushes the quantity of pizzas produced to its efficient level of 10,000 a day. If production is less than 10,000 pizzas a day, a shortage raises the price, which increases production. If production exceeds 10,000 pizzas a day, a surplus of pizzas lowers the price, which decreases production. So a competitive pizza market is efficient.

Figure 5.5(a) also shows the consumer surplus and producer surplus. The sum of consumer surplus and producer surplus is called **total surplus**. When the efficient quantity is produced, total surplus is maximized. Buyers and sellers acting in their self-interest end up promoting the social interest.

FIGURE 5.5   An Efficient Market for Pizza

(a) Equilibrium and surpluses

(b) Efficiency

Competitive equilibrium in part (a) occurs when the quantity demanded equals the quantity supplied. Resources are used efficiently in part (b) when marginal social benefit, MSB, equals marginal social cost, MSC. Total surplus, which is the sum of consumer surplus (the green triangle) and producer surplus (the blue triangle) is maximized.

The efficient quantity in part (b) is the same as the equilibrium quantity in part (a). The competitive pizza market produces the efficient quantity of pizzas.

—— MyEconLab Animation and Draw Graph ——

ECONOMICS IN ACTION

Seeing the Invisible Hand

Adam Smith said that a seller in a competitive market is "led by *an invisible hand* to promote an end which was no part of his intention" (see p. 8). Smith believed that the invisible hand sends resources to the uses in which they have the highest value.

You can't *see* the invisible hand, but you can imagine it, and you can see its consequences in the cartoon and in today's world.

Umbrella for Sale The cold drinks vendor has cold drinks and shade and he has a marginal cost and a minimum supply-price of each. The reader on the park bench has a marginal benefit and willingness to pay for each. The reader's marginal benefit from shade exceeds the vendor's marginal cost; but the vendor's marginal cost of a cold drink exceeds the reader's marginal benefit. They trade the umbrella. The vendor gets a producer surplus from selling the shade for more than its marginal cost, and the reader gets a consumer surplus from buying the shade for less than its marginal benefit. Both are better off and the umbrella has moved to a higher-valued use.

The Invisible Hand at Work Today Many of the markets in which you trade work like that in the cartoon to achieve an efficient allocation of resources.

When you order a pizza for home delivery, you make a choice about how scarce resources will be used. You make your choice in your self-interest. The pizza cook and the person who delivers your pizza also make their choices in their self-interest.

The pizza market coordinates these choices. You buy the quantity of pizza that makes the price you pay equal to your marginal benefit. And the pizza producer sells the quantity at which the price equals his marginal cost. Total surplus is maximized in an efficient pizza market.

Market Failure

Markets are not always efficient, and when a market is inefficient, we call the outcome **market failure**. In a market failure, either too little (underproduction) or too much (overproduction) of an item is produced.

Underproduction In Fig. 5.6(a), the quantity of pizzas produced is 5,000 a day. At this quantity, consumers are willing to pay $20 for a pizza that costs only $10 to produce. The quantity produced is inefficient—there is underproduction—and total surplus is smaller than its maximum possible level.

We measure the scale of inefficiency by **deadweight loss**, which is the decrease in total surplus that results from an inefficient level of production. The gray triangle in Fig. 5.6(a) shows the deadweight loss.

Overproduction In Fig. 5.6(b), the quantity of pizzas produced is 15,000 a day. At this quantity, consumers are willing to pay only $10 for a pizza that costs $20 to produce. By producing the 15,000th pizza, $10 of resources are wasted. Again, the gray triangle shows the deadweight loss, which reduces the total surplus to less than its maximum.

Inefficient production creates a deadweight loss that is borne by the entire society: It is a social loss.

Sources of Market Failure

Obstacles to efficiency that bring market failure are

- Price and quantity regulations
- Taxes and subsidies
- Externalities
- Public goods and common resources
- Monopoly
- High transactions costs

Price and Quantity Regulations A *price regulation*, either a price cap or a price floor, blocks the price adjustments that balance the quantity demanded and the quantity supplied and lead to underproduction. A *quantity regulation* that limits the amount that a farm is permitted to produce also leads to underproduction.

Taxes and Subsidies *Taxes* increase the prices paid by buyers, lower the prices received by sellers, and lead to underproduction. *Subsidies*, which are payments by the government to producers, decrease the prices paid by buyers, increase the prices received by sellers, and lead to overproduction.

FIGURE 5.6   Underproduction and Overproduction

(a) Underproduction

(b) Overproduction

If 5,000 pizzas a day are produced, in part (a), total surplus (the sum of the green and blue areas) is smaller than its maximum by the amount of the deadweight loss (the gray triangle). At all quantities below 10,000 pizzas a day, the benefit from one more pizza exceeds its cost.

If 15,000 pizzas a day are produced, in part (b), total surplus is also smaller than its maximum by the amount of the deadweight loss. At all quantities in excess of 10,000 pizzas a day, the cost of one more pizza exceeds its benefit.

——— MyEconLab Animation and Draw Graph ———

Externalities An *externality* is a cost or a benefit that affects someone other than the seller or the buyer. An *external cost* arises when an electric utility burns coal and emits carbon dioxide. The utility doesn't consider the cost of climate change when it decides how much power to produce. The result is overproduction. An *external benefit* arises when an apartment owner installs a smoke detector and decreases her neighbor's fire risk. She doesn't consider the benefit to her neighbor when she decides how many detectors to install. The result is underproduction.

Public Goods and Common Resources A *public good* is a good or service from which everyone benefits and no one can be excluded. National defense is an example. A competitive market would underproduce national defense because everyone would try to free ride on everyone else.

A *common resource* is owned by no one but is available to be used by everyone. Atlantic salmon is an example. It is in everyone's self-interest to ignore the costs they impose on others when they decide how much of a common resource to use: It is overused.

Monopoly A *monopoly* is a firm that is the sole provider of a good or service. Local water supply and cable television are supplied by firms that are monopolies. The monopoly's self-interest is to maximize its profit, and because it has no competitors, it produces too little and charges too high a price: It underproduces.

High Transactions Costs When you buy your first house, you will also buy the services of an agent and a lawyer to do the transaction. Economists call the costs of the services that enable a market to bring buyers and sellers together **transactions costs**. It is costly to operate *any* market, but some markets are so costly to operate that they simply don't. For example, there's no market in time slots on a local tennis court. Instead, the court uses first-come, first-served: You hang around until the court becomes vacant and "pay" with your waiting time. When transactions costs are high, the market might underproduce.

You now know the conditions under which resource allocation is efficient. You've seen how a competitive market can be efficient, and you've seen some obstacles to efficiency. Can alternative allocation methods improve on the market?

Alternatives to the Market

When a market is inefficient, can one of the alternative nonmarket methods that we described at the beginning of this chapter do a better job? Sometimes it can.

Often, majority rule might be used in an attempt to improve the allocation of resources. But majority rule has its own shortcomings. A group that pursues the self-interest of its members can become the majority. For example, a price or quantity regulation that creates inefficiency is almost always the result of a self-interested group becoming the majority and imposing costs on the minority. Also, with majority rule, votes must be translated into actions by bureaucrats who have their own agendas based on their self-interest.

Managers in firms issue commands and avoid the transactions costs that they would incur if they went to a market every time they needed a job done.

First-come, first-served works best in some situations. Think about the scene at a busy ATM. Instead of waiting in line people might trade places at a "market" price. But someone would need to ensure that trades were honored. At a busy ATM, first-come, first-served is the most efficient arrangement.

There is no one efficient mechanism that allocates all resources efficiently. But markets, when supplemented by other mechanisms such as majority rule, command systems, and first-come, first-served, do an amazingly good job.

◆ REVIEW QUIZ

1 Do competitive markets use resources efficiently? Explain why or why not.
2 What is deadweight loss and under what conditions does it occur?
3 What are the obstacles to achieving an efficient allocation of resources in the market economy?

Work these questions in Study Plan 5.3 and get instant feedback. Do a Key Terms Quiz.   MyEconLab

Is an efficient allocation of resources also a fair allocation? Does the competitive market provide people with fair incomes for their work? Do people always pay a fair price for the things they buy? Don't we need the government to step into some competitive markets to prevent the price from rising too high or falling too low? Let's now study these questions.

◆ Is the Competitive Market Fair?

When a natural disaster strikes, such as a severe winter storm or a hurricane, the prices of many essential items jump. The reason prices jump is that the demand and willingness to pay for these items has increased, but the supply has not changed. So the higher prices achieve an efficient allocation of scarce resources. News reports of these price hikes almost never talk about efficiency. Instead, they talk about equity or fairness. The claim that is often made is that it is unfair for profit-seeking dealers to cheat the victims of natural disaster.

Similarly, when low-skilled people work for a wage that is below what most would regard as a "living wage," the media and politicians talk of employers taking unfair advantage of their workers.

How do we decide whether something is fair or unfair? You know when you *think* something is unfair, but how do you *know?* What are the *principles* of fairness?

Philosophers have tried for centuries to answer this question. Economists have offered their answers too. But before we look at the proposed answers, you should know that there is no universally agreed upon answer.

Economists agree about efficiency. That is, they agree that it makes sense to make the economic pie as large as possible and to produce it at the lowest possible cost. But they do not agree about equity. That is, they do not agree about what are fair shares of the economic pie for all the people who make it. The reason is that ideas about fairness are not exclusively economic ideas. They touch on politics, ethics, and religion. Nevertheless, economists have thought about these issues and have a contribution to make. Let's examine the views of economists on this topic.

To think about fairness, think of economic life as a game—a serious game. All ideas about fairness can be divided into two broad groups. They are

- It's not fair if the *result* isn't fair.
- It's not fair if the *rules* aren't fair.

It's Not Fair if the *Result* Isn't Fair

The earliest efforts to establish a principle of fairness were based on the view that the result is what matters. The general idea was that it is unfair if people's incomes are too unequal. For example, it is unfair

that a bank president earns millions of dollars a year while a bank teller earns only thousands of dollars. It is unfair that a store owner makes a larger profit and her customers pay higher prices in the aftermath of a winter storm.

During the nineteenth century, economists thought they had made an incredible discovery: Efficiency requires equality of incomes. To make the economic pie as large as possible, it must be cut into equal pieces, one for each person. This idea turns out to be wrong. But there is a lesson in the reason that it is wrong, so this idea is worth a closer look.

Utilitarianism The nineteenth-century idea that only equality brings efficiency is called *utilitarianism*. **Utilitarianism** is a principle that states that we should strive to achieve "the greatest happiness for the greatest number." The people who developed this idea were known as utilitarians. They included the most eminent thinkers, such as Jeremy Bentham and John Stuart Mill.

Utilitarians argued that to achieve "the greatest happiness for the greatest number," income must be transferred from the rich to the poor up to the point of complete equality—to the point at which there are no rich and no poor.

They reasoned in the following way: First, everyone has the same basic wants and a similar capacity to enjoy life. Second, the greater a person's income, the smaller is the marginal benefit of a dollar. The millionth dollar spent by a rich person brings a smaller marginal benefit to that person than the marginal benefit that the thousandth dollar spent brings to a poorer person. So by transferring a dollar from the millionaire to the poorer person, more is gained than is lost. The two people added together are better off.

Figure 5.7 illustrates this utilitarian idea. Tom and Jerry have the same marginal benefit curve, *MB*. (Marginal benefit is measured on the same scale of 1 to 3 for both Tom and Jerry.) Tom is at point *A*. He earns $5,000 a year, and his marginal benefit from a dollar is 3 units. Jerry is at point *B*. He earns $45,000 a year, and his marginal benefit from a dollar is 1 unit. If a dollar is transferred from Jerry to Tom, Jerry loses 1 unit of marginal benefit and Tom gains 3 units. So together, Tom and Jerry are better off—they are sharing the economic pie more efficiently. If a second dollar is transferred, the same thing happens: Tom gains more than Jerry loses. And the same is true for every dollar transferred until they both reach point *C*. At point *C*, Tom and Jerry have $25,000

FIGURE 5.7   Utilitarian Fairness

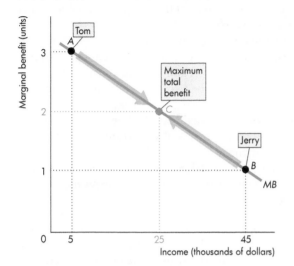

Tom earns $5,000 and has 3 units of marginal benefit at point A. Jerry earns $45,000 and has 1 unit of marginal benefit at point B. If income is transferred from Jerry to Tom, Jerry's loss is less than Tom's gain. Only when each of them has $25,000 and 2 units of marginal benefit (at point C) can the sum of their total benefit increase no further.

MyEconLab Animation

each and a marginal benefit of 2 units. Now they are sharing the economic pie in the most efficient way. It brings the greatest happiness to Tom and Jerry.

The Big Tradeoff One big problem with the utilitarian ideal of complete equality is that it ignores the costs of making income transfers. Recognizing the costs of making income transfers leads to what is called the **big tradeoff**, which is a tradeoff between efficiency and fairness.

The big tradeoff is based on the following facts. Income can be transferred from people with high incomes to people with low incomes only by taxing the high incomes. Taxing people's income from employment makes them work less. It results in the quantity of labor being less than the efficient quantity. Taxing people's income from capital makes them save less. It results in the quantity of capital being less than the efficient quantity. With smaller quantities of both labor and capital, the quantity of goods and services produced is less than the efficient quantity. The economic pie shrinks.

The tradeoff is between the size of the economic pie and the degree of equality with which it is shared. The greater the amount of income redistribution through income taxes, the greater is the inefficiency—the smaller is the economic pie.

There is a second source of inefficiency. A dollar taken from a rich person does not end up as a dollar in the hands of a poorer person. Some of the dollar is spent on administration of the tax and transfer system. The cost of tax-collecting agencies, such as the Internal Revenue Service (IRS), and welfare-administering agencies, such as the Centers for Medicare & Medicaid Services (CMS), must be paid with some of the taxes collected. Also, taxpayers hire accountants, auditors, and lawyers to help them ensure that they pay the correct amount of taxes. These activities use skilled labor and capital resources that could otherwise be used to produce goods and services that people value.

When all these costs are taken into account, taking a dollar from a rich person does not give a dollar to a poor person. It is possible that with high taxes, people with low incomes might end up being worse off. Suppose, for example, that highly taxed entrepreneurs decide to work less hard and shut down some of their businesses. Low-income workers get fired and must seek other, perhaps even lower-paid, work.

Today, because of the big tradeoff, no one says that fairness requires complete equality of incomes.

Make the Poorest as Well Off as Possible A new solution to the big-tradeoff problem was proposed by philosopher John Rawls in a classic book entitled *A Theory of Justice*, published in 1971. Rawls says that, taking all the costs of income transfers into account, the fair distribution of the economic pie is the one that makes the poorest person as well off as possible. The incomes of rich people should be taxed, and after paying the costs of administering the tax and transfer system, what is left should be transferred to the poor. But the taxes must not be so high that they make the economic pie shrink to the point at which the poorest person ends up with a smaller piece. A bigger share of a smaller pie can be less than a smaller share of a bigger pie. The goal is to make the piece enjoyed by the poorest person as big as possible. Most likely, this piece will not be an equal share.

The "fair results" idea requires a change in the results after the game is over. Some economists say that these changes are themselves unfair and propose a different way of thinking about fairness.

It's Not Fair if the *Rules* Aren't Fair

The idea that it's not fair if the rules aren't fair is based on a fundamental principle that seems to be hardwired into the human brain: the symmetry principle. The **symmetry principle** is the requirement that people in similar situations be treated similarly. It is the moral principle that lies at the center of all the big religions and that says, in some form or other, "Behave toward other people in the way you expect them to behave toward you."

In economic life, this principle translates into *equality of opportunity*. But equality of opportunity to do what? This question is answered by the philosopher Robert Nozick in a book entitled *Anarchy, State, and Utopia*, published in 1974.

Nozick argues that the idea of fairness as an outcome or result cannot work and that fairness must be based on the fairness of the rules. He suggests that fairness obeys two rules:

1. The state must enforce laws that establish and protect private property.
2. Private property may be transferred from one person to another only by voluntary exchange.

The first rule says that everything that is valuable must be owned by individuals and that the state must ensure that theft is prevented. The second rule says that the only legitimate way a person can acquire property is to buy it in exchange for something else that the person owns. If these rules, which are the only fair rules, are followed, then the result is fair. It doesn't matter how unequally the economic pie is shared, provided that the pie is made by people, each one of whom voluntarily provides services in exchange for the share of the pie offered in compensation.

These rules satisfy the symmetry principle. If these rules are not followed, the symmetry principle is broken. You can see these facts by imagining a world in which the laws are not followed.

First, suppose that some resources or goods are not owned. They are common property. Then everyone is free to participate in a grab to use them. The strongest will prevail. But when the strongest prevails, the strongest effectively *owns* the resources or goods in question and prevents others from enjoying them.

Second, suppose that we do not insist on voluntary exchange for transferring ownership of resources from one person to another. The alternative is *involuntary* transfer. In simple language, the alternative is theft.

Both of these situations violate the symmetry principle. Only the strong acquire what they want. The weak end up with only the resources and goods that the strong don't want.

In a majority-rule political system, the strong are those in the majority or those with enough resources to influence opinion and achieve a majority.

In contrast, if the two rules of fairness are followed, everyone, strong and weak, is treated in a similar way. All individuals are free to use their resources and human skills to create things that are valued by themselves and others and to exchange the fruits of their efforts with all others. This set of arrangements is the only one that obeys the symmetry principle.

Fair Rules and Efficiency If private property rights are enforced and if voluntary exchange takes place in a competitive market with none of the obstacles described above (p. 114), resources will be allocated efficiently.

According to the Nozick fair-rules view, no matter how unequal is the resulting distribution of income and wealth, it will be fair.

It would be better if everyone were as well off as those with the highest incomes, but scarcity prevents that outcome and the best attainable outcome is the efficient one.

Case Study: A Generator Shortage in a Natural Disaster

Hurricane Katrina shut down electricity supplies over a wide area and increased the demand for portable generators. What is the fair way to allocate the available generators?

If the market price is used, the outcome is efficient. Sellers *and buyers* are better off and no one is worse off. But people who own generators make a larger profit and the generators go to those who want them most and can afford them. Is that fair?

On the Nozick rules view, the outcome is fair. On the fair outcome view, the outcome might be considered unfair. But what are the alternatives? They are command; majority rule; contest; first-come, first-served; lottery; personal characteristics; and force. Except by chance, none of these methods delivers an allocation of generators that is either fair or efficient. It is unfair in the rules view because the distribution involves involuntary transfers of resources among citizens. It is unfair in the results view because the poorest don't end up being made as well off as possible.

AT **ISSUE**

Price Gouging

Price gouging is the practice of offering an essential item for sale following a natural disaster at a price much higher than its normal price.

In the aftermath of Hurricane Katrina, John Shepperson bought 19 generators and rented a U-Haul truck to transport them from his Kentucky home to a town in Mississippi that had lost its electricity supply. He offered the generators to eager buyers at twice the price he had paid for them. But before Mr. Shepperson had made a sale, the Mississippi police confiscated the generators and put him in jail for four days for price gouging.

In **Favor of a Law Against Price Gouging**

Supporters of laws against price gouging say

- It unfairly exploits vulnerable needy buyers.
- It unfairly rewards unscrupulous sellers.
- In situations of extraordinary shortage, prices should be regulated to prevent these abuses and scarce resources should be allocated by one of the non-market mechanisms such as majority vote or equal shares for all.

Should the price that this seller of generators may charge be regulated?

The **Economist's Response**

Economists say that preventing a voluntary market transaction leads to inefficiency—it makes some people worse off without making anyone better off.

- In the figure below, when the demand for generators increases from D_0 to D_1, the equilibrium price rises from $200 to $600.
- Calling the price rise "gouging" and blocking it with a law prevents additional units from being made available and creates a deadweight loss.

The Effects of a Price-Gouging Law

REVIEW QUIZ

1 What are the two big approaches to thinking about fairness?

2 What is the utilitarian idea of fairness and what is wrong with it?

3 Explain the big tradeoff. What idea of fairness has been developed to deal with it?

4 What is the idea of fairness based on fair rules?

Work these questions in Study Plan 5.4 and get instant feedback. Do a Key TermsQuiz.   MyEconLab

◆ You've now studied efficiency and equity (fairness), the two biggest issues that run through the whole of economics. *Economics in the News* on pp. 120–121 looks at an example of an *inefficiency* in our economy today. At many points throughout this book—and in your life—you will return to and use the ideas you've learned in this chapter. We start to apply these ideas in the next chapter where we study some sources of *in*efficiency and *un*fairness.

Making Traffic Flow Efficiently

A Fundamental Law of Road Congestion

American Economic Review
October, 2011

It is not an everyday occurrence for economic research to make the news. But an article in the *American Economic Review* by Gilles Duranton and Matthew A. Turner of the University of Toronto entitled "The Fundamental Law of Road Congestion: Evidence from U.S. Cities," caught the attention of several newspapers and magazines for its eyepopping findings and implicit recommendation.

Noting that an average American household spends almost 3 hours a day in a passenger vehicle achieving an average speed of less than 30 miles per hour, Professors Duranton and Turner wanted to find out how it might be possible to end the rush-hour crawl, ease traffic congestion, and make the nation's highways more productive.

To get the answers, they studied traffic flows and highways in all the major U.S. cities in 1983, 1993, and 2003 to determine the effect of adding highway capacity on traffic volumes and flows.

Their startling discovery is that on interstate highways, increasing highway capacity increases vehicle miles traveled by the same percentage. Residents and businesses drive more, and better highways attract inward migration.

Durant and Turner also found that increasing the capacity of one type of road diverts little traffic from other types of roads.

And they found that increasing the provision of public transportation does not lower congestion.

They concluded that the only candidate for improving traffic flow is to use a congestion pricing system.

Source of information: "The Fundamental Law of Road Congestion: Evidence from US Cities", *American Economic Review*, 101(6): 2616-52, (October, 2011).

MyEconLab More Economics in the News

ESSENCE OF THE STORY

- Economists Gilles Duranton and Matthew Turner discovered that adding a lane to a highway does not ease congestion.

- Highway use increases in proportion to the available roadways.

- Increasing the capacity of one road does not reduce congestion on others.

- Duranton and Turner say that congestion pricing is the only available solution to overcrowded highways.

ECONOMIC ANALYSIS

- The discovery that adding a highway does not ease congestion points to congestion pricing as a solution. Let's see how a congestion price works.

- A highway has the marginal social cost curve MSC in the figures. The highway can carry only 10,000 vehicles per hour with no congestion.

- At off-peak times, the demand curve and marginal benefit curve is $D_o = MSB_o$; and the peak time demand curve and marginal benefit curve is $D_p = MSB_p$.

- Figure 1 illustrates inefficient road use. At off-peak, the outcome is efficient but at the peak demand time, at a zero price, 40,000 vehicles per hour enter the road. The marginal social cost is $6 per vehicle-hour and there is a deadweight loss (of time and gasoline) shown by the gray triangle.

- Figure 2 illustrates efficient road use at the peak period. Imposing a congestion charge of $3 per vehicle-hour brings an equilibrium at 25,000 vehicles per hour, which is the efficient quantity. Total surplus, the sum of consumer surplus (green) *plus* producer surplus (blue), is maximized.

- Congestion charges would be paid by all road users, regardless of whether they are rich or poor, but they don't have to leave the poor worse off.

- Revenue raised from congestion charges can be redistributed to low-income households if there is a fairness problem.

- So long as road users pay the marginal social cost of their decision, road use is efficient.

- London has a simple system of congestion pricing that imposes a charge when a vehicle enters a central congestion zone.

- Singapore has the world's most sophisticated congestion pricing with the price displayed on gantries (see photo), and the price rises as congestion increases and falls as congestion eases.

- Advances in technology make congestion pricing an attractive alternative to congestion.

Figure 1 Inefficient Rush-Hour Road Use

While traffic grinds to a halt on U.S. freeways, Electronic Road Pricing (ERP) keeps vehicles moving in Singapore.

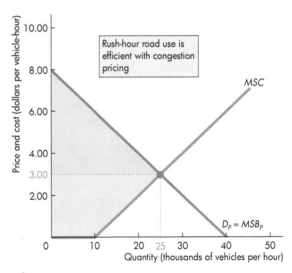

Figure 2 Efficient Rush-Hour Road Use

121

SUMMARY

Key Points

Resource Allocation Methods (pp. 106–107)

- Because resources are scarce, some mechanism must allocate them.
- The alternative allocation methods are market price; command; majority rule; contest; first-come, first-served; lottery; personal characteristics; and force.

Working Study Plan Problem 1 will give you a better understanding of resource allocation methods.

Benefit, Cost, and Surplus (pp. 108–111)

- The maximum price willingly paid is marginal benefit, so a demand curve is also a marginal benefit curve.
- The market demand curve is the horizontal sum of the individual demand curves and is the marginal social benefit curve.
- Value is what people are *willing to* pay; price is what people *must* pay.
- Consumer surplus is the excess of the benefit received from a good or service over the amount paid for it.
- The minimum supply-price is marginal cost, so a supply curve is also a marginal cost curve.
- The market supply curve is the horizontal sum of the individual supply curves and is the marginal social cost curve.
- Cost is what producers pay; price is what producers receive.

- Producer surplus is the excess of the amount received from the sale of a good or service over the cost of producing it.

Working Study Plan Problems 2 to 7 will give you a better understanding of benefit, cost, and surplus.

Is the Competitive Market Efficient? (pp. 112–115)

- In a competitive equilibrium, marginal social benefit equals marginal social cost and resource allocation is efficient.
- Buyers and sellers acting in their self-interest end up promoting the social interest.
- Total surplus, consumer surplus plus producer surplus, is maximized.
- Producing less than or more than the efficient quantity creates deadweight loss.
- Price and quantity regulations; taxes and subsidies; externalities; public goods and common resources; monopoly; and high transactions costs can lead to market failure.

Working Study Plan Problem 8 will give you a better understanding of the efficiency of competitive markets.

Is the Competitive Market Fair? (pp. 116–119)

- Ideas about fairness can be divided into two groups: fair *results* and fair *rules*.
- Fair-results ideas require income transfers from the rich to the poor.
- Fair-rules ideas require property rights and voluntary exchange.

Working Study Plan Problems 9 and 10 will give you a better understanding of the fairness of competitive markets.

Key Terms

MyEconLab Key Terms Quiz

Big tradeoff, 117
Command system, 106
Consumer surplus, 109
Deadweight loss, 114

Market failure, 114
Producer surplus, 111
Symmetry principle, 118
Total surplus, 112

Transactions costs, 115
Utilitarianism, 116

◆ WORKED PROBLEM

MyEconLab   You can work this problem in Chapter 5 Study Plan.

The figure illustrates the market for sunscreen.

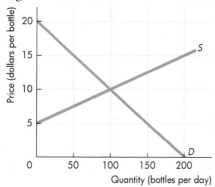

Questions

1. At the market equilibrium, calculate
   (a) consumer surplus and (b) producer surplus.
2. Is the market for sunscreen efficient? Why?
3. What is deadweight loss? Calculate it if factories produce only 50 bottles of sunscreen.

Solutions

1. (a) Consumer surplus is the excess of the benefit received over the amount buyers paid for it. The demand curve tells us the benefit, so consumer surplus equals the area under the demand curve above the market price, summed over the quantity bought. The price paid is $10 a bottle, the quantity bought is 100 bottles, so consumer surplus equals the area of the green triangle in the figure below.

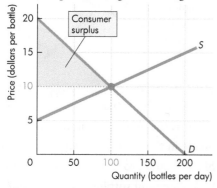

Area of the triangle = (Base × Height) ÷ 2. The base is the quantity bought (100 bottles) and the height the maximum price ($20 a bottle) *minus* the market price ($10 a bottle). Consumer surplus equals 100 × ($20 − $10) ÷ 2, which is $500.

Key Point: Consumer surplus equals the area under the demand curve above the market price.

1. (b) Producer surplus is the excess of the amount received by sellers over the cost of production.

The supply curve tells us the cost of producing the good, so producer surplus is equal to the area under the market price above the supply curve, summed over the quantity sold.

Producer surplus is equal to the area of the blue triangle in the following figure.

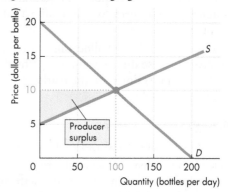

In this triangle, the base is the quantity sold (100 bottles), the height is the market price ($10 a bottle) *minus* the minimum cost ($5 a bottle), so producer surplus is 100 × ($10 − $5) ÷ 2, or $250.

Key Point: Producer surplus equals the area under the market price above the supply curve.

2. Total surplus (consumer surplus plus producer surplus) is a maximum, so the market is efficient.

Key Point: A competitive market is always efficient.

3. When factories produce *less* than the efficient quantity (100 bottles), some total surplus is lost. This loss is called the deadweight loss and it is equal to the area of the gray triangle in the following figure.

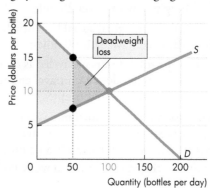

MyEconLab Interactive Animation

The base is the benefit of the 50th bottle *minus* the cost of producing it ($7.50), the height is quantity not produced (50 bottles), so deadweight loss equals ($15 − $7.50) × 50 ÷ 2, which is $187.50.

Key Point: Underproduction creates a deadweight loss.

STUDY PLAN PROBLEMS AND APPLICATIONS

MyEconLab   You can work Problems 1 to 10 in Chapter 5 Study Plan and get instant feedback.

Resource Allocation Methods (Study Plan 5.1)

1. At Chez Panisse, a restaurant in Berkeley, reservations are essential. At Mandarin Dynasty, a restaurant near the University of California San Diego, reservations are recommended. At Eli Cannon's, a restaurant in Middletown, Connecticut, reservations are not accepted.

   Describe the method of allocating scarce table resources at these three restaurants. Why do you think restaurants don't use the market price to allocate their tables?

Benefit, Cost, and Surplus (Study Plan 5.2)

Use the following table to work Problems 2 to 4.
The table gives the demand schedules for train travel for the only buyers in the market, Ann, Beth, and Cy.

Price (dollars per mile)	Quantity demanded (miles)		
	Ann	Beth	Cy
3	30	25	20
4	25	20	15
5	20	15	10
6	15	10	5
7	10	5	0
8	5	0	0
9	0	0	0

2. a. Construct the market demand schedule.

   b. What is the maximum price that each traveler is willing to pay to travel 20 miles? Why?

3. a. What is the marginal social benefit when the total distance traveled is 60 miles?

   b. When the total distance traveled is 60 miles, how many miles does each travel and what is their marginal private benefit?

4. What is each traveler's consumer surplus when the price is $4 a mile? What is the market consumer surplus when the price is $4 a mile?

Use the table in the next column to work Problems 5 to 7.

The table gives the supply schedules of the only sellers of hot air balloon rides: Xavier, Yasmin, and Zack.

5. a. Construct the market supply schedule.

   b. What are the minimum prices that Xavier, Yasmin, and Zack are willing to accept to supply 20 rides? Why?

Price (dollars per ride)	Quantity supplied (rides per week)		
	Xavier	Yasmin	Zack
100	30	25	20
90	25	20	15
80	20	15	10
70	15	10	5
60	10	5	0
50	5	0	0
40	0	0	0

6. a. What is the marginal social cost when the total number of rides is 30?

   b. What is the marginal cost for each supplier when the total number of rides is 30 and how many rides does each of the sellers supply?

7. When the price is $70 a ride, what is each seller's producer surplus? What is the market producer surplus?

Is the Competitive Market Efficient? (Study Plan 5.3)

8. The figure shows the competitive market for cellphones.

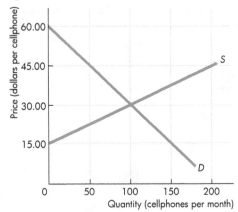

   a. What is the market equilibrium?

   b. Shade in the consumer surplus and label it.

   c. Shade in the producer surplus and label it.

   d. Calculate total surplus.

   e. Is the market for cellphones efficient?

Is the Competitive Market Fair? (Study Plan 5.4)

9. Explain why the allocation method used by each restaurant in Problem 1 is fair or not fair.

10. In the Worked Problem (p. 123), how can the 50 bottles available be allocated to beach-goers? Would the possible methods be fair or unfair?

ADDITIONAL PROBLEMS AND APPLICATIONS

MyEconLab   You can work these problems in MyEconLab if assigned by your instructor.

Resource Allocation Methods

11. At McDonald's, no reservations are accepted; at Panorama at St. Louis Art Museum, reservations are accepted; at the Bissell Mansion restaurant, reservations are essential. Describe the method of allocating tables in these three restaurants. Why do restaurants have different reservations policies?

Benefit, Cost, and Surplus

Use the following table to work Problems 12 to 15. The table gives the supply schedules for jet-ski rides by the only suppliers: Rick, Sam, and Tom.

Price (dollars per ride)	Quantity supplied (rides per day)		
	Rick	Sam	Tom
10.00	0	0	0
12.50	5	0	0
15.00	10	5	0
17.50	15	10	5
20.00	20	15	10

12. What is each owner's minimum supply-price of 10 rides a day?
13. Which owner has the largest producer surplus when the price of a ride is $17.50? Explain.
14. What is the marginal social cost of 45 rides a day?
15. Construct the market supply schedule of jet-ski rides.
16. The table gives the demand and supply schedules for sandwiches.

Price (dollars per sandwich)	Quantity demanded	Quantity supplied
	(sandwiches per hour)	
0	300	0
1	250	50
2	200	100
3	150	150
4	100	200
5	50	250
6	0	300

a. What is the maximum price that consumers are willing to pay for the 200th sandwich?
b. What is the minimum price that producers are willing to accept for the 200th sandwich?
c. If 200 sandwiches a day are available, what is the total surplus?

17. **Home Heating Bills Surge Amid Record Cold**
If there's one thing that can set home heating costs soaring, it's a long, frigid blast from one of the coldest winters in 20 years and people are going to use 10 to 12 percent more natural gas this year than they have normally.

Source: CBC News, March 3, 2014

a. How is the price of natural gas determined?
b. When demand increases, explain the process by which the market adjusts.
c. On a graph, show the effect of the increase in demand on consumer surplus and producer surplus.

Is the Competitive Market Efficient?

18. Use the data in the table in Problem 16.
a. If the sandwich market is efficient, what is the consumer surplus, what is the producer surplus, and what is the total surplus?
b. If the demand for sandwiches increases and sandwich makers produce the efficient quantity, what happens to producer surplus and deadweight loss?

Use the following news clip to work Problems 19 to 21.

The Right Price for Digital Music
Apple's $1.29-for-the-latest-songs model isn't perfect and isn't it too much to pay for music that appeals to just a few people? We need a system that will be profitable but fair to music lovers. The solution: Price song downloads according to demand. The more people who download a particular song, the higher will be the price of that song; the fewer people who buy a particular song, the lower will be the price of that song. That is a free-market solution—the market would determine the price.

Source: Slate, December 5, 2005

Assume that the marginal social cost of downloading a song from the iTunes Store is zero. (This assumption means that the cost of operating the iTunes Store doesn't change if people download more songs.)

19. a. Draw a graph of the market for downloadable music with a price of $1.29 for all the latest songs. On your graph, show consumer surplus and producer surplus.

b. With a price of $1.29 for all the latest songs, is the market efficient or inefficient? If it is inefficient, show the deadweight loss on your graph.

20. If the pricing scheme described in the news clip were adopted, how would consumer surplus, producer surplus, and the deadweight loss change?

21. a. If the pricing scheme described in the news clip were adopted, would the market be efficient or inefficient? Explain.

    b. Is the pricing scheme described in the news clip a "free-market solution"? Explain.

22. Only 1 percent of the world supply of water is fit for human consumption. Some places have more water than they can use; some could use much more than they have. The 1 percent available would be sufficient if only it were in the right place.

    a. What is the major problem in achieving an efficient use of the world's water?

    b. If there were a global market in water, like there is in oil, how do you think the market would be organized?

    c. Would a free world market in water achieve an efficient use of the world's water resources? Explain why or why not.

Is the Competitive Market Fair?

23. Use the information in Problem 22. Would a free world market in water achieve a fair use of the world's water resources? Explain why or why not and be clear about the concept of fairness that you are using.

24. The winner of the men's and women's tennis singles at the U.S. Open is paid twice as much as the runner-up, but it takes two players to have a singles final. Is the compensation arrangement fair?

25. **The Scandal of Phone Call Price Gouging by Prisons**

    In most U.S. states, the phone company guarantees the prison a commission of a percentage on every call. The average commission is 42% of the cost of the call, but in some states it is 60%. So 60% of what families pay to receive a collect call from their imprisoned relative has nothing to do with the cost of the phone service. Also, the phone company that offers the highest commission is often the company to get the prison contract.

    Source: *The Guardian*, May 23, 2012

a. Who is practicing price gouging: the prison, the phone company, or both? Explain.

b. Evaluate the "fairness" of the prison's commission.

Economics in the News

26. After you have studied *Economics in the News* on pp. 120–121, answer the following questions.

    a. What is the method used to allocate highway space in the United States and what is the method used in Singapore?

    b. Who benefits from the U.S. method of highway resource allocation? Explain your answer using the ideas of marginal social benefit, marginal social cost, consumer surplus, and producer surplus.

    c. Who benefits from the Singaporean method of highway resource allocation? Explain your answer using the ideas of marginal social benefit, marginal social cost, consumer surplus, and producer surplus.

    d. If road use were rationed by limiting drivers with even-date birthdays to drive only on even days (and odd-date birthdays to drive only on odd days), would highway use be more efficient? Explain your answer.

27. **Fight over Water Rates; Escondido Farmers Say Increase Would Put Them Out of Business**

    Agricultural users of water pay less than residential and business users. Since 1993, water rates have increased by more than 90 percent for residential customers and by only 50 percent for agricultural users.

    Source: *The San Diego Union-Tribune*, June 14, 2006

a. Do you think that the allocation of water between agricultural and residential users is likely to be efficient? Explain your answer.

b. If agricultural users paid a higher price, would the allocation of resources be more efficient?

c. If agricultural users paid a higher price, what would happen to consumer surplus and producer surplus from water?

d. Is the difference in price paid by agricultural and residential users fair?

6 GOVERNMENT ACTIONS IN MARKETS

After studying this chapter, you will be able to:

◆ Explain how a rent ceiling creates a housing shortage

◆ Explain how a minimum wage law creates unemployment

◆ Explain the effects of a tax

◆ Explain the effects of production quotas and subsidies

◆ Explain how markets for illegal goods work

In New York City, where food servers and grocery clerks earn the minimum wage of $7.25 an hour, a budget one-bedroom apartment rents for $1,000 a month. For the lowest paid, that leaves $160 a month for food, clothing, and other necessities. What can governments do to help these people?

This chapter explains the effects of minimim wage laws and rent ceilings, and *Economics in the News* at the end of the chapter looks at some recent changes in state minimum wages. The chapter also explains the effects of taxes, production quotas and subsidies, and laws that make trading in some things illegal.

A Housing Market with a Rent Ceiling

We spend more of our income on housing than on any other good or service, so it isn't surprising that rents can be a political issue. When rents are high, or when they jump by a large amount, renters might lobby the government for limits on rents.

A government regulation that makes it illegal to charge a price higher than a specified level is called a **price ceiling** or **price cap**.

The effects of a price ceiling on a market depend crucially on whether the ceiling is imposed at a level that is above or below the equilibrium price.

A price ceiling set *above the equilibrium price* has no effect. The reason is that the price ceiling does not constrain the market forces. The force of the law and the market forces are not in conflict. But a price ceiling *below the equilibrium price* has powerful effects on a market. The reason is that the price ceiling attempts to prevent the price from regulating the quantities demanded and supplied. The force of the law and the market forces are in conflict.

When a price ceiling is applied to a housing market, it is called a **rent ceiling**. A rent ceiling set below the equilibrium rent creates

- A housing shortage
- Increased search activity
- A black market

A Housing Shortage

At the equilibrium price, the quantity demanded equals the quantity supplied. In a housing market, when the rent is at the equilibrium level, the quantity of housing supplied equals the quantity of housing demanded and there is neither a shortage nor a surplus of housing.

But at a rent set below the equilibrium rent, the quantity of housing demanded exceeds the quantity of housing supplied—there is a shortage. So if a rent ceiling is set below the equilibrium rent, there will be a shortage of housing.

When there is a shortage, the quantity available is the quantity supplied, and somehow this quantity must be allocated among the frustrated demanders. One way in which this allocation occurs is through increased search activity.

Increased Search Activity

The time spent looking for someone with whom to do business is called **search activity**. We spend some time in search activity almost every time we make a purchase. When you're shopping for the latest hot new cellphone, and you know four stores that stock it, how do you find which store has the best deal? You spend a few minutes on the Internet, checking out the various prices. In some markets, such as the housing market, people spend a lot of time checking the alternatives available before making a choice.

When a price is regulated and there is a shortage, search activity increases. In the case of a rent-controlled housing market, frustrated would-be renters scan the newspapers, not only for housing ads but also for death notices! Any information about newly available housing is useful, and apartment seekers race to be first on the scene when news of a possible supplier breaks.

The *opportunity cost* of a good is equal not only to its price but also to the value of the search time spent finding the good. So the opportunity cost of housing is equal to the rent (a regulated price) plus the time and other resources spent searching for the restricted quantity available. Search activity is costly. It uses time and other resources, such as phone calls, automobiles, and gasoline that could have been used in other productive ways.

A rent ceiling controls only the rent portion of the cost of housing. The cost of increased search activity might end up making the full cost of housing *higher* than it would be without a rent ceiling.

A Black Market

A rent ceiling also encourages illegal trading in a **black market**, an illegal market in which the equilibrium price exceeds the price ceiling. Black markets occur in rent-controlled housing and many other markets. For example, scalpers run black markets in tickets for big sporting events and rock concerts.

When a rent ceiling is in force, frustrated renters and landlords constantly seek ways of increasing rents. One common way is for a new tenant to pay a high price for worthless fittings, such as charging $2,000 for threadbare drapes. Another is for the tenant to pay an exorbitant price for new locks and keys—called "key money."

The level of a black market rent depends on how tightly the rent ceiling is enforced. With loose enforcement, the black market rent is close to the unregulated rent. But with strict enforcement, the black market rent is equal to the maximum price that a renter is willing to pay.

Figure 6.1 illustrates the effects of a rent ceiling. The demand curve for housing is *D* and the supply curve is *S*. A rent ceiling is imposed at $800 a month. Rents that exceed $800 a month are in the gray-shaded illegal region in the figure. You can see that the equilibrium rent, where the demand and supply curves intersect, is in the illegal region.

At a rent of $800 a month, the quantity of housing supplied is 60,000 units and the quantity demanded is 100,000 units. So with a rent of $800 a month, there is a shortage of 40,000 units of housing.

To rent the 60,000th unit, someone is willing to pay $1,200 a month. They might pay this amount by incurring search costs that bring the total cost of housing to $1,200 a month, or they might pay a black market price of $1,200 a month. Either way, they end up incurring a cost that exceeds what the equilibrium rent would be in an unregulated market.

Inefficiency of a Rent Ceiling

A rent ceiling set below the equilibrium rent results in an inefficient underproduction of housing services. The *marginal social benefit* of housing exceeds its *marginal social cost* and a deadweight loss shrinks the producer surplus and consumer surplus (Chapter 5, pp. 112–114).

Figure 6.2 shows this inefficiency. The rent ceiling ($800 per month) is below the equilibrium rent ($1,000 per month) and the quantity of housing supplied (60,000 units) is less than the efficient quantity (80,000 units).

Because the quantity of housing supplied (the quantity available) is less than the efficient quantity, there is a deadweight loss, shown by the gray triangle. Producer surplus shrinks to the blue triangle and consumer surplus shrinks to the green triangle. The red rectangle represents the potential loss from increased search activity. This loss is borne by consumers and the full loss from the rent ceiling is the sum of the deadweight loss and the increased cost of search.

FIGURE 6.1   A Rent Ceiling

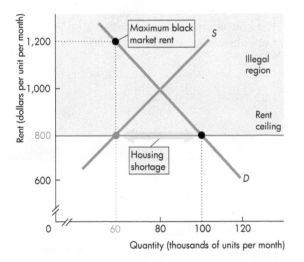

A rent above the rent ceiling of $800 a month is illegal (in the gray-shaded illegal region). At a rent of $800 a month, the quantity of housing supplied is 60,000 units. Frustrated renters spend time searching for housing and they make deals with landlords in a black market. Someone is willing to pay $1,200 a month for the 60,000th unit.

MyEconLab Animation and Draw Graph

FIGURE 6.2   The Inefficiency of a Rent Ceiling

Without a rent ceiling, the market produces an efficient 80,000 units of housing at a rent of $1,000 a month. A rent ceiling of $800 a month decreases the quantity of housing supplied to 60,000 units. Producer surplus and consumer surplus shrink and a deadweight loss arises. The red rectangle represents the cost of resources used in increased search activity. The full loss from the rent ceiling equals the sum of the red rectangle and gray triangle.

MyEconLab Animation and Draw Graph

Are Rent Ceilings Fair?

Rent ceilings might be inefficient, but don't they achieve a fairer allocation of scarce housing? Let's explore this question.

Chapter 5 (pp. 116–118) reviews two key ideas about fairness. According to the *fair-rules* view, anything that blocks voluntary exchange is unfair, so rent ceilings are unfair. But according to the *fair-result* view, a fair outcome is one that benefits the less well off. So according to this view, the fairest outcome is the one that allocates scarce housing to the poorest. To see whether rent ceilings help to achieve a fairer outcome in this sense, we need to consider how the market allocates scarce housing resources in the face of a rent ceiling.

Blocking rent adjustments doesn't eliminate scarcity. Rather, because it decreases the quantity of housing available, it creates an even bigger challenge for the housing market. Somehow, the market must ration a smaller quantity of housing and allocate that housing among the people who demand it.

When the rent is not permitted to allocate scarce housing, what other mechanisms are available, and are *they* fair? Some possible mechanisms are:

- A lottery
- First-come, first-served
- Discrimination

A lottery allocates housing to those who are lucky, not to those who are poor. First-come, first-served (a method used to allocate housing in England after World War II) allocates housing to those who have the greatest foresight and who get their names on a list first, not to the poorest. Discrimination allocates scarce housing based on the views and self-interest of the owner of the housing. In the case of public housing, what counts is the self-interest of the bureaucracy that administers the allocation.

In principle, self-interested owners and bureaucrats could allocate housing to satisfy some criterion of fairness, but they are not likely to do so. Discrimination based on friendship, family ties, and criteria such as race, ethnicity, or sex is more likely to enter the equation. We might make such discrimination illegal, but we cannot prevent it from occurring.

It is hard, then, to make a case for rent ceilings on the basis of fairness. When rent adjustments are blocked, other methods of allocating scarce housing resources operate that do not produce a fair outcome.

ECONOMICS IN ACTION
Rent Control Winners: The Rich and Famous

New York, San Francisco, London, and Paris, four of the world's great cities, have rent ceilings in some part of their housing markets. Boston had rent ceilings for many years but abolished them in 1997. Many other U.S. cities do not have, and have never had, rent ceilings. Among them are Atlanta, Baltimore, Chicago, Dallas, Philadelphia, Phoenix, and Seattle.

To see the effects of rent ceilings in practice we can compare the housing markets in cities with ceilings with those without ceilings. We learn two main lessons from such a comparison.

First, rent ceilings definitely create a housing shortage. Second, they do lower the rents for some but raise them for others.

A survey* conducted in 1997 showed that the rents of housing units *actually available for rent* were 2.5 times the average of all rents in New York but equal to the average rent in Philadelphia. The winners from rent ceilings are the families that have lived in a city for a long time. In New York, these families include some rich and famous ones. The voting power of the winners keeps the rent ceilings in place. Mobile newcomers are the losers in a city with rent ceilings.

The bottom line is that, in principle and in practice, rent ceilings are inefficient and unfair.

---

* William Tucker, "How Rent Control Drives Out Affordable Housing," Cato Policy Analysis No. 274, May 21, 1997, Cato Institute.

◆ REVIEW QUIZ

1. What is a rent ceiling and what are its effects if it is set above the equilibrium rent?
2. What are the effects of a rent ceiling that is set below the equilibrium rent?
3. How are scarce housing resources allocated when a rent ceiling is in place?
4. Why does a rent ceiling create an inefficient and unfair outcome in the housing market?

Work these questions in Study Plan 6.1 and get instant feedback. Do a Key Terms Quiz.   MyEconLab

You now know how a price ceiling (rent ceiling) works. Next, we'll learn about the effects of a price floor by studying a minimum wage in a labor market.

A Labor Market with a Minimum Wage

For each one of us, the labor market is the market that influences the jobs we get and the wages we earn. Firms decide how much labor to demand, and the lower the wage rate, the greater is the quantity of labor demanded. Households decide how much labor to supply, and the higher the wage rate, the greater is the quantity of labor supplied. The wage rate adjusts to make the quantity of labor demanded equal to the quantity supplied.

When wage rates are low, or when they fail to keep up with rising prices, labor unions might turn to governments and lobby for a higher wage rate.

A government regulation that makes it illegal to charge a price lower than a specified level is called a **price floor**.

The effects of a price floor on a market depend crucially on whether the floor is imposed at a level that is above or below the equilibrium price.

A price floor set *below the equilibrium price* has no effect. The reason is that the price floor does not constrain the market forces. The force of the law and the market forces are not in conflict. But a price floor set *above the equilibrium price* has powerful effects on a market. The reason is that the price floor attempts to prevent the price from regulating the quantities demanded and supplied. The force of the law and the market forces are in conflict.

When a price floor is applied to a labor market, it is called a **minimum wage**. A minimum wage imposed at a level that is above the equilibrium wage creates unemployment. Let's look at the effects of a minimum wage.

Minimum Wage Brings Unemployment

At the equilibrium price, the quantity demanded equals the quantity supplied. In a labor market, when the wage rate is at the equilibrium level, the quantity of labor supplied equals the quantity of labor demanded: There is neither a shortage of labor nor a surplus of labor.

But at a wage rate above the equilibrium wage, the quantity of labor supplied exceeds the quantity of labor demanded—there is a surplus of labor. So when a minimum wage is set above the equilibrium wage, there is a surplus of labor. The demand for labor determines the level of employment, and the surplus of labor is unemployed.

FIGURE 6.3   Minimum Wage and Unemployment

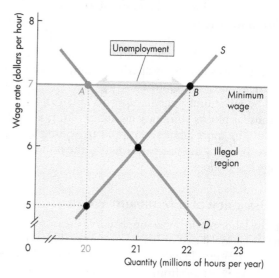

The minimum wage rate is set at $7 an hour. Any wage rate below $7 an hour is illegal (in the gray-shaded illegal region). At the minimum wage of $7 an hour, 20 million hours are hired but 22 million hours are available. Unemployment—AB—of 2 million hours a year is created. With only 20 million hours demanded, someone is willing to supply the 20 millionth hour for $5.

MyEconLab Animation and Draw Graph

Figure 6.3 illustrates the effect of the minimum wage on unemployment. The demand for labor curve is *D* and the supply of labor curve is *S*. The horizontal red line shows the minimum wage set at $7 an hour. A wage rate below this level is illegal, in the gray-shaded illegal region of the figure. At the minimum wage rate, 20 million hours of labor are demanded (point *A*) and 22 million hours of labor are supplied (point *B*), so 2 million hours of available labor are unemployed.

With only 20 million hours demanded, someone is willing to supply that 20 millionth hour for $5. Frustrated unemployed workers spend time and other resources searching for hard-to-find jobs.

Is the Minimum Wage Fair?

The minimum wage is unfair on both views of fairness: It delivers an unfair *result* and imposes an unfair *rule*.

The *result* is unfair because only those people who have jobs and keep them benefit from the minimum wage. The unemployed end up worse off than they would be with no minimum wage. Some of those who search for jobs and find them end up worse off because of the increased cost of job search they incur. Also those who search and find jobs aren't always the least well off. When the wage rate doesn't allocate labor, other mechanisms determine who finds a job. One such mechanism is discrimination, which is yet another source of unfairness.

The minimum wage imposes an unfair *rule* because it blocks voluntary exchange. Firms are willing to hire more labor and people are willing to work more, but they are not permitted by the minimum wage law to do so.

Inefficiency of a Minimum Wage

In the labor market, the supply curve measures the marginal social cost of labor to workers. This cost is leisure forgone. The demand curve measures the marginal social benefit from labor. This benefit is the value of the goods and services produced. An unregulated labor market allocates the economy's scarce labor resources to the jobs in which they are valued most highly. The market is efficient.

The minimum wage frustrates the market mechanism and results in unemployment and increased job search. At the quantity of labor employed, the marginal social benefit of labor exceeds its marginal social cost and a deadweight loss shrinks the firms' surplus and the workers' surplus.

Figure 6.4 shows this inefficiency. The minimum wage ($7 an hour) is above the equilibrium wage ($6 an hour) and the quantity of labor demanded and employed (20 million hours) is less than the efficient quantity (21 million hours).

Because the quantity of labor employed is less than the efficient quantity, there is a deadweight loss, shown by the gray triangle. The firms' surplus shrinks to the blue triangle and the workers' surplus shrinks to the green triangle. The red rectangle shows the potential loss from increased job search, which is borne by workers. The full loss from the minimum wage is the sum of the deadweight loss and the increased cost of job search.

◆ AT **ISSUE**

Does the Minimum Wage Cause Unemployment?

In the United States, the federal government's Fair Labor Standards Act sets the minimum wage, which has fluctuated between 35 percent and 50 percent of the average wage, and in 2014 it was $7.25 an hour, a level set in 2009. Most states have minimum wages that exceed the federal minimum.

Does the minimum wage result in unemployment, and if so, how much unemployment does it create?

No, It Doesn't	Yes, It Does
David Card of the University of California at Berkeley and Alan Krueger of Princeton University say:	Most economists are skeptical about Card and Krueger's conclusion.

No, It Doesn't

David Card of the University of California at Berkeley and Alan Krueger of Princeton University say:

- An increase in the minimum wage *increases teenage employment* and *decreases unemployment*.
- Their study of minimum wages in California, New Jersey, and Texas found that the employment rate of low-income workers increased following an increase in the minimum wage.
- A higher wage *increases* employment by making workers more conscientious and productive as well as less likely to quit, which lowers unproductive labor turnover.
- A higher wage rate also encourages managers to seek ways to increase labor productivity.

Yes, It Does

Most economists are skeptical about Card and Krueger's conclusion.

- The consensus view is that a 10 percent rise in the minimum wage *decreases teenage employment* by between 1 and 3 percent.
- Firms freely pay wage rates above the equilibrium wage to encourage more productive work habits.
- Daniel Hamermesh of the University of Texas at Austin says that firms anticipate the rise and cut employment *before* the minimum wage goes up.
- Finis Welch of Texas A&M University and Kevin Murphy of the University of Chicago say the employment effects that Card and Krueger found are caused by regional differences in economic growth and not by a rise in the minimum wage.

FIGURE 6.4   The Inefficiency of a Minimum Wage

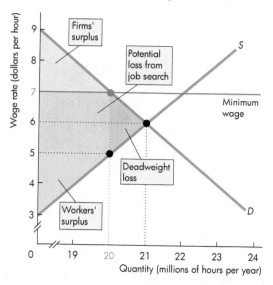

A minimum wage decreases employment. Firms' surplus (blue area) and workers' surplus (green area) shrink and a deadweight loss (gray area) arises. Job search increases and the red area shows the loss from this activity.

————— MyEconLab Animation —————

◆ REVIEW QUIZ

1 What is a minimum wage and what are its effects if it is set above the equilibrium wage?

2 What are the effects of a minimum wage set below the equilibrium wage?

3 Explain how scarce jobs are allocated when a minimum wage is in place.

4 Explain why a minimum wage creates an inefficient allocation of labor resources.

5 Explain why a minimum wage is unfair.

Work these questions in Study Plan 6.2 and get instant feedback. Do a Key Terms Quiz.   MyEconLab

Next we're going to study a more widespread government action in markets: taxes. We'll see how taxes change prices and quantities. You will discover the surprising fact that while the government can impose a tax, it can't decide who will pay the tax! You will also see that a tax creates a deadweight loss.

Taxes

Everything you earn and almost everything you buy is taxed. Income taxes and Social Security taxes are deducted from your earnings and sales taxes are added to the bill when you buy something. Employers also pay a Social Security tax for their workers, and producers of tobacco products, alcoholic drinks, and gasoline pay a tax every time they sell something.

Who *really* pays these taxes? Because the income tax and Social Security tax are deducted from your pay, and the sales tax is added to the prices that you pay, isn't it obvious that *you* pay these taxes? And isn't it equally obvious that your employer pays the employer's contribution to the Social Security tax and that tobacco producers pay the tax on cigarettes?

You're going to discover that it isn't obvious who *really* pays a tax and that lawmakers don't make that decision. We begin with a definition of tax incidence.

Tax Incidence

Tax incidence is the division of the burden of a tax between buyers and sellers. When the government imposes a tax on the sale of a good,* the price paid by buyers might rise by the full amount of the tax, by a lesser amount, or not at all. If the price paid by buyers rises by the full amount of the tax, then the burden of the tax falls entirely on buyers—the buyers pay the tax. If the price paid by buyers rises by a lesser amount than the tax, then the burden of the tax falls partly on buyers and partly on sellers. And if the price paid by buyers doesn't change at all, then the burden of the tax falls entirely on sellers.

Tax incidence does not depend on the tax law. The law might impose a tax on sellers or on buyers, but the outcome is the same in either case. To see why, let's look at the tax on cigarettes in New York City.

A Tax on Sellers

On July 1, 2002, Mayor Bloomberg put a tax of $1.50 a pack on cigarettes sold in New York City. To work out the effects of this tax on the sellers of cigarettes, we begin by examining the effects on demand and supply in the market for cigarettes.

———————————————

*These outcomes also apply to services and factors of production (land, labor, and capital).

In Fig. 6.5, the demand curve is *D*, and the supply curve is *S*. With no tax, the equilibrium price is $3 per pack and 350 million packs a year are bought and sold.

A tax on sellers is like an increase in cost, so it decreases supply. To determine the position of the new supply curve, we add the tax to the minimum price that sellers are willing to accept for each quantity sold. You can see that without the tax, sellers are willing to offer 350 million packs a year for $3 a pack. So with a $1.50 tax, they will offer 350 million packs a year only if the price is $4.50 a pack. The supply curve shifts to the red curve labeled *S + tax on sellers*.

Equilibrium occurs where the new supply curve intersects the demand curve at 325 million packs a year. The price paid by buyers rises by $1 to $4 a pack. And the price received by sellers falls by 50¢ to $2.50 a pack. So buyers pay $1 of the tax and sellers pay the other 50¢.

A Tax on Buyers

Suppose that instead of taxing sellers, New York City taxes cigarette buyers $1.50 a pack.

A tax on buyers lowers the amount they are willing to pay sellers, so it decreases demand and shifts the demand curve leftward. To determine the position of this new demand curve, we subtract the tax from the maximum price that buyers are willing to pay for each quantity bought. You can see, in Fig. 6.6, that without the tax, buyers are willing to buy 350 million packs a year for $3 a pack. So with a $1.50 tax, they are willing to buy 350 million packs a year only if the price including the tax is $3 a pack, which means that they're willing to pay sellers only $1.50 a pack. The demand curve shifts to become the red curve labeled *D – tax on buyers*.

Equilibrium occurs where the new demand curve intersects the supply curve at a quantity of 325 million packs a year. The price received by sellers is $2.50 a pack, and the price paid by buyers is $4.

Equivalence of Tax on Buyers and Sellers

You can see that the tax on buyers in Fig. 6.6 has the same effects as the tax on sellers in Fig. 6.5. In both cases, the equilibrium quantity decreases to 325 million packs a year, the price paid by buyers rises to $4 a pack, and the price received by sellers falls to $2.50 a pack. Buyers pay $1 of the $1.50 tax, and sellers pay the other 50¢ of the tax.

FIGURE 6.5   A Tax on Sellers

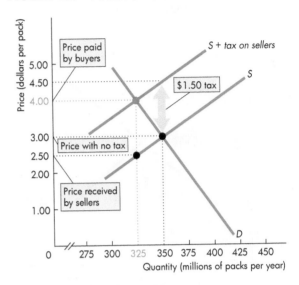

With no tax, 350 million packs a year are bought and sold at $3 a pack. A tax on sellers of $1.50 a pack shifts the supply curve from *S* to *S + tax on sellers*. The equilibrium quantity decreases to 325 million packs a year, the price paid by buyers rises to $4 a pack, and the price received by sellers falls to $2.50 a pack. The tax raises the price paid by buyers by less than the tax and lowers the price received by sellers, so buyers and sellers share the burden of the tax.

MyEconLab Animation and Draw Graph

Can We Share the Burden Equally? Suppose that Mayor Bloomberg wants the burden of the cigarette tax to fall equally on buyers and sellers and declares that a 75¢ tax be imposed on each. Is the burden of the tax then shared equally?

You can see that it is not. The tax is still $1.50 a pack. You've seen that the tax has the same effect regardless of whether it is imposed on sellers or buyers. So imposing half the tax on sellers and half on buyers is like an average of the two cases you've just examined. (Draw the demand-supply graph and work out what happens in this case. The demand curve shifts downward by 75¢ and the supply curve shifts upward by 75¢. The new equilibrium quantity is still 325 million packs a year. Buyers pay $4 a pack, of which 75¢ is tax. Sellers receive $3.25 from buyers, but pay a 75¢ tax, so sellers net $2.50 a pack.)

When a transaction is taxed, there are two prices: the price paid by buyers, which includes the tax; and the price received by sellers, which excludes the tax.

FIGURE 6.6   A Tax on Buyers

With no tax, 350 million packs a year are bought and sold at $3 a pack. A tax on buyers of $1.50 a pack shifts the demand curve from D to D – tax on buyers. The equilibrium quantity decreases to 325 million packs a year, the price paid by buyers rises to $4 a pack, and the price received by sellers falls to $2.50 a pack. The tax raises the price paid by buyers by less than the tax and lowers the price received by sellers, so buyers and sellers share the burden of the tax.

MyEconLab Animation

Buyers respond to the price that *includes* the tax and sellers respond to the price that *excludes* the tax.

A tax is like a wedge between the price buyers pay and the price sellers receive. The size of the wedge determines the effects of the tax, not the side of the market on which the government imposes the tax.

The Social Security Tax The Social Security tax is an example of a tax that Congress imposes equally on both buyers and sellers. But the principles you've just learned apply to this tax too. The market for labor, not Congress, decides how the burden of the Social Security tax is divided between firms and workers.

In the New York City cigarette tax example, buyers bear twice the burden of the tax borne by sellers. In special cases, either buyers or sellers bear the entire burden. The division of the burden of a tax between buyers and sellers depends on the elasticities of demand and supply, as you will now see.

Tax Incidence and Elasticity of Demand

The division of the tax between buyers and sellers depends in part on the elasticity of demand. There are two extreme cases:

- Perfectly inelastic demand—buyers pay.
- Perfectly elastic demand—sellers pay.

Perfectly Inelastic Demand Figure 6.7 shows the market for insulin, a vital daily medication for those with diabetes. Demand is perfectly inelastic at 100,000 doses a day, regardless of the price, as shown by the vertical demand curve D. That is, a diabetic would sacrifice all other goods and services rather than not consume the insulin dose that provides good health. The supply curve of insulin is S. With no tax, the price is $2 a dose and the quantity is 100,000 doses a day.

If insulin is taxed at 20¢ a dose, we must add the tax to the minimum price at which drug companies are willing to sell insulin. The result is the new supply curve S + tax. The price rises to $2.20 a dose, but the quantity does not change. Buyers pay the entire tax of 20¢ a dose.

FIGURE 6.7   Tax with Perfectly Inelastic Demand

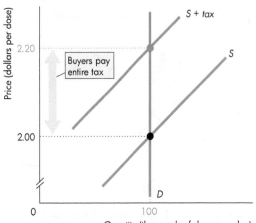

In this market for insulin, demand is perfectly inelastic. With no tax, the price is $2 a dose and the quantity is 100,000 doses a day. A tax of 20¢ a dose shifts the supply curve to S + tax. The price rises to $2.20 a dose, but the quantity bought does not change. Buyers pay the entire tax.

MyEconLab Animation

Perfectly Elastic Demand Figure 6.8 shows the market for pink marker pens. Demand is perfectly elastic at $1 a pen, as shown by the horizontal demand curve *D*. If pink pens are less expensive than the other colors, everyone uses pink. If pink pens are more expensive than other colors, no one uses pink. The supply curve is *S*. With no tax, the price of a pink pen is $1 and the quantity is 4,000 pens a week.

Suppose that the government imposes a tax of 10¢ a pen on pink marker pens but not on other colors. The new supply curve is *S + tax*. The price remains at $1 a pen, and the quantity decreases to 1,000 pink pens a week. The 10¢ tax leaves the price paid by buyers unchanged but lowers the amount received by sellers by the full amount of the tax. Sellers pay the entire tax of 10¢ a pink pen.

We've seen that when demand is perfectly inelastic, buyers pay the entire tax and when demand is perfectly elastic, sellers pay the entire tax. In the usual case, demand is neither perfectly inelastic nor perfectly elastic and the tax is split between buyers and sellers. But the division depends on the elasticity of demand: The more inelastic the demand, the larger is the amount of the tax paid by buyers.

FIGURE 6.8   Tax with Perfectly Elastic Demand

In this market for pink pens, demand is perfectly elastic. With no tax, the price of a pen is $1 and the quantity is 4,000 pens a week. A tax of 10¢ a pink pen shifts the supply curve to *S + tax*. The price remains at $1 a pen, and the quantity of pink pens sold decreases to 1,000 a week. Sellers pay the entire tax.

——— MyEconLab Animation ———

Tax Incidence and Elasticity of Supply

The division of the tax between buyers and sellers also depends, in part, on the elasticity of supply. Again, there are two extreme cases:

- Perfectly inelastic supply—sellers pay.
- Perfectly elastic supply—buyers pay.

Perfectly Inelastic Supply Figure 6.9(a) shows the market for water from a mineral spring that flows at a constant rate that can't be controlled. Supply is perfectly inelastic at 100,000 bottles a week, as shown by the supply curve *S*. The demand curve for the water from this spring is *D*. With no tax, the price is 50¢ a bottle and the quantity is 100,000 bottles.

Suppose this spring water is taxed at 5¢ a bottle. The supply curve does not change because the spring owners still produce 100,000 bottles a week, even though the price they receive falls. But buyers are willing to buy the 100,000 bottles only if the price is 50¢ a bottle, so the price remains at 50¢ a bottle. The tax reduces the price received by sellers to 45¢ a bottle, and sellers pay the entire tax.

Perfectly Elastic Supply Figure 6.9(b) shows the market for sand from which computer-chip makers extract silicon. Supply of this sand is perfectly elastic at a price of 10¢ a pound, as shown by the supply curve *S*. The demand curve for sand is *D*. With no tax, the price is 10¢ a pound and 5,000 pounds a week are bought.

If this sand is taxed at 1¢ a pound, we must add the tax to the minimum supply-price. Sellers are now willing to offer any quantity at 11¢ a pound along the curve *S + tax*. A new equilibrium is determined where the new supply curve intersects the demand curve: at a price of 11¢ a pound and a quantity of 3,000 pounds a week. The tax has increased the price buyers pay by the full amount of the tax—1¢ a pound—and has decreased the quantity sold. Buyers pay the entire tax.

We've seen that when supply is perfectly inelastic, sellers pay the entire tax, and when supply is perfectly elastic, buyers pay the entire tax. In the usual case, supply is neither perfectly inelastic nor perfectly elastic and the tax is split between buyers and sellers. But how the tax is split depends on the elasticity of supply: The more elastic the supply, the larger is the amount of the tax paid by buyers.

FIGURE 6.9   Tax and the Elasticity of Supply

(a) Perfectly inelastic supply

(b) Perfectly elastic supply

Part (a) shows the market for water from a mineral spring. Supply is perfectly inelastic. With no tax, the price is 50¢ a bottle. With a tax of 5¢ a bottle, the price remains at 50¢ a bottle. The number of bottles bought remains the same, but the price received by sellers decreases to 45¢ a bottle. Sellers pay the entire tax.

Part (b) shows the market for sand. Supply is perfectly elastic. With no tax, the price is 10¢ a pound. A tax of 1¢ a pound increases the minimum supply-price to 11¢ a pound. The supply curve shifts to *S + tax*. The price increases to 11¢ a pound. Buyers pay the entire tax.

MyEconLab Animation

Taxes and Efficiency

A tax drives a wedge between the buying price and the selling price and results in inefficient underproduction. The price buyers pay is also the buyers' willingness to pay, which measures *marginal social benefit*. The price sellers receive is also the sellers' minimum supply-price, which equals *marginal social cost*.

A tax makes marginal social benefit exceed marginal social cost, shrinks the producer surplus and consumer surplus, and creates a deadweight loss.

Figure 6.10 shows the inefficiency of a tax on MP3 players. The demand curve, *D*, shows marginal social benefit, and the supply curve, *S*, shows marginal social cost. Without a tax, the market produces the efficient quantity (5,000 players a week).

With a tax, the sellers' minimum supply-price rises by the amount of the tax and the supply curve shifts to *S + tax*. This supply curve does *not* show marginal social cost. The tax component isn't a *social* cost of

FIGURE 6.10   Taxes and Efficiency

With no tax, 5,000 players a week are produced. With a $20 tax, the buyers' price rises to $210, the sellers' price falls to $190, and the quantity decreases to 4,000 players a week. Consumer surplus shrinks to the green area, and the producer surplus shrinks to the blue area. Part of the loss of consumer surplus and producer surplus goes to the government as tax revenue (the purple area) and part becomes a deadweight loss (the gray area).

MyEconLab Animation

production. It is a transfer of resources to the government. At the new equilibrium quantity (4,000 players a week), both consumer surplus and producer surplus shrink. Part of each surplus goes to the government in tax revenue—the purple area; part becomes a deadweight loss—the gray area.

Only in the extreme cases of perfectly inelastic demand and perfectly inelastic supply does a tax not change the quantity bought and sold so that no deadweight loss arises.

Taxes and Fairness

We've examined the incidence and the efficiency of taxes. But when political leaders debate tax issues, it is fairness, not incidence and efficiency, that gets the most attention. Democrats complain that Republican tax cuts are unfair because they give the benefits of lower taxes to the rich. Republicans counter that it is fair that the rich get most of the tax cuts because they pay most of the taxes. No easy answers are available to the questions about the fairness of taxes.

Economists have proposed two conflicting principles of fairness to apply to a tax system:

- The benefits principle
- The ability-to-pay principle

The Benefits Principle The *benefits principle* is the proposition that people should pay taxes equal to the benefits they receive from the services provided by government. This arrangement is fair because it means that those who benefit most pay the most taxes. It makes tax payments and the consumption of government-provided services similar to private consumption expenditures.

The benefits principle can justify high fuel taxes to pay for freeways, high taxes on alcoholic beverages and tobacco products to pay for public healthcare services, and high rates of income tax on high incomes to pay for the benefits from law and order and from living in a secure environment, from which the rich might benefit more than the poor.

The Ability-to-Pay Principle The *ability-to-pay principle* is the proposition that people should pay taxes according to how easily they can bear the burden of the tax. A rich person can more easily bear the burden than a poor person can, so the ability-to-pay principle can reinforce the benefits principle to justify high rates of income tax on high incomes.

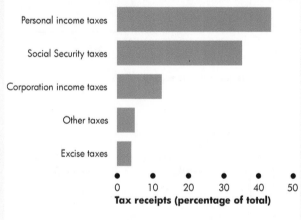
Your next task is to study production quotas and subsidies, tools that are used to influence the markets for farm products.

Production Quotas and Subsidies

An early or late frost, a hot dry summer, and a wet spring present just a few of the challenges that fill the lives of farmers with uncertainty and sometimes with economic hardship. Fluctuations in the weather bring fluctuations in farm output and prices and sometimes leave farmers with low incomes. To help farmers avoid low prices and low incomes, governments intervene in the markets for farm products.

Price floors that work a bit like the minimum wage that you've already studied might be used. But as you've seen, this type of government action creates a surplus and is inefficient. These same conclusions apply to the effects of a price floor for farm products.

Governments often use two other methods of intervention in the markets for farm products:

■ Production quotas
■ Subsidies

Production Quotas

In the markets for sugarbeets, tobacco leaf, and cotton (among others), governments have, from time to time, imposed production quotas. A **production quota** is an upper limit to the quantity of a good that may be produced in a specified period. To discover the effects of a production quota, let's look at what a quota does to the market for sugarbeets.

Suppose that the growers of sugarbeets want to limit total production to get a higher price. They persuade the government to introduce a production quota on sugarbeets.

The effect of the production quota depends on whether it is set below or above the equilibrium quantity. If the government introduced a production quota above the equilibrium quantity, nothing would change because sugarbeet growers would already be producing less than the quota. But a production quota set *below the equilibrium quantity* has big effects, which are

■ A decrease in supply
■ A rise in price
■ A decrease in marginal cost
■ Inefficient underproduction
■ An incentive to cheat and overproduce

Figure 6.11 illustrates these effects.

FIGURE 6.11   The Effects of a Production Quota

With no quota, growers produce 60 million tons a year and the price is $30 a ton. A production quota of 40 million tons a year restricts total production to that amount. The quantity produced decreases to 40 million tons a year, the price rises to $50 a ton, and the farmers' marginal cost falls to $20 a ton. Because marginal social cost (on the supply curve) is less than marginal social benefit (on the demand curve), a deadweight loss arises from the underproduction.

MyEconLab Animation

A Decrease in Supply A production quota on sugarbeets decreases the supply of sugarbeets. Each grower is assigned a production limit that is less than the amount that would be produced—and supplied—without the quota. The total of the growers' limits equals the quota, and any production in excess of the quota is illegal.

The quantity supplied becomes the amount permitted by the production quota, and this quantity is fixed. The supply of sugarbeets becomes perfectly inelastic at the quantity permitted under the quota.

In Fig. 6.11, with no quota, growers would produce 60 million tons of sugarbeets a year—the market equilibrium quantity. With a production quota set at 40 million tons a year, the gray-shaded area shows the illegal region. As in the case of price ceilings and price floors, market forces and political forces are in conflict in this illegal region.

The vertical red line labeled "Quota" becomes the supply curve of sugarbeets at prices above $20 a ton.

A Rise in Price The production quota raises the price of sugarbeets. When the government sets a production quota, it leaves market forces free to determine the price. Because the quota decreases the supply of sugarbeets, it raises the price. In Fig. 6.11, with no quota, the price is $30 a ton. With a quota of 40 million tons, the price rises to $50 a ton.

A Decrease in Marginal Cost The production quota lowers the marginal cost of growing sugarbeets. Marginal cost decreases because growers produce less and stop using the resources with the highest marginal cost. Sugarbeet growers slide down their supply (and marginal cost) curves. In Fig. 6.11, marginal cost decreases to $20 a ton.

Inefficiency The production quota results in inefficient underproduction. Marginal social benefit at the quantity produced is equal to the market price, which has increased. Marginal social cost at the quantity produced has decreased and is less than the market price. So marginal social benefit exceeds marginal social cost and a deadweight loss arises.

An Incentive to Cheat and Overproduce The production quota creates an incentive for growers to cheat and produce more than their individual production limit. With the quota, the price exceeds marginal cost, so the grower can get a larger profit by producing one more unit. Of course, if all growers produce more than their assigned limit, the production quota becomes ineffective, and the price falls to the equilibrium (no quota) price.

To make the production quota effective, growers must set up a monitoring system to ensure that no one cheats and overproduces. But it is costly to set up and operate a monitoring system and it is difficult to detect and punish producers who violate their quotas.

Because of the difficulty of operating a quota, producers often lobby governments to establish a quota and provide the monitoring and punishment systems that make it work.

Subsidies

In the United States, the producers of peanuts, sugarbeets, milk, wheat, and many other farm products receive subsidies. A **subsidy** is a payment made by the government to a producer. A large and controversial Farm Bill passed by Congress in 2008 renewed and extended a wide range of subsidies.

The effects of a subsidy are similar to the effects of a tax but they go in the opposite directions. These effects are

- An increase in supply
- A fall in price and increase in quantity produced
- An increase in marginal cost
- Payments by government to farmers
- Inefficient overproduction

Figure 6.12 illustrates the effects of a subsidy to peanut farmers.

An Increase in Supply In Fig. 6.12, with no subsidy, the demand curve D and the supply curve S determine the price of peanuts at $40 a ton and the quantity of peanuts at 40 million tons a year.

Suppose that the government introduces a subsidy of $20 a ton to peanut farmers. A subsidy is like a negative tax. A tax is equivalent to an increase in cost, so a subsidy is equivalent to a decrease in cost. The subsidy brings an increase in supply.

To determine the position of the new supply curve, we subtract the subsidy from the farmers' minimum supply-price. In Fig. 6.12, with no subsidy, farmers are willing to offer 40 million tons a year at a price of $40 a ton. With a subsidy of $20 a ton, they will offer 40 million tons a year if the price is as low as $20 a ton. The supply curve shifts to the red curve labeled $S - subsidy$.

A Fall in Price and Increase in Quantity Produced The subsidy lowers the price of peanuts and increases the quantity produced. In Fig. 6.12, equilibrium occurs where the new supply curve intersects the demand curve at a price of $30 a ton and a quantity of 60 million tons a year.

An Increase in Marginal Cost The subsidy lowers the price paid by consumers but increases the marginal cost of producing peanuts. Marginal cost increases because farmers grow more peanuts, which means that they must begin to use some resources that are less ideal for growing peanuts. Peanut farmers slide up their supply (and marginal cost) curves. In Fig. 6.12, marginal cost increases to $50 a ton.

Payments by Government to Farmers The government pays a subsidy to peanut farmers on each ton of peanuts produced. In this example, farmers increase production to 60 million tons a year and receive a

FIGURE 6.12   The Effects of a Subsidy

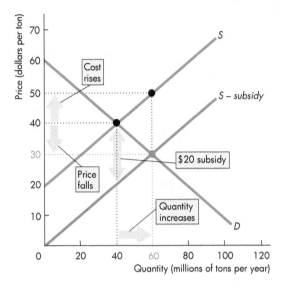

With no subsidy, farmers produce 40 million tons a year at $40 a ton. A subsidy of $20 a ton shifts the supply curve rightward to *S – subsidy*. The equilibrium quantity increases to 60 million tons a year, the price falls to $30 a ton, and the price plus the subsidy received by farmers rises to $50 a ton. In the new equilibrium, marginal social cost (on the supply curve) exceeds marginal social benefit (on the demand curve) and the subsidy results in inefficient overproduction.

MyEconLab Animation

subsidy of $20 a ton. So peanut farmers receive payments from the government that total $1,200 million a year.

Inefficient Overproduction The subsidy results in inefficient overproduction. At the quantity produced with the subsidy, marginal social benefit is equal to the market price, which has fallen. Marginal social cost has increased and it exceeds the market price. Because marginal social cost exceeds marginal social benefit, the increased production brings inefficiency.

Subsidies spill over to the rest of the world. Because a subsidy lowers the domestic market price, subsidized farmers will offer some of their output for sale on the world market. The increase in supply on the world market lowers the price in the rest of the world. Faced with lower prices, farmers in other countries decrease production and receive smaller revenues.

ECONOMICS IN ACTION
Rich High-Cost Farmers the Winners

Farm subsidies are a major obstacle to achieving an efficient use of resources in the global markets for farm products and are a source of tension between the United States, Europe, and developing nations.

The United States and the European Union are the world's two largest and richest economies. They also pay their farmers the biggest subsidies, which create inefficient overproduction of food in these rich economies.

At the same time, U.S. and European subsidies make it more difficult for farmers in the developing nations of Africa, Asia, and Central and South America to compete in global food markets. Farmers in these countries can often produce at a lower opportunity cost than the U.S. and European farmers.

Two rich countries, Australia and New Zealand, have stopped subsidizing farmers. The result has been an improvement in the efficiency of farming in these countries. New Zealand is so efficient at producing lamb and dairy products that it has been called the Saudi Arabia of milk (an analogy with Saudi Arabia's huge oil reserve and production.)

International opposition to U.S. and European farm subsidies is strong. Opposition to farm subsidies inside the United States and Europe is growing, but it isn't as strong as the pro-farm lobby, so don't expect an early end to these subsidies.

◆ REVIEW QUIZ

1. Summarize the effects of a production quota on the market price and the quantity produced.
2. Explain why a production quota is inefficient.
3. Explain why a voluntary production quota is difficult to operate.
4. Summarize the effects of a subsidy on the market price and the quantity produced.
5. Explain why a subsidy is inefficient.

Work these questions in Study Plan 6.4 and get instant feedback. Do a Key Terms Quiz.   MyEconLab

Governments intervene in some markets by making it illegal to trade in a good. Let's now see how these markets work.

Markets for Illegal Goods

The markets for many goods and services are regulated, and buying and selling some goods is illegal. The best-known examples of such goods are drugs such as marijuana, cocaine, ecstasy, and heroin.

Despite the fact that these drugs are illegal, trade in them is a multibillion-dollar business. This trade can be understood by using the same economic model and principles that explain trade in legal goods. To study the market for illegal goods, we're first going to examine the prices and quantities that would prevail if these goods were not illegal. Next, we'll see how prohibition works. Then we'll see how a tax might be used to limit the consumption of these goods.

A Free Market for a Drug

Figure 6.13 shows the market for a drug. The demand curve, *D,* shows that, other things remaining the same, the lower the price of the drug, the larger is the quantity of the drug demanded. The supply curve, *S,* shows that, other things remaining the same, the lower the price of the drug, the smaller is the quantity supplied. If the drug were not illegal, the quantity bought and sold would be Q_C and the price would be P_C.

A Market for an Illegal Drug

When a good is illegal, the cost of trading in the good increases. By how much the cost increases and who bears the cost depend on the penalties for violating the law and the degree to which the law is enforced. The larger the penalties and the better the policing, the higher are the costs. Penalties might be imposed on sellers, buyers, or both.

Penalties on Sellers Drug dealers in the United States face large penalties if their activities are detected. Penalties for convicted dealers range from jail terms of 10 years to life and fines that might be as large as $2 million.

These penalties are part of the cost of supplying illegal drugs, and they bring a decrease in supply—a leftward shift in the supply curve. To determine the new supply curve, we add the cost of breaking the law to the minimum price that drug dealers are willing to accept.

In Fig. 6.13, the cost of breaking the law by selling drugs (*CBL*) is added to the minimum price

FIGURE 6.13   A Market for an Illegal Good

The demand curve for drugs is *D,* and the supply curve is *S.* If drugs are not illegal, the quantity bought and sold is Q_C at a price of P_C—point *E.* If selling drugs is illegal, the cost of breaking the law by selling drugs (*CBL*) is added to the minimum supply-price and supply decreases to $S + CBL$. The market moves to point *F.* If buying drugs is illegal, the cost of breaking the law is subtracted from the maximum price that buyers are willing to pay, and demand decreases to $D - CBL$. The market moves to point *G.* With both buying and selling illegal, the supply curve and the demand curve shift and the market moves to point *H.* The market price remains at P_C, but the market price plus the penalty for buying rises—point *J*—and the market price minus the penalty for selling falls—point *K.*

MyEconLab Animation

that dealers will accept and the supply curve shifts leftward to $S + CBL$. If penalties were imposed only on sellers, the market equilibrium would move from point *E* to point *F.*

Penalties on Buyers In the United States, it is illegal to *possess* drugs such as marijuana, cocaine, ecstasy, and heroin. Possession of marijuana can bring a prison term of 1 year, and possession of heroin can bring a prison term of 2 years. Penalties fall on buyers, and the cost of breaking the law must be subtracted from the value of the good to determine the maximum price buyers are willing to pay for the drugs. Demand decreases, and the demand curve shifts leftward. In Fig. 6.13, the demand curve shifts to $D - CBL$. If penalties were imposed only on buyers, the market equilibrium would move from point E to point G.

Penalties on Both Sellers and Buyers If penalties are imposed on both sellers *and* buyers, both supply and demand decrease and both the supply curve and the demand curve shift. In Fig. 6.13, the costs of breaking the law are the same for both buyers and sellers, so both curves shift leftward by the same amount. The market equilibrium moves to point H. The market price remains at the competitive market price P_C, but the quantity bought decreases to Q_P. Buyers pay P_C plus the cost of breaking the law, which equals P_B. Sellers receive P_C minus the cost of breaking the law, which equals P_S.

The larger the penalties and the greater the degree of law enforcement, the larger is the decrease in demand and/or supply. If the penalties are heavier on sellers, the supply curve shifts farther than the demand curve and the market price rises above P_C. If the penalties are heavier on buyers, the demand curve shifts farther than the supply curve and the market price falls below P_C. In the United States, the penalties on sellers are larger than those on buyers, so the quantity of drugs traded decreases and the market price increases compared with a free market.

With high enough penalties and effective law enforcement, it is possible to decrease demand and/or supply to the point at which the quantity bought is zero. But in reality, such an outcome is unusual. It does not happen in the United States in the case of illegal drugs. The key reason is the high cost of law enforcement and insufficient resources for the police to achieve effective enforcement. Because of this situation, some people suggest that drugs (and other illegal goods) should be legalized and sold openly but also taxed at a high rate in the same way that legal drugs such as alcohol are taxed. How would such an arrangement work?

Legalizing and Taxing Drugs

From your study of the effects of taxes, it is easy to see that the quantity bought of a drug could be decreased if the drug were legalized and taxed. Imposing a sufficiently high tax could decrease the supply, raise the price, and achieve the same decrease in the quantity bought as does a prohibition on drugs. The government would collect a large tax revenue.

Illegal Trading to Evade the Tax It is likely that an extremely high tax rate would be needed to cut the quantity of drugs bought to the level prevailing with a prohibition. It is also likely that many drug dealers and consumers would try to cover up their activities to evade the tax. If they did act in this way, they would face the cost of breaking the law—the tax law. If the penalty for tax law violation is as severe and as effectively policed as drug-dealing laws, the analysis we've already conducted applies also to this case. The quantity of drugs bought would depend on the penalties for law breaking and on the way in which the penalties are assigned to buyers and sellers.

Taxes Versus Prohibition: Some Pros and Cons Which is more effective: prohibition or taxes? In favor of taxes and against prohibition is the fact that the tax revenue can be used to make law enforcement more effective. It can also be used to run a more effective education campaign against illegal drug use. In favor of prohibition and against taxes is the fact that prohibition sends a signal that might influence preferences, decreasing the demand for illegal drugs. Also, some people intensely dislike the idea of the government profiting from trade in harmful substances.

◆ REVIEW QUIZ

1 How does the imposition of a penalty for selling an illegal drug influence demand, supply, price, and the quantity of the drug consumed?
2 How does the imposition of a penalty for possessing an illegal drug influence demand, supply, price, and the quantity of the drug consumed?
3 How does the imposition of a penalty for selling *or* possessing an illegal drug influence demand, supply, price, and the quantity of the drug consumed?
4 Is there any case for legalizing drugs?

Work these questions in Study Plan 6.5 and get instant feedback.   MyEconLab

◆ You now know how to use the demand and supply model to predict prices, to study government actions in markets, and to study the sources and costs of inefficiency. In *Economics in the News* on pp. 144–145, you will see how to apply what you've learned by looking at the effects of the minimum wage rate in the market for low-skilled labor.

Push to Raise the Minimum Wage

Most State Minimum Wages Rising to Exceed the Federal Minimum

Bureau of Labor Statistics and National Conference of State Legislatures

The recovery from the 2008–2009 recession has not seen much growth in wage rates, and the spread between the top and bottom earnings has widened. Budget-strained low-paid workers and their political supporters think the minimum wage should rise.

The Bureau of Labor Statistics (BLS) reports that in 2013, 1.5 million earned the federal minimum wage of $7.25 an hour and about 1.8 million had wages below the federal minimum. These 3.3 million workers represented 4.3 percent of hourly paid workers, which compares to 4.7 percent in 2012 and 13.4 percent in 1979.

Federal law-makers are not moving, but most state legislatures agree that the minimum wage should rise. According to the National Conference of State Legislatures, 38 states introduced minimum wage bills during the 2014 session and 34 states considered increases to the state minimum wage rate. Ten states (Connecticut, Delaware, Hawaii, Maryland, Massachusetts, Michigan, Minnesota, Rhode Island, Vermont, and West Virginia) and D.C. have increased their minimum wage rate during the 2014 session.

As of August 1, 2014, 23 states and D.C. have minimum wage rates above the federal minimum wage and 18 states have minimum wage rates the same as the federal minimum wage of $7.25 an hour. A few states have minimum wage rates below the federal minimum wage, so the federal minimum thus applies in these cases.

Most economists think that a higher minimum wage will lower employment.

BLS Reports March 2014 Report 1048 *Characteristics of Minimum Wage Workers, 2013*, http://www.bls.gov/cps/minwage2013.pdf, and National Conference of State Legislatures, http://www.ncsl.org/research/labor-and-employment/state-minimum-wage-chart.aspx#1

ESSENCE OF THE STORY

- In 2014, 34 states considered raising the state minimum wage rate.

- In 2014, state minimum wage rates were higher than the federal rate of $7.25 an hour in 23 states and DC.

- Another 18 states have a minimum wage rate equal to the federal minimum.

- The Bureau of Labor Statistics reports that 3.3 million or 4.3 percent of hourly- paid workers were paid at or below the federal minimum in 2013.

- Supporters of minimum-wage hikes say that low-paid workers have fallen further behind.

- Economists say a higher minimum wage will cost jobs.

MyEconLab More Economics in the News

ECONOMIC ANALYSIS

- The state minimum wage rate exceeds the federal minimum wage rate in 23 states.

- The state average minimum wage in 2014 was $8.25 an hour, $1 more than the federal minimum of $7.25 an hour, set in 2009.

- Other wage rates have risen and the cost of living has increased, and there was a widely held view that the minimum wage rate needed to rise.

- With disagreement leading to inaction in Washington, an increasing number of state governments began to raise their state minimum wage rates to levels that exceeded the federal minimum wage.

- Supporters of the increases believed that employment would not be adversely affected, while opponents argued that the higher minimum wage would bring job losses.

- The figures illustrate these two opinions about the effect of a higher minimum wage rate.

- Figure 1 illustrates a market for low-skilled labor in which the equilibrium wage rate exceeds the minimum wage.

- The demand for labor is D_0 and the supply of labor is S_0, so the equilibrium wage rate is $8.75 an hour.

- The minimum wage rate is $8.25 an hour, so no one earns the minimum wage.

- Because the equilibrium wage rate exceeds the minimum wage rate, the quantity of labor demanded equals the quantity of labor supplied and the minimum wage rate has no effect on the market outcome.

- Figure 2 illustrates a market for low-skilled labor in which the equilibrium wage rate is lower than the minimum wage rate.

- The demand for labor is D_1 and the supply of labor is S_1, so the equilibrium wage rate is $7.75 an hour.

- The minimum wage rate is $8.25 an hour, and the quantity of labor employed equals the quantity demanded at the minimum wage rate.

- The quantity of labor demanded and employed is 3.6 million—the quantity estimated by the Bureau of Labor Statistics.

- At the equilibrium wage rate, the quantity of labor supplied is 3.7 million (an assumed quantity) and 0.1 million workers are unemployed.

- With the equilibrium wage rate less than the minimum wage rate, the quantity of labor demanded is less than the quantity of labor supplied and the minimum wage rate brings an increase in unemployment.

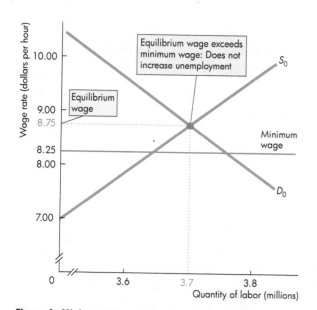

Figure 1 Minimum Wage Below Equilibrium Wage

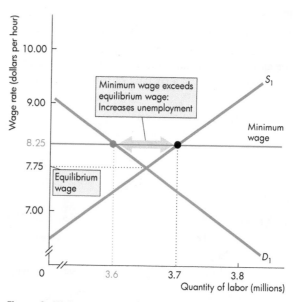

Figure 2 Minimum Wage Above Equilibrium Wage

SUMMARY

Key Points

A Housing Market with a Rent Ceiling (pp. 128–130)

- A rent ceiling that is set above the equilibrium rent has no effect.
- A rent ceiling that is set below the equilibrium rent creates a housing shortage, increased search activity, and a black market.
- A rent ceiling that is set below the equilibrium rent is inefficient and unfair.

Working Problems 1 and 2 will give you a better understanding of a housing market with a rent ceiling.

A Labor Market with a Minimum Wage (pp. 131–133)

- A minimum wage set below the equilibrium wage rate has no effect.
- A minimum wage set above the equilibrium wage rate creates unemployment and increases the amount of time people spend searching for a job.
- A minimum wage set above the equilibrium wage rate is inefficient, unfair, and hits low-skilled young people hardest.

Working Problems 3 and 4 will give you a better understanding of a labor market with a minimum wage.

Taxes (pp. 133–138)

- A tax raises the price paid by buyers, but usually by less than the tax.
- The elasticity of demand and the elasticity of supply determine the share of a tax paid by buyers and sellers.

- The less elastic the demand or the more elastic the supply, the larger is the share of the tax paid by buyers.
- If demand is perfectly elastic or supply is perfectly inelastic, sellers pay the entire tax. And if demand is perfectly inelastic or supply is perfectly elastic, buyers pay the entire tax.

Working Problem 5 will give you a better understanding of taxes.

Production Quotas and Subsidies (pp. 139–141)

- A production quota leads to inefficient underproduction, which raises the price.
- A subsidy is like a negative tax. It lowers the price, increases the cost of production, and leads to inefficient overproduction.

Working Problems 6 and 7 will give you a better understanding of production quotas and subsidies.

Markets for Illegal Goods (pp. 142–143)

- Penalties on sellers increase the cost of selling the good and decrease the supply of the good.
- Penalties on buyers decrease their willingness to pay and decrease the demand for the good.
- Penalties on buyers and sellers decrease the quantity of the good, raise the price buyers pay, and lower the price sellers receive.
- Legalizing and taxing can achieve the same outcome as penalties on buyers and sellers.

Working Problem 8 will give you a better understanding of markets for illegal goods.

Key Terms

MyEconLab Key Terms Quiz

Black market, 128
Minimum wage, 131
Price cap, 128
Price ceiling, 128

Price floor, 131
Production quota, 139
Rent ceiling, 128
Search activity, 128

Subsidy, 140
Tax incidence, 133

WORKED PROBLEM

MyEconLab   You can work this problem in Chapter 6 Study Plan.

The table shows the demand and supply schedules for tickets to a concert in the park.

Price (dollars per ticket)	Quantity demanded	Quantity supplied
	(tickets per concert)	
5	600	200
6	500	300
7	400	400
8	300	500
9	200	600
10	100	700

Questions

1. If there is no tax on concert tickets, what is the price of a ticket and how many tickets are bought?

If a sales tax of $2 a ticket is imposed on sellers of concert tickets

2. What is the price a concert-goer pays for a ticket and how many tickets are bought?
3. Who pays the tax and what is the government's tax revenue?
4. Is the market for concert tickets efficient? Explain.

Solutions

1. With no sales tax on concert tickets, the price of a ticket is the market equilibrium price, which is $7 a ticket. At $7 a ticket, the quantity of tickets bought is 400 per concert.
2. With a sales tax of $2 a ticket imposed on sellers, the supply of tickets decrease. The reason it that at any ticket price paid by buyers, concert organizers will receive $2 less per ticket.

   For example, concert organizers are willing to supply 700 tickets per concert if they receive $10 a ticket. But with a tax of $2 a ticket, concert organizers will receive only $8 a ticket after paying the government the $2 tax per ticket. So concert organizers will not be willing to supply 700 tickets at the after-tax price of $8 a ticket. The table above tells us that concert organizers are willing to supply only 500 tickets per concert when they receive $8 a ticket.

   We need to create the new supply schedule. We have already found one point on the new supply schedule: At a market price of $10 a ticket, concert organizers are willing to supply 500 tickets.

   The table in the next column shows the new supply schedule.

Price (dollars per ticket)	Quantity demanded	New quantity supplied
	(tickets per concert)	
6	500	
7	400	200
8	300	300
9	200	400
10	100	500

   Check that you can explain why, at a market price of $7 a ticket, concert organizers are willing to supply 400 tickets when tickets are not taxed but only 200 tickets when tickets are taxed $2 per ticket.

   With the $2 tax, concert-goers pay $8 a ticket and buy 300 tickets.

Key Point: A sales tax raises the market price and the quantity bought decreases.

3. If a sales tax of $2 a ticket is imposed on concert tickets, the price concert-goers pay rises from $7 a ticket to $8 a ticket. So concert-goers pay $1 of the $2 tax. Concert organizers pay the other $1 of tax. The government's tax revenue is $2 × 300, or $600.

Key Point: Some of the tax is paid by buyers and some by sellers.

4. With no tax, 400 tickets per concert is efficient. With the tax, the ticket price rises and the quantity bought decreases to 300 per concert. The outcome is inefficient and a deadweight loss arises.

Key Point: A sales tax that decreases the quantity sold is inefficient and creates a deadweight loss.

Key Figure

MyEconLab Interactive Animation

STUDY PLAN PROBLEMS AND APPLICATIONS

MyEconLab   You can work Problems 1 to 8 in Chapter 6 Study Plan and get instant feedback.

A Housing Market with a Rent Ceiling (Study Plan 6.1)

Use the following graph of the market for rental housing in Townsville to work Problems 1 and 2.

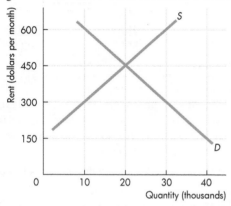

1. a. What are the equilibrium rent and the quantity of housing rented?

   b. If a rent ceiling is set at $600 a month, what is the rent paid? What is the shortage of housing?

2. If the rent ceiling is $300 a month, what is the quantity rented, the shortage of housing, and the maximum price that someone is willing to pay for the last unit of housing available?

A Labor Market with a Minimum Wage (Study Plan 6.2)

Use the following data on the demand and supply schedules of teenage labor to work Problems 3 and 4.

Wage rate (dollars per hour)	Quantity demanded	Quantity supplied
	(hours per month)	
5	2,500	1,500
6	2,000	2,000
7	1,500	2,500
8	1,000	3,000

3. Calculate the equilibrium wage rate, the hours worked, and the quantity of unemployment.

4. The minimum wage for teenagers is $7 an hour.
   a. How many hours are unemployed?
   b. If the demand for teenage labor increases by 500 hours a month, what is the wage rate and how many hours are unemployed?

Taxes (Study Plan 6.3)

5. The table in the next column sets out the demand and supply schedules for chocolate brownies.

Price (cents per brownie)	Quantity demanded	Quantity supplied
	(millions per day)	
50	5	3
60	4	4
70	3	5
80	2	6

   a. If sellers are taxed 20¢ a brownie, what is the price and who pays the tax?
   b. If buyers are taxed 20¢ a brownie, what is the price and who pays the tax?

Production Quotas and Subsidies (Study Plan 6.4)

Use the following data to work Problems 6 and 7. The demand and supply schedules for rice are

Price (dollars per box)	Quantity demanded	Quantity supplied
	(boxes per week)	
1.20	3,000	1,500
1.30	2,750	2,000
1.40	2,500	2,500
1.50	2,250	3,000
1.60	2,000	3,500

Calculate the price, the marginal cost of rice, and the quantity produced if the government

6. Sets a production quota of 2,000 boxes a week.
7. Introduces a subsidy of $0.30 a box.

Markets for Illegal Goods (Study Plan 6.5)

8. The figure shows the market for an illegal good.

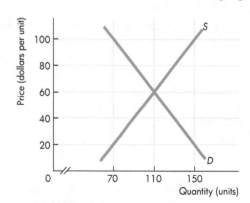

Calculate the market price and the quantity bought if a penalty of $20 a unit is imposed on
a. Sellers only or buyers only.
b. Both sellers and buyers.

ADDITIONAL PROBLEMS AND APPLICATIONS

MyEconLab   You can work these problems in MyEconLab if assigned by your instructor.

A Housing Market with a Rent Ceiling

Use the following table to work Problems 9 and 10. The table sets out the demand and supply schedules for college meals:

Price (dollars per meal)	Quantity demanded	Quantity supplied
	(meals per week)	
4	3,000	1,500
5	2,750	2,000
6	2,500	2,500
7	2,250	3,000
8	2,000	3,500

9. a. What are the equilibrium meal price and equilibrium quantity of meals?

   b. If the college put a price ceiling on meals at $7 a meal, what is the price students pay for a meal? How many meals do they buy?

10. If the college put a price ceiling on meals at $4 a meal, what is the quantity bought, the shortage of meals, and the maximum price that someone is willing to pay for the last meal available?

A Labor Market with a Minimum Wage

Use the following news clip to work Problems 11 and 12.

Malaysia Passes Its First Minimum Wage Law

About 3.2 million low-income workers across Malaysia are expected to benefit from the country's first minimum wage, which the government says will transform Malaysia into a high-income nation. Employer groups argue that paying the minimum wage, which is not based on productivity or performance, would raise their costs and reduce business profits.

Source: *The New York Times*, May 1, 2012

11. On a graph of the market for low-skilled labor, show the effect of the minimum wage on the quantity of labor employed.

12. Explain the effects of the minimum wage on the workers' surplus, the firms' surplus, and the efficiency of the market for low-skilled workers.

Taxes

13. Use the news clip in Problem 11.
    a. If the Malaysian government cut the tax on business profits, would it offset the effect of the minimum wage on employment? Explain.

   b. Would a cut in the Social Security tax that small businesses pay offset the effect of the higher minimum wage on employment? Explain.

14. The demand and supply schedules for tulips are

Price (dollars per bunch)	Quantity demanded	Quantity supplied
	(bunches per week)	
10	100	40
12	90	60
14	80	80
16	70	100
18	60	120

   a. If tulips are not taxed, what is the price and how many bunches are bought?

   b. If tulips are taxed $6 a bunch, what are the price and quantity bought? Who pays the tax?

15. **Cigarette Taxes, Black Markets, and Crime: Lessons from New York's 50-Year Losing Battle**

New York City has the highest cigarette taxes in the country. During the four months following the recent tax hike, sales of taxed cigarettes in the city fell by more than 50 percent as consumers turned to the city's bustling black market. The thriving illegal market for cigarettes has diverted billions of dollars from legitimate businesses and governments to criminals.

Source: Cato Institute, February 6, 2003

   a. How has the market for cigarettes in New York City responded to the high cigarette taxes?

   b. How does the emergence of a black market impact the elasticity of demand in a legal market?

   c. Why might an increase in the tax rate actually cause a decrease in the tax revenue?

Production Quotas and Subsidies

Use the following news clip to work Problems 16 to 18.

Crop Prices Erode Farm Subsidy Program

High corn and soybean prices mean farmers are making the most money in their lives. The reason: Grain prices are far too high to trigger payouts under the U.S. primary farm-subsidy program's "price support" formula. The market has done what Congress couldn't do and that is "slash farm subsidies."

Source: *The Wall Street Journal*, July 25, 2011

16. a. Why are U.S. soybean farmers subsidized?

b. Explain how a subsidy paid to soybean farmers affects the price of soybean and the marginal cost of producing it.

17. Show in a graph how a subsidy paid to soybean farmers affects the consumer surplus and the producer surplus from soybean. Does the subsidy make the soybean market more efficient or less efficient? Explain.

18. In the market for corn with a price support, explain why the corn price has risen and ended up being too high to "trigger payouts."

Use the following figure, which shows the market for tomatoes, to work Problems 19 and 20.

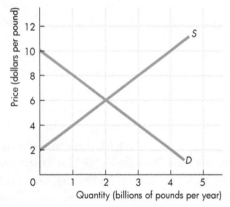

19. If the government subsidizes growers at $4 a pound, what is the quantity produced, the quantity demanded, and the subsidy paid to growers?

20. If the government subsidizes growers at $4 a pound, who gains and who loses from the subsidy? What is the deadweight loss? Could the subsidy be regarded as being fair?

Markets for Illegal Goods

21. The table gives the demand and supply schedules for an illegal drug.

Price (dollars per unit)	Quantity demanded	Quantity supplied
	(units per day)	
50	500	300
60	400	400
70	300	500
80	200	600
90	100	700

a. What is the price and how many units are bought if there is no penalty on drugs?

b. If the penalty on sellers is $20 a unit, what are the price and quantity consumed?

c. If the penalty on buyers is $20 a unit, what are the price and quantity consumed?

Economics in the News

22. After you have studied *Economics in the News* on pp. 144–145, answer the following questions.

a. When a state raises its minimum wage above the federal minimum, what would you expect to happen to unemployment in that state? Illustrate your answer with a graph.

b. The news article reports that the percentage of hourly paid workers paid the minimum wage or less decreased from 13.4 percent in 1979 to 4.3 percent in 2013. Would you expect the rise in the minimum wage to have a smaller effect on unemployment today than in 1979?

c. The news article reports that during the recovery from the 2008–2009 recession, wage rates grew slowly and the bottom wage rates grew slower than top wage rates, straining the budgets of low-paid workers. How would you expect this fact to have influenced the effect of the minimum wage on unemployment?

23. **Hollywood: Organized Crime Hits the Movies**

The Mexican army seized 1,180 disc burners and 3.14 million copies of movies and TV shows from 23 warehouses in a move to fight piracy that costs Hollywood about $590 million a year.

Source: Bloomberg *Businessweek*, April 7, 2011

Assume that the marginal cost of producing a DVD (legal or illegal) is a constant $3 and that legal DVDs bear an additional marginal cost of $5 each in royalty payments to film studios.

a. Draw a graph of the market for counterfeit DVDs, assuming that there are no effective penalties on either buyers or sellers for breaking the law.

b. How do the events reported in the news clip change the market outcome? Show the effects in your graph.

c. With no penalty on buyers, if a penalty for breaking the law is imposed on sellers at more than $5 a disc, how does the market work and what is the equilibrium price?

d. With no penalty on sellers, if a penalty for breaking the law is imposed on buyers at more than $5 a disc, how does the market work and what is the equilibrium price?

e. What is the marginal benefit of an illegal DVD in the situations described in parts (c) and (d)?

f. In light of your answer to part (e), why does law enforcement usually focus on sellers rather than buyers?

7 GLOBAL MARKETS IN ACTION

After studying this chapter, you will be able to:

- ◆ Explain how markets work with international trade
- ◆ Identify the gains from international trade and its winners and losers
- ◆ Explain the effects of international trade barriers
- ◆ Explain and evaluate arguments used to justify restricting international trade

iPhones, Wii games, and Nike shoes are just three of the items that you might buy that are not produced in the United States. Why don't we produce phones, games, and shoes in America? Isn't the globalization of production killing good American jobs?

You will find the answers in this chapter. And you will see why global trade is a win-win deal for buyers and sellers. You will also see why governments restrict trade, and in *Economics in the News* at the end of the chapter, why it is difficult for the United States to make a free-trade deal with Japan.

But first, we study the gains from international trade.

◢ How Global Markets Work

Because we trade with people in other countries, the goods and services that we can buy and consume are not limited by what we can produce. The goods and services that we buy from other countries are our **imports**; and the goods and services that we sell to people in other countries are our **exports**.

International Trade Today

Global trade today is enormous. In 2013, global exports and imports were $23 trillion, which is one third of the value of global production. The United States is the world's largest international trader and accounts for 10 percent of world exports and 12 percent of world imports. Germany and China, which rank 2 and 3 behind the United States, lag by a large margin.

In 2013, total U.S. exports were $2.3 trillion, which is about 14 percent of the value of U.S. production. Total U.S. imports were $2.7 trillion, which is about 17 percent of total expenditure in the United States.

We trade both goods and services. In 2013, exports of services were about one third of total exports and imports of services were about one fifth of total imports.

What Drives International Trade?

Comparative advantage is the fundamental force that drives international trade. Comparative advantage (see Chapter 2, p. 40) is a situation in which a person can perform an activity or produce a good or service at a lower opportunity cost than anyone else. This same idea applies to nations. We can define *national comparative advantage* as a situation in which a nation can perform an activity or produce a good or service at a lower opportunity cost than any other nation.

The opportunity cost of producing a T-shirt is lower in China than in the United States, so China has a comparative advantage in producing T-shirts. The opportunity cost of producing an airplane is lower in the United States than in China, so the United States has a comparative advantage in producing airplanes.

You saw in Chapter 2 how Liz and Joe reap gains from trade by specializing in the production of the good at which they have a comparative advantage and then trading with each other. Both are better off.

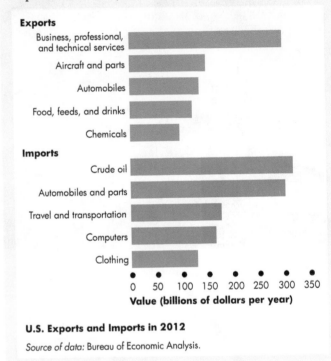
This same principle applies to trade among nations. Because China has a comparative advantage at producing T-shirts and the United States has a comparative advantage at producing airplanes, the people of both countries can gain from specialization and trade. China can buy airplanes from the United States at a lower opportunity cost than that at which Chinese firms can produce them. And Americans can buy T-shirts from China for a lower opportunity cost than that at which U.S. firms can produce them. Also, through international trade, Chinese producers can get higher prices for their T-shirts and Boeing can sell airplanes for a higher price. Both countries gain from international trade.

Let's now illustrate the gains from trade that we've just described by studying demand and supply in the global markets for T-shirts and airplanes.

Why the United States Imports T-Shirts

The United States imports T-shirts because the rest of the world has a comparative advantage in producing T-shirts. Figure 7.1 illustrates how this comparative advantage generates international trade and how trade affects the price of a T-shirt and the quantities produced and bought.

The demand curve D_{US} and the supply curve S_{US} show the demand and supply in the U.S. domestic market only. The demand curve tells us the quantity of T-shirts that Americans are willing to buy at various prices. The supply curve tells us the quantity of T-shirts that U.S. garment makers are willing to sell at various prices—that is, the quantity supplied at each price when all T-shirts sold in the United States are produced in the United States.

Figure 7.1(a) shows what the U.S. T-shirt market would be like with no international trade. The price

of a shirt would be $8 and 40 million shirts a year would be produced by U.S. garment makers and bought by U.S. consumers.

Figure 7.1(b) shows the market for T-shirts with international trade. Now the price of a T-shirt is determined in the world market, not the U.S. domestic market. The world price of a T-shirt is less than $8, which means that the rest of the world has a comparative advantage in producing T-shirts. The world price line shows the world price at $5 a shirt.

The U.S. demand curve, D_{US}, tells us that at $5 a shirt, Americans buy 60 million shirts a year. The U.S. supply curve, S_{US}, tells us that at $5 a shirt, U.S. garment makers produce 20 million T-shirts a year. To buy 60 million T-shirts when only 20 million are produced in the United States, we must import T-shirts from the rest of the world. The quantity of T-shirts imported is 40 million a year.

FIGURE 7.1   A Market with Imports

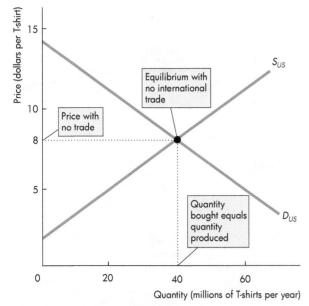

(a) Equilibrium with no international trade

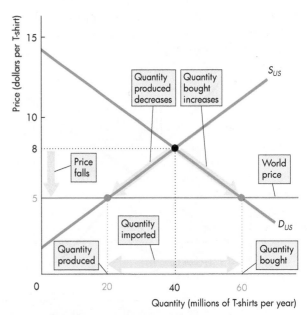

(b) Equilibrium in a market with imports

Part (a) shows the U.S. market for T-shirts with no international trade. The U.S. domestic demand curve D_{US} and U.S. domestic supply curve S_{US} determine the price of a T-shirt at $8 and the quantity of T-shirts produced and bought in the United States at 40 million a year.

Part (b) shows the U.S. market for T-shirts with

international trade. World demand for and world supply of T-shirts determine the world price of a T-shirt, which is $5. The price in the U.S. market falls to $5 a shirt. U.S. purchases of T-shirts increase to 60 million a year, and U.S. production of T-shirts decreases to 20 million a year. The United States imports 40 million T-shirts a year.

Why the United States Exports Airplanes

Figure 7.2 illustrates international trade in airplanes. The demand curve D_{US} and the supply curve S_{US} show the demand and supply in the U.S. domestic market only. The demand curve tells us the quantity of airplanes that U.S. airlines are willing to buy at various prices. The supply curve tells us the quantity of airplanes that U.S. aircraft makers are willing to sell at various prices.

Figure 7.2(a) shows what the U.S. airplane market would be like with no international trade. The price of an airplane would be $100 million and 400 airplanes a year would be produced by U.S. aircraft makers and bought by U.S. airlines.

Figure 7.2(b) shows the U.S. airplane market with international trade. Now the price of an airplane is determined in the world market and the world price of an airplane is higher than $100 million, which means that the United States has a comparative advantage in producing airplanes. The world price line shows the world price at $150 million.

The U.S. demand curve, D_{US}, tells us that at $150 million an airplane, U.S. airlines buy 200 airplanes a year. The U.S. supply curve, S_{US}, tells us that at $150 million an airplane, U.S. aircraft makers produce 700 airplanes a year. The quantity produced in the United States (700 a year) minus the quantity purchased by U.S. airlines (200 a year) is the quantity of airplanes exported, which is 500 airplanes a year.

◆ REVIEW QUIZ

1   Describe the situation in the market for a good or service that the United States imports.
2   Describe the situation in the market for a good or service that the United States exports.

You can work these questions in Study Plan 7.1 and get instant feedback. Do a Key Terms Quiz.   MyEconLab

---

FIGURE 7.2   A Market with Exports

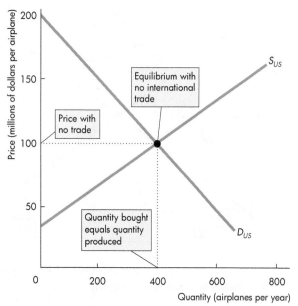

(a) Equilibrium without international trade

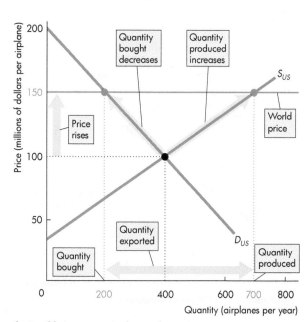

(b) Equilibrium in a market with exports

In part (a), the U.S. market with no international trade, the U.S. domestic demand curve D_{US} and the U.S. domestic supply curve S_{US} determine the price of an airplane at $100 million and 400 airplanes are produced and bought each year.

In part (b), the U.S. market with international trade, world demand and world supply determine the world price, which is $150 million per airplane. The price in the U.S. market rises. U.S. airplane production increases to 700 a year, and U.S. purchases of airplanes decrease to 200 a year. The United States exports 500 airplanes a year.

MyEconLab Animation

Winners, Losers, and the Net Gain from Trade

In Chapter 1 (see p. 6), we asked whether globalization is in the self-interest of the low-wage worker in Malaysia who sews your new running shoes and the displaced shoemaker in Atlanta? Is it in the social interest? We're now going to answer these questions. You will learn why producers complain about cheap foreign imports, but consumers of imports never complain.

Gains and Losses from Imports

We measure the gains and losses from imports by examining their effect on consumer surplus, producer surplus, and total surplus. In the importing country the winners are those whose surplus increases and the losers are those whose surplus decreases.

Figure 7.3(a) shows what consumer surplus and producer surplus would be with no international trade in T-shirts. U.S. domestic demand, D_{US}, and U.S. domestic supply, S_{US}, determine the price and quantity. The green area shows consumer surplus and the blue area shows producer surplus. Total surplus is the sum of consumer surplus and producer surplus.

Figure 7.3(b) shows how these surpluses change when the U.S. market opens to imports. The U.S. price falls to the world price. The quantity bought increases to the quantity demanded at the world price and consumer surplus expands from A to the larger green area $A + B + D$. The quantity produced in the United States decreases to the quantity supplied at the world price and producer surplus shrinks to the smaller blue area C.

Part of the gain in consumer surplus, the area B, is a loss of producer surplus—a redistribution of total surplus. But the other part of the increase in consumer surplus, the area D, is a net gain. This increase in total surplus results from the lower price and increased purchases and is the gain from imports.

FIGURE 7.3   Gains and Losses in a Market with Imports

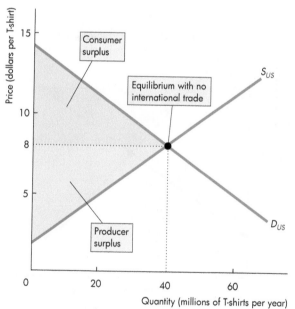

(a) Consumer surplus and producer surplus with no international trade

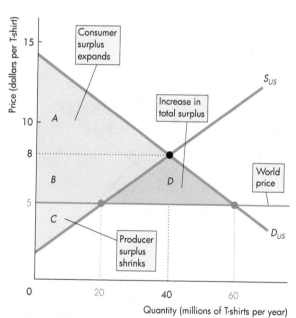

(b) Gains and losses from imports

In part (a), with no international trade, the green area shows the consumer surplus and the blue area shows the producer surplus.

In part (b), with international trade, the price falls to the world price of $5 a shirt. Consumer surplus expands from area A to the area $A + B + D$. Producer surplus shrinks to area C. Area B is a transfer of surplus from producers to consumers. Area D is an increase in total surplus—the gain from imports.

Gains and Losses from Exports

We measure the gains and losses from exports just like we measured those from imports, by their effect on consumer surplus, producer surplus, and total surplus.

Figure 7.4(a) shows the situation with no international trade. Domestic demand, D_{US}, and domestic supply, S_{US}, determine the price and quantity, the consumer surplus, and the producer surplus.

Figure 7.4(b) shows how the consumer surplus and producer surplus change when the good is exported. The price rises to the world price. The quantity bought decreases to the quantity demanded at the world price and the consumer surplus shrinks to the green area A. The quantity produced increases to the quantity supplied at the world price and the producer surplus expands to the blue area $B + C + D$.

Part of the gain in producer surplus, the area B, is a loss in consumer surplus—a redistribution of the total surplus. But the other part of the increase in producer surplus, the area D, is a net gain. This increase in total surplus results from the higher price and increased production and is the gain from exports.

Gains for All

You've seen that both imports and exports bring gains. Because one country's exports are other countries' imports, international trade brings gain for all countries. International trade is a win-win game.

◆ REVIEW QUIZ

1 How is the gain from imports distributed between consumers and domestic producers?
2 How is the gain from exports distributed between consumers and domestic producers?
3 Why is the net gain from international trade positive?

Work these questions in Study Plan 7.2 and get instant feedback.   MyEconLab

---

FIGURE 7.4   Gains and Losses in a Market with Exports

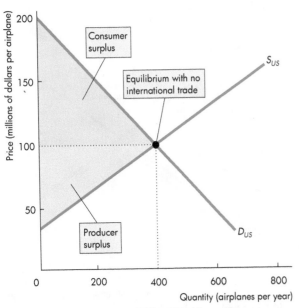

(a) Consumer surplus and producer surplus with no international trade

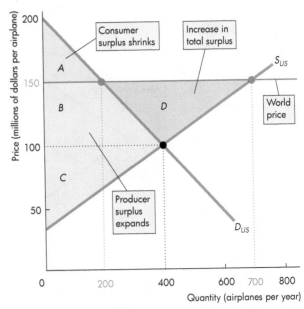

(b) Gains and losses from exports

In part (a), the U.S. market with no international trade, the green area shows the consumer surplus and the blue area shows the producer surplus. In part (b), the U.S. market with international trade, the price rises to the world price.

Consumer surplus shrinks to area A. Producer surplus expands from area C to the area B + C + D. Area B is a transfer of surplus from consumers to producers. Area D is an increase in total surplus—the gain from exports.

◥ International Trade Restrictions

Governments use four sets of tools to influence international trade and protect domestic industries from foreign competition. They are

- Tariffs
- Import quotas
- Other import barriers
- Export subsidies

Tariffs

A **tariff** is a tax on a good that is imposed by the importing country when an imported good crosses its international boundary. For example, the government of India imposes a 100 percent tariff on wine imported from California. So when an Indian imports a $10 bottle of Californian wine, he pays the Indian government a $10 import duty.

Tariffs raise revenue for governments and serve the self-interest of people who earn their incomes in import-competing industries. But as you will see, restrictions on free international trade decrease the gains from trade and are not in the social interest.

The Effects of a Tariff To see the effects of a tariff, let's return to the example in which the United States imports T-shirts. With free trade, the T-shirts are imported and sold at the world price. Then, under pressure from U.S. garment makers, the U.S. government imposes a tariff on imported T-shirts. Buyers of T-shirts must now pay the world price plus the tariff. Several consequences follow and Fig. 7.5 illustrates them.

Figure 7.5(a) shows the situation with free international trade. The United States produces 20 million T-shirts a year and imports 40 million a year at the world price of $5 a shirt. Figure 7.5(b) shows what happens with a tariff set at $2 per T-shirt.

FIGURE 7.5   The Effects of a Tariff

(a) Free trade

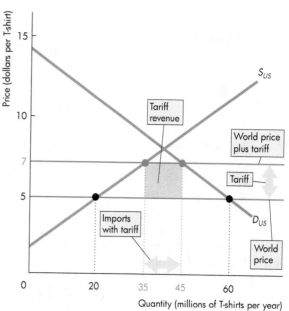

(b) Market with tariff

The world price of a T-shirt is $5. With free trade in part (a), Americans buy 60 million T-shirts a year. U.S. garment makers produce 20 million T-shirts a year and the United States imports 40 million a year.

With a tariff of $2 per T-shirt in part (b), the price in the U.S. market rises to $7 a T-shirt. U.S. production increases, U.S. purchases decrease, and the quantity imported decreases. The U.S. government collects a tariff revenue of $2 on each T-shirt imported, which is shown by the purple rectangle.

The following changes occur in the market for T-shirts:

- The price of a T-shirt in the United States rises by $2.
- The quantity of T-shirts bought in the United States decreases.
- The quantity of T-shirts produced in the United States increases.
- The quantity of T-shirts imported into the United States decreases.
- The U.S. government collects a tariff revenue.

Rise in Price of a T-Shirt To buy a T-shirt, Americans must pay the world price plus the tariff, so the price of a T-shirt rises by the $2 tariff to $7. Figure 7.5(b) shows the new domestic price line, which lies $2 above the world price line. The price rises by the full amount of the tariff. The buyer pays the entire tariff because supply from the rest of the world is perfectly elastic (see Chapter 6, pp. 136–137).

Decrease in Purchases The higher price of a T-shirt brings a decrease in the quantity demanded along the demand curve. Figure 7.5(b) shows the decrease from 60 million T-shirts a year at $5 a shirt to 45 million a year at $7 a shirt.

Increase in Domestic Production The higher price of a T-shirt stimulates domestic production, and U.S. garment makers increase the quantity supplied along the supply curve. Figure 7.5(b) shows the increase from 20 million T-shirts at $5 a shirt to 35 million a year at $7 a shirt.

Decrease in Imports T-shirt imports decrease by 30 million, from 40 million to 10 million a year. Both the decrease in purchases and the increase in domestic production contribute to this decrease in imports.

Tariff Revenue The government's tariff revenue is $20 million—$2 per shirt on 10 million imported shirts—shown by the purple rectangle.

Winners, Losers, and the Social Loss from a Tariff A tariff on an imported good creates winners and losers and a social loss. When the U.S. government imposes a tariff on an imported good,

- U.S. consumers of the good lose.
- U.S. producers of the good gain.
- U.S. consumers lose more than U.S. producers gain.
- Society loses: a deadweight loss arises.

U.S. Consumers of the Good Lose Because the price of a T-shirt in the United States rises, the quantity of T-shirts demanded decreases. The combination of a higher price and smaller quantity bought decreases consumer surplus—the loss to U.S. consumers that arises from a tariff.

ECONOMICS IN ACTION

U.S. Tariffs Almost Gone

The Smoot-Hawley Act, which was passed in 1930, took U.S. tariffs to a peak average rate of 20 percent in 1933. (One third of imports was subject to a 60 percent tariff.) The **General Agreement on Tariffs and Trade (GATT)** was established in 1947. Since then tariffs have fallen in a series of negotiating rounds, the most significant of which are identified in the figure. Tariffs are now as low as they have ever been but import quotas and other trade barriers persist.

Tariffs: 1930–2013

Sources of data: U.S. Bureau of the Census, *Historical Statistics of the United States, Colonial Times to 1970*, Bicentennial Edition, Part 1 (Washington, D.C., 1975); Series U-212: updated from *Statistical Abstract of the United States:* various editions.

U.S. Producers of the Good Gain Because the price of an imported T-shirt rises by the amount of the tariff, U.S. T-shirt producers are now able to sell their T-shirts for the world price plus the tariff. At the higher price, the quantity of T-shirts supplied by U.S. producers increases. The combination of a higher price and larger quantity produced increases producer surplus—the gain to U.S. producers from the tariff.

U.S. Consumers Lose More Than U.S. Producers Gain
Consumer surplus decreases for four reasons: Some becomes producer surplus, some is lost in a higher cost of production (domestic producers have higher costs than foreign producers), some is lost because imports decrease, and some goes to the government as tariff revenue. Figure 7.6 shows these sources of lost consumer surplus.

Figure 7.6(a) shows the consumer surplus and producer surplus with free international trade in T-shirts. Figure 7.6(b) shows the consumer surplus and producer surplus with a $2 tariff on imported T-shirts. By comparing Fig. 7.6(b) with Fig. 7.6(a), you can see how a tariff changes these surpluses.

Consumer surplus—the green area—shrinks for four reasons. First, the higher price transfers surplus from consumers to producers. The blue area *B* represents this loss (and gain of producer surplus). Second, domestic production costs more than imports. The supply curve S_{US} shows the higher cost of production and the gray area *C* shows this loss of consumer surplus. Third, some of the consumer surplus is transferred to the government. The purple area *D* shows this loss (and gain of government revenue). Fourth, some of the consumer surplus is lost because imports decrease. The gray area *E* shows this loss.

Society Loses: A Deadweight Loss Arises Some of the loss of consumer surplus is transferred to producers and some is transferred to the government and spent on government programs that people value. But the increase in production cost and the loss from decreased imports is transferred to no one: It is a social loss—a deadweight loss. The gray areas labeled *C* and *E* represent this deadweight loss. Total surplus decreases by the area *C + E*.

FIGURE 7.6 The Winners and Losers from a Tariff

(a) Free trade

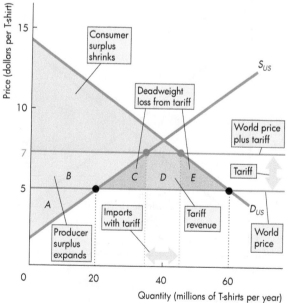

(b) Market with tariff

The world price of a T-shirt is $5. In part (a), with free trade, the United States imports 40 million T-shirts. Consumer surplus, producer surplus, and the gains from free trade are as large as possible.

In part (b), a tariff of $2 per T-shirt raises the U.S. price

of a T-shirt to $7. The quantity imported decreases. Consumer surplus shrinks by the areas B, C, D, and E. Producer surplus expands by area B. The government's tariff revenue is area D, and the tariff creates a deadweight loss equal to the area C + E.

Import Quotas

We now look at the second tool for restricting trade: import quotas. An **import quota** is a restriction that limits the quantity of a good that may be imported in a given period.

Most countries impose import quotas on a wide range of items. The United States imposes them on food products such as sugar and bananas and manufactured goods such as textiles and paper.

Import quotas enable the government to satisfy the self-interest of the people who earn their incomes in the import-competing industries. But you will discover that, like a tariff, an import quota decreases the gains from trade and is not in the social interest.

The Effects of an Import Quota The effects of an import quota are similar to those of a tariff. The price rises, the quantity bought decreases, and the quantity produced in the United States increases. Figure 7.7 illustrates the effects.

Figure 7.7(a) shows the situation with free international trade. Figure 7.7(b) shows what happens with an import quota of 10 million T-shirts a year. The U.S. supply curve of T-shirts becomes the domestic supply curve, S_{US}, plus the quantity that the import quota permits. So the supply curve becomes $S_{US} + quota$. The price of a T-shirt rises to $7, the quantity of T-shirts bought in the United States decreases to 45 million a year, the quantity of T-shirts produced in the United States increases to 35 million a year, and the quantity of T-shirts imported into the United States decreases to the quota quantity of 10 million a year. All the effects of this quota are identical to the effects of a $2 per shirt tariff, as you can check in Fig. 7.5(b).

Winners, Losers, and the Social Loss from an Import Quota An import quota creates winners and losers that are similar to those of a tariff but with an interesting difference.

FIGURE 7.7   The Effects of an Import Quota

(a) Free trade

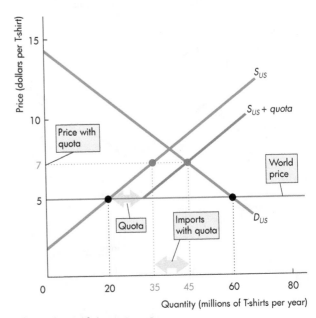

(b) Market with import quota

With free international trade, in part (a), Americans buy 60 million T-shirts at the world price. The United States produces 20 million T-shirts and imports 40 million a year. With an import quota of 10 million T-shirts a year, in part (b),

the supply of T-shirts in the United States is shown by the curve $S_{US} + quota$. The price in the United States rises to $7 a T-shirt. U.S. production increases, U.S. purchases decrease, and the quantity of T-shirts imported decreases.

MyEconLab Animation

When the government imposes an import quota,

- U.S. consumers of the good lose.
- U.S. producers of the good gain.
- Importers of the good gain.
- Society loses: a deadweight loss arises.

Figure 7.8 shows these gains and losses from a quota. By comparing Fig. 7.8(b) with a quota and Fig. 7.8(a) with free trade, you can see how an import quota of 10 million T-shirts a year changes the consumer and producer surpluses.

Consumer surplus—the green area—shrinks. This decrease is the loss to consumers from the import quota. The decrease in consumer surplus is made up of four parts. First, some of the consumer surplus is transferred to producers. The blue area B represents this loss of consumer surplus (and gain of producer surplus). Second, part of the consumer surplus is lost because the domestic cost of production is higher than the world price. The gray area C represents this loss. Third, part of the consumer surplus is transferred to importers who buy T-shirts for $5 (the world price) and sell them for $7 (the U.S. domestic price). The two blue areas D represent this loss of consumer surplus and profit for importers. Fourth, part of the consumer surplus is lost because imports decrease. The gray area E represents this loss.

The loss of consumer surplus from the higher cost of production and the decrease in imports is a social loss—a deadweight loss. The gray areas labeled C and E represent this deadweight loss. Total surplus decreases by the area $C + E$.

You can now see the one difference between a quota and a tariff. A tariff brings in revenue for the government while a quota brings a profit for the importers. All the other effects are the same, provided the quota is set at the same quantity of imports that results from the tariff.

FIGURE 7.8   The Winners and Losers from an Import Quota

(a) Free trade

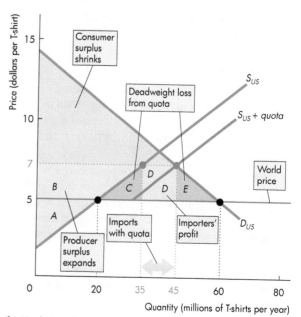

(b) Market with import quota

The world price of a T-shirt is $5. In part (a), with free trade, the United States produces 20 million T-shirts a year and imports 40 million T-shirts. Consumer surplus, producer surplus, and the gain from free international trade (darker green area) are as large as possible.

In part (b), the import quota raises the price of a T-shirt to $7. The quantity imported decreases. Consumer surplus shrinks by the areas B, C, D, and E. Producer surplus expands by area B. Importers' profit is the two areas D, and the quota creates a deadweight loss equal to $C + E$.

ECONOMICS IN THE NEWS

The Changing Market for Coat Hangers

Your Dry Cleaning Bill Is About to Get Worse
The price of wire hangers is a big deal for a dry cleaner, and that price will rise when the Commerce Department puts a 21 percent tariff on hangers made in Vietnam. The tariff is in response to a wire-hanger export subsidy paid to producers in Vietnam.

Source: CNN Money, June 4, 2012

SOME FACTS

Albert J. Parkhouse invented the wire hanger in Jackson, Michigan, in 1903 and for almost 100 years, the United States produced and exported wire hangers. During the past 20 years, China and Vietnam have become the major lowest-cost producers.

THE PROBLEM

Explain why the United States has switched from exporting to importing wire hangers. Also explain the effects of the 21 percent tariff. Does Vietnam's export subsidy make the tariff efficient? Illustrate your explanations with a graph.

THE SOLUTION

- Initially, the opportunity cost of producing a wire hanger was lower in the United States than in the rest of the world. The United States had a comparative advantage in producing wire hangers and exported them.

- Today, the opportunity cost of producing a wire hanger is lower in China and Vietnam than in the United States (and other countries). China and Vietnam have a comparative advantage in producing wire hangers, so the United States imports them.

- By imposing a 21 percent tariff on wire hangers, the price in the United States rises above the world price by this percentage.

- The higher price decreases the quantity of wire hangers demanded in the United States, increases the quantity that U.S. producers supply, and decreases U.S. imports of wire hangers.

- The figure illustrates the U.S. market for wire hangers. The demand curve D_{US} and the supply curve S_{US} are assumed not to change. The U.S. price with no international trade is 10 cents per hanger.

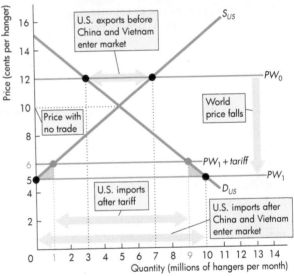

U.S. Market for Wire Hangers

- With a world price PW_0 of 12 cents a hanger, the United States had a comparative advantage in hangers, so it produced 7 million hangers a month, used 3 million, and exported 4 million. The figure shows the quantity of U.S. exports.

- When the world price falls to PW_1 at 5 cents a hanger, the United States stops producing hangers and imports 10 million a month.

- With a 21 percent tariff, the price in the United States rises to $PW_1 + tariff$. U.S. hanger production now becomes 1 million a month, the quantity used decreases to 9 million, and imports decrease to 8 million.

- The fact that the tariff is a response to Vietnam's export subsidy does not make the tariff efficient. It creates a deadweight loss shown by the two gray triangles.

Other Import Barriers

Two sets of policies that influence imports are

- Health, safety, and regulation barriers
- Voluntary export restraints

Health, Safety, and Regulation Barriers Thousands of detailed health, safety, and other regulations restrict international trade. For example, U.S. food imports are examined by the Food and Drug Administration to determine whether the food is "pure, wholesome, safe to eat, and produced under sanitary conditions." The discovery of BSE (mad cow disease) in just one U.S. cow in 2003 was enough to close down international trade in U.S. beef. The European Union bans imports of most genetically modified foods, such as U.S.-produced soybeans. Although regulations of the type we've just described are not designed to limit international trade, they have that effect.

Voluntary Export Restraints A *voluntary export restraint* is like a quota allocated to a foreign exporter of a good. This type of trade barrier isn't common. It was initially used during the 1980s when Japan voluntarily limited its exports of car parts to the United States.

Export Subsidies

A *subsidy* is a payment by the government to a producer. You studied the effects of a subsidy on the quantity produced and the price of a subsidized farm product in Chapter 6, pp. 140–141.

An *export subsidy* is a payment by the government to the producer of an exported good. Export subsidies are illegal under a number of international agreements, including the North American Free Trade Agreement (NAFTA), and the rules of the World Trade Organization (WTO).

Although export subsidies are illegal, the subsidies that the U.S. and European Union governments pay to farmers end up increasing domestic production, some of which gets exported. These exports of subsidized farm products make it harder for producers in other countries, notably in Africa and Central and South America, to compete in global markets. Export subsidies bring gains to domestic producers, but they result in inefficient underproduction in the rest of the world and create a deadweight loss.

ECONOMICS IN ACTION
Self-Interest Beats the Social Interest

The **World Trade Organization** (**WTO**) is an international body established by the world's major trading nations for the purpose of supervising international trade and lowering the barriers to trade.

In 2001, at a meeting of trade ministers from all the WTO member-countries held in Doha, Qatar, an agreement was made to begin negotiations to lower tariff barriers and quotas that restrict international trade in farm products and services. These negotiations are called the **Doha Development Agenda** or the **Doha Round**.

In the period since 2001, thousands of hours of conferences in Cancún in 2003, Geneva in 2004, and Hong Kong in 2005, and ongoing meetings at WTO headquarters in Geneva, costing millions of taxpayers' dollars, have made disappointing progress.

Rich nations, led by the United States, the European Union, and Japan, want greater access to the markets of developing nations in exchange for allowing those nations greater access to the markets of the rich world, especially those for farm products.

Developing nations, led by Brazil, China, India, and South Africa, want access to the markets of farm products of the rich world, but they also want to protect their infant industries.

With two incompatible positions, these negotiations are stalled and show no signs of a breakthrough. The self-interests of rich nations and developing nations are preventing the achievement of the social interest.

◆ REVIEW QUIZ

1 What are the tools that a country can use to restrict international trade?
2 Explain the effects of a tariff on domestic production, the quantity bought, and the price.
3 Explain who gains and who loses from a tariff and why the losses exceed the gains.
4 Explain the effects of an import quota on domestic production, consumption, and price.
5 Explain who gains and who loses from an import quota and why the losses exceed the gains.

Work these questions in Study Plan 7.3 and get instant feedback. Do a Key Terms Quiz. MyEconLab

◥ The Case Against Protection

You've just seen that free trade promotes prosperity and protection is inefficient. Yet trade is restricted with tariffs, quotas, and other barriers. Why? Seven arguments for trade restrictions are that protecting domestic industries from foreign competition

- Helps an infant industry grow.
- Counteracts dumping.
- Saves domestic jobs.
- Allows us to compete with cheap foreign labor.
- Penalizes lax environmental standards.
- Prevents rich countries from exploiting developing countries.
- Reduces offshore outsourcing that sends good U.S. jobs to other countries.

Helps an Infant Industry Grow

Comparative advantages change with on-the-job experience—*learning-by-doing*. When a new industry or a new product is born—an *infant industry*—it is not as productive as it will become with experience. It is argued that such an industry should be protected from international competition until it can stand alone and compete.

It is true that learning-by-doing can change comparative advantage, but this fact doesn't justify protecting an infant industry. Firms anticipate and benefit from learning-by-doing without protection from foreign competition.

When Boeing started to build airplanes, productivity was at first low. But after a period of learning-by-doing, huge productivity gains followed. Boeing didn't need a tariff to achieve these productivity gains.

Counteracts Dumping

Dumping occurs when a foreign firm sells its exports at a lower price than its cost of production. Dumping might be used by a firm that wants to gain a global monopoly. In this case, the foreign firm sells its output at a price below its cost to drive domestic firms out of business. When the domestic firms have gone, the foreign firm takes advantage of its monopoly position and charges a higher price for its product. Dumping is illegal under the rules of the World Trade Organization and is usually regarded as a justification for temporary tariffs, which are called *countervailing duties*.

But it is virtually impossible to detect dumping because it is hard to determine a firm's costs. As a result, the test for dumping is whether a firm's export price is below its domestic price. But this test is weak because it is rational for a firm to charge a low price in a market in which the quantity demanded is highly sensitive to price and a higher price in a market in which demand is less price-sensitive.

Saves Domestic Jobs

First, free trade does destroy some jobs, but it also creates other jobs. It brings about a global rationalization of labor and allocates labor resources to their highest-valued activities. International trade in textiles has cost tens of thousands of U.S. jobs as U.S. textile mills and other factories closed. But tens of thousands of jobs have been created in other countries as textile mills opened. And tens of thousands of U.S. workers have better-paying jobs than as textile workers because U.S. export industries have expanded and created new jobs. More jobs have been created than destroyed.

Although protection can save particular jobs, it does so at a high cost. For example, until 2005, U.S. textile jobs were protected by an international agreement called the Multifiber Arrangement. The U.S. International Trade Commission (ITC) has estimated that because of import quotas, 72,000 jobs existed in the textile industry that would otherwise have disappeared and that the annual clothing expenditure in the United States was $15.9 billion ($160 per family) higher than it would have been with free trade. Equivalently, the ITC estimated that each textile job saved cost $221,000 a year.

Imports don't only destroy jobs. They create jobs for retailers that sell imported goods and for firms that service those goods. Imports also create jobs by creating income in the rest of the world, some of which is spent on U.S.-made goods and services.

Allows Us to Compete with Cheap Foreign Labor

With the removal of tariffs on trade between the United States and Mexico, people said we would hear a "giant sucking sound" as jobs rushed to Mexico. That didn't happen. Why?

It didn't happen because low-wage labor is low-productivity labor. If a U.S. autoworker earns $30 an hour and produces 15 units of output an hour, the average labor cost of a unit of output is $2. If a Mexican auto-worker earns $3 an hour and produces 1 unit of output an hour, the average labor cost of a unit of output is $3. Other things remaining the same, the higher a worker's productivity, the higher is the worker's wage rate. High-wage workers have high productivity; low-wage workers have low productivity.

It is *comparative advantage*, not wage differences, that drive international trade and that enable us to compete with Mexico and Mexico to compete with us.

Penalizes Lax Environmental Standards

Another argument for protection is that it provides an incentive to poor countries to raise their environmental standards—free trade with the richer and "greener" countries is a reward for improved environmental standards.

This argument for protection is weak. First, a poor country cannot afford to be as concerned about its environmental standard as a rich country can. Today, some of the worst pollution of air and water is found in China, Mexico, and the former communist countries of Eastern Europe. But only a few decades ago, London and Los Angeles topped the pollution league chart. The best hope for cleaner air in Beijing and Mexico City is rapid income growth, which free trade promotes. As incomes in developing countries grow, they have the *means* to match their desires to improve their environment. Second, a poor country may have a comparative advantage at doing "dirty" work, which helps it to raise its income and at the same time enables the global economy to achieve higher environmental standards than would otherwise be possible.

Prevents Rich Countries from Exploiting Developing Countries

Another argument for protection is that international trade must be restricted to prevent the people of the rich industrial world from exploiting the poorer people of the developing countries and forcing them to work for slave wages.

Child labor and near-slave labor are serious problems. But by trading with poor countries, we increase the demand for the goods that these countries produce and increase the demand for their labor. When the demand for labor in developing countries increases, the wage rate rises. So, rather than exploiting people in developing countries, trade can improve their opportunities and increase their incomes.

Reduces Offshore Outsourcing that Sends Good U.S. Jobs to Other Countries

Offshore outsourcing—buying goods, components, or services from firms in other countries—brings gains from trade identical to those of any other type of trade. We could easily change the names of the items traded from T-shirts and airplanes (the examples in the previous sections of this chapter) to banking services and call-center services (or any other pair of services). A U.S. bank might export banking services to Indian firms, and Indians might provide call-center services to U.S. firms. This type of trade would benefit both Americans and Indians, provided the United States has a comparative advantage in banking services and India has a comparative advantage in call-center services.

Despite the gain from specialization and trade that offshore outsourcing brings, many people believe that it also brings costs that eat up the gains. Why?

A major reason is that it seems to send good U.S. jobs to other countries. It is true that some manufacturing and service jobs are going overseas. But others are expanding at home. The United States imports call-center services, but it exports education, health-care, legal, financial, and a host of other types of services. The number of jobs in these sectors is expanding and will continue to expand.

The exact number of jobs that have moved to lower-cost offshore locations is not known, and estimates vary. But even the highest estimate is small compared to the normal rate of job creation and labor turnover.

Gains from trade do not bring gains for every single person. Americans, on average, gain from offshore outsourcing, but some people lose. The losers are those who have invested in the human capital to do a specific job that has now gone offshore.

Unemployment benefits provide short-term temporary relief for these displaced workers. But the long-term solution requires retraining and the acquisition of new skills.

Beyond bringing short-term relief through unemployment benefits, government has a larger role to play. By providing education and training, it can enable the labor force of the twenty-first century to engage in the ongoing learning and sometimes rapid retooling that jobs we can't foresee today will demand.

Schools, colleges, and universities will expand and become better at doing their job of producing a more highly educated and flexible labor force.

◆ AT **ISSUE**

Is Offshore Outsourcing Bad or Good for America?

Citibank, Bank of America, Apple, Nike, and Wal-Mart engage in offshore outsourcing when they buy finished goods, components, or services from firms in other countries. Buying goods and components has been going on for centuries, but buying *services* such as customer support call-center services, is new and is made possible by the development of low-cost telephone and Internet service.

Should this type of offshore outsourcing be discouraged and penalized with taxes and regulations?

Bad

- In his 2012 *State of the Union Address*, President Obama said, "A business that wants to outsource jobs shouldn't get a tax deduction for doing it. ... It is time to stop rewarding businesses that ship jobs overseas, and start rewarding companies that create jobs right here in America."

- A survey conducted in 2004 found that 69 percent of Americans think outsourcing hurts the U.S. economy and only 17 percent think it helps.

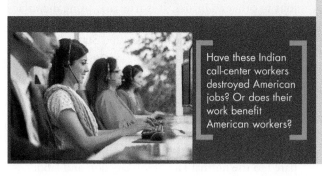

Have these Indian call-center workers destroyed American jobs? Or does their work benefit American workers?

Good

- Economist N. Gregory Mankiw, when Chair of President George W. Bush's Council of Economic Advisers, said, "I think outsourcing ... is probably a plus for the economy in the long run."

- Mankiw went on to say that it doesn't matter whether "items produced abroad come on planes, ships, or over fiber-optic cables ... the economics is basically the same."

- What Greg Mankiw is saying is that the economic analysis of the gains from international trade—exactly the same as what you have studied on pp. 153–156—applies to all types of international trade.

- Offshore outsourcing, like all other forms of international trade, is a source of gains for all.

Avoiding Trade Wars

We have reviewed the arguments commonly heard in favor of protection and the counterarguments against it. But one counterargument to protection that is general and quite overwhelming is that protection invites retaliation and can trigger a trade war.

A trade war is a contest in which when one country raises its import tariffs, other countries retaliate with increases of their own, which trigger yet further increases from the first country.

A trade war occurred during the Great Depression of the 1930s when the United States introduced the Smoot-Hawley tariff. Country after country retaliated with its own tariff, and in a short period, world trade had almost disappeared. The costs to all countries were large and led to a renewed international resolve to avoid such self-defeating moves in the future. The costs also led to attempts to liberalize trade following World War II.

Why Is International Trade Restricted?

Why, despite all the arguments against protection, is trade restricted? There are two key reasons:

- Tariff revenue
- Rent seeking

Tariff Revenue Government revenue is costly to collect. In developed countries such as the United States, a well-organized tax collection system is in place that can generate billions of dollars of income tax and sales tax revenues.

But governments in developing countries have a difficult time collecting taxes from their citizens. Much economic activity takes place in an informal economy with few financial records. The one area in which economic transactions are well recorded is international trade. So tariffs on international trade are a convenient source of revenue in these countries.

Rent Seeking Rent seeking is the major reason why international trade is restricted. **Rent seeking** is lobbying for special treatment by the government to create economic profit or to divert consumer surplus or producer surplus away from others. Free trade increases consumption possibilities *on average*, but not everyone shares in the gain and some people even lose. Free trade brings benefits to some and imposes costs on others, with total benefits exceeding total costs. The uneven distribution of costs and benefits is the principal obstacle to achieving more liberal international trade.

Returning to the example of trade in T-shirts and airplanes, the benefits from free trade accrue to all the producers of airplanes and to those producers of T-shirts that do not bear the costs of adjusting to a smaller garment industry. These costs are transition costs, not permanent costs. The costs of moving to free trade are borne by the garment producers and their employees who must become producers of other goods and services in which the United States has a comparative advantage.

The number of winners from free trade is large, but because the gains are spread thinly over a large number of people, the gain per person is small. The winners could organize and become a political force lobbying for free trade. But political activity is costly. It uses time and other scarce resources and the gains per person are too small to make the cost of political activity worth bearing.

In contrast, the number of losers from free trade is small, but the loss per person is large. Because the loss per person is large, the people who lose *are* willing to incur considerable expense to lobby against free trade.

Both the winners and losers weigh benefits and costs. Those who gain from free trade weigh the benefits it brings against the cost of achieving it. Those who lose from free trade and gain from protection weigh the benefit of protection against the cost of maintaining it. The protectionists undertake a larger quantity of political lobbying than the free traders.

Compensating Losers

If, in total, the gains from free international trade exceed the losses, why don't those who gain compensate those who lose so that everyone is in favor of free trade?

Some compensation does take place. When Congress approved the North American Free Trade

Agreement (NAFTA) with Canada and Mexico, it set up a $56 million fund to support and retrain workers who lost their jobs as a result of the new trade agreement. During NAFTA's first six months, only 5,000 workers applied for benefits under this scheme. The losers from international trade are also compensated indirectly through the normal unemployment compensation arrangements. But only limited attempts are made to compensate those who lose.

The main reason full compensation is not attempted is that the costs of identifying all the losers and estimating the value of their losses would be enormous. Also, it would never be clear whether a person who has fallen on hard times is suffering because of free trade or for other reasons that might be largely under her or his control. Furthermore, some people who look like losers at one point in time might, in fact, end up gaining. The young autoworker who loses his job in Michigan and becomes a computer assembly worker in Minneapolis might resent the loss of work and the need to move. But a year later, looking back on events, he counts himself fortunate.

Because we do not, in general, compensate the losers from free international trade, protectionism is a popular and permanent feature of our national economic and political life.

◆ REVIEW QUIZ

1 What are the infant industry and dumping arguments for protection? Are they correct?

2 Can protection save jobs and the environment and prevent workers in developing countries from being exploited?

3 What is offshore outsourcing? Who benefits from it and who loses?

4 What are the main reasons for imposing a tariff?

5 Why don't the winners from free trade win the political argument?

Work these questions in Study Plan 7.4 and get instant feedback. Do a Key Terms Quiz.   MyEconLab

◆ We end this chapter on global markets in action with *Economics in the News* on pp. 168–169, where we apply what you've learned by looking at the benefits of and obstacles to a U.S. free-trade deal with Japan.

Obstacles to Free Trade

Obama and Abe Fail to Reach Trade Deal

Thw Financial Times
April 25, 2014

… Despite encouraging statements from Mr. Obama and Japanese prime minister Shinzo Abe, negotiators failed to overcome differences on Japanese agricultural tariffs and the automobile trade. …

In their joint statement, Mr. Obama and Mr. Abe said the progress made marked a "key milestone in the Trans Pacific Partnership (TPP) negotiations and will inject fresh momentum into the broader talks." But neither side provided any details about what was achieved.

…

"All of us have to move out of our comfort zones and not just expect that we are going to get access to somebody else's market without providing access to our own," Mr. Obama said on Thursday.

The talks between the United States and Japan have been focused on agriculture and cars. The United States has been seeking greater access to Japan's automotive and agricultural markets although Japan has vowed to do what it can to protect politically sensitive products such as beef, pork, and rice. In exchange, Japan wants the United States to remove its existing tariffs on imported cars and light trucks.

The significance of a breakthrough, however, would be much broader, said Jeffrey Schott, a close watcher of the TPP and U.S. trade policy at the Washington-based Peterson Institute for International Economics.

Chief negotiators from all 12 TPP countries are due to gather in Vietnam in May and their trade ministers are expected to meet shortly afterwards in China. Both encounters are seen as important for efforts to wrap up the TPP. Not having a U.S.-Japan deal before then would be a setback.

Any deal with Japan would also help the Obama administration in its efforts to secure so-called "fast track" negotiating authority from Congress. Senior Democrats have been reluctant to back the U.S. president's plan.

Jonathan Soble and Shawn Donnan, "Obama and Abe Fail to Reach Trade Deal," *The Financial Times*, April 25, 2014.

MyEconLab More Economics in the News

ESSENCE OF THE STORY

- The United States and Japan are attempting to make a trade agreement as a component of the broad TPP.

- Negotiations have focused on agriculture and cars.

- The United States wants greater access to Japan's auto and agricultural markets.

- Japan wants to protect beef, pork, and rice.

- Japan wants the United States to remove tariffs on imported cars and light trucks.

- Not having a U.S.-Japan deal before broader negotiations among the 12 TPP nations would be a setback.

ECONOMIC ANALYSIS

- Twelve Pacific-rim nations are attempting to reach a trade deal that lowers barriers to trade.

- The United States and Japan, the two largest of the economies, are seeking agreement ahead of the broader negotiations, but obstacles stand in the way of a deal.

- The core of the problem is Japan's wish to protect its farmers, and especially its rice farmers.

- Figure 1 shows how Japan is protecting its rice farmers but damaging its consumers' interest.

- The demand curve is D_J and the supply curve is S_J. With a total ban on rice imports (an import quota of zero), the price of rice is $4,000 per ton and 10 million tons are produced and consumed per year.

- If Japan opened up its rice market to free international trade, the price of rice would fall. In Fig. 1, the price falls to the world price (assumed) of $2,800 per ton, shown by the line PW.

- With free trade, Japan can buy rice for $2,800 per ton and the price in Japan falls to that level. The quantity of rice demanded increases to 16 million tons, the quantity supplied decreases to 6 million tons, and 10 million tons are imported. (Assumed quantities.)

- The Japanese rice producers' surplus shrinks and the Japanese consumer surplus expands by the amount of the light green area. Consumer surplus also increases and total surplus increases by the darker green area.

- The farm lobby in Japan is strong and the government is unwilling to risk losing votes by permitting free trade in rice. But it has moved in that direction in its deal with Australia, and it is expected to move further in a deal with the United States.

- Figure 2 shows why the United States is interested in this deal. The demand curve for rice is D_{US} and the supply curve is S_{US}. If there were no international trade in rice, the price in the United States would be $1,600 per ton and 4 million tons would be produced and consumed each year.

- With free trade, the United States can sell rice at the world price of $2,800 per ton and the price in the United States rises to that level. The quantity of rice demanded decreases to 2 million tons, the quantity supplied increases to 8 million tons, and 6 million tons are exported. (Assumed quantities.)

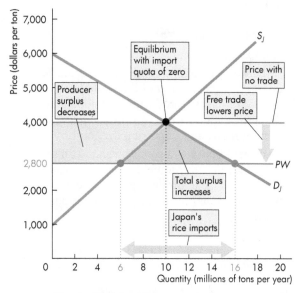

Figure 1 The Market for Rice in Japan

Figure 2 The Market for Rice in the United States

- The U.S. consumer surplus shrinks and the U.S. rice producers' surplus expands by the amount of the light blue area. Producer surplus also increases and total surplus increases by the darker blue area.

SUMMARY

Key Points

How Global Markets Work (pp. 152–154)

- Comparative advantage drives international trade.
- If the world price of a good is lower than the domestic price, the rest of the world has a comparative advantage in producing that good and the domestic country gains by producing less, consuming more, and importing the good.
- If the world price of a good is higher than the domestic price, the domestic country has a comparative advantage in producing that good and gains by producing more, consuming less, and exporting the good.

Working Problems 1 to 3 will give you a better understanding of how global markets work.

Winners, Losers, and the Net Gain from Trade (pp. 155–156)

- Compared to a no-trade situation, in a market with imports, consumer surplus is larger, producer surplus is smaller, and total surplus is larger with free international trade.
- Compared to a no-trade situation, in a market with exports, consumer surplus is smaller, producer surplus is larger, and total surplus is larger with free international trade.

Working Problem 4 will give you a better understanding of winners, losers, and the net gains from trade.

International Trade Restrictions (pp. 157–163)

- Countries restrict international trade by imposing tariffs, import quotas, and other import barriers.
- Trade restrictions raise the domestic price of imported goods, lower the quantity imported, decrease consumer surplus, increase producer surplus, and create a deadweight loss.

Working Problems 5 to 11 will give you a better understanding of international trade restrictions.

The Case Against Protection (pp. 164–167)

- Arguments that protection helps an infant industry to grow and counteracts dumping are weak.
- Arguments that protection saves jobs, allows us to compete with cheap foreign labor, is needed to penalize lax environmental standards, and prevents exploitation of developing countries are flawed.
- Offshore outsourcing is just a new way of reaping gains from trade and does not justify protection.
- Trade restrictions are popular because protection brings a small loss per person to a large number of people and a large gain per person to a small number of people. Those who gain have a stronger political voice than those who lose and it is too costly to identify and compensate losers.

Working Problem 12 will give you a better understanding of the case against protection.

Key Terms

MyEconLab Key Terms Quiz

Dumping, 164
Exports, 152
Import quota, 160
Imports, 152

Offshore outsourcing, 165
Rent seeking, 167
Tariff, 157

WORKED PROBLEM

MyEconLab   You can work this problem in Chapter 7 Study Plan.

The table shows the U.S. demand schedule for honey and the supply schedule of honey by U.S. producers. The world price of honey is $8 a jar.

Price (dollars per jar)	Quantity demanded	Quantity supplied
	(millions of jars per year)	
5	10	0
6	8	3
7	6	6
8	4	9
9	2	12
10	0	15

Questions

1. With no international trade, what is the price of honey and the quantity bought and sold in the United States? Does the United States have a comparative advantage in producing honey and with free international trade, does the United States export or import honey?

2. With free international trade, what is the U.S. price of honey, the quantity bought by Americans, the quantity produced in the United States, and the quantity of honey exported or imported?

3. Do Americans gain from international trade in honey? Do all Americans gain? If not, who loses and do the gains exceed the losses?

Solutions

1. With no international trade, the price of honey is that at which the U.S. quantity demanded equals the U.S quantity supplied. The table shows that this price is $7 a jar at which the equilibrium quantity is 6 million jars a year.

   The price of honey in the United States is less than the world price, which means that the opportunity cost of producing a jar of honey in the United States is *less* than the opportunity cost of producing it in the rest of the world. So U.S. producers have a comparative advantage in producing honey and with free international trade, the United States exports honey.

Key Point: Comparative advantage is determined by comparing the opportunity cost of producing the good in the United States to the world price.

2. With free international trade, the price of honey in the United States rises to the world price of $8 a jar. Americans cut their consumption of honey

to 4 million jars a year while U.S. honey producers expand production to 9 million jars a year. The United States exports 5 million jars a year.

   The figure shows the quantities bought and produced in the United States and the quantity exported.

Key Point: As the domestic price rises to the world price, the quantity demanded decreases and the quantity supplied increases, and the difference is exported.

3. With free international trade, the United States gains from exporting honey because the higher price and the larger quantity of honey produced increase U.S. total surplus from honey.

   Consumers lose because the price of honey rises and they buy less honey. Consumer surplus from honey decreases. But the higher price and the larger quantity produced increase producer surplus from honey. The United States gains because the increase in producer surplus is greater than the loss in consumer surplus.

   The figure shows that with no trade, consumer surplus equals area $A + B$ and producer surplus equals area C. With free trade, consumer surplus shrinks to area A, producer surplus expands to area $B + C + D$, and total surplus (the gains from trade in honey) increases by area D.

Key Point: Free trade increases the total surplus, but for an exporting country some consumer surplus is transferred to producers of the exported good.

Key Figure

MyEconLab Interactive Graph

STUDY PLAN PROBLEMS AND APPLICATIONS

MyEconLab   You can work Problems 1 to 11 in Chapter 7 Study Plan and get instant feedback.

How Global Markets Work (Study Plan 7.1)

Use the following data to work Problems 1 to 3. Wholesalers buy and sell roses in containers that hold 120 stems. The table provides information about the wholesale market for roses in the United States. The demand schedule is the wholesalers' demand and the supply schedule is the U.S. rose growers' supply.

Price (dollars per container)	Quantity demanded	Quantity supplied
	(millions of containers per year)	
100	15	0
125	12	2
150	9	4
175	6	6
200	3	8
225	0	10

Wholesalers can buy roses at auction in Aalsmeer, Holland, for $125 per container.

1. a. Without international trade, what would be the price of a container of roses and how many containers of roses a year would be bought and sold in the United States?

   b. At the price in your answer to part (a), does the United States or the rest of the world have a comparative advantage in producing roses?

2. If U.S. wholesalers buy roses at the lowest possible price, how many do they buy from U.S. growers and how many do they import?

3. Draw a graph to illustrate the U.S. wholesale market for roses. Show the equilibrium in that market with no international trade and the equilibrium with free trade. Mark the quantity of roses produced in the United States, the quantity imported, and the total quantity bought.

Winners, Losers, and the Net Gain from Trade
(Study Plan 7.2)

4. Use the information on the U.S. wholesale market for roses in Problem 1 to

   a. Explain who gains and who loses from free international trade in roses compared to a situation in which Americans buy only roses grown in the United States.

   b. Draw a graph to illustrate the gains and losses from free trade.

   c. Calculate the gain from international trade.

International Trade Restrictions (Study Plan 7.3)

Use the information on the U.S. wholesale market for roses in Problem 1 to work Problems 5 to 10.

5. If the United States puts a tariff of $25 per container on imports of roses, explain how the U.S. price of roses, the quantity of roses bought, the quantity produced in the United States, and the quantity imported change.

6. Who gains and who loses from this tariff?

7. Draw a graph of the U.S. market for roses to illustrate the gains and losses from the tariff and on the graph identify the gains and losses, the tariff revenue, and the deadweight loss created.

8. If the United States puts an import quota on roses of 5 million containers, what happens to the U.S. price of roses, the quantity of roses bought, the quantity produced in the United States, and the quantity imported?

9. Who gains and who loses from this quota?

10. Draw a graph to illustrate the gains and losses from the import quota and on the graph identify the gains and losses, the importers' profit, and the deadweight loss.

The Case Against Protection (Study Plan 7.4)

11. **Chinese Tire Maker Rejects Charge of Defects**
    U.S. regulators ordered the recall of more than 450,000 faulty tires. The Chinese producer of the tires disputed the allegations and hinted that the recall might be an effort to hamper Chinese exports to the United States.
    Source: *International Herald Tribune*,
    June 26, 2007

    a. What does the news clip imply about the comparative advantage of producing tires in the United States and China?

    b. Could product quality be a valid argument against free trade? If it could, explain how.

ADDITIONAL PROBLEMS AND APPLICATIONS

MyEconLab   You can work these problems in MyEconLab if assigned by your instructor.

How Global Markets Work

12. Suppose that the world price of sugar is 10 cents a pound, the United States does not trade internationally, and the equilibrium price of sugar in the United States is 20 cents a pound. The United States then begins to trade internationally.

   a. How does the price of sugar in the United States change?

   b. Do U.S. consumers buy more or less sugar?

   c. Do U.S. sugar growers produce more or less sugar?

   d. Does the United States export or import sugar and why?

13. Suppose that the world price of steel is $100 a ton, India does not trade internationally, and the equilibrium price of steel in India is $60 a ton. India then begins to trade internationally.

   a. How does the price of steel in India change?

   b. How does the quantity of steel produced in India change?

   c. How does the quantity of steel bought by India change?

   d. Does India export or import steel and why?

14. A semiconductor is a key component in your laptop, cellphone, and iPod. The table provides information about the market for semiconductors in the United States.

Price (dollars per unit)	Quantity demanded	Quantity supplied
	(billions of units per year)	
10	25	0
12	20	20
14	15	40
16	10	60
18	5	80
20	0	100

Producers of semiconductors can get $18 a unit on the world market.

   a. With no international trade, what would be the price of a semiconductor and how many semiconductors a year would be bought and sold in the United States?

   b. Does the United States have a comparative advantage in producing semiconductors?

15. **Act Now, Eat Later**

   The hunger crisis in poor countries has its roots in U.S. and European policies of subsidizing the diversion of food crops to produce biofuels like corn-based ethanol. That is, doling out subsidies to put the world's dinner into the gas tank.

   Source: *Time*, May 5, 2008

   a. What is the effect on the world price of corn of the increased use of corn to produce ethanol in the United States and Europe?

   b. How does the change in the world price of corn affect the quantity of corn produced in a poor developing country with a comparative advantage in producing corn, the quantity it consumes, and the quantity that it either exports or imports?

Winners, Losers, and the Net Gain from Trade

16. Draw a graph of the market for corn in the poor developing country in Problem 15(b) to show the changes in consumer surplus, producer surplus, and deadweight loss.

Use the following news clip to work Problems 17 and 18.

South Korea to Resume U.S. Beef Imports

South Korea will reopen its market to most U.S. beef. South Korea banned imports of U.S. beef in 2003 amid concerns over a case of mad cow disease in the United States. The ban closed what was then the third-largest market for U.S. beef exporters.

Source: CNN, May 29, 2008

17. a. Explain how South Korea's import ban on U.S. beef affected beef producers and consumers in South Korea.

   b. Draw a graph of the market for beef in South Korea to illustrate your answer to part (a). Identify the changes in consumer surplus, producer surplus, and deadweight loss.

18. a. Assuming that South Korea is the only importer of U.S. beef, explain how South Korea's import ban on U.S. beef affected beef producers and consumers in the United States.

   b. Draw a graph of the market for beef in the United States to illustrate your answer to part (a). Identify the changes in consumer surplus, producer surplus, and deadweight loss.

International Trade Restrictions

Use the following information to work Problems 19 to 21.

Before 1995, trade between the United States and Mexico was subject to tariffs. In 1995, Mexico joined NAFTA and all U.S. and Mexican tariffs have gradually been removed.

19. Explain how the price that U.S. consumers pay for goods from Mexico and the quantity of U.S. imports from Mexico have changed. Who are the winners and who are the losers from this free trade?

20. Explain how the quantity of U.S. exports to Mexico and the U.S. government's tariff revenue from trade with Mexico have changed.

21. Suppose that this year tomato growers in Florida lobby the U.S. government to impose an import quota on Mexican tomatoes. Explain who in the United States would gain and who would lose from such a quota.

Use the following information to work Problems 22 and 23.

Suppose that in response to huge job losses in the U.S. textile industry, Congress imposes a 100 percent tariff on imports of textiles from China.

22. Explain how the tariff on textiles will change the price that U.S. buyers pay for textiles, the quantity of textiles imported, and the quantity of textiles produced in the United States.

23. Explain how the U.S. and Chinese gains from trade will change. Who in the United States will lose and who will gain?

Use the following information to work Problems 24 and 25.

With free trade between Australia and the United States, Australia would export beef to the United States. But the United States imposes an import quota on Australian beef.

24. Explain how this quota influences the price that U.S. consumers pay for beef, the quantity of beef produced in the United States, and the U.S. and the Australian gains from trade.

25. Explain who in the United States gains from the quota on beef imports and who loses.

The Case Against Protection

26. **Trading Up**

The cost of protecting jobs in uncompetitive sectors through tariffs is high: Saving a job in the sugar industry costs American consumers $826,000 in higher prices a year; saving a dairy industry job costs $685,000 per year; and saving a job in the manufacturing of women's handbags costs $263,000.

Source: *The New York Times*, June 26, 2006

a. What are the arguments for saving the jobs mentioned in this news clip? Explain why these arguments are faulty.

b. Is there any merit to saving these jobs?

Economics in the News

27. After you have studied *Economics in the News* on pp. 168–169, answer the following questions.

a. What is the TPP?

b. Who in the United States would benefit and who would lose from a successful TPP?

c. Illustrate your answer to part (b) with an appropriate graphical analysis assuming that tariffs are not completely eliminated.

d. Who in Japan and other TPP nations would benefit and who would lose from a successful TPP?

e. Illustrate with an appropriate graphical analysis who in Japan would benefit and who would lose from a successful TPP, assuming that all Japan's import quotas and tariffs are completely eliminated.

28. E.U. Agrees to Trade Deal with South Korea

Italy has dropped its resistance to a E.U. trade agreement with South Korea, which will wipe out $2 billion in annual duties on E.U. exports. Italians argued that the agreement, which eliminates E.U. duties on South Korean cars, would put undue pressure on its own automakers.

Source: *The Financial Times*, September 16, 2010

a. What is a free trade agreement? What is its aim?

b. Explain how a tariff on E.U. car imports changes E.U. production of cars, purchases of cars, and imports of cars. Illustrate your answer with an appropriate graphical analysis.

c. Show on your graph the changes in consumer surplus and producer surplus that result from free trade in cars.

d. Explain why Italian automakers opposed cuts in car import tariffs.

The Amazing Market

PART TWO

UNDERSTANDING HOW MARKETS WORK

The five chapters that you've just studied explain how markets work. The market is an amazing instrument. It enables people who have never met and who know nothing about each other to interact and do business. It also enables us to allocate our scarce resources to the uses that we value most highly. Markets can be very simple or highly organized. Markets are ancient and they are modern.

A simple and ancient market is one that the American historian Daniel J. Boorstin describes in *The Discoverers* (p. 161). In the late fourteenth century,

> *The Muslim caravans that went southward from Morocco across the Atlas Mountains arrived after twenty days at the shores of the Senegal River. There the Moroccan traders laid out separate piles of salt, of beads from Ceutan coral, and cheap manufactured goods. Then they retreated out of sight. The local tribesmen, who lived in the strip mines where they dug their gold, came to the shore and put a heap of gold beside each pile of Moroccan goods. Then they, in turn, went out of view, leaving the Moroccan traders either to take the gold offered for a particular pile or to reduce the pile of their merchandise to suit the offered price in gold. Once again the Moroccan traders withdrew, and the process went on. By this system of commercial etiquette, the Moroccans collected their gold.*

Auctions on eBay and U.S. government auctions of the airwaves that cellphone companies use are examples of organized and modern markets. Susan Athey, whom you will meet on the following page, is a world-renowned expert on the design of auctions.

Everything and anything that can be exchanged is traded in markets to the benefit of both buyers and sellers.

Alfred Marshall *(1842–1924) grew up in an England that was being transformed by the railroad and by the expansion of manufacturing. Mary Paley was one of Marshall's students at Cambridge, and when Alfred and Mary married, in 1877, celibacy rules barred Alfred from continuing to teach at Cambridge. By 1884, with more liberal rules, the Marshalls returned to Cambridge, where Alfred became Professor of Political Economy.*

Many economists had a hand in refining the demand and supply model, but the first thorough and complete statement of the model as we know it today was set out by Alfred Marshall, with the help of Mary Paley Marshall. Published in 1890, this monumental treatise, The Principles of Economics, *became the textbook on economics on both sides of the Atlantic for almost half a century.*

"The forces to be dealt with are ... so numerous, that it is best to take a few at a time. ... Thus we begin by isolating the primary relations of supply, demand, and price."

ALFRED MARSHALL
The Principles of Economics

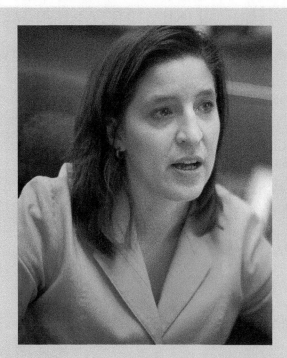

SUSAN ATHEY is Professor of Economics at Harvard University. Born in 1970, she completed high school in three years, wrapped up three majors—in economics, mathematics, and computer science—at Duke University at 20, completed her Ph.D. at Stanford University at 24, and was voted tenure at MIT and Stanford at 29. After teaching at MIT for six years and Stanford for five years, she moved to Harvard in 2006. Among her many honors and awards, the most prestigious is the John Bates Clark Medal given to the best economist under 40. She is the first woman to receive this award.

Professor Athey's research is broad both in scope and style. A government that wants to auction natural resources will turn to her fundamental discoveries (and possibly consult with her) before deciding how to organize the auction. An economist who wants to test a theory using a large data set will use her work on statistics and econometrics.

Michael Parkin talked with Susan Athey about her research, what economists have learned about designing markets, and her advice to students.

Professor Athey, what sparked your interest in economics?

I was studying mathematics and computer science, but I felt that the subjects were not as relevant as I would like. I discovered economics through a research project with a professor who was working on auctions. I had a summer job working for a firm that sold computers to the government through auctions. Eventually my professor, Bob Marshall, wrote two articles on the topic and testified before Congress to help reform the system for government procurement of computers. That really inspired me and showed me the power of economic ideas to change the world and to make things work more efficiently.

What is the connection between an auction and the supply and demand model?

The basic laws of supply and demand can be seen in evidence in an auction market like eBay. The more sellers that are selling similar products, the lower the prices they can expect to achieve. Similarly, the more buyers there are demanding those objects, the higher the prices the sellers can achieve.

*Read the full interview with Susan Athey in MyEconLab.

An important thing for an auction marketplace is to attract a good balance of buyers and sellers so that both the buyers and the sellers find it more profitable to transact in that marketplace rather than using some other mechanism. From a seller's perspective, the more bidders there are on the platform, the greater the demand and the higher the prices. And from the buyer's perspective, the more sellers there are on the platform, the greater the supply and the lower the prices.

> The basic laws of supply and demand can be seen in evidence in an auction market like eBay.

Can we think of an auction as a mechanism for finding the equilibrium price and quantity?

Exactly. We can think of the whole collection of auctions on eBay as being a mechanism to discover a market clearing price, and individual items might sell a little higher or a little lower but over all we believe that the prices on eBay auctions will represent equilibrium prices.

8

UTILITY AND DEMAND

After studying this chapter, you will be able to:

◆ Explain the limits to consumption and describe preferences using the concept of utility

◆ Explain the marginal utility theory of consumer choice

◆ Use marginal utility theory to predict the effects of changes in prices and incomes and to explain the paradox of value

◆ Describe some new ways of explaining consumer choices

You enjoy sugary drinks and sometimes, perhaps, drink more than is good for your health. What determines our choices about the quantity of sugary drinks we consume?

You know that diamonds are expensive and water is cheap. Doesn't that seem odd? Why do we place a higher value on useless diamonds than on essential-to-life water?

The theory of consumer choice that you're going to study in this chapter answers questions like the ones we've just posed. *Economics in the News* at the end of the chapter applies what you learn to a debate about whether sugary drinks should be banned or taxed to discourge their consumption.

Consumption Choices

The choices that you make as a buyer of goods and services—your consumption choices—are influenced by many factors. We can summarize them under two broad headings:

- Consumption possibilities
- Preferences

Consumption Possibilities

Your consumption possibilities are all the things that you can afford to buy. You can afford many different combinations of goods and services, but they are all limited by your income and by the prices that you must pay. For example, you might decide to spend a big part of your income on a gym membership and personal trainer and little on movies and music, or you might spend lots on movies and music and use the free gym at school.

The easiest way to describe consumption possibilities is to consider a model consumer who buys only two items. That's what we'll now do. We'll study the consumption possibilities of Lisa, who buys only movies and soda.

A Consumer's Budget Line Consumption possibilities are limited by income and by the prices of movies and soda. When Lisa spends all her income, she reaches the limits to her consumption possibilities. We describe this limit with a **budget line,** which marks the boundary between those combinations of goods and services that a household can afford to buy and those that it cannot afford.

Figure 8.1 illustrates Lisa's consumption possibilities of movies and soda and her budget line. Lisa has an income of $40 a month, the price of a movie is $8, and the price of soda is $4 a case. Rows *A* through *F* in the table show six possible ways of allocating $40 to these two goods. For example, in row *A* Lisa buys 10 cases of soda and sees no movies; in row *F* she sees 5 movies and buys no soda; and in row *C* she sees 2 movies and buys 6 cases of soda.

Points *A* through *F* in the graph illustrate the possibilities presented in the table, and the line passing through these points is Lisa's budget line.

The budget line constrains choices: It marks the boundary between what is affordable and unaffordable. Lisa can afford all the points on the budget line and inside it. Points outside the line are unaffordable.

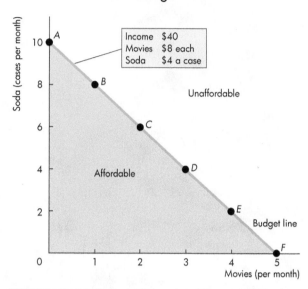

FIGURE 8.1   Lisa's Budget Line

Income	$40
Movies	$8 each
Soda	$4 a case

| | Movies | | Soda | |
Possibility	Quantity	Expenditure (dollars)	Cases	Expenditure (dollars)
A	0	0	10	40
B	1	8	8	32
C	2	16	6	24
D	3	24	4	16
E	4	32	2	8
F	5	40	0	0

The graph and the table show six possible ways in which Lisa can allocate $40 to movies and soda. In row *C* and at point *C*, she sees 2 movies and buys 6 cases of soda. The line *AF* is Lisa's budget line and is a boundary between what she can afford and what she cannot afford. Her choices must lie along the line *AF* or inside the orange area.

—————— MyEconLab Animation and Draw Graph ——————

Changes in Consumption Possibilities Consumption possibilities change when income or prices change. A rise in income shifts the budget line outward but leaves its slope unchanged. A change in a price changes the slope[1] of the line. Our goal is to predict the effects of such changes on consumption choices. To do so, we must determine the choice a consumer makes. The budget line shows what is possible; preferences determine which possibility is chosen. We'll now describe a consumer's preferences.

——————
[1] Chapter 9 explains an alternative model of consumer choice and pp. 203–204 provides some detail on how changes in income and prices change the budget line.

Preferences

Lisa's income and the prices that she faces limit her consumption choices, but she still has lots of choice. The choice that she makes depends on her **preferences**—a description of her likes and dislikes.

You saw one way that economists use to describe preferences in Chapter 2 (p. 36), the concept of *marginal benefit* and the *marginal benefit curve*. But you also saw in Chapter 5 (p. 108) that a marginal benefit curve is also a demand curve. The goal of a theory of consumer choice is to derive the demand curve from a deeper account of how consumers make their buying plans. That is, we want to *explain what determines demand and marginal benefit.*

To achieve this goal, we need a deeper way of describing preferences. One approach to this problem uses the idea of utility, and defines **utility** as the benefit or satisfaction that a person gets from the consumption of goods and services. We distinguish two utility concepts:

- Total utility
- Marginal utility

Total Utility The total benefit that a person gets from the consumption of all the different goods and services is called **total utility.** Total utility depends on the level of consumption—more consumption generally gives more total utility.

To illustrate the concept of total utility, think about Lisa's choices. We tell Lisa that we want to measure her utility from movies and soda. We can use any scale that we wish to measure her total utility and we give her two starting points: (1) We will call the total utility from no movies and no soda zero utility; and (2) we will call the total utility she gets from seeing 1 movie a month 50 units.

We then ask Lisa to tell us, using the same scale, how much she would like 2 movies, and more, up to 10 movies a month. We also ask her to tell us, on the same scale, how much she would like 1 case of soda a month, 2 cases, and more, up to 10 cases a month.

In Table 8.1, the columns headed "Total utility" show Lisa's answers. Looking at those numbers, you can say a lot about how much Lisa likes soda and movies. She says that 1 case of soda gives her 75 units of utility—50 percent more than the utility that she gets from seeing 1 movie. You can also see that her total utility from soda climbs more slowly than her total utility from movies. This difference turns on the second utility concept: *marginal utility.*

TABLE 8.1 Lisa's Utility from Movies and Soda

	Movies			Soda	
Quantity (per month)	Total utility	Marginal utility	Cases (per month)	Total utility	Marginal utility
0	0		0	0	
		 50			 75
1	50		1	75	
		 40			 48
2	90		2	123	
		 32			 36
3	122		3	159	
		 28			 24
4	150		4	183	
		 26			 22
5	176		5	205	
		 24			 20
6	200		6	225	
		 22			 13
7	222		7	238	
		 20			 10
8	242		8	248	
		 17			 7
9	259		9	255	
		 16			 5
10	275		10	260	

Marginal Utility We define **marginal utility** as the *change* in total utility that results from a one-unit increase in the quantity of a good consumed.

In Table 8.1, the columns headed "Marginal utility" show Lisa's marginal utility from movies and soda. You can see that if Lisa increases the soda she buys from 1 to 2 cases a month, her total utility from soda increases from 75 units to 123 units. For Lisa, the marginal utility from the second case each month is 48 units (123 − 75).

The marginal utility numbers appear midway between the quantities of soda because it is the *change* in the quantity she buys from 1 to 2 cases that produces the marginal utility of 48 units.

Marginal utility is *positive,* but it *diminishes* as the quantity of a good consumed increases.

Positive Marginal Utility All the things that people enjoy and want more of have a positive marginal utility. Some objects and activities can generate negative marginal utility—and lower total utility. Two examples are hard labor and polluted air. But all the goods and services that people value and that we are thinking about here have positive marginal utility: Total utility increases as the quantity consumed increases.

Diminishing Marginal Utility As Lisa sees more movies, her total utility from movies increases but her marginal utility from movies decreases. Similarly, as she

FIGURE 8.2   Total Utility and Marginal Utility

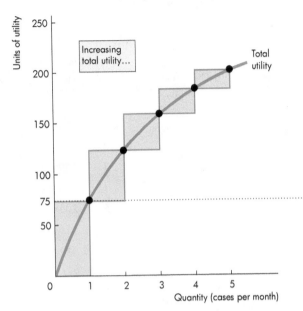

The figure graphs Lisa's total utility and marginal utility from soda based on the numbers for the first 5 cases of soda a month in Table 8.1. Part (a) shows her total utility—increasing total utility. The bars along the total utility curve show the extra total utility from each additional case of soda—marginal utility. Part (b) shows Lisa's diminishing marginal utility from soda.

(a) Total utility   **(b) Marginal utility**

MyEconLab Animation

---

consumes more soda, her total utility from soda increases but her marginal utility from soda decreases.

The tendency for marginal utility to decrease as the consumption of a good increases is so general and universal that we give it the status of a *principle*—the principle of **diminishing marginal utility.**

You can see Lisa's diminishing marginal utility by calculating a few numbers. Her marginal utility from soda decreases from 75 units from the first case to 48 units from the second case and to 36 units from the third. Her marginal utility from movies decreases from 50 units for the first movie to 40 units for the second and 32 units for the third. Lisa's marginal utility diminishes as she buys more of each good.

Your Diminishing Marginal Utility You've been studying all day and into the evening, and you've been too busy finishing an assignment to shop for soda. A friend drops by with a can of soda. The utility you get from that soda is the marginal utility from your first soda of the day—from *one* can. On another day you've been on a soda binge. You've been working on an assignment, but you've guzzled 10 cans of soda while doing so, and are now totally wired. You are happy enough to have one more can, but the thrill that you get from it is not very large. It is the marginal utility from the *eleventh* can in a day.

Graphing Lisa's Utility Schedules Figure 8.2(a) illustrates Lisa's total utility from soda. The more soda Lisa consumes in a month, the more total utility she gets. Her total utility curve slopes upward.

Figure 8.2(b) illustrates Lisa's marginal utility from soda. It is a graph of the marginal utility numbers in Table 8.1. This graph shows Lisa's diminishing marginal utility from soda. Her marginal utility curve slopes downward as she consumes more soda.

We've described Lisa's consumption possibilities and preferences. Your next task is to see how Lisa chooses what to consume.

◆ REVIEW QUIZ

1 Explain how a consumer's income and the prices of goods limit consumption possibilities.
2 What is utility and how do we use the concept of utility to describe a consumer's preferences?
3 What is the distinction between total utility and marginal utility?
4 What is the key assumption about marginal utility?

Work these questions in Study Plan 8.1 and get instant feedback. Do a Key Terms Quiz.   MyEconLab

Utility-Maximizing Choice

Consumers want to get the most utility possible from their limited resources. They make the choice that maximizes utility. To discover this choice, we combine the constraint imposed by the budget and the consumer's preferences and find the point on the budget line that gives the consumer the maximum attainable utility. Let's find Lisa's utility-maximizing choice.

A Spreadsheet Solution

Lisa's most direct way of finding the quantities of movies and soda that maximize her utility is to make a table in a spreadsheet with the information and calculations shown in Table 8.2. Let's see what that table tells us.

Find the Just-Affordable Combinations Table 8.2 shows the combinations of movies and soda that Lisa can afford and that exhaust her $40 income. For example, in row A, Lisa buys only soda and at $4 a case she can buy 10 cases. In row B, Lisa sees 1 movie and buys 8 cases of soda. She spends $8 on the movie. At $4 a case, she spends $32 on soda and can buy 8 cases. The combination in row B just exhausts her $40. The combinations shown in the table are the same as those plotted on her budget line in Fig. 8.1.

We noted that the budget line shows that Lisa can also afford any combination *inside* the budget line. The quantities in those combinations would be smaller than the ones shown in Table 8.2 and they do not exhaust her $40. But smaller quantities don't maximize her utility. Why? The marginal utilities of movies and soda are positive, so the more of each that Lisa buys, the more total utility she gets.

Find the Total Utility for Each Just-Affordable Combination Table 8.2 shows the total utility that Lisa gets from the just-affordable quantities of movies and soda. The second and third columns show the numbers for movies and the fourth and fifth columns show those for soda. The center column adds the total utility from movies to the total utility from soda. This number, the total utility from movies *and* soda, is what Lisa wants to maximize.

In row A of the table, Lisa sees no movies and buys 10 cases of soda. She gets no utility from movies and 260 units of utility from soda. Her total utility from movies and soda (the center column) is 260 units.

TABLE 8.2 Lisa's Utility-Maximizing Choice

	Movies $8		Total utility from movies and soda	Soda $4	
	Quantity (per month)	Total utility		Total utility	Cases (per month)
A	0	0	260	260	10
B	1	50	298	248	8
C	2	90	315	225	6
D	3	122	305	183	4
E	4	150	273	123	2
F	5	176	176	0	0

In row C of the table, Lisa sees 2 movies and buys 6 cases of soda. She gets 90 units of utility from movies and 225 units of utility from soda. Her total utility from movies and soda is 315 units. This combination of movies and soda maximizes Lisa's total utility. That is, given the prices of movies and soda, Lisa's best choice when she has $40 to spend is to see 2 movies and buy 6 cases of soda.

If Lisa sees 1 movie, she can buy 8 cases of soda, but she gets only 298 units of total utility—17 units less than the maximum attainable. If she sees 3 movies, she can buy only 4 cases of soda. She gets 305 units of total utility—10 units less than the maximum attainable.

Consumer Equilibrium We've just described Lisa's consumer equilibrium. A **consumer equilibrium** is a situation in which a consumer has allocated all of his or her available income in the way that maximizes his or her total utility, given the prices of goods and services. Lisa's consumer equilibrium is 2 movies and 6 cases of soda.

To find Lisa's consumer equilibrium, we did something that an economist might do but that a consumer is not likely to do: We measured her total utility from all the affordable combinations of movies and soda and then, by inspection of the numbers, selected the combination that gives the highest total utility. There is a more natural way of finding a consumer's equilibrium—a way that uses the idea that choices are made at the margin, as you first met in Chapter 1. Let's look at this approach.

Choosing at the Margin

When you go shopping you don't do utility calculations. But you do decide how to allocate your budget, and you do so in a way that you think is best for you. If you could make yourself better off by spending a few more dollars on an extra unit of one item and the same number of dollars less on something else, you would make that change. So, when you've allocated your budget in the best possible way, you can't make yourself better off by spending more on one item and less on others.

Marginal Utility per Dollar Economists interpret your best possible choice by using the idea of marginal utility per dollar. *Marginal utility* is the increase in total utility that results from consuming *one more unit* of a good. **Marginal utility per dollar** is the *marginal utility* from a good that results from spending *one more dollar* on it.

The distinction between these two marginal concepts is clearest for a good that is infinitely divisible, such as gasoline. You can buy gasoline by the smallest fraction of a gallon and literally choose to spend one more or one less dollar at the pump. The increase in total utility that results from spending one more dollar at the pump is the marginal utility per dollar from gasoline. When you buy a movie ticket or a case of soda, you must spend your dollars in bigger lumps. To buy our marginal movie ticket or case of soda, you must spend the price of one unit and your total utility increases by the marginal utility from that item. So to calculate the marginal utility per dollar for movies (or soda), we must divide marginal utility from the good by its price.

Call the marginal utility from movies MU_M and the price of a movie P_M. Then the *marginal utility per dollar from movies* is

$$MU_M/P_M.$$

Call the marginal utility from soda MU_S and the price of a case of soda P_S. Then the *marginal utility per dollar from soda* is

$$MU_S/P_S.$$

By comparing the marginal utility per dollar from all the goods that a person buys, we can determine whether the budget has been allocated in the way that maximizes total utility.

Let's see how we use the marginal utility per dollar to define a utility-maximizing rule.

Utility-Maximizing Rule A consumer's total utility is maximized by following the rule:

- Spend all the available income.
- Equalize the marginal utility per dollar for all goods.

Spend All the Available Income Because more consumption brings more utility, only those choices that exhaust income can maximize utility. For Lisa, combinations of movies and soda that leave her with money to spend don't give her as much total utility as those that exhaust her $40 per month income.

Equalize the Marginal Utility per Dollar The basic idea behind this rule is to move dollars from good B to good A if doing so increases the utility from good A by more than it decreases the utility from good B. Such a utility-increasing move is possible if the marginal utility per dollar from good A *exceeds* that from good B.

But buying more of good A decreases its marginal utility. And buying less of good B increases its marginal utility. So by moving dollars from good B to good A, total utility rises, and the gap between the marginal utilities per dollar gets smaller.

As long as the gap exists—as long as the marginal utility per dollar from good A exceeds that from good B—total utility can be increased by spending more on A and less on B. But when enough dollars have been moved from B to A to make the two marginal utilities per dollar equal, total utility cannot be increased further. Total utility is maximized.

Lisa's Marginal Calculation Let's apply the basic idea to Lisa. To calculate Lisa's marginal utility per dollar, we divide her marginal utility numbers for each quantity of each good by the price of the good. The table in Fig. 8.3 shows these calculations for Lisa, and the graph illustrates the situation on Lisa's budget line. The rows of the table are three of her affordable combinations of movies and soda.

Too Much Soda and Too Few Movies In row B, Lisa sees 1 movie a month and consumes 8 cases of soda a month. Her marginal utility from seeing 1 movie a month is 50 units. Because the price of a movie is $8, Lisa's marginal utility per dollar from movies is 50 units divided by $8, or 6.25 units of utility per dollar.

Lisa's marginal utility from soda when she consumes 8 cases of soda a month is 10 units. Because the price of soda is $4 a case, Lisa's marginal utility per dollar from soda is 10 units divided by $4, or 2.50 units of utility per dollar.

When Lisa sees 1 movie and consumes 8 cases of soda a month, her marginal utility per dollar from soda is *less than* her marginal utility per dollar from movies. That is,

$$MU_S/P_S < MU_M/P_M.$$

If Lisa spent an extra dollar on movies and a dollar less on soda, her total utility would increase. She would get 6.25 units from the extra dollar spent on movies and lose 2.50 units from the dollar less spent on soda. Her total utility would increase by 3.75 units (6.25 − 2.50).

Too Little Soda and Too Many Movies In row *D*, Lisa sees 3 movies a month and consumes 4 cases of soda. Her marginal utility from seeing the third movie a month is 32 units. At a price of $8 a movie, Lisa's marginal utility per dollar from movies is 32 units divided by $8, or 4 units of utility per dollar.

Lisa's marginal utility from soda when she buys 4 cases a month is 24 units. At a price of $4 a case, Lisa's marginal utility per dollar from soda is 24 units divided by $4, or 6 units of utility per dollar.

When Lisa sees 3 movies and consumes 4 cases of soda a month, her marginal utility per dollar from soda *exceeds* her marginal utility per dollar from movies. That is,

$$MU_S/P_S > MU_M/P_M.$$

If Lisa spent an extra dollar on soda and a dollar less on movies, her total utility would increase. She would get 6 units from the extra dollar spent on soda and she would lose 4 units from the dollar less spent on movies. Her total utility would increase by 2 units (6 − 4).

Utility-Maximizing Movies and Soda In Fig. 8.3, if Lisa moves from row *B* to row *C*, she increases the movies she sees from 1 to 2 a month and decreases the soda she consumes from 8 to 6 cases a month. Her marginal utility per dollar from movies falls to 5 and her marginal utility per dollar from soda rises to 5.

Similarly, if Lisa moves from row *D* to row *C*, she decreases the movies she sees from 3 to 2 a month and increases the soda she consumes from 4 to 6 cases a month. Her marginal utility per dollar from movies rises to 5 and her marginal utility per dollar from soda falls to 5.

When Lisa sees 2 movies and consumes 6 cases of soda a month, her marginal utility per dollar from soda *equals* her marginal utility per dollar from

FIGURE 8.3 Equalizing Marginal Utilities per Dollar

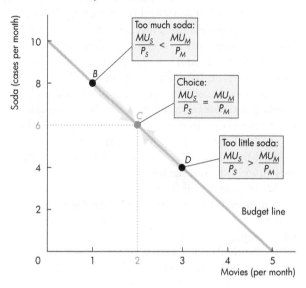

The graph shows Lisa's budget line and identifies three points on it. The rows of the table describe these points.

At point *B* (row *B*), with 1 movie and 8 cases of soda, Lisa's marginal utility per dollar from soda is less than that from movies: Buy less soda and see more movies.

At point *D* (row *D*), with 3 movies and 4 cases of soda, Lisa's marginal utility per dollar from soda is greater than that from movies: Buy more soda and see fewer movies.

At point *C* (row *C*), with 2 movies and 6 cases of soda, Lisa's marginal utility per dollar from soda is equal to that from movies: Lisa's utility is maximized.

MyEconLab Animation and Draw Graph

	Movies ($8 each)			Soda ($4 per case)		
	Quantity	Marginal utility	Marginal utility per dollar	Cases	Marginal utility	Marginal utility per dollar
B	1	50	6.25	8	10	2.50
C	2	40	5.00	6	20	5.00
D	3	32	4.00	4	24	6.00

movies. That is,

$$MU_S/P_S = MU_M/P_M.$$

Lisa can't move from this allocation of her budget without making herself worse off.

The Power of Marginal Analysis

The method we've just used to find Lisa's utility-maximizing choice of movies and soda is an example of the power of marginal analysis. Lisa doesn't need a computer and a spreadsheet program to maximize utility. She can achieve this goal by comparing the marginal gain from having more of one good with the marginal loss from having less of another good.

The rule that she follows is simple: If the marginal utility per dollar from movies exceeds the marginal utility per dollar from soda, see more movies and buy less soda; if the marginal utility per dollar from soda exceeds the marginal utility per dollar from movies, buy more soda and see fewer movies.

More generally, if the marginal gain from an action exceeds the marginal loss, take the action. You will meet this principle time and again in your study of economics, and you will find yourself using it when you make your own economic choices, especially when you must make big decisions.

Revealing Preferences

When we introduced the idea of utility, we arbitrarily chose 50 units as Lisa's total utility from 1 movie, and we pretended that we asked Lisa to tell us how many units of utility she got from different quantities of soda and movies.

You're now about to discover that we don't need to ask Lisa to tell us her preferences. We can figure them out for ourselves by observing what she buys at various prices.

Also, the units in which we measure Lisa's preferences don't matter. Any arbitrary units will work. In this respect, utility is like temperature. Predictions about the freezing point of water don't depend on the temperature scale; and predictions about a household's consumption choice don't depend on the units of utility.

Lisa's Preferences In maximizing total utility by making the marginal utility per dollar equal for all goods, the units in which utility is measured do not matter.

You've seen that when Lisa maximizes her total utility, her marginal utility per dollar from soda, MU_S/P_S, equals her marginal utility per dollar from movies, MU_M/P_M. That is,

$$MU_S/P_S = MU_M/P_M.$$

Multiply both sides of this equation by the price of soda, P_S, to obtain

$$MU_S = MU_M \times (P_S/P_M).$$

This equation says that the marginal utility from soda, MU_S, is equal to the marginal utility from movies, MU_M, multiplied by the ratio of the price of soda, P_S, to the price of a movie, P_M.

The ratio P_S/P_M is the relative price of soda in terms of movies: It is the number of movies that must be forgone to get 1 case of soda. It is also the opportunity cost of soda. (See Chapter 2, p. 33 and Chapter 3, p. 56.)

For Lisa, when $P_M = \$8$ and $P_S = \$4$ we observe that in a month she goes to the movies twice and buys 6 cases of soda. So we know that her MU_S from 6 cases of soda equals her MU_M from 2 movies multiplied by $\$4/\$8$ or 0.5. That is, for Lisa, the marginal utility from 6 cases of soda equals one-half of the marginal utility from 2 movies.

If we observe the choices that Lisa makes at more prices, we can find more rows in her utility schedule. By her choices, Lisa reveals her preferences.

Units of Utility Don't Matter Lisa's marginal utility from 6 cases of soda is one-half of her marginal utility from 2 movies. So if the marginal utility from the second movie is 40 units, then the marginal utility from the sixth case of soda is 20 units. But if we call the marginal utility from the second movie 50 units, then the marginal utility from the sixth case of soda is 25 units. The units of utility are arbitrary.

◆ REVIEW QUIZ

1 Why does a consumer spend the entire budget?
2 What is the marginal utility per dollar and how is it calculated?
3 What two conditions are met when a consumer is maximizing utility?
4 Explain why equalizing the marginal utility per dollar for all goods maximizes utility.

Work these questions in Study Plan 8.2 and get instant feedback. Do a Key Terms Quiz.   MyEconLab

You now understand the marginal utility theory of consumer choices. Your next task is to see what the theory predicts.

Predictions of Marginal Utility Theory

We're now going to use marginal utility theory to make some predictions. You will see that marginal utility theory predicts the law of demand. The theory also predicts that a fall in the price of a substitute of a good decreases the demand for the good and that for a normal good, a rise in income increases demand. All these effects, which in Chapter 3 we simply assumed, are predictions of marginal utility theory.

To derive these predictions, we will study the effects of three events:

- A fall in the price of a movie
- A rise in the price of soda
- A rise in income

A Fall in the Price of a Movie

With the price of a movie at $8 and the price of soda at $4, Lisa is maximizing utility by seeing 2 movies and buying 6 cases of soda each month. Then, with no change in her $40 income and no change in the price of soda, the price of a movie falls from $8 to $4. How does Lisa change her buying plans?

Finding the New Quantities of Movies and Soda
You can find the effect of a fall in the price of a movie on the quantities of movies and soda that Lisa buys in a three-step calculation.

1. Determine the just-affordable combinations of movies and soda at the new prices.
2. Calculate the new marginal utilities per dollar from the good whose price has changed.
3. Determine the quantities of movies and soda that make their marginal utilities per dollar equal.

Affordable Combinations The lower price of a movie means that Lisa can afford more movies or more soda. Table 8.3 shows her new affordable combinations. In row *A*, if she continues to see 2 movies a month, she can now afford 8 cases of soda and in row *B*, if she continues to buy 6 cases of soda, she can now afford 4 movies. Lisa can afford any of the combinations shown in the rows of Table 8.3.

The next step is to find her new marginal utilities per dollar from movies.

New Marginal Utilities per Dollar from Movies A person's preferences don't change just because a price has changed. With no change in her preferences, Lisa's marginal utilities in Table 8.3 are the same as those in Table 8.1. But because the price of a movie has changed, the marginal utility *per dollar* from movies changes. In fact, with a halving of the price of a movie from $8 to $4, the marginal utility per dollar from movies has doubled.

The numbers in Table 8.3 show Lisa's new marginal utility per dollar from movies for each quantity of movies. The table also shows Lisa's marginal utility per dollar from soda for each quantity.

Equalizing the Marginal Utilities per Dollar You can see that if Lisa continues to see 2 movies a month and buy 6 cases of soda, her marginal utility per dollar from movies (row *A*) is 10 units and her marginal utility per dollar from soda (row *B*) is 5 units. Lisa is buying too much soda and too few movies. If she spends a dollar more on movies and a dollar less on soda, her total utility increases by 5 units (10 − 5).

If Lisa continues to buy 6 cases of soda and increases the number of movies to 4 (row *B*), her

TABLE 8.3 How a Change in the Price of Movies Affects Lisa's Choices

	Movies ($4 each)			Soda ($4 per case)		
	Quantity	Marginal utility	Marginal utility per dollar	Cases	Marginal utility	Marginal utility per dollar
	0	0		10	5	1.25
	1	50	12.50	9	7	1.75
A	2	40	**10.00**	8	10	2.50
	3	32	8.00	7	13	3.25
B	4	28	7.00	**6**	20	**5.00**
	5	26	6.50	5	22	5.50
C	6	24	6.00	4	24	6.00
	7	22	5.50	3	36	9.00
	8	20	5.00	2	48	12.00
	9	17	4.25	1	75	18.75
	10	16	4.00	0	0	

marginal utility per dollar from movies falls to 7 units, but her marginal utility per dollar from soda is 5 units. Lisa is still buying too much soda and seeing too few movies. If she spends a dollar more on movies and a dollar less on soda, her total utility increases by 2 units $(7 - 5)$.

But if Lisa sees 6 movies and buys 4 cases of soda a month (row C), her marginal utility per dollar from movies (6 units) equals her marginal utility per dollar from soda and she is maximizing utility. If Lisa moves from this allocation of her budget in either direction, her total utility decreases.

Lisa's increased purchases of movies results from a substitution effect—she substitutes the now lower-priced movies for soda—and an income effect—she can afford more movies.

A Change in the Quantity Demanded Lisa's increase in the quantity of movies that she sees is a change in the quantity demanded. It is the change in the quantity of movies that she plans to see each month when the price of a movie changes and all other influences on buying plans remain the same. We illustrate a change in the quantity demanded by a movement along a demand curve.

Figure 8.4(a) shows Lisa's demand curve for movies. When the price of a movie is $8, Lisa sees 2 movies a month. When the price of a movie falls to $4, she sees 6 movies a month. Lisa moves downward along her demand curve for movies.

The demand curve traces the quantities that maximize utility at each price, with all other influences remaining the same. You can also see that utility-maximizing choices generate a downward-sloping demand curve. Utility maximization with diminishing marginal utility implies the law of demand.

A Change in Demand The decrease in the quantity of soda that Lisa buys is the change in the quantity of soda that she plans to buy at a given price of soda when the price of a movie changes. It is a change in her demand for soda. We illustrate a change in demand by a shift of a demand curve.

Figure 8.4(b) shows Lisa's demand curve for soda. The price of soda is fixed at $4 a case. When the price of a movie is $8, Lisa buys 6 cases of soda on demand curve D_0. When the price of a movie falls to $4, Lisa buys 4 cases of soda on demand curve D_1. The fall in the price of a movie decreases Lisa's demand for soda. Her demand curve for soda shifts leftward. For Lisa, soda and movies are substitutes.

FIGURE 8.4   A Fall in the Price of a Movie

(a) Demand for movies

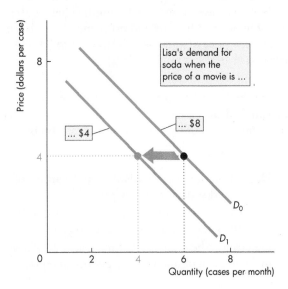

(b) Demand for soda

When the price of a movie falls and the price of soda remains the same, the quantity of movies demanded by Lisa increases, and in part (a), Lisa moves along her demand curve for movies. Also, when the price of a movie falls, Lisa's demand for soda decreases, and in part (b), her demand curve for soda shifts leftward. For Lisa, soda and movies are substitutes.

MyEconLab Animation

A Rise in the Price of Soda

Now suppose that with the price of a movie at $4, the price of soda rises from $4 to $8 a case. How does this price change influence Lisa's buying plans? We find the answer by repeating the three-step calculation with the new price of soda.

Table 8.4 shows Lisa's new affordable combinations. In row *A*, if she continues to buy 4 cases of soda a month she can afford to see only 2 movies; and in row *B*, if she continues to see 6 movies a month, she can afford only 2 cases of soda.

Table 8.4 show Lisa's marginal utility per dollar from soda for each quantity of soda when the price is $8 a case. The table also shows Lisa's marginal utility per dollar from movies for each quantity.

If Lisa continues to buy 4 cases of soda (row *A*), her marginal utility per dollar from soda is 3. But she must cut the movies she sees to 2, which increases her marginal utility per dollar from movies to 10. Lisa is buying too much soda and too few movies. If she spends a dollar less on soda and a dollar more on movies, her utility increases by 7 units (10 − 3).

But if Lisa sees 6 movies a month and cuts her soda to 2 cases (row *B*), her marginal utility per dollar from movies (6 units) equals her marginal utility per dollar from soda. She is maximizing utility.

Lisa's decreased purchases of soda results from an income effect—she can afford fewer cases and she buys fewer cases. But she continues to buy the same quantity of movies.

Lisa's Demand for Soda Now that we've calculated the effect of a change in the price of soda on Lisa's buying plans when income and the price of movies remain the same, we have found two points on her demand curve for soda: When the price of soda is $4 a case, Lisa buys 4 cases a month; and when the price of soda is $8 a case, she buys 2 cases a month.

Figure 8.5 shows these points on Lisa's demand curve for soda. It also shows the change in the quantity of soda demanded when the price of soda rises and all other influences on Lisa's buying plans remain the same.

In this example, Lisa continues to buy the same quantity of movies, but this outcome does not always occur. It is a consequence of Lisa's preferences. With different marginal utilities, she might have decreased or increased the quantity of movies that she sees when the price of soda changes.

You've seen that marginal utility theory predicts the law of demand—the way in which the quantity demanded of a good changes when its price changes. Next, we'll see how marginal utility theory predicts the effect of a change in income on demand.

TABLE 8.4 How a Change in the Price of Soda Affects Lisa's Choices

	Movies ($4 each)			Soda ($8 per case)		
	Quantity	Marginal utility	Marginal utility per dollar	Cases	Marginal utility	Marginal utility per dollar
	0	0		5	22	2.75
A	2	40	10.00	**4**	24	**3.00**
	4	28	7.00	3	36	4.50
B	6	24	6.00	2	48	6.00
	8	20	5.00	1	75	9.38
	10	16	4.00	0	0	

FIGURE 8.5 A Rise in the Price of Soda

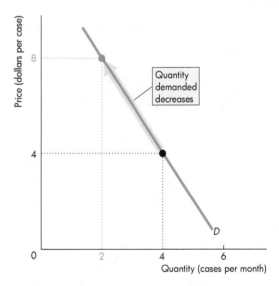

When the price of soda rises and the price of a movie and Lisa's income remain the same, the quantity of soda demanded by Lisa decreases. Lisa moves along her demand curve for soda.

A Rise in Income

Suppose that Lisa's income increases from $40 to $56 a month and that the price of a movie is $4 and the price of soda is $4 a case. With these prices and with an income of $40 a month, Lisa sees 6 movies and buys 4 cases of soda a month (Table 8.3). How does the increase in Lisa's income from $40 to $56 change her buying plans?

Table 8.5 shows the calculations needed to answer this question. If Lisa continues to see 6 movies a month, she can now afford to buy 8 cases of soda (row *A*); if she continues to buy 4 cases of soda, she can now afford to see 10 movies (row *C*).

In row *A*, Lisa's marginal utility per dollar from movies is greater than her marginal utility per dollar from soda. She is buying too much soda and too few movies. In row *C*, Lisa's marginal utility per dollar from movies is less than her marginal utility per dollar from soda. She is buying too little soda and too many movies. But in row *B*, when Lisa sees 8 movies a month and buys 6 cases of soda, her marginal utility per dollar from movies equals that from soda. She is maximizing utility.

Figure 8.6 shows the effects of the rise in Lisa's income on her demand curves for movies and soda. The price of each good is $4. When Lisa's income

TABLE 8.5   Lisa's Choices with an Income of $56 a Month

	Movies ($4 each)			Soda ($4 per case)		
	Quantity	Marginal utility	Marginal utility per dollar	Cases	Marginal utility	Marginal utility per dollar
	4	28	7.00	10	5	1.25
	5	26	6.50	9	7	1.75
A	6	24	**6.00**	8	10	2.50
	7	22	5.50	7	13	3.25
B	8	20	5.00	6	20	5.00
	9	17	4.25	5	22	5.50
C	10	16	4.00	4	24	**6.00**

rises to $56 a month, she sees 2 more movies and buys 2 more cases of soda. Her demand curves for both movies and soda shift rightward—her demand for both movies and soda increases. With a larger income, the consumer always buys more of a *normal* good. For Lisa, movies and soda are normal goods.

FIGURE 8.6   The Effects of a Rise in Income

(a) Demand for movies

(b) Demand for soda

When Lisa's income increases, her demand for movies and her demand for soda increase. Lisa's demand curves

for movies, in part (a), and for soda, in part (b), shift rightward. For Lisa, movies and soda are normal goods.

The Paradox of Value

The price of water is low and the price of a diamond is high, but water is essential to life while diamonds are used mostly for decoration. How can valuable water be so cheap while a relatively useless diamond is so expensive? This so-called *paradox of value* has puzzled philosophers for centuries. Not until the theory of marginal utility had been developed could anyone give a satisfactory answer.

The Paradox Resolved The paradox is resolved by distinguishing between *total* utility and *marginal* utility. The total utility that we get from water is enormous. But remember, the more we consume of something, the smaller is its marginal utility.

We use so much water that its marginal utility—the benefit we get from one more glass of water or another 30 seconds in the shower—diminishes to a small value.

Diamonds, on the other hand, have a small total utility relative to water, but because we buy few diamonds, they have a high marginal utility.

When a household has maximized its total utility, it has allocated its income in the way that makes the marginal utility per dollar equal for all goods. That is, the marginal utility from a good divided by the price of the good is equal for all goods.

This equality of marginal utilities per dollar holds true for diamonds and water: Diamonds have a high price and a high marginal utility. Water has a low price and a low marginal utility. When the high marginal utility from diamonds is divided by the high price of a diamond, the result is a number that equals the low marginal utility from water divided by the low price of water. The marginal utility per dollar is the same for diamonds and water.

Value and Consumer Surplus Another way to think about the paradox of value and illustrate how it is resolved uses *consumer surplus*. Figure 8.7 explains the paradox of value by using this idea. The supply of water in part (a) is perfectly elastic at price P_W, so the quantity of water consumed is Q_W and the large green area shows the consumer surplus from water. The supply of diamonds in part (b) is perfectly inelastic at the quantity Q_D, so the price of a diamond is P_D and the small green area shows the consumer surplus from diamonds. Water is cheap, but brings a large consumer surplus; diamonds are expensive, but bring a small consumer surplus.

FIGURE 8.7 The Paradox of Value

(a) Water

(b) Diamonds

Part (a) shows the demand for and supply of water. Supply is perfectly elastic at the price P_W. At this price, the quantity of water consumed is Q_W and the large green triangle shows consumer surplus. Part (b) shows the demand for and supply of diamonds. Supply is perfectly inelastic at the quantity Q_D. At this quantity, the price of a diamond is P_D and the small green triangle shows consumer surplus. Water is valuable—has a large consumer surplus—but cheap. Diamonds are less valuable than water—have a smaller consumer surplus—but are expensive.

MyEconLab Animation and Draw Graph

Temperature: An Analogy

Utility is similar to temperature—both are abstract concepts. You can't *observe* temperature. You can observe water turning to steam if it is hot enough or turning to ice if it is cold enough. You can also construct an instrument—a thermometer—that can help you to predict when such changes will occur. We call the scale on the thermometer *temperature* and we call the units of temperature *degrees*. But like the units of utility, these degree units are arbitrary. We can use Celsius units or Fahrenheit units or some other units.

The concept of utility helps us to make predictions about consumption choices in much the same way that the concept of temperature helps us to make predictions about physical phenomena.

Admittedly, marginal utility theory does not enable us to predict how buying plans change with the same precision that a thermometer enables us to predict when water will turn to ice or steam. But the theory provides important insights into buying plans and has some powerful implications. It helps us to understand why people buy more of a good or service when its price falls and why people buy more of most goods when their incomes increase. It also resolves the paradox of value.

We're going to end this chapter by looking at some new ways of studying individual economic choices and consumer behavior.

◆ REVIEW QUIZ

1 When the price of a good falls and the prices of other goods and a consumer's income remain the same, explain what happens to the consumption of the good whose price has fallen and to the consumption of other goods.

2 Elaborate on your answer to the previous question by using demand curves. For which good does demand change and for which good does the quantity demanded change?

3 If a consumer's income increases and if all goods are normal goods, explain how the quantity bought of each good changes.

4 What is the paradox of value and how is the paradox resolved?

5 What are the similarities between utility and temperature?

Work these questions in Study Plan 8.3 and get instant feedback.   MyEconLab

ECONOMICS IN ACTION

Maximizing Utility from Recorded Music

In 2012, Americans spent $7 billion on recorded music, down from more than $14 billion in 2000. But the combined quantity of discs and downloads bought increased from 1 billion in 2000 to 1.6 billion in 2012 and the average price of a unit of recorded music fell from $14.00 to $3.90.

The average price fell because the mix of formats bought changed dramatically. In 2001, we bought 900 million CDs; in 2012, we bought only 211 million CDs and downloaded 1.4 billion music files. Figure 1 shows the longer history of the changing formats of recorded music.

The music that we buy isn't just one good—it is several goods. Singles and albums are different goods; downloads and discs are different goods; and downloads to a computer and downloads to a cellphone are different goods. There are five major categories and the table shows the quantities of each that we bought in 2012 (excluding DVDs and cassettes).

Format	Singles	Albums
	(millions in 2012)	
Disc	211	241
Download	1,400	105
Mobile	116	–

Source of data: Recording Industry Association of America.

Most people buy all their music in digital form, but many still buy physical CDs and some people buy both downloads and CDs.

We get utility from the singles and albums that we buy, and the more songs and albums we have, the more utility we get. But our marginal utility from songs and albums decreases as the quantity that we own increases.

We also get utility from convenience. A song that we can buy with a mouse click and play with the spin of a wheel is more convenient both to buy and to use than a song on a CD. The convenience of songs downloaded over the Internet means that, song for song, we get more utility from a song downloaded than we get from a song on a physical CD.

But most albums are still played at home on a CD player. So for most people, a physical CD is a more convenient medium for delivering an album. Album for album, people on average get more utility from a CD than from a download.

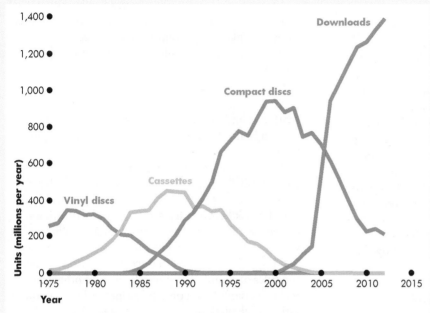

Figure 1 Changing Formats of Recorded Music

Sources of data: U.S. Census Bureau, *The 2012 Statistical Abstract*, Table 1140; and the Recording Industry Association of America.

In the 1970s, recorded music came on vinyl discs. Cassettes gradually replaced vinyl, then compact discs (CDs) gradually replaced cassettes, and today, digital files downloaded to computers and mobile devices are replacing physical CDs.

When we decide how many singles and albums to download and how many to buy on CD, we compare the marginal utility per dollar from each type of music in each format. We make the marginal utility per dollar from each type of music in each format equal, as the equations below show.

The market for single downloads has created an enormous consumer surplus. Figure 2 shows the demand curve for singles. One point on the demand curve is the 2001 price and quantity—100 million singles were bought at an average price of $5.00. Another point on the demand curve is that for 2012—1,400 million singles downloaded at $1.20 each.

If the demand curve has not shifted and is linear (assumed here), we can calculate the increase in consumer surplus generated by the fall in the price and the increase in the quantity demanded. The green area of the figure shows this increase in consumer surplus.

Consumer surplus increases by ($5.00 − $1.20) = $3.80 on the first 100 million and by $3.80 × 1,300/2 on the additional 1,300 singles. So the increase in consumer surplus is $2.85 billion.

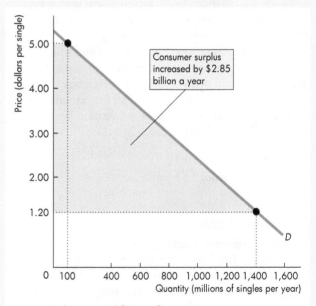

Figure 2 The Demand for Singles

$$\frac{MU_{single\ downloads}}{P_{single\ downloads}} = \frac{MU_{album\ downloads}}{P_{album\ downloads}} = \frac{MU_{physical\ singles}}{P_{physical\ singles}} = \frac{MU_{physical\ albums}}{P_{physical\ albums}} = \frac{MU_{mobile}}{P_{mobile}}$$

$$\frac{MU_{single\ downloads}}{\$1.20} = \frac{MU_{album\ downloads}}{\$10.99} = \frac{MU_{physical\ singles}}{\$4.76} = \frac{MU_{physical\ albums}}{\$9.99} = \frac{MU_{mobile}}{\$2.39}$$

▶ New Ways of Explaining Consumer Choices

When William Stanley Jevons developed marginal utility theory in the 1860s, he would have loved to look inside people's brains and "see" their utility. But he believed that the human brain was the ultimate black box that could never be observed directly. For Jevons, and for most economists today, the purpose of marginal utility theory is to explain our *actions*, not what goes on inside our brains.

Economics has developed over the past 150 years with little help from and paying little attention to advances being made in psychology. Both economics and psychology seek to explain human behavior, but they have developed different ways of attacking the challenge.

A few researchers *have* paid attention to the potential payoff from exploring economic problems by using the tools of psychology. These researchers, some economists and some psychologists, think that marginal utility theory is based on a view of how people make choices that attributes too much to reason and rationality. They propose an alternative approach based on the methods of psychology.

Other researchers, some economists and some neuroscientists, are using new tools to look inside the human brain and open up Jevons' "black box."

This section provides a very brief introduction to these new and exciting areas of economics. We'll explore the two related research agendas:

- Behavioral economics
- Neuroeconomics

Behavioral Economics

Behavioral economics studies the ways in which limits on the human brain's ability to compute and implement rational decisions influences economic behavior—both the decisions that people make and the consequences of those decisions for the way markets work.

Behavioral economics starts with observed behavior. It looks for anomalies—choices that do not seem to be rational. It then tries to account for the anomalies by using ideas developed by psychologists that emphasize features of the human brain that limit rational choice.

In behavioral economics, instead of being rational utility maximizers, people are assumed to have three impediments that prevent rational choice: bounded rationality, bounded willpower, and bounded self-interest.

Bounded Rationality Bounded rationality is rationality that is limited by the computing power of the human brain. We can't always work out the rational choice.

For Lisa, choosing between movies and soda, it seems unlikely that she would have much trouble figuring out what to buy. But toss Lisa some uncertainty and the task becomes harder. She's read the reviews of *Ironman 2* on Fandango, but does she really want to see that movie? How much marginal utility will it give her? Faced with uncertainty, people might use rules of thumb, listen to the views of others, and make decisions based on gut instinct rather than on rational calculation.

Bounded Willpower Bounded willpower is the less-than-perfect willpower that prevents us from making a decision that we know, at the time of implementing the decision, we will later regret.

Lisa might be feeling particularly thirsty when she passes a soda vending machine. Under Lisa's rational utility-maximizing plan, she buys her soda at the discount store, where she gets it for the lowest possible price. Lisa has already bought her soda for this month, but it is at home. Spending $1 on a can now means giving up a movie later this month.

Lisa's rational choice is to ignore the temporary thirst and stick to her plan. But she might not possess the willpower to do so—sometimes she will and sometimes she won't.

Bounded Self-Interest Bounded self-interest is the limited self-interest that results in sometimes suppressing our own interests to help others.

A hurricane hits the Florida coast and Lisa, feeling sorry for the victims, donates $10 to a fund-raiser. She now has only $30 to spend on movies and soda this month. The quantities that she buys are not, according to her utility schedule, the ones that maximize her utility.

The main applications of behavioral economics are in two areas: finance, where uncertainty is a key factor in decision making, and savings, where the future is a key factor. But one behavior observed by behavioral economists is more general and might affect your choices. It is called the endowment effect.

The Endowment Effect The endowment effect is the tendency for people to value something more highly simply because they own it. If you have allocated your income to maximize utility, then the price you would be willing to accept to give up something that you own (for example, your coffee mug) should be the same as the price you are willing to pay for an identical one.

In experiments, students seem to display the endowment effect: The price they are willing to pay for a coffee mug that is identical to the one they own is less than the price they would be willing to accept to give up the coffee mug that they own. Behavioral economists say that this behavior contradicts marginal utility theory.

Neuroeconomics

Neuroeconomics is the study of the activity of the human brain when a person makes an economic decision. The discipline uses the observational tools and ideas of neuroscience to obtain a better understanding of economic decisions.

Neuroeconomics is an experimental discipline. In an experiment, a person makes an economic decision and the electrical or chemical activity of the person's brain is observed and recorded using the same type of equipment that neurosurgeons use to diagnose brain disorders.

The observations provide information about which regions of the brain are active at different points in the process of making an economic decision.

Observations show that some economic decisions generate activity in the area of the brain (called the prefrontal cortex) where we store memories, analyze data, and anticipate the consequences of our actions. If people make rational utility-maximizing decisions, it is in this region of the brain that the decision occurs.

But observations also show that some economic decisions generate activity in the region of the brain (called the hippocampus) where we store memories of anxiety and fear. Decisions that are influenced by activity in this part of the brain might not be rational but instead be driven by fear or panic.

Neuroeconomists are also able to observe the amount of a brain hormone (called dopamine), the quantity of which increases in response to pleasurable events and decreases in response to disappointing events. These observations might one day enable neuroeconomists to actually measure utility and shine a bright light inside what was once believed to be the ultimate black box.

Controversy

The new ways of studying consumer choice that we've briefly described here are being used more widely to study business decisions and decisions in financial markets, and this type of research is surely going to become more popular.

But behavioral economics and neuroeconomics generate controversy. Most economists hold the view of Jevons that the goal of economics is to explain the decisions that we observe people making and not to explain what goes on inside people's heads.

Most economists would prefer to probe apparent anomalies more deeply and figure out why they are not anomalies after all.

Economists also point to the power of marginal utility theory and its ability to explain consumer choice and demand as well as resolve the paradox of value.

◆ REVIEW QUIZ

1 Define behavioral economics.
2 What are the three limitations on human rationality that behavioral economics emphasizes?
3 Define neuroeconomics.
4 What do behavioral economics and neuroeconomics seek to achieve?

Work these questions in Study Plan 8.4 and get instant feedback. Do a Key Terms Quiz.   MyEconLab

---

◆ You have now completed your study of marginal utility theory and some new ideas about how people make economic choices. You can see marginal utility theory in action once again in *Economics in the News* on pp. 194–195, where it is used to compare the effects of a tax on big cups of sugary soft drinks versus an outright ban.

Influencing Consumer Choice for Sugary Drinks

Drinks Groups Sue Over NY "Supersize" Ban

The Financial Times
October 13, 2012

The U.S. beverage industry is taking the administration of Michael Bloomberg, New York mayor, to court over its decision to ban sales of "supersized" sugary drinks.

Trade groups led by the American Beverage Association filed a lawsuit late on Friday in New York state court attempting to block the rule, which is set to be imposed next spring.

Last month, New York's board of health voted to approve a proposal made by Mr. Bloomberg in May that would prohibit restaurants, theaters, and stadiums from selling sugary drinks in portions bigger than 16 fl oz. …

The lawsuit comes as the soda industry is locked in an increasingly contentious battle with regulators over labeling and taxation of their products. Industry groups are currently fighting soda tax proposals in two California cities and have successfully pushed back several other similar efforts. …

Marc La Vorgna, a spokesman for Mr. Bloomberg, called the lawsuit baseless and suggested that the drinks industry would fail to stop the ban.

"For 100 years, major public health decisions—the posting of calorie counts, the ban of transfats, the sanitation of the sewage system, the fluoridation of the water system, and much more—have been left to a board of health professionals and it has benefited the health of New Yorkers," he said. "The mayor's plan to limit the size of sugary beverages—the leading contributor to the obesity epidemic—has spurred a long overdue national dialogue on obesity."

Alan Rappeport, "Drinks Groups Sue Over NY 'Supersize' Ban," *The Financial Times*, October 13, 2012.

MyEconLab More Economics in the News

ESSENCE OF THE STORY

- New York City mayor Michael Bloomberg has banned the sale of sweetened drinks larger than 16 ounces at many venues.

- Two cities in California are considering placing a tax on sugar-sweetened beverages.

- Trade groups that sell these drinks are seeking court orders to block the ban and taxes.

- A spokesman for mayor Bloomberg says sugary drinks are the leading contributor to obesity and the ban is a public health measure like the sanitation system.

ECONOMIC ANALYSIS

- Concerned that people are choosing to consume more sugary soda than is healthy, New York mayor Michael Bloomberg wants to ban large servings and the city of Richmond, CA, is considering a 1-penny-per-ounce tax.

- Consumers choose to buy the quantity of sugary drinks that maximizes utility.

- To do so, they make the marginal utility per dollar for all other goods and services equal to the marginal utility per dollar for sugary drinks. That is:

$$\frac{MU_O}{P_O} = \frac{MU_S}{P_S}.$$

- Because of the way in which drinks are sold, there isn't a single price. The table shows some prices in St. Louis in June 2012.

Prices of Sugary Drinks

Size (ounces)	At the movies	At a 7-Eleven
20	4.00	1.09
32	4.50	1.29
44	5.00	1.49
52	5.50	1.69
104	[free refill]	

- These prices tell us that people who buy their drinks in big cups pay a lower price per ounce.

- Because a person who buys a 52-ounce cup gets a free refill, the price of the marginal ounce for that person is zero. With a price of zero, the buyer drinks the quantity at which marginal utility is also zero.

- The suggestions for decreasing the consumption of sugary drinks are ways of raising the price.

- A tax raises the price because the tax is added to the price received by the seller. A ban on large cups raises the price because the price per ounce is higher for small cups than for large cups. Both have a similar outcome.

- Faced with a higher price of sugary drinks, a consumer maximizes utility by consuming a smaller quantity of sugary drinks.

- The reason is that consumer equilibrium becomes

$$\frac{MU_O}{P_O} = \frac{MU_S}{(P_S + tax)}.$$

- When a tax is imposed, the price doesn't rise by the entire amount of the tax, but generally $P_S + tax$ is greater than the price before that tax was imposed.

- Because $P_S + tax$ is greater than P_S, MU_S must rise to restore the equality of the marginal utilities per dollar. But to increase MU_S, the quantity of sugary drinks consumed must decrease.

- Figure 1 illustrates and makes clear why consumption of sugary drinks decreases.

- Suppose that with no tax, the budget line is BL_0 and to make the marginal utilities per dollar equal, the consumer buys 60 ounces of drinks and 100 units of other goods and services per day.

- A tax raises the price to $P_S + tax$ and the budget line becomes steeper as BL_1.

- If the consumer continues to drink 60 ounces per day, the quantity of other items bought must fall to 50 units a day. MU_O rises and

$$\frac{MU_O}{P_O} > \frac{MU_S}{(P_S + tax)}.$$

- To restore maximum utility, the consumer buys a smaller quantity of sugary drinks, which increases MU_S, and a greater quantity of other goods, which decreases MU_O. A movement up along the budget line BL_1 shows these changes in quantities consumed.

- The consumer substitutes other goods and services for sugary drinks until

$$\frac{MU_O}{P_O} = \frac{MU_S}{(P_S + tax)}.$$

- At this point, the consumer is again maximizing utility.

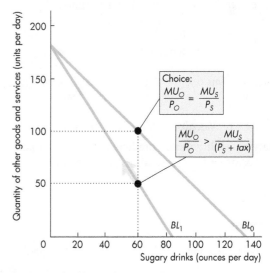

Figure 1 The Effect of a Tax

SUMMARY

Key Points

Consumption Choices (pp. 178–180)

- A household's consumption choices are determined by its consumption possibilities and preferences.
- A budget line defines a household's consumption possibilities.
- A household's preferences can be described by a utility schedule that lists the total utility and marginal utility derived from various quantities of goods and services consumed.
- The principle of diminishing marginal utility is that the marginal utility from a good or service decreases as consumption of the good or service increases.

Working Problems 1 to 5 will give you a better understanding of consumption choices.

Utility-Maximizing Choice (pp. 181–184)

- A consumer's objective is to maximize total utility.
- Total utility is maximized when all the available income is spent and when the marginal utility per dollar from all goods is equal.
- If the marginal utility per dollar for good *A* exceeds that for good *B*, total utility increases if the quantity purchased of good *A* increases and the quantity purchased of good *B* decreases.

Working Problems 6 to 8 will give you a better understanding of a consumer's utility-maximizing choice.

Predictions of Marginal Utility Theory (pp. 185–191)

- Marginal utility theory predicts the law of demand. That is, other things remaining the same, the

higher the price of a good, the smaller is the quantity demanded of that good.
- Marginal utility theory also predicts that, other things remaining the same, an increase in the consumer's income increases the demand for a normal good.
- Marginal utility theory resolves the paradox of value.
- Total value is *total* utility or consumer surplus. But price is related to *marginal* utility.
- Water, which we consume in large amounts, has a high total utility and a large consumer surplus, but the price of water is low and the marginal utility from water is low.
- Diamonds, which we buy in small quantities, have a low total utility and a small consumer surplus, but the price of a diamond is high and the marginal utility from diamonds is high.

Working Problems 9 to 13 will give you a better understanding of the predictions of marginal utility theory.

New Ways of Explaining Consumer Choices
(pp. 192–193)

- Behavioral economics studies limits on the ability of the human brain to compute and implement rational decisions.
- Bounded rationality, bounded willpower, and bounded self-interest are believed to explain some choices.
- Neuroeconomics uses the ideas and tools of neuroscience to study the effects of economic events and choices inside the human brain.

Working Problems 14 and 15 will give you a better understanding of the new ways of explaining consumer choices.

Key Terms

MyEconLab Key Terms Quiz

Behavioral economics, 192
Budget line, 178
Consumer equilibrium, 181
Diminishing marginal utility, 180

Marginal utility, 179
Marginal utility per dollar, 182
Neuroeconomics, 193
Preferences, 179

Total utility, 179
Utility, 179

WORKED PROBLEM

MyEconLab   You can work this problem in Chapter 8 Study Plan.

Jake has a budget of $10 per week to spend on song downloads and cookies. The table shows his marginal utility from each good.

Quantity per week	Marginal utility from a song	Marginal utility from a cookie
1	14	20
2	12	16
3	11	12
4	10	8
5	9	4
6	8	3
7	7	2
8	6	1

Questions

1. If the price of a song is $1 and the price of a cookie is $2, what are the quantities of songs and cookies that exhaust Jake's budget?

2. How does Jake allocate his $10 between songs and cookies?

3. If the price of a song rises to $2 and the price of a cookie remains at $2, does Jake buy fewer songs and cookies, or only fewer songs?

Solutions

1. The price of a cookie is twice that of a song, so each additional cookie Jake buys costs him 2 fewer songs—the opportunity cost of a cookie is 2 songs. So Jake can buy either 8 songs and 1 cookie, or 6 songs and 2 cookies, or 4 songs and 3 cookies, or 2 songs and 4 cookies, or 0 songs and 5 cookies.

Key Point: To exhaust the budget, all income is spent.

2. Jake buys the quantities of songs and cookies that maximize his total utility. He buys the quantities that make the marginal utility per dollar the same for the two goods.

To calculate the marginal utility per dollar, make a table in which each row is an affordable combination of songs and cookies. Show the marginal utility for each good and then calculate the marginal utility per dollar for each row.

The table in the next column shows the calculations. Check the calculation on row B, with 4 songs and 3 cookies. The marginal utility of a song is 10 units and because the price of a song is $1, the marginal utility per dollar is also 10 units.

	Songs ($1 each)			Cookies ($2 each)		
	Quantity	Marginal utility	Marginal utility per dollar	Quantity	Marginal utility	Marginal utility per dollar
A	2	12	12	4	8	4
B	4	10	10	3	12	6
C	6	8	8	2	16	8
D	8	6	6	1	20	10

The marginal utility of a cookie is 12 units and because the price of a cookie is $2, the marginal utility per dollar is 6 units.

Because the marginal utility per dollar from 4 songs *exceeds* that from 3 cookies, Jake can increase his total utility by buying more songs and fewer cookies.

In the highlighted row C, the marginal utilities per dollar are equal and total utility is maximized. So Jake buys 6 songs and 2 cookies to maximize utility.

Key Point: Total utility is maximized when the marginal utility per dollar is the same for all goods.

3. If the price of a song rises to $2, the affordable combinations shrink. Jake can now afford combinations of quantities that total 5. The table below shows the new combinations that exhaust Jake's budget and the marginal utility per dollar for each possibility.

	Songs ($2 each)			Cookies ($2 each)		
	Quantity	Marginal utility	Marginal utility per dollar	Quantity	Marginal utility	Marginal utility per dollar
A	1	14	7	4	8	4
B	2	12	6	3	12	6
C	3	11	5.5	2	16	8
D	4	10	5	1	20	10

To maximize his utility, Jake now buys only 2 songs and increases his consumption of cookies to 3 per week in row B.

Key Point: When the price of a good rises, the utility-maximizing quantity of that good decreases, but the quantity of other goods bought might increase or decrease.

MyEconLab   You can work Problems 1 to 15 in Chapter 8 Study Plan and get instant feedback.

Consumption Choices (Study Plan 8.1)

Jerry has $12 a week to spend on yogurt and berries. The price of yogurt is $2, and berries are $4 a box.

1. List the combinations of yogurt and berries that Jerry can afford. Draw a graph of his budget line with the quantity of berries plotted on the x-axis.

2. How do Jerry's consumption possibilities change if, other things remaining the same, (i) the price of berries falls and (ii) Jerry's income increases?

Use the following data to work Problems 3 to 5.

Max has $35 a day to spend on windsurfing and snorkeling and he can spend as much time as he likes doing them. The price of renting equipment for windsurfing is $10 an hour and for snorkeling is $5 an hour. The table shows the total utility Max gets from each activity.

Hours per day	Total utility from windsurfing	Total utility from snorkeling
1	120	40
2	220	76
3	300	106
4	360	128
5	396	140
6	412	150
7	422	158

3. Calculate Max's marginal utility from windsurfing at each number of hours per day. Does Max's marginal utility from windsurfing obey the principle of diminishing marginal utility?

4. Calculate Max's marginal utility from snorkeling at each number of hours per day. Does Max's marginal utility from snorkeling obey the principle of diminishing marginal utility?

5. Which does Max enjoy more: his 6th hour of windsurfing or his 6th hour of snorkeling?

Utility-Maximizing Choice (Study Plan 8.2)

Use the data in Problem 3 to work Problems 6 to 8.

6. Make a table of the combinations of hours spent windsurfing and snorkeling that Max can afford.

7. Add two columns to your table in Problem 6 and list Max's marginal utility per dollar from windsurfing and from snorkeling.

8. a. To maximize his utility, how many hours a day does Max spend on each activity?
   b. If Max spent a dollar more on windsurfing

and a dollar less on snorkeling than in part (a), how would his total utility change?

   c. If Max spent a dollar less on windsurfing and a dollar more on snorkeling than in part (a), how would his total utility change?

Predictions of Marginal Utility Theory (Study Plan 8.3)

Use the data in Problem 3 to work Problems 9 to 13.

9. If the price of renting windsurfing equipment is cut to $5 an hour, how many hours a day does Max spend on each activity?

10. Draw Max's demand curve for rented windsurfing equipment. Over the price range $5 to $10 an hour, is Max's demand elastic or inelastic?

11. How does Max's demand for snorkeling equipment change when the price of windsurfing equipment falls? What is Max's cross elasticity of demand for snorkeling with respect to the price of windsurfing? Are windsurfing and snorkeling substitutes or complements for Max?

12. If Max's income increases from $35 to $55 a day, how does his demand for windsurfing equipment change? Is windsurfing a normal good? Explain.

13. If Max's income increases from $35 to $55 a day, how does his demand for snorkeling equipment change? Is snorkeling a normal good? Explain.

New Ways of Explaining Consumer Choices
(Study Plan 8.4)

Use the following news clip to work Problems 14 and 15.

Eating Away the Innings in Baseball's Cheap Seats

Baseball and gluttony, two of America's favorite pastimes, are merging, with Major League Baseball stadiums offering all-you-can-eat seats. Some fans try to "set personal records" during their first game, but by the third time in such seats they eat normally.

Source: *USA Today*, March 6, 2008

14. What conflict might exist between utility-maximization and setting "personal records" for eating? What does the fact that fans eat less at subsequent games indicate about their marginal utility from ballpark food as they consume more?

15. How can setting personal records for eating be reconciled with marginal utility theory? Which ideas of behavioral economics are consistent with the information in the news clip?

ADDITIONAL PROBLEMS AND APPLICATIONS

MyEconLab   You can work these problems in MyEconLab if assigned by your instructor.

Consumption Choices

16. Tim buys 2 pizzas and sees 1 movie a week when he has $16 to spend, a movie ticket is $8, and a pizza is $4. Draw Tim's budget line. If the price of a movie ticket falls to $4, describe how Tim's consumption possibilities change.

17. Cindy has $70 a month to spend, and she can spend as much time as she likes playing golf and tennis. The price of an hour of golf is $10, and the price of an hour of tennis is $5. The table shows Cindy's marginal utility from each sport.

Hours per month	Marginal utility from golf	Marginal utility from tennis
1	80	40
2	60	36
3	40	30
4	30	10
5	20	5
6	10	2
7	6	1

Make a table that shows Cindy's affordable combinations of hours playing golf and tennis. If Cindy increases her expenditure to $100, describe how her consumption possibilities change.

Utility-Maximizing Choice

Use the information in Problem 17 to work Problems 18 to 24.

18. a. How many hours of golf and how many hours of tennis does Cindy play to maximize her utility?

    b. Compared to part (a), if Cindy spent a dollar more on golf and a dollar less on tennis, by how much would her total utility change?

    c. Compared to part (a), if Cindy spent a dollar less on golf and a dollar more on tennis, by how much would her total utility change?

19. Explain why, if Cindy equalized the marginal utility per hour of golf and tennis, she would *not* maximize her utility.

Predictions of Marginal Utility Theory

Cindy's tennis club raises its price of an hour of tennis from $5 to $10, other things remaining the same.

20. a. List the combinations of hours spent playing golf and tennis that Cindy can now afford and her marginal utility per dollar from golf and from tennis.

    b. How many hours does Cindy now spend playing golf and how many hours does she spend playing tennis?

21. Use the information in Problem 20 to draw Cindy's demand curve for tennis. Over the price range of $5 to $10 an hour of tennis, is Cindy's demand for tennis elastic or inelastic?

22. Explain how Cindy's demand for golf changed when the price of an hour of tennis increased from $5 to $10 in Problem 20. What is Cindy's cross elasticity of demand for golf with respect to the price of tennis? Are tennis and golf substitutes or complements for Cindy?

23. Cindy loses her math tutoring job and the amount she has to spend on golf and tennis falls from $70 to $35 a month. With the price of an hour of golf at $10 and of tennis at $5, calculate the change in the hours she spends playing golf. For Cindy, is golf a normal good or an inferior good? Is tennis a normal good or an inferior good?

24. Cindy takes a Club Med vacation, the cost of which includes unlimited sports activities. With no extra charge for golf and tennis, Cindy allocates a total of 4 hours a day to these activities.

    a. How many hours does Cindy play golf and how many hours does she play tennis?

    b. What is Cindy's marginal utility from golf and from tennis?

    c. Why does Cindy equalize the marginal utilities rather than the marginal utility per dollar from golf and from tennis?

25. Jim has made his best affordable choice of muffins and coffee. He spends all of his income on 10 muffins at $1 each and 20 cups of coffee at $2 each. Now the price of a muffin rises to $1.50 and the price of coffee falls to $1.75 a cup.

    a. Will Jim now be able to buy 10 muffins and 20 coffees?

b. If Jim changes the quantities he buys, will he buy more or fewer muffins and more or less coffee? Expain your answer.

26. Ben spends $50 a year on 2 bunches of flowers and $50 a year on 10,000 gallons of tap water. Ben is maximizing utility and his marginal utility from water is 0.5 unit per gallon.
   a. Are flowers or water more valuable to Ben?
   b. Explain how Ben's expenditure on flowers and water illustrates the paradox of value.

New Ways of Explaining Consumer Choices

Use the following news clip to work Problems 27 to 29.

Putting a Price on Human Life

Researchers at Stanford and the University of Pennsylvania estimated that a healthy human life is worth about $129,000. Using Medicare records on treatment costs for kidney dialysis as a benchmark, the authors tried to pinpoint the threshold beyond which ensuring another "quality" year of life was no longer financially worthwhile. The study comes amid debate over whether Medicare should start rationing healthcare on the basis of cost effectiveness.

Source: *Time*, June 9, 2008

27. Why might Medicare ration healthcare according to treatment that is "financially worthwhile" as opposed to providing as much treatment as is needed by a patient, regardless of costs?

28. What conflict might exist between a person's valuation of his or her own life and the rest of society's valuation of that person's life?

29. How does the potential conflict between self-interest and the social interest complicate setting a financial threshold for Medicare treatments?

Economics in the News

30. After you have studied *Economics in the News* (pp. 194–195), answer the following questions.
   a. If big cups of sugary drinks are banned at restaurants, theaters, and stadiums,
      (i) How will the price of an ounce of sugary drink change?
      (ii) How will consumers respond to the change in price?

   b. If a tax is imposed on sugary drinks, how does
      (i) The marginal utility of a sugary drink change?
      (ii) The consumer surplus in the market for sugary drinks change?

31. **Five Signs You Have Too Much Money**
   When a bottle of water costs $38, it's hard not to agree that bottled water is a fool's drink. The drink of choice among image-conscious status seekers and high-end tee-totalers in L.A. is Bling H_2O. It's not the water that accounts for the cost of the $38, but the "limited edition" bottle decked out in Swarovski crystals.

   Source: CNN, January 17, 2006

   a. Assuming that the price of a bottle of Bling H_2O is $38 in all the major U.S. cities, what might its popularity in Los Angeles reveal about consumers' incomes or preferences in Los Angeles relative to other major U.S. cities?
   b. Why might the marginal utility from a bottle of Bling H_2O decrease more rapidly than the marginal utility from ordinary bottled water?

32. **How to Buy Happiness. Cheap**
   On any day, the rich tend to be a bit happier than the poor, but increases in average living standards don't seem to make people happier. The average American's income is up 80% since 1972, but the percentage describing themselves as "very happy" (roughly a third) hasn't changed. As living standards increase, most of us respond by raising our own standards: Things that once seemed luxuries now are necessities and we work harder to buy stuff that satisfies us less and less.

   Source: CNN, October 1, 2004

   According to the news clip,
   a. How do widespread increases in living standards influence total utility?
   b. How do total utility and marginal utility from consumption change over time?

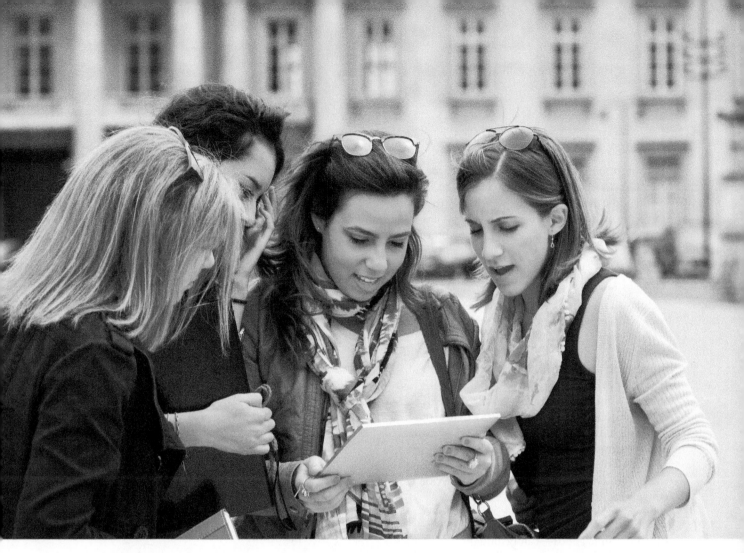

9 POSSIBILITIES, PREFERENCES, AND CHOICES

After studying this chapter,
you will be able to:

◆ Describe a household's budget line and show how it changes when prices or income change

◆ Use indifference curves to map preferences and explain the principle of diminishing marginal rate of substitution

◆ Predict the effects of changes in prices and income on consumption choices

The iPad has revolutionized the way we read magazines and books and check our grades. Yet the magazine racks and bookstore shelves are still stuffed with traditional printed paper. Similarly, low-priced on-demand movies and DVD rentals have made it easier to watch a movie at home. Yet we're also going to movie theaters in ever-greater numbers.

In this chapter, we're going to study a model that explains the choices we make and applies it to choices about using new and old technologies. At the end of the chapter in *Economics in the News*, we use the model to explain why e-books are taking off and replacing printed books.

Consumption Possibilities

Consumption choices are limited by income and by prices. A household has a given amount of income to spend and cannot influence the prices of the goods and services it buys. A household's **budget line** describes the limits to its consumption choices. Let's look at Lisa's budget line.*

Budget Line

Lisa has an income of $40 a month to spend. She buys two goods: movies and soda. The price of a movie is $8, and the price of soda is $4 a case.

Figure 9.1 shows alternative combinations of movies and soda that Lisa can afford. In row A, she sees no movies and buys 10 cases of soda. In row F, she sees 5 movies and buys no soda. Both of these combinations of movies and soda exhaust the $40 available. Check that the combination of movies and soda in each of the other rows also exhausts Lisa's $40 of income. The numbers in the table and the points A through F in the graph describe Lisa's consumption possibilities.

Divisible and Indivisible Goods Some goods—called divisible goods—can be bought in any quantity desired. Examples are gasoline and electricity. We can best understand household choice if we suppose that all goods and services are divisible. For example, Lisa can see half a movie a month on average by seeing one movie every two months. When we think of goods as being divisible, the consumption possibilities are not only the points A through F shown in Fig. 9.1, but also all the intermediate points that form the line running from A to F. This line is Lisa's budget line.

Affordable and Unaffordable Quantities Lisa's budget line is a constraint on her choices. It marks the boundary between what is affordable and what is unaffordable. She can afford any point on the line and inside it. She cannot afford any point outside the line. The constraint on her consumption depends on the prices and her income, and the constraint changes when the price of a good or her income changes. To see how, we use a budget equation.

---

*If you have studied Chapter 8 on marginal utility theory, you have already met Lisa. This tale of her thirst for soda and zeal for movies will sound familiar to you—up to a point. In this chapter, we're going to explore her budget line in more detail and use a different method for representing preferences—one that does not require the idea of utility.

FIGURE 9.1   The Budget Line

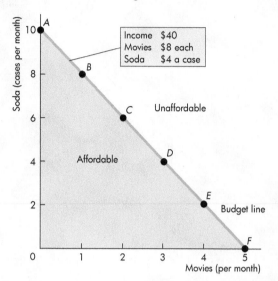

Consumption possibility	Movies (per month)	Soda (cases per month)
A	0	10
B	1	8
C	2	6
D	3	4
E	4	2
F	5	0

Lisa's budget line shows the boundary between what she can and cannot afford. The rows of the table list Lisa's affordable combinations of movies and soda when her income is $40, the price of soda is $4 a case, and the price of a movie is $8. For example, row A tells us that Lisa spends all of her $40 income when she buys 10 cases of soda and sees no movies. The figure graphs Lisa's budget line. Points A through F in the graph represent the rows of the table. For divisible goods, the budget line is the continuous line AF. To calculate the equation for Lisa's budget line, start with expenditure equal to income:

$$\$4Q_S + \$8Q_M = \$40.$$

Divide by $4 to obtain

$$Q_S + 2Q_M = 10.$$

Subtract $2Q_M$ from both sides to obtain

$$Q_S = 10 - 2Q_M.$$

MyEconLab Animation

Budget Equation

We can describe the budget line by using a *budget equation*. The budget equation starts with the fact that

Expenditure = Income.

Expenditure is equal to the sum of the price of each good multiplied by the quantity bought. For Lisa,

Expenditure = (Price of soda × Quantity of soda)
+ (Price of a movie × Quantity of movies).

Call the price of soda P_S, the quantity of soda Q_S, the price of a movie P_M, the quantity of movies Q_M, and income Y. We can now write Lisa's budget equation as

$$P_S Q_S + P_M Q_M = Y.$$

Or, using the prices Lisa faces, $4 a case of soda and $8 a movie, and Lisa's income, $40, we get

$$\$4Q_S + \$8Q_M = \$40.$$

Lisa can choose any quantities of soda (Q_S) and movies (Q_M) that satisfy this equation. To find the relationship between these quantities, divide both sides of the equation by the price of soda (P_S) to get

$$Q_S + \frac{P_M}{P_S} \times Q_M = \frac{Y}{P_S}.$$

Now subtract the term (P_M/P_S) × Q_M from both sides of this equation to get

$$Q_S = \frac{Y}{P_S} - \frac{P_M}{P_S} \times Q_M.$$

For Lisa, income (Y) is $40, the price of a movie (P_M) is $8, and the price of soda (P_S) is $4 a case. So Lisa must choose the quantities of movies and soda to satisfy the equation

$$Q_S = \frac{\$40}{\$4} - \frac{\$8}{\$4} \times Q_M,$$

or

$$Q_S = 10 - 2Q_M.$$

To interpret the equation, look at the budget line in Fig. 9.1 and check that the equation delivers that budget line. First, set Q_M equal to zero. The budget equation tells us that Q_S, the quantity of soda, is Y/P_S, which is 10 cases. This combination of Q_M and Q_S is the one shown in row A of the table in Fig. 9.1. Next set Q_M equal to 5. Q_S now equals zero (row F of the table). Check that you can derive the other rows.

The budget equation contains two variables chosen by the household (Q_M and Q_S) and two variables that the household takes as given (Y/P_S and P_M/P_S). Let's look more closely at these variables.

Real Income A household's **real income** is its income expressed as a quantity of goods that the household can afford to buy. Expressed in terms of soda, Lisa's real income is Y/P_S. This quantity is the maximum quantity of soda that she can buy. It is equal to her money income divided by the price of soda. Lisa's money income is $40 and the price of soda is $4 a case, so her real income in terms of soda is 10 cases, which is shown in Fig. 9.1 as the point at which the budget line intersects the y-axis.

Relative Price A **relative price** is the price of one good divided by the price of another good. In Lisa's budget equation, the variable P_M/P_S is the relative price of a movie in terms of soda. For Lisa, P_M is $8 a movie and P_S is $4 a case, so P_M/P_S is equal to 2 cases of soda per movie. That is, to see 1 movie, Lisa must give up 2 cases of soda.

You've just calculated Lisa's opportunity cost of seeing a movie. Recall that the opportunity cost of an action is the best alternative forgone. For Lisa to see 1 more movie a month, she must forgo 2 cases of soda. You've also calculated Lisa's opportunity cost of soda. For Lisa to buy 2 more cases of soda a month, she must forgo seeing 1 movie. So her opportunity cost of 2 cases of soda is 1 movie.

The relative price of a movie in terms of soda is the magnitude of the slope of Lisa's budget line. To calculate the slope of the budget line, recall the formula for slope (see the Chapter 1 Appendix): Slope equals the change in the variable measured on the y-axis divided by the change in the variable measured on the x-axis as we move along the line. In Lisa's case (Fig. 9.1), the variable measured on the y-axis is the quantity of soda and the variable measured on the x-axis is the quantity of movies. Along Lisa's budget line, as soda decreases from 10 to 0 cases, movies increase from 0 to 5. So the magnitude of the slope of the budget line is 10 cases divided by 5 movies, or 2 cases of soda per movie. The magnitude of this slope is exactly the same as the relative price we've just calculated. It is also the opportunity cost of a movie.

A Change in Prices When prices change, so does the budget line. The lower the price of the good measured on the x-axis, other things remaining the same, the flatter is the budget line. For example, if the price of a movie falls from $8 to $4, real income

FIGURE 9.2   Changes in Prices and Income

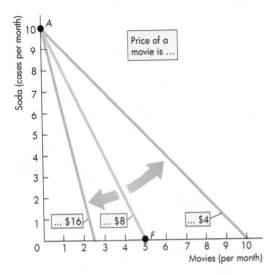

(a) A change in price

(b) A change in income

In part (a), the price of a movie changes. A fall in the price from $8 to $4 rotates the budget line outward and makes it flatter. A rise in the price from $8 to $16 rotates the budget line inward and makes it steeper.

In part (b), income falls from $40 to $20 while the prices of movies and soda remain the same. The budget line shifts leftward, but its slope does not change.

MyEconLab Animation and Draw Graph

in terms of soda does not change but the relative price of a movie falls. The budget line rotates outward and becomes flatter, as Fig. 9.2(a) illustrates. The higher the price of the good measured on the *x*-axis, other things remaining the same, the steeper is the budget line. For example, if the price of a movie rises from $8 to $16, the relative price of a movie increases. The budget line rotates inward and becomes steeper, as Fig. 9.2(a) illustrates.

A Change in Income A change in money income changes real income but does not change the relative price. The budget line shifts, but its slope does not change. An increase in money income increases real income and shifts the budget line rightward. A decrease in money income decreases real income and shifts the budget line leftward.

Figure 9.2(b) shows the effect of a change in money income on Lisa's budget line. The initial budget line when Lisa's income is $40 is the same as in Fig. 9.1. The new budget line shows how much Lisa can buy if her income falls to $20 a month. The two budget lines have the same slope because the relative price is the same. The new budget line is closer to the origin because Lisa's real income has decreased.

◆ REVIEW QUIZ

1 What does a household's budget line show?
2 How does the relative price and a household's real income influence its budget line?
3 If a household has an income of $40 and buys only bus rides at $2 each and magazines at $4 each, what is the equation of the household's budget line?
4 If the price of one good changes, what happens to the relative price and the slope of the household's budget line?
5 If a household's money income changes and prices do not change, what happens to the household's real income and budget line?

Work these questions in Study Plan 9.1 and get instant feedback. Do a Key Terms Quiz.   MyEconLab

We've studied the limits to what a household can consume. Let's now learn how we can describe preferences and make a map that contains a lot of information about a household's preferences.

Preferences and Indifference Curves

You are going to discover a very cool idea: that of drawing a map of a person's preferences. A preference map is based on the intuitively appealing idea that people can sort all the possible combinations of goods into three groups: preferred, not preferred, and indifferent. To make this idea more concrete, let's ask Lisa to tell us how she ranks various combinations of movies and soda.

Figure 9.3 shows part of Lisa's answer. She tells us that she currently sees 2 movies and buys 6 cases of soda a month at point C. She then lists all the combinations of movies and soda that she says are just as acceptable to her as her current situation. When we plot these combinations of movies and soda, we get the green curve in Fig. 9.3(a). This curve is the key element in a preference map and is called an indifference curve.

An **indifference curve** is a line that shows combinations of goods among which a consumer is *indifferent*. The indifference curve in Fig. 9.3(a) tells us that Lisa is just as happy to see 2 movies and buy 6 cases of soda a month at point C as she is to have the combination of movies and soda at point G or at any other point along the curve.

Lisa also says that she prefers all the combinations of movies and soda above the indifference curve in Fig. 9.3(a)—the yellow area—to those on the indifference curve. And she prefers any combination on the indifference curve to any combination in the gray area below the indifference curve.

The indifference curve in Fig. 9.3(a) is just one of a whole family of such curves. This indifference curve appears again in Fig. 9.3(b), labeled I_1. The curves labeled I_0 and I_2 are two other indifference curves. Lisa prefers any point on indifference curve I_2 to any point on indifference curve I_1, and she prefers any point on I_1 to any point on I_0. We refer to I_2 as being a higher indifference curve than I_1 and I_1 as being higher than I_0.

A preference map is a series of indifference curves that resemble the contour lines on a map. By looking at the shape of the contour lines on a map, we can draw conclusions about the terrain. Similarly, by looking at the shape of the indifference curves, we can draw conclusions about a person's preferences.

Let's learn how to "read" a preference map.

FIGURE 9.3   A Preference Map

(a) An indifference curve

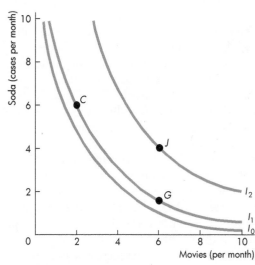

(b) Lisa's preference map

Part (a) shows one of Lisa's indifference curves. She is indifferent between point C (with 2 movies and 6 cases of soda) and all other points on the green indifference curve, such as G. She prefers points above the indifference curve (in the yellow area) to points on it, and she prefers points on the indifference curve to points below it (in the gray area). Part (b) shows three of the indifference curves—I_0, I_1, and I_2—in Lisa's preference map. She prefers point J to point C or G, and she prefers all the points on I_2 to those on I_1.

Marginal Rate of Substitution

The **marginal rate of substitution** (*MRS*) is the rate at which a person will give up good *y* (the good measured on the *y*-axis) to get an additional unit of good *x* (the good measured on the *x*-axis) while remaining indifferent (remaining on the same indifference curve). The magnitude of the slope of an indifference curve measures the marginal rate of substitution.

■ If the indifference curve is *steep*, the marginal rate of substitution is *high*. The person is willing to give up a large quantity of good *y* to get an additional unit of good *x* while remaining indifferent.

■ If the indifference curve is *flat*, the marginal rate of substitution is *low*. The person is willing to give up a small amount of good *y* to get an additional unit of good *x* while remaining indifferent.

Figure 9.4 shows you how to calculate the marginal rate of substitution.

At point *C* on indifference curve *I*₁, Lisa buys 6 cases of soda and sees 2 movies. Her marginal rate of substitution is the magnitude of the slope of the indifference curve at point *C*. To measure this magnitude, place a straight line against, or tangent to, the indifference curve at point *C*. Along that line, as the quantity of soda decreases by 10 cases, the number of movies increases by 5—or 2 cases per movie. At point *C*, Lisa is willing to give up soda for movies at the rate of 2 cases per movie—a marginal rate of substitution of 2.

At point *G* on indifference curve *I*₁, Lisa buys 1.5 cases of soda and sees 6 movies. Her marginal rate of substitution is measured by the slope of the indifference curve at point *G*. That slope is the same as the slope of the tangent to the indifference curve at point *G*. Now, as the quantity of soda decreases by 4.5 cases, the number of movies increases by 9—or 1/2 case per movie. At point *G*, Lisa is willing to give up soda for movies at the rate of 1/2 case per movie—a marginal rate of substitution of 1/2.

As Lisa sees more movies and buys less soda, her marginal rate of substitution diminishes. Diminishing marginal rate of substitution is the key assumption about preferences. A **diminishing marginal rate of substitution** is a general tendency for a person to be willing to give up less of good *y* to get one more unit of good *x*, while at the same time remaining indifferent as the quantity of *x* increases. In Lisa's case, she is less willing to give up soda to see one more movie as the number of movies she sees increases.

FIGURE 9.4   The Marginal Rate of Substitution

The magnitude of the slope of an indifference curve is called the marginal rate of substitution (MRS). The red line at point *C* tells us that Lisa is willing to give up 10 cases of soda to see 5 movies. Her marginal rate of substitution at point *C* is 10 divided by 5, which equals 2. The red line at point *G* tells us that Lisa is willing to give up 4.5 cases of soda to see 9 movies. Her marginal rate of substitution at point *G* is 4.5 divided by 9, which equals 1/2.

MyEconLab Animation and Draw Graph

Your Diminishing Marginal Rate of Substitution

Think about your own diminishing marginal rate of substitution. Imagine that in a week, you drink 10 cases of soda and see no movies. Most likely, you are willing to give up a lot of soda so that you can see just 1 movie. But now imagine that in a week, you buy 1 case of soda and see 6 movies. Most likely, you will now not be willing to give up much soda to see a seventh movie. As a general rule, the greater the number of movies you see, the smaller is the quantity of soda you are willing to give up to see one additional movie.

The shape of a person's indifference curves incorporates the principle of the diminishing marginal rate of substitution because the curves are bowed toward the origin. The tightness of the bend of an indifference curve tells us how willing a person is to substitute one good for another while remaining indifferent. Let's look at some examples that make this point clear.

Degree of Substitutability

Most of us would not regard movies and soda as being *close* substitutes, but they are substitutes. No matter how much you love soda, some increase in the number of movies you see will compensate you for being deprived of a can of soda. Similarly, no matter how much you love going to the movies, some number of cans of soda will compensate you for being deprived of seeing one movie. A person's indifference curves for movies and soda might look something like those for most ordinary goods and services shown in Fig. 9.5(a).

Close Substitutes   Some goods substitute so easily for each other that most of us do not even notice which we are consuming. The different brands of marker pens and pencils are examples. Most people don't care which brand of these items they use or where they buy them. A marker pen from the campus bookstore is just as good as one from the local grocery store. You would be willing to forgo a pen from the campus store if you could get one more pen from the local grocery store. When two goods are perfect substitutes, their indifference curves are straight lines that slope downward, as Fig. 9.5(b) illustrates. The marginal rate of substitution is constant.

Complements   Some goods do not substitute for each other at all. Instead, they are complements. The complements in Fig. 9.5(c) are left and right running shoes. Indifference curves of perfect complements are L-shaped. One left running shoe and one right running shoe are as good as one left shoe and two right shoes. Having two of each is preferred to having one of each, but having two of one and one of the other is no better than having one of each.

The extreme cases of perfect substitutes and perfect complements shown here don't often happen in reality, but they do illustrate that the shape of the indifference curve shows the degree of substitutability between two goods. The closer the two goods are to perfect substitutes, the closer the marginal rate of substitution is to being constant (a straight line), rather than diminishing (a curved line). Indifference

---

FIGURE 9.5   The Degree of Substitutability

(a) Ordinary goods   **(b) Perfect substitutes**   **(c) Perfect complements**

The shape of the indifference curves reveals the degree of substitutability between two goods. Part (a) shows the indifference curves for two ordinary goods: movies and soda. To drink less soda and remain indifferent, one must see more movies. The number of movies that compensates for a reduction in soda increases as less soda is consumed. Part (b) shows the indifference curves for two perfect substitutes. For the consumer to remain indifferent, one fewer marker pen from the local grocery store must be replaced by one extra marker pen from the campus bookstore. Part (c) shows two perfect complements—goods that cannot be substituted for each other at all. Having two left running shoes with one right running shoe is no better than having one of each. But having two of each is preferred to having one of each.

MyEconLab Animation

"With the pork I'd recommend an Alsatian white or a Coke."

© The New Yorker Collection 1988
Robert Weber from cartoonbank.com. All Rights Reserved.

curves for poor substitutes are tightly curved and lie between the shapes of those shown in Figs. 9.5(a) and 9.5(c).

As you can see in the cartoon, according to the waiter's preferences, Coke and Alsatian white wine are perfect substitutes and each is a complement of pork. We hope the customers agree with him.

◆ REVIEW QUIZ

1 What is an indifference curve and how does a preference map show preferences?

2 Why does an indifference curve slope downward and why is it bowed toward the origin?

3 What do we call the magnitude of the slope of an indifference curve?

4 What is the key assumption about a consumer's marginal rate of substitution?

Work these questions in Study Plan 9.2 and get instant feedback. Do a Key Terms Quiz.   MyEconLab

The two components of the model of household choice are now in place: the budget line and the preference map. We will now use these components to work out a household's choice and to predict how choices change when prices and income change.

◆ Predicting Consumer Choices

We are now going to predict the quantities of movies and soda that Lisa chooses to buy. We're also going to see how these quantities change when a price changes or when Lisa's income changes. Finally, we're going to see how the *substitution effect* and the *income effect*, two ideas that you met in Chapter 3 (see p. 57), guarantee that for a normal good, the demand curve slopes downward.

Best Affordable Choice

When Lisa makes her best affordable choice of movies and soda, she spends all her income and is on her highest attainable indifference curve. Figure 9.6 illustrates this choice: The budget line is from Fig. 9.1 and the indifference curves are from Fig. 9.3(b). Lisa's best affordable choice is 2 movies and 6 cases of soda at point *C*—the *best affordable point*.

FIGURE 9.6   The Best Affordable Choice

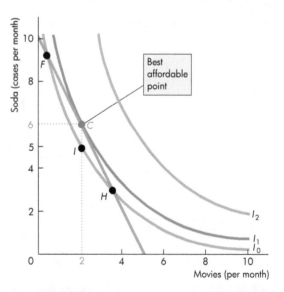

Lisa's best affordable choice is at point *C*, the point on her budget line and on her highest attainable indifference curve. At point *C*, Lisa's marginal rate of substitution between movies and soda (the magnitude of the slope of the indifference curve *I₁*) equals the relative price of movies and soda (the slope of the budget line).

—— **MyEconLab** Animation and Draw Graph ——

On the Budget Line The best affordable point is on the budget line. For every point inside the budget line, such as point *I*, there are points on the budget line that Lisa prefers. For example, she prefers all the points on the budget line between *F* and *H* to point *I*, so she chooses a point on the budget line.

On the Highest Attainable Indifference Curve Every point on the budget line lies on an indifference curve. For example, points *F* and *H* lie on the indifference curve I_0. By moving along her budget line from either *F* or *H* toward *C*, Lisa reaches points on ever-higher indifference curves that she prefers to points *F* or *H*. When Lisa gets to point *C*, she is on the highest attainable indifference curve.

Marginal Rate of Substitution Equals Relative Price
At point *C*, Lisa's marginal rate of substitution between movies and soda (the magnitude of the slope of the indifference curve) is equal to the relative price of movies and soda (the magnitude of the slope of the budget line). Lisa's willingness to pay for a movie equals her opportunity cost of a movie.

Let's now see how Lisa's choices change when a price changes.

A Change in Price

The effect of a change in the price of a good on the quantity of the good consumed is called the **price effect**. We will use Fig. 9.7(a) to work out the price effect of a fall in the price of a movie. We start with the price of a movie at $8, the price of soda at $4 a case, and Lisa's income at $40 a month. In this situation, she buys 6 cases of soda and sees 2 movies a month at point *C*.

Now suppose that the price of a movie falls to $4. With a lower price of a movie, the budget line rotates outward and becomes flatter. The new budget line is the darker orange one in Fig. 9.7(a). For a refresher on how a price change affects the budget line, check back to Fig. 9.2(a).

Lisa's best affordable point is now point *J*, where she sees 6 movies and drinks 4 cases of soda. Lisa drinks less soda and watches more movies now that movies are cheaper. She cuts her soda purchases from 6 to 4 cases and increases the number of movies she sees from 2 to 6 a month. When the price of a movie falls and the price of soda and her income remain constant, Lisa substitutes movies for soda.

FIGURE 9.7   Price Effect and Demand Curve

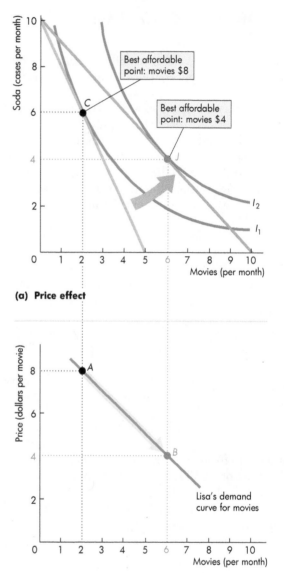

(a) Price effect

(b) Demand curve

Initially, Lisa's best affordable point is *C* in part (a). If the price of a movie falls from $8 to $4, Lisa's best affordable point is *J*. The move from *C* to *J* is the price effect.

At a price of $8 a movie, Lisa sees 2 movies a month, at point *A* in part (b). At a price of $4 a movie, she sees 6 movies a month, at point *B*. Lisa's demand curve for movies traces out her best affordable quantity of movies as the price of a movie varies.

— MyEconLab Animation —

ECONOMICS IN ACTION

Best Affordable Choice of Movies and DVDs

Between 2005 and 2014, box-office receipts rose by more than ticket prices, which means that moviegoing has increased.

Why has moviegoing increased? One answer is that the consumer's experience has improved. Movies in 3-D such as *Godzilla* play better on the big screen than at home. Also, movie theaters are able to charge a higher price for 3-D films and other big hits, which further boosts receipts. But there is another answer, and at first thought an unlikely one: Events in the market for DVD rentals have impacted going to the movies. To see why, let's look at the recent history of the DVD rentals market.

Back in 2005, Blockbuster was the main player and the price of a DVD rental was around $4 a night. Redbox was a fledgling. It had started a year earlier with just 140 kiosks in selected McDonald's restaurants. But Redbox expanded rapidly and in 2014 had outlets across the nation renting DVDs at a price of $1.20 a night. Blockbuster was history.

The easy access to DVDs at $1.20 a night transformed the markets for movie watching and the figure shows why.

A student has a budget of $50 a month to allocate to movies. To keep the story clear, we'll suppose that it cost $10 to go to a movie in both 2005 and 2014. The price of a DVD rental in 2005 was $4, so the student's budget line is the one that runs from 5 movies on the *y*-axis to 12.5 DVD rentals on the *x*-axis. The student's best affordable point is 7 rentals and 2 movies a month.

In 2014, the price of a rental falls to $1.20 a night but the price of a movie ticket remains at $10. So the budget line rotates outward. The student's best affordable point is now at 17 rentals and 3 movies a month. (This student loves movies!)

Many other things changed between 2005 and 2014 that influenced the markets for movies and DVD rentals, but the fall in the price of a DVD rental was the biggest influence.

Best Affordable Movies and DVD Rentals

The Demand Curve In Chapter 3, we asserted that the demand curve slopes downward. We can now derive a demand curve from a consumer's budget line and indifference curves. By doing so, we can see that the law of demand and the downward-sloping demand curve are consequences of a consumer's choosing her or his best affordable combination of goods.

To derive Lisa's demand curve for movies, lower the price of a movie and find her best affordable point at different prices. We've just done this for two movie prices in Fig. 9.7(a). Figure 9.7(b) highlights these two prices and two points that lie on Lisa's demand curve for movies. When the price of a movie is $8, Lisa sees 2 movies a month at point A. When the price falls to $4, she increases the number of movies she sees to 6 a month at point B. The demand curve is made up of these two points plus all the other points that tell us Lisa's best affordable quantity of movies at each movie price, with the price of soda and Lisa's income remaining the same. As you can see, Lisa's demand curve for movies slopes downward—the lower the price of a movie, the more movies she sees. This is the law of demand.

Next, let's see how Lisa changes her purchases of movies and soda when her income changes.

A Change in Income

The effect of a change in income on buying plans is called the **income effect**. Let's work out the income effect by examining how buying plans change when income changes and prices remain constant. Figure 9.8 shows the income effect when Lisa's income falls. With an income of $40, the price of a movie at $4, and the price of soda at $4 a case, Lisa's best affordable point is J—she buys 6 movies and 4 cases of soda. If her income falls to $28, her best affordable point is K—she sees 4 movies and buys 3 cases of soda. When Lisa's income falls, she buys less of both goods. Movies and soda are normal goods.

The Demand Curve and the Income Effect A change in income leads to a shift in the demand curve, as shown in Fig. 9.8(b). With an income of $40, Lisa's demand curve for movies is D_0, the same as in Fig. 9.7(b). But when her income falls to $28, she plans to see fewer movies at each price, so her demand curve shifts leftward to D_1.

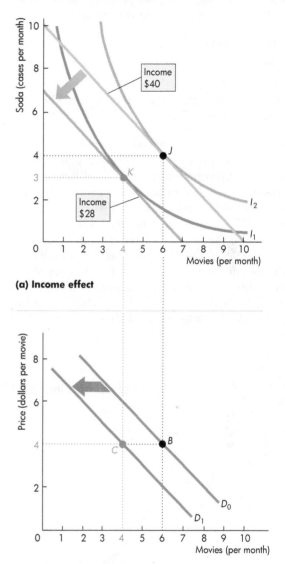

FIGURE 9.8 Income Effect and Change in Demand

(a) Income effect

(b) Demand curve for movies

A change in income shifts the budget line, changes the best affordable point, and changes demand.

In part (a), when Lisa's income decreases from $40 to $28, she sees fewer movies and buys less soda.

In part (b), when Lisa's income is $40, her demand curve for movies is D_0. When Lisa's income falls to $28, her demand curve for movies shifts leftward to D_1. For Lisa, going to the movies is a normal good. Her demand for movies decreases because she now sees fewer movies at each price.

MyEconLab Animation

Substitution Effect and Income Effect

For a normal good, a fall in its price *always* increases the quantity bought. We can prove this assertion by dividing the price effect into two parts:

- Substitution effect
- Income effect

Figure 9.9(a) shows the price effect and Figs. 9.9(b) and 9.9(c) show the two parts into which we separate the price effect.

Substitution Effect The **substitution effect** is the effect of a change in price on the quantity bought when the consumer (hypothetically) remains indifferent between the original situation and the new one. To work out Lisa's substitution effect when the price of a movie falls, we must lower her income by enough to keep her on the same indifference curve as before.

Figure 9.9(a) shows the price effect of a fall in the price of a movie from $8 to $4. The number of movies increases from 2 to 6 a month. When the price falls, suppose (hypothetically) that we cut Lisa's income to $28. What's special about $28? It is the

income that is just enough, at the new price of a movie, to keep Lisa's best affordable point on the same indifference curve (I_1) as her original point C. Lisa's budget line is now the medium orange line in Fig. 9.9(b). With the lower price of a movie and a smaller income, Lisa's best affordable point is K. The move from C to K along indifference curve I_1 is the substitution effect of the price change. The substitution effect of the fall in the price of a movie is an increase in the quantity of movies from 2 to 4. The direction of the substitution effect never varies: When the relative price of a good falls, the consumer substitutes more of that good for the other good.

Income Effect To calculate the substitution effect, we gave Lisa a $12 pay cut. To calculate the income effect, we give Lisa back her $12. The $12 increase in income shifts Lisa's budget line outward, as shown in Fig. 9.9(c). The slope of the budget line does not change because both prices remain the same. This change in Lisa's budget line is similar to the one illustrated in Fig. 9.8. As Lisa's budget line shifts outward, her consumption possibilities expand and her best afford-

---

FIGURE 9.9   Substitution Effect and Income Effect

(a) Price effect

(b) Substitution effect

When the price of a movie falls from $8 to $4, Lisa moves from point C to point J in part (a). The price effect is an increase in the number of movies from 2 to 6 a month. This price effect is separated into a substitution effect in part (b) and an income effect in part (c).

To isolate the substitution effect, we confront Lisa with the new price but keep her on her original indifference curve, I_1. The substitution effect is the move from C to K along indifference curve I_1 — an increase from 2 to 4 movies a month.

able point becomes J on indifference curve I_2. The move from K to J is the income effect of the price change.

As Lisa's income increases, she sees more movies. For Lisa, a movie is a normal good. For a normal good, the income effect *reinforces* the substitution effect. Because the two effects work in the same direction, we can be sure that the demand curve slopes downward. But some goods are inferior goods. What can we say about the demand for an inferior good?

Inferior Goods Recall that an *inferior good* is a good for which *demand decreases* when *income increases*. For an inferior good, the income effect is negative, which means that a lower price does not inevitably lead to an increase in the quantity demanded. The substitution effect of a fall in the price increases the quantity demanded, but the negative income effect works in the opposite direction and offsets the substitution effect to some degree. The key question is to what degree.

If the negative income effect *equals* the positive substitution effect, a fall in price leaves the quantity bought the same. When a fall in price leaves the quantity demanded unchanged, the demand curve is vertical and demand is perfectly inelastic.

If the negative income effect *is smaller than* the positive substitution effect, a fall in price increases the quantity bought and the demand curve still slopes downward like that for a normal good. But the demand for an inferior good might be less elastic than that for a normal good.

If the negative income effect *exceeds* the positive substitution effect, a fall in the price *decreases* the quantity bought and the demand curve *slopes upward*. This case does not appear to occur in the real world.

You can apply the indifference curve model that you've studied in this chapter to explain the changes in the way we buy recorded music, see movies, and make all our other consumption choices. We allocate our budgets to make our best affordable choices. Changes in prices and incomes change our best affordable choices and change consumption patterns.

◆ **REVIEW QUIZ**

1 When a consumer chooses the combination of goods and services to buy, what is she or he trying to achieve?

2 Explain the conditions that are met when a consumer has found the best affordable combination of goods to buy. (Use the terms *budget line*, *marginal rate of substitution*, and *relative price* in your explanation.)

3 If the price of a normal good falls, what happens to the quantity demanded of that good?

4 Into what two effects can we divide the effect of a price change?

5 For a normal good, does the income effect reinforce the substitution effect or does it partly offset the substitution effect?

Work these questions in Study Plan 9.3 and get instant feedback. Do a Key Terms Quiz.   MyEconLab

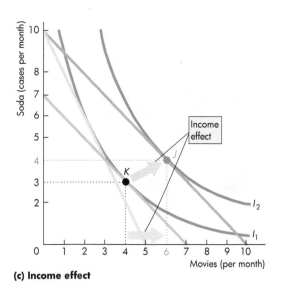

(c) Income effect

To isolate the income effect, we confront Lisa with the new price of movies but increase her income so that she can move from the original indifference curve, I_1, to the new one, I_2. The income effect is the move from K to J—an increase from 4 to 6 movies a month.

MyEconLab Animation and Draw Graph

◆ *Economics in the News* on pp. 214–215 applies the theory of household choice to explain how people chose whether to buy their books in electronic or paper format and why e-books boomed in 2011.

In the chapters that follow, we study the choices that firms make in their pursuit of profit and how those choices determine the supply of goods and services and the demand for productive resources.

Paper Books Versus e-Books

It's the End of Books As You Knew Them: e-Books Out-Sell Hardbound

ZDNet
June 18, 2012

If you follow the book trade, you knew this was coming. e-books, no matter whether you read them on an Amazon Kindle, a Barnes & Noble Nook, or your iPad are selling like crazy. We may complain about their high prices and even take e-book publishers to court for their prices and hardware lock-in, but we love our e-books. In fact, we love them so much that for the first time adult e-book sales were higher than adult hardcover sales.

It wasn't even close. The Association of American Publishers reported that in the first quarter of 2012, adult e-book sales were up to $282.3 million while adult hardcover sales came to only $229.6 million. In last year's first quarter, hardcover sales accounted for $223 million in sales while e-books logged $220.4 million.

So where are the e-book buyers coming from? The answer is trade and mass-market paperbacks. Trade paperback sales fell from $335-million to $299.8-million. That's a drop of 10.5%. Mass market paperbacks sales had it even worse. They plummeted $124.8-million to $98.9-million in the same quarter last year. That's a fall of 20.8%.

The conventional wisdom had been that e-books would eat up hardbound book sales. That's not happening. Instead, while e-books will certainly by year's end be the most popular book format, it's paperback books that are really taking a hit. Perhaps that's because when you're buying a hardcover, you're buying not just a story, but an artifact, an object with more value than just as a way to get to the story. ...

© 2012 ZDNet.

ESSENCE OF THE STORY

- In the first quarter of 2012, adult e-books out-sold adult hardcover books for the first time.

- The Association of American Publishers reported first quarter 2012, adult e-book sales at $282.3 million and adult hardcover sales at $229.6 million.

- First quarter 2011 numbers were e-books $220.4 million and hardcovers $223 million.

- Trade paperback sales fell from $335 million to $299.8 million—a 10.5 percent fall.

- Mass market paperback sales fell from $124.8 million to $98.9 million—a 20.8 percent fall.

ECONOMIC ANALYSIS

- Sales of e-books are growing rapidly because of the choices that millions of consumers are making. One of these consumers is Andy.

- Andy loves reading, but he also enjoys music. His budget for books and music is limited. So he must choose among the many alternative combinations of books and albums that he can afford.

- Figure 1 shows Andy's indifference curves for books (of all types) and albums.

- Andy's annual budget for albums and books is $600. The price of an album is $10, the price of a print book is $20, and the price of an e-book is $10.

- Figure 1 shows two budget lines: one if Andy buys print books and albums and another if he buys e-books and albums.

- In Fig. 1, the price of an e-book reader is $200. Andy must spend this amount on a reader if he is to buy e-books, which leaves him with $400 for albums and e-books. If he buys 15 e-books, he can afford 25 albums [(15 × $10) + (25 × $10) = $400].

- If Andy buys print books and albums, he can afford 15 print books and 30 albums [(15 × $20) + (30 × $10) = $600].

- This combination is Andy's best affordable choice—15 print books and 30 albums shown at point A. Andy doesn't buy e-books.

- Now the price of an e-book reader falls, and today Andy can buy a reader that previously cost $200 for $100.

- Figure 2 shows what happens to Andy's budget line and his choices.

- If Andy buys print books and albums, nothing changes. He can still afford 15 print books and 30 albums [(15 × $20) + (30 × $10) = $600].

- But if he buys e-books, his situation has changed. After spending $100 on an e-book reader, Andy is left with $500 for albums and e-books. If he buys 15 e-books he can now afford 35 albums [(15 × $10) + (35 × $10) = $500].

- Andy can now afford more albums if he buys the same number of books that he bought when the reader cost $200. But that's not Andy's best affordable combination of albums and books.

- The price of an e-book is lower than the price of a print book, so for Andy the relative price of a book has fallen and he can benefit by substituting books for albums.

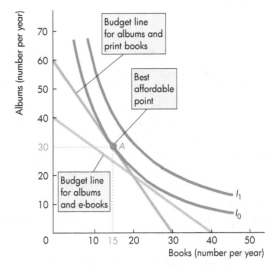

Figure 1 When the Price of a Reader Is $200

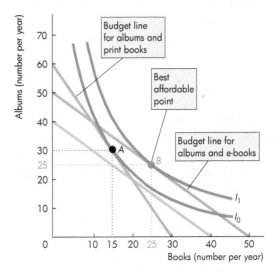

Figure 2 When the Price of a Reader Is $100

- Andy moves along his budget line to the point at which his marginal rate of substitution of books for albums equals the relative price.

- This point occurs at B where Andy buys 25 e-books and 25 albums [(25 × $10) + (25 × $10) = $500].

- The surge in e-book sales is the consequence of Andy and other rational consumers responding to the incentive of a change in relative prices and, in particular, a fall in the price of an e-book reader.

SUMMARY

Key Points

Consumption Possibilities (pp. 202–204)

- The budget line is the boundary between what a household can and cannot afford, given its income and the prices of goods.
- The point at which the budget line intersects the *y*-axis is the household's real income in terms of the good measured on that axis.
- The magnitude of the slope of the budget line is the relative price of the good measured on the *x*-axis in terms of the good measured on the *y*-axis.
- A change in the price of one good changes the slope of the budget line. A change in income shifts the budget line but does not change its slope.

Working Problems 1 to 5 will give you a better understanding of consumption possibilities.

Preferences and Indifference Curves (pp. 205–208)

- A consumer's preferences can be represented by indifference curves. The consumer is indifferent among all the combinations of goods that lie on an indifference curve.
- A consumer prefers any point above an indifference curve to any point on it and prefers any point on an indifference curve to any point below it.
- The magnitude of the slope of an indifference curve is called the marginal rate of substitution.
- The marginal rate of substitution diminishes as consumption of the good measured on the *y*-axis

decreases and consumption of the good measured on the *x*-axis increases.

Working Problems 6 and 7 will give you a better understanding of preferences and indifference curves.

Predicting Consumer Choices (pp. 208–213)

- A household consumes at its best affordable point. This point is on the budget line and on the highest attainable indifference curve and has a marginal rate of substitution equal to relative price.
- The effect of a price change (the price effect) can be divided into a substitution effect and an income effect.
- The substitution effect is the effect of a change in price on the quantity bought when the consumer (hypothetically) remains indifferent between the original choice and the new choice.
- The substitution effect always results in an increase in consumption of the good whose relative price has fallen.
- The income effect is the effect of a change in income on consumption.
- For a normal good, the income effect reinforces the substitution effect. For an inferior good, the income effect works in the opposite direction to the substitution effect.

Working Problems 8 to 11 will give you a better understanding of predicting consumer choices.

Key Terms

MyEconLab Key Terms Quiz

Budget line, 202
Diminishing marginal rate of
   substitution, 206
Income effect, 211

Indifference curve, 205
Marginal rate of substitution, 206
Price effect, 209
Real income, 203

Relative price, 203
Substitution effect, 212

◆ WORKED PROBLEM

MyEconLab   You can work this problem in Chapter 9 Study Plan.

Wendy drinks 10 sugary drinks and 4 smoothies a week. Smoothies are $5 each and sugary drinks were $2 each. This week, things are different: The government has slapped a tax on sugary drinks and their price has doubled to $4. But it's not all bad news for Wendy. The government has also revised the income tax, so Wendy's drinks budget has increased. She can now just afford to buy her usual 10 sugary drinks and 4 smoothies a week.

Questions

1. What was Wendy's drinks budget last week and what is it this week?
2. What was Wendy's opportunity cost of a sugary drink last week and what is it this week?
3. Does Wendy buy 10 sugary drinks and 4 smoothies this week? Explain.
4. Is Wendy better off this week than last week? Explain.

Solutions

1. To find Wendy's drinks budget, use the fact that Income (available for drinks) = Expenditure.

   Expenditure = (Price of a sugary drink × Quantity of sugary drinks) + (Price of a smoothie × Quantity of smoothies).

   Last week, her income was ($2 × 10) + ($5 × 4) = $40.

   This week, her income is ($4 × 10) + ($5 × 4) = $60.

Key Point: Income limits expenditure and expenditure equals price multiplied by quantity, summed over the goods consumed.

2. Wendy's opportunity cost of a sugary drink is the number of smoothies she must forgo to get 1 sugary drink. Wendy's opportunity cost equals the relative price of a sugary drink, which is the price of a sugary drink divided by the price of a smoothie.

   Last week, Wendy's opportunity cost of a sugary drink was $2 ÷ $5 = 2/5 or 0.4 smoothies.

   This week, it is $4 ÷ $5 = 4/5 or 0.8 smoothies.

Key Point: A relative price is an opportunity cost.

3. Wendy does not buy 10 sugary drinks and 4 smoothies this week because it is not her best affordable choice.

At her best affordable choice, Wendy's marginal rate of substitution (*MRS*) between sugary drinks and smoothies is equal to the relative price of sugary drinks and smoothies.

Last week, when she chose 10 sugary drinks and 4 smoothies, her *MRS* was 0.4, equal to last week's relative price of 0.4 smoothies per sugary drink. This week, the relative price is 0.8 smoothies per sugary drink, so Wendy changes her choice to make her *MRS* equal 0.8.

To increase her *MRS* from 0.4 to 0.8, Wendy buys fewer sugary drinks and more smoothies. We know how she changes her choice but not the new quantities she buys. To get the quantities, we would need to know Wendy's preferences as described by her indifference curves.

Key Point: When the relative price of a good rises, the consumer buys less of that good to make the *MRS* increase to equal the higher relative price.

4. Wendy is better off! She can still buy her last week's choice but, at that choice, she is not at her best affordable point. So by buying more smoothies, she moves along her budget line to a higher indifference curve at which *MRS* equals 0.8.

Key Point: When both income and the relative price of a good change so that the old choice is still available, the consumer's best affordable choice changes.

Key Figure

MyEconLab Interactive Animation

STUDY PLAN PROBLEMS AND APPLICATIONS

MyEconLab   You can work Problems 1 to 11 in Chapter 9 Study Plan and get instant feedback.

Consumption Possibilities (Study Plan 9.1)

Use the following data to work Problems 1 and 2.

Sara's income is $12 a week. The price of popcorn is $3 a bag, and the price of a smoothie is $3.

1. Calculate Sara's real income in terms of smoothies. Calculate her real income in terms of popcorn. What is the relative price of smoothies in terms of popcorn? What is the opportunity cost of a smoothie?

2. Calculate the equation for Sara's budget line (with bags of popcorn on the left side). Draw a graph of Sara's budget line with the quantity of smoothies on the x-axis. What is the slope of Sara's budget line? What determines its value?

Use the following data to work Problems 3 and 4.

Sara's income falls from $12 to $9 a week, while the price of popcorn is unchanged at $3 a bag and the price of a smoothie is unchanged at $3.

3. What is the effect of the fall in Sara's income on her real income in terms of (a) smoothies and (b) popcorn?

4. What is the effect of the fall in Sara's income on the relative price of a smoothie in terms of popcorn? What is the slope of Sara's new budget line if it is drawn with smoothies on the x-axis?

5. Sara's income is $12 a week. The price of popcorn rises from $3 to $6 a bag, and the price of a smoothie is unchanged at $3. Explain how Sara's budget line changes with smoothies on the x-axis.

Preferences and Indifference Curves (Study Plan 9.2)

6. Draw figures that show your indifference curves for the following pairs of goods:
   - Right gloves and left gloves
   - Coca-Cola and Pepsi
   - Desktop computers and laptop computers
   - Strawberries and ice cream

For each pair, are the goods perfect substitutes, perfect complements, substitutes, complements, or unrelated?

7. Discuss the shape of the indifference curve for each of the following pairs of goods:
   - Orange juice and smoothies
   - Baseballs and baseball bats

- Left running shoe and right running shoe
- Eyeglasses and contact lenses

Explain the relationship between the shape of the indifference curve and the marginal rate of substitution as the quantities of the two goods change.

Predicting Consumer Choices (Study Plan 9.3)

Use the following data to work Problems 8 and 9.

Pam has made her best affordable choice of cookies and granola bars. She spends all of her weekly income on 30 cookies at $1 each and 5 granola bars at $2 each. Next week, she expects the price of a cookie to fall to 50¢ and the price of a granola bar to rise to $5.

8. a. Will Pam be able to buy and want to buy 30 cookies and 5 granola bars next week?

   b. Which situation does Pam prefer: cookies at $1 and granola bars at $2 or cookies at 50¢ and granola bars at $5?

9. a. If Pam changes how she spends her weekly income, will she buy more or fewer cookies and more or fewer granola bars?

   b. When the prices change next week, will there be an income effect, a substitution effect, or both at work?

Use the following news clip to work Problems 10 and 11.

Boom Time for "Gently Used" Clothes

Most retailers are blaming the economy for their poor sales, but one store chain that sells used name-brand children's clothes, toys, and furniture is boldly declaring that an economic downturn can actually be a boon for its business. Last year, the company took in $20 million in sales, up 5% from the previous year.

Source: CNN, April 17, 2008

10. a. According to the news clip, is used clothing a normal good or an inferior good? If the price of used clothing falls and income remains the same, explain how the quantity of used clothing bought changes.

   b. Describe the substitution effect and the income effect that occur.

11. Use a graph of a family's indifference curves for used clothing and other goods. Then draw two budget lines to show the effect of a fall in income on the quantity of used clothing purchased.

◆ ADDITIONAL PROBLEMS AND APPLICATIONS

 MyEconLab   You can work these problems in MyEconLab if assigned by your instructor.

Consumption Possibilities

Use the following data to work Problems 12 to 15.

Marc has a budget of $20 a month to spend on root beer and DVDs. The price of root beer is $5 a bottle, and the price of a DVD is $10.

12. What is the relative price of root beer in terms of DVDs and what is the opportunity cost of a bottle of root beer?

13. Calculate Marc's real income in terms of root beer. Calculate his real income in terms of DVDs.

14. Calculate the equation for Marc's budget line (with the quantity of root beer on the left side).

15. Draw a graph of Marc's budget line with the quantity of DVDs on the *x*-axis. What is the slope of Marc's budget line? What determines its value?

Use the following data to work Problems 16 to 19.

Amy has $20 a week to spend on coffee and cake. The price of coffee is $4 a cup, and the price of cake is $2 a slice.

16. Calculate Amy's real income in terms of cake. Calculate the relative price of cake in terms of coffee.

17. Calculate the equation for Amy's budget line (with cups of coffee on the left side).

18. If Amy's income increases to $24 a week and the prices of coffee and cake remain unchanged, describe the change in her budget line.

19. If the price of cake doubles while the price of coffee remains at $4 a cup and Amy's income remains at $20, describe the change in her budget line.

Use the following news clip to work Problems 20 and 21.

Gas Prices Straining Budgets

With gas prices rising, many people say they are staying in and scaling back spending to try to keep within their budget. They are driving as little as possible, cutting back on shopping and eating out, and reducing other discretionary spending.

Source: CNN, February 29, 2008

20. a. Sketch a budget line for a household that spends its income on only two goods: gasoline and restaurant meals. Identify the combinations of gasoline and restaurant meals that are affordable and those that are unaffordable.

   b. Sketch a second budget line to show how a rise in the price of gasoline changes the affordable and unaffordable combinations of gasoline and restaurant meals. Describe how the household's consumption possibilities change.

21. How does a rise in the price of gasoline change the relative price of a restaurant meal? How does a rise in the price of gasoline change real income in terms of restaurant meals?

Preferences and Indifference Curves

Use the following information to work Problems 22 and 23.

Rashid buys only books and CDs and the figure shows his preference map.

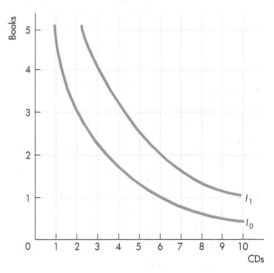

22. a. If Rashid chooses 3 books and 2 CDs, what is his marginal rate of substitution?

   b. If Rashid chooses 2 books and 6 CDs, what is his marginal rate of substitution?

23. Do Rashid's indifference curves display diminishing marginal rate of substitution? Explain why or why not.

24. **You May Be Paid More (or Less) Than You Think**

It's so hard to put a price on happiness, isn't it? But if you've ever had to choose between a job you like and a better-paying one that you like less, you probably wished some economist would tell you how much job satisfaction is worth. Trust in management is by far the biggest component to consider. Say you get a new boss and your trust in management goes up a bit (say, up 1 point on a 10-point scale). That's like getting a 36-percent pay raise. In other words, that increased level of trust will boost your level of overall satisfaction in life by about the same amount as a 36-percent raise would.

Source: CNN, March 29, 2006

a. Measure trust in management on a 10-point scale, measure pay on the same 10-point scale, and think of them as two goods. Sketch an indifference curve (with trust on the *x*-axis) that is consistent with the news clip.

b. What is the marginal rate of substitution between trust in management and pay according to this news clip?

c. What does the news clip imply about the principle of diminishing marginal rate of substitution? Is that implication likely to be correct?

Predicting Consumer Choices

Use the following data to work Problems 25 and 26.
Jim has made his best affordable choice of muffins and coffee. He spends all of his income on 10 muffins at $1 each and 20 cups of coffee at $2 each. Now the price of a muffin rises to $1.50 and the price of coffee falls to $1.75 a cup.

25. a. Will Jim now be able and want to buy 10 muffins and 20 coffees?

b. Which situation does Jim prefer: muffins at $1 and coffee at $2 a cup or muffins at $1.50 and coffee at $1.75 a cup?

26. a. If Jim changes the quantities that he buys, will he buy more or fewer muffins and more or less coffee? Explain your answer.

b. When the prices change, will there be an income effect, a substitution effect, or both at work? Explain your answer.

Use the following data and figure to work Problems 27 to 29.
Sara's income is $12 a week. The price of popcorn is $3 a bag, and the price of cola is $1.50 a can. The figure shows Sara's preference map for popcorn and cola.

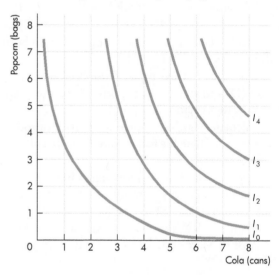

27. What quantities of popcorn and cola does Sara buy? What is Sara's marginal rate of substitution at the point at which she consumes?

28. Suppose that the price of cola rises from $1.50 to $3.00 a can while the price of popcorn and Sara's income remain the same. What quantities of cola and popcorn does Sara now buy? What are two points on Sara's demand curve for cola? Draw Sara's demand curve.

29. Suppose that the price of cola rises to $3.00 a can and the price of popcorn and Sara's income remain the same.

a. What is the substitution effect of this price change and what is the income effect of the price change?

b. Is cola a normal good or an inferior good? Explain.

Economics in the News

30. After you have studied *Economics in the News* on pp. 214–215, answer the following questions.

a. How do you buy books?

b. Sketch your budget line for books and other goods.

c. Sketch your indifference curves for books and other goods.

d. Identify your best affordable point.

Making the Most of Life

PART THREE

UNDERSTANDING HOUSEHOLDS' CHOICES

The powerful forces of demand and supply shape the fortunes of families, businesses, nations, and empires in the same unrelenting way that the tides and winds shape rocks and coastlines. You saw in Chapters 3 through 7 how these forces raise and lower prices, increase and decrease quantities bought and sold, cause revenues to fluctuate, and send resources to their most valuable uses.

These powerful forces begin quietly and privately with the choices that each one of us makes. Chapters 8 and 9 probe these individual choices, offering two alternative approaches to explaining both consumption plans and the allocation of time. These explanations of consumption plans can also explain "non-economic" choices, such as whether to marry and how many children to have. In a sense, there are no non-economic choices. If there is scarcity, there must be choice, and economics studies all choices.

The earliest economists (Adam Smith and his contemporaries) did not have a very deep understanding of households' choices. It was not until the nineteenth century that progress was made in this area when Jeremy Bentham (below) introduced the concept of utility and applied it to the study of human choices. Today, Steven Levitt, whom you will meet on the following page, is one of the most influential students of human behavior.

Jeremy Bentham *(1748–1832), who lived in London, was the son and grandson of lawyers and was himself trained as a barrister. But Bentham rejected the opportunity to maintain the family tradition and, instead, spent his life as a writer, activist, and Member of Parliament in the pursuit of rational laws that would bring the greatest happiness to the greatest number of people.*

Bentham, whose embalmed body is preserved to this day in a glass cabinet in the University of London, was the first person to use the concept of utility to explain human choices. But in Bentham's day, the distinction between explaining and prescribing was not a sharp one, and Bentham was ready to use his ideas to tell people how they ought to behave. He was one of the first to propose pensions for the retired, guaranteed employment, minimum wages, and social benefits such as free education and free medical care.

"... It is the greatest happiness of the greatest number that is the measure of right and wrong."

JEREMY BENTHAM
Fragment on Government

I think of economics as being primarily about a way of looking at the world and a set of tools for thinking clearly.

STEVEN D. LEVITT is William B. Ogden Distinguished Service Professor of Economics at the University of Chicago. Born in Minneapolis, he was an undergraduate at Harvard and a graduate student at MIT. Among his many honors, he was recently awarded the John Bates Clark Medal, given to the best economist under 40.

Professor Levitt has studied an astonishingly wide range of human choices and their outcomes. He has examined the effects of policing on crime, shown that real estate agents get a higher price when they sell their own homes than when they sell other people's, devised a test to detect cheating teachers, and studied the choices of drug dealers and gang members. Much of this research has been popularized in *Freakonomics* (Steven D. Levitt and Stephen J. Dubner, HarperCollins, 2005). What unifies this apparently diverse body of research is the use of natural experiments. Professor Levitt has an incredible ability to find just the right set of events and the data the events have generated to enable him to isolate the effect he's looking for.

Michael Parkin talked with Steven Levitt about his work and what economists have discovered about how people respond to incentives.

Why did you become an economist?

As a freshman in college, I took introductory economics. All the ideas made perfect sense to me—it was the way I naturally thought. My friends were befuddled. I thought, "This is the field for me!"

The idea of rational choice made at the margin lies at the heart of economics. Would you say that your work generally supports that idea or challenges it? Can you provide some examples?

I don't like the word "rational" in this context. I think economists model agents as being rational just for convenience. What really matters is whether people respond to incentives. My work very much supports the idea that humans in all types of circumstances respond strongly to incentives. I've seen it with drug dealers, auto thieves, sumo wrestlers, real estate agents, and elementary school teachers, just to name a few examples.

Drug dealers, for instance, want to make money, but they also want to avoid being arrested or even killed. In the data we have on drug sellers, we see that when the drug trade is more lucrative, dealers are willing to take greater risks of arrest to carve out a share of the market…. Sumo wrestlers, on the other hand, care mostly about their official ranking. Sometimes matches occur where one wrestler has more to lose or gain than the other wrestler. We find that sumo wrestlers make corrupt deals to make sure the wrestler who wins is the one who needs to win.

Why is an economist interested in crime and cheating?

I think of economics as being primarily about a way of looking at the world and a set of tools for thinking clearly. The topics you apply these tools to are unlimited. That is why I think economics has been so powerful. If you understand economics and use the tools wisely, you will be a better business person, doctor, public servant, parent.

*Read the full interview with Steven Levitt in MyEconLab.

10

ORGANIZING PRODUCTION

After studying this chapter,
you will be able to:

◆ Explain the economic problem that all firms face

◆ Distinguish between technological efficiency and
economic efficiency

◆ Define and explain the principal–agent problem

◆ Distinguish among different types of markets

◆ Explain why markets coordinate some economic
activities and why firms coordinate others

In 1990, a British scientist named Tim Berners-Lee
invented the World Wide Web, a remarkable idea
that paved the way for the creation of thousands of
profitable firms among which are Facebook, Twitter,
Google, Amazon, and eBay.

What are the decisions that firms must make?
That's the question you study in this chapter. In
Economics in the News at the end of the chapter,
we'll look at some decisions made by Facebook and
Google in the Internet advertising market.

◆ The Firm and Its Economic Problem

The 20 million firms in the United States differ in size and in the scope of what they do, but they all perform the same basic economic functions. Each **firm** is an institution that hires factors of production and organizes those factors to produce and sell goods and services. Our goal is to predict firms' behavior. To do so, we need to know a firm's goal and the constraints it faces. We start with the goal.

The Firm's Goal

When economists ask entrepreneurs what they are trying to achieve, they get many different answers. Some talk about making a high-quality product, others about business growth, others about market share, others about the job satisfaction of their workforce, and an increasing number today talk about social and environmental responsibility. All of these goals are pursued by firms, but they are not the fundamental goal: They are the means to that goal.

A firm's goal is to maximize profit. A firm that does not seek to maximize profit is either eliminated or taken over by a firm that does seek that goal.

What is the profit that a firm seeks to maximize? To answer this question, we'll look at Campus Sweaters, Inc., a small producer of knitted sweaters owned and operated by Cindy.

Accounting Profit

In 2012, Campus Sweaters received $400,000 for the sweaters it sold and paid out $80,000 for wool, $20,000 for utilities, $120,000 for wages, $5,000 for the lease of a computer, and $5,000 in interest on a bank loan. These expenses total $230,000, so the firm had a cash surplus of $170,000.

To measure the profit of Campus Sweaters, Cindy's accountant subtracted $20,000 for the depreciation of buildings and knitting machines from the $170,000 cash surplus. *Depreciation* is the fall in the value of a firm's capital. To calculate depreciation, accountants use Internal Revenue Service rules based on standards established by the Financial Accounting Standards Board. Using these rules, Cindy's accountant calculated that Campus Sweaters made a profit of $150,000 in 2012.

Economic Accounting

Accountants measure a firm's profit to ensure that the firm pays the correct amount of income tax and to show its investors how their funds are being used.

Economists measure a firm's profit to enable them to predict the firm's decisions, and the goal of these decisions is to maximize *economic profit*. **Economic profit** is equal to total revenue minus total cost, with total cost measured as the *opportunity cost of production*.

A Firm's Opportunity Cost of Production

The *opportunity cost* of any action is the highest-valued alternative forgone. The *opportunity cost of production* is the value of the best alternative use of the resources that a firm uses in production.

A firm's opportunity cost of production is the value of real alternatives forgone. We express opportunity cost in money units so that we can compare and add up the value of the alternatives forgone.

A firm's opportunity cost of production is the sum of the cost of using resources

- Bought in the market
- Owned by the firm
- Supplied by the firm's owner

Resources Bought in the Market A firm incurs an opportunity cost when it buys resources in the market. The amount spent on these resources is an opportunity cost of production because the firm could have bought different resources to produce some other good or service. For Campus Sweaters, the resources bought in the market are wool, utilities, labor, a leased computer, and a bank loan. The $230,000 spent on these items in 2012 could have been spent on something else, so it is an opportunity cost of producing sweaters.

Resources Owned by the Firm A firm incurs an opportunity cost when it uses its own capital. The cost of using capital owned by the firm is an opportunity cost of production because the firm could sell the capital that it owns and rent capital from another firm. When a firm uses its own capital, it implicitly rents it from itself. In this case, the firm's opportunity cost of using the capital it owns is called the **implicit rental rate** of capital. The implicit rental rate of capital has two components: economic depreciation and forgone interest.

Economic Depreciation Accountants measure *depreciation*, the fall in the value of a firm's capital, using formulas that are unrelated to the change in the market value of capital. **Economic depreciation** is the fall in the *market value* of a firm's capital over a given period. It equals the market price of the capital at the beginning of the period minus the market price of the capital at the end of the period.

Suppose that Campus Sweaters could have sold its buildings and knitting machines on January 1, 2012, for $400,000 and that it can sell the same capital on December 31, 2012, for $375,000. The firm's economic depreciation during 2012 is $25,000 ($400,000 – $375,000). This forgone $25,000 is an opportunity cost of production.

Forgone Interest The funds used to buy capital could have been used for some other purpose, and in their next best use, they would have earned interest. This forgone interest is an opportunity cost of production.

Suppose that Campus Sweaters used $300,000 of its own funds to buy capital. If the firm invested its $300,000 in bonds instead of a knitting factory (and rented the capital it needs to produce sweaters), it would have earned $15,000 a year in interest. This forgone interest is an opportunity cost of production.

Resources Supplied by the Firm's Owner A firm's owner might supply *both* entrepreneurship and labor.

Entrepreneurship The factor of production that organizes a firm and makes its decisions might be supplied by the firm's owner or by a hired entrepreneur. The return to entrepreneurship is profit, and the profit that an entrepreneur earns *on average* is called **normal profit**. Normal profit is the cost of entrepreneurship and is an opportunity cost of production.

If Cindy supplies entrepreneurial services herself, and if the normal profit she can earn on these services is $45,000 a year, this amount is an opportunity cost of production at Campus Sweaters.

Owner's Labor Services *In addition* to supplying entrepreneurship, the owner of a firm might supply labor but not take a wage. The opportunity cost of the owner's labor is the wage income forgone by not taking the best alternative job.

If Cindy supplies labor to Campus Sweaters, and if the wage she can earn on this labor at another firm is $55,000 a year, this amount of wages forgone is an opportunity cost of production at Campus Sweaters.

Economic Accounting: A Summary

Table 10.1 summarizes the economic accounting. Campus Sweaters' total revenue is $400,000; its opportunity cost of production is $370,000; and its economic profit is $30,000.

Cindy's personal income is the $30,000 of economic profit plus the $100,000 that she earns by supplying resources to Campus Sweaters.

The Firm's Decisions

To achieve the objective of maximum economic profit, a firm must make five decisions:

1. What to produce and in what quantities
2. How to produce
3. How to organize and compensate its managers and workers
4. How to market and price its products
5. What to produce itself and buy from others

In all these decisions, a firm's actions are limited by the constraints that it faces. Your next task is to learn about these constraints.

TABLE 10.1   Economic Accounting

Item		Amount
Total Revenue		**$400,000**
Cost of Resources Bought in Market		
Wool	$80,000	
Utilities	20,000	
Wages	120,000	
Computer lease	5,000	
Bank interest	5,000	$230,000
Cost of Resources Owned by Firm		
Economic depreciation	$25,000	
Forgone interest	15,000	$40,000
Cost of Resources Supplied by Owner		
Cindy's normal profit	$45,000	
Cindy's forgone wages	55,000	$100,000
Opportunity Cost of Production		**$370,000**
Economic Profit		**$30,000**

━━━━━━━━━━━━━━━ MyEconLab Animation ━━━

The Firm's Constraints

Three features of a firm's environment limit the maximum economic profit it can make. They are

- Technology constraints
- Information constraints
- Market constraints

Technology Constraints Economists define technology broadly. A **technology** is any method of producing a good or service. Technology includes the detailed designs of machines and the layout of the workplace. It includes the organization of the firm. For example, the shopping mall is one technology for producing retail services. It is a different technology from the catalog store, which in turn is different from the downtown store.

It might seem surprising that a firm's profit is limited by technology because it seems that technological advances are constantly increasing profit opportunities. Almost every day, we learn about some new technological advance that amazes us. With computers that speak and recognize our own speech and cars that can find the address we need in a city we've never visited, we can accomplish more than ever.

Technology advances over time. But at each point in time, to produce more output and gain more revenue, a firm must hire more resources and incur greater costs. The increase in profit that a firm can achieve is limited by the technology available. For example, by using its current plant and workforce, Ford can produce some maximum number of cars per day. To produce more cars per day, Ford must hire more resources, which increases its costs and limits the increase in profit that it can make by selling the additional cars.

Information Constraints We never possess all the information we would like to have to make decisions. We lack information about both the future and the present. For example, suppose you plan to buy a new computer. When should you buy it? The answer depends on how the price is going to change in the future. Where should you buy it? The answer depends on the prices at hundreds of different computer stores. To get the best deal, you must compare the quality and prices in every store. But the opportunity cost of this comparison exceeds the cost of the computer!

A firm is constrained by limited information about the quality and efforts of its workforce, the current and future buying plans of its customers, and the plans of its competitors. Workers might make too little effort, customers might switch to competing suppliers, and a competitor might enter the market and take some of the firm's business.

To address these problems, firms create incentives to boost workers' efforts even when no one is monitoring them; conduct market research to lower uncertainty about customers' buying plans; and "spy" on each other to anticipate competitive challenges. But these efforts don't eliminate incomplete information and uncertainty, which limit the economic profit that a firm can make.

Market Constraints The quantity each firm can sell and the price it can obtain are constrained by its customers' willingness to pay and by the prices and marketing efforts of other firms. Similarly, the resources that a firm can buy and the prices it must pay for them are limited by the willingness of people to work for and invest in the firm. Firms spend billions of dollars a year marketing and selling their products. Some of the most creative minds strive to find the right message that will produce a knockout television advertisement. Market constraints and the expenditures firms make to overcome them limit the profit a firm can make.

◆ REVIEW QUIZ

1 What is a firm's fundamental goal and what happens if the firm doesn't pursue this goal?
2 Why do accountants and economists calculate a firm's costs and profit in different ways?
3 What are the items that make opportunity cost differ from the accountant's measure of cost?
4 Why is normal profit an opportunity cost?
5 What are the constraints that a firm faces? How does each constraint limit the firm's profit?

Work these questions in Study Plan 10.1 and get instant feedback. Do a Key Terms Quiz.   MyEconLab

In the rest of this chapter and in Chapters 11 through 14, we study the choices that firms make. You're going to learn how we can predict a firm's decisions as those that maximize profit given the constraints the firm faces. We begin by taking a closer look at a firm's technology constraints.

Technological and Economic Efficiency

Microsoft employs a large workforce, and most Microsoft workers possess a large amount of human capital. But the firm uses a small amount of physical capital. In contrast, a coal-mining company employs a huge amount of mining equipment (physical capital) and almost no labor. Why? The answer lies in the concept of efficiency. There are two concepts of production efficiency: technological efficiency and economic efficiency. **Technological efficiency** occurs when the firm produces a given output by using the least amount of inputs. **Economic efficiency** occurs when the firm produces a given output at the least cost. Let's explore the two concepts of efficiency by studying an example.

Suppose that there are four alternative techniques for making TVs:

A. *Robot production.* One person monitors the entire computer-driven process.

B. *Production line.* Workers specialize in a small part of the job as the emerging TV passes them on a production line.

C. *Hand-tool production.* A single worker uses a few hand tools to make a TV.

D. *Bench production.* Workers specialize in a small part of the job but walk from bench to bench to perform their tasks.

Table 10.2 sets out the amounts of labor and capital required by each of these four methods to make 10 TVs a day.

Which of these alternative methods are technologically efficient?

Technological Efficiency

Recall that *technological efficiency* occurs when the firm produces a given output by using the least amount of inputs. Look at the numbers in the table and notice that method *A* uses the most capital and the least labor. Method *C* uses the most labor and the least capital. Method *B* and method *D* lie between the two extremes. They use less capital and more labor than method *A* and less labor but more capital than method *C*.

Compare methods *B* and *D*. Method *D* requires 100 workers and 10 units of capital to produce 10

TABLE 10.2   Four Ways of Making 10 TVs a Day

		Quantities of inputs	
	Method	Labor	Capital
A	Robot production	1	1,000
B	Production line	10	10
C	Hand-tool production	1,000	1
D	Bench production	100	10

TVs. Method *B* can produce those same 10 TVs by using 10 workers and the same 10 units of capital. Because method *D* uses the same amount of capital and more labor than method *B*, method *D* is not technologically efficient.

Are any of the other methods not technologically efficient? The answer is no. Each of the other methods is technologically efficient. Method *A* uses more capital but less labor than method *B*, and method *C* uses more labor but less capital than method *B*.

Which of the methods are economically efficient?

Economic Efficiency

Recall that *economic efficiency* occurs when the firm produces a given output at the least cost.

Method *D*, which is technologically inefficient, is also economically inefficient. It uses the same amount of capital as method *B* but 10 times as much labor, so it costs more. A technologically inefficient method is never economically efficient.

One of the three technologically efficient methods is economically efficient. The other two are economically inefficient. But which method is economically efficient depends on factor prices.

In Table 10.3(a), the wage rate is $75 per day and the rental rate of capital is $250 per day. By studying Table 10.3(a), you can see that method *B* has the lowest cost and is the economically efficient method.

In Table 10.3(b), the wage rate is $150 a day and the rental rate of capital is $1 a day. Looking at Table 10.3(b), you can see that method *A* has the lowest cost and is the economically efficient method. In this case, capital is so cheap relative to labor that the

TABLE 10.3   The Costs of Different Ways of Making 10 TVs a Day

(a) Wage rate $75 per day; Capital rental rate $250 per day

Method	Inputs Labor	Capital	Labor cost ($75 per day)		Capital cost ($250 per day)		Total cost
A	1	1,000	$75	+	$250,000	=	$250,075
B	10	10	750	+	2,500	=	3,250
C	1,000	1	75,000	+	250	=	75,250

(b) Wage rate $150 per day; Capital rental rate $1 per day

Method	Inputs Labor	Capital	Labor cost ($150 per day)		Capital cost ($1 per day)		Total cost
A	1	1,000	$150	+	$1,000	=	$1,150
B	10	10	1,500	+	10	=	1,510
C	1,000	1	150,000	+	1	=	150,001

(c) Wage rate $1 per day; Capital rental rate $1,000 per day

Method	Inputs Labor	Capital	Labor cost ($1 per day)		Capital cost ($1,000 per day)		Total cost
A	1	1,000	$1	+	$1,000,000	=	$1,000,001
B	10	10	10	+	10,000	=	10,010
C	1,000	1	1,000	+	1,000	=	2,000

method that uses the most capital is the economically efficient method.

In Table 10.3(c), the wage rate is $1 a day and the rental rate of capital is $1,000 a day. You can see that method *C* has the lowest cost and is the economically efficient method. In this case, labor is so cheap relative to capital that the method that uses the most labor is the economically efficient method.

Economic efficiency depends on the relative costs of resources. The economically efficient method is the one that uses a smaller amount of the more expensive resource and a larger amount of the less expensive resource.

A firm that is not economically efficient does not maximize profit. Natural selection favors efficient firms and inefficient firms disappear. Inefficient firms go out of business or are taken over by firms that produce at lower costs.

◆ REVIEW QUIZ

1 Is a firm technologically efficient if it uses the latest technology? Why or why not?

2 Is a firm economically inefficient if it can cut its costs by producing less? Why or why not?

3 Explain the key distinction between technological efficiency and economic efficiency.

4 Why do some firms use large amounts of capital and small amounts of labor while others use small amounts of capital and large amounts of labor?

Work these questions in Study Plan 10.2 and get instant feedback. Do a Key Terms Quiz.   MyEconLab

Next we study the information constraints that firms face and the wide array of organization structures these constraints generate.

◗ Information and Organization

Each firm organizes the production of goods and services using a combination of two systems:

- Command systems
- Incentive systems

Command Systems

A **command system** is a method of organizing production that uses a managerial hierarchy. Commands pass downward through the hierarchy, and information passes upward.

The military uses the purest form of command system. A commander-in-chief makes the big decisions about strategic goals. Beneath this highest level, generals organize their military resources. Beneath the generals, successively lower ranks organize smaller and smaller units but pay attention to ever-increasing degrees of detail. At the bottom of the hierarchy are the people who operate weapons systems.

Command systems in firms are not as rigid as those in the military, but they share some similar features. A chief executive officer (CEO) sits at the top of a firm's command system. Senior executives specialize in managing production, marketing, finance, and personnel. Beneath these senior managers are the people who supervise the day-to-day operations of the business and beneath them, the people who operate the firm's machines and who make and sell the firm's products.

Managers try to be well informed, but they almost always have incomplete information about what is happening in the divisions for which they are responsible. For this reason, firms also use incentive systems.

Incentive Systems

An **incentive system** is a method of organizing production that uses a market-like mechanism inside the firm. Instead of issuing commands, senior managers create compensation schemes to induce workers to perform in ways that maximize the firm's profit.

Incentive systems operate at all levels in a firm. The compensation plan of a CEO might include a share in the firm's profit, factory floor workers sometimes receive compensation based on the quantity they produce, and salespeople, who spend most of their working time alone, are induced to work hard by being paid a small salary and a large performance-related bonus.

The Principal–Agent Problem

The **principal–agent problem** is the problem of devising compensation rules that induce an *agent* to act in the best interest of a *principal*. For example, the stockholders of Texaco are *principals,* and the firm's managers are *agents*. The stockholders (the principals) must induce the managers (agents) to act in the stockholders' best interest. Similarly, Mark Zuckerberg (a principal) must induce the designers who are working on the next generation Facebook (agents) to work efficiently.

Agents, whether they are managers or workers, pursue their own goals and often impose costs on a principal. For example, the goal of stockholders of Citicorp (principals) is to maximize the firm's profit—its true profit, not some fictitious paper profit. But the firm's profit depends on the actions of its managers (agents), and they have their own goals. Perhaps a bank manager takes a customer to a ball game on the pretense that she is building customer loyalty, when in fact she is simply enjoying on-the-job leisure. This same manager is also a principal, and her tellers are agents. The manager wants the tellers to work hard and attract new customers so that she can meet her operating targets. But the workers slack off and take on-the-job leisure.

Coping with the Principal–Agent Problem

A principal must create incentives that induce each agent to work in the interests of the principal. Three ways of coping with the principal–agent problem are

- Ownership
- Incentive pay
- Long-term contracts

Ownership By assigning ownership (or part-ownership) of a business to managers or workers, it is sometimes possible to induce a job performance that increases a firm's profits. Part-ownership is quite common for senior managers but less common for workers. When United Airlines was running into problems a few years ago, it made most of its employees owners of the company.

Incentive Pay Incentive pay—pay related to performance—is very common. Incentives are based on a variety of performance criteria such as profits, production, or sales targets. Promoting an employee for good performance is another example of the use of incentive pay.

Long-Term Contracts Long-term contracts tie the long-term fortunes of managers and workers (agents) to the success of the principal(s)—the owner(s) of the firm. For example, a multiyear employment contract for a CEO encourages that person to take a long-term view and devise strategies that achieve maximum profit over a sustained period.

These three ways of coping with the principal–agent problem give rise to different types of business organization.

Types of Business Organization

The three main types of business organization are

- Proprietorship
- Partnership
- Corporation

Proprietorship A *proprietorship* is a firm with a single owner—a proprietor—who has unlimited liability. *Unlimited liability* is the legal responsibility for all the

---

◆ ECONOMICS IN THE NEWS

Principals and Agents Get It Wrong

JPMorgan Pay May Be Clawed Back

In May 2012, JPMorgan Chase announced that traders in London had incurred losses of $2 billion. CEO Jamie Dimon said the losses arose from a "flawed, complex, poorly reviewed, poorly executed, and poorly monitored" trading strategy. JPMorgan Chase's stock price fell on the news. One top executive took early retirement. JPMorgan executives and traders are compensated by results with bonus payments in cash and stock options. Dimon said "It's likely that there will be clawbacks" of compensation.

Sources: *AP, Bloomberg,* and *Reuters,* May/June, 2012

THE QUESTIONS

- Who are the principals and who are the agents?
- How did JPMorgan try to cope with its principal–agent problem?
- On the occasion reported here, how did JPMorgan get it wrong?
- What role did JPMorgan's share price play?

THE ANSWERS

- The JPMorgan stockholders are principals and Jamie Dimon is their agent.
- Jamie Dimon, as CEO, is a principal and the top executives are agents.
- JPMorgan top executives are principals, and the traders who incurred the losses are agents.
- JPMorgan tried to cope with the principal–agent problem by compensating agents with performance bonuses, profit shares through stock options, and with the possibility of clawbacks for poor performance.
- We don't know the details but, based on what

Figure 1 JPMorgan Share Price

Jamie Dimon said, it seems that the specific trading activities that incurred a $2 billion loss were complex and not properly understood either by the traders (the agents at the end of the line) or the managers who designed the trading activities.

- The fall in JPMorgan's stock price not only lowered the wealth of stockholders but also lowered the compensation of Jamie Dimon and the other executives compensated with stock options.

MyEconLab More Economics in the News

debts of a firm up to an amount equal to the entire personal wealth of the owner. Farmers, computer programmers, and artists are often proprietorships.

The proprietor makes management decisions, receives the firm's profits, and is responsible for its losses. Profits from a proprietorship are taxed at the same rate as other sources of the proprietor's personal income.

Partnership A *partnership* is a firm with two or more owners who have unlimited liability. Partners must agree on an appropriate management structure and on how to divide the firm's profits among themselves. The profits of a partnership are taxed as the personal income of the owners, but each partner is legally liable for all the debts of the partnership (limited only by the wealth of that individual partner). Liability for the full debts of the partnership is called *joint unlimited liability*. Most law firms are partnerships.

Corporation A *corporation* is a firm owned by one or more limited liability stockholders. *Limited liability* means that the owners have legal liability only for the value of their initial investment. This

limitation of liability means that if the corporation becomes bankrupt, its owners do not use their personal wealth to pay the corporation's debts.

Corporations' profits are taxed independently of stockholders' incomes. Stockholders pay a capital gains tax on the profit they earn when they sell a stock for a higher price than they paid for it. Corporate stocks generate capital gains when a corporation retains some of its profit and reinvests it in profitable activities. So retained earnings are taxed twice because the capital gains they generate are taxed. Dividend payments are also taxed but at a lower rate than other sources of income.

Pros and Cons of Different Types of Firms

The different types of business organization arise from firms trying to cope with the principal–agent problem. Each type has advantages in particular situations and because of its special advantages, each type continues to exist. Each type of business organization also has disadvantages.

Table 10.4 summarizes these and other pros and cons of the different types of firms.

TABLE 10.4 The Pros and Cons of Different Types of Firms

Type of Firm	Pros	Cons
Proprietorship	■ Easy to set up ■ Simple decision making ■ Profits taxed only once as owner's income	■ Bad decisions not checked; no need for consensus ■ Owner's entire wealth at risk ■ Firm dies with owner ■ Cost of capital and labor is high relative to that of a corporation
Partnership	■ Easy to set up ■ Diversified decision making ■ Can survive withdrawal of partner ■ Profits taxed only once as owners' incomes	■ Achieving consensus may be slow and expensive ■ Owners' entire wealth at risk ■ Withdrawal of partner may create capital shortage ■ Cost of capital and labor is high relative to that of a corporation
Corporation	■ Owners have limited liability ■ Large-scale, low-cost capital available ■ Professional management not restricted by ability of owners ■ Perpetual life ■ Long-term labor contracts cut labor costs	■ Complex management structure can make decisions slow and expensive ■ Retained profits taxed twice: as company profit and as stockholders' capital gains

ECONOMICS IN ACTION

Types of Firms in the Economy

Three types of firms operate in the United States: proprietorships, partnerships, and corporations.

Which type of firm dominates? Which produces most of the output of the U.S. economy?

Proprietorships Most Common Three quarters of the firms in the United States are proprietorships and they are mainly small businesses. Almost one fifth of the firms are corporations, and only a twentieth are partnerships (see Fig.1).

Corporations Produce Most Corporations generate almost 90 percent of business revenue. Revenue is a measure of the value of production, so corporations produce most of the output in the U.S. economy.

Variety Across Industries In agriculture, forestry, and fishing, proprietorships generate about 40 percent of the total revenue. Proprietorships also generate a significant percentage of the revenue in services, construction, and retail trade. Partnerships account for a small percentage of revenue in all sectors and feature most in agriculture, forestry, and fishing; services; and mining. Corporations dominate all sectors and have the manufacturing industries almost to themselves.

Why do corporations dominate the business scene? Why do the other types of businesses survive? And why are proprietorships and partnerships more prominent in some sectors? The answers lie in the pros and cons of the different types of business organization. Corporations dominate where a large amount of capital is used; proprietorships dominate where flexibility in decision making is critical.

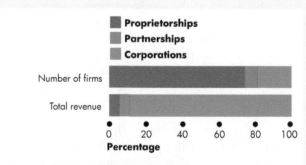

Figure 1 Number of Firms and Total Revenue

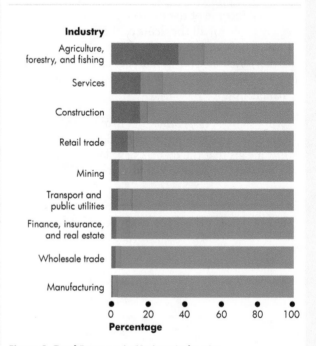

Figure 2 Total Revenue in Various Industries

Source of data: U.S. Bureau of the Census, Statistical Abstract of the United States, 2001.

◆ **REVIEW QUIZ**

1 Explain the distinction between a command system and an incentive system.
2 What is the principal–agent problem? What are three ways in which firms try to cope with it?
3 What are the three types of firms? Explain the major advantages and disadvantages of each.

Work these questions in Study Plan 10.3 and get instant feedback. Do a Key Terms Quiz.   MyEconLab

You've now seen how technology constraints and information constraints influence the way firms operate. You've seen why some firms operate with a large amount of labor and human capital and a small amount of physical capital. You've also seen how firms use a mixture of command and incentive systems and employ different types of business organization to cope with the principal–agent problem.

Your next task is to look at the variety of market situations in which firms operate and classify the different market environments in which firms do business.

Markets and the Competitive Environment

The markets in which firms operate vary a great deal. Some are highly competitive, and profits in these markets are hard to come by. Some appear to be almost free from competition, and firms in these markets earn large profits. Some markets are dominated by fierce advertising campaigns in which each firm seeks to persuade buyers that it has the best products. And some markets display the character of a strategic game.

Economists identify four market types:

1. Perfect competition
2. Monopolistic competition
3. Oligopoly
4. Monopoly

Perfect competition arises when there are many firms, each selling an identical product, many buyers, and no restrictions on the entry of new firms into the industry. The many firms and buyers are all well informed about the prices of the products of each firm in the industry. The worldwide markets for wheat, corn, rice, and other grain crops are examples of perfect competition.

Monopolistic competition is a market structure in which a large number of firms compete by making similar but slightly different products. Making a product slightly different from the product of a competing firm is called **product differentiation**. Product differentiation gives a firm in monopolistic competition an element of market power. The firm is the sole producer of the particular version of the good in question. For example, in the market for pizzas, hundreds of firms make their own version of the perfect pizza. Each of these firms is the sole producer of a particular brand. Differentiated products are not necessarily different products. What matters is that consumers perceive them to be different. For example, different brands of potato chips and ketchup might be almost identical but be perceived by consumers to be different.

Oligopoly is a market structure in which a small number of firms compete. Computer software, airplane manufacture, and international air transportation are examples of oligopolistic industries. Oligopolies might produce almost identical products, such as the colas produced by Coke and Pepsi. Or they might produce differentiated products such as Boeing and Airbus aircraft.

Monopoly arises when there is one firm, which produces a good or service that has no close substitutes and in which the firm is protected by a barrier preventing the entry of new firms. In some places, the phone, gas, electricity, cable television, and water suppliers are local monopolies—monopolies restricted to a given location. Microsoft Corporation, the software developer that created Windows, the operating system for the personal computer, is an example of a global monopoly.

Perfect competition is the most extreme form of competition. Monopoly is the most extreme absence of competition. The other two market types fall between these extremes.

Many factors must be taken into account to determine which market structure describes a particular real-world market. One of these factors is the extent to which a small number of firms dominates the market. To measure this feature of markets, economists use indexes called measures of concentration. Let's look at these measures.

Measures of Concentration

Economists use two measures of concentration:

- The four-firm concentration ratio
- The Herfindahl-Hirschman Index

The Four-Firm Concentration Ratio The **four-firm concentration ratio** is the percentage of the value of sales accounted for by the four largest firms in an industry. The range of the concentration ratio is from almost zero for perfect competition to 100 percent for monopoly. This ratio is the main measure used to assess market structure.

Table 10.5 shows two calculations of the four-firm concentration ratio: one for tire makers and one for printers. In this example, 14 firms produce tires. The largest four have 80 percent of the sales, so the four-firm concentration ratio is 80 percent. In the printing industry, with 1,004 firms, the largest four firms have only 0.5 percent of the sales, so the four-firm concentration ratio is 0.5 percent.

A low concentration ratio indicates a high degree of competition, and a high concentration ratio indicates an absence of competition. A monopoly has a concentration ratio of 100 percent—the largest (and only) firm has 100 percent of the sales. A four-firm concentration ratio that exceeds 60 percent is regarded as an indication of a market that is highly concentrated and dominated by a few firms in an oligopoly. A ratio of less than 60 percent is regarded as an indication of a competitive market.

The Herfindahl-Hirschman Index The **Herfindahl-Hirschman Index**—also called the HHI—is the square of the percentage market share of each firm summed over the largest 50 firms (or summed over all the firms if there are fewer than 50) in a market. For example, if there are four firms in a market and the market shares of the firms are 50 percent, 25 percent, 15 percent, and 10 percent, the Herfindahl-Hirschman Index is:

$$HHI = 50^2 + 25^2 + 15^2 + 10^2 = 3,450.$$

TABLE 10.5   Calculating the Four-Firm Concentration Ratio

Tire makers		Printers	
Firm	Sales (millions of dollars)	Firm	Sales (millions of dollars)
Top, Inc.	200	Fran's	2.5
ABC, Inc.	250	Ned's	2.0
Big, Inc.	150	Tom's	1.8
XYZ, Inc.	100	Jill's	1.7
Largest 4 firms	700	Largest 4 firms	8.0
Other 10 firms	175	Other 1,000 firms	1,592.0
Industry	875	Industry	1,600.0

Four-firm concentration ratios:

Tire makers: $\dfrac{700}{875} \times 100 = 80$ percent   Printers: $\dfrac{8}{1,600} \times 100 = 0.5$ percent

ECONOMICS IN ACTION
Concentration in the U.S. Economy

The U.S. Department of Commerce calculates and publishes data showing concentration ratios and the HHI for each industry in the United States. The bars in the figure show the four-firm concentration ratio and the number at the end of each bar is the HHI.

Cigarette and battery manufacturing are two of the most concentrated industries. A very small number of firms dominate the markets for these products and their competitors are small firms that have small market shares.

Glass containers, trucks, breakfast cereals, and major appliances are highly concentrated industries. They are oligopolies.

Cookies and crackers, motor vehicles, and soft drinks are moderately concentrated industries. They are examples of monopolistic competition.

Snack food, ice cream, milk, cheese, commercial printing, canvas bags manufacturing, quick printers, and bakers have low concentration measures and are highly competitive industries.

Concentration measures are useful indicators of the degree of competition in a market, but they must be supplemented by other information to determine the structure of the market.

Newspapers and automobiles are examples of how the concentration measures give a misleading reading of the degree of competition. Most newspapers are local. They serve a single city or even a smaller area. So despite the low concentration measure, newspapers are concentrated in their own local areas. Automobiles are traded internationally and foreign cars are freely imported into the United States. Despite the moderately high U.S. concentration measure, the automobile industry is competitive.

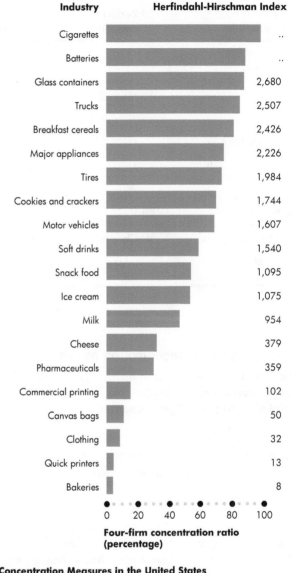

Concentration Measures in the United States

Source of data: Concentration Ratios in Manufacturing (Washington, D.C.: U.S. Department of Commerce, 2007).

In perfect competition, the HHI is small. For example, if each of the largest 50 firms in an industry has a market share of 0.1 percent, then the HHI is $0.1^2 \times 50 = 0.5$. In a monopoly, the HHI is 10,000. The firm has 100 percent of the market: $100^2 = 10,000$.

The HHI became a popular measure of the degree of competition during the 1980s, when the Justice Department used it to classify markets. A market in which the HHI is less than 1,500 is regarded as being competitive. A market in which the HHI lies between 1,500 and 2,500 is regarded as being moderately competitive. But a market in which the HHI exceeds 2,500 is regarded as being uncompetitive.

Table 10.6 summarizes the characteristics of the types of market structure, along with the measures of concentration and some examples of each type.

TABLE 10.6   Market Structure

Characteristics	Perfect competition	Monopolistic competition	Oligopoly	Monopoly
Number of firms in industry	Many	Many	Few	One
Product	Identical	Differentiated	Either identical or differentiated	No close substitutes
Barriers to entry	None	None	Moderate	High
Firm's control over price	None	Some	Considerable	Considerable or regulated
Concentration ratio	0	Low	High	100
HHI (approx. ranges)	Close to 0	Less than 2,500	More than 2,500	10,000
Examples	Wheat, corn	Food, clothing	Computer chips	Local water supply

Limitations of a Concentration Measure

The three main limitations of using only concentration measures as determinants of market structure are their failure to take proper account of

- The geographical scope of the market
- Barriers to entry and firm turnover
- The correspondence between a market and an industry

Geographical Scope of the Market Concentration measures take a national view of the market. Many goods are sold in a *national* market, but some are sold in a *regional* market and some in a *global* one. The concentration measures for newspapers are low, indicating competition, but in most cities the newspaper industry is highly concentrated. The concentration measures for automobiles are high, indicating little competition, but the three biggest U.S. car makers compete with foreign car makers in a highly competitive global market.

Barriers to Entry and Firm Turnover Some markets are highly concentrated but entry is easy and the turnover of firms is large. For example, small towns have few restaurants, but no restrictions hinder a new restaurant from opening and many attempt to do so.

Also, a market with only a few firms might be competitive because of *potential entry*. The few firms in a market face competition from the many potential firms that will enter the market if economic profit opportunities arise.

Market and Industry Correspondence To calculate concentration ratios, the Department of Commerce classifies each firm as being in a particular industry. But markets do not always correspond closely to industries for three reasons.

First, markets are often narrower than industries. For example, the pharmaceutical industry, which has a low concentration ratio, operates in many separate markets for individual products—for example, measles vaccine and AIDS-fighting drugs. These drugs do not compete with each other, so this industry, which looks competitive, includes firms that are monopolies (or near monopolies) in markets for individual drugs.

Second, most firms make several products. For example, Westinghouse makes electrical equipment and, among other things, gas-fired incinerators and plywood. So this one firm operates in at least three separate markets, but the Department of Commerce classifies Westinghouse as being in the electrical goods and equipment industry. The fact that Westinghouse competes with other producers of plywood does not

ECONOMICS IN ACTION

A Competitive Environment

How competitive are markets in the United States? Do most U.S. firms operate in competitive markets, in monopolistic competition, in oligopoly, or in monopoly markets?

The data needed to answer these questions are hard to get. The last attempt to answer the questions, in a study by William G. Shepherd, an economics professor at the University of Massachusetts at Amherst, covered the years from 1939 to 1980. The figure shows what he discovered.

In 1980, three quarters of the value of goods and services bought and sold in the United States was traded in markets that are essentially competitive—markets that have almost perfect competition or monopolistic competition. Monopoly and the dominance of a single firm accounted for about 5 percent of sales. Oligopoly, which is found mainly in manufacturing, accounted for about 18 percent of sales.

Over the period studied, the U.S. economy became increasingly competitive. The percentage of output sold by firms operating in competitive markets (blue bars) has expanded most, and has shrunk most in oligopoly markets (red bars).

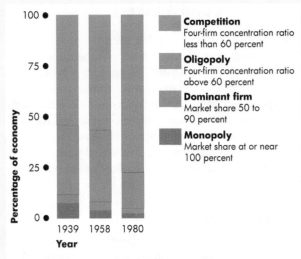

The Market Structure of the U.S. Economy

Source of data: William G. Shepherd, "Causes of Increased Competition in the U.S. Economy, 1939–1980," *Review of Economics and Statistics*, Vol 64, No 4 (November, 1982), pp. 613–626. © 1982 by the President and Fellows of Harvard College. Reprinted with permission.

But also during the past decades, the U.S. economy has become much more exposed to competition from the rest of the world. The data used by William G. Shepherd don't capture this international competition, so the data probably understate the degree of true competition in the U.S. economy.

show up in the concentration numbers for the plywood market.

Third, firms switch from one market to another depending on profit opportunities. For example, Motorola, which today produces cellular telephones and other communications products, has diversified from being a TV and computer chip maker. Motorola no longer produces TVs. Publishers of newspapers, magazines, and textbooks are today rapidly diversifying into Internet and multimedia products. These switches among markets show that there is much scope for entering and exiting a market, and so measures of concentration have limited usefulness.

Despite their limitations, concentration measures do provide a basis for determining the degree of competition in a market when they are combined with information about the geographical scope of the market, barriers to entry, and the extent to which large, multiproduct firms straddle a variety of markets.

◆ REVIEW QUIZ

1 What are the four market types? Explain the distinguishing characteristics of each.

2 What are the two measures of concentration? Explain how each measure is calculated.

3 Under what conditions do the measures of concentration give a good indication of the degree of competition in a market?

4 Is the U.S. economy competitive? Is it becoming more competitive or less competitive?

Work these questions in Study Plan 10.4 and get instant feedback. Do a Key Terms Quiz.   MyEconLab

You now know the variety of market types and how we identify them. Our final question in this chapter is: What determines the things that firms decide to buy from other firms rather than produce for themselves?

◆ Produce or Outsource? Firms and Markets

To produce a good or service, even a simple one such as a shirt, factors of production must be hired and their activities coordinated. To produce a good as complicated as an iPhone, an enormous range of specialist factors of production must be coordinated.

Factors of production can be coordinated either by firms or markets. We'll describe these two ways of organizing production and then see why firms play a crucial role in achieving an efficient use of resources.

Firm Coordination

Firms hire labor, capital, and land, and by using a mixture of command systems and incentive systems (see p. 229) organize and coordinate their activities to produce goods and services.

Firm coordination occurs when you take your car to the garage for service such as an oil change and brake check. The garage owner hires a mechanic and tools and coordinates all the activities that get your car serviced. Firms also coordinate the production of cornflakes, golf clubs, and a host of other items.

Market Coordination

Markets coordinate production by adjusting prices and making the decisions of buyers and sellers of factors of production and components consistent.

Market coordination occurs to produce a rock concert. A promoter books a stadium, rents some stage equipment, hires some audio and video recording engineers and technicians, and engages some rock groups, a superstar, a publicity agent, and a ticket agent. The promoter sells tickets to thousands of rock fans, audio rights to a recording company, and video and broadcasting rights to a television network. All these transactions take place in markets that coordinate the buying and selling of this huge variety of factors of production.

Outsourcing, buying parts or products from other firms, is another example of market coordination. Dell outsources the production of all the components of its computers. Automakers outsource the production of windshields, windows, transmission systems, engines, tires, and many other auto parts. Apple outsources the entire production of iPods, iPads, and iPhones.

Why Firms?

What determines whether a firm or a market coordinates a particular set of activities? How does a firm decide whether to buy an item from another firm or manufacture it itself? The answer is cost. Taking account of the opportunity cost of time as well as the costs of the other inputs, a firm uses the method that costs least. In other words, it uses the economically efficient method.

If a task can be performed at a lower cost by markets than by a firm, markets will do the job, and any attempt to set up a firm to replace such market activity will be doomed to failure.

Firms coordinate economic activity when a task can be performed more efficiently by a firm than by markets. In such a situation, it is profitable to set up a firm. Firms are often more efficient than markets as coordinators of economic activity because they can achieve

- Lower transactions costs
- Economies of scale
- Economies of scope
- Economies of team production

Lower Transactions Costs Firms eliminate transactions costs. **Transactions costs** are the costs that arise from finding someone with whom to do business, of reaching an agreement about the price and other aspects of the exchange, and of ensuring that the terms of the agreement are fulfilled. Market transactions require buyers and sellers to get together and to negotiate the terms and conditions of their trading. Sometimes, lawyers have to be hired to draw up contracts. A broken contract leads to still more expense. A firm can lower such transactions costs by reducing the number of individual transactions undertaken.

Imagine getting your car fixed using market coordination. You hire a mechanic to diagnose the problems and make a list of the parts and tools needed to fix them. You buy the parts from several dealers, rent the tools from ABC Rentals, hire an auto mechanic, return the tools, and pay your bills. You can avoid all these transactions and the time they cost you by letting your local garage fix the car.

Economies of Scale When the cost of producing a unit of a good falls as its output rate increases, **economies of scale** exist. An automaker experiences economies of scale because as the scale of production increases, the firm can use cost-saving equipment and

ECONOMICS IN ACTION

Apple Doesn't Make the iPhone!

Apple designed the iPhone and markets it, but Apple doesn't manufacture it. Why? Apple wants to produce the iPhone at the lowest possible cost. Apple achieves its goal by assigning the production task to more than 30 firms, some of which are listed in the table opposite. These 30 firms produce the components in Asia, Europe, and North America and then the components are assembled in its sleek, iconic case by Foxconn and Quanta in Taiwan.

Most electronic products—TVs, DVD players, iPods and iPads, and personal computers—are produced in a similar way to the iPhone with a combination of firm and market coordination. Hundreds of little-known firms compete fiercely to get their components into well-known consumer products.

Altus Technology	Taiwan
Balda	Germany
Broadcom	United States
Cambridge Silicon Radio	UK
Catcher	Taiwan
Cyntec	Taiwan
Delta Electronics	Taiwan
Epson	Japan
Foxconn	Taiwan
Infineon Technologies	Germany
Intel	United States
Largan Precision	Taiwan
Lite-On	Taiwan
Marvell	United States
Micron	United States
National Semiconductor	United States
Novatek	Taiwan
Primax	Taiwan
Quanta	Taiwan
Samsung	Korea
Sanyo	Japan
Sharp	Japan
Taiwan Semiconductor	Taiwan
TMD	Japan

highly specialized labor. An automaker that produces only a few cars a year must use hand-tool methods that are costly. Economies of scale arise from specialization and the division of labor that can be reaped more effectively by firm coordination rather than market coordination.

Economies of Scope A firm experiences **economies of scope** when it uses specialized (and often expensive) resources to produce a *range of goods and services*. For example, Toshiba uses its designers and specialized equipment to make the hard drive for the iPod. But it makes many different types of hard drives and other related products. As a result, Toshiba produces the iPod hard drive at a lower cost than a firm making only the iPod hard drive could achieve.

Economies of Team Production A production process in which the individuals in a group specialize in mutually supportive tasks is *team production*. Sports provide the best examples of team activity. In baseball, some team members specialize in pitching and others in fielding. In basketball, some team members specialize in defense and some in offense. The production of goods and services offers many examples of team activity. For example, production lines in a TV manufacturing plant work most efficiently when individual activity is organized in teams, each worker specializing in a few tasks. You can also think of an entire firm as being a team. The team has buyers of raw materials and other inputs, production workers, and salespeople. Each individual member of the team

specializes, but the value of the output of the team and the profit that it earns depend on the coordinated activities of all the team's members.

Because firms can economize on transactions costs, reap economies of scale and economies of scope, and organize efficient team production, it is firms rather than markets that coordinate most of our economic activity.

◆ REVIEW QUIZ

1   What are the two ways in which economic activity can be coordinated?
2   What determines whether a firm or markets coordinate production?
3   What are the main reasons why firms can often coordinate production at a lower cost than markets can?

Work these questions in Study Plan 10.5 and get instant feedback. Do a Key Terms Quiz.   MyEconLab

◆   *Economics in the News* on pp. 240–241 explores the market for Internet advertising. In the next four chapters, we continue to study firms and the decisions they make. In Chapter 11, we learn about the relationships between cost and output at different output levels. These relationships are common to all types of firms in all types of markets. We then turn to problems that are specific to firms in different types of markets.

Battling for Markets in Internet Advertising

Facebook Rolls Out Real-Time Ad Platform

The Financial Times
September 13, 2012

Some of the world's largest advertising companies have signed up to Facebook's new real-time advertising platform, in a move that the social network hopes will bolster its revenue streams.

On Thursday, Facebook officially launched the platform, called Facebook Ad Exchange, or FBX, following months of testing. The system allows marketers to bid in real-time to buy ad impressions on the social networking site, and deliver their ads to users based on their immediate web-browsing habits, or linked to current events, such as sports results.

"Real-time marketing is getting to be a really important component of digital advertising," said Rebecca Lieb, an analyst with the Altimeter Group. "We'll see a lot of event-triggered marketing in the upcoming election cycle."

The ads use information gathered from computer browsing histories to target individual Facebook users, and the ad prices fluctuate as in an auction-style bidding system. So a user who looks at shoes on a retail site could then see an ad for the same brand when clicking back to Facebook.

The capacity will help Facebook compete more directly with advertising rivals Google and Yahoo, which have long provided real-time bidding to advertisers....

Within one tenth of a second, the system notifies when an ad space is available, evaluates 2,000 data points to determine the most relevant ad, calculates a price and prompts the ad to appear.

The global real-time bidding sector is estimated to be worth some $3bn–$4bn, but industry observers expect this to reach as much as $20bn by 2015....

Mark Wembridge and April Dembosky, "Facebook Rolls Out Real-Time Ad Platform," *The Financial Times*, September 13, 2012.

MyEconLab More Economics in the News

ESSENCE OF THE STORY

- Facebook is under pressure to generate advertising revenue.
- Real-time bidding is widely used for Internet advertising and its market share is growing rapidly.
- Facebook and Google are getting better at capturing user activity.
- A new Facebook system will target ads at the user's current interests.
- Advertisers will bid to get their ads in front of the right users.

ECONOMIC ANALYSIS

- Like all firms, Facebook and Google aim to maximize profit.

- Facebook provides social networking services and Google provides search services, a variety of other services, and with Google+ is offering a social networking service.

- Facebook and Google face constraints imposed by the market and technology.

- People who use social networks demand their services, and at the latest count Facebook and another 200-odd firms supply social networking services.

- People looking for information demand Internet search services, and Google and more than 100 other firms supply Internet search services.

- The equilibrium price of social networking services and of Internet search services is zero, and the equilibrium quantity of each is the quantity demanded at a zero price.

- Social network and Internet search providers enjoy economies of scope: They produce advertising services as well as their other service.

- Unlike social networking and search, Internet advertising is a big revenue and profit generator.

- Because the providers of social networking and search know a lot about their users, they can offer advertisers access to potential customers and charge a high price for this precision.

- Google has been enormously successful at delivering advertising based on a user's search activity, and its revenue has grown from $1 billion in 2003 to $56 billion in 2013 (see Fig.1). Google's profit in 2013 was $13 billion (see Fig. 2).

- Facebook is still learning how to tap its advertising potential and the news article describes its innovation in 2012: real-time bidding for advertising based on a user's browsing.

- Facebook's revenue is beginning to grow, but by 2013 it had reached only $8 billion (see Fig. 1).

- Providing a social networking service or search service doesn't guarantee success in generating advertising revenue and profit.

- Yahoo is an example of a firm that hasn't performed as well as its owners would wish.

- As Google and Facebook have seen explosive growth in users and revenues, Yahoo has struggled.

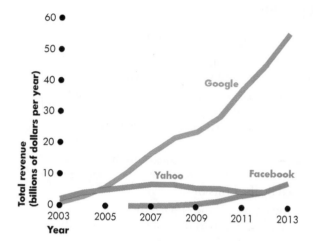

Figure 1 Total Revenue Comparison

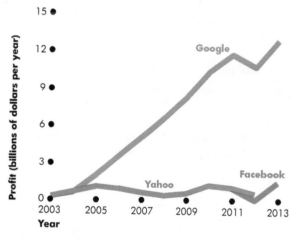

Figure 2 Profit Comparison

- Figure 1 shows that Yahoo's revenue peaked in 2008 and has been falling while Google's has soared and Facebook's has grown to overtake that of Yahoo.

- Figure 2 shows that Yahoo's profit has been flat while Google's has soared. Facebook's profit remains modest.

- The data shown in Figs.1 and 2 suggest that so far, Internet search is a more effective tool for generating revenue and profit than social networking. Perhaps Facebook's new revenue model will change that.

- The data also suggest that Facebook's and Google's expansion is tightening the market constraint that Yahoo faces.

SUMMARY

Key Points

The Firm and Its Economic Problem (pp. 224–226)

- Firms hire and organize factors of production to produce and sell goods and services.
- A firm's goal is to maximize economic profit, which is total revenue minus total cost measured as the opportunity cost of production.
- A firm's opportunity cost of production is the sum of the cost of resources bought in the market, using the firm's own resources, and resources supplied by the firm's owner.
- Normal profit is the opportunity cost of entrepreneurship and is part of the firm's opportunity cost.
- Technology, information, and markets limit the economic profit that a firm can make.

Working Problems 1 and 2 will give you a better understanding of the firm and its economic problem.

Technological and Economic Efficiency (pp. 227–228)

- A method of production is technologically efficient when a firm uses the least amount of inputs to produce a given output.
- A method of production is economically efficient when the cost of producing a given output is as low as possible.

Working Problem 3 will give you a better understanding of technological and economic efficiency.

Information and Organization (pp. 229–232)

- Firms use a combination of command systems and incentive systems to organize production.
- Faced with incomplete information and uncertainty, firms induce managers and workers to perform in ways that are consistent with the firms' goals.
- Proprietorships, partnerships, and corporations use ownership, incentive pay, and long-term contracts to cope with the principal–agent problem.

Working Problem 4 will give you a better understanding of information and organization.

Markets and the Competitive Environment (pp. 233–237)

- In perfect competition, many sellers offer an identical product to many buyers and entry is free.
- In monopolistic competition, many sellers offer slightly different products to many buyers and entry is free.
- In oligopoly, a small number of sellers compete and barriers to entry limit the number of firms.
- In monopoly, one firm produces an item that has no close substitutes and the firm is protected by a barrier to entry that prevents the entry of competitors.

Working Problems 5 and 6 will give you a better understanding of markets and the competitive environment.

Produce or Outsource? Firms and Markets (pp. 238–239)

- Firms coordinate economic activities when they can perform a task more efficiently—at lower cost—than markets can.
- Firms economize on transactions costs and achieve the benefits of economies of scale, economies of scope, and economies of team production.

Working Problem 7 will give you a better understanding of firms and markets.

Key Terms

MyEconLab Key Terms Quiz

Command system, 229
Economic depreciation, 225
Economic efficiency, 227
Economic profit, 224
Economies of scale, 238
Economies of scope, 239
Firm, 224

Four-firm concentration ratio, 234
Herfindahl-Hirschman Index, 234
Implicit rental rate, 224
Incentive system, 229
Monopolistic competition, 233
Monopoly, 233
Normal profit, 225

Oligopoly, 233
Perfect competition, 233
Principal–agent problem, 229
Product differentiation, 233
Technological efficiency, 227
Technology, 226
Transactions costs, 238

WORKED PROBLEM

MyEconLab   You can work this problem in Chapter 10 Study Plan.

Mike operates a bike retail store and repair shop, Mike's Bikes.

Some data about the firm and industry:

- Last year, the market value of the firm's showroom and workshop increased from $600,000 to $675,000; the market value of the inventory of unsold bikes decreased from $400,000 to $320,000; and the market value of the firm's tools remained constant at $5,000.
- The firm paid manufacturers $770,000 for bikes.
- The cost of electricity and IT services was $25,000.
- The wages paid to shop assistants were $50,000.
- Mike is the firm's entrepreneur. He also works part-time at a bike manufacturer that pays $40 per hour. The manufacturer wants Mike to work full time, but instead he does repairs at Mike's Bikes for 10 hours a week.
- Normal profit in bike retailing is $40,000 per year.
- The interest rate is 5 percent per year.

Questions

1. What was the cost of the resources Mike's Bikes bought in the marketplace last year?
2. What was Mike's Bikes' opportunity cost of using resources owned by the firm last year?
3. What was Mike's Bikes' opprtunity cost of using resources supplied by Mike last year?
4. What was Mike's Bikes' opportunity cost of production last year?

Solutions

1. The firm bought bikes for $770,000; electricity and IT services for $25,000; and paid wages to shop assistants of $50,000. The total cost of these resources bought in the marketplace was $845,000.

Key Point: The cost of resources bought in the market is the total amount paid for them.

2. The resources owned by Mike's Bikes are the tools, the inventory of bikes, and the showroom and workshop.

The opportunity cost of using these resources is economic depreciation and forgone interest.

Economic depreciation is the change in the market value of the firm's resources. The market value of the inventory of bikes fell by $80,000 but the market value of the showroom and workshop increased by

$75,000, so the total economic depreciation was $80,000 − $75,000, or $5,000.

Forgone interest is the interest that could be earned on the market value of the firm's resources. That value is $675,000 (showroom and workshop), $320,000 (bikes), and $5,000 (tools), which total $1,000,000. The interest forgone is 5 percent of the $1,000,000, which equals $50,000.

So the opportunity cost of using resources owned by the firm was $5,000 + $50,000, or $55,000.

Key Point: The cost of using resources owned by the firm is part of the firm's opportunity costs.

3. The resources supplied by Mike are his entrepreneurial services and his labor. The opportunity cost of his entrepreneurial services is normal profit of $40,000 and of his labor is $20,000 (10 hours a week at his opportunity cost of $40 per hour, for 50 weeks). These two items total $60,000.

Key Point: The cost of using resources supplied by the owner is part of the firm's opportunity costs.

4. The opportunity cost of production is the sum of three components of the opportunity cost of the resources used, $845,000 + $55,000 + $60,000, which was $960,000.

Key Point: The firm's opportunity cost of production is the sum of the cost of all the resources used.

Key Table

Item		Amount
Cost of Resources Bought in Market		
Bikes	$770,000	
Electricity and IT services	25,000	
Wages	50,000	845,000
Cost of Resources Owned by Firm		
Economic depreciation	$5,000	
Forgone interest	50,000	$55,000
Cost of Resources Supplied by Owner		
Mike's normal profit	$40,000	
Mike's forgone wages	20,000	$60,000
Opportunity Cost of Production		**$960,000**

MyEconLab Interactive Animation

STUDY PLAN PROBLEMS AND APPLICATIONS

MyEconLab   You can work Problems 1 to 7 in Chapter 10 Study Plan and get instant feedback.

The Firm and Its Economic Problem (Study Plan 10.1)

1. One year ago, Jack and Jill set up a vinegar-bottling firm (called JJVB). Use the following data to calculate JJVB's opportunity cost of production during its first year of operation:
   - Jack and Jill put $50,000 of their own money into the firm and bought equipment for $30,000.
   - They hired one worker at $20,000 a year.
   - Jack quit his old job, which paid $30,000 a year, and worked full-time for JJVB.
   - Jill kept her old job, which paid $30 an hour, but gave up 500 hours of leisure a year to work for JJVB.
   - JJVB bought $10,000 of goods and services.
   - The market value of the equipment at the end of the year was $28,000.
   - Jack and Jill have a $100,000 home loan on which they pay interest of 6 percent a year.

2. Joe, who has no skills, no job experience, and no alternative employment, runs a shoeshine stand. Other operators of shoeshine stands earn $10,000 a year. Joe pays rent of $2,000 a year, and his total revenue is $15,000 a year. Joe spent $1,000 on equipment, which he used his credit card to buy. The interest on a credit card balance is 20 percent a year. At the end of the year, Joe was offered $500 for his business and all its equipment. Calculate Joe's opportunity cost of production and his economic profit.

Technological and Economic Efficiency (Study Plan 10.2)

3. Four ways of laundering 100 shirts are:

Method	Labor (hours)	Capital (machines)
A	1	10
B	5	8
C	20	4
D	50	1

   a. Which methods are technologically efficient?
   b. Which method is economically efficient if the hourly wage rate and the implicit rental rate of capital are (i) wage rate $1, rental rate $100; (ii) wage rate $5, rental rate $50; and (iii) wage rate $50, rental rate $5?

Information and Organization (Study Plan 10.3)

4. **Executive Pay**

   Executive compensation, based on performance, can theoretically constrain pay, but companies are paying their top executives more and more. The median compensation of a CEO in 2013 was $13.9 million, up 9 percent from 2012.

   Source: CNBC, April 28, 2014

   What is the economic problem that CEO compensation schemes are designed to solve? Would paying executives with stock align their interests with shareholders'?

Markets and the Competitive Environment

(Study Plan 10.4)

5. Sales of the firms in the tattoo industry are:

Firm	Sales (dollars per year)
Bright Spots	450
Freckles	325
Love Galore	250
Native Birds	200
Other 15 firms	800

   Calculate the four-firm concentration ratio. What is the structure of the tattoo industry?

6. **GameStop Racks Up the Points**

   No retailer has more cachet among gamers than GameStop. For now, only Wal-Mart has a larger share—21.3% last year. GameStop's share was 21.1% last year, and may well overtake Wal-Mart this year. But if new women gamers prefer shopping at Target to GameStop, Wal-Mart and Target might erode GameStop's market share.

   Source: *Fortune*, June 9, 2008

   Estimate a range for the four-firm concentration ratio and the HHI for the U.S. game market based on the data provided in this news clip.

Produce or Outsource? Firms and Markets

(Study Plan 10.5)

7. FedEx contracts independent truck operators to pick up and deliver its packages and pays them on the volume of packages carried. Why doesn't FedEx buy more trucks and hire more drivers? What incentive problems might arise from this arrangement?

ADDITIONAL PROBLEMS AND APPLICATIONS

MyEconLab   You can work these problems in MyEconLab if assigned by your instructor.

The Firm and Its Economic Problem

Use the following data to work Problems 8 and 9.

Lee is a computer programmer who earned $35,000 in 2011. But on January 1, 2012, Lee opened a body board manufacturing business. At the end of the first year of operation, he submitted the following information to his accountant:

- He stopped renting out his cottage for $3,500 a year and used it as his factory. The market value of the cottage increased from $70,000 to $71,000.
- He spent $50,000 on materials, phone, etc.
- He leased machines for $10,000 a year.
- He paid $15,000 in wages.
- He used $10,000 from his savings account, which earns 5 percent a year interest.
- He borrowed $40,000 at 10 percent a year.
- He sold $160,000 worth of body boards.
- Normal profit is $25,000 a year.

8. Calculate Lee's opportunity cost of production and his economic profit.

9. Lee's accountant recorded the depreciation on his cottage during 2012 as $7,000. According to the accountant, what profit did Lee make?

10. In 2011, Toni taught music and earned $20,000. She also earned $4,000 by renting out her basement. On January 1, 2012, she quit teaching, stopped renting out her basement, and began to use it as the office for her new Web site design business. She took $2,000 from her savings account to buy a computer. During 2012, she paid $1,500 for the lease of a Web server and $1,750 for high-speed Internet service. She received a total revenue from Web site designing of $45,000 and earned interest at 5 percent a year on her savings account balance. Normal profit is $55,000 a year. At the end of 2012, Toni could have sold her computer for $500. Calculate Toni's opportunity cost of production and her economic profit in 2012.

11. **The Colvin Interview: Chrysler**

The key driver of profitability will be that the focus of the company isn't on profitability. Our focus is on the customer. If we can find a way to give customers what they want better than anybody else, then what can stop us?

Source: *Fortune*, April 14, 2008

a. In spite of what Chrysler's vice chairman and co-president claims, why is Chrysler's focus actually on profitability?

b. What would happen to Chrysler if it didn't focus on maximizing profit, but instead focused its production and pricing decisions to "give customers what they want"?

12. **Must Watches**

Stocks too volatile? Bonds too boring? Then try an alternative investment—one you can wear on your wrist. ... [The] typical return on a watch over five to ten years is roughly 10%. [One could] do better in an index fund, but ... what other investment is so wearable?

Source: *Fortune*, April 14, 2008

a. What is the cost of buying a watch?

b. What is the opportunity cost of owning a watch?

c. Does owning a watch create an economic profit opportunity?

Technological and Economic Efficiency

Use the following data to work Problems 13 and 14.

Four methods of completing a tax return and the time taken by each method are with a PC, 1 hour; with a pocket calculator, 12 hours; with a pocket calculator and paper and pencil, 12 hours; and with a pencil and paper, 16 hours. The PC and its software cost $1,000, the pocket calculator costs $10, and the pencil and paper cost $1.

13. Which, if any, of the methods is technologically efficient?

14. Which method is economically efficient if the wage rate is (i) $5 an hour, (ii) $50 an hour, and (iii) $500 an hour?

15. **A Medical Sensation**

Hospitals are buying da Vinci surgical robots. Surgeons, sitting comfortably at a da Vinci console, can use various robotic attachments to perform even the most complex procedures.

Source: *Fortune*, April 28, 2008

a. Assume that performing a surgery with a surgical robot requires fewer surgeons and nurses. Is using the surgical robot technologically efficient?

b. What additional information would you need to be able to say that switching to surgical robots is economically efficient for a hospital?

Information and Organization

16. Wal-Mart has more than 3,700 stores, more than one million employees, and total revenues of close to a quarter of a trillion dollars in the United States alone. Sarah Frey-Talley runs the family-owned Frey Farms in Illinois and supplies Wal-Mart with pumpkins and other fresh produce.

    a. How does Wal-Mart coordinate its activities? Is it likely to use mainly a command system or also to use incentive systems? Explain.

    b. How do you think Sarah Frey-Talley coordinates the activities of Frey Farms? Is she likely to use mainly a command system or also to use incentive systems? Explain.

    c. Describe, compare, and contrast the principal–agent problems faced by Wal-Mart and Frey Farms. How might these firms cope with their principal–agent problems?

17. **Where Does Google Go Next?**

    Google gives its engineers one day a week to work on whatever project they want. A couple of colleagues did what many of the young geniuses do at Google: They came up with a cool idea. At Google, you often end up with a laissez-faire mess instead of resource allocation.

    Source: *Fortune*, May 26, 2008

    a. Describe Google's method of organizing production with their software engineers.

    b. What are the potential gains and opportunity costs associated with this method?

Markets and the Competitive Environment

18. Market shares of chocolate makers are:

Firm	Market share (percent)
Truffles, Inc.	25
Magic, Inc.	20
Mayfair, Inc.	15
All Natural, Inc.	15
Gold, Inc.	15
Bond, Inc.	10

    Calculate the Herfindahl-Hirschman Index. What is the structure of the chocolate industry?

Produce or Outsource? Firms and Markets

Use the following information to work Problems 19 to 21.

Two leading design firms, Astro Studios of San Francisco and Hers Experimental Design Laboratory, Inc. of Osaka, Japan, worked with Microsoft to design the Xbox 360 video game console. IBM, ATI, and SiS designed the Xbox 360's hardware. Three firms—Flextronics, Wistron, and Celestica—manufactured the Xbox 360 at their plants in China and Taiwan.

19. Describe the roles of market coordination and coordination by firms in the design, manufacture, and marketing of the Xbox 360.

20. a. Why do you think Microsoft works with a large number of other firms, rather than performing all the required tasks itself?

    b. What are the roles of transactions costs, economies of scale, economies of scope, and economies of team production in the design, manufacture, and marketing of the Xbox?

21. Why do you think the Xbox is designed in the United States and Japan but built in China?

Economics in the News

22. After you have studied *Economics in the News* on pp. 240–241, answer the following questions.

    a. What products do Facebook and Google sell?

    b. In what types of markets do Facebook and Google compete?

    c. How do social networks and Internet search providers generate revenue?

    d. What is special about social networking sites that make them attractive to advertisers?

    e. What is special about Internet search providers that make them attractive to advertisers?

    f. What technological changes might increase the profitability of social networks compared to Internet search providers?

23. **Long Reviled, Merit Pay Gains Among Teachers**

    School districts in many states experiment with plans that compensate teachers partly based on classroom performance, rather than their years on the job and coursework completed. Working with mentors to improve their instruction and getting bonuses for raising student achievement encourages efforts to raise teaching quality.

    Source: *The New York Times*, June 18, 2007

    How does "merit pay" attempt to cope with the principal–agent problem in public education?

11

OUTPUT AND COSTS

After studying this chapter, you will be able to:

- Distinguish between the short run and the long run
- Explain and illustrate a firm's short-run product curves
- Explain and derive a firm's short-run cost curves
- Explain and derive a firm's long-run average cost curve

Behind the scenes of your favorite Starbucks coffee shop, many economic decisions have been made that affect the firm's cost of production. Starbucks has decided how much to produce, how many people to employ, and how much and what type of equipment to use. How does a firm make these decisions?

We are going to answer this question in this chapter. And in *Economics in the News* at the end of the chapter, we'll look at how recent expansion decisions by Starbucks affect the firm's production costs. But first, we'll study the costs of a simpler, smaller firm, Campus Sweaters, a (fictional) producer of knitwear.

◆ Decision Time Frames

People who operate firms make many decisions, and all of their decisions are aimed at achieving one overriding goal: maximum attainable profit. But not all decisions are equally critical. Some decisions are big ones. Once made, they are costly (or impossible) to reverse. If such a decision turns out to be incorrect, it might lead to the failure of the firm. Other decisions are small. They are easily changed. If one of these decisions turns out to be incorrect, the firm can change its actions and survive.

The biggest decision that an entrepreneur makes is in what industry to establish a firm. For most entrepreneurs, their background knowledge and interests drive this decision. But the decision also depends on profit prospects—on the expectation that total revenue will exceed total cost.

Cindy has decided to set up Campus Sweaters. She has also decided the most effective method of organizing the firm. But she has not decided the quantity to produce, the factors of production to hire, or the price to charge for sweaters.

Decisions about the quantity to produce and the price to charge depend on the type of market in which the firm operates. Perfect competition, monopolistic competition, oligopoly, and monopoly all confront the firm with *different* problems. Decisions about *how* to produce a given output do not depend on the type of market in which the firm operates. *All* types of firms in *all* types of markets make similar decisions about how to produce.

The actions that a firm can take to influence the relationship between output and cost depend on how soon the firm wants to act. A firm that plans to change its output rate tomorrow has fewer options than one that plans to change its output rate six months or six years in the future.

To study the relationship between a firm's output decision and its costs, we distinguish between two decision time frames:

- The short run
- The long run

The Short Run

The **short run** is a time frame in which the quantity of at least one factor of production is fixed. For most firms, capital, land, and entrepreneurship are fixed factors of production and labor is the variable factor of

production. We call the fixed factors of production the firm's *plant*: In the short run, a firm's plant is fixed.

For Campus Sweaters, the fixed plant is its factory building and its knitting machines. For an electric power utility, the fixed plant is its buildings, generators, computers, and control systems.

To increase output in the short run, a firm must increase the quantity of a variable factor of production, which is usually labor. So to produce more output, Campus Sweaters must hire more labor and operate its knitting machines for more hours a day. Similarly, an electric power utility must hire more labor and operate its generators for more hours a day.

Short-run decisions are easily reversed. The firm can increase or decrease its output in the short run by increasing or decreasing the amount of labor it hires.

The Long Run

The **long run** is a time frame in which the quantities of *all* factors of production can be varied. That is, the long run is a period in which the firm can change its *plant*.

To increase output in the long run, a firm can change its plant as well as the quantity of labor it hires. Campus Sweaters can decide whether to install more knitting machines, use a new type of machine, reorganize its management, or hire more labor. Long-run decisions are *not* easily reversed. Once a plant decision is made, the firm usually must live with it for some time. To emphasize this fact, we call the past expenditure on a plant that has no resale value a **sunk cost**. A sunk cost is irrelevant to the firm's current decisions. The only costs that influence its current decisions are the short-run cost of changing its labor inputs and the long-run cost of changing its plant.

◆ REVIEW QUIZ

1 Distinguish between the short run and the long run.
2 Why is a sunk cost irrelevant to a firm's current decisions?

Work these questions in Study Plan 11.1 and get instant feedback. Do a Key Terms Quiz.   MyEconLab

We're going to study costs in the short run and the long run. We begin with the short run and describe a firm's technology constraint.

Short-Run Technology Constraint

To increase output in the short run, a firm must increase the quantity of labor employed. We describe the relationship between output and the quantity of labor employed by using three related concepts:

1. Total product
2. Marginal product
3. Average product

These product concepts can be illustrated either by product schedules or by product curves. Let's look first at the product schedules.

Product Schedules

Table 11.1 shows some data that describe Campus Sweaters' total product, marginal product, and average product. The numbers tell us how the quantity of sweaters produced increases as Campus Sweaters employs more workers. The numbers also tell us about the productivity of the labor that Campus Sweaters employs.

Focus first on the columns headed "Labor" and "Total product." **Total product** is the maximum output that a given quantity of labor can produce. You can see from the numbers in these columns that as Campus Sweaters employs more labor, total product increases. For example, when 1 worker is employed, total product is 4 sweaters a day, and when 2 workers are employed, total product is 10 sweaters a day. Each increase in employment increases total product.

The **marginal product** of labor is the increase in total product that results from a one-unit increase in the quantity of labor employed, with all other inputs remaining the same. For example, in Table 11.1, when Campus Sweaters increases employment from 2 to 3 workers and does not change its capital, the marginal product of the third worker is 3 sweaters—total product increases from 10 to 13 sweaters.

Average product tells how productive workers are on average. The **average product** of labor is equal to total product divided by the quantity of labor employed. For example, in Table 11.1, the average product of 3 workers is 4.33 sweaters per worker—13 sweaters a day divided by 3 workers.

If you look closely at the numbers in Table 11.1, you can see some patterns. As Campus Sweaters hires more labor, marginal product increases initially, and

TABLE 11.1 Total Product, Marginal Product, and Average Product

	Labor (workers per day)	Total product (sweaters per day)	Marginal product (sweaters per additional worker)	Average product (sweaters per worker)
A	0	0		
			 4	
B	1	4		4.00
			 6	
C	2	10		5.00
			 3	
D	3	13		4.33
			 2	
E	4	15		3.75
			 1	
F	5	16		3.20

Total product is the total amount produced. Marginal product is the change in total product that results from a one-unit increase in labor. For example, when labor increases from 2 to 3 workers a day (row *C* to row *D*), total product increases from 10 to 13 sweaters a day. The marginal product of going from 2 to 3 workers is 3 sweaters. Average product is total product divided by the quantity of labor employed. For example, the average product of 3 workers is 4.33 sweaters per worker (13 sweaters a day divided by 3 workers).

then begins to decrease. For example, marginal product increases from 4 sweaters a day for the first worker to 6 sweaters a day for the second worker and then decreases to 3 sweaters a day for the third worker. Average product also increases at first and then decreases. You can see the relationships between the quantity of labor hired and the three product concepts more clearly by looking at the product curves.

Product Curves

The product curves are graphs of the relationships between employment and the three product concepts you've just studied. They show how total product, marginal product, and average product change as employment changes. They also show the relationships among the three concepts. Let's look at the product curves.

Total Product Curve

Figure 11.1 shows Campus Sweaters' total product curve, *TP*, which is a graph of the total product schedule. Points *A* through *F* correspond to rows *A* through *F* in Table 11.1. To graph the entire total product curve, we vary labor by hours rather than whole days.

Notice the shape of the total product curve. As employment increases from zero to 1 worker a day, the curve becomes steeper. Then, as employment increases to 3, 4, and 5 workers a day, the curve becomes less steep.

The total product curve is similar to the *production possibilities frontier* (explained in Chapter 2). It separates the attainable output levels from those that are unattainable. All the points that lie above the curve are unattainable. Points that lie below the curve, in the orange area, are attainable, but they are inefficient—they use more labor than is necessary to produce a given output. Only the points *on* the total product curve are technologically efficient.

FIGURE 11.1   Total Product Curve

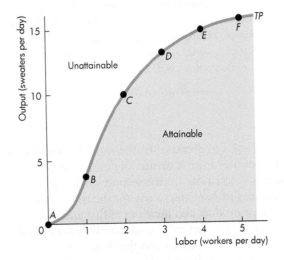

The total product curve, *TP*, is based on the data in Table 11.1. The total product curve shows how the quantity of sweaters produced changes as the quantity of labor employed changes. For example, 2 workers can produce 10 sweaters a day (point *C*). Points *A* through *F* on the curve correspond to the rows of Table 11.1. The total product curve separates attainable outputs from unattainable outputs. Points below the *TP* curve are inefficient.

MyEconLab Animation

Marginal Product Curve

Figure 11.2 shows Campus Sweaters' marginal product of labor. Part (a) reproduces the total product curve from Fig. 11.1 and part (b) shows the marginal product curve, *MP*.

In part (a), the orange bars illustrate the marginal product of labor. The height of a bar measures marginal product. Marginal product is also measured by the slope of the total product curve. Recall that the slope of a curve is the change in the value of the variable measured on the *y*-axis—output—divided by the change in the variable measured on the *x*-axis—labor—as we move along the curve. A one-unit increase in labor, from 2 to 3 workers, increases output from 10 to 13 sweaters, so the slope from point *C* to point *D* is 3 sweaters per additional worker, the same as the marginal product we've just calculated.

Again varying the amount of labor in the smallest units possible, we can draw the marginal product curve shown in Fig. 11.2(b). The *height* of this curve measures the *slope* of the total product curve at a point. Part (a) shows that an increase in employment from 2 to 3 workers increases output from 10 to 13 sweaters (an increase of 3). The increase in output of 3 sweaters appears on the *y*-axis of part (b) as the marginal product of going from 2 to 3 workers. We plot that marginal product at the midpoint between 2 and 3 workers. Notice that the marginal product shown in Fig. 11.2(b) reaches a peak at 1.5 workers, and at that point, marginal product is 6 sweaters per additional worker. The peak occurs at 1.5 workers because the total product curve is steepest when employment increases from 1 worker to 2 workers.

The total product and marginal product curves differ across firms and types of goods. GM's product curves are different from those of PennPower, whose curves in turn are different from those of Campus Sweaters. But the shapes of the product curves are similar because almost every production process has two features:

- Increasing marginal returns initially
- Diminishing marginal returns eventually

Increasing Marginal Returns   Increasing marginal returns occur when the marginal product of an additional worker exceeds the marginal product of the previous worker. Increasing marginal returns arise from increased specialization and division of labor in the production process.

FIGURE 11.2   Total Product and Marginal Product

(a) Total product

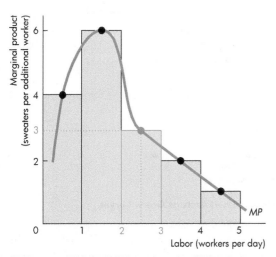

(b) Marginal product

Marginal product is illustrated by the orange bars. For example, when labor increases from 2 to 3 workers a day, marginal product is the orange bar whose height is 3 sweaters. (Marginal product is shown midway between the quantities of labor to emphasize that marginal product results from *changing* the quantity of labor.) The steeper the slope of the total product curve (*TP*) in part (a), the larger is marginal product (*MP*) in part (b). Marginal product increases to a maximum (in this example when 1.5 workers a day are employed) and then declines—diminishing marginal product.

MyEconLab Animation

For example, if Campus Sweaters employs one worker, that person must learn all the aspects of sweater production: running the knitting machines, fixing breakdowns, packaging and mailing sweaters, buying and checking the type and color of the wool. All these tasks must be performed by that one person.

If Campus Sweaters hires a second person, the two workers can specialize in different parts of the production process and can produce more than twice as much as one worker. The marginal product of the second worker is greater than the marginal product of the first worker. Marginal returns are increasing.

Diminishing Marginal Returns Most production processes experience increasing marginal returns initially, but all production processes eventually reach a point of *diminishing* marginal returns. **Diminishing marginal returns** occur when the marginal product of an additional worker is less than the marginal product of the previous worker.

Diminishing marginal returns arise from the fact that more and more workers are using the same capital and working in the same space. As more workers are added, there is less and less for the additional workers to do that is productive. For example, if Campus Sweaters hires a third worker, output increases but not by as much as it did when it hired the second worker. In this case, after two workers are hired, all the gains from specialization and the division of labor have been exhausted. By hiring a third worker, the factory produces more sweaters, but the equipment is being operated closer to its limits. There are even times when the third worker has nothing to do because the machines are running without the need for further attention. Hiring more and more workers continues to increase output but by successively smaller amounts. Marginal returns are diminishing. This phenomenon is such a pervasive one that it is called a "law"—the law of diminishing returns. The **law of diminishing returns** states that

> As a firm uses more of a variable factor of production with a given quantity of the fixed factor of production, the marginal product of the variable factor eventually diminishes.

You are going to return to the law of diminishing returns when we study a firm's costs, but before we do that, let's look at the average product of labor and the average product curve.

Average Product Curve

Figure 11.3 illustrates Campus Sweaters' average product of labor and shows the relationship between average product and marginal product. Points *B* through *F* on the average product curve *AP* correspond to those same rows in Table 11.1. Average product increases from 1 to 2 workers (its maximum value at point *C*) but then decreases as yet more workers are employed. Notice also that average product is largest when average product and marginal product are equal. That is, the marginal product curve cuts the average product curve at the point of maximum average product. For the number of workers at which marginal product exceeds average product, average product is *increasing*. For the number of workers at which marginal product is less than average product, average product is *decreasing*.

The relationship between the average product and marginal product is a general feature of the relationship between the average and marginal values of any variable—even your grades.

FIGURE 11.3   Average Product

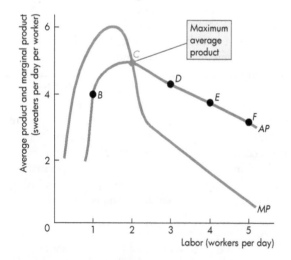

The figure shows the average product of labor and the connection between average product and marginal product. With 1 worker, marginal product exceeds average product, so average product is increasing. With 2 workers, marginal product equals average product, so average product is at its maximum. With more than 2 workers, marginal product is less than average product, so average product is decreasing.

MyEconLab Animation

ECONOMICS IN ACTION

How to Pull Up Your Average

Do you want to pull up your average grade? Then make sure that your grade this semester is better than your current average! This semester is your marginal semester. If your marginal grade exceeds your average grade (like the second semester in the figure), your average will rise. If your marginal grade equals your average grade (like the third semester in the figure), your average won't change. If your marginal grade is below your average grade (like the fourth semester in the figure), your average will fall.

The relationship between your marginal and average grades is exactly the same as that between marginal product and average product.

Marginal and Average Grade Curves

◆ REVIEW QUIZ

1 Explain how the marginal product and average product of labor change as the labor employed increases (a) initially and (b) eventually.
2 What is the law of diminishing returns? Why does marginal product eventually diminish?
3 Explain the relationship between marginal product and average product.

Work these questions in Study Plan 11.2 and get instant feedback. Do a Key Terms Quiz.   MyEconLab

Campus Sweaters' product curves influence its costs, as you are now going to see.

Short-Run Cost

To produce more output in the short run, a firm must employ more labor, which means that it must increase its costs. We describe the relationship between output and cost by using three cost concepts:

- Total cost
- Marginal cost
- Average cost

Total Cost

A firm's **total cost** (*TC*) is the cost of *all* the factors of production it uses. We separate total cost into total *fixed* cost and total *variable* cost.

Total fixed cost (*TFC*) is the cost of the firm's fixed factors. For Campus Sweaters, total fixed cost includes the cost of renting knitting machines and *normal profit*, which is the opportunity cost of Cindy's entrepreneurship (see Chapter 10, p. 225). The quantities of fixed factors don't change as output changes, so total fixed cost is the same at all outputs.

Total variable cost (*TVC*) is the cost of the firm's variable factors. For Campus Sweaters, labor is the variable factor, so this component of cost is its wage bill. Total variable cost changes as output changes.

Total cost is the sum of total fixed cost and total variable cost. That is,

$$TC = TFC + TVC.$$

The table in Fig. 11.4 shows total costs. Campus Sweaters rents one knitting machine for $25 a day, so its *TFC* is $25. To produce sweaters, the firm hires labor, which costs $25 a day. *TVC* is the number of workers multiplied by $25. For example, to produce 13 sweaters a day, in row *D*, the firm hires 3 workers and *TVC* is $75. *TC* is the sum of *TFC* and *TVC*, so to produce 13 sweaters a day, *TC* is $100. Check the calculations in the other rows of the table.

Figure 11.4 shows Campus Sweaters' total cost curves, which graph total cost against output. The green *TFC* curve is horizontal because total fixed cost ($25 a day) does not change when output changes. The purple *TVC* curve and the blue *TC* curve both slope upward because to increase output, more labor must be employed, which increases total variable cost. Total fixed cost equals the vertical distance between the *TVC* and *TC* curves.

Let's now look at a firm's marginal cost.

FIGURE 11.4   Total Cost Curves

Labor (workers per day)	Output (sweaters per day)	Total fixed cost (*TFC*)	Total variable cost (*TVC*)	Total cost (*TC*)
		(dollars per day)		
A 0	0	25	0	25
B 1	4	25	25	50
C 2	10	25	50	75
D 3	**13**	**25**	**75**	**100**
E 4	15	25	100	125
F 5	16	25	125	150

Campus Sweaters rents a knitting machine for $25 a day, so this cost is the firm's total fixed cost. The firm hires workers at a wage rate of $25 a day, and this cost is its total variable cost. For example, in row *D*, Campus Sweaters employs 3 workers and its total variable cost is 3 × $25, which equals $75. Total cost is the sum of total fixed cost and total variable cost. For example, when Campus Sweaters employs 3 workers, total cost is $100—total fixed cost of $25 plus total variable cost of $75.

The graph shows Campus Sweaters' total cost curves. Total fixed cost is constant—the *TFC* curve is a horizontal line. Total variable cost increases as output increases, so the *TVC* curve and the *TC* curve increase as output increases. The vertical distance between the *TC* curve and the *TVC* curve equals total fixed cost, as illustrated by the two arrows.

MyEconLab Animation

Marginal Cost

Figure 11.4 shows that total variable cost and total cost increase at a decreasing rate at small outputs but eventually, as output increases, total variable cost and total cost increase at an increasing rate. To understand this pattern in the change in total cost as output increases, we need to use the concept of *marginal cost*.

A firm's **marginal cost** is the increase in total cost that results from a one-unit increase in output. We calculate marginal cost as the increase in total cost divided by the increase in output. The table in Fig. 11.5 shows this calculation. When, for example, output increases from 10 sweaters to 13 sweaters, total cost increases from $75 to $100. The change in output is 3 sweaters, and the change in total cost is $25. The marginal cost of one of those 3 sweaters is ($25 ÷ 3), which equals $8.33.

Figure 11.5 graphs the marginal cost data in the table as the red marginal cost curve, *MC*. This curve is U-shaped because when Campus Sweaters hires a second worker, marginal cost decreases, but when it hires a third, a fourth, and a fifth worker, marginal cost successively increases.

At small outputs, marginal cost decreases as output increases because of greater specialization and the division of labor. But as output increases further, marginal cost eventually increases because of the *law of diminishing returns*. The law of diminishing returns means that the output produced by each additional worker is successively smaller. To produce an additional unit of output, ever more workers are required, and the cost of producing the additional unit of output—marginal cost—must eventually increase.

Marginal cost tells us how total cost changes as output increases. The final cost concept tells us what it costs, on average, to produce a unit of output. Let's now look at Campus Sweaters' average costs.

Average Cost

Ther are three average costs of production:

1. Average fixed cost
2. Average variable cost
3. Average total cost

Average fixed cost (*AFC*) is total fixed cost per unit of output. **Average variable cost** (*AVC*) is total variable cost per unit of output. **Average total cost** (*ATC*) is total cost per unit of output. The average cost concepts are calculated from the total cost concepts as follows:

$$TC = TFC + TVC.$$

Divide each total cost term by the quantity produced, Q, to get

$$\frac{TC}{Q} = \frac{TFC}{Q} + \frac{TVC}{Q},$$

or

$$ATC = AFC + AVC.$$

The table in Fig. 11.5 shows the calculation of average total cost. For example, in row C, output is 10 sweaters. Average fixed cost is ($25 ÷ 10), which equals $2.50, average variable cost is ($50 ÷ 10), which equals $5.00, and average total cost is ($75 ÷ 10), which equals $7.50. Note that average total cost is equal to average fixed cost ($2.50) plus average variable cost ($5.00).

Figure 11.5 shows the average cost curves. The green average fixed cost curve (*AFC*) slopes downward. As output increases, the same constant total fixed cost is spread over a larger output. The blue average total cost curve (*ATC*) and the purple average variable cost curve (*AVC*) are U-shaped. The vertical distance between the average total cost and average variable cost curves is equal to average fixed cost—as indicated by the two arrows. That distance shrinks as output increases because average fixed cost declines with increasing output.

Marginal Cost and Average Cost

The marginal cost curve (*MC*) intersects the average variable cost curve and the average total cost curve *at their minimum points*. When marginal cost is less than average cost, average cost is decreasing, and when marginal cost exceeds average cost, average cost is increasing. This relationship holds for both the *ATC* curve and the *AVC* curve. It is another example of the relationship you saw in Fig. 11.3 for average product and marginal product and in your average and marginal grades.

Why the Average Total Cost Curve Is U-Shaped

Average total cost is the sum of average fixed cost and average variable cost, so the shape of the *ATC* curve

FIGURE 11.5   Marginal Cost and Average Costs

Marginal cost is calculated as the change in total cost divided by the change in output. When output increases from 4 to 10 sweaters, an increase of 6 sweaters, total cost increases by $25. Marginal cost is $25 ÷ 6, which is $4.17.

Each average cost concept is calculated by dividing the related total cost by output. When 10 sweaters are produced, AFC is $2.50 ($25 ÷ 10), AVC is $5 ($50 ÷ 10), and ATC is $7.50 ($75 ÷ 10).

The graph shows that the MC curve is U-shaped and intersects the AVC curve and the ATC curve at their minimum points. The average fixed cost curve (AFC) is downward sloping. The ATC curve and AVC curve are U-shaped. The vertical distance between the ATC curve and the AVC curve is equal to average fixed cost, as illustrated by the two arrows.

	Labor (workers per day)	Output (sweaters per day)	Total fixed cost (TFC)	Total variable cost (TVC)	Total cost (TC)	Marginal cost (MC) (dollars per additional sweater)	Average fixed cost (AFC)	Average variable cost (AVC)	Average total cost (ATC)
			(dollars per day)				(dollars per sweater)		
A	0	0	25	0	25		—	—	—
						.... 6.25			
B	1	4	25	25	50		6.25	6.25	12.50
						.... 4.17			
C	2	10	25	50	75		2.50	5.00	7.50
						.... 8.33			
D	3	13	25	75	100		1.92	5.77	7.69
						.......12.50			
E	4	15	25	100	125		1.67	6.67	8.33
						.......25.00			
F	5	16	25	125	150		1.56	7.81	9.38

MyEconLab Animation and Draw Graph

combines the shapes of the *AFC* and *AVC* curves. The U shape of the *ATC* curve arises from the influence of two opposing forces:

1. Spreading total fixed cost over a larger output
2. Eventually diminishing returns

When output increases, the firm spreads its total fixed cost over a larger output and so its average fixed cost decreases—its *AFC* curve slopes downward.

Diminishing returns means that as output increases, ever-larger amounts of labor are needed to produce an additional unit of output. So as output increases, average variable cost decreases initially but

eventually increases, and the *AVC* curve slopes upward. The *AVC* curve is U-shaped.

The shape of the *ATC* curve combines these two effects. Initially, as output increases, both average fixed cost and average variable cost decrease, so average total cost decreases. The *ATC* curve slopes downward.

But as output increases further and diminishing returns set in, average variable cost starts to increase. With average fixed cost decreasing more quickly than average variable cost is increasing, the *ATC* curve continues to slope downward. Eventually, average variable cost starts to increase more quickly than average fixed cost decreases, so average total cost starts to increase. The *ATC* curve slopes upward.

Cost Curves and Product Curves

The technology that a firm uses determines its costs. A firm's cost curves come directly from its product curves. You've used this link in the tables in which we have calculated total cost from the total product schedule and information about the prices of the factors of production. We're now going to get a clearer view of the link between the product curves and the cost curves. We'll look first at the link between total cost and total product and then at the links between the average and marginal product and cost curves.

Total Product and Total Variable Cost Figure 11.6 shows the links between the firm's total product curve, *TP*, and its total *variable* cost curve, *TVC*. The graph is a bit unusual in two ways. First, it measures two variables on the *x*-axis—labor and variable cost. Second, it graphs the *TVC* curve but with variable cost on the *x*-axis and output on the *y*-axis. The graph can show labor and cost on the *x*-axis because variable cost is proportional to labor. One worker costs $25 a day. Graphing output against labor gives the *TP* curve and graphing variable cost against output gives the *TVC* curve.

FIGURE 11.6   Total Product and Total Variable Cost

The figure shows the total product curve, *TP*, as a graph of output (sweaters per day) plotted against labor (workers per day). It also shows the total variable cost curve, *TVC*, as a graph of total variable cost (dollars per day) against output. The only difference between the *TVC* curve here and that in Fig. 11.4 is that we've switched the *x*-axis and *y*-axis.

MyEconLab Animation

Checkout Cost Curves

Walmart Adds iPhone Scan-and-Checkout Feature to 12 More Markets

Walmart is tripling the number of stores that lets shoppers scan items with their iPhones and pay at self-checkout counters. Walmart's "Scan & Go" program will soon be in more than 200 stores.

Source: Reuters, March 20, 2013

DATA AND ASSUMPTIONS

A grocery store paid $20,000 to install 5 worker-operated checkout lines. With a life of 9 years and operating for 10 hours a day, these machines have an *implicit rental rate* of $1.00 an hour. Checkout clerks can be hired for $10 an hour. The total product schedule (checkouts per hour) for this store is

Checkout clerks	1	2	3	4	5
Checkouts per hour	12	22	30	36	40

Another grocery store has converted to all self-checkout. It paid $100,000 to install a 5-line self-operated system. With a 5-year life and operating for 10 hours a day, the system has an *implicit rental rate* of $7.00 an hour. It hires checkout assistants to help customers at $10 an hour—the same wage as paid to checkout clerks. The total product schedule for this store is

Checkout assistants	1	1	1	2
Checkouts per hour	12	22	30	36

That is, one checkout assistant can help shoppers check out up to a rate of 30 an hour and a second assistant can boost output to 36 an hour. (Shoppers using self-checkout aren't as quick as clerks, so the fastest rate at which this store can check out customers is 36 an hour.)

THE PROBLEM

- Which checkout system has the lower average total cost (*ATC*)? Which system has the lower marginal cost (*MC*)? Sketch the *ATC* and *MC* curves for the two systems.

THE SOLUTION

- Start with the worker-operated checkout system. Fixed cost is $1.00 per hour and variable cost is $10.00 per clerk. So the total cost schedule is

Checkout clerks	1	2	3	4	5
Checkouts per hour	12	22	30	36	40
Total cost (*TC*) per hour	11	21	31	41	51

- Calculate *MC* as the change in *TC* divided by the change in output (change in number of checkouts) and calculate *ATC* as *TC* divided by output to get

Checkouts per hour	12	22	30	36	40
Marginal cost (MC)	0.83	1.00	1.25	1.67	2.50
Average total cost (ATC)	0.92	0.95	1.03	1.14	1.28

- Figure 1 graphs the *MC* and *ATC* values at each output rate.

Figure 1 Operator Checkout

- Now do similar calculations for the self-checkout system. Fixed cost is $7.00 per hour and variable cost is $10.00 per clerk hour. So the total cost schedule is

Checkout assistants	1	1	1	2
Checkouts per hour	12	22	30	36
Total cost (TC) per hour	17	17	17	27

- Calculate *MC* and *ATC* in the same way as before to get

Checkouts per hour	12	22	30	36
Marginal cost (MC)	0.83	0	0	1.67
Average total cost (ATC)	1.42	0.77	0.57	0.75

- Figure 2 graphs the *MC* and *ATC* values at each output rate.
- Figure 3 compares the *ATC* of the two systems. You can see that the self-checkout system has higher *ATC* at low output rates and lower *ATC* at higher output rates. The reason is that self-checkout has a higher fixed cost and lower variable cost than the worker-operated system.

Figure 3 ATC Compared

Figure 2 Self-Checkout

Average and Marginal Product and Cost Figure 11.7 shows the links between the firm's average and marginal product curves and its average and marginal cost curves. The upper graph shows the average product curve, *AP*, and the marginal product curve, *MP*—like those in Fig. 11.3. The lower graph shows the average variable cost curve, *AVC*, and the marginal cost curve, *MC*—like those in Fig. 11.5.

As labor increases up to 1.5 workers a day (upper graph), output increases to 6.5 sweaters a day (lower graph). Marginal product and average product rise and marginal cost and average variable cost fall. At the point of maximum marginal product, marginal cost is at a minimum.

As labor increases from 1.5 workers to 2 workers a day (upper graph), output increases from 6.5 sweaters to 10 sweaters a day (lower graph). Marginal product falls and marginal cost rises, but average product continues to rise and average variable cost continues to fall. At the point of maximum average product, average variable cost is at a minimum. As labor increases further, output increases. Average product diminishes and average variable cost increases.

Shifts in the Cost Curves

The position of a firm's short-run cost curves depends on two factors:

- Technology
- Prices of factors of production

Technology A technological change that increases productivity increases the marginal product and average product of labor. With a better technology, the same factors of production can produce more output, so the technological advance lowers the costs of production and shifts the cost curves downward.

For example, advances in robot production techniques have increased productivity in the automobile industry. As a result, the product curves of Chrysler, Ford, and GM have shifted upward and their cost curves have shifted downward. But the relationships between their product curves and cost curves have not changed. The curves are still linked in the way shown in Figs. 11.6 and 11.7.

Often, as in the case of robots producing cars, a technological advance results in a firm using more capital, a fixed factor, and less labor, a variable factor.

FIGURE 11.7   Average and Marginal Product Curves and Cost Curves

A firm's *MP* curve is linked to its *MC* curve. If, as the firm increases its labor from 0 to 1.5 workers a day, the firm's marginal product rises, its marginal cost falls. If marginal product is at a maximum, marginal cost is at a minimum. If, as the firm hires more labor, its marginal product diminishes, its marginal cost rises.

A firm's *AP* curve is linked to its *AVC* curve. If, as the firm increases its labor to 2 workers a day, its average product rises, its average variable cost falls. If average product is at a maximum, average variable cost is at a minimum. If, as the firm hires more labor, its average product diminishes, its average variable cost rises.

MyEconLab Animation

TABLE 11.2   A Compact Glossary of Costs

Term	Symbol	Definition	Equation
Fixed cost		Cost that is independent of the output level; cost of a fixed factor of production	
Variable cost		Cost that varies with the output level; cost of a variable factor of production	
Total fixed cost	TFC	Cost of the fixed factors of production	
Total variable cost	TVC	Cost of the variable factors of production	
Total cost	TC	Cost of all factors of production	$TC = TFC + TVC$
Output (total product)	TP	Total quantity produced (output Q)	
Marginal cost	MC	Change in total cost resulting from a one-unit increase in total product	$MC = \Delta TC \div \Delta Q$
Average fixed cost	AFC	Total fixed cost per unit of output	$AFC = TFC \div Q$
Average variable cost	AVC	Total variable cost per unit of output	$AVC = TVC \div Q$
Average total cost	ATC	Total cost per unit of output	$ATC = AFC + AVC$

Another example is the use of ATMs by banks to dispense cash. ATMs, which are fixed capital, have replaced tellers, which are variable labor. Such a technological change decreases total cost but increases fixed costs and decreases variable cost. This change in the mix of fixed cost and variable cost means that at small outputs, average total cost might increase, while at large outputs, average total cost decreases.

Prices of Factors of Production An increase in the price of a factor of production increases the firm's costs and shifts its cost curves. How the curves shift depends on which factor price changes.

An increase in rent or some other component of *fixed* cost shifts the *TFC* and *AFC* curves upward and shifts the *TC* curve upward but leaves the *AVC* and *TVC* curves and the *MC* curve unchanged. For example, if the interest expense paid by a trucking company increases, the fixed cost of transportation services increases.

An increase in wages, gasoline, or another component of *variable* cost shifts the *TVC* and *AVC* curves upward and shifts the *MC* curve upward but leaves

the *AFC* and *TFC* curves unchanged. For example, if truck drivers' wages or the price of gasoline increases, the variable cost and marginal cost of transportation services increase.

You've now completed your study of short-run costs. All the concepts that you've met are summarized in a compact glossary in Table 11.2.

◆ REVIEW QUIZ

1 What relationships do a firm's short-run cost curves show?
2 How does marginal cost change as output increases (a) initially and (b) eventually?
3 What does the law of diminishing returns imply for the shape of the marginal cost curve?
4 What is the shape of the *AFC* curve and why does it have this shape?
5 What are the shapes of the *AVC* curve and the *ATC* curve and why do they have these shapes?

Work these questions in Study Plan 11.3 and get instant feedback. Do a Key Terms Quiz.   MyEconLab

◗ Long-Run Cost

We are now going to study the firm's long-run costs. In the long run, a firm can vary both the quantity of labor and the quantity of capital, so in the long run, all the firm's costs are variable.

The behavior of long-run cost depends on the firm's *production function*, which is the relationship between the maximum output attainable and the quantities of both labor and capital.

The Production Function

Table 11.3 shows Campus Sweaters' production function. The table lists total product schedules for four different quantities of capital. The quantity of capital identifies the plant size. The numbers for plant 1 are for a factory with 1 knitting machine—the case we've just studied. The other three plants have 2, 3, and 4 machines. If Campus Sweaters uses plant 2 with 2 knitting machines, the various amounts of labor can produce the outputs shown in the second column of the table. The other two columns show the outputs of yet larger quantities of capital. Each column of the table could be graphed as a total product curve for each plant.

Diminishing Returns Diminishing returns occur with each of the four plant sizes as the quantity of labor increases. You can check that fact by calculating the marginal product of labor in each of the plants with 2, 3, and 4 machines. With each plant size, as the firm increases the quantity of labor employed, the marginal product of labor (eventually) diminishes.

Diminishing Marginal Product of Capital
Diminishing returns also occur with each quantity of labor as the quantity of capital increases. You can check that fact by calculating the marginal product of capital at a given quantity of labor. The *marginal product of capital* is the change in total product divided by the change in capital when the quantity of labor is constant—equivalently, the change in output resulting from a one-unit increase in the quantity of capital. For example, if Campus Sweaters has 3 workers and increases its capital from 1 machine to 2 machines, output increases from 13 to 18 sweaters a day. The marginal product of the second machine is 5 sweaters a day. If Campus Sweaters continues to employ 3 workers

TABLE 11.3   The Production Function

Labor (workers per day)	Output (sweaters per day)			
	Plant 1	Plant 2	Plant 3	Plant 4
1	4	10	13	15
2	10	15	18	20
3	13	18	22	24
4	15	20	24	26
5	16	21	25	27
Knitting machines (number)	1	2	3	4

The table shows the total product data for four quantities of capital (plant sizes). The greater the plant size, the larger is the output produced by any given quantity of labor. For a given plant size, the marginal product of labor diminishes as more labor is employed. For a given quantity of labor, the marginal product of capital diminishes as the quantity of capital used increases.

and increases the number of machines from 2 to 3, output increases from 18 to 22 sweaters a day. The marginal product of the third machine is 4 sweaters a day, down from 5 sweaters a day for the second machine.

Let's now see what the production function implies for long-run costs.

Short-Run Cost and Long-Run Cost

As before, Campus Sweaters can hire workers for $25 a day and rent knitting machines for $25 a day. Using these factor prices and the data in Table 11.3, we can calculate the average total cost and graph the *ATC* curves for factories with 1, 2, 3, and 4 knitting machines. We've already studied the costs of a factory with 1 machine in Figs. 11.4 and 11.5. In Fig. 11.8, the average total cost curve for that case is ATC_1. Figure 11.8 also shows the average total cost curve for a factory with 2 machines, ATC_2, with 3 machines, ATC_3, and with 4 machines, ATC_4.

You can see, in Fig. 11.8, that the plant size has a big effect on the firm's average total cost.

FIGURE 11.8   Short-Run Costs of Four Different Plants

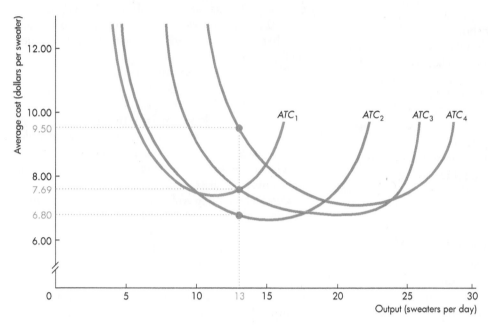

The figure shows short-run average total cost curves for four different quantities of capital at Campus Sweaters. The firm can produce 13 sweaters a day with 1 knitting machine on ATC_1 or with 3 knitting machines on ATC_3 for an average cost of $7.69 a sweater. The firm can produce 13 sweaters a day by using 2 machines on ATC_2 for $6.80 a sweater or by using 4 machines on ATC_4 for $9.50 a sweater.

If the firm produces 13 sweaters a day, the least-cost method of production, *the long-run method*, is with 2 machines on ATC_2.

MyEconLab Animation

In Fig. 11.8, two things stand out:

1. Each short-run *ATC* curve is U-shaped.
2. For each short-run *ATC* curve, the larger the plant, the greater is the output at which average total cost is at a minimum.

Each short-run *ATC* curve is U-shaped because, as the quantity of labor increases, its marginal product initially increases and then diminishes. This pattern in the marginal product of labor, which we examined in some detail for the plant with 1 knitting machine on pp. 254–255, occurs at all plant sizes.

The minimum average total cost for a larger plant occurs at a greater output than it does for a smaller plant because the larger plant has a higher total fixed cost and therefore, for any given output, a higher average fixed cost.

Which short-run *ATC* curve a firm operates on depends on the plant it has. In the long run, the firm can choose its plant and the plant it chooses is the one that enables it to produce its planned output at the lowest average total cost.

To see why, suppose that Campus Sweaters plans to produce 13 sweaters a day. In Fig. 11.8, with 1 machine, the average total cost curve is ATC_1 and the

average total cost of 13 sweaters a day is $7.69 a sweater. With 2 machines, on ATC_2, average total cost is $6.80 a sweater. With 3 machines, on ATC_3, average total cost is $7.69 a sweater, the same as with 1 machine. Finally, with 4 machines, on ATC_4, average total cost is $9.50 a sweater.

The economically efficient plant for producing a given output is the one that has the lowest average total cost. For Campus Sweaters, the economically efficient plant to use to produce 13 sweaters a day is the one with 2 machines.

In the long run, Cindy chooses the plant that minimizes average total cost. When a firm is producing a given output at the least possible cost, it is operating on its *long-run average cost curve.*

The **long-run average cost curve** is the relationship between the lowest attainable average total cost and output when the firm can change both the plant it uses and the quantity of labor it employs.

The long-run average cost curve is a planning curve. It tells the firm the plant and the quantity of labor to use at each output to minimize average cost. Once the firm chooses a plant, the firm operates on the short-run cost curves that apply to that plant.

The Long-Run Average Cost Curve

Figure 11.9 shows how a long-run average cost curve is derived. The long-run average cost curve *LRAC* consists of pieces of the four short-run *ATC* curves. For outputs up to 10 sweaters a day, average total cost is the lowest on ATC_1. For outputs between 10 and 18 sweaters a day, average total cost is the lowest on ATC_2. For outputs between 18 and 24 sweaters a day, average total cost is the lowest on ATC_3. And for outputs in excess of 24 sweaters a day, average total cost is the lowest on ATC_4. The piece of each *ATC* curve with the lowest average total cost is highlighted in dark blue in Fig. 11.9. This dark blue scallop-shaped curve made up of the pieces of the four *ATC* curves is the *LRAC* curve.

Economies and Diseconomies of Scale

Economies of scale are features of a firm's technology that make average total cost *fall* as output increases. When economies of scale are present, the *LRAC* curve slopes downward. In Fig. 11.9, Campus Sweaters has economies of scale for outputs up to 15 sweaters a day.

Greater specialization of both labor and capital is the main source of economies of scale. For example, if GM produces 100 cars a week, each worker must perform many different tasks and the capital must be general-purpose machines and tools. But if GM produces 10,000 cars a week, each worker specializes in a small number of tasks, uses task-specific tools, and becomes highly proficient.

Diseconomies of scale are features of a firm's technology that make average total cost *rise* as output increases. When diseconomies of scale are present, the *LRAC* curve slopes upward. In Fig. 11.9, Campus Sweaters experiences diseconomies of scale at outputs greater than 15 sweaters a day.

The challenge of managing a large enterprise is the main source of diseconomies of scale.

Constant returns to scale are features of a firm's technology that keep average total cost constant as output increases. When constant returns to scale are present, the *LRAC* curve is horizontal.

Economies of Scale at Campus Sweaters The economies of scale and diseconomies of scale at Campus Sweaters arise from the firm's production function in Table 11.3. With 1 machine and 1 worker, the firm produces 4 sweaters a day. With 2 machines and 2 workers, total cost doubles but

---

FIGURE 11.9   Long-Run Average Cost Curve

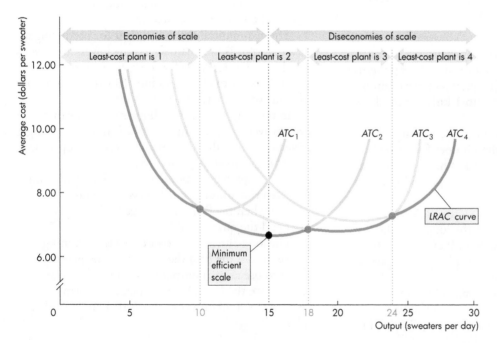

The long-run average cost curve traces the lowest attainable *ATC* when both labor and capital change. The green arrows highlight the output range over which each plant achieves the lowest *ATC*. Within each range, to change the quantity produced, the firm changes the quantity of labor it employs.

Along the *LRAC* curve, economies of scale occur if average cost falls as output increases; diseconomies of scale occur if average cost rises as output increases. Minimum efficient scale is the output at which average cost is lowest, 15 sweaters a day.

ECONOMICS IN ACTION
Produce More to Cut Cost

Why do GM, Ford, and the other automakers have expensive equipment lying around that isn't fully used? You can answer this question with what you've learned in this chapter.

The basic answer is that auto production enjoys economies of scale. A larger output rate brings a lower long-run average cost—the firm's *LRAC* curve slopes downward.

An auto producer's average total cost curves look like those in the figure. To produce 20 vehicles an hour, the firm installs the plant with the short-run average total cost curve ATC_1. The average cost of producing a vehicle is $20,000.

Producing 20 vehicles an hour doesn't use the plant at its lowest possible average total cost. If the firm could sell enough cars for it to produce 40 vehicles an hour, the firm could use its current plant and produce at an average cost of $15,000 a vehicle.

But if the firm planned to produce 40 vehicles an hour, it would not stick with its current plant. The firm would install a bigger plant with the short-run average total cost curve ATC_2, and produce 40 vehicles an hour for $10,000 a car.

Automobile Plant Average Cost Curves

output more than doubles to 15 sweaters a day, so average cost decreases and Campus Sweaters experiences economies of scale. With 4 machines and 4 workers, total cost doubles again but output less than doubles to 26 sweaters a day, so average cost increases and the firm experiences diseconomies of scale.

Minimum Efficient Scale A firm's **minimum efficient scale** is the *smallest* output at which long-run average cost reaches its lowest level. At Campus Sweaters, the minimum efficient scale is 15 sweaters a day.

The minimum efficient scale plays a role in determining market structure. In a market in which the minimum efficient scale is small relative to market demand, the market has room for many firms, and the market is competitive. In a market in which the minimum efficient scale is large relative to market demand, only a small number of firms, and possibly only one firm, can make a profit and the market is either an oligopoly or monopoly. We will return to this idea in the next three chapters.

REVIEW QUIZ

1 What does a firm's production function show and how is it related to a total product curve?
2 Does the law of diminishing returns apply to capital as well as labor? Explain why or why not.
3 What does a firm's *LRAC* curve show? How is it related to the firm's short-run *ATC* curves?
4 What are economies of scale and diseconomies of scale? How do they arise? What do they imply for the shape of the *LRAC* curve?
5 What is a firm's minimum efficient scale?

Work these questions in Study Plan 11.4 and get instant feedback. Do a Key Terms Quiz.   MyEconLab

Economics in the News on pp. 264–265 applies what you've learned about a firm's cost curves. It looks at Starbucks' cost curves and explains how increasing plant size by adding stores can lower average total cost.

Expanding Capacity at Starbucks

Starbucks Canada to Open 150 New Outlets, Biggest Expansion Ever

Financial Post
February 8, 2013

Thanks in part to Target, Starbucks Canada will be undertaking the biggest expansion effort in its history this year, with plans to open more than 150 new locations across the country.

…

The subsidiary of Seattle-based Starbucks Corp. will open outlets inside many of the 124 Target locations opening in Canada in 2013 beginning next month—but the exact number is still a secret, Starbucks Canada president Annie Young-Scrivner said Friday.

The growth is also a response to company's successful bid to tap into the Canadian palate with its burgeoning Blonde roast coffee in a way that it had not before, bringing a host of new customers through its doors, she said in an interview on Friday. …

After the first nine months, Blonde grew to represent 12% of Starbucks Canada brewed coffee sales. Since the company began a sampling and marketing push last month in Canada, the lighter blend now accounts for 20% of those sales. Typically 38% of Starbucks Canada customers drink dark roast and 42% drink medium roast, she said. "Some people thought our roast was too dark before. We had a lot of customers who would come to us for their lattes, but would go somewhere else for their coffee. I think our mix will continue to shift more towards the Blonde roast." …

MyEconLab More Economics in the News

ESSENCE OF THE STORY

- Starbucks plans to open more than 150 new locations across Canada.

- Many of the new outlets will be inside Target stores.

- Starbucks has expanded its number of customers with a successful Blonde roast coffee variety.

- Canadians prefer lighter roasts, and Starbucks expects continued growth of business with ongoing shift towards the Blonde roast.

ECONOMIC ANALYSIS

- Starbucks can increase output by hiring more labor, or by increasing its plant size. Or it can both increase its plant size and hire more labor.

- Starbucks can increase its plant size by either replacing an existing café with a larger one, or expanding the number of cafés.

- The decision turns on comparing costs, and Starbucks has figured that it minimizes cost by expanding the number of cafés and hiring more labor.

- We don't know Starbucks' costs, but we can gain insight into the firm's decision with an example.

- The table shows an assumed total product schedule for a Starbucks café. It also shows Starbucks' total cost (*TC*), marginal cost (*MC*), and average total cost, (*ATC*).

- Figure 1 graphs the marginal cost and average total cost curves.

- If Starbucks wants to increase production in a café to above 1,000 coffees per day, marginal cost rises sharply.

- But if Starbucks opens a new café, a given quantity of labor can produce a greater output.

- With a bigger capacity, fixed cost increases, so at low output levels, average total cost also increases.

- But at higher output levels, because *average* fixed cost decreases, average total cost also decreases.

- Figure 2 shows Starbucks original *ATC* curve, ATC_0, and the new *ATC* curve, ATC_1, which shows average total cost when the firm has added one more café.

Labor (workers per day)	Output (coffees per day)	Total cost (*TC*) (dollars per day)	Marginal cost (*MC*)	Average total cost (*ATC*)
			(dollars per coffee)	
A	0	0	1,000	—
				. . . . . 2.00
B	10	400	1,800	4.50
				. . . . . 1.33
C	20	1,000	2,600	2.60
				. . . . . 2.67
D	30	1,300	3,400	2.62
				. . . . . 4.00
E	40	1,500	4,200	2.80
				. . . . . 8.00
F	50	1,600	5,000	3.13

- Increasing output with a larger plant size avoids the sharply rising marginal cost of the original café.

- In this example, Starbucks can now hire more labor to operate two cafés and average total cost falls as output increases above 1,000 coffees per day.

- Figure 2 also shows Starbucks long-run average cost curve (*LRAC*).

- If the firm wants to expand output yet further and avoid the rising costs along ATC_1, it can open additional cafés and move along its long-run average cost curve.

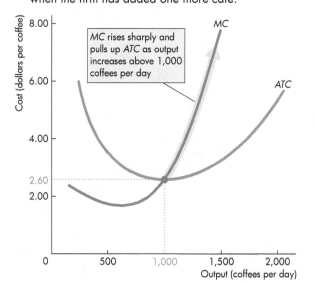

Figure 1 Starbucks' Short-Run Cost Curves

Figure 2 Starbucks' Long-Run Cost Curve

265

◆ SUMMARY

Key Points

Decision Time Frames (p. 248)

- In the short run, the quantity of at least one factor of production is fixed and the quantities of the other factors of production can be varied.
- In the long run, the quantities of all factors of production can be varied.

Working Problem 1 will give you a better understanding of a firm's decision time frames.

Short-Run Technology Constraint (pp. 249–252)

- A total product curve shows the quantity a firm can produce with a given quantity of capital and different quantities of labor.
- Initially, the marginal product of labor increases as the quantity of labor increases, because of increased specialization and the division of labor.
- Eventually, marginal product diminishes because an increasing quantity of labor must share a fixed quantity of capital—the law of diminishing returns.
- Initially, average product increases as the quantity of labor increases, but eventually average product diminishes.

Working Problems 2 to 6 will give you a better understanding of a firm's short-run technology constraint.

Short-Run Cost (pp. 253–259)

- As output increases, total fixed cost is constant, and total variable cost and total cost increase.
- As output increases, average fixed cost decreases and average variable cost, average total cost, and marginal cost decrease at low outputs and increase at high outputs. These cost curves are U-shaped.

Working Problems 7 to 11 will give you a better understanding of a firm's short-run cost.

Long-Run Cost (pp. 260–263)

- A firm has a set of short-run cost curves for each different plant. For each output, the firm has one least-cost plant. The larger the output, the larger is the plant that will minimize average total cost.
- The long-run average cost curve traces out the lowest attainable average total cost at each output when both capital and labor inputs can be varied.
- With economies of scale, the long-run average cost curve slopes downward. With diseconomies of scale, the long-run average cost curve slopes upward.

Working Problems 12 to 14 will give you a better understanding of a firm's long-run cost.

Key Terms

MyEconLab Key Terms Quiz

Average fixed cost, 254
Average product, 249
Average total cost, 254
Average variable cost, 254
Constant returns to scale, 262
Diminishing marginal returns, 251
Diseconomies of scale, 262

Economies of scale, 262
Law of diminishing returns, 251
Long run, 248
Long-run average cost curve, 261
Marginal cost, 254
Marginal product, 249
Minimum efficient scale, 263

Short run, 248
Sunk cost, 248
Total cost, 253
Total fixed cost, 253
Total product, 249
Total variable cost, 253

WORKED PROBLEM

The table provides data about a firm's short-run cost. It shows the firm's total cost, TC, and marginal cost, MC, at five levels of output, including zero output.

Output	MC	TC	TFC	TVC	ATC	AFC	AVC
0		$12	?	?			
	$10						
1		?	?	?	?	?	?
	$2						
2		?	?	?	?	?	?
	$6						
3		?	?	?	?	?	?
	$22						
4		?	?	?	?	?	?

Questions

1. Fill in the cells marked "?" to record the firm's costs: TC, TFC, TVC, ATC, AFC, and AVC at each output.
2. Draw a graph of the total cost curves, and a graph of the average and marginal cost curves.

Solutions

1a. Begin by using the fact that marginal cost, MC, is the change in total cost, TC, when output increases by 1 unit. This fact means that TC at 1 unit equals TC at zero units plus MC of the first unit. TC is $12 at zero and MC of the first unit is $10, so TC at 1 unit equals $22. The rest of the TC column is calculated in the same way. For example, TC at 4 units is $52, which equals $30 + $22.

1b. TFC equals TC at zero output, so you can fill in the TFC column as $12 at each quantity of output.

1c. Because $TC = TFC + TVC$, you can fill in the TVC column as $TVC = TC - TFC$. For example, at 1 unit of output, $TVC = $22 - $12 = $10.

1d. Average cost equals $TC \div$ output, so to fill in the ATC, AFC, and AVC columns, divide the numbers for TC, TFC, and TVC by the output level. For example, ATC at 3 units of output is $30 \div 3 = $10.

Output	MC	TC	TFC	TVC	ATC	AFC	AVC
0		$12	$12	0			
	$10						
1		$22	$12	$10	$22	$12	$10
	$2						
2		$24	$12	$12	$12	$6	$6
	$6						
3		$30	$12	$18	$10	$4	$6
	$22						
4		$52	$12	$40	$13	$3	$10

Key Point: Given a firm's total cost at zero output and its marginal cost at each output, by using the relationships among the cost concepts, we can calculate the total costs and the average costs at each output.

2. The key figure (a) graphs the total cost curves and the key figure (b) graphs the marginal and average cost curves.

Key Point: The marginal cost curve intersects the average cost curves at their minimum points.

Key Figure

(a) Total Cost Curves

(b) Average and Marginal Cost Curves

STUDY PLAN PROBLEMS AND APPLICATIONS

MyEconLab   You can work Problems 1 to 14 in Chapter 11 Study Plan and get instant feedback.

Decision Time Frames (Study Plan 11.1)

1. Which of the following news items involves a short-run decision and which involves a long-run decision? Explain.

   January 31, 2008: Starbucks will open 75 more stores abroad than originally predicted, for a total of 975.

   February 25, 2008: For three hours on Tuesday, Starbucks will shut down every single one of its 7,100 stores so that baristas can receive a refresher course.

   June 2, 2008: Starbucks replaces baristas with vending machines.

   July 18, 2008: Starbucks is closing 616 stores by the end of March.

Short-Run Technology Constraint (Study Plan 11.2)

Use the following table to work Problems 2 to 6. The table sets out Sue's Surfboards' total product schedule.

Labor (workers per week)	Output (surfboards per week)
1	30
2	70
3	120
4	160
5	190
6	210
7	220

2. Draw the total product curve.
3. Calculate the average product of labor and draw the average product curve.
4. Calculate the marginal product of labor and draw the marginal product curve.
5. a. Over what output range does Sue's Surfboards enjoy the benefits of increased specialization and division of labor?

   b. Over what output range does the firm experience diminishing marginal product of labor?

   c. Over what output range does the firm experience an increasing average product of labor but a diminishing marginal product of labor?

6. Explain how it is possible for a firm to experience simultaneously an increasing *average* product but a diminishing *marginal* product.

Short-Run Cost (Study Plan 11.3)

Use the following data to work Problems 7 to 11. Sue's Surfboards, in Problem 2, hires workers at $500 a week and its total fixed cost is $1,000 a week.

7. Calculate total cost, total variable cost, and total fixed cost of each output in the table. Plot these points and sketch the short-run total cost curves.
8. Calculate average total cost, average fixed cost, average variable cost, and marginal cost of each output in the table. Plot these points and sketch the short-run average and marginal cost curves.
9. Illustrate the connection between Sue's *AP*, *MP*, *AVC*, and *MC* curves in graphs like those in Fig. 11.7.
10. Sue's Surfboards rents a factory. If the rent rises by $200 a week and other things remain the same, how do Sue's Surfboards' short-run average cost curves and marginal cost curve change?
11. Workers at Sue's Surfboards negotiate a wage increase of $100 a week per worker. If other things remain the same, explain how Sue's Surfboards' short-run average cost curves and marginal cost curve change.

Long-Run Cost (Study Plan 11.4)

Use the following data to work Problems 12 to 14. Jackie's Canoe Rides rents canoes at $100 per day and pays $50 per day for each canoe operator it hires. The table shows the firm's production function.

Labor (workers per day)	Output (rides per day)			
	Plant 1	Plant 2	Plant 3	Plant 4
10	20	40	55	65
20	40	60	75	85
30	65	75	90	100
40	75	85	100	110
Canoes	10	20	30	40

12. Graph the *ATC* curves for Plant 1 and Plant 2. Explain why these *ATC* curves differ.
13. Graph the *ATC* curves for Plant 3 and Plant 4. Explain why these *ATC* curves differ.
14. a. On Jackie's *LRAC* curve, what is the average cost of producing 40, 75, and 85 rides a week?

    b. What is Jackie's minimum efficient scale?

    c. Does Jackie's production function feature economies of scale or diseconomies of scale?

ADDITIONAL PROBLEMS AND APPLICATIONS

MyEconLab   You can work these problems in MyEconLab if assigned by your instructor.

Decision Time Frames

15. A Bakery on the Rise

Some 500 customers a day line up to buy Avalon's breads, scones, muffins, and coffee. Staffing and management are worries. Avalon now employs 35 and plans to hire 15 more. Its payroll will climb by 30 percent to 40 percent. The new CEO has executed an ambitious agenda that includes the move to a larger space, which will increase the rent from $3,500 to $10,000 a month.

Source: CNN, March 24, 2008

a. Which of Avalon's decisions described in the news clip is a short-run decision and which is a long-run decision?

b. Why is Avalon's long-run decision riskier than its short-run decision?

16. The Sunk-Cost Fallacy

You have good tickets to a basketball game an hour's drive away. There's a blizzard raging outside, and the game is being televised. You can sit warm and safe at home and watch it on TV, or you can bundle up, dig out your car, and go to the game. What do you do?

Source: *Slate*, September 9, 2005

a. What type of cost is your expenditure on tickets?

b. Why is the cost of the ticket irrelevant to your current decision about whether to stay at home or go to the game?

Short-Run Technology Constraint

17. Terri runs a rose farm. One worker produces
1,000 roses a week; hiring a second worker doubles her total product; hiring a third worker doubles her output again; hiring a fourth worker increased her total product but by only 1,000 roses. Construct Terri's marginal product and average product schedules. Over what range of workers do marginal returns increase?

Short-Run Cost

18. Use the events described in the news clip in
Problem 15. By how much will Avalon's short-run decision increase its total variable cost? By how much will Avalon's long-run decision increase its monthly total fixed cost? Sketch Avalon's short-run *ATC* curve before and after the events described in the news clip.

19. Bill's Bakery has a fire and Bill loses some of his
cost data. The bits of paper that he recovers after the fire provide the information in the following table (all the cost numbers are dollars).

TP	AFC	AVC	ATC	MC
10	120	100	220	
				80
20	*A*	*B*	150	
				90
30	40	90	130	
				130
40	30	*C*	*D*	
				E
50	24	108	132	

Bill asks you to come to his rescue and provide the missing data in the five spaces identified as *A*, *B*, *C*, *D*, and *E*.

Use the following table to work Problems 20 and 21. ProPainters hires students at $250 a week to paint houses. It leases equipment at $500 a week. The table sets out its total product schedule.

Labor (students)	Output (houses painted per week)
1	2
2	5
3	9
4	12
5	14
6	15

20. If ProPainters paints 12 houses a week, calculate its
total cost, average total cost, and marginal cost. At what output is average total cost a minimum?

21. Explain why the gap between ProPainters' total
cost and total variable cost is the same no matter how many houses are painted.

22. For Pepsi, a Business Decision with Social Benefit

PepsiCo has done a deal with 300 small Mexican farmers close to their two factories to buy corn at a guaranteed price. PepsiCo saves transportation costs and the use of local farms assures it access to the type of corn best suited to its products and processes. "That gives us great leverage because corn prices don't fluctuate so much, but transportation costs do," said Pedro Padierna, president of PepsiCo in Mexico.

Source: *The New York Times*, February 21, 2011

a. How do fluctuations in the price of corn and in transportation costs influence PepsiCo's short-run cost curves?

b. How does the deal with the farmers to avoid fluctuations in costs benefit PepsiCo?

Long-Run Cost

Use the table in Problem 20 and the following information to work Problems 23 and 24.

If ProPainters doubles the number of students it hires and doubles the amount of equipment it leases, it experiences diseconomies of scale.

23. Explain how the *ATC* curve with one unit of equipment differs from that when ProPainters uses double the amount of equipment.

24. Explain what might be the source of the diseconomies of scale that ProPainters experiences.

Use the following information to work Problems 25 to 27.

The table shows the production function of Bonnie's Balloon Rides. Bonnie's pays $500 a day for each balloon it rents and $25 a day for each balloon operator it hires.

Labor (workers per day)	Output (rides per day)			
	Plant 1	Plant 2	Plant 3	Plant 4
10	6	10	13	15
20	10	15	18	20
30	13	18	22	24
40	15	20	24	26
50	16	21	25	27
Balloons (number)	1	2	3	4

25. Graph the *ATC* curves for Plant 1 and Plant 2. Explain why these *ATC* curves differ.

26. Graph the *ATC* curves for Plant 3 and Plant 4. Explain why these *ATC* curves differ.

27. a. On Bonnie's *LRAC* curve, what is the average cost of producing

    (i) 15 rides a day?

    (ii) 18 rides a day?

    b. Explain how Bonnie's uses its long-run average cost curve to decide how many balloons to rent.

Economics in the News

28. After you have studied *Economics in the News* on pp. 264–265, answer the following questions.

    a. Explain the distinction between the short run and the long run and identify when Starbucks would want to make each type of change.

    b. Explain economies of scale. Does Starbucks reap economies of scale in the example on p. 265?

    c. Draw a graph to illustrate Starbucks' cost curves as it opens more and more cafés in Target stores.

    d. Explain why Starbucks is opening cafés in Target stores rather than stand alone cafés.

29. **Starbucks Unit Brews Up Self-Serve Espresso Bars**

    Coinstar has installed automated, self-serve espresso kiosks in grocery stores. Kiosks cost just under $40,000 each and Coinstar provides maintenance. The self-serve kiosk removes the labor costs of having a barista serve Starbucks' coffee, and store personnel refill the machine.

    Source: MSNBC, June 1, 2008

    a. What is Coinstar's total fixed cost of operating one self-serve kiosk? What are its variable costs of providing coffee at a self-serve kiosk?

    b. Assume that a coffee machine operated by a barista costs less than $40,000. Explain how the fixed costs, variable costs, and total costs of barista-served and self-served coffee differ.

    c. Sketch the marginal cost and average cost curves implied by your answer to part (b).

Use the following news clip to work Problems 30 and 31.

Gap Will Focus on Smaller Scale Stores

Gap has too many stores that are 12,500 square feet. The target store size is 6,000 square feet to 10,000 square feet, so Gap plans to combine previously separate concept stores. Some Gap body, adult, maternity, baby and kids stores will be combined in one store.

Source: CNN, June 10, 2008

30. Thinking of a Gap store as a production plant, explain why Gap is making a decision to reduce the size of its stores. Is Gap's decision a long-run decision or a short-run decision?

31. How might Gap take advantage of economies of scale by combining concept stores into one store?

12

PERFECT COMPETITION

After studying this chapter, you will be able to:

◆ Define perfect competition

◆ Explain how a firm makes its output decision

◆ Explain how price and output are determined in perfect competition

◆ Explain why firms enter and leave a market

◆ Predict the effects of technological change in a competitive market

◆ Explain why perfect competition is efficient

A million "apps" have been created for smartphones and tablets. Most of these apps are the work of individuals in intense competition with each other. No single app writer can influence the price of an app, but each writer can and must decide how many hours to work and how many apps to produce.

In this chapter, we study producers who, like small app developers, are in intense competition—in *perfect competition*. At the end of the chapter, in *Economics in the News*, we apply the perfect competition model to the highly competitive market in apps.

◗ What Is Perfect Competition?

The firms that you study in this chapter face the force of raw competition. We call this extreme form of competition perfect competition. **Perfect competition** is a market in which

- Many firms sell identical products to many buyers.
- There are no restrictions on entry into the market.
- Established firms have no advantage over new ones.
- Sellers and buyers are well informed about prices.

Farming, fishing, wood pulping and paper milling, the manufacture of paper cups and shopping bags, grocery and fresh flower retailing, photo finishing, lawn services, plumbing, painting, dry cleaning, and laundry services are all examples of highly competitive industries.

How Perfect Competition Arises

Perfect competition arises if the minimum efficient scale of a single producer is small relative to the market demand for the good or service. In this situation, there is room in the market for many firms. A firm's *minimum efficient scale* is the smallest output at which long-run average cost reaches its lowest level. (See Chapter 11, p. 263.)

In perfect competition, each firm produces a good that has no unique characteristics, so consumers don't care which firm's good they buy.

Price Takers

Firms in perfect competition are price takers. A **price taker** is a firm that cannot influence the market price because its production is an insignificant part of the total market.

Imagine that you are a wheat farmer in Kansas. You have a thousand acres planted—which sounds like a lot. But compared to the millions of acres in Colorado, Oklahoma, Texas, Nebraska, and the Dakotas, as well as the millions more in Canada, Argentina, Australia, and Ukraine, your thousand acres are a drop in the ocean. Nothing makes your wheat any better than any other farmer's, and all the buyers of wheat know the price at which they can do business.

If the market price of wheat is $4 a bushel, then that is the highest price you can get for your wheat. Ask for $4.10 and no one will buy from you. Offer it for $3.90 and you'll be sold out in a flash and have given away 10¢ a bushel. You take the market price.

Economic Profit and Revenue

A firm's goal is to maximize *economic profit*, which is equal to total revenue minus total cost. Total cost is the *opportunity cost* of production, which includes *normal profit*. (See Chapter 10, p. 225.)

A firm's **total revenue** equals the price of its output multiplied by the number of units of output sold (price × quantity). **Marginal revenue** is the change in total revenue that results from a one-unit increase in the quantity sold. Marginal revenue is calculated by dividing the change in total revenue by the change in the quantity sold.

Figure 12.1 illustrates these revenue concepts. In part (a), the market demand curve, D, and market supply curve, S, determine the market price. The market price is $25 a sweater. Campus Sweaters is just one of many producers of sweaters, so the best it can do is to sell its sweaters for $25 each.

Total Revenue   Total revenue is equal to the price multiplied by the quantity sold. In the table in Fig. 12.1, if Campus Sweaters sells 9 sweaters, its total revenue is $225 (9 × $25).

Figure 12.1(b) shows the firm's total revenue curve (TR), which graphs the relationship between total revenue and the quantity sold. At point A on the TR curve, the firm sells 9 sweaters and has a total revenue of $225. Because each additional sweater sold brings in a constant amount—$25—the total revenue curve is an upward-sloping straight line.

Marginal Revenue   Marginal revenue is the change in total revenue that results from a one-unit increase in quantity sold. In the table in Fig. 12.1, when the quantity sold increases from 8 to 9 sweaters, total revenue increases from $200 to $225, so marginal revenue is $25 a sweater.

Because the firm in perfect competition is a price taker, the change in total revenue that results from a one-unit increase in the quantity sold equals the market price. *In perfect competition, the firm's marginal revenue equals the market price.* Figure 12.1(c) shows the firm's marginal revenue curve (MR) as the horizontal line at the market price.

Demand for the Firm's Product   The firm can sell any quantity it chooses at the market price. So the demand curve for the firm's product is a horizontal line at the market price, the same as the firm's marginal revenue curve.

FIGURE 12.1 Demand, Price, and Revenue in Perfect Competition

(a) Sweater market

(b) Campus Sweaters' total revenue

(c) Campus Sweaters' marginal revenue

Quantity sold (Q) (sweaters per day)	Price (P) (dollars per sweater)	Total revenue (TR = P × Q) (dollars)	Marginal revenue (MR = ΔTR/ΔQ) (dollars per additional sweater)
8	25	200	
			 25
9	25	225	
			 25
10	25	250	

In part (a), market demand and market supply determine the market price (and quantity). Part (b) shows the firm's total revenue curve (*TR*). Point A corresponds to the second row of the table—Campus Sweaters sells 9 sweaters at $25 a sweater, so total revenue is $225. Part (c) shows the firm's marginal revenue curve (*MR*). This curve is also the demand curve for the firm's sweaters. The demand for sweaters from Campus Sweaters is perfectly elastic at the market price of $25 a sweater.

MyEconLab Animation

A horizontal demand curve illustrates a perfectly elastic demand, so the demand for the firm's product is perfectly elastic. A sweater from Campus Sweaters is a *perfect substitute* for a sweater from any other factory. But the *market* demand for sweaters is *not* perfectly elastic: Its elasticity depends on the substitutability of sweaters for other goods and services.

The Firm's Decisions

The goal of the competitive firm is to maximize economic profit, given the constraints it faces. To achieve its goal, a firm must decide

1. How to produce at minimum cost
2. What quantity to produce
3. Whether to enter or exit a market

You've already seen how a firm makes the first decision. It does so by operating with the plant that minimizes long-run average cost—by being on its long-run average cost curve. We'll now see how the firm makes the other two decisions. We start by looking at the firm's output decision.

The Firm's Output Decision

A firm's cost curves (total cost, average cost, and marginal cost) describe the relationship between its output and costs (see Chapter 11, pp. 253–259). And a firm's revenue curves (total revenue and marginal revenue) describe the relationship between its output and revenue (pp. 272–273). From the firm's cost curves and revenue curves, we can find the output that maximizes the firm's economic profit.

Figure 12.2 shows how to do this for Campus Sweaters. The table lists the firm's total revenue and total cost at different outputs, and part (a) of the figure shows the firm's total revenue curve, *TR*, and total cost curve, *TC*. These curves are graphs of

numbers in the first three columns of the table.

Economic profit equals total revenue minus total cost. The fourth column of the table in Fig. 12.2 shows the economic profit made by Campus Sweaters, and part (b) of the figure graphs these numbers as its economic profit curve, *EP*.

Campus Sweaters maximizes its economic profit by producing 9 sweaters a day: Total revenue is $225, total cost is $183, and economic profit is $42. No other output rate achieves a larger profit.

At outputs of less than 4 sweaters and more than 12 sweaters a day, Campus Sweaters would incur an economic loss. At either 4 or 12 sweaters a day, Campus Sweaters would make zero economic profit, called a *break-even point*.

FIGURE 12.2   Total Revenue, Total Cost, and Economic Profit

(a) Revenue and cost

(b) Economic profit and loss

Quantity (Q) (sweaters per day)	Total revenue (TR) (dollars)	Total cost (TC) (dollars)	Economic profit (TR – TC) (dollars)
0	0	22	–22
1	25	45	–20
2	50	66	–16
3	75	85	–10
4	100	100	0
5	125	114	11
6	150	126	24
7	175	141	34
8	200	160	40
9	225	183	42
10	250	210	40
11	275	245	30
12	300	300	0
13	325	360	–35

The table lists Campus Sweaters' total revenue, total cost, and economic profit. Part (a) graphs the total revenue and total cost curves, and part (b) graphs economic profit.

Campus Sweaters makes maximum economic profit, $42 a day ($225 – $183), when it produces 9 sweaters a day. At outputs of 4 sweaters and 12 sweaters a day, Campus Sweaters makes zero economic profit—these are break-even points. At an output less than 4 sweaters and greater than 12 sweaters a day, Campus Sweaters incurs an economic loss.

Marginal Analysis and the Supply Decision

Another way to find the profit-maximizing output is to use marginal analysis, which compares marginal revenue, *MR*, with marginal cost, *MC*. As output increases, the firm's marginal revenue is constant but its marginal cost eventually increases.

If marginal revenue exceeds marginal cost (*MR* > *MC*), then the revenue from selling one more unit exceeds the cost of producing it and an increase in output increases economic profit. If marginal revenue is less than marginal cost (*MR* < *MC*), then the revenue from selling one more unit is less than the cost of producing that unit and a *decrease* in output *increases* economic profit. If marginal revenue equals marginal cost (*MR* = *MC*), then the revenue from selling one more unit equals the cost incurred to produce that unit. Economic profit is maximized and either an increase or a decrease in output decreases economic profit.

Figure 12.3 illustrates these propositions. If Campus Sweaters increases its output from 8 sweaters to 9 sweaters a day, marginal revenue ($25) exceeds marginal cost ($23), so by producing the 9th sweater economic profit increases by $2 from $40 to $42 a day. The blue area in the figure shows the increase in economic profit when the firm increases production from 8 to 9 sweaters per day.

If Campus Sweaters increases its output from 9 sweaters to 10 sweaters a day, marginal revenue ($25) is less than marginal cost ($27), so by producing the 10th sweater, economic profit decreases. The last column of the table shows that economic profit decreases from $42 to $40 a day. The red area in the figure shows the economic loss that arises from increasing production from 9 to 10 sweaters a day.

Campus Sweaters maximizes economic profit by producing 9 sweaters a day, the quantity at which marginal revenue equals marginal cost.

A firm's profit-maximizing output is its quantity supplied at the market price. The quantity supplied at a price of $25 a sweater is 9 sweaters a day. If the price were higher than $25 a sweater, the firm would increase production. If the price were lower than $25 a sweater, the firm would decrease production. These profit-maximizing responses to different market prices are the foundation of the law of supply:

Other things remaining the same, the higher the market price of a good, the greater is the quantity supplied of that good.

FIGURE 12.3   Profit-Maximizing Output

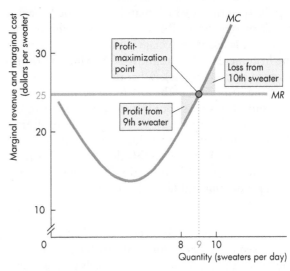

Quantity (Q) (sweaters per day)	Total revenue (TR) (dollars)	Marginal revenue (MR) (dollars per additional sweater)	Total cost (TC) (dollars)	Marginal cost (MC) (dollars per additional sweater)	Economic profit (TR − TC) (dollars)
7	175		141		34
		25		19	
8	200		160		40
		25		23	
9	225		183		42
		25		27	
10	250		210		40
		25		35	
11	275		245		30

The firm maximizes profit by producing the output at which marginal revenue equals marginal cost and marginal cost is increasing. The table and figure show that marginal cost equals marginal revenue and economic profit is maximized when Campus Sweaters produces 9 sweaters a day. The table shows that if Campus Sweaters increases output from 8 to 9 sweaters, marginal cost is $23, which is less than the marginal revenue of $25. If output increases from 9 to 10 sweaters, marginal cost is $27, which exceeds the marginal revenue of $25. If marginal revenue exceeds marginal cost, an increase in output increases economic profit. If marginal revenue is less than marginal cost, an increase in output decreases economic profit. If marginal revenue equals marginal cost, economic profit is maximized.

MyEconLab Animation and Draw Graph

Temporary Shutdown Decision

You've seen that a firm maximizes profit by producing the quantity at which marginal revenue (price) equals marginal cost. But suppose that at this quantity, price is less than average total cost. In this case, the firm incurs an economic loss. Maximum profit is a loss (a minimum loss). What does the firm do?

If the firm expects the loss to be permanent, it goes out of business. But if it expects the loss to be temporary, the firm must decide whether to shut down temporarily and produce no output, or to keep producing. To make this decision, the firm compares the loss from shutting down with the loss from producing and takes the action that minimizes its loss.

Loss Comparisons A firm's economic loss equals total fixed cost, *TFC*, plus total variable cost minus total revenue. Total variable cost equals average variable cost, *AVC*, multiplied by the quantity produced, *Q*, and total revenue equals price, *P*, multiplied by the quantity *Q*. So:

$$\text{Economic loss} = TFC + (AVC - P) \times Q.$$

If the firm shuts down, it produces no output ($Q = 0$). The firm has no variable costs and no revenue but it must pay its fixed costs, so its economic loss equals total fixed cost.

If the firm produces, then in addition to its fixed costs, it incurs variable costs. But it also receives revenue. Its economic loss equals total fixed cost—the loss when shut down—plus total variable cost minus total revenue. If total variable cost exceeds total revenue, this loss exceeds total fixed cost and the firm shuts down. Equivalently, if average variable cost *exceeds* price, this loss exceeds total fixed cost and the firm *shuts down*.

The Shutdown Point A firm's **shutdown point** is the price and quantity at which it is indifferent between producing and shutting down. The shutdown point occurs at the price and the quantity at which average variable cost is a minimum. At the shutdown point, the firm is minimizing its loss and its loss equals total fixed cost. If the price falls below minimum average variable cost, the firm shuts down temporarily and continues to incur a loss equal to total fixed cost. At prices above minimum average variable cost but below average total cost, the firm produces the loss-minimizing output and incurs a loss, but a loss that is less than total fixed cost.

Figure 12.4 illustrates the firm's shutdown decision and the shutdown point that we've just described for Campus Sweaters.

The firm's average variable cost curve is *AVC* and the marginal cost curve is *MC*. Average variable cost has a minimum of $17 a sweater when output is 7 sweaters a day. The *MC* curve intersects the *AVC* curve at its minimum. (We explained this relationship in Chapter 11; see pp. 254–255.)

The figure shows the marginal revenue curve *MR* when the price is $17 a sweater, a price equal to min-imum average variable cost. Marginal revenue equals marginal cost at 7 sweaters a day, so this quantity maximizes economic profit (minimizes economic loss). The *ATC* curve shows that the firm's average total cost of producing 7 sweaters a day is $20.14 a sweater. The firm incurs a loss equal to $3.14 a sweater on 7 sweaters a day, so its loss is $22 a day. The table in Fig. 12.2 shows that Campus Sweaters' loss equals its total fixed cost.

FIGURE 12.4   The Shutdown Decision

The shutdown point is at minimum average variable cost. At a price below minimum average variable cost, the firm shuts down and produces no output. At a price equal to minimum average variable cost, the firm is indifferent between shutting down and producing no output or producing the output at minimum average variable cost. Either way, the firm minimizes its economic loss and incurs a loss equal to total fixed cost.

The Firm's Supply Curve

A perfectly competitive firm's supply curve shows how its profit-maximizing output varies as the market price varies, other things remaining the same. The supply curve is derived from the firm's marginal cost curve and average variable cost curves. Figure 12.5 illustrates the derivation of the supply curve.

When the price *exceeds* minimum average variable cost (more than $17), the firm maximizes profit by producing the output at which marginal cost equals price. If the price rises, the firm increases its output—it moves up along its marginal cost curve.

When the price is *less than* minimum average variable cost (less than $17 a sweater), the firm maximizes profit by temporarily shutting down and producing no output. The firm produces zero output at all prices below minimum average variable cost.

When the price *equals* minimum average variable cost, the firm maximizes profit *either* by temporarily shutting down and producing no output *or* by producing the output at which average variable cost is a minimum—the shutdown point, T. The firm never produces a quantity between zero and the quantity at the shutdown point T (a quantity greater than zero and less than 7 sweaters a day).

The firm's supply curve in Fig. 12.5(b) runs along the y-axis from a price of zero to a price equal to minimum average variable cost, jumps to point T, and then, as the price rises above minimum average variable cost, follows the marginal cost curve.

◆ REVIEW QUIZ

1 Why does a firm in perfect competition produce the quantity at which marginal cost equals price?
2 What is the lowest price at which a firm produces an output? Explain why.
3 What is the relationship between a firm's supply curve, its marginal cost curve, and its average variable cost curve?

Work these questions in Study Plan 12.2 and get instant feedback. Do a Key Terms Quiz.   MyEconLab

So far, we've studied a single firm in isolation. We've seen that the firm's profit-maximizing decision depends on the market price, which it takes as given. How is the market price determined? Let's find out.

FIGURE 12.5   A Firm's Supply Curve

(a) Marginal cost and average variable cost

(b) Campus Sweaters' short-run supply curve

Part (a) shows the firm's profit-maximizing output at various market prices. At $25 a sweater, it produces 9 sweaters, and at $17 a sweater, it produces 7 sweaters. At all prices below $17 a sweater, Campus Sweaters produces nothing. Its shutdown point is T. Part (b) shows the firm's supply curve—the quantity of sweaters it produces at each price. Its supply curve is made up of the marginal cost curve at all prices above minimum average variable cost and the vertical axis at all prices below minimum average variable cost.

____ MyEconLab Animation and Draw Graph ____

Output, Price, and Profit in the Short Run

To determine the price and quantity in a perfectly competitive market, we need to know how market demand and market supply interact. We start by studying a perfectly competitive market in the short run. The short run is a situation in which the number of firms is fixed.

Market Supply in the Short Run

The **short-run market supply curve** shows the quantity supplied by all the firms in the market at each price when each firm's plant and the number of firms remain the same.

You've seen how an individual firm's supply curve is determined. The market supply curve is derived from the individual supply curves. The quantity supplied by the market at a given price is the sum of the quantities supplied by all the firms in the market at that price.

Figure 12.6 shows the supply curve for the competitive sweater market. In this example, the market consists of 1,000 firms exactly like Campus Sweaters. At each price, the quantity supplied by the market is 1,000 times the quantity supplied by a single firm.

The table in Fig. 12.6 shows the firm's and the market's supply schedules and how the market supply curve is constructed. At prices below $17 a sweater, every firm in the market shuts down; the quantity supplied by the market is zero. At $17 a sweater, each firm is indifferent between shutting down and producing nothing or operating and producing 7 sweaters a day. Some firms will shut down, and others will supply 7 sweaters a day. The quantity supplied by each firm is *either* 0 or 7 sweaters, and the quantity supplied by the market is *between* 0 (all firms shut down) and 7,000 (all firms produce 7 sweaters a day each).

The market supply curve is a graph of the market supply schedules, and the points on the supply curve *A* through *D* represent the rows of the table.

To construct the market supply curve, we sum the quantities supplied by all the firms at each price. Each of the 1,000 firms in the market has a supply schedule like Campus Sweaters. At prices below $17 a sweater, the market supply curve runs along the *y*-axis. At $17 a sweater, the market supply curve is horizontal—supply is perfectly elastic. As the price

FIGURE 12.6   Short-Run Market Supply Curve

Price (dollars per sweater)	Quantity supplied by Campus Sweaters (sweaters per day)	Quantity supplied by market (sweaters per day)
A	17	0 or 7	0 to 7,000
B	20	8	8,000
C	25	9	9,000
D	31	10	10,000

The market supply schedule is the sum of the supply schedules of all the individual firms. A market that consists of 1,000 identical firms has a supply schedule similar to that of one firm, but the quantity supplied by the market is 1,000 times as large as that of the one firm (see the table). The market supply curve is S_M. Points *A*, *B*, *C*, and *D* correspond to the rows of the table. At the shutdown price of $17 a sweater, each firm produces either 0 or 7 sweaters a day and the quantity supplied by the market is between 0 and 7,000 sweaters a day. The market supply is perfectly elastic at the shutdown price.

MyEconLab Animation

rises above $17 a sweater, each firm increases its quantity supplied and the quantity supplied by the market increases by 1,000 times that of one firm.

Short-Run Equilibrium

Market demand and short-run market supply determine the market price and market output. Figure 12.7(a) shows a short-run equilibrium. The short-run supply curve, S, is the same as S_M in Fig. 12.6. If the market demand curve is D_1, the market price is $20 a sweater. Each firm takes this price as given and produces its profit-maximizing output, which is 8 sweaters a day. Because the market has 1,000 identical firms, the market output is 8,000 sweaters a day.

A Change in Demand

Changes in demand bring changes to short-run market equilibrium. Figure 12.7(b) shows these changes.

If demand increases and the demand curve shifts rightward to D_2, the market price rises to $25 a sweater. At this price, each firm maximizes profit by increasing its output to 9 sweaters a day. The market output increases to 9,000 sweaters a day.

If demand decreases and the demand curve shifts leftward to D_3, the market price falls to $17. At this

price, each firm maximizes profit by decreasing its output. If each firm produces 7 sweaters a day, the market output decreases to 7,000 sweaters a day.

If the demand curve shifts farther leftward than D_3, the market price remains at $17 a sweater because the market supply curve is horizontal at that price. Some firms continue to produce 7 sweaters a day, and others temporarily shut down. Firms are indifferent between these two activities, and whichever they choose, they incur an economic loss equal to total fixed cost. The number of firms continuing to produce is just enough to satisfy the market demand at a price of $17 a sweater.

Profits and Losses in the Short Run

In short-run equilibrium, although the firm produces the profit-maximizing output, it does not necessarily end up making an economic profit. It might do so, but it might alternatively break even or incur an economic loss. Economic profit (or loss) per sweater is price, P, minus average total cost, ATC. So economic profit (or loss) is $(P - ATC) \times Q$. If price

FIGURE 12.7   Short-Run Equilibrium

(a) Equilibrium

(b) Change in equilibrium

In part (a), the market supply curve is S and the market demand curve is D_1. The market price is $20 a sweater. At this price, each firm produces 8 sweaters a day and the market produces 8,000 sweaters a day.

In part (b), if the market demand increases to D_2, the

price rises to $25 a sweater. Each firm produces 9 sweaters a day and market output is 9,000 sweaters. If market demand decreases to D_3, the price falls to $17 a sweater and each firm decreases its output. If each firm produces 7 sweaters a day, the market output is 7,000 sweaters a day.

equals average total cost, a firm breaks even—the entrepreneur makes normal profit. If price exceeds average total cost, a firm makes an economic profit. If price is less than average total cost, a firm incurs an economic loss. Figure 12.8 shows these three possible short-run profit outcomes for Campus Sweaters. These outcomes correspond to the three different levels of market demand that we've just examined.

Three Possible Short-Run Outcomes

Figure 12.8(a) corresponds to the situation in Fig. 12.7(a) where the market demand is D_1. The equilibrium price of a sweater is $20 and the firm produces 8 sweaters a day. Average total cost is $20 a sweater. Price equals average total cost (ATC), so the firm breaks even (makes zero economic profit).

Figure 12.8(b) corresponds to the situation in Fig. 12.7(b) where the market demand is D_2. The equilibrium price of a sweater is $25 and the firm produces 9 sweaters a day. Here, price exceeds average total cost, so the firm makes an economic profit. Its economic profit is $42 a day, which equals $4.67 per sweater ($25.00 − $20.33) multiplied by 9, the

profit-maximizing number of sweaters produced. The blue rectangle shows this economic profit. The height of that rectangle is profit per sweater, $4.67, and the length is the quantity of sweaters produced, 9 a day. So the area of the rectangle is economic profit of $42 a day.

Figure 12.8(c) corresponds to the situation in Fig. 12.7(b) where the market demand is D_3. The equilibrium price of a sweater is $17. Here, the price is less than average total cost, so the firm incurs an economic loss. Price and marginal revenue are $17 a sweater, and the profit-maximizing (in this case, loss-minimizing) output is 7 sweaters a day. Total revenue is $119 a day (7 × $17). Average total cost is $20.14 a sweater, so the economic loss is $3.14 per sweater ($20.14 − $17.00). This loss per sweater multiplied by the number of sweaters is $22. The red rectangle shows this economic loss. The height of that rectangle is economic loss per sweater, $3.14, and the length is the quantity of sweaters produced, 7 a day. So the area of the rectangle is the firm's economic loss of $22 a day. If the price dips below $17 a sweater, the firm temporarily shuts down and incurs an economic loss equal to total fixed cost.

FIGURE 12.8   Three Short-Run Outcomes for the Firm

(a) Break even

(b) Economic profit

(c) Economic loss

In the short run, the firm might break even (make zero economic profit), make an economic profit, or incur an economic loss. In part (a), the price equals minimum average total cost. At the profit-maximizing output, the firm breaks even and makes zero economic profit. In part (b), the market price is $25 a sweater. At the profit-maximizing output,

the price exceeds average total cost and the firm makes an economic profit, which is equal to the area of the blue rectangle. In part (c), the market price is $17 a sweater. At the profit-maximizing output, the price is below minimum average total cost and the firm incurs an economic loss, which is equal to the area of the red rectangle.

ECONOMICS IN ACTION

Production Cutback and Temporary Shutdown

The high price of gasoline and anxiety about unemployment and future incomes brought a decrease in the demand for luxury goods including high-end motorcycles such as Harley-Davidsons.

Harley-Davidson's profit-maximizing response to the decrease in demand was to cut production and lay off workers. Some of the production cuts and lay-offs were temporary and some were permanent.

Harley-Davidson's bike production plant in York County, Pennsylvania, was temporarily shut down in the summer of 2008 because total revenue was insufficient to cover total variable cost.

The firm also permanently cut its workforce by 300 people. This permanent cut was like that at Campus Sweaters when the market demand for sweaters decreased from D_1 to D_3 in Fig. 12.7(b).

Work these questions in Study Plan 12.3 and get instant feedback. Do a Key Terms Quiz.

◆ REVIEW QUIZ

1 How do we derive the short-run market supply curve in perfect competition?
2 In perfect competition, when market demand increases, explain how the price of the good and the output and profit of each firm changes in the short run.
3 In perfect competition, when market demand decreases, explain how the price of the good and the output and profit of each firm changes in the short run.

MyEconLab

▶ Output, Price, and Profit in the Long Run

In short-run equilibrium, a firm might make an economic profit, incur an economic loss, or break even. Although each of these three situations is a short-run equilibrium, only one of them is a long-run equilibrium. The reason is that in the long run, firms can enter or exit the market.

Entry and Exit

Entry occurs in a market when new firms come into the market and the number of firms increases. Exit occurs when existing firms leave a market and the number of firms decreases.

Firms respond to economic profit and economic loss by either entering or exiting a market. New firms enter a market in which existing firms are making an economic profit. Firms exit a market in which they are incurring an economic loss. Temporary economic profit and temporary economic loss don't trigger entry and exit. It's the prospect of persistent economic profit or loss that triggers entry and exit.

Entry and exit change the market supply, which influences the market price, the quantity produced by each firm, and its economic profit (or loss).

If firms enter a market, supply increases and the market supply curve shifts rightward. The increase in supply lowers the market price and eventually eliminates economic profit. When economic profit reaches zero, entry stops.

If firms exit a market, supply decreases and the market supply curve shifts leftward. The market price rises and economic loss decreases. Eventually, economic loss is eliminated and exit stops.

To summarize:

- New firms enter a market in which existing firms are making an economic profit.
- As new firms enter a market, the market price falls and the economic profit of each firm decreases.
- Firms exit a market in which they are incurring an economic loss.
- As firms leave a market, the market price rises and the economic loss incurred by the remaining firms decreases.
- Entry and exit stop when firms make zero economic profit.

A Closer Look at Entry

The sweater market has 800 firms with cost curves like those in Fig. 12.9(a). The market demand curve is D, the market supply curve is S_1, and the price is $25 a sweater in Fig. 12.9(b). Each firm produces 9 sweaters a day and makes an economic profit.

This economic profit is a signal for new firms to enter the market. As entry takes place, supply increases and the market supply curve shifts rightward toward S^*. As supply increases with no change in demand, the market price gradually falls from $25 to $20 a sweater. At this lower price, each firm makes zero economic profit and entry stops.

Entry results in an increase in market output, but each firm's output *decreases*. Because the price falls, each firm moves down its supply curve and produces less. Because the number of firms increases, the market produces more.

A Closer Look at Exit

The sweater market has 1,200 firms with cost curves like those in Fig. 12.9(a). The market demand curve is D, the market supply curve is S_2, and the price is $17 a sweater in Fig. 12.9(b). Each firm produces 7 sweaters a day and incurs an economic loss.

This economic loss is a signal for firms to exit the market. As exit takes place, supply decreases and the market supply curve shifts leftward toward S^*. As supply decreases with no change in demand, the market price gradually rises from $17 to $20 a sweater. At this higher price, losses are eliminated, each firm makes zero economic profit, and exit stops.

Exit results in a decrease in market output, but each firm's output *increases*. Because the price rises, each firm moves up its supply curve and produces more. Because the number of firms decreases, the market produces less.

FIGURE 12.9   Entry, Exit, and Long-Run Equilibrium

(a) Campus Sweaters

(b) The sweater market

Each firm has cost curves like those of Campus Sweaters in part (a). The market demand curve is D in part (b).

When the market supply curve in part (b) is S_1, the price is $25 a sweater. In part (a), each firm produces 9 sweaters a day and makes an economic profit. Profit triggers the entry of new firms and as new firms enter, the market supply curve shifts rightward, from S_1 toward S^*. The price falls from $25 to $20 a sweater, and the quantity produced increases from 7,200 to 8,000 sweaters. Each firm decreases its output to 8

sweaters a day and its economic profit falls to zero.

When the market supply curve is S_2, the price is $17 a sweater. In part (a), each firm produces 7 sweaters a day and incurs an economic loss. Loss triggers exit and as firms exit, the market supply curve shifts leftward, from S_2 toward S^*. The price rises from $17 to $20 a sweater, and the quantity produced decreases from 8,400 to 8,000 sweaters. Each firm increases its output from 7 to 8 sweaters a day and its economic profit rises to zero.

ECONOMICS IN ACTION

Entry and Exit

An example of entry and falling prices occurred during the 1980s and 1990s in the personal computer market. When IBM introduced its first PC in 1981, IBM had little competition. The price was $7,000 (about $16,850 in today's money) and IBM made a large economic profit selling the new machine.

Observing IBM's huge success, new firms such as Gateway, NEC, Dell, and a host of others entered the market with machines that were technologically identical to IBM's. In fact, they were so similar that they came to be called "clones." The massive wave of entry into the personal computer market increased the market supply and lowered the price. The economic profit for all firms decreased.

Today, a $400 computer is vastly more powerful than its 1981 ancestor that cost 42 times as much.

The same PC market that saw entry during the 1980s and 1990s has seen some exit more recently. In 2001, IBM, the firm that first launched the PC, announced that it was exiting the market. The intense competition from Gateway, NEC, Dell, and others that entered the market following IBM's lead has lowered the price and eliminated the economic profit. So IBM now concentrates on servers and other parts of the computer market.

IBM exited the PC market because it was incurring economic losses. Its exit decreased market supply and made it possible for the remaining firms in the market to make zero economic profit.

International Harvester, a manufacturer of farm equipment, provides another example of exit. For decades, people associated the name "International Harvester" with tractors, combines, and other farm machines. But International Harvester wasn't the only maker of farm equipment. The market became intensely competitive, and the firm began to incur economic losses. Now the firm has a new name, Navistar International, and it doesn't make tractors any more. After years of economic losses and shrinking revenues, it got out of the farm-machine business in 1985 and started to make trucks.

International Harvester exited because it was incurring an economic loss. Its exit decreased supply and made it possible for the remaining firms in the market to break even.

Long-Run Equilibrium

You've now seen how economic profit induces entry, which in turn eliminates the profit. You've also seen how economic loss induces exit, which in turn eliminates the loss.

When economic profit and economic loss have been eliminated and entry and exit have stopped, a competitive market is in *long-run equilibrium*.

You've seen how a competitive market adjusts toward its long-run equilibrium. But a competitive market is rarely *in* a state of long-run equilibrium. Instead, it is constantly and restlessly evolving toward long-run equilibrium. The reason is that the market is constantly bombarded with events that change the constraints that firms face.

Markets are constantly adjusting to keep up with changes in tastes, which change demand, and changes in technology, which change costs.

In the next sections, we're going to see how a competitive market reacts to changing tastes and technology and how the market guides resources to their highest-valued use.

◆ REVIEW QUIZ

1 What triggers entry in a competitive market? Describe the process that ends further entry.

2 What triggers exit in a competitive market? Describe the process that ends further exit.

Work these questions in Study Plan 12.4 and get instant feedback.   MyEconLab

Changes in Demand and Supply as Technology Advances

The arrival of high-speed Internet service increased the demand for personal computers and the demand for music and movie downloads. At the same time, the arrival of these technologies decreased the demand for the retail services of record stores.

What happens in a competitive market when the demand for its product changes? The perfect competition model can answer this question.

An Increase in Demand

Producers of computer components are in long-run equilibrium making zero economic profit when the arrival of the high-speed Internet brings an increase in the demand for computers and the components from which they are built. The equilibrium price of a component rises and producers make economic profits. New firms start to enter the market. Supply

increases and the price stops rising and then begins to fall. Eventually, enough firms have entered for the supply and the increased demand to be in balance at a price that enables the firms in the market to return to zero economic profit—long-run equilibrium.

Figure 12.10 illustrates. In the market in part (a), demand is D_0, supply is S_0, price is P_0, and market output is Q_0. At the firm in part (b), profit is maximized with marginal revenue, MR_0, equal to marginal cost, MC, at output q_0. Economic profit is zero.

Market demand increases and the demand curve shifts rightward to D_1, in Fig. 12.10(a). The price rises to P_1, and the quantity supplied increases from Q_0 to Q_1 as the market moves up along its short-run supply curve S_0. In Fig. 12.10(b), the firm maximizes profit by producing q_1, where marginal revenue MR_1 equals MC. The market is now in short-run equilibrium in which each firm makes an economic profit.

The economic profit brings entry and short-run supply increases—the market supply curve starts to shift rightward. The increase in supply lowers the

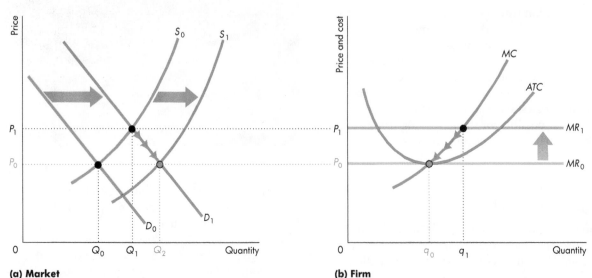

FIGURE 12.10   An Increase in Demand

(a) Market

(b) Firm

A market starts out in long-run competitive equilibrium. Part (a) shows the market demand curve D_0, the market supply curve S_0, the market price P_0, and the equilibrium quantity Q_0. Each firm sells its output at the price P_0, so its marginal revenue curve is MR_0 in part (b). Each firm produces q_0 and makes zero economic profit.

Market demand increases from D_0 to D_1 in part (a) and the market price rises to P_1. Each firm maximizes profit by increasing its output to q_1 in part (b), and the market output

increases to Q_1 in part (a). Firms now make economic profits. New firms enter the market, and as they do so, the market supply curve gradually shifts rightward, from S_0 toward S_1. This shift gradually lowers the market price from P_1 back to P_0. While the price is above P_0, firms make economic profits, so new firms keep entering the market. Once the price has returned to P_0, each firm makes zero economic profit and there is no incentive for firms to enter. Each firm produces q_0, and the market output is Q_2.

MyEconLab Animation

price and firms decrease output—move down along their marginal cost or supply curve in Fig. 12.10(b).

Eventually, entry shifts the supply curve to S_1 in Fig. 12.10(a). The market price has returned to its original level, P_0. At this price, each firm produces q_0, the same as the quantity produced before the increase in demand. Market output is Q_2 in a long-run equilibrium.

The difference between the initial long-run equilibrium and the new long-run equilibrium is the number of firms in the market. An increase in demand has increased the number of firms. In the

process of moving from the initial equilibrium to the new one, each firm makes an economic profit.

A Decrease in Demand

A *decrease* in demand triggers a similar response to the one you've just studied but in the opposite direction. A decrease in demand brings a lower price, economic losses, and exit. Exit decreases supply, which raises the price to its original level and economic profit returns to zero in a new long-run equilibrium. *Economics in the News* below looks at an example.

ECONOMICS IN THE NEWS

Record Stores Exit

Iconic Central Texas Record Store Set to Close

Bobby Barnard opened Sundance Records & Tapes in San Marcos in 1977. But the customers stopped coming, so in 2012 this oldest continually operating music store in Central Texas closed its doors.

Source: Associated Press, March 28, 2012

THE PROBLEM

Provide a graphical analysis to explain why Sundance exited the market and the effects of exit on the market for record store services.

THE SOLUTION

- With demand D_0 and supply S_0, Q_0 customers are served at a price P_0 in part (a) of Fig. 1.
- With marginal revenue MR_0 and marginal cost MC, a record store serves q_0 customers in long-run equilibrium in part (b) of Fig. 1.

- Demand decreases to D_1, the price falls to P_1, and marginal revenue falls to MR_1. Customers decrease to q_1 (and Q_1) and stores incur economic losses.
- Faced with economic loss, Sundance and other stores exit and the market supply decreases to S_1.
- The decrease in supply raises the price and firms remaining return to zero economic profit.

(a) Market

(b) Individual record store

Figure 1 The Market for Record Store Services

Technological Advances Change Supply

We've studied the effects of technological change on demand and to isolate those effects we've kept the individual firm's cost curves unchanged. But new technologies also lower production costs. We now study those effects of advancing technology.

Starting from a long-run equilibrium, when a new technology becomes available that lowers production costs, the first firms to use it make economic profit. But as more firms begin to use the new technology, market supply increases and the price falls. At first, new-technology firms continue to make positive economic profits, so more enter. But firms that continue to use the old technology incur economic losses. Why? Initially they were making zero economic profit and now with the lower price they incur economic losses. So old-technology firms exit.

Eventually, all the old-technology firms have exited and enough new-technology firms have entered to increase the market supply to a level that lowers the price to equal the minimum average total cost using the new technology. In this situation, all the firms, all of which are now new-technology firms, are making zero economic profit.

Figure 12.11 illustrates the process that we've just described. Part (a) shows the market demand and supply curves and market equilibrium. Part (b) shows the cost and revenue curves for a firm using the original old technology. Initially these are the only firms. Part (c) shows the cost and revenue curves for a firm using a new technology after it becomes available.

In part (a), the demand curve is D and initially the supply curve is S_0, so the price is P_0 and the equilibrium quantity is Q_0.

In part (b), marginal revenue is MR_0 and each firm produces q_0 where MR_0 equals MC_{Old}. Economic profit is zero and firms are producing at minimum average total cost on the curve ATC_{Old}.

When a new technology becomes available, average total cost and marginal cost of production fall, and firms that use the new technology produce with the average total cost curve ATC_{New} and marginal cost curve MC_{New} in part (c).

When one firm adopts the new technology, it is too small to influence supply, so the price remains at P_0 and the firm makes an economic profit. But economic profit brings entry of new-technology firms. Market supply increases and the price falls.

FIGURE 12.11   A Technological Advance Lowers Production Costs

(a) Market   **(b) Old-technology firm**   **(c) New-technology firm**

In part (a), the demand curve is D and initially the supply curve is S_0. The price is P_0 and the equilibrium quantity is Q_0. In part (b), marginal revenue is MR_0 and each firm produces q_0 where MR_0 equals MC_{Old}. Economic profit is zero.

A new technology becomes available with lower costs of ATC_{New} and MC_{New} in part (c). A firm that uses this technology produces q_0 where MR_0 equals MC_{New}.

As more firms use this technology, market supply

increases and the price falls. With price below P_0 and above P_1, old-technology firms incur economic losses and exit and new-technology firms make economic profits and new firms enter the market.

In the new long-run equilibrium, the old-technology firms have gone. New-technology firms increase the market supply to S_1. The price falls to P_1, marginal revenue is MR_1, and each firm produces q_1 where MR_1 equals MC_{New}.

ECONOMICS IN THE NEWS

The Falling Cost of Sequencing DNA

Company Announces Low-Cost DNA Decoding Machine

Life Technologies Corp. announced it has developed a $149,000 machine that can decode a person's DNA in a day, at a long-sought price goal of $1,000, making a person's genome useful for medical care.

Source: *USA Today*, January 11, 2012

SOME DATA

The graph shows how the cost of sequencing a person's entire genome has fallen. Life Technologies (in the news clip) is one of around 40 firms competing to develop a machine that can lower that cost from the current $5,000 to $1,000 or less. Many dozens of firms operate DNA sequencing machines and sell their services in a competitive market.

THE QUESTIONS

- What are the competitive markets in the news clip?
- Are any of these markets in long-run equilibrium?
- Are any firms in these markets likely to be making an economic profit?
- Are any of the firms in these markets likely to be incurring an economic loss?
- Are these markets likely to be experiencing entry, exit, or both? If both, which is likely to be greater?
- Who gains from the advances in DNA sequencing technology in the short run and in the long run: producers, or consumers, or both?

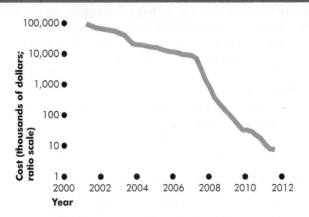

Figure 1 Cost per Genome

Source of data: National Human Genome Research Institute.

THE ANSWERS

- The markets are for DNA sequencing machines and for DNA sequencing services.
- With massive ongoing technological change, neither market is likely to be in long-run equilibrium.
- Firms using the latest technology are likely to be making economic profit.
- Firms using the older technology are likely to be incurring economic loss.
- New-technology firms are entering and old-technology firms are exiting, but with a falling price, there is more entry than exit.
- In the short run, firms gain from higher profit and consumers gain from the lower price. In the long run, economic profit will be zero but consumers will continue to gain from the low price.

MyEconLab More Economics in the News

With price below P_0, old-technology firms incur an economic loss and exit. With price above P_1, new-technology firms make an economic profit and enter. When a new long-run equilibrium is achieved, the old-technology firms have gone. The number of new-technology firms that have entered have shifted the supply curve to S_1. The price is P_1, marginal revenue is MR_1, and each firm in Fig. 12.11(c) produces q_1 using the new technology where MR_1 equals MC_{New}.

Technological change brings only temporary gains to producers. But the lower prices and better products that technological advances bring are permanent gains for consumers.

REVIEW QUIZ

Describe what happens to output, price, and economic profit in the short run and in the long run in a competitive market following

1 An increase in demand
2 A decrease in demand
3 The adoption of a new technology that lowers production costs.

Work these questions in Study Plan 12.5 and get instant feedback.   MyEconLab

Competition and Efficiency

You've seen how firms in perfect competition decide the quantity to produce in the short run and in the long run. You've also seen how these individual decisions determine the market supply that interacts with market demand to determine the equilibrium price and quantity.

We're now going to use what you've learned to gain a deeper understanding of why competition achieves an efficient allocation of resources.

Efficient Use of Resources

Resource use is efficient when we produce the goods and services that people value most highly (see Chapter 2, pp. 35–37, and Chapter 5, p. 112). If it is possible to make someone better off without anyone else becoming worse off, resources are *not* being used efficiently. For example, suppose we produce a computer that no one wants and no one will ever use and, at the same time, some people are clamoring for more video games. If we produce fewer computers and reallocate the unused resources to produce more video games, some people will be better off and no one will be worse off. So the initial resource allocation was inefficient.

We can test whether resources are allocated efficiently by comparing marginal social benefit and marginal social cost. In the computer and video games example, the marginal social benefit of a video game exceeds its marginal social cost; the marginal social cost of a computer exceeds its marginal social benefit. So by producing fewer computers and more video games, we move resources toward a higher-valued use.

Choices, Equilibrium, and Efficiency

We can use what you have learned about the decisions of consumers and firms and equilibrium in a competitive market to describe an efficient use of resources.

Choices Consumers allocate their budgets to get the most value possible out of them. We derive a consumer's demand curve by finding how the best budget allocation changes as the price of a good changes. So consumers get the most value out of their resources at all points along their demand curves. If the people who consume a good or service are the

only ones who benefit from it, then the market demand curve measures the benefit to the entire society and is the marginal social benefit curve.

Competitive firms produce the quantity that maximizes profit. We derive the firm's supply curve by finding the profit-maximizing quantity at each price. So firms get the most value out of their resources at all points along their supply curves. If the firms that produce a good or service bear all the costs of producing it, then the market supply curve measures the marginal cost to the entire society and the market supply curve is the marginal social cost curve.

Equilibrium and Efficiency Resources are used efficiently when marginal social benefit equals marginal social cost. Competitive equilibrium achieves this efficient outcome because, with no externalities, price equals marginal social benefit for consumers, and price equals marginal social cost for producers.

The gains from trade are the sum of consumer surplus and producer surplus. The gains from trade for consumers are measured by *consumer surplus*, which is the area below the demand curve and above the price paid. (See Chapter 5, p. 109.) The gains from trade for producers are measured by *producer surplus*, which is the area above the supply curve and below the price received. (See Chapter 5, p. 111.) The total gains from trade equals *total surplus*—the sum of consumer surplus and producer surplus. When the market for a good or service is in equilibrium, the gains from trade are maximized.

Efficiency in the Sweater Market Figure 12.12 illustrates the efficiency of perfect competition in the sweater market. Part (a) shows the market, and part (b) shows Campus Sweaters.

In part (a), consumers get the most value from their budgets at all points on the market demand curve, $D = MSB$. Producers get the most value from their resources at all points on the market supply curve, $S = MSC$. At the equilibrium quantity and price, marginal social benefit equals marginal social cost, and resources are allocated efficiently. Consumer surplus is the green area, producer surplus is the blue area, and *total surplus* (the sum of producer surplus and consumer surplus) is maximized.

In part (b) Campus Sweaters (and every other firm) makes zero economic profit, and each firm has the plant that enables it to produce at the lowest possible average total cost. Consumers are as well off as

FIGURE 12.12   Efficiency of Perfect Competition

(a) The sweater market

(b) Campus Sweaters

In part (a), market demand, *D*, and market supply, *S*, determine the equilibrium price and quantity. Consumers have made the best available choices on the demand curve, and firms are producing at least cost on the supply curve.

Marginal social benefit, *MSB*, equals marginal social cost, *MSC*, so resources are used efficiently. In part (b), Campus Sweaters produces at the lowest possible long-run average total cost and makes zero economic profit.

MyEconLab Animation and Draw Graph

possible because the good cannot be produced at a lower cost and the equilibrium price equals that least possible cost.

When firms in perfect competition are away from long-run equilibrium, either entry or exit moves the market toward the situation depicted in Fig. 12.12. During this process, the market is efficient because marginal social benefit equals marginal social cost. But it is only in long-run equilibrium that economic profit is driven to zero and consumers pay the lowest feasible price.

◆ You've now completed your study of perfect competition. *Economics in the News* on pp. 290–291 gives you an opportunity to use what you have learned to understand the market for smartphone and tablet computer "apps."

Although many markets approximate the model of perfect competition, many do not. In Chapter 13, we study markets at the opposite extreme of market power: monopoly. Then in the following chapters we'll study markets that lie between perfect competition

and monopoly. In Chapter 14, we study monopolistic competition and in Chapter 15, we study oligopoly. When you have completed this study, you'll have a tool kit that will enable you to understand the variety of real-world markets.

◆ REVIEW QUIZ

1 State the conditions that must be met for resources to be allocated efficiently.

2 Describe the choices that consumers make and explain why consumers are efficient on the market demand curve.

3 Describe the choices that producers make and explain why producers are efficient on the market supply curve.

4 Explain why resources are used efficiently in a competitive market.

Work these questions in Study Plan 12.6 and get instant feedback.   MyEconLab

Perfect Competition in Smart Phone Apps

From Zero to 75 Billion in Six Years

When Apple launched its App Store in July 2008, it had 10 million downloads in the first weekend. That number grew to 100 million in the first two months, 500 million in the first six months, and 1 billion in the first nine months. By mid-2014, downloads hit 75 billion and were growing at 800 apps per second.

At its launch, the store had just 552 apps, but within six months, that number had grown to 15,000 and the pace of growth accelerated. Total apps passed the million mark in October 2013 and hit 1.2 million by mid-2014 and continue to grow at a pace of 25,000 to 30,000 new apps a month.

As the app market grew, so did the number of app developers, which had reached 6.1 million by mid-2013 and 9 million by June 2014.

Developers began to see cash flowing in. Although Apple takes a 30 percent cut, it had paid developers $1 billion by June 2010, $10 billion by June 2013, and $13 billion by June 2014.

Google's app store opened three months later than Apples', but it grew even-more spectacularly to top 1.3 million apps in 2014.

Most apps (62 percent) are free, and of those that are not free the most common price is 99 cents. But one gaming app costs $999.99.

Games represent 18 percent of apps and education another 11 percent.

Sources of information: Sarah Perez, "iTunes App Store Now Has 1.2 Million Apps, Has Seen 75 Billion Downloads to Date," *TechCrunch* June 2, 2014; Chuck Jones, "Apples App Store About To Hit 1 Million Apps," *Forbes*, December 11 2013; apps-world.net, July 11, 2013; and statistica.com, August 28, 2014.

MyEconLab More Economics in the News

ESSENCE OF THE STORY

- Apple has 1.2 million apps, a number that is growing by 25,000 to 30,000 per month.

- 75 billion apps have been downloaded.

- Nine million people have registered as Apple app developers, up from 6.1 million a year earlier.

- Apple has paid $13 billion to app developers.

- App prices range from zero (for 62 percent of apps) to $999.99, and the most common price is 99 cents.

- Google (Android) apps are also growing and its store offers 1.3 million apps.

ECONOMIC ANALYSIS

- The iPhone, iPad, and Android smartphones and tablet computers have created a large demand for apps.

- Although apps are not like corn or sweaters and come in thousands of varieties, the market for apps is highly competitive and we can use the perfect competition model to explain what is happening in that market.

- The market began to operate in 2008, when the first app developers got to work using a software development kit made available by Apple.

- During 2009 through 2014, the number of iPhones and Android smartphones increased dramatically. By the end of 2013, 420 million iPhones and 750 million Android phones had been sold.

- The increase in the number of devices in use increased the demand for apps.

- Thousands of developers, most of them individuals, saw a profit opportunity and got to work creating apps. Their entry into the market increased the supply of apps.

- But the demand for apps kept growing and despite the entry of more developers, profit opportunities remained.

- Figure 1 illustrates the market for apps. In 2013, the demand for apps was D_0 and the supply was S_0. The equilibrium price was P_0 and the quantity was Q_0.

- Figure 2 illustrates the cost and revenue curves of an individual app developer. With marginal revenue MR and marginal cost MC, the developer maximizes profit by producing an app that sells q_0 units.

- Average total cost of an app (on the ATC curve) is less than the price, so the developer makes an economic profit.

- Economic profit brings entry, so in Fig. 1, supply increases in 2014 to S_1. But the demand for apps also keeps increasing and in 2014 the demand curve is D_1.

- The equilibrium quantity increases to Q_1, and this quantity is produced by an increased number of developers—each producing q_0 units and each continuing to make an economic profit.

- The developer's cost curves in Fig. 2 are unchanged, but as development tools improve, development costs will fall and the cost curves will shift downward, which will further increase supply.

- At some future date, market supply will increase by enough to eliminate economic profit and the market for apps will be in long-run equilibrium. That date is unknown but likely to be a long way off.

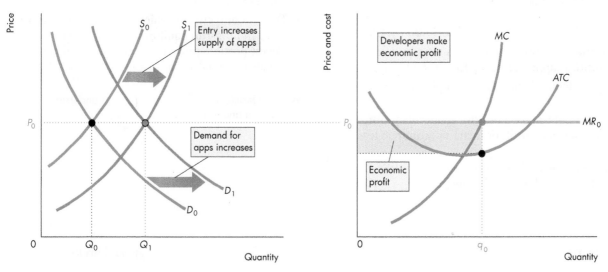

Figure 1 The Market for Apps

Figure 2 An Individual App Developer

SUMMARY

Key Points

What Is Perfect Competition? (pp. 272–273)

- In perfect competition, many firms sell identical products to many buyers; there are no restrictions on entry; sellers and buyers are well informed about prices.
- A perfectly competitive firm is a price taker.
- A perfectly competitive firm's marginal revenue always equals the market price.

Working Problem 1 will give you a better understanding of perfect competition.

The Firm's Output Decision (pp. 274–277)

- The firm produces the output at which marginal revenue (price) equals marginal cost.
- In short-run equilibrium, a firm can make an economic profit, incur an economic loss, or break even.
- If price is less than minimum average variable cost, the firm temporarily shuts down.
- At prices below minimum average variable cost, a firm's supply curve runs along the y-axis; at prices above minimum average variable cost, a firm's supply curve is its marginal cost curve.

Working Problems 2 to 5 will give you a better understanding of a firm's output decision.

Output, Price, and Profit in the Short Run (pp. 278–281)

- The market supply curve shows the sum of the quantities supplied by each firm at each price.
- Market demand and market supply determine price.
- A firm might make a positive economic profit, a zero economic profit, or incur an economic loss.

Working Problem 6 will give you a better understanding of output, price, and profit in the short run.

Output, Price, and Profit in the Long Run (pp. 281–283)

- Economic profit induces entry and economic loss induces exit.
- Entry increases supply and lowers price and profit. Exit decreases supply and raises price and profit.
- In long-run equilibrium, economic profit is zero. There is no entry or exit.

Working Problem 7 will give you a better understanding of output, price, and profit in the long run.

Changes in Demand and Supply as Technology Advances (pp. 284–287)

- A permanent increase in demand leads to a larger market output and a larger number of firms. A permanent decrease in demand leads to a smaller market output and a smaller number of firms.
- New technologies lower the cost of production, increase supply, and in the long run lower the price and increase the quantity.

Working Problem 8 will give you a better understanding of changes in demand and supply as technology advances.

Competition and Efficiency (pp. 288–289)

- Resources are used efficiently when we produce goods and services in the quantities that people value most highly.
- Perfect competition achieves an efficient allocation. In long-run equilibrium, consumers pay the lowest possible price and marginal social benefit equals marginal social cost.

Working Problem 9 will give you a better understanding of competition and efficiency.

Key Terms

MyEconLab Key Terms Quiz

Marginal revenue, 272
Perfect competition, 272
Price taker, 272

Short-run market supply curve, 278
Shutdown point, 276
Total revenue, 272

WORKED PROBLEM

MyEconLab   You can work this problem in Chapter 12 Study Plan.

The table provides data on a market demand schedule (top two rows) and a firm's average and marginal cost schedules (bottom four rows).

Price P ($)	24	20	16	12	8
Quantity	3,000	4,000	5,000	6,000	7,000
Firm's output	1	2	3	4	5
MC ($)	11.00	11.13	12.00	13.63	16.00
ATC ($)	13.50	12.25	12.00	12.19	12.70
AVC ($)	11.25	11.13	11.25	11.63	12.25

Questions

1. What is the firm's shutdown point?
2. If there are 1,000 identical firms in the market, what is the market price and quantity?
3. With 1,000 firms, will firms enter or exit?
4. What is the long-run equilibrium price, quantity, and number of firms?

Solutions

1. The firm will stop producing if the market price falls below minimum *AVC*. In the table, *AVC* is at a minimum of $11.13 when 2 units are produced, so that is the shutdown point.

Key Point: A firm shuts down if the market price is *less* than minimum *AVC*.

2. The first step is to find the market supply schedule. The firm supplies the quantity at which marginal cost equals market price and its supply curve is its *MC* curve above the shutdown point. The market supply curve is the sum of the 1,000 firms' supply curves. For example, at a price (*MC*) of $12, the quantity supplied is 3,000 units—one point on the supply curve.

The second step is to find the price at which the quantity supplied by 1,000 firms equals quantity demanded. When the price (*MC*) is $16, each firm produces 5 units, so the quantity supplied by the market is 5,000 units. At $16, the quantity demanded is 5,000 units, so the market price is $16 and the quantity is 5,000 units.

Key Point: Each firm supplies the quantity at which marginal cost equals market price.

3. Firms will enter if the price exceeds *ATC* and exit if the price is below *ATC*. In the equilibrium above, *P* is $16 and *ATC* is $12.70, so firms enter.

Key Point: Firms enter when $P > ATC$.

4. In long-run equilibrium, economic profit is zero, so $P = ATC$. Firms maximize profit, so $P = MC$. This outcome occurs at minimum *ATC*. From the table, minimum *ATC* is $12 and the firm's output is 3 units. At $12, 6,000 units are demanded, so firms enter until this quantity is supplied. The number of firms increases to 2,000 (6,000 units divided by 3 units per firm).

Key Point: In long-run equilibrium, economic profit is zero and the market price equals minimum *ATC*.

Key Figure

MyEconLab Interactive Animation

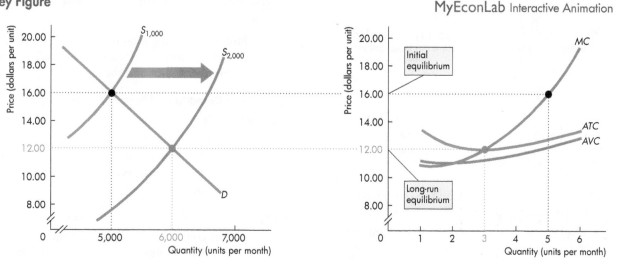

(a) Market

(b) Individual firm

STUDY PLAN PROBLEMS AND APPLICATIONS

MyEconLab   You can work Problems 1 to 9 in Chapter 12 Study Plan and get instant feedback.

What Is Perfect Competition? (Study Plan 12.1)

1. Lin's makes fortune cookies. Anyone can make and sell fortune cookies, so there are dozens of producers. All fortune cookies are the same and buyers and sellers know this fact. In what type of market does Lin's operate? What determines the price of fortune cookies? What determines Lin's marginal revenue?

The Firm's Output Decision (Study Plan 12.2)

Use the following table to work Problems 2 to 4. Pat's Pizza Kitchen is a price taker and the table shows its costs of production.

Output (pizzas per hour)	Total cost (dollars per hour)
0	10
1	21
2	30
3	41
4	54
5	69

2. Calculate Pat's profit-maximizing output and economic profit if the market price is (i) $14 a pizza, (ii) $12 a pizza, and (iii) $10 a pizza.
3. What is Pat's shutdown point and what is Pat's economic profit if it shuts down temporarily?
4. Derive Pat's supply curve.
5. The market for paper is perfectly competitive and 1,000 firms produce paper. The table sets out the market demand schedule for paper.

Price (dollars per box)	Quantity demanded (thousands of boxes per week)
3.65	500
5.20	450
6.80	400
8.40	350
10.00	300
11.60	250
13.20	200

The table in the next column sets out the costs of each producer of paper.

Calculate the market price, the market output, the quantity produced by each firm, and the firm's economic profit or loss.

Output (boxes per week)	Marginal cost (dollars per additional box)	Average variable cost	Average total cost
		(dollars per box)	
200	6.40	7.80	12.80
250	7.00	7.00	11.00
300	7.65	7.10	10.43
350	8.40	7.20	10.06
400	10.00	7.50	10.00
450	12.40	8.00	10.22
500	20.70	9.00	11.00

Output, Price, and Profit in the Short Run

(Study Plan 12.3)

6. In Problem 5, the market demand decreases and the demand schedule becomes:

Price (dollars per box)	Quantity demanded (thousands of boxes per week)
2.95	500
4.13	450
5.30	400
6.48	350
7.65	300
8.83	250
10.00	200
11.18	150

If firms have the same costs set out in Problem 5, what is the market price and the firm's economic profit or loss in the short run?

Output, Price, and Profit in the Long Run

(Study Plan 12.5)

7. In Problem 5, in the long run what is the market price and the quantity of paper produced? What is the number of firms in the market?

Changes in Demand and Supply as Technology

Advances (Study Plan 12.5)

8. If the market demand for paper remains the same as in Problem 6, calculate the market price, market output, and the economic profit or loss of each firm.

Competition and Efficiency (Study Plan 12.6)

9. In perfect competition in long-run equilibrium, can consumer surplus or producers surplus be increased? Explain your answer.

ADDITIONAL PROBLEMS AND APPLICATIONS

MyEconLab   You can work these problems in MyEconLab if assigned by your instructor.

What Is Perfect Competition?

Use the following news clip to work Problems 10 to 12.

Money in the Tank

Two gas stations stand on opposite sides of the road: Rutter's Farm Store and Sheetz gas station. Rutter's doesn't even have to look across the highway to know when Sheetz changes its price for a gallon of gas. When Sheetz raises the price, Rutter's pumps are busy. When Sheetz lowers prices, there's not a car in sight. Both gas stations survive, but each has no control over the price.

Source: *The Mining Journal*, May 24, 2008

10. In what type of market do these gas stations operate? What determines the price of gasoline and the marginal revenue from gasoline?

11. Describe the elasticity of demand that each of these gas stations faces.

12. Why does each of these gas stations have so little control over the price of the gasoline it sells?

The Firm's Output Decision

13. The figure shows the costs of Quick Copy, one of many copy shops near campus.

If the market price of copying is 10¢ a page, calculate Quick Copy's
a. Profit-maximizing output
b. Economic profit

14. The market for smoothies is perfectly competitive. The table in the next column sets out the market demand schedule.

Price (dollars per smoothie)	Quantity demanded (smoothies per hour)
1.90	1,000
2.00	950
2.20	800
2.91	700
4.25	550
5.25	400
5.50	300

Each of the 100 producers of smoothies has the following costs when it uses its least-cost plant:

Output (smoothies per hour)	Marginal cost (dollars per additional smoothie)	Average variable cost	Average total cost
		(dollars per smoothie)	
3	2.50	4.00	7.33
4	2.20	3.53	6.03
5	1.90	3.24	5.24
6	2.00	3.00	4.67
7	2.91	2.91	4.34
8	4.25	3.00	4.25
9	8.00	3.33	4.44

a. What is the market price of a smoothie?
b. What is the market quantity of smoothies?
c. How many smoothies does each firm sell?
d. What is the economic profit made or economic loss incurred by each firm?

15. **Chevy Volt Production Temporarily Shut Down**
GM will temporarily lay off 1,300 employees as the company stops production of the electric car, Chevy Volt, for five weeks. GM had hoped to sell 10,000 Volts last year, but ended up selling just 7,671. It plans to maintain inventory levels by adjusting production to match demand.

Source: *Politico*, March 2, 2012

a. Explain how the shutdown decision will affect GM Chevy Volt's *TFC, TVC,* and *TC.*
b. Under what conditions would this shutdown decision maximize Chevy Volt's economic profit (or minimize its loss)? Explain your answer.
c. Under what conditions will GM start producing the Chevy Volt again? Explain your answer.

Output, Price, and Profit in the Short Run

16. **Big Drops in Prices for Crops Make It Tough Down on the Farm**

    Grain prices have fallen roughly 50 percent from earlier this year. With better-than-expected crop yields, world grain production this year will rise 5 percent from 2007 to a record high.

    Source: *USA Today*, October 23, 2008

    Why did grain prices fall in 2008? Draw a graph to show that short-run effect on an individual farmer's economic profit.

Output, Price, and Profit in the Long Run

17. In Problem 14, do firms enter or exit the market for smoothies in the long run? What is the market price and the equilibrium quantity in the long run?

18. In Problem 15, under what conditions would GM stop producing the Chevy Volt and exit the market for electric cars? Explain your answer.

19. **Exxon Mobil Selling All Its Retail Gas Stations**

    Exxon Mobil is not alone among Big Oil exiting the retail gas business, a market where profits have gotten tougher as crude oil prices have risen. Gas station owners say they're struggling to turn a profit because while wholesale gasoline prices have risen sharply, they've been unable to raise pump prices fast enough to keep pace.

    Source: *Houston Chronicle*, June 12, 2008

    a. Is Exxon Mobil making a shutdown or exit decision in the retail gasoline market?

    b. Under what conditions will this decision maximize Exxon Mobil's economic profit?

    c. How might Exxon Mobil's decision affect the economic profit of other gasoline retailers?

Changes in Demand and Supply as Technology Advances

20. **Another DVD Format, but It's Cheaper**

    New Medium Enterprises claims that its new system, HD VMD, is equal to Blu-ray's but at $199 it's cheaper than the $300 Blu-ray player. The Blu-ray Disc Association says New Medium will fail because it believes that Blu-ray technology will always be more expensive. But mass production will cut the cost of a Blu-ray player to $90.

    Source: *The New York Times*, March 10, 2008

    a. Explain how technological change in Blu-ray production might support the prediction of lower prices in the long run. Illustrate your explanation with a graph.

    b. Even if Blu-ray prices do drop to $90 in the long run, why might the HD VMD still end up being less expensive at that time?

Competition and Efficiency

21. In a perfectly competitive market, each firm maximizes its profit by choosing only the quantity to produce. Regardless of whether the firm makes an economic profit or incurs an economic loss, the short-run equilibrium is efficient. Is the statement true? Explain why or why not.

Economics in the News

22. After you have studied *Economics in the News* on pp. 290–291, answer the following questions.

    a. What are the features of the market for apps that make it competitive?

    b. Does the information provided in the news article suggest that the app market is in long-run equilibrium? Explain why or why not.

    c. How would an advance in development technology that lowered a developer's costs change the market supply and the developer's marginal revenue, marginal cost, average total cost, and economic profit?

    d. Illustrate your answer to part (c) with an appropriate graphical analysis.

23. **Smartphones: 2.6 Billion and Rising**

    Smartphone subscriptions increased by 40 percent in 2013 to reach 2.6 billion. This number is expected to rise to 5.6 billion by 2019. Emerging markets, especially China and India, provide most of the growth as many people buy their first smartphone.

    Source: CNET News, November 11, 2013

    a. Explain the effects of the increase in global demand for smartphones on the market for smartphones and on an individual smartphone producer in the short run.

    b. Draw a graph to illustrate your explanation in part (a).

    c. Explain the long-run effects of the increase in global demand for smartphones on the market for smartphones.

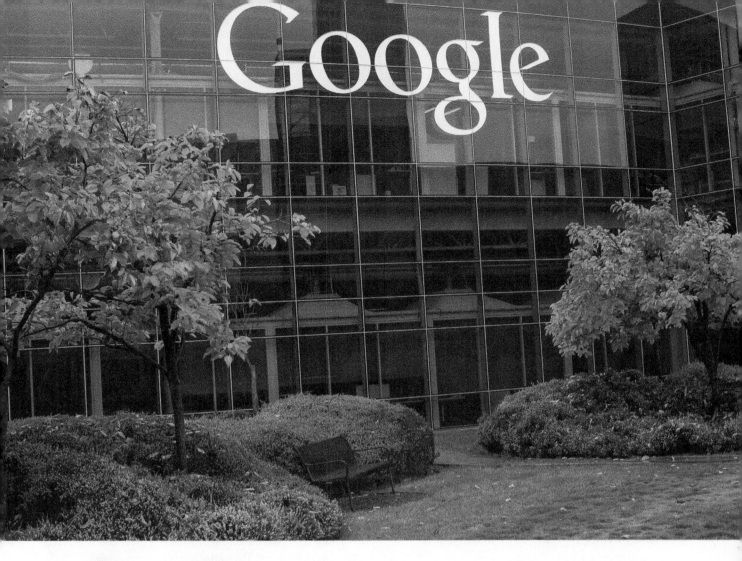

13 MONOPOLY

After studying this chapter, you will be able to:

◆ Explain how monopoly arises

◆ Explain how a single-price monopoly determines its output and price

◆ Compare the performance and efficiency of single-price monopoly and competition

◆ Explain how price discrimination increases profit

◆ Explain how monopoly regulation influences output, price, economic profit, and efficiency

Google and Microsoft are big players in the markets for Web search and advertising and for computer operating systems, markets that are obviously not perfectly competitive.

In this chapter, we study markets dominated by one big firm. We call such a market *monopoly*. We study the performance and the efficiency of monopoly and compare it with perfect competition.

In *Economics in the News* at the end of the chapter, we look at the remarkable success of Google and ask whether Google is serving the social interest or violating U.S. and European antitrust laws.

Monopoly and How It Arises

A **monopoly** is a market with a single firm that produces a good or service with no close substitutes and that is protected by a barrier that prevents other firms from entering that market.

How Monopoly Arises

Monopoly arises for two key reasons:

- No close substitutes
- Barrier to entry

No Close Substitutes If a good has a close substitute, even though only one firm produces it, that firm effectively faces competition from the producers of the substitute. A monopoly sells a good or service that has no good substitutes. Tap water and bottled water are close substitutes for drinking, but tap water has no effective substitutes for showering or washing a car and a local public utility that supplies tap water is a monopoly.

Barrier to Entry A constraint that protects a firm from potential competitors is called a **barrier to entry.** There are three types of barrier to entry:

- Natural
- Ownership
- Legal

Natural Barrier to Entry A natural barrier to entry creates a **natural monopoly**: a market in which economies of scale enable one firm to supply the entire market at the lowest possible cost. The firms that deliver gas, water, and electricity to our homes are examples of natural monopoly.

Figure 13.1 illustrates a natural monopoly. The market demand curve for electric power is *D*, and the long-run average cost curve is *LRAC*. Economies of scale prevail over the entire length of the *LRAC* curve. At a price of 5 cents per kilowatt-hour, the quantity demanded is 4 million kilowatt-hours and one firm can produce that quantity at a cost of 5 cents per kilowatt-hour. If two firms shared the market equally, it would cost each of them 10 cents per kilowatt-hour to produce a total of 4 million kilowatt-hours.

Ownership Barrier to Entry An ownership barrier to entry occurs if one firm owns a significant portion of a key resource. An example of this type of monopoly occurred during the last century when De Beers

FIGURE 13.1 Natural Monopoly

The market demand curve for electric power is *D*, and the long-run average cost curve is *LRAC*. Economies of scale exist over the entire *LRAC* curve. One firm can distribute 4 million kilowatt-hours at a cost of 5 cents a kilowatt-hour. This same total output costs 10 cents a kilowatt-hour with two firms. One firm can meet the market demand at a lower cost than two or more firms can. The market is a natural monopoly.

MyEconLab Animation

controlled up to 90 percent of the world's supply of diamonds. (Today, its share is only 65 percent.)

Legal Barrier to Entry A legal barrier to entry creates a **legal monopoly**: a market in which competition and entry are restricted by the granting of a public franchise, government license, patent, or copyright.

A *public franchise* is an exclusive right granted to a firm to supply a good or service. An example is the U.S. Postal Service, which has the exclusive right to carry first-class mail. A *government license* controls entry into particular occupations, professions, and industries. Examples of this type of barrier to entry occur in medicine, law, dentistry, schoolteaching, architecture, and many other professional services. Licensing does not always create a monopoly, but it does restrict competition.

A *patent* is an exclusive right granted to the inventor of a product or service. A *copyright* is an exclusive right granted to the author or composer of a literary, musical, dramatic, or artistic work. Patents and copyrights are valid for a limited time period that varies from country to country. In the United States, a patent is valid for 20 years. Patents encourage the *invention* of new products and production methods. They also stimulate *innovation*—the use of new inventions—by encouraging inventors to publicize their discoveries and offer them for use under license. Patents have stimulated innovations in areas as diverse as soybean seeds, pharmaceuticals, memory chips, and video games.

ECONOMICS IN ACTION
Information-Age Monopolies

Information-age technologies have created three big natural monopolies—firms with large plant costs but almost zero marginal cost, so they experience economies of scale.

These firms are Microsoft, Google, and Facebook. The operating system of 87 percent of personal computers is some version of Windows; Google performs 67 percent of Internet searches and 58 percent of Web browsing is done using Chrome; and Facebook has a 50 percent share of the social media market.

These same information-age technologies have also destroyed monopolies. FedEx, UPS, the fax machine, and e-mail have weakened the monopoly of the U.S. Postal Service; and the satellite dish has weakened cable television monopolies.

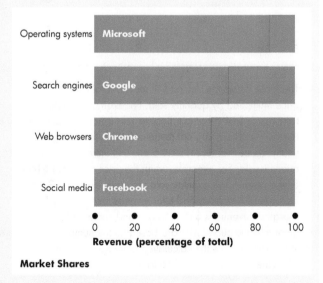

Market Shares

Monopoly Price-Setting Strategies

A major difference between monopoly and competition is that a monopoly sets its own price. In doing so, the monopoly faces a market constraint: To sell a larger quantity, the monopoly must set a lower price. There are two monopoly situations that create two pricing strategies:

- Single price
- Price discrimination

Single Price A **single-price monopoly** is a firm that must sell each unit of its output for the same price to all its customers. De Beers sells diamonds (of a given size and quality) for the same price to all its customers. If it tried to sell at a low price to some customers and at a higher price to others, only the low-price customers would buy from De Beers. Others would buy from De Beers' low-price customers. De Beers is a *single-price* monopoly.

Price Discrimination When a firm practices **price discrimination**, it sells different units of a good or service for different prices. Many firms price discriminate. Microsoft sells its Windows and Office software at different prices to different buyers. Computer manufacturers who install the software on new machines, students and teachers, governments, and businesses all pay different prices. Pizza producers offer a second pizza for a lower price than the first one. These are examples of *price discrimination*.

When a firm price discriminates, it looks as though it is doing its customers a favor. In fact, it is charging the highest possible price for each unit sold and making the largest possible profit.

▶ REVIEW QUIZ

1 How does monopoly arise?
2 How does a natural monopoly differ from a legal monopoly?
3 Distinguish between a price-discriminating monopoly and a single-price monopoly.

Work these questions in Study Plan 13.1 and get instant feedback. Do a Key Terms Quiz.   MyEconLab

We start with a single-price monopoly and see how it makes its decisions about the quantity to produce and the price to charge to maximize its profit.

A Single-Price Monopoly's Output and Price Decision

To understand how a single-price monopoly makes its output and price decision, we must first study the link between price and marginal revenue.

Price and Marginal Revenue

Because in a monopoly there is only one firm, the demand curve facing the firm is the market demand curve. Let's look at Bobbie's Barbershop, the sole supplier of haircuts in Cairo, Nebraska. The table in Fig. 13.2 shows the market demand schedule. At a price of $20, Bobbie sells no haircuts. The lower the price, the more haircuts per hour she can sell. For example, at $12, consumers demand 4 haircuts per hour (row *E*).

Total revenue (*TR*) is the price (*P*) multiplied by the quantity sold (*Q*). For example, in row *D*, Bobbie sells 3 haircuts at $14 each, so total revenue is $42. *Marginal revenue* (*MR*) is the change in total revenue (ΔTR) resulting from a one-unit increase in the quantity sold. For example, if the price falls from $16 (row *C*) to $14 (row *D*), the quantity sold increases from 2 to 3 haircuts. Total revenue increases from $32 to $42, so the change in total revenue is $10. Because the quantity sold increases by 1 haircut, marginal revenue equals the change in total revenue and is $10. Marginal revenue is placed between the two rows to emphasize that marginal revenue relates to the *change* in the quantity sold.

Figure 13.2 shows the market demand curve and marginal revenue curve (*MR*) and also illustrates the calculation we've just made. Notice that at each level of output, marginal revenue is less than price—the marginal revenue curve lies *below* the demand curve.

Why is marginal revenue *less* than price? It is because when the price is lowered to sell one more unit, two opposing forces affect total revenue. The lower price results in a revenue loss on the original units sold and a revenue gain on the increased quantity sold. For example, at a price of $16 a haircut, Bobbie sells 2 haircuts (point *C*). If she lowers the price to $14, she sells 3 haircuts and has a revenue gain of $14 on the third haircut. But she now receives only $14 on each of the first 2 haircuts—$2 less than before. As a result, she loses $4 of revenue on the first 2 haircuts. To calculate marginal revenue, she must deduct this amount from the revenue gain of $14. So marginal revenue is $10, which is less than the price.

FIGURE 13.2   Demand and Marginal Revenue

	Price (P) (dollars per haircut)	Quantity demanded (Q) (haircuts per hour)	Total revenue (TR = P × Q) (dollars)	Marginal revenue (MR = ΔTR/ΔQ) (dollars per haircut)
A	20	0	0	
				18
B	18	1	18	
				14
C	16	2	32	
				10
D	14	3	42	
				6
E	12	4	48	
				2
F	10	5	50	

The table shows the demand schedule. Total revenue (*TR*) is price multiplied by quantity sold. For example, in row *C*, the price is $16 a haircut, Bobbie sells 2 haircuts, and total revenue is $32. Marginal revenue (*MR*) is the change in total revenue that results from a one-unit increase in the quantity sold. For example, when the price falls from $16 to $14 a haircut, the quantity sold increases from 2 to 3, an increase of 1 haircut, and total revenue increases by $10. Marginal revenue is $10. The demand curve and the marginal revenue curve, *MR*, are based on the numbers in the table and illustrate the calculation of marginal revenue when the price falls from $16 to $14 a haircut.

MyEconLab Animation and Draw Graph

Marginal Revenue and Elasticity

A single-price monopoly's marginal revenue is related to the *elasticity of demand* for its good. The demand for a good can be *elastic* (the elasticity is greater than 1), *inelastic* (the elasticity is less than 1), or *unit elastic* (the elasticity is equal to 1). Demand is *elastic* if a 1 percent fall in the price brings a greater than 1 percent increase in the quantity demanded. Demand is *inelastic* if a 1 percent fall in the price brings a less than 1 percent increase in the quantity demanded. Demand is *unit elastic* if a 1 percent fall in the price brings a 1 percent increase in the quantity demanded. (See Chapter 4, pp. 84–86.)

If demand is elastic, a fall in the price brings an increase in total revenue—the revenue gain from the increase in quantity sold outweighs the revenue loss from the lower price—and marginal revenue is *positive*. If demand is inelastic, a fall in the price brings a decrease in total revenue—the revenue gain from the increase in quantity sold is outweighed by the revenue loss from the lower price—and marginal revenue is *negative*. If demand is unit elastic, total revenue does not change—the revenue gain from the increase in the quantity sold offsets the revenue loss from the lower price—and marginal revenue is *zero*. (See Chapter 4, p. 88.)

Figure 13.3 illustrates the relationship between marginal revenue, total revenue, and elasticity. As the price gradually falls from $20 to $10 a haircut, the quantity demanded increases from 0 to 5 haircuts an hour. Over this output range, marginal revenue is positive in part (a), total revenue increases in part (b), and the demand for haircuts is elastic. As the price falls from $10 to $0 a haircut, the quantity of haircuts demanded increases from 5 to 10 an hour. Over this output range, marginal revenue is negative in part (a), total revenue decreases in part (b), and the demand for haircuts is inelastic. When the price is $10 a haircut, marginal revenue is zero in part (a), total revenue is at a maximum in part (b), and the demand for haircuts is unit elastic.

In Monopoly, Demand Is Always Elastic

The relationship between marginal revenue and elasticity of demand that you've just discovered implies that a profit-maximizing monopoly never produces an output in the inelastic range of the market demand curve. If it did so, it could charge a higher price, produce a smaller quantity, and increase its profit. Let's now look at a monopoly's price and output decision.

FIGURE 13.3   Marginal Revenue and Elasticity

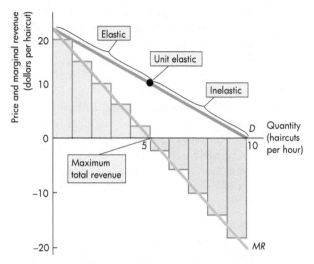

(a) Demand and marginal revenue curves

(b) Total revenue curve

In part (a), the demand curve is *D* and the marginal revenue curve is *MR*. In part (b), the total revenue curve is *TR*. Over the range 0 to 5 haircuts an hour, a price cut increases total revenue, so marginal revenue is positive—as shown by the blue bars. Demand is elastic. Over the range 5 to 10 haircuts an hour, a price cut decreases total revenue, so marginal revenue is negative—as shown by the red bars. Demand is inelastic. At 5 haircuts an hour, total revenue is maximized and marginal revenue is zero. Demand is unit elastic.

MyEconLab Animation

Price and Output Decision

A monopoly sets its price and output at the levels that maximize economic profit. To determine this price and output level, we need to study the behavior of both cost and revenue as output varies. A monopoly faces the same types of technology and cost constraints as a competitive firm, so its costs (total cost, average cost, and marginal cost) behave just like those of a firm in perfect competition. And a monopoly's revenues (total revenue, price, and marginal revenue) behave in the way we've just described.

Table 13.1 provides information about Bobbie's costs, revenues, and economic profit, and Fig. 13.4 shows the same information graphically.

Maximizing Economic Profit You can see in Table 13.1 and Fig. 13.4(a) that total cost (*TC*) and total revenue (*TR*) both rise as output increases, but *TC* rises at an increasing rate and *TR* rises at a decreasing rate. Economic profit, which equals *TR* minus *TC*, increases at small output levels, reaches a maximum, and then decreases. The maximum profit ($12) occurs when Bobbie sells 3 haircuts for $14 each. If she sells 2 haircuts for $16 each or 4 haircuts for $12 each, her economic profit will be only $8.

Marginal Revenue Equals Marginal Cost You can see Bobbie's marginal revenue (*MR*) and marginal cost (*MC*) in Table 13.1 and Fig. 13.4(b).

When Bobbie increases output from 2 to 3 haircuts, *MR* is $10 and *MC* is $6. *MR* exceeds *MC* by $4 and Bobbie's profit increases by that amount. If Bobbie increases output yet further, from 3 to 4 haircuts, *MR* is $6 and *MC* is $10. In this case, *MC* exceeds *MR* by $4, so profit decreases by that amount. When *MR* exceeds *MC*, profit increases if output increases. When *MC* exceeds *MR*, profit increases if output *decreases*. When *MC* equals *MR*, profit is maximized.

Figure 13.4(b) shows the maximum profit as price (on the demand curve *D*) minus average total cost (on the *ATC* curve) multiplied by the quantity produced—the blue rectangle.

Maximum Price the Market Will Bear Unlike a firm in perfect competition, a monopoly influences the price of what it sells. But a monopoly doesn't set the price at the maximum *possible* price. At the maximum possible price, the firm would be able to sell only one unit of output, which in general is less than the profit-maximizing quantity. Rather, a monopoly produces the profit-maximizing quantity and sells that quantity for the highest price it can get.

TABLE 13.1   A Monopoly's Output and Price Decision

Price (P) (dollars per haircut)	Quantity demanded (Q) (haircuts per hour)	Total revenue (TR = P × Q) (dollars)	Marginal revenue (MR = ΔTR/ΔQ) (dollars per haircut)	Total cost (TC) (dollars)	Marginal cost (MC = ΔTC/ΔQ) (dollars per haircut)	Profit (TR − TC) (dollars)
20	0	0		20		−20
			 18		 1	
18	1	18		21		−3
			 14		 3	
16	2	32		24		+8
			 10		 6	
14	3	42		30		+12
			 6		 10	
12	4	48		40		+8
			 2		 15	
10	5	50		55		−5

This table gives the information needed to find the profit-maximizing output and price. Total revenue (*TR*) equals price multiplied by the quantity sold. Profit equals total revenue minus total cost (*TC*). Profit is maximized when 3 haircuts are sold at a price of $14 each. Total revenue is $42, total cost is $30, and economic profit is $12 ($42 − $30).

FIGURE 13.4 A Monopoly's Output and Price

(a) Total revenue and total cost curves

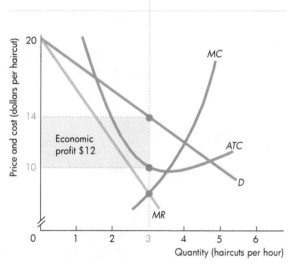

(b) Demand and marginal revenue and cost curves

In part (a), economic profit is the vertical distance equal to total revenue (*TR*) minus total cost (*TC*) and it is maximized at 3 haircuts an hour.

In part (b), economic profit is maximized when marginal cost (*MC*) equals marginal revenue (*MR*). The profit-maximizing output is 3 haircuts an hour. The price is determined by the demand curve (*D*) and is $14 a haircut. The average total cost of a haircut is $10, so economic profit, the blue rectangle, is $12—the profit per haircut ($4) multiplied by 3 haircuts.

—— MyEconLab Animation and Draw Graph ——

All firms maximize profit by producing the output at which marginal revenue equals marginal cost. For a competitive firm, price equals marginal revenue, so price also equals marginal cost. For a monopoly, price exceeds marginal revenue, so price also exceeds marginal cost.

A monopoly charges a price that exceeds marginal cost, but does it always make an economic profit? In Fig. 13.4(b), Bobbie produces 3 haircuts an hour. Her average total cost is $10 (on the *ATC* curve) and her price is $14 (on the *D* curve), so her profit per haircut is $4 ($14 minus $10). Bobbie's economic profit is shown by the area of the blue rectangle, which equals the profit per haircut ($4) multiplied by the number of haircuts (3), for a total of $12.

If firms in a perfectly competitive market make a positive economic profit, new firms enter. That does *not* happen in monopoly. Barriers to entry prevent new firms from entering the market, so a monopoly can make a positive economic profit and might continue to do so indefinitely. Sometimes that economic profit is large, as in the international diamond business.

Bobbie makes a positive economic profit. But suppose that Bobbie's landlord increases the rent on her salon. If Bobbie pays an additional $12 an hour for rent, her fixed cost increases by $12 an hour. Her marginal cost and marginal revenue don't change, so her profit-maximizing output remains at 3 haircuts an hour. Her profit decreases by $12 an hour to zero. If Bobbie's salon rent increases by more than $12 an hour, she incurs an economic loss. If this situation were permanent, Bobbie would go out of business.

◆ REVIEW QUIZ

1 What is the relationship between marginal cost and marginal revenue when a single-price monopoly maximizes profit?

2 How does a single-price monopoly determine the price it will charge its customers?

3 What is the relationship between price, marginal revenue, and marginal cost when a single-price monopoly is maximizing profit?

4 Why can a monopoly make a positive economic profit even in the long run?

Work these questions in Study Plan 13.2 and get instant feedback.   MyEconLab

Single-Price Monopoly and Competition Compared

Imagine a market that is made up of many small firms operating in perfect competition. Then imagine that a single firm buys out all these small firms and creates a monopoly.

What will happen in this market? Will the price rise or fall? Will the quantity produced increase or decrease? Will economic profit increase or decrease? Will either the original competitive situation or the new monopoly situation be efficient?

These are the questions we're now going to answer. First, we look at the effects of monopoly on the price and quantity produced. Then we turn to the questions about efficiency.

Comparing Price and Output

Figure 13.5 shows the market we'll study. The market demand curve is D. The demand curve is the same regardless of how the industry is organized. But the supply side and the equilibrium are different in monopoly and competition. First, let's look at the case of perfect competition.

Perfect Competition Initially, with many small perfectly competitive firms in the market, the market supply curve is S. This supply curve is obtained by summing the supply curves of all the individual firms in the market.

In perfect competition, equilibrium occurs where the supply curve and the demand curve intersect. The price is P_C, and the quantity produced by the industry is Q_C. Each firm takes the price P_C and maximizes its profit by producing the output at which its own marginal cost equals the price. Because each firm is a small part of the total industry, there is no incentive for any firm to try to manipulate the price by varying its output.

Monopoly Now suppose that this industry is taken over by a single firm. Consumers do not change, so the market demand curve remains the same as in the case of perfect competition. But now the monopoly recognizes this demand curve as a constraint on the price at which it can sell its output. The monopoly's marginal revenue curve is MR.

The monopoly maximizes profit by producing the quantity at which marginal revenue equals marginal cost. To find the monopoly's marginal cost curve, first

recall that in perfect competition, the market supply curve is the sum of the supply curves of the firms in the industry. Also recall that each firm's supply curve is its marginal cost curve (see Chapter 12, p. 277). So when the market is taken over by a single firm, the competitive market's supply curve becomes the monopoly's marginal cost curve. To remind you of this fact, the supply curve is also labeled MC.

The output at which marginal revenue equals marginal cost is Q_M. This output is smaller than the competitive output Q_C. And the monopoly charges the price P_M, which is higher than P_C. We have established that

> Compared to a perfectly competitive market, a single-price monopoly produces a smaller output and charges a higher price.

We've seen how the output and price of a monopoly compare with those in a competitive market. Let's now compare the efficiency of the two types of market.

FIGURE 13.5   Monopoly's Smaller Output and Higher Price

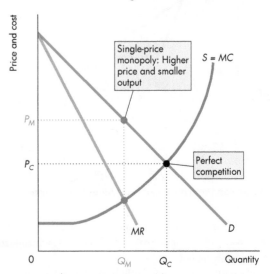

A competitive market produces the quantity Q_C at price P_C. A single-price monopoly produces the quantity Q_M at which marginal revenue equals marginal cost and sells that quantity for the price P_M. Compared to perfect competition, a single-price monopoly produces a smaller output and charges a higher price.

MyEconLab Animation

Efficiency Comparison

Perfect competition (with no externalities) is efficient. Figure 13.6(a) illustrates the efficiency of perfect competition and serves as a benchmark against which to measure the inefficiency of monopoly. Along the demand and marginal social benefit curve ($D = MSB$), consumers are efficient. Along the supply curve and marginal social cost curve ($S = MSC$), producers are efficient. In competitive equilibrium, the price is P_C, the quantity is Q_C, and marginal social benefit equals marginal social cost.

Consumer surplus is the green triangle under the demand curve and above the equilibrium price (see Chapter 5, p. 109). *Producer surplus* is the blue area above the supply curve and below the equilibrium price (see Chapter 5, p. 111). Total surplus (consumer surplus and producer surplus) is maximized.

Also, in long-run competitive equilibrium, entry and exit ensure that each firm produces its output at the minimum possible long-run average cost.

To summarize: At the competitive equilibrium, marginal social benefit equals marginal social cost; total surplus is maximized; firms produce at the lowest possible long-run average cost; and resource use is efficient.

Figure 13.6(b) illustrates the inefficiency of monopoly and the sources of that inefficiency. A monopoly produces Q_M and sells its output for P_M. The smaller output and higher price drive a wedge between marginal social benefit and marginal social cost and create a *deadweight loss*. The gray triangle shows the deadweight loss and its magnitude is a measure of the inefficiency of monopoly.

Consumer surplus shrinks for two reasons. First, consumers lose by having to pay more for the good. This loss to consumers is a gain for monopoly and increases the producer surplus. Second, consumers lose by getting less of the good, and this loss is part of the deadweight loss.

Although the monopoly gains from a higher price, it loses some producer surplus because it produces a smaller output. That loss is another part of the deadweight loss.

A monopoly produces a smaller output than perfect competition and faces no competition, so it does not produce at the lowest possible long-run average cost. As a result, monopoly damages the consumer interest in three ways: A monopoly produces less, increases the cost of production, and raises the price by more than the increased cost of production.

FIGURE 13.6   Inefficiency of Monopoly

(a) Perfect competition

(b) Monopoly

In perfect competition in part (a), output is Q_C and the price is P_C. Marginal social benefit (*MSB*) equals marginal social cost (*MSC*); total surplus, the sum of consumer surplus (the green triangle) and producer surplus (the blue area), is maximized; and in the long run, firms produce at the lowest possible average cost. Monopoly in part (b) produces Q_M and raises the price to P_M. Consumer surplus shrinks, the monopoly gains, and a deadweight loss (the gray triangle) arises.

MyEconLab Animation and Draw Graph

Redistribution of Surpluses

You've seen that monopoly is inefficient because marginal social benefit exceeds marginal social cost and there is deadweight loss—a social loss. But monopoly also brings a *redistribution* of surpluses.

Some of the lost consumer surplus goes to the monopoly. In Fig. 13.6, the monopoly takes the difference between the higher price, P_M, and the competitive price, P_C, on the quantity sold, Q_M. So the monopoly takes that part of the consumer surplus. This portion of the loss of consumer surplus is not a loss to society. It is a redistribution from consumers to the monopoly producer.

Rent Seeking

You've seen that monopoly creates a deadweight loss and is inefficient. But the social cost of monopoly can exceed the deadweight loss because of an activity called rent seeking. Any surplus—consumer surplus, producer surplus, or economic profit—is called **economic rent.** The pursuit of wealth by capturing economic rent is called **rent seeking.**

You've seen that a monopoly makes its economic profit by diverting part of consumer surplus to itself—by converting consumer surplus into economic profit. So the pursuit of economic profit by a monopoly is rent seeking. It is the attempt to capture consumer surplus.

Rent seekers pursue their goals in two main ways. They might

- Buy a monopoly
- Create a monopoly

Buy a Monopoly To rent seek by buying a monopoly, a person searches for a monopoly that is for sale at a lower price than the monopoly's economic profit. Trading of taxicab licenses is an example of this type of rent seeking. In some cities, taxicabs are regulated. The city restricts both the fares and the number of taxis that can operate so that operating a taxi results in economic profit. A person who wants to operate a taxi must buy a license from someone who already has one. People rationally devote time and effort to seeking out profitable monopoly businesses to buy. In the process, they use up scarce resources that could otherwise have been used to produce goods and services. The value of this lost production is part of the social cost of monopoly. The amount paid for a monopoly is not a social cost because the payment is just a transfer of an existing producer surplus from the buyer to the seller.

Create a Monopoly Rent seeking by creating a monopoly is mainly a political activity. It takes the form of lobbying and trying to influence the political process. Such influence might be sought by making campaign contributions in exchange for legislative support or by indirectly seeking to influence political outcomes through publicity in the media or more direct contacts with politicians and bureaucrats. An example of a monopoly created in this way is the government-imposed restrictions on the quantities of textiles that may be imported into the United States. Another is a regulation that limits the number of oranges that may be sold in the United States. These are regulations that restrict output and increase price.

This type of rent seeking is a costly activity that uses up scarce resources. Taken together, firms spend billions of dollars lobbying Congress, state legislators, and local officials in the pursuit of licenses and laws that create barriers to entry and establish a monopoly.

Rent-Seeking Equilibrium

Barriers to entry create monopoly. But there is no barrier to entry into rent seeking. Rent seeking is like perfect competition. If an economic profit is available, a new rent seeker will try to get some of it. And competition among rent seekers pushes up the price that must be paid for a monopoly, to the point at which the rent seeker makes zero economic profit by operating the monopoly. For example, competition for the right to operate a taxi in New York City leads to a price of more than $100,000 for a taxi license, which is sufficiently high to eliminate the economic profit made by a taxi operator.

Figure 13.7 shows a rent-seeking equilibrium. The cost of rent seeking is a fixed cost that must be added to a monopoly's other costs. Rent seeking and rent-seeking costs increase to the point at which no economic profit is made. The average total cost curve, which includes the fixed cost of rent seeking, shifts upward until it just touches the demand curve. Economic profit is zero. It has been lost in rent seeking.

Consumer surplus is unaffected, but the deadweight loss from monopoly is larger. The deadweight loss now includes the original deadweight loss triangle plus the lost producer surplus, shown by the enlarged gray area in Fig. 13.7.

FIGURE 13.7   Rent-Seeking Equilibrium

With competitive rent seeking, a single-price monopoly uses all its economic profit to maintain its monopoly. The firm's rent-seeking costs are fixed costs. They add to total fixed cost and to average total cost. The *ATC* curve shifts upward until, at the profit-maximizing price, the firm breaks even.

MyEconLab Animation

REVIEW QUIZ

1 Why does a single-price monopoly produce a smaller output and charge more than the price that would prevail if the market were perfectly competitive?

2 How does a monopoly transfer consumer surplus to itself?

3 Why is a single-price monopoly inefficient?

4 What is rent seeking and how does it influence the inefficiency of monopoly?

Work these questions in Study Plan 13.3 and get instant feedback. Do a Key Terms Quiz.   MyEconLab

So far, we've considered only a single-price monopoly. But many monopolies do not operate with a single price. Instead, they price discriminate. Let's now see how a price-discriminating monopoly works.

⬤ Price Discrimination

You encounter *price discrimination*—selling a good or service at a number of different prices—when you travel, go to the movies, get your hair cut, visit an art museum or theme park, or buy pizza. These are all examples of firms with market power, setting the prices of an identical good or service at different levels for different customers.

Not all price *differences* are price *discrimination*: they reflect differences in production costs. For example, real-time meters for electricity enable power utilities to charge a different price at peak-load times than during the night. But it costs more per kilowatt-hour to generate electricity at peak-load times so this price difference reflects production cost differences and is not price discrimination.

At first sight, price discrimination appears to be inconsistent with profit maximization. Why would a movie theater allow children to see movies at a discount? Why would a hairdresser charge students and senior citizens less? Aren't these firms losing profit by being nice to their customers? The answer, as you are about to discover, is that price discrimination is profitable: It increases economic profit.

But to be able to price discriminate, the firm must sell a product that cannot be resold; and it must be possible to identify and separate different buyer types.

Two Ways of Price Discriminating

Firms price discriminate in two broad ways. They discriminate

- Among groups of buyers
- Among units of a good

Discriminating Among Groups of Buyers People differ in the value they place on a good—their marginal benefit and willingness to pay. Some of these differences are correlated with features such as age, employment status, and other easily distinguished characteristics. When such a correlation is present, firms can profit by price discriminating among the different groups of buyers.

For example, salespeople and other business travelers know that a face-to-face sales meeting with a customer might bring a large and profitable order. So for these travelers, the marginal benefit from a trip is large and the price that such a traveler is willing to pay for a trip is high. In contrast, for a leisure traveler, any of several different trips and even no trip at all are options. So for leisure travelers, the marginal benefit of a trip is small and the price that such a traveler is willing to pay for a trip is low. Because the price that business travelers are willing to pay exceeds what leisure travelers are willing to pay, it is possible for an airline to price discriminate between these two groups and increase its profit. We'll return to this example of price discrimination below.

Discriminating Among Units of a Good Everyone experiences diminishing marginal benefit, so if all the units of the good are sold for a single price, buyers end up with a consumer surplus equal to the value they get from each unit minus the price paid for it.

A firm that price discriminates by charging a buyer one price for a single item and a lower price for a second or third item can capture some of the consumer surplus. Buy one pizza and get a second one for a lower price is an example of this type of price discrimination.

Increasing Profit and Producer Surplus

By getting buyers to pay a price as close as possible to their maximum willingness to pay, a monopoly captures the consumer surplus and converts it into producer surplus. And more producer surplus means more economic profit.

To see why more producer surplus means more economic profit, recall some definitions. With total revenue *TR* and total cost *TC*,

$$Economic\ profit = TR - TC.$$

Producer surplus is total revenue minus the area under the marginal cost curve. But the area under the marginal cost curve is total *variable* cost, *TVC*. So producer surplus equals total revenue minus *TVC*, or

$$Producer\ surplus = TR - TVC.$$

You can see that the difference between economic profit and producer surplus is the same as the difference between *TC* and *TVC*. But *TC* minus *TVC* equals total *fixed* cost, *TFC*. So

$$Economic\ profit = Producer\ surplus - TFC.$$

For a given level of total fixed cost, anything that increases producer surplus also increases economic profit.

Let's now see how price discrimination works by looking at a price-discriminating airline.

A Price-Discriminating Airline

Inter-City Airlines has a monopoly on passenger flights between two cities. Figure 13.8 shows the market demand curve, *D*, for travel on this route. It also shows Inter-City Airline's marginal revenue curve, *MR*, and marginal cost curve, *MC*. Inter-City's marginal cost is a constant $40 per trip. (It is easier to see how price discrimination works for a firm with constant marginal cost.)

Single-Price Profit Maximization As a single-price monopoly, Inter-City maximizes profit by producing the quantity of trips at which *MR* equals *MC*, which is 8,000 trips a week, and charging $120 a trip. With a marginal cost of $40 a trip, producer surplus is $80 a trip, and Inter-City's producer surplus is $640,000 a week, shown by the area of the blue rectangle. Inter-City's customers enjoy a consumer surplus shown by the area of the green triangle.

FIGURE 13.8   A Single Price of Air Travel

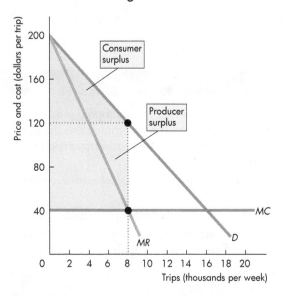

Inter-City Airlines has a monopoly on an air route with a market demand curve D. Inter-City's marginal cost, MC, is $40 per trip. As a single-price monopoly, Inter-City's marginal revenue curve is MR. Profit is maximized by selling 8,000 trips a week at $120 a trip. Producer surplus is $640,000 a week—the blue rectangle—and Inter-City's customers enjoy a consumer surplus—the green triangle.

Discrimination Between Two Types of Travelers

Inter-City surveys its customers and discovers that they are all business travelers. It also surveys people who are *not* its customers and discovers that they are mainly people who travel for leisure. These people travel by bus or car, but would travel by air at a low fare. Inter-City would like to attract some of these travelers and knows that to do so, it must offer a fare below the current $120 a trip. How can it do that?

Inter-City digs more deeply into its survey results and discovers that its current customers always plan their travel less than two weeks before departure. In contrast, the people who travel by bus or car know their travel plans at least two weeks ahead of time.

Inter-City sees that it can use what it has discovered about its current and potential new customers to separate the two types of travelers into two markets: one market for business travel and another for leisure travel.

Figure 13.9 shows Inter-City's two markets. Part (a), the market for business travel, is the same as Fig. 13.8. Part (b) shows the market for leisure travel. No leisure traveler is willing to pay the business fare of $120 a trip, so at that price, the quantity demanded in part (b) is zero. The demand curve D_L is the demand for travel on this route after satisfying the demand of business travelers. Inter-City's marginal cost remains at $40 a trip, so its marginal revenue curve is MR_L. Inter-City maximizes profit by setting the leisure fare at $80 a trip and attracting 4,000 leisure travelers a week. Inter-City's producer surplus increases by $160,000 a week—the area of the blue rectangle in Fig. 13.9(b)—and leisure travelers enjoy a consumer surplus—the area of the green triangle.

Inter-City announces its new fare schedule: no restrictions, $120 and 14-day advance purchase, $80. Inter-City increases its passenger count by 50 percent and increases its producer surplus by $160,000.

FIGURE 13.9   Price Discrimination

(a) Business travel

(b) Leisure travel

Inter-City separates its market into two types of travel: business travel with no restrictions in part (a) and leisure travel that requires a 14-day advance purchase in part (b). For business travel, the profit-maximizing price is $120 a trip with 8,000 trips a week. For leisure travel, the profit-maximizing price is $80 a trip with 4,000 trips a week.

Inter-City continues to make the same producer surplus on business travel as it did with a single price and business travelers continue to enjoy the same consumer surplus. But in part (b), Inter-City sells 4,000 trips to leisure travelers, which increases its producer surplus—the blue rectangle—and increases consumer surplus—the green triangle.

Discrimination Among Several Types of Travelers

Pleased with the success of its price discrimination between business and leisure travelers, Inter-City sees that it might be able to profit even more by dividing its customers into a larger number of types. So it does another customer survey, which reveals that some business travelers are willing to pay $160 for a fully-refundable, unrestricted ticket while others are willing to pay only $120 for a nonrefundable ticket. So applying the same principles as it used to discriminate between business and leisure travelers, Inter-City now discriminates between business travelers who want a refundable ticket and those who want a non-refundable ticket.

Another survey of leisure travelers reveals that they fall into two goups: those who are able to plan 14 days ahead and others who can plan 21 days ahead. So Inter-City discriminates between these two groups with two fares: an $80 and a $60 fare.

By offering travelers four different fares, the airline increases its producer surplus and increases its economic profit. But why only four fares? Why not keep looking for ever more traveler types and offer even more fares?

Perfect Price Discrimination

Firms try to capture an ever larger part of consumer surplus by devising a host of special conditions, each one of which appeals to a tiny segment of the market but at the same time excludes others from taking advantage of a lower price. The more consumer surplus a firm is able to capture, the closer it gets to the extreme case called **perfect price discrimination**, which occurs if a firm can sell each unit of output for the highest price someone is willing to pay for it. In this extreme (hypothetical) case consumer surplus is eliminated and captured as producer surplus.

With perfect price discrimination, something special happens to marginal revenue—the market demand curve becomes the marginal revenue curve. The reason is that when the monopoly cuts the price to sell a larger quantity, it sells only the marginal unit at the lower price. All the other units continue to be sold for the highest price that each buyer is willing to pay. So for the perfect price discriminator, marginal revenue *equals* price and the market demand curve becomes the monopoly's marginal revenue curve.

With marginal revenue equal to price, Inter-City can obtain even greater producer surplus by increasing output up to the point at which price (and marginal revenue) equals marginal cost.

So Inter-City seeks new travelers who will not pay as much as $60 a trip but who will pay more than $40, its marginal cost. Inter-City offers a variety of vacation specials at different low fares that appeal only to new travelers. Existing customers continue to pay the higher fares and some, with further perks and frills that have no effect on cost, are induced to pay fares going all the way up to $200 a trip.

With all these special conditions and fares, Inter-City increases its output to the quantity demanded at marginal cost, extracts the entire consumer surplus on that quantity, and maximizes economic profit.

Figure 13.10 shows the outcome with perfect price discrimination and compares it with the single-price monopoly outcome. The range of business-class fares extract the entire consumer surplus from this group. The new leisure-class fares going down to $40 a trip attract an additional 8,000 travelers and take the entire consumer surplus of leisure travelers. Inter-City makes the maximum possible economic profit.

FIGURE 13.10   Perfect Price Discrimination

Dozens of fares discriminate among many different types of business travelers, and many new low fares with restrictions appeal to leisure travelers. With perfect price discrimination, the market demand curve becomes Inter-City's marginal revenue curve. Producer surplus is maximized when the lowest fare equals marginal cost. Inter-City sells 16,000 trips and makes the maximum possible economic profit.

MyEconLab Animation

*Would it bother you to hear how
little I paid for this flight?*

From William Hamilton, "Voodoo Economics," © 1992 by
The Chronicle Publishing Company, p. 3.
Reprinted with permission of Chronicle Books.

Efficiency and Rent Seeking with Price Discrimination

With perfect price discrimination, output increases to the point at which price equals marginal cost. This output is identical to that of perfect competition. Perfect price discrimination pushes consumer surplus to zero but increases the monopoly's producer surplus to equal the total surplus in perfect competition. With perfect price discrimination, no deadweight loss is created, so perfect price discrimination achieves efficiency.

> The more perfectly the monopoly can price discriminate, the closer its output is to the competitive output and the more efficient is the outcome.

But the outcomes of perfect competition and perfect price discrimination differ. First, the distribution of the total surplus is not the same. In perfect competition, total surplus is shared by consumers and producers, while with perfect price discrimination, the monopoly takes it all. Second, because the monopoly takes all the total surplus, rent seeking is profitable.

People use resources in pursuit of economic rent, and the bigger the rents, the more resources are used in pursuing them. With free entry into rent seeking, the long-run equilibrium outcome is that rent seekers use up the entire producer surplus.

Real-world airlines are as creative as Inter-City Airlines, as you can see in the cartoon! Disney Corporation is creative too in extracting consumer surplus, as *Economics in Action* shows.

We next study some key monopoly policy issues.

ECONOMICS IN ACTION
Attempting Perfect Price Discrimination

If you want to spend a day at Disney World, it will cost you $99. You can spend a second consecutive day for an extra $89. A third day will cost you $86. But for a fourth day, you'll pay only $20 and for more days all the way up to 10, you'll pay only $10 a day.

The Disney Corporation hopes that it has read your willingness to pay correctly and not left you with too much consumer surplus.

Disney's Ticket Prices

◆ REVIEW QUIZ

1 What is price discrimination and how is it used to increase a monopoly's profit?
2 Explain how consumer surplus changes when a monopoly price discriminates.
3 Explain how consumer surplus, economic profit, and output change when a monopoly perfectly price discriminates.
4 What are some of the ways that real-world airlines price discriminate?

Work these questions in Study Plan 13.4 and get instant feedback. Do a Key Terms Quiz.   MyEconLab

ECONOMICS IN THE NEWS

Microsoft Monopoly

Microsoft Windows 8 to Go on Sale in October

Microsoft announced that its Windows 8 operating system will be released in October 2012, three years after Windows 7 went public. Windows 8 will be available in 109 languages across 231 markets worldwide.

Source: Associated Press, July 9, 2012

SOME DATA

Microsoft Windows 8 Versions and U.S. Prices

Version	Price
Full from Microsoft	249.99
Upgrade from Microsoft	199.99
Full from Amazon	162.99
OEM	148.95
Student from Microsoft	69.99

Microsoft sold 180 million Windows 8 licenses at different prices in different national markets.

THE QUESTIONS

- Is Microsoft a monopoly?
- Is Microsoft a natural monopoly or a legal monopoly?
- Does Microsoft price discriminate or do the different prices of Windows reflect cost differences?
- Sketch a demand curve for Windows, Microsoft's marginal cost curve, and the distribution of the total surplus between consumers and Microsoft.

THE ANSWERS

- Microsoft controls 87 percent of the market for computer operating systems, and almost 100 percent of the non-Apple market, which makes it an effective monopoly.
- Microsoft is a natural monopoly. It has large fixed costs and almost zero marginal cost, so its long-run average cost curve ($LRAC$) slopes downward and economies of scale are achieved when the $LRAC$ curve intersects the demand curve.
- Microsoft sells Windows for a number of different prices to different market segments and the marginal cost of a Windows license is the same for all market segments, so Microsoft is a price-discriminating monopoly.

- The figure illustrates the demand curve, D, and marginal cost curve, MC, for Windows licenses.
- Using the U.S. prices in the data table, the figure shows how Microsoft converts consumer surplus into producer surplus by price discriminating.
- Because Microsoft also price discriminates among its different national markets, it gains even more producer surplus than the figure illustrates.

Microsoft Grabs Consumer Surplus

Windows 8 has 109 foreign language versions, which expands Microsoft's scope for price discrimination.

Monopoly Regulation

Natural monopoly presents a dilemma. With economies of scale, it produces at the lowest possible cost. But with market power, it has an incentive to raise the price above the competitive price and produce too little—to operate in the self-interest of the monopolist and not in the social interest.

Regulation—rules administered by a government agency to influence prices, quantities, entry, and other aspects of economic activity in a firm or industry—is a possible solution to this dilemma.

To implement regulation, the government establishes agencies to oversee and enforce the rules. For example, the Surface Transportation Board regulates prices on interstate railroads, some trucking and bus lines, and water and oil pipelines. By the 1970s, almost a quarter of the nation's output was produced by regulated industries (far more than just natural monopolies) and a process of deregulation began.

Deregulation is the process of removing regulation of prices, quantities, entry, and other aspects of economic activity in a firm or industry. During the past 30 years, deregulation has occurred in domestic air transportation, telephone service, interstate trucking, and banking and financial services. Cable TV was deregulated in 1984, re-regulated in 1992, and deregulated again in 1996.

Regulation is a possible solution to the dilemma presented by natural monopoly but not a guaranteed solution. There are two theories about how regulation actually works: the *social interest theory* and the *capture theory*.

The **social interest theory** is that the political and regulatory process relentlessly seeks out inefficiency and introduces regulation that eliminates deadweight loss and allocates resources efficiently.

The **capture theory** is that regulation serves the self-interest of the producer, who captures the regulator and maximizes economic profit. Regulation that benefits the producer but creates a deadweight loss gets adopted because the producer's gain is large and visible while each individual consumer's loss is small and invisible. No individual consumer has an incentive to oppose the regulation, but the producer has a big incentive to lobby for it.

We're going to examine efficient regulation that serves the social interest and see why it is not a simple matter to design and implement such regulation.

Efficient Regulation of a Natural Monopoly

A cable TV company is a *natural monopoly*—it can supply the entire market at a lower price than two or more competing firms can. Cox Communications, based in Atlanta, provides cable TV to households in 20 states. The firm has invested heavily in satellite receiving dishes, cables, and control equipment and so has large fixed costs. These fixed costs are part of the firm's average total cost. Its average total cost decreases as the number of households served increases because the fixed cost is spread over a larger number of households.

Unregulated, Cox produces the quantity that maximizes profit. Like all single-price monopolies, the profit-maximizing quantity is less than the efficient quantity, and underproduction results in a deadweight loss.

How can Cox be regulated to produce the efficient quantity of cable TV service? The answer is by being regulated to set its price equal to marginal cost, known as the **marginal cost pricing rule.** The quantity demanded at a price equal to marginal cost is the efficient quantity—the quantity at which marginal benefit equals marginal cost.

Figure 13.11 illustrates the marginal cost pricing rule. The demand curve for cable TV is *D*. Cox's marginal cost curve is *MC*. That marginal cost curve is (assumed to be) horizontal at $10 per household per month—that is, the cost of providing each additional household with a month of cable programming is $10. The efficient outcome occurs if the price is regulated at $10 per household per month with 10 million households served.

But there is a problem: At the efficient output, average total cost exceeds marginal cost, so a firm that uses marginal cost pricing incurs an economic loss. A cable TV company that is required to use a marginal cost pricing rule will not stay in business for long. How can the firm cover its costs and, at the same time, obey a marginal cost pricing rule?

There are two possible ways of enabling the firm to cover its costs: price discrimination and a two-part price (called a *two-part tariff*).

For example, Verizon offers plans at a fixed monthly price that give access to the cellphone network and unlimited free calls. The price of a call (zero) equals Verizon's marginal cost of a call. Similarly, a cable TV operator can charge a one-time connection fee that covers its fixed cost and then charge a monthly fee equal to marginal cost.

FIGURE 13.11   Regulating a Natural Monopoly

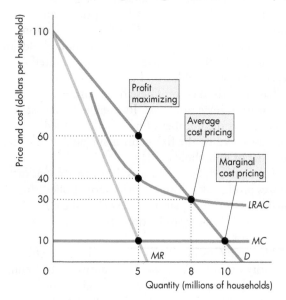

A natural monopoly cable TV supplier faces the demand curve *D*. The firm's marginal cost is constant at $10 per household per month, as shown by the curve labeled *MC*. The long-run average cost curve is *LRAC*.

Unregulated, as a profit-maximizer, the firm serves 5 million households at a price of $60 a month. An efficient marginal cost pricing rule sets the price at $10 a month. The monopoly serves 10 million households and incurs an economic loss. A second-best average cost pricing rule sets the price at $30 a month. The monopoly serves 8 million households and earns zero economic profit.

MyEconLab Animation

Second-Best Regulation of a Natural Monopoly

A natural monopoly cannot always be regulated to achieve an efficient outcome. There are two possible ways of enabling a regulated monopoly to avoid an economic loss:

■ Average cost pricing
■ Government subsidy

Average Cost Pricing The **average cost pricing rule** sets price equal to average total cost. With this rule the firm produces the quantity at which the average

total cost curve cuts the demand curve. This rule results in the firm making zero economic profit—breaking even. But because for a natural monopoly average total cost exceeds marginal cost, the quantity produced is less than the efficient quantity and a deadweight loss arises.

Figure 13.11 illustrates the average cost pricing rule. The price is $30 a month and 8 million households get cable TV.

Government Subsidy A government subsidy is a direct payment to the firm equal to its economic loss. To pay a subsidy, the government must raise the revenue by taxing some other activity. You saw in Chapter 6 that taxes themselves generate deadweight loss.

And the Second-Best Is ... Which is the better option, average cost pricing or marginal cost pricing with a government subsidy? The answer depends on the relative magnitudes of the two deadweight losses. Average cost pricing generates a deadweight loss in the market served by the natural monopoly. A subsidy generates deadweight losses in the markets for the items that are taxed to pay for the subsidy. The smaller deadweight loss is the second-best solution to regulating a natural monopoly. Making this calculation in practice is too difficult, so average cost pricing is generally preferred to a subsidy.

Implementing average cost pricing presents the regulator with a challenge because it is not possible to be sure what a firm's costs are. So regulators use one of two practical rules:

■ Rate of return regulation
■ Price cap regulation

Rate of Return Regulation Under **rate of return regulation,** a firm must justify its price by showing that its return on capital doesn't exceed a specified target rate. This type of regulation can end up serving the self-interest of the firm rather than the social interest. The firm's managers have an incentive to inflate costs by spending on items such as private jets, free baseball tickets (disguised as public relations expenses), and lavish entertainment. Managers also have an incentive to use more capital than the efficient amount. The rate of return on capital is regulated but not the total return on capital, and the greater the amount of capital, the greater is the total return.

Price Cap Regulation For the reason that we've just examined, rate of return regulation is increasingly being replaced by price cap regulation. A **price cap regulation** is a price ceiling—a rule that specifies the highest price the firm is permitted to set. This type of regulation gives a firm an incentive to operate efficiently and keep costs under control. Price cap regulation has become common for the electricity and telecommunications industries and is replacing rate of return regulation.

To see how a price cap works, let's suppose that the cable TV operator is subject to this type of regulation. Figure 13.12 shows that without regulation, the firm maximizes profit by serving 5 million households and charging a price of $60 a month. If a price cap is set at $30 a month, the firm is permitted to sell

any quantity it chooses at that price or at a lower price. At 5 million households, the firm now incurs an economic loss. It can decrease the loss by increasing output to 8 million households. To increase output above 8 million households, the firm would have to lower the price and again it would incur a loss. So the profit-maximizing quantity is 8 million households—the same as with average cost pricing.

Notice that a price cap lowers the price and increases output. This outcome is in sharp contrast to the effect of a price ceiling in a competitive market that you studied in Chapter 6 (pp. 128–130). The reason is that in a monopoly, the unregulated equilibrium output is less than the competitive equilibrium output, and the price cap regulation replicates the conditions of a competitive market.

In Fig. 13.12, the price cap delivers average cost pricing. In practice, the regulator might set the cap too high. For this reason, price cap regulation is often combined with *earnings sharing regulation*—a regulation that requires firms to make refunds to customers when profits rise above a target level.

FIGURE 13.12 Price Cap Regulation

A natural monopoly cable TV supplier faces the demand curve *D*. The firm's marginal cost is constant at $10 per household per month, as shown by the curve labeled *MC*. The long-run average cost curve is *LRAC*.

Unregulated, the firm serves 5 million households at a price of $60 a month. A price cap sets the maximum price at $30 a month. The firm has an incentive to minimize cost and serve the quantity of households that demand service at the price cap. The price cap regulation lowers the price and increases the quantity.

MyEconLab Animation

REVIEW QUIZ

1 What is the pricing rule that achieves an efficient outcome for a regulated monopoly? What is the problem with this rule?
2 What is the average cost pricing rule? Why is it not an efficient way of regulating monopoly?
3 What is a price cap? Why might it be a more effective way of regulating monopoly than rate of return regulation?
4 Compare the consumer surplus, producer surplus, and deadweight loss that arise from average cost pricing with those that arise from profit-maximization pricing and marginal cost pricing.

Work these questions in Study Plan 13.5 and get instant feedback. Do a Key Terms Quiz.   *MyEconLab*

◆ You've now completed your study of monopoly. *Economics in the News* on pp. 316–317 looks at Google's dominant position in the market for Internet search advertising.

In the next chapter, we study markets that lie between the extremes of perfect competition and monopoly and that blend elements of the two.

Is Google Misusing Monopoly Power?

Google and E.U. Agree to Settle Search Row

The Financial Times
February 5, 2014

Google ended its three-year tangle with antitrust regulators on Wednesday, as it reached a deal with Brussels which critics claimed would cement its dominance of some of the most valuable commercial activity on the web.

Following the U.S. Federal Trade Commission closing a similar case last year, regulators on both sides of the Atlantic have now largely cleared Google's practice of overriding its own algorithmically chosen results to put paid-for links at the top of its pages.

The European Commission went further than U.S. regulators by extracting a concession that will require the internet group to give rival Internet services a showing alongside its own preferred results, provided they bid against each other for the space.

Rivals immediately panned the approach as "worse than nothing" as it gave Brussels' blessing to Google sucking traffic from other Internet sites for some of the most valuable searches on the web, such as users looking for digital cameras or hotels. …

Joaquín Almunia, the E.U. competition chief, said … "Google should not be prevented from trying to provide users with what they're looking for." … "What Google should do is also give rivals a prominent space … in a visual format which will attract users."…

Although it still faces an investigation in Canada, the deal effectively brings the curtain down on Google's first showdown with the world's leading antitrust regulators. Unlike Microsoft, which became embroiled in a 10-year battle with Brussels, it chose to settle rather than risk large fines or tying up senior management attention in a fight. …

…

Alex Barker and Richard Waters, "Google and E.U. Agree to Settle Search Row," *Financial Times*, February 14, 2014.

MyEconLab More Economics in the News

ESSENCE OF THE STORY

- Google reached a settlement with the European Union antitrust regulators.

- It settled a similar case with the U.S. Federal Trade Commission 2013 but still faces an investigation in Canada.

- The European regulators require Google display rival Internet services alongside its preferred results, provided they bid against each other for the space.

- Competitors say the regulations are too weak and enable Google to capture traffic from other Internet sites for some of the most valuable searches.

ECONOMIC ANALYSIS

- Google gets its revenue by selling advertisements associated with search keywords.

- Google sells keywords based on a combination of willingness-to-pay and the number of clicks an advertisement receives, with bids starting at 5 cents per click.

- Google has steadily improved its search engine and refined and simplified its interface with both searchers and advertisers to make searches more powerful and advertising more effective.

- Figure 1 shows Google's extraordinary success in terms of its revenue, cost, and profit.

- Google could have provided a basic search engine with none of the features of today's Google.

- If Google had followed this strategy, people seeking information would have used other search engines and advertisers would have been willing to pay lower prices for Google ads.

- Google would have faced the market described in Fig. 2 and earned a small economic profit.

- Instead, Google improved its search engine and the effectiveness of advertising. The demand for Google ads increased.

- By selling keywords to the highest bidder, Google is able to achieve perfect price discrimination.

- Figure 3 shows the consequences of Google's successful strategy. With perfect price discrimination, Google's producer surplus is maximized. Google produces the efficient quantity of search and advertising by accepting ads at prices that exceed or equal marginal cost.

- Google does not appear to be acting against the social interest: There is no antitrust case to answer.

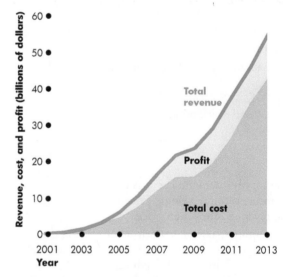

Figure 1 Google's Revenue, Cost, and Profit

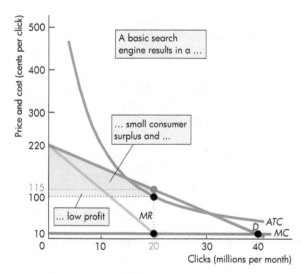

Figure 2 Basic Search Engine

Figure 3 Google with AdWords and Other Features

317

SUMMARY

Key Points

Monopoly and How It Arises (pp. 298–299)

- A monopoly is a market with a single supplier of a good or service that has no close substitutes and in which barriers to entry prevent competition.
- Barriers to entry may be legal (public franchise, license, patent, or copyright), ownership (one firm controls a resource), or natural (created by economies of scale).
- A monopoly might be able to price discriminate when there is no resale possibility.
- Where resale is possible, a firm charges one price.

Working Problem 1 will give you a better understanding of monopoly and how it arises.

A Single-Price Monopoly's Output and Price Decision

(pp. 300–303)

- A monopoly's demand curve is the market demand curve and a single-price monopoly's marginal revenue is less than price.
- A monopoly maximizes profit by producing the output at which marginal revenue equals marginal cost and by charging the maximum price that consumers are willing to pay for that output.

Working Problems 2 to 4 will give you a better understanding of a single-price monopoly's output and price decision.

Single-Price Monopoly and Competition Compared

(pp. 304–307)

- A single-price monopoly charges a higher price and produces a smaller quantity than a perfectly competitive market.
- A single-price monopoly restricts output and creates a deadweight loss.

- The total loss that arises from monopoly equals the deadweight loss plus the cost of the resources devoted to rent seeking.

Working Problem 5 will give you a better understanding of the comparison of single-price monopoly and perfect competition.

Price Discrimination (pp. 307–312)

- Price discrimination converts consumer surplus into economic profit.
- Perfect price discrimination extracts the entire consumer surplus; each unit is sold for the maximum price that each consumer is willing to pay; the quantity produced is the efficient quantity.
- Rent seeking with perfect price discrimination might eliminate the entire consumer surplus and producer surplus.

Working Problem 6 will give you a better understanding of price discrimination.

Monopoly Regulation (pp. 313–315)

- Monopoly regulation might serve the social interest or the interest of the monopoly (the monopoly captures the regulator).
- Price equal to marginal cost achieves efficiency but results in economic loss.
- Price equal to average cost enables the firm to cover its cost but is inefficient.
- Rate of return regulation creates incentives for inefficient production and inflated cost.
- Price cap regulation with earnings sharing regulation can achieve a more efficient outcome than rate of return regulation.

Working Problems 7 to 9 will give you a better understanding of monopoly regulation.

Key Terms

MyEconLab Key Terms Quiz

Average cost pricing rule, 314
Barrier to entry, 298
Capture theory, 313
Deregulation, 313
Economic rent, 306
Legal monopoly, 298

Marginal cost pricing rule, 313
Monopoly, 298
Natural monopoly, 298
Perfect price discrimination, 310
Price cap regulation, 315
Price discrimination, 299

Rate of return regulation, 314
Regulation, 313
Rent seeking, 306
Single-price monopoly, 299
Social interest theory, 313

WORKED PROBLEM

MyEconLab   You can work this problem in Chapter 13 Study Plan.

Tanya's Tattoos is local monopoly. Columns 1 and 2 of the table set out the market demand schedule and columns 2 and 3 set out the total cost schedule.

Price (dollars per tattoo)	Quantity (tattoos per hour)	Total cost (dollars per hour)
60	0	30
50	1	50
40	2	70
30	3	90
20	4	110

Questions

1. If Tanya's Tattoos is a single-price monopoly, what is Tanya's profit-maximizing quantity? What price does Tanya's charge? What are its economic profit and producer surplus?

2. If Tanya's Tattoos perfectly price discriminates, what quantity does Tanya's produce? What are its economic profit and producer surplus?

Solutions

1. The profit-maximizing quantity is that at which marginal cost equals marginal revenue. Marginal cost—the increase in total cost when output increases by one unit—is $20 at all output levels. Marginal revenue—the change in total revenue when output increases by one unit—is calculated in the table at the top of the next column.

   Marginal revenue equals marginal cost of $20 at 2 tattoos per hour (midway between $30 and $10). So this quantity maximizes profit. The

Demand schedule

Price (dollars per tattoo)	Quantity (tattoos per hour)	Total revenue (dollars per hour)	Marginal revenue (dollars per tattoo)
60	0	0	
			⋯⋯ 50
50	1	50	
			⋯⋯ 30
40	2	80	
			⋯⋯ 10
30	3	90	
			⋯⋯ −10
20	4	80	

highest price at which 2 tattoos an hour can be sold is $40 per tattoo, so total revenue is $80. Total cost is $70, so economic profit is $10. *TFC* (*TC* at zero output) is $30, so *TVC* is $40. Producer surplus (*TR* − *TVC*) is $40 an hour.

Key Point: Profit is maximized when marginal cost equals marginal revenue.

2. If Tanya can perfectly price discriminate, she produces 4 tattoos an hour and sells one for $50, one for $40, one for $30, and one for $20. Total revenue is $140 and total cost is $110, so economic profit is $30 an hour. Producer surplus (*TR* − *TVC*) = $140 − $80 = $60 an hour.

Key Point: With perfect price discrimination, a firm charges the highest price that each buyer is willing to pay and increases production to the quantity at which the lowest price equals marginal cost.

The key figure illustrates the two outcomes.

Key Figure

MyEconLab Interactive Animation

(a) Single-price monopoly

(b) Price-discriminating monopoly

STUDY PLAN PROBLEMS AND APPLICATIONS

MyEconLab   You can work problems 1 to 9 in Chapter 13 Study Plan and get instant feedback.

Monopoly and How It Arises (Study Plan 13.1)

1. The U.S. Postal Service has a monopoly on non-urgent First Class Mail. Pfizer Inc. makes LIPI-TOR, a prescription drug that lowers cholesterol. Cox Communications is the sole provider of cable television service in some parts of San Diego.

   Are any these firms protected by a barrier to entry? Do any of these firms produce a good or service that has a substitute? Might any of them be able to profit from price discrimination? Explain your answers.

A Single-Price Monopoly's Output and Price Decision

(Study Plan 13.2)

Use the following table to work Problems 2 to 4. Minnie's Mineral Springs is a single-price monopoly. Columns 1 and 2 of the table set out the market demand schedule for Minnie's water and columns 2 and 3 set out Minnie's total cost schedule.

Price (dollars per bottle)	Quantity (bottles per hour)	Total cost (dollars per hour)
10	0	1
8	1	3
6	2	7
4	3	13
2	4	21
0	5	31

2. Calculate Minnie's marginal revenue schedule and draw a graph of the market demand curve and Minnie's marginal revenue curve. Explain why Minnie's marginal revenue is less than the price.

3. At what price is Minnie's total revenue maximized and over what price range is the demand for water elastic? Why will Minnie not produce a quantity at which the market demand is inelastic?

4. Calculate Minnie's profit-maximizing output and price and economic profit.

Single-Price Monopoly and Competition Compared

(Study Plan 13.3)

5. Use the data in Problem 2 to work Problem 5.
   a. Use a graph to illustrate the producer surplus generated from Minnie's Mineral Springs' water production and consumption.

   b. Is Minnie's an efficient producer of water? Explain your answer.
   c. Suppose that new wells were discovered nearby to Minnie's and Minnie's faced competition from new producers. Explain what would happen to Minnie's output, price, and profit.

Price Discrimination (Study Plan 13.4)

6. La Bella Pizza can produce a pizza for a marginal cost of $2. Its price of a pizza is $15.
   a. Could La Bella Pizza make a larger economic profit by offering a second pizza for $5? Use a graph to illustrate your answer.
   b. How might La Bella Pizza make even more economic profit? Would it then be more efficient than when it charged $15 for each pizza?

Monopoly Regulation (Study Plan 13.5)

Use the following figure to work Problems 7 to 9. The figure shows Calypso, a U.S. natural gas distributor. It is a natural monopoly that cannot price discriminate.

What quantity will Calypso produce, what price will it charge, and what will be the total surplus and deadweight loss if Calypso is

7. An unregulated profit-maximizing firm?
8. Regulated to make zero economic profit?
9. Regulated to be efficient?

ADDITIONAL PROBLEMS AND APPLICATIONS

MyEconLab   You can work these problems in MyEconLab if assigned by your instructor.

Monopoly and How It Arises

Use the following list, which gives some information about seven firms, to answer Problems 10 and 11.

- Coca-Cola cuts its price below that of Pepsi-Cola in an attempt to increase its market share.
- A single firm, protected by a barrier to entry, produces a personal service that has no close substitutes.
- A barrier to entry exists, but the good has some close substitutes.
- A firm offers discounts to students and seniors.
- A firm can sell any quantity it chooses at the going price.
- The government issues Nike an exclusive license to produce golf balls.
- A firm experiences economies of scale even when it produces the quantity that meets the entire market demand.

10. In which of the seven cases might monopoly arise?
11. Which of the seven cases are natural monopolies and which are legal monopolies? Which can price discriminate, which cannot, and why?

A Single-Price Monopoly's Output and Price Decision

Use the following information to work Problems 12 to 16.

Hot Air Balloon Rides is a single-price monopoly. Columns 1 and 2 of the table set out the market demand schedule and columns 2 and 3 set out the total cost schedule.

Price (dollars per ride)	Quantity (rides per month)	Total cost (dollars per month)
220	0	80
200	1	160
180	2	260
160	3	380
140	4	520
120	5	680

12. Construct Hot Air's total revenue and marginal revenue schedules.
13. Draw a graph of the market demand curve and Hot Air's marginal revenue curve.
14. Find Hot Air's profit-maximizing output and price and calculate the firm's economic profit.

15. If the government imposes a tax on Hot Air's profit, how do its output and price change?
16. If instead of taxing Hot Air's profit, the government imposes a sales tax on balloon rides of $30 a ride, what are the new profit-maximizing quantity, price, and economic profit?
17. The figure illustrates the situation facing the publisher of the only newspaper containing local news in an isolated community.

a. On the graph, mark the profit-maximizing quantity and price and the publisher's total revenue per day.
b. At the price charged, is the demand for this newspaper elastic or inelastic? Why?

Single-Price Monopoly and Competition Compared

18. Show on the graph in Problem 17 the consumer surplus from newspapers and the deadweight loss created by the monopoly. Explain why this market might encourage rent seeking.
19. If the newspaper market in Problem 17 were perfectly competitive, what would be the quantity, price, consumer surplus, and producer surplus? Mark each on the graph.
20. **What the Apple-Samsung Verdict Means for Your Smartphone**

A California jury found Samsung guilty of violating the majority of the patents in question, including software features like double-tap zooming and scrolling. It recommended that Apple be awarded more than $1 billion in damages. This verdict could significantly affect both smartphone users and producers.

Source: CNN Money, August 26, 2012

a. If Apple became a monopoly in the smartphone market, who would benefit and who would lose?

b. Compared to a smartphone monopoly, who would benefit and who would lose if the smartphone market became perfectly competitive?

c. Explain which market would be efficient: a perfectly competitive one or a monopoly.

Price Discrimination

21. **AT&T Moves Away from Unlimited-Data Pricing**

AT&T said it will eliminate its $30 unlimited data plan as the crush of data use from the iPhone has hurt call quality. AT&T is introducing new plans costing $15 a month for 200 megabytes of data traffic or $25 a month for 2 gigabytes. AT&T says those who exceed 2 gigabytes of usage will pay $10 a month for each additional gigabyte. AT&T hopes that these plans will attract more customers.

Source: The Wall Street Journal, June 2, 2010

a. Explain why AT&T's new plans might be price discrimination.

b. Draw a graph to illustrate the original plan and the new plans.

Monopoly Regulation

22. **iSurrender**

In 2008, getting your hands on the new iPhone meant signing a two-year AT&T contract. Some markets, because of the costs of being a player, tend toward either a single firm or a small number of firms. Everyone hoped the wireless market would be different. A telephone monopoly has been the norm for most of American telecommunication history, except for what may turn out to have been a brief experimental period from 1984 through 2012, or so. It may be that telephone monopolies in America are a national tradition.

Source: Slate, June 10, 2008

a. How did AT&T, the exclusive provider of wireless service for the iPhone in 2008, influence the wireless telecommunication market?

b. Explain why the wireless market might "tend toward either a single firm or a small number of firms." Why might this justify allowing a regulated monopoly to exist in this market?

Economics in the News

23. After you have studied *Economics in the News* on pp. 316–317, answer the following questions.

a. Why did the European regulators say that Google was misusing its monopoly power? Do you agree? Explain why or why not.

b. Explain why it would be inefficient to regulate Google to make it charge the same price per keyword click to all advertisers.

c. Explain why selling keywords to the highest bidder can lead to an efficient allocation of advertising resources.

24. **F.C.C. Planning Rules to Open Cable Market**

The Federal Communications Commission (F.C.C.) is setting new regulations to open the cable television market to independent programmers and rival video services. The new rules will make it easier for small independent programmers to lease access to cable channels, and the size of the nation's largest cable companies will be capped at 30 percent of the market.

Source: The New York Times, November 10, 2007

a. What barriers to entry exist in the cable television market?

b. Are high cable prices evidence of monopoly power?

c. Draw a graph to illustrate the effects of the F.C.C.'s new regulations on the price, quantity, total surplus, and deadweight loss.

25. **Antitrust Inquiry Launched into Intel**

Intel, the world's largest chipmaker, holds 80 percent of the microprocessor market. Advanced Micro Devices complains that Intel stifles competition, but Intel says that the 42.4 percent fall in prices between 2000 and 2007 shows that this industry is fiercely competitive.

Source: The Washington Post, June 7, 2008

a. Is Intel a monopoly in the chip market?

b. Evaluate the argument made by Intel that the fall in prices "shows that this industry is fiercely competitive."

14

MONOPOLISTIC COMPETITION

After studying this chapter, you will be able to:

◆ Define and identify monopolistic competition

◆ Explain how a firm in monopolistic competition determines its price and output in the short run and the long run

◆ Explain why advertising costs are high and why firms in monopolistic competition use brand names

At tennis-warehouse.com, you have a choice of racquets made by 19 producers. The top five have 265 different racquets to choose among. Tennis racquet producers compete, but each has a monopoly on its own special kind of racquet—the market is an example of monopolistic competition.

The model of monopolistic competition helps us to understand the competition that we see every day. And in *Economics in the News*, at the end of the chapter, we apply the model to the market for tennis racquets.

What Is Monopolistic Competition?

You have studied perfect competition, in which a large number of firms produce at the lowest possible cost, make zero economic profit, and are efficient. You've also studied monopoly, in which a single firm restricts output, produces at a higher cost and price than in perfect competition, and is inefficient.

Most real-world markets are competitive but not perfectly competitive, because firms in these markets have some power to set their prices, as monopolies do. We call this type of market *monopolistic competition*.

Monopolistic competition is a market structure in which

- A large number of firms compete.
- Each firm produces a differentiated product.
- Firms compete on product quality, price, and marketing.
- Firms are free to enter and exit the industry.

Large Number of Firms

In monopolistic competition, as in perfect competition, the industry consists of a large number of firms. The presence of a large number of firms has three implications for the firms in the industry.

Small Market Share   In monopolistic competition, each firm supplies a small part of the total industry output. Consequently, each firm has only limited power to influence the price of its product. Each firm's price can deviate from the average price of other firms by only a relatively small amount.

Ignore Other Firms   A firm in monopolistic competition must be sensitive to the average market price of the product, but the firm does not pay attention to any one individual competitor. Because all the firms are relatively small, no one firm can dictate market conditions, and so no one firm's actions directly affect the actions of the other firms.

Collusion Impossible   Firms in monopolistic competition would like to be able to conspire to fix a higher price—called *collusion*. But because the number of firms in monopolistic competition is large, coordination is difficult and collusion is not possible.

Product Differentiation

A firm practises **product differentiation** if it makes a product that is slightly different from the products of competing firms. A differentiated product is one that is a close substitute but not a perfect substitute for the products of the other firms. Some people are willing to pay more for one variety of the product, so when its price rises, the quantity demanded of that variety decreases, but it does not (necessarily) decrease to zero. For example, Adidas, Asics, Diadora, Etonic, Fila, New Balance, Nike, Puma, and Reebok all make differentiated running shoes. If the price of Adidas running shoes rises and the prices of the other shoes remain constant, Adidas sells fewer shoes and the other producers sell more. But Adidas shoes don't disappear unless the price rises by a large enough amount.

Competing on Quality, Price, and Marketing

Product differentiation enables a firm to compete with other firms in three areas: product quality, price, and marketing.

Quality   The quality of a product is the physical attributes that make it different from the products of other firms. Quality includes design, reliability, the service provided to the buyer, and the buyer's ease of access to the product. Quality lies on a spectrum that runs from high to low. Some firms—such as Dell Computer Corp.—offer high-quality products. They are well designed and reliable, and the customer receives quick and efficient service. Other firms offer a lower-quality product that is poorly designed, that might not work perfectly, and that is not supported by effective customer service.

Price   Because of product differentiation, a firm in monopolistic competition faces a downward-sloping demand curve. So, like a monopoly, the firm can set both its price and its output. But there is a tradeoff between the product's quality and price. A firm that makes a high-quality product can charge a higher price than a firm that makes a low-quality product.

Marketing   Because of product differentiation, a firm in monopolistic competition must market its product. Marketing takes two main forms: advertising and packaging. A firm that produces a high-quality

ECONOMICS IN ACTION

Monopolistic Competition Today

These ten industries operate in monopolistic competition. The number of firms in the industry is shown in parentheses after the name of the industry. The red bars show the percentage of industry sales by the 4 largest firms. The green bars show the percentage of industry sales by the next 4 largest firms, and the blue bars show the percentage of industry sales by the next 12 largest firms. So the entire length of the combined red, green, and blue bars shows the percentage of industry sales by the 20 largest firms. The Herfindahl-Hirschman Index is shown on the right.

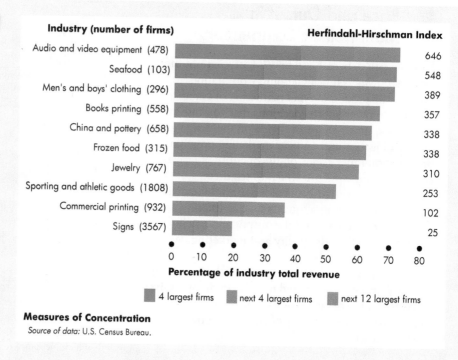

Measures of Concentration
Source of data: U.S. Census Bureau.

product wants to sell it for a suitably high price. To be able to do so, it must advertise and package its product in a way that convinces buyers that they are getting the higher quality for which they are paying a higher price. For example, pharmaceutical companies advertise and package their brand-name drugs to persuade buyers that these items are superior to the lower-priced generic alternatives. Similarly, a low-quality producer uses advertising and packaging to persuade buyers that although the quality is low, the low price more than compensates for this fact.

Entry and Exit

Monopolistic competition has no barriers to prevent new firms from entering the industry in the long run. Consequently, a firm in monopolistic competition cannot make an economic profit in the long run. When existing firms make an economic profit, new firms enter the industry. This entry lowers prices and eventually eliminates economic profit. When firms incur economic losses, some firms leave the industry in the long run. This exit increases prices and eventually eliminates the economic loss.

In long-run equilibrium, firms neither enter nor leave the industry and the firms in the industry make zero economic profit.

Examples of Monopolistic Competition

Economics in Action below shows 10 industries that are good examples of monopolistic competition. These industries have a large number of firms, which is shown in parentheses. In the market for audio and video equipment, the 4 largest firms produce only 41 percent of the industry's total sales and the 20 largest firms produce 72 percent of total sales. The number on the right is the Herfindahl-Hirschman Index (see Chapter 10, p. 234).

◆ REVIEW QUIZ

1 What are the distinguishing characteristics of monopolistic competition?
2 How do firms in monopolistic competition compete?
3 Provide some examples of industries near your school that operate in monopolistic competition (excluding those in the figure below).

Work these questions in Study Plan 14.1 and get instant feedback. Do a Key Terms Quiz.   MyEconLab

Price and Output in Monopolistic Competition

Suppose you've been hired by VF Corporation, the firm that owns Nautica Clothing Corporation, to manage the production and marketing of Nautica jackets. Think about the decisions that you must make at Nautica. First, you must decide on the design and quality of jackets and on your marketing program. Second, you must decide on the quantity of jackets to produce and the price at which to sell them.

We'll suppose that Nautica has already made its decisions about design, quality, and marketing and now we'll concentrate on the output and pricing decisions. We'll study quality and marketing decisions in the next section.

For a given quality of jackets and marketing activity, Nautica faces given costs and market conditions. Given its costs and the demand for its jackets, how does Nautica decide the quantity of jackets to produce and the price at which to sell them?

The Firm's Short-Run Output and Price Decision

In the short run, a firm in monopolistic competition makes its output and price decision just like a monopoly firm does. Figure 14.1 illustrates this decision for Nautica jackets.

The demand curve for Nautica jackets is *D*. This demand curve tells us the quantity of Nautica jackets demanded at each price, given the prices of other jackets. It is not the demand curve for jackets in general.

The *MR* curve shows the marginal revenue curve associated with the demand curve for Nautica jackets. It is derived just like the marginal revenue curve of a single-price monopoly that you studied in Chapter 13.

The *ATC* curve and the *MC* curve show the average total cost and the marginal cost of producing Nautica jackets.

Nautica's goal is to maximize its economic profit. To do so, it produces the output at which marginal revenue equals marginal cost. In Fig. 14.1, this output is 125 jackets a day. Nautica charges the price that buyers are willing to pay for this quantity, which is determined by the demand curve. This price is $75 per jacket. When Nautica produces 125 jackets a day, its average total cost is $25 per jacket and it makes an economic profit of $6,250 a day ($50 per jacket

FIGURE 14.1   Economic Profit in the Short Run

Nautica maximizes profit by producing the quantity at which marginal revenue equals marginal cost, 125 jackets a day, and charging the price of $75 a jacket. This price exceeds the average total cost of $25 a jacket, so the firm makes an economic profit of $50 a jacket. The blue rectangle illustrates economic profit, which equals $6,250 a day ($50 a jacket multiplied by 125 jackets a day).

_____ MyEconLab Animation and Draw Graph _____

multiplied by 125 jackets a day). The blue rectangle shows Nautica's economic profit.

Profit Maximizing Might Be Loss Minimizing

Figure 14.1 shows that Nautica is making a large economic profit. But such an outcome is not inevitable. A firm might face a level of demand for its product that is too low for it to make an economic profit.

Excite@Home was such a firm. Offering high-speed Internet service over the same cable that provides television, Excite@Home hoped to capture a large share of the Internet portal market in competition with AOL, MSN, and a host of other providers.

Figure 14.2 illustrates the situation facing Excite@Home in 2001. The demand curve for its portal service is *D*, the marginal revenue curve is *MR*, the average total cost curve is *ATC*, and the marginal cost curve is *MC*. Excite@Home maximized profit—

FIGURE 14.2   Economic Loss in the Short Run

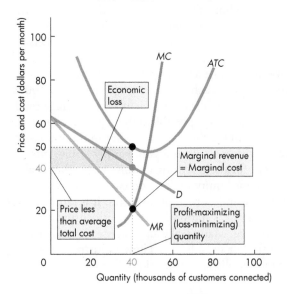

Profit is maximized where marginal revenue equals marginal cost. The loss-minimizing quantity is 40,000 customers. The price of $40 a month is less than the average total cost of $50 a month, so the firm incurs an economic loss of $10 a customer. The red rectangle illustrates economic loss, which equals $400,000 a month ($10 a customer multiplied by 40,000 customers).

——————— MyEconLab Animation ———————

equivalently, it minimized its loss—by producing the output at which marginal revenue equals marginal cost. In Fig. 14.2, this output is 40,000 customers. Excite@Home charged the price that buyers were willing to pay for this quantity, which was determined by the demand curve and which was $40 a month. With 40,000 customers, Excite@Home's average total cost was $50 per customer, so it incurred an economic loss of $400,000 a month ($10 a customer multiplied by 40,000 customers). The red rectangle shows Excite@Home's economic loss.

So far, the firm in monopolistic competition looks like a single-price monopoly. It produces the quantity at which marginal revenue equals marginal cost and then charges the price that buyers are willing to pay for that quantity, as determined by the demand curve. The key difference between monopoly and monopolistic competition lies in what happens next when firms either make an economic profit or incur an economic loss.

Long Run: Zero Economic Profit

A firm like Excite@Home is not going to incur an economic loss for long. Eventually, it goes out of business. Also, there is no restriction on entry into monopolistic competition, so if firms in an industry are making economic profit, other firms have an incentive to enter that industry.

As the Gap and other firms start to make jackets similar to those made by Nautica, the demand for Nautica jackets decreases. The demand curve for Nautica jackets and the marginal revenue curve shift leftward. As these curves shift leftward, the profit-maximizing quantity and price fall.

Figure 14.3 shows the long-run equilibrium. The demand curve for Nautica jackets and the marginal revenue curve have shifted leftward. The firm produces 75 jackets a day and sells them for $25 each. At this output level, average total cost is also $25 per jacket.

FIGURE 14.3   Output and Price in the Long Run

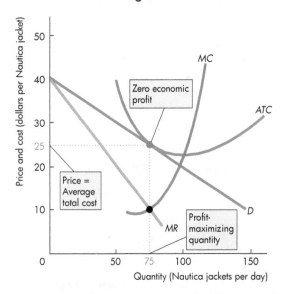

Economic profit encourages entry, which decreases the demand for each firm's product. When the demand curve touches the ATC curve at the quantity at which MR equals MC, the market is in long-run equilibrium. The output that maximizes profit is 75 jackets a day, and the price is $25 per jacket. Average total cost is also $25 per jacket, so economic profit is zero.

——————— MyEconLab Animation ———————

So Nautica is making zero economic profit on its jackets. When all the firms in the industry are making zero economic profit, there is no incentive for new firms to enter.

If demand is so low relative to costs that firms incur economic losses, exit will occur. As firms leave an industry, the demand for the products of the remaining firms increases and their demand curves shift rightward. The exit process ends when all the firms in the industry are making zero economic profit.

Monopolistic Competition and Perfect Competition

Figure 14.4 compares monopolistic competition and perfect competition and highlights two key differences between them:

- Excess capacity
- Markup

Excess Capacity A firm has **excess capacity** if it produces less than its **efficient scale**, which is the quantity at which average total cost is a minimum—the quantity at the bottom of the U-shaped *ATC* curve. In Fig. 14.4, the efficient scale is 100 jackets a day. Nautica in part (a) produces 75 Nautica jackets a day and has *excess capacity* of 25 jackets a day. But if all jackets are alike and are produced by firms in perfect competition, each firm in part (b) produces 100 jackets a day, which is the efficient scale. Average total cost is the lowest possible only in *perfect* competition.

You can see the excess capacity in monopolistic competition all around you. Family restaurants (except for the truly outstanding ones) almost always have some empty tables. You can always get a pizza delivered in less than 30 minutes. It is rare that every pump at a gas station is in use with customers waiting in line. Many real estate agents are ready to help you find or sell a home. These industries are examples of monopolistic competition. The firms have excess

---

FIGURE 14.4   Excess Capacity and Markup

(a) Monopolistic competition

(b) Perfect competition

The efficient scale is 100 jackets a day. In monopolistic competition in the long run, because the firm faces a downward-sloping demand curve for its product, the quantity produced is less than the efficient scale and the firm has excess capacity. Price exceeds marginal cost by the amount of the markup.

In contrast, because in perfect competition the demand for each firm's product is perfectly elastic, the quantity produced in the long run equals the efficient scale and price equals marginal cost. The firm produces at the least possible cost and there is no markup.

capacity. They could sell more by cutting their prices, but they would then incur losses.

Markup A firm's **markup** is the amount by which price exceeds marginal cost. Figure 14.4(a) shows Nautica's markup. In perfect competition, price always equals marginal cost and there is no markup. Figure 14.4(b) shows this case. In monopolistic competition, buyers pay a higher price than in perfect competition and also pay more than marginal cost.

Is Monopolistic Competition Efficient?

Resources are used efficiently when marginal social benefit equals marginal social cost. Price equals marginal social benefit and the firm's marginal cost equals marginal social cost (assuming there are no external benefits or costs). So if the price of a Nautica jacket exceeds the marginal cost of producing it, the quantity of Nautica jackets produced is less than the efficient quantity. And you've just seen that in long-run equilibrium in monopolistic competition, price *does* exceed marginal cost. So is the quantity produced in monopolistic competition less than the efficient quantity?

Making the Relevant Comparison Two economists meet in the street, and one asks the other, "How is your husband?" The quick reply is "Compared to what?" This bit of economic wit illustrates a key point: Before we can conclude that something needs fixing, we must check out the available alternatives.

The markup that drives a gap between price and marginal cost in monopolistic competition arises from product differentiation. It is because Nautica jackets are not quite the same as jackets from Banana Republic, CK, Diesel, DKNY, Earl Jackets, Gap, Levi's, Ralph Lauren, or any of the other dozens of producers of jackets that the demand for Nautica jackets is not perfectly elastic. The only way in which the demand for jackets from Nautica might be perfectly elastic is if there were only one kind of jacket and all firms made it. In this situation, Nautica jackets are indistinguishable from all other jackets. They don't even have identifying labels.

If there were only one kind of jacket, the total benefit of jackets would almost certainly be less than it is with variety. People value variety—not only because it enables each person to select what he or she likes best but also because it provides an external benefit. Most of us enjoy seeing variety in the choices of others. Contrast a scene from the China of the 1960s, when everyone wore a Mao tunic, with the China of today, where everyone wears the clothes of their own choosing. Or contrast a scene from the Germany of the 1930s, when almost everyone who could afford a car owned a first-generation Volkswagen Beetle, with the world of today with its enormous variety of styles and types of automobiles.

If people value variety, why don't we see infinite variety? The answer is that variety is costly. Each different variety of any product must be designed, and then customers must be informed about it. These initial costs of design and marketing—called setup costs—mean that some varieties that are too close to others already available are just not worth creating.

The Bottom Line Product variety is both valued and costly. The efficient degree of product variety is the one for which the marginal social benefit of product variety equals its marginal social cost. The loss that arises because the quantity produced is less than the efficient quantity is offset by the gain that arises from having a greater degree of product variety. So compared to the alternative—product uniformity—monopolistic competition might be efficient.

◆ REVIEW QUIZ

1 How does a firm in monopolistic competition decide how much to produce and at what price to offer its product for sale?
2 Why can a firm in monopolistic competition make an economic profit only in the short run?
3 Why do firms in monopolistic competition operate with excess capacity?
4 Why is there a price markup over marginal cost in monopolistic competition?
5 Is monopolistic competition efficient?

Work these questions in Study Plan 14.2 and get instant feedback. Do a Key Terms Quiz.   MyEconLab

You've seen how the firm in monopolistic competition determines its output and price in both the short run and the long run when it produces a given product and undertakes a *given* marketing effort. But how does the firm choose its product quality and marketing effort? We'll now study these decisions.

▶ Product Development and Marketing

When Nautica made its price and output decision that we've just studied, it had already made its product quality and marketing decisions. We'll now look at these decisions and see how they influence the firm's output, price, and economic profit.

Product Development

The prospect of new firms entering the industry keeps firms in monopolistic competition on their toes! To enjoy economic profits, they must continually seek ways of keeping one step ahead of imitators—other firms who imitate the success of profitable firms.

To maintain economic profit, a firm must either develop an entirely new product, or develop a significantly improved product that provides it with a competitive edge, even if only temporarily. A firm that introduces a new or improved and more differentiated product faces a demand that is less elastic and is able to increase its price and make an economic profit. Eventually, imitators will make close substitutes for the firm's new product and compete away the economic profit arising from an initial advantage. So to restore economic profit, the firm must develop another new or seriously improved product.

Profit-Maximizing Product Development The decision to develop a new or improved product is based on the same type of profit-maximizing calculation that you've already studied.

Product development is a costly activity, but it also brings in additional revenues. The firm must balance the cost and revenue at the margin.

The marginal dollar spent on developing a new or improved product is the marginal cost of product development. The marginal dollar that the new or improved product earns for the firm is the marginal revenue of product development. At a low level of product development, the marginal revenue from a better product exceeds the marginal cost. At a high level of product development, the marginal cost of a better product exceeds the marginal revenue.

When the marginal cost and marginal revenue of product development are equal, the firm is undertaking the profit-maximizing amount of product development.

Efficiency and Product Development Is the profit-maximizing amount of product development also the efficient amount? Efficiency is achieved if the marginal social benefit of a new and improved product equals its marginal social cost.

The marginal social benefit of an improved product is the increase in price that consumers are willing to pay for it. The marginal social cost is the amount that the firm must pay to make the improvement. Profit is maximized when marginal *revenue* equals marginal cost. But in monopolistic competition, marginal revenue is less than price, so product development is probably not pushed to its efficient level.

Monopolistic competition brings many product changes that cost little to implement and are purely cosmetic, such as improved packaging or a new scent in laundry powder. Even when there is a truly improved product, it is never as good as the consumer would like and for which the consumer is willing to pay a higher price. For example, "The Legend of Zelda: Skyward Sword" is regarded as an almost perfect and very cool game, but users complain that it isn't quite perfect. It is a game whose features generate a marginal revenue equal to the marginal cost of creating them.

Advertising

A firm with a differentiated product needs to ensure that its customers know how its product is different from the competition. A firm also might attempt to create a consumer perception that its product is different, even when that difference is small. Firms use advertising and packaging to achieve this goal.

Advertising Expenditures Firms in monopolistic competition incur huge costs to ensure that buyers appreciate and value the differences between their own products and those of their competitors. So a large proportion of the price that we pay for a good covers the cost of selling it, and this proportion is increasing. Advertising in newspapers and magazines and on radio, television, and the Internet is the main selling cost. But it is not the only one. Selling costs include the cost of shopping malls that look like movie sets, glossy catalogs and brochures, and the salaries, airfares, and hotel bills of salespeople.

Advertising expenditures affect the profits of firms in two ways: They increase costs, and they change demand. Let's look at these effects.

ECONOMICS IN ACTION

The Cost of Selling a Pair of Shoes

When you buy a pair of running shoes that cost you $70, you're paying $9 for the materials from which the shoes are made, $2.75 for the services of the Malaysian worker who made the shoes, and $5.25 for the production and transportation services of a manufacturing firm in Asia and a shipping company. These numbers total $17. You pay $3 to the U.S. government in import duty. So we've now accounted for a total of $20. Where did the other $50 go? It is the cost of advertising, retailing, and other sales and distribution services.

The selling costs associated with running shoes are not unusual. Almost everything that you buy includes a selling cost component that exceeds one half of the total cost. Your clothing, food, electronic items, DVDs, magazines, and even your textbooks cost more to sell than they cost to manufacture.

Advertising costs are only a part, and often a small part, of total selling costs. For example, Nike spends about $4 on advertising per pair of running shoes sold.

For the U.S. economy as a whole, there are some 20,000 advertising agencies, which employ more than 200,000 people and have sales of $45 billion. These numbers are only part of the total cost of advertising because firms have their own internal advertising departments, the costs of which we can only guess.

But the biggest part of selling costs is not the cost of advertising. It is the cost of retailing services. The retailer's selling costs (and economic profit) are often as much as 50 percent of the price you pay.

Raw materials $9 Production costs $8 Import duty $3 Selling costs $50

Selling Costs and Total Cost Selling costs are fixed costs and they increase the firm's total cost. So like the fixed cost of producing a good, advertising costs per unit decrease as the quantity produced increases.

Figure 14.5 shows how selling costs change a firm's average total cost. The blue curve shows the average total cost of production. The red curve shows the firm's average total cost of production plus advertising. The height of the red area between the two curves shows the average fixed cost of advertising. The *total* cost of advertising is fixed. But the *average* cost of advertising decreases as output increases.

Figure 14.5 shows that if advertising increases the quantity sold by a large enough amount, it can lower average total cost. For example, if the quantity sold increases from 25 jackets a day with no advertising to 100 jackets a day with advertising, average total cost falls from $60 to $40 a jacket. The reason is that although the *total* fixed cost has increased, the greater fixed cost is spread over a greater output, so average total cost decreases.

FIGURE 14.5   Selling Costs and Total Cost

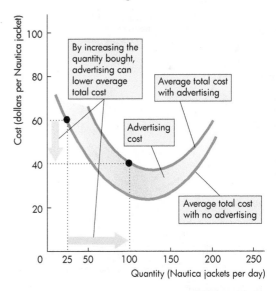

By increasing the quantity bought, advertising can lower average total cost

Average total cost with advertising

Advertising cost

Average total cost with no advertising

Selling costs such as the cost of advertising are fixed costs. When added to the average total cost of production, selling costs increase average total cost by a greater amount at small outputs than at large outputs. If advertising enables sales to increase from 25 jackets a day to 100 jackets a day, average total cost *falls* from $60 to $40 a jacket.

MyEconLab Animation

Selling Costs and Demand Advertising and other selling efforts change the demand for a firm's product. But how? Does demand increase or does it decrease? The most natural answer is that advertising increases demand. By informing people about the quality of its products or by persuading people to switch from the products of other firms, a firm might expect to increase the demand for its own products.

But all firms in monopolistic competition advertise, and all seek to persuade customers that they have the best deal. If advertising enables a firm to survive, the number of firms in the market might increase. And to the extent that the number of firms does increase, advertising *decreases* the demand faced by any one firm. It also makes the demand for any one firm's product more elastic. So advertising can end up not only lowering average total cost but also lowering the markup and the price.

Figure 14.6 illustrates this possible effect of advertising. In part (a), with no advertising, the demand for Nautica jackets is not very elastic. Profit is maximized at 75 jackets per day, and the markup is large. In part (b), advertising, which is a fixed cost, increases average total cost from ATC_0 to ATC_1 but leaves marginal cost unchanged at MC. Demand becomes much more elastic, the profit-maximizing quantity increases, and the markup shrinks.

Using Advertising to Signal Quality

Some advertising, like the Roger Federer Rolex watch ad in glossy magazines or the huge number of dollars that Coke and Pepsi spend, seems hard to understand. There doesn't seem to be any concrete information about a watch in a tennis player's smile. And surely everyone knows about Coke and Pepsi. What is the gain from pouring millions of dollars into advertising these well-known colas?

One answer is that advertising is a signal to the consumer of a high-quality product. A **signal** is an action taken by an informed person (or firm) to send a message to uninformed people. Think about two colas:

FIGURE 14.6   Advertising and the Markup

(a) No firms advertise

(b) All firms advertise

If no firms advertise, demand for each firm's product is low and not very elastic. The profit-maximizing output is small, the markup is large, and the price is high.

Advertising increases average total cost and shifts the *ATC* curve upward from ATC_0 to ATC_1. If all firms advertise, the demand for each firm's product becomes more elastic. Output increases, the price falls, and the markup shrinks.

MyEconLab Animation

Coke and Oke. Oke knows that its cola is not very good and that its taste varies a lot depending on which cheap batch of unsold cola it happens to buy each week. So Oke knows that while it could get a lot of people to try Oke by advertising, they would all quickly discover what a poor product it is and switch back to the cola they bought before. Coke, in contrast, knows that its product has a high-quality, consistent taste and that once consumers have tried it, there is a good chance they'll never drink anything else. On the basis of this reasoning, Oke doesn't advertise but Coke does. And Coke spends a lot of money to make a big splash.

Cola drinkers who see Coke's splashy ads know that the firm would not spend so much money advertising if its product were not truly good. So consumers reason that Coke is indeed a really good product. The flashy expensive ad has signaled that Coke is really good without saying anything about Coke.

Notice that if advertising is a signal, it doesn't need any specific product information. It just needs to be expensive and hard to miss. That's what a lot of advertising looks like. So the signaling theory of advertising predicts much of the advertising that we see.

Brand Names

Many firms create and spend a lot of money promoting a brand name. Why? What benefit does a brand name bring to justify the sometimes high cost of establishing it?

The basic answer is that a brand name provides information to consumers about the quality of a product, and is an incentive to the producer to achieve a high and consistent quality standard.

To see how a brand name helps the consumer, think about how you use brand names to get information about quality. You're on a road trip, and it is time to find a place to spend the night. You see roadside advertisements for Holiday Inn, Joe's Motel, and Annie's Driver's Stop. You know about Holiday Inn because you've stayed in it before. You've also seen their advertisements and know what to expect. You have no information at all about Joe's and Annie's. They might be better than the lodgings you do know about, but without that knowledge, you're not going to try them. You use the brand name as information and stay at Holiday Inn.

This same story explains why a brand name provides an incentive to achieve high and consistent quality. Because no one would know whether Joe's and Annie's were offering a high standard of service, they

have no incentive to do so. But equally, because everyone expects a given standard of service from Holiday Inn, a failure to meet a customer's expectation would almost surely lose that customer to a competitor. So Holiday Inn has a strong incentive to deliver what it promises in the advertising that creates its brand name.

Efficiency of Advertising and Brand Names

To the extent that advertising and brand names provide consumers with information about the precise nature of product differences and product quality, they benefit the consumer and enable a better product choice to be made. But the opportunity cost of the additional information must be weighed against the gain to the consumer.

The final verdict on the efficiency of monopolistic competition is ambiguous. In some cases, the gains from extra product variety offset the selling costs and the extra cost arising from excess capacity. The tremendous varieties of books, magazines, clothing, food, and drinks are examples of such gains. It is less easy to see the gains from being able to buy a brand-name drug with the identical chemical composition to that of a generic alternative, but many people willingly pay more for the brand-name alternative.

◆ REVIEW QUIZ

1 How, other than by adjusting price, do firms in monopolistic competition compete?
2 Why might product development be efficient and why might it be inefficient?
3 Explain how selling costs influence a firm's cost curves and its average total cost.
4 Explain how advertising influences the demand for a firm's product.
5 Are advertising and brand names efficient?

Work these questions in Study Plan 14.3 and get instant feedback. Do a Key Terms Quiz.   MyEconLab

◆ Monopolistic competition is one of the most common market structures that you encounter in your daily life. *Economics in the News* on pp. 334–335 applies the model of monopolistic competition to the market for tennis racquets and shows why you can expect continual improvement and the introduction of new racquets from Babolat, Wilson, Head, Prince, Dunlop, and other racquet producers.

Product Differentiation in Tennis Racquets

Big Serves, Big Data: The First Connected Tennis Racquet

Popular Mechanics
November 7, 2013

Tennis players know all about the feel of hitting the sweet spot in the strings. Now they can back up that feeling with facts. The first tennis racquet with an on/off switch is also the first racquet to track stroke data, including where the ball hits the string bed.

The Babolat Play Pure Drive Set will launch on Dec. 12. Babolat, a French racquet manufacturer founded in 1875, revealed the racquet to PopMech early, showing off the culmination of a 10-year project.

CEO Eric Babolat envisioned the connected racquet a decade ago, but it took time for sensor technology to shrink down and lighten up enough so that he wouldn't have to strap a backpack and wires to players. …

Babolat teamed with French firm Movea, the company behind the Nintendo Wii remote, to build the digital guts. Inside the otherwise-hollow grip they placed an accelerometer and gyroscope along with a 6-hour battery, USB port, Bluetooth connectivity, and enough memory to hold 150 hours of play data. …

The Babolat Play detects stroke type—forehand, backhand, smash, and first and second serves—measures spin and power, tracks rally length and play time, and maps out the location the ball strikes the string bed. The racquet saves all that data, which is available for download to an app via either Bluetooth to Android or Apple mobile devices, or USB to a computer. In two test sessions, the app distilled the information accurately. …

The app saves training and match sessions, shares information in a community setting, and compares data head-to-head with friends or top players—so you can see how well you stack up against a champion like Nadal. …

"The oldest company in tennis is making tennis cool," Eric Babolat says. All with an on/off switch.

Copyright Popular Mechanics 2013.

ESSENCE OF THE STORY

- Babolat, a French tennis recquet manufacturer, has created a tennis racquet that tracks and stores stroke data.

- Babolat started making tennis racquets in 1875.

- CEO Eric Babolat envisioned the racquet 10 years ago, but the technology needed was not then available.

- Babolat worked with the company behind the Nintendo Wii remote to create the new racquet.

- The oldest company in tennis is at the forefront of racquet technology.

MyEconLab More Economics in the News

ECONOMIC ANALYSIS

- The market for tennis racquets is an example of monopolistic competition.

- Nineteen firms compete in a market with up to 1,000 differentiated racquets.

- Although the racquets are differentiated, most of them are close substitutes for each other.

- Close substitutes have highly elastic demand, so markups are low and economic profit is competed away.

- To make an economic profit, a firm must keep innovating.

- The market for tennis racquets has seen a sequence of innovation: metal frame (Wilson, 1967), oversize frame (Prince, 1976), and graphite frame (Prince, 1980).

- Today's innovation is Babolat's Play Pure Drive electronic racquet described in the news article.

- By creating a substantially differentiated product, Babolat was able to bring to the market a product more clearly differentiated from its competitors.

- The monopolistic competition model explains what is now happening at Babolat and what the future holds.

- Figure 1 shows the market for Babolat's electronic racquet. (The numbers are assumptions.)

- Because Babolat's smart racquet differs from other racquets and has features that users value, the demand curve, *D*, and marginal revenue curve, *MR*, provide a large short-run profit opportunity.

- The marginal cost curve is *MC* and the average total cost curve is *ATC*. Babolat maximizes its economic profit by producing the quantity at which marginal revenue equals marginal cost.

- This quantity of racquets can be sold for $400 each.

- The blue rectangle shows Babolat's economic profit.

- Because Babolat makes an economic profit, entry will take place. Dunlop, Head, Prince, and Wilson will enter the smart racquet market.

- Figure 2 shows the consequences of entry for Babolat.

- The demand for the Babolat racquet decreases as the market is shared with the other racquets.

- Babolat's profit-maximizing price for the electronic racquet falls, and in the long run economic profit is eliminated.

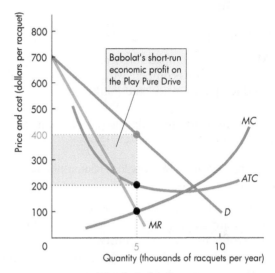

Figure 1 Economic Profit in the Short Run

Figure 2 Zero Economic Profit in the Long Run

- With zero economic profit, Babolat (along with the other producers) has an incentive to develop an even better differentiated racquet and start the cycle described here again, making an economic profit with a new racquet in the short run.

335

SUMMARY

Key Points

What Is Monopolistic Competition? (pp. 324–325)

- Monopolistic competition occurs when a large number of firms compete with each other on product quality, price, and marketing.

Working Problems 1 and 2 will give you a better understanding of what monopolistic competition is.

Price and Output in Monopolistic Competition

(pp. 326–329)

- Each firm in monopolistic competition faces a downward-sloping demand curve and produces the profit-maximizing quantity.
- Entry and exit result in zero economic profit and excess capacity in long-run equilibrium.

Working Problems 3 to 8 will give you a better understanding of price and output in monopolistic competition.

Product Development and Marketing (pp. 330–333)

- Firms in monopolistic competition innovate and develop new products.
- Advertising expenditures increase total cost, but average total cost might fall if the quantity sold increases by enough.
- Advertising expenditures might increase demand, but demand might decrease if competition increases.
- Whether monopolistic competition is inefficient depends on the value we place on product variety.

Working Problem 9 will give you a better understanding of product development and marketing.

Key Terms

Efficient scale, 328
Excess capacity, 328

Markup, 329
Monopolistic competition, 324

MyEconLab Key Terms Quiz

Product differentiation, 324
Signal, 332

WORKED PROBLEM

MyEconLab   You can work this problem in Chapter 14 Study Plan.

The table provides information about Prue's Personal Trainer Service, a firm that is in monopolistic competition with similar firms that offer slightly differentiated services.

Demand schedule		Production costs	
Price (dollars per session)	Quantity (sessions per hour)	MC (dollars per session)	ATC (dollars per session)
45	0		..
		 12	
40	1		33
		 5	
35	2		19
		 7	
30	3		15
		 27	
25	4		18

Questions

1. What is Prue's profit-maximizing quantity? What is Prue's price?
2. What is Prue's markup and does she have excess capacity?
3. Is Prue in a long-run equilibrium?

Solutions

1. The profit-maximizing quantity is that at which marginal cost equals marginal revenue. The table above provides the marginal cost data. For example, the marginal cost of the 4th session per hour is $27. The table below shows the calculation of marginal revenue. Mutliply quantity by price to find total revenue (third column) and then calculate the change in total revenue when the quantity increases by 1 session (fourth column).

Demand schedule		Total revenue (dollars per hour)	Marginal revenue (dollars per session)
Price (dollars per session)	Quantity (sessions per hour)		
45	0	0	
			 40
40	1	40	
			 30
35	2	70	
			 20
30	3	90	
			 10
25	4	100	

When the number of sessions increases from 2 to 3 an hour, marginal revenue ($20) exceeds marginal cost ($7), so profit increases. But when the number of sessions increases from 3 to 4 an hour, marginal cost ($27) exceeds marginal revenue ($10), so profit decreases. So 3 sessions an hour maximizes Prue's profit. The highest price at which 3 sessions an hour can be sold is $30 a session, which is the profit-maximizing price.

Key Point: To maximize profit, increase production if $MR > MC$ and decrease production if $MR < MC$.

2. To find Prue's markup, we compare price to marginal cost. Use the fact that $MC = ATC$ at minimum ATC and notice that minimum ATC is $15 a session at 3 sessions an hour. The price is $30 a session, so the markup is 100 percent. Prue is producing at minimum ATC, which is the efficient scale, so she has no excess capacity.

Key Point: Markup is the amount by which price exceeds marginal cost; and excess capacity is the gap between output and the efficient scale.

3. In the long run, entry decreases demand and drives economic profit to zero. Prue is making a profit of $45 an hour (price of $30 a session minus ATC of $15 a session, multiplied by 3 sessions an hour). So Prue is not in a long-run equilibrium.

Key Point: Entry decreases the demand for the firm's good or service and economic profit falls to zero. The key figure illustrates Prue's short-run equilibrium situation.

Key Figure   MyEconLab Interactive Animation

STUDY PLAN PROBLEMS AND APPLICATIONS

MyEconLab   You can work Problems 1 to 9 in Chapter 14 Study Plan and get instant feedback.

What Is Monopolistic Competition? (Study Plan 14.1)

1. Which of the following items are sold by firms in monopolistic competition? Explain your selections.
   - Cable television service
   - Wheat
   - Athletic shoes
   - Soda
   - Toothbrushes
   - Ready-mix concrete

2. The four-firm concentration ratio for audio equipment makers is 30 and for electric lamp makers it is 89. The HHI for audio equipment makers is 415 and for electric lamp makers it is 2,850. Which of these markets is an example of monopolistic competition?

Price and Output in Monopolistic Competition

(Study Plan 14.2)

Use the following information to work Problems 3 and 4.

Sara is a dot.com entrepreneur who has established a Web site at which people can design and buy sweatshirts. Sara pays $1,000 a week for her Web server and Internet connection. The sweatshirts that her customers design are made to order by another firm, and Sara pays this firm $20 a sweatshirt. Sara has no other costs. The table sets out the demand schedule for Sara's sweatshirts.

Price (dollars per sweatshirt)	Quantity demanded (sweatshirts per week)
0	100
20	80
40	60
60	40
80	20
100	0

3. Calculate Sara's profit-maximizing output, price, and economic profit.
4. a. Do you expect other firms to enter the Web sweatshirt business and compete with Sara?
   b. What happens to the demand for Sara's sweatshirts in the long run? What happens to Sara's economic profit in the long run?

Use the following figure, which shows the situation facing Flight Inc., a producer of running shoes, to work Problems 5 to 8.

5. What quantity does Flight produce, what price does it charge, and what is its economic profit?
6. In the long run, how does Flight change its price and the quantity it produces? What happens to the market output of running shoes?
7. Does Flight have excess capacity in the long run? If it has excess capacity in the long run, why doesn't it decrease its capacity?
8. Is the market for running shoes efficient or inefficient in the long run? Explain your answer.

Product Development and Marketing (Study Plan 14.3)

9. Suppose that Tommy Hilfiger's marginal cost of a jacket is a constant $100 and the total fixed cost at one of its stores is $2,000 a day. This store sells 20 jackets a day, which is its profit-maximizing number of jackets. Then the stores nearby start to advertise their jackets. The Tommy Hilfiger store now spends $2,000 a day advertising its jackets, and its profit-maximizing number of jackets sold jumps to 50 a day.
   a. What is this store's average total cost of a jacket sold (i) before the advertising begins and (ii) after the advertising begins?
   b. Can you say what happens to the price of a Tommy Hilfiger jacket, Tommy's markup, and Tommy's economic profit? Why or why not?

ADDITIONAL PROBLEMS AND APPLICATIONS

MyEconLab   You can work these problems in MyEconLab if assigned by your instructor

What Is Monopolistic Competition?

10. Which of the following items are sold by firms in monopolistic competition? Explain your selection.
    - Orange juice
    - Canned soup
    - PCs
    - Chewing gum
    - Breakfast cereals
    - Corn

11. The HHI for automobiles is 2,350, for sporting goods it is 161, for batteries it is 2,883, and for jewelry it is 81. Which of these markets is an example of monopolistic competition?

Price and Output in Monopolistic Competition

Use the following data to work Problems 12 and 13. Lorie teaches singing. Her fixed costs are $1,000 a month, and it costs her $50 of labor to give one class. The table shows the demand schedule for Lorie's singing lessons.

Price (dollars per lesson)	Quantity demanded (lessons per month)
0	250
50	200
100	150
150	100
200	50
250	0

12. Calculate Lorie's profit-maximizing output, price, and economic profit.

13. a. Do you expect other firms to enter the singing lesson business and compete with Lorie?

    b. What happens to the demand for Lorie's lessons in the long run? What happens to Lorie's economic profit in the long run?

Use the figure in the next column, which shows the situation facing Mike's Bikes, a producer of mountain bikes, to work Problems 14 to 18. The demand and costs of other mountain bike producers are similar to those of Mike's Bikes.

14. What quantity does the firm produce and what is its price? Calculate the firm's economic profit or economic loss.

15. What will happen to the number of firms producing mountain bikes in the long run?

16. a. How will the price of a mountain bike and the number of bikes produced by Mike's Bikes change in the long run?

    b. How will the quantity of mountain bikes produced by all firms change in the long run?

17. Is there any way for Mike's Bikes to avoid having excess capacity in the long run?

18. Is the market for mountain bikes efficient or inefficient in the long run? Explain your answer.

Use the following news clip to work Problems 19 and 20.

Groceries for the Gourmet Palate

No food, it seems, is safe from being repackaged to look like an upscale product. Samuel Adams' $120 Utopias, in a ridiculous copper-covered 24-oz. bottle meant to resemble an old-fashioned brew kettle, is barely beer. It's not carbonated like a Bud, but aged in oak barrels like scotch. It has a vintage year, like a Bordeaux, is light, complex, and free of any alcohol sting, despite having six times as much alcohol content as a regular can of brew.

Source: *Time*, April 14, 2008

19. a. Explain how Samuel Adams has differentiated its Utopias to compete with other beer brands in terms of quality, price, and marketing.

    b. Predict whether Samuel Adams produces at, above, or below the efficient scale in the short run.

20. a. Predict whether the $120 price tag on the Utopias is at, above, or below marginal cost
    (i) In the short run   (ii) In the long run
  b. Do you think that Samuel Adams' Utopias makes the market for beer inefficient?

Use the following news clip to work Problems 21 and 22.

Swinging for Female Golfers

One of the hottest areas of innovation is in clubs for women, who now make up nearly a quarter of the 24 million golfers in the United States. Callaway and Nike, two of the leading golf-equipment manufacturers, recently released new clubs designed for women.

Source: *Time*, April 21, 2008

21. a. How are Callaway and Nike attempting to maintain economic profit?
  b. Draw a graph to illustrate the cost curves and revenue curves of Callaway or Nike in the market for golf clubs for women.
  c. Show on your graph in part (b) the short-run economic profit.

22. a. Explain why the economic profit that Callaway and Nike make on golf clubs for women is likely to be temporary.
  b. Draw a graph to illustrate the cost curves and revenue curves of Callaway or Nike in the market for golf clubs for women in the long run. Mark the firm's excess capacity.

Product Development and Marketing

Use the following data to work Problems 23 to 25. Bianca bakes delicious cookies. Her total fixed cost is $40 a day, and her average variable cost is $1 a bag. Few people know about Bianca's Cookies, and she is maximizing her profit by selling 10 bags a day for $5 a bag. Bianca thinks that if she spends $50 a day on advertising, she can increase her market share and sell 25 bags a day for $5 a bag.

23. If Bianca's advertising works as she expects, can she increase her economic profit by advertising?

24. If Bianca advertises, will her average total cost increase or decrease at the quantity produced?

25. If Bianca advertises, will she continue to sell her cookies for $5 a bag or will she change her price?

Use the following news clip to work Problems 26 and 27.

A Thirst for More Champagne

Champagne exports have tripled in the past 20 years. That poses a problem for northern France, where the bubbly hails from—not enough grapes. So French authorities have unveiled a plan to extend the official Champagne grape-growing zone to cover 40 new villages. This revision has provoked debate. The change will take several years to become effective. In the meantime the vineyard owners whose land values will jump markedly if the changes are finalized certainly have reason to raise a glass.

Source: *Fortune*, May 12, 2008

26. a. Why is France so strict about designating the vineyards that can use the Champagne label?
  b. Explain who most likely opposes this plan.

27. Assuming that vineyards in these 40 villages are producing the same quality of grapes with or without this plan, why will their land values "jump markedly" if this plan is approved?

28. **Under Armour's Big Step Up**
    Under Armour, the red-hot athletic-apparel brand, has joined Nike, Adidas, and New Balance as a major player in the market for athletic footwear. Under Armour plans to revive the long-dead cross-training category. But will young athletes really spend $100 for a cross training shoe to lift weights in?

    Source: *Time*, May 26, 2008

    What factors influence Under Armour's ability to make an economic profit in the cross-training shoe market?

Economics in the News

29. After you have studied *Economics in the News* on pp. 334–335, answer the following questions.
  a. Why do you think Babolat worked with the firm that helped Nintendo develop the Wii remote?
  b. How would Babolat's cost curves (*MC* and *ATC*) have been different if they had not worked with the Wii developer?
  c. How do you think the launch of Babolat's new-technology racquet has influenced the demand for other firms' racquets?
  d. Explain the effects of the introduction of the new-technology racquet on Prince and other firms in the market for tennis racquets.
  e. Draw a graph to illustrate your answer to part (c). Explain your answer.
  f. What do you predict will happen to the markup in the market for smart racquets?
  g. What do you predict will happen to excess capacity in the market for smart racquets? Explain your answer.

15 OLIGOPOLY

After studying this chapter, you will be able to:

◆ Define and identify oligopoly

◆ Use game theory to explain how price and output are determined in oligopoly

◆ Use game theory to explain other strategic decisions

◆ Describe the antitrust laws that regulate oligopoly

Chances are that your cellphone service provider is Verizon or AT&T. Two thirds of Americans have plans with these two firms. Similarly, the chip in your computer was made by either Intel or AMD; the battery in your TV remote by Duracell or Energizer; and the airplane that takes you on a long-distance trip by Boeing or the European firm Airbus.

How does a market work when only two or a handful of firms compete? To answer this question, we use the model of oligopoly.

At the end of the chapter, in *Economics in the News*, we'll look at the market for cellphone service and see how Verizon and AT&T battle to maximize profit.

What Is Oligopoly?

Oligopoly, like monopolistic competition, lies between perfect competition and monopoly. The firms in oligopoly might produce an identical product and compete only on price, or they might produce a differentiated product and compete on price, product quality, and marketing. **Oligopoly** is a market structure in which

- Natural or legal barriers prevent the entry of new firms.
- A small number of firms compete.

Barriers to Entry

Natural or legal barriers to entry can create oligopoly. You saw in Chapter 13 how economies of scale and demand form a natural barrier to entry that can create a *natural monopoly*. These same factors can create a *natural oligopoly*.

Figure 15.1 illustrates two natural oligopolies. The demand curve, D (in both parts of the figure), shows the demand for taxi rides in a town. If the average

total cost curve of a taxi company is ATC_1 in part (a), the market is a natural **duopoly**—an oligopoly market with two firms. You can probably see some examples of duopoly where you live. Some cities have only two taxi companies, two car rental firms, two copy centers, or two college bookstores.

The lowest price at which the firm would remain in business is $10 a ride. At that price, the quantity of rides demanded is 60 a day, the quantity that can be provided by just two firms. There is no room in this market for three firms. But if there were only one firm, it would make an economic profit and a second firm would enter to take some of the business and economic profit.

If the average total cost curve of a taxi company is ATC_2 in part (b), the efficient scale of one firm is 20 rides a day. This market is large enough for three firms.

A legal oligopoly arises when a legal barrier to entry protects the small number of firms in a market. A city might license two taxi firms or two bus companies, for example, even though the combination of demand and economies of scale leaves room for more than two firms.

FIGURE 15.1   Natural Oligopoly

(a) Natural duopoly

(b) Natural oligopoly with three firms

The minimum average total cost of producing a ride is $10, so $10 a ride is the lowest possible price that a firm can charge. When a firm produces the efficient scale of 30 rides a day, two firms can satisfy the market demand. This market is

a natural oligopoly with two firms—a natural duopoly. When the efficient scale of one firm is 20 rides per day, three firms can satisfy the market demand at the lowest possible price. This natural oligopoly has three firms.

ECONOMICS IN ACTION

Oligopoly Today

These markets are oligopolies. Although in some of them the number of firms (in parentheses) is large, the share of the market held by the four largest firms (the red bars) is close to 100 percent.

The most concentrated markets—batteries, glass containers, breakfast cereals, computer hard drives, and light bulbs—are dominated by a handful of firms.

If you want to buy a battery for your TV remote or toothbrush, you'll find it hard to avoid buying a Duracell or an Energizer.

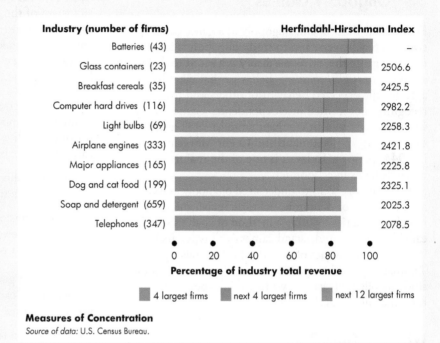

Industry (number of firms)	Herfindahl-Hirschman Index
Batteries (43)	–
Glass containers (23)	2506.6
Breakfast cereals (35)	2425.5
Computer hard drives (116)	2982.2
Light bulbs (69)	2258.3
Airplane engines (333)	2421.8
Major appliances (165)	2225.8
Dog and cat food (199)	2325.1
Soap and detergent (659)	2025.3
Telephones (347)	2078.5

Percentage of industry total revenue

■ 4 largest firms ■ next 4 largest firms ■ next 12 largest firms

Measures of Concentration
Source of data: U.S. Census Bureau.

Small Number of Firms

Because barriers to entry exist, oligopoly consists of a small number of firms, each of which has a large share of the market. Such firms are interdependent, and they face a temptation to cooperate to increase their joint economic profit.

Interdependence With a small number of firms in a market, each firm's actions influence the profits of all the other firms. When Penny Stafford opened her coffee shop in Bellevue, Washington, a nearby Starbucks coffee shop took a hit. Within days, Starbucks began to attract Penny's customers with enticing offers and lower prices. Starbucks survived, but Penny eventually went out of business. Penny Stafford and Starbucks were interdependent.

Temptation to Cooperate When a small number of firms share a market, they can increase their profits by forming a cartel and acting like a monopoly. A **cartel** is a group of firms acting together—colluding—to limit output, raise price, and increase economic profit. Cartels are illegal, but they do operate in some markets. But for reasons that you'll discover in this chapter, cartels tend to break down.

Examples of Oligopoly

Economics in Action above shows some examples of oligopoly. The dividing line between oligopoly and monopolistic competition is hard to pin down. As a practical matter, we identify oligopoly by looking at concentration ratios, the Herfindahl-Hirschman Index, and information about the geographical scope of the market and barriers to entry. The HHI that divides oligopoly from monopolistic competition is generally taken to be 2,500. An HHI below 2,500 is usually an example of monopolistic competition, and a market in which the HHI exceeds 2,500 is usually an example of oligopoly.

◆ REVIEW QUIZ

1. What are the two distinguishing characteristics of oligopoly?
2. Why are firms in oligopoly interdependent?
3. Why do firms in oligopoly face a temptation to collude?
4. Can you think of some examples of oligopolies that you buy from?

Work these questions in Study Plan 15.1 and get instant feedback. Do a Key Terms Quiz.   MyEconLab

Oligopoly Games

Economists think about oligopoly as a game between two or a few players, and to study oligopoly markets they use game theory. **Game theory** is a set of tools for studying *strategic behavior*—behavior that takes into account the expected behavior of others and the recognition of mutual interdependence. Game theory was invented by John von Neumann in 1937 and extended by von Neumann and Oskar Morgenstern in 1944 (p. 367). Today, it is one of the major research fields in economics.

Game theory seeks to understand oligopoly as well as other forms of economic, political, social, and even biological rivalries by using a method of analysis specifically designed to understand games of all types, including the familiar games of everyday life (see Talking with Thomas Hubbard on p. 368). To lay the foundation for studying oligopoly games, we first think about the features that all games share.

What Is a Game?

What is a game? At first thought, the question seems silly. After all, there are many different games. There are ball games and parlor games, games of chance and games of skill. But what is it about all these different activities that makes them games? What do all these games have in common? All games share four common features:

- Rules
- Strategies
- Payoffs
- Outcome

We're going to look at these features of games by playing a game called "the prisoners' dilemma." The prisoners' dilemma game displays the essential features of many games, including oligopoly games, and it gives a good illustration of how game theory works and generates predictions.

The Prisoners' Dilemma

Art and Bob have been caught red-handed stealing a car. Facing airtight cases, they will receive a sentence of two years each for their crime. During his interviews with the two prisoners, the district attorney begins to suspect that he has stumbled on the two people who were responsible for a multimillion-dollar bank robbery some months earlier. But this is just a suspicion. He has no evidence on which he can convict them of the greater crime unless he can get them to confess. But how can he extract a confession? The answer is by making the prisoners play a game. The district attorney makes the prisoners play the following game.

Rules Each prisoner (player) is placed in a separate room and cannot communicate with the other prisoner. Each is told that he is suspected of having carried out the bank robbery and that

> If both of them confess to the larger crime, each will receive a sentence of 3 years for both crimes.
>
> If he alone confesses and his accomplice does not, he will receive only a 1-year sentence while his accomplice will receive a 10-year sentence.

Strategies In game theory, **strategies** are all the possible actions of each player. Art and Bob each have two possible actions:

1. Confess to the bank robbery.
2. Deny having committed the bank robbery.

Because there are two players, each with two strategies, there are four possible outcomes:

1. Both confess.
2. Both deny.
3. Art confesses and Bob denies.
4. Bob confesses and Art denies.

Payoffs Each prisoner can work out his *payoff* in each of these situations, and we can tabulate the four possible payoffs for each of the prisoners in what is called a payoff matrix for the game. A **payoff matrix** is a table that shows the payoffs for every possible action by each player for every possible action by each other player.

Table 15.1 shows a payoff matrix for Art and Bob. The squares show the payoffs for each prisoner—the red triangle in each square shows Art's and the blue triangle shows Bob's. If both prisoners confess (top left), each gets a prison term of 3 years. If Bob confesses but Art denies (top right), Art gets a 10-year sentence and Bob gets a 1-year sentence. If Art confesses and Bob denies (bottom left), Art gets a 1-year sentence and Bob gets a 10-year sentence. Finally, if both of them deny (bottom right), neither can be convicted of the bank robbery charge but both are sentenced for the car theft—a 2-year sentence.

Outcome The choices of both players determine the outcome of the game. To predict that outcome, we use an equilibrium idea proposed by John Nash of Princeton University (who received the Nobel Prize for Economic Science in 1994 and was the subject of the 2001 movie *A Beautiful Mind*). In **Nash equilibrium**, player *A* takes the best possible action given the action of player *B* and player *B* takes the best possible action given the action of player *A*.

In the case of the prisoners' dilemma, the Nash equilibrium occurs when Art makes his best choice given Bob's choice and when Bob makes his best choice given Art's choice.

To find the Nash equilibrium, we compare all the possible outcomes associated with each choice and eliminate those that are dominated—that are not as good as some other choice. Let's find the Nash equilibrium for the prisoners' dilemma game.

Finding the Nash Equilibrium Look at the situation from Art's point of view. If Bob confesses (top row), Art's best action is to confess because in that case, he is sentenced to 3 years rather than 10 years. If Bob denies (bottom row), Art's best action is still to confess because in that case, he receives 1 year rather than 2 years. So Art's best action is to confess.

Now look at the situation from Bob's point of view. If Art confesses (left column), Bob's best action is to confess because in that case, he is sentenced to 3 years rather than 10 years. If Art denies (right column), Bob's best action is still to confess because in that case, he receives 1 year rather than 2 years. So Bob's best action is to confess.

Because each player's best action is to confess, each does confess, each goes to jail for 3 years, and the district attorney has solved the bank robbery. This is the Nash equilibrium of the game.

The Nash equilibrium for the prisoners' dilemma is called a **dominant-strategy equilibrium**, which is an equilibrium in which the best strategy of each player is to cheat (confess) *regardless of the strategy of the other player*.

The Dilemma The dilemma arises as each prisoner contemplates the consequences of his decision and puts himself in the place of his accomplice. Each knows that it would be best if both denied. But each also knows that if he denies it is in the best interest of the other to confess. So each considers whether to deny and rely on his accomplice to deny or to confess

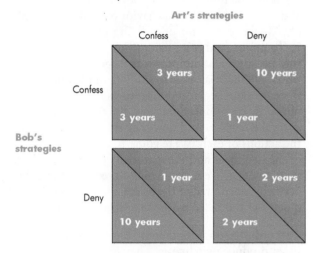

TABLE 15.1 Prisoners' Dilemma Payoff Matrix

Each square shows the payoffs for the two players, Art and Bob, for each possible pair of actions. In each square, the red triangle shows Art's payoff and the blue triangle shows Bob's. For example, if both confess, the payoffs are in the top left square. The equilibrium of the game is for both players to confess and each gets a 3-year sentence.

MyEconLab Animation

hoping that his accomplice denies but expecting him to confess. The dilemma leads to the equilibrium of the game.

A Bad Outcome For the prisoners, the equilibrium of the game, with each confessing, is not the best outcome. If neither of them confesses, each gets only 2 years for the lesser crime. Isn't there some way in which this better outcome can be achieved? It seems that there is not, because the players cannot communicate with each other. Each player can put himself in the other player's place, and so each player can figure out that there is a best strategy for each of them. The prisoners are indeed in a dilemma. Each knows that he can serve 2 years *only* if he can trust the other to deny. But each prisoner also knows that it is *not* in the best interest of the other to deny. So each prisoner knows that he must confess, thereby delivering a bad outcome for both.

The firms in an oligopoly are in a similar situation to Art and Bob in the prisoners' dilemma game. Let's see how we can use this game to understand oligopoly.

An Oligopoly Price-Fixing Game

We can use game theory and a game like the prisoners' dilemma to understand price fixing, price wars, and other aspects of the behavior of firms in oligopoly. We'll begin with a price-fixing game.

To understand price fixing, we're going to study the special case of duopoly—an oligopoly with two firms. Duopoly is easier to study than oligopoly with three or more firms, and it captures the essence of all oligopoly situations. Somehow, the two firms must share the market. And how they share it depends on the actions of each. We're going to describe the costs of the two firms and the market demand for the item they produce. We're then going to see how game theory helps us to predict the prices charged and the quantities produced by the two firms in a duopoly.

Cost and Demand Conditions Two firms, Trick and Gear, produce switchgears. They have identical costs. Figure 15.2(a) shows their average total cost curve (*ATC*) and marginal cost curve (*MC*). Figure 15.2(b) shows the market demand curve for switchgears (*D*). The two firms produce identical switchgears, so one firm's switchgear is a perfect substitute for the other's, and the market price of each firm's product is identical. The quantity demanded depends on that price—the higher the price, the smaller is the quantity demanded.

This industry is a natural duopoly. Two firms can produce this good at a lower cost than either one firm or three firms can. For each firm, average total cost is at its minimum when production is 3,000 units a week. When price equals minimum average total cost, the total quantity demanded is 6,000 units a week, and two firms can just produce that quantity.

Collusion We'll suppose that Trick and Gear enter into a collusive agreement. A **collusive agreement** is an agreement between two (or more) producers to form a cartel to restrict output, raise the price, and increase profits. Such an agreement is illegal in the United States and is undertaken in secret. The firms in a cartel can pursue two startegies:

- Comply
- Cheat

A firm that complies carries out the agreement. A firm that cheats breaks the agreement to its own benefit and to the cost of the other firm.

Because each firm has two strategies, there are four possible combinations of actions for the firms:

1. Both firms comply.
2. Both firms cheat.
3. Trick complies and Gear cheats.
4. Gear complies and Trick cheats.

FIGURE 15.2   Costs and Demand

(a) Individual firm

(b) Industry

The average total cost curve for each firm is *ATC*, and the marginal cost curve is *MC* (part a). Minimum average total cost is $6,000 a unit, and it occurs at a production of 3,000 units a week.

Part (b) shows the market demand curve. At a price of $6,000, the quantity demanded is 6,000 units per week. The two firms can produce this output at the lowest possible average cost. If the market had one firm, it would be profitable for another to enter. If the market had three firms, one would exit. There is room for only two firms in this industry. It is a natural duopoly.

Colluding to Maximize Profits Let's work out the payoffs to the two firms if they collude to make the maximum profit for the cartel by acting like a monopoly. The calculations that the two firms perform are the same calculations that a monopoly performs. (You can refresh your memory of these calculations by looking at Chapter 13, pp. 302–303.) The only thing that the firms in duopoly must do beyond what a monopoly does is to agree on how much of the total output each of them will produce.

Figure 15.3 shows the price and quantity that maximize industry profit for the duopoly. Part (a) shows the situation for each firm, and part (b) shows the situation for the industry as a whole. The curve labeled MR is the industry marginal revenue curve. This marginal revenue curve is like that of a single-price monopoly (Chapter 13, p. 300). The curve labeled MC_I is the industry marginal cost curve if each firm produces the same quantity of output. This curve is constructed by adding together the outputs of the two firms at each level of marginal cost. Because the two firms are the same size, at each level of marginal cost the industry output is twice the output of one firm. The curve MC_I in part (b) is twice as far to the right as the curve MC in part (a).

To maximize industry profit, the firms in the duopoly agree to restrict output to the rate that makes the industry marginal cost and marginal revenue equal. That output rate, as shown in part (b), is 4,000 units a week. The demand curve shows that the

highest price for which the 4,000 switchgears can be sold is $9,000 each. Trick and Gear agree to charge this price.

To hold the price at $9,000 a unit, production must be 4,000 units a week. So Trick and Gear must agree on output rates for each of them that total 4,000 units a week. Let's suppose that they agree to split the market equally so that each firm produces 2,000 switchgears a week. Because the firms are identical, this division is the most likely.

The average total cost (ATC) of producing 2,000 switchgears a week is $8,000, so the profit per unit is $1,000 and economic profit is $2 million (2,000 units × $1,000 per unit). The economic profit of each firm is represented by the blue rectangle in Fig. 15.3(a).

We have just described one possible outcome for a duopoly game: The two firms collude to produce the monopoly profit-maximizing output and divide that output equally between themselves. From the industry point of view, this solution is identical to a monopoly. A duopoly that operates in this way is indistinguishable from a monopoly. The economic profit that is made by a monopoly is the maximum total profit that can be made by the duopoly when the firms collude.

But with price greater than marginal cost, either firm might think of trying to increase profit by cheating on the agreement and producing more than the agreed amount. Let's see what happens if one of the firms does cheat in this way.

FIGURE 15.3   Colluding to Make Monopoly Profits

(a) Individual firm   (b) Industry

The industry marginal cost curve, MC_I in part (b), is the horizontal sum of the two firms' marginal cost curves, MC in part (a). The industry marginal revenue curve is MR. To maximize profit, the firms produce 4,000 units a week (the quantity at which marginal revenue equals marginal cost). They sell that output for $9,000 a unit. Each firm produces 2,000 units a week. Average total cost is $8,000 a unit, so each firm makes an economic profit of $2 million (blue rectangle)—2,000 units multiplied by $1,000 profit a unit.

One Firm Cheats on a Collusive Agreement To set the stage for cheating on their agreement, Trick convinces Gear that demand has decreased and that it cannot sell 2,000 units a week. Trick tells Gear that it plans to cut its price so that it can sell the agreed 2,000 units each week. Because the two firms produce an identical product, Gear matches Trick's price cut but still produces only 2,000 units a week.

In fact, there has been no decrease in demand. Trick plans to increase output, which it knows will lower the price, and Trick wants to ensure that Gear's output remains at the agreed level.

Figure 15.4 illustrates the consequences of Trick's cheating. Part (a) shows Gear (the complier); part (b) shows Trick (the cheat); and part (c) shows the industry as a whole. Suppose that Trick increases output to 3,000 units a week. If Gear sticks to the agreement to produce only 2,000 units a week, total output is now 5,000 a week, and given demand in part (c), the price falls to $7,500 a unit.

Gear continues to produce 2,000 units a week at a cost of $8,000 a unit and incurs a loss of $500 a unit, or $1 million a week. This economic loss is shown by the red rectangle in part (a). Trick produces 3,000 units a week at a cost of $6,000 a unit. With a price

of $7,500, Trick makes a profit of $1,500 a unit and therefore an economic profit of $4.5 million. This economic profit is the blue rectangle in part (b).

We've now described a second possible outcome for the duopoly game: One of the firms cheats on the collusive agreement. In this case, the industry output is larger than the monopoly output and the industry price is lower than the monopoly price. The total economic profit made by the industry is also smaller than the monopoly's economic profit. Trick (the cheat) makes an economic profit of $4.5 million, and Gear (the complier) incurs an economic loss of $1 million. The industry makes an economic profit of $3.5 million. This industry profit is $0.5 million less than the economic profit that a monopoly would make, but it is distributed unevenly. Trick makes a bigger economic profit than it would under the collusive agreement, while Gear incurs an economic loss.

A similar outcome would arise if Gear cheated and Trick complied with the agreement. The industry profit and price would be the same, but in this case, Gear (the cheat) would make an economic profit of $4.5 million and Trick (the complier) would incur an economic loss of $1 million.

Let's next see what happens if both firms cheat.

FIGURE 15.4   One Firm Cheats

(a) Complier   **(b) Cheat**   **(c) Industry**

One firm, shown in part (a), complies with the agreement and produces 2,000 units. The other firm, shown in part (b), cheats on the agreement and increases its output to 3,000 units a week. Given the market demand curve, shown in part (c), and with a total production of 5,000 units a week,

the price falls to $7,500 a unit. At this price, the complier in part (a) incurs an economic loss of $1 million ($500 per unit × 2,000 units), shown by the red rectangle. In part (b), the cheat makes an economic profit of $4.5 million ($1,500 per unit × 3,000 units), shown by the blue rectangle.

Both Firms Cheat Suppose that both firms cheat and that each firm behaves like the cheating firm that we have just analyzed. Each tells the other that it is unable to sell its output at the going price and that it plans to cut its price. But because both firms cheat, each will propose a successively lower price. As long as price exceeds marginal cost, each firm has an incentive to increase its production—to cheat. Only when price equals marginal cost is there no further incentive to cheat. This situation arises when the price has reached $6,000. At this price, marginal cost equals price. Also, price equals minimum average total cost. At a price less than $6,000, each firm incurs an economic loss. At a price of $6,000, each firm covers all its costs and makes zero economic profit. Also, at a price of $6,000, each firm wants to produce 3,000 units a week, so the industry output is 6,000 units a week. Given the demand conditions, 6,000 units can be sold at a price of $6,000 each.

Figure 15.5 illustrates the situation just described. Each firm, in part (a), produces 3,000 units a week, and its average total cost is a minimum ($6,000 per unit). The market as a whole, in part (b), operates at the point at which the market demand curve (D) intersects the industry marginal cost curve (MC_I). Each firm has lowered its price and increased its output to try to gain an advantage over the other firm. Each has pushed this process as far as it can without incurring an economic loss.

We have now described a third possible outcome of this duopoly game: Both firms cheat. If both firms

cheat on the collusive agreement, the output of each firm is 3,000 units a week and the price is $6,000 a unit. Each firm makes zero economic profit.

The Payoff Matrix Now that we have described the strategies and payoffs in the duopoly game, we can summarize the strategies and the payoffs in the form of the game's payoff matrix. Then we can find the Nash equilibrium.

Table 15.2 sets out the payoff matrix for this game. It is constructed in the same way as the payoff matrix for the prisoners' dilemma in Table 15.1. The squares show the payoffs for the two firms—Gear and Trick. In this case, the payoffs are profits. (For the prisoners' dilemma, the payoffs were losses.)

The table shows that if both firms cheat (top left), they achieve the perfectly competitive outcome— each firm makes zero economic profit. If both firms comply (bottom right), the industry makes the monopoly profit and each firm makes an economic profit of $2 million. The top right and bottom left squares show the payoff if one firm cheats while the other complies. The firm that cheats makes an economic profit of $4.5 million, and the one that complies incurs a loss of $1 million.

Nash Equilibrium in the Duopolists' Dilemma The duopolists have a dilemma like the prisoners' dilemma. Do they comply or cheat? To answer this question, we must find the Nash equilibrium.

FIGURE 15.5 Both Firms Cheat

(a) Individual firm   (b) Industry

If both firms cheat by increasing production, the collusive agreement collapses. The limit to the collapse is the competitive equilibrium. Neither firm will cut its price below $6,000 (minimum average total cost) because to do so will result in losses. In part (a), each firm produces 3,000 units a week at an average total cost of $6,000. In part (b), with a total production of 6,000 units, the price falls to $6,000. Each firm now makes zero economic profit. This output and price are the ones that would prevail in a competitive industry.

TABLE 15.2   Duopoly Payoff Matrix

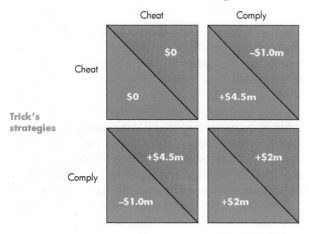

Each square shows the payoffs from a pair of actions. For example, if both firms comply with the collusive agreement, the payoffs are recorded in the bottom right square. The red triangle shows Gear's payoff, and the blue triangle shows Trick's. In Nash equilibrium, both firms cheat.

—— MyEconLab Animation ——

Look at things from Gear's point of view. Gear reasons as follows: Suppose that Trick cheats. If I comply, I will incur an economic loss of $1 million. If I also cheat, I will make zero economic profit. Zero is better than *minus* $1 million, so I'm better off if I cheat. Now suppose Trick complies. If I cheat, I will make an economic profit of $4.5 million, and if I comply, I will make an economic profit of $2 million. A $4.5 million profit is better than a $2 million profit, so I'm better off if I cheat. So regardless of whether Trick cheats or complies, it pays Gear to cheat. Cheating is Gear's best strategy.

Trick comes to the same conclusion as Gear because the two firms face an identical situation. So both firms cheat. The Nash equilibrium of the duopoly game is that both firms cheat. And although the industry has only two firms, they charge the same price and produce the same quantity as those in a competitive industry. Also, as in perfect competition, each firm makes zero economic profit.

Economics in Action (on this page) and *Economics in the News* (p. 353) look at some other prisoners' dilemma games. But not all games are prisoners' dilemmas, as you'll now see.

ECONOMICS IN ACTION
A Game in the Market for Tissues

Anti-Viral Kleenex and Puffs Plus Lotion didn't get developed because Kimberly-Clark (Kleenex) and P&G (Puffs) were thinking about helping you cope with a miserable cold. These new-style tissues and other innovations in the quality of facial tissues are the product of a costly research and development (R&D) game.

The table below illustrates the game (with hypothetical numbers). Each firm can spend either $25 million or nothing on R&D. If neither firm spends, Kimberly-Clark makes an economic profit of $70 million and P&G of $30 million (bottom right). If each firm spends on R&D, Kimberly-Clark's economic profit is $45 million and P&G's is $5 million (top left). The other parts of the matrix show the economic profits for each when one spends on R&D and the other doesn't.

Confronted with these payoffs, Kimberly-Clark sees that it gets a bigger profit if it spends on R&D regardless of what P&G does. P&G reaches the same conclusion: It, too, gets a bigger profit by spending on R&D regardless of what Kimberly-Clark does.

Because R&D is the best strategy for both players, it is the Nash equilibrium—a *dominant-strategy Nash equilibrium*.

The outcome of this game is that both firms conduct R&D. They make less profit than they would if they could collude to achieve the cooperative outcome of no R&D. But you get a better Kleenex or Puffs tissue.

Kleenex Versus Puffs: An R&D Game

A Game of Chicken

The Nash equilibrium for the prisoners' dilemma is unique: both players cheat (confess). Not all games have a unique equilibrium, and one that doesn't is a game called "chicken."

An Example of the Game of Chicken A graphic, if disturbing, version of "chicken" has two cars racing toward each other. The first driver to swerve and avoid a crash is the "chicken." The payoffs are a big loss for both if no one "chickens out;" zero for both if both "chicken out;" and zero for the chicken and a gain for the one who stays the course. If player 1 swerves, player 2's best strategy is to stay the course; and if player 1 stays the course, player 2's best strategy is to swerve.

An Economic Example of Chicken An economic game of chicken can arise when research and development (R&D) creates a new technology that cannot be kept secret or patented, so both firms benefit from the R&D of either firm. The chicken in this case is the firm that does the R&D.

Suppose, for example, that either Apple or Nokia spends $9 million developing a new touch-screen technology that both would end up being able to use regardless of which of them developed it.

Table 15.3 illustrates a payoff matrix for the game that Apple and Nokia play. Each firm has two strategies: Do the R&D ("chicken out") or do not do the R&D. Each entry shows the additional profit (the profit from the new technology minus the cost of the research), given the strategies adopted.

If neither firm does the R&D, each makes zero additional profit. If both firms conduct the R&D, each firm makes an additional $5 million. If one of the firms does the R&D ("chickens out"), the chicken makes $1 million and the other firm makes $10 million. Confronted with these payoffs the two firms calculate their best strategies. Nokia is better off doing R&D if Apple does no R&D. Apple is better off doing R&D if Nokia does no R&D. There are two Nash equilibrium outcomes: Only one of them does the R&D, but we can't predict which one.

You can see that an outcome with no firm doing R&D isn't a Nash equilibrium because one firm would be better off doing it. Also both firms doing R&D isn't a Nash equilibrium because one firm would be better off *not* doing it. To decide *which* firm does the R&D, the firms might toss a coin, called a mixed strategy.

TABLE 15.3 An R&D Game of Chicken

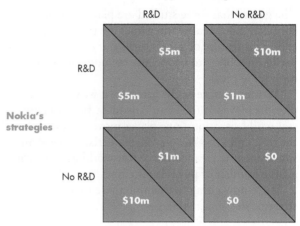

If neither firm does the R&D, their payoffs are in the bottom right square. When one firm "chickens out" and does the R&D while the other does no R&D, their payoffs are in the top right and bottom left squares. When both "chicken out" and do the R&D, the payoffs are in the top left square. The red triangle shows Apple's payoff, and the blue triangle shows Nokia's. The equilibrium for this R&D game of chicken is for only one firm to undertake the R&D. We cannot tell which firm will do the R&D and which will not.

◆ REVIEW QUIZ

1 What are the common features of all games?
2 Describe the prisoners' dilemma game and explain why the Nash equilibrium delivers a bad outcome for both players.
3 Why does a collusive agreement to restrict output and raise the price create a game like the prisoners' dilemma?
4 What creates an incentive for firms in a collusive agreement to cheat and increase output?
5 What is the equilibrium strategy for each firm in a duopolists' dilemma and why do the firms not succeed in colluding to raise the price and profits?
6 Describe the payoffs for an R&D game of chicken and contrast them with the payoffs in a prisoners' dilemma game.

Work these questions in Study Plan 15.2 and get instant feedback. Do a Key Terms Quiz.   MyEconLab

Repeated Games and Sequential Games

The games that we've studied are played just once. In contrast, many real-world games are played repeatedly. This feature of games turns out to enable real-world duopolists to cooperate, collude, and make a monopoly profit.

Another feature of the games that we've studied is that the players move simultaneously. But in many real-world situations, one player moves first and then the other moves—the play is sequential rather than simultaneous. This feature of real-world games creates a large number of possible outcomes.

We're now going to examine these two aspects of strategic decision making.

A Repeated Duopoly Game

If two firms play a game repeatedly, one firm has the opportunity to penalize the other for previous "bad" behavior. If Gear cheats this week, perhaps Trick will cheat next week. Before Gear cheats this week, won't it consider the possibility that Trick will cheat next week? What is the equilibrium of this game?

Actually, there is more than one possibility. One is the Nash equilibrium that we have just analyzed. Both players cheat, and each makes zero economic profit forever. In such a situation, it will never pay one of the players to start complying unilaterally because to do so would result in a loss for that player and a profit for the other. But a **cooperative equilibrium** in which the players make and share the monopoly profit is possible.

A cooperative equilibrium might occur if cheating is punished. There are two extremes of punishment. The smallest penalty is called "tit for tat." A *tit-for-tat strategy* is one in which a player cooperates in the current period if the other player cooperated in the previous period, but cheats in the current period if the other player cheated in the previous period. The most severe form of punishment is called a trigger strategy. A *trigger strategy* is one in which a player cooperates if the other player cooperates but plays the Nash equilibrium strategy forever thereafter if the other player cheats.

In the duopoly game between Gear and Trick, a tit-for-tat strategy keeps both players cooperating and making monopoly profits. Let's see why with an example.

Table 15.4 shows the economic profit that Trick and Gear will make over a number of periods under two alternative sequences of events: colluding and cheating with a tit-for-tat response by the other firm.

If both firms stick to the collusive agreement in period 1, each makes an economic profit of $2 million. Suppose that Trick contemplates cheating in period 1. The cheating produces a quick $4.5 million economic profit and inflicts a $1 million economic loss on Gear. But a cheat in period 1 produces a response from Gear in period 2. If Trick wants to get back into a profit-making situation, it must return to the agreement in period 2 even though it knows that Gear will punish it for cheating in period 1. So in period 2, Gear punishes Trick and Trick cooperates. Gear now makes an economic profit of $4.5 million, and Trick incurs an economic loss of $1 million. Adding up the profits over two periods of play, Trick would have made more profit by cooperating—$4 million compared with $3.5 million.

What is true for Trick is also true for Gear. Because each firm makes a larger profit by sticking with the collusive agreement, both firms do so and the monopoly price, quantity, and profit prevail.

In reality, whether a cartel works like a one-play game or a repeated game depends primarily on the

TABLE 15.4   Cheating with Punishment

Period of play	Collude		Cheat with tit-for-tat	
	Trick's profit	Gear's profit	Trick's profit	Gear's profit
	(millions of dollars)		(millions of dollars)	
1	2	2	4.5	−1.0
2	2	2	−1.0	4.5
3	2	2	2.0	2.0
4	⋮	⋮	⋮	⋮

If duopolists repeatedly collude, each makes a profit of $2 million per period of play. If one player cheats in period 1, the other player plays a tit-for-tat strategy and cheats in period 2. The profit from cheating can be made for only one period and must be paid for in the next period by incurring a loss. Over two periods of play, the best that a duopolist can achieve by cheating is a profit of $3.5 million, compared to an economic profit of $4 million by colluding.

ECONOMICS IN THE NEWS

Airbus Versus Boeing

Boeing Strikes Back in Single-Aisle Market

Airbus and Boeing are in fierce competition in the narrow-body passenger jet market. Airbus got moving first with its A320neo for which it has 1,400 orders. Boeing responded with the 737 Max for which it had 549 orders in mid-2012 and an aim for 1,000 orders by the end of 2012.

Boeing rejected suggestions that it was in a price war with Airbus over the A320neo and 737 Max but confirmed it would woo some airline customers of its European rival.

Source: *Financial Times*, July 9, 2012

SOME DATA

Aircraft	List price
Airbus Neo	$96.7 million
Boeing Max	$96.0 million

ASSUMPTIONS

- Assume that the performance and operating costs of the A320neo and the Max are identical.
- At list prices, Airbus and Boeing can get another 200 orders each and make $2 billion each in economic profit.
- At discounted prices, Airbus and Boeing can get another 225 orders each and make $1 billion each in economic profit.
- If one of them holds the list price and the other discounts, the discounter can get 450 new orders and make $3 billion and the other will get no new orders.

THE QUESTIONS

- In what type of market are Airbus and Boeing competing?
- How did moving first benefit Airbus?
- Given the assumptions above, will the airplane producers discount their prices or stick to the list prices? To answer this question, set out the payoff matrix for the game that Airbus and Boeing are playing and find the Nash equilibrium.
- If the game could be played repeatedly, how might the strategies and equilibrium change?

THE ANSWERS

- Airbus and Boeing are a duopoly.
- By moving first, Airbus had a temporary monopoly and was able to grab a large market share.

- The table illustrates the payoff matrix for the game between Airbus and Boeing.
- The outcome is a dominant-strategy Nash equilibrium. Both firms discount their prices and get 225 new orders each. If one firm held the list price, the other would discount and take the 450 new orders.
- If the game could be played repeatedly, the discounter could be punished and a cooperative equilibrium would arise in which neither discounts.

Airbus' strategies

	Discount	List
Discount	225 / $1b (Airbus) 225 / $1b (Boeing)	0 / $0 (Airbus) 450 / $3b (Boeing)
List	450 / $3b (Airbus) 0 / $0 (Boeing)	200 / $2b (Airbus) 200 / $2b (Boeing)

Boeing's strategies

Duopoly Game: Market for Airplanes

Are the A320neo and Max in a price war?

number of players and the ease of detecting and punishing cheating. The larger the number of players, the harder it is to maintain a cartel.

Games and Price Wars A repeated duopoly game can help us understand real-world behavior and, in particular, price wars. Some price wars can be interpreted as the implementation of a tit-for-tat strategy. But the game is a bit more complicated than the one we've looked at because the players are uncertain about the demand for the product.

Playing a tit-for-tat strategy, firms have an incentive to stick to the monopoly price. But fluctuations in demand lead to fluctuations in the monopoly price, and sometimes, when the price changes, it might seem to one of the firms that the price has fallen because the other has cheated. In this case, a price war will break out. The price war will end only when each firm is satisfied that the other is ready to cooperate again. There will be cycles of price wars and the restoration of collusive agreements. Fluctuations in the world price of oil might be interpreted in this way.

Some price wars arise from the entry of a small number of firms into an industry that had previously been a monopoly. Although the industry has a small number of firms, the firms are in a prisoners' dilemma and they cannot impose effective penalties for price cutting. The behavior of prices and outputs in the computer chip industry during 1995 and 1996 can be explained in this way. Until 1995, the market for Pentium chips for IBM-compatible computers was dominated by one firm, Intel Corporation, which was able to make maximum economic profit by producing the quantity of chips at which marginal cost equaled marginal revenue. The price of Intel's chips was set to ensure that the quantity demanded equaled the quantity produced. Then in 1995 and 1996, with the entry of a small number of new firms, the industry became an oligopoly. If the firms had maintained Intel's price and shared the market, together they could have made economic profits equal to Intel's profit. But the firms were in a prisoners' dilemma, so prices fell toward the competitive level.

Let's now study a sequential game. There are many such games, and the one we'll examine is among the simplest. It has an interesting implication and it will give you the flavor of this type of game. The sequential game that we'll study is an entry game in a contestable market.

A Sequential Entry Game in a Contestable Market

If two firms play a sequential game, one firm makes a decision at the first stage of the game and the other makes a decision at the second stage.

We're going to study a sequential game in a **contestable market**—a market in which firms can enter and leave so easily that firms in the market face competition from *potential* entrants. Examples of contestable markets are routes served by airlines and by barge companies that operate on the major waterways. These markets are contestable because firms could enter if an opportunity for economic profit arose and could exit with no penalty if the opportunity for economic profit disappeared.

If the Herfindahl-Hirschman Index (p. 234) is used to determine the degree of competition, a contestable market appears to be uncompetitive. But a contestable market can behave as if it were perfectly competitive. To see why, let's look at an entry game for a contestable air route.

A Contestable Air Route Agile Air is the only firm operating on a particular route. Demand and cost conditions are such that there is room for only one airline to operate. Wanabe Inc. is another airline that could offer services on the route.

We describe the structure of a sequential game by using a *game tree* like that in Fig. 15.6. At the first stage, Agile Air must set a price. Once the price is set and advertised, Agile can't change it. That is, once set, Agile's price is fixed and Agile can't react to Wanabe's entry decision. Agile can set its price at either the monopoly level or the competitive level.

At the second stage, Wanabe must decide whether to enter or to stay out. Customers have no loyalty (there are no frequent-flyer programs) and they buy from the lowest-price firm. So if Wanabe enters, it sets a price just below Agile's and takes all the business.

Figure 15.6 shows the payoffs from the various decisions (Agile's in the red triangles and Wanabe's in the blue triangles).

To decide on its price, Agile's CEO reasons as follows: Suppose that Agile sets the monopoly price. If Wanabe enters, it earns 90 (think of all payoff numbers as thousands of dollars). If Wanabe stays out, it earns nothing. So Wanabe will enter. In this case Agile will lose 50.

Now suppose that Agile sets the competitive price. If Wanabe stays out, it earns nothing, and if it enters,

FIGURE 15.6 Agile Versus Wanabe: A Sequential Entry Game in a Contestable Market

If Agile sets the monopoly price, Wanabe makes 90 (thousand dollars) by entering and earns nothing by staying out. So if Agile sets the monopoly price, Wanabe enters.

If Agile sets the competitive price, Wanabe earns nothing if it stays out and incurs a loss if it enters. So if Agile sets the competitive price, Wanabe stays out.

━━━━━ MyEconLab Animation ━━━━━

it loses 10, so Wanabe will stay out. In this case, Agile will make zero economic profit.

Agile's best strategy is to set its price at the competitive level and make zero economic profit. The option of earning 100 by setting the monopoly price with Wanabe staying out is not available to Agile. If Agile sets the monopoly price, Wanabe enters, undercuts Agile, and takes all the business.

In this example, Agile sets its price at the competitive level and makes zero economic profit. A less costly strategy, called **limit pricing**, sets the price at the highest level that inflicts a loss on the entrant. Any loss is big enough to deter entry, so it is not always necessary to set the price as low as the competitive price. In the example of Agile and Wanabe, at the competitive price, Wanabe incurs a loss of 10 if it enters. A smaller loss would still keep Wanabe out.

This game is interesting because it points to the possibility of a monopoly behaving like a competitive industry and serving the social interest without regulation. But the result is not general and depends on one crucial feature of the setup of the game: At the second stage, Agile is locked in to the price set at the first stage.

If Agile could change its price in the second stage, it would want to set the monopoly price if Wanabe stayed out—100 with the monopoly price beats zero with the competitive price. But Wanabe can figure out what Agile would do, so the price set at the first stage

has no effect on Wanabe. Agile sets the monopoly price and Wanabe might either stay out or enter.

We've looked at two of the many possible repeated and sequential games, and you've seen how these types of games can provide insights into the complex forces that determine prices and profits.

> ### ◆ REVIEW QUIZ
>
> 1 If a prisoners' dilemma game is played repeatedly, what punishment strategies might the players employ and how does playing the game repeatedly change the equilibrium?
>
> 2 If a market is contestable, how does the equilibrium differ from that of a monopoly?
>
> Work these questions in Study Plan 15.3 and get instant feedback. Do a Key Terms Quiz.   MyEconLab

So far, we've studied oligopoly with unregulated market power. Firms like Trick and Gear are free to collude to maximize their profit with no concern for the consumer or the law.

But when firms collude to achieve the monopoly outcome, they also have the same effects on efficiency and the social interest as monopoly. Profit is made at the expense of consumer surplus and a deadweight loss arises. Your next task is to see how U.S. antitrust law limits market power.

▶ Antitrust Law

Antitrust law is the law that regulates oligopolies and prevents them from becoming monopolies or behaving like monopolies. Two government agencies cooperate to enforce the antitrust laws: the Federal Trade Commission and the Antitrust Division of the U.S. Department of Justice.

The Antitrust Laws

The United States has two main antitrust laws:

- The Sherman Act, 1890
- The Clayton Act, 1914

The Sherman Act The Sherman Act made it a felony to create or attempt to create a monopoly or a cartel.

During the 1880s, lawmakers and the general public were outraged and disgusted by the practices of some of the big-name leaders of American business. The actions of J.P. Morgan, John D. Rockefeller, and W.H. Vanderbilt led to them being called the "robber barons." It turns out that the most lurid stories of the actions of these great American capitalists were not of their creation of monopoly power to exploit consumers but of their actions to damage each other.

Nevertheless, monopolies that damaged the consumer interest did emerge. For example, John D. Rockefeller had a virtual monopoly in the market for oil.

Table 15.5 summarizes the two main provisions of the Sherman Act. Section 1 of the act is precise:

TABLE 15.5   The Sherman Act of 1890

Section 1:

Every contract, combination in the form of trust or otherwise, or conspiracy, in restraint of trade or commerce among the several States, or with foreign nations, is hereby declared to be illegal.

Section 2:

Every person who shall monopolize, or attempt to monopolize, or combine or conspire with any other person or persons, to monopolize any part of the trade or commerce among the several States, or with foreign nations, shall be deemed guilty of a felony.

Conspiring with others to restrict competition is illegal. But Section 2 is general and imprecise. Just what is an "attempt to monopolize"?

The Clayton Act The Clayton Act, which was passed in response to a wave of mergers that occurred at the beginning of the twentieth century, provided the answer to the question left dangling by the Sherman Act: It defined the "attempt to monopolize." The Clayton Act supplemented the Sherman Act and strengthened and clarified the antitrust law.

When Congress passed the Clayton Act, it also established the Federal Trade Commission, the federal agency charged with the task of preventing monopoly practices that damage the consumer interest.

Two amendments to the Clayton Act—the Robinson-Patman Act of 1936 and the Celler-Kefauver Act of 1950—outlaw specific practices and provide even greater precision to the antitrust law. Table 15.6 describes these practices and summarizes the main provisions of these three acts.

TABLE 15.6   The Clayton Act and Its Amendments

Clayton Act	**1914**
Robinson-Patman Act	**1936**
Celler-Kefauver Act	**1950**

These acts prohibit the following practices *only if* they substantially lessen competition or create monopoly:

1. Price discrimination

2. Contracts that require other goods to be bought from the same firm (called *tying arrangements*)

3. Contracts that require a firm to buy all its requirements of a particular item from a single firm (called *requirements contracts*)

4. Contracts that prevent a firm from selling competing items (called *exclusive dealing*)

5. Contracts that prevent a buyer from reselling a product outside a specified area (called *territorial confinement*)

6. Acquiring a competitor's shares or assets

7. Becoming a director of a competing firm

Price Fixing Always Illegal

Colluding with competitors to fix the price is *always* a violation of the antitrust law. If the Justice Department can prove the existence of a price fixing cartel, also called a *horizontal price fixing agreement*, defendants can offer no acceptable excuse.

The predictions of the effects of price fixing that you saw in the previous sections of this chapter provide the reasons for the unqualified attitude toward price fixing. A duopoly cartel can maximize profit and behave like a monopoly. To achieve the monopoly outcome, the cartel restricts production and fixes the price at the monopoly level. The consumer suffers because consumer surplus shrinks. And the outcome is inefficient because a deadweight loss arises.

It is for these reasons that the law declares that all price fixing is illegal. No excuse can justify the practice.

Other practices raise antitrust concerns but are more controversial and generate debate among lawyers and economists. We'll examine three of these practices.

Three Antitrust Policy Debates

Some practices that engender antitrust policy debate are

- Resale price maintenance
- Tying arrangements
- Predatory pricing

Resale Price Maintenance Most manufacturers sell their products to the final consumer indirectly through a wholesale and retail distribution system. **Resale price maintenance** occurs when a distributor agrees with a manufacturer to resell a product *at or above a specified minimum price*.

A resale price maintenance agreement, also called a *vertical price fixing agreement*, is *not* illegal under the Sherman Act provided it is not anticompetitive. Nor is it illegal for a manufacturer to refuse to supply a retailer who doesn't accept guidance on what the minimum price should be.

In 2007, the Supreme Court ruled that a handbag manufacturer could impose a minimum retail price on a Dallas store, Kay's Kloset. Since that ruling, many manufacturers have imposed minimum retail prices. The practice is judged on a case-by-case basis.

Does resale price maintenance create an inefficient or efficient use of resources? Economists can be found on both sides of this question.

Inefficient Resale Price Maintenance Resale price maintenance is inefficient if it enables dealers to charge the monopoly price. By setting and enforcing the resale price, the manufacturer might be able to achieve the monopoly price.

Efficient Resale Price Maintenance Resale price maintenance might be efficient if it enables a manufacturer to induce dealers to provide the efficient standard of service. Suppose that SilkySkin wants shops to demonstrate the use of its new unbelievable moisturizing cream in an inviting space. With resale price maintenance, SilkySkin can offer all the retailers the same incentive and compensation. Without resale price maintenance, a cut-price drug store might offer SilkySkin products at a low price. Buyers would then have an incentive to visit a high-price shop for a product demonstration and then buy from the low-price shop. The low-price shop would be a free rider (like the consumer of a public good in Chapter 16, p. 374), and an inefficient level of service would be provided.

SilkySkin could pay a fee to retailers that provide good service and leave the resale price to be determined by the competitive forces of supply and demand. But it might be too costly for SilkySkin to monitor shops and ensure that they provide the desired level of service.

Tying Arrangements A **tying arrangement** is an agreement to sell one product only if the buyer agrees to buy another, different product. With tying, the only way the buyer can get the one product is to also buy the other product. Microsoft has been accused of tying Internet Explorer and Windows. Textbook publishers sometimes tie a Web site and a textbook and force students to buy both. (You can't buy the book you're now reading, new, without the Web site. But you can buy the Web site access without the book, so these products are not tied.)

Could textbook publishers make more money by tying a book and access to a Web site? The answer is sometimes but not always. Suppose that you and other students are willing to pay $80 for a book and $20 for access to a Web site. The publisher can sell these items separately for these prices or bundled for $100. The publisher does not gain from bundling.

But now suppose that you and only half of the students are willing to pay $80 for a book and $20 for a Web site and the other half of the students are willing to pay $80 for a Web site and $20 for a book. Now if the two items are sold separately, the publisher can charge $80 for the book and $80 for the Web site. Half the students buy the book but not the Web site, and the other half buy the Web site but not the book. But if the book and Web site are bundled for $100, everyone buys the bundle and the publisher makes an extra $20 per student. In this case, bundling has enabled the publisher to price discriminate.

There is no simple, clear-cut test of whether a firm is engaging in tying or whether, by doing so, it has increased its market power and profit and created inefficiency.

Predatory Pricing **Predatory pricing** is setting a low price to drive competitors out of business with the intention of setting a monopoly price when the competition has gone. John D. Rockefeller's Standard Oil Company was the first to be accused of this practice in the 1890s, and it has been claimed often in antitrust cases since then. Predatory pricing is an attempt to create a monopoly and as such it is illegal under Section 2 of the Sherman Act.

It is easy to see that predatory pricing is an idea, not a reality. Economists are skeptical that predatory pricing occurs. They point out that a firm that cuts its price below the profit-maximizing level loses during the low-price period. Even if it succeeds in driving its competitors out of business, new competitors will enter as soon as the price is increased, so any potential gain from a monopoly position is temporary. A high and certain loss is a poor exchange for a temporary and uncertain gain. No case of predatory pricing has been definitively found.

ECONOMICS IN ACTION

The United States Versus Microsoft

In 1998, the Antitrust Division of the U.S. Department of Justice along with the Departments of Justice of a number of states charged Microsoft, the world's largest producer of software for personal computers, with violations of both sections of the Sherman Act.

A 78-day trial followed that pitched two prominent MIT economics professors against each other, Franklin Fisher for the government and Richard Schmalensee for Microsoft.

The Case Against Microsoft The claims against Microsoft were that it

- Possessed monopoly power.
- Used predatory pricing and tying arrangements.
- Used other anticompetitive practices.

It was claimed that with 80 percent of the market for PC operating systems, Microsoft had excessive monopoly power. This monopoly power arose from two barriers to entry: economies of scale and network economies. Microsoft's average total cost falls as production increases (economies of scale) because the fixed cost of developing an operating system such as Windows is large while the marginal cost of producing one copy of Windows is small. Further, as the number of Windows users increases, the range of Windows applications expands (network economies), so a potential competitor would need to produce not only a competing operating system but also an entire range of supporting applications as well.

When Microsoft entered the Web browser market with its Internet Explorer, it offered the browser for a zero price. This price was viewed as predatory pricing. Microsoft integrated Internet Explorer with Windows so that anyone who uses this operating system would not need a separate browser such as Netscape Navigator. Microsoft's competitors claimed that this practice was an illegal tying arrangement.

Microsoft's Response Microsoft challenged all these claims. It said that Windows was vulnerable to competition from other operating systems such as Linux and Apple's Mac OS and that there was a permanent threat of competition from new entrants.

Microsoft claimed that integrating Internet Explorer with Windows provided a single, unified product of greater consumer value like a refrigerator with a chilled water dispenser or an automobile with a CD player.

The Outcome The court agreed that Microsoft was in violation of the Sherman Act and ordered that it be broken into two firms: an operating systems producer and an applications producer. Microsoft successfully appealed this order. In the final judgment, though, Microsoft was ordered to disclose to other software developers details of how its operating system works, so that they could compete effectively against Microsoft. In the summer of 2002, Microsoft began to comply with this order.

ECONOMICS IN ACTION

No Cellphone Service Merger

The FTC used its HHI guidelines (summarized in the figure) to block a proposed merger in the market for cellphone service. In 2011, AT&T wanted to buy T-Mobile from the German Deutsch Telecommunication. But the market for cellphone service is highly concentrated. Verizon is the largest service provider with close to 40 percent of the market share. AT&T has a 30 percent share and Sprint and T-Mobile about 12 percent each. Another 14 small firms share the remaining market. So the four largest firms in this market have a 94 percent market share. The HHI is around 2,800.

The figure shows how the HHI would have changed with the merger of AT&T and T-Mobile. It would have increased the HHI by around 700 points. With an HHI of 2,800 and an increase of 700, there was a presumption that the merger would give AT&T too much market power, so the FTC decided to block it.

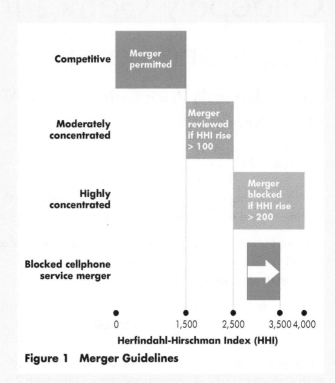

Figure 1   Merger Guidelines

Mergers and Acquisitions

Mergers, which occur when two or more firms agree to combine to create one larger firm, and *acquisitions*, which occur when one firm buys another firm, are common events. Mergers occurred when Chrysler and the German auto producer Daimler-Benz combined to form DaimlerChrysler and when the Belgian beer producer InBev bought the U.S. brewing giant Anheuser-Busch and created a new combined company, Anheuser-Busch InBev. An acquisition occurred when Rupert Murdoch's News Corp bought Myspace.

The mergers and acquisitions that occur don't create a monopoly. But two (or more) firms might be tempted to try to merge so that they can gain market power and operate like a monopoly. If such a situation arises, the Federal Trade Commission (FTC) takes an interest in the move and stands ready to block the merger. To determine which mergers it will examine and possibly block, the FTC uses guidelines, one of which is the Herfindahl-Hirschman Index (HHI) (see Chapter 10, pp. 234–235).

A market in which the HHI is less than 1,500 is regarded as competitive. An index between 1,500 and 2,500 indicates a moderately concentrated market, and a merger in this market that would increase the index by 100 points is challenged by the FTC. An index above 2,500 indicates a concentrated market, and a merger in this market that would increase the index by 200 points is generally blocked. You can see an application of these guidelines in *Economics in Action* above.

◆ Oligopoly is a market structure that you often encounter in your daily life. *Economics in the News* on pp. 360–361 looks at a game played in the market for cellphone service.

Oligopoly Games in Cellphone Service

AT&T Extends Price Cuts in Battle With T-Mobile for Data Users

Bloomberg
March 8, 2014

AT&T is cutting mobile-phone subscription charges for the second time in two months, seeking to hold on to smartphone customers amid a price war with T-Mobile.

Starting tomorrow, AT&T customers can sign up for a Shared Value plan with 2 gigabytes of data for $65 a month, down from $80. Adding a second phone to the plan brings the price up to $90, down from $105. ...

The price reduction comes a day after T-Mobile said it will double to 1 gigabyte the amount of data allotted to its $50-a-month Simple Choice package. AT&T cut its shared data plan for families by $40 last month as it seeks to keep pace with T-Mobile's aggressive pricing strategy. T-Mobile gained 2.1 million customers in the past three quarters, reversing its performance in 2012. The company offers a plan with 2.5 gigabytes of data for $60 a month for one phone or $90 a month for two phones.

Over the past year, Bellevue, Washington-based T-Mobile introduced a series of pricing changes to shake up the industry, becoming the first carrier to offer customers quicker phone upgrades, payment financing, and international data and text-messaging at no extra charge. It also started a $450 credit program for users who switch from other providers.

AT&T, based in Dallas, is the second-largest U.S. wireless carrier, trailing Verizon Communications Inc. T-Mobile is fourth, behind Sprint Corp. Competition between AT&T and T-Mobile, which abandoned a merger attempt in 2011, has intensified in part because they use similar technology, making it easier for customers to switch devices between their networks.

Scott Moritz, "AT&T Extends Price Cuts in Battle With T-Mobile for Data Users," *Bloomberg*, March 8, 2014"

MyEconLab More Economics in the News

ESSENCE OF THE STORY

- AT&T and T-Mobile use similar technology, which makes it easy for customers to switch devices between their networks.

- The two firms are in a smartphone-service price war.

- T-Mobile has gained 2.1 million customers by increasing the value of its plans without raising prices.

- AT&T has cut the prices of its plans.

ECONOMIC ANALYSIS

- The U.S. market in cellphone service is dominated by four firms: Verizon, AT&T Mobility, Sprint, and T-Mobile.

- Figure 1 shows the shares in this market. You can see that Verizon has 35 percent of the market; AT&T has 33 percent, Sprint has 16 percent; and T-Mobile has 14 percent. Another nine small firms share the remaining 2 percent.

- In 2013, T-Mobile and AT&T increased the intensity of their competition.

- T-Mobile increased the value and cost of production of its plans but held prices, and so decreased its profit.

- AT&T cut its prices, which decreased its profit.

- We can interpret this competition as a prisoners' dilemma game.

- Table 1 shows the payoff matrix (millions of dollars of profit) for the game played by T-Mobile and AT&T. (The numbers are hypothetical.)

- This game is a prisoners' dilemma like that on p. 345 and has a dominant-strategy Nash equilibrium.

- If T-Mobile offers an increased value of service, AT&T avoids a larger loss by cutting its price; and if T-Mobile does nothing different (no change), AT&T increases its profit by cutting its prices and gaining market share.

- So AT&T's best strategy is to cut prices.

- If AT&T cuts its prices, T-Mobile avoids a larger loss by incurring a higher cost of offering its customers greater value plans; and if AT&T *doesn't* cut its price (no change),

T-Mobile increases profit by offering its customers greater value plans.

- So T-Mobile's best strategy is to incur the higher cost of offering its customers greater value plans.

- Because the best strategy for AT&T is to cut price and for T-Mobile to incur the higher cost of offering its customers greater value plans, that is the equilibrium of the game.

- The firms are in a prisoners' dilemma because each would be better off avoiding the contest on quality of service and price.

- But each firm can see that if it doesn't take its best action, the other firm will gain and it will lose.

- The game we've just described is played only once, and both firms move at the same time.

- But in the game played by T-Mobile and AT&T, the firms move sequentially and repeatedly.

- If T-Mobile and AT&T adopt a tit-for-tat punishment strategy, it is possible that the current war between them will end and they will return to higher prices and larger profits.

- This market is one that affects everyone, and one that will expand as cellphones become ever smarter and used for more data-intensive activities.

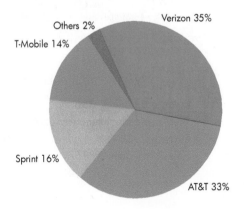

Figure 1 Market Shares in Cellphone Service

Table 1 T-Mobile and AT&T in a Prisoners' Dilemma

361

SUMMARY

Key Points

What Is Oligopoly? (pp. 342–343)

■ Oligopoly is a market in which a small number of firms compete.

Working Problems 1 to 3 will give you a better understanding of what oligopoly is.

Oligopoly Games (pp. 344–351)

■ Oligopoly is studied by using game theory, which is a method of analyzing strategic behavior.

■ In a prisoners' dilemma game, two prisoners acting in their own self-interest harm their joint interest.

■ An oligopoly (duopoly) price-fixing game is a prisoners' dilemma in which the firms might collude or cheat.

■ In Nash equilibrium, both firms cheat and output and price are the same as in perfect competition.

■ Firms' decisions about advertising and R&D can be studied by using game theory.

Working Problems 4 to 6 will give you a better understanding of oligopoly games.

Repeated Games and Sequential Games (pp. 352–355)

■ In a repeated game, a punishment strategy can produce a cooperative equilibrium in which price and output are the same as in a monopoly.

■ In a sequential contestable market game, a small number of firms can behave like firms in perfect competition.

Working Problem 7 will give you a better understanding of repeated and sequential games.

Antitrust Law (pp. 356–359)

■ The first antitrust law, the Sherman Act, was passed in 1890, and the law was strengthened in 1914 when the Clayton Act was passed and the Federal Trade Commission was created.

■ All price-fixing agreements are violations of the Sherman Act, and no acceptable excuse exists.

■ Resale price maintenance might be efficient if it enables a producer to ensure the efficient level of service by distributors.

■ Tying arrangements can enable a monopoly to price discriminate and increase profit, but in many cases, tying would not increase profit.

■ Predatory pricing is unlikely to occur because it brings losses and only temporary potential gains.

■ The Federal Trade Commission uses guidelines such as the Herfindahl-Hirschman Index to determine which mergers to investigate and possibly block.

Working Problem 8 will give you a better understanding of antitrust law.

Key Terms

◆ WORKED PROBLEM

MyEconLab You can work this problem in Chapter 15 Study Plan.

Black and White are the two and only producers of piano keys. The firms are identical. They have the same technologies and costs, and they produce the same quantities of piano keys. Their keys are identical too, so they sell for the same price regardless of whether Black or White produces them.

The firms are busy and operating at capacity output. But profit margins are thin and they are making zero economic profit.

Despite it being illegal, the two firms decide to collude: to restrict output and raise the price. The deal is that each of them cuts output to 50 percent of the current level and raises the price.

With the deal in place, the firms can earn the maximum monopoly profit and share it equally.

But each firm wants a bigger share of the market and to get back to the original output level. They each know, though, that if only one of them increases output, profit will increase for the one with larger output and the other will incur an economic loss. They also know that if both of them increase production, they will be back in the situation before the deal.

Questions

1. Describe the game played by Black and White.
2. Make up some profit numbers for Black and White that are consistent with the above account of their situation. Construct a payoff matrix for the game they are playing, and find the equilibrium of the game.

Solutions

1. The game played by Black and White is a duopoly prisoners' dilemma cartel game.
   Each player has two strategies: 1) keep the cartel agreement and 2) break the cartel agreement.
   The payoffs are symmetric.
   If both keep the agreement, they each earn 50 percent of the maximum attainable monopoly profit.
   If both break the agreement, they each earn zero economic profit.
   If one of them breaks the agreement, the breaker earns a profit that is larger than 50 percent of the monopoly profit and the other incurs a loss.
   The game is a prisoners' dilemma because each knows that the joint best outcome requires

keeping the agreement and that the other has an incentive to break it.

Key Point: A duopoly price-fixing game is a prisoners' dilemma in which the firms might keep or break an agreement to collude—might comply or cheat.

2. The table below shows a payoff matrix with profit (and loss) numbers that are consistent with the story about Black and White.
   If both break the agreement (top left), they earn zero economic profit ($0 in the table).
   If both keep the agreement (bottom right), they earn a monopoly profit and share it equally ($10m each in the table).
   If one keeps the agreement and the other breaks it (top right and bottom left), the keeper incurs a loss (−$5m in the table) and the breaker gets a profit larger than half the monopoly profit ($14m in the table).
   The Nash equilibrium is for both firms to break the agreement and make zero economic profit.
   For each firm, breaking the agreement is the best strategy regardless of the strategy of the other player.
   If the other firm keeps the agreement, then the firm that breaks it increases its profit by $4m.
   But if the other firm also breaks the agreement, then breaking the agreement avoids economic loss.

Key Point: The Nash equilibrium of a prisoners' dilemma is not the best joint outcome.

Key Table

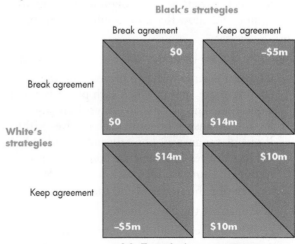

Black's strategies

	Break agreement	Keep agreement
White's strategies Break agreement	$0 / $0	−$5m / $14m
Keep agreement	$14m / −$5m	$10m / $10m

MyEconLab Interactive Animation

STUDY PLAN PROBLEMS AND APPLICATIONS

MyEconLab   You can work Problems 1 to 8 in Chapter 15 Study Plan and get instant feedback.

What Is Oligopoly? (Study Plan 15.1)

1. Intel and Advanced Micro Devices make most of the chips that power a PC. What makes the market for PC chips a duopoly? Sketch the market demand and cost curves that describe the situation in the market and that prevent firms from entering.

2. **Sparks Fly for Energizer**

   Energizer is gaining market share against competitor Duracell and its profit is rising despite the sharp rise in the price of zinc, a key battery ingredient.

   Source: www.businessweek.com, August 2007

   In what type of market are batteries sold? Explain your answer.

3. **Oil City**

   In the 1990s, Reliance spent $6 billion to build a world-class oil refinery at Jamnagar, India. Now Reliance's expansion will make it the world's biggest producer of gasoline—1.2 million gallons per day, or about 5% of global capacity. Reliance plans to sell the gasoline in the United States and Europe where it's too expensive and politically difficult to build new refineries. The bulked-up Jamnagar will be able to move the market and Singapore traders expect a drop in fuel prices as soon as it's going at full steam.

   Source: *Fortune*, April 28, 2008

   a. Explain why the news clip implies that the gasoline market is not perfectly competitive.

   b. What barriers to entry might limit competition and allow Reliance to influence the price?

Oligopoly Games (Study Plan 15.2)

4. Consider a game with two players who cannot communicate, and in which each player is asked a question. The players can answer honestly or lie. If both answer honestly, each receives $100. If one player answers honestly and the other lies, the liar receives $500 and the honest player gets nothing. If both lie, then each receives $50.

   a. Describe the strategies and the payoffs.

   b. Construct the payoff matrix.

   c. What is the equilibrium of this game?

   d. Compare this game to the prisoners' dilemma. Are the games similar or different? Explain.

5. Soapy Inc. and Suddies Inc., the only soap-powder producers, collude and agree to share the market equally. If neither firm cheats, each makes $1 million. If one firm cheats, it makes $1.5 million, while the complier incurs a loss of $0.5 million. If both cheat, they break even. Neither firm can monitor the other's actions.

   a. What are the strategies in this game? Construct the payoff matrix for this game.

   b. If the game is played only once what is the equilibrium? Is it a dominant-strategy equilibrium? Explain.

6. **The World's Largest Airline**

   United Airlines and Continental Airlines announced a $3 billion merger to create the world's biggest airline. The new airline will be able to better compete with low-cost domestic and foreign airlines. Travelers could face higher fares, although the merged airline has no such plans. But one rationale for any merger is to cut capacity.

   Source: *The New York Times*, June 7, 2010

   a. Explain how this airline merger might (i) increase air travel prices or (ii) lower air travel production costs.

   b. Explain how cost savings arising from a cut in capacity might be passed on to travelers or boost producers' profits. Which might happen from this airline merger and why?

Repeated Games and Sequential Games

(Study Plan 15.3)

7. If Soapy Inc. and Suddies Inc. play the game in Problem 5 repeatedly, on each round of play

   a. What strategies might each firm adopt?

   b. Can the firms adopt a strategy that gives the game a cooperative equilibrium?

   c. Would one firm still be tempted to cheat in a cooperative equilibrium? Explain your answer.

Antitrust Law (Study Plan 15.4)

8. AT&T offers iPhone users a $15 a month plan for 200 megabytes of data and a $25 a month plan for 2 gigabytes of data. It won't take Verizon Wireless long to begin offering data plans too.

   Source: Cnet News, June 3, 2010

   a. Is AT&T likely to be using predatory pricing?

   b. If a price war develops, who benefits most?

ADDITIONAL PROBLEMS AND APPLICATIONS

MyEconLab   You can work these problems in MyEconLab if assigned by your instructor.

What Is Oligopoly?

9. **An Energy Drink with a Monster of a Stock**

   The $5.7 billion energy-drink category, in which Monster holds the No. 2 position behind industry leader Red Bull, has slowed down as copycat brands jostle for shelf space. Over the past five years Red Bull's market share in dollar terms has gone from 91 percent to well under 50 percent and much of that loss has been Monster's gain.

   Source: *Fortune*, December 25, 2006

   a. Describe the structure of the energy-drink market. How has that structure changed over the past few years?

   b. If Monster and Red Bull formed a cartel, how would the price charged for energy drinks and the profits made change?

Oligopoly Games

Use the following data to work Problems 10 and 11. Bud and Wise are the only two producers of aniseed beer, a New Age product designed to displace root beer. Bud and Wise are trying to figure out how much of this new beer to produce. They know

   (i) If they both produce 10,000 gallons a day, they will make the maximum attainable joint economic profit of $200,000 a day, or $100,000 a day each.

   (ii) If either firm produces 20,000 gallons a day while the other produces 10,000 gallons a day, the one that produces 20,000 gallons will make an economic profit of $150,000 and the other will incur an economic loss of $50,000.

   (iii) If both produce 20,000 gallons a day, each firm will make zero economic profit.

10. Construct a payoff matrix for the game that Bud and Wise must play.

11. Find the Nash equilibrium of the game that Bud and Wise play.

12. **Asian Rice Exporters to Discuss Cartel**

   The Asian rice-exporting nations planned to discuss a proposal that they form a cartel. Ahead of the meeting, the countries said that the purpose of the rice cartel would be to contribute to ensuring food stability, not just in an individual country but also to address food shortages in the region and the world. The cartel will not hoard rice and raise prices when there are shortages.

   The Philippines says that it is a bad idea. It will create an oligopoly, and the cartel could price the grain out of reach for millions of people.

   Source: CNN, May 6, 2008

   a. Assuming the rice-exporting nations become a profit-maximizing colluding oligopoly, explain how they would influence the global market for rice and the world price of rice.

   b. Assuming the rice-exporting nations become a profit-maximizing colluding oligopoly, draw a graph to illustrate their influence on the global market for rice.

   c. Even in the absence of international antitrust laws, why might it be difficult for this cartel to successfully collude? Use the ideas of game theory to explain.

13. Suppose that Mozilla and Microsoft each develop their own versions of an amazing new Web browser that allows advertisers to target consumers with great precision. Also, the new browser is easier and more fun to use than existing browsers. Each firm is trying to decide whether to sell the browser or to give it away. What are the likely benefits from each action? Which action is likely to occur?

14. Why do Coca-Cola and PepsiCo spend huge amounts on advertising? Do they benefit? Does the consumer benefit? Explain your answer by constructing a game to illustrate the choices Coca-Cola and PepsiCo make.

Use the following news clip to work Problems 15 and 16.

PS4 vs. Xbox One Battle Means Gamers Win, Sony Says

Microsoft's latest move in the PlayStation 4 vs. Xbox One battle was to lower the price of Xbox One to $399—the same price as the PS4.

   Source: *GameSpot*, July 1, 2014

15. a. Thinking about the competition between Sony and Microsoft in the market for game consoles as a game, describe the firms' strategies concerning design, marketing, and price.

   b. What, based on the information provided, turned out to be the equilibrium of the game?

16. Can you think of reasons why the two consoles are different?

Repeated Games and Sequential Games

17. If Bud and Wise in Problems 10 and 11 play the game repeatedly, what is the equilibrium of the game?

18. Agile Airlines' profit on a route on which it has a monopoly is $10 million a year. Wanabe Airlines is considering entering the market and operating on this route. Agile warns Wanabe to stay out and threatens to cut the price so that if Wanabe enters it will make no profit. Wanabe determines that the payoff matrix for the game in which it is engaged with Agile is shown in the table.

Does Wanabe believe Agile's assertion? Does Wanabe enter or not? Explain.

19. **Oil Trading Probe May Uncover Manipulation**

Amid soaring oil prices the Commodity Futures Trading Commission (CFTC) is looking into manipulation of the oil market—withholding oil in an attempt to drive prices higher. The CFTC has found such evidence in the past and it's likely it will find evidence again. But it is unlikely that a single player acting alone would be able to run the price up from $90 to $135.

Source: CNN, May 30, 2008

What type of market does the news clip imply best describes the U.S. oil market?

Antitrust Law

Use the following news clip to work Problems 20 and 21.

Gadgets for Sale ... or Not

How come the prices of some gadgets, like the iPod, are the same no matter where you shop? No, the answer isn't that Apple illegally manages prices. In reality, Apple uses an accepted retail strategy called minimum advertised price to discourage resellers from discounting. The minimum advertised price (MAP) is the absolute lowest price of a product that resellers can advertise. Marketing subsidies offered by a manufacturer to its resellers usually keep the price at

or above the MAP. Stable prices are important to the company that is both a manufacturer and a retailer. If Apple resellers advertised the iPod below cost, they could squeeze the Apple Stores out of their own markets. The downside to the price stability is that by limiting how low sellers can go, MAP keeps prices artificially high (or at least higher than they might otherwise be with unfettered price competition).

Source: *Slate*, December 22, 2006

20. a. Describe the practice of resale price maintenance that violates the Sherman Act.

    b. Describe the MAP strategy used by Apple and explain how it differs from a resale price maintenance agreement that would violate the Sherman Act.

21. Why might the MAP strategy be against the social interest and benefit only the producer?

Economics in the News

22. After you have studied *Economics in the News* on pp. 360–361, answer the following questions.

    a. What are the strategies of T-Mobile and AT&T in the market for cellphone service?

    b. Why, according to the news article, is it that AT&T and T-Mobile are in a fierce battle?

    c. Why wouldn't AT&T stick with its high price and leave T-Mobile to incur the cost of offering higher-valued plans?

    d. Could T-Mobile do something that would make it the market leader? Would that action maximize T-Mobile's profit?

23. **Boeing and Airbus Predict Asian Sales Surge**

Airlines in the Asia-Pacific region are emerging as the biggest customers for aircraft makers Boeing and Airbus. The two firms predict that over the next 20 years, more than 8,000 planes worth up to $1.2 trillion will be sold there.

Source: BBC News, February 3, 2010

    a. In what type of market are big airplanes sold?

    b. Thinking of competition between Boeing and Airbus as a game, what are the strategies and the payoffs?

    c. Set out a hypothetical payoff matrix for the game you've described in part (b). What is the equilibrium of the game?

    d. Do you think the market for big airplanes is efficient? Explain and illustrate your answer.

Managing Change and Limiting Market Power

Our economy is constantly changing. Every year, new goods appear and old ones disappear. New firms are born, and old ones die. This process of change is initiated and managed by firms operating in markets.

When a new product appears, just one or two firms sell it: Apple and IBM were the only producers of personal computers; Microsoft was (and almost still is) the only producer of the PC operating system; Intel was the only producer of the PC chip. These firms had enormous power to determine the quantity to produce and the price of their products.

In many markets, entry eventually brings competition. Even with just two rivals, the industry changes its face in a dramatic way. *Strategic interdependence* is capable of leading to an outcome like perfect competition.

With the continued arrival of new firms in an industry, the market becomes competitive. But in most markets, the competition isn't perfect: it becomes *monopolistic competition* with each firm selling its own differentiated product.

Often, an industry that is competitive becomes less so as the bigger and more successful firms in the industry begin to swallow up the smaller firms, either by driving them out of business or by acquiring their assets. Through this process, an industry might return to oligopoly or even monopoly. You can see such a movement in the auto and banking industries today.

By studying firms and markets, we gain a deeper understanding of the forces that allocate resources and begin to see the invisible hand at work.

John von Neumann *was one of the great minds of the twentieth century. Born in Budapest, Hungary, in 1903, Johnny, as he was known, showed early mathematical brilliance. He was 25 when he published the article that changed the social sciences and began a flood of research on* **game theory**—*a flood that has not subsided. In that article, von Neumann proved that in a zero-sum game (such as sharing a pie), there exists a best strategy for each player.*

Von Neumann did more than invent game theory: He also invented and built the first practical computer, and he worked on the Manhattan Project, which developed the atomic bomb during World War II.

Von Neumann believed that the social sciences would progress only if they used their own mathematical tools, not those of the physical sciences.

"Real life consists of bluffing, of little tactics of deception, of asking yourself what is the other man going to think I mean to do."

JOHN VON NEUMANN, told to Jacob Bronowski (in a London taxi) and reported in *The Ascent of Man.*

THOMAS HUBBARD is the John L. and Helen Kellogg Distinguished Professor of Management and Strategy at the Kellogg School of Management, Northwestern University and a research fellow at the National Bureau of Economic Research.

Professor Hubbard is an empirical economist. His work is driven by data. The central problems that unify much of his work are the limits to information and the fact that information is costly to obtain. Professor Hubbard studies the ways in which information problems influence the organization of firms; the extent to which firms make or buy what they sell; and the structure and performance of markets.

His work appears in the leading journals such as the *American Economic Review*, the *Quarterly Journal of Economics*, and the *Rand Journal of Economics*. He is a co-editor of the *Journal of Industrial Economics*.

Michael Parkin talked with Thomas Hubbard about his research and what we learn from it about the choices that firms make and their implications for market structure and performance.

Professor Hubbard, you have made important contributions to our understanding of outsourcing: whether a firm will make it or buy it. Can you summarize what economists know about this issue?

If there is one thing that Coase (Ronald Coase, see p. 417) taught us about the boundaries of the firm, it is that when thinking about whether to do something internally or to outsource it, a very useful starting point is to make the decision on a transaction-by-transaction basis.

The way I like to think about it is to boil it down to the theory of markets and incentives. Markets provide strong incentives but not necessarily good incentives. So when you outsource something, you rely on a market mechanism rather than on something within a firm that is less than a market mechanism. By outsourcing, you expose people to a strong market incentive. Now that can be good, and it is good most of the time. Strong market incentives get people to do things that the market rewards. Market rewards are generally quite valuable, but in some circumstances what the market rewards isn't

> Markets provide strong incentives but not necessarily good incentives.

what the buyer would want to reward. So there's a tradeoff. Strong incentives are sometimes good and sometimes bad. Therefore, keeping things inside the firm provides a weaker incentive. Sometimes that is good.

Can you provide an example?

Think about McDonald's. McDonald's is not one firm. It is many firms because a lot of the outlets are owned and managed by franchisees and some are owned and managed internally by McDonald's.

McDonald's thinks about whether to run one of its restaurants itself or to franchise it out.

One thing that it has in mind is that if it franchises it out, then the franchisee is going to be exposed to very strong market incentives. Now under some circumstances this is great. The franchisee treats the business as if he owns it. So the good part about it is the franchisee works hard to try to develop his business.

But a flip side to the franchisee's treating the business as his own is that it can be harmful for the McDonald's brand.

*Read the full interview with Thomas Hubbard in MyEconLab.

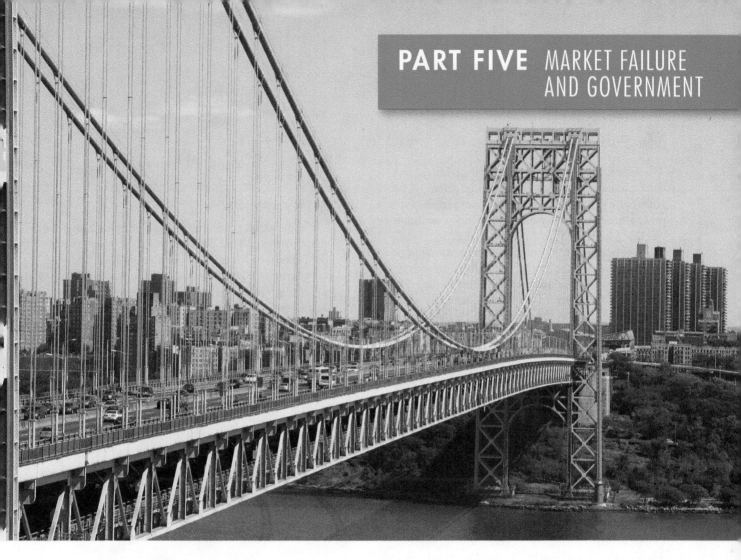

16 PUBLIC CHOICES, PUBLIC GOODS, AND HEALTHCARE

After studying this chapter, you will be able to:

◆ Explain why some choices are *public* choices and how they are made in a political marketplace

◆ Explain how the free-rider problem arises and how the quantity of public goods is determined

◆ Explain why governments provide healthcare and how our healthcare markets work

The George Washington Bridge that links New York and New Jersey is one of 607,380 road bridges in the United States built and maintained by governments. Healthcare along with a wide array of other goods and services are also provided by governments. But why governments? Why not private firms?

Are governments efficient in their provision of bridges, healthcare, and other goods and services?

These are the questions we study in this chapter. In *Economics in the News* at the end of the chapter, we return to bridges and look at the problem of keeping them safe.

Public Choices

All economic choices are made by individuals, but some choices are *private* and some are *public*. A *private choice* is a decision that has consequences for the person making it. Your decision to buy a textbook or work at McDonald's is a private choice.

A **public choice** is a decision that has consequences for many people and perhaps for an entire society. The decision by members of Congress to pass the Affordable Care Act—Obamacare—and the decisions that created the enrollment website Healthcare.gov are examples of public choices.

Some of the things we care most about are decided by people making public choices, and very large quantities of scarce resources get used as a result of these choices. *Economics in Action* opposite provides a snapshot of what our federal, state, and local governments buy.

Why do governments allocate a large quantity of resources? The economic theory of government answers this question.

Why Governments?

Governments perform three economic functions: They establish and maintain property rights, provide nonmarket mechanisms for allocating scarce resources, and redistribute income and wealth.

Property rights and the legal system that enforces them are the foundation of the market economy, which, in many situations, functions well and allocates scarce resources efficiently. But sometimes the market fails (see Chapter 5, pp. 114–115).

When market failure occurs, choices made in the pursuit of self-interest have not served the social interest.

The market economy also delivers a distribution of income and wealth that most people regard as unfair. Equity requires some redistribution.

Replacing markets with government resource-allocation decisions is no simple matter. Just as there can be market failure, there can also be government failure. **Government failure** is a situation in which government actions lead to inefficiency—to either underprovision or overprovision.

Government failure can arise because government is made up of many individuals, each with their own economic objectives. Public choices are the outcome of the choices made by these individuals. To analyze these choices, economists have developed a public choice theory of the political marketplace.

ECONOMICS IN ACTION
The Goods and Services Provided by Governments

The U.S. federal government spent $2 trillion on goods and services in 2013. The state and local governments spent another $1.8 trillion. The total of $3.8 trillion is one quarter of all expenditure in the U.S. economy.

The figure shows what our governments buy. The biggest item is healthcare, with education not far behind. National defense comes next. The total spent on the nation's highways and bridges (transportation), police and fire services (protection), and government itself is about one fifth of government expenditure.

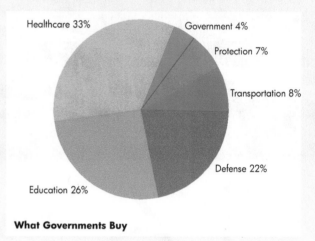

What Governments Buy

Public Choice and the Political Marketplace

The four groups of decision makers shown in Fig. 16.1 interact in the political marketplace. They are

- Voters
- Firms
- Politicians
- Bureaucrats

Voters Voters evaluate politicians' policy proposals, benefit from public goods and services, and pay some of the taxes. They support the politicians whose policy proposals make them better off and express their demand for public goods and services by voting, helping in political campaigns, lobbying, and making campaign contributions.

Firms Firms also evaluate politicians' policy proposals, benefit from public goods and services, and pay some of the taxes. Although firms don't vote, they

FIGURE 16.1   The Political Marketplace

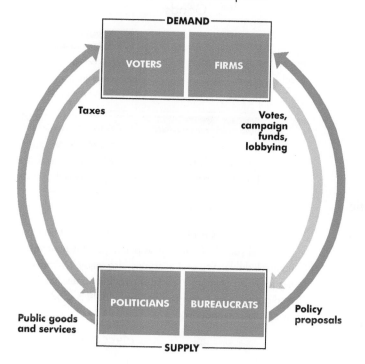

Voters and firms demand public goods and services and policies that serve their self-interest.

Voters support the policies they like with their votes. And voters and firms support policies they like with campaign contributions and by lobbying.

Politicians and bureaucrats supply public goods and services, set taxes, and make policy proposals that serve their self-interest.

Politicians want to attract enough votes to get them elected and keep them in office. Bureaucrats want to get the largest possible budget for their departments.

A political equilibrium balances all these public choices.

MyEconLab Animation

do make campaign contributions and are a major source of funds for political parties. Firms also engage in lobbying activity to persuade politicians to propose policies that benefit them.

Politicians   Politicians are the elected persons in the federal, state, and local governments. The goal of a politician is to get elected and to remain in office. Votes to a politician are like profit to a firm. Politicians also direct bureaucrats.

Bureaucrats   Bureaucrats are the public servants who work in government departments. They administer tax collection, the delivery of public goods and services, and the administration of rules and regulations.

The self-interest of a bureaucrat is served when the budget of her or his department is maximized. The bigger the budget of a department, the greater is the prestige of its chief and the greater are the opportunities for promotion for people farther down the bureaucratic ladder. This economic assumption implies that in doing what they perceive to be a good job in the public interest, they take care of their own self-interest too.

Political Equilibrium

Voters, firms, politicians, and bureaucrats make their economic choices in their own self-interest. Public choices, like private choices, are constrained by what is feasible. Each person's public choices are also constrained by the public choices of others.

The balance of forces in the political marketplace determines the outcome of all the public choices that people make. In a **political equilibrium** the choices of voters, firms, politicians, and bureaucrats are all compatible and no group can see a way of improving its position by making a different choice.

Ideally, the political equilibrium achieves allocative efficiency and serves the social interest, but this outcome is not guaranteed, as you'll see in this chapter.

We make public choices because some situations just don't permit private choices. The core of the reason we can't always make private choices is that some goods and services (and some factors of production) have a public nature—they are *public* goods and services.

Your next task is to see exactly what we mean by a *public* good or service.

What Is a Public Good?

To see what makes a good a *public* good, we distinguish between two features of all goods: the extent to which people can be *excluded* from consuming them and the extent to which one person's consumption *rivals* someone else's consumption.

Excludable A good is **excludable** if it is possible to prevent someone from enjoying its benefits. Brink's security services, East Point Seafood's fish, and a U2 concert are examples. People must pay to benefit from them.

A good is **nonexcludable** if it is impossible (or extremely costly) to prevent anyone from benefiting from it. The services of the LAPD, fish in the Pacific Ocean, and a concert on network television are examples. When an LAPD cruiser enforces the speed limit, everyone on the highway benefits; anyone with a boat can fish in the ocean; and anyone with a TV can watch a network broadcast.

Rival A good is **rival** if one person's use of it decreases the quantity available for someone else. A Brink's truck can't deliver cash to two banks at the same time. A fish can be consumed only once.

A good is **nonrival** if one person's use of it does not decrease the quantity available for someone else. The services of the LAPD and a concert on network television are nonrival. One person's benefit doesn't lower the benefit of others.

A Fourfold Classification

Figure 16.2 classifies goods, services, and resources into four types.

Private Goods A **private good** is both rival and excludable. A can of Coke and a fish on East Point Seafood's farm are examples of private goods.

Public Goods A **public good** is both nonrival and nonexcludable. A public good simultaneously benefits everyone, and no one can be excluded from its benefits. National defense is the best example of a public good.

Common Resources A **common resource** is rival and nonexcludable. A unit of a common resource can be used only once, but no one can be prevented from using what is available. Ocean fish are a common resource. They are rival because a fish taken by one person isn't available for anyone else, and they are nonexcludable because it is difficult to prevent people from catching them.

FIGURE 16.2   Fourfold Classification of Goods

	Excludable	Nonexcludable
Rival	**Private goods** Food and drink Car House	**Common resources** Fish in ocean Atmosphere National parks
Nonrival	**Natural monopoly goods** Internet Cable television Bridge or tunnel	**Public goods** National defense The law Air traffic control

A private good is rival and excludable: You must pay to get it and you alone enjoy it. A public good is nonrival and nonexcludable: You and everyone else enjoy it without paying for it. A common resource is rival but nonexcludable. And a good that is nonrival but excludable is produced by a natural monopoly.

MyEconLab Animation

Natural Monopoly Goods A **natural monopoly good** is nonrival but excludable. Potential consumers can be excluded if they don't pay but adding one more user doesn't rival other users, so marginal cost is zero. Examples of natural monopoly goods are the Internet, cable television, and an uncongested bridge or tunnel. Why is a nonrival but excludable good a natural monopoly good? It is because there is a fixed cost of producing it. With a zero marginal cost, average total cost falls as output increases so economies of scale exist over the entire range of output for which there is a demand, and one firm can produce the good at a lower cost than can two or more firms (see p. 298).

The Things Our Governments Buy

Of the things that our governments buy, shown in *Economics in Action* on p. 370, national defense, protection, and constructing and maintaining the transportation infrastructure fit the definition of a public good. They are nonrival and nonexcludable. But what about healthcare and education, the two biggest items? They don't look like public goods. A person can be excluded from a hospital or college. And one person's use of a hospital bed or place in college rivals another's. So aren't healthcare and education private goods? Why do governments provide them?

ECONOMICS IN ACTION
Is a Lighthouse a Public Good?

Built on Little Brewster Island in 1716 to guide ships into and out of the Boston Harbor, Boston Lighthouse was the first light station in North America.

For two centuries, economists used the lighthouse as an example of a public good. No one can be prevented from seeing its warning light—*nonexcludable*—and one person seeing its light doesn't prevent someone else from doing so too—*nonrival*.

Ronald Coase, who won the 1991 Nobel Prize for ideas he first developed when he was an undergraduate at the London School of Economics, discovered that before the nineteenth century, lighthouses in England were built and operated by private corporations that earned profits by charging tolls on ships docking at nearby ports. A ship that refused to pay the lighthouse toll was *excluded* from the port.

So the benefit arising from the services of a lighthouse is *excludable*. Because the services provided by a lighthouse are nonrival but excludable, a lighthouse is an example of a natural monopoly good and not a public good.

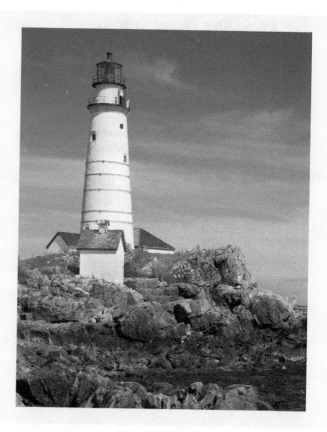

Healthcare Healthcare is two goods: care supplied by doctors and other professionals, and insurance. Governments provide both healthcare services and health insurance because, left to the market alone, they would be inefficiently underprovided and unfairly distributed. For a majority of voters, it is unfair and unethical to allocate scarce healthcare resources only to those who can afford them—those who are willing and able to pay. Most people want the government to provide a single mother who is living in poverty with access to a doctor or hospital when she needs those services.

To work well, a market needs buyers and sellers who are well informed about the item being traded. In the case of healthcare services, doctors and healthcare professionals are better informed than patients about the service and treatment needed. And in the case of health insurance, the insured is better informed than the insurer about the risks faced.

Also, lacking the relevant information about risk, fit and healthy people often take too short a view and don't buy enough insurance.

Education Governments provide public education because it brings benefits that spill over to others—called *external benefits*. Everyone benefits from living in an educated society where friends and neighbors share a common heritage.

The rest of this chapter studies the public choices that must be made to avoid the underprovision of public goods and healthcare. Chapter 17 studies the ways of coping with externalities, including those arising from education, and the challenge of conserving common resources.

◆ REVIEW QUIZ

1 List the economic functions of governments.
2 Describe the political marketplace: Who are the participants, what do they do, and what is a political equilibrium?
3 Distinguish among public goods, private goods, common resources, and natural monopoly goods.
4 Why are healthcare and education not public goods and why do governments play a large role in the markets for these services?

Work these questions in Study Plan 16.1 and get instant feedback. Do a Key Terms Quiz.   MyEconLab

Providing Public Goods

Why do governments provide firefighting services? Why don't the people of California buy brush firefighting services from Firestorm, a private firm that competes for our dollars in the marketplace in the same way that McDonald's does? The answer is that firefighting is a public good. It is nonexcludable and nonrival and it has a free-rider problem.

The Free-Rider Problem

A free rider enjoys the benefits of a good or service without paying for it. Because a public good is provided for everyone to use and no one can be excluded from its benefits, no one has an incentive to pay his or her share of the cost. Everyone has an incentive to free ride. The **free-rider problem** is that the economy would provide an inefficiently small quantity of a public good. Marginal social benefit from the public good would exceed its marginal social cost and a deadweight loss would arise.

Let's look at the marginal social benefit and marginal social cost of a public good.

Marginal Social Benefit from a Public Good

Lisa and Max (the only people in a society) value fire-fighting airplanes. Figures 16.3(a) and 16.3(b) graph their marginal benefits from the airplanes as MB_L for Lisa and MB_M for Max. The marginal benefit from a public good (like that from a private good) diminishes as the quantity of the good increases.

Figure 16.3(c) shows the marginal *social* benefit curve, *MSB*. Because everyone gets the same quantity of a public good, its marginal social benefit is the sum of the marginal benefits of all the individuals at each *quantity*. So the marginal social benefit curve is the *vertical* sum of the individual marginal benefit curves. The curve *MSB* is the marginal social benefit curve for the economy made up of Lisa and Max. For each airplane, Lisa's marginal benefit is added to Max's marginal benefit.

Contrast the *MSB* curve for a public good with that of a private good. To obtain the economy's *MSB* curve for a private good, we sum the *quantities demanded* by all the individuals at each *price*—we sum the individual marginal benefit curves *horizontally* (see Chapter 5, pp. 108–109).

FIGURE 16.3 Benefits of a Public Good

(a) Lisa's marginal benefit

(b) Max's marginal benefit

(c) Economy's marginal social benefit

The marginal social benefit at each quantity of the public good is the sum of the marginal benefits of all individuals. The marginal benefit curves are MB_L for Lisa and MB_M for Max. The economy's marginal social curve is *MSB*.

MyEconLab Animation

Marginal Social Cost of a Public Good

The marginal social cost of a public good is determined in exactly the same way as that of a private good—see Chapter 5, p. 110. The principle of increasing marginal cost applies to the marginal cost of a public good, so the marginal social cost increases as the quantity of the public good increases.

Efficient Quantity of a Public Good

To determine the efficient quantity of a public good, we use the principles that you learned in Chapter 5. The efficient quantity is that at which marginal social benefit equals marginal social cost.

Figure 16.4 shows the marginal social benefit curve, *MSB*, and the marginal social cost curve, *MSC*, for firefighting airplanes. (We'll now think of society as consisting of Lisa and Max and the other 39 million Californians.)

If marginal social benefit exceeds marginal social cost, as it does with 2 airplanes, resources can be used more efficiently by increasing the number of airplanes. The extra benefit exceeds the extra cost. If marginal social cost exceeds marginal social benefit, as it does with 4 airplanes, resources can be used more efficiently by decreasing the number of airplanes. The cost saving exceeds the loss of benefit.

If marginal social benefit equals marginal social cost, as it does with 3 airplanes, resources are allocated efficiently. Resources cannot be used more efficiently because to provide more than 3 airplanes increases cost by more than the extra benefit, and to provide fewer airplanes lowers the benefit by more than the cost saving.

Inefficient Private Provision

Could a private firm—Firestorm—deliver the efficient quantity of firefighting airplanes? Most likely it couldn't, because no one would have an incentive to buy his or her share of the airplanes. Everyone would reason as follows: The number of airplanes provided by Firestorm is not affected by my decision to pay my share or not. But my own private consumption will be greater if I free ride and do not pay my share of the cost of the airplanes. If I don't pay, I enjoy the same level of fire protection and I can buy more private goods. I will spend my money on private goods and free ride on fire

FIGURE 16.4   The Efficient Quantity of a Public Good

With fewer than 3 airplanes, marginal social benefit, *MSB*, exceeds marginal social cost, *MSC*. With more than 3 airplanes, *MSC* exceeds *MSB*. Only with 3 airplanes is *MSC* equal to *MSB* and the number of airplanes is efficient.

MyEconLab Animation

protection. Such reasoning is the free-rider problem. If everyone reasons the same way, Firestorm has no revenue and so provides no airplanes. Because the efficient number of airplanes is 3, private provision is inefficient.

Efficient Public Provision

The outcome of the political process might be efficient or inefficient. We look first at an efficient outcome. There are two political parties: Fears and Hopes. They agree on all issues except the number of firefighting airplanes: The Fears want 4, and the Hopes want 2. Both parties want to get elected, so they run a voter survey and discover the marginal social benefit curve of Fig. 16.5. They also consult with airplane producers to establish the marginal cost curve. The parties then do a "what-if" analysis. If the Fears propose 4 airplanes and the Hopes propose 2, the voters will be equally unhappy with both parties. Compared to the efficient quantity, the Hopes want an underprovision of 1 airplane and the Fears want an overprovision of 1 airplane. The deadweight losses are equal and the election would be too close to call.

Contemplating this outcome, the Fears realize that they are too fearful to get elected. They figure that, if they scale back to 3 airplanes, they will win the election if the Hopes stick with 2. The Hopes reason in a similar way and figure that, if they increase the number of airplanes to 3, they can win the election if the Fears propose 4.

So they both propose 3 airplanes. The voters are indifferent between the parties, and each party receives 50 percent of the vote. But regardless of which party wins the election, 3 airplanes are provided and this quantity is efficient. Competition in the political marketplace results in the efficient provision of a public good.

The Principle of Minimum Differentiation The **principle of minimum differentiation** is the tendency for competitors (including political parties) to make themselves similar to appeal to the maximum number of clients or voters. This principle describes the behavior of political parties. It also explains why fast-food restaurants cluster in the same block. For example, if Domino's opens a new pizza outlet, it is likely that Pizza Hut will soon open nearby.

FIGURE 16.5   An Efficient Political Outcome

The Hopes would like to provide 2 airplanes and the Fears would like to provide 4 airplanes. The political outcome is 3 airplanes because unless each party proposes 3 airplanes, the other party will beat it in an election.

MyEconLab Animation

ECONOMICS IN ACTION
Fighting Colorado's Wildfires

The 2012 wildfire season was extreme. Colorado had its worst season in a decade with major fires that devastated communities in and around Colorado Springs. And across the Western states, close to half a million acres (780 square miles) of land were burned.

Wildfires are natural and vital for the ecosystem, but some fires are started by human action, and some both human-made and naturally occurring fires, like the 2012 fires in Colorado, burn close to where people live. So protection against wildfires is a vital *public good*.

But not all fire protection services are *produced* by government. *Private* wildfire service contractors supply around 40 percent of wildfire suppression services. So fighting wildfires is an example of a public good that is *provided* by government and paid for with tax revenues, but in part *produced* by private firms.

Firestorm Wildfire Suppression Inc. is one such firm. Operating from Chico, CA, Firestorm hires and trains firefighters and produces firefighting services to maximize its profit. To achieve this goal, the firm must produce firefighting services at the lowest possible cost.

But if Firestorm (and its competitors) tried to sell their services to each individual homeowner in the wildfire regions, they wouldn't get enough revenue to remain in business. There would be a free-rider problem. The free-rider problem is avoided because governments buy the services of Firestorm.

For the political process to deliver the efficient outcome, voters must be well informed, evaluate the alternatives, and vote in the election. Political parties must be well informed about voter preferences. As the next section shows, we can't expect to achieve this outcome.

Inefficient Public Overprovision

If competition between two political parties is to deliver the efficient quantity of a public good, bureaucrats must cooperate and help to achieve this outcome. But bureaucrats might have a different idea and end up frustrating rather than facilitating an efficient outcome. Their actions might bring *government failure*.

Objective of Bureaucrats Bureaucrats want to maximize their department's budget because a bigger budget brings greater status and more power. So the Emergency Services Department's objective is to maximize the budget for firefighting airplanes.

Figure 16.6 shows the outcome if the bureaucrats are successful in the pursuit of their goal. They might try to persuade the politicians that 3 airplanes cost more than the originally budgeted amount; or they might press their position more strongly and argue for more than 3 airplanes. In Fig. 16.6, the Emergency Services Department persuades the politicians to provide 4 airplanes.

Why don't the politicians block the bureaucrats? Won't overproviding airplanes cost future votes? It will if voters are well informed and know what is best for them. But voters might not be well informed, and well-informed interest groups might enable the bureaucrats to achieve their objective and overcome the objections of the politicians.

Rational Ignorance A principle of the economic analysis of public choices is that it is rational for a voter to be ignorant about an issue unless that issue has a perceptible effect on the voter's economic welfare. Each voter knows that he or she can make virtually no difference to the fire protection policy of the government of California and that it would take an enormous amount of time and effort to become even moderately well informed about alternative fire-protection technologies. Rationally uninformed voters enable bureaucrats and special interest groups to overprovide public goods.

FIGURE 16.6 Bureaucratic Overprovision

Well-informed bureaucrats want to maximize their budget and rationally ignorant voters enable the bureaucrats to go some way toward achieving their goal. A public good might be inefficiently overprovided with a deadweight loss.

MyEconLab Animation

◆ REVIEW QUIZ

1 What is the free-rider problem? Why do free riders make the private provision of a public good inefficient?

2 Under what conditions will competition among politicians for votes result in an efficient provision of a public good?

3 How do rationally ignorant voters and budget-maximizing bureaucrats prevent the political marketplace from delivering the efficient quantity of a public good?

4 Explain why public choices might lead to the overprovision rather than the underprovision of a public good.

Work these questions in Study Plan 16.2 and get instant feedback. Do a Key Terms Quiz.   *MyEconLab*

You've seen how the political marketplace provides public goods and why it might *over*provide them. Your next task is to see how the political marketplace provides healthcare.

The Economics of Healthcare

Governments spend more on healthcare than on any other item. (see *Economics in Action* on p. 370). The key reason why governments play a large role in healthcare is that it would be underprovided and unfairly distributed if left to the market alone.

You are now going to see how governments influence the provision of healthcare, how healthcare markets in the United States compare with those in some other countries, and how it might be possible to improve on our current healthcare programs.

We begin by seeing why the market would underprovide healthcare—why there would be a healthcare market failure.

Healthcare Market Failure

Healthcare consists of healthcare services (the services of physicians, specialists, nurses, other professionals, and hospitals) and health insurance. Both would be underprovided and unfairly distributed without some government action.

The *social* benefit of healthcare exceeds the benefit perceived by its consumers, which means that the *marginal social benefit* of healthcare exceeds the willingness and ability to pay for it.

Three problems make healthcare a special good: Consumers and potential consumers of healthcare

- Underestimate its benefit
- Underestimate their future needs
- Can't afford the care they need

Underestimate Benefit People don't have enough information to value the benefit of healthcare correctly. Most people lack the medical knowledge to determine their treatment needs. And many (especially healthy and young people) optimistically underestimate the health risks that they face. So they undervalue the insurance policies that can help them pay for healthcare; and they undervalue the healthcare resources that stand ready to help them when needed.

Underestimate Future Needs People take too short a view of the benefits of healthcare. The young and healthy know that they will become old and less healthy and will likely become big consumers of healthcare. But the time horizon over which they plan doesn't stretch that far into the future. The end result is that many people perceive too small a marginal benefit from health insurance, and are not willing to pay what it is actually worth to them.

Can't Afford For many people, the price of health insurance is beyond their ability to pay for it. Two groups of people are unable to afford adequate health insurance: those with a long-term health problem and the aged. But these are the people with the greatest need for healthcare.

Most people want to live in a society that treats these less healthy, older, and poorer people with compassion and ensure that they are provided with access to affordable healthcare. So there is an additional social benefit from healthcare for less healthy, older, and poorer people.

Because the marginal social benefit of healthcare exceeds the marginal benefit perceived by its consumers, a competitive market in healthcare would underprovide it. And this underprovision has two dimensions. It is

- Inefficient, and
- Unfair

Inefficient Figure 16.7 illustrates the inefficient underprovision of a competitive market in healthcare.

The curve $D = MB$ shows the demand for healthcare, which is determined by the willingness and ability to pay for it, which in turn is determined by its *perceived* marginal benefit, MB.

The curve $S = MSC$ shows the supply of healthcare. The supply curve is also the marginal cost curve, which we will assume correctly measures the marginal social cost, MSC.

The equilibrium quantity of healthcare is at the intersection of the demand curve, $D = MB$, and the supply curve, $S = MSC$. In Fig. 16.7, that quantity is 0.3 billion patients per year.

The curve MSB shows the marginal social benefit of healthcare, which, for the reasons explained above, exceeds the willingness and ability to pay.

The efficient quantity of healthcare is that at which $MSB = MSC$. In Fig. 16.7, that quantity is 0.7 billion patients per year.

Because the efficient quantity exceeds the market quantity, the market underprovides healthcare. The marginal social benefit that patients who fail to get care would generate exceeds the marginal social cost of providing care, so the underprovision creates the deadweight loss shown by the gray triangle.

Unfair Not only is there deadweight loss, but also there is an unfair distribution of the loss. The people who receive healthcare are the ones who are willing and able to pay for it. They are people who are normally fit and healthy and able to earn an average or

FIGURE 16.7 Healthcare Market Failure

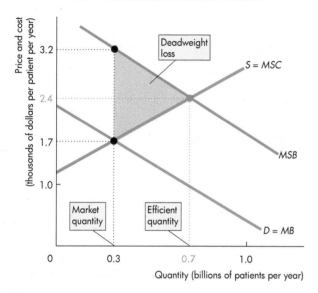

The demand curve, *D = MB*, shows the marginal benefit and willingness to pay for healthcare, and the supply curve, *S = MSC*, shows the marginal social cost of providing healthcare. A competitive market would provide care for 0.3 billion patients. The curve *MSB* shows the marginal social benefit of healthcare. The efficient quantity is that at which *MSB = MSC* and is 0.7 billion patients. The gray triangle shows the deadweight loss from underprovision.

MyEconLab Animation Draw Graph.

better than average income. The people who don't receive healthcare and who bear the deadweight loss are the long-term sick and the aged who can't afford the cost of healthcare.

Because the market would deliver an inefficient and unfair outcome, healthcare is provided by the *public* choices of governments. But there are alternative methods and scales of public provision, so governments must consider the effects of the alternatives in making their choices.

Alternative Public Choice Solutions

We're now going to examine the public choices that deliver healthcare services. You can see in *Economics in Action* on this page that there is a wide range of levels of public funding of healthcare. Public choices pay 83 percent of the healthcare bills in the United Kingdom, 70 percent in Canada, and 46 percent in the United States. But among these three countries, public expenditure per person is highest in the United States.

ECONOMICS IN ACTION

U.S. Healthcare Expenditures in Global Perspective

The best U.S. healthcare is the best in the world, but it is costly. Americans spend 18 percent of income—almost $9,000 per person per year—on healthcare. This amount is *more than double* the average spent in other rich countries. And this expenditure is projected to rise as the U.S. population ages and the "baby boom" generation retires.

The figure below compares U.S. healthcare costs with those of 13 other countries: some rich and some not so rich.

The figure shows that even rich countries such as Canada, Germany, and France spend barely a half as much, per person, on healthcare as do Americans. And health outcomes measured by life expectancy and quality of health are as good as or better in these other rich countries than those in the United States.

Another feature of U.S. healthcare expenditure is its very large public component (the blue bars in the figure). Government expenditure per person on healthcare in the United States is the second highest in the world, exceeded only by that of the Netherlands. It exceeds that in Canada, where selling private health insurance is illegal, and in Germany and France, where there is a greater acceptance of high taxes and big government than in the United States.

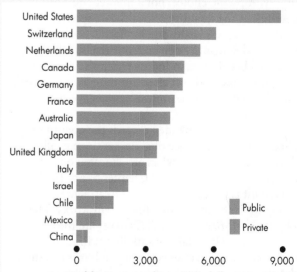

Healthcare Expenditures in 14 Countries

Different public choice solutions lead to these differences in healthcare expenditures. And the different solutions have implications for both the efficiency and the cost of healthcare.

We examine three approaches to supplementing or replacing the market: one used in Canada and the United Kingdom and two used in the United States. The three approaches are

- Universal coverage, single payer
- Private and government insurance
- Subsidized private insurance: Obamacare

Universal Coverage, Single Payer In Canada and the United Kingdom, healthcare is provided by a system with two key features: universal coverage and a single payer.

Universal coverage means that everyone is covered by health insurance, with no exceptions and no excluded preconditions.

Single payer means that the government alone pays the healthcare bills. The government pays the doctors, nurses, and hospitals, and it pays for prescription drugs.

In the United Kingdom, most of the doctors are employed by the government and most of the hospitals are government owned. In Canada, the doctors and hospitals are independent private agents, but they may not sell their services other than to the government.

Because the government is the sole buyer of healthcare services, it chooses the quantity of care to supply. A public choice, not a market equilibrium, determines the quantity of healthcare service.

Patients access healthcare services at a zero (or low) price, so the quantity demanded is that at which the marginal benefit is zero (or low). But the demand for healthcare has no direct effect on the quantity actually available, which is determined by the government's supply decision.

The quantity demanded exceeds the quantity supplied and in the absence of a market price to allocate the scarce resources, services are allocated on a first-come, first-served basis (see Chapter 5, pp. 106–107). The result is a long wait time for treatment.

Figure 16.8 shows how this system works. The $D = MB$, MSB, and $S = MSC$ curves are the same as in Fig. 16.7. The quantity supplied is fixed at a level that exceeds the market equilibrium but is less than the efficient quantity, so a deadweight loss arises.

The area of the gray triangle shows the smallest possible amount of deadweight loss, which would be the loss if patients were treated in the order of their

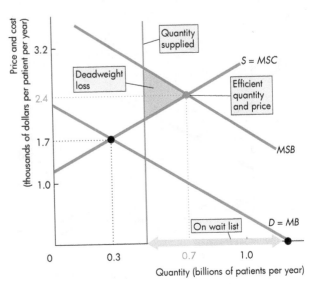

FIGURE 16.8 Public Production with Waiting

The government produces a fixed quantity of healthcare that exceeds the market quantity at the intersection of the $D = MB$ and $S = MSC$ curves but is less than the efficient quantity at the intersection of the MSB and $S = MSC$ curves. Patients face a zero price, so the quantity of healthcare demanded exceeds the quantity supplied. The available healthcare resources are allocated by doctors and patients wait for their treatment.

MyEconLab Animation

willingness to pay. But some people who are waiting in a long line are willing to pay more than the cost of the attention their health problem needs—their marginal benefit exceeds the marginal cost. Others get service even if their marginal benefit is less than the marginal cost. So the full deadweight loss exceeds the area of the gray triangle.

Defenders of this system say that inefficiencies are small and worth accepting because the outcome is fair as everyone has equal access to services. But it isn't exactly true that everyone has equal access. Some people are better at playing the system than others and are able to jump the line.

Private and Government Insurance In the United States, most healthcare services are produced by private doctors and hospitals that receive their incomes from three sources: private health insurance, governments, and patients. Private health insurance pays 41 percent of the bills, government Medicare, Medicaid, and other programs pay 46 percent, and the remaining 13 percent comes from patients. Patients' out-of-pocket payments arise because some

ECONOMICS IN ACTION

How We Pay for Our Healthcare Services

Total healthcare expenditure in the United States is around $3 trillion a year—18 percent of total income. Governments, both federal and state, spend 46 percent of the healthcare dollars. Private insurance companies pay 41 percent and the remaining 13 percent comes directly from the patient's pocket.

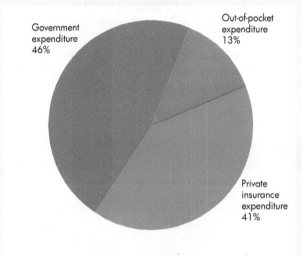

Sources of Expenditure on Healthcare

people are uninsured, and those who are insured face deductibles in their private insurance policies or co-payments for services provided under Medicare and Medicaid.

The scale of out-of-pocket costs combined with conditions set out in insurance plans and the demand for healthcare service determine the quantity of healthcare service provided. Measured by visits to a physician's office, that quantity is 1 billion patients per year. (The average number of physician visits is 3 per person per year.)

Inefficient Overproduction? We don't know whether private insurance together with Medicare and Medicaid provides the efficient quantity of healthcare. But relative to what is spent in other rich countries, the scale of expenditure on these programs suggests that they do overprovide. That is what we will assume in examining how the market works.

Figure 16.9 shows the market for healthcare services. Again, the *D = MB, MSB,* and *S = MSC* curves are the same as those in Fig. 16.7.

The quantity provided is the quantity demanded by patients and supplied by doctors at the out-of-pocket cost to patients.

FIGURE 16.9   Private and Public Inefficient Overproduction and Uncontrolled Expenditure

(a) Inefficiency

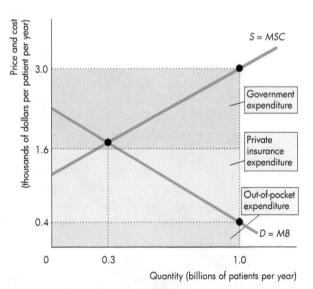

(b) Uncontrolled public expenditure

The quantity of healthcare service is determined by the quantity demanded at the out-of-pocket price. In both parts of the figure, this quantity is 1 billion patients per year.

In part (a), the quantity of healthcare service exceeds the efficient quantity and creates a deadweight loss. In part (b), out-of-pocket payments, private insurance, and government expenditure meet the cost of the quantity of care demanded of $3,000 per patient per year.

MyEconLab Animation

Doctors and hospitals negotiate fees with the government that equal marginal cost, which also equals marginal social cost. Marginal social cost of the quantity provided exceeds marginal benefit, so the over-provision creates the deadweight loss shown by the area of the gray triangle in Fig. 16.9(a).

Uncontrolled Expenditure Figure 16.9(b) illustrates the sources of expenditure: patients' out-of-pocket expenditure (red), expenditure by private insurers (blue), and government expenditure (purple).

Government expenditure is determined by the quantity of care demanded, not by a fixed budget. And without changes in the Medicare and Medicaid programs, this expenditure will grow as the aged population grows. *At Issue* below suggests a solution to this problem.

Obamacare The Patient Protection and Affordable Care Act, 2010 (Obamacare) has created a Health Insurance Marketplace to provide subsidized insurance.

On the supply side of the new marketplace are private insurers. On the demand side are the uninsured and those who want to find a better plan than their current one.

To qualify for subsidies, plans offered through the marketplace must cover pre-existing conditions, preventive services, and 10 essential health benefits.

The premium paid depends on family size and income. An example: A couple both aged 31 with two children and earning the median family income of $51,371 receive a subsidy (as a tax credit) of $5,534 leaving them to pay $3,562 for a $9,096 policy.

◆ AT **ISSUE**

Is Obamacare the Solution to U.S. Healthcare Problems?

The *Patient Protection and Affordable Care Act, 2010* (Obamacare) has created a Health Insurance Marketplace to provide subsidized insurance. By the end of April 2014, 8 million families had signed up for Obamacare. The Act remains controversial, and alternative solutions to the healthcare problem have been proposed. So, *is* Obamacare the solution?

Yes

- A Whitehouse *Fact Sheet* says the *Affordable Care Act* keeps healthcare costs low, promotes prevention, and holds insurance companies accountable.

- It stops insurance companies denying coverage of pre-existing conditions.

- It makes preventive care such as mammograms and wellness visits for seniors free of charge.

- It makes quality, affordable, private health-insurance plans available for those currently uninsured.

The Healthcare Fix

Universal Insurance for All Americans

Laurence J. Kotlikoff

Professor Laurence J. Kotlikoff of Boston University; author of *The Healthcare Fix* and creator of *Medicare Part C for All*.

No

- Laurence Kotlikoff, an economics professor at Boston University, says Obamacare has no effective mechanism for containing costs.

- He proposes a universal private health-insurance Basic Plan that creates incentives to improve health and deliver healthcare services efficiently.

- Each year, each American gets a voucher to buy health insurance from a company of their choice.

- The voucher's value equals the expected cost of covering the person, which is determined by health indicators. (Example: An 80-year-old diabetic might get a $70,000 voucher while a healthy 14-year-old girl might get a $3,000 voucher.)

- The total value of vouchers does not exceed 10 percent of total U.S. income.

- Public expenditure on healthcare grows as income grows, and an Independent Panel adds procedures and technologies covered by the Basic Plan but at a slower pace than in the current system.

Families with no health insurance in 2014 are required to pay a monthly fee of $95 per adult and $47.50 per child or 1 percent of income, whichever is higher, with a maximum family fee of $285 ($3,420 a year).

Figure 16.10 illustrates how the Obamacare subsidy works. The demand and marginal benefit curve $D = MB$ and the supply and marginal social cost curve $S = MSC$ determine the market quantity of 2 million insured at a price of $6,000 per family.

A subsidy of $5,000 puts a gap between the price paid of $4,000 and the price received by the insurer, $9,000. The government pays the subsidy and the total payment, the blue rectangle, is the subsidy per family multiplied by the number of families receiving the subsidy.

The numbers in Fig. 16.10 are calibrated approximately to the actual premiums and subsidies in Obamacare. The median household receives a subsidy of about $5,000, and (in 2014) 8 million families signed up through the Obamacare marketplace. The total subsidy paid by the government is around $40 billion ($5,000 × 8 million = $40 billion).

To determine whether the outcome of the Obamacare subsidy achieves an efficient outcome, we would need to have an estimate of the extent to which the marginal social benefit of health insurance for the affected families exceeds their ability and willingness to pay. The subsidy might be too large, too small, or just right.

Vouchers a Better Solution?

The power of the market leads economists to seek a market solution to all resource allocation problems, and healthcare is no exception.

When a market failure arises because marginal social benefit exceeds the ability and willingness to pay, economists say that vouchers should be used. A **voucher** is a token that can be used to buy only the item that the voucher specifies. So a healthcare voucher could be used only to buy health insurance.

Laurence Kotlikoff (see *At Issue* on the previous page) suggests that every American be given a health care voucher, the value of which is tied to each individual's health profile.

The voucher program would replace Medicare, Medicaid, Obamacare, and some other smaller government programs. The total value of vouchers would be limited, and the government, not the consumer of healthcare services, would be in control of the healthcare budget.

The markets for health insurance and healthcare services would be free to work like any other competitive market to seek an efficient outcome.

FIGURE 16.10   Subsidized Health Insurance

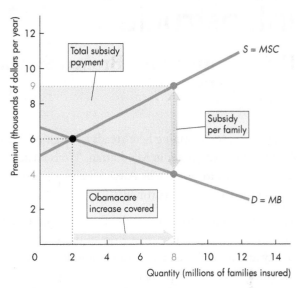

In the market for health insurance, the demand and marginal private benefit curve, $D = MB$, and the supply and marginal social cost curve, $S = MSC$, would deliver an equilibrium with too many people uninsured. A subsidy puts a gap between what the insured pays and the insurer receives and increases the number of families covered. The outcome is efficient if the subsidy brings marginal social benefit into equality with marginal social cost.

───── MyEconLab Animation ─────

◆ REVIEW QUIZ

1 What is special about healthcare that makes it a good provided by government?
2 Why would the market economy produce too little healthcare?
3 How do Canada and the United Kingdom deliver healthcare and what is the problem left unresolved?
4 What are the problems with Medicare and Medicaid?
5 What is the problem that Obamacare seeks to solve and how does the solution work?

Work these questions in Study Plan 16.3 and get instant feedback. Do a Key Terms Quiz.   MyEconLab

◆ *Economics in the News* on pp. 384–385 returns to public goods and looks at the challenge of maintaining our transportation infrastructure.

Maintaining the Transportation Infrastructure

U.S. Infrastructure: Broken System

The Financial Times
April 24, 2014

"Thank you for shopping here" reads the sign on the old gas station at the corner of 10th Avenue and 24th Street in Manhattan. "Your custom is appreciated." But there was not sufficient custom to save the business. The plot is surrounded by wooden hoardings and is to be redeveloped as luxury apartments.

The station, most recently run by Russia's Lukoil, closed last year – one of thousands across the United States to have drawn down the shutters. A combination of increasing fuel efficiency and a steady reduction in the number of miles Americans drive each year has cut into the country's demand to fill up.

The declining fuel sales do not only threaten the narrow world of gas station owners and attendants. For every gallon pumped at the 10th Avenue station, the U.S. federal government received 18.4 cents toward its Highway Trust Fund, which disburses tens of billions of dollars annually to pay for the construction and upkeep of roads, bridges, and other infrastructure in U.S. states. The State of New York took another 69.6 cents. With fewer gallons being pumped, there is less revenue to keep the U.S. transportation system in good shape. ...

A barrier to mobilizing support for greater investment is that past scandals over the misuse of infrastructure funds are better remembered than tragedies resulting from underfunding. ...

The best-known tragedy is the collapse of a freeway bridge over the Mississippi in August 2007 in Minneapolis, which killed 13 people. ...

Copyright 2014 The Financial Times. Reprinted with permission. Further reproduction is prohibited.

ESSENCE OF THE STORY

- Americans are driving fewer miles and in more fuel-efficient vehicles, so the quantity of gasoline consumed is falling.

- The federal and state governments get funds from the gas tax to maintain the highway system, and these funds are now too small to do the job required.

- Underfunding results in inadequate maintenance that sometimes leads to tragedy such as the collapse of a bridge in Minneapolis.

- Scandals over the misuse of infrastructure funds are a barrier to mobilizing support for greater investment.

MyEconLab More Economics in the News

ECONOMIC ANALYSIS

- The road transportation infrastructure of the United States consists of 4 million miles of roads, 47,000 miles of interstate highways, and 607,000 bridges.

- As the news article explains, the gas tax is the main source of funds for maintaining this vast stock of transportation capital, and declining gas use is decreasing these funds.

- The result is too little expenditure on maintaining the infrastructure.

- Bridge collapse is the most visible and worrying consequence of inadequate maintenance.

- The American Society of Civil Engineers says that one in nine (that's 67,487) bridges are structurally deficient.

- A spending increase of $8 billion annually is needed to bring the nation's bridges to a safe standard by 2028.

- You can explain the problem of bridge maintenance by using the tools you've learned in this chapter.

- In Fig. 1, the *x*-axis measures the number of bridges repaired per year and the *y*-axis measures the marginal benefit and cost of repairing a bridge.

- The *MSC* curve shows the marginal social cost of repairing a bridge and the *MSB* curve shows the marginal social benefit.

- The efficient use of resources occurs when 6,000 bridges per year are repaired at a cost of $3 million per bridge, with a total expenditure of $18 billion per year.

- Restricted funds block this efficient outcome. The actual number of bridges repaired is 4,000 per year at a cost of $2.5 million per bridge, with a total expenditure of $10 billion per year. (The numbers are in the region of the actual U.S. data but are assumptions.)

- Because the number of bridges repaired per year is less than the efficient quantity, there is a deadweight loss.

- If Fig. 1 is a correct description of the problem, a political party can propose a bridge repair and tax program that achieves an efficient outcome.

- The problem is that taxes are collected now and bridges are repaired later, so the political party must be able to credibly commit to doing the work after it has collected the funds.

Figure 1 **Underprovision of Infrastructure**

The collapsed freeway bridge over the Mississippi in Minneapolis in August 2007.

385

SUMMARY

Key Points

Public Choices (pp. 370–373)

- Governments establish and maintain property rights, provide nonmarket mechanisms for allocating scarce resources, and redistribute income and wealth.
- Public choice theory explains how voters, firms, politicians, and bureaucrats interact in the political marketplace and why government failure might occur.
- A private good is a good or service that is rival and excludable.
- A public good is a good or service that is nonrival and nonexcludable.
- Healthcare and education are private goods that governments provide on the basis of need rather than on the ability and willingness to pay.

Working Problems 1 and 2 will give you a better understanding of public choices.

Providing Public Goods (pp. 374–377)

- Because a public good is a good or service that is *nonrival* and *nonexcludable*, it creates a *free-rider* problem: No one has an incentive to pay their share of the cost of providing a public good.
- The efficient level of provision of a public good is that at which marginal social benefit equals marginal social cost.

- Competition between political parties can lead to the efficient scale of provision of a public good.
- Bureaucrats who maximize their budgets and voters who are rationally ignorant can lead to the inefficient overprovision of a public good—government failure.

Working Problems 3 to 6 will give you a better understanding of providing public goods.

The Economics of Healthcare (pp. 378–383)

- Governments provide healthcare because people underestimate its value, don't plan far enough into the future, and many can't afford its cost.
- The marginal social benefit of healthcare exceeds the willingness and ability to pay for it.
- A competitive market would underprovide healthcare.
- In some countries, governments provide healthcare at a zero or low price and ration with wait times.
- U.S. private insurance, Medicare, and Medicaid possibly overprovide for those covered.
- Obamacare provides subsidized insurance and compels everyone to make a minimum contribution for health coverage.

Working Problems 7 to 10 will give you a better understanding of the economics of healthcare.

Key Terms

MyEconLab Key Terms Quiz

Common resource, 372
Excludable, 372
Free-rider problem, 374
Government failure, 370
Natural monopoly good, 372

Nonexcludable, 372
Nonrival, 372
Political equilibrium, 371
Principle of minimum
    differentiation, 376

Private good, 372
Public choice, 370
Public good, 372
Rival, 372
Voucher, 383

WORKED PROBLEM

MyEconLab You can work this problem in Chapter 16 Study Plan.

The table sets out the marginal benefits that Ann, Sue, and Zack receive from spraying their shared swamp to control mosquitos. The marginal social cost (*MSC*) is a constant $12 per spray.

Number of sprays per season	Marginal benefit		
	Ann	Sue	Zack
	(dollars per spray)		
0	5	10	15
1	4	8	12
2	3	6	9
3	2	4	6
4	1	2	3
5	0	0	0

Questions

1. What is the marginal social benefit from mosquito control at each quantity of sprays?
2. What is the efficient number of sprays per season?

Solutions

1. Mosquito control is a public good, so its marginal social benefit (*MSB*) is found by summing the marginal benefits of the three people at each quantity of sprays.

   The table below records the calculations. At 2 sprays per season, for example, marginal social benefit is $18 per spray, which is the sum of $3 (Ann), $6 (Sue), and $9 Zack). The other rows of the table show the marginal social benefit for other quantities of sprays.

   Figure 1 illustrates the calculation and constructs the *MSB* curve.

Number of sprays per season	Marginal benefit			Marginal social benefit
	Ann	Sue	Zack	
	(dollars per spray)			
0	5	10	15	30
1	4	8	12	24
2	3	6	9	18
3	2	4	6	12
4	1	2	3	6
5	0	0	0	0

Key Point: The marginal social benefit curve of a public good is the *vertical* sum of the individual marginal benefit curves.

2. To find the efficient number of sprays, we need to determine the number of sprays per season at which the *MSB* equals the *MSC* of $12 per spray.

   From the table above, *MSB* equals $12 per spray at 3 sprays per season, so that is the efficient quantity.

Key Point: The efficient quantity of a public good is that at which its marginal social benefit equals its marginal social cost.

Key Figures

Figure 1 Marginal Social Benefit

Figure 2 Efficient Quantity

MyEconLab Interactive Animation

STUDY PLAN PROBLEMS AND APPLICATIONS

MyEconLab   You can work Problems 1 to 10 in Chapter 16 Study Plan and get instant feedback.

Public Choices (Study Plan 16.1)

1. Classify each of the following items as excludable, nonexcludable, rival, or nonrival. Explain your answer.
   - A Big Mac
   - Brooklyn bridge
   - A view of the Statue of Liberty
   - A hurricane warning system

2. Classify each of the following items as a public good, a private good, a natural monopoly good, or a common resource. Explain your answer.
   - Highway patrol services
   - Internet service
   - Fish in the Atlantic ocean
   - UPS courier service

Providing Public Goods (Study Plan 16.2)

3. For each of the following goods, explain why a free-rider problem arises or how it is avoided.
   - July 4th fireworks display
   - Interstate 81 in Virginia
   - Wireless Internet access in hotels
   - The public library in your city

4. The table sets out the benefits that Terri and Sue receive from on-campus police at night:

| Police officers on duty (number per night) | Marginal benefit | |
| | Terri | Sue |
	(dollars per police officer)	
1	18	22
2	14	18
3	10	14
4	6	10
5	2	6

Suppose that Terri and Sue are the only students on campus at night. Draw a graph to show the marginal social benefit from the on-campus police at night.

Use the data on mosquito control in the table in the next column to work Problems 5 and 6.

5. What quantity of spraying would a private firm provide? What is the efficient quantity of spraying? In a single-issue election on mosquito control, what quantity would the winner provide?

| Quantity (square miles sprayed per day) | Marginal social cost | Marginal social benefit |
	(thousands of dollars per day)	
1	2	10
2	4	8
3	6	6
4	8	4
5	10	2

6. If the government appoints a bureaucrat to run the program, would mosquito spraying most likely be underprovided, overprovided, or provided at the efficient quantity?

The Economics of Healthcare (Study Plan 16.3)

Use the following figure, which shows the marginal benefit from health insurance and the willingness and ability to pay for it, to work Problems 7 to 10.

The marginal cost of insurance is a constant $6,000 per family per year. Marginal social benefit from insurance exceeds the willingness and ability to pay by a constant $4,000 per family per year.

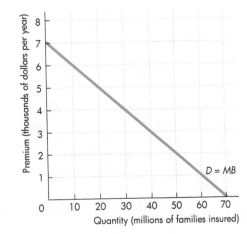

7. With no public health insurance market, how many families buy insurance, what is the premium, and is the coverage efficient?

8. If the government provides healthcare to achieve the efficient coverage, how many families are covered and how much must taxpayers pay?

9. If the government subsidizes private insurers, what subsidy will achieve the efficient coverage?

10. If the government gave coverage to everyone, what problems would arise in the related market for healthcare services?

ADDITIONAL PROBLEMS AND APPLICATIONS

MyEconLab   You can work these problems in MyEconLab if assigned by your instructor.

Public Choices

11. Classify each of the following items as excludable, nonexcludable, rival, or nonrival.
    - Homeland security
    - A Starbucks coffee
    - A view of the Liberty Bell
    - The Appalachian Trail
    - A Google search

12. Classify each of the following items as a public good, a private good, a natural monopoly good, or a common resource. Explain your answer.
    - Measles vaccinations
    - Tuna in the Pacific Ocean
    - Airline service in the United States
    - Local storm-water system

13. Classify each of the following goods as a private good, a public good, a natural monopoly good, or none of the above.
    - Chewing gum
    - Cable TV
    - The New York City subway
    - A skateboard
    - The Santa Monica beach

Providing Public Goods

14. The table sets out the marginal benefits that Sam and Nick receive from the town's street lighting:

| Number of street lights | Marginal benefit | |
| | Sam | Nick |
	(dollars per street light)	
1	10	12
2	8	9
3	6	6
4	4	3
5	2	0

   a. Is the town's street lighting a private good or a public good?
   b. Suppose that Sam and Nick are the only residents of the town. Draw a graph to show the marginal social benefit from the town's street lighting.

15. What is the principle of diminishing marginal benefit? In Problem 14, does Sam's, Nick's, or the society's marginal benefit diminish faster?

Use the following news clip to work Problems 16 and 17.

A Bridge Too Far Gone

The gas taxes paid for much of America's post-war freeway system. Now motorists pay about one-third in gas taxes to drive a mile as they did in the 1960s. Yet raising such taxes is politically tricky. This would matter less if private cash was flooding into infrastructure, or if new ways were being found to control demand. Neither is happening, and private companies building toll roads brings howls of outrage.

Source: *The Economist*, August 9, 2007

16. Why is it "politically tricky" to raise gas taxes to finance infrastructure?

17. What in the news clip points to the distinction between public *production* of a public good and public *provision*? Give examples of three public goods that are *produced* by private firms but *provided* by government and paid for with taxes.

18. **Vaccination Dodgers**

    Doctors struggle to eradicate polio worldwide, but one of the biggest problems is persuading parents to vaccinate their children. Since the discovery of the vaccine, polio has been eliminated from Europe and the law requires everyone to be vaccinated. People who refuse to be vaccinated are "free riders."

    Source: *USA Today*, March 12, 2008

    a. Explain why someone in a rich country who has not opted out on medical or religious grounds and refuses to be vaccinated is a "free rider."
    b. Polio in poor countries such as Myanmar has reappeared in 2010 and is increasing. Are people who are too poor to afford the vaccination "free riders"? Should vaccinations be compulsory? Explain your answer.

The Economics of Healthcare

19. **Obamacare Hits Enrollment Goal**

    A last-minute enrollment surge enabled the White House to meet its 7 million sign-up target for the Affordable Care Act. President Barack Obama said on Tuesday that 7.1 million people had signed up on federal or state exchanges for coverage under the healthcare law.

    Source: *CNN*, April 1, 2014

a. If the White House target was to enroll the efficient quantity of families in Obamacare, how would it have determined that target?

b. Draw a graph to illustrate the health-insurance market and illustrate how the Obamacare subsidy influences the number of families covered.

c. How would the demand for health insurance change if the penalty for not signing up for Obamacare were abolished? Draw a graph to illustrate the outcome

Use the following information and figure to work Problems 20 to 22.

The marginal cost of health insurance is a constant $8,000 a year and the figure shows the marginal benefit and willingness and ability to pay curve. Suppose that the marginal social benefit of insurance exceeds the willingness and ability to pay by a constant $2,000 per family per year.

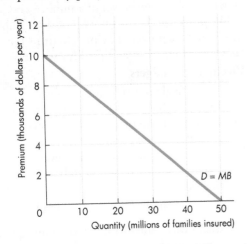

20. If all health insurance is private and the market for insurance is competitive, how many families are covered, what is the premium, and what is the deadweight loss created?

21. If the government decides to provide public health insurance (like Canada), what healthcare fee does it charge to achieve an efficient coverage? How much will taxpayers have to pay?

22. If the government decides to subsidize health insurance (like Obamacare), what subsidy will achieve the efficient coverage?

Economics in the News

23. After you have studied *Economics in the News* on pp. 384–385, answer the following questions.

a. What is the source of revenue for constructing and maintaining the transportation infrastructure?

b. Why has that revenue source not grown fast enough to deliver an efficient scale of infrastructure provision?

c. What other revenue sources can you suggest that could provide a solution to underprovision?

d. How would you expect population growth to influence the marginal social benefit of highways and bridges?

e. Illustrate your answer to (d) by drawing a version of the figure on p. 385 that shows the effect of an increase in the population.

24. **Who's Hiding Under Our Umbrella?**

Students of the Cold War learn that, to deter possible Soviet aggression, the United States placed a "strategic umbrella" over NATO Europe and Japan, with the United States providing most of their national security. Under President Ronald Reagan, the United States spent 6 percent of total income on defense, whereas the Europeans spent only 2 to 3 percent and the Japanese spent only 1 percent, although all faced a common enemy. Thus the U.S. taxpayer paid a disproportionate share of the overall defense spending, whereas NATO Europe and Japan spent more on consumer goods or saved.

Source: *International Herald Tribune*, January 30, 2008

a. Explain the free-rider problem described in this news clip.

b. Does the free-rider problem in international defense mean that the world has too little defense against aggression?

c. How do nations try to overcome the free-rider problem among nations?

17

EXTERNALITIES

After studying this chapter, you will be able to:

◆ Explain how externalities arise

◆ Explain why external costs bring market failure and overproduction and how property rights and public choices might achieve an efficient outcome

◆ Explain the tragedy of the commons and its possible solutions

◆ Explain why external benefits bring market failure and underproduction and public choices might achieve an efficient outcome

How can we use less coal to generate electricity and reduce carbon emissions that bring climate change? What can we do to conserve the ocean's fish stocks and save them from extinction? How can we ensure that we spend enough on our schools and colleges?

These are the questions we study in this chapter. They arise because some of our choices impose costs on or bring benefits to others that we don't think about when we make those choices.

In *Economics in the News* at the end of the chapter, we look at the Obama administration's ideas on how to counter carbon emissions and climate change.

⬛▶ Externalities In Our Lives

An **externality** is a cost of or a benefit from an action that falls on someone other than the person or firm choosing the action. We call an externality that imposes a cost a **negative externality**; and we call an externality that provides a benefit a **positive externality**.

We identify externalities as four types:

- Negative production externalities
- Positive production externalities
- Negative consumption externalities
- Positive consumption externalities

Negative Production Externalities

Burning coal to generate electricity emits carbon dioxide that is warming the planet. Logging and the clearing of forests is destroying the habitat of wildlife and also adding carbon dioxide to the atmosphere. These activities are negative production externalities, the costs of which are borne by everyone, and even by future generations.

Noise is another negative production externality. When the U.S. Open tennis tournament is being played at Flushing Meadows, players, spectators, and television viewers around the world share a cost that New Yorkers experience every day: the noise of airplanes taking off from LaGuardia Airport. Aircraft noise imposes a cost on millions of people who live under the flight paths to airports in every major city.

Positive Production Externalities

To produce orange blossom honey, Honey Run Honey of Chico, California, locates beehives next to an orange orchard. The honeybees collect pollen and nectar from the orange blossoms to make the honey. At the same time, they transfer pollen between the blossoms, which helps to fertilize the blossoms. Two positive production externalities are present in this example. Honey Run Honey gets a positive production externality from the owner of the orange orchard; and the orange grower gets a positive production externality from Honey Run.

Negative Consumption Externalities

Negative consumption externalities are a source of irritation for most of us. Smoking tobacco in a confined space creates fumes that many people find unpleasant and that pose a health risk. So smoking in restaurants and on airplanes generates a negative

externality. To avoid this negative externality, many restaurants and all airlines ban smoking. But while a smoking ban avoids a negative consumption externality for most people, it imposes a negative external cost on smokers who would prefer to enjoy the consumption of tobacco while dining or taking a plane trip.

Noisy parties and outdoor rock concerts are other examples of negative consumption externalities. They are also examples of the fact that a simple ban on an activity is not a solution. Banning noisy parties avoids the external cost on sleep-seeking neighbors, but it results in the sleepers imposing an external cost on the fun-seeking partygoers.

Permitting dandelions to grow in lawns, not picking up leaves in the fall, allowing a dog to bark loudly or to foul a neighbor's lawn, and letting a cellphone ring in class are other examples of negative consumption externalities.

Positive Consumption Externalities

When you get a flu vaccination, you lower your risk of being infected. If you avoid the flu, your neighbor, who didn't get vaccinated, has a better chance of remaining healthy. Flu vaccinations generate positive consumption externalities.

When the owner of a historic building restores it, everyone who sees the building gets pleasure from it. Similarly, when someone erects a spectacular home—such as those built by Frank Lloyd Wright during the 1920s and 1930s—or other exciting building—such as the Chrysler and Empire State Buildings in New York or the Walt Disney Concert Hall in Los Angeles—an external consumption benefit flows to everyone who has an opportunity to view it.

Education, which we examine in more detail in this chapter, is a major example of this type of externality.

◆ REVIEW QUIZ

1 What are the four types of externality?
2 Provide an example of each type of externality that is different from the ones described above.

Work these questions in Study Plan 17.1 and get instant feedback. Do a Key Terms Quiz.   MyEconLab

We're now going to examine the market failure that arises from an externality and the ways in which it can be avoided. We begin by looking at the negative production externality, pollution.

ECONOMICS IN ACTION

Opposing Trends: Success and Failure

The trends in local U.S. air quality and global greenhouse gas concentrations are starkly opposing. The concentrations of air pollutants in U.S. cities is decreasing, as it has done so for the past 32 years. In contrast, the concentration of greenhouse gases (mainly carbon dioxide) in the global atmosphere is increasing and posing an ever more urgent problem.

Air Pollution Trends Figure 1 shows the trends in the concentrations of the six main pollutants of the air in the United States between 1980 and 2012. The concentrations of all these pollutants decreased.

The Clean Air Act has brought regulations that almost eliminated lead and cut emissions of carbon monoxide, sulfur dioxide, and nitrogen dioxide to below 40 percent and ozone to 80 percent of their 1980 levels, and particulate matter to 64 percent of its 2000 level. And economic actions that you will learn about in this chapter have almost eliminated lead from highway vehicles and industrial processes.

These reductions in air pollution are even more impressive seen against the trends in economic activity. Between 1980 and 2012, total production in the United States increased by 145 percent, vehicle miles traveled increased by 95 percent, and the population increased by 40 percent.

Global CO₂ and Temperature Trends Figure 2 shows the global trends in carbon dioxide (CO_2) concentration and temperature.

Both trends are starkly upward. CO_2 concentration has increased by almost 40 percent since 1850, and global temperature has been rising for more than 100 years.

Scientists agree that the scale on which we burn fossil fuels is the major source of the rising CO_2 trend. There is more uncertainty about the effect of the increase in CO_2 on global temperature, but the consensus is that the effect is significant.

Stopping the rising CO_2 trend requires joint action by the governments of every nation. But a binding agreement among nations to reduce greenhouse gas emissions, the *Kyoto Protocol*, excluded the major developing countries and the United States refused to ratify it. You will see in this chapter why global warming is a much harder problem to solve than reducing air pollution in the United States.

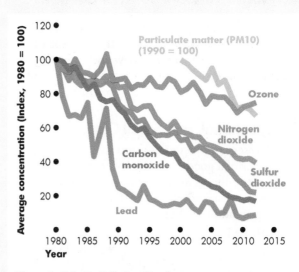

Figure 1 U.S. Air Pollution Trends
Source of data: United States Environmental Protection Agency.

Los Angeles still has a smoggy dawn on some days

Figure 2 Global Warming Trends
Sources of data: Temperature: Met Office Hadley Centre (combined land and oceans); CO₂: Scripps Institution of Oceanography, Mauna Loa Observatory, Hawaii, data since 1960 and ice-core estimates before 1960.

Negative Externality: Pollution

To see the effects and possible remedies for a negative production externality, we'll look at the example of production activities that pollute. We begin by distinguishing among three costs: private, external, and social.

Private, External, and Social Cost

A *private cost* of production is a cost that is borne by the producer of a good or service. *Marginal cost* is the cost of producing an *additional unit* of a good or service. So **marginal private cost** (MC) is the cost of producing an additional unit of a good or service that is borne by its producer.

An *external cost* is a cost of producing a good or service that is *not* borne by the producer but borne by other people. A **marginal external cost** is the cost of producing an additional unit of a good or service that falls on people other than the producer.

Marginal social cost (MSC) is the marginal cost incurred by the producer and by everyone else on whom the cost falls—by society. It is the sum of marginal private cost and marginal external cost. That is,

$$MSC = MC + \text{Marginal external cost.}$$

We express costs in dollars, but we must always remember that a cost is an opportunity cost—something real, such as clean air or a clean river, is given up to get something.

Valuing an External Cost Economists use market prices to put a dollar value on the external cost of pollution. For example, suppose that there are two similar rivers, one polluted and the other clean. Ten identical homes are built along the side of each river. The homes on the clean river rent for $2,000 per month, and those on the polluted river rent for $1,500 per month. If the pollution is the only detectable difference between the two rivers and the two locations, the rent difference of $500 per month is the pollution cost per home. With 10 homes on the side of a polluted river, the external cost of pollution is $5,000 per month.

External Cost and Output Figure 17.1 shows an example of the relationship between output and cost in a paint industry that pollutes rivers. The marginal cost curve, MC, describes the marginal private cost borne by the paint producers, which increases as the quantity of paint produced increases.

FIGURE 17.1   An External Cost

The MC curve shows the marginal private cost borne by the factories that produce paint. The MSC curve shows the sum of marginal private cost and marginal external cost. When output is 3 million gallons of paint per month, marginal private cost is $1.00 per gallon, marginal external cost is 75¢ per gallon, and marginal social cost is $1.75 per gallon.

MyEconLab Animation

If a firm pollutes a river, it imposes an external cost borne by other users of the river. Pollution and its marginal external cost increase with the amount of paint produced.

The marginal social cost curve, MSC, is found by adding marginal external cost to marginal private cost. So a point on the MSC curve shows the sum of the marginal private cost and marginal external cost at a given level of output.

For example, if 3 million gallons of paint per month are produced, marginal private cost is $1.00 per gallon, marginal external cost is 75¢ per gallon, and marginal social cost is $1.75 per gallon.

Let's now see how much paint gets produced and how much pollution gets created.

Equilibrium and Amount of Pollution Equilibrium in the market for paint determines the amount of pollution. Figure 17.2 has the same MC and MSC curves as Fig. 17.1 and also has a market demand and marginal social benefit curve, $D = MSB$. Equilibrium occurs at a price of $1.00 per gallon and 3 million

FIGURE 17.2 Inefficiency with an External Cost

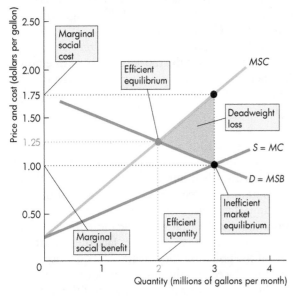

The factories' marginal private cost curve is the market supply curve, S = MC. The market demand curve is the marginal social benefit curve, D = MSB. The market equilibrium occurs at a price of $1.00 per gallon and 3 million gallons per month. This outcome is inefficient because marginal social cost exceeds marginal social benefit. The efficient quantity of paint is 2 million gallons per month. The gray triangle shows the deadweight loss created by the pollution.

MyEconLab Animation and Draw Graph

gallons per month. This equilibrium is one with *inefficient overproduction* (Chapter 5, p. 114) because marginal social cost at $1.75 per gallon exceeds marginal social benefit at $1.00 per gallon.

The efficient equilibrium occurs where marginal social benefit *equals* marginal social cost at 2 million gallons of paint per month. Too much paint is produced, too much pollution is created, and the area of the deadweight loss triangle measures the society's loss.

The deadweight loss arises because the paint factories only take their private cost into account when making their production decision. If some method can be found to get paint factories to create less pollution and eliminate the deadweight loss, everyone—the owners of paint factories and the residents of the riverside homes—can gain. So, what can be done to fix the inefficiency that arises from an external

cost? Three approaches are available and we will examine each of them. They are

- Establish property rights
- Mandate clean technology
- Tax or price pollution

Establish Property Rights

Property rights are legally established titles to the ownership, use, and disposal of factors of production and goods and services that are enforceable in the courts. Property rights are a foundation stone of the market economy. But they don't apply to all property. Establishing property rights can confront producers with the costs of their actions and provide the incentives that allocate resources efficiently.

To see how property rights work, suppose that the paint producers have property rights on a river and the homes alongside it—they *own* the river and the homes. The rental income that the paint producers are able to make on the homes depends on the amount of pollution they create. Using the earlier example, people are willing to pay a rent of $2,000 a month to live alongside a pollution-free river but only $1,500 a month to live with the pollution created by producing 3 million gallons of paint per month.

The forgone rental income from homes alongside a polluted river is an opportunity cost of producing paint. The paint producers must now decide how to respond to this cost. There are two possible responses:

- Use an abatement technology
- Produce less and pollute less

Use an Abatement Technology An **abatement technology** is a production technology that reduces or prevents pollution. The catalytic converter in every U.S. car is an example of an abatement technology. Its widespread adoption (with lead-free gasoline) has dramatically reduced pollution from highway vehicles and helped to achieve the trends in U.S. air quality shown on p. 393.

Abatement technologies exist to eliminate or reduce pollution from electricity generation and many industrial processes, including the manufacture of paint.

Produce Less and Pollute Less An alternative to incurring the cost of using an abatement technology is to use the polluting technology but cut production, reduce pollution, and get a higher income from renting homes by the river. The decision turns on cost: Firms will choose the least-cost alternative.

Efficient Market Equilibrium Figure 17.3 illustrates the efficient market outcome. With property rights in place, the paint producers face the pollution costs or the abatement costs, whichever is lower. The *MSC* curve includes the cost of producing paint plus *either* the cost of abatement *or* the cost of pollution (forgone rent), whichever is lower. This curve, labeled $S = MC = MSC$, is now the market supply curve.

Market equilibrium occurs at a price of $1.25 per gallon and 2 million gallons of paint per month. This outcome is efficient.

If the forgone rent is less than the abatement cost, the factories will still create some pollution, but it will be the efficient quantity. If the abatement cost is lower than the forgone rent, the factories will stop polluting. But they will produce the efficient quantity because marginal cost includes the abatement cost.

The Coase Theorem Does it matter whether the polluter or the victim of the pollution owns the resource that might be polluted? Until 1960, everyone thought that it did matter. But in 1960, Ronald Coase (see p. 417) had a remarkable insight that we now call the Coase theorem.

The **Coase theorem** is the proposition that if property rights exist and the transactions costs of enforcing them are low, then private transactions are efficient and it doesn't matter who has the property rights.

Application of the Coase Theorem Suppose that instead of the paint factories owning the homes, the residents own their homes and the river. Now the factories must pay a fee to the homeowners for the right to dump their waste. The greater the quantity of waste dumped into the river, the more the factories must pay. So again, the factories face the opportunity cost of the pollution they create. The quantity of paint produced and the amount of waste dumped are the same whoever owns the homes and the river. If the factories own them, they bear the cost of pollution because they receive a lower income from home rents. If the residents own the homes and the river, the factories bear the cost of pollution because they must pay a fee to the homeowners. In both cases, the factories bear the cost of their pollution and dump the efficient amount of waste into the river.

The Coase solution works only when transactions costs are low. **Transactions costs** are the opportunity costs of conducting a transaction. For example, when you buy a house, you pay an agent to help you find the best place and a lawyer to run checks that assure you that the seller owns the property and that after you've paid for it, the ownership has been properly transferred to you. These costs are transactions costs.

In the example of the homes alongside a river, the transactions costs that are incurred by a small number of paint factories and a few homeowners might be low enough to enable them to negotiate the deals that produce an efficient outcome. But in many situations, transactions costs are so high that it would be inefficient to incur them. In these situations, the Coase solution is not available.

FIGURE 17.3   Property Rights Achieve an Efficient Outcome

With property rights, the marginal cost curve that excludes pollution and abatement costs shows only part of the producers' marginal cost. The marginal cost of producing paint now includes the cost of pollution—the external cost—or the cost of abatement. So the market supply curve is $S = MC = MSC$. Market equilibrium occurs at a price of $1.25 per gallon and 2 million gallons of paint per month. Marginal social cost equals marginal social benefit, so the outcome is efficient.

Mandate Clean Technology

When property rights are too difficult to define and enforce, public choices are made. Regulation is a government's most likely response.

Most countries regulate what may be dumped in rivers and lakes and emitted into the atmosphere. The environmental resources of the United States are heavily regulated.

An example of environmental regulation is the Clean Air Act of 1970 and its later amendments, which give the Environmental Protection Agency (EPA) the authority to issue regulations that limit emissions and achieve defined air quality standards.

The EPA has issued thousands of regulations that require chemical plants, utilities, and steel mills to adopt best-practice pollution abatement technologies and limit their emissions of specified air pollutants. Other regulations have been issued that govern road vehicle emission limits, which must be met by the vehicle manufacturers.

In 2007, the Supreme Court ruled that the EPA has authority to regulate greenhouse gas emissions.

Although direct regulation can and has reduced emissions and improved air quality, economists are generally skeptical about this approach. Abatement is not always the least-cost solution. Also, government agencies are not well placed to find the cost-minimizing solution to a pollution problem. Individual firms seeking to minimize cost and maximize profit and responding to price signals are more likely to achieve an efficient outcome. We'll now examine these other approaches to pollution.

Tax or Cap and Price Pollution

Governments use two main methods of confronting polluters with the costs of their decisions:

- Taxes
- Cap-and-trade

Taxes Governments can use taxes as an incentive for producers to cut back the pollution they create. Taxes used in this way are called **Pigovian taxes**, in honor of Arthur Cecil Pigou, the British economist who first worked out this method of dealing with external costs during the 1920s.

By setting the tax equal to the marginal external cost (or marginal abatement cost if it is lower), firms can be made to behave in the same way as they would if they bore the cost of the externality directly.

To see how government actions can change the outcome in a market with external costs, let's return to the example of paint factories and the river. Assume that the government has assessed the marginal external cost of pollution accurately and

imposes a tax on the factories that exactly equals this cost. The producers are now confronted with the social cost of their actions. The market equilibrium is one in which price equals marginal social cost—an efficient outcome.

Figure 17.4 illustrates the effects of a Pigovian tax on paint factory pollution. The curve $D = MSB$ is the market demand and the marginal social benefit curve. The curve MC is the marginal cost curve. The tax equals the marginal external cost of the pollution. We add this tax to the marginal private cost to find the market supply curve, the curve labeled $S = MC + tax = MSC$. This curve is the market supply curve because it tells us the quantity supplied at each price, given the factories' marginal cost and the tax they must pay. This curve is also the marginal social cost curve because the pollution tax has been set equal to the marginal external cost.

FIGURE 17.4   A Pollution Tax to Achieve an Efficient Outcome

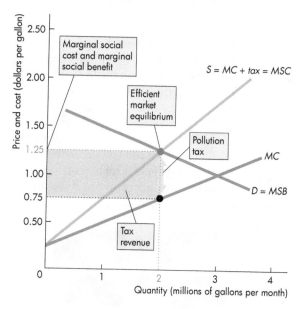

When the government imposes a pollution tax equal to the marginal external cost of pollution, the market supply curve becomes the marginal private cost curve, MC, plus the tax—the curve $S = MC + tax$. Market equilibrium occurs at a price of $1.25 per gallon and a quantity of 2 million gallons of paint per month. This equilibrium is efficient because marginal social cost equals marginal social benefit. The purple rectangle shows the government's tax revenue.

—— MyEconLab Animation and Draw Graph ——

ECONOMICS IN ACTION

Taxing Carbon Emissions

British Columbia, Ireland, and the United Kingdom are making their carbon footprints smaller.

British Columbia's Carbon Tax Introduced in 2008 at $10 per metric ton of carbon emitted, British Columbia's tax increased each year to its final rate of $30 per metric ton in 2012. The tax applies to all forms of carbon emission from coal, oil, and natural gas. The tax is revenue-neutral, which means that other taxes, personal and corporate income taxes, are cut by the amount raised by the carbon tax. Between 2008 and 2012, carbon emissions fell by 17 percent.

Ireland's Carbon Tax Since 2010, Ireland has taxed kerosene, gas oil, liquid petroleum gas, fuel oil, natural gas, and solid fuels. The tax rate in 2013 was 10 euros ($13) per metric ton of CO_2 emitted and 20 euros ($26) per ton in 2014. Emissions have fallen since the tax was introduced, but recession as well as the carbon tax brought this fall.

U.K. Tax on Gasoline The United Kingdom doesn't call its gasoline tax a carbon tax, but it has the same effect on drivers. The figure shows the U.K. price of gasoline compared with that in three other countries. The enormous differences arise almost entirely from tax differences. An effect of these price differences is that cars in the United Kingdom get an average of 38 miles per gallon while in the United States, the average is 23 miles per gallon. A high gas tax cuts carbon emissions by inducing people to drive smaller cars and to drive less.

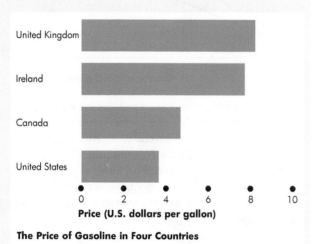

The Price of Gasoline in Four Countries

Demand and supply now determine the market equilibrium price at $1.25 per gallon and a quantity of 2 million gallons of paint a month. At this quantity of paint production, the marginal social cost is $1.25 and the marginal social benefit is $1.25, so the market outcome is efficient. The factories incur a marginal private cost of 75¢ per gallon and pay a pollution tax of 50¢ per gallon. The government collects tax revenue of $1 million per month.

Cap-and-Trade A cap is an upper limit. You met the idea of a government imposing an upper limit when you learned about production quotas (Chapter 6, p. 139) and import quotas (Chapter 7, p. 160). A cap is a quota—a pollution quota.

A government that uses this method must first estimate the efficient quantity of pollution and set the overall cap at that level.

Just like a production or import quota, a pollution quota or cap must somehow be allocated to individual firms (and possibly even households). In an efficient allocation of pollution quotas, each firm has the same marginal social cost. So to make an efficient allocation of the cap across firms, the government would need to know each firm's marginal production cost and marginal abatement cost.

A Pigovian tax achieves an efficient allocation of pollution across firms because each firm chooses how much to produce and pollute taking the tax into account, and produces the quantity at which marginal social cost equals price. Because all firms face the same market price, they also incur the same marginal social cost.

The government solves the allocation problem by making an initial distribution of the cap across firms and allowing them to trade in a market for pollution permits. Firms that have a low marginal abatement cost sell permits and make big cuts in pollution. Firms that have a high marginal abatement cost buy permits and make smaller cuts or perhaps even no cuts in pollution.

The market in permits determines the equilibrium price of pollution and each firm, confronted with that price, maximizes profit by setting its marginal pollution cost or marginal abatement cost, whichever is lower, equal to the market price of a permit.

By confronting polluters with a price of pollution, trade in pollution permits can achieve the same efficient outcome as a Pigovian tax.

◆ AT **ISSUE**

Should We be Doing More to Reduce Carbon Emissions?

Economists agree that tackling the global-warming problem requires changes in the incentives that people face. The cost of carbon-emitting activities must rise and the cost of clean-energy technologies must fall.

Disagreement centers on *how* to change incentives. Should more countries set targets for cutting carbon emissions at a faster rate? Should they introduce a carbon tax, emissions charges, or cap-and-trade to cut emissions? Should clean energy research and development be subsidized?

Yes: *The Stern Review*

- Confronting emitters with a tax or price on carbon imposes low present costs for high future benefits.

- The cost of reducing greenhouse gas emissions to safe levels can be kept to 1 percent of global income each year.

- The future benefits are incomes at least 5 percent and possibly 20 percent higher than they will be with inaction every year forever.

- Climate change is a global problem that requires an international coordinated response.

- Unlike most taxes, which bring deadweight loss, a carbon tax eliminates (or reduces) deadweight loss.

- Strong, deliberate policy action is required to change the incentives that emitters face.

- Policy actions should include:

  1. Emissions limits and emissions trading
  2. Increased subsidies for energy research and development, including the development of low-cost clean technology for generating electricity
  3. Reduced deforestation and research into new drought and flood-resilient crop varieties

No: **The Copenhagen Consensus**

- Confronting emitters with a tax or price on carbon imposes high present costs and low future benefits.

- Unless the entire world signs on to an emissions reduction program, free riders will increase their emissions and carbon leakage will occur.

- A global emissions reduction program and carbon tax would lower living standards in the rich countries and slow the growth rate of living standards in developing countries.

- Technology is already advancing and the cost of cleaner energy is falling.

- Fracking technology has vastly expanded the natural gas deposits that can be profitably exploited and replacing coal with gas halves the carbon emissions from electricity generation.

- Free-market price signals will allocate resources to the development of new technologies that stop and eventually reverse the upward trend in greenhouse gasses.

Economist Nicholas Stern, principal author of *The Stern Review on the Economics of Climate Change.* Greenhouse gas emission is "the greatest market failure the world has ever seen."

To avoid the risk of catastrophic climate change, the upward CO_2 trend must be stopped.

Bjørn Lomborg, President of the Copenhagen Consensus and author of *The Skeptical Environmentalist.* "For little environmental benefit, we could end up sacrificing growth, jobs, and opportunities for the big majority, especially in the developing world."

ECONOMICS IN ACTION
A Global Prisoners' Dilemma

China, the United States, and the European Union create 52 percent of global carbon emissions. Another six large countries create a further 21 percent (see Fig. 1).

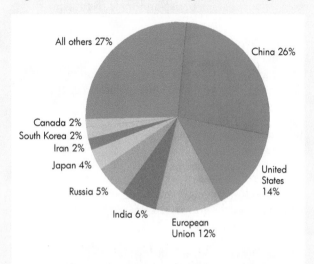

Figure 1 The Global Distribution of CO₂ Emissions

Cutting global carbon emissions is a *prisoners' dilemma* (see pp. 344–345). The payoff matrix illustrates the dilemma. The strategies for the United States and other countries are to keep increasing carbon emissions or to cut them.

Cutting emissions requires using production technologies with higher private costs. But higher private costs make the nation's exporters less competitive in world markets. By letting others cut their emissions and continuing to use low-cost carbon emitting technologies, a nation can gain a competitive advantage.

In the payoff matrix below, China is better off increasing emissions regardless of what others do; and the others are better off increasing their emissions regardless of what China does. The *Nash equilibrium* (see p. 345) is for all countries to keep increasing their emissions. But the world is better off if all cut.

The challenge is to find a cooperative outcome that avoids this prisoners' dilemma.

Figure 2 The Global Prisoners' Dilemma

Coping with Global Externalities

The United States has cut the emissions of local air pollutants and made its own air cleaner by adopting the measures you've just seen. But one country, even a big country such as the United States that accoounts for 20 percent of the value of global production and 14 percent of carbon emissions, can't solve the problem of global warming and climate change alone. Coping with this problem requires public choices at a *global* level, choices by all governments, which are much harder to make and coordinate.

A lower CO_2 concentration in the world's atmosphere is a global *public good*. And like all public goods, it brings a *free-rider problem* (see Chapter 16, p. 374). Without a mechanism to ensure participation in a global carbon reduction program, countries are in a *prisoners' dilemma* (see *Economics in Action* above).

Your next task is to study another negative production externality, the tragedy of the commons, and the arrangements that can achieve the efficient use of common resources.

Negative Externality: The Tragedy of the Commons

Overgrazing the pastures around a village in Middle Ages England, and overfishing the Southern Bluefin tuna, Pacific Yellowfin tuna, Atlantic cod, and Minke whales during the recent past are tragedies of the commons. Other current tragedies are the destruction of tropical rainforests in Africa and the Amazon basin of South America.

The **tragedy of the commons** is the overuse of a common resource that arises when its users have no incentive to conserve it and use it sustainably and efficiently.

To study the tragedy of the commons and its possible remedies, we'll focus on one of the recent and current tragedies – overfishing and depleting the stock of tuna. You're about to discover that there are two problems that give rise to the tragedy of the commons:

- Unsustainable use of a common resource
- Inefficient use of a common resource

Unsustainable Use of a Common Resource

Many common resources are renewable—they replenish themselves by the birth and growth of new members of the population. Fish, trees, and the fertile soil are all examples of this type of resource. At any given time, there is a stock of the resource and a rate at which it is being used.

A common resource is being used *unsustainably* if its rate of use persistently decreases its stock. A common resource is being used *sustainably* if its rate of use is less than or equal to its rate of renewal so that the stock available either grows or remains constant.

Focusing on the example of fish, a species is being used unsustainably if the catch persistently decreases the stock and it is being used sustainably if the catch is less than or equal to the rate of renewal of the fish population.

The sustainable catch depends on the stock of fish and in the way illustrated by the sustainable catch curve, *SCC*, in Fig. 17.5.

Along the *SCC* curve, with a small stock of fish the quantity of new fish born is also small, so the sustainable catch is small.

With a large stock of fish many fish are born but they must compete with each other for food, so only a few survive to reproduce and to grow large enough to catch, and again the sustainable catch is small.

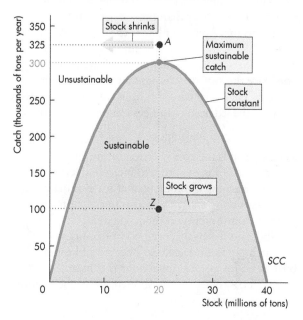

FIGURE 17.5   Sustainable Catch

As the fish stock increases (on the *x*-axis), the sustainable catch (on the *y*-axis) increases to a maximum. As the stock increases further, the fish must compete for food and the sustainable catch falls. If the catch exceeds the sustainable catch, such as at point *A*, the fish stock diminishes. If the catch is less than the sustainable catch, such as at point *Z*, the fish stock increases.

MyEconLab Animation

Between a small and a large stock is a stock of fish that maximizes the sustainable catch. In Fig. 17.5, this stock is 20 million tons and the maximum sustainable catch is 300,000 tons per year.

The maximum sustainable catch arises from a balancing of the birth of new fish from the stock and the availability of food to sustain the fish population. If the quantity of fish caught is less than the sustainable catch, at a point such as *Z*, the fish stock grows. If the quantity caught equals the sustainable catch, at any point on the *SCC*, the fish stock remains constant and is available for future generations of fishers in the same quantity that is available today.

But if the quantity caught exceeds the sustainable catch, at a point such as *A*, the fish stock shrinks and, unchecked, eventually falls to zero.

You now understand the problem of using a common renewable natural resource sustainably. But another problem is using it efficiently.

Inefficient Use of a Common Resource

In an unregulated market, even if the catch is sustainable, it will be bigger than the efficient catch: overfishing occurs. And most likely, the catch will not be sustainable. Why does overfishing occur? The answer is that fishers face only their own private cost and don't face the cost they impose on others—the external cost. The social cost of fishing combines the private cost and the external cost. Let's examine these costs.

Marginal Private Cost The *marginal private cost* of catching fish is the cost incurred by keeping a boat and crew at sea for long enough to increase the catch by one ton. Keeping a fishing boat at sea eventually runs into *diminishing marginal returns* (see Chapter 11, p. 251). As the crew gets tired, the storage facilities get overfull, and the boat's speed is cut to conserve fuel, the catch per hour decreases. The cost of keeping the boat at sea for an additional hour is constant, so the marginal cost of catching fish increases as the quantity caught increases.

You've just seen that the *principle of increasing marginal cost* applies to catching fish just as it applies to other production activities: Marginal private cost increases as the quantity of fish caught increases.

The marginal private cost of catching fish determines an indiviual fisher's supply of fish. A profit-maximizing fisher is willing to supply the quantity at which the market price of fish covers the marginal private cost. And the market supply is the sum of the quantities supplied by each individual fisher.

Marginal External Cost The marginal external cost of catching fish is the cost per additional ton that one fisher's production imposes on all other fishers. This additional cost arises because one fisher's catch decreases the remaining stock, which in turn decreases the renewal rate of the stock and makes it harder for others to find and catch fish.

Marginal external cost also increases as the quantity of fish caught increases. If the quantity of fish caught is so large that it drives the species to near extinction, the marginal external cost becomes infinitely large.

Marginal Social Cost The *marginal social cost* of catching fish is the marginal private cost plus the marginal external cost. Because both components of marginal social cost increase as the quantity caught increases, marginal social cost also increases with the quantity of fish caught.

Marginal Social Benefit and Demand The marginal social benefit from fish is the price that consumers are willing to pay for an additional pound of fish. Marginal social benefit decreases as the quantity of fish consumed increases, so the market demand curve, which is also the marginal social benefit curve, slopes downward.

Overfishing Equilibrium Figure 17.6 illustrates overfishing and how it arises. The market demand curve for fish is the marginal social benefit curve, *MSB*. The market supply curve is the marginal *private* cost curve, *MC*. Market equilibrium occurs at the intersection point of these two curves. The equilibrium quantity is 800,000 tons of fish per year and the equilibrium price is $10 per pound. At this market equilibrium, overfishing occurs.

FIGURE 17.6   Why Overfishing Occurs

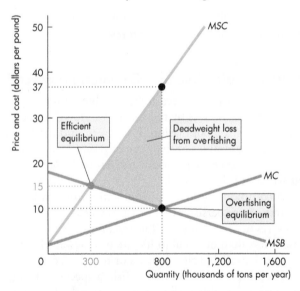

The market supply curve is the marginal private cost curve, MC. The market demand curve is the marginal social benefit curve, MSB. Market equilibrium occurs at a quantity of 800,000 tons per year and a price of $10 per pound.

The marginal social cost curve is MSC and at the market equilibrium there is overfishing—marginal social cost exceeds marginal social benefit.

The quantity at which MSC equals MSB is the efficient quantity, 300,000 tons per year. The area of the gray triangle measures the deadweight loss from overfishing.

MyEconLab Animation

Figure 17.6 illustrates why overfishing occurs. At the market equilibrium quantity, marginal social benefit (and willingness to pay) is $10 per pound, but the marginal social cost ($37 per pound) exceeds this amount. The marginal external cost is the cost of running down the fish stock.

Efficient Equilibrium What is the efficient use of a common resource? It is the use of the resource that makes the marginal social benefit from the resource equal to the marginal social cost of using it.

In Fig. 17.6, the efficient quantity of fish is 300,000 tons per year—the quantity that makes marginal social cost (on the *MSC* curve) equal to marginal social benefit (on the *MSB* curve). At this quantity, the marginal catch of each individual fisher costs society what people are willing to pay for it.

Deadweight Loss from Overfishing Deadweight loss measures the cost of overfishing. The area of the gray triangle in Fig. 17.6 illustrates this loss. It is the marginal social cost minus the marginal social benefit from all the fish caught in excess of the efficient quantity.

ECONOMICS IN ACTION
The Original Tragedy of the Commons

The term "tragedy of the commons" comes from 14th-century England, where areas of rough grassland surrounding villages were overgrazed and the quantity of cows and sheep that they could feed kept falling.

During the 16th century, the price of wool increased, sheep farming became profitable, and sheep owners wanted to control the land they used. So the commons were gradually privatized and land use became more efficient.

One of Today's Tragedies of the Commons

Before 1970, Atlantic cod was abundant, despite the fact that it had been fished for many centuries and was a major food source for the first European settlers in North America. By 1620, there were more than 1,000 fishing boats catching large quantities of cod in the northwest Atlantic off the coast of what is now New England and Newfoundland. Most of the fishing during these years was done using lines and productivity was low. But low productivity limited the catch and enabled cod to be caught sustainably over hundreds of years.

The situation changed dramatically during the 1960s with the introduction of huge nets, sonar technology to find fish concentrations, and large ships with efficient processing and storage facilities. These technological advances brought soaring cod harvests and cod landings almost tripled in a decade.

This volume of cod could not be taken without a serious collapse in the remaining stock and by the 1980s it became vital to regulate cod fishing. But regulation was of limited success and stocks continued to decline. In 1992, a total ban on cod fishing in the North Atlantic stabilized the population but at a very low level. Two decades of ban have enabled the species to repopulate, and it is now hoped that one day cod fishing will return but at a low and sustainable rate.

The Atlantic Cod Catch: 1850–2005

Achieving an Efficient Outcome

Defining the conditions under which a common resource is used efficiently is easier than delivering those conditions. To use a common resource efficiently, it is necessary to design an incentive mechanism that confronts the users of the resource with the marginal *social* consequences of their actions. The same principles apply to common resources as those that you met earlier in this chapter when you studied the external cost of pollution.

The three main methods that might be used to achieve the efficient use of a common resource are

- Property rights
- Production quotas
- Individual transferable quotas (ITQs)

Property Rights A common resource that no one owns and that anyone is free to use contrasts with *private property*, which is a resource that *someone* owns and has an incentive to use in the way that maximizes its value. One way of overcoming the tragedy of the commons is to convert a common resource to private property. By assigning private property rights to what was previously a common resource, its owner faces the same conditions as society faces. It doesn't matter who owns the resource. The users of the resource will be confronted with the full cost of using it because they either own it or pay a fee to the owner for permission to use it.

When private property rights over a resource are established and enforced, the *MSC* curve becomes the marginal *private* cost curve, and the use of the resource is efficient.

Figure 17.3, which illustrates an efficient outcome with property rights when confronted with pollution, also applies to the over-fishing problem. The supply curve $S = MC = MSC$ and the demand curve $D = MSB$ determine the equilibrium price and quantity. The price equals both marginal social benefit and marginal social cost and the fish catch is efficient.

The private property solution to the tragedy of the commons *is* available in some cases. It was the solution to the original tragedy of the commons in England's Middle Ages. It is also a solution that has been used to prevent overuse of the airwaves that carry cellphone services. The right to use this space (called the frequency spectrum) has been auctioned by governments to the highest bidders. The owner of each part of the spectrum is the only one permitted to use it (or to license someone else to use it).

But assigning private property rights is not always feasible. It would be difficult to assign private property rights to the oceans because the cost of enforcing them would be too high. In the absence of property rights, some form of government intervention is used. One such intervention is a production quota.

Production Quotas A *production quota* is an upper limit to the quantity of a good that may be produced in a specified period. Each individual producer is allocated a quota.

You studied the effects of a production quota in Chapter 6 (pp. 139–140) and learned that a quota can drive a wedge between marginal social benefit and marginal social cost and create deadweight loss. In that earlier example, the market was efficient without a quota. But in the case of common resources, the market overuses the resource and produces an inefficient quantity. A production quota in this market brings a move toward a more efficient outcome. But implementing a production quota has two problems.

First, it is in every fisher's self-interest to catch more fish than the quantity permitted under the quota. The reason is that price exceeds marginal private cost, so by catching more fish, a fisher gets a higher income. If enough fishers break the quota, overfishing and the tragedy of the commons remain.

Second, marginal cost is not, in general, the same for all producers—as we're assuming here. Efficiency requires that the quota be allocated to the producers with the lowest marginal cost. But bureaucrats who allocate quotas do not have information about the marginal cost of individual producers. Even if they tried to get this information, producers would have an incentive to lie about their costs so as to get a bigger quota.

So where producers are difficult, or very costly, to monitor or where marginal cost varies across producers, a production quota cannot achieve an efficient outcome.

Individual Transferable Quotas Where producers are difficult to monitor or where marginal cost varies across producers, a more sophisticated quota system can be effective. It is an **individual transferable quota (ITQ)**, which is a production limit that is assigned to an individual who is then free to transfer (sell) the quota to someone else. A market in ITQs emerges and ITQs are traded at their market price. (Cap-and-trade to limit pollution is an ITQ for pollution).

The market price of an ITQ is the highest price that someone is willing to pay for one. That price is marginal social benefit minus marginal cost. The price of an ITQ will rise to this level because fishers who don't have a quota would be willing to pay this amount to get one.

A fisher with an ITQ could sell it for the market price, so by not selling the ITQ the fisher incurs an opportunity cost. The marginal cost of fishing, which now includes the opportunity cost of the ITQ, equals the marginal social benefit from the efficient quantity.

Figure 17.7 illustrates how ITQs work. Each fisher receives an allocation of ITQs and the total catch permitted by the ITQs is 300,000 tons per year. Fishers trade ITQs: Those with low marginal cost buy ITQs from those with high marginal cost, and the market price of an ITQ settles at $10 per pound of fish. The marginal private cost of fishing now becomes the original marginal private cost, *MC*, plus the cost of the ITQ. The marginal private cost curve shifts upward from *MC* to *MC* + *price of ITQ* and each fisher is confronted with the marginal *social* cost of fishing. No one has an incentive to exceed the quota because to do so would send marginal cost above price and result in a loss on the marginal catch. The outcome is efficient.

ECONOMICS IN ACTION
ITQs Work

Iceland introduced the first ITQs in 1984 to conserve its stocks of lobster. In 1986, New Zealand and a bit later Australia introduced ITQs to conserve fish stocks in the South Pacific and Southern Oceans. And this system was introduced in Alaska to manage halibut stocks during the 1990s.

The evidence from these cases suggests that ITQs work well when they are properly enforced.

ITQs help maintain fish stocks, but they also reduce the size of the fishing industry. This consequence of ITQs puts them against the self-interest of fishers. In all countries, the fishing industry opposes restrictions on its activities, but in Iceland, Australia, New Zealand, and Alaska the opposition is not strong enough to block ITQs.

In the United States, other than Alaska, the opposition has been harder to overcome, and in 1996 Congress passed the Sustainable Fishing Act that put a moratorium on ITQs. This moratorium was lifted in 2004 and since then, ITQs have been applied to 28 fisheries from the Gulf of Alaska to the Gulf of Mexico.

Economists have studied the effects of ITQs extensively and agree that in most cases they work and offer an effective tool for achieving an efficient use of the stock of ocean fish.

But in some situations, ITQs have been unsuccessful. The main reasons for failure of an ITQ system are that the total permitted catch might be set too large; some fish species migrate and get overfished outside the regions covered by the ITQs; and sometimes the monitoring and enforcement of quotas is inadequate.

FIGURE 17.7   ITQs to Use a Common Resource Efficiently

ITQs are issued on a scale that keeps output at the efficient level. The market price of an ITQ equals the marginal social benefit minus marginal cost. Because each user of the common resource faces the opportunity cost of using the resource, self-interest achieves the social interest.

— MyEconLab Animation —

REVIEW QUIZ

1 What is the tragedy of the commons? Give two examples, including one from your state.
2 Describe the conditions under which a common resource is used efficiently.
3 Review three methods that might achieve the efficient use of a common resource and explain the obstacles to efficiency.

Work these questions in Study Plan 17.3 and get instant feedback. Do a Key Terms Quiz.   MyEconLab

◆ Positive Externality: Knowledge

Knowledge comes from education and research. And both bring external benefits. To keep the explanation of the problems that arise from external benefits and the possible solutions to those problems as clear as possible, we will focus on just one aspect of the production of knowledge, the provision of college education.

We begin by distinguishing between private benefits and social benefits.

Private Benefits and Social Benefits

A *private benefit* is a benefit that the consumer of a good or service receives. For example, expanded job opportunities and a higher income are private benefits of a college education.

Marginal benefit is the benefit from an *additional unit* of a good or service. So **marginal private benefit** (*MB*) is the benefit that the consumer of a good or service receives from an additional unit of it. When one additional student attends college, the benefit that student receives is the marginal private benefit from college education.

The *external benefit* from a good or service is the benefit that someone other than the consumer of the good or service receives. College graduates generate many external benefits. On average, they are better citizens, have lower crime rates, and are more tolerant of the views of others. They enable the success of high-quality newspapers and television broadcasts, music, theater, and other organized social activities that bring benefits to many other people.

A **marginal external benefit** is the benefit from an additional unit of a good or service that people *other than its consumer* enjoy. The benefit that your friends and neighbors get from your college education is the marginal external benefit of your college education.

Marginal social benefit (*MSB*) is the marginal benefit enjoyed by society—by the consumer of a good or service (marginal private benefit) and by others (the marginal external benefit). That is,

$$MSB = MB + \text{Marginal external benefit.}$$

Figure 17.8 shows an example of the relationship between marginal private benefit, marginal external benefit, and marginal social benefit. The marginal benefit curve, *MB*, describes the marginal private benefit enjoyed by the people who receive a college education. Marginal private benefit decreases as the number of students enrolled in college increases.

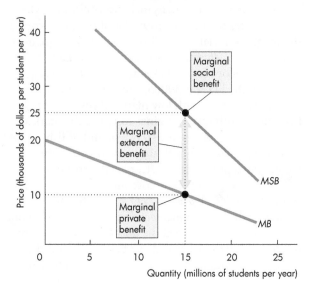

FIGURE 17.8   An External Benefit

The *MB* curve shows the marginal private benefit enjoyed by the people who receive a college education. The *MSB* curve shows the sum of marginal private benefit and marginal external benefit. When 15 million students attend college, the marginal private benefit is $10,000 per student, the marginal external benefit is $15,000 per student, and the marginal social benefit is $25,000 per student.

MyEconLab Animation

In the example in Fig. 17.8, when 15 million students enroll in college, the marginal external benefit is $15,000 per student per year. The marginal social benefit curve, *MSB*, is the sum of marginal private benefit and marginal external benefit at each number of students. For example, when 15 million students a year enroll in college, the marginal private benefit is $10,000 per student and the marginal external benefit is $15,000 per student, so the marginal social benefit is $25,000 per student.

When people make schooling decisions, they ignore its external benefits and consider only its private benefits. So if education were provided by private schools that charged full-cost tuition, there would be too few college graduates.

Figure 17.9 illustrates this private underprovision. The supply curve is the marginal social cost curve, *S = MSC*. The demand curve is the marginal *private* benefit curve, *D = MB*. Market equilibrium occurs at a tuition of $15,000 per student per year and

7.5 million students per year. At this equilibrium, the marginal social benefit of $38,000 per student exceeds the marginal social cost by $23,000 per student. Too few students are enrolled in college. The efficient number is 15 million per year, where marginal social benefit equals marginal social cost. The gray triangle shows the deadweight loss created.

To get closer to producing the efficient quantity of a good with an external benefit, we make public choices, through governments, to modify the market outcome.

Government Actions in the Market with External Benefits

To encourage more students to enroll in college—to achieve an efficient quantity of college education—students must be confronted with a lower market price and the taxpayer must somehow pay for the costs not covered by what the student pays.

FIGURE 17.9   Inefficiency with an External Benefit

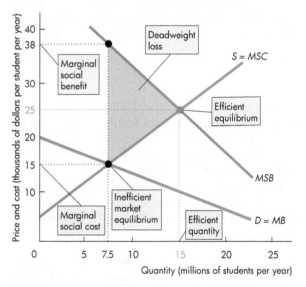

The market demand curve is the marginal private benefit curve, $D = MB$. The supply curve is the marginal social cost curve, $S = MSC$. Market equilibrium at a tuition of $15,000 a year and 7.5 million students is inefficient because marginal social benefit exceeds marginal social cost. The efficient quantity is 15 million students. A deadweight loss arises (gray triangle) because too few students enroll in college.

MyEconLab Animation and Draw Graph

Three devices that governments can use to achieve a more efficient allocation of resources in the presence of external benefits are

- Public production
- Private subsidies
- Vouchers

Public Production With **public production**, a good or service is produced by a public authority that receives its revenue from the government. The education services produced by state universities and colleges and public schools are examples of public production.

Private Subsidies A **subsidy** is a payment that the government makes to private producers. By making the subsidy depend on the level of output, the government can induce private decision makers to consider external benefits when they make their choices.

Vouchers A **voucher** is a token that the government provides to households, which they can use to buy specified goods or services. Food stamps are examples of vouchers. The vouchers (food stamps) can be spent only on food and are designed to improve the diet and health of extremely poor families.

School vouchers have been advocated as a means of improving the quality of education and are used in Washington, D.C. A school voucher allows parents to choose the school their children will attend and to use the voucher to pay part of the cost. The school cashes the vouchers to pay its bills. A voucher could be provided to a college student in a similar way, and although technically not a voucher, a federal Pell Grant has a similar effect.

Because vouchers can be spent only on a specified item, they increase the willingness to pay for that item and so increase the demand for it.

Illustrating an Efficient Outcome

Figure 17.10 illustrates an efficient outcome. With marginal social cost curve *MSC* and marginal social benefit curve *MSB*, the efficient number of college students is 15,000. The marginal *private* benefit curve *MB* tells us that 15,000 students will enroll only if the tuition is $10,000 per year. But the marginal social cost of 15,000 students is $25,000 per year. To enable the marginal social cost to be paid, taxpayers must pay the balance of $15,000 per student per year.

To achieve the efficient outcome with public production, public colleges receive funds from government equal to $15,000 per student per year, charge tuition of $10,000 per student per year, and enroll 15 million students.

To achieve the efficient outcome with private provision, private colleges receive a government subsidy of $15,000 per student per year. This subsidy reduces the colleges' costs and would make their marginal cost equal to $10,000 per student at the efficient quantity. Tuition of $10,000 covers this cost, and the subsidy of $15,000 per student covers the balance of the cost.

To achieve an efficient outcome with vouchers, government provides a voucher to each student with a value equal to the marginal external benefit at the efficient number of students. In Fig. 17.10, the efficient number of students is 15 million and the voucher is valued at $15,000 per student. Each student pays $10,000 tuition and gives the college a $15,000 voucher. The colleges receive $25,000 per student, which equals their marginal cost.

Bureaucratic Inefficiency and Government Failure

You've seen three government actions that achieve an efficient provision of a good with an external benefit. In each case, if the government estimates the marginal external benefit correctly and makes marginal social benefit equal to marginal social cost, the outcome is efficient.

Does the comparison that we've just made mean that pubic provision, subsidized private provision, and vouchers are equivalent? It does not. And the reason lies in something that you've already encountered in your study of public goods in Chapter 16—the behavior of bureaucrats combined with rational ignorance that leads to government failure.

Problems with Public Production Public colleges and schools are operated by a bureaucracy and are subject to the same problems as the provision of public goods. Bureaucrats seek to maximize their budgets, which brings inefficient overspending.

In the case of colleges and schools, overspending doesn't mean *overprovision*. Just the opposite: People complain about *underprovision*. The overspending is budget padding and waste.

Education bureaucrats incur costs that exceed the minimum efficient cost. They might hire more assistants than the number needed to do their work efficiently; give themselves sumptuous offices; get generous expense allowances; build schools in the wrong places where land costs are too high.

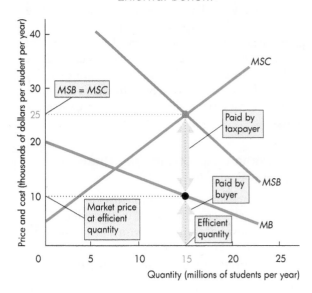

FIGURE 17.10   An Efficient Outcome with an External Benefit

The efficient number of college students is 15 million, where marginal social benefit equals marginal social cost. With the demand and marginal private benefit curve, $D = MB$, the price at which the efficient number will enroll is $10,000 per year. If students pay this price, the taxpayer must somehow pay the rest, which equals the marginal external benefit at the efficient quantity—$15,000 per student per year.

————— MyEconLab Animation and Draw Graph —————

Economists have compared the costs of private and public schools and have found that the costs per student of public schools are on the order of *three times* the costs of comparable private schools (see Talking with Carolyn Hoxby on p. 418.)

But bureaucracy can be limited and public production made more efficient. Charter schools (see *Economics in Action* on p. 409) are showing one way of cutting costs even while improving quality.

Problems with Private Subsidies Subsidizing private producers might overcome some of the problems created by public production. A private producer has an incentive to produce at minimum cost and avoid the budget padding of a bureaucratic producer. But two problems arise with private subsidies.

First, the subsidy budget must be allocated by a bureau. A national, state, or local department of education must lobby for its own budget and allocate this budget between school subsidies and its own administration costs. To the extent that the bureaucrats succeed in maximizing their own administration budget, they siphon off resources from schools and a problem similar to that of public production arises.

Second, it is in the self-interest of subsidized producers to maximize their subsidy. These producers might even spend some of the subsidy they receive lobbying for an even bigger one.

So subsidized private provision is unlikely to achieve an efficient allocation of resources. What about the third method: vouchers?

Are Vouchers the Solution? Vouchers have four advantages over the other two approaches:

1. Vouchers can be used with public production, private provision, or competition between the two.
2. Governments can set the value of vouchers and the total voucher budget to overcome bureaucratic overprovision and budget padding.
3. Vouchers spread the public contribution thinly across millions of consumers, so no one consumer has an interest in wasting part of the value received in lobbying for overprovision.
4. By giving the buying power to the final consumer, producers must compete for business and provide a high standard of service at the lowest attainable cost.

For these four reasons, vouchers are popular with economists. But they are controversial and opposed by most education administrators and teachers.

In *The Economics of School Choice,* a book edited by Caroline M. Hoxby, economists study the effect of school choice on student achievement and school productivity and show how vouchers can be designed to achieve their goals while avoiding their potential pitfalls. Caroline Hoxby is confident that she can design a voucher that best achieves any educational and school performance objective.

◆ *Economics in the News* on pp. 410–411 looks at the economics of President Obama's proposals for lowering carbon emissions.

The next two chapters examine the third big question of economics: For whom are goods and services produced? We examine the markets for factors of production and discover how factor incomes and the distribution of income are determined.

ECONOMICS IN ACTION
Education Quality and Cost: Charter Schools

A *charter school* is a public school, so it is funded like a regular public school but is free to make its own education policy. Around 4,000 charter schools in 40 states, teaching more than 1 million students, are in operation today. When the demand for places in a charter school exceeds the supply, students are chosen by lottery. This method of selection provides rich data for testing the performance of charter schools.

Are charter schools succeeding? Success has two dimensions: educational standards attained and cost per student. Charter schools perform well on both dimensions. They achieve higher standards and cost less. Charter school students achieve better test scores in math and reading than equivalent students who apply to but randomly don't get into a charter school.

Charter schools also achieve this higher standard at lower cost. For example, in Detroit, cost per student in charter schools is 25 percent less than in regular public schools in equivalent areas.

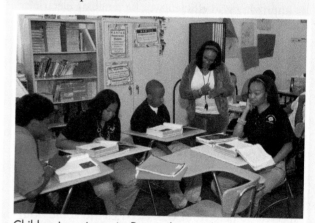

Children in an inner-city Detroit charter school

◆ REVIEW QUIZ

1 Why would the market economy produce too little education?
2 How might governments achieve an efficient provision of education?
3 What are the key differences among public production, private subsidies, and vouchers?
4 Why do economists generally favor vouchers to achieve an efficient outcome?

Work these questions in Study Plan 17.4 and get instant feedback. Do a Key Terms Quiz.   MyEconLab

A Carbon Reduction Plan

Obama Proposes Biggest Ever U.S. Push for Carbon Cuts

The Financial Times
June 2, 2014

The Obama administration has launched the most ambitious plan to combat climate change in U.S. history by proposing to … cut carbon dioxide emissions from power stations by 30 percent by 2030 from 2005 levels. …

The Environmental Protection Agency, the regulator that drew up the plan, said it would create tens of thousands of jobs and lead to lower household electricity bills because of improvements in energy efficiency.

But business groups, with representatives of the coal industry in the forefront, warned that the plans would raise bills, cause job losses, and increase the risk of blackouts. …

Under the plan, each U.S. state is given a different target for cutting carbon emissions from its power sector. They will decide how to achieve the cuts by switching to cleaner energy sources such as natural gas, nuclear, or wind power, by improving grid efficiency or by reducing electricity consumption. …

When burnt for power generation, coal creates roughly twice as much CO_2 as gas, and coal miners and power plants would be hurt the most by the administration's plan.

The EPA said its proposals could cut demand for coal by up to 27 percent and prices by up to 17 percent.

Despite Republican accusations that Mr. Obama is waging a "war on coal," the administration said it still expected 30 percent of U.S. electricity to come from coal by 2030.

The proposals would benefit other sources of generation, including gas, renewables, and nuclear power. …

MyEconLab More Economics in the News

ESSENCE OF THE STORY

- The Environmental Protection Agency (EPA) has a plan that cuts carbon dioxide emissions from power stations to 30 percent below their 2005 levels by 2030.

- Using coal to generate electricity creates twice as much CO_2 as using gas, and states will hit targets by switching from coal to natural gas, nuclear, and wind power, or by cutting electricity consumption.

- The EPA says the plan creates jobs and cuts electricity bills because of improvements in energy efficiency.

- Business groups say the plan raises electricity bills, destroys jobs, and increases the risk of blackouts.

- The EPA says its plan cuts coal use by up to 27 percent and lowers the price of coal by up to 17 percent

ECONOMIC ANALYSIS

- Because coal used to generate electricity creates twice as much CO_2 as gas, by converting from coal to gas, CO_2 emissions can be cut without lowering the amount of electricity consumed.

- A switch from coal to gas can be achieved by mandating power utilities or by confronting them with a price for carbon emissions that makes a switch in their self-interest.

- Regardless of the method used, a switch from coal to gas decreases the demand for coal and increases the demand for gas. The price of coal falls and the price of gas rises.

- The inefficiency arising from carbon emissions is measured by the deadweight loss it creates. Switching from coal to gas decreases the deadweight loss from using coal, increases the deadweight loss from using gas, and decreases the overall deadweight loss.

- But deadweight loss remains unless the consumption of electricity is cut to the point at which its marginal benefit and price equals its marginal *social* cost.

- The figures illustrate what will happen if the EPA plan is achieved.

- In Fig. 1, the demand for and marginal social benefit of electricity generated using coal is $D = MSB$. The supply of coal and the marginal private cost curve is $S = MC$, and the marginal social benefit curve is MSC. The efficient quantity of coal-generated electricity is 1.2 terawatt-hours per year. But the equilibrium quantity is 1.6 terawatt-hours per year, so overproduction brings a deadweight loss as shown by the area of the gray triangle.

- The EPA plan decreases the use of coal. In Fig. 1, the EPA target for coal generators is the efficient quantity, so the deadweight loss is eliminated.

- Figure 2 illustrates the effects of the switch from coal to gas. Gas generators are a bit more costly to operate than coal generators, so the marginal cost of producing electricity increases from MC_0 to MC_1 when gas generators replace coal generators.

- But gas is cleaner than coal, so emissions decrease and the marginal external cost falls. The marginal social cost falls from MSC_0 to MSC_1.

- Because the marginal cost of generating electricity increases, supply of electricity decreases, the price rises, and the equilibrium quantity decreases.

- The deadweight loss from generating electricity decreases from the area of the light gray triangle to the area of the dark gray triangle.

Figure 1 Making Coal Generation Efficient

Figure 2 More Efficient but Remains Inefficient

- The success of this plan to lower carbon emissions will depend on the ways in which incentives are changed. The cost of using coal must rise to induce power utilities to find the most efficient substitutes for coal.

- The planned changes in the quantity and price of electricity leave a large amount of carbon emissions in place.

SUMMARY

Key Points

Externalities in Our Lives (pp. 392–393)

- An externality can arise from either a production activity or a consumption activity.
- A negative externality imposes an external cost. A positive externality provides an external benefit.

Working Problems 1 and 2 will give you a better understanding of the externalities in our lives.

Negative Externality: Pollution (pp. 394–400)

- A competitive market would produce too much of a good that has external production costs.
- External costs are costs of production that fall on people other than the producer of a good or service. Marginal social cost equals marginal private cost plus marginal external cost.
- Producers take account only of marginal private cost and produce more than the efficient quantity when there is a marginal external cost.
- Sometimes it is possible to overcome a negative externality by assigning a property right.
- When property rights cannot be assigned, governments might overcome externalities by using taxes or cap-and-trade.

Working Problems 3 and 4 will give you a better understanding of the external costs of pollution.

Negative Externality: The Tragedy of the Commons (pp. 401–405)

- Common resources create a problem that is called the tragedy of the commons—no one has a private incentive to conserve the resources and use them at an efficient rate.
- A common resource is used to the point at which the marginal private benefit equals the marginal cost.
- A common resource might be used efficiently by creating a private property right, setting a quota, or issuing individual transferable quotas.

Working Problems 5 and 6 will give you a better understanding of the tragedy of the commons.

Positive Externality: Knowledge (pp. 406–409)

- External benefits are benefits that are received by people other than the consumer of a good or service. Marginal social benefit equals marginal private benefit plus marginal external benefit.
- External benefits from education arise because better-educated people tend to be better citizens, commit fewer crimes, and support social activities.
- Vouchers or subsidies to schools or the provision of public education below cost can achieve a more efficient provision of education.

Working Problems 7 to 9 will give you a better understanding of the external benefit from knowledge.

Key Terms

MyEconLab Key Terms Quiz

Abatement technology, 395
Coase theorem, 396
Externality, 392
Individual transferable
    quota (ITQ), 404
Marginal external benefit, 406
Marginal external cost, 394

Marginal privavte benefit, 406
Marginal private cost, 394
Marginal social benefit, 406
Marginal social cost, 394
Negative externality, 392
Pigovian taxes, 397
Positive externality, 392

Property rights, 395
Public production, 407
Subsidy, 407
Tragedy of the commons, 401
Transactions costs, 396
Voucher, 407

WORKED PROBLEM

MyEconLab   You can work this problem in Chapter 17 Study Plan.

The first two columns of the table show the demand schedule for fitness sessions with independent coaches; the second and third columns show the coaches' marginal cost. Fitness creates an external benefit and the marginal external benefit is $10 per session. The market for fitness sessions is competitive.

Price (dollars per session)	Quantity (sessions per month)	Marginal cost (dollars per session)
10	800	30
15	600	25
20	400	20
25	200	15
30	0	10

Questions

1. What is the market-determined quantity of fitness sessions per month and what is the price of a session?
2. Calculate the marginal social benefit from fitness sessions at each quantity of sessions.
3. What is the efficient number of fitness sessions per month?

Solutions

1. In the market for fitness sessions the supply schedule is the same as the marginal cost schedule. The quantity of sessions is that at which marginal private benefit equals marginal cost. Marginal private benefit is the same as price, so the number of sessions per month is 400 and the price of a session is $20.

Key Point: The market outcome is determined by marginal private benefit and marginal cost.

2. Marginal social benefit (*MSB*) equals the sum of marginal private benefit (*MB*), which equals price, and the marginal external benefit of $10 per session.

The table below shows the calculations.

Quantity (sessions per month)	MB (dollars per session)	MSB (dollars per session)
800	10	20
600	15	25
400	20	30
200	25	35
0	-	-

For example, the marginal social benefit from 600 sessions per month equals the marginal private benefit of $15 per session plus the marginal external benefit of $10 per session, which equals $25 per session.

Key Point: The marginal social benefit from a service that creates a positive externality is the sum of the marginal private benefit and the marginal external benefit.

3. To find the efficient number of sessions, we need to determine the number of sessions per month at which the marginal social benefit (*MSB*) equals marginal cost (*MC*).

The table below combines the data from the other two tables.

Quantity (sessions per month)	MSB (dollars per session)	MC (dollars per session)
800	20	30
600	25	25
400	30	20
200	35	15
0	-	10

By inspecting the table above, you can see that *MSB* equals *MC* at 600 sessions per month, so that is the efficient quantity.

Key Point: The efficient quantity of a service that creates a positive externality is the quantity at which marginal social benefit from the service equals the marginal cost of producing the service.

Key Figure

MyEconLab Interactive Animation

STUDY PLAN PROBLEMS AND APPLICATIONS

MyEconLab   You can work Problems 1 to 9 in Chapter 17 Study Plan and get instant feedback.

Externalities in Our Lives (Study Plan 17.1)

1. Describe three consumption activities that create external costs.

2. Describe three production activities that create external benefits.

Negative Externality: Pollution (Study Plan 17.2)

Use the following figure, which illustrates the market for cotton, to work Problems 3 and 4.

Suppose that the cotton growers use a chemical to control insects and waste flows into the town's river. The marginal social cost of producing the cotton is double the marginal private cost.

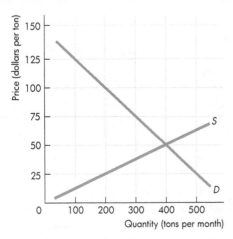

3. If no one owns the river and the town takes no action to control the waste, what is the quantity of cotton and the deadweight loss created?

4. If the town owns the river and taxes cotton growers so that the efficient quantity is grown, how much tax revenue does the town receive? Is the quantity of waste zero? Explain your answer.

Negative Externality: Tragedy of the Commons

(Study Plan 17.3)

Use the figure in the next column to work Problems 5 and 6.

The figure illustrates the market for North Atlantic tuna.

5. a. What is the quantity of tuna that fishers catch and the price of tuna? Is the tuna stock being used efficiently? Explain why or why not.

   b. What would be the price of tuna, if the stock of tuna were used efficiently?

6. With a quota of 40 tons a month for the tuna fishing industry, what is the price of tuna and the quantity caught? Does overfishing occur?

Positive Externality: Knowledge (Study Plan 17.4)

Use the following figure, which shows the demand for college education, to work Problems 7 to 9.

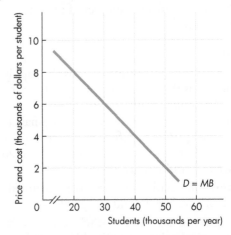

The marginal cost is a constant $6,000 per student per year. The marginal external benefit from a college education is a constant $4,000 per student per year.

7. What is the efficient number of students? If all colleges are private, how many people enroll in college and what is the tuition?

8. If the government provides public colleges, what tuition will achieve the efficient number of students? How much will taxpayers have to pay?

9. If the government offers students vouchers, what is the value of the voucher that will achieve the efficient number of students?

ADDITIONAL PROBLEMS AND APPLICATIONS

MyEconLab You can work these problems in MyEconLab if assigned by your instructor.

Externalities in Our Lives

10. What externalities arise from smoking tobacco products and how do we deal with them?

11. What externalities arise from beautiful and ugly buildings and how do we deal with them?

Negative Externality: Pollution

12. Betty and Anna work at the same office in Philadelphia and they have to attend a meeting in Pittsburgh. They decide to drive to the out-of-town meeting together. Betty is a cigarette smoker and her marginal benefit from smoking a pack of cigarettes a day is $40. Cigarettes are $6 a pack. Anna dislikes cigarette smoke, and her marginal benefit from a smoke-free environment is $50 a day. What is the outcome if
    a. Betty drives her car with Anna as a passenger?
    b. Anna drives her car with Betty as a passenger?

Use the following data and the figure, which illustrates the market for a pesticide with no government intervention, to work Problems 13 to 16.

When factories produce pesticide, they also create waste, which they dump into a lake on the outskirts of the town. The marginal external cost of the waste is equal to the marginal private cost of producing the pesticide (that is, the marginal social cost of producing the pesticide is double the marginal private cost).

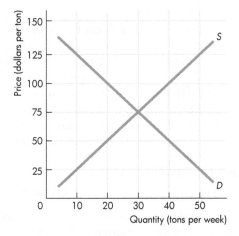

13. What is the quantity of pesticide produced if no one owns the lake and what is the efficient quantity of pesticide?

14. If the town owns the lake, what is the quantity of pesticide produced and how much does the town charge the factories to dump waste?

15. If the pesticide factories own the lake, how much pesticide is produced?

16. If no one owns the lake and the government levies a pollution tax, what is the tax that achieves the efficient outcome?

Use the following table to work Problems 17 to 19.

The first two columns of the table show the demand schedule for electricity from a coal burning utility; the second and third columns show the utility's cost of producing electricity. The marginal external cost of the pollution created equals the marginal cost.

Price (cents per kilowatt)	Quantity (kilowatts per day)	Marginal cost (cents per kilowatt)
4	500	10
8	400	8
12	300	6
16	200	4
20	100	2

17. With no government action to control pollution, what is the quantity of electricity produced, the price of electricity, and the marginal external cost of the pollution generated?

18. With no government action to control pollution, what is the marginal social cost of the electricity generated and the deadweight loss created?

19. If the government levies a pollution tax such that the utility produces the efficient quantity, what is the price of electricity, the tax levied, and the government's tax revenue per day?

Negative Externality: The Tragedy of the Commons

20. **Polar Ice Cap Shrinks Further and Thins**
    With the warming of the planet, the polar ice cap is shrinking and the Arctic Sea is expanding. As the ice cap shrinks further, more and more underwater mineral resources will become accessible. Many countries are staking out territorial claims to parts of the polar region.
    Source: *The Wall Street Journal*, April 7, 2009

    Explain how ownership of these mineral resources will influence the amount of damage done to the Arctic Sea and its wildlife.

Use the following figure to work Problems 21 to 23.

A spring runs under a village. Everyone can sink a well on her or his land and take water from the spring. The figure shows the marginal social benefit from and the marginal cost of taking water.

21. What is the quantity of water taken and what is the private cost of the water taken?

22. What is the efficient quantity of water taken and the marginal social cost at the efficient quantity?

23. If the village council sets a quota on the total amount of water such that the spring is used efficiently, what would be the quota and the market value of the water taken per day?

24. If hikers and other visitors were required to pay a fee to use the Appalachian Trail,
    a. Would the use of this common resource be more efficient?
    b. Would it be even more efficient if the most popular spots along the trail had the highest prices?
    c. Why do you think we don't see more market solutions to the tragedy of the commons?

Positive Externality: Knowledge

Use the following data to work Problems 25 to 28. The table shows the demand for college education. The marginal cost of educating a student is a

Price (dollars per student)	Quantity (students per year)
6,000	10,000
5,000	20,000
4,000	30,000
3,000	40,000
2,000	50,000

constant $4,000 a year and education creates an external benefit of a constant $2,000 per student per year.

25. If all colleges are private and the market for education is competitive, calculate the number of students, the tuition, and the deadweight loss.

26. If all colleges are public colleges, calculate the tuition that will achieve the efficient number of students. How much will taxpayers have to pay?

27. If the government decides to subsidize private colleges, what subsidy will achieve the efficient number of college students?

28. If all colleges are private and the government offers vouchers to those who enroll at a college, calculate the value of the voucher that will achieve the efficient number of students.

Economics in the News

29. After you have studied *Economics in the News* on pp. 410–411, answer the following questions.
    a. What are the marginal private costs of and marginal private benefits from using gas rather than coal to generate electricity?
    b. What are the marginal social costs of and marginal social benefits from using gas rather than coal to generate electricity?
    c. How will the EPA's plan for power utilities to switch from coal to gas change the price that households pay for electricity?
    d. How will the EPA's plan for utilities to switch from coal to gas change the efficiency of electricity production?

30. **Where the Tuna Roam**
    To the first settlers, the Great Plains posed the same problem as the oceans today: a vast, open area where there seemed to be no way to protect animals. But animals thrived once the settlers divvied up the land and devised ways to protect their livestock. Today, the oceans are much like an open range. Fishers catch as much as they can, even if they are overfishing. They figure any fish they don't take for themselves will just be taken by someone else.
    Source: *The New York Times*, November 4, 2006

    a. What are the similarities between the problems faced by the earliest settlers in the West and today's fishers?
    b. Can the tragedy of the commons in the oceans be eliminated in the same manner used by the early settlers on the plains?
    c. How can ITQs change the short-term outlook of fishers to a long-term outlook?

We, the People, …

UNDERSTANDING MARKET FAILURE AND GOVERNMENT

Thomas Jefferson knew that creating a government of the people, by the people, and for the people was a huge enterprise and one that could easily go wrong. Creating a constitution that made despotic and tyrannical rule impossible was relatively easy. The founding fathers did their best to practice sound economics. They designed a sophisticated system of incentives—of carrots and sticks—to make the government responsive to public opinion and to limit the ability of individual self-interests to gain at the expense of the majority. But they were not able to create a constitution that effectively blocks the ability of special interest groups to capture the consumer and producer surpluses that result from specialization and exchange.

We have created a system of government to deal with four market failures: (1) monopoly; (2) externalities; (3) public goods; and (4) common resources.

Government might help cope with these market failures, but as the founding fathers knew well, government does not eliminate the pursuit of self-interest. Voters, politicians, and bureaucrats pursue their self-interest, sometimes at the expense of the social interest, and instead of market failure, we get government failure.

Many economists have thought long and hard about the problems discussed in this part. But none has had as profound an effect on our ideas in this area as Ronald Coase.

Ronald Coase *(1910–2013) was born in England and educated at the London School of Economics, where he was deeply influenced by his teacher, Arnold Plant, and by the issues of his youth: communist central planning versus free markets.*

Professor Coase lived in the United States from 1951 until his death in 2013. He first visited America as a 20-year-old on a traveling scholarship during the depths of the Great Depression. It was on this visit, and before he had completed his bachelor's degree, that he conceived the ideas that 60 years later were to earn him the 1991 Nobel Prize for Economic Science.

Ronald Coase discovered and clarified the significance of transactions costs and property rights for the functioning of the economy. He revolutionized the way we think about property rights and externalities and opened up the growing field of law and economics.

"The question to be decided is: Is the value of fish lost greater or less than the value of the product which contamination of the stream makes possible?"

RONALD H. COASE
The Problem of Social Cost

CAROLINE M. HOXBY is the Allie S. Freed Professor of Economics at Harvard University. Born in Cleveland, Ohio, she was an undergraduate at Harvard and a graduate student at Oxford and MIT.

Professor Hoxby is a leading scholar of the economics of education. She has written many articles on this topic and has published books entitled *The Economics of School Choice* and *College Choices* (both University of Chicago Press, 2003 and 2004, respectively). She is Program Director of the Economics of Education Program at the National Bureau of Economic Research, serves on several other national boards that study education issues, and has advised or provided testimony to several state legislatures and the United States Congress.

Michael Parkin talked with Caroline Hoxby about her work and the progress that economists have made in understanding how the financing and the provision of education influence the quality of education and the equality of access to it.

Why did you decide to become an economist?

I've wanted to be an economist from about the age of 13. That was when I took my first class in economics (an interesting story in itself) and discovered that all of the thoughts swimming around in my head belonged to a "science" and there was an entire body of people who understood this science—a lot better than I did, anyway. I can still recall reading *The Wealth of Nations* for the first time; it was a revelation.

What drew you to study the economics of education?

We all care about education, perhaps because it is the key means by which opportunity is (or should be) extended to all in the United States. Also, nearly everyone now acknowledges that highly developed countries like the United States rely increasingly on education as the engine of economic growth. Thus, one reason I was drawn to education is its importance. However, what primarily drew me was that education issues were so clearly begging for economic analysis and that there was so little of it. I try hard to understand educational institutions and problems, but I insist on bringing economic logic to bear on educational issues.

What can economists say about the alternative methods of financing education? Is there a voucher solution that could work?

There is definitely a voucher solution that could work because vouchers are inherently an extremely flexible policy. …

> **Economists should say to policy makers: "Tell me your goals; I'll design you a voucher."**

Any well-designed voucher system will give schools an incentive to compete. However, when designing vouchers, we can also build in remedies for a variety of educational problems. Vouchers can be used to ensure that disabled children get the funding they need and the program choices they need.

Compared to current school finance programs, vouchers can do a better job of ensuring that low-income families have sufficient funds to invest in the child's education. Well-designed vouchers can encourage schools to make their student bodies socio-economically diverse.

Economists should say to policy makers: "Tell me your goals; I'll design you a voucher."

*Read the full interview with Caroline Hoxby in MyEconLab.

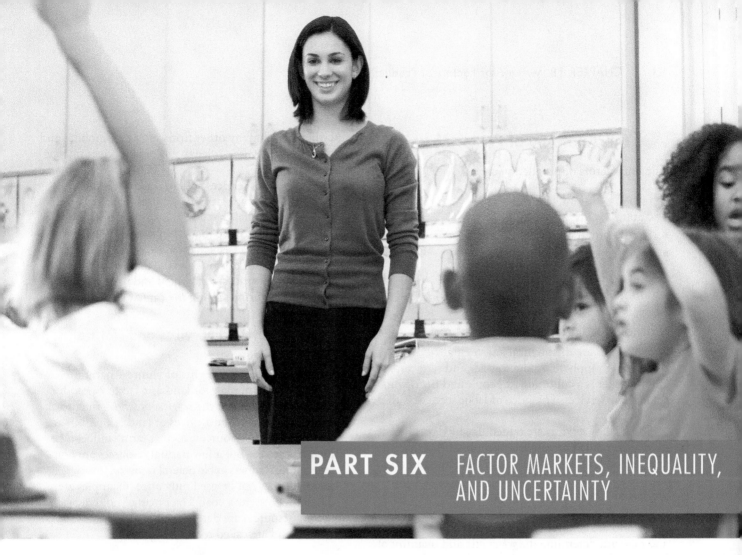

PART SIX FACTOR MARKETS, INEQUALITY, AND UNCERTAINTY

18 MARKETS FOR FACTORS OF PRODUCTION

After studying this chapter, you will be able to:

◆ Describe the anatomy of factor markets
◆ Explain how the value of marginal product determines the demand for a factor of production
◆ Explain how wage rates and employment are determined and how labor unions influence labor markets
◆ Explain how capital and land rental rates and natural resource prices are determined

A teacher in a public school earns much more than an equally good teacher in a charter school, and your college basketball coach earns much more than your economics professor. Why? What determines the wages that people earn? Wages are important, but finding a job is important too. Why are so many manufacturing jobs disappearing and what new jobs are being created?

In this chapter, we study labor markets as well as markets for capital and natural resources. In *Economics in the News* at the end of the chapter we answer the question about teachers' pay.

▶ The Anatomy of Factor Markets

The four factors of production are

- Labor
- Capital
- Land (natural resources)
- Entrepreneurship

Let's take a brief look at the anatomy of the markets in which these factors of production are traded.

Markets for Labor Services

Labor services are the physical and mental work effort that people supply to produce goods and services. A labor market is a collection of people and firms who trade labor services. The price of labor services is the wage rate.

Some labor services are traded day by day. These services are called *casual labor*. People who pick fruit and vegetables often just show up at a farm and take whatever work is available that day. But most labor services are traded on a job contract.

Most labor markets have many buyers and many sellers and are competitive. In these markets, supply and demand determine the wage rate and quantity of labor employed. Jobs expand when demand increases and jobs disappear when demand decreases.

In some labor markets, a labor union operates like a monopoly on the supply-side of the labor market. In this type of labor market, a bargaining process between the union and the employer determines the wage rate.

We'll study both competitive labor markets and labor unions in this chapter.

Markets for Capital Services

Capital consists of the tools, instruments, machines, buildings, and other constructions that have been produced in the past and that businesses now use to produce goods and services. These physical objects are themselves goods—capital goods. Capital goods are traded in goods markets, just as bottled water and toothpaste are. The price of a dump truck, a capital good, is determined by supply and demand in the market for dump trucks. This market is not a market for capital services.

A market for *capital services* is a *rental market*—a market in which the services of capital are hired.

An example of a market for capital services is the vehicle rental market in which Avis, Budget, Hertz, U-Haul, and many other firms offer automobiles and trucks for hire. The price in a capital services market is a *rental rate*.

Most capital services are not traded in a market. Instead, a firm buys capital and uses it itself. The services of the capital that a firm owns and operates have an implicit price that arises from depreciation and interest costs (see Chapter 10, pp. 224–225). You can think of this price as the implicit rental rate of capital. Firms that buy capital and use it themselves are *implicitly* renting the capital to themselves.

Markets for Land Services and Natural Resources

Land consists of all the gifts of nature—natural resources. The market for land as a factor of production is the market for the *services of land*—the use of land. The price of the services of land is a rental rate.

Most natural resources, such as farm land, can be used repeatedly. But a few natural resources are non-renewable. **Nonrenewable natural resources** are resources that can be used only once. Examples are oil, natural gas, and coal. The prices of nonrenewable natural resources are determined in global *commodity markets* and are called *commodity prices*.

Entrepreneurship

Entrepreneurial services are not traded in markets. Entrepreneurs receive the profit or bear the loss that results from their business decisions.

◆ REVIEW QUIZ

1 What are the factors of production and their prices?
2 What is the distinction between capital and the services of capital?
3 What is the distinction between the price of capital equipment and the rental rate of capital?

Work these questions in Study Plan 18.1 and get instant feedback. Do a Key Term Quiz.   MyEconLab

---

The rest of this chapter explores the influences on the demand and supply of factors of production. We begin by studying the demand for a factor of production.

The Demand for a Factor of Production

The demand for a factor of production is a **derived demand**—it is derived from the demand for the goods and services that the labor produces. You've seen, in Chapters 10 through 15, how a firm determines its profit-maximizing output. The quantities of factors of production demanded are a consequence of the firm's output decision. A firm hires the quantities of factors of production that produce the firm's profit-maximizing output.

To decide the quantity of a factor of production to hire, a firm compares the cost of hiring an additional unit of the factor with its value to the firm. The cost of hiring an additional unit of a factor of production is the factor price. The value to the firm of hiring one more unit of a factor of production is called the factor's **value of marginal product**. We calculate the value of marginal product as the price of a unit of output multiplied by the marginal product of the factor of production.

To study the demand for a factor of production, we'll use labor as the example. But what you learn here about the demand for labor applies to the demand for all factors of production.

Value of Marginal Product

Table 18.1 shows you how to calculate the value of marginal product of labor at Angelo's Bakery.

The first two columns show Angelo's total product schedule—the number of loaves per hour that each quantity of labor can produce. The third column shows the marginal product of labor—the change in total product that results from a one-unit increase in the quantity of labor employed. (See Chapter 11, pp. 249–252 for a refresher on product schedules.)

Angelo can sell bread at the going market price of $2 a loaf. Given this information, we can calculate the value of marginal product (fourth column). It equals price multiplied by marginal product. For example, the marginal product of hiring the second worker is 6 loaves. Each loaf sold brings in $2, so the value of marginal product of the second worker is $12 (6 loaves at $2 each).

A Firm's Demand for Labor

The value of marginal product of labor tells us what an additional worker is worth to a firm. It tells us the revenue that the firm earns by hiring one more worker. The wage rate tells us what an additional worker costs a firm.

The value of marginal product of labor and the wage rate together determine the quantity of labor demanded by a firm. Because the value of marginal product decreases as the quantity of labor employed increases, there is a simple rule for maximizing profit: Hire the quantity of labor at which the value of marginal product equals the wage rate.

If the value of marginal product of labor exceeds the wage rate, a firm can increase its profit by hiring

---

TABLE 18.1   Value of Marginal Product at Angelo's Bakery

	Quantity of labor (L) (workers)	Total product (TP) (loaves per hour)	Marginal product ($MP = \Delta TP/\Delta L$) (loaves per worker)	Value of marginal product ($VMP = MP \times P$) (dollars per worker)
A	0	0		
			7	14
B	1	7		
			6	**12**
C	**2**	13		
			5	10
D	3	18		
			4	8
E	4	22		
			3	6
F	5	25		

The value of marginal product of labor equals the price of the product multiplied by marginal product of labor. If Angelo's hires 2 workers, the marginal product of the second worker is 6 loaves (in the third column). The price of a loaf is $2, so the value of marginal product of the second worker is $2 a loaf multiplied by 6 loaves, which is $12 (in fourth column).

one more worker. If the wage rate exceeds the value of marginal product of labor, a firm can increase its profit by firing one worker. But if the wage rate equals the value of marginal product of labor, the firm cannot increase its profit by changing the number of workers it employs. The firm is making the maximum possible profit. So

> The quantity of labor demanded by a firm is the quantity at which the value of marginal product of labor equals the wage rate.

A Firm's Demand for Labor Curve

A firm's demand for labor curve is derived from its value of marginal product curve. Figure 18.1 shows these two curves. Figure 18.1(a) shows the value of marginal product curve at Angelo's Bakery. The blue bars graph the numbers in Table 18.1. The curve labeled *VMP* is Angelo's value of marginal product curve.

If the wage rate falls and other things remain the same, a firm hires more workers. Figure 18.1(b) shows Angelo's demand for labor curve.

Suppose the wage rate is $10 an hour. You can see in Fig.18.1(a) that if Angelo hires 2 workers, the value of the marginal product of labor is $12 an hour. At a wage rate of $10 an hour, Angelo makes a profit of $2 an hour on the second worker. If Angelo hires a third worker, the value of marginal product of that worker is $10 an hour. So on this third worker, Angelo breaks even.

If Angelo hired 4 workers, his profit would fall. The fourth worker generates a value of marginal product of only $8 an hour but costs $10 an hour, so Angelo does not hire the fourth worker. When the wage rate is $10 an hour, the quantity of labor demanded by Angelo is 3 workers.

Figure 18.1(b) shows Angelo's demand for labor curve, *D*. At $10 an hour, the quantity of labor demanded by Angelo is 3 workers. If the wage rate increased to $12 an hour, Angelo would decrease the quantity of labor demanded to 2 workers. If the wage rate decreased to $8 an hour, Angelo would increase the quantity of labor demanded to 4 workers.

A change in the wage rate brings a change in the quantity of labor demanded and a movement along the demand for labor curve.

A change in any other influence on a firm's labor-hiring plans changes the demand for labor and shifts the demand for labor curve.

FIGURE 18.1   The Demand for Labor at Angelo's Bakery

(a) Value of marginal product

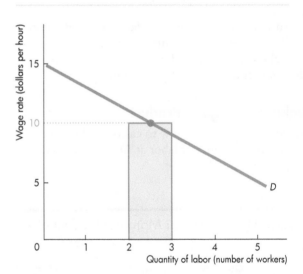

(b) Demand for labor

Angelo's Bakery can sell any quantity of bread at $2 a loaf. The blue bars in part (a) represent the firm's value of marginal product of labor (based on Table 18.1). The line labeled *VMP* is the firm's value of marginal product curve. Part (b) shows Angelo's demand for labor curve. Angelo hires the quantity of labor that makes the value of marginal product equal to the wage rate. The demand for labor curve slopes downward because the value of marginal product diminishes as the quantity of labor employed increases.

_____ **MyEconLab** Animation and Draw Graph _____

Changes in a Firm's Demand for Labor

A firm's demand for labor depends on

- The price of the firm's output
- The prices of other factors of production
- Technology

The Price of the Firm's Output The higher the price of a firm's output, the greater is the firm's demand for labor. The price of output affects the demand for labor through its influence on the value of marginal product of labor. A higher price for the firm's output increases the value of marginal product of labor. A change in the price of a firm's output leads to a shift in the firm's demand for labor curve. If the price of the firm's output increases, the demand for labor increases and the demand for labor curve shifts rightward.

For example, if the price of bread increased to $3 a loaf, the value of marginal product of Angelo's fourth worker would increase from $8 an hour to $12 an hour. At a wage rate of $10 an hour, Angelo would now hire 4 workers instead of 3.

The Prices of Other Factors of Production If the price of using capital decreases relative to the wage rate, a firm substitutes capital for labor and increases the quantity of capital it uses. Usually, the demand for labor will decrease when the price of using capital falls. For example, if the price of a bread-making machine falls, Angelo might decide to install one machine and lay off a worker. But the demand for labor could increase if the lower price of capital led to a sufficiently large increase in the scale of production. For example, with cheaper machines available, Angelo might install a machine and hire more labor to operate it. This type of factor substitution occurs in the long run when the firm can change the size of its plant.

Technology New technologies decrease the demand for some types of labor and increase the demand for other types. For example, if a new automated bread-making machine becomes available, Angelo might install one of these machines and fire most of his workforce—a decrease in the demand for bakery workers. But the firms that manufacture and service automated bread-making machines hire more labor, so there is an increase in the demand for this type of labor. An event similar to this one occurred during the 1990s when the introduction of electronic telephone exchanges decreased the demand for telephone operators and increased the demand for computer programmers and electronics engineers.

Table 18.2 summarizes the influences on a firm's demand for labor.

TABLE 18.2   A Firm's Demand for Labor

The Law of Demand

(Movements along the demand curve for labor)

The quantity of labor demanded by a firm

Decreases if:	Increases if:
■ The wage rate increases	■ The wage rate decreases

Changes in Demand

(Shifts in the demand curve for labor)

A firm's demand for labor

Decreases if:	Increases if:
■ The price of the firm's output decreases	■ The price of the firm's output increases
■ The price of a substitute for labor falls	■ The price of a substitute for labor rises
■ The price of a complement of labor rises	■ The price of a complement of labor falls
■ A new technology or new capital decreases the marginal product of labor	■ A new technology or new capital increases the marginal product of labor

---

◆ REVIEW QUIZ

1 What is the value of marginal product of labor?
2 What is the relationship between the value of marginal product of labor and the marginal product of labor?
3 How is the demand for labor derived from the value of marginal product of labor?
4 What are the influences on the demand for labor?

Work these questions in Study Plan 18.2 and get instant feedback. Do a Key Terms Quiz.   MyEconLab

Labor Markets

Labor services are traded in many different labor markets. Examples are markets for bakery workers, van drivers, crane operators, computer support specialists, air traffic controllers, surgeons, and economists. Some of these markets, such as the market for bakery workers, are local. They operate in a given neighborhood or town. Some labor markets, such as the market for air traffic controllers, are national. Firms and workers search across the nation for the right match of worker and job. And some labor markets are global, such as the market for superstar hockey, basketball, baseball, and soccer players.

We'll look at a local market for bakery workers as an example. First, we'll look at a *competitive* labor market. Then, we'll see how monopoly elements can influence a labor market.

A Competitive Labor Market

A competitive labor market is one in which many firms demand labor and many households supply labor.

Market Demand for Labor Earlier in the chapter, you saw how an individual firm decides how much labor to hire. The market demand for labor is derived from the demand for labor by individual firms. We determine the market demand for labor by adding together the quantities of labor demanded by all the firms in the market at each wage rate. (The market demand for a good or service is derived in a similar way—see Chapter 5, pp. 108–109.)

Because each firm's demand for labor curve slopes downward, the market demand for labor curve also slopes downward.

The Market Supply of Labor The market supply of labor is derived from the supply of labor decisions made by individual households.

Individual's Labor Supply Decision People can allocate their time to two broad activities: labor supply and leisure. (Leisure is a catch-all term. It includes all activities other than supplying labor.) For most people, leisure is more fun than work so to induce them to work they must be offered a wage.

Think about the labor supply decision of Jill, one of the workers at Angelo's Bakery. Let's see how the wage rate influences the quantity of labor she is willing to supply.

Reservation Wage Rate Jill enjoys her leisure time, and she would be pleased if she didn't have to spend her time working at Angelo's Bakery. But Jill wants to earn an income, and as long as she can earn a wage rate of at least $5 an hour, she's willing to work. This wage is called her *reservation wage*. At any wage rate above her reservation wage, Jill supplies some labor.

The wage rate at Angelo's is $10 an hour, and at that wage rate, Jill chooses to work 30 hours a week. At a wage rate of $10 an hour, Jill regards this use of her time as the best available. Figure 18.2 illustrates.

Backward-Bending Labor Supply Curve If Jill were offered a wage rate between $5 and $10 an hour, she would want to work fewer hours. If she were offered a wage rate above $10 an hour, she would want to work more hours, but only up to a point. If Jill could

FIGURE 18.2   Jill's Labor Supply Curve

Jill's labor supply curve is S. Jill supplies no labor at wage rates below her reservation wage of $5 an hour. As the wage rate rises above $5 an hour, the quantity of labor that Jill supplies increases to a maximum of 40 hours a week at a wage rate of $25 an hour. As the wage rate rises above $25 an hour, Jill supplies a decreasing quantity of labor: her labor supply curve bends backward. The income effect on the demand for leisure dominates the substitution effect.

MyEconLab Animation

earn $25 an hour, she would be willing to work 40 hours a week (and earn $1,000 a week). But at a wage rate above $25 an hour, with the goods and services that Jill can buy for $1,000, her priority would be a bit more leisure time. So if the wage rate increased above $25 an hour, Jill would cut back on her work hours and take more leisure. Jill's labor supply curve eventually bends backward.

Jill's labor supply decisions are influenced by a substitution effect and an income effect.

Substitution Effect At wage rates below $25 an hour, the higher the wage rate Jill is offered, the greater is the quantity of labor that she supplies. Jill's wage rate is her *opportunity cost of leisure*. If she quits work an hour early to catch a movie, the cost of that extra hour of leisure is the wage rate that Jill forgoes. The higher the wage rate, the less willing Jill is to forgo the income and take the extra leisure time. This tendency for a higher wage rate to induce Jill to work longer hours is a *substitution effect*.

Income Effect The higher Jill's wage rate, the higher is her income. A higher income, other things remaining the same, induces Jill to increase her demand for most goods and services. Leisure is one of those goods. Because an increase in income creates an increase in the demand for leisure, it also creates a decrease in the quantity of labor supplied.

Market Supply Curve The market supply curve shows the quantity of labor supplied by all households in a particular job market. It is found by adding together the quantities of labor supplied by all households to a given job market at each wage rate, so the greater the number of households (the greater is the working-age population), the greater is the market supply of labor.

Despite the fact that an individual's labor supply curve eventually bends backward, the market supply curve of labor slopes upward. The higher the wage rate for bakery workers, the greater is the quantity of bakery workers supplied in that labor market.

One reason why the market supply curve doesn't bend backward is that different households have different reservation wage rates and different wage rates at which their labor supply curves bend backward.

Also, along a supply curve in a particular job market, the wage rates available in other job markets remain the same. For example, along the supply curve of bakers, the wage rates of salespeople and all other types of labor are constant.

Let's now look at labor market equilibrium.

Competitive Labor Market Equilibrium Labor market equilibrium determines the wage rate and employment. In Fig. 18.3, the market demand curve for bakery workers is *D* and the market supply curve of bakery workers is *S*. The equilibrium wage rate is $10 an hour, and the equilibrium quantity is 300 bakery workers. If the wage rate exceeded $10 an hour, there would be a surplus of bakery workers. More people would be looking for jobs in bakeries than firms were willing to hire. In such a situation, the wage rate would fall as firms found it easy to hire people at a lower wage rate. If the wage rate were less than $10 an hour, there would be a shortage of bakery workers. Firms would not be able to fill all the positions they had available. In this situation, the wage rate would rise as firms found it necessary to offer higher wages to attract labor. Only at a wage rate of $10 an hour are there no forces operating to change the wage rate.

FIGURE 18.3   The Market for
Bakery Workers

A competitive labor market coordinates firms' and households' plans. The market is in equilibrium—the quantity of labor demanded equals the quantity supplied at a wage rate of $10 an hour when 300 workers are employed. If the wage rate exceeds $10 an hour, the quantity supplied exceeds the quantity demanded and the wage rate will fall. If the wage rate is below $10 an hour, the quantity demanded exceeds the quantity supplied and the wage rate will rise.

MyEconLab Animation

ECONOMICS IN ACTION
Wage Rates in the United States

In 2013, the average weekly wage in the United States was $776. The figure shows the *median weekly wage rates* for 20 jobs selected from the more than 700 jobs for which the Bureau of Labor Statistics reports wage rate data.

You can see that a chief executive, on average, earns more than 5 times as much per week as a fast-food worker and twice as much as a high-school teacher. Remember that these numbers are medians. Some chief executives earn much more and some earn less than the median.

Many more occupations earn a wage rate below the national average than above it. Most of the occupations that earn more than the national average require a college degree and postgraduate training.

Earning differences are explained by differences in the value of the marginal product of the skills in the various occupations and in market power.

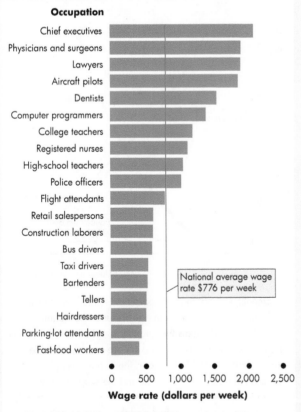

Weekly Wage Rates in 20 Jobs

Source of data: Bureau of Labor Statistics.

Differences and Trends in Wage Rates

You can use what you've learned about labor markets to explain some of the differences in wage rates across occupations and the trends in wage rates.

Wage rates are unequal, and *Economics in Action* on this page shows a sample of the inequality in wages in 2013. The differences in wage rates across occupations—including college professors and basketball coaches—are driven by differences in demand and supply in labor markets. The highest wage rates are earned in occupations where the value of marginal product is highest and where few people have the ability and training to perform the job.

Rising Wage Rates Wage rates increase over time and trend upward. The reason is that the value of marginal product of labor also increases over time. Technological change and the new types of capital that it brings make workers more productive. With greater labor productivity, the demand for labor increases, which increases the wage rate. Even jobs in which physical productivity doesn't increase experience increases in the *value* of marginal product. Child care is an example. A child-care worker can't care for an increasing number of children, but an increasing number of parents who earn high wages are willing to hire child-care workers. The *value* of marginal product of these workers increases, so the demand for their services increases, and so does their wage rate.

Increased Wage Inequality In recent years wage inequality has increased. High wage rates have increased more rapidly than the low ones, and some low wage rates have stagnated or even fallen. The reasons are complex and not fully understood, but the best explanation is that there is an interaction between technology and education.

The new information technologies of the 1990s and 2000s made well-educated, skilled workers more productive, so it raised their wage rates. For example, the computer created the jobs and increased the wage rates of computer programmers and electronic engineers.

These same technologies destroyed some low-skilled jobs. For example, the ATM took the jobs and lowered the wage rate of bank tellers, and automatic telephones took the jobs of telephone operators.

Another reason for increased inequality is that globalization has brought increased competition for low-skilled workers and at the same time opened global markets for high-skilled workers.

ECONOMICS IN THE NEWS

College Major and Job Prospects

The Most Valuable College Major

Which college major is most likely to land you a well-paying job right out of school? Katie Bardaro, an economist at PayScale, a compensation research firm, says biomedical engineering is your best bet. The median salary starts at $53,800 and by mid-career reaches $84,700 and keeps rising. The median salary for all biomedical engineers in 2012 was $88,000.

Some other science and engineering jobs pay more but don't have as good an outlook for jobs growth. The Bureau of Labor Statistics projects that the number of jobs for biomedical engineers will increase from today's 20,000 to 32,000 in 2020—an increase of more than 60 percent. In contrast, the working-age population will increase by only 8 percent by 2020.

Sources: The Bureau of Labor Statistics and
Forbes, May 15, 2012

THE QUESTIONS

- Why is the number of jobs for biomedical engineering graduates increasing?
- What determines the demand for biomedical engineers and why might it be increasing?
- What determines the supply of biomedical engineers and why might it be increasing?
- What determines whether the wage rate of biomedical engineers will rise?
- Provide a graphical illustration of the market for biomedical engineers in 2012 and 2020.

Biomedical engineers design and build replacement parts for the human body.

MyEconLab More Economics in the News

THE ANSWERS

- The number of jobs for biomedical engineers is growing because *both* demand for and supply of biomedical engineers are increasing.
- The demand for biomedical engineers is *derived* from the demand for biomedical products. The demand for replacement parts for the human body is increasing because technological advances are creating new and improved products.
- The supply of biomedical engineers is determined by the working-age population and the number of people who decide to major in the subject. The supply is increasing because the working-age population is increasing and good job prospects are attracting a larger percentage of people to study biomedical engineering.
- The wage rate of biomedical engineers will rise if the demand for their services increases faster than supply.
- The figure illustrates the market for biomedical engineers in 2012 and in 2020.
- Demand is expected to increase from D_{12} to D_{20}.
- Supply is expected to increase from S_{12} to S_{20}.
- The increase in demand is much greater than the increase in supply.
- The equilibrium quantity (the number of jobs) increases from 20,000 in 2012 to 32,000 in 2020.
- Because demand increases by more than supply, the equilibrium wage rate rises. (The 2020 wage rate is an assumption.)

The Market for Biomedical Engineers in 2012 and 2020

A Labor Market with a Union

A **labor union** is an organized group of workers that aims to increase the wage rate and influence other job conditions. Let's see what happens when a union enters a competitive labor market.

Influences on Labor Supply One way of raising the wage rate is to decrease the supply of labor. In some labor markets, a union can restrict supply by controlling entry into apprenticeship programs or by influencing job qualification standards. Markets for skilled workers, doctors, dentists, and lawyers are the easiest ones to control in this way.

If there is an abundant supply of nonunion labor, a union can't decrease supply. For example, in the market for farm labor in southern California, the flow of nonunion labor from Mexico makes it difficult for a union to control the supply.

On the demand side of the labor market, the union faces a tradeoff: The demand for labor curve slopes downward, so restricting supply to raise the wage rate costs jobs. For this reason, unions also try to influence the demand for union labor.

Influences on Labor Demand A union tries to increase the demand for the labor of its members in four main ways:

1. Increasing the value of marginal product of its members by organizing and sponsoring training schemes and apprenticeship programs, and by professional certification.
2. Lobbying for import restrictions and encouraging people to buy goods made by unionized workers.
3. Supporting minimum wage laws, which increase the cost of employing low-skilled labor and lead firms to substitute high-skilled union labor for low-skilled nonunion labor.
4. Lobbying for restrictive immigration laws to decrease the supply of foreign workers.

Labor Market Equilibrium with a Union Figure 18.4 illustrates what happens to the wage rate and employment when a union successfully enters a competitive labor market. With no union, the demand curve is D_C, the supply curve is S_C, the wage rate is $10 an hour, and 300 workers have jobs.

Now a union enters this labor market. First, look at what happens if the union has sufficient control over the supply of labor to be able to restrict supply

FIGURE 18.4   A Union Enters a Competitive Labor Market

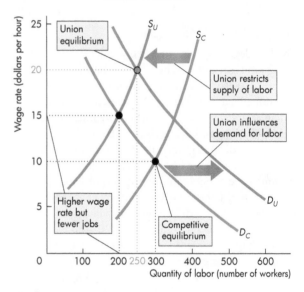

In a competitive labor market, the demand curve is D_C and the supply curve is S_C. The wage rate is $10 an hour and 300 workers are employed. If a union decreases the supply of labor and the supply of labor curve shifts to S_U, the wage rate rises to $15 an hour and employment decreases to 200 workers. If the union can also increase the demand for labor and shift the demand for labor curve to D_U, the wage rate rises to $20 an hour and 250 workers are employed.

——— MyEconLab Animation and Draw Graph ———

below its competitive level—to S_U. If that is all the union is able to do, employment falls to 200 workers and the wage rate rises to $15 an hour.

Suppose now that the union is also able to increase the demand for labor to D_U. The union can get an even bigger increase in the wage rate and with a smaller fall in employment. By maintaining the restricted labor supply at S_U, the union increases the wage rate to $20 an hour and achieves an employment level of 250 workers.

Because a union restricts the supply of labor in the market in which it operates, the union's actions spill over into nonunion markets. Workers who can't get union jobs must look elsewhere for work. This action increases the supply of labor in nonunion markets and lowers the wage rate in those markets. This spillover effect further widens the gap between union and nonunion wages.

Monopsony in the Labor Market Not all labor markets in which unions operate are competitive. Rather, some are labor markets in which the employer possesses market power and the union enters to try to counteract that power.

A market in which there is a single buyer is called a **monopsony**. A monopsony labor market has one employer. In some parts of the country, managed healthcare organizations are the major employer of healthcare professionals. In some communities, Wal-Mart is the main employer of salespeople. These firms have monopsony power.

A monopsony acts on the buying side of a market in a similar way to a monopoly on the selling side. The firm maximizes profit by hiring the quantity of labor that makes the marginal cost of labor equal to the value of marginal product of labor and by paying the lowest wage rate at which it can attract this quantity of labor.

Figure 18.5 illustrates a monopsony labor market. Like all firms, a monopsony faces a downward-sloping value of marginal product curve, *VMP,* which is its demand for labor curve, *D*—the curve labeled *VMP = D* in the figure.

What is special about monopsony is the marginal cost of labor. For a firm in a competitive labor market, the marginal cost of labor is the wage rate. For a monopsony, the marginal cost of labor exceeds the wage rate. The reason is that being the only buyer in the market, the firm faces an upward-sloping supply of labor curve—the curve *S* in the figure.

To attract one more worker, the monopsony must offer a higher wage rate. But it must pay this higher wage rate to all its workers, so the marginal cost of a worker is the wage rate plus the increased wage bill that arises from paying all the workers the higher wage rate.

The supply curve is now the average cost of labor curve and the relationship between the supply curve and the marginal cost of labor curve, *MCL,* is similar to that between a monopoly's demand curve and marginal revenue curve (see p. 300). The relationship between the supply curve and the *MCL* curve is also similar to that between a firm's average cost curve and marginal cost curve (see pp. 258–259).

To find the profit-maximizing quantity of labor to hire, the monopsony sets the marginal cost of labor equal to the value of marginal product of labor. In Fig. 18.5, this outcome occurs when the firm employs 100 workers.

To hire 100 workers, the firm must pay $10 an hour (on the supply of labor curve). Each worker is paid $10 an hour, but the value of marginal product of labor is $20 an hour, so the firm makes an economic profit of $10 an hour on the marginal worker.

If the labor market in Fig. 18.5 were competitive, the equilibrium wage rate and employment would be determined by the demand and supply curves. The wage rate would be $15 an hour, and 150 workers would be employed. So compared with a competitive labor market, a monopsony pays a lower wage rate and employs fewer workers.

A Union and a Monopsony A union is like a monopoly. If the union (monopoly seller) faces a monopsony buyer, the situation is called **bilateral monopoly**. An example of bilateral monopoly is the Writers Guild of America that represents film, television, and radio

---

FIGURE 18.5   A Monopsony Labor Market

A monopsony is a market structure in which there is a single buyer. A monopsony in the labor market has a value of marginal product curve *VMP = D*, and faces a labor supply curve *S*. The marginal cost of labor curve is *MCL*. Making the marginal cost of labor equal to the value of marginal product of labor maximizes profit. The monopsony hires 100 hours of labor and pays the lowest wage rate for which that quantity of labor will work—$10 an hour.

MyEconLab Animation

◆ AT **ISSUE**

Monopoly Power for Evil or Good?

The standard view of economists is that monopoly is bad. It prevents resources from being used efficiently, and on any criterion of fairness or equity, monopoly is unfair. It fails to serve the social interest.

We normally think of a monopoly as a big firm that gouges its customers. But a surprising monopoly (and monopsony) has attracted attention—the National Collegiate Athletic Association (NCAA).

Does the NCAA do a good job at efficiently allocating the talents of college athletes and providing those athletes with a fair return for their efforts?

The standard economist's view is that the NCAA doesn't serve the social interest. But there is an opposing view.

Let's look at both sides of this argument.

The **Standard View**

Robert Barro expresses the standard economist view. While acknowledging that the NCAA has boosted the productivity of college sports programs, he says that the NCAA monopoly

- Suppresses financial competition in college sports.

- Restricts scholarships and other payments to college athletes.

- Prevents college basketball players who come from poor families from accumulating wealth during a college career.

- Keeps poor students poor.

Despite doing these bad things, the NCAA manages to convince most people that the bad guys are the colleges that violate NCAA rules by attempting to pay their athletes competitive wages.

An **Opposing View**

Richard B. McKenzie of the University of California, Irvine, and Dwight R. Lee of the University of Georgia, in their book, *In Defense of Monopoly: How Market Power Fosters Creative Production* (University of Michigan Press, 2008), say the NCAA

- Helps its members to cooperate to everyone's benefit.
- Has enabled healthy growth of college athletics over the past 50 years.
- Has generated economic profits for member schools.
- Does not lower student athletes' wages.
- Has stimulated the demand for student athletes and increased their wages and employment opportunities.

Permitting NCAA colleges to pay athletes competitive wages is misguided.

The contenders for best monopoly in America include the Post Office, Microsoft, and the NCAA. And the winner is ... the NCAA.

Robert Barro, "The Best Little Monopoly in America," *BusinessWeek,* December 9, 2002

The Connecticut Huskies celebrate their victory at the 2014 NCAA National Championship writers, and an employers' alliance that represents CBS, MGM, NBC, and other entertainment companies. Every three years, the Writers Guild and the employers' alliance negotiate a pay deal.

In bilateral monopoly, the outcome is determined by bargaining, which depends on the costs that each party can inflict on the other. The firm can shut down temporarily and lock out its workers, and the workers can shut down the firm by striking. Each party estimates the other's strength and what it will lose if it does not agree to the other's demands.

Usually, an agreement is reached without a strike or a lockout. The threat is usually enough to bring the bargaining parties to an agreement. When a strike or lockout does occur, it is because one party has misjudged the costs each party can inflict on the other. Such an event occurred in November 2007 when the writers and entertainment producers failed to agree on a compensation deal. A 100-day strike followed that ended up costing the entertainment industry an estimated $2 billion.

In the example in Fig. 18.5, if the union and employer are equally strong, and each party knows the strength of the other, they will agree to split the gap between $10 (the wage rate on the supply curve) and $20 (the wage rate on the demand curve) and agree to a wage rate of $15 an hour.

You've now seen that in a monopsony, a union can bargain for a higher wage rate without sacrificing jobs. A similar outcome can arise in a monopsony labor market when a minimum wage law is enforced. Let's look at the effect of a minimum wage.

Monopsony and the Minimum Wage In a competitive labor market, a minimum wage that exceeds the equilibrium wage decreases employment (see Chapter 6, pp. 131–132). In a monopsony labor market, a minimum wage can increase both the wage rate and employment. Let's see how.

Figure 18.6 shows a monopsony labor market without a union. The wage rate is $10 an hour and 100 workers are employed.

A minimum wage law is passed that requires employers to pay at least $15 an hour. The monopsony now faces a perfectly elastic supply of labor at $15 an hour up to 150 workers (along the minimum wage line). To hire more than 150 workers, a wage rate above $15 an hour must be paid (along the supply curve). Because the wage rate is $15 an hour up to 150 workers, so is the marginal cost of labor $15 an hour up to 150 workers. To maximize profit, the monopsony sets the marginal cost of labor equal to the value of marginal product of

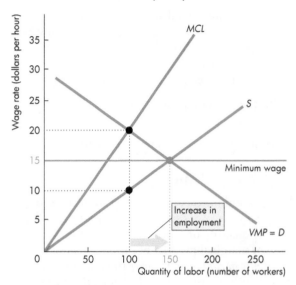

FIGURE 18.6 Minimum Wage Law in Monopsony

In a monopsony labor market, the wage rate is $10 an hour and 100 workers are hired. If a minimum wage law increases the wage rate to $15 an hour, the wage rate rises to this level and employment increases to 150 workers.

MyEconLab Animation and Draw Graph

labor (on the demand curve). That is, the monopsony hires 150 workers and pays $15 an hour. The minimum wage law has succeeded in raising the wage rate and increasing the number of workers employed.

◆ REVIEW QUIZ

1 What determines the amount of labor that households plan to supply?
2 How are the wage rate and employment determined in a competitive labor market?
3 How do labor unions influence wage rates?
4 What is a monopsony and why is a monopsony able to pay a lower wage rate than a firm in a competitive labor market?
5 How is the wage rate determined when a union faces a monopsony?
6 What is the effect of a minimum wage law in a monopsony labor market?

Work these questions in Study Plan 18.3 and get instant feedback. Do a Key Terms Quiz. MyEconLab

Capital and Natural Resource Markets

The markets for capital and land can be understood by using the same basic ideas that you've seen when studying a competitive labor market. But markets for nonrenewable natural resources are different. We'll now examine three groups of factor markets:

- Capital rental markets
- Land rental markets
- Nonrenewable natural resource markets

Capital Rental Markets

The demand for capital is derived from the *value of marginal product of capital*. Profit-maximizing firms hire the quantity of capital services that makes the value of marginal product of capital equal to the *rental rate of capital*. The *lower* the rental rate of capital, other things remaining the same, the *greater* is the quantity of capital demanded. The supply of capital responds in the opposite way to the rental rate. The *higher* the rental rate, other things remaining the same, the *greater* is the quantity of capital supplied. The equilibrium rental rate makes the quantity of capital demanded equal to the quantity supplied.

Figure 18.7 illustrates the rental market for tower cranes—capital used to construct high-rise buildings. The value of marginal product and the demand curve is *VMP = D*. The supply curve is *S*. The equilibrium rental rate is $1,000 per day and 100 tower cranes are rented.

Rent-Versus-Buy Decision Some capital services are obtained in a rental market like the market for tower cranes. And as with tower cranes, many of the world's large airlines rent their airplanes. But not all capital services are obtained in a rental market. Instead, firms buy the capital equipment that they use. You saw in Chapter 10 (pp. 224–225) that the cost of the services of the capital that a firm owns and operates itself is an implicit rental rate that arises from depreciation and interest costs. Firms that buy capital *implicitly* rent the capital to themselves.

The decision to obtain capital services in a rental market rather than buy capital and rent it implicitly is made to minimize cost. The firm compares the cost of explicitly renting the capital and the cost of buying and implicitly renting it. This decision is the same as

FIGURE 18.7   A Rental Market for Capital

The value of marginal product of tower cranes, *VMP*, determines the demand, *D*, for tower crane rentals. With the supply curve *S*, the equilibrium rental rate is $1,000 a day and 100 cranes are rented.

——— MyEconLab Animation ———

the one that a household makes in deciding whether to rent or buy a home.

To make a rent-versus-buy decision, a firm must compare a cost incurred in the *present* with a stream of rental costs incurred over some *future* period. The Mathematical Note (pp. 438–439) explains how to make this comparison by calculating the *present value* of a future amount of money. If the *present value* of the future rental payments of an item of capital equipment exceeds the cost of buying the capital, the firm will buy the equipment. If the *present value* of the future rental payments of an item of capital equipment is less than the cost of buying the capital, the firm will rent (or lease) the equipment.

Land Rental Markets

The demand for land is based on the same factors as the demand for labor and the demand for capital— the *value of marginal product of land*. Profit-maximizing firms rent the quantity of land at which the value of marginal product of land is equal to the *rental rate of land*. The *lower* the rental rate, other things remaining the same, the *greater* is the quantity of land demanded.

But the supply of land is special: Its quantity is fixed, so the quantity supplied cannot be changed by people's decisions. The supply of each particular block of land is perfectly inelastic.

The equilibrium rental rate makes the quantity of land demanded equal to the quantity available. Figure 18.8 illustrates the market for a 10-acre block of land on 42nd Street in New York City. The quantity supplied is fixed and the supply curve is *S*. The value of marginal product and the demand curve is $VMP = D$. The equilibrium rental rate is $1,000 an acre per day.

The rental rate of land is high in New York because the willingness to pay for the services produced by that land is high, which in turn makes the *VMP* of land high. A Big Mac costs more at McDonald's on 42nd Street, New York, than at McDonald's on Jefferson Avenue, St. Louis, but not because the rental rate of land is higher in New York. The rental rate of land is higher in New York because of the greater willingness to pay for a Big Mac (and other goods and services) in New York.

FIGURE 18.8   A Rental Market for Land

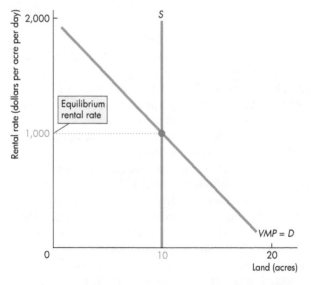

The value of marginal product of a 10-acre block, *VMP*, determines the rental demand, *D*, for this land. With the supply curve *S*, this block rents for $1,000 per acre per day.

MyEconLab Animation

Nonrenewable Natural Resource Markets

The nonrenewable natural resources are oil, gas, and coal. Burning one of these fuels converts it to energy and other by-products, and the used resource cannot be re-used. The natural resources that we use to make metals are also nonrenewable, but they can be used again, at some cost, by recycling them.

Oil, gas, and coal are traded in global commodity markets. The price of a given grade of crude oil is the same in New York, London, and Singapore. Traders, linked by telephone and the Internet, operate these markets around the clock every day of the year.

Demand and supply determine the prices and the quantities traded in these commodity markets. We'll look at the influences on demand and supply by considering the global market for crude oil.

The Demand for Oil The two key influences on the demand for oil are

1. The *value of marginal product* of oil
2. The expected future price of oil

The value of marginal product of oil is the *fundamental* influence on demand. It works in exactly the same way for a nonrenewable resource as it does for any other factor of production. The greater the quantity of oil used, the smaller is the value of marginal product of oil. Diminishing value of marginal product makes the demand curve slope downward. The lower the price, the greater is the quantity demanded.

The higher the expected future price of oil, the greater is the present demand for oil. The expected future price is a *speculative* influence on demand. Oil in the ground and oil in storage tanks are inventories that can be held or sold. A trader might plan to buy oil to hold now and to sell it later for a profit. Instead of buying oil to hold and sell later, the trader could buy a bond and earn interest. The interest forgone is the opportunity cost of holding the oil. If the price of oil is expected to rise by a bigger percentage than the interest rate, a trader will hold oil and incur the opportunity cost. In this case, the return from holding oil exceeds the return from holding bonds.

The Supply of Oil The three key influences on the supply of oil are

1. The known oil reserves
2. The scale of current oil production facilities
3. The expected future price of oil

Known oil reserves are the oil that has been discovered and can be extracted with today's technology. This quantity increases over time because advances in technology enable ever-less accessible sources to be discovered. The greater the size of known reserves, the greater is the supply of oil. But this influence on supply is small and indirect. It operates by changing the expected distant future price of oil. Even a major new discovery of oil would have a negligible effect on current supply of oil.

The scale of current oil production facilities is the *fundamental* influence on the supply of oil. Producing oil is like any production activity: It is subject to increasing marginal cost. The increasing marginal cost of extracting oil means that the supply curve of oil slopes upward. The higher the price of oil, the greater is the quantity supplied. When new oil wells are sunk or when new faster pumps are installed, the supply of oil increases. When existing wells run dry, the supply of oil decreases. Over time, the factors that increase supply are more powerful than those that decrease supply, so changes in the scale of current oil production facilities increase the supply of oil.

Speculative forces based on expectations about the future price also influence the supply of oil. The *higher* the expected future price of oil, the *smaller* is the present supply of oil. A trader with an oil inventory might plan to sell now or to hold and sell later. You've seen that interest forgone is the opportunity cost of holding the oil. If the price of oil is expected to rise by a bigger percentage than the interest rate, it is profitable to incur the opportunity cost of holding oil rather than selling it immediately.

The Equilibrium Price of Oil

The demand for oil and the supply of oil determine the equilibrium price and quantity traded. Figure 18.9 illustrates the market equilibrium.

The value of marginal product of oil, *VMP*, is the *fundamental determinant of demand*, and the marginal cost of extraction, *MC*, is the *fundamental determinant of supply*. Together, they determine the *market fundamentals price*.

If expectations about the future price are also based on fundamentals, the equilibrium price is the market fundamentals price. But if expectations about the future price of oil depart from what the market fundamentals imply, *speculation* can drive a wedge between the equilibrium price and the market fundamentals price.

FIGURE 18.9   A Nonrenewable Natural Resource Market

The value of marginal product of a natural resource, *VMP*, and the marginal cost of extraction, *MC*, determine the *market fundamentals* price. Demand, *D*, and supply, *S*, which determine the equilibrium price, are influenced by the expected future price. Speculation can bring a gap between the market fundamentals price and the equilibrium price.

MyEconLab Animation

The Hotelling Principle

Harold Hotelling, an economist at Columbia University, had an incredible idea: Traders expect the price of a nonrenewable natural resource to rise at a rate equal to the interest rate. We call this idea the **Hotelling principle**. Let's see why it is correct.

You've seen that the interest rate is the opportunity cost of holding an oil inventory. If the price of oil is expected to rise at a rate that exceeds the interest rate, it is profitable to hold a bigger inventory. Demand increases, supply decreases, and the price rises. If the interest rate exceeds the rate at which the price of oil is expected to rise, it is not profitable to hold an oil inventory. Demand decreases, supply increases, and the price falls. But if the price of oil is expected to rise at a rate equal to the interest rate, holding an inventory of oil is just as good as holding bonds. Demand and supply don't change and the price does not change. Only when the price of oil is expected to rise at a rate equal to the interest rate is the price at its equilibrium.

ECONOMICS IN ACTION

The World and U.S. Markets for Oil

The world produced 85 million barrels of oil per day in 2013 and the price was steady at around $110 a barrel.

Although the United States imports oil from other countries, most of it comes from close to home and domestic production has increased in recent years. Figure 1 provides the details: Only 12 percent of the U.S. oil supply comes from the Middle East and one third comes from Canada, Mexico, and other Western Hemisphere countries.

Even if the United States produced all its own oil, it would still face a fluctuating global price. U.S. producers would not willingly sell to U.S. buyers for a price below the world price. So energy independence doesn't mean an independent oil price.

The Hotelling principle tells us that we must expect the price of oil to rise at a rate equal to the interest rate. But expecting the price to rise at a rate equal to the interest rate doesn't mean that the price will rise at this rate. As you can see in Fig. 2, the price of oil over the past 50 or so years has not followed the path predicted by the Hotelling principle.

The forces that influence expectations are not well understood. The expected future price of oil depends on its expected future rate of use and the rate of discovery of new sources of supply. One person's expectation about a future price also depends on guesses about other people's expectations. These guesses can change abruptly and become self-reinforcing. When the expected future price of oil changes for whatever

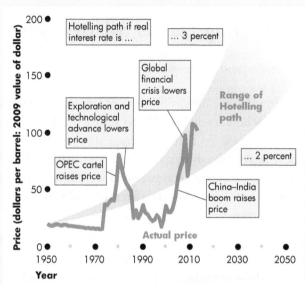

Figure 2 The Price of Oil and Its Hotelling Path
Source of data: U.S. Energy Information Administration.

reason, demand and supply change, and so does the price. Prices in speculative markets are always volatile.

◆ REVIEW QUIZ

1 What determines demand and supply in rental markets for capital and land?
2 What determines the demand for a nonrenewable natural resource?
3 What determines the supply of a nonrenewable natural resource?
4 What is the market fundamentals price and how might it differ from the equilibrium price?
5 Explain the Hotelling principle.

Work these questions in Study Plan 18.4 and get instant feedback. Do a Key Terms Quiz.   MyEconLab

◆ *Economics in the News* on pp. 436–437 contrasts the outcomes in competitive and union labor markets for teachers.

The next chapter looks more closely at the distribution of income and its trends. The chapter also looks at the efforts by governments to redistribute income and modify the market outcome.

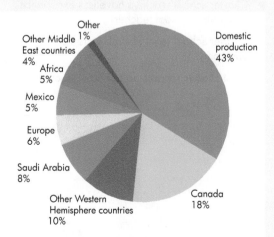

Figure 1 Our Diverse Sources of Oil
Source of data: U.S. Energy Information Administration.

Labor Markets in Action

Comparing Teacher Salaries by School Type

Illinois Network of Charter Schools, National Center on School Choice, Vanderbilt University, and journalgazette.net

Reported on the Illinois Network of Charter Schools' web site (http://incschools.org/), charter school teachers in Illinois with 1 to 3 years experience earn $44,500 on average. That is $9,500 less than the average salary for similarly experienced traditional public school teachers. And the difference grows. For teachers with 10 to 12 years experience, a charter school teacher earns an average of $56,600 per year while a traditional public school teacher earns $81,800 per year—a difference of $25,200 per year or 45 percent of a charter school teacher's pay.

Research by David Stuit and Thomas M. Smith of the National Center on School Choice at Vanderbilt Univer sity shows that teacher turnover rates at charter schools substantially exceed those at traditional public schools. Stuit and Smith found that the odds of a charter school teacher leaving to take a job outside teaching were 130 percent greater than those of a traditional public school teacher. And the odds of a charter school teacher leaving to take a job in another school were 76 percent greater.

Because charter school teachers are more likely to quit than are traditional public school teachers, the average years of teaching experience is less in charter schools than in public schools.

Charter school leaders interviewed by journalgazette.net (of Fort Wayne, Indiana) say that while restricted budgets make it impossible to match traditional public school salaries, there is a supply of teachers "drawn to charters out of an appreciation of their mission, a love for the kids they serve, and a desire for autonomy not granted in tra-ditional public school environments."

Most charter schools hire non-union teachers and are free from many of the restrictions arising from teachers' unions and regulation.

MyEconLab More Economics in the News

ESSENCE OF THE STORY

- In Illinois, experienced charter school teachers earn an average of $56,600 per year and traditional public school teachers earn an aver-age of $81,800 per year, a gap of $25,200 per year.

- Charter schools have substantially higher teacher turnover rates than traditional public schools.

- Charter schools have smaller budgets than traditional public schools.

- Charter school teachers have less experience than public school teachers.

- Charter school teachers value greater autonomy.

- Most charter schools do not have teachers' unions.

ECONOMIC ANALYSIS

- Teachers in charter schools are paid much lower salaries (wage rates), on average, than teachers in traditional public schools for three main reasons:
  1. Charter school teachers are less experienced.
  2. Charter schools have tighter budgets than traditional public schools.
  3. Charter school teachers are not (usually) unionized.

- Charter school teachers are, on average, less experienced than public school teachers, so their marginal product is less than that of traditional public school teachers, which means that their *VMP* is lower and the demand for their services is reduced.

- Because charter schools have tighter budgets than public schools, the market values the services of charter school teachers at a lower (implicit) price, which further lowers their *VMP* and reduces the charter schools' demand for teachers.

- Some teachers say that they value the freedom and autonomy that a charter school gives them. This preference for working in a charter school increases the supply of charter school teachers (relative to what it would be without the autonomy.)

- The combination of a reduced demand and greater supply lowers the equilibrium wage rate of charter school teachers. Figure 1 illustrates.

- If teachers in charter schools had the same experience as those in traditional public schools and if charter school budgets were as big as traditional public school budgets, the charter schools' demand curve for teachers would be D_P.

- If charter school teachers didn't have the autonomy they enjoy, the supply curve of charter school teachers would be S_P. The equilibrium wage rate would be $70,000 per year. (This wage rate is an assumption.)

- The factors discussed above decrease demand to D_C, increase supply to S_C, and lower the equilibrium wage rate to $60,000 per year.

- The fact that traditional public school teachers are unionized and most charter school teachers are not makes the wage gap even bigger.

- In Fig. 2, the teachers' union at traditional public schools boosts the demand for teachers by lobbying for bigger school budgets and the union restricts the supply of teachers by raising qualification requirements.

- The demand for public school teachers increases from its competitive level, D_P, to D_U and the supply decreases

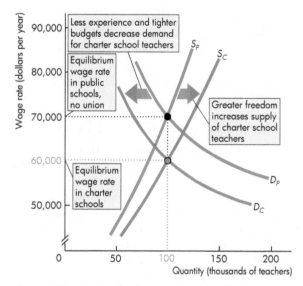

Figure 1 The Market for Charter School Teachers

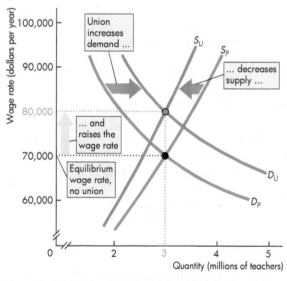

Figure 2 The Market for Unionized Public School Teachers

from its competitive level, S_P, to S_U. The equilibrium wage rate rises to $80,000 per year.

- When a traditional public school is replaced by a charter school, the teachers who remain in the charter school take a very large wage cut.

- The wage cut explains the higher teacher turnover rate of charter schools. The wage cut is too big for some teachers, so they search for an alternative better paying job and quit teaching.

437

MATHEMATICAL NOTE

Present Value and Discounting

Rent-Versus-Buy Decision

To decide whether to rent an item of capital equipment or to buy the capital and implicitly rent it, a firm must compare the present expenditure on the capital with the future rental cost of the capital.

Comparing Current and Future Dollars

To compare a present expenditure with a future expenditure, we convert the future expenditure to its "present value."

The present value of a future amount of money is the amount that, if invested today, will grow to be as large as that future amount when the interest that it will earn is taken into account.

So the present value of a future amount of money is smaller than the future amount. The calculation that we use to convert a future amount of money to its present value is called discounting.

The easiest way to understand discounting and present value is to first consider its opposite: How a present value grows to a future amount of money because of *compound interest*.

Compound Interest

Compound interest is the interest on an initial investment plus the interest on the interest that the investment has previously earned. Because of compound interest, a present amount of money (a present value) grows into a larger future amount. The future amount is equal to the present amount (present value) plus the interest it will earn in the future. That is,

Future amount = Present value + Interest income.

The interest in the first year is equal to the present value multiplied by the interest rate, r, so

Amount after 1 year = Present value +
$\qquad$ (r × Present value).

or

Amount after 1 year = Present value × $(1 + r)$.

If you invest $100 today and the interest rate is 10 percent a year ($r = 0.1$), 1 year from today you will have $110—the original $100 plus $10 interest.

Check that the above formula delivers that answer:

$$\$100 \times 1.1 = \$110.$$

If you leave this $110 invested to earn 10 percent during a second year, at the end of that year you will have

Amount after 2 years = Present value × $(1 + r)^2$.

With the numbers of the previous example, you invest $100 today at an interest rate of 10 percent a year ($r = 0.1$). After 1 year, you will have $110—the original $100 plus $10 interest. And after 2 years, you will have $121. In the second year, you earned $10 on your initial $100 plus $1 on the $10 interest that you earned in the first year.

Check that the above formula delivers that answer:

$$\$100 \times (1.1)^2 = \$100 \times 1.21 = \$121.$$

If you leave your $100 invested for n years, it will grow to

Amount after n years = Present value × $(1 + r)^n$.

With an interest rate of 10 percent a year, your $100 will grow to $195 after 7 years ($n = 7$)—almost double the present value of $100.

Discounting a Future Amount

We have just calculated future amounts 1 year, 2 years, and n years in the future, knowing the present value and the interest rate. To calculate the present value of these future amounts, we just work backward.

To find the present value of an amount 1 year in the future, we divide the future amount by $(1 + r)$.

That is,

$$\text{Present value} = \frac{\text{Amount of money one year in future}}{(1 + r)}.$$

Let's check that we can use the present value formula by calculating the present value of $110 1 year from now when the interest rate is 10 percent a year.

You'll be able to guess that the answer is $100 because we just calculated that $100 invested today at 10 percent a year becomes $110 in one year. So the present value of $110 to be received 1 year from today is $100. But let's use the formula. Putting the numbers into the above formula, we have

$$\text{Present value} = \frac{\$110}{(1 + 0.1)}$$
$$= \frac{\$110}{1.1} = \$100.$$

To calculate the present value of an amount of money 2 years in the future, we use the formula:

$$\text{Present value} = \frac{\text{Amount of money two years in future}}{(1 + r)^2}$$

Use this formula to calculate the present value of $121 to be received 2 years from now at an interest rate of 10 percent a year. With these numbers, the formula gives

$$\text{Present value} = \frac{\$121}{(1 + 0.1)^2}$$
$$= \frac{\$121}{(1.1)^2}$$
$$= \frac{\$121}{1.21}$$
$$= \$100.$$

We can calculate the present value of an amount of money n years in the future by using the general formula

$$\text{Present value} = \frac{\text{Amount of money } n \text{ years in future}}{(1 + r)^n}$$

For example, if the interest rate is 10 percent a year, $100 to be received 10 years from now has a present value of $38.55. That is, if $38.55 is invested today at 10 percent a year it will accumulate to $100 in 10 years.

Present Value of a Sequence of Future Amounts

You've seen how to calculate the present value of an amount of money to be received 1 year, 2 years, and n years in the future. Most practical applications of present value calculate the present value of a sequence of future amounts of money that are spread over several years. An airline's payment of rent for the lease of airplanes is an example.

To calculate the present value of a sequence of amounts over several years, we use the formula you have learned and apply it to each year. We then sum the present values for all the years to find the present value of the sequence of amounts.

For example, suppose that a firm expects to pay $100 a year for each of the next 5 years and the interest rate is 10 percent a year ($r = 0.1$). The present value (PV) of these five payments of $100 each is calculated by using the following formula:

$$PV = \frac{\$100}{1.1} + \frac{\$100}{1.1^2} + \frac{\$100}{1.1^3} + \frac{\$100}{1.1^4} + \frac{\$100}{1.1^5},$$

which equals

$$PV = \$90.91 + \$82.64 + \$75.13 + \$68.30 + \$62.09$$
$$= \$379.07.$$

You can see that the firm pays $500 over 5 years. But because the money is paid in the future, it is not worth $500 today. Its present value is only $379.07. And the farther in the future the money is paid, the smaller is its present value. The $100 paid 1 year in the future is worth $90.91 today, but the $100 paid 5 years in the future is worth only $62.09 today.

The Decision

If this firm could lease a machine for 5 years at $100 a year or buy the machine for $500, it would jump at leasing. Only if the firm could buy the machine for less than $379.07 would it want to buy.

Many personal and business decisions turn on calculations like the one you've just made. A decision to buy or rent an apartment, to buy or lease a car, and to pay off a student loan or let the loan run another year can all be made using the above calculation.

SUMMARY

Key Points

The Anatomy of Factor Markets (p. 420)

- The factor markets are job markets for labor; rental markets (often implicit rental markets) for capital and land; and global commodity markets for nonrenewable natural resources.
- The services of entrepreneurs are not traded on a factor market.

Working Problem 1 will give you a better understanding of the anatomy of factor markets.

The Demand for a Factor of Production

(pp. 421–423)

- The value of marginal product determines the demand for a factor of production.
- The value of marginal product decreases as the quantity of the factor employed increases.
- The firm employs the quantity of each factor of production that makes the value of marginal product equal to the factor price.

Working Problems 2 to 6 will give you a better understanding of the demand for a factor of production.

Labor Markets (pp. 424–431)

- The value of marginal product of labor determines the demand for labor. A rise in the wage rate brings a decrease in the quantity demanded.
- The quantity of labor supplied depends on the wage rate. At low wage rates, a rise in the wage rate increases the quantity supplied. Beyond a high enough wage rate, a rise in the wage rate decreases the quantity supplied—the supply curve eventually bends backward.

- Demand and supply determine the wage rate in a competitive labor market.
- A labor union can raise the wage rate by restricting the supply or increasing the demand for labor.
- A monopsony can lower the wage rate below the competitive level.
- A union or a minimum wage in a monopsony labor market can raise the wage rate without a fall in employment.

Working Problems 7 to 9 will give you a better understanding of labor markets.

Capital and Natural Resource Markets (pp. 432–435)

- The value of marginal product of capital (and land) determines the demand for capital (and land).
- Firms make a rent-versus-buy decision by choosing the option that minimizes cost.
- The supply of land is inelastic and the demand for land determines the rental rate.
- The demand for a nonrenewable natural resource depends on the value of marginal product and on the expected future price.
- The supply of a nonrenewable natural resource depends on the known reserves, the cost of extraction, and the expected future price.
- The price of nonrenewable natural resources can differ from the market fundamentals price because of speculation based on expectations about the future price.
- The price of a nonrenewable natural resource is expected to rise at a rate equal to the interest rate.

Working Problem 10 will give you a better understanding of capital and natural resource markets.

Key Terms

MyEconLab Key Terms Quiz

Bilateral monopoly, 429
Derived demand, 421
Hotelling principle, 434

Labor union, 428
Monopsony, 429

Nonrenewable natural
resources, 420
Value of marginal product, 421

WORKED PROBLEM

MyEconLab   You can work this Problem in Chapter 18 Study Plan.

Tom hires workers to pack the tomatoes he grows. The market for tomatoes is perfectly competitive, and the price of tomatoes is $2 a box. The labor market is competitive, and the market wage rate is $16 an hour. The table shows the workers' total product schedule.

Number of workers	Quantity produced (boxes packed per hour)
1	14
2	26
3	36
4	44
5	50

Questions

1. Calculate the marginal product of the third worker hired and that worker's value of marginal product.

2. How many workers will Tom hire to maximize profit and what will the workers produce?

3. If the market wage rate rises to $20 an hour, how many workers will Tom hire?

Solutions

1. Marginal product (*MP*) of the 3rd worker equals the total product (*TP*) of 3 workers (36 boxes) minus the *TP* of 2 workers (26 boxes), so the *MP* of the 3rd worker is 10 boxes of tomatoes.

   The 3rd worker's value of marginal product (*VMP*) equals the 3rd worker's *MP* (10 boxes of tomatoes an hour) multiplied by the price of a box of tomatoes ($2), so the *VMP* of the 3rd worker equals $20 an hour.

   The figure shows the *VMP* of each worker.

Key Point: The value of marginal product of labor is the marginal product of labor multiplied by the market price of the good produced by the labor.

2. Tom maximizes profit by hiring the number of workers at which *VMP* equals the market wage rate. The table in the next column shows the calculations.

   The market wage rate is $16 an hour, so Tom hires the number of workers at which the *VMP* equals $16 an hour. You can see in the table that *VMP* equal $16 an hour when Tom hires the 4th worker. So Tom maximizes profit when he hires

Number of workers	TP (boxes per hour)	MP (boxes per worker)	VMP (dollars per hour)
1	14		
		12	24
2	26		
		10	20
3	36		
		 8	16
4	44		
		 6	12
5	50		

4 workers who produce 44 boxes of tomatoes. Tom sells the tomatoes for $88 and pays the wages of $64, so his profit is $24 an hour. The figure shows this equality.

Key Point: The firm maximizes profit by hiring the quantity of labor at which the value of marginal product of labor equals the market wage rate.

3. If the market wage rate rises to $20 an hour, the *VMP* of labor does not change and remains the same as in the table above. But now with a market wage rate of $20 an hour, Tom hires fewer workers. *VMP* equals $20 an hour when Tom hire the 3rd worker. So Tom cuts the number of workers to 3.

Key Point: When the market wage rate rises, the firm maximizes profit by hiring fewer workers.

Key Figure

MyEconLab Interactive Animation

STUDY PLAN PROBLEMS AND APPLICATIONS

MyEconLab   You can work Problems 1 to 10 in Chapter 18 Study Plan and get instant feedback.

The Anatomy of Factor Markets (Study Plan 18.1)

1. Tim is opening a new online store. He plans to hire two workers at $10 an hour. Tim is also considering buying or leasing some new computers. The purchase price of a computer is $900 and after three years it is worthless. The annual cost of leasing a computer is $450.
   a. In which factor markets does Tim operate?
   b. What is the price of the capital equipment and the rental rate of capital?

The Demand for a Factor of Production

(Study Plan 18.2)

Use the following data to work Problems 2 to 6. Wanda's is a fish store that hires students to pack the fish. Students can pack the following amounts of fish:

Number of students	Quantity of fish packed (pounds)
1	20
2	50
3	90
4	120
5	145
6	165
7	180
8	190

The fish market is competitive and the price of fish is 50¢ a pound. The market for packers is competitive and their market wage rate is $7.50 an hour.

2. Calculate the value of marginal product of labor and draw the value of marginal product curve.
3. a. Find Wanda's demand for labor curve.
   b. How many students does Wanda's employ?

Use the following additional data to work Problems 4 and 5.

The market price of fish falls to 33.33¢ a pound, but the packers' wage rate remains at $7.50 an hour.

4. How does the students' marginal product change? How does the value of marginal product of labor change?
5. How does Wanda's demand for labor change? What happens to the number of students that Wanda employs?

6. At Wanda's fish store, packers' wages increase to $10 an hour, but the price of fish remains at 50¢ a pound.
   a. What happens to the value of marginal product of labor?
   b. What happens to Wanda's demand for labor curve?
   c. How many students does Wanda's employ?

Labor Markets (Study Plan 18.3)

Use the following news clip to work Problems 7 to 9.

In Modern Rarity, Workers Form Union at Small Chain

In New York's low-income neighborhoods, labor unions have virtually no presence. But after a year-long struggle, 95 workers at a chain of 10 sneaker stores have formed a union. After months of negotiations, the two sides signed a three-year contract that sets the wage rate at $7.25 an hour.

Source: *The New York Times*, February 5, 2006

7. Why are labor unions scarce in New York's low-income neighborhoods?
8. Who wins from this union contract? Who loses?
9. How can this union try to change the demand for labor?

Capital and Natural Resource Markets

(Study Plan 18.4)

10. **Land Prices Reflect High Commodity Prices**
   As their family grows, the Steens are finding it more difficult for the next generation to stay in ranching. "The problem is they don't create any more land," Steen said. As the prices for cattle, corn, and other commodities climb, so does the value of land in South Dakota.

   Source: *Rapid City Journal*, January 30, 2012

   a. Why does the price of land in South Dakota keep rising? In your answer include a discussion of the demand for and supply of land.
   b. Use a graph to show why the price of land in South Dakota increased over the past decade.
   c. Is the supply of land in South Dakota perfectly inelastic?

ADDITIONAL PROBLEMS AND APPLICATIONS

MyEconLab   You can work these problems in MyEconLab if assigned by your instructor.

The Anatomy of Factor Markets

11. Venus is opening a tennis school. She plans to hire a marketing graduate to promote and manage the school at $20 an hour. Venus is also considering buying or leasing a new tennis ball machine. The purchase price of the machine is $1,000 and after three years it is worthless. The annual cost of leasing the machine is $500.
    a. In which factor markets does Venus operate?
    b. What is the price of the capital equipment and the rental rate of capital?

The Demand for a Factor of Production

Use the following data to work Problems 12 to 15. Kaiser's Ice Cream Parlor hires workers to produce milk shakes. The market for milk shakes is perfectly competitive, and the price of a milk shake is $4. The labor market is competitive, and the wage rate is $40 a day. The table shows the workers' total product schedule.

Number of workers	Quantity produced (milk shakes per day)
1	7
2	21
3	33
4	43
5	51
6	55

12. Calculate the marginal product of hiring the fourth worker and the fourth worker's value of marginal product.
13. How many workers will Kaiser's hire to maximize its profit and how many milk shakes a day will Kaiser's produce?
14. If the price of a milk shake rises to $5, how many workers will Kaiser's hire?
15. Kaiser's installs a new machine for making milk shakes that increases the productivity of workers by 50 percent. If the price of a milk shake remains at $4 and the wage rises to $48 a day, how many workers does Kaiser's hire?
16. **Detroit Oil Refinery Expansion Approved**
    Marathon Oil Saturday started work on a $1.9 billion expansion of its gasoline refinery in Detroit. Marathon will employ 800 construction workers and add 135 permanent jobs to the existing 480 workers at the refinery.
    Source: *United Press International*, June 21, 2008
    a. Explain how rising gasoline prices influence the market for refinery labor.
    b. Draw a graph to illustrate the effects of rising gasoline prices on the market for refinery labor.

Labor Markets

Use the following news clip to work Problems 17 and 18.

Miner Sacks 17,000 Workers Over Pay Dispute
Impala Platinum has sacked 17,000 South African miners at its Rustenburg mine because they took part in an illegal strike. The miners refused to have their union negotiate in the two-week pay dispute with the world's second largest platinum producer. Mining provides a quarter of all jobs in Rustenburg.
Source: abc.com.au, February 3, 2012

17. How would the wage rate and employment for the Rustenburg miners be determined in a competitive market?
18. a. Explain how it is possible that the mine workers were being paid less than the wage that would be paid in a competitive labor market.
    b. What would be the effect of a minimum wage law in the market for miners?

Use the following news clip to work Problems 19 to 22.

The New War over Wal-Mart
Today, Wal-Mart employs more people—1.7 million—than any other private employer in the world. With size comes power: Wal-Mart's prices are lower and United Food and Commercial Workers International Union argues that Wal-Mart's wages are also lower than its competitors. Last year, the workers at a Canadian outlet joined the union and Wal-Mart immediately closed the outlet. But does Wal-Mart behave any worse than its competitors? When it comes to payroll, Wal-Mart's median hourly wage tracks the national median wage for general retail jobs.
Source: *The Atlantic*, June 2006

19. a. Assuming that Wal-Mart has market power in a labor market, explain how the firm could use that market power in setting wages.

b. Draw a graph to illustrate how Wal-Mart might use labor market power to set wages.

20. a. Explain how a union of Wal-Mart's employees would attempt to counteract Wal-Mart's wage offers (a bilateral monopoly).

b. Explain the response by the Canadian Wal-Mart to the unionization of employees.

21. Based upon evidence presented in this article, does Wal-Mart function as a monopsony in labor markets, or is the market for retail labor more competitive? Explain.

22. If the market for retail labor is competitive, explain the potential effect of a union on the wage rates. Draw a graph to illustrate your answer.

Capital and Natural Resource Markets

23. New technology has allowed oil to be pumped from much deeper offshore oil fields than before. For example, 28 deep ocean rigs operate in the deep waters of the Gulf of Mexico.

a. What effect do you think deep ocean sources have had on the world oil price?

b. Who will benefit from drilling for oil in the Gulf of Mexico? Explain your answer.

24. Water is a natural resource that is plentiful in Canada but not plentiful in Arizona.

a. If Canadians start to export bulk water to Arizona, what do you predict will be the effect on the price of bulk water?

b. Will Canada eventually run out of water?

c. Do you think the Hotelling principle applies to Canada's water? Explain why or why not.

25. **Gas Prices Create Land Rush**

There is a land rush going on across Pennsylvania, but buyers aren't interested in the land itself. Buyers are interested in what lies beneath the earth's surface—mineral rights to natural gas deposits. Record high natural gas prices have pushed up drilling activity across the state, but drilling companies have discovered a new technology that will enable deep gas-bearing shale to be exploited. Development companies, drilling companies, and speculators have been trying to lease mineral rights from landowners. The new drilling techniques might recover about 10 percent of those reserves, and that would ring up at a value of $1 trillion.

Source: *Erie Times-News*, June 15, 2008

a. Explain why the demand for land in Pennsylvania has increased.

b. If companies are responding to the higher prices for natural gas by drilling right now wherever they can, what does that imply about their assumptions about the future price of natural gas in relation to current interest rates?

c. What could cause the price of natural gas to fall in the future?

Economics in the News

26. After you have studied *Economics in the News* on pp. 436–437, answer the following questions.

a. Is the average difference in the salaries of charter school and regular public school teachers greater or smaller than the difference at the top end of the pay scales?

b. What are the influences on the demand for the highest-paid teachers that explain their high wage rates?

c. What are the influences on the supply of the highest-paid teachers that explain their high wage rates?

d. Draw a graph of the market for the highest-paid teachers.

e. If all charter school teachers became unionized, how would the market for these teachers change? Illustrate your answer with a graph.

f. How would you expect unionization of charter school teachers to influence the unionized market for regular public school teachers?

g. If the public school systems were able to break the teachers' union, how would the market for regular public school teachers change? Illustrate your answer with a graph.

Mathematical Note

27. Keshia is opening a new bookkeeping service. She is considering buying or leasing some new laptop computers. The purchase price of a laptop is $1,500 and after three years it is worthless. The annual lease rate is $550 per laptop. The value of marginal product of one laptop is $700 a year. The value of marginal product of a second laptop is $625 a year. The value of marginal product of a third laptop is $575 a year. And the value of marginal product of a fourth laptop is $500 a year.

a. How many laptops will Keshia lease or buy?

b. If the interest rate is 4 percent a year, will Keshia lease or buy her laptops?

c. If the interest rate is 6 percent a year, will Keshia lease or buy her laptops?

19

ECONOMIC
INEQUALITY

After studying this chapter,
you will be able to:

◆ Describe the distributions of income and wealth and
the trends in economic inequality in the United States

◆ Describe the distribution of income and the trends in
inequality in selected countries and the world

◆ Explain the sources of economic inequality and its
trends

◆ Describe the scale of government income redistribution in the United States

When Apple hired Angela Ahrendts to manage its
retail stores, it paid her a signing bonus worth $67
million. Other top-earning women include Marissa
Mayer at Yahoo! and Sheryl Sandberg at Facebook.
At the other end of the pay scale are the thousands
of fast-food workers calling for a rise in the minimum
wage. Why do a few people get enormous incomes,
while most struggle to get by on a few dollars an
hour? In this chapter, we study economic inequality—
its extent, its sources, and the things governments do
to make it less extreme. In *Economics in the News* at
the end of the chapter, we return to Angela Ahrendts
and see why Apple thinks she is worth so much.

Economic Inequality in the United States

The most commonly used measure of economic inequality is the distribution of annual income. The Census Bureau defines income as **money income**, which equals *market income* plus cash payments to households by government. **Market income** equals wages, interest, rent, and profit earned in factor markets, before paying income taxes.

The Distribution of Income

Figure 19.1 shows the distribution of annual income across the 122 million households in the United States in 2012. Note that the *x*-axis measures household money income and the *y*-axis measures the percentage of households.

The most common household income is called the *mode* income. In 2012, almost 6 percent of the households had incomes of between $15,000 and $20,000. The value of $15,000 marked on the figure is an estimate.

The middle level of household income in 2012, called the *median* income, was $51,017. Fifty percent of households have an income that exceeds the median and fifty percent have an income below the median.

The average household money income in 2012, called the *mean* income, was $71,274. This number equals total household income, about $8.7 trillion, divided by the 122 million households. You can see in Fig. 19.1 that the mode is less than the median and that the median is less than the mean. This feature of the distribution of income tells us that there are more households with low incomes than with high incomes. It also tells us that some of the high incomes are very high.

The income distribution in Fig. 19.1 is called a *positively skewed* distribution, which means that it has a long tail of high values. This distribution contrasts with the bell that describes the distribution of people's heights. In a bell-shaped distribution, the mean, median, and mode are all equal.

Another way of looking at the distribution of income is to measure the percentage of total income received by each given percentage of households. Data are reported for five groups—called *quintiles* or fifth shares—each consisting of 20 percent of households.

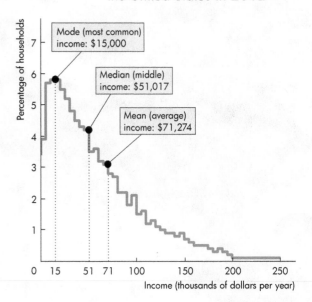

FIGURE 19.1   The Distribution of Income in the United States in 2012

The distribution of income is positively skewed. The mode (most common) income is less than the median (middle) income, which in turn is less than the mean (average) income. The distribution shown here ends at $250,000 because data above that level are not available, but the distribution goes up to several million dollars a year.

Source of data: DeNavas-Walt, Carmen, Bernadette D. Proctor, and Jessica C. Smith, U.S. Census Bureau, Current Population Reports, P60–245, Income, Poverty, and Health Insurance Coverage in the United States: 2012, U.S. Government Printing Office, Washington, DC, 2013.

MyEconLab Animation

Figure 19.2 shows the distribution based on these shares in 2012. The poorest 20 percent of households received 3.2 percent of total income; the second poorest 20 percent received 8.3 percent of total income; the middle 20 percent received 14.4 percent of total income; the next highest 20 percent received 23.0 percent of total income; and the highest 20 percent received 51.1 percent of total income.

The distribution of income in Fig. 19.1 and the quintile shares in Fig. 19.2 tell us that income is distributed unequally. But we need a way of comparing the distribution of income in different periods and using different measures. A clever graphical tool called the *Lorenz curve* enables us to make such comparisons.

FIGURE 19.2   U.S. Quintile Shares in 2012

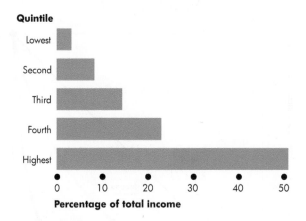

Households (quintile)	Income (percentage of total income)
Lowest	3.2
Second	8.3
Third	14.4
Fourth	23.0
Highest	51.1

In 2012, the lowest quintile of households received 3.2 percent of total income; the second quintile received 8.3 percent; the third quintile received 14.4 percent; the fourth quintile received 23.0 percent; and the highest quintile received 51.1 percent.

Source of data: See Fig. 19.1.

——— MyEconLab *Animation* ———

The Income Lorenz Curve

The income **Lorenz curve** graphs the cumulative percentage of income against the cumulative percentage of households. Figure 19.3 shows the income Lorenz curve using the quintile shares from Fig. 19.2. The table shows the percentage of income of each quintile group. For example, row *A* tells us that the lowest quintile of households receives 3.2 percent of total income. The table also shows the *cumulative* percentages of households and income. For example, row *B* tells us that the lowest two quintiles (lowest 40 percent) of households receive 11.5 percent of total income (3.2 percent for the lowest quintile plus 8.3 percent for the next lowest).

FIGURE 19.3   The Income Lorenz Curve in 2012

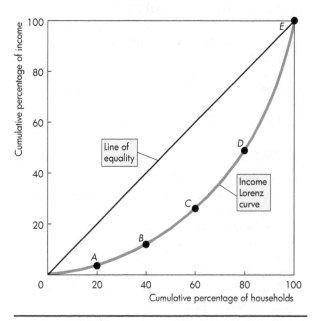

	Households		Income	
	Quintile	Cumulative percentage	Percentage	Cumulative percentage
A	Lowest	20	3.2	3.2
B	Second	40	8.3	11.5
C	Third	60	14.4	25.9
D	Fourth	80	23.0	48.9
E	Highest	100	51.1	100.0

The cumulative percentage of income is graphed against the cumulative percentage of households. Points *A* through *E* on the Lorenz curve correspond to the rows of the table. If incomes were distributed equally, each quintile of households would receive 20 percent of total income and the Lorenz curve would fall along the line of equality. The Lorenz curve shows that income is unequally distributed.

Source of data: See Fig. 19.1.

——— MyEconLab *Animation and Draw Graph* ———

The Lorenz curve provides a direct visual clue about the degree of income inequality by comparing it with the line of equality. This line, identified in Fig. 19.3, shows what the Lorenz curve would be if everyone had the same level of income.

If income were distributed equally across all the households, each quintile would receive 20 percent of total income and the cumulative percentages of income received would equal the cumulative percentages of households, so the Lorenz curve would be the straight line labeled "Line of equality."

The actual distribution of income shown by the curve labeled "Income Lorenz curve" can be compared with the line of equality. The closer the Lorenz curve is to the line of equality, the more equal is the distribution of income.

The Distribution of Wealth

The distribution of wealth provides another way of measuring economic inequality. A household's **wealth** is the value of the things that it owns at a *point in time*. In contrast, income is the amount that the household receives over a given *period of time*.

Figure 19.4 shows the Lorenz curve for wealth in the United States in 2010 (the most recent year for which we have wealth distribution data). The median household wealth in 2010 was $77,300. Wealth is extremely unequally distributed, and for this reason, the data are grouped by five unequal groups of households. The poorest 25 percent of households have no wealth and the next poorest 25 percent own only 1.1 percent of total wealth (row B' in the table in Fig. 19.4). Even the third richest 25 percent own only 8.5 percent of total wealth. The richest 25 percent of households own 90.4 percent of wealth, and within this wealthiest group the richest 10 percent of households own 74.5 percent of total wealth.

Figure 19.4 shows the income Lorenz curve (from Fig. 19.3) alongside the wealth Lorenz curve. You can see that the Lorenz curve for wealth is much farther away from the line of equality than is the Lorenz curve for income, which means that the distribution of wealth is much more unequal than the distribution of income.

Wealth or Income?

We've seen that wealth is much more unequally distributed than is income. Which distribution provides the better description of the degree of inequality? To answer this question, we need to think about the connection between wealth and income.

Wealth is a stock of assets, and income is the flow of earnings that results from the stock of wealth. Suppose that a person owns assets worth

---

FIGURE 19.4   Lorenz Curves for Income and Wealth

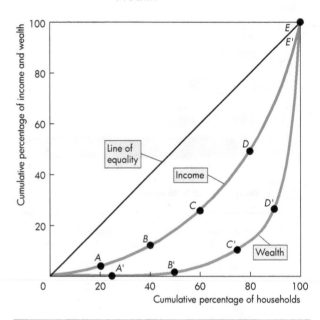

Households		Wealth	
Percentage	**Cumulative percentage**	**Percentage**	**Cumulative percentage**
A' Lowest 25	25	0.0	0.0
B' Next 25	50	1.1	1.1
C' Next 25	75	8.5	9.6
D' Next 15	90	15.9	25.5
E' Highest 10	100	74.5	100.0

The cumulative percentage of wealth is graphed against the cumulative percentage of households. Points A' through E' on the Lorenz curve for wealth correspond to the rows of the table. By comparing the Lorenz curves for income and wealth, we can see that wealth is distributed much more unequally than is income.

Sources of data: For the income distribution data, see Fig. 19.1. The wealth distribution data are calculated from the Federal Reserve Board's Survey of Consumer Finances for 2010, reported in Jesse Bricker, Arthur B. Kennickell, Kevin B. Moore, and John Sabelhaus, with assistance from Samuel Ackerman, Robert Argento, Gerhard Fries, and Richard A. Windle, "Changes in U.S. Family Finances from 2007 to 2010: Evidence from the Survey of Consumer Finances," *Federal Reserve Bulletin*, June 2012, Vol. 98, No. 2.

MyEconLab Animation

$1 million—has a wealth of $1 million. If the rate of return on assets is 5 percent a year, then this person receives an income of $50,000 a year from those assets. We can describe this person's economic condition by using either the wealth of $1 million or the income of $50,000. When the rate of return is 5 per cent a year, $1 million of wealth equals $50,000 of income in perpetuity. Wealth and income are just different ways of looking at the same thing.

But in Fig. 19.4, the distribution of wealth is more unequal than the distribution of income. Why? It is because the wealth data do not include the value of human capital, while the income data measure income from all wealth, including human capital.

Think about Lee and Peter, two people with equal income and equal wealth. Lee's wealth is human capital and his entire income is from employment. Peter's wealth is in the form of investments in stocks and bonds and his entire income is from these investments.

When a Census Bureau agent interviews Lee and Peter in a national income and wealth survey, their incomes are recorded as being equal, but Lee's wealth is recorded as zero, while Peter's wealth is recorded as the value of his investments. Peter looks vastly more wealthy than Lee in the survey data.

Because the national survey of wealth excludes human capital, the income distribution is a more accurate measure of economic inequality than the wealth distribution.

Annual or Lifetime Income and Wealth?

A typical household's income changes over its life cycle. Income starts out low, grows to a peak when the household's workers reach retirement age, and then falls after retirement. Also, a typical household's wealth changes over time. Like income, it starts out low, grows to a peak at the point of retirement, and falls after retirement.

Think about three households with identical lifetime incomes, one young, one middle-aged, and one retired. The middle-aged household has the highest income and wealth, the retired household has the lowest, and the young household falls in the middle. The distributions of annual income and wealth in a given year are unequal, but the distributions of lifetime income and wealth are equal.

The data on inequality share the bias that you've just seen. Inequality in annual income and wealth data overstates lifetime inequality because households are at different stages in their life cycles.

Trends in Inequality

To see trends in the income distribution, we use a measure called the Gini ratio. The **Gini ratio** equals the area between the Lorenz curve and the line of equality divided by the entire area beneath the line of equality. The more the Lorenz curve bows away from the line of equality, the larger is the Gini ratio. And the larger the Gini ratio, the greater is the degree of income inequality. If income is equally distributed, the Lorenz curve is the same as the line of equality, so the Gini ratio is zero. If most people have an income close to zero and a few people have very large incomes, the Gini ratio is close to 1.

Figure 19.5 shows the U.S. Gini ratio from 1972 to 2012. You can see that the Gini ratio has steadily increased, which means that incomes have become less equal.

FIGURE 19.5   The U.S. Gini Ratio: 1972–2012

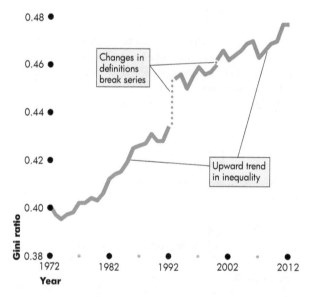

Measured by the Gini ratio, the distribution of income in the United States became more unequal from 1972 to 2012. The percentage of income earned by the richest households increased through these years. Changes in definitions make the numbers before and after 1992 and before and after 2000 not comparable. Despite the breaks in the data, the trends are still visible.

Source of data: See Fig. 19.1.

MyEconLab Animation

ECONOMICS IN ACTION

The Rich Get Richer, but School Still Pays

American incomes have been getting steadily more unequal, and 67 percent of Americans told the Gallup poll that they think incomes in 2012 are too unequal. Twenty-one years earlier, in 1991, only 21 percent of Americans thought there were too many people who were too rich.

A key feature of rising inequality is the trend in the incomes of the super rich. Emmanuel Saez of the University of California, Berkeley, used tax returns data to get the numbers graphed in Fig. 1.

After decades of a falling share, starting in 1981, the share of income received by the richest one percent began a steady climb. By 2012 (the latest year in the database), the richest one percent were earning 19.3 percent of the nation's income.

The bottom quintile gets 3.2 percent of total income, so an average household in the top one percent receives more than 120 times the average income of a household in the lowest quintile.

Movie stars, sports stars, and the CEOs of large corporations are among the super rich. People who scratch out a living doing seasonal work on farms earn the lowest incomes. Aside from these extremes, what are the characteristics of the people who earn high incomes and the people who earn low incomes? Figure 2 below answers this question. (The data are for 2012, but the patterns are persistent).

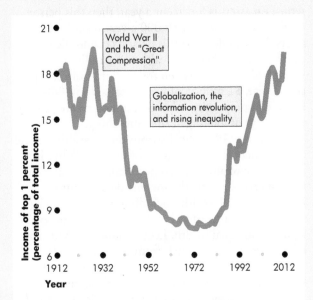

Figure 1 The Income Shares of the Top One Percent

Source of data: Alvaredo, Facundo, Anthony B. Atkinson, Thomas Piketty, and Emmanuel Saez, The World Top Incomes Database, http://g-mond.parisschoolofeconomics.eu/topincomes, 12/08/2012.

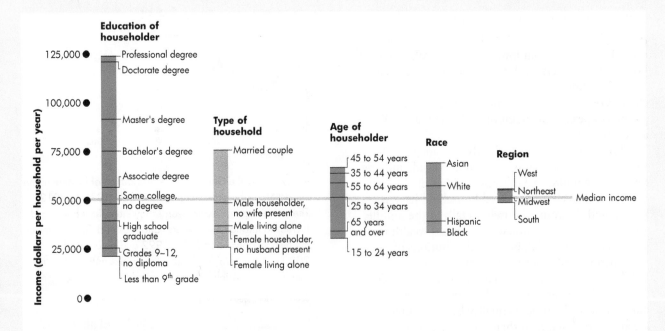

Figure 2 The Distribution of Income by Selected Household Characteristics

Source of data: See Fig. 19.1.

Education A postgraduate education is the main source of a high income. A person with a professional degree (such as a medical or law degree) earns, on average, $121,000—more than double the median income. Just completing high school raises a person's income by more than $12,000 a year; and getting a bachelor's degree adds another $30,000 a year. The average income of people who have not completed 9th grade is $22,000—less than half the median income.

Type of Household Married couples earn more, on average, than people who live alone. A married couple earns about $76,000. In contrast, men who live alone earn about $37,000, and women who live alone earn only $26,000.

Age of Householder Households with the oldest and youngest householders have lower incomes than do those with middle-aged householders. When the householder is aged between 45 and 54, household income

averages $66,000. And when the householder is aged between 35 and 44, household income averages $64,000. When the householder is aged between 15 and 24, average household income is $31,000. And for householders over 65, the average household income is $34,000.

Race and Ethnicity White Americans have an average income of $57,000, while black Americans have an average income of $33,000. People of Hispanic origin are a bit better off, with an average income of $39,000. Asians are best off with an average income of $69,000.

Region People who live in the West and Northeast earn more, on average, than people who live in the Midwest and the South. While the region does make a difference, its magnitude is small compared to the dominating effect of education.

The bottom line: School pays and so does marriage.

Poverty

Households at the bottom of the income distribution are so poor that they are considered to be living in poverty. **Poverty** is a situation in which a household's income is too low to be able to buy the quantities of food, shelter, and clothing that are deemed necessary. This concept of poverty is relative: People are poor compared to what is regarded as normal or average, and so poor that their situation is regarded as a problem that needs attention.

A different poverty concept is *absolute poverty*—poverty so extreme that it challenges survival. For millions of people living in Africa and Asia, poverty is absolute. The poorest struggle to survive on incomes of less than $400 a year.

Official U.S. Poverty Measure In the United States, the poverty level is calculated each year by the Social Security Administration. In 2012, the poverty level for a four-person household was an income of $23,492. Other income levels apply to households of different sizes.

Amount of Poverty About 46 million Americans—15 percent of the population—live in households that have incomes below the poverty level. The incidence of poverty varies by race, age, work experience, physical ability, and household status.

We'll look at each of these influences on poverty.

Race The poverty rate among white Americans is 13 percent compared to 26 percent for Hispanic-origin Americans and 27 percent of black Americans.

But the absolute number of white Americans in poverty, 31 million, is greater than the number of minority households—11 million black and 14 million Hispanic.

Age Poverty rates are 22 percent for children, 14 percent for people aged 18 to 64, and 9 percent for seniors aged 65 and over.

Work Experience Americans with a job, either full time or part time, are much less likely to be living in poverty than those without a job. The poverty rate for those with jobs is 7 percent and for those without jobs is 33 percent.

Physical Ability The poverty rate among people with disabilities is very high—29 percent. These people often have no jobs and no easy access to care.

Household Status More than 28 percent of households in which the householder is a female with no husband present have incomes below the poverty level.

The overall poverty rate and the averages for the groups we've just examined have increased during the past few years following a major economic recession. But aside from this recent upturn in the poverty rate, it has been remarkably constant.

ECONOMICS IN ACTION

Is the American Dream Still Alive?

The "American Dream" is that with hard work and fair play, everyone can expect to be rewarded with a better and a rising standard of living. Is this idea alive and well today?

Of the several ways in which we might test whether the dream is still alive, the one that we'll examine here is the mobility that occurs up and down the income distribution. Can households in the third,

downward movement to about a quarter of households, even moved all the way to the lowest quintile.

Part (b) shows that a majority of households remained in the same quintile, and at both extremes more remained than moved. A majority of the third quintile moved, but in roughly equal numbers in both directions.

So what do these data say about the dream? It is alive for some: It is possible to move up the income ladder. But it is also possible to move down. There is two-way mobility for American households.

(a) Income mobility

Income Mobility and Immobility 2007–2009

Sources of data: See Fig. 19.4.

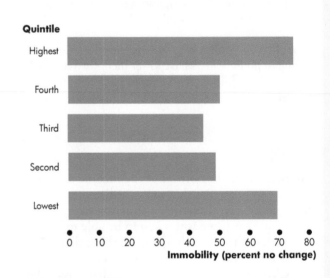

(b) Income immobility

second, and lowest quintiles move up to a higher quintile?

The graphs, which show data for 2007 to 2009, provide an answer to this question. Part (a) shows that about a quarter of the households in the third quintile moved up one quintile and a few moved up two quintiles to the highest. Some households in the second and lowest quintiles also moved up two, three, and even four quintiles.

But by the definition of an income distribution, for all the movements up there must be some movements down. Households in the highest quintile don't have a permanent right to be at the top. And as you can see in the graph, close to one fifth of the highest quintile moved down one quintile and a few, bringing the total

REVIEW QUIZ

1. Which is distributed more unequally, income or wealth? Why? Which is the better measure?
2. How has the distribution of income changed in the past few decades?
3. What are the main characteristics of high-income and low-income households?
4. What is poverty and how does its incidence vary across the races?
5. How much mobility has there been through the income quintiles since 2007?

Work these questions in Study Plan 19.1 and get instant feedback. Do a Key Terms Quiz. MyEconLab

Inequality in the World Economy

Which countries have the greatest economic inequality and which have the least and the greatest equality? Where does the United States rank? Is it one of the most equal or most unequal, or is it somewhere in the middle? And how much inequality is there in the world as a whole when we consider the entire world as a single global economy?

We'll answer these questions by first looking at the income distribution in a selection of countries and then by examining features of the global distribution of income.

Income Distributions in Selected Countries

By inspecting the income distribution data for every country, we can compare the degree of income inequality and identify the countries with the most inequality and those with the least inequality.

Figure 19.6 summarizes some extremes and shows where the United States lies in the range of degrees of income inequality.

Look first at the numbers in the table. They tell us that in Brazil and South Africa, the lowest quintile of households receive only 2 percent of total income while the highest quintile receive 65 percent of total income. An average person in the highest quintile receives 32.5 times the income of an average person in the lowest quintile.

Contrast these numbers with those for Finland and Sweden. In these countries, the lowest quintile receives 8 percent of total income and the highest quintile receives 35 percent. So an average person in the highest quintile receives 4.4 times the income of an average person in the lowest quintile.

The numbers for the United States lie between these extremes with an average person in the highest quintile receiving just under 10 times the amount received by an average person in the lowest quintile.

Brazil and South Africa are extremes not matched in any other major country or region. Inequality is large in these countries because they have a relatively small but rich European population and a large and relatively poor indigenous population.

Finland and Sweden are extremes, but they are not unusual. Income distributions similar to these are found in many European countries in which governments pursue aggressive income redistribution policies.

We look next at the global income distribution.

FIGURE 19.6   Lorenz Curves Compared

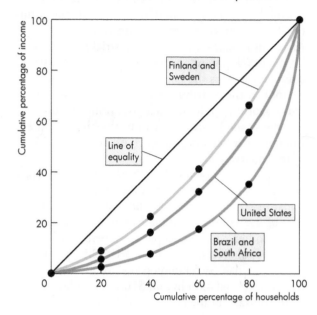

The table shows the percentages of total income received by each quintile. The figure shows the cumulative percentage of income graphed against the cumulative percentage of households. The data and the Lorenz curves show that income is distributed most unequally in Brazil and South Africa and least unequally in Finland and Sweden. The degree of income inequality in the United States lies between these extremes.

Households (quintile)	Percentage of total income[1]		
	Brazil and South Africa	United States	Finland and Sweden
Lowest	2	5	8
Second	5	11	14
Third	10	16	20
Fourth	18	24	23
Highest	65	44	35

Sources of data: Brazil, South Africa, Finland, and Sweden, Klaus W. Deininger and Lyn Squire, Measuring Income Inequality Database, World Bank, http://go.worldbank.org/. United States, see Fig. 19.1.

[1]The data are based on income *after* redistribution. See pp. 459–461 for an account of income redistribution in the United States.

MyEconLab Animation

Global Inequality and Its Trends

The global distribution of income is much more unequal than the distribution within any one country. The reason is that many countries, especially in Africa and Asia, are in a pre-industrial stage of economic development and are poor, while industrial countries such as the United States are rich. When we look at the distribution of income across the entire world population that goes from the low income of the poorest African to the high income of the richest American, we observe a very large degree of inequality.

To put some raw numbers on this inequality, start with the poorest. Measured in the value of the U.S. dollar in 2005, a total of 3 billion people or 50 percent of the world population live on $2.50 a day or less. Another 2 billion people or 30 percent of the world population live on more than $2.50 but less than $10 a day. So 5 billion people or 80 percent of the world population live on $10 a day or less.

In contrast, in the rich United States, the *average* person has an income of $115 per day and an average person in the highest income quintile has an income of $460 a day.

So the average American earns 46 times the income of one of the world's 3 billion poorest people and more than 11.5 times the income of 80 percent of the people who live in developing economies. An American with the average income in the highest quintile earns 184 times that of the world's poorest people but only 16 times that of an average bottom quintile American.

World Gini Ratio   We can compare world inequality with U.S. inequality by comparing Gini ratios. You saw that the U.S. Gini ratio in 2012 was about 0.47. The world Gini ratio is about 0.61. Recalling the interpretation of the Gini ratio in terms of the Lorenz curve, the world Lorenz curve lies much farther from the line of equality than does the U.S. Lorenz curve.

World Trend   You saw (in Fig. 19.5 on p. 449) that incomes have become more unequal in the United States—the Gini ratio has increased. The same trends are found in most economies. Increased income inequality is a big issue in two of the world's largest and poor nations, China and India. In these two economies, urban middle classes are getting richer at a faster pace than the rural farmers.

Despite greater inequality within countries, the world is becoming *less* unequal. Figure 19.7 shows

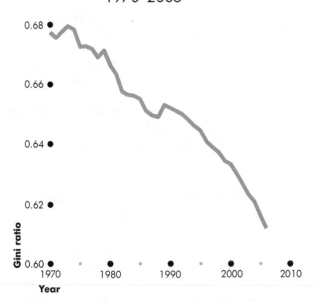

FIGURE 19.7   The World Gini Ratio: 1970–2005

Measured by the Gini ratio, the distribution of income in the entire world became more equal between 1970 and 2005.

Source of data: Xavier Sala-i-Martin and Maxim Pinkovskiy, "Parametric estimations of the world distribution of income," 22 January 2010, http://www.voxeu.org/article/parametric-estimations-world-distribution-income.

MyEconLab Animation

this trend toward less inequality as measured by the world Gini ratio. How can the world income distribution become less unequal while individual countries become more unequal? The answer is that average incomes in poorer countries are rising much faster than average incomes in rich countries. While the gap between rich and poor is widening within countries, it is narrowing across countries.

REVIEW QUIZ

1   In which countries are incomes distributed most unequally and least unequally?
2   Which income distribution is more unequal and why: the income distribution in the United States or in the entire world?
3   How can incomes become *more* unequally distributed within countries and *less* unequally distributed across countries?

Work these questions in Study Plan 19.2 and get instant feedback.   MyEconLab

The Sources of Economic Inequality

We've described some key facts about economic inequality and its trends and our task now is to explain those facts. We began this task in Chapter 18 by learning about the forces that influence demand and supply in the markets for labor, capital, and land. We're now going to deepen our understanding of these forces.

Inequality arises from unequal labor market outcomes and from unequal ownership of capital. We'll begin by looking at labor markets and three features of them that contribute to differences in income:

- Human capital
- Discrimination
- Contests among superstars

Human Capital

A clerk in a law firm earns less than a tenth of the amount earned by the attorney he assists. An operating room assistant earns less than a tenth of the amount earned by the surgeon with whom she works. A bank teller earns less than a tenth of the amount earned by the bank's CEO. Some of the differences in these earnings arise from differences in human capital.

To see the influence of human capital on labor incomes, consider the example of a law clerk and the attorney he assists. (The same reasoning can be applied to an operating room assistant and surgeon, or a bank teller and bank CEO.)

Demand, Supply, and Wage Rates An attorney performs many tasks that a law clerk cannot perform. Imagine an untrained law clerk cross-examining a witness in a complicated trial. The tasks that the attorney performs are valued highly by her clients who willingly pay for her services. Using a term that you learned in Chapter 18, an attorney has a *high value of marginal product*, and a higher value of marginal product than her law clerk. But you also learned in Chapter 18 that the value of marginal product of labor determines (is the same as) the demand for labor. So, because an attorney has a higher value of marginal product, the demand for attorney services is greater than the demand for law-clerk services.

To become an attorney, a person must acquire human capital. But human capital is costly to acquire. This cost—an opportunity cost—includes expenditures on tuition and textbooks. It also includes forgone earnings during the years spent in college and law school. It might also include low earnings doing on-the-job training in a law office during the summer.

Because the human capital needed to supply attorney services is costly to acquire, a person's willingness to supply these services reflects this cost. The supply of attorney services is smaller than the supply of law-clerk services.

The demand for and supply of each type of labor determine the wage rate that each type of labor earns. Attorneys earn a higher wage rate than law clerks because the demand for attorneys is greater and the supply of attorneys is smaller. The gap between the wage rates reflects the higher value of marginal product of an attorney (demand) and the cost of acquiring human capital (supply).

Trends in Wage Inequality You've seen that high-income households have earned an increasing share of total income while low-income households have earned a decreasing share: The distribution of income in the United States has become more unequal. Technological change and globalization are two possible sources of this increased inequality.

Technological Change Information technologies such as computers and laser scanners are *substitutes in production* for low-skilled labor: They perform tasks that previously were performed by low-skilled labor. The introduction of these technologies has lowered the marginal product and the demand for low-skilled labor. These same technologies require high-skilled labor to design, program, and run them. High-skilled labor and the information technologies are *complements in production*. So these new technologies have increased the marginal product and demand for high-skilled labor.

Figure 19.8 illustrates the effects of information technologies on wages and employment. The supply of low-skilled labor in part (a) and that of high-skilled labor in part (b) are S, and initially, the demand in each market is D_0. The low-skill wage rate is $5 an hour, and the high-skill wage rate is $10 an hour. The demand for low-skilled labor decreases to D_1 in part (a) and the demand for high-skilled labor increases to D_1 in part (b). The low-skill wage rate falls to $4 an hour and the high-skill wage rate rises to $15 an hour.

Globalization The entry of China and other developing countries into the global economy has

FIGURE 19.8   Explaining the Trend in Income Distribution

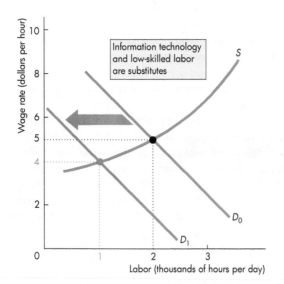

(a) A decrease in demand for low-skilled labor

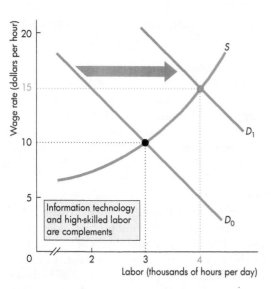

(b) An increase in demand for high-skilled labor

Low-skilled labor and information technologies are substitutes in production. In part (a), advances in information technology decrease the demand for low-skilled labor and lower its wage rate. High-skilled labor and information technologies are complements in production. In part (b), advances in information technology increase the demand for high-skilled labor and raise its wage rate.

MyEconLab Animation

lowered the prices of many manufactured goods. Lower prices for the firm's output lowers the value of marginal product of the firm's workers and decreases the demand for their labor. A situation like that in Fig. 19.8(a) occurs. The wage rate falls, and employment shrinks.

At the same time, the growing global economy increases the demand for services that employ high-skilled workers, and the value of marginal product and the demand for high-skilled labor increases. A situation like that in Fig. 19.8(b) occurs. The wage rate rises, and employment opportunities for high-skilled workers expand.

Discrimination

Human capital differences can explain some of the economic inequality that we observe. Discrimination is another possible source of inequality.

Suppose that black females and white males have identical abilities as investment advisors. If everyone is free of race and sex prejudice, the market determines the same wage rate for both groups. But if customers are prejudiced against women and minorities, this prejudice is reflected in the wage rates—white men earn more than black women.

Counteracting Forces Economists disagree about whether prejudice actually causes wage differentials, and one line of reasoning implies that it does not. In the above example, customers who buy from white men pay a higher service charge for investment advice than do the customers who buy from black women. This price difference acts as an incentive to encourage people who are prejudiced to buy from the people against whom they are prejudiced. This force could be strong enough to eliminate the effects of discrimination altogether. Suppose, as is true in manufacturing, that a firm's customers never meet its workers. If such a firm discriminates against women or minorities, it can't compete with firms who hire these groups because its costs are higher than those of the nonprejudiced firms. Only firms that do not discriminate survive in a competitive industry.

Whether because of discrimination or from some other source, women and visible minorities do earn lower incomes than white males. Another possible source of lower wage rates of women arises from differences in the relative degree of specialization of women and men.

Differences in the Degree of Specialization Couples must choose how to allocate their time between working for a wage and doing jobs in the home, such as cooking, cleaning, shopping, organizing vacations, and, most important, bearing and raising children. Let's look at the choices of Bob and Sue.

Bob might specialize in earning an income and Sue in taking care of the home. Or Sue might specialize in earning an income and Bob in taking care of the home. Or both of them might earn an income and share home production jobs.

The allocation they choose depends on their preferences and on their earning potential. The choice of an increasing number of households is for each person to diversify between earning an income and doing some household chores. But in most households, Bob will specialize in earning an income and Sue will both earn an income and bear a larger share of the task of running the home. With this allocation, Bob will probably earn more than Sue. If Sue devotes time and effort to ensuring Bob's mental and physical well-being, the quality of Bob's market labor will be higher than it would be if he were diversified. If the roles were reversed, Sue would be able to supply market labor that earns more than Bob's.

To test whether the degree of specialization accounts for earnings differences between the sexes, economists have compared the incomes of never-married men and women. They have found that, on the average, with equal amounts of human capital, the wages of these two groups are the same.

Contests Among Superstars

The differences in income that arise from differences in human capital are important and affect a large proportion of the population. But human capital differences can't account for some of the really large income differences.

The super rich—those in the top one percent of the income distribution whose income share has been rising—earn vastly more than can be explained by human capital differences. What makes a person super rich?

A clue to the answer is provided by thinking about the super rich in tennis and golf. What makes tennis players and golfers special is that their earnings depend on where they finish in a tournament. When Rafael Nadal won the U.S. Open Tennis Championship in 2013, he received $2,600,000. The runner-up in this event, Novak Djokovic,

received $1,300,000. So Rafa earned double the amount earned by Novak. And he earned 81 times the amount received by the players who lost in the first round of the tournament.

It is true that Rafael Nadal has a lot of human capital. He practices hard and long and is a remarkable athlete. But anyone who is good enough to get into a tennis Grand Slam tournament is similarly well equipped with human capital and has spent a similar number of long hours in training and practice. It isn't human capital that explains the differences in earnings. It is the tournament and the prize differences that accounts for the large differences in earnings.

Three questions jump out: First, why do we reward superstar tennis players (and golfers) with prizes for winning a contest? Second, why are the prizes so different? And third, do the principles that apply on the tennis court (and golf course) apply more generally to corporations?

Why Prizes for a Contest? The answer to this question (which was noted in Chapter 5, p. 106) is that contests with prizes do a good job of allocating scarce resources efficiently when the efforts of the participants are hard to monitor and reward directly. There is only one winner, but many people work hard in an attempt to be that person. So a great deal of diligent effort is induced by a contest.

Why Are Prizes So Different? The prizes need to be substantially different to induce enough effort. If the winner received 10 percent more than the runner up, the gain from being the winner would be insufficient to encourage anyone to work hard enough. Someone would win but no one would put in much effort. Tennis matches would be boring, golf scores would be high, and no one would be willing to pay to see these sports. Big differences are necessary to induce a big enough effort to generate the quality of performance that people are willing to pay to see.

Does the Principle Apply More Generally? Winner-takes-all isn't confined to tennis and golf. Movie stars; superstars in baseball, basketball, football, and ice hockey; and top corporate executives can all be viewed as participants in contests that decide the winners. The prize for the winner is an income at least double that of the runner up and many multiples of the incomes of those who drop out earlier in the tournament.

Do Contests Among Superstars Explain the Trend?
Contests among superstars can explain large differences in incomes. But can contests explain the trend toward greater inequality with an increasing share of total income going to the super rich as shown on p. 450?

An idea first suggested by University of Chicago economist Sherwin Rosen suggests that a winner-takes-all contest can explain the trend. The key is that globalization has increased the market reach of the winner and increased the spread between the winner and the runners-up.

Global television audiences now watch all the world's major sporting events and the total revenue generated by advertising spots during these events has increased. Competition among networks and cable and satellite television distributors has increased the fees that event organizers receive. And to attract the top star performers, prize money has increased and the winner gets the biggest share of the prize pot.

So the prizes in sports have become bigger and the share of income going to the "winner" has increased.

A similar story can be told about superstars and the super rich in business. As the cost of doing business on a global scale has fallen, more and more corporations have become global in their reach. Not only are large multinational corporations sourcing their inputs from far afield and selling in every country, they are also recruiting their top executives from a global talent pool. With a larger source of talent, and a larger total revenue, firms must make the "prize"—the reward for the top job—more attractive to compete for the best managers.

We've examined some sources of inequality in the labor market. Let's now look at the way inequality arises from unequal ownership of capital.

Unequal Wealth

You've seen that wealth inequality—excluding human capital—is much greater than income inequality. This greater wealth inequality arises from two sources: life-cycle saving patterns and transfers of wealth from one generation to the next.

Life-Cycle Saving Patterns Over a family's life cycle, wealth starts out at zero or perhaps less than zero. A student who has financed education all the way through graduate school might have lots of human capital and an outstanding student loan of $60,000. This person has negative wealth. Gradually loans get

paid off and a retirement fund is accumulated. At the point of retiring from full-time work, the family has maximum wealth. Then, during its retirement years, the family spends its wealth. This life-cycle pattern means that much of the wealth is owned by people in their sixties.

Intergenerational Transfers Some households inherit wealth from the previous generation. Some save more than enough on which to live during retirement and transfer wealth to the next generation. But these intergenerational transfers of wealth do not always increase wealth inequality. If a generation that has a high income saves a large part of that income and leaves wealth to a succeeding generation that has a lower income, this transfer decreases the degree of inequality. But one feature of intergenerational transfers of wealth leads to increased inequality: wealth concentration through marriage.

Marriage and Wealth Concentration People tend to marry within their own socioeconomic class—a phenomenon called *assortative mating*. In everyday language, "like attracts like." Although there is a good deal of folklore that "opposites attract," perhaps such Cinderella tales appeal to us because they are so rare in reality. Wealthy people seek wealthy partners.

Because of assortative mating, wealth becomes more concentrated in a small number of families and the distribution of wealth becomes more unequal.

◆ REVIEW QUIZ

1 What role does human capital play in accounting for income inequality?
2 What role might discrimination play in accounting for income inequality?
3 What role might contests among superstars play in accounting for income inequality?
4 How might technological change and globalization explain trends in the distribution of income?
5 Does inherited wealth make the distribution of income less equal or more equal?

Work these questions in Study Plan 19.3 and get instant feedback.   MyEconLab

Next, we're going to see how U.S. taxes and government programs redistribute income and decrease the degree of economic inequality.

Income Redistribution

The three main ways in which governments in the United States redistribute income are

- Income taxes
- Income maintenance programs
- Subsidized services

Income Taxes

Income taxes may be progressive, regressive, or proportional. A **progressive income tax** is one that taxes income at an average rate that increases as income increases. A **regressive income tax** is one that taxes income at an average rate that decreases as income increases. A **proportional income tax** (also called a *flat-rate income tax*) is one that taxes income at a constant rate, regardless of the level of income.

The income tax rates that apply in the United States are composed of two parts: federal and state taxes. Some cities, such as New York City, also have an income tax. There is variety in the detailed tax arrangements in the individual states, but the tax system, at both the federal and state levels, is progressive. The poorest working households receive money from the government through an earned income tax credit. Successively higher-income households pay 10 percent, 15 percent, 25 percent, 28 percent, 33 percent, and 35 percent of each additional dollar earned.

Income Maintenance Programs

Three main types of programs redistribute income by making direct payments (in cash, services, or vouchers) to people in the lower part of the income distribution. They are

- Social Security programs
- Unemployment compensation
- Welfare programs

Social Security Programs The main Social Security program is OASDHI—Old Age, Survivors, Disability, and Health Insurance. Monthly cash payments to retired or disabled workers or their surviving spouses and children are paid for by compulsory payroll taxes on both employers and employees.

In 2013, total Social Security expenditure was budgeted at $1.3 trillion, and the average monthly Social Security check was $1,230 or $14,760 per year.

The other component of Social Security is Medicare, which provides hospital and health insurance for the elderly and disabled.

Unemployment Compensation To provide an income to unemployed workers, every state has established an unemployment compensation program. Under these programs, a tax is paid that is based on the income of each covered worker and such a worker receives a benefit when he or she becomes unemployed. The details of the benefits vary from state to state.

Welfare Programs The purpose of welfare is to provide incomes for people who do not qualify for Social Security or unemployment compensation. They are

1. Supplementary Security Income (SSI) program, designed to help the neediest elderly, disabled, and blind people
2. Temporary Assistance for Needy Households (TANF) program, designed to help households that have inadequate financial resources
3. Food Stamp program, designed to help the poorest households obtain a basic diet
4. Medicaid, designed to cover the costs of medical care for households receiving help under the SSI and TANF programs

Subsidized Services

A great deal of redistribution takes place in the United States through the provision of subsidized services—services provided by the government at prices below the cost of production. The taxpayers who consume these goods and services receive a transfer in kind from the taxpayers who do not consume them. The two most important areas in which this form of redistribution takes place are healthcare and education—both kindergarten through grade 12 and college and university.

In 2013–2014, students enrolled in the University of California system paid annual tuition and fees of $13,200. The cost of providing a year's education at the University of California was probably about $40,000. So a household with just one member enrolled in one of these institutions received a benefit from the government of $26,800 a year.

ECONOMICS IN ACTION

Income Redistribution: Only the Richest Pay

A household's *market income* tells us what a household earns in the absence of government redistribution. You've seen that market income is *not* the official basis for measuring the distribution of income that we've used in this chapter. The Census Bureau's measure is *money income* (market income plus cash transfers from the government). But market income is the correct starting point for measuring the scale of income redistribution.

We begin with market income and then subtract taxes and add the amounts received in benefits. The result is the distribution of income after taxes and benefits. The data available on benefits exclude the value of subsidized services such as college, so the resulting distribution might understate the total amount of redistribution from the rich to the poor.

The figures show the scale of redistribution in 2001, the most recent year for which the Census Bureau has provided these data. In Fig. 1, the blue Lorenz curve describes the market distribution of income and the green Lorenz curve shows the distribution of income after all taxes and benefits, including Medicaid and Medicare benefits. (The Lorenz curve based on money income in Fig. 19.3 lies between these two curves.)

The distribution after taxes and benefits is less unequal than is the market distribution. The lowest quintile of households received only 0.7 percent of market income but 4.6 percent of income after taxes and benefits. The highest quintile of households received 54 percent of market income, but only 44.4 percent of income after taxes and benefits.

Figure 2 highlights the percentage of total income redistributed among the five groups. The share of total income received by the lowest 60 percent of households increased. The share received by the fourth quintile barely changed, but the share received by the highest quintile fell by 9.6 percent.

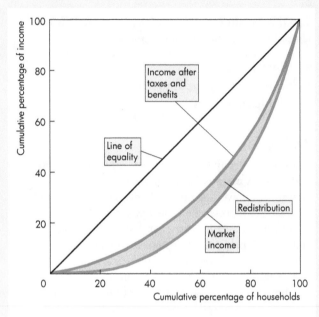

Figure 1   Income Distribution Before and After Redistribution

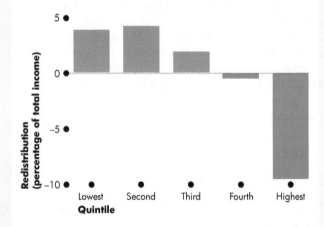

Figure 2   The Scale of Redistribution

Source of data: U.S. Bureau of the Census, Current Population Survey Annual Social and Economic Supplement, Effect of Benefits and Taxes on Income and Poverty, Table 1 Income Distribution Measures, by Definition of Income: 2009.

Government provision of healthcare services has grown to the scale of private provision. Programs such as Medicaid and Medicare bring high-quality and high-cost healthcare to millions of people who earn too little to buy such services themselves.

The Big Tradeoff

The redistribution of income creates what has been called the **big tradeoff**, a tradeoff between equity and efficiency. The big tradeoff arises because redistribution uses scarce resources and weakens incentives.

A dollar collected from a rich person does not translate into a dollar received by a poor person. Some of it gets used up in the process of redistribution. Tax-collecting agencies such as the Internal Revenue Service and welfare-administering agencies (as well as tax accountants and lawyers) use skilled labor, computers, and other scarce resources to do their work. The bigger the scale of redistribution, the greater is the opportunity cost of administering it.

But the cost of collecting taxes and making welfare payments is a small part of the total cost of redistribution. A bigger cost arises from the inefficiency (deadweight loss) of taxes and benefits. Greater equality can be achieved only by taxing productive activities such as work and saving. Taxing people's income from their work and saving lowers the after-tax income they receive. This lower after-tax income makes them work and save less, which in turn results in smaller output and less consumption not only for the rich who pay the taxes but also for the poor who receive the benefits.

It is not only taxpayers who face weaker incentives to work. Benefit recipients also face weaker incentives. In fact, under the welfare arrangements that prevailed before the 1996 reforms, households that benefited from welfare faced the weakest incentives to work. When a welfare recipient got a job, benefits were withdrawn and eligibility for programs such as Medicaid ended, so the household in effect paid a tax of more than 100 percent on its earnings. This arrangement locked poor households in a welfare trap.

So the agencies that determine the scale and methods of income redistribution must pay close attention to the incentive effects of taxes and benefits. Let's close this chapter by looking at one way in which lawmakers are tackling the big tradeoff today.

A Major Welfare Challenge Young women who have not completed high school, have a child (or children), live without a partner, and more likely are black or Hispanic are among the poorest people in the United States today. They and their children present a major welfare challenge.

First, their numbers are large. In 2012, there were 15.5 million single-mother families, 5 million of which were in poverty. In 2009 (the most recent year with census data), single mothers were owed $35 billion in child support and 30 percent of the women received no support from their children's fathers.

The long-term solution to the problem these women face is education and job training—acquiring human capital. The short-term solutions are enforcing child support payments by absent fathers and former spouses and providing welfare.

Welfare must be designed to minimize the disincentive to pursue the long-term goal of becoming self-supporting. The current welfare program in the United States tries to walk this fine line.

Passed in 1996, the Personal Responsibility and Work Opportunities Reconciliation Act strengthened the Office of Child Support Enforcement and increased the penalties for nonpayment of support. The act also created the Temporary Assistance for Needy Households (TANF) program. TANF is a block grant paid to the states, which administer payments to individuals. It is not an open-ended entitlement program. An adult member of a household that is receiving assistance must either work or perform community service, and there is a five-year limit for assistance.

◆ REVIEW QUIZ

1 How do governments in the United States redistribute income?
2 Describe the scale of redistribution in the United States.
3 What is one of the major welfare challenges today and how is it being tackled in the United States?

Work these questions in Study Plan 19.4 and get instant feedback. Do a Key Terms Quiz.   MyEconLab

◆ We've examined economic inequality in the United States. We've seen how inequality arises and that inequality has been increasing. *Economics in the News* on pp. 462–463 looks at the increasing inequality that began during the early 1980s and continues today.

The next chapter focuses on some problems for the market economy that arise from uncertainty and incomplete information. But unlike the cases we studied in Chapters 16 and 17, this time the market does a good job of coping with the problems.

Trends in Incomes of the Super Rich

Apple Gives Ex-Burberry CEO Potential $67M Signing Bonus as She Takes Reins as Retail Boss

New York Daily News
May 7, 2014

Now that's some golden apple.

Apple is handing over a whopping signing bonus potentially worth as much as $67 million to its new retail boss, Angela Ahrendts, according to a regulatory filing.

The massive payday, in the form of restricted stock, makes the ex-Burberry CEO the highest-paid female exec at a public U.S. company and among the best paid in the country, according to compensation research firm Equilar.

"If you put her on a list of the highest-paid executives of public traded companies in 2013, she is likely in the top five," Aaron Boyd, director of governance research at Equilar, told the *Daily News*.

Ahrendts' payday is even bigger than the $60 million package handed to Marissa Mayer to lure her to the top spot at Yahoo!. ...

Apple is known for handing out generous pay packages to its execs. Ahrendts is the only female on Apple's 10-person executive team. She reports to Apple CEO Tim Cook. The computer giant was willing to pay up for a seasoned retail vet who can potentially give its 400-plus stores a lift.

Ahrendts took the helm at Burberry in 2006 and is widely credited with sprucing up the fabled British brand and taking it more upscale.

Apple's new retail boss will be tasked with boosting its retail stores.

During her tenure, sales more than doubled and Burberry's stock price tripled. She won props for using social media to tout the fashion house. ...

© 2014 The New York Daily News.

MyEconLab More Economics in the News

ESSENCE OF THE STORY

- Angela Ahrendts, Apple's retail boss, got a signing bonus that could be worth $67 million.

- Ahrendts' task is to increase sales in Apple's retail stores.

- Her previous job was CEO at Burberry, an upscale British brand.

- During her tenure at Burberry, the firm's sales more than doubled and its stock price tripled.

- Ahrendts is in the top five highest-paid executives at a public U.S. company and the top female.

ECONOMIC ANALYSIS

- The news article reports the extremely high incomes received by two top female executives. These high incomes are not rare today and have been getting less rare.

- Economists Thomas Piketty of l'Ecole d'économie de Paris—Paris School of Economics and Emmanuel Saez of U.C. Berkeley examined the tax returns of the super rich and found the trend shown in Fig. 1.

- Figure 1 shows the income share (percentage of total income) received by the top 0.01 percent of the population.

- The top 0.01 percent includes the top corporate executives and in 2008 was made up of 15,246 families with incomes that exceeded $9,141,000.

- The average family in the top 0.01 percent received 296 times the income of the average family in the bottom quintile. This ratio was 27 in 1965. These ratios are in line with the trend reported in the news article.

- Why are executives like Angela Ahrendts paid so much? And why have top incomes risen so much? Isn't there an abundance of talent around? Could not and should not these people be paid much less?

- It is true that there is an abundance of talent. Globalization has made the entire world the talent pool that large corporations tap for their top executive spots.

- But it is because of the abundance of talent that executive pay has become so high.

- You saw on p. 457 that we can view top executives as the winners of a contest among potential superstars.

- Contests induce high effort and productivity from managers at all levels as they compete for the top job.

- How hard people compete (how productive they are) depends on the size of the prize and the probability of winning it.

- You can think of the contest in terms of the pyramids in Fig. 2. The talent pool is the base of the pyramid and the contest delivers a winner who gets to the top.

- When the talent pool is small, as it was in 1965, the chance of being the winner is large enough for a moderate prize to induce enough effort.

- When the talent pool is large, as it is today, the chance of being the winner is very small, so to induce the same amount of effort, the prize is very large.

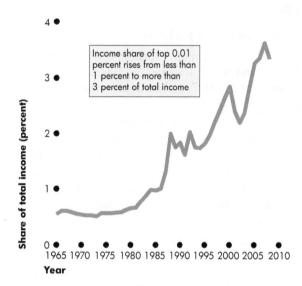

Income share of top 0.01 percent rises from less than 1 percent to more than 3 percent of total income

Figure 1 Income Share of the Top 0.01 Percent

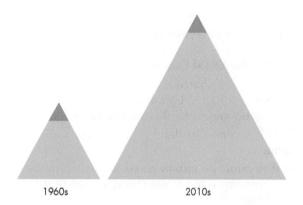

1960s   2010s

Figure 2 Bigger Pyramid Means Bigger Prizes for Getting to Top

Source of data: Figure 1, Emmanuel Saez, "Striking it Richer: The Evolution of Top Incomes in the United States," *Pathways*, Winter 2008 issue.

- This superstar contest idea explains the direction of change—why top executives' earnings have increased relative to the average wage.

- It also explains why Angela Ahrendts and Marissa Mayer earn such enormous incomes.

SUMMARY

Key Points

Economic Inequality in the United States (pp. 446–452)

- In 2012, the mode money income was between $15,000 and $20,000 a year, the median money income was $51,017, and the mean money income was $71,274.
- The income distribution is positively skewed.
- In 2012, the poorest 20 percent of households received 3.2 percent of total income and the wealthiest 20 percent received 51.1 percent of total income.
- Wealth is distributed more unequally than money income because the wealth data exclude the value of human capital.
- Since 1972, the distribution of income has become more unequal.
- Education, type of household, age of householder, and race all influence household income.

Working Problems 1 and 2 will give you a better understanding of economic inequality in the United States.

Inequality in the World Economy (pp. 453–454)

- Incomes are distributed most unequally in Brazil and South Africa and least unequally in Finland, Sweden, and some other European economies.
- The U.S. income distribution lies between the extremes.
- The distribution of income across individuals in the global economy is much more unequal than in the United States.
- The global income distribution has been getting less unequal as rapid income growth in China and India has lifted millions from poverty.

Working Problems 3 to 5 will give you a better understanding of economic inequality in the world economy.

The Sources of Economic Inequality (pp. 455–458)

- Inequality arises from differences in human capital and from contests among superstars.
- Trends in the distribution of human capital and in the rewards to superstars that arise from technological change and globalization can explain some of the trend in increased inequality.
- Inequality might arise from discrimination.
- Inequality between men and women might arise from differences in the degree of specialization.
- Intergenerational transfers of wealth lead to increased inequality because people can't inherit debts and assortative mating tends to concentrate wealth.

Working Problem 6 will give you a better understanding of the sources of economic inequality.

Income Redistribution (pp. 459–461)

- Governments redistribute income through progressive income taxes, income maintenance programs, and subsidized services.
- Redistribution increases the share of total income received by the lowest 60 percent of households and decreases the share of total income received by the highest quintile. The share of the fourth quintile barely changes.
- Because the redistribution of income weakens incentives, it creates a tradeoff between equity and efficiency.
- Effective redistribution seeks to support the long-term solution to low income, which is education and job training—acquiring human capital.

Working Problems 7 and 8 will give you a better understanding of income redistribution.

Key Terms

MyEconLab Key Terms Quiz

Big tradeoff, 460
Gini ratio, 449
Lorenz curve, 447
Market income, 446

Money income, 446
Poverty, 451
Progressive income tax, 459
Proportional income tax, 459

Regressive income tax, 459
Wealth, 448

WORKED PROBLEM

MyEconLab   You can work this problem in Chapter 19 Study Plan.

The table shows the quintile shares of income in South Africa and Norway

Households (quintile)	Norway	South Africa
	(percentage of total income)	
Lowest	10	3
Second	16	5
Third	19	8
Fourth	22	16
Highest	33	68

Questions

1. Make a table to show the cumulative percentage of income against the cumulative percentage of households in Norway and find five points on the Lorenz curve for Norway.

2. Is income in Norway distributed more equally or less equally than in South Africa? Explain.

3. If the government of South Africa redistributed income so that its distribution matched that of Norway, which quintiles would see their incomes increase and which would decrease?

Solutions

1. To make a cumulative distribution table (below), start with the lowest quintile (20 percent of households) who receive 10 percent of income. Now add the income share of the second quintile to show that the lowest 40 percent of households receive $10 + 16 = 26$ percent of income. Repeating: the lowest 60 percent households receive $26 + 19 = 45$ percent of income, the lowest 80 percent receive $45 + 22 = 67$ percent of income, and 100 percent receive $67 + 33 = 100$ percent of income.

Households		Income	
Quintile	Cumulative percentage	Percentage	Cumulative percentage
Lowest	20	10	10
Second	40	16	26
Third	60	19	45
Fourth	80	22	67
Highest	100	33	100

The Lorenz curve shows the percentages of total income received by the cumulative percentages of

households. The rows of the following table shows the five points.

Households (percentage)	Cumulative percentage
Lowest 20	10
Lowest 40	26
Lowest 60	45
Lowest 80	67
All 100	100

Key Point: To calculate the cumulative distribution, start with the lowest quintile's share and gradually add the next higher quintile's share.

2. Each quintile in Norway except the highest one receives a larger percentage of total income than does the corresponding quintile in South Africa. So income in Norway is more equally distributed than in South Africa. Compare the Lorenz curves in the figure.

3. To make the South African distribution match Norway's, the lowest quintile would have to receive and additional 7 percent. The second quintile would have to receive an additional 11 percent, the third quintile and additional 11 percent and the fourth quintile and additional 6 percent.

   The second and third quintiles would receive the biggest increase and only the highest quintile would have a smaller share of income.

Key Point: To make the distribution more equal, redistribute income from higher to lower quintiles.

Key Figure   MyEconLab Interactive Animation

STUDY PLAN PROBLEMS AND APPLICATIONS

MyEconLab   You can work Problems 1 to 8 in Chapter 19 Study Plan and get instant feedback.

Economic Inequality in the United States

(Study Plan 19.1)

1. What is money income? Describe the U.S. distribution of money income in 2012.

2. The table shows money income shares in the United States in 2001.

Households (quintile)	Money income (percentage of total)
Lowest	3.5
Second	8.8
Third	14.5
Fourth	23.1
Highest	50.1

Draw a U.S. Lorenz curve in 2001. Was the U.S. distribution of income more equal in 2001 than in 2012 (see p. 447)? Explain your answer.

Inequality in the World Economy (Study Plan 19.2)

3. Incomes in China and India are a small fraction of U.S. income, but incomes in China and India are growing at more than twice the rate of U.S. incomes.

   a. Explain how economic inequality in China and India is changing relative to that in the United States.

   b. How is the world Lorenz curve and world Gini ratio changing?

Use the following table to work Problems 4 and 5. The table shows the income shares in the United States, Canada, and the United Kingdom in 2009.

Households (quintile)	United States	Canada	United Kingdom
	(percentage of total income)		
Lowest	3	7	3
Second	8	13	5
Third	15	18	14
Fourth	24	25	25
Highest	50	37	53

4. Draw the Lorenz curves for the United States and Canada. In which country was money income less equally distributed in 2009?

5. Draw the Lorenz curves for the United States and the United Kingdom. In which country was income less equally distributed in 2009?

The Sources of Economic Inequality (Study Plan 19.3)

6. The following figure shows the market for low-skilled labor.

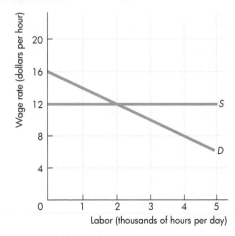

The value of marginal product of high-skilled workers is $16 an hour greater than that of low-skilled workers at each quantity of labor. The cost of acquiring human capital adds $12 an hour to the wage that must be offered to attract high-skilled labor.

Compare the equilibrium wage rates of low-skilled labor and high-skilled labor. Explain why the difference between these wage rates equals the cost of acquiring human capital.

Income Redistribution (Study Plan 19.4)

Use the following table to work Problems 7 and 8. The table shows three redistribution schemes.

Before-tax income (dollars)	Plan A tax (dollars)	Plan B tax (dollars)	Plan C tax (dollars)
10,000	1,000	1,000	2,000
20,000	2,000	4,000	2,000
30,000	3,000	9,000	2,000

7. Which scheme has
   (i) a proportional tax?
   (ii) a regressive tax?
   (iii) a progressive tax?

8. Which scheme will
   (i) increase economic inequality?
   (ii) reduce economic inequality?
   (iii) have no effect on economic inequality?

ADDITIONAL PROBLEMS AND APPLICATIONS

MyEconLab   You can work these problems in MyEconLab if assigned by your instructor.

Economic Inequality in the United States

Use the following table to work Problems 9 and 10. The table shows the distribution of market income in the United States in 2007.

Households (quintile)	Market income (percentage of total)
Lowest	1.1
Second	7.1
Third	13.9
Fourth	22.8
Highest	55.1

9. a. What is the definition of market income?

   b. Draw the Lorenz curve for the distribution of market income.

10. Compare the distribution of market income with the distribution of money income shown in Fig. 19.3 on p. 447. Which distribution is more unequal and why?

Inequality in the World Economy

Use the following table to work Problems 11 to 13. The table shows shares of income in Australia.

Households (quintile)	Income share (percentage of total)
Lowest	7
Second	13
Third	18
Foourth	24
Highest	38

11. Draw the Lorenz curves for the income distribution in Australia and in Brazil and South Africa (use the data in Fig. 19.6 on p. 453). Is income distributed more equally or less equally in Brazil and South Africa than in Australia?

12. Is the Gini ratio for Australia larger or smaller than that for Brazil and South Africa? Explain your answer.

13. What are some reasons for the differences in the distribution of income in Australia and in Brazil and South Africa?

The Sources of Economic Inequality

14. The figure shows the market for a group of workers who are discriminated against. Suppose

that other workers in the same industry are not discriminated against and their value of marginal product is perceived to be twice that of the workers who are discriminated against. Suppose also that the supply of these other workers is 2,000 hours per day less at each wage rate.

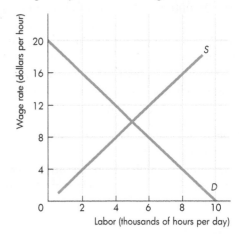

a. What is the wage rate of the workers who are discriminated against?

b. For workers who are discriminated against, what quantity of labor is employed?

c. What is the wage rate of the workers who do not face discrimination?

d. For workers who do not face discrimination, what quantity of labor is employed?

15. **Where Women's Pay Trumps Men's**
Men work more than women on the job, at least in terms of overall hours. That's just one reason why in most fields, men's earnings exceed women's earnings. But Warren Farrell found 39 occupations in which women's median earnings exceeded men's earnings by at least 5 percent and in some cases by as much as 43 percent. In fields like engineering, a company may get one woman and seven men applying for a job. If the company wants to hire the woman, it might have to pay a premium to get her. Also, where women can combine technical expertise with people skills—such as those required in sales and where customers prefer dealing with a woman—that's likely to contribute to a premium in pay.

Source: CNN, March 2, 2006

a. Draw a graph to illustrate why discrimination

could result in female workers getting paid more than male workers for some jobs.

b. Explain how market competition could potentially eliminate this wage differential.

c. If customers "prefer dealing with a woman" in some markets, how might that lead to a persistent wage differential between men and women?

Use the following data to work Problems 16 and 17.

In 2010, 828,000 Americans had full-time management jobs that paid an average of $96,450 a year while 4.3 million Americans had full-time retail sales jobs that paid an average of $20,670 a year.

Managers require a high school certificate while retail sales people don't but they undergo training.

Source: Bureau of Labor Statistics

16. Explain why managers are paid more than retail salespeople.

17. If the online shopping trend continues, how do you think the market for salespeople will change in coming years?

Income Redistribution

18. Use the information provided in Problem 9 and in Fig. 19.3 on p. 447.
   a. What is the percentage of total income that is redistributed from the highest income group?
   b. What percentages of total income are redistributed to the lower income groups?

19. Describe the effects of increasing the amount of income redistribution in the United States to the point at which the lowest income group receives 15 percent of total income and the highest income group receives 30 percent of total income.

Use the following news clip to work Problems 20 and 21.

The Tax Debate We Should be Having

A shrinking number of Americans are bearing an even bigger share of the nation's income tax burden. In 2005, the bottom 40 percent of Americans by income had an effective tax rate that's negative: Their households received more money through the income tax system than they paid. The top 50% of taxpayers pay 97% of total income tax and the top 10% of taxpayers pay 70%. The top 1% paid almost 40% of all income tax, a proportion that has jumped dramatically since 1986.

Given the U.S. tax system, any tax cut must benefit the rich, but in terms of the change in effective tax rates: The bottom 50% got a much bigger tax cut under the Bush tax cut than the top 1%. Did the dollar value of Bush's tax cuts go mostly to the wealthy? Absolutely.

Source: *Fortune*, April 14, 2008

20. Explain why tax cuts in a progressive income tax system are consistently criticized for favoring the wealthy.

21. How might the benefits of tax cuts "trickle down" to others whose taxes are not cut?

Economics in the News

22. After you have studied *Economics in the News* on pp. 462–463, answer the following questions.
   a. What is the trend in top executive pay?
   b. How can the idea of a contest among potential top executives explain their high pay?
   c. How can the idea of a contest among potential top executives explain the trend in their pay?
   d. If the contest among potential top executives is the correct explanation for their high pay, what would be the effects of a cap on top executive pay?

23. **The Best and Worst College Degrees by Salary**

Business administration is always a strong contender for honors as the most popular college major. This is no surprise since students think business is the way to make big bucks. But is business administration really as lucrative as students and their parents believe? Nope.

In a new survey by PayScale, Inc. of salaries by college degree, business administration didn't even break into the list of the top 10 or 20 most lucrative college degrees. A variety of engineering majors claim eight of the top 10 salary spots with chemical engineering ($65,700) winning best for starting salaries. Out of 75 undergrad college majors, business administration ($42,900) came in 35th, behind such degrees as occupational therapy ($61,300), information technology ($49,400), and economics ($48,800).

Source: moneywatch.com, July 21, 2009

a. Why do college graduates with different majors have drastically different starting salaries?

b. Draw a graph of the labor markets for economics majors and business administration majors to illustrate your explanation of the differences in the starting salaries of these two groups.

20

UNCERTAINTY AND INFORMATION

After studying this chapter,
you will be able to:

◆ Explain how people make decisions when they are uncertain about the consequences

◆ Explain how markets enable people to buy and sell risk

◆ Explain how markets cope when buyers and sellers have private information

◆ Explain how uncertainty and incomplete information influence the efficiency of markets

You want an A in your economics course and you want to graduate with a high GPA. But what if grades are inflated and you along with everyone else gets an A? What happens in the job market for college graduates? And how do accurate grades help the market work?

The job market for college graduates is an example of a market with uncertainty and incomplete information. Can this market achieve an efficient outcome? This chapter answers these questions. In *Economics in the News* at the end of the chapter, you will see why grade inflation is not in your best interest.

Decisions in the Face of Uncertainty

Tania, a student, is trying to decide which of two summer jobs to take. She can work as a house painter and earn enough to save $2,000 by the end of the summer. There is no uncertainty about the income from this job. If Tania takes it, she will definitely have $2,000 in her bank account at the end of the summer. The other job, working as a telemarketer selling subscriptions to a magazine, is risky. If Tania takes this job, her bank balance at the end of the summer will depend on her success at selling. She will earn enough to save $5,000 if she is successful but only $1,000 if she turns out to be a poor salesperson. Tania has never tried selling, so she doesn't know how successful she'll be. But some of her friends have done this job, and 50 percent of them do well and 50 percent do poorly. Basing her expectations on this experience, Tania thinks there is a 50 percent chance that she will earn $5,000 and a 50 percent chance that she will earn $1,000.

Tania is equally as happy to paint as she is to make phone calls. She cares only about the money. Which job does she prefer: the one that provides her with $2,000 for sure or the one that offers her a 50 percent chance of making $5,000 but a 50 percent risk of making only $1,000?

To answer this question, we need a way of comparing the two outcomes. One comparison is the expected wealth that each job creates.

Expected Wealth

Expected wealth is the money value of what a person expects to own at a given point in time. An expectation is an average calculated by using a formula that weights each possible outcome with the probability (chance) that it will occur.

For Tania, the probability that she will have $5,000 is 0.5 (a 50 percent chance). The probability that she will have $1,000 is also 0.5. Notice that the probabilities sum to 1. Using these numbers, we can calculate Tania's expected wealth, EW, which is

$$EW = (\$5,000 \times 0.5) + (\$1,000 \times 0.5) = \$3,000.$$

Notice that expected wealth decreases if the risk of a poor outcome increases. For example, if Tania has a

20 percent chance of success (and 80 percent chance of failure), her expected wealth falls to $1,800—

$$(\$5,000 \times 0.2) + (\$1,000 \times 0.8) = \$1,800.$$

Tania can now compare the expected wealth from each job—$3,000 for the risky job and $2,000 for the non-risky job.

So does Tania prefer the risky job because it gives her a greater expected wealth? The answer is we don't know because we don't know how much Tania dislikes risk.

Risk Aversion

Risk aversion is the dislike of risk. Almost everyone is risk averse but some more than others. In football, running is less risky than passing. Coach John Harbaugh of the Baltimore Ravens, who favors a cautious running game, is risk averse. Denver quarterback Peyton Manning, who favors a risky passing game, is less risk averse. But almost everyone is risk averse to some degree.

We can measure the degree of risk aversion by the compensation needed to make a given amount of risk acceptable. Returning to Tania: If she needs to be paid more than $1,000 to take on the risk arising from the telemarketing job, she will choose the safe painting job and take the $2,000 non-risky income. But if she thinks that the extra $1,000 of expected income is enough to compensate her for the risk, she will take the risky job.

To make this idea concrete, we need a way of thinking about how a person values different levels of wealth. The concept that we use is *utility*. We apply the same idea that explains how people make expenditure decisions (see Chapter 8) to explain risk aversion and decisions in the face of risk.

Utility of Wealth

Wealth (money in the bank and other assets of value) is like all good things. It yields utility. The more wealth a person has, the greater is that person's total utility. But each additional dollar of wealth brings a diminishing increment in total utility—the marginal utility of wealth diminishes as wealth increases.

Diminishing marginal utility of wealth means that the gain in utility from an increase in wealth is smaller than the loss in utility from an equal decrease in wealth. Stated differently, *the pain from a loss is greater than the pleasure from a gain of equal size.*

Figure 20.1 illustrates Tania's utility of wealth. Each point *A* through *F* on Tania's utility of wealth curve corresponds to the value identified by the same letter in the table. For example, at point *C*, Tania's wealth is $2,000, and her total utility is 70 units. As Tania's wealth increases, her total utility increases and her marginal utility decreases. Her marginal utility is 25 units when wealth increases from $1,000 to $2,000, but only 13 units when wealth increases from $2,000 to $3,000.

We can use a person's utility of wealth curve to calculate expected utility and the cost of risk.

Expected Utility

Expected utility is the utility value of what a person expects to own at a given point in time. Like expected wealth, it is calculated by using a formula that weights each possible outcome with the probability that it will occur. But it is the utility outcome, not the money outcome, that is used to calculate expected utility.

Figure 20.2 illustrates the calculation for Tania. Wealth of $5,000 gives 95 units of utility and wealth of $1,000 gives 45 units of utility. Each outcome has a probability of 0.5 (a 50 percent chance). Using these numbers, we can calculate Tania's expected utility, *EU*, which is

$$EU = (95 \times 0.5) + (45 \times 0.5) = 70.$$

FIGURE 20.1   The Utility of Wealth

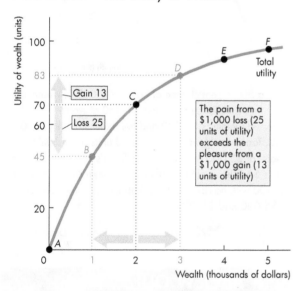

	Wealth (dollars)	Total utility (units)	Marginal utility (units)
A	0	0	
			45
B	1,000	45	
			25
C	**2,000**	**70**	
			13
D	3,000	83	
			8
E	4,000	91	
			4
F	5,000	95	

The table shows Tania's utility of wealth schedule, and the figure shows her utility of wealth curve. Utility increases as wealth increases, but the marginal utility of wealth diminishes.

—— MyEconLab Animation ——

FIGURE 20.2   Expected Utility

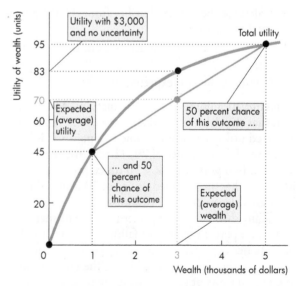

Tania has a 50 percent chance of having $5,000 of wealth and a total utility of 95 units. She also has a 50 percent chance of having $1,000 of wealth and a total utility of 45 units. Tania's expected wealth is $3,000 (the average of $5,000 and $1,000) and her expected utility is 70 units (the average of 95 and 45). With a wealth of $3,000 and no uncertainty, Tania's total utility is 83 units. For a given expected wealth, the greater the range of uncertainty, the smaller is expected utility.

—— MyEconLab Animation ——

Expected utility decreases if the risk of a poor outcome increases. For example, if Tania has a 20 percent chance of success (and an 80 percent chance of failure), her expected utility is 55 units—

$$(95 \times 0.2) + (45 \times 0.8) = 55.$$

Notice how the range of uncertainty affects expected utility. Figure 20.2 shows that with $3,000 of wealth and no uncertainty, total utility is 83 units. But with the same expected wealth and Tania's uncertainty—a 50 percent chance of having $5,000 and a 50 percent chance of having $1,000—expected utility is only 70 units. Tania's uncertainty lowers her expected utility by 13 units.

Expected utility combines expected wealth and risk into a single index.

Making a Choice with Uncertainty

Faced with uncertainty, a person chooses the action that maximizes expected utility. To select the job that gives her the maximum expected utility, Tania must:

1. Calculate the expected utility from the risky telemarketing job
2. Calculate the expected utility from the safe painting job
3. Compare the two expected utilities

Figure 20.3 illustrates the calculations. You've just seen that the risky telemarketing job gives Tania an expected utility of 70 units. The safe painting job also gives Tania a utility of 70. That is, the total utility of $2,000 with no risk is 70 units. So with either job, Tania has an expected utility of 70 units. She is indifferent between these two jobs.

If Tania had only a 20 percent chance of success and an 80 percent chance of failure in the telemarketing job, her expected utility would be 55 (calculated above). In this case, she would take the painting job and get 70 units of utility. But if the probabilities were reversed and she had an 80 percent chance of success and only a 20 percent chance of failure in the telemarketing job, her expected utility would be 85 units—$(95 \times 0.8) + (45 \times 0.2) = 85$. In this case, she would take the risky telemarketing job.

We can calculate the cost of risk by comparing the expected wealth in a given risky situation with the wealth that gives the same total utility but no risk. Using this principle, we can find Tania's cost of bearing the risk that arises from the telemarketing job. That cost, highlighted in Fig. 20.3, is $1,000.

FIGURE 20.3   Choice Under Uncertainty

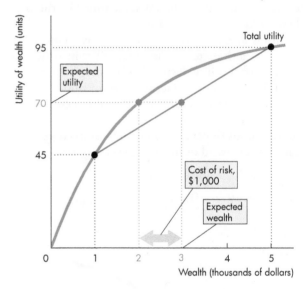

With a 50 percent chance of having $5,000 of wealth and a 50 percent chance of having $1,000 of wealth, Tania's expected wealth is $3,000 and her expected utility is 70 units. Tania would have the same 70 units of total utility with wealth of $2,000 and no risk, so Tania's cost of bearing this risk is $1,000. Tania is indifferent between the job that pays $2,000 with no risk and the job that offers an equal chance of $5,000 and $1,000.

—— MyEconLab Animation and Draw Graph ——

◆ REVIEW QUIZ

1 What is the distinction between expected wealth and expected utility?
2 How does the concept of utility of wealth capture the idea that pain of loss exceeds the pleasure of gain?
3 What do people try to achieve when they make a decision under uncertainty?
4 How is the cost of the risk calculated when making a decision with an uncertain outcome?

Work these questions in Study Plan 20.1 and get instant feedback. Do a Key Terms Quiz.   MyEconLab

You've now seen how a person makes a risky decision. In the next section, we'll see how markets enable people to reduce the risks they face.

Buying and Selling Risk

You've seen at many points in your study of markets how both buyers and sellers gain from trade. Buyers gain because they value what they buy more highly than the price they must pay—they receive a *consumer surplus*. And sellers gain because they face costs that are less than the price at which they can sell—they receive a *producer surplus*.

Just as buyers and sellers gain from trading goods and services, so they can also gain by trading risk. But risk is a bad, not a good. The good that is traded is risk avoidance. A buyer of risk avoidance can gain because the value of avoiding risk is greater than the price that must be paid to someone else to get them to bear the risk. The seller of risk avoidance faces a lower cost of risk than the price that people are willing to pay to avoid the risk.

We're going to put some flesh on the bare bones of this brief account of how people can gain from trading risk by looking at insurance markets.

Insurance Markets

Insurance plays a huge role in our economic lives. We'll explain

- How insurance reduces risk
- Why people buy insurance
- How insurance companies earn a profit

How Insurance Reduces Risk Insurance reduces the risk that people face by sharing or pooling the risks. When people buy insurance against the risk of an unwanted event, they pay an insurance company a *premium*. If the unwanted event occurs, the insurance company pays out the amount of the insured loss.

Think about auto collision insurance. The probability that any one person will have a serious auto accident is small. But a person who does have an auto accident incurs a large loss. For a large population, the probability of one person having an accident is the proportion of the population that has an accident. But this proportion is known, so the probability of an accident occurring and the total cost of accidents can be predicted. An insurance company can pool the risks of a large population and enable everyone to share the costs. It does so by collecting premiums from everyone and paying out benefits to those who suffer a loss. An insurance company that remains in business collects at least as much in premiums as it pays out in benefits.

Why People Buy Insurance People buy insurance and insurance companies earn a profit by selling insurance because people are risk averse. To see why people buy insurance and why it is profitable, let's consider an example. Dan owns a car worth $10,000, and that is his only wealth. There is a 10 percent chance that Dan will have a serious accident that makes his car worth nothing. So there is a 90 percent chance that Dan's wealth will remain at $10,000 and a 10 percent chance that his wealth will be zero. Dan's expected wealth is $9,000—($10,000 × 0.9) + ($0 × 0.1).

Dan is risk averse (just like Tania in the previous example). Because Dan is risk averse, he will be better off by buying insurance to avoid the risk that he faces, if the insurance premium isn't too high.

Without knowing some details about just how risk averse Dan is, we don't know the most that he would be willing to pay to avoid this risk. But we do know that he would pay more than $1,000. If Dan did pay $1,000 to avoid the risk, he would have $9,000 of wealth and face no uncertainty about his wealth. If he does not have an accident, his wealth is the $10,000 value of his car minus the $1,000 he pays the insurance company. If he does lose his car, the insurance company pays him $10,000, so he still has $9,000. Being risk averse, Dan's expected utility from $9,000 with no risk is greater than his expected utility from an expected $9,000 with risk. So Dan would be willing to pay more than $1,000 to avoid this risk.

How Insurance Companies Earn a Profit For the insurance company, $1,000 is the minimum amount at which it would be willing to insure Dan and other people like him. With say 50,000 customers all like Dan, 5,000 customers (50,000 × 0.1) lose their cars and 45,000 don't. Premiums of $1,000 give the insurance company a total revenue of $50,000,000. With 5,000 claims of $10,000, the insurance company pays out $50,000,000. So a premium of $1,000 enables the insurance company to break even (make zero economic profit) on this business.

But Dan (and everyone else) is willing to pay more than $1,000, so insurance is a profitable business and there is a gain from trading risk.

The gain from trading risk is shared by Dan (and the other people who buy insurance) and the insurance company. The exact share of the gain depends on the state of competition in the market for insurance.

If the insurance market is a monopoly, the insurance company can take all the gains from trading risk. But if the insurance market is competitive, economic profit will induce entry and profits will be competed away. In this case, Dan (and the other buyers of insurance) gets the gain.

A Graphical Analysis of Insurance

We can illustrate the gains from insurance by using a graph of Dan's utility of wealth curve. We begin, in Fig. 20.4, with the situation if Dan doesn't buy insurance and decides to bear the risk he faces.

Risk-Taking Without Insurance With no accident, Dan's wealth is $10,000 and his total utility is 100 units. If Dan has an accident, his car is worthless: he has no wealth and no utility. Because the chance of an accident is 10 percent (or 0.1), the chance of not having an accident is 90 percent (or 0.9). Dan's expected wealth is $9,000—($10,000 × 0.9) + ($0 × 0.1)—and his expected utility is 90 units—(100 × 0.9) + (0 × 0.1).

You've just seen that without insurance, Dan gets 90 units of utility. But Dan also gets 90 units of utility if he faces no uncertainty with a smaller amount of wealth.

We're now going to see how much Dan will pay to avoid uncertainty.

The Value and Cost of Insurance Figure 20.5 shows the situation when Dan buys insurance. You can see that for Dan, having $7,000 with no risk is just as good as facing a 90 percent chance of having $10,000 and a 10 percent chance of having no wealth. So if Dan pays $3,000 for insurance, he has $7,000 of wealth, faces no uncertainty, and gets 90 units of utility. The amount of $3,000 is the maximum that Dan is willing to pay for insurance. It is the value of insurance to Dan.

Figure 20.5 also shows the cost of insurance. With a large number of customers each of whom has a 10 percent chance of making a $10,000 claim for the loss of a vehicle, the insurance company can provide insurance at a cost of $1,000 (10 percent of $10,000). If Dan pays only $1,000 for insurance, his

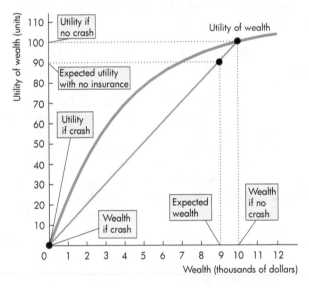

**FIGURE 20.4   Taking a Risk
Without Insurance**

Dan's wealth (the value of his car) is $10,000, which gives him 100 units of utility.

With no insurance, if Dan has a crash, he has no wealth and no utility.

With a 10 percent chance of a crash, Dan's expected wealth is $9,000 and his expected utility is 90 units.

MyEconLab Animation

wealth is $9,000 (the $10,000 value of his car minus the $1,000 he pays for insurance), and his utility from $9,000 of wealth with no uncertainty is about 98 units.

Gains from Trade Because Dan is willing to pay up to $3,000 for insurance that costs the insurance company $1,000, there is a gain from trading risk of $2,000 per insured person. How the gains are shared depends on the nature of the market. If the insurance market is competitive, entry will increase supply and lower the price to $1,000 (plus normal profit and operating costs). Dan (and the other buyers of insurance) enjoys a consumer surplus. If the insurance market is a monopoly, the insurance company takes the $2,000 per insured person as economic profit.

FIGURE 20.5   The Gains from Insurance

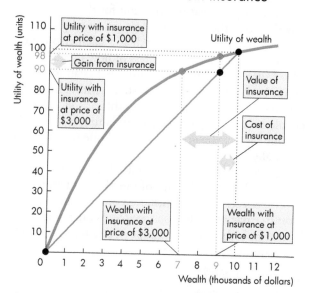

If Dan pays $3,000 for insurance, his wealth is $7,000 and his utility is 90 units—the same utility as with no insurance—so $3,000 is the value of insurance for Dan.

If Dan pays $1,000 for insurance, which is the insurance company's cost of providing insurance, his wealth is $9,000 and his utility is about 98 units.

Dan and the insurance company share the gain from insurance.

————— MyEconLab Animation —————

Risk That Can't Be Insured

The gains from auto collision insurance that we've studied here apply to all types of insurance. Examples are property and casualty insurance, life insurance, and healthcare insurance. One person's risks associated with driving, life, and health are independent of other persons'. That's why insurance is possible. The risks are spread across a population.

But not all risks can be insured. To be insurable, risks must be independent. If an event causes everyone to be a loser, it isn't possible to spread and pool the risks. For example, flood insurance is often not available for people who live on a floodplain because if one person incurs a loss, most likely all do.

Also, to be insurable, a risky event must be observable to both the buyer and seller of insurance. But much of the uncertainty that we face arises

ECONOMICS IN ACTION
Insurance in the United States

We spend 7 percent of our income on private insurance. That's more than we spend on cars or food. The figure shows the relative sizes of the four main types of private insurance. More than 80 percent of Americans have life insurance, and most have private health insurance.

In addition, we buy Medicare, Medicaid, Social Security, and unemployment insurance through our taxes.

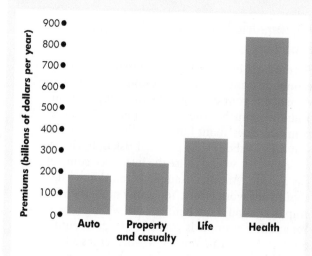

The U.S. Insurance Industry

Sources of data: U.S. Bureau of the Census, National Institute for Healthcare Management, and the American Council of Life Insurers.

◆ REVIEW QUIZ

1 How does insurance reduce risk?
2 How do we determine the value (willingness to pay) for insurance?
3 How can an insurance company offer people a deal worth taking? Why do both the buyers and the sellers of insurance gain?
4 What kinds of risks can't be insured?

Work these questions in Study Plan 20.2 and get instant feedback.   MyEconLab

because we know less (or more) than others with whom we do business. In the next section, we look at the way markets cope when buyers and sellers have different information.

◆ Private Information

In all the markets that you've studied so far, the buyers and the sellers are well informed about the good, service, or factor of production being traded. But in some markets, either the buyers or the sellers—usually the sellers—are better informed about the value of the item being traded than the person on the other side of the market. Information about the value of the item being traded that is possessed by only buyers or sellers is called **private information**. And a market in which the buyers or sellers have private information has **asymmetric information**.

Asymmetric Information: Examples and Problems

Asymmetric information affects many of your own economic transactions. One example is your knowledge about your driving skills and temperament. You know much more than your auto insurance company does about how carefully and defensively you drive—about your personal risk of having an accident that would cause the insurance company to pay a claim. Another example is your knowledge about your work effort. You know more than your employer about how hard you are willing to work. Yet another example is your knowledge about the quality of your car. You know whether it's a lemon, but the person to whom you are about to sell it does not know and can't find out until after he or she has bought it.

Asymmetric information creates two problems:

- Adverse selection
- Moral hazard

Adverse Selection   **Adverse selection** is the tendency for people to *enter into agreements* in which they can use their private information to their own advantage and to the disadvantage of the uninformed party.

For example, if Jackie offers her salespeople a fixed wage, she will attract lazy salespeople. Hardworking salespeople will prefer not to work for Jackie because they can earn more by working for someone who pays by results. The fixed-wage contract adversely selects those with private information (knowledge about their work habits) who can use that knowledge to their own advantage and to the disadvantage of the other party.

Moral Hazard   **Moral hazard** is the tendency for people with private information, *after entering into an agreement*, to use that information for their own benefit and at the cost of the less-informed party. For example, Jackie hires Mitch as a salesperson and pays him a fixed wage regardless of how much he sells. Mitch faces a moral hazard. He has an incentive to put in the least possible effort, benefiting himself and lowering Jackie's profits. For this reason, salespeople are usually paid by a formula that makes their income higher, the greater is the volume (or value) of their sales.

A variety of devices have evolved that enable markets to function in the face of moral hazard and adverse selection. We've just seen one, the use of incentive payments for salespeople. We're going to look at how three markets cope with adverse selection and moral hazard. They are

- The market for used cars
- The market for loans
- The market for insurance

The Market for Used Cars

When a person buys a car, it might turn out to be a lemon. If the car is a lemon, it is worth less to the buyer than if it has no defects. Does the used car market have two prices reflecting these two values—a low price for lemons and a higher price for cars without defects? It turns out that it does. But it needs some help to do so and to overcome what is called the **lemons problem**—the problem that in a market in which it is not possible to distinguish reliable products from lemons, there are too many lemons and too few reliable products traded.

To see how the used car market overcomes the lemons problem, we'll first look at a used car market that has a lemons problem.

The Lemons Problem in a Used Car Market
To explain the lemons problem as clearly as possible, we'll assume that there are only two kinds of cars: defective cars—lemons—and cars without defects that we'll call good cars. Whether or not a car is a lemon is private information that is available only to the current owner. The buyer of a used car can't tell whether he is buying a lemon until after he has bought the car and learned as much about it as its current owner knows.

Some people with low incomes and the time and ability to fix cars are willing to buy lemons as long as they know what they're buying and pay an appropriately low price. Suppose that a lemon is worth $5,000 to a buyer. More people want to buy a good car and we'll assume that a good car is worth $25,000 to a buyer.

But the buyer can't tell the difference between a lemon and a good car. Only the seller has this information. And telling the buyer that a car is not a lemon does not help. The seller has no incentive to tell the truth.

So the most that the buyer knows is the probability of buying a lemon. If half of the used cars sold turn out to be lemons, the buyer knows that he has a 50 percent chance of getting a good car and a 50 percent chance of getting a lemon.

The price that a buyer is willing to pay for a car of unknown quality is more than the value of a lemon because the car might be a good one. But the price is less than the value of a good car because it might turn out to be a lemon.

Now think about the sellers of used cars, who know the quality of their cars. Someone who owns a good car is going to be offered a price that is less than the value of that car to the buyer. Many owners will

be reluctant to sell for such a low price. So the quantity of good used cars supplied will not be as large as it would be if people paid the price they are worth.

In contrast, someone who owns a lemon is going to be offered a price that is greater than the value of that car to the buyer. So owners of lemons will be eager to sell and the quantity of lemons supplied will be greater than it would be if people paid the price that a lemon is worth.

Figure 20.6 illustrates the used car market that we've just described. Part (a) shows the demand for used cars, D, and the supply of used cars, S. The market equilibrium occurs at a price of $10,000 per car with 400 cars traded each month.

Some cars are good ones and some are lemons, but buyers can't tell the difference until it is too late to influence their decision to buy. But buyers do know what a good car and a lemon are worth to them, and sellers know the quality of the cars they are offering for sale. Figure 20.6(b) shows the demand curve for good cars, D_G, and the supply curve of good cars, S_G. Figure 20.6(c) shows the demand curve for lemons, D_L, and the supply curve of lemons, S_L.

At the market price of $10,000 per car, owners of good cars supply 200 cars a month for sale. Owners

FIGURE 20.6   The Lemons Problem

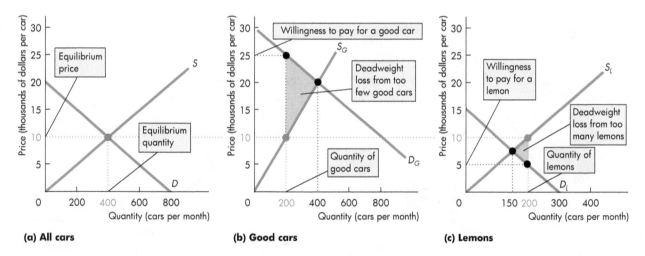

(a) All cars   **(b) Good cars**   **(c) Lemons**

Buyers can't tell a good used car from a lemon. Demand and supply determine the price and quantity of used cars traded in part (a). In part (b), D_G is the demand curve for good used cars and S_G is the supply curve. At the market price, too few

good cars are available, which brings a deadweight loss. In part (c), D_L is the demand curve for lemons and S_L is the supply curve. At the market price, too many lemons are available, which brings a deadweight loss.

MyEconLab Animation

of lemons also supply 200 cars a month for sale. The used car market is inefficient because there are too many lemons and not enough good cars. Figure 20.6 makes this inefficiency clear by using the concept of deadweight loss (see Chapter 5, pp. 114–115).

At the quantity of good cars supplied, buyers are willing to pay $25,000 for a good car. They are willing to pay more than a good car is worth to its current owner for all good cars up to 400 cars a month. The gray triangle shows the deadweight loss that results from there being too few good used cars.

At the quantity of lemons supplied, buyers are willing to pay $5,000 for a lemon. They are willing to pay less than a lemon is worth to its current owner for all lemons above 150 cars a month. The gray triangle shows the deadweight loss that results from there being too many lemons.

You can see *adverse selection* in this used car market because there is a greater incentive to offer a lemon for sale. You can see *moral hazard* because the owner of a lemon has little incentive to take good care of it. The market for used cars is not working well. Too many lemons and too few good cars are traded.

A Used Car Market with Dealers' Warranties

How can used car dealers convince buyers that a car isn't a lemon? The answer is by giving a guarantee in the form of a warranty. By providing warranties only on good cars, dealers signal which cars are good ones and which are lemons.

Signaling occurs when an informed person takes actions that send information to uninformed persons. The grades and degrees that a university awards students are signals. They inform potential (uninformed) employers about the ability of the people they are considering hiring.

In the market for used cars, dealers send signals by giving warranties on the used cars they offer for sale. The message in the signal is that the dealer agrees to pay the costs of repairing the car if it turns out to have a defect.

Buyers believe the signal because the cost of sending a false signal is high. A dealer who gives a warranty on a lemon ends up bearing a high cost of repairs—and gains a bad reputation. A dealer who gives a warranty only on good cars has no repair costs and a reputation that gets better and better. It pays

---

FIGURE 20.7   Warranties Make the Used Car Market Efficient

(a) Good cars

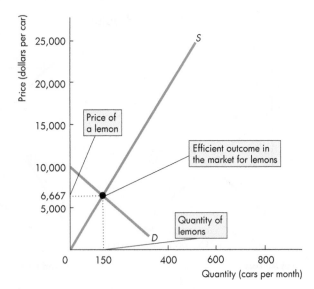

(b) Lemons

With dealers' warranties as signals, the equilibrium price of a good used car is $20,000 and 400 cars are traded. The market for good used cars is efficient. Because the signal

enables buyers to spot a lemon, the price of a lemon is $6,667 and 150 lemons are traded. The market for lemons is efficient.

dealers to send an accurate signal, and it is rational for buyers to believe the signal.

So a car with a warranty is a good car; a car without a warranty is a lemon. Warranties solve the lemons problem and enable the used car market to function efficiently with two prices: one for lemons and one for good cars.

Figure 20.7 illustrates this outcome. In part (a) the demand for and supply of good cars determine the price of a good car. In part (b), the demand for and supply of lemons determine the price of a lemon. Both markets are efficient.

Pooling Equilibrium and Separating Equilibrium

You've seen two outcomes in the market for used cars. Without warranties, there is only one message visible to the buyer: All cars look the same. So there is one price regardless of whether the car is a good car or a lemon. We call the equilibrium in a market when only one message is available and an uninformed person cannot determine quality a **pooling equilibrium.**

But in a used car market with warranties, there are two messages: Good cars have warranties and lemons don't. So there are two car prices for the two types of cars. We call the equilibrium in a market when signaling provides full information to a previously uninformed person a **separating equilibrium.**

The Market for Loans

When you buy a tank of gasoline and swipe your credit card, you are taking a loan from the bank that issued your card. You demand and your bank supplies a loan. Have you noticed the interest rate on an unpaid credit card balance? In 2014, it ranged between 7 percent a year and 36 percent a year. Why are these interest rates so high? And why is there such a huge range?

The answer is that when banks make loans, they face the risk that the loan will not be repaid. The risk that a borrower, also known as a creditor, might not repay a loan is called **credit risk** or **default risk.** For credit card borrowing, the credit risk is high and it varies among borrowers. The highest-risk borrowers pay the highest interest rate.

Interest rates and the price of credit risk are determined in the market for loans. The lower the interest rate, the greater is the quantity of loans demanded and for a given level of credit risk, the higher the interest rate, the greater is the quantity of loans supplied. Demand and supply determine the interest rate and the price of credit risk.

If lenders were unable to charge different interest rates to reflect different degrees of credit risk, there would be a pooling equilibrium and an inefficient loans market.

Inefficient Pooling Equilibrium

To see why a pooling equilibrium would be inefficient, suppose that banks can't identify the individual credit risk of their borrowers: they have no way of knowing how likely it is that a given loan will be repaid. In this situation, every borrower pays the same interest rate and the market is in a pooling equilibrium.

If all borrowers pay the same interest rate, the market for loans has the same problem as the used car market. Low-risk customers borrow less than they would if they were offered the low interest rate appropriate for their low credit risk. High-risk customers borrow more than they would if they faced the high interest rate appropriate for their high credit risk. So banks face an *adverse selection* problem. Too many borrowers are high risk and too few are low risk.

Signaling and Screening in the Market for Loans

Lenders don't know how likely it is that a given loan will be repaid, but the borrower does know. Low-risk borrowers have an incentive to signal their risk by providing lenders with relevant information. Signals might include information about the length of time a person has been in the current job or has lived at the current address, home ownership, marital status, age, and business record.

High-risk borrowers might be identified simply as those who have failed to signal low risk. These borrowers have an incentive to mislead lenders; and lenders have an incentive to induce high-risk borrowers to reveal their risk level. Inducing an informed party to reveal relevant private information is called **screening.**

By not lending to people who refuse to reveal relevant information, banks are able to screen as well as receive signals that help them to separate their borrowers into a number of credit-risk categories. If lenders succeed, the market for loans comes to a separating equilibrium with a high interest rate for high-risk borrowers and a low interest rate for low-risk borrowers. Signaling and screening in the market for loans act like warranties in the used car market and work to avoid the deadweight loss of a pooling equilibrium.

ECONOMICS IN ACTION
The Sub-Prime Credit Crisis

A sub-prime mortgage is a loan to a homebuyer who has a high risk of default. Figure 1 shows that between 2001 and 2005, the price of risk was low. Figure 2 shows why: The supply of credit, S_0, was large and so was the amount of risk taking. In 2007, the supply of credit decreased to S_1. The price of risk jumped and, faced with a higher interest rate, many sub-prime borrowers defaulted. Defaults in the sub-prime mortgage market spread to other markets that supplied the funds that financed mortgages.

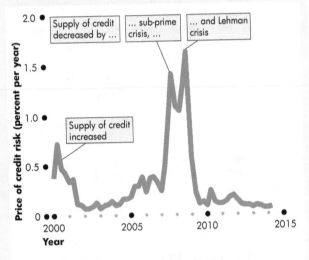

Figure 1 The Price of Commercial Credit Risk

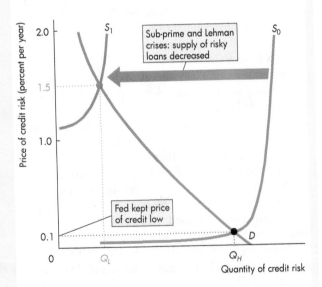

Figure 2 The Market for Risky Loans

The Market for Insurance

People who buy insurance face moral hazard, and insurance companies face adverse selection. *Moral hazard* arises because a person with insurance against a loss has less incentive than an uninsured person to avoid the loss. For example, a business with fire insurance has less incentive to install a fire alarm or sprinkler system than a business with no fire insurance does. *Adverse selection* arises because people who create greater risks are more likely to buy insurance. For example, a person with a history of driving infringements is more likely to buy collision insurance than is a person with a history of good driving.

Insurance companies have an incentive to find ways around the moral hazard and adverse selection problems. By doing so, they can lower premiums for low-risk people and raise premiums for high-risk people.

One way in which auto insurance companies separate high-risk and low-risk customers is with a *no-claim bonus*. A driver accumulates a no-claim bonus by driving safely and avoiding accidents. The greater the bonus, the greater is the incentive to drive carefully. Insurance companies also use a *deductible*. A deductible is the amount of a loss that the insured person agrees to bear. The premium is smaller, the larger is the deductible, and the decrease in the premium is more than proportionate to the increase in the deductible. By offering insurance with full coverage—no deductible—on terms that are attractive only to the high-risk people and by offering coverage with a deductible on more favorable terms that are attractive to low-risk people, insurance companies can do profitable business with everyone. High-risk people choose policies with a low deductible and a high premium; low-risk people choose policies with a high-deductible and a low premium.

◆ REVIEW QUIZ

1 How does private information create adverse selection and moral hazard?
2 How do markets for cars use warranties to cope with private information?
3 How do markets for loans use signaling and screening to cope with private information?
4 How do markets for insurance use no-claim bonuses to cope with private information?

Work these questions in Study Plan 20.3 and get instant feedback. Do a Key Terms Quiz.   MyEconLab

Uncertainty, Information, and the Invisible Hand

A recurring theme throughout microeconomics is the big question: When do choices made in the pursuit of *self-interest* also promote the *social interest?* When does the invisible hand work well and when does it fail us? You've learned about the concept of efficiency, a major component of what we mean by the social interest. And you've seen that while competitive markets generally do a good job in helping to achieve efficiency, impediments such as monopoly and the absence of well-defined property rights can prevent the attainment of an efficient use of resources.

How do uncertainty and incomplete information affect the ability of self-interested choices to lead to a social interest outcome? Are these features of economic life another reason why markets fail and why some type of government intervention is required to achieve efficiency?

These are hard questions, and there are no definitive answers. But there are some useful things that we can say about the effects of uncertainty and a lack of complete information on the efficiency of resource use. We'll begin our brief review of this issue by thinking about information as just another good.

Information as a Good

More information is generally useful, and less uncertainty about the future is generally useful. Think about information as one of the goods that we want more of.

The most basic lesson about efficiency that you learned in Chapter 2 can be applied to information. Along our production possibilities frontier, we face a tradeoff between information and all other goods and services. Information, like everything else, can be produced at an increasing opportunity cost—an increasing marginal cost. For example, we could get more accurate weather forecasts, but only at increasing marginal cost, as we increased the amount of information that we gather from the atmosphere and the amount of money that we spend on supercomputers to process the data.

The principle of decreasing marginal benefit also applies to information. More information is valuable, but the more you know, the less you value another increment of information. For example, knowing that it will rain tomorrow is valuable information.

Knowing the amount of rain to within an inch is even more useful. But knowing the amount of rain to within a millimeter probably isn't worth much more.

Because the marginal cost of information is increasing and the marginal benefit is decreasing, there is an efficient amount of information. It would be inefficient to be overinformed.

In principle, competitive markets in information might deliver this efficient quantity. Whether they actually do so is hard to determine.

Monopoly in Markets that Cope with Uncertainty

There are probably large economies of scale in providing services that cope with uncertainty and incomplete information. The insurance industry, for example, is highly concentrated. Where monopoly elements exist, exactly the same inefficiency issues arise as occur in markets where uncertainty and incomplete information are not big issues. So it is likely that in some information markets, including insurance markets, there is underproduction arising from the attempt to maximize monopoly profit.

◆ REVIEW QUIZ

1 Thinking about information as a good, what determines the information that people are willing to pay for?
2 Why is it inefficient to be overinformed?
3 Why are some of the markets that provide information likely to be dominated by monopolies?

Work these questions in Study Plan 20.4 and get instant feedback.   MyEconLab

◆ You've seen how people make decisions when faced with uncertainty and how markets work when there is asymmetric information. *Economics in the News* on pp. 482–483 looks at the way markets in human capital and labor use grades as signals that sort students by ability so that employers can hire the type of labor they seek. You'll see why grade deflation can be efficient and grade inflation is inefficient. Discriminating grades are in the social interest and in the self-interest of universities and students.

Grades as Signals

Dean Says Median Grade at Harvard College Is A-, Most Common Grade Is A

The Crimson
December 4, 2013

The median grade at Harvard College is an A-, and the most frequently awarded mark is an A, Dean of Undergraduate Education Jay M. Harris said on Tuesday afternoon, supporting suspicions that the College employs a softer grading standard than many of its peer institutions. ...

"A little bird has told me that the most frequently given grade at Harvard College right now is an A-," Mansfield said during the meeting's question period. "If this is true or nearly true, it represents a failure on the part of this faculty and its leadership to maintain our academic standards."...

...Classics Department chair Mark J. Schiefsky, ... said he was surprised by how high the median grade was.

"I don't know what should be done about it, but it seems to me troubling," Schiefsky said. "One has a range of grades to give and one would presumably expect a wider distribution."...

The issue of grade inflation has taken center stage at some of Harvard's peer institutions as well. In 2004, Princeton substantially restructured its grading system, instructing professors to award grades in the A-range to no more than 35 percent of their students in undergraduate coursework and no more than 55 percent of students in junior and senior year independent study. ...

Yale has initiated its own discussion about grading policies in the last year, forming an ad hoc committee on the subject. In a review last spring, that committee found that 62 percent of grades awarded at Yale College from 2010 to 2012 were in the A-range.

Copyright © 2014 The Harvard Crimson, Inc.

Matthew Q. Clarida and Nicholas P. Fandos "Substantiating Fears of Grade Inflation, Dean Says Median Grade at Harvard College Is A-, Most Common Grade Is A". The Harvard Crimson. 2 December 2013.

MyEconLab More Economics in the News

ESSENCE OF THE STORY

- The median grade at Harvard is an A-.

- The most frequently awarded grade is an A.

- Harvard's Dean of Undergraduate Education Jay suspects the College employs a softer grading standard than many similar institutions.

- Harvard's Classics Department Chair Mark J. Schiefsky says the high grades are troubling and he would "expect a wider distribution."

- Princeton has set guidelines that limit the percentage of grades in the A-range.

- At Yale, 62 percent of grades between 2010 and 2012 were in the A-range and the school has created a committee to review the matter.

ECONOMIC ANALYSIS

- Accurate grades provide valuable information to students and potential employers about a student's ability.

- Harvard, Princeton, and Yale (and most schools) want to provide accurate information and avoid grade inflation—awarding a high grade to most students.

- The labor market for new college graduates works badly with grade inflation and works well with accurate grading.

- Figure 1 shows a labor market for new college graduates when there is grade inflation.

- Students with high ability are not distinguished from other students, and the supply curve represents the supply of students of all ability levels.

- The demand curve shows the employers' willingness to hire new workers without knowledge of their true ability.

- Students get hired for a low wage rate. Eventually, they get sorted by ability as employers discover the true ability of their workers from on-the-job performance.

- Figures 2 and 3 show the outcome with accurate grading.

- In Fig. 2, students with high grades get high-wage jobs and in Fig. 3, students with low grades get low-wage jobs.

- The outcomes in Figs. 2 and 3 that arise immediately with accurate grading occur eventually with grade inflation as employers accumulate information about the abilities of the workers.

- But the cost to the student and the employer of discovering true ability is greater with grade inflation than with accurate grading.

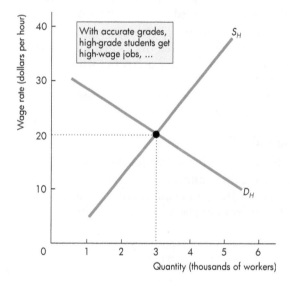

Figure 2 The Market for A Students

Figure 1 Market with Grade Inflation

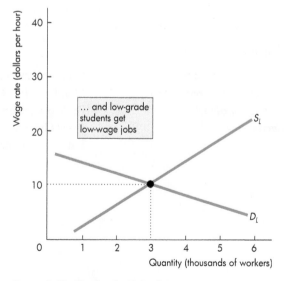

Figure 3 The Market for D Students

SUMMARY

Key Points

Decisions in the Face of Uncertainty (pp. 470–472)

- To make a rational choice under uncertainty, people choose the action that maximizes the expected utility of wealth.
- A decreasing marginal utility of wealth makes people risk averse. A sure outcome with a given expected wealth is preferred to a risky outcome with the same expected wealth—risk is costly.
- The cost of risk is found by comparing the expected wealth in a given risky situation with the wealth that gives the same utility but with no risk.

Working Problem 1 will give you a better understanding of decisions in the face of uncertainty.

Buying and Selling Risk (pp. 473–475)

- People trade risk in markets for insurance.
- By pooling risks, insurance companies can reduce the risks people face (from insured activities) at a lower cost than the value placed on the lower risk.

Working Problems 2 and 3 will give you a better understanding of buying and selling risk.

Private Information (pp. 476–480)

- Asymmetric information creates adverse selection and moral hazard problems.

- When it is not possible to distinguish good-quality products from lemons, too many lemons and too few good-quality products are traded in a pooling equilibrium.
- Signaling can overcome the lemons problem.
- In the market for used cars, warranties signal good cars and an efficient separating equilibrium occurs.
- Private information about credit risk is overcome by using signals and screening based on personal characteristics.
- Private information about risk in insurance markets is overcome by using the no-claim bonus and deductibles.

Working Problems 4 and 5 will give you a better understanding of private information.

Uncertainty, Information, and the Invisible Hand (p. 481)

- Less uncertainty and more information can be viewed as a good that has increasing marginal cost and decreasing marginal benefit.
- Competitive information markets might be efficient, but economies of scale might bring inefficient underproduction of information and insurance.

Working Problem 6 will give you a better understanding of uncertainty, information, and the invisible hand.

Key Terms

MyEconLab Key Terms Quiz

Adverse selection, 476
Asymmetric information, 476
Credit risk or default risk, 479
Expected utility, 471
Expected wealth, 470

Lemons problem, 476
Moral hazard, 476
Pooling equilibrium, 479
Private information, 476
Risk aversion, 470

Screening, 479
Separating equilibrium, 479
Signaling, 478

◆ WORKED PROBLEM

MyEconLab   You can work this problem in Chapter 20 Study Plan.

Lou is offered a risky summer lawn-mowing job. If he takes this job, there is a 50 percent chance that at the end of the summer he will have $5,000 and a 50 percent chance that he will have only $1,000. The table shows Lou's utility from his end-of-summer wealth.

Wealth (dollars)	Utility (units)
0	0
1,000	8
2,000	14
3,000	17
4,000	19
5,000	20
6,000	21

Questions

1. What is Lou's expected end-of-summer wealth from taking this job?

2. What is Lou's expected utility from taking this job?

3. Another firm offers Lou a job with no risk. How much end-of-summer wealth would Lou need from that job for him to take it in preference to the risky lawn-mowing job?

4. What is Lou's cost of risk?

Solutions

1. With a 50 percent chance of having $5,000 and a 50 percent chance of having $1,000, Lou's expected wealth equals $(5,000 \times 0.5) + (1,000 \times 0.5)$, which equals $3,000.

Key Point: Expected wealth is the average wealth calculated by using a formula that weights each possible outcome with the probablity (chance) that it will occur.

2. Lou's expected utility from taking this job depends on his utility from the two outcomes. Lou's utility from $5,000 is 20 units and his utility from $1,000 is 8 units. Each possibility occurs with a probability of 0.5, so his expected utility equals $(20 \times 0.5) + (8 \times 0.5) = 14$ units.

Key Point: Expected utility is the average utility calculated by using a formula that weights the utility from each outcome with the probablity (chance) that it will occur.

3. For Lou to take the no-risk job rather than the risky lawn-mowing job, he would need to get an end-of-summer utility that exceeds his expected utility of 14 units from the risky lawn-mowing job.

   From the data in the table, for Lou to have the same utility at the end of the summer as he'd get from the risky job, he would need the no-risk job to give him $2,000 of wealth.

Key Point: A risky outcome must have a larger expected wealth than a no-risk outcome to give the same expected utility.

4. Lou's cost of risk from taking the lawn-mowing job equals his expected wealth from taking the risky job ($3,000) minus the wealth from the no-risk job that gives him the same utility ($2,000) as the risky job. So for Lou, the cost of risk is $1,000.

Key Point: The cost of risk equals the amount that a person would have to be offered to create the incentive to bear the risk.

Key Figure

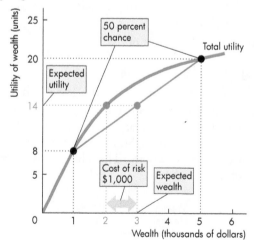

MyEconLab Interactive Animation

STUDY PLAN PROBLEMS AND APPLICATIONS

MyEconLab   You can work Problems 1 to 6 in Chapter 20 Study Plan and get instant feedback.

Decisions in the Face of Uncertainty (Study Plan 20.1)

1. The figure shows Lee's utility of wealth curve.

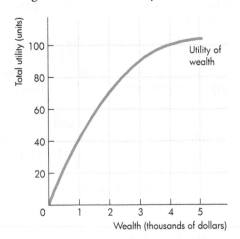

Lee is offered a job as a salesperson in which there is a 50 percent chance that she will make $4,000 a month and a 50 percent chance that she will make nothing.

a. What is Lee's expected income from taking this job?

b. What is Lee's expected utility from taking this job?

c. How much would another firm have to offer Lee with certainty to persuade her not to take the risky sales job?

d. What is Lee's cost of risk?

Buying and Selling Risk (Study Plan 20.2)

Use the following data to work Problems 2 and 3.
Larry lives in a neighborhood in which 20 percent of the cars are stolen every year. Larry's car, which he parks on the street overnight, is worth $20,000. (This is Larry's only wealth.) The table shows Larry's utility of wealth schedule.

Wealth (dollars)	Utility (units)
20,000	400
16,000	350
12,000	280
8,000	200
4,000	110
0	0

2. If Larry cannot buy auto theft insurance, what is his expected wealth and his expected utility?

3. High-Crime Auto Theft, an insurance company, offers to sell Larry insurance at $8,000 a year and promises to provide Larry with a replacement car worth $20,000 if his car is stolen. Is Larry willing to buy this insurance? If not, is he willing to pay $4,000 a year for such insurance?

Private Information (Study Plan 20.3)

4. Suppose that there are three national soccer leagues: Time League, Goal Difference League, and Bonus for Win League. The leagues are of equal quality, but the players are paid differently. Players in the Time League are paid by the hour for time spent practicing and playing. Players in the Goal Difference League are paid an amount that depends on the goals scored by the team minus the goals scored against it. Players in the Bonus for Win League are paid one wage for a loss, a higher wage for a tie, and the highest wage of all for a win.

a. Describe the predicted differences in the quality of the games played by each of the leagues.

b. Which league is the most attractive to players?

c. Which league will generate the largest profits?

5. You can't buy insurance against the risk of being sold a lemon. Why isn't there such a market? How does the market provide a buyer with some protection against being sold a lemon? What are the main ways in which markets overcome the lemons problem?

Uncertainty, Information, and the Invisible Hand

(Study Plan 20.4)

6. **Show Us Our Money**
I have no clue what my colleagues make and I consider my salary my own business. It turns out that could be a huge mistake. What if employers made all employee salaries known? If you think about it, who is served by all the secrecy? Knowing what other workers make might be more ammunition to gun for a raise.

Source: *Time*, May 12, 2008

Explain why a worker might be willing to pay for the salary information of other workers.

ADDITIONAL PROBLEMS AND APPLICATIONS

MyEconLab   You can work these problems in MyEconLab if assigned by your instructor.

Decisions in the Face of Uncertainty

Use the following table, which shows Jimmy's and Zenda's utility of wealth schedules, to work Problems 7 to 9.

Wealth	Jimmy's utility	Zenda's utility
0	0	0
100	200	512
200	300	640
300	350	672
400	375	678
500	387	681
600	393	683
700	396	684

7. What are Jimmy's and Zenda's expected utilities from a bet that gives them a 50 percent chance of having a wealth of $600 and a 50 percent chance of having nothing?

8. a. Calculate Jimmy's and Zenda's marginal utility of wealth schedules.

   b. Who is more risk averse, Jimmy or Zenda? How do you know?

9. Suppose that Jimmy and Zenda each have $400 and are offered a business investment opportunity that involves committing the entire $400 to the project. The project could return $600 (a profit of $200) with a probability of 0.85 or $200 (a loss of $200) with a probability of 0.15. Who goes for the project and who hangs on to the initial $400?

Use the following information to work Problems 10 to 12.

Two students, Jim and Kim, are offered summer jobs managing a student house-painting business. There is a 50 percent chance that either of them will be successful and end up with $21,000 of wealth to get them through the next school year. But there is also a 50 percent chance that either will end up with only $3,000 of wealth. Each could take a completely safe but back-breaking job picking fruit that would leave them with a guaranteed $9,000 at the end of the summer. The table in the next column shows Jim's and Kim's utility of wealth schedules.

Wealth	Jim's utility	Kim's utility
0	0	0
3,000	100	200
6,000	200	350
9,000	298	475
12,000	391	560
15,000	482	620
18,000	572	660
21,000	660	680

10. Does anyone take the painting job? If so, who takes it and why? Does anyone take the job picking fruit? If so, who takes it and why?

11. In Problem 10, what is each student's maximized expected utility? Who has the larger expected wealth? Who ends up with the larger wealth at the end of the summer?

12. In Problem 10, if one of the students takes the risky job, how much more would the fruit-picking job have needed to pay to attract that student?

Buying and Selling Risk

Use the following table, which shows Chris's utility of wealth schedule, to work Problems 13 and 14.

Chris's wealth is $5,000 and it consists entirely of her share in a risky ice cream business. If the summer is cold, the business will fail, and she will have no wealth. Where Chris lives there is a 50 percent chance each year that the summer will be cold.

Wealth (dollars)	Utility (units)
5,000	150
4,000	140
3,000	120
2,000	90
1,000	50
0	0

13. If Chris cannot buy cold-summer insurance, what is her expected wealth and what is her expected utility?

14. Business Loss Recovery, an insurance company, is willing to sell Chris cold-summer insurance at a price of $3,000 a year and promises to pay her

$5,000 if the summer is cold and the business fails. Is Chris willing to buy this loss insurance? If she is, is she willing to pay $4,000 a year for it?

Private Information

Use the following information to work Problems 15 to 17.

Larry has a good car that he wants to sell; Harry has a lemon that he wants to sell. Each knows what type of car he is selling. You are looking at used cars and plan to buy one.

15. If both Larry and Harry are offering their cars for sale at the same price, from whom would you most want to buy, Larry or Harry, and why?

16. If you made an offer of the same price to Larry and Harry, who would sell to you and why? Describe the adverse selection problem that arises if you offer the same price to Larry and Harry.

17. How can Larry signal that he is selling a good car so that you are willing to pay Larry the price that he knows his car is worth, and a higher price than what you are willing to offer Harry?

18. Pam is a safe driver and Fran is a reckless driver. Each knows what type of driver she is, but no one else knows. What might an automobile insurance company do to get Pam to signal that she is a safe driver so that it can offer her insurance at a lower premium than it offers to Fran?

19. Why do you think it is not possible to buy insurance against having to put up with a low-paying, miserable job? Explain why a market in insurance of this type would be valuable to workers but unprofitable for an insurance provider and so would not work.

Uncertainty, Information, and the Invisible Hand

Use the following news clip to work Problems 20 and 21.

Why We Worry About the Things We Shouldn't … and Ignore the Things We Should

We pride ourselves on being the only species that understands the concept of risk, yet we have a confounding habit of worrying about mere possibilities while ignoring probabilities, building barricades against perceived dangers while leaving ourselves exposed to real ones: 20% of all adults still smoke; nearly 20% of drivers and more than 30% of back-seat passengers don't use seat belts; two thirds of us

are overweight or obese. We dash across the street against the light and build our homes in hurricane-prone areas—and when they're demolished by a storm, we rebuild in the same spot.

Source: *Time*, December 4, 2006

20. Explain how "worrying about mere possibilities while ignoring probabilities" can result in people making decisions that not only fail to satisfy social interest, but also fail to satisfy self-interest.

21. How can information be used to improve people's decision making?

Economics in the News

22. After you have studied *Economics in the News* on pp. 482–483, answer the following questions.

a. What information do accurate grades provide that grade inflation hides?

b. If grade inflation became widespread in high schools, colleges, and universities, what new arrangements do you predict would emerge to provide better information about student ability?

c. Do you think grade inflation is in anyone's self-interest? Explain who benefits and how they benefit from grade inflation.

d. How do you think grade inflation might be controlled?

23. **Are You Paid What You're Worth?**

How do you know if your pay adequately reflects your contributions to your employer's profits? In many instances, you don't. Your employer has more and better information than you do about how your salary and bonus compare to others in your field, to others in your office, and relative to the company's profits in any given year. You can narrow the information gap a bit if you're willing to buy salary reports from compensation sources. For example, at $200, a quick-call salary report from Economic Research Institute will offer you compensation data for your position based on your years of experience, your industry and the place where your company is located.

Source: CNN, April 3, 2006

a. Explain the role that asymmetric information can play in worker wages.

b. What adverse selection problem exists if a firm offers lower wages to current workers?

c. What will determine how much a worker should actually pay for a detailed salary report?

For Whom?

PART SIX

During the past 35 years, the gap between the richest and the poorest in America has widened. But millions in Asia have been lifted from poverty and are now enjoying a high and rapidly rising standard of living. What are the forces that generate these trends? The answer to this question is the forces of demand and supply in factor markets. These forces determine wages, interest rates, rents, and the prices of natural resources. These forces also determine people's incomes.

In America, human capital and entrepreneurship are the most prized resources, and their incomes have grown most rapidly. In Asia, labor has seen its wage rates transformed. And in all regions rich in oil, incomes have risen on the back of high and fast-rising energy prices.

Many outstanding economists have advanced our understanding of factor markets and the role they play in helping to resolve the conflict between the demands of humans and the resources available. One of them is Thomas Robert Malthus.

Another is Harold Hotelling, whose prediction of an ever-rising price of nonrenewable natural resources implies an ever-falling rate of their use and an intensifying search for substitutes.

Yet another is Julian Simon, who challenged both the Malthusian gloom and the Hotelling Principle. He believed that people are the "ultimate resource" and predicted that a rising population lessens the pressure on natural resources. A bigger population provides a larger number of resourceful people who can discover more efficient ways of using scarce resources.

Thomas Robert Malthus *(1766–1834), an English clergyman and economist, was an extremely influential social scientist. In his best-selling* Essay on the Principle of Population, *published in 1798, he predicted that population growth would outstrip food production and said that wars, famine, and disease were inevitable unless population growth was held in check by marrying at a late age and living a celibate life. (He married at 38 a wife of 27, marriage ages that he recommended for others.)*

Malthus had a profound influence on Charles Darwin, who got the key idea that led him to the theory of natural selection from the Essay on the Principle of Population. *But it was also Malthus's gloomy predictions that made economics the "dismal science."*

> "The passion between the sexes has appeared in every age to be so nearly the same, that it may always be considered, in algebraic language, as a given quantity."
>
> **THOMAS ROBERT MALTHUS**
> *An Essay on the Principle of Population*

RAJ CHETTY is the William Henry Bloomberg Professor of Economics, at Harvard University, where he was also an undergraduate, earning his BA summa cum laude in 2000, and graduate student, completing his PhD in 2003.

Professor Chetty is also Director of Harvard's Lab for Economic Applications and Policy, Co-Director of the Public Economics Program or the National Bureau of Economic Research, a member of the Congressional Budget Office Panel of Economic Advisers, and editor of the Journal of Public Economics.

His list of honors is extraordinarily long and includes the 2013 John Bates Clark Medal of the American Economic Association, awarded to the best economist under 40 years of age, the National Tax Association Best Dissertation Prize in 2003, and the Harris, Hoopes, and Williams Prizes for the best thesis and undergraduate in economics at Harvard, in 2000.

He has published more than 20 papers in leading journals on a wide range of policy issues and come up with interesting answers, some of which he describes here.

Michael Parkin talked with Raj Chetty about his research and what we learn from it about how to design more effective government economic policies.

Every economics student learns that tax incidence and deadweight loss depend on the elasticities of supply and demand, and that one of the most crucial elasticities is that of the supply of labor. What does your work tell us about this elasticity? Is labor supply elastic or inelastic?

It is true that the labor supply elasticity is a key determinant of the deadweight loss from income taxation. If people are very responsive in how much they work, that is, if labor supply is very elastic with respect to tax rates, then having high tax rates will generate a lot of inefficiency.

My work has shown that the picture is actually quite a bit more complicated than that because there are many other factors that affect how people respond to tax changes beyond what we have in standard economic models.

> ... labor supply might be somewhat elastic in the long run ... [but in the short run] may not be very elastic.

To take one example, we usually assume that people perfectly understand and pay attention to the complicated income tax system that we face in the United States today. But we have a number of studies showing that in fact many people aren't aware of tax rates they face, don't really pay attention to tax changes, and may not, at least in the short run, respond by changing the amount they work when the tax code is changed in complicated ways.

The bottom line is that labor supply might be somewhat elastic in the long run if you've got very high tax rates, say, as in European economies for 50 years consistently. People might start to think "Oh, I don't get to keep so much of my paycheck, maybe it doesn't pay to work." With a short-run tax increase of 5 or 10 percent, our growing sense is that people may not respond as much, and labor supply may not be very elastic.

*Read the full interview with Raj Chetty in MyEconLab.

Abatement technology A production technology that reduces or prevents pollution. (p. 395)

Absolute advantage A person has an absolute advantage if that person is more productive than another person. (p. 40)

Adverse selection The tendency for people to *enter into agreements* in which they can use their private information to their own advantage and to the disadvantage of the uninformed party. (p. 476)

Allocative efficiency A situation in which goods and services are produced at the lowest possible cost and in the quantities that provide the greatest possible benefit. We cannot produce more of any good without giving up some of another good that we *value more highly*. (p. 35)

Antitrust law A law that regulates oligopolies and prevents them from becoming monopolies or behaving like monopolies. (p. 356)

Asymmetric information A market in which buyers or sellers have private information. (p. 476)

Average cost pricing rule A rule that sets price to cover cost including normal profit, which means setting the price equal to average total cost. (p. 314)

Average fixed cost Total fixed cost per unit of output. (p. 254)

Average product The average product of a factor of production. It equals total product divided by the quantity of the factor employed. (p. 249)

Average total cost Total cost per unit of output. (p. 254)

Average variable cost Total variable cost per unit of output. (p. 254)

Barrier to entry A natural or legal constraint that protects a firm from potential competitors. (p. 298)

Behavioral economics A study of the ways in which limits on the human brain's ability to compute and implement rational decisions influences economic behavior—both the decisions that people make and the consequences of those decisions for the way markets work. (p. 192)

Benefit The benefit of something is the gain or pleasure that it brings and is determined by preferences. (p. 9)

Big tradeoff The tradeoff between efficiency and fairness. (pp. 117, 460)

Bilateral monopoly A situation in which a monopoly seller faces a monopsony buyer. (p. 429)

Black market An illegal market in which the equilibrium price exceeds the legally imposed price ceiling. (p. 128)

Budget line The limit to a household's consumption choices. It marks the boundary between those combinations of goods and services that a household can afford to buy and those that it cannot afford. (pp. 178, 202)

Capital The tools, equipment, buildings, and other constructions that businesses use to produce goods and services. (p. 4)

Capital accumulation The growth of capital resources, including *human capital*. (p. 38)

Capture theory A theory that regulation serves the self-interest of the producer, who captures the regulator and maximizes economic profit. (p. 313)

Cartel A group of firms acting together—colluding— to limit output, raise the price, and increase economic profit. (p. 343)

Ceteris paribus Other things being equal—all other relevant things remaining the same. (p. 24)

Change in demand A change in buyers' plans that occurs when some influence on those plans other than the price of the good changes. It is illustrated by a shift of the demand curve. (p. 58)

Change in supply A change in sellers' plans that occurs when some influence on those plans other than the price of the good changes. It is illustrated by a shift of the supply curve. (p. 63)

Change in the quantity demanded A change in buyers' plans that occurs when the price of a good changes but all other influences on buyers' plans remain unchanged. It is illustrated by a movement along the demand curve. (p. 61)

Change in the quantity supplied A change in sellers' plans that occurs when the price of a good changes but all other influences on sellers' plans remain unchanged. It is illustrated by a movement along the supply curve. (p. 64)

Coase theorem The proposition that if property rights exist, if only a small number of parties are involved, and transactions costs are low, then private transactions are efficient, and it doesn't matter who has the property rights. (p. 396)

Collusive agreement An agreement between two (or more) producers to form a cartel to restrict output, raise the price, and increase profits. (p. 346)

Command system A method of allocating resources by the order (command) of someone in authority. In a firm a managerial hierarchy organizes production. (pp. 106, 229)

Common resource A resource that is rival and nonexcludable. (p. 372)

Comparative advantage A person or country has a comparative advantage in an activity if that person or country can perform the activity at a lower opportunity cost than anyone else or any other country. (p. 40)

Competitive market A market that has many buyers and many sellers, so no single buyer or seller can influence the price. (p. 56)

Complement A good that is used in conjunction with another good. (p. 59)

Constant returns to scale Features of a firm's technology that lead to constant long-run average cost as output increases. When constant returns to scale are present, the *LRAC* curve is horizontal. (p. 262)

Consumer equilibrium A situation in which a consumer has allocated all his or her available income in the way that, given the prices of goods and services, maximizes his or her total utility. (p. 181)

Consumer surplus The excess of the benefit received from a good over the amount paid for it. It is calculated as the marginal benefit (or value) of a good minus its price, summed over the quantity bought. (p. 109)

Contestable market A market in which firms can enter and leave so easily that firms in the market face competition from *potential* entrants. (p. 354)

Cooperative equilibrium The outcome of a game in which the players make and share the monopoly profit. (p. 352)

Credit risk The risk that a borrower, also known as a creditor, might not repay a loan. (p. 479)

Cross elasticity of demand The responsiveness of the demand for a good to a change in the price of a substitute or complement, other things remaining the same. It is calculated as the percentage change in the quantity demanded of the good divided by the percentage change in the price of the substitute or complement. (p. 92)

Deadweight loss A measure of inefficiency. It is equal to the decrease in total surplus that results from an inefficient level of production. (p. 114)

Default risk The risk that a borrower might not repay a loan. (p. 479)

Demand The entire relationship between the price of the good and the quantity demanded of it when all other influences on buyers' plans remain the same. It is illustrated by a demand curve and described by a demand schedule. (p. 57)

Demand curve A curve that shows the relationship between the quantity demanded of a good and its price when all other influences on consumers' planned purchases remain the same. (p. 58)

Deregulation The process of removing regulation of prices, quantities, entry, and other aspects of economic activity in a firm or industry. (p. 313)

Derived demand Demand for a factor of production—it is derived from the demand for the goods and services produced by that factor. (p. 421)

Diminishing marginal rate of substitution The general tendency for a person to be willing to give up

less of good y to get one more unit of good x, while at the same time remaining indifferent as the quantity of good x increases. (p. 206)

Diminishing marginal returns The tendency for the marginal product of an additional unit of a factor of production to be less than the marginal product of the previous unit of the factor. (p. 251)

Diminishing marginal utility The tendency for marginal utility to decrease as the quantity consumed of a good increases. (p. 180)

Direct relationship A relationship between two variables that move in the same direction. (p. 18)

Diseconomies of scale Features of a firm's technology that make average total cost rise as output increases—the *LRAC* curve slopes upward. (p. 262)

Dominant strategy equilibrium An equilibrium in which the best strategy for each player is to cheat *regardless of the strategy of the other player*. (p. 345)

Dumping The sale by a foreign firm of exports at a lower price than the cost of production. (p. 164)

Duopoly An oligopoly market in which two producers of a good or service compete. (p. 342)

Economic depreciation The *fall* in the market value of a firm's capital over a given period. (p. 225)

Economic efficiency A situation that occurs when the firm produces a given output at the least cost. (p. 227)

Economic growth The expansion of production possibilities. (p. 38)

Economic model A description of some aspect of the economic world that includes only those features of the world that are needed for the purpose at hand. (p. 11)

Economic profit A firm's total revenue minus its total cost, with total cost measured as the opportunity cost of production. (p. 224)

Economic rent Any surplus—consumer surplus, producer surplus, or economic profit. (p. 306)

Economics The social science that studies the *choices* that individuals,

businesses, governments, and entire societies make as they cope with *scarcity* and the *incentives* that influence and reconcile those choices. (p. 2)

Economies of scale Features of a firm's technology that make average total cost fall as output increases—the *LRAC* curve slopes downward. (pp. 238, 262)

Economies of scope Decreases in average total cost that occur when a firm uses specialized resources to produce a range of goods and services. (p. 239)

Efficient Resource use is efficient if it is *not* possible to make someone better off without making someone else worse off. (p. 5)

Efficient scale The quantity at which average total cost is a minimum—the quantity at the bottom of the U-shaped *ATC* curve. (p. 328)

Elastic demand Demand with a price elasticity greater than 1; other things remaining the same, the percentage change in the quantity demanded exceeds the percentage change in price. (p. 86)

Elasticity of supply The responsiveness of the quantity supplied of a good to a change in its price, other things remaining the same. (p. 94)

Entrepreneurship The human resource that organizes the other three factors of production: labor, land, and capital. (p. 4)

Equilibrium price The price at which the quantity demanded equals the quantity supplied. (p. 66)

Equilibrium quantity The quantity bought and sold at the equilibrium price. (p. 66)

Excess capacity A firm has excess capacity if it produces below its efficient scale. (p. 328)

Excludable A good or service or a resource is excludable if it is possible to prevent someone from enjoying the benefit of it. (p. 372)

Expected utility The utility value of what a person expects to own at a given point in time. (p. 471)

Expected wealth The money value of what a person expects to own at a given point in time. (p. 470)

Exports The goods and services that we sell to people in other countries. (p. 152)

Externality A cost of or a benefit from an action that falls on someone other than the person or firm choosing the action. (p. 392)

Factors of production The productive resources used to produce goods and services. (p. 3)

Firm An economic unit that hires factors of production and organizes those factors to produce and sell goods and services. (pp. 44, 224)

Four-firm concentration ratio A measure of market power that is calculated as the percentage of the value of sales accounted for by the four largest firms in an industry. (p. 234)

Free-rider problem The problem that the market would provide an inefficiently small quantity of a public good. (p. 374)

Game theory A set of tools for studying strategic behavior—behavior that takes into account the expected behavior of others and the recognition of mutual interdependence. (p. 344)

Gini ratio The ratio of the area between the line of equality and the Lorenz curve to the entire area beneath the line of equality. (p. 449)

Goods and services The objects that people value and produce to satisfy human wants. (p. 3)

Government failure A situation in which government actions lead to inefficiency—to either underprovision or overprovision. (p. 370)

Herfindahl–Hirschman Index A measure of market power that is calculated as the square of the market share of each firm (as a percentage) summed over the largest 50 firms (or over all firms if there are fewer than 50) in a market. (p. 234)

Hotelling Principle The idea that traders expect the price of a non-renewable natural resource to rise at a rate equal to the interest rate. (p. 434)

Human capital The knowledge and skill that people obtain from education, on-the-job training, and work experience. (p. 3)

Implicit rental rate The firm's opportunity cost of using its own capital. (p. 224)

Import quota A restriction that limits the maximum quantity of a good that may be imported in a given period. (p. 160)

Imports The goods and services that we buy from people in other countries. (p. 152)

Incentive A reward that encourages an action or a penalty that discourages one. (p. 2)

Incentive system A method of organizing production that uses a market-like mechanism inside the firm. (p. 229)

Income effect The effect of a change in income on buying plans, other things remaining the same. (p. 211)

Income elasticity of demand The responsiveness of demand to a change in income, other things remaining the same. It is calculated as the percentage change in the quantity demanded divided by the percentage change in income. (p. 91)

Indifference curve A line that shows combinations of goods among which a consumer is *indifferent*. (p. 205)

Individual transferable quota (ITQ) A production limit that is assigned to an individual who is free to transfer (sell) the quota to someone else. (p. 404)

Inelastic demand A demand with a price elasticity between 0 and 1; the percentage change in the quantity demanded is less than the percentage change in price. (p. 85)

Inferior good A good for which demand decreases as income increases. (p. 60)

Interest The income that capital earns. (p. 4)

Inverse relationship A relationship between variables that move in opposite directions. (p. 19)

Keynesian A macroeconomist who believes that left alone, the economy would rarely operate at full employment and that to achieve full employment, active help from fiscal policy and monetary policy is required. (p. 662)

Keynesian cycle theory A theory that fluctuations in investment driven by fluctuations in business confidence—summarized by the phrase "animal spirits"—are the main source of fluctuations in aggregate demand. (p. 712)

Labor The work time and work effort that people devote to producing goods and services. (p. 3)

Labor union An organized group of workers that aims to increase the wage rate and influence other job conditions. (p. 428)

Land The "gifts of nature" that we use to produce goods and services. (p. 3)

Law of demand Other things remaining the same, the higher the price of a good, the smaller is the quantity demanded of it; the lower the price of a good, the larger is the quantity demanded of it. (p. 57)

Law of diminishing returns As a firm uses more of a variable factor of production with a given quantity of the fixed factor of production, the marginal product of the variable factor of production eventually diminishes. (p. 251)

Law of supply Other things remaining the same, the higher the price of a good, the greater is the quantity supplied of it; the lower the price of a good, the smaller is the quantity supplied. (p. 62)

Legal monopoly A market in which competition and entry are restricted by the granting of a public franchise, government license, patent, or copyright. (p. 298)

Lemons problem The problem that in a market in which it is not possible to distinguish reliable products from lemons, there are too many lemons and too few reliable products traded. (p. 476)

Limit pricing The practice of setting the price at the highest level that inflicts a loss on an entrant. (p. 355)

Linear relationship A relationship between two variables that is illustrated by a straight line. (p. 18)

Long run The time frame in which the quantities of *all* factors of production can be varied. (p. 248)

Long-run average cost curve The relationship between the lowest attainable average total cost and output when the firm can change both the plant it uses and the quantity of labor it employs. (p. 261)

Lorenz curve A curve that graphs the cumulative percentage of income or wealth against the cumulative percentage of households. (p. 447)

Macroeconomics The study of the performance of the national economy and the global economy. (p. 2)

Margin When a choice is made by comparing a little more of something with its cost, the choice is made at the margin. (p. 10)

Marginal benefit The benefit that a person receives from consuming one more unit of a good or service. It is measured as the maximum amount that a person is willing to pay for one more unit of the good or service. (pp. 10, 36)

Marginal benefit curve A curve that shows the relationship between the marginal benefit of a good and the quantity of that good consumed. (p. 36)

Marginal cost The *opportunity cost* of producing *one* more unit of a good or service. It is the best alternative forgone. It is calculated as the increase in total cost divided by the increase in output. (pp. 10, 35, 254)

Marginal cost pricing rule A rule that sets the price of a good or service equal to the marginal cost of producing it. (p. 313)

Marginal external benefit The benefit from an additional unit of a good or service that people other than the consumer enjoy. (p. 406)

Marginal external cost The cost of producing an additional unit of a good or service that falls on people other than the producer. (p. 394)

Marginal private benefit The benefit from an additional unit of a good or

service that the consumer of that good or service receives. (p. 406)

Marginal private cost The cost of producing an additional unit of a good or service that is borne by the producer of that good or service. (p. 394)

Marginal product The increase in total product that results from a one-unit increase in the variable input, with all other inputs remaining the same. It is calculated as the increase in total product divided by the increase in the variable input employed, when the quantities of all other inputs remain the same. (p. 249)

Marginal rate of substitution The rate at which a person will give up good *y* (the good measured on the *y*-axis) to get an additional unit of good *x* (the good measured on the *x*-axis) while at the same time remaining indifferent (remaining on the same indifference curve) as the quantity of *x* increases. (p. 206)

Marginal revenue The change in total revenue that results from a one-unit increase in the quantity sold. It is calculated as the change in total revenue divided by the change in quantity sold. (p. 272)

Marginal social benefit The marginal benefit enjoyed by society—by the consumer of a good or service (marginal private benefit) plus the marginal benefit enjoyed by others (marginal external benefit). (p. 406)

Marginal social cost The marginal cost incurred by the producer and by everyone else on whom the cost falls—by society. It is the sum of marginal private cost and marginal external cost. (p. 394)

Marginal utility The *change* in total utility resulting from a one-unit increase in the quantity of a good consumed. (p. 179)

Marginal utility per dollar The marginal utility from a good that results from spending one more dollar on it. It is calculated as the marginal utility from the good divided by its price. (p. 182)

Market Any arrangement that enables buyers and sellers to get information and to do business with each other. (p. 44)

Market failure A situation in which a market delivers an inefficient outcome. (p. 114)

Market income The wages, interest, rent, and profit earned in factor markets and before paying income taxes. (p. 446)

Markup The amount by which the firm's price exceeds its marginal cost. (p. 329)

Microeconomics The study of the choices that individuals and businesses make, the way these choices interact in markets, and the influence of governments. (p. 2)

Minimum efficient scale The *smallest* quantity of output at which the long-run average cost reaches its lowest level. (p. 263)

Minimum wage A regulation that makes the hiring of labor below a specified wage rate illegal. The lowest wage at which a firm may legally hire labor. (p. 131)

Money Any commodity or token that is generally acceptable as a means of payment. (p. 44)

Money income Market income plus cash payments to households by the government. (p. 446)

Money price The number of dollars that must be given up in exchange for a good or service. (p. 56)

Monopolistic competition A market structure in which a large number of firms make similar but slightly different products and compete on product quality, price, and marketing, and firms are free to enter or exit the market. (pp. 233, 324)

Monopoly A market structure in which there is one firm, which produces a good or service that has no close substitutes and in which the firm is protected from competition by a barrier preventing the entry of new firms. (pp. 233, 298)

Monopsony A market in which there is a single buyer. (p. 429)

Moral hazard A tendency for people with private information, *after entering into an agreement*, to use that information for their own benefit and at the cost of the less-informed party. (p. 476)

Nash equilibrium The outcome of a game that occurs when player A takes the best possible action given the action of player B and player B takes the best possible action given the action of player A. (p. 345)

Natural monopoly A market in which economies of scale enable one firm to supply the entire market at the lowest possible cost. (p. 298)

Natural monopoly good A good that is nonrival and excludable. When buyers can be excluded if they don't pay but the good is nonrival, marginal cost is zero. (p. 372)

Negative externality An externality that arises from either production or consumption and that imposes an external cost. (p. 392)

Negative relationship A relationship between variables that move in opposite directions. (p. 19)

Neuroeconomics The study of the activity of the human brain when a person makes an economic decision. (p. 193)

Nonexcludable A good or service or a resource is nonexcludable if it is impossible (or extremely costly) to prevent someone from enjoying its benefits. (p. 372)

Nonrenewable natural resources Natural resources that can be used only once. (p. 420)

Nonrival A good or service or a resource is nonrival if its use by one person does not decrease the quantity available for someone else. (p. 372)

Normal good A good for which demand increases as income increases. (p. 60)

Normal profit The return to entrepreneurship is normal profit and it is the profit that an entrepreneur earns *on average*. (p. 225)

Offshore outsourcing A U.S. firm buys finished goods, components, or services from firms in other countries. (p. 165)

Oligopoly A market structure in which a small number of firms compete. (pp. 233, 342)

Opportunity cost The highest-valued alternative that we must give up to get something. (pp. 9, 33)

Payoff matrix A table that shows the payoffs for every possible action by each player for every possible action by each other player. (p. 344)

Perfect competition A market in which there are many firms each selling an identical product; there are many buyers; there are no restrictions on entry into the industry; firms in the industry have no advantage over potential new entrants; and firms and buyers are well informed about the price of each firm's product. (pp. 233, 272)

Perfectly elastic demand Demand with an infinite price elasticity; the quantity demanded changes by an infinitely large percentage in response to a tiny price change. (p. 85)

Perfectly inelastic demand Demand with a price elasticity of zero; the quantity demanded remains constant when the price changes. (p. 85)

Perfect price discrimination Price discrimination that occurs when a firm sells each unit of output for the highest price that anyone is willing to pay for it. The firm extracts the entire consumer surplus. (p. 310)

Pigovian taxes Taxes that are used as an incentive for producers to cut back on an activity that creates an external cost. (p. 397)

Political equilibrium The situation in which the choices of voters, firms, politicians, and bureaucrats are all compatible and no group can see a way of improving its position by making a different choice. (p. 371)

Pooling equilibrium The equilibrium in a market when only one message is available and an uninformed person cannot determine quality. (p. 479)

Positive externality An externality that arises from either production or consumption and that creates an external benefit. (p. 392)

Positive relationship A relationship between two variables that move in the same direction. (p. 18)

Poverty A state in which a household's income is too low to be able to buy the quantities of food, shelter, and clothing that are deemed necessary. (p. 451)

Predatory pricing Setting a low price to drive competitors out of business with the intention of setting a monopoly price when the competition has gone. (p. 358)

Preferences A description of a person's likes and dislikes and the intensity of those feelings. (pp. 9 36, 179)

Price cap A regulation that makes it illegal to charge a price higher than a specified level. (p. 128)

Price cap regulation A rule that specifies the highest price that the firm is permitted to set—a price ceiling. (p. 315)

Price ceiling A regulation that makes it illegal to charge a price higher than a specified level. (p. 128)

Price discrimination The practice of selling different units of a good or service for different prices. (p. 299)

Price effect The effect of a change in the price of a good on the quantity of the good consumed, other things remaining the same. (p. 209)

Price elasticity of demand A units-free measure of the responsiveness of the quantity demanded of a good to a change in its price, when all other influences on buyers' plans remain the same. (p. 84)

Price floor A regulation that makes it illegal to trade at a price lower than a specified level. (p. 131)

Price taker A firm that cannot influence the price of the good or service it produces. (p. 272)

Principal–agent problem The problem of devising compensation rules that induce an *agent* to act in the best interest of a *principal*. (p. 229)

Principle of minimum differentiation The tendency for competitors to make themselves similar to appeal to the maximum number of clients or voters. (p. 376)

Private good A good or service that is both rival and excludable. (p. 372)

Private information Information about the value of an item being traded that is possessed by only buyers or sellers. (p. 476)

Producer surplus The excess of the amount received from the sale of a good or service over the cost of producing it. It is calculated as the price of a good minus the marginal cost (or minimum supply-price), summed over the quantity sold. (p. 111)

Product differentiation Making a product slightly different from the product of a competing firm. (pp. 233, 324)

Production efficiency A situation in which goods and services are produced at the lowest possible cost. (p. 33)

Production possibilities frontier The boundary between those combinations of goods and services that can be produced and those combinations that cannot. (p. 32)

Production quota An upper limit to the quantity of a good that may be produced in a specified period. (p. 139)

Profit The income earned by entrepreneurship. (p. 4)

Progressive income tax A tax on income at an average rate that increases as income increases. (p. 459)

Property rights The social arrangements that govern the ownership, use, and disposal of anything that people value. Property rights are enforceable in the courts. (pp. 44, 395)

Proportional income tax A tax on income at a constant rate, regardless of the level of income. (p. 459)

Public choice A decision that has consequences for many people and perhaps for the entire society. (p. 370)

Public good A good or service that is both nonrival and nonexcludable. It can be consumed simultaneously by everyone and no one can be excluded from enjoying its benefits. (p. 372)

Public production The production of a good or service by a public authority that receives its revenue from the government. (p. 407)

Quantity demanded The amount of a good or service that consumers plan to buy during a given time period at a particular price. (p. 57)

Quantity supplied The amount of a good or service that producers plan to sell during a given time period at a particular price. (p. 62)

Rate of return regulation A regulation that requires the firm to justify its price by showing that its return on capital doesn't exceed a specified target rate. (p. 314)

Rational choice A choice that compares costs and benefits and achieves the greatest benefit over cost for the person making the choice. (p. 9)

Real income A household's income expressed as a quantity of goods that the household can afford to buy. (p. 203)

Regressive income tax A tax on income at an average rate that decreases as income increases. (p. 459)

Regulation Rules administered by a government agency to influence prices, quantities, entry, and other aspects of economic activity in a firm or industry. (p. 313)

Relative price The ratio of the price of one good or service to the price of another good or service. A relative price is an opportunity cost. (pp. 56, 203)

Rent The income that land earns. (p. 4)

Rent ceiling A regulation that makes it illegal to charge a rent higher than a specified level. (p. 128)

Rent seeking The lobbying for special treatment by the government to create economic profit or to divert consumer surplus or producer surplus away from others. The pursuit of wealth by capturing economic rent. (pp. 167, 306)

Resale price maintenance A distributor's agreement with a manufacturer to resell a product *at or above a specified minimum price*. (p. 357)

Risk aversion The dislike of risk. (p. 470)

Rival A good, service, or a resource is rival if its use by one person decreases the quantity available for someone else. (p. 372)

Scarcity Our inability to satisfy all our wants. (p. 2)

Scatter diagram A graph that plots the value of one variable against the value of another variable for a number of different values of each variable. (p. 16)

Screening Inducing an informed party to reveal relevant private information. (p. 479)

Search activity The time spent looking for someone with whom to do business. (p. 128)

Self-interest The choices that you think are the best ones available for you are choices made in your self-interest. (p. 5)

Separating equilibrium The equilibrium in a market when signaling provides full information to a previously uninformed person. (p. 479)

Short run The time frame in which the quantity of at least one factor of production is fixed and the quantities of the other factors can be varied. The fixed factor is usually capital—that is, the firm uses a given plant. (p. 248)

Short-run market supply curve A curve that shows the quantity supplied in a market at each price when each firm's plant and the number of firms remain the same. (p. 278)

Shutdown point The price and quantity at which the firm is indifferent between producing the profit-maximizing output and shutting down temporarily. The shutdown point occurs at the price and the quantity at which average variable cost is a minimum. (p. 276)

Signal An action taken by an informed person (or firm) to send a message to uninformed people. (p. 332)

Signaling A situation in which an informed person takes actions that send information to uninformed persons. (p. 478)

Single-price monopoly A monopoly that must sell each unit of its output for the same price to all its customers. (p. 299)

Slope The change in the value of the variable measured on the y-axis divided by the change in the value of the variable measured on the x-axis. (p. 22)

Social interest Choices that are the best ones for society as a whole. (p. 5)

Social interest theory A theory that the political and regulatory process relentlessly seeks out inefficiency and introduces regulation that eliminates deadweight loss and allocates resources efficiently. (p. 313)

Strategies All the possible actions of each player in a game. (p. 344)

Subsidy A payment made by the government to a producer. (pp. 140, 407)

Substitute A good that can be used in place of another good. (p. 59)

Substitution effect The effect of a change in price of a good or service on the quantity bought when the consumer (hypothetically) remains indifferent between the original and the new consumption situations—that is, the consumer remains on the same indifference curve. (p. 212)

Sunk cost The past expenditure on a plant that has no resale value. (p. 248)

Supply The entire relationship between the price of a good and the quantity supplied of it when all other influences on producers' planned sales remain the same. It is described by a supply schedule and illustrated by a supply curve. (p. 62)

Supply curve A curve that shows the relationship between the quantity supplied of a good and its price when all other influences on producers' planned sales remain the same. (p. 62)

Symmetry principle A requirement that people in similar situations be treated similarly. (p. 118)

Tariff A tax that is imposed by the importing country when an imported good crosses its international boundary. (p. 157)

Tax incidence The division of the burden of the tax between the buyer and the seller. (p. 133)

Technological change The development of new goods and of better ways of producing goods and services. (p. 38)

Technological efficiency A situation that occurs when the firm produces a given output by using the least amount of inputs. (p. 227)

Technology Any method of producing a good or service. (p. 226)

Total cost The cost of all the productive resources that a firm uses. (p. 253)

Total fixed cost The cost of the firm's fixed inputs. (p. 253)

Total product The maximum output that a given quantity of labor can produce. (p. 249)

Total revenue The value of a firm's sales. It is calculated as the price of the good multiplied by the quantity sold. (pp. 88, 272)

Total revenue test A method of estimating the price elasticity of demand by observing the change in total revenue that results from a change in the price, when all other influences on the quantity sold remain the same. (p. 88)

Total surplus The sum of consumer surplus and producer surplus. (p. 112)

Total utility The total benefit that a person gets from the consumption of all the different goods and services. (p. 179)

Total variable cost The cost of all the firm's variable inputs. (p. 253)

Tradeoff A constraint that involves giving up one thing to get something else. (p. 9)

Tragedy of the commons The absence of incentives to prevent the overuse and depletion of a commonly owned resource. (p. 401)

Transactions costs The opportunity costs of making trades in a market.

The costs that arise from finding someone with whom to do business, of reaching an agreement about the price and other aspects of the exchange, and of ensuring that the terms of the agreement are fulfilled. (pp. 115, 238, 396)

Tying arrangement An agreement to sell one product only if the buyer agrees to buy another, different product. (p. 357)

Unit elastic demand Demand with a price elasticity of 1; the percentage change in the quantity demanded equals the percentage change in price. (p. 85)

Utilitarianism A principle that states that we should strive to achieve "the greatest happiness for the greatest number of people." (p. 116)

Utility The benefit or satisfaction that a person gets from the consumption of goods and services. (p. 179)

Value of marginal product The value to the firm of hiring one more unit of a factor of production. It is calculated as the price of a unit of output multiplied by the marginal product of the factor of production. (p. 421)

Voucher A token that the government provides to households, which they can use to buy specified goods and services. (pp. 383, 407)

Wages The income that labor earns. (p. 4)

Wealth The value of all the things that people own—the market value of their assets—at a point in time. (p. 448)

Abel/Bernanke/Croushore
Macroeconomics*

Acemoglu/Laibson/List
Economics*

Bade/Parkin
Foundations of Economics*

Berck/Helfand
*The Economics of the
Environment*

Bierman/Fernandez
*Game Theory with
Economic Applications*

Blanchard
Macroeconomics*

Blau/Ferber/Winkler
*The Economics of Women,
Men, and Work*

**Boardman/Greenberg/
Vining/ Weimer**
Cost-Benefit Analysis

Boyer
*Principles of Transportation
Economics*

Branson
*Macroeconomic Theory
and Policy*

Bruce
*Public Finance and the
American Economy*

Carlton/Perloff
*Modern Industrial
Organization*

Case/Fair/Oster
Principles of Economics*

Chapman
*Environmental Economics:
Theory, Application,
and Policy*

Cooter/Ulen
Law & Economics

Daniels/VanHoose
*International Monetary &
Financial Economics*

Downs
*An Economic Theory
of Democracy*

Ehrenberg/Smith
Modern Labor Economics

Farnham
Economics for Managers

Folland/Goodman/Stano
*The Economics of Health
and Health Care*

Fort
Sports Economics

Froyen
Macroeconomics

Fusfeld
The Age of the Economist

Gerber
International Economics*

González-Rivera
*Forecasting for Economics
and Business*

Gordon
Macroeconomics*

Greene
Econometric Analysis

Gregory
Essentials of Economics

Gregory/Stuart
*Russian and Soviet
Economic Performance
and Structure*

Hartwick/Olewiler
*The Economics of Natural
Resource Use*

Heilbroner/Milberg
*The Making of the
Economic Society*

Heyne/Boettke/Prychitko
*The Economic Way
of Thinking*

Holt
*Markets, Games, and
Strategic Behavior*

Hubbard/O'Brien
Economics*

*Money, Banking, and the
Financial System**

**Hubbard/O'Brien/
Rafferty**
Macroeconomics*

Hughes/Cain
American Economic History

Husted/Melvin
International Economics

Jehle/Reny
*Advanced Microeconomic
Theory*

Johnson-Lans
*A Health Economics
Primer*

Keat/Young/Erfle
Managerial Economics

Klein
*Mathematical Methods
for Economics*

Krugman/Obstfeld/Melitz
*International Economics:
Theory & Policy**

Laidler
The Demand for Money

Leeds/von Allmen
The Economics of Sports

**Leeds/von Allmen/
Schiming**
Economics*

Lynn
*Economic Development:
Theory and Practice for
a Divided World*

Miller
Economics Today*

*Understanding Modern
Economics*

Miller/Benjamin
*The Economics of Macro
Issues*

Miller/Benjamin/North
*The Economics of Public
Issues*

Mills/Hamilton
Urban Economics

Mishkin
*The Economics of Money,
Banking, and Financial
Markets**

*The Economics of Money,
Banking, and Financial
Markets, Business School
Edition**

*Macroeconomics: Policy
and Practice**

Murray
*Econometrics: A Modern
Introduction*

O'Sullivan/Sheffrin/Perez
*Economics: Principles,
Applications and Tools**

Parkin
Economics*

Perloff
Microeconomics*

*Microeconomics: Theory
and Applications with
Calculus**

Perloff/Brander
*Managerial Economics
and Strategy**

Phelps
Health Economics

Pindyck/Rubinfeld
Microeconomics*

**Riddell/Shackelford/
Stamos/ Schneider**
*Economics: A Tool for
Critically Understanding
Society*

Roberts
*The Choice: A Fable
of Free Trade and Protection*

Rohlf
*Introduction to Economic
Reasoning*

Roland
Development Economics

Scherer
*Industry Structure, Strategy,
and Public Policy*

Schiller
*The Economics of Poverty
and Discrimination*

Sherman
Market Regulation

Stock/Watson
Introduction to Econometrics

Studenmund
*Using Econometrics:
A Practical Guide*

Tietenberg/Lewis
*Environmental and
Natural Resource
Economics Environmental
Economics and Policy*

Todaro/Smith
Economic Development

Waldman/Jensen
*Industrial Organization:
Theory and Practice*

**Walters/Walters/Appel/
Callahan/Centanni/
Maex/O'Neill**
*Econversations: Today's
Students Discuss Today's
Issues*

Weil
Economic Growth

Williamson
Macroeconomics

* denotes MyEconLab titles   Visit www.myeconlab.com to learn more

Taken from: *Microeconomics*, Fifth Edition, by R. Glenn Hubbard and Anthony Patrick O'Brien

CHAPTER
8

Firms, the Stock Market, and Corporate Governance

Chapter Outline and Learning Objectives

Facebook Learns the Benefits and Costs of Becoming a Publicly Owned Firm

When Mark Zuckerberg started Facebook in 2004, he was a sophomore in college. Just nine years later, Facebook had 1.1 billion active users worldwide. Zuckerberg started Facebook because he believed that people were less interested in meeting new friends online—the assumption built into other social networking sites—than they were in staying in touch with the friends they already had. On Facebook, pages are typically visible only to people the user has linked to, or "friended," which reduces the problem of fake identities that plagued other sites.

By the fall of 2011, Zuckerberg faced a decision: Any business experiencing the runaway success of Facebook needs to raise funds quickly to finance its expansion. Some businesses raise funds by borrowing from banks. Large firms, as Facebook has become, have the ability to sell stocks and bonds to investors in financial markets. Firms that sell stock that is traded in financial markets such as the New York Stock Exchange are called public firms, while firms that do not sell stock are called private firms. For Zuckerberg, turning Facebook into a public firm and selling stock would raise revenue, but buyers of the stock would have partial ownership of the firm and a claim on its profits and might question Zuckerberg's leadership. Zuckerberg would retain control but feared that he might no longer have a completely free hand to continue Facebook's expansion.

Finally, in May 2012, Facebook sold shares of stock to the general public. Many individual investors were eager to buy shares at the initial price of $38 per share. During the following year, though, as more people began using Facebook on smartphones and tablets than on computers, Facebook had difficulty selling advertisements, and its revenue grew more slowly than expected. As a result, Facebook's stock price fluctuated. In 2013, Facebook's stock finally rose above its initial price of $38 per share, providing investors who had bought at that price with significant gains.

As we will see in this chapter, financial markets are an important source of funds to many firms and an important source of investment opportunities to households. More generally, a well-functioning financial system is crucial to the health of the economy.

Sources: Based on Jessi Hempel, "How Facebook Is Taking over Our Lives," *Fortune*, March 11, 2009; Khadeeja Safdar, "Facebook, One Year Later: What Really Happened in the Biggest IPO Flop Ever," *Atlantic*, May 20, 2013; and Evelyn Rusli, "After IPO, Facebook Gets Serious about Making Money," *Wall Street Journal*, May 16, 2013.

Economics in Your Life

Do Corporate Managers Act in the Best Interests of Shareholders?

Although stockholders legally own corporations, managers often have a great deal of freedom in deciding how corporations are run. As a result, managers can make decisions, such as spending money on large corporate headquarters or decorating their offices with expensive paintings, that are in their interests but not in the interests of the shareholders. If managers make decisions that waste money and lower the profits of a firm, the price of the firm's stock will fall, which hurts the investors who own the stock. Suppose you are considering buying stock in a corporation. Why will it be difficult to get the managers to act in your interests rather than in their own? Given this problem, should you ever take on the risk of buying stock? As you read this chapter, try to answer these questions. You can check your answers against those we provide on **page 255** at the end of this chapter.

I n this chapter, we look at firms: how they are organized, how they raise funds, and the information they provide to investors. As we have discussed in earlier chapters, firms in a market system are responsible for organizing the factors of production to produce goods and services. Firms are the vehicles entrepreneurs use to earn profits. To succeed, entrepreneurs must meet consumers' wants by producing new or better goods and services or by finding ways to produce existing goods and services at a lower cost so that they can be sold at a lower price. Entrepreneurs also need access to sufficient funds, and they must be able to efficiently organize production. As the typical firm in many industries has become larger over the past 100 years, the task of efficiently organizing production has become more difficult. In the final section of this chapter, we look at problems of *corporate governance* that have occurred in recent years. We also look at the steps firms and the government have taken to avoid similar problems in the future.

Categorize the major types of firms in the United States.

Sole proprietorship A firm owned by a single individual and not organized as a corporation.

Partnership A firm owned jointly by two or more persons and not organized as a corporation.

Corporation A legal form of business that provides owners with protection from losing more than their investment should the business fail.

Asset Anything of value owned by a person or a firm.

Limited liability The legal provision that shields owners of a corporation from losing more than they have invested in the firm.

Types of Firms

In studying a market economy, it is important to understand the basics of how firms operate. In the United States, there are three main categories of firms: *sole proprietorships*, *partnerships*, and *corporations*. A **sole proprietorship** is a firm owned by a single individual. Although most sole proprietorships are small, some employ many workers and earn large profits. **Partnerships** are firms owned jointly by two or more—sometimes many—persons. Most law and accounting firms are partnerships. Some of them can be quite large. For instance, in 2013, the Baker & McKenzie law firm based in Chicago had 1,400 partners. Most large firms, though, are organized as *corporations*. A **corporation** is a legal form of business that provides owners with protection from losing more than their investment in the firm should the business fail.

Who Is Liable? Limited and Unlimited Liability

A key distinction among the three types of firms is that the owners of sole proprietorships and partnerships have unlimited liability, which means that there is no legal distinction between the personal assets of the owners of the firm and the assets of the firm. An **asset** is anything of value owned by a person or a firm. If a sole proprietorship or a partnership owes a lot of money to the firm's suppliers or employees, the suppliers and employees have a legal right to sue the firm for payment, even if in order to pay their debts the firm's owners have to sell some of their personal assets, such as stocks or bonds. In other words, with sole proprietorships and partnerships, the owners are not legally distinct from the firms they own.

It may only seem fair that the owners of a firm be responsible for the firm's debts. But early in the nineteenth century, it became clear to many state legislatures in the United States that unlimited liability was a significant problem for any firm that was attempting to raise funds from large numbers of investors. An investor might be interested in making a relatively small investment in a firm but be unwilling to become a partner in the firm, for fear of placing at risk all of his or her personal assets if the firm were to fail. To get around this problem, state legislatures began to pass *general incorporation laws*, which allowed firms to be organized as corporations. Under the corporate form of business, the owners of a firm have **limited liability**, which means that if the firm fails, the owners can never lose more than the amount they have invested in the firm. The personal assets of the owners of the firm are not affected by the failure of the firm. In fact, in the eyes of the law, a corporation is a legal "person," separate from its owners. Limited liability has made it possible for corporations to raise funds by issuing shares of stock to large numbers of investors. For example, if you buy a share of Facebook stock, you are a part owner of the firm, but even if Facebook were to go bankrupt, you would

	Sole Proprietorship	Partnership	Corporation
Advantages	• Control by owner • No layers of management	• Ability to share work • Ability to share risks	• Limited personal liability • Greater ability to raise funds
Disadvantages	• Unlimited personal liability • Limited ability to raise funds	• Unlimited personal liability • Limited ability to raise funds	• Costly to organize • Possible double taxation of income

Table 8.1

Differences among Business Organizations

not be personally responsible for any of Facebook's debts. Therefore, you could not lose more than the amount you paid for the stock.

Organizing a firm as a corporation also has some disadvantages. In the United States, corporate profits are taxed twice—once at the corporate level and again when investors in the firm receive a share of the firm's profits. Corporations generally are larger than sole proprietorships and partnerships and are therefore more difficult to organize and run. Table 8.1 reviews the advantages and disadvantages of different forms of business organization.   MyEconLab Concept Check

Corporations Earn the Majority of Revenue and Profits

Figure 8.1 gives basic statistics on the three types of business organizations. Panel (a) shows that almost three-quarters of all firms are sole proprietorships. Panels (b) and (c) show that although only 18 percent of all firms are corporations, they account for a majority of the revenue and profits earned by all firms. *Profit* is the difference between revenue and the total cost to a firm of producing the goods and services it offers for sale.

There are more than 5.8 million corporations in the United States, but only 35,000 have annual revenues of more than $50 million. We can think of these 35,000 firms—including Apple, McDonald's, and Facebook—as representing "big business." These large firms earn more than 80 percent of the total profits of all corporations in the United States.   MyEconLab Concept Check

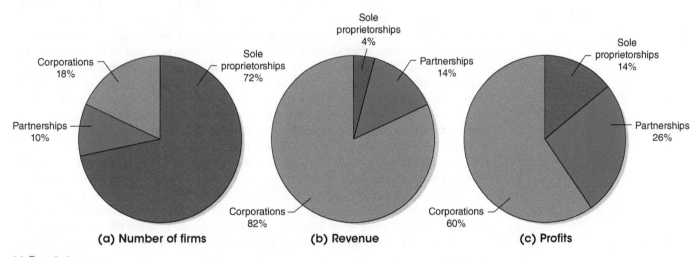

(a) Number of firms   **(b) Revenue**   **(c) Profits**

MyEconLab Animation

Figure 8.1   **Business Organizations: Sole Proprietorships, Partnerships, and Corporations**

The three types of firms in the United States are sole proprietorships, partnerships, and corporations. Panel (a) shows that only 18 percent of all firms are corporations. Yet, as panels (b) and (c) show, corporations account for a majority of the revenue and profits earned by all firms.

Source: Internal Revenue Service, *Statistics on Income.*

How Important Are Small Businesses to the U.S. Economy?

We have seen that although a large majority of all firms are sole proprietorships, they account for only a small fraction of total revenues and profits earned by all firms. In addition, as the following figure shows, more than 70 percent of people work at firms that have 50 or more employees. Does this mean that small businesses are not important to the U.S. economy?

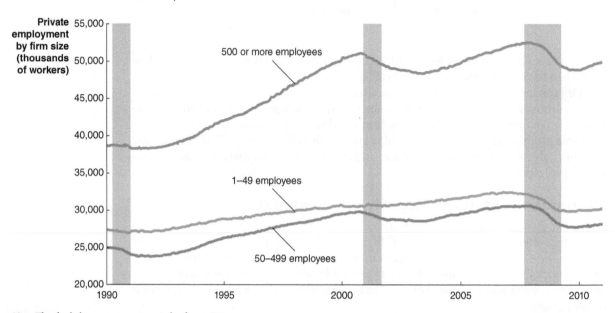

Note: The shaded areas represent periods of recession.

Source: U.S. Bureau of Labor Statistics, "Experimental Size Class Employment, Hours, and Earnings Series from the Current Employment Statistics Survey," July 26, 2012.

On the contrary, most economists would argue that small firms are vital to the health of the economy. Starting a small firm provides an entrepreneur with a vehicle for bringing a new product or process to market. Finding funds to start a small firm is often difficult, though, because a new firm lacks a record of operating profitably, so banks and other lenders worry that the firm won't be able to pay back borrowed money. As a result, more than 80 percent of small firms are started using funds provided by the founders and their families, by borrowing on credit cards, or by taking out loans against the value of the founders' homes. While anyone starting a new firm hopes to become successful, perhaps even wealthy, founding a company can also provide employment opportunities for workers and new goods and services for consumers. In most years, more than 600,000 new firms open in the United States, and, of these, more than 95 percent employ fewer than 20 workers. In a typical year, new small firms create 3.3 million jobs. Forty percent of all new jobs are created by small firms, and in some years more than half are. Strikingly, more than 85 percent of all jobs created by new firms of all sizes are created by small firms.

Although, on average, jobs at small firms pay lower wages than jobs at large firms and are less likely to provide fringe benefits, such as health insurance and retirement accounts, workers at small firms tend to be younger, and the first job for many workers is often with a small firm. Small firms are also less likely than large firms to lay off workers during a recession.

Entrepreneurs founding small firms have been the source of many important new goods and services, even though large firms spend much more on research and development than do small firms. Some economists have argued that although spending on research and development by large firms frequently leads to important improvements in existing products, innovative new products are often introduced by small firms. For instance, during the late nineteenth and early twentieth centuries, Thomas Edison, Henry Ford, and the Wright Brothers were all responsible for introducing important products shortly after starting what were initially very small firms. In more recent years, Bill Gates, Steve Jobs, Michael Dell, and Mark Zuckerberg decided that the best way to develop their ideas was by founding Microsoft, Apple, Dell Computer, and Facebook, rather than by choosing to work for large corporations. Each of these firms began with a handful of employees, and the key products and processes they pioneered were developed long before they evolved into the large firms they are today.

Sources: David Neumark, Brandon Wall, and Junfu Zhang, "Do Small Businesses Create More Jobs? New Evidence for the United States from the National Establishment Time Series," *Review of Economics and Statistics*, Vol. 93, No. 1, February 2011, pp. 16–29; Ben Casselman, "Small Business Tops in Job Creation, but Also Job Cuts," *Wall Street Journal*, January 29, 2013; Amar Bhidé, *The Origins and Evolution of New Businesses*, New York: Oxford University Press, 2003; Giuseppe Moscarini and Fabien Postel-Vinay, "The Contribution of Large and Small Employers to Job Creation at Times of High and Low Unemployment," *American Economic Review*, Vol. 102, No. 6, October 2012, pp. 2509–2539; data are from *The Statistical Abstract of the United States*; the U.S. Small Business Administration; and the U.S. Bureau of Labor Statistics.

Your Turn: Test your understanding by doing related problems 1.8 and 1.9 on page 256 at the end of this chapter.

MyEconLab Study Plan

The Structure of Corporations and the Principal–Agent Problem

Describe the typical management structure of corporations and understand the concepts of separation of ownership from control and the principal–agent problem.

Because large corporations account for a majority of sales and profits in the economy, it is important to know how they are managed. Most large corporations have a similar management structure. The way in which a corporation is structured and the effect that structure has on the corporation's behavior is referred to as **corporate governance**.

Corporate Structure and Corporate Governance

Corporate governance The way in which a corporation is structured and the effect that structure has on the corporation's behavior.

Corporations are legally owned by their *shareholders*, the owners of the corporation's stock. Unlike with a sole proprietorship, a corporation's shareholders, although they are the firm's owners, do not manage the firm directly. Instead, they elect a *board of directors* to represent their interests. The board of directors appoints a *chief executive officer* (CEO) to run the day-to-day operations of the corporation. Sometimes the board of directors also appoints other members of *top management*, such as the *chief financial officer* (CFO). At other times, the CEO appoints other members of top management. Members of top management, including the CEO and CFO, often serve on the board of directors. They are called *inside directors*. Members of the board of directors who do not have a direct management role in the firm are called *outside directors*. The outside directors are intended to act as a check on the decisions of top managers, but the distinction between an outside director and an inside director is not always clear. For example, the CEO of a firm that sells a good or service to a large corporation may sit on the corporation's board of directors. Although technically an outside director, this person may be reluctant to oppose the top managers because they have the power to stop purchasing from his or her firm. In some instances, top managers have effectively controlled their firms' boards of directors.

Unlike the owners of family businesses, the top management of a large corporation does not generally own a large share of the firm's stock, so large corporations have a **separation of ownership from control**. Although the shareholders actually own the firm, the top management controls the firm's day-to-day operations. Because top managers own only a small percentage of the firm's stock, they may decrease the firm's profits by spending money to purchase private jets or schedule management meetings at luxurious resorts. Economists refer to the conflict between the interests of shareholders and the interests of the top management as a **principal–agent problem**.[1] This problem occurs when agents—in this case, a firm's top management—pursue their own interests rather than the interests of the principal who hired them—in this case, the shareholders

Separation of ownership from control A situation in a corporation in which the top management, rather than the shareholders, controls day-to-day operations.

Principal–agent problem A problem caused by an agent pursuing his own interests rather than the interests of the principal who hired him.

[1]In Chapter 7, we saw that the principal–agent problem arises from moral hazard that can occur because of asymmetric information. In this case, the asymmetric information involves top managers knowing more about how the firm is actually run than do the firm's shareholders.

of the corporation. To reduce the effect of the principal–agent problem, many boards of directors in the 1990s began to tie the salaries of top managers to the profits of the firm or to the price of the firm's stock. They hoped this step would give top managers an incentive to make the firm as profitable as possible, thereby benefiting its shareholders. Sometimes, though, top managers act in ways that increase the profits of the firm in the short run—and the salaries and bonuses of the top managers—but that actually reduce the profits of the firm in the long run.   MyEconLab Concept Check

Solved Problem 8.2   MyEconLab Interactive Animation

Should a Firm's CEO Also Be the Chairman of the Board?

James Dimon has served as both CEO of JP Morgan Chase bank and the chairman of the firm's board of directors. A resolution at the 2013 shareholders' meeting proposed separating the two positions so that one person could not serve in both roles. Jeffrey Sonnenfeld, a professor at the Yale School of Management, argued against the resolution, contending that it is easier for a CEO to provide strong leadership to a firm if he or she is also the chairman of the board: "In the town square of villages in almost every nation, there is a statue celebrating not a board committee but a courageous individual leader." Briefly discuss whether you believe the shareholders of JP Morgan Chase should have approved the resolution.

Solving the Problem

Step 1: **Review the chapter material.** This problem is about the principal–agent problem, so you may want to review the section "Corporate Structure and Corporate Governance" on page 241.

Step 2: **Answer the question by discussing the pros and cons of having the positions of CEO and chairman of the board held by different people.** Corporations face a principal–agent problem because their top managers run the firm but rarely own more than a small amount of the firm's stock. This separation of ownership from control may result in CEOs taking actions that are in their interests but not in the interest of the shareholders.

The argument in favor of having two people fill these positions is that the role of the board of directors is to monitor the CEO and other top managers. If the CEO runs the board of directors as its chair, it may be more difficult for the board to effectively monitor that person. Jeffrey Sonnenfeld and others argue, though, that unless the CEO is also the chairman, the CEO will lack the undivided authority to make decisions and successfully lead the firm.

Economists disagree about how to structure a corporation: Some economists argue that the CEO should not also serve as chairman, while other economists recommend that one person should fill both roles.

Extra Credit: JP Morgan Chase's shareholders rejected the proposal to require different people to serve in the two positions. Fewer than 25 percent of the 500 largest U.S. firms have an independent director serving as chairman of the board.

Source: Jeffrey A. Sonnenfeld, "The Jamie Dimon Witch Hunt," *New York Times*, May 8, 2013.

MyEconLab Study Plan   **Your Turn:** For more practice, do related problems 2.7 and 2.8 on page 257 at the end of this chapter.

8.3 LEARNING OBJECTIVE

Explain how firms raise the funds they need to operate and expand.

How Firms Raise Funds

Owners and managers of firms try to earn a profit. To earn a profit, a firm must raise funds to pay for its operations, including paying its employees and buying or renting computers and other machinery and equipment. Indeed, a central challenge for anyone running a firm, whether that person is a sole proprietor or a top manager of a large corporation, is raising the funds needed to operate and expand the business. Suppose you decide to open an online social networking site using $100,000 you have saved in a bank. You use the $100,000 to rent an office for your firm, buy computers, and pay other startup expenses. Your firm is a great success, and you decide to expand it by moving to a larger office and buying more computers. As the owner of a small business, you can raise the funds for this expansion in three ways:

1. If you are making a profit, you could reinvest the profits back into your firm. Profits that are reinvested in a firm rather than taken out of the firm and paid to the firm's owners are referred to as *retained earnings*.
2. You could raise funds by recruiting additional owners to invest in the firm. This arrangement would increase the firm's *financial capital*.
3. Finally, you could borrow the funds from relatives, friends, or a bank.

The managers of a large public firm have some additional ways to raise funds, as we will see in the next section.

Sources of External Funds

Unless firms rely on retained earnings, they have to raise the *external funds* they need from those who have funds available to invest. It is the role of an economy's *financial system* to transfer funds from savers to borrowers.

Most firms raise external funds in two ways. The first way, called **indirect finance**, relies on financial intermediaries such as banks. If you put $1,000 in a checking account or in a certificate of deposit (CD), the bank will loan most of those funds to borrowers. The bank will combine your funds with those of other depositors and, for example, make a $100,000 loan to a local business. Small businesses rely heavily on bank loans as their primary source of external funds.

A second way for firms to acquire external funds is through *financial markets*. Raising funds in these markets, such as the New York Stock Exchange on Wall Street in New York City, is called **direct finance**. Direct finance usually takes the form of the borrower selling the lender a *financial security*. A financial security is a document—sometimes in electronic form—that states the terms under which the funds are passed from the buyer of the security (who is lending funds) to the borrower. *Bonds* and *stocks* are the two main types of financial securities. Typically, only large corporations are able to sell bonds and stocks on financial markets. Investors are generally unwilling to buy securities issued by small and medium-sized firms because the investors lack sufficient information on the financial health of smaller firms.

Bonds **Bonds** are financial securities that represent promises to repay a fixed amount of funds. When Apple sells a bond to raise funds, it promises to pay the purchaser of the bond an interest payment each year for the term of the bond, as well as a payment of the loan amount, or the *principal*, at the end of the term. Apple may need to raise many millions of dollars to build new offices, but each individual bond has a principal, or *face value*, of $1,000, which is the amount each bond purchaser is lending Apple. So, Apple must sell many bonds to raise all the funds it needs. Suppose Apple promises it will pay interest of $40 per year to anyone who buys one of its bonds. The interest payments on a bond are called **coupon payments**. The **interest rate** is the cost of borrowing funds, usually expressed as a percentage of the amount borrowed. We can calculate the interest rate on the bond, called the *coupon rate*, by dividing the coupon by the face value of the bond. In this case, the coupon rate is:

$$\frac{\$40}{\$1,000} = 0.04, \text{ or } 4\%.$$

Many bonds that corporations issue have terms, or *maturities*, of 30 years. In this example, if you bought a bond from Apple, Apple would pay you $40 per year for 30 years, and at the end of the thirtieth year, Apple would repay the $1,000 principal to you.

The interest rate that a borrower selling a bond has to pay depends on how likely bond buyers—investors—think that the bond seller is to default, or not make the

Indirect finance A flow of funds from savers to borrowers through financial intermediaries such as banks. Intermediaries raise funds from savers to lend to firms (and other borrowers).

Direct finance A flow of funds from savers to firms through financial markets, such as the New York Stock Exchange.

Bond A financial security that represents a promise to repay a fixed amount of funds.

Coupon payment An interest payment on a bond.

Interest rate The cost of borrowing funds, usually expressed as a percentage of the amount borrowed.

promised coupon or principal payments. The higher the *default risk* on a bond, the higher the interest rate will be. For example, investors see the federal government as being very unlikely to default on its bonds, so federal government bonds pay a lower interest rate than do bonds of a firm such as Apple. In turn, Apple pays a lower interest rate on its bonds than does a corporation that investors believe is not as likely to make its bond payments.

Making the Connection MyEconLab Video	The Rating Game: Is the U.S. Treasury Likely to Default on Its Bonds?

Federal regulations require that before they can sell bonds to investors, firms and governments must first have bonds rated by one of the credit-rating agencies. The three largest rating agencies are Moody's Investors Service, Standard & Poor's Corporation, and Fitch Ratings. These private firms rate bonds by giving them letter grades—AAA or Aaa being the highest—that reflect the likelihood that the firm or government will be able to make the payments on the bond. The following table shows the ratings:

	Moody's Investors Service	Standard & Poor's (S&P)	Fitch Ratings	Meaning of the Ratings
Investment-grade bonds	Aaa	AAA	AAA	Highest credit quality
	Aa	AA	AA	Very high credit quality
	A	A	A	High credit quality
	Baa	BBB	BBB	Good credit quality
Non-investment-grade bonds	Ba	BB	BB	Speculative
	B	B	B	Highly speculative
	Caa	CCC	CCC	Substantial default risk
	Ca	CC	CC	Very high levels of default risk
	C	C	C	Exceptionally high levels of default risk
	—	D	D	Default

Note: The entries in the "Meaning of the Ratings" column are slightly modified from those that Fitch uses. The other two rating agencies have similar descriptions. For each rating from Aa to Caa, Moody's adds a numerical modifier of 1, 2, or 3. The rating Aa1 is higher than the rating Aa2, and the rating Aa2 is higher than the rating Aa3. Similarly, Standard & Poor's and Fitch Ratings add a plus (+) or minus (−) sign. The rating AA+ is higher than the rating AA, and the rating AA is higher than the rating AA−.

Source: *Money, Banking, and the Financial System*, 2nd edition by R. Glenn Hubbard and Anthony P. O'Brien. Copyright © 2014 by Pearson Education, Inc. Reprinted and electronically reproduced by permission of Pearson Education, Inc., Upper Saddle River, New Jersey.

Investors can use the ratings in deciding how much risk they are willing to accept when buying a bond. Generally, the lower the rating, the higher the interest rate an investor will receive, but also the higher the risk that the issuer of the bond will default.

The rating agencies charge firms and governments—rather than investors—for their services. This arrangement raises the question of whether rating agencies face a conflict of interest. Because firms issuing bonds can choose which of the agencies to hire to rate their bonds, the agencies may have an incentive to give higher ratings than might be justified in order to keep the firms' business. During the housing boom of the mid-2000s, some financial firms issued *mortgage-backed bonds*. These bonds were similar to regular corporate bonds except that the interest payments came from mortgage loans people had taken out to buy houses. The money from those mortgage payments was passed along to investors who had bought the mortgage-backed bonds. The rating agencies gave many of these bonds AAA ratings, even though when housing prices began to decline in 2006, many homeowners stopped making their mortgage payments and the value of the bonds declined sharply. Some economists and policymakers believe the rating agencies provided the high ratings primarily to ensure that the firms that issued the bonds would continue to hire them.

Standard & Poor's (S&P) became involved in another controversy in August 2011, when it downgraded U.S. Treasury bonds from AAA to AA+. Never before had a rating agency given Treasury bonds less than a AAA rating. S&P downgraded the Treasury's rating because of the size of the federal government's budget deficit. Whenever the federal government runs a budget deficit, the Treasury must borrow an amount equal to the deficit by issuing bonds. In 2011, the federal government was spending much more than it was collecting in taxes, which resulted in a large budget deficit. The budget deficit reflected the lower tax receipts and increased government spending resulting from the 2007–2009 economic recession. But forecasts from the U.S. Congressional Budget Office indicated that even after the effects of the recession had disappeared, large budget deficits would remain because spending on Social Security, Medicare, Medicaid, and other government programs were expected to increase faster than tax revenues. When prolonged negotiations between President Barack Obama and Congress failed to make much of a dent in the problem, S&P announced the rating downgrade. In the months following the announcement, interest rates on Treasury bonds actually fell rather than rose, as might have been expected if investors had believed that a default was possible.

So, is it likely that the U.S. Treasury will default on its bonds? S&P argued that while a default is still unlikely, the continuing large deficits increased the chance that someday the Treasury might not make the interest payments on its bonds. As the federal deficit shrank during 2013, most economists believed that the chance of a Treasury default was low. Like the Ghost of Christmas Yet to Come in Charles Dickens's *A Christmas Carol*, S&P was giving a warning of something that might happen rather than something that necessarily must happen.

Sources: Mary Williams Walsh, "Credit Ratings Services Give Mixed Reviews to Tax Deal," *New York Times*, January 3, 2013; and Andrew Ross Sorkin, "S.E.C. Urges Changes to Ratings-Agency Rules," *New York Times*, August 29, 2010.

Your Turn: Test your understanding by doing related problem 3.8 on page 258 at the end of this chapter.

MyEconLab Study Plan

Stocks When you buy a newly issued bond from a firm, you are lending funds to that firm. When you buy **stock** issued by a firm, you are actually buying part ownership of the firm. When a corporation sells stock, it is doing the same thing the owner of a small business does when he or she takes on a partner: The firm is increasing its financial capital by bringing additional owners into the firm. Any one shareholder usually owns only a small fraction of the total shares of stock issued by a corporation.

> **Stock** A financial security that represents partial ownership of a firm.

Many small investors buy shares of *mutual funds* rather than directly buying stocks of companies. Mutual funds, such as Fidelity Investment's Magellan Fund, sell shares to investors and use the funds to invest in a portfolio of financial assets, such as stocks and bonds. By buying shares in a mutual fund, small investors reduce the costs they would pay to buy many individual stocks and bonds. Small savers who have only enough money to buy a few individual stocks and bonds can also lower their investment risk by buying shares in a mutual fund because most mutual funds hold a large number of stocks and bonds. If a firm issuing a stock or bond declares bankruptcy, causing the stock or bond to lose all of its value, the effect on a mutual fund's portfolio is likely to be small. The effect might be devastating, though, to a small investor who had invested most of his or her savings in the stock or bond. Because mutual funds are willing to buy back their shares at any time, they also provide savers with easy access to their money.

A shareholder is entitled to a portion of the corporation's profits, if there are any. Corporations generally keep some of their profits as retained earnings to finance future expansion. The remaining profits are paid to shareholders as **dividends**. If a firm uses its retained earnings to grow and earn economic profits, its share price rises, which provides a *capital gain* for investors. If a corporation is unable to make a profit, it usually does not pay a dividend. Under the law, corporations must make payments on any debt they have before making payments to their owners. That is, a corporation must make promised payments to bondholders before it can make any dividend payments to shareholders. Unlike bonds, stocks do not have a maturity date, so the firm is not obliged to return the investor's funds at any particular date.   MyEconLab Concept Check

> **Dividends** Payments by a corporation to its shareholders.

Stock and Bond Markets Provide Capital—and Information

The original purchasers of stocks and bonds may resell them to other investors. In fact, most of the buying and selling of stocks and bonds that takes place each day involves investors reselling existing stocks and bonds to each other rather than corporations selling new stocks and bonds to investors. The buyers and sellers of stocks and bonds together make up the *stock and bond markets*. There is no single place where stocks and bonds are bought and sold. Some trading of stocks and bonds takes place in buildings known as *exchanges*, such as the New York Stock Exchange or the Tokyo Stock Exchange. In the United States, the stocks and bonds of the largest corporations are traded on the New York Stock Exchange. The development of computer technology has spread the trading of stocks and bonds outside exchanges to *securities dealers* linked by computers. These dealers comprise the *over-the-counter market*. The stocks of many computer and other high-technology firms—including Apple, Google, and Facebook—are traded in the most important of the over-the-counter markets, the *National Association of Securities Dealers Automated Quotations* system, which is referred to by its acronym, NASDAQ.

Shares of stock represent claims on the profits of the firms that issue them. Therefore, as the fortunes of the firms change and they earn more or less profit, the prices of the stock the firms have issued should also change. Similarly, bonds represent claims to receive coupon payments and one final payment of the principal. Therefore, a particular bond that was issued in the past may have its price go up or down, depending on whether the coupon payments being offered on newly issued bonds are higher or lower than those on existing bonds. If you hold a bond with a coupon of $30 per year, and newly issued bonds have coupons of $40 per year, the price of your bond will fall because it is less attractive to investors. The price of a bond will also be affected by changes in *default risk*, which reflects investors' perceptions of the issuing firm's ability to make the coupon payments. For example, if investors begin to believe that a firm may soon go out of business and stop making coupon payments to its bondholders, the price of the firm's bonds will fall to very low levels.

Changes in the value of a firm's stocks and bonds offer important information for a firm's managers, as well as for investors. An increase in the stock price means that investors are

Don't Let This Happen to You

When Facebook Shares Are Sold, Facebook Doesn't Get the Money

Facebook is a popular investment, with investors buying and selling shares often as their views about the value of the firm shift. That's great for Facebook, right? Think of Facebook collecting all that money as shares change hands and the stock price goes up. *Wrong.* Facebook raises funds in a primary market, but its shares trade in a secondary market. Those trades don't put money into Facebook's hands, but they do give important information to the firm's managers. Let's see why.

Primary markets are those in which firms sell newly issued stocks and bonds to initial buyers. Businesses can raise funds in a primary financial market in two ways— by borrowing (selling bonds) or selling shares of stock— which result in different types of claims on the borrowing firm's future income. Although you may hear about the stock market fluctuations every day in news updates, bonds actually account for more of the funds raised by borrowers. The total value of bonds in the United States is typically about twice the value of stocks.

In *secondary markets*, stocks and bonds that have already been issued are sold by one investor to another. If Facebook sells shares to the public, it is turning to a primary market for new funds. Once Facebook shares are issued, investors trade the shares in the secondary market. Facebook does not receive any new funds when its shares are traded on secondary markets. The initial seller of a stock or bond raises funds from an investor only in the primary market. Secondary markets convey information to firms' managers and investors by determining the price of stocks and bonds. For example, a major increase in Facebook's stock price conveys the market's good feelings about the firm, and the firm may decide to raise funds to expand. So, secondary markets are valuable sources of information for corporations that are considering raising funds.

Primary and secondary markets are both important, but they play different roles. As an investor, you principally trade stocks and bonds in a secondary market. As a corporate manager, you may help decide how to raise new funds to expand the firm where you work.

MyEconLab Study Plan

Your Turn: Test your understanding by doing related problem 3.11 on page 258 at the end of this chapter.

more optimistic about the firm's profit prospects, and the firm's managers might want to expand the firm's operations as a result. By contrast, a decrease in the firm's stock price indicates that investors are less optimistic about the firm's profit prospects, so management may want to shrink the firm's operations. Similarly, changes in the value of the firm's bonds imply changes in the cost of external funds to finance the firm's investment in research and development or in new factories. A higher bond price indicates a lower cost of new external funds, while a lower bond price indicates a higher cost of new external funds.   MyEconLab Concept Check

Why Do Stock Prices Fluctuate So Much?

The performance of the U.S. stock market is often measured using *stock market indexes*. Stock market indexes are averages of stock prices, with the value of the index set equal to 100 in a particular year, called the *base year*. Because the stock indexes are intended to show movements in prices from one year to the next, rather than the actual dollar values of the underlying stocks, the year chosen for the base year is unimportant. Figure 8.2 shows movements from January 1996 to June 2013 in the three most widely followed stock indexes:

- The Dow Jones Industrial Average, which is an index of the stock prices of 30 large U.S. corporations.

- The S&P 500, which is an index prepared by Standard & Poor's Corporation and includes the stock prices of 500 large U.S. firms.

- The NASDAQ Composite Index, which includes the stock prices of more than 4,000 firms whose shares are traded in the NASDAQ stock market. NASDAQ is an over-the-counter market, meaning that buying and selling on NASDAQ is carried out between dealers who are linked together by computer. The listings on NASDAQ are dominated by high-tech firms such as Apple, Facebook, and Google.

As we have seen, ownership of a firm's stock represents a claim on the firm's profits. So, the larger the firm's profits are, the higher its stock price will be. When the overall economy is expanding, incomes, employment, and spending will all increase, as will corporate profits. When the economy is in a recession, incomes, employment, and spending will fall, as will corporate profits. Therefore, we would expect that stock prices will rise when the economy is expanding and fall when the economy is in recession. We see this pattern reflected in the three stock market indexes shown in Figure 8.2. All three indexes follow a roughly similar pattern: increases in stock prices during the

MyEconLab Real-time data

Figure 8.2   Movements in Stock Market Indexes, January 1996 to June 2013

The performance of the U.S. stock market is often measured by market indexes, which are averages of stock prices. The three most important indexes are the Dow Jones Industrial Average, the S&P 500, and the NASDAQ. During the period from 1996 to 2013, the three indexes followed similar patterns, rising when the U.S. economy was expanding and falling when the economy was in recession. Note that in all three panels the vertical axis does not start at zero.

economic expansion of the late 1990s, declines after the "dot-com crash" of 2000 and the recession of 2001, increases from late 2001 to late 2007, declines as the U.S. economy entered a recession at the end of 2007, and then increases beginning in early 2009.

The stock prices of many early Internet companies soared in the late 1990s, as some analysts made what turned out to be overly optimistic predictions about how rapidly online retailing would grow. In 2000, when investors came to believe that many dot-coms would never be profitable, their stock prices crashed. Because the NASDAQ is dominated by high-tech stocks, it experienced greater swings during the dot-com boom and bust of the late 1990s and early 2000s than did the other two indexes. The sharp declines in all three indexes beginning in late 2007 reflected the severity of the recession that began in December of that year. The severity of the recession was due in part to problems with financial firms, which we will discuss later in this chapter. During 2013, as recovery from the recession continued, the Dow Jones Industrial Average and the S&P 500 both reached their highest values ever.   MyEconLab Concept Check

Making the Connection
MyEconLab Video

Following Abercrombie & Fitch's Stock Price in the Financial Pages

If you read the online stock listings on the *Wall Street Journal*'s Web site or on another site, you will notice that the listings pack into a small space a lot of information about what happened to stocks during the previous day's trading. The following figure reproduces a small portion of the listings from the *Wall Street Journal* on June 8, 2013, for stocks listed on the New York Stock Exchange. The listings provide information on the buying and selling of stocks of five firms during the previous day. Let's focus on the highlighted listing for Abercrombie & Fitch, the clothing store, and examine the information in each column:

- The first column gives the name of the company.
- The second column gives the firm's "ticker" symbol (ANF), which you may have seen scrolling along the bottom of the screen on cable financial news channels.
- The third column (Open) gives the price (in dollars) of the stock at the time when trading began, which is 9:30 A.M., on the New York Stock Exchange. Abercrombie & Fitch opened for trading at a price of $51.11.
- The fourth column (High) and the fifth column (Low) give the highest price and the lowest price the stock sold for during that day.
- The sixth column (Close) gives the price the stock sold for the last time it was traded before the close of trading (4:00 P.M.), which in this case was $51.70.
- The seventh column (Net Chg) gives the amount by which the closing price changed from the closing price the day before. In this case, the price of Abercrombie & Fitch's stock had risen by $2.10 per share from its closing price the day before. Changes in Abercrombie & Fitch's stock price give the firm's managers a signal that they may want to expand or contract the firm's operations.
- The eighth column (%Chg) gives the change in the price in percentage terms rather than in dollar terms.
- The ninth column (Vol) gives the number of shares of stock traded on the previous day.
- The tenth column (52-Week High) and the eleventh column (52-Week Low) give, the highest price the stock has sold for and the lowest price the stock has sold for during the previous year. These numbers tell how *volatile* the stock price is—how much it fluctuates over the course of the year. In this case, Abercrombie's stock had been quite volatile, rising as high as $55.23 per share and falling as low as $28.64 per share. These large fluctuations in price are an indication of how risky investing in the stock market can be.
- The twelfth column (Div) gives the dividend, expressed in dollars. In this case, 0.80 means that Abercrombie paid a dividend of $0.80 per share.

- The thirteenth column (Yield) gives the *dividend yield*, which is calculated by dividing the dividend by the *closing price* of the stock—the price at which Abercrombie's stock last sold before the close of trading on the previous day.
- The fourteenth column (PE) gives the *P–E ratio* (or *price–earnings ratio*), which is calculated by dividing the price of the firm's stock by its earnings per share. (Remember that because firms retain some earnings, earnings per share is not necessarily the same as dividends per share.) Abercrombie's P–E ratio was 27, meaning that its price per share was 27 times its earnings per share. So, you would have to pay $27 to buy $1 of Abercrombie & Fitch's earnings.
- The final column (Year-to-Date %Chg) gives the percentage change in the price of the stock from the beginning of the year to the previous day. In this case, the price of Abercrombie's stock had increased by 7.8 percent since the beginning of 2013.

	Symbol	Open	High	Low	Close	Net Chg	%Chg	Vol	52-Week High	52-Week Low	Div	Yield	PE	Year-to-Date % Chg
Abbott Laboratories	ABT	36.95	37.55	36.90	37.51	0.87	2.37	5,971,945	38.77	29.22	0.56	1.49	11.25	19.69
AbbVie	ABBV	43.72	44.27	43.50	44.00	0.50	1.15	5,421,935	48.00	32.51	1.60	3.64	...	28.81
Abercrombie & Fitch	ANF	51.11	52.25	51.07	51.70	2.10	4.23	2,060,682	55.23	28.64	0.80	1.55	27.27	7.78
ABM Industries	ABM	24.85	24.90	24.51	24.66	0.02	0.08	196,680	26.38	17.85	0.60	2.43	18.54	23.61
Acadia Realty Trust	AKR	26.44	26.64	25.96	26.40	0.05	0.19	415,048	29.32	22.27	0.84	3.18	...	5.26

Source: "Closing Quote Tables" from *Wall Street Journal*. Copyright © 2013 by Dow Jones & Company, Inc. Reproduced with permission of Dow Jones & Company, Inc.

Your Turn: Test your understanding by doing related problems 3.12 and 3.13 on page 258 at the end of this chapter.

MyEconLab Study Plan

Using Financial Statements to Evaluate a Corporation

To raise funds, a firm's managers must persuade potential lenders or investors that it will be profitable. Before a firm can sell new issues of stocks or bonds, it must first provide investors and financial regulators with information about its finances. To borrow from a bank, the firm must also provide the bank with financial information.

In most high-income countries, government agencies require firms to disclose specific financial information to the public before they are allowed to sell securities such as stocks or bonds in financial markets. In the United States, the Securities and Exchange Commission (SEC) requires publicly owned firms to report their performance in financial statements prepared using standard accounting methods, often referred to as *generally accepted accounting principles*. Such disclosure reduces the cost to investors of gathering information about firms, but it doesn't eliminate these costs—for two reasons. First, some firms may be too young to have much information for potential investors to evaluate. Second, managers may try to present the required information in the most favorable way so that investors will overvalue their securities.

Private firms also collect information on business borrowers and sell the information to lenders and investors. If the information-gathering firms do a good job, lenders and investors purchasing the information will be better able to judge the quality of borrowing firms. Some firms—including Moody's Investors Service, Standard & Poor's Corporation, Value Line, and Dun & Bradstreet—collect information from businesses and sell it to subscribers. Buyers include individual investors, libraries, and financial intermediaries. You can find some of these publications in your college library or through online information services.

What kind of information do investors and firm managers need? A firm must answer three basic questions: What to produce? How to produce it? What price to charge? To answer these questions, a firm's managers need two pieces of information: The first is the firm's revenues and costs, and the second is the value of the property and other assets the firm owns and the firm's debts, or other **liabilities**, that it owes to households and other firms. Potential investors in the firm also need this information to decide whether to buy the firm's stocks or bonds. The information can be found in the firm's *financial statements*, principally its income statement and balance sheet, which we discuss next.

MyEconLab Concept Check

> **Liability** Anything owed by a person or a firm.

The Income Statement

A firm's **income statement** shows its revenues, costs, and profit over a period of time. Corporations issue annual income statements, although the 12-month *fiscal year* covered may be different from the calendar year to better represent the seasonal pattern of the business. We explore income statements in greater detail in the appendix to this chapter.

> **Income statement** A financial statement that shows a firm's revenues, costs, and profit over a period of time.

Accounting Profit An income statement shows a firm's revenue, costs, and profit for the firm's fiscal year. To determine profitability, the income statement starts with the firm's revenue and subtracts its operating expenses and taxes paid. The remainder, *net income*, is the **accounting profit** of the firm.

> **Accounting profit** A firm's net income, measured as revenue minus operating expenses and taxes paid.

Economic Profit Accounting profit provides information on a firm's current net income, measured according to accepted accounting standards. Accounting profit is not, however, the ideal measure of a firm's profits because it neglects some of the firm's costs. *Economic profit* provides a better indication than accounting profit of how successful a firm is because economic profit is calculated using all of a firm's costs. Firms making an economic profit will remain in business and may even expand. Firms making an *economic loss* are unlikely to remain in business in the long run. To understand how economic profit is calculated, remember that economists always measure cost as *opportunity cost*. The **opportunity cost** of any activity is the highest-valued alternative that must be given up to engage in that activity. Costs are either *explicit* or *implicit*. When a firm spends money, an **explicit cost** results. If a firm incurs an opportunity cost but does not spend money, an **implicit cost** results. For example, firms incur an explicit labor cost when they pay wages to employees. Firms have many other explicit costs as well, such as the cost of the electricity used to light their buildings or the costs of advertising or insurance.

> **Opportunity cost** The highest-valued alternative that must be given up to engage in an activity.

> **Explicit cost** A cost that involves spending money.

> **Implicit cost** A nonmonetary opportunity cost.

Some costs are implicit, however. The most important of these is the opportunity cost to investors of the funds they have invested in the firm. Economists use the term *normal rate of return* to refer to the minimum amount that investors must earn on the funds they invest in a firm, expressed as a percentage of the amount invested. If a firm fails to provide investors with at least a normal rate of return, it will not be able to remain in business over the long run because investors will not continue to invest their funds in the firm. For example, Borders was once the second-largest bookstore chain in the United States and a very profitable firm, with stock that sold for more than $40 per share. By 2010, investors became convinced that the firm's difficulty competing with Amazon and other online booksellers and its loss of sales to e-books meant that the firm would never be able to provide investors with a normal rate of return. Many investors expected that the firm would eventually have to declare bankruptcy, and as a result, the price of Border's stock plummeted to less than $1 per share. Within a year, the firm declared bankruptcy, and its remaining assets were sold off. The return (in dollars) that investors require to continue investing in a firm is a true cost to the firm and should be subtracted from the firm's revenues to calculate its profits.

The rate of return that investors require to continue investing in a firm varies from firm to firm. If the investment is risky—as would be the case with a biotechnology startup—investors may require a high rate of return to compensate them for the risk. Investors in firms in more established industries, such as electric utilities, may require lower rates of return. The exact rate of return investors require to invest in any particular firm is difficult to calculate, which also makes it difficult for an accountant to include the return as a cost on an income statement. Firms have other implicit costs, besides the return investors require, that can also be difficult to calculate. As a result, the rules of accounting generally require that only explicit costs be included in the firm's financial records. *Economic costs* include both explicit costs *and* implicit costs. **Economic profit** is equal to a firm's revenues minus its economic costs. Because accounting profit excludes some implicit costs, it is larger than economic profit.   MyEconLab Concept Check

Economic profit A firm's revenues minus all of its implicit and explicit costs.

The Balance Sheet

A firm's **balance sheet** sums up its financial position on a particular day, usually the end of a quarter or year. Recall that an asset is anything of value that a firm owns and a liability is a debt or an obligation owed by a firm. Subtracting the value of a firm's liabilities from the value of its assets leaves its *net worth*. We can think of the net worth as what the firm's owners would be left with if the firm were closed, its assets were sold, and its liabilities were paid off. Investors can determine a firm's net worth by inspecting its balance sheet. We analyze a balance sheet in more detail in the appendix to this chapter.   MyEconLab Concept Check

Balance sheet A financial statement that sums up a firm's financial position on a particular day, usually the end of a quarter or year.

MyEconLab Study Plan

Corporate Governance Policy and the Financial Crisis of 2007–2009

8.5 LEARNING OBJECTIVE

Discuss the role that corporate governance problems may have played in the financial crisis of 2007–2009.

A firm's financial statements provide important information on the firm's ability to create value for investors and the economy. Accurate and easy-to-understand financial statements are inputs to decisions by the firm's managers and by investors. In fact, the information in financial statements helps guide resource allocation in the economy.

Firms disclose financial statements in periodic filings to the federal government and in *annual reports* to shareholders. An investor is more likely to buy a firm's stock if the firm's income statement shows a large after-tax profit and if its balance sheet shows a large net worth. The top management of a firm has at least two reasons to attract investors and keep the firm's stock price high. First, a higher stock price increases the funds the firm can raise when it sells a given amount of stock. Second, to reduce the principal-agent problem, boards of directors often tie the salaries of top managers to the firm's stock price or to the profitability of the firm.

Top managers clearly have an incentive to maximize the profits reported on the income statement and the net worth reported on the balance sheet. If top managers make good decisions, the firm's profits will be high, and the firm's assets will be large relative to its liabilities. Problems that surfaced during the early 2000s, however, revealed that some top managers have inflated profits and hidden liabilities that should have been listed on their balance sheets. At other firms, managers took on more risk than they disclosed to investors. We will explore recent problems with corporate governance and the government's reaction to these problems by discussing the accounting scandals of the early 2000s and problems that many financial firms encountered during 2007–2009.

The Accounting Scandals of the Early 2000s

In the early 2000s, the top managers of several well-known firms, including Enron, an energy trading firm, and WorldCom, a telecommunications firm, falsified their firms' financial statements in order to mislead investors about how profitable the firms actually were. Several top managers were sentenced to long jail terms, and some of the firms, including Enron, went out of business.

How was it possible for corporations such as Enron and WorldCom to falsify their financial statements? The federal government regulates how financial statements are prepared, but this regulation cannot by itself guarantee the accuracy of the statements. All firms that issue stock to the public have certified public accountants working for outside firms *audit* their financial statements. Unfortunately, as the Enron and WorldCom scandals revealed, top managers who are determined to deceive investors about the true financial condition of their firms can also deceive outside auditors.

To guard against future scandals, new federal legislation was enacted in 2002. The landmark *Sarbanes-Oxley Act* of 2002 requires that CEOs personally certify the accuracy of financial statements. The Sarbanes-Oxley Act also requires that financial analysts and auditors disclose whether any conflicts of interest might exist that would limit their independence in evaluating a firm's financial condition. On balance, most observers acknowledge that the Sarbanes-Oxley Act increased confidence in the U.S. corporate governance system. However, as we will discuss in the next section, problems during 2007–2009 at financial firms again raised questions of whether corporations were adequately disclosing information to investors.   MyEconLab Concept Check

The Financial Crisis of 2007–2009

Beginning in 2007 and lasting into 2009, the U.S. economy suffered the worst financial crisis since the Great Depression of the 1930s. At the heart of the crisis was a problem in the market for home mortgages. When people buy houses, they typically borrow the money by taking out a mortgage loan from a bank or another financial institution. The house they are buying is pledged as collateral for the loan, meaning that the bank can take possession of the house and sell it if the borrower defaults by failing to make the payments on the loan.

For many years, a bank or other financial institution granting a mortgage would keep the loan until the borrower had paid it off. Beginning in the 1970s, financial institutions began *securitizing* some mortgage loans, which means that groups of mortgages were bundled together and sold to investors. These *mortgage-backed securities* are very similar to bonds in that the investor who buys one receives regular interest payments, which in this case come from the payments being made on the original mortgage loans. At first, the securitization process was carried out by the Federal National Mortgage Association ("Fannie Mae") and the Federal Home Loan Mortgage Corporation ("Freddie Mac"), which Congress had established to help increase the volume of lending in the home mortgage market. Fannie Mae and Freddie Mac would buy mortgages granted to creditworthy borrowers and bundle them into securities that were then sold to investors.

Beginning in the 1990s, private financial firms, primarily investment banks, started to securitize mortgages. By the early 2000s, many mortgages were being granted by banks and other financial institutions to "subprime" borrowers, whose credit histories include failures to make payments on bills, and "Alt-A" borrowers, who failed to document that their incomes were high enough to afford their mortgage payments. Both subprime and Alt-A borrowers were more likely to default on loans than were conventional borrowers. Fueled by the ease of obtaining a mortgage, housing prices in the United States soared before beginning a sharp downturn in mid-2006. By 2007, many borrowers—particularly subprime and Alt-A borrowers—began to default on their mortgages. These defaults were bad news for anyone owning mortgage-backed securities because the value of these securities depended on steady payments being made on the underlying mortgages. As prices of these securities plunged, many financial institutions suffered heavy losses, and some of the largest of them remained in business only because they received aid from the federal government.

During the financial crisis, many investors complained that they weren't aware of the riskiness of some of the assets—particularly mortgage-backed securities—on the balance sheets of financial firms. Some observers believed that the managers of many financial firms had intentionally misled investors about the riskiness of these assets. Others argued that the managers themselves had not understood how risky the assets were. In the fall of 2008, Fannie Mae and Freddie Mac were brought under direct control of the government. As the crisis passed, in July 2010, Congress overhauled the regulation of the financial system with the passage of the **Wall Street Reform and Consumer Protection Act**, referred to as the **Dodd-Frank Act**. Among its provisions, the act created the Consumer Financial Protection Bureau, housed in the Federal Reserve—the central bank of the United States—to write rules intended to protect consumers in their borrowing and investing activities. The act also established the Financial Stability Oversight Council, which includes representatives from all the major federal financial regulatory bodies, including the SEC and the Federal Reserve. The council is intended to identify and act on risks to the financial system. Economists are divided in their opinions about whether the Dodd-Frank Act will significantly reduce the risk of future financial crises.　　　　　MyEconLab Concept Check

Wall Street Reform and Consumer Protection Act (Dodd-Frank Act) Legislation passed during 2010 that was intended to reform regulation of the financial system.

Did Principal–Agent Problems Help Cause the 2007–2009 Financial Crisis?

As we have seen, the process of securitizing mortgages played an important role in the financial crisis of 2007–2009. Beginning in the 1990s, private investment banks began to securitize mortgages. Unlike commercial banks, whose main activities are accepting deposits and making loans, investment banks had traditionally concentrated on providing advice to corporations on selling new stocks and bonds and on *underwriting* the issuance of stocks and bonds by guaranteeing a price to the firm selling them. Investment banking is considered riskier than commercial banking because investment banks can suffer substantial losses on underwriting. To address this greater risk, Congress passed the *Glass-Steagall Act* in 1933. The act prevented financial firms from being both commercial banks and investment banks.

Some economists and policymakers argued that Glass-Steagall reduced competition for investment banking services by prohibiting commercial banks from offering these services. Congress repealed the Glass-Steagall Act in 1999, after which some commercial banks began engaging in investment banking. Many of the largest, best-known investment banks, such as Lehman Brothers, Bear Stearns, Goldman Sachs, Merrill Lynch, and Morgan Stanley, remained exclusively investment banks. The mortgage-backed securities originated by the investment banks were mostly sold to investors, but some were retained as investments by these firms. As a result, when the prices of these securities declined beginning in 2007, the investment banks suffered heavy losses. Lehman Brothers was forced to declare bankruptcy; Merrill Lynch and Bear Stearns were sold to commercial banks in deals arranged by the U.S. government; and Goldman Sachs and Morgan Stanley became bank holding companies, which allowed them to engage in commercial banking activity.

Why did investment banks take on so much risk by originating securities backed by mortgages granted to borrowers who had a high likelihood of defaulting on the loans? Michael Lewis, a financial journalist and former Wall Street bond salesman, has argued that a key reason was a change in how the investment banks were organized. Traditionally, large Wall Street investment banks had been organized as partnerships, but by 2000 they had all converted to being publicly traded corporations. As we have seen, in a partnership the funds of the relatively small group of owners are put directly at risk, and the principal–agent problem is reduced because there is little separation of ownership from control. With a publicly traded corporation, on the other hand, the principal–agent problem can be severe. Lewis argues:

> No investment bank owned by its employees would have . . . bought and held $50 billion in [exotic mortgage-backed securities]. . . . or even allow [these securities] to be sold to its customers. The hoped-for short-term gain would not have justified the long-term hit.

Issues of corporate governance will clearly continue to be a concern for economists, policymakers, and investors.　　　　　MyEconLab Concept Check

The Ups and Downs of Investing in Facebook

The first time a company sells stock, the sale is called an *initial public offering* (IPO). In 2012, Mark Zuckerberg announced his plan to take Facebook public with an IPO. There was widespread anticipation among both ordinary investors and institutional investors, such as managers of mutual funds. Many small investors hoped they would be getting in on the ground floor of a high-tech company whose profits—and stock price—would soar, as had happened with firms like Microsoft and Apple. Unfortunately, as the following graph shows, during the year following the IPO these investors were disappointed.

Investors who bought at the IPO price of $38 per share found that the price of the stock had fallen by 10 percent by the second day of trading. More than a year later, in mid-June 2013, Facebook stock was selling for about $23 per share, a decline of nearly 40 percent from the IPO price. But then the stock price began to rise and by October 2013 reached $54 per share, well above the IPO price. What explains the swings in Facebook's stock?

First, stock prices are very difficult to predict. As we have seen, the price of a firm's stock reflects the firm's profitability. But it is not just the firm's current profitability—which is known—that counts; the firm's future profitability—which is not known with certainty—matters even more. Investors are willing to pay much higher prices for stock issued by firms that they expect to be highly profitable in the future than they are for stock issued by firms that they expect will be less profitable. Many investors were willing to pay the IPO price of $38 per share because they expected that Facebook's rapid growth of the previous few years and increasing profits would continue into the future. In fact, though, Facebook was beginning to encounter difficulties because more people were accessing the site on their phones or tablets and Facebook was having trouble selling advertising on the mobile version of its site. When it appeared that Facebook's profits would not be increasing as rapidly as many investors had expected, the firm's stock price dropped well below the IPO level and stayed there. But then, unexpectedly, in July 2013 Facebook reported that its revenue from ads on the mobile version of its site had soared. As a result, Facebook's stock price rose more than 30 percent in one day.

There was still controversy, though, about Facebook's IPO. Some investors argued that Facebook was aware that its future profits were likely to be lower than expected and had made this information available before the IPO to the Morgan Stanley investment bank, which was underwriting the IPO, and to some investment analysts at other financial firms. Although Facebook and Morgan Stanley argued that Facebook had made all relevant information publicly available before the IPO, some investors filed lawsuits because they believed the company had taken advantage of them. The SEC launched an investigation. Morgan Stanley, without admitting or denying guilt, agreed to pay the state of Massachusetts a $5 million fine to settle a lawsuit brought by the secretary of the commonwealth of Massachusetts.

In late 2013, the outcome of the SEC's investigation of the Facebook IPO remained uncertain. Because Facebook's stock price eventually rose above its IPO price, investors had become less critical of the firm. Some investors, though, continued to doubt whether firms launching IPOs were fully disclosing information. The question remained important as Twitter and other firms prepared for IPOs.

Sources: Vindu Goel, "Facebook's Stock Soars Amid Rosy Growth Expectations," *New York Times*, July 25, 2013; Paul Vigna, "Facebook IPO Anniversary: No Sugarcoating It," *Wall Street Journal*, May 17, 2013; Jessica E. Lessin, Pui-Wing Tam, and Telis Demos, "Pace Picks Up on Tech IPOs," *Wall Street Journal*, May 16, 2013; and Susanne Craig and Ben Protess, "Massachusetts Fines Morgan Stanley over Facebook IPO," *New York Times*, December 17, 2012.

Your Turn: Test your understanding by doing related problem 5.6 on page 260 at the end of this chapter.   MyEconLab Study Plan

---

Continued from page 237

Economics in Your Life

Do Corporate Managers Act in the Best Interests of Shareholders?

At the beginning of the chapter, we asked you to consider two questions: Why is it difficult to get the managers of a firm to act in your interests rather than in their own? and Given this problem, should you ever take on the risk of buying stock? The reason managers may not act in shareholders' interest is that in large corporations there is separation of ownership from control: The shareholders own the firm, but the top managers actually control it. This results in the principal–agent problem discussed in the chapter. The principal–agent problem clearly adds to the risk you would face by buying stock rather than doing something safe with your money, such as putting it in the bank. But the rewards to owning stock can also be substantial, potentially earning you far more over the long run than if you keep your money in a bank account.

Buying the stock of well-known firms, such as Google, that are closely followed by Wall Street investment analysts helps to reduce the principal–agent problem. It is less likely that the managers of these firms will take actions that are clearly not in the best interests of shareholders because the managers' actions are difficult to conceal. Buying the stock of large, well-known firms certainly does not completely eliminate the risk from the principal–agent problem, however. Enron, WorldCom, and some of the other firms that were involved in the scandals discussed in this chapter were all well known and closely followed by Wall Street analysts, as were the large financial firms that ran into difficulties during the financial crisis of 2007–2009, but their stock turned out to be very poor investments.

Conclusion

In a market system, firms make independent decisions about which goods and services to produce, how to produce them, and what prices to charge. In modern high-income countries, such as the United States, large corporations account for a majority of the sales and profits earned by firms. Generally, the managers of these corporations do a good job of representing the interests of stockholders while providing the goods and services demanded by consumers. As the business scandals of the early 2000s and the problems with financial firms in 2007–2009 showed, however, the principal–agent problem can sometimes become severe. Economists debate the costs and benefits of regulations proposed to address these problems.

Visit MyEconLab for a news article and analysis related to the concepts in this chapter.

Chapter Summary and Problems

Key Terms

Accounting profit, p. 250

Asset, p. 238

Balance sheet, p. 251

Bond, p. 243

Corporate governance, p. 241

Corporation, p. 238

Coupon payment, p. 243

Direct finance, p. 243

Dividends, p. 245

Economic profit, p. 251

Explicit cost, p. 250

Implicit cost, p. 250

Income statement, p. 250

Indirect finance, p. 243

Interest rate, p. 243

Liability, p. 250

Limited liability, p. 238

Opportunity cost, p. 250

Partnership, p. 238

Principal–agent problem, p. 241

Separation of ownership from control, p. 241

Sole proprietorship, p. 238

Stock, p. 245

Wall Street Reform and Consumer Protection Act (Dodd-Frank Act), p. 253

| 8.1 | Types of Firms, pages 238–241 |

LEARNING OBJECTIVE: Categorize the major types of firms in the United States.

Summary

There are three types of firms: A **sole proprietorship** is a firm owned by a single individual and not organized as a corporation. A **partnership** is a firm owned jointly by two or more persons and not organized as a corporation. A **corporation** is a legal form of business that provides the owners with limited liability. An **asset** is anything of value owned by a person or a firm. The owners of sole proprietorships and partnerships have unlimited liability, which means there is no legal distinction between the personal assets of the owners of the business and the assets of the business. The owners of corporations have **limited liability**, which means they can never lose more than their investment in the firm. Although only 18 percent of firms are corporations, they account for the majority of revenue and profits earned by all firms.

 Visit **www.myeconlab.com** to complete these exercises online and get instant feedback.

Review Questions

1.1 What are the three major types of firms in the United States? Briefly discuss the most important characteristics of each type.

1.2 What is limited liability? Why does the government grant limited liability to the owners of corporations?

1.3 Why is limited liability more important for firms trying to raise funds from a large number of investors than for firms trying to raise funds from a small number of investors?

Problems and Applications

1.4 Suppose that shortly after graduating from college, you decide to start your own business. Will you be likely to organize the business as a sole proprietorship, a partnership, or a corporation? Explain your reasoning.

1.5 How would the establishment of limited liability for the owners of corporations affect the production possibilities frontier of a country over time?

1.6 Evaluate the following argument:

I would like to invest in the stock market, but I think that buying shares of stock in a corporation is too risky. Suppose I buy $10,000 of Facebook stock, and the company ends up going bankrupt. Because as a stockholder I'm part owner of the company, I might be responsible for paying hundreds of thousands of dollars of the company's debts.

1.7 According to an article in the *Economist* magazine, historian David Faure has argued that the Chinese economy failed to grow rapidly during the nineteenth century because "family-run companies . . . could not raise sufficient capital to exploit the large-scale opportunities tied to the rise of the steam engine, notably railways and (with limited exceptions) global shipping and automated manufacturing." How did the United States solve the problem of firms raising enough funds to operate railroads and other large-scale businesses?
Source: "The PCCW Buy-Out in Court," *Economist*, April 21, 2009.

1.8 **[Related to the** Making the Connection **on page 240]** Why might large existing firms be more likely to focus on improving existing goods and services than on introducing new ones? Why might small new firms take the opposite approach?

1.9 **[Related to the** Making the Connection **on page 240]** Muhammad Yunus is a Ph.D. economist and winner of the Nobel Peace Prize in 2006. He founded the Grameen Bank and was an innovator in using microcredit, or small loans—often of $100 or less—to spur growth in developing countries. "Yunus realized that very small loans to very poor people could make a big difference" in the ability of entrepreneurs in developing countries to start new businesses. Why would the funding to start small firms be more difficult in developing countries than in the United States? How do most entrepreneurs in the United States obtain funds to start new firms?
Source: William Easterly, *The White Man's Burden: Why the West's Efforts to Aid the Rest Have Done So Much Ill and So Little Good,* New York: Penguin Books, 2006, pp. 58–59.

The Structure of Corporations and the Principal–Agent Problem, pages 241–242
LEARNING OBJECTIVE: Describe the typical management structure of corporations and understand the concepts of separation of ownership from control and the principal–agent problem.

Summary

Corporate governance refers to the way in which a corporation is structured and the effect a corporation's structure has on the firm's behavior. Most corporations have a similar management structure: The shareholders elect a board of directors that appoints the corporation's top managers, such as the chief executive officer (CEO). Because top managers often do not own a large fraction of the stock in the corporation, large corporations have a **separation of ownership from control**. When top managers have less incentive to increase the corporation's profits than to increase their own salaries and their own enjoyment, corporations can suffer from the **principal–agent problem**. The principal–agent problem exists when the principals—in this case, the shareholders of the corporation—have difficulty getting the agent—the corporation's top management—to carry out their wishes.

MyEconLab   Visit **www.myeconlab.com** to complete these exercises online and get instant feedback.

Review Questions

2.1 What does it mean to say that there is a separation of ownership from control in large corporations?

2.2 How is the separation of ownership from control related to the principal–agent problem?

2.3 Why is it important for a board of directors to have outside directors, as opposed to only inside directors?

Problems and Applications

2.4 The principal–agent problem arises almost everywhere in the business world, and it also crops up even closer to home. Discuss the principal–agent problem that exists in the college classroom. Who is the principal? Who is the agent? What potential conflicts in objectives exist between this principal and this agent?

2.5 In a public corporation, the principal–agent problem between ownership and top management results from asymmetric information. What information, if known, would prevent this principal–agent problem?

2.6 Sales personnel, whether selling life insurance, automobiles, or pharmaceuticals, typically get paid on commission instead of a straight hourly wage. How does paying a commission help solve the principal–agent problem between the owners of a business and the sales force?

2.7 **[Related to** Solved Problem 8.2 **on page 242]** Briefly explain whether you agree with the following argument: "The separation of ownership from control in large corporations and the principal–agent problem mean that top managers can work short days, take long vacations, and otherwise slack off."

2.8 **[Related to** Solved Problem 8.2 **on page 242]** The members of many corporate boards of directors have to be reelected by the firm's stockholders every year. Some corporations, though, have staggered elections for their boards of directors, with only one-half or one-third of the members being up for election each year. According to an article in the *Economist* magazine, studies have found that firms that have staggered elections for their boards of directors are less profitable than similar firms where all members of the boards of directors are elected each year. Provide a possible explanation for this finding.
Source: "A Different Class," *Economist*, February 18, 2011.

2.9 Private equity firms, such as Blackstone and Kohlberg Kravis Roberts & Co., search for firms where the managers appear not to be maximizing profits. A private equity firm can buy stock in these firms and have its employees elected to the firms' boards of directors and may even acquire control of the targeted firm and replace the top management. Does the existence of private equity firms reduce any problems in corporate governance? Briefly explain.

 How Firms Raise Funds, pages 242–249
LEARNING OBJECTIVE: Explain how firms raise the funds they need to operate and expand.

Summary

Firms rely on retained earnings—which are profits retained by the firm and not paid out to the firm's owners—or on using the savings of households for the funds they need to operate and expand. With **direct finance**, the savings of households flow directly to businesses when investors buy **stocks** and **bonds** in financial markets. With **indirect finance**, savings flow indirectly to businesses when households deposit money in saving and checking accounts in banks and the banks lend these funds to businesses. Federal, state, and local governments also sell bonds in financial markets, and households also borrow funds from banks. When a firm sells a bond, it is borrowing money from the buyer of the bond. Firms make **coupon payments** to buyers of bonds. The **interest rate** is the cost of borrowing funds, usually expressed as a percentage of the amount borrowed. When a firm sells stock, it is selling part ownership of the firm to the buyer of the stock. **Dividends** are payments by a corporation to its shareholders. The original purchasers of stocks and bonds may resell them in stock and bond markets, such as the New York Stock Exchange. The performance of the U.S. stock market is often measured using stock market indexes. The three most widely followed stock indexes are the Dow Jones Industrial Average, the S&P 500, and the NASDAQ Composite Index.

MyEconLab   Visit **www.myeconlab.com** to complete these exercises online and get instant feedback.

Review Questions

3.1 What is the difference between direct finance and indirect finance? If you borrow money from a bank to buy a new car, are you using direct finance or indirect finance?

3.2 Why is a bond considered to be a loan but a share of stock is not? Why do corporations issue both bonds and shares of stock?

3.3 How do the stock and bond markets provide information to businesses? Why do stock and bond prices change over time?

Problems and Applications

3.4 Suppose that a firm in which you have invested is losing money. Would you rather own the firm's stock or the firm's bonds? Briefly explain.

3.5 Suppose you originally invested in a firm when it was small and unprofitable. Now the firm has grown to be large and profitable. Would you be better off if you had bought the firm's stock or the firm's bonds? Briefly explain.

3.6 If you deposit $20,000 in a savings account at a bank, you might earn 1 percent interest per year. Someone who borrows $20,000 from a bank to buy a new car might have to pay an interest rate of 6 percent per year on the loan. Knowing this, why don't you just lend your money directly to the car buyer, cutting out the bank?

3.7 **[Related to the** Chapter Opener **on page 237]** Were the shares of stock issued as a result of Facebook's initial public offering (IPO) sold in a primary market or a secondary market? Was the IPO an example of direct finance or indirect finance?

3.8 **[Related to the** Making the Connection **on page 244]** In 2013, the government of Thailand was suffering large losses on a rice subsidy program introduced to raise the incomes of rice farmers. An article in the *Wall Street Journal* reported that: "Moody's Investors Service on Monday warned that losses from the subsidy could threaten Thailand's stable Baa1 rating."
  a. What is Moody's top bond rating? Why might Thailand not have received this rating even before the Thai government began to suffer large losses on the rice subsidy program?
  b. If Moody's decides to downgrade Thailand's debt rating, what will be the likely result for the interest rate the Thai government will have to pay when it sells bonds? Briefly explain.
  Source: James Hookway and Sameer Mohindru, "Thailand's Credibility Risks Beating over Rice Dispute," *Wall Street Journal*, June 7, 2013.

3.9 What effect would the following events be likely to have on the price of Google's stock?
  a. A competitor launches a search engine that is better than Google's.
  b. The corporate income tax is abolished.
  c. Google's board of directors becomes dominated by close friends and relatives of its top management.

  d. The price of wireless Internet connections in developing countries unexpectedly drops, so more and more people world wide use the Internet.
  e. Google announces a profit of $10 billion, but investors anticipated that Google would earn a profit of $11 billion.

3.10 The following appeared in an article in the *Wall Street Journal* about the bond market in high-income (or developed) countries (that is, the United States and countries in Europe) and the emerging-market countries (that is, Latin American and Asian countries):
  "In the developed markets, it's been about analyzing the business cycle, and in emerging markets, it's been about solvency," says David Rolley, the co-manager of the Loomis Sayles Global Bond fund. "Now it's not. You have to do both for both." . . . It could ultimately mean that developed economies, the U.S. included, could face extra penalties for the perceived, even if ever-so-slight, risk that they may not repay their debts.
  a. What does it mean to say that the emerging markets have been about "solvency"?
  b. What are the "extra penalties" the developed economies could face from the increase in perceived risk?
  Source: Matthieu Wirz and Matt Phillips, "Sea Change in Map of Global Risk," *Wall Street Journal*, August 1, 2011.

3.11 **[Related to the** Don't Let This Happen to You **on page 246]** Briefly explain whether you agree with the following statement: "The total value of the shares of Microsoft stock traded on the NASDAQ last week was $250 million, so the firm actually received more revenue from stock sales than from selling software."

3.12 **[Related to the** Making the Connection **on page 248]** Loans from banks are the most important external source of funds to businesses because most businesses are too small to borrow in financial markets by issuing stocks or bonds. Most investors are reluctant to buy the stocks or bonds of small businesses because of the difficulty of gathering accurate information on the financial strength and profitability of these businesses. Nevertheless, news about the stock market is included in nearly every network news program and is often the lead story in the business section of most newspapers. Is there a contradiction here? Why is the average viewer of TV news or the average reader of a newspaper interested in the fluctuations in prices in the stock market?

3.13 **[Related to the** Making the Connection **on page 248]** The following table shows information on June 7, 2013 on the stock price of Starbucks Corporation:
  a. How much did the price of Starbucks' stock change from the day before?
  b. Did the Starbucks' stock price vary much during this day's trading?
  c. Did the price of Starbucks' stock vary much over the preceding 52 weeks?
  d. How many shares of Starbucks' stock were traded on this day?

Symbol	Open	High	Low	Close	Net Chg	Volume	52-Week High	52-Week Low	Div
SBUX	63.41	65.09	63.41	65.04	0.01	6,794,623	65.09	43.04	0.84

Using Financial Statements to Evaluate a Corporation, pages 249–251

LEARNING OBJECTIVE: Understand the information provided in corporations' financial statements.

Summary

A firm's **income statement** sums up its revenues, costs, and profit over a period of time. A firm's **balance sheet** sums up its financial position on a particular day, usually the end of a quarter or year. A balance sheet records a firm's assets and liabilities. A **liability** is anything owed by a person or a firm. Firms report their **accounting profit** on their income statements. Accounting profit does not always include all of a firm's **opportunity cost**. **Explicit cost** is a cost that involves spending money. **Implicit cost** is a nonmonetary opportunity cost. Because accounting profit excludes some implicit costs, it is larger than **economic profit**.

MyEconLab   Visit www.myeconlab.com to complete these exercises online and get instant feedback.

Review Questions

4.1 What is the difference between a firm's assets and its liabilities? Give an example of an asset and an example of a liability.

4.2 What is the difference between a firm's balance sheet and its income statement?

4.3 Distinguish between a firm's explicit costs and its implicit costs and between a firm's accounting profit and its economic profit.

4.4 Would a business be expected to survive in the long run if it earned a positive accounting profit but a negative economic profit? Briefly explain.

Problems and Applications

4.5 Paolo currently has $100,000 invested in bonds that earn him 10 percent interest per year. He wants to open a pizza restaurant and is considering either selling the bonds and using the $100,000 to start his restaurant or borrowing $100,000 from a bank, which would charge him an annual interest rate of 7 percent. He finally decides to sell the bonds and not take out the bank loan. He reasons, "Because I already have the $100,000 invested in the bonds, I don't have to pay anything to use the money. If I take out the bank loan, I have to pay interest, so my costs of producing pizza will be higher if I take out the loan than if I sell the bonds." What do you think of Paolo's reasoning?

4.6 Paolo and Alfredo are twins who both want to open pizza restaurants. Their parents have always liked Alfredo best, and they buy two pizza ovens and give both to him. Unfortunately, Paolo must buy his own pizza ovens. Does Alfredo have a lower cost of producing pizza than Paolo does because Alfredo received his pizza ovens as a gift, while Paolo had to pay for his? Briefly explain.

4.7 Dane decides to give up a job earning $200,000 per year as a corporate lawyer and converts the duplex that he owns into a UFO museum. (He had been renting out the duplex for $20,000 a year.) His direct expenses include $75,000 per year paid to his assistants and $10,000 per year for utilities. Fans flock to the museum to see his collection of extraterrestrial paraphernalia, which he could easily sell on eBay for $1,000,000. Over the course of the year, the museum brings in revenues of $200,000.
  a. How much is Dane's accounting profit for the year?
  b. Is Dane earning an economic profit? Explain.

4.8 The Securities and Exchange Commission requires that every firm that wishes to issue stocks and bonds to the public make available its balance sheet and income statement. Briefly explain how information useful to investors can be found in these financial statements.

Corporate Governance Policy and the Financial Crisis of 2007–2009, pages 251–255

LEARNING OBJECTIVE: Discuss the role that corporate governance problems may have played in the financial crisis of 2007–2009.

Summary

Because their compensation often rises with the profitability of the corporation, top managers have an incentive to overstate the profits reported on their firm's income statements. During the early 2000s, it became clear that the top managers of several large corporations had done this, even though intentionally falsifying financial statements is illegal. The *Sarbanes-Oxley Act* of 2002 took several steps intended to increase the accuracy of financial statements and increase the penalties for falsifying them. The financial crisis of 2007–2009 revealed that many financial firms held assets that were far riskier than investors had realized. Congress passed the **Wall Street Reform and Consumer Protection Act (Dodd-Frank Act)** in July 2010 to address some of the issues raised by the financial crisis of 2007–2009.

MyEconLab   Visit www.myeconlab.com to complete these exercises online and get instant feedback.

Review Questions

5.1 What is the Sarbanes-Oxley Act? Why was it passed?

5.2 What was the source of the problems encountered by many financial firms during the crisis of 2007–2009?

Problems and Applications

5.3 The following is from an article in *USA Today*:

> In what some call a worldwide corporate-governance movement, shareholders are pushing

for stronger corporate-governance laws, teaming with investors from different countries and negotiating behind the scenes with businesses.

What is corporate governance? Why would shareholders push for stronger corporate governance laws?

Source: Edward Iwata, "Corporate Governance Gets More Transparent Worldwide," *USA Today*, February 17, 2008.

5.4 According to an article in the *Wall Street Journal*: "Companies in Standard & Poor's 500 stock index elected the smallest number of new directors last year [2012] in 10 years . . . ." Is having members of boards of directors serve for longer periods likely to be good news or bad news for corporate governance? Briefly explain.

Source: Joann S. Lublin, "The 40-Year Club: America's Longest-Serving Directors," *Wall Street Journal*, July 16, 2013.

5.5 An article in the *Wall Street Journal* observes: "Being on the board of directors of a publicly traded company isn't as much fun as it used to be. You're tied up in accounting red tape as a result of reforms under the Sarbanes-Oxley Act of 2002 . . . ." Is it possible to put a dollar value on the benefits to the economy of corporations complying with Sarbanes-Oxley? Which groups are likely to receive the most benefits from Sarbanes-Oxley: investors, corporations, or some other group?

Source: Jason Zweig, "Would You Want to Be a Director of This Company?" *Wall Street Journal*, July 24, 2013.

5.6 **[Related to the** Making the Connection **on page 254]** Jay Ritter, a professor at the University of Florida, was quoted in the *Wall Street Journal* as saying about Facebook: "It's entirely possible for a company to have solid growth prospects while its stock is overvalued."
a. What does it mean to say that a stock is "overvalued"?
b. Why might a firm's stock be overvalued despite the firm having "solid growth prospects"?

Source: Mark Hulbert, "A Year after Its Debut, Facebook Still Looks Overpriced," *Wall Street Journal*, May 17, 2013.

5.7 An article about corporate fraud on forbes.com stated that "misleading accounting and disclosure practices weaken the integrity of capital markets." The article noted that

using incentive contracts for top managers can create a "'perverse' incentive to manipulate stock prices because their (executive) total package is based on stock price appreciation."
a. Why do financial markets depend on accurate accounting and disclosure practices? Why can misleading accounting and disclosure practices weaken the integrity of financial markets?
b. Why do corporate boards of directors sometimes link top managers' compensation to the corporations' stock prices? Briefly explain how tying compensation too closely to stock prices might create an incentive for corporate fraud.

Source: John Wasik, "How Corporate Fraud Costs You Money: Four Red Flags," forbes.com, June 17, 2013.

Real-Time-Data Exercises

D8.1 **[The stock market and recessions]** Go to the Web site of the Federal Reserve Bank of St. Louis (FRED) (research.stlouisfed.org/fred2/) and download and graph the data series for the S&P 500 stock index (SP500) from January 1957 until the most recent day available. Go to the Web site of the National Bureau of Economic Research (nber.org) and find the dates for business cycle peaks and troughs (the period between a business cycle peak and trough is a recession). Describe how stock prices move just before, during, and just after a recession. Is the pattern the same across recessions?

D8.2 **[Exploring dividends]** Go to wsj.com and find the dividend per share for each of the following firms:
a. Microsoft
b. Apple
c. Coca-Cola
d. Facebook
To find the dividend per share, enter the company's name in the search box on the home page. Which pays the highest dividend? Which has the highest dividend yield? Which does not pay a dividend? Why might a firm not pay a dividend? Why would investors buy the stock of a firm that does not pay a dividend?

Appendix

Tools to Analyze Firms' Financial Information

8A LEARNING OBJECTIVE

Understand the concept of present value and the information contained on a firm's income statement and balance sheet.

As we saw in the chapter, modern business firms are not just "black boxes" transforming inputs into output. The majority of business revenues and profits are earned by large corporations. Unlike founder-dominated firms, the typical large corporation is run by managers who generally do not own a controlling interest in the firm. Large firms raise funds from outside investors, and outside investors seek information on firms and the assurance that the managers of firms will act in the interests of the investors.

This chapter shows how corporations raise funds by issuing stocks and bonds. This appendix provides more detail to support that discussion. We begin by analyzing *present value* as a key concept in determining the prices of financial securities. We then provide greater information on *financial statements* issued by corporations, using Facebook as an example.

Using Present Value to Make Investment Decisions

Firms raise funds by selling equity (stock) and debt (bonds and loans) to investors and lenders. If you own shares of stock or a bond, you will receive payments in the form of dividends or coupons over a number of years. Most people value funds they already have more highly than funds they will receive some time in the future. For example, you would probably not trade $1,000 you already have for $1,000 you will not receive for one year. The longer you have to wait to receive a payment, the less value it will have for you. One thousand dollars you will not receive for two years is worth less to you than $1,000 you will receive after one year. The value you give today to money you will receive in the future is called the future payment's **present value**. The present value of $1,000 you will receive in one year will be less than $1,000.

Present value The value in today's dollars of funds to be paid or received in the future.

Why is the $1,000 you will not receive for one year less valuable to you than the $1,000 you already have? The most important reason is that if you have $1,000 today, you can use that $1,000 today. You can buy goods and services with the money and receive enjoyment from them. The $1,000 you receive in one year does not have direct use to you now.

Also, prices will likely rise during the year you are waiting to receive your $1,000. So, when you finally do receive the $1,000 in one year, you will not be able to buy as much with it as you could with $1,000 today. Finally, there is some risk that you will not receive the $1,000 in one year. The risk may be very great if an unreliable friend borrows $1,000 from you and vaguely promises to pay you back in one year. The risk may be very small if you lend money to the federal government by buying a U.S. Treasury bond. In either case, though, there is at least some risk that you will not receive the funds promised.

When someone lends money, the lender expects to be paid back both the amount of the loan and some additional interest. Say that you decide that you are willing to lend your $1,000 today if you are paid back $1,100 one year from now. In this case, you are charging $100/$1,000 = 0.10, or 10 percent interest on the funds you have loaned. Economists would say that you value $1,000 today as equivalent to the $1,100 to be received one year in the future.

Notice that $1,100 can be written as $1,000(1 + 0.10). That is, the value of money received in the future is equal to the value of money in the present multiplied by 1 plus the interest rate, with the interest rate expressed as a decimal. Or:

$$\$1,100 = \$1,000(1 + 0.10).$$

Notice, also, that if we divide both sides by $(1 + 0.10)$, we can rewrite this formula as:

$$\$1,000 = \frac{\$1,100}{(1 + 0.10)}.$$

The rewritten formula states that the present value is equal to the future value to be received in one year divided by 1 plus the interest rate. This formula is important because you can use it to convert any amount to be received in one year into its present value. Writing the formula generally, we have:

$$\text{Present value} = \frac{\text{Future value}_1}{(1 + i)}.$$

The present value of funds to be received in one year—Future value$_1$—can be calculated by dividing the amount of those funds to be received by 1 plus the interest rate. With an interest rate of 10 percent, the present value of $\$1,000,000$ to be received one year from now is:

$$\frac{\$1,000,000}{(1 + 0.10)} = \$909,090.91.$$

This formula allows us to calculate the value today of funds that will be received in one year. But financial securities such as stocks and bonds involve promises to pay funds over many years. Therefore, it would be useful if we could expand this formula to calculate the present value of funds to be received more than one year in the future.

This expansion is easy to do. Go back to the original example, where we assumed you were willing to loan out your $\$1,000$ for one year, provided that you received 10 percent interest. Suppose you are asked to lend the funds for two years and that you are promised 10 percent interest per year for each year of the loan. That is, you are lending $\$1,000$, which at 10 percent interest will grow to $\$1,100$ after one year, and you are agreeing to loan that $\$1,100$ out for a second year at 10 percent interest. So, after two years, you will be paid back $\$1,100(1 + 0.10)$, or $\$1,210$. Or:

$$\$1,210 = \$1,000(1 + 0.10)(1 + 0.10),$$

or:

$$\$1,210 = \$1,000(1 + 0.10)^2.$$

This formula can also be rewritten as:

$$\$1,000 = \frac{\$1.210}{(1 + 0.10)^2}.$$

To put this formula in words, the $\$1,210$ you receive two years from now has a present value equal to $\$1,210$ divided by the quantity 1 plus the interest rate squared. If you agree to lend out your $\$1,000$ for three years at 10 percent interest, you will receive:

$$\$1,331 = \$1,000(1 + 0.10)^3.$$

Notice, again, that:

$$\$1,000 = \frac{\$1,331}{(1 + 0.10)^3}.$$

You can probably see a pattern here. We can generalize the concept to say that the present value of funds to be received n years in the future—whether n is 1, 20, or 85 does not matter—equals the amount of the funds to be received divided by the quantity 1 plus the interest rate raised to the nth power. For instance, with an interest rate of 10 percent, the value of $\$1,000,000$ to be received 25 years in the future is:

$$\text{Present value} = \frac{\$1,000,000}{(1 + 0.10)^{25}} = \$92,296.$$

Or, more generally:

$$\text{Present value} = \frac{\text{Future value}_n}{(1 + i)^n}$$

where Future value$_n$ represents funds that will be received in n years.

Solved Problem 8A.1

How to Receive Your Contest Winnings

Suppose you win a contest and are given the choice of the following prizes:

Prize 1: $50,000 to be received right away, with four additional payments of $50,000 to be received each year for the next four years
Prize 2: $175,000 to be received right away

Explain which prize you would choose and the basis for your decision.

Solving the Problem

Step 1: **Review the material.** This problem involves applying the concept of present value, so you may want to review the section "Using Present Value to Make Investment Decisions" which begins on page 261.

Step 2: **Explain the basis for choosing the prize.** Unless you need cash immediately, you should choose the prize with the highest present value.

Step 3: **Calculate the present value of each prize.** Prize 2 consists of one payment of $175,000 received right away, so its present value is $175,000. Prize 1 consists of five payments spread out over time. To find the present value of the prize, we must find the present value of each of these payments and add them together. To calculate present value, we must use an interest rate. Let's assume an interest rate of 10 percent. In that case, the present value of Prize 1 is:

$$\$50,000 + \frac{\$50,000}{(1 + 0.10)} + \frac{\$50,000}{(1 + 0.10)^2} + \frac{\$50,000}{(1 + 0.10)^3} + \frac{\$50,000}{(1 + 0.10)^4}$$

$$= \$50,000 + \$45,454.55 + \$41,322.31 + \$37,565.74 + \$34,150.67$$

$$= \$208,493.$$

Step 4: **State your conclusion.** Prize 1 has the greater present value, so you should choose it rather than Prize 2.

Your Turn: For more practice, do related problems 8A.6, 8A.7, 8A.8, and 8A.9 on page 268 at the end of this appendix.

Using Present Value to Calculate Bond Prices

Anyone who buys stocks or bonds is really buying a promise to receive certain payments—dividends in the case of stocks or coupons in the case of bonds. The price investors are willing to pay for a financial asset should be equal to the value of the payments they will receive as a result of owning the asset. Because most of the coupon or dividend payments will be received in the future, it is their present value that matters. Put another way, we have the following important idea: *The price of a financial asset should be equal to the present value of the payments to be received from owning that asset.*

Let's consider an example. Suppose that in 1986, General Electric issued a bond with an $80 coupon that will mature in 2016. It is now 2014, and that bond has been bought and sold by investors many times. You are considering buying it. If you buy the bond, you will receive two years of coupon payments plus a final payment of the bond's principal, or face value, of $1,000. Suppose, once again, that you need an interest rate of 10 percent to invest your funds. If the bond has a coupon of $80, the present value of the payments you receive from owning the bond—and, therefore, the present value of the bond—will be:

$$\text{Present value} = \frac{\$80}{(1 + 0.10)} + \frac{\$80}{(1 + 0.10)^2} + \frac{\$1,000}{(1 + 0.10)^2} = \$965.29.$$

That is, the present value of the bond will equal the present value of the three payments you will receive during the two years you own the bond. You should, therefore, be willing to pay $965.29 to own this bond and have the right to receive these payments from GE. This process of calculating present values of future payments is used to determine bond prices, with one qualification: The relevant interest rate used by investors in the bond market to calculate the present value and, therefore, the price of an existing bond is usually the coupon rate on comparable newly issued bonds. Therefore, the general formula for the price of a bond is:

$$\text{Bond price} = \frac{\text{Coupon}_1}{(1 + i)} + \frac{\text{Coupon}_2}{(1 + i)^2} + \cdots + \frac{\text{Coupon}_n}{(1 + i)^n} + \frac{\text{Face value}}{(1 + i)^n},$$

where Coupon_1 is the coupon payment to be received after one year, Coupon_2 is the coupon payment to be received after two years, up to Coupon_n, which is the coupon payment received in the year the bond matures. The ellipsis takes the place of the coupon payments—if any—received between the second year and the year when the bond matures. Face value is the amount that will be received when the bond matures. The interest rate on comparable newly issued bonds is i. MyEconLab Concept Check

Using Present Value to Calculate Stock Prices

When you own a firm's stock, you are legally entitled to your share of the firm's profits. Remember that the profits a firm pays out to its shareholders are referred to as *dividends*. The price of a share of stock should be equal to the present value of the dividends investors expect to receive as a result of owning that stock. Therefore, the general formula for the price of a stock is:

$$\text{Stock price} = \frac{\text{Dividend}_1}{(1 + i)} + \frac{\text{Dividend}_2}{(1 + i)^2} + \cdots$$

Notice that this formula looks very similar to the one we used to calculate the price of a bond, with a couple of important differences. First, unlike a bond, a share of stock has no maturity date, so we have to calculate the present value of an infinite number of dividend payments. At first, it may seem that the stock's price must be infinite as well, but remember that dollars you don't receive for many years are worth very little today. For instance, a dividend payment of $10 that will be received 40 years in the future is worth only a little more than $0.20 today at a 10 percent interest rate. The second difference between the stock price formula and the bond price formula is that the coupon payments you receive from owning the bond are known with certainty—they are set when the bond is issued and cannot be changed—you don't know for sure what the dividend payments from owning a stock will be. How large a dividend payment you will receive depends on how profitable the company will be in the future.

Although it is possible to forecast the future profitability of a company, this cannot be done with perfect accuracy. To emphasize this point, some economists rewrite the basic stock price formula by adding a superscript e to each dividend term to emphasize that these are *expected* dividend payments. Because the future profitability of companies is often very difficult to forecast, it is not surprising that differences of opinion exist over what the price of a particular stock should be. Some investors will be very optimistic about the future profitability of a company and will, therefore, believe that the company's stock should have a high price. Other investors might be very pessimistic and believe that the company's stock should have a low price.   MyEconLab Concept Check

A Simple Formula for Calculating Stock Prices

It is possible to simplify the formula for determining the price of a stock, if we assume that dividends will grow at a constant rate:

$$\text{Stock price} = \frac{\text{Dividend}}{(i - \text{Growth rate})}.$$

In this equation, Dividend is the dividend expected to be received one year from now, and Growth rate is the rate at which those dividends are expected to grow. If a company pays a dividend of $1 per share to be received one year from now and Growth rate is 10 percent, the company is expected to pay a dividend of $1.10 the following year, $1.21 the year after that, and so on.

Now suppose that IBM will pay a dividend of $5 per share at the end of year, the consensus of investors is that these dividends will increase at a rate of 5 percent per year for the indefinite future, and the interest rate is 10 percent. Then the price of IBM's stock should be:

$$\text{Stock price} = \frac{\$5.00}{(0.10 - 0.05)} = \$100.00.$$

Particularly during the years 1999 and 2000, there was much discussion of whether the high prices of many Internet stocks—such as the stock of Amazon.com—were justified, given that many of these companies had not made any profit yet and so had not paid any dividends. Is there any way that a rational investor would pay a high price for the stock of a company currently not earning profits? The formula for determining stock prices shows that it is possible, provided that the investor's assumptions are optimistic enough! For example, during 1999, one stock analyst predicted that Amazon.com would soon be earning $10 per share of stock. That is, Amazon.com's total earnings divided by the number of shares of its stock outstanding would be $10. Suppose Amazon.com pays out that $10 in dividends and that the $10 will grow rapidly over the years, by, say, 7 percent per year. Then the formula indicates that the price of Amazon.com stock should be:

$$\text{Stock price} = \frac{\$10.00}{(0.10 - 0.07)} = \$333.33.$$

If you are sufficiently optimistic about the future prospects of a company, a high stock price can be justified even if the company is not currently earning a profit. But investors in stocks must be careful. Suppose investors decide that growth prospects for Amazon are only 4 percent per year instead of 7 percent because the firm turns out not to be as profitable as initially believed. Then our formula indicates that the price of Amazon.com stock should be:

$$\text{Stock price} = \frac{\$10.00}{(0.10 - 0.04)} = \$166.67.$$

This price is only half the price determined assuming a more optimistic growth rate. Hence investors use information about a firm's profitability and growth prospects to determine what the firm is worth.   MyEconLab Concept Check

Going Deeper into Financial Statements

Corporations disclose substantial information about their business operations and financial position to actual and potential investors. Some of this information meets the demands of participants in financial markets and of information-collection agencies, such as Moody's Investors Service, which develops credit ratings that help investors judge how risky corporate bonds are. Other information meets the reporting requirements of the U.S. Securities and Exchange Commission.

Key sources of information about a corporation's profitability and financial position are its principal financial statements—the *income statement* and the *balance sheet*. These important information sources were first introduced in the chapter. In the following section we go into more detail, using recent data for Facebook as an example.

Analyzing Income Statements

As discussed in the chapter, a firm's income statement summarizes its revenues, costs, and profit over a period of time. Figure 8A.1 shows Facebook's income statement for 2012.

Facebook's income statement presents the results of the company's operations during the year. Listed first are the revenues it earned, largely from selling advertising on its Web site, from January 1, 2012, to December 31, 2012: $5,089 million. Listed next are Facebook's operating expenses, the most important of which is its *cost of revenue*—which is commonly known as *cost of sales* or *cost of goods sold*: $1,364 million. Cost of revenue is the direct cost of producing the products sold, including in this case the salaries of the computer programmers Facebook hires to write the software for its Web site. Facebook also has substantial costs for researching and developing its products ($1,399 million) and for advertising and marketing them ($896 million). General and administrative expenses ($892 million) include costs such as the salaries of top managers.

The difference between a firm's revenue and its costs is its profit. Profit shows up in several forms on an income statement. A firm's *operating income* is the difference between its revenue and its operating expenses. Most corporations, including Facebook, also have interest expenses and income from investments, such as government and corporate bonds. In this case, Facebook paid $44 million more in interest expenses than it earned on its investments, so its *income before taxes* was $494 million. The federal government taxes the profits of corporations. During 2012, Facebook paid $441 million in taxes. *Net income* after taxes was $53 million. That this level of profits is low considering the price of Facebook's stock is another indication that investors were expecting Facebook's profits to

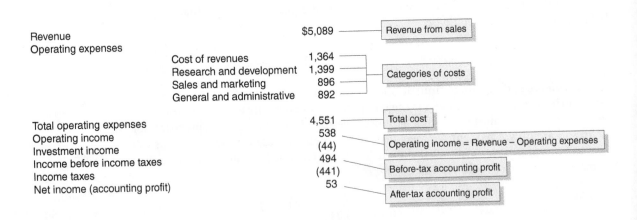

Note: All numbers are in millions of dollars.

Figure 8A.1 **Facebook's Income Statement for 2012**

MyEconLab Real-time data

Facebook's income statement shows the company's revenue, costs, and profit for 2012. The difference between its revenue ($5,089 million) and its operating expenses ($4,551 million) is its operating income ($538 million). Most corporations also have interest expenses and income from investments, such as government and corporate bonds. In this case, Facebook paid $44 million more in interest expenses than it

earned on its investments, so its *income before taxes* was $494 million. After paying taxes of $441 million, Facebook was left with a net income, or accounting profit, of $53 million for the year.

Note: Negative values are shown in parentheses.

Source: Facebook 2012 10-K Annual Report. SEC EDGAR Web site www.sec.gov/edgar.shtml.

be much larger in the future. The net income that firms report on their income statements is referred to as their after-tax *accounting profit*.   MyEconLab Concept Check

Analyzing Balance Sheets

As discussed in the chapter, while a firm's income statement reports the firm's activities for a period of time, a firm's balance sheet summarizes its financial position on a particular day, usually the end of a quarter or year. To understand how a balance sheet is organized, first recall that an asset is anything of value that the firm owns, and a liability is a debt or an obligation that the firm owes. Subtracting the value of a firm's liabilities from the value of its assets leaves its *net worth*. Because a corporation's stockholders are its owners, net worth is often listed as **stockholders' equity** on a balance sheet. Using these definitions, we can state the balance sheet equation (also called the basic accounting equation) as follows:

$$\text{Assets} - \text{Liabilities} = \text{Stockholders' Equity,}$$

or:

$$\text{Assets} = \text{Liabilities} + \text{Stockholders' Equity.}$$

Stockholders' equity The difference between the value of a corporation's assets and the value of its liabilities; also known as *net worth*.

This equation tells us that the value of a firm's assets must equal the value of its liabilities plus the value of stockholders' equity. An important accounting rule dating back to the beginning of modern bookkeeping in fifteenth-century Italy holds that balance sheets should list assets on the left side and liabilities and net worth, or stockholders' equity, on the right side. Notice that this means that *the value of the left side of the balance sheet must always equal the value of the right side*. Figure 8A.2 shows Facebook's balance sheet as of December 31, 2012.

A couple of the entries on the asset side of the balance sheet may be unfamiliar: *Current assets* are assets that the firm could convert into cash quickly, such as the balance in its checking account or its accounts receivable, which is money currently owed to the firm for products that have been delivered but not yet paid for. *Goodwill* represents the difference between the purchase price of a company and the market value of its assets. It represents the ability of a business to earn an economic profit from its assets. For example, if you buy a restaurant that is located on a busy intersection and you employ a chef with a reputation for preparing delicious food, you may pay more than the market value of the tables, chairs, ovens, and other assets. This additional amount you pay will be entered on the asset side of your balance sheet as goodwill.

Current liabilities are short-term debts such as accounts payable, which is money owed to suppliers for goods received but not yet paid for, or bank loans that will be paid back in less than one year. Long-term bank loans and the value of outstanding corporate bonds are *long-term liabilities*.

MyEconLab Study Plan

Assets		Liabilities and Stockholders' Equity	
Current assets	$11,267	Current liabilities	$1,052
Property and equipment	2,391	Long-term liabilities	2,296
Goodwill	1,388	Total liabilities	3,348
Other long-term assets	57	Stockholders' equity	11,755
Total assets	$15,103	Total liabilities and stockholders' equity	$15,103

Note: All values are in millions of dollars.

Figure 8A.2

Facebook's Balance Sheet as of December 31, 2012

Corporations list their assets on the left of their balance sheets and their liabilities on the right. The difference between the value of a firm's assets and the value of its liabilities equals the net worth of the firm, or stockholders' equity. Stockholders' equity is listed on the right side of the balance sheet. Therefore, the value of the left side of the balance sheet must always equal the value of the right side.
Source: Facebook 2012 10-K Annual Report. SEC EDGAR Web site www.sec.gov/edgar.shtml.

Key Terms

Present value, p. 261   Stockholders' equity, p. 267

 Tools to Analyze Firms' Financial Information, pages 261–267

LEARNING OBJECTIVE: Understand the concept of present value and the information contained on a firm's income statement and balance sheet.

Review Questions

8A.1 Why is money you receive at some future date worth less to you than money you receive today? If the interest rate rises, what effect does this have on the present value of payments you receive in the future?

8A.2 Give the formula for calculating the present value of a bond that will pay a coupon of $100 per year for 10 years and that has a face value of $1,000.

8A.3 Compare the formula for calculating the present value of the payments you will receive from owning a bond to the formula for calculating the present value of the payments you will receive from owning a stock. What are the key similarities? What are the key differences?

8A.4 How is operating income calculated? How does operating income differ from net income? How does net income differ from accounting profit?

8A.5 What is the key difference between a firm's income statement and its balance sheet? What is listed on the left side of a balance sheet? What is listed on the right side?

Problems and Applications

8A.6 [Related to Solved Problem 8A.1 **on page 263**] If the interest rate is 10 percent, what is the present value of a bond that matures in two years, pays $85 one year from now, and pays $1,085 two years from now?

8A.7 [Related to Solved Problem 8A.1 **on page 263**] Before the 2013 season, the Los Angeles Angels signed outfielder Josh Hamilton to a contract that would pay him an immediate $10 million signing bonus and the following amounts: $15 million for the 2013 season, $15 million for the 2014 season, $23 million for the 2015 season, $30 million for the 2016 season, and $30 million for the 2017 season. The contract also specified that $2 million would be given to a charity. Assume that Hamilton receives each of his five seasonal salaries as a lump-sum payment at the end of the season.
  a. Some newspaper reports described Hamilton as having signed a $125 million contract with the Angels. Do you agree that $125 million was the value of this contract? Briefly explain.
  b. What was the present value of Hamilton's contract at the time he signed it (assuming an interest rate of 10 percent)? For simplicity, you can ignore the $2 million given to charity.

  c. If you use an interest rate of 5 percent, what was the present value of Hamilton's contract?
  Source: Drew Silva, "Breaking Down Josh Hamilton's Five-Year, $125M Contract," hardballtalk.nbcsports.com, December 15, 2012.

8A.8 [Related to Solved Problem 8A.1 **on page 263**] A winner of the Pennsylvania Lottery was given the choice of receiving $18 million at once or $1,440,000 per year for 25 years.
  a. If the winner had opted for the 25 annual payments, how much in total would she have received?
  b. At an interest rate of 10 percent, what would be the present value of the 25 payments?
  c. At an interest rate of 5 percent, what would be the present value of the 25 payments?
  d. What interest rate would make the present value of the 25 payments equal to the one payment of $18 million? (This question is difficult and requires the use of a financial calculator or a spreadsheet. *Hint:* If you are familiar with the Excel spreadsheet program, use the RATE function. You can answer parts (b) and (c) by using the Excel PV [Present Value] function.)

8A.9 [Related to Solved Problem 8A.1 **on page 263**] Before the start of the 2000 baseball season, the New York Mets decided they didn't want Bobby Bonilla playing for them any longer. But Bonilla had a contract with the Mets for the 2000 season that would have obliged the Mets to pay him $5.9 million. When the Mets released Bonilla, he agreed to take the following payments in lieu of the $5.9 million the Mets would have paid him in the year 2000: He would receive 25 equal payments of $1,193,248.20 each July 1 from 2011 to 2035. If you were Bobby Bonilla, which would you rather have had, the lump-sum $5.9 million in 2000 or the 25 payments beginning in 2011? Explain the basis for your decision.
  Source: Mike Sielski, "There's No Accounting for This," *Wall Street Journal*, July 1, 2010.

8A.10 Suppose that eLake, an online auction site, is paying a dividend of $2 per share. You expect this dividend to grow 2 percent per year, and the interest rate is 10 percent. What is the most you would be willing to pay for a share of stock in eLake? If the interest rate is 5 percent, what is the most you would be willing to pay? When interest rates in the economy decline, would you expect stock prices in general to rise or fall? Briefly explain.

8A.11 Suppose you buy the bond of a large corporation at a time when the inflation rate is very low. If the inflation rate increases during the time you hold the bond, what is likely to happen to the price of the bond?

8A.12 Use the information in the following table for calendar year 2012 to prepare an income statement for McDonald's Corporation. Be sure to include entries for operating income and net income.

Revenue from company restaurants	$18,603 million
Revenue from franchised restaurants	8,965 million
Cost of operating company-owned restaurants	15,224 million
Income taxes	2,614 million
Interest expense	517 million
General and administrative cost	2,455 million
Cost of restaurant leases	1,527 million

Source: McDonalds Corp. 2012 10-K Annual Report. SEC EDGAR Web site, www.sec.gov/edgar.shtml.

8A.13 Use the information in the following table on the financial situation of Starbucks Corporation as of December 31, 2012, to prepare a balance sheet for the firm. Be sure to include an entry for stockholders' equity.

Current assets	$4,220 million
Current liabilities	2,210 million
Property and equipment	2,659 million
Long-term liabilities	895 million
Goodwill	399 million
Other assets	962 million

Source: Starbucks Corp. (2012) 10-K Annual Report. SEC EDGAR Web site (www.sec.gov/edgar.shtml).

8A.14 The *current ratio* is equal to a firm's current assets divided by its current liabilities. Use the information in Figure 8A.2 on page 267 to calculate Facebook's current ratio on December 31, 2012. Investors generally prefer that a firm's current ratio be greater than 1.5. What problems might a firm encounter if the value of its current assets is low relative to the value of its current liabilities?

CREDITS

Photo

page 236, Reuters/Landov

Text

page 253, Michael Lewis, "The End," *Portfolio*, December 2008.

Chapter

1 WHAT IS ECONOMICS?

Answers to the Review Quiz

Page 2

1. List some examples of the scarcity that you face.

    Examples of scarcity common to students include not enough income to afford both tuition and a nice car, not enough learning capacity to study for both an economics exam and a chemistry exam in one night, and not enough time to allow extensive studying and extensive socializing.

3. Find an example of the distinction between microeconomics and macroeconomics in today's headlines.

    Microeconomics: On May 6, 2014 a headline in *The New York Times* was "Bayer Buys Merck's Consumer Business for $14.2 Billion." This story covers a microeconomic topic because it discusses how two pharmaceutical firms have decided to transfer ownership of the unit producing over-the-counter consumer products for Merck. *Macroeconomics*: On May 6, 2014, a headline in *The* Wall Street Journal was "U.S. Trade Gap Narrows as Demand Grows Here and Abroad." This story covers a macroeconomic topic because it concerns the total amount of international trade in the entire economy.

Page 7

1. Describe the broad facts about *what, how*, and *for whom* goods and services are produced.

    What gets produced is significantly different today than in the past. Today the U.S. economy produces more services, such as medical operations, teaching, and hair styling, than goods, such as pizza, automobiles, and computers. How goods and services are produced is by businesses determining how the factors of production, land, labor, capital and entrepreneurship, are combined to make the goods and services we consume. Land includes all natural resources, both renewable natural resources such as wood, and nonrenewable natural resources such as natural gas. Labor's quality depends on people's human capital. In the U.S. economy, human capital obtained through schooling has increased over the years with far more people completing high school and attending college than in past years. Finally, for whom are goods and services to be produced depends on the way income is distributed to U.S. citizens. This distribution is not equal; the 20 percent of people with the lowest income earn about 5 percent of the nation's total income while the 20 percent of people with the highest incomes earn about 50 percent of total income. On the average, men earn more than women, whites more than non-whites, and college graduates more than high school graduates.

Page 10

1. Explain the idea of a tradeoff and think of three tradeoffs that you have made today.

    A tradeoff reflects the point that when someone gets one thing, something else must be given up. What is given up is the opportunity cost of whatever is obtained. Three examples of tradeoffs that are common to students include: a) When a student sleeps in rather than going to his or her early morning economics class, the student trades off additional sleep for study time. The opportunity cost of the decision is a lower grade on the exam. b) When a student running late for class parks his or her car illegally, the student trades off saving time for the risk of a ticket. The potential opportunity cost of the decision is the goods and services that cannot be purchased if the student receives an expensive parking ticket. c) A student trades off higher income by spending time during the day working at a part-time job for less time spent at leisure time and study. The opportunity cost for the higher income is less leisure and lower grades in classes.

3.   Explain why opportunity cost is the best forgone alternative and provide examples of some opportunity costs that you have faced today.

When a decision to undertake one activity is made, often many alternative activities are no longer possible. Often these activities are mutually exclusive so only the highest valued alternative is actually forgone. For instance, the decision to go to a student's 8:30 AM class eliminates the possibility of sleeping in during the hour and of jogging during the hour. But in this case, it is impossible to *both* sleep in and to jog during the hour, so the opportunity cost cannot be both activities. What is lost is *only* the activity that otherwise would have been chosen—*either* sleeping in *or* jogging—which is whatever activity would have been chosen, that is, the most highly valued of the forgone alternatives. For students, attending class, doing homework, studying for a test are all activities with opportunity costs.

5.   Explain why choices respond to incentives and think of three incentives to which you have responded today.

People making rational decisions compare the marginal benefits of different actions to their marginal costs. Therefore people's choices change when their incentives, that is the marginal benefit and/or marginal cost, of the choice changes. Just as everyone else, students respond to incentives; a) A student studies because of the incentives offered by grades. b) A student is more likely to attend a class if attendance is factored into the grade. c) A student might attend a meeting of a club if the student's significant other is eager to attend the meeting.

Page 11

1.   Distinguish between a positive statement and a normative statement and provide examples.

A *positive* statement is a description of how the world *is*. It is testable. A *normative* statement is a description of how the world *ought to be*. It is, by its very nature, not testable because there is no universally approved criterion by which the statement can be judged. "I will receive an A for this course," is a positive statement made by an economics student—it might not be true, but it is testable. "I will receive a good grade for this course," is a normative statement. Whether someone agrees with it depends on his or her interpretation of what makes for a "good" grade.

3.   How do economists try to disentangle cause and effect?

Economists use models to understand some aspect of the economic world. Testing the predictions of models makes it necessary to disentangle cause and effect. To overcome this problem, economists have three methods of testing their models: Using a natural experiment, using a statistical investigation, and using economic experiments. A natural experiment is a situation that arises in the ordinary course of life in which one factor being studied varies and the other factors are the same. This method allows the economist to focus on the effect from the factor that differs between the two situations. A statistical investigation looks for correlations between variables but then determining whether the correlation actually reflects causation can be difficult. An economic experiment puts people into decision making situations and then varies the relevant factors one at a time to determine each factor's effect.

Answers to the Study Plan Problems and Applications

1. Apple Inc. decides to make iTunes freely available in unlimited quantities.

    a. Does Apple's decision change the incentives that people face?

    Apple's decision changes people's incentives. For example, it increases people's incentives to buy an iPod to take advantage of the newly "free" music available on iTunes.

    b. Is Apple's decision an example of a microeconomic or a macroeconomic issue?

    Apple's decision is a microeconomic decision because it affects a single company and a single market.

3. Explain how the following news headlines concern self-interest and the social interest.

    a. Starbucks Expands in China

    Starbucks' expansion is a decision made by Starbucks to further Starbucks' interest. Thus the decision is directly in Srarbucks' self interest. The social interest is affected because Starbucks' expansion will have an effect in China. For instance, more Chinese citizens might drink coffee rather than tea and fewer coffee shops run by Chinese firms might open.

    b. McDonald's Moves into Gourmet Coffee

    McDonald's decision to serve gourmet coffee is a decision made by McDonald's to further McDonald's interest. Thus the decision is directly in McDonald's self interest. The social interest is affected because more people will drink coffee rather than other drinks such as sodas.

    c. Food Must Be Labeled with Nutrition Data

    The decision to require that food must be labeled with nutrition information is made in the social interest. This decision is not made by any one single firm and so does not (necessarily) reflect anyone's self interest.

5. Cost of Sochi Winter Olympics

    The Russian government spent $6.7 billion on Olympic facilities and $16.7 billion upgrading Sochi area infrastructure. Sponsors spent $27.6 billion on hotels and facilities hoping to turn Sochi into a year-round tourist magnet.

    Source: *The Washington Post*, February 11, 2014

    Was the opportunity cost of the Sochi Olympics $6.7, $23.4, or $51 billion? Explain your answer.

    The $6.7 billion spent on Olympic facilities is definitely an opportunity cost of the Sochi Olympics. The $16.7 billion spent upgrading the Sochi area infrastructure and the $27.6 billion spent on hotels and facilities are an opportunity cost of the Sochi Olympics *if* the funds would not have spent otherwise. However, if there were already plans underway to upgrade the Sochi area infrastructure then the cost is not an opportunity cost of the Sochi Olympics because the cost would have been paid even if Sochi did not host the Olympics. Similarly, if there were already plans underway to build hotels and facilities in Sochi then the cost is not an opportunity cost of the Sochi Olympics because the cost would have been paid even if Sochi did not host the Olympics.

Answers to Additional Problems and Applications

7. **Rapper Offers Free Tickets for Concert**

Eminem will hit the road with Rihanna offering an awesome deal—buy one and get one free!

Source: *Mstars News*, February 24, 2014

When Eminem gave away tickets, what was free and what was scarce? Explain your answer.

The seats in the arenas are scarce—there are only a limited number. Also scarce is the time the enthusiastic fans spend in line to acquire the tickets. In addition, if the fans who with the "free" ticket attended the concert rather than sell their free tickets, they incurred the opportunity cost of the foregone ticket price. So the concert was far from "free" for the concert-goers. The publicity that Eminem receives is free to him but the publicity used reporters' scarce time to report on the lines for the tickets rather than reporting on other news worthy events.

9. How does a successful movie illustrate self-interested choices that are also in the social interest?

The a successful movie increases the income of the people involved with the movie. Hence these people's choices are driven largely by self interest. However the creation of a successful movie also increases the quantity of widely enjoyed entertainment. The amount of entertainment available in the economy increases which benefits society. So the choices the people made in their self interest also reflected choices made in the social interest.

11. What might be an incentive for you to take a class in summer school? List some of the benefits and costs involved in your decision. Would your choice be rational?

Early graduation, smaller class sizes, and/or retaining eligibility for a scholarship are examples of incentives that encourage taking summer classes. The benefits of taking summer classes might include early graduation, more personal attention from the instructor, retained eligibility for a scholarship, and increased knowledge about some aspect of the world. Costs potentially include forgone summer jobs or internships, less time to spend with friends, and additional tuition and other class-related expenses if the class I not one that would be taken otherwise. The choice is rational as long as the student determines that taking summer classes offers the highest benefit over cost for the use of his or time and efforts.

13. Provide two microeconomic statements and two macroeconomic statements. Classify your statements as positive or normative, and explain your classifications.

Microeconomic statements are: Fewer deep water oil wells should be drilled in the Gulf of Mexico. If less oil is produced, the price of oil will rise. The first statement is normative because it relies on what the person thinks "should" be done. The second statement is positive because it is possible to test the effect of less oil being produced.

Macroeconomic statements are: The currently unemployment rate is too high. The current unemployment rate is higher for blacks than for whites. The first statement is normative because it depends on what is deemed "too high." The second statement is positive because it can be checked to determine its validity.

Chapter

2 THE ECONOMIC PROBLEM

Answers to the Review Quizzes

Page 34

1. How does the production possibilities frontier illustrate scarcity?

   The unattainable combinations of production that lie *beyond* the *PPF* illustrate the concept of *scarcity*. There simply are not enough resources to produce any of these combinations of outputs. Additionally, while moving along the *PPF* to increase the production of one good requires that the production of another good be reduced, which also illustrates scarcity.

3. How does the production possibilities frontier show that every choice involves a tradeoff?

   Movements along the *PPF* frontier illustrate that producing more of one good requires producing less of other good. This observation reflects the result that a *tradeoff* must be made when producing output efficiently.

5. Why is opportunity cost a ratio?

   The slope of the *PPF* is a *ratio* that expresses the quantity of lost production of the good on the *y*-axis to the increase in the production of the good on the *x*-axis moving downward along the *PPF*. The steeper the slope, the greater ratio, and the greater is the opportunity cost of increasing the output of the good measured on the horizontal axis.

Page 37

1. What is marginal cost? How is it measured?

   Marginal cost is the opportunity cost of producing *one more unit* of a good or service. Along a *PPF* marginal cost is reflected in the absolute value of the slope of the *PPF*. In particular, the magnitude of the slope of the *PPF* is the marginal cost of a unit of the good measured along the *x*-axis. As the magnitude of the slope changes moving along the *PPF*, the marginal cost changes.

3. How does the marginal benefit from a good change as the quantity produced of that good increases?

   As the more of a good is consumed, the marginal benefit received from each unit is smaller than the marginal benefit received from the unit consumed immediately before it, and is larger than the marginal benefit from the unit consumed immediately after it. This set of results is known as the principle of *decreasing marginal benefit* and is often assumed by economists to be a common characteristic of an individual's preferences over most goods and services in the economy.

5. What conditions must be satisfied if resources are used efficiently?

   Resources are used efficiently when more of one good or service cannot be produced without producing less of some of another good or service that is *valued more highly*. This is known as *allocative efficiency* and it occurs when: 1) production efficiency is achieved, and 2) the marginal benefit received from the last unit produced is equal to the marginal cost of producing the last unit.

Page 39

1. What generates economic growth?

   The two key factors that generate economic growth are *technological change* and *capital accumulation*. Technological change allows an economy to produce more with the same amount of limited resources, Capital accumulation, the growth of capital resources including human capital, means that an economy has increased its available resources for production.

3. What is the opportunity cost of economic growth?

   When a society devotes more of its scarce resources to research and development of new technologies, or devotes additional resources to produce more capital equipment, both decisions lead to increased consumption opportunities in future periods at the cost of less consumption today. The loss of consumption today is the opportunity cost borne by society for creating economic growth.

5. Does economic growth overcome scarcity?

   Scarcity reflects the inability to satisfy all our wants. Regardless of the amount of economic growth, scarcity will remain present because it will never be possible to satisfy all our wants. For instance it will never be possible to satisfy all the wants of the several thousand people who all would like to ski the best slopes on Vail with only their family and a few best friends present. So economic growth allows more wants to be satisfied but it does not eliminate scarcity.

Page 43

1. What gives a person a comparative advantage?

   A person has a comparative advantage in an activity if that person can perform the activity at a lower opportunity cost than anyone else, If the person gives up the least amount of other goods and services to produce a particular good or service, the person has the lowest opportunity cost of producing that good or service.

3. Why do people specialize and trade?

   People can compare consumption possibilities from producing all goods and services through *self-sufficiency* against specializing in producing only those goods and services that reflect their comparative advantage and trading their output with others who do the same. People can then see that the consumption possibilities from specialization and trade are greater than under self-sufficiency. Therefore it is in people's own *self-interest* to specialize. It was Adam Smith who first pointed out in the *Wealth of Nations* how individuals *voluntarily* engage in this socially beneficial and cooperative activity through the pursuit of their own self-interest, rather than for society's best interests.

5. What is the source of the gains from trade?

   As long as people have different opportunity costs of producing goods or services, total output is higher with specialization and trade than if each individual produced goods and services under self-sufficiency. This increase in output is the gains from trade.

Page 45

1. Why are social institutions such as firms, markets, property rights, and money necessary?

   These social institutions factors necessary for a decentralized economy to coordinate production. *Firms* are necessary to allow people to specialize. Without firms, specialization would be limited because a person would need to specialize in the *entire* production of a good or service. With firms people are able to specialize in producing particular bits of a good or service. For a society to enjoy the fruits of specialization and trade, the individuals who comprise that society must voluntarily desire to specialize in the first place. Discovering trade opportunities after a person has specialized in his or her comparative advantage in production is what allows that person to gain from his or her own specialization efforts. Trading opportunities can only take place if a *market* exists where people observe prices to discover available trade opportunities. *Money* is necessary to allow low-cost trading in markets. Without money, goods would need to be directly exchanged for other goods, a difficult and unwieldy situation. Finally people must enjoy social recognition of and government protection of *property rights* to have confidence that their commitments to trade arrangements will be respected by everyone in the market.

3.   What are the flows in the market economy that go from firms to households and the flows from households to firms?

On the real side of the economy, goods and services flow from firms to households. On the monetary side of the economy, payments for factors of production, wages, rent, interest, and profits, flow from firms to households. Flowing from households to firms on the monetary side of the economy are the expenditures on goods and services and on the real side are the factors of production, labor, land, capital, and entrepreneurship.

Answers to the Study Plan Problems and Applications

Use the following data to work Problems 1 and 3. Brazil produces ethanol from sugar, and the land used to grow sugar can be used to grow food crops. The table to the right sets out Brazil's production possibilities for ethanol and food crops.

Ethanol (barrels per day)		Food crops (tons per day)
70	and	0
64	and	1
54	and	2
40	and	3
22	and	4
0	and	5

1. a. Draw a graph of Brazil's **PPF** and explain how your graph illustrates scarcity.

   Figure 2.1 shows Brazil's PPF. The production possibilities frontier indicates scarcity because it shows the limits to what can be produced. In particular, production combinations of ethanol and food crops that lie outside the production possibilities frontier are not attainable.

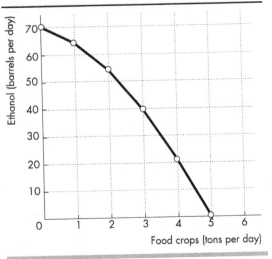

FIGURE **2.1**
Problem 1

   b. If Brazil produces 40 barrels of ethanol a day, how much food must it produce to achieve production efficiency?

   If Brazil produces 40 barrels of ethanol per day, it achieves production efficiency if it also produces 3 tons of food per day.

   c. Why does Brazil face a tradeoff on its **PPF**?

   Brazil faces a tradeoff on its PPF because Brazil's resources and technology are limited. For Brazil to produce more of one good, it must shift factors of production away from the other good. Therefore to increase production of one good requires decreasing production of the other, which reflects a tradeoff.

3. Does Brazil face an increasing opportunity cost of ethanol? What feature of Brazil's PPF illustrates increasing opportunity cost?

   Brazil faces an increasing opportunity cost of ethanol production. For instance, when increasing ethanol production from 0 barrels per day to 22 barrels the opportunity cost of a barrel of ethanol is 1/22 of a ton of food while increasing ethanol production another 18 barrels per day (to a total of 40 barrels per day) has an opportunity cost of 1/18 of a ton of food per barrel of ethanol. The PPF's bowed outward shape reflects the increasing opportunity cost.

Use the above table (for Problems 1 and 3) to work Problem 5.

5. Define marginal benefit. Explain how it is measured and why the data in the table does not enable you to calculate Brazil's marginal benefit from food.

   The marginal benefit of a good is the benefit received from consuming one more unit of the good. The marginal benefit of a good or service is measured by the most people are willing to pay for one more unit of it. The data in the table do not provide information on how much people are willing to pay for an additional unit of food. The table has no information on the marginal benefit of food.

7. A farm grows wheat and produces pork. The marginal cost of producing each of these products increases as more of it is produced.

   a. Make a graph that illustrates the farm's *PPF*.

   The *PPF* is illustrated in Figure 2.2 as PPF_0. Because the marginal cost of both wheat and pork increase as more of the good is produced, the *PPF* displays increasing opportunity cost so it has the "conventional" bowed-outward shape.

   b. The farm adopts a new technology that allows it to use fewer resources to fatten pigs. On your graph sketch the impact of the new technology on the farm's **PPF**.

   The new technology rotates the *PPF* outward from PPF_0 to PPF_1.

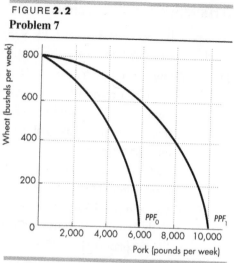

FIGURE **2.2**
Problem 7

   c. With the farm using the new technology described in part (b), has the opportunity cost of producing a ton of wheat increased, decreased, or remained the same? Explain and illustrate your answer.

   The opportunity cost of producing wheat has increased. The opportunity cost of a bushel of wheat is equal to the magnitude of 1/(slope of the *PPF*). As illustrated in Figure 2.2, for each quantity of wheat the slope of PPF_1 has a smaller magnitude than the slope of PPF_0 so the opportunity cost of a bushel of wheat is higher along PPF_1. For a specific example, the opportunity cost of increasing wheat product from 600 bushels per week to 800 bushels per week along PPF_1 is 6,000 pounds of pork but is only 3,000 pounds of pork along PPF_0.

   d. Is the farm more efficient with the new technology than it was with the old one? Why?

   The farm is able to produce more with the new technology than with the old, but it is not necessarily more efficient. If the farm was producing on its *PPF* before the new technology and after, the farm was production efficient both before the new technology and after.

9. Suppose that Tessa buys a new machine for making jackets that enables her to make 20 jackets an hour. (She can still make only 80 caps per hour.)

   a. Who now has a comparative advantage in producing jackets?

   Sue forgoes 40 caps to produce 4 jackets, so Sue's opportunity cost of producing one jacket is (40 caps)/(4 jackets) or 10 caps per jacket. Tessa forgoes 80 caps to produce 20 jackets, so Tessa's opportunity cost of producing one jacket is (80 caps)/(20 jackets) or 4 caps per jacket. Tessa has the comparative advantage in producing jackets because her opportunity cost of a jacket is lower than Sue's opportunity cost.

   b. Can Sue and Tessa still gain from trade?

   Tessa and Sue can still gain from trade because Tessa (now) has a comparative advantage in producing jackets and Sue (now) has a comparative advantage in producing caps. Tessa will produce jackets and Sue will produce caps.

   c. Would Sue and Tessa still be willing to trade 1 jacket for 15 caps? Explain your answer.

   Sue and Tessa will not be willing to trade 1 jacket for 15 caps. In particular, Sue, whose comparative advantage lies in producing caps, can produce 1 jacket at an opportunity cost of only 10 caps. So Sue will be unwilling to pay any more than 10 caps per jacket.

Answers to Additional Problems and Applications

Use the table to work Problem 11. Suppose that Yucatan's production possibilities are given in the table.

Food (pounds per month)		Sunscreen (gallons per month)
300	and	0
200	and	50
100	and	100
0	and	150

11. a. Draw a graph of Yucatan's PPF and explain how your graph illustrates a tradeoff.

   Yucatan's PPF is illustrated in Figure 2.3. The figure illustrates a tradeoff because moving along Yucatan's PPF producing more of one good requires producing less of the other good. Yucatan trades off more production of one good for less production of the other.

FIGURE 2.3
Problem 11a

   b. If Yucatan produces 150 pounds of food per month, how much sunscreen must it produce if it achieves production efficiency?

   If Yucatan produces 150 pounds of food per month, then the point labeled A on the PPF in Figure 2.11 shows that Yucatan must produce 75 gallons of sunscreen per month to achieve production efficiency.

   c. What is Yucatan's opportunity cost of producing (i) 1 pound of food and (ii) 1 gallon of sunscreen?

   Yucatan's PPF is linear so the opportunity cost of producing 1 pound of food is the same at all quantities. Calculate the opportunity cost of producing 1 pound of food when increasing the production of food from 0 to 100 pounds per month. Between these two ranges of production, the quantity of sunscreen produced falls from 150 gallons per month to 100 gallons per month, a decrease of 50 gallons. The opportunity cost is 50 gallons of sunscreen to gain 100 pounds of food. The opportunity cost per pound of food equals (50 gallons of sunscreen)/(100 pounds of food), or an opportunity cost of 0.5 gallon of sunscreen per pound of food.

   Yucatan's PPF is linear so the opportunity cost of producing 1 gallon of sunscreen is the same at all quantities. Calculate the opportunity cost of producing 1 gallon of sunscreen when increasing the production of sunscreen from 0 to 50 gallons per month. Between these two ranges of production, the quantity of food produced falls from 300 pounds per month to 200 pounds per month, a decrease of 100 pounds. The opportunity cost is 100 pounds of food to gain 50 gallons of sunscreen, or (100 pounds of food)/(50 gallons of sunscreen) which yields an opportunity cost of 2.0 pounds of food per gallon of sunscreen.

   e. What is the relationship between your answers to part (c)?

   Answers (c) and (d) reflect the fact that opportunity cost is a ratio. The opportunity cost of gaining a unit of a good moving along the PPF equals the quantity of the other good or service forgone divided by the quantity of the good or service gained. The opportunity cost of one good, food, is equal to the inverse of the opportunity cost of the other good, sunscreen.

13. In problem 11, what is the marginal cost of 1 pound of food in Yucatan when the quantity produced is 150 pounds per day? What is special about the marginal cost of food in Yucatan?

> The marginal cost of a pound of food in Yucatan is constant at all points along Yucatan's *PPF* and is equal to 0.5 gallons of sunscreen per pound of food. The special point about Yucatan's marginal cost is the fact that the marginal cost is constant. This result reflects Yucatan's linear *PPF*.

15. **U.K. Music Stores Squeezed off Main Street**

Music retailing is changing: Sony Music and Amazon are selling online, discount stores are selling at low prices, and Main Street music retailers are all struggling.

Source: *The Economist*, 20 January 2007

a. Draw the *PPF* curves for Main Street music retailers and online music retailers before and after the Internet became available.

> Before there was an Internet, there were no online retailers and the production possibilities frontier was PPF_0 in Figure 2.4. After the Internet was developed, online retailers were created and started to sell songs. The Internet is a technological advance that rotates the production possibilities frontier outward to PPF_1 in Figure 2.4.

FIGURE **2.4**

Problem 15a

b. Draw the marginal cost and marginal benefit curves for Main Street music retailers and online music retailers before and after the Internet became available.

> Online music retailers have a lower marginal cost of delivering recorded music than do main street music retailers. The marginal benefit for recorded music is the same regardless of whether the music came from an online store or a main street store. Therefore in Figure 2.5 the marginal benefit curve for recorded music is MB, the marginal cost of main street stores is MC_0, and the marginal cost of online stores is MC_1.

FIGURE **2.5**

Problem 15b

c. Explain how changes in production possibilities, preferences or both have changed the way in which recorded music is retailed.

> The change in production possibilities, which created lower-cost online recorded music stores, have changed the way recorded music is purchased. Because the marginal cost of buying recorded music is less using an online store, today most recorded music is purchased from online stores. Consequently main street music stores are disappearing as they go bankrupt and fail.

Use the following news clip to work Problem 17.

Malaria Eradication Back on the Table

In response to the Gates Malaria Forum in October 2007, countries are debating the pros and cons of eradication. Dr. Arata Kochi of the World Health Organization believes that with enough money malaria cases could be cut by 90 percent, but it would be very expensive to eliminate the remaining10 percent of cases, so countries should not strive to eradicate malaria.

Source: *The New York Times*, March 4, 2008

17.   Make a graph with the percentage of malaria cases eliminated on the *x*-axis and the marginal cost and marginal benefit of driving down malaria cases on the *y*-axis. On your graph:

(i)   Draw a marginal cost curve and marginal benefit curve that are consistent with Dr. Kochi's opinion.

(ii)   Identify the quantity of malaria eradicated that achieves allocative efficiency.

FIGURE **2.6**
Problem 17

Figure 2.6 shows a marginal cost curve and a marginal benefit curve that are consistent with Dr. Kochi's views. Dr. Kochi believes that the last 10 percent of malaria would be very expensive to eradicate. The marginal cost curve in the figure reflects this view because the marginal cost curve rises rapidly after 90 percent of malaria is eradicated. The marginal benefit curve is downward sloping, reflecting diminishing marginal benefit from malaria eradication. The allocatively efficient quantity of malaria eradicated is 90 percent because that is the quantity for which the marginal benefit of eradication equals the marginal cost of eradication. This outcome demonstrates Dr. Kochi's conclusion that countries should not attempt to completely.

19.   **Toyota Plans to Build a Better Company**

Toyota will continue to produce 3 million cars per year and use the balance of its resources to upgrade its workers' skills and create new technology. In three years' time, Toyota plans to produce better cars and be more productive.

Source: *Financial Post*, April 7, 2014

a.   What is the opportunity cost of upgrading its workers' skills and creating new technology?

The opportunity cost of upgrading workers' skills and creating new technology is the next best alternative forgone by these changes. The story indicates that the next best alternative for Toyota is building new cars, so the opportunity cost of upgrading workers' skills and creating new technology is the current production of new cars that are forgone.

b. Sketch Toyota's *PPF* and mark its production point in 2014. Now show on your graph Toyota's *PPF* in 2018.

Figure 2.7 shows Toyota's *PPF* in 2014 and in 2018. The upgrade in workers' skills and the new technology shift Toyota's *PPF* outward so that its *PPF* in 2018 lies beyond its *PPF* in 2014. Toyota's production point in 2014 is labeled A.

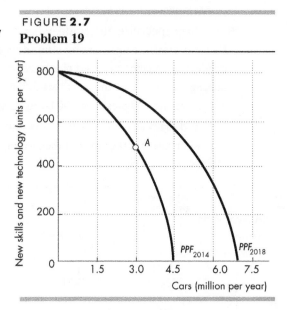

FIGURE **2.7**
Problem 19

Use the following data to work Problem 21.

Kim can produce 40 pies or 400 cakes an hour. Liam can produce 100 pies or 200 cakes an hour.

21. a   Draw a graph of Kim's *PPF* and Liam's *PPF* and show the point at which each produces when they spend 30 minutes of each hour producing pies and 30 minutes producing cakes.

FIGURE **2.8**
Problem 21a

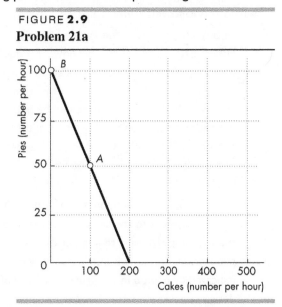

FIGURE **2.9**
Problem 21a

Kim's *PPF* is illustrated in Figure 2.8; Liam's *PPF* is illustrated in Figure 2.9.

Point *A* in both figures shows their production points when each spends 30 minutes making cakes and 30 minutes making pies.

b. On your graph, show what Kim produces and what Liam produces when they specialize.

Kim will specialize in cakes and Liam will specialize in pies. Point B in both figures shows the production points when each specializes.

c. When they specialize and trade, what are the total gains from trade?

Kim will specialize in cakes and Liam will specialize in pies. If they specialize and trade, the total production of *both* cakes and pies increase. When each spends 30 minutes making cakes and 30 minutes making pies, together they produce 300 cakes and 70 pies. When they specialize, together they produce 400 cakes and 100 pies. The 100 increase in cakes and the 30 increase pies is the gains from trade.

d. If Kim and Liam share the total gains equally, what trade takes place between them?

Kim will trade 50 cakes (half of the gain in cake production) to Liam in exchange for 15 pies (half of the increase in pie production).

Tony's Production Possibilities			Patty's Production Possibilities		
Snowboards (units per week)		Skis (units per week)	Snowboards (units per week)		Skis (units per week)
25	and	0	20	and	0
20	and	10	10	and	5
15	and	20	0	and	10
10	and	30			
5	And	40			
0	And	50			

23. Indicate on a graph of the circular flows in the market economy, the real and money flows in which the following items belong:

a. You buy an iPad from the Apple Store.

FIGURE **2.10**
Problem 23

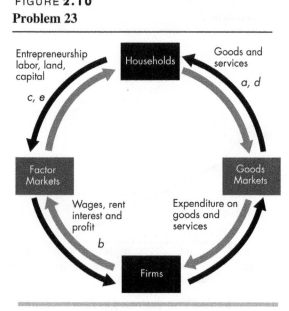

Figure 2.10 shows the circular flows in a market economy. Your purchase of an iPad from Apple is the purchase of a good from a firm. This flow is in the black arrow indicated by point *a* in the figure. When you pay for the iPad, the corresponding money flow is in the grey arrow in the opposite direction to the black arrow labeled *a*.

b. Apple Inc. pays the designers of the iPad.

Apple's payment to the designers of the iPad is the payment of a wage to a factor of production. This flow is in the grey arrow indicated by point *b* in the figure. The flow of design services from the designer to Apple is in the black arrow in the opposite direction to the grey arrow labeled *b*.

d. Apple Inc. decides to expand and rents an adjacent building.

Apple's decision to expand by renting a building means that Apple is increasing the capital it uses. This flow is in the black arrow indicated by point c in the figure. The flow of the payment for the rental services of the building is in the grey arrow in the opposite direction to the black arrow labeled c.

d. You buy a new e-book from Amazon.

Your purchase of an e-book from Amazon is the purchase of a good from a firm. This flow is in the black arrow indicated by point d in the figure. When you pay for the e-book, the corresponding money flow is in the grey arrow in the opposite direction to the black arrow labeled d.

e. Apple Inc. hires a student as an intern during the summer.

Apple's decision to hire a student intern is Apple increasing the labor it uses. The flow of labor services is in the black arrow indicated by point e in the figure. The flow of the payment for the labor services is in the grey arrow in the opposite direction to the black arrow labeled c.

Economics in the News

2 5 . **Lots of Little Screens**

Inexpensive broadband access has created a generation of television producers for whom the Internet is their native medium. As they redirect the focus from TV to computers, cell phones, and iPods, the video market is developing into an open digital network.

Source: *The New York Times*, December 2, 2007

a. How has inexpensive broadband changed the production possibilities of video entertainment and other goods and services?

Inexpensive broadband has increased the production possibilities.

b. Sketch a *PPF* for video entertainment and other goods and services before broadband.

The *PPF* should have video entertainment on one axis and other goods and services on the other as illustrated in Figure 2.11 by PPF_0. The *PPF* is bowed outward as a conventional *PPF*.

c. Show how the arrival of inexpensive broadband has changed the *PPF*.

The arrival of inexpensive broadband shifts the *PPF* outward as shown by the change from PPF_0 to PPF_1 in Figure 2.11. The intersection of the new *PPF* along the axis measuring video entertainment increases and the intersection of the new *PPF* along the axis measuring other goods and services does not change.

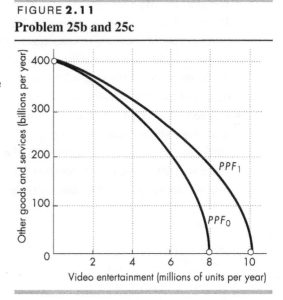

FIGURE **2.11**
Problem 25b and 25c

© 2016 Pearson Education, Inc.

d. Sketch a marginal benefit curve for video entertainment.

    The marginal benefit curve should be a conventional downward-sloping marginal benefit curve as shown in Figure 2.12. The marginal benefit from video entertainment is measured along the vertical axis and the quantity of video entertainment is measured along the horizontal axis.

e. Show how the new generation of TV producers for whom the Internet is their native medium might have changed the marginal benefit from video entertainment.

    The marginal benefit increases because these new producers will be better able to take advantage of the Internet since it is their native medium. Because they will be able to create entertainment designed for the Internet, the marginal benefit from video entertainment increases. In Figure 2.12, the marginal benefit curve shifts rightward from the initial marginal benefit curve, MB_0, to the new marginal benefit curve, MB_1.

f. Explain how the efficient quantity of video entertainment has changed.

    The arrival of broadband has decreased the marginal cost of providing video entertainment, so the marginal cost curve shifts rightward. This shift is illustrated in the Figure 2.13 by the rightward shift of the marginal cost curve from MC_0 to MC_1. As Figure 2.13 shows, the allocatively efficient quantity of video entertainment increases. In Figure 2.13, the allocatively efficient quantity increases from 5 million units per year to 8 million units per year.

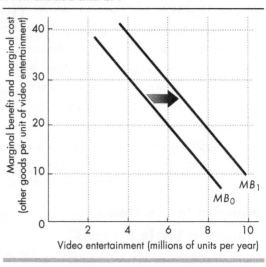

FIGURE **2.12**

Problem 25d and 25e

FIGURE **2.13**

Problem 25f

3 DEMAND AND SUPPLY

Answers to the Review Quizzes

Page 56

1. What is the distinction between a money price and a relative price?

   The money price of a good is the dollar amount that must be paid for it. The relative price of a good is its money price expressed as a ratio to the money price of another good. Thus the relative price is the amount of the other good that must be foregone to purchase a unit of the first good.

3. Think of examples of goods whose relative price has risen or fallen by a large amount.

   Some examples of items where both the money price and the relative price have risen over time are gasoline, college tuition, and food. Some examples of items where both the money price and the relative price have fallen over time are personal computers, HD televisions, and calculators.

Page 61

1. Define the quantity demanded of a good or service.

   The *quantity demanded* of a good or service is the amount that consumers plan to buy during a given time period at a particular price.

3. What does the demand curve tell us about the price that consumers are willing to pay?

   For any fixed quantity of a good available, the vertical distance of the demand curve from the *x*-axis shows the *maximum price* that consumers are willing to pay for that quantity of the good. The price on the demand curve at this quantity indicates the marginal benefit to consumers of the last unit consumed at that quantity.

5. Why does demand not change when the price of a good changes with no change in the other influences on buying plans?

   If the price of a good falls and nothing else changes, then the *quantity of the good demanded* increases and there is a movement down along the demand curve, but the *demand* for the good remains unchanged and the demand curve does not shift.

Page 65

1. Define the quantity supplied of a good or service.

   The quantity supplied of a good or service is the amount of the good or service that firms plan to sell in a given period of time at a specified price.

3. What does the supply curve tell us about the producer's minimum supply price?

   For any quantity, the vertical distance between the supply curve and the *x*-axis shows the *minimum price* that suppliers must receive to produce that quantity of output. As a result, the price is the marginal cost of the last unit produced at this level of output.

5.   What happens to the quantity of cell phones supplied and the supply of cell phones if the price of a cell phone falls?

> If the price of cell phones falls and nothing else changes, then the *quantity of cell phones supplied* will decrease and there is a movement down along the supply curve for cell phones. The *supply* of cell phones, however, remains unchanged and the supply curve does not shift.

Page 67

1.   What is the equilibrium price of a good or service?

> The *equilibrium price* is the price at which the quantity demanded by the buyers is equal to the quantity supplied by the sellers.

3.   Over what range of prices does a surplus arise? What happens to the price when there is a surplus?

> A surplus arises at market prices above the equilibrium price. A *surplus* causes the price to fall, decreasing quantity supplied and increasing quantity demanded until the equilibrium price is attained.

5.   Why is the equilibrium price the best deal available for both buyers and sellers?

> The equilibrium price reflects that the highest price consumers are willing to pay for that amount of the good or service and is just equal to the minimum price that suppliers require for delivering it. Demanders would prefer to pay a lower price, but suppliers are unwilling to supply that quantity at a lower price. Suppliers would prefer a higher price, but demanders are unwilling to pay a higher price for that quantity. Hence neither demanders not suppliers can do business at a better price.

Page 73

What is the effect on the price and quantity of MP3 players (such as the iPod) if

1.   The price of a PC falls or the price of an MP3 download rises? (Draw the diagrams!)

> A fall in the price of a PC decreases the demand for MP3 players because a PC is a *substitute* for an MP3 player. The demand curve for MP3 players shifts leftward. Supply remains unchanged. The price of an MP3 player falls and the quantity of MP3 players decreases.

> A rise in the price of an MP3 download decreases the demand for MP3 players because an MP3 download is a *complement* of an MP3 player. The demand curve for MP3 players shifts leftward. Supply remains unchanged. The price of an MP3 player falls and the quantity of MP3 players decreases.

3.   Any two of these events in questions 1 and 2 occur together? (Draw the diagrams!)
        There are six combinations:

            (1) If the price of a PC falls and the price of an MP3 download rises, demand decreases, supply is
            unchanged, so the price falls and the quantity decreases.

            (2) If the price of a PC falls and more firms produce MP3 players, demand decreases and supply
            increases so the price falls and the quantity might increase, decrease, or not change.

            (3) If the price of PC falls and the wages paid electronic workers rise, demand decreases and
            supply decreases so the quantity decreases and the price might rise, fall, or not change.

            (4) If the price of an MP3 download rises and more firms produce MP3 players, demand
            decreases and supply increases so the price falls and quantity might increase or decrease or
            remain the same.

            (5) If the price of an MP3 download falls and the wages paid electronic workers rise, demand
            decreases and supply decreases so the quantity decreases and the price might rise or fall or
            remain the same.

            (6) If more firms produce MP3 players and the wages paid electronics workers rise, supply might
            increase or decrease or remain unchanged, demand is unchanged, so the outcome cannot be
            predicted.

Answers to the Study Plan Problems and Applications

1. In April 2014, the money price of a carton of milk was $2.01 and the money price of gallon of gasoline was $3.63. Calculate the relative price of a gallon of gasoline in terms of milk.

    The relative price of a gallon of gasoline in terms of milk equals ($3.63 per gallon of gasoline)/($2.01 per carton of milk) = 1.81 cartons of milk per gallon of gasoline.

3. Which of the following goods are likely substitutes and which are likely complements? (You may use an item in more than once.):

    coal, oil, natural gas, wheat, corn, pasta, pizza, sausage, skateboard, roller blades, video game, laptop, iPad, cellphone, text message, email

    Substitutes include: coal and oil; coal and natural gas; oil and natural gas; wheat and corn; pasta and pizza; pasta and sausage; pizza and sausage (they type of sausage that cannot be used as a topping on pizza); skateboard and roller blades; skateboard and video game; roller blades and video game; laptop and iPad; and, text message and email.

    Complements include: pizza and sausage (the type of sausage that can be used as a topping on pizza); skateboard and iPad; roller blades and iPad; video game (those played on a computer) and laptop; cellphone and text message; and, cellphone (smart cellphone) and email.

5. In 2013, the price of corn fell and some corn farmers will switch from growing corn in 2014 to growing soybeans.

    a. Does this fact illustrate the law of demand or the law of supply? Explain your answer.

        This fact illustrates the law of supply: the lower price of corn decreases the quantity of corn grown.

    b. Why would a corn farmer grow soybeans?

        Corn and soybeans are substitutes in production and soybeans have become more profitable. A corn farmer would switch to soybeans because the profit from growing soybeans exceeds that from growing corn.

7. The demand and supply schedules for gum are in the table.

    a. Suppose that the price of gum is 70¢ a pack. Describe the situation in the gum market and explain how the price adjusts.

Price (cents per pack)	Quantity demanded	Quantity supplied
	(millions of packs a week)	
20	180	60
40	140	100
60	100	140
80	60	180

    At 70 cents a pack, there is a surplus of gum and the price falls. At 70 cents a pack, the quantity demanded is 80 million packs a week and the quantity supplied is 160 million packs a week. There is a surplus of 80 million packs a week. The price falls until market equilibrium is restored at a price of 50 cents a pack.

    b. Suppose that the price of gum is 30¢ a pack. Describe the situation in the gum market and explain how the price adjusts.

        At 30 cents a pack, there is a shortage of gum and the price rises. At 30 cents a pack, the quantity demanded is 160 million packs a week and the quantity supplied is 80 million packs a week. There is a shortage of 80 million packs a week. The price rises until market equilibrium is restored at a price of 50 cents a pack.

9. In Problem 7, a fire destroys some factories
    that produce gum and the quantity of gum
    supplied decreases by 40 million packs a week
    at each price.

    a. Explain what happens in the market for gum
        and draw a graph to illustrate the changes.

        As the number of gum-producing factories
        decreases, the supply of gum decreases. There is
        a new supply schedule and, in Figure 3.1, the
        supply curves shifts leftward by 40 million packs
        at each price to the new supply curve S_1. After
        the fire, the quantity supplied at 50 cents is now
        only 80 million packs, and there is a shortage of
        gum. The price rises to 60 cents a pack, at
        which the new quantity supplied equals the
        quantity demanded. The new equilibrium price
        is 60 cents and the new equilibrium quantity is
        100 million packs a week.

    b. If, at the time as the fire the teenage
        population increases and the quantity of
        gum demanded increases 40 million packs a
        week at each price. What is the new market
        equilibrium? Show the changes on your graph.

        The new price is 70 cents a pack, and the
        quantity is 120 million packs a week. The
        demand for gum increases and the demand
        curve shifts rightward by 40 million packs at
        each price. Supply decreases by 40 millions
        packs a week and the supply curve shifts
        leftward by 40 million packs at each price. These
        changes are shown in Figure 3.2 by the shift of
        the demand curve from D to D_1 and the shift of
        the supply curve from S to S_1. At any price
        below 70 cents a pack there is a shortage of
        gum. The price of gum rises until the shortage is
        eliminated.

FIGURE **3.1**
Problem 9

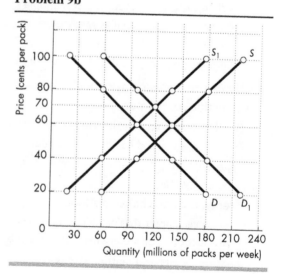

FIGURE **3.2**
Problem 9b

Answers to Additional Problems and Applications

11.   What features of the world market for crude oil make it a competitive market?

The world oil market is a competitive market because there are a large number of sellers and a large number of buyers. There are so many sellers and so many buyers that no individual seller or individual buyer can influence he price of oil.

13.   The price of gasoline has increased during the past year.

a.   Explain why the law of demand applies to gasoline just as it does to all other goods and services.

When the price of gasoline rises, people decrease the quantity of gasoline they demand. Both the substitution effect and the income effect lead consumers to decrease the quantity of gasoline demanded.

b.   Explain how the substitution effect influences gasoline purchases and provide some examples of substitutions that people might make when the price of gasoline rises and other things remain the same.

When the price of gasoline rises, people substitute other goods and services for gasoline. For instance, people substitute public transport (such as buses), carpools, motorcycles, walking, and bicycles for driving alone in a car to work.

c.   Explain how the income effect influences gasoline purchases and provide some examples of the income effects that might occur when the price of gasoline rises and other things remain the same.

When the price of gasoline rises, people's real incomes fall. People respond by decreasing their demand for normal goods, such as gasoline. In the gasoline market, some people trade in large, fuel guzzling cars because they can no longer afford to fuel the large vehicle. Others will not purchase a car or truck because they are not able to afford the gasoline necessary to use it.

15.   Classify the following pairs of goods and services as substitutes in production, complements in production, or neither.

a.   Bottled water and health club memberships

Bottled water and health club memberships are neither substitutes in production nor complements in production. (For consumers, these are complements because people in health clubs drink a lot of bottled water.)

b.   French fries and baked potatoes

For a restaurant that produces both French fries and baked potatoes, they are substitutes in production. (For a consumer, they are substitutes.)

c.   Leather boots and leather shoes

Leather boots and leather shoes are substitutes in production.

d.   Hybrids and SUVs

For an auto company that produces both on the same assembly line, they are substitutes in production. (For a consumer, hybrids and SUVs are substitutes.)

e.   Diet coke and regular coke

For a soda company that produces both on the same assembly line, they are substitutes in production. (For a consumer, Diet coke and regular coke are substitutes.)

17.   **New Maple Syrup Sap Method**

With the new way to tap maple trees, farmers could produce 10 times as much maple syrup per acre.

Source: cbc.ca, February 5, 2014

Will the new method change the supply of maple syrup or the quantity supplied of maple syrup, other things remaining the same. Explain.

> The new technology increases the supply of maple syrup. At each price, the new technology increases the quantity that will be supplied. The supply curve shifts rightward.

Use Figure 3.4 to work Problem 19.

19. a.   If the price of a pizza is $12, is there a shortage or a surplus and does the price rise or fall?

> If the price of a pizza is $12, there is a shortage of pizza; the quantity demanded of pizzas exceeds the quantity supplied. The shortage forces the price higher to the equilibrium price of $14 a pizza.

b.   Buyers want to pay the lowest possible price, so why would they be willing to pay more than $12 for a pizza?

> If the price of a pizza is $12 the shortage means that not all buyers can buy a pizza. From their perspective they would rather pay more than $12 and be able to purchase a pizza than to keep the price at $12 and leave them without a pizza.

FIGURE **3.4**
Problem 19

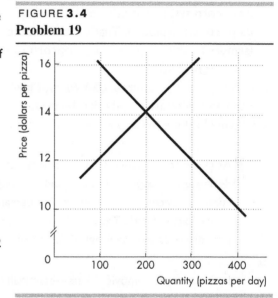

21.   A new dip increases the quantity of potato chips that people want to buy by 30 million bags per week at each price.

a.   Does the demand for chips change? Does the supply of chips change? Describe the change.

> As the new dip comes onto the market, the demand for potato chips increases. Supply does not change. The demand curves shifts rightward.

b.   How do the equilibrium price and equilibrium quantity of chips change?

> Demand increases by 30 million bags a week. The demand curve shifts rightward as shown in Figure 3.6 by the shift from D to D_1. The quantity demanded at each price increases by 30 million bags. The quantity demanded at 65¢ is now 175 million bags a week of potato chips. The price rises to 80¢ a bag, at which the quantity supplied equals the quantity demanded (160 million bags a week). The new equilibrium price is 80¢ per bag and the new equilibrium quantity is 160 million bags.

FIGURE **3.6**
Problem 21b

23. If the virus hits just as the new dip in Problem 21 comes onto the market, how do the equilibrium price and equilibrium quantity of chips change?

> The result by itself of the new dip entering the market is a price of 80¢ a bag and a quantity of 160 million bags. But now with the virus affecting the market, at this price there is a shortage of potato chips. The price of potato chips rises until the shortage is eliminated. The new equilibrium price is 100¢ a bag, and the new equilibrium quantity is 140 million bags a week.

25. **"Popcorn Movie" Experience Gets Pricier**
Cinemas are raising the price of popcorn. Demand for field corn, which is used for animal feed, corn syrup, and ethanol, has increased and its price has exploded. That's caused some farmers to shift from growing popcorn to easier-to-grow field corn.

> Source: *USA Today*, May 24, 2008

Explain and illustrate graphically the events described in the news clip in the market for

a. Popcorn

> As illustrated in Figure 3.7, the farmers' actions decrease the supply of popcorn and the supply curve of popcorn shifts leftward. The demand curve does not shift. The equilibrium price of popcorn rises and the quantity decreases.

b. Movie tickets

> In the market for movie tickets—essentially the market for viewing movies in the theater—popcorn and viewing movies are complements. The increase in the price of popcorn decreases the demand for attending movies in the theater. As a result, Figure 3.8 shows the demand curve shifting leftward. The equilibrium price of attending a movie in the theater falls and the equilibrium quantity decreases.

FIGURE **3.7**
Problem 25a

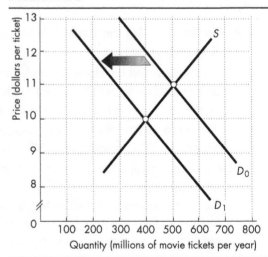

FIGURE **3.8**
Problem 25b

Economics in the News

27.   After you have studied *Economics in the news* on pp. 74–75, answer the following questions:

a.   What would happen to the price of bananas if TR4 spread to Central America?

The price of bananas would rise.

b.   What are some of the substitutes for bananas and what would happen to demand, supply, price, and quantity in the markets for these items if TR4 were to come to America?

Banana consumers could substitute other fruits, such as apples, peaches, or apricots. These changes would not change the supply of these products. The demand for these products, however, would increase, thereby raising their price and quantity.

c.   What are some of the complements of bananas and what would happen to demand, supply, price, and quantity in the markets for these items if TR4 were to come to America?

The classic complement for bananas is cereal. A rise in the price of bananas decreases the demand for cereal, so the demand curve for cereal shifts leftward. The supply of cereal is unaffected. The decrease in the demand for cereal lowers the equilibrium price of cereal and decreases the equilibrium quantity of cereal.

d.   When the price of bananas increased in 2008, did it rise by as much as the rise in the rise in the price of oil? Why or why not?

In 2008 the price of oil rose by about 70 percent, so the 20 percent price hike in the price of bananas was much less than the rise in price of oil. The price of oil is a cost of producing bananas. When the price of oil rose, the cost of producing bananas rose, so that the supply of bananas decreased. In response, the price of bananas rose. But there are other costs of producing bananas. The other costs did not rise by as much as the price of oil, so the decrease in the supply of bananas was smaller and, accordingly, the rise in the price of bananas was less than of oil.

e.   Why would the expectation of the future arrival of TR4 in the Americas have little or no effect on today's price of bananas?

If TR4 arrives in the Americas, the supply of bananas will decrease, thereby raising the price. The rise in the future expected for some goods can decrease the current supply and increase the current demand. But these changes assume that the good is storable. For example, the current supply decreases when the expected future price rises because producers store the product to sell in the future when its price is expected to be higher. Bananas, however, are not storable. Therefore producers (and demanders) do not respond to the higher expected future price.

Chapter
4 ELASTICITY

Answers to the Review Quizzes

Page 90

1. Why do we need a units-free measure of the responsiveness of the quantity demanded of a good or service to a change in its price?

    The elasticity of demand is a units-free measure. Compare it as a measure of the responsiveness to some other candidate that depends on the units, such as the slope. The slope of the demand curve changes as the units measuring the same quantity of the good change (going from pounds to ounces, for example). The value of the elasticity is independent of the units used to measure the price and quantity of the product. As a result, the elasticity can be compared across the same good when quantity is measured in different units and/or the price is measured in different currencies. The elasticities of different goods also can be compared even though they are measured in different units.

3. What makes the demand for some goods elastic and the demand for other goods inelastic?

    The magnitude of the price elasticity of demand for a good depends on three main influences:

    - ☐ *Closeness of substitutes.* The more easily people can substitute other items for a particular good, the larger is the price elasticity of demand for that good.

    - ☐ *The proportion of income spent on the good.* The larger the portion of the consumer's budget being spent on a good, the greater is the price elasticity of demand for that good.

    - ☐ *The time elapsed since a price change.* Usually, the more time that has passed after a price change, the greater is the price elasticity of demand for a good.

5. What is the total revenue test?

    The total revenue test is a method of estimating the price elasticity of demand by observing the change in total revenue, given a change in price, holding all other things constant. The total revenue test shows that a price cut increases total revenue if demand is elastic, decreases total revenue if demand is inelastic, and does not change total revenue if demand is unit elastic.

Page 94

1. What does the income elasticity of demand measure?

    The income elasticity of demand measures how the quantity demanded of a good responds to a change in income. The formula for the income elasticity of demand is the percentage change in the quantity of the good demanded divided by the percentage change in income.

3. What does the cross elasticity of demand measure?

    The cross elasticity of demand measures how the quantity demanded of one good responds to a change in the price of another good. The formula for the cross elasticity of demand is the percentage change in the quantity of the good demanded divided by the percentage change in the price of the related good.

Page 96

1. Why do we need a units-free measure of the responsiveness of the quantity supplied of a good or service to a change in its price?

    The elasticity of supply is a units-free measure. We need a units-free measure of the elasticity of supply for the same reason we need a units-free measure of the elasticity of demand: Because the value of the elasticity of supply is independent of the units used to measure the price and quantity of the good, the elasticity of supply can be compared across the same good when quantity is measured in different units and/or the price is measured in different currencies. In addition, the elasticities of supply of different goods also can be compared even though they are measured in different units.

3. What are the main influences on the elasticity of supply that make the supply of some goods elastic and the supply of other goods inelastic?

    The main influences on the elasticity of supply are:

    ☐ *Resource substitution possibilities*: the greater the suppliers' ability to substitute resources, the greater will be their ability to react to price changes and the greater the elasticity of supply.

    ☐ *Time frame for the supply decision*: the greater the amount of time available after the price change, the greater is the suppliers' ability to adjust quantity supplied, and the greater the elasticity of supply.

5. How does the time frame over which a supply decision is made influence the elasticity of supply? Explain your answer.

    The momentary supply, short-run supply, and long-run supply all illustrate the response of suppliers to changes in the price, but they differ according to how much time has elapsed after the price change.

    ☐ The *momentary supply* is frequently the least elastic and shows how suppliers cannot easily respond to a price change immediately after the price change occurs. Changing the quantity produced means changing the inputs into the production process, which takes time to complete. Sometimes the momentary supply is *perfectly inelastic*.

    ☐ The *short-run supply* shows suppliers' response after enough time has elapsed for some, but not all, of the possible technological adjustments have occurred. Short-run supply generally is intermediate in elasticity between the momentary supply and the long-run supply.

    ☐ The *long-run supply* shows how suppliers react after enough time has passed that *all* possible adjustments to factors of production have been made to accommodate the price change. It usually is the most elastic of the three supplies.

Answers to the Study Plan Problems and Applications

1. Rain spoils the strawberry crop, the price rises from $4 to $6 a box, and the quantity demanded decreases from 1,000 to 600 boxes a week.

    a. Calculate the price elasticity of demand over this price range.

    The price elasticity of demand is 1.25. The price elasticity of demand equals the percentage change in the quantity demanded divided by the percentage change in the price. The price rises from $4 to $6 a box, a rise of $2 a box. The average price is $5 a box. So the percentage change in the price is $2 divided by $5 and then multiplied by 100, which equals 40 percent. The quantity decreases from 1,000 to 600 boxes, a decrease of 400 boxes. The average quantity is 800 boxes. So the percentage change in quantity is 400 divided by 800, which equals 50 percent. The price elasticity of demand for strawberries is 50 percent divided by 40 percent, which equals 1.25.

    b. Describe the demand for strawberries.

    The price elasticity of demand exceeds 1, so the demand for strawberries is elastic.

3. The demand schedule for hotel rooms is in the table.

    a. What happens to total revenue when the price falls from $400 to $250 a room per night and from $250 to $200 a room per night?

    When the price is $400, the total revenue is equal to $400 × 50 million rooms, or $20 billion. When the price is $250, the total revenue is equal to $250 × 80 million rooms, or $20 billion. So the total revenue does not change when the price falls from $400 to $250 a night.

Price (dollars per night)	Quantity demanded (millions of rooms per night)
200	100
250	80
400	50
500	40
800	25

    When the price is $250, the total revenue is equal to $250 × 80 million rooms, or $20 billion. When the price is $200, the total revenue is equal to $200 × 100 million rooms, or $20 billion. So the total revenue does not change when the price falls from $400 to $250 a night.

    b. Is the demand for hotel rooms elastic, inelastic or unit elastic?

    The total revenue is the same at all prices, $20 billion. Because a change in price does not change the total revenue at *any* price, the demand is unit elastic at all prices.

5. In 2003, when music downloading first took off, Universal Music slashed the average price of a CD from $21 to $15. The company expected the price cut to boost the quantity of CDs sold by 30 percent, other things remaining the same.

    a. What was Universal Music's estimate of the price elasticity of demand for CDs?

    Using the data in the question, the price elasticity of demand is 0.90. The change in the price is $6 and the average of the two prices is $18, so the percentage change in the price is ($6/$18) × 100, which equals 33.3 percent. The increase in the quantity demanded was estimated to be 30 percent. The price elasticity of demand equals (30.0 percent)/(33.3 percent), or 0.90.

    b. If you were making the pricing decision at Universal Music, what would be your pricing decision? Explain your decision.

    The demand is inelastic, so if nothing else changes the price cut leads to a decrease in Universal Music's total revenue. However, downloaded music and CDs are substitutes for each other and the quantity of downloaded music was forecast to rise substantially. Effectively, the price of downloading music fell as more people gained access to the Internet and download sites proliferated. The fall in the price of the substitute, downloaded music, decreases the demand for Universal Music's CDs, so the decision to cut prices most likely was forced as the result of the (forecasted) decrease in demand for CDs.

7.   If a 12 percent rise in the price of orange juice decreases the quantity of orange juice demanded by 22 percent and increases the quantity of apple juice demanded by 14 percent, calculate the

   a.   Price elasticity of demand for orange juice.

     The price elasticity of demand for orange juice is 1.83. The price elasticity of demand is the percentage change in the quantity demanded of the good divided by the percentage change in the price of the good. So the price elasticity of demand equals 22 percent divided by 12 percent, which is 1.83.

   b.   Cross elasticity of demand for apple juice with respect to the price of orange juice.

     The cross elasticity of demand between orange juice and apple juice is 1.17. The cross elasticity of demand is the percentage change in the quantity demanded of one good divided by the percentage change in the price of another good. So the cross elasticity of demand is the percentage change in the quantity demanded of apple juice divided by the percentage change in the price of orange juice. The cross elasticity equals 14 percent divided by 12 percent, which is 1.17.

9.   The table sets out the supply schedule of jeans.

Price (dollars per pair)	Quantity supplied (millions of pairs per year)
120	24
125	28
130	32
135	36

   a.   Calculate the elasticity of supply when the price rises from $125 to $135 a pair.

     The elasticity of supply equals the percentage change in the quantity supplied divided by the percentage change in price. The percentage change in the quantity demanded equals [(36 − 28)/32] × 100, which is 25.0 percent. The percentage change in the price equals [($135− $125)/$130] × 100, which is 7.7 percent. The elasticity of supply equals (25.0 percent/7.7 percent), which is 3.25.

   b.   Calculate the elasticity of supply when the average price is $125 a pair.

     To find the elasticity at an average price of $125 a pair, change the price such that $125 is the average price—for example, a rise in the price from $120 to $130 a pair. To calculate the elasticity when the average price is $125, calculate the elasticity over the price range from $120 to $130. The percentage change in the quantity demanded equals [(32 − 24)/28] × 100, which is 28.6 percent. The percentage change in the price equals [($130 − $120)/$125] × 100, which is 8.0 percent. The elasticity of supply equals (28.6 percent/8.0 percent), which is 3.58.

   c.   Is the supply of jeans elastic, inelastic, or unit elastic?

     The supply of jeans is elastic.

Answers to Additional Problems and Applications

11.   Figure 4.2 shows the demand for DVD rentals.

a.   Calculate the elasticity of demand when the price of a DVD rental rises from $3 to $5.

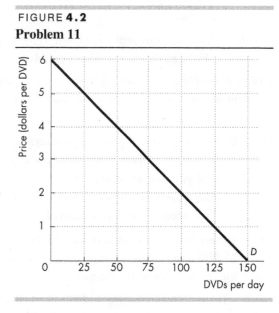

FIGURE **4.2**
Problem 11

The price elasticity of demand is 2. When the price of a DVD rental rises from $3 to $5, the quantity demanded of DVDs decreases from 75 to 25 a day. The price elasticity of demand equals the percentage change in the quantity demanded divided by the percentage change in the price. The price increases from $3 to $5, an increase of $2 a DVD. The average price is $4 per DVD. So the percentage change in the price equals $2 divided by $4 and then multiplied by 100, which equals 50 percent. The quantity decreases from 75 to 25 DVDs, a decrease of 50 DVDs. The average quantity is 50 DVDs. So the percentage change in quantity demanded equals 50 divided by 50 and then multiplied by 100, which equals 100 percent. The price elasticity of demand for DVD rentals equals 100 percent divided by 50 percent, which is 2.

b.   At what price is the elasticity of demand for DVD rentals equal to 1?

The price elasticity of demand equals 1 at $3 a DVD. The price elasticity of demand equals 1 at the price halfway between the origin and the price at which the demand curve intersects the y-axis. That price is $3 a DVD.

Use the following table to work Problem 13.
The demand schedule for computer chips is in the table.

Price (dollars per chip)	Quantity demanded (millions of chips per year)
200	50
250	45
300	40
350	35
400	30

13.   At an average price of $350, is the demand for chips elastic, inelastic, or unit elastic? Use the total revenue test to answer this question.

The demand for chips is unit elastic. The total revenue test says that if the price changes and total revenue remains the same, the demand is unit elastic at the average price. For an average price of $350 a chip, cut the price from $400 to $300 a chip. When the price of a chip falls from $400 to $300, the total revenue remains at $12,000 million. So at the average price of $350 a chip, demand is unit elastic.

15.   Your price elasticity of demand for bananas is 4. If the price of bananas rises by 5 percent, what is

a.   The percentage change in the quantity of bananas you buy?

The quantity of bananas you buy decreases by 20 percent. The price elasticity of demand equals the percentage change in the quantity demanded divided by the percentage change in the price. Rearranging this formula shows that the percentage change in the quantity demanded equals the price elasticity of demand multiplied by the percentage change in the price. The percentage change in the quantity demanded equals 4 × 5 percent, which is 20 percent.

b. The change in your expenditure on bananas?

> Your total expenditure decreases because your demand is elastic. The fall in expenditure is *approximately* 15 percent, the 5 percent rise in price offset by the 20 percent decrease in the quantity purchased.

Use this information to work Problem 17.

Economy Forces Many to Shorten Holiday Plans

This year Americans are taking fewer exotic holidays by air and instead are visiting local scenic places by car. The global financial crisis has encouraged many Americans to cut their holiday budgets.

Source: *USA Today*, May 22, 2009

17. Given the prices of the two holidays, is the income elasticity of demand for exotic holidays positive or negative? Are exotic holidays a normal good or an inferior good? Are local holidays a normal good or an inferior good?

> The income elasticity of demand for exotic holidays is positive so exotic holidays are a normal good. The income elasticity of demand for local holidays is negative so local holidays are an inferior good.

19. When Alex's income was $3,000, he bought 4 bagels and 12 donuts a month. Now his income is $5,000 and he buys 8 bagels and 6 donuts a month. Calculate Alex's income elasticity of demand for (a) bagels and (b) donuts.

a. The income elasticity of demand equals the percentage change in the quantity demanded divided by the percentage change in income. The change in income is $2,000 and the average income is $4,000, so the percentage change in income equals 50 percent. The change in the quantity demanded is 4 bagels and the average quantity demanded is 6 bagels, so the percentage change in the quantity demanded equals 66.67 percent. The income elasticity of demand for bagels equals (66.67 percent)/(50 percent), which is 1.33.

b. From part (a), the percentage change in income is 50 percent. The change in the quantity demanded is −6 donuts and the average quantity demanded is 9 donuts, so the percentage change in the quantity demanded is −66.67 percent. The income elasticity of demand for donuts equals (−66.67 percent)/(50 percent), which is −1.33.

21. If a 5 percent fall in the price of chocolate sauce increases the quantity demanded of chocolate sauce by 10 percent and increases the quantity of ice cream demanded by 15 percent, calculate the:

a. Price elasticity of demand for chocolate sauce.

> The price elasticity of demand for chocolate sauce equals the percentage change in the quantity of chocolate sauce demanded divided by the percentage change in the price of chocolate sauce. Using the data in the problem, the price elasticity of demand equals (10 percent)/(−5 percent), which is 2.0.

b. Cross elasticity of demand for ice cream with respect to the price of chocolate sauce.

> The cross elasticity of demand for ice cream with respect to the price of chocolate sauce equals the percentage change in the quantity of ice cream demanded divided by the percentage change in the price of chocolate sauce. Using the data in the problem, the cross elasticity of demand equals (15 percent)/(−5 percent), which is −3.0. Ice cream and chocolate sauce are complements.

23. The table sets out the supply schedule of long-distance phone calls. Calculate the elasticity of supply when

Price (cents per minute)	Quantity supplied (millions of minutes per day)
10	200
20	400
30	600
40	800

a. The price falls from 40¢ to 30¢ a minute.

The elasticity of supply is 1. The elasticity of supply is the percentage change in the quantity supplied divided by the percentage change in the price. When the price falls from 40 cents to 30 cents, the change in the price is 10 cents and the average price is 35 cents. The percentage change in the price is 28.57 percent. When the price falls from 40 cents to 30 cents, the quantity supplied decreases from 800 to 600 calls. The change in the quantity supplied is 200 calls, and the average quantity is 700 calls, so the percentage change in the quantity supplied is 28.57 percent. The elasticity of supply equals (28.57 percent)/(28.57 percent), which is 1.

b. The average price is 20¢ a minute.

The elasticity of supply is 1. The formula for the elasticity of supply calculates the elasticity at the average price. So to find the elasticity at an average price of 20 cents a minute, change the price such that 20 cents is the average price—for example, a fall in the price from 30 cents to 10 cents a minute. When the price falls from 30 cents to 10 cents, the change in the price is 20 cents and the average price is 20 cents. The percentage change in the price is 100 percent. When the price falls from 30 cents to 10 cents, the quantity supplied decreases from 600 to 200 calls. The change in the quantity supplied is 400 calls and the average quantity is 400 calls. The percentage change in the quantity supplied is 100 percent. The elasticity of supply is the percentage change in the quantity supplied divided by the percentage change in the price. The elasticity of supply is 1.

Economics in the News

25. After you have studied *Economics in the News* on pp. 98–99, answer the following questions.

a. Looking at Fig. 1 on p. 99, explain what must have happened in 2014 to the supply of coffee.

The price of coffee soared in 2014, which indicates that the supply of coffee decreased.

b. Given the information in Fig. 1 and the estimated elasticity of demand for coffee, by what percentage did the quantity of coffee change in 2014 and in which direction?

The price of coffee rose from $1.00 per pound to $1.60 per pound. Therefore the percentage increase in the price of coffee is ($1.60 − $1.00)/$1.30 = 46 percent. The price elasticity of demand is 0.26. Therefore the quantity of coffee decreased by 0.26 × 46 percent, which is 12 percent.

c. The news article says that farmers' revenue shrank as the price of coffee fell. Explain why this fact tells us that the demand for coffee is inelastic.

The total revenue test shows that total revenue falls when the price falls only if the demand for the product is inelastic. Therefore, because farmers' total revenue from coffee fell when the price of coffee fell, the total revenue test means that the demand for coffee must be inelastic.

d. How does the total revenue test work for a rise in the price? What do you predict happened to total revenue in 2014? Why?

If the demand for a product is inelastic and the price rises, the total revenue increases. Therefore, in 2014 when the price of coffee rose, coffee farmers' total revenue increased.

e.   Coffee isn't just coffee. It comes in different varieties, the main two being Arabica and Robusta. Would you expect the elasticity of demand for Arabica to be the same as the elasticity of demand for coffee? Explain why or why not.

There are more close substitutes for the specific type of coffee, Arabica, than there are for coffee in general, so the price elasticity of demand for Arabica is larger than the price elasticity of demand for coffee.

5 EFFICIENCY AND EQUITY

Answers to the Review Quizzes

Page 107

1. Why do we need methods of allocating scarce resources?

    Because resources are scare, it is not possible to fulfill everyone's wants. As a result, some method of deciding which wants will be fulfilled and which will not—that is, some method of allocating resources—must be utilized.

3. Provide an example of each allocation method that illustrates when it works well.

    Below are examples of when each allocation scheme works well:

    *   Market price: Generally works well in competitive markets and for most goods and services. An example is the allocation of cat food.
    *   Command: Generally works well in organizations where lines of authority are clear and it is easy to monitor subordinates. An example is in a fast food restaurant when the supervisor tells a worker to clean the tables.
    *   Majority rule: Generally works well when large numbers of people are affected by the allocation. An example is an election in which people vote whether or not to support a tax to build more parks.
    *   Contest: Generally works well when the efforts of the participates are hard to monitor. An example is the contest run by Pfizer in which three top managers competed to see who would be appointed CEO.
    *   First-come, first-served: Generally works well when a resource can be used by only one user at a time. An example is a line at a movie ticket booth.
    *   Lottery: Generally works well when there is no way to easily distinguish which user of a resource would use it most effectively. An example is the lottery used to allocate cell phone frequencies.
    *   Personal characteristics: Generally works well when resource use is such that different people consume the same resources. An example is the decision whom to marry.
    *   Force: Generally works well when used to uphold the rule of law. An example is the state imprisoning thieves and thereby preventing resource allocation by the thief stealing the resource.

Page 111

1. What is the relationship between the marginal benefit, value, and demand?

    The value of one more unit of a good is its marginal benefit. The marginal benefit of a good or service is measured by the maximum amount that consumers are willing to pay for one more unit of a good or service. The demand curve shows the maximum consumers are willing to pay for each additional unit, so the demand curve is the same as the marginal benefit curve.

3. What is consumer surplus? How is it measured?

    Consumer surplus is the excess of the benefit received from a good over the amount paid for it. The total consumer surplus is the sum of the consumer surpluses on all the units purchased. It is measured as the area under the demand curve and above the price.

5. What is the relationship between individual supply and market supply?

    The market supply equals the sum of the individual quantities supplied by all the producers at each price. The market supply curve is equal to the horizontal sum of all the individual supply curves.

Page 115

1. Do competitive markets use resources efficiently? Explain why or why not.

    In the absence of the obstacles mentioned earlier in the chapter, competitive markets use society's resources efficiently. For resources to be used efficiently they must be allocated to produce the quantity of a good or service where the marginal cost of the last unit produced in the market is equal to the marginal benefit. This condition will be met in a competitive market because the quantity occurs where the demand curve (which equals the marginal social benefit curve) intersects the supply curve (which equals the marginal social cost curve).

3. What are the obstacles to achieving an efficient allocation of resources in the market economy?

    Markets with price or quantity regulations, taxes or subsidies, externalities, public goods or common resources, monopoly power, or high transactions costs will not produce the efficient quantity of a good or service. In each of these situations, the market prices charged or quantities produced and sold will not result in the efficient allocation of resources. Efficiency requires that the marginal social benefit of the last unit produced be equal to the marginal social cost. The equilibrium at the intersection of the demand and supply curves in the competitive market creates this result. When the market price or quantity is pulled away from the market equilibrium, the marginal social benefit of the last unit produced does not equal its marginal social cost.

Page 119

1. What are the two big approaches to thinking about fairness?

    The two big approaches to thinking about fairness are:

    ☐ "It's not fair if the *result* isn't fair," or *utilitarianism*.
    ☐ "It's not fair if the *rules* aren't fair," or *equality of opportunity*.

3. Explain the big tradeoff. What idea of fairness has been developed to deal with it?

    The big tradeoff is the tradeoff between *efficiency* and *fairness*. Redistributing incomes changes the incentives facing producers and consumers. Taxing income decreases producer surplus and taxing purchases decreases consumer surplus. Producers produce less and consumers consume less, and total economic activity declines, such that the size of the economic pie decreases. The big tradeoff has led to the idea that the fairest distribution is that which makes the poorest person as well off as possible.

Answers to the Study Plan Problems and Applications

1. At Chez Panisse, a restaurant in Berkeley, reservations are essential. At Mandarin Dynasty, a restaurant near the University of California San Diego, reservations are recommended. At Eli Cannon's, a restaurant in Middletown, Connecticut, reservations are not accepted.

   Describe the method of allocating scarce table resources at these three restaurants. Why do you think restaurants don't use the market price to allocate their tables?

> All these restaurants use a first-come, first-serve system. Eli Cannon's uses this system directly. Chez Panisse uses a first-come, first-serve system because the first person to call to make a reservation at a particular time is allocated the table at that time. Mandarin Dynasty uses a combination of the immediate first-come, first-serve system and the reservation based first-come, first-serve system.

> Market allocation requires that customers pay for a table and the price would fluctuate from one hour to the next depending on the number of customers who arrive. Customers would be highly uncertain about the price they would need to pay and such uncertainty decreases the demand for meals from the restaurant. The decreased demand lowers the restaurant's profit.

Use the following table to work Problem 3.

The table gives the demand schedules for train travel for the only buyers in the market, Ann, Beth, and Cy.

Price (dollars per mile)	Quantity demanded (miles)		
	Ann	Beth	Cy
3	30	25	20
4	25	20	15
5	20	15	10
6	15	10	5
7	10	5	0
8	5	0	0
9	0	0	0

3. a. What is the marginal social benefit when the total distance travelled is 60 miles?

   The marginal social benefit when the quantity is 60 miles is $4 per mile. The marginal social benefit is determined from the consumers' demand schedules and equals the maximum price that consumers will pay for the quantity. The demand schedule shows that the maximum price consumers will pay for 60 miles is $4 per mile and this price equals the marginal social benefit.

   b. When the total distance traveled is 60 miles, how many miles does each travel and what is their marginal private benefit?

   > The three travel a total distance of 60 miles when the price is $4 a mile. Each person's marginal benefit is $4 per mile. At this price Ann travels 25 miles, Beth travels 20 miles, and Cy travels 15 miles.

Use the following table to work Problems 5 and 7.

The table gives the supply schedules of hot air balloon rides for the only sellers in the market, Xavier, Yasmin, and Zack.

Price (dollars per ride)	Quantity supplied (rides per week)		
	Xavier	Yasmin	Zack
100	30	25	20
90	25	20	15
80	20	15	10
70	15	10	5
60	10	5	0
50	5	0	0
40	0	0	0

5. a. Construct the market supply schedule.

   The market supply schedule shows the sum of the quantities supplied by Xavier, Yasmin, and Zack at each price. When the price is $100 per ride, the market quantity supplied is 75 rides; when the price is $90 per ride, the market quantity supplied is 60 rides; when the price is $80 per ride, the market quantity supplied is 45 rides; when the price is $70 per ride, the market quantity supplied is 30 rides; when the price is $60 per ride, the market quantity supplied is 15 rides; when the price is $50 per ride, the market quantity supplied is 5 rides; and when the price is $40 per ride, the market quantity supplied is 0 rides.

b. What are the minimum prices that Xavier, Yasmin, and Zack are willing to accept to supply 20 rides? Why?

The minimum supply-price equals the lowest price at which a producer is willing to produce the given quantity. The supply schedule tells us the minimum supply-price. Xavier's minimum supply-price for 20 rides is $80; Yasmin's minimum supply-price is $90; and, Zack's minimum supply-price is $100.

7. When the price is $70 a ride, what is each firm's producer surplus? What is the market producer surplus?

Xavier's producer surplus is $225; Yasmin's is $100; and, Zack's is $25.

When the price is $70 per ride, Xavier supplies 15 rides. Xavier's producer surplus is the triangular area under the price and above his supply curve. The supply curve is linear, so Xavier's producer surplus is $1/2 \times (\$70 - \$40) \times 15$, which equals $225.

When the price is $70 per ride, Yasmin supplies 10 rides. Yasmin's producer surplus is the triangular area under the price and above his supply curve. The supply curve is linear, so Yasmin's producer surplus is $1/2 \times (\$70 - \$50) \times 10$, which equals $100.

When the price is $70 per ride, Zack supplies 5 rides. Zack's producer surplus is the triangular area under the price and above his supply curve. The supply curve is linear, so Zack's producer surplus is $1/2 \times (\$70 - \$60) \times 5$, which equals $25.

The market producer surplus is equal to the sum of Xavier's producer surplus, Yasmin's producer surplus, and Zack's producer surplus, which is $225 + $100 + $25 or $350.

9. Explain why the allocation method used by each restaurant in Problem 1 is fair or not fair.

According to the "fair rules" approach, all of the methods are fair because everyone faces the same rules and therefore the same chance of obtaining a table. According to the "fair results" approach, none of the methods are fair because in each case some people get a table and others do not.

Answers to Additional Problems and Applications

11. At McDonald's, no reservations are accepted; at Panorama at St. Louis Art Museum, reservations are accepted; at the Bissell Mansion restaurant, reservations are essential. Describe the method of allocating tables in these three restaurants. Why do restaurants have different reservations policies?

    All these restaurants use a first-come, first-serve system. McDonald's uses this system directly. Bissell Mansion uses a first-come, first-serve because the first person to call to make a reservation at a particular time is allocated the table at that time. Puck's uses a combination of the immediate first-come, first-serve system and the reservation based first-come, first-serve system.

    The speed with which tables turn over at the different restaurants probably is quite different and the customers probably have quite different values of time. Bissell Mansion has a low turnover rate—only 1 or 2 groups of customers can use a table each night—and its customers have a high value of time. If Bissell Mansion refused to take reservations, its customers would need to wait an inefficiently long time and would go elsewhere so that Bissell Mansion profits would be lower. At McDonald's, the tables have a high turnover rate (indeed, many customers do not use the tables at all, buying their food to go) and the customers have a lower value of time. Allowing reservations would be costly for McDonald's and would spare its customers only a slight wait at most so that allowing reservations would decrease McDonald's profits. At Puck's, the turnover rate of the tables is between that at Bissell Mansion and McDonald's, so it uses a combination of phone reservation first-come, first-serve and appear in person first-come, first-serve.

Use the following table to work Problems 13 and 15.

The table gives the supply schedules for jet-ski rides by the only suppliers: Rick, Sam, and Tom.

Price (dollars per ride)	Quantity supplied (rides per week)		
	Rick	Sam	Tom
10.00	0	0	0
12.50	5	0	0
15.00	10	5	0
17.50	15	10	5
20.00	20	15	10

13. Which owner has the largest producer surplus when the price of a ride is $17.50? Explain.

    Rick has the largest producer surplus when the price is $17.50. Rick's producer surplus is largest because he produces the largest quantity and his costs are lower than those of the other producers. More formally, each supplier's producer surplus is equal to the area under the price and above that producer's supply curve. Calculating these areas of producer surplus, Rick's producer surplus is $56.25, Sam's producer surplus is $25.00, and Tom's producer surplus is $6.25.

15. Construct the market supply schedule of jet-ski rides.

    When the price is $10.00, the quantity of rides supplied is 0; when the price is $12.50, the quantity supplied is 5 rides; when the price is $15.00, the quantity supplied is 15; when the price is $17.50, the quantity supplied is 30; and, when the price is $20, the quantity supplied is 45.

17. **Home Heating Bills Surge Amid Record Cold**

If there's one thing that can set home heating costs soaring, it's a long, frigid blast from one of the coldest winters in 20 years and people are going to use 10 to 12 per cent more natural gas this year than they have normally.

Source: CBC News, March 3, 2014

a. How is the price of natural gas determined?

The price of natural gas is determined in the market for natural gas by demand and supply.

b. When demand increases, explain the process by which the market adjusts.

When demand increases, at the initial equilibrium price there is a shortage. The shortage forces the price to rise. As the price rises, the quantity demanded decreases and the quantity supplied increases. The price continues to rise until the quantity demanded equals the quantity supplied. That price is the new equilibrium price. Once that price is reached, there are no further changes.

FIGURE **5.3a**
Problem 17

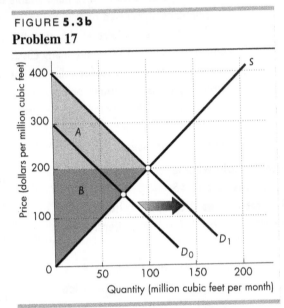

FIGURE **5.3b**
Problem 17

c. On a graph, show the effect of the increase in demand on consumer surplus and producer surplus.

Figure 5.3a shows the initial in consumer surplus (labeled A) and producer surplus (labeled B). After the increase in demand, Figure 5.3b shows the new consumer surplus (again labeled A) and the new producer surplus (again labeled B).

Use the following news clip to work Problems 19 and 21.

The Right Price for Digital Music

Apple's $1.29-for-the-latest-songs model isn't perfect and isn't it too much to pay for music that appeals to just a few people? What we need is a system that will be profitable but fair to music lovers. The solution: Price song downloads according to demand. The more people who download a particular song, the higher will be the price of that song; the fewer people who buy a particular song, the lower will be the price of that song. That is a free-market solution—the market would determine the price.

Source: *Slate*, December 5, 2005

Assume that the marginal social cost of downloading a song from the iTunes Store is zero. (This assumption means that the cost of operating the iTunes Store doesn't change if people download more songs.)

19. a.   Draw a graph of the market for downloadable music with a price of $1.29 for all the latest songs. On your graph, show consumer surplus and producer surplus.

   Figure 5.4 shows this market. The marginal social cost curve runs along the horizontal axis. The consumer surplus is area A and the producer surplus is area B.

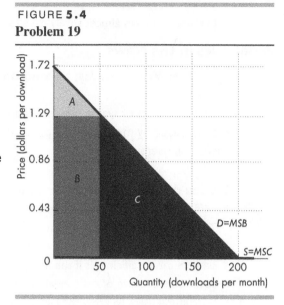

FIGURE **5.4**
Problem 19

   b.   With a price of $1.29 for all the latest songs, is the market efficient or inefficient? If it is inefficient, show the deadweight loss on your graph.

   The market is inefficient. Efficiency requires that the amount be the quantity for which the marginal social benefit equals the marginal social cost, which in this case is the quantity at which the marginal social benefit curve intersects the horizontal axis. The deadweight loss is area C in Figure 5.4.

21. a.   If the pricing scheme described in the news clip were adopted, would the market be efficient or inefficient? Explain.

   The market would likely become more inefficient because the inefficiency of the popular songs—the songs most people want—increases. The price exceeds the marginal social cost.

   b.   Is the pricing scheme described in the news clip a "free-market solution"? Explain.

   With a pure free-market solution the price is determined by supply and demand. The pricing method discussed in the clip uses only demand and so it is not the same as a pure free-market solution. A pure free market solution produces the efficient quantity, 200 downloads in the figure, with the price equal to zero.

23.   Would a free world market in water achieve a fair use of the world's water resources? Explain why or why not and be clear about the concept of fairness that you are using.

   A "fair results" approach to fairness would argue that in third world countries, very poor inhabitants (for example, nomads) would not be able to afford "enough" water and so some redistribution is needed for the sake of fairness. A "fair rules" approach to fairness asserts that a competitive market is enough to insure fairness because the exchange of water is voluntary.

25.   **The Scandal of Phone Call Price Gouging by Prisons**
   In most states, the phone company guarantees the prison a commission of a percentage on every call. The average commission is 42% of the cost of the call, but in some states it is 60%. So 60% of what families pay to receive a collect call from their imprisoned relative has nothing to do with the cost of the phone service. Also, the phone company that offers the highest commission is often the company to get the prison contract.

   Source: *The Guardian*, May 23, 2012

   a.   Who is practicing price gouging: the prison, the phone company, or both? Explain.

   Although the phone company alone appears to be price gouging, both the phone company and the prison are price gouging. The phone company is gouging because it charges a higher price on collect calls by its captive customers, the prisoners, than it charges its ordinary customers who are free to make calls using other methods. The prison is price gouging because it charges the phone company a high commission but does not share any of the revenue with the prisoners.

b. Evaluate the "fairness" of the prison's commission.

According to the "rules" view of fairness, the commission is fair because the prisoners' decisions to call are voluntary. According to the "results" view of fairness, the commission is almost surely unfair because prisoners almost surely have lower-than-average income.

Economics in the News

27. **Fight Over Water Rates; Escondido Farmers Say Increase Would Put Them Out of Business**

Agricultural users of water pay less than residential and business users. Since 1993, water rates have increased by more than 90 percent for residential customers and by only 50 percent for agricultural users.

Source: *The San Diego Union-Tribune*, June 14, 2006

a. Do you think that the allocation of water between agricultural and residential users is likely to be efficient? Explain your answer.

The allocation of water is almost surely inefficient. If the marginal social cost curve of distributing water is the same for agricultural and residential users, as is probably the case, the only way that the allocation scheme can be efficient is if the marginal social benefit curve of agricultural lies below the marginal social benefit curve of residential users. Such a situation seems unlikely because water is necessary for agricultural users to grow their crops so the marginal social benefit of water to farmers probably exceeds that for residential users.

b. If agricultural users paid a higher price, would the allocation of resources be more efficient?

If agricultural users paid a higher rate for water, probably the allocation of resources would be more efficient. Efficiency requires that marginal social benefit equals marginal social cost. Currently it is likely the case that the marginal social benefit of the last unit of water for agricultural users is less than the marginal social cost of producing the last unit of water.

c. If agricultural users paid a higher price, what would happen to consumer surplus and producer surplus from water?

If the price paid by agricultural users rises, the consumer surplus of agricultural users decreases and the producer surplus increases.

d. Is the difference in price paid by agricultural and residential users fair?

According to the "fair results" approach, the difference in price is fair only if agricultural users are poorer than residential users. If, however, agricultural users are wealthier than or comparable to residential users, the difference in price is not fair. The difference in price is not fair according to the "fair rules" approach because the price of water is not determined in competitive markets.

6 GOVERNMENT ACTIONS IN MARKETS

Answers to the Review Quizzes

Page 130

1. What is a rent ceiling and what are its effects if it is set above the equilibrium rent?

    A rent ceiling is a specific example of a price ceiling. A rent ceiling is a government imposed regulation that makes it illegal to charge a rent higher than a specified level. If a rent ceiling is set above the equilibrium rent, it has no effect because it does not make the equilibrium rent illegal.

3. How are scarce housing resources allocated when a rent ceiling is in place?

    With an effective rent ceiling, some means for allocation of housing units (other than by price) becomes necessary. Some What housing is allocated by first-come, first-serve. Other housing is allocated by discrimination. Black markets also develop, where housing units are allocated at a rent higher than the regulated rent.

Page 133

1. What is a minimum wage and what are its effects if it is set above the equilibrium wage?

    A *minimum wage* is a price floor applied to the labor market. A minimum wage is a government imposed regulation that makes it illegal to charge (or pay) a wage rate lower than a specified level. If the minimum wage is set above the equilibrium wage, it creates a surplus of labor—unemployment—and decreases workers' and firms' surplus.

3. Explain how scarce jobs are allocated when a minimum wage is in place.

    If a minimum wage is set *above* the equilibrium wage, the ability of the competitive market to allocate resources is thwarted and other means must be used. Sometimes the method used is first-come, first-served so that those who are first in line to apply for openings are given the jobs. Other times discrimination is used so that those from favored groups are allocated the jobs.

5. Explain why a minimum wage is unfair.

    Workers who receive wage hikes and retain their jobs gain from the minimum wage but workers who lose their jobs and workers who must extensively search for a job lose. Those who keep (or find) jobs are not necessarily the least well off, so the minimum wage fails the fair results approach to fairness. And the minimum wage also fails the fair rules approach to fairness because the minimum wage blocks voluntary transactions that otherwise would occur.

Page 138

1. How does the elasticity of demand influence the incidence of a tax, the tax revenue, and the deadweight loss?

    The more elastic the demand for a given supply, the smaller the increase in the price paid by the buyers and the greater the decrease in the price received by the sellers, which means that the incidence on buyers is smaller. Additionally, the more elastic the demand, the smaller the quantity bought so the smaller the tax revenue; and the larger the deadweight loss.

3.   Why is a tax inefficient?

The imposition of a tax on a market causes a wedge to be driven between the price received by the seller and the price paid by the buyer. This causes the marginal social benefit from the last unit sold to be higher than its marginal social cost, and the market will under-produce the good or service being taxed. If more of the good or service were produced, the marginal social benefit gained would be greater than the marginal social cost incurred, and the net benefit to society would increase.

5.   What are the two principles of fairness that are applied to tax systems?

The two principles of fairness are the benefits principle and the ability-to-pay principle. The benefits principle asserts that people should pay taxes equal to the benefits they receive from the government provided services. The ability-to-pay principle asserts that people should pay taxes according to how easily they can bear the burden of the tax.

Page 141

1.   Summarize the effects of a production quota on the market price and the quantity produced.

A production quota set below the equilibrium quantity raises the price and decreases the quantity.

3.   Explain why a voluntary production quota is difficult to operate.

A voluntary quota is difficult to operate because a production quota results in a massive incentive to "cheat" on the production quota by increasing production. A production quota decreases the quantity produced. By decreasing the quantity produced, a production quota raises the price and reduces the marginal social cost of the last unit produced. Because the price exceeds the marginal social cost, producers have an incentive to increase their production (beyond the quota amount) to boost their profit.

5.   Explain why a subsidy is inefficient.

A subsidy creates inefficiency because a subsidy leads to a lower price and increased production. Marginal social benefit equals the price and so the lower price signals that the marginal social benefit falls. And the increased production means that the marginal social cost of production rises. So at the level of production with a subsidy, the marginal social benefit is less than the marginal social cost and inefficiency is created.

Page 143

1.   How does the imposition of a penalty for selling an illegal drug influence demand, supply, price, and the quantity of the drug consumed?

If the penalty is levied on the *seller*, the penalty is added to the *minimum price required* for supplying the good or service. The demand curve remains unchanged but the supply curve shifts leftward, so that the vertical distance between the initial supply curve and the supply curve with the penalty equals the dollar value of the penalty. In this case, the equilibrium price of the good rises and the equilibrium quantity decreases.

3.   How does the imposition of a penalty for selling *or* possessing an illegal drug influence demand, supply, price, and the quantity of the drug consumed?

If *buyers and sellers* face penalties, both the demand and supply curves shift leftward. If the shift of the supply curve is larger, the equilibrium price rises and quantity decreases; if the shift of the demand curve is larger, the price falls and quantity decreases; if the shifts are the same magnitude, the price is unchanged and the quantity decreases.

Answers to the Study Plan Problems and Applications

Use Figure 6.1, which shows the market for rental housing in Townsville, to work Problem 1.

1. a. What are the equilibrium rent and equilibrium quantity of rental housing?

    The equilibrium rent is $450 a month and the equilibrium quantity is 20,000 housing units.

    b. If a rent ceiling is set at $600 a month, what is the rent paid? What is the shortage of housing?

    If the rent ceiling is set at $600 per month, it is above the equilibrium rent and so is ineffective because renters still pay the equilibrium rent, $450 per month. There is no shortage of housing units: The quantity of housing demanded, 20,000 units, equals the quantity of units supplied.

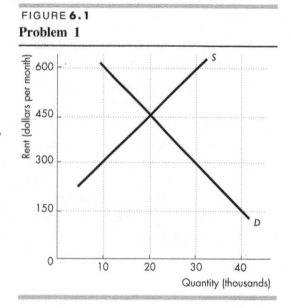

FIGURE **6.1**

Problem 1

Use the following data on the demand and supply schedules of teenage labor to work Problem 3.

3. Calculate the equilibrium wage rate, the hours worked, and the quantity of unemployment.

    The equilibrium wage rate is $6 an hour and 2,000 hours a month are worked. Unemployment is zero. Everyone who wants to work for $6 an hour is employed.

Wage rate (dollars per hour)	Quantity demanded	Quantity supplied
	(hours per month)	
5	2,500	1,500
6	2,000	2,000
7	1,500	2,500
8	1,000	3,000

5. The table sets out the demand and supply schedules for chocolate brownies.

    a. If sellers are taxed 20¢ a brownie, what is the price and who pays the tax?

    The price paid by buyers, including the tax, is 70 cents a brownie. The price received by sellers, excluding the tax, is 50 cents a brownie. If there is no tax, the price is 60 cents a brownie, so consumers and sellers each pay 10 cents of the tax on a brownie.

    b. If buyers are taxed 20¢ a brownie, what is the price and who pays the tax?

    The price received by sellers, excluding the tax, is 50 cents a brownie, and 3 million brownies a day are consumed. The price paid by buyers, including the tax, is 70 cents a brownie. Consumers and sellers each pay 10 cents of the tax.

Price (cents per brownie)	Quantity demanded	Quantity supplied
	(millions per day)	
50	5	3
60	4	4
70	3	5
80	2	6

Use the following data to work Problem 7.
The demand and supply schedules for rice are in the table.

Calculate the price, the marginal cost of rice, and the quantity produced if the government

7.   Introduces a subsidy of $0.30 a box.

     With a subsidy of $0.30 a box for rice, the price is $1.20 a box, the marginal cost $1.50 a box, and the quantity produced is 3,000 boxes a week. The subsidy of $0.30 lowers the price at which each quantity in the table is supplied. For example, rice farmers will supply 3,000 boxes a week if the price is $1.50 minus $0.30, which is $1.20. With a subsidy, the market equilibrium occurs at a price of $1.20 a box. At this price, the quantity demanded is 3,000 boxes and the quantity supplied is 3,000 boxes. The marginal cost of producing rice is given by the supply schedule and is $1.50 a box.

Price (dollars per box)	Quantity demanded	Quantity supplied
	(boxes per week)	
1.20	3,000	1,500
1.30	2,750	2,000
1.40	2,500	2,500
1.50	2,250	3,000
1.60	2,000	3,500

Answers to Additional Problems and Applications

The table sets out the demand and supply schedules for college meals.

9. a. **What are the equilibrium meal price and equilibrium quantity of meals?**

    The equilibrium price of a meal is $6 per meal and the equilibrium quantity is 2,500 meals per week.

    b. **If the college put a price ceiling on meals at $7 a meal, what is the price students pay for a meal? How many meals do they buy?**

    The price ceiling is above the equilibrium price, so it is ineffective. The price of a meal remains at $6 per meal and students buy 2,500 meals per week.

Price (dollars per meal)	Quantity demanded	Quantity supplied
	(meals per week)	
4	3,000	1,500
5	2,750	2,000
6	2,500	2,500
7	2,250	3,000
8	2,000	3,500
9	1,750	4,000
10	1,500	4,500

Use the following news clip to work Problems 11.

Malaysia Passes Its First Minimum Wage Law

About 3.2 million low-income workers across Malaysia are expected to benefit from the country's first minimum wage, which the government says will transform Malaysia into a high-income nation. Employer groups argue that paying the minimum wage, which is not based on productivity or performance, would raise their costs and reduce business profits.

Source: *The New York Times*, May 1, 2012

11. **On a graph of the market for low-skilled labor, show the effect of the minimum wage on the quantity of labor employed.**

    Figure 6.4 shows the effect in the labor market. Before the hike in the minimum wage, the equilibrium wage rate was 3 ringgits per hour and equilibrium employment was 3.4 million workers. After the imposition of the minimum wage, assumed to 5.5 ringgits an hour, employment falls to 3.2 million and unemployment equals 0.3 million workers (the difference between 3.5 million workers, the quantity of labor supplied at a wage rate of 5.5 ringgits an hour, and quantity of labor demanded at the same wage rate.)

FIGURE **6.4**
Problem 11

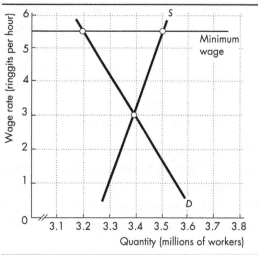

13. Use the news clip in Problem 11.

    a. **If the Malaysian government cut the tax on business profits, would it offset the effect of the minimum wage on employment? Explain.**

    The tax cut on small businesses would offset some of the harm imposed on small businesses but it would not offset much of the decrease in employment. The higher wage rate leads firms to decrease the quantity of labor they demand. If a tax cut increases firms' profitability and they respond by increasing their production, then the demand for labor increases. This increase would offset some of the initial fall in employment. But the offset likely would be small because the cut in taxes will be shared between the businesses and the consumers.

b. Would a cut in the Social Security tax that small businesses pay offset the effect of the higher minimum wage on employment? Explain.

> A cut in the Social Security tax imposed on small businesses could offset the effect the minimum wage hike had on decreasing employment. If Social Security taxes are cut, firms' demand for labor would increase which would result in an increase in employment. Of course the size of the offset would depend on the size of the cut in the Social Security tax and the elasticity of demand for labor and the elasticity supply of labor. Because the supply of labor is probably quite inelastic, most of the benefit of the cut in Social Security tax would be received by workers, which also makes the potential offset small.

15. **Cigarette Taxes, Black Markets, and Crime: Lessons from New York's 50-Year Losing Battle**

New York City has the highest cigarette taxes in the country. During the four months following the recent tax hike, sales of taxed cigarettes in the city fell by more than 50 percent as consumers turned to the city's bustling black market. The thriving illegal market for cigarettes has diverted billions of dollars from legitimate businesses and governments to criminals.

Source: Cato Institute, February 6, 2003

a. How has the market for cigarettes in New York City responded to the high cigarette taxes?

> Consumers (and some suppliers!) have turned to the black market. In the black market taxes are not collected so the price to consumers is significantly lower. So the tax decreases the quantity demanded in the legal market and increases demand in the black market.

b. How does the emergence of a black market impact the elasticity of demand in a legal market?

> The black market is a close substitute for the legal market, so the emergence of the black market increased the price elasticity of demand in the legal market.

c. Why might an increase in the tax rate actually cause a decrease in the tax revenue?

> If the demand is elastic, then the decrease in the equilibrium quantity from the tax is large enough so that the government collects less tax revenue. More specifically, if the magnitude of the percentage decrease in the quantity exceeds the percentage increase in the tax rate, then the tax revenue collected by the government decreases.

Use the following to work problem 17.

Crop Prices Erode Farm Subsidy Program

High corn and soybean prices mean farmers are making the most money in their lives. The reason: Grain prices are far too high to trigger payouts under the U.S. primary farm-subsidy program's "price support" formula. The market has done what Congress couldn't do and that is "slash farm subsidies."

Source: The Wall Street Journal, July 25, 2011

17. Show in a graph how a subsidy paid to soybean farmers affects the consumer surplus and the producer surplus from soybean. Does the subsidy make the soybean market more efficient or less efficient? Explain.

> In Figure 6.5, with no subsidy, the equilibrium price is $16 per bushel and 350 million bushels are produced. The total surplus is the triangular area *abc*. The upper half of the triangle is the consumer surplus and the lower half is the producer surplus. With the subsidy the price falls to $12 per bushel and the equilibrium quantity rises to 370 million bushels. There is a deadweight loss, equal to the area of the grey triangle. The total surplus with the subsidy is the initial total surplus minus the total

deadweight loss (in Figure 6.5, the two areas are the same size, so the total surplus—the sum of the consumer surplus plus the producer surplus—is $0.) With the subsidy, the expanded level of production means that marginal social cost exceeds marginal social benefit so the subsidy makes the market less efficient.

FIGURE **6.5**
Problem 17

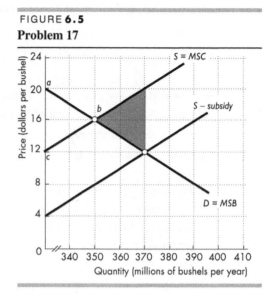

Quantity (millions of bushels per year)

Use the following figure, which shows the market for tomatoes, to work Problem 19.

19. If the government subsidizes growers at $4 a pound, what is the quantity produced, the quantity demanded, and the subsidy paid to growers?

  If the government subsidizes growers at $4 a pound, the supply increases. As shown in Figure 6.7, the supply curve shifts downward by $4. The demand does not change. The new price is $4 per pound and at this price the quantity produced is 3 billion pounds and the quantity demanded is 3 billion pounds. The government pays ($4 a pound) × (3 billion pounds), which is $12 billion.

FIGURE **6.6**
Problems 19 and 20

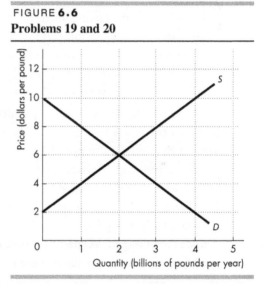

Quantity (billions of pounds per year)

21. The table gives the demand and supply schedules for an illegal drug.

  a. What is the price and how many units are bought if there is no penalty on drugs?

  The price is $60 per unit and 400 units are consumed.

  b. If the penalty on sellers is $20 a unit, what are the price and quantity consumed?

  The price is $70 per unit and 300 units are consumed.

  c. If the penalty on buyers is $20 a unit, what are the price and quantity consumed?

  The price $50 per unit and 300 units are consumed.

Price (dollars per unit)	Quantity demanded	Quantity supplied
	(units per day)	
50	500	300
60	400	400
70	300	500
80	200	600
90	100	700

23.   **Hollywood: Organized Crime Hits the Movies**

The Mexican army seized 1,180 disc burners and 3.14 million copies of movies and TV shows from 23 warehouses in a move to fight piracy that costs Hollywood about $590 million a year.

Source: Bloomberg *Businessweek*, April 7, 2011

Assume that the marginal cost of producing a DVD (legal or illegal) is a constant $3 and that legal DVDs bear an additional marginal cost of $5 each in royalty payments to film studios.

a.   Draw a graph of the market for counterfeit DVDs, assuming that there are no effective penalties on either buyers or sellers for breaking the law.

FIGURE **6.9**

Problem 23

Figure 6.9 shows the market for illegal DVDs. With no penalties the supply curve is *S* and the demand curve is *D*. In the figure, the equilibrium price is $3.00 per DVD and the equilibrium quantity is 5 million DVDs.

b.   How do the events reported in the news clip change the market outcome? Show the effects in your graph.

The seizure of the (approximately) 3 million discs decreases (at least temporarily) the supply. In Figure 6.9, the supply curve shifts from *S* to $S_{Seizure}$. The price rises, in the market to $6 per disc, and the quantity decreases, to 2 million discs.

c.   With no penalty on buyers, if a penalty for breaking the law is imposed on sellers at more than $5 a disc, how does the market work and what is the equilibrium price?

The marginal cost of producing illegal discs increases from $3.00 per disc to $3.00 per disc + penalty. The supply curve shifts upward by the amount of the penalty so it becomes a horizontal line at a price higher than $8. For instance, if a $6 penalty was imposed, the supply curve would shift upward by $6 from the initial supply curve *S*. With the demand and supply curves in Figure 6.9, the new equilibrium price for an illegal DVD paid by buyers becomes $9, the equilibrium price received by sellers becomes $3, and the equilibrium quantity becomes 1 million.

d.   With no penalty on sellers, if a penalty for breaking the law is imposed on buyers at more than $5 a disc, how does the market work and what is the equilibrium price?

With a penalty imposed on buyers of more than $5.00 per disc, the demand curve for illegal discs shifts downward by the amount of the penalty, that is, shifts downward by more than $5.00. If the penalty imposed is, say, $6, the demand curve shifts downward by $6. With the demand and supply curves in Figure 6.9, the new equilibrium price for an illegal DVD paid by buyers becomes $9, the equilibrium price received by sellers becomes $3, and the equilibrium quantity becomes 1 million.

e.   What is the marginal benefit of an illegal DVD in the situations described in parts (c) and (d)?

The marginal benefit of an illegal DVD is determined by the demand curve. In both parts (c) and (d), in Figure 6.9 the marginal benefit of a DVD with 1 million DVDs being transacted is $9.00.

f.   In light of your answer to part (e), why does law enforcement usually focus on sellers rather than buyers?

Law enforcement typically focuses on sellers because there are fewer sellers and their locations are easier to find.

Chapter

7 GLOBAL MARKETS IN ACTION

Answers to the Review Quizzes

Page 154

1.   Describe the situation in the market for a good or service that the United States imports.

The goods and services the United States will import are those in which the United States has a higher opportunity cost of production relative to other countries. In those markets the U.S. no-trade price is higher than the world price. With trade the quantity produced in the United States is less than the quantity consumed and the difference is imported.

Page 156

1.   How is the gain from imports distributed between consumers and domestic producers?

Consumers gain consumer surplus from imports and domestic producers lose producer surplus from imports.

3.   Why is the net gain from international trade positive?

The net gain from international trade is positive because the gain to the winners exceeds the losses to the losers. For instance, in the case of an imported good, *all* the loss of producer surplus is transferred to consumers as consumer surplus. In addition, however, consumers also gain additional consumer surplus from the units imported. The total gain of consumer surplus exceeds the loss of producer surplus so that the net surplus increases. The situation is similar for exports: The total gain of producer surplus exceeds the loss of consumer surplus.

Page 163

1.   What are the tools that a country can use to restrict international trade?

A country can use tariffs, import quotas, other import barriers such as health, safety, and regulation barriers, and voluntary export restraints to restrict international trade. Export subsidies given by a nation decrease other countries' exports and thereby restrict their international trade.

3.   Explain who gains and who loses from a tariff and why the losses exceed the gains.

Domestic consumers lose consumer surplus from the tariff. Domestic producers gain producer surplus from the tariff. The government also gains revenue from the tariff. But the gain in producer surplus plus the gain in government revenue is less than the loss of consumer surplus, so on net a tariff creates a deadweight loss.

5.   Explain who gains and who loses from an import quota and why the losses exceed the gains.

Domestic consumers lose consumer surplus from the import quota. Domestic producers gain producer surplus from the import quota. The importers also gain additional profit from the import quota. But the gain in producer surplus plus the importers' profits is less than the loss of consumer surplus, so on net an import quota creates a deadweight loss.

© 2016 Pearson Education, Inc.

Page 167

1. What are the infant industry and dumping arguments for protection? Are they correct?

    The attempt to stimulate the growth of new industries is the *infant-industry argument* for protection, which states that it is necessary to protect a new industry from import competition to facilitate the growth of that industry, making it competitive in the world markets. This argument is based on the idea that as firms mature they become more productive. However this argument for protection only works if the benefits also spill over into other industries and other parts of the economy. This is rarely the case, as the entrepreneurs of infant industries and their financial supporters take this risk into account and all returns usually accrue only to them, not to other industries. And it is more efficient to subsidize the infant industry needing protection than it is to protect it by restricting trade.

    The *dumping argument* for protection states that a foreign firm is selling its exports at a lower price than its cost of production. Foreign firms trying to monopolize the international market may use this practice. Once the competition is gone, the foreign firm will raise prices and reap profits. This argument fails for several reasons. First, it is virtually impossible to detect the occurrence of dumping since it is impossible to verify a firm's production costs. The test most commonly used is if the firm's price when it exports is lower than its domestic price. This test only examines the supply side of the two markets and ignores the demand side. If the domestic market is inelastic and the export market is elastic (which is almost always the case) then it is natural for a firm to price the domestic goods higher than the exports. Second, it is difficult to see how a global firm could have a monopoly for the goods or services it exports. There are too many foreign suppliers (and potential suppliers), making global competition too extensive for a monopoly to exist in the global market. And, even if there is global monopoly it is more efficient to regulate it than to impose trade restrictions on its products.

3. What is offshore outsourcing? Who benefits from it and who loses?

    Offshore outsourcing occurs when a firm in the United States buys finished goods, components, or services from firms in other countries. Workers who have skills for jobs that have been sent abroad lose from offshore outsourcing. Consumers who consume the goods and services produced abroad and imported into the United States benefit.

5. Why don't the winners from free trade win the political argument?

    Trade restrictions are enacted despite the inherent inefficiency because of the political actions of rent seeking groups, which fear that foreign competition might have a negative impact on their industry, firm, or jobs. The anti-trade groups are easily organized and have much to gain from trade restrictions, whereas the vast millions of consumers, who would win from free trade, are difficult to organize because each individual has only a small amount of loss when trade restrictions are imposed. Hence the winners from trade restrictions frequently out-lobby the winners from free trade.

Answers to the Study Plan Problems and Applications

Use the following data to work Problems 1 and 3. Wholesalers buy and sell roses in containers that hold 120 stems. The table provides information about the wholesale market for roses in the United States. The demand schedule is the wholesalers' demand and the supply schedule is the U.S. rose growers' supply. Wholesalers can buy roses at auction in Aalsmeer, Holland, for $125 per container.

Price (dollars per container)	Quantity demanded	Quantity supplied
	(millions of containers per year)	
100	15	0
125	12	2
150	9	4
175	6	6
200	3	8
225	0	10

1. a. Without international trade, what would be the price of a container of roses and how many containers of roses a year would be bought and sold in the United States?

   Without international trade, in the United States the price of a container of roses is $175 and 6 million containers of roses are bought and sold.

   b. At the price in your answer to part (a), does the United States or the rest of the world have a comparative advantage in producing roses?

   The price of roses in the United States exceeds the price in the rest of the world, so the rest of the world has a comparative advantage in producing roses.

3. Draw a graph to illustrate the U.S. wholesale market for roses. Show the equilibrium in that market with no international trade and the equilibrium with free trade. Mark the quantity of roses produced in the United States, the quantity imported, and the total quantity bought.

   In Figure 7.1, the equilibrium without international trade is determined at the intersection of the demand curve and the supply curve. Without international trade the equilibrium price is $175 per container and 6 million containers per year are bought and produced. With international trade the world price is $125 per container, as shown in Figure 7.1. The quantity produced in the United States is 2 million containers and the quantity bought in the United States is 12 million containers. Imports into the United States account for the difference between the quantity bought and the quantity produced, 10 million containers.

FIGURE **7.1**
Problem 3

Use the information on the U.S. wholesale market for roses in Problem 1 to work Problems 5, 7 and 9.

5. If the United States puts a tariff of $25 per container on imports of roses, explain how the U.S. price of roses, the quantity of roses bought, the quantity produced in the United States, and the quantity imported changed.

   The U.S. price of roses rises from $125 per container (the price with free trade) to $150 per container. The quantity of roses produced in the United States increases from 2 million containers (the quantity produced with free trade) to 4 million containers. The quantity of roses consumed in the United States decreases from 12 million containers (the quantity consumed with free trade) to 9 million containers. The quantity imported decreases from 10 million containers to 5 million containers.

7.   Draw a graph of the U.S. market for roses to illustrate the gains and losses from the tariff and on the graph identify the gains and losses, the tariff revenue, and the deadweight loss created.

FIGURE **7.3**

Problem 7

Figure 7.3 shows the effect of the tariff. The amount of the tariff per container is equal to the height of the light gray arrow. Before the tariff U.S. consumer surplus was equal to area A + area B + area C + area E + area F. After the tariff U.S. consumer surplus is equal to area A. U.S. consumers lose consumer surplus equal to area B + area C + area E + area F. Before the tariff U.S. producer surplus was equal to area G. After the tariff U.S. producer surplus is equal to area G + area B. U.S. producers gain producer surplus equal to area B. After the tariff the U.S. government gains tariff revenue equal to area E. The deadweight loss from the tariff is equal to area C + area F.

9.   Who gains and who loses from this quota?

U.S. rose growers and importers of roses gain from the quota. U.S. rose wholesalers lose from the quota.

11.   **Chinese Tire Maker Rejects Charge of Defects**

U.S. regulators ordered the recall of more than 450,000 faulty tires. The Chinese producer of the tires disputed the allegations and hinted that the recall might be an effort to hamper Chinese exports to the United States.

Source: *International Herald Tribune*, June 26, 2007

a.   What does the news clip imply about the comparative advantage of producing tires in the United States and China?

Because the tires were produced in China, the news clip suggests that China has the comparative advantage in producing tires.

b.   Could product quality be a valid argument against free trade? If it could, explain how.

Product quality is not a valid argument against free trade. Quality is a valid concern for consumers. If consumers cannot judge quality themselves, then government inspection might be necessary. But in that case government inspection of both imported and domestically produced goods is required. To single out imported goods or services makes little sense. And, by questioning the quality of tires, U.S. producers create questions in the minds of U.S. consumers regarding the safety of imported tires, thereby increasing the demand for domestically produced tires.

Answers to Additional Problems and Applications

13. Suppose that the world price of steel is $100 a ton, India does not trade internationally, and the equilibrium price of steel in India is $60 a ton. India then begins to trade internationally.

   a. How does the price of steel in India change?

   The price of steel in India rises to equal the world price.

   b. How does the quantity of steel produced in India change?

   Producers respond to the higher price by increasing the quantity of steel produced.

   c. How does the quantity of steel bought by India change?

   Steel users in India respond to the higher price by decreasing the quantity of steel bought.

   d. Does India export or import steel and why?

   Because the price of steel in India is lower than the world, India has a comparative advantage in the production of steel. India will export steel.

15. **Act Now, Eat Later**

   The hunger crisis in poor countries has its roots in U.S. and European policies of subsidizing the diversion of food crops to produce biofuels like corn-based ethanol. That is, doling out subsidies to put the world's dinner into the gas tank.

   Source: *Time*, May 5, 2008

   a. What is the effect on the world price of corn of the increased use of corn to produce ethanol in the United States and Europe?

   The use of corn to produce ethanol increased the demand for corn, thereby raising the price of corn.

   b. How does the change in the world price of corn affect the quantity of corn produced in a poor developing country with a comparative advantage in producing corn, the quantity it consumes, and the quantity that it either exports or imports?

   The higher world price of corn decreases the consumption of corn and increases the production of corn in poor developing countries. Because the country has a comparative advantage it will export corn. The higher price leads the country to increase its exports.

Use the following news clip to work Problem 17.

South Korea to Resume U.S. Beef Imports

South Korea will reopen its market to most U.S. beef. South Korea banned imports of U.S. beef in 2003 amid concerns over a case of mad cow disease in the United States. The ban closed what was then the third-largest market for U.S. beef exporters.

Source: CNN, May 29, 2008

17. a. Explain how South Korea's import ban on U.S. beef affected beef producers and consumers in South Korea.

   The South Korean ban raised the price of beef in South Korea. The higher price led to increased production in South Korea, which made South Korean producers better off. The higher price also led to decreased consumption in South Korea, which made South Korean consumers worse off.

b.   Draw a graph of the market for beef in South Korea to illustrate your answer to part (a). Identify the changes in consumer surplus, producer surplus, and deadweight loss.

Figure 7.6 shows the effect of South Korea's import ban. Prior to the ban the price of beef in South Korea was $4 per pound. At this price the quantity consumed in South Korea was 12 million tons of beef per year and the quantity produced in South Korea was 2 million tons of beef per year. The difference, 10 million tons of beef per year, was imported from the United States. Consumer surplus in South Korea was equal to area A + area B + area C and producer surplus in South Korea was equal to area E. With the import ban, the price of beef in South Korea rises to $6 per pound. At this price 6 million tons of beef per year are consumed in South Korea and 6 million tons of beef per year are produced in South Korea. There are no imports. Consumer surplus is South Korea shrinks to only area A and producer surplus grows to equal area B + area E. There is now a deadweight loss which is equal to area C.

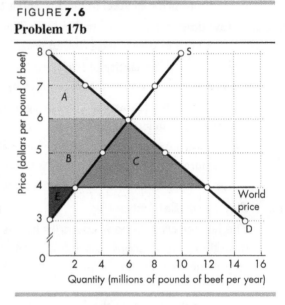

FIGURE 7.6
Problem 17b

Use the following information to work Problems 19 to 21.
Before 1995, trade between the United States and Mexico was subject to tariffs. In 1995, Mexico joined NAFTA and all U.S. and Mexican tariffs have gradually been removed.

19.   Explain how the price that U.S. consumers pay for goods from Mexico and the quantity of U.S. imports from Mexico have changed. Who are the winners and who are the losers from this free trade?

With NAFTA, the prices that U.S. consumers pay for goods from Mexico have fallen and, as a result, the quantity of imports from Mexico have increased. Winners from this free trade are Mexican producers of goods exported to the United States and U.S. consumers of these goods. Losers are Mexican consumers of the goods and U.S. producers of the goods.

21.   Suppose that in 2015 tomato growers in Florida lobby the U.S. government to impose an import quota on Mexican tomatoes. Explain who in the United States would gain and who would lose from such a quota.

U.S. tomato growers gain from such a quota. The importers who hold the quota rights also gain. U.S. consumers of tomatoes lose from such a quota.

Use the following information to work Problem 23.
Suppose that in response to huge job losses in the U.S. textile industry, Congress imposes a 100 percent tariff on imports of textiles from China.

23.   Explain how the U.S. and Chinese gains from trade will change. Who in the United States will lose and who will gain?

The decrease in trade means that the U.S. and Chinese gains from trade decrease. In the United States, U.S. producers gain from the tariff. The U.S. government also gains revenue from the tariff. U.S. textile consumers lose.

Use the following information to work Problem 25.
With free trade between Australia and the United States, Australia would export beef to the United States. But the United States imposes an import quota on Australian beef.

25.   Explain who in the United States gains from the quota on beef imports and who loses.
         U.S. beef producers gain from the quota. The people who hold the import quota rights also
         gain. U.S. beef consumers lose from the quota.

Economics in the News

27.   After you have studied *Economics in the News* on pp. 168–169, answer the following questions.
   a.   What is the TPP?
         The TTP is the Trans Pacific Partnership, a trade agreement among 12 nations.
   b.   Who in the United States would benefit and who would lose from a successful TPP?
         U.S. exporters of goods whose tariffs are reduced and U.S. consumers of imported goods whose tariffs
         are reduced benefit from a successful TPP. U.S. consumers of exported goods whose tariffs are reduced
         and U.S. producers of imported goods whose tariffs are reduced lose from a successful TPP. The
         government might gain or lose tariff revenue depending on the magnitudes of the consumption and
         production changes.
   c.   Illustrate your answer to part (b) with an appropriate graphical analysis assuming that tariffs are
         not completely eliminated.

         Figure 7.8a shows the effect in the United States of lowering the U.S. tariff on a good. Initially the price
         in the United States was $90 per unit. Consumer surplus was equal to area *A* and producer surplus was
         equal to area *B* + area *F*. When the tariff is lowered, the price in the United States becomes $70 per
         unit. Consumer surplus increases and equals area *A* + area *B* + area *C*. Producer surplus, however,
         decreases to area *F*. The government's tariff revenue equals area *E*.

         Figure 7.8b shows the effect in the United States of lowering the Japanese tariff on rice. Initially the
         price in the United States was $300 per ton. Consumer surplus was equal to area *A* + area *B* and
         producer surplus was equal to area *E*. When the tariff is lowered so that the Japanese now import rice,
         the price in the United States rises to become the world price of $500 per ton. Consumer surplus
         decreases and equals area *A*. Producer surplus, however, increases to area *B* + area *C* + area *E*.

FIGURE **7.8a**
Problem 27(c)

FIGURE **7.8b**
Problem 27(c)

d.   Who in Japan and other TPP nations would benefit and who would lose from a successful TPP?
     In other TPP nations and particularly in Japan, consumers of rice and other farm products would benefit
     from a successful TPP. In other TPP nations and particularly in Japan, producers of rice and other farm
     products would lose from a successful TPP. The Japanese government would lose tariff revenue.

e.   Illustrate with an appropriate graphical analysis who in Japan would benefit and who would lose
     from a successful TPP assuming that all Japan's import quotas and tariffs are completely
     eliminated.

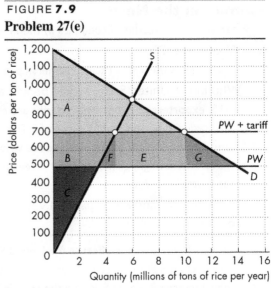

FIGURE **7.9**

Problem 27(e)

Figure 7.9 shows the effect in Japan of
eliminating Japan's tariffs and import quotas.
Figure 7.9 shows the effect in the market for
rice; the effect in other markets is similar.
Before the tariffs and import quotas are
eliminated, the price in Japan was $700 per ton
of rice. The consumer surplus is equal to area A,
the producer surplus was equal to area B + area
C and the government's tariff revenue (and/or
importers' economic profit) was equal to area
E. After the tariffs and import quotas are
removed, the price falls to $500 per ton of rice.
Consumer surplus increases and equals area A +
area B + area F + area E + area G. Producer
surplus, however, decreases to area C. The
government's tariff revenue (and/or importers'
economic profit) disappears. Consumers benefit because their consumer surplus increases; producers
lose because their producer surplus decreases; the government (and/or importers) loses because their
tariff revenue (or economic profit) is eliminated.

8 UTILITY AND DEMAND

Answers to the Review Quizzes

Page 180

1. Explain how a consumer's income and the prices of goods limit consumption possibilities.

    A consumer's consumption possibilities are limited by the consumer's income and the prices of the goods. The consumer is unable to consume limitless quantities of goods and services because the consumer must pay a price for each good or service consumed and the consumer's income is limited. If the consumer's income increases and/or the prices of the goods and services fall, the quantity of goods and services the consumer can afford increases, thereby increasing the consumer's consumption possibilities.

3. What is the distinction between total utility and marginal utility?

    Total utility is the entire amount of satisfaction an individual obtains from the total amount of goods and services consumed. Marginal utility is the change in total utility from a one-unit increase in the consumption of a good or service.

Page 184

1. Why does a consumer spend the entire budget?

    The more goods and services a person consumes, the higher the person's utility. By spending his or her entire budget, the person is consuming the maximum quantity of goods and services, which means the utility can be at its maximum.

3. What two conditions are met when a consumer is maximizing utility?

    The two conditions that must be met to ensure that a consumer is maximizing his or her utility are: i) all available income is spent, and ii) the marginal utility per dollar spent is equal for all goods and services consumed.

Page 190

1. When the price of a good falls and the prices of other goods and a consumer's income remain the same, explain what happens to the consumption of the good whose price has fallen and to the consumption of other goods.

    When the price of a good falls, the marginal utility per dollar for that good increases. The marginal utility per dollar for other goods does not change. To maximize total utility, a consumer makes marginal utility per dollar equal for all goods, so the consumer buys more of the good that has experienced the fall in price and less of the goods whose marginal utilities per dollar have not changed.

3. If a consumer's income increases and if all goods are normal goods, explain how the quantity bought of each good changes.

    If the consumer's income increases and all the goods consumed are normal goods, then the consumption of all goods increase. With the increase in income, the initial consumption possibility is now affordable with money left over. If the consumer's utility for all goods increases with consumption, because the consumer seeks to maximize utility subject to prices and available income, he or she will use the money left over from the initial bundle to increase the quantity consumed for all goods and services. By doing so the consumer increases his or her total utility. This increase occurs while the price of these goods and services remained unchanged, which indicates there is a rightward shift of the demand curve for all goods and services.

5.   What are the similarities between utility and temperature?

The scales of both utility and temperature are arbitrary. The units used to measure both can be changed without changing their predictive abilities. For instance, the scale used to "measure" utility can be changed without consequence and the scale used to measure temperature (such as Celsius, Fahrenheit, or Kelvin) also can be changed without consequence. Additionally, although neither utility nor temperature can be directly observed, both can be used to make predictions about the observable world.

Page 193

1.   Define behavioral economics.

Behavioral economics studies the ways that limits on the ability of people's brains to compute and implement rational decisions influence their economic actions.

3.   Define neuroeconomics.

Neuroeconomics studies the activity of the human brain when it makes an economic decision.

Answers to the Study Plan Problems and Applications

Jerry has $12 a week to spend on yogurt and berries. The price of yogurt is $2, and berries are $4 a box.

1. List the combinations of yogurt and berries that Jerry can afford. Draw a graph of Jerry's budget line with the quantity of berries plotted on the x-axis.

    Jerry can buy 6 yogurts and 0 boxes of berries; 4 yogurts and 1 box of berries; 2 yogurts and 2 boxes of berries; and, 0 yogurts and 3 boxes of berries. Figure 8.1 shows Jerry's budget line.

FIGURE **8.1**
Problem 1

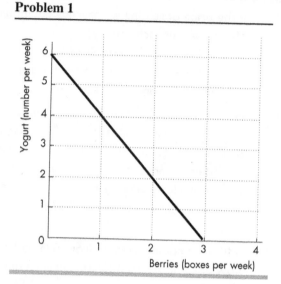

Use the following data to work Problems 3, 5, 7 and 9.

Max has $35 a day to spend on windsurfing and snorkeling and he can spend as much time as he likes doing them. The price of renting equipment for windsurfing is $10 an hour and for snorkeling is $5 an hour. The table shows the total utility Max gets from each activity.

Hours per day	Total utility from windsurfing	Total utility from snorkeling
1	120	40
2	220	76
3	300	106
4	360	128
5	396	140
6	412	150
7	422	158

3. Calculate Max's marginal utility from windsurfing at each number of hours per day. Does Max's marginal utility from windsurfing obey the principle of diminishing marginal utility?

    Max's marginal utility from windsurfing 1 hour per day is 120; from windsurfing 2 hours per day is 100; from windsurfing 3 hours per day is 80; from windsurfing 4 hours per day is 60; from windsurfing 5 hours per day is 36; from windsurfing 6 hours per day is 16; and, from windsurfing 7 hours per day is 10. Max's marginal utility from windsurfing obeys the principle of diminishing marginal utility because it decreases as consumption increases.

5. Which does Max enjoy more: his 6th hour of windsurfing or his 6th hour of snorkeling?

    Max's marginal utility from his 6th hour of windsurfing is 16 and his marginal utility from his 6th hour of snorkeling is 10. Max enjoys his 6th hour of windsurfing more than his 6th hour of snorkeling.

7.   Add two columns to your table in Problem 6 and list Max's marginal utility per dollar from windsurfing and from snorkeling.

   The columns are in the table, in the second and fourth columns.

Use the data in Problem 3 to work Problems 9, 11 and 13.

9.   If the price of renting windsurfing equipment is cut to $5 an hour, how many hours a day does Max spend on each activity?

   Max will now maximize his total utility by spending 5 hours windsurfing and 2 hours snorkeling. This combination of windsurfing and snorkeling uses all of Max's income and sets the marginal utility per dollar from windsurfing equal to the marginal utility per dollar from snorkeling.

11.   How does Max's demand for snorkeling equipment change when the price of windsurfing equipment falls? What is Max's cross elasticity of demand for snorkeling with respect to the price of windsurfing? Are windsurfing and snorkeling substitutes or complements for Max?

   When the price of windsurfing falls, Max increases the hours he snorkels from 1 hour to 2 hours. Max's demand for snorkeling increases when the price of windsurfing falls. Max's cross elasticity of demand equals (1 hour/1.5 hours)/($5/$7.50) = −1.00. Windsurfing and snorkeling are complements for Max.

13.   If Max's income increases from $35 to $55 a day, how does his demand for snorkeling equipment change? Is snorkeling a normal good? Explain.

   Max's demand for rented snorkeling equipment increases. The quantity of snorkeling equipment demanded at a price of $5 per hour increases from 1 hour (problem 8 (a)) to 3 hours (this problem). As a result Max's demand curve for rented snorkeling equipment shifts rightward as illustrated in Figure 8.4 by the shift from D_1 to D_2. Snorkeling equipment is a normal good.

FIGURE **8.4**

Problem 13

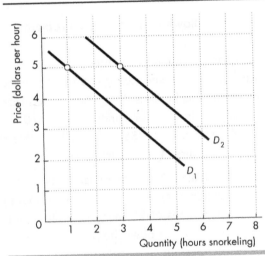

Use the following news clip to work Problem 15.

Eating Away the Innings in Baseball's Cheap Seats
Baseball and gluttony, two of America's favorite pastimes, are merging, with Major League Baseball stadiums offering all-you-can-eat seats. Some fans try to "set personal records" during their first game, but by the third time in such seats they eat normally.

Source: *USA Today*, March 6, 2008

15.   How can setting personal records for eating be reconciled with marginal utility theory? Which ideas of behavioral economics are consistent with the information in the news clip?

> The marginal utility of food consumption includes not only the "usual utility" from food but also the utility from setting a food-eating record.
>
> Bounded willpower seems very consistent with the information. Undoubtedly the people who "set personal records" in the stadium regret their decisions at later dates when they either have less income to spend than they desire and/or need to lose weight.

Answers to Additional Problems and Applications

17. Cindy has $70 a month to spend, and she can spend as much time as she likes playing golf and tennis. The price of an hour of golf is $10, and the price of an hour of tennis is $5. The table shows Cindy's marginal utility from each sport.

Make a table that shows Cindy's affordable combinations of hours playing golf and tennis. If Cindy increases her expenditure to $100, describe how her consumption possibilities change.

Hours per month	Marginal utility from golf	Marginal utility from tennis
1	80	40
2	60	36
3	40	30
4	30	10
5	20	5
6	10	2
7	6	1

The table showing Cindy's affordable combinations of hours playing golf and tennis is to the right. If Cindy increases her expenditure, then for each entry of tennis hours in the table, her hours of playing golf increase by 3 hours. Alternatively, for each entry of golf hours in the table her hours of playing tennis increase by 6. In terms of a diagram, Cindy's budget line shifts to the right and its slope does not change.

Hours playing golf	Hours playing tennis
7	0
6	2
5	4
4	6
3	8
2	10
1	12
0	14

Use the information in Problem 17 to work Problems 19, 21 and 23.

19. Explain why, if Cindy equalized the marginal utility per hour of golf and tennis, she would *not* maximize her utility.

Cindy would not maximize her utility by equalizing the marginal utility per hour of golf and tennis because golf and tennis have different prices. Golf is twice as expensive as tennis, so effectively every unit of utility that Cindy buys from playing golf costs her twice as much as buying a unit of utility from playing tennis. Equalizing the marginal utilities means that the marginal utility per dollar from tennis is greater than her marginal utility per dollar from golf. This inequality means that Cindy can increase her utility if she spends a dollar less on golf and a dollar more on tennis.

Cindy's tennis club raises its price of an hour of tennis from $5 to $10, other things remaining the same.

Hours playing golf	Marginal utility per dollar from golf	Hours playing tennis	Marginal utility per dollar from tennis
7	0.6	0	
6	1.0	1	4.0
5	2.0	2	3.6
4	3.0	3	3.0
3	4.0	4	1.0
2	6.0	5	0.5
1	8.0	6	0.2
0		7	0.1

21. Use the information in the table to draw Cindy's demand curve for tennis. Over the price range of $5 to $10 an hour of tennis, is Cindy's demand for tennis elastic or inelastic?

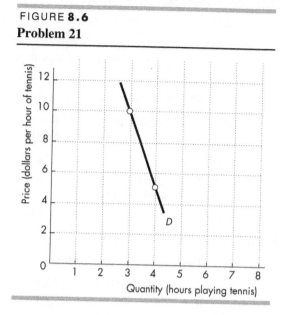

FIGURE **8.6**
Problem 21

> One point on her demand curve is 4 hours of tennis when the price is $5 per hour. Another point is 3 hours of tennis when the price is $10 per hour. Cindy's demand curve is in Figure 8.6. The price elasticity of demand between these two points on her demand curve is 0.43, so Cindy's demand is inelastic.

23. Cindy loses her math tutoring job and the amount she has to spend on golf and tennis falls from $70 to $35 a month. With the price of an hour of golf at $10 and of tennis $5, calculate the change in the hours she spends playing golf. For Cindy, is golf a normal good or an inferior good? Is tennis a normal good or an inferior good?

> With an income of $35, Cindy now plays golf for 2 hours and tennis for 3 hours to maximize her utility. This combination allocates (spends) all her income and sets the marginal utility per dollar from golf equal to the marginal utility per dollar from tennis. Golf is a normal good because the fall in income leads to a decrease in Cindy's demand for hours spent playing golf from 5 hours to 2 hours. Tennis is a normal good because the fall in income leads to a decrease in Cindy's demand for hours spent playing tennis from 4 hours to 3 hours.

25. Jim has made his best affordable choice of muffins and coffee. He spends all of his income on 10 muffins at $1 each and 20 cups of coffee at $2 each. Now the price of a muffin rises to $1.50 and the price of coffee falls to $1.75 a cup.

   a. Will Jim now be able to buy 10 muffins and 20 coffees?

   > Before the changes in price, Jim spent all his income on muffins and coffee. Therefore Jim's income is (10 muffins) × ($1 each) + (20 cups of coffee) × ($2 each) = $50. After the change in prices, the cost of 10 muffins and 20 coffees is (10 muffins) × ($1.50 each) + (20 cups of coffee) × ($1.75 each), which is $50. Therefore Jim can buy 10 muffins and 20 coffees.

   b. If Jim changes the quantities he buys, will he buy more or fewer muffins and more or less coffee? Explain your answer.

   > If Jim changes the quantities he buys, he will buy more coffee and fewer muffins. He will make these changes because coffee has fallen in relative price while muffins have risen in relative price.

Use the following news clip to work Problems 27 and 29.

Putting a Price on Human Life

Researchers at Stanford and the University of Pennsylvania estimated that a healthy human life is worth about $129,000. Using Medicare records on treatment costs for kidney dialysis as a benchmark, the authors tried to pinpoint the threshold beyond which ensuring another "quality" year of life was no longer financially worthwhile. The study comes amid debate over whether Medicare should start rationing health care on the basis of cost effectiveness.

Source: *Time*, June 9, 2008

27. Why might Medicare ration health care according to treatment that is "financially worthwhile" as opposed to providing as much treatment as is needed by a patient, regardless of costs?

Increasing the quantity of health care lowers the marginal utility from the last unit of health care. At some amount of health care the point is reached such that the marginal utility per dollar of health care is less than the marginal utility per dollar from other goods and services. At that point the quantity of health care being provided is too much and society would be better off with less health care.

29. How does the potential conflict between self-interest and the social interest complicate setting a financial threshold for Medicare treatments?

Each individual has a very high marginal utility from an additional year of life. Hence each individual's marginal utility per dollar from extending their life is extremely high and so their self-interested demand will be very high. But the rest of society's marginal utility per dollar from an additional year of the person's life is much lower and the socially interested demand will be much lower.

Economics in the News

31. **Five Signs You Have Too Much Money**

When a bottle of water costs $38, it's hard not to agree that bottled water is a fool's drink. The drink of choice among image-conscious status seekers and high-end tee-totalers in L.A. is Bling H_2O. It's not the water that accounts for the cost of the $38, but the "limited edition" bottle decked out in Swarovski crystals.

Source: CNN, January 17, 2006

a. Assuming that the price of a bottle of Bling H_2O is $38 in all the major U.S. cities, what might its popularity in Los Angeles reveal about consumers' incomes or preferences in Los Angeles relative to other U.S. cities?

If Bling H_2O is a normal good, then the increased popularity in Los Angeles indicates that incomes in Los Angeles are higher than elsewhere. In addition, the increased popularity of the drink in Los Angeles indicates that the marginal utility of Bling H_2O is higher in Los Angeles than elsewhere.

b. Why might the marginal utility from a bottle of Bling H_2O decrease more rapidly than the marginal utility from ordinary bottled water?

One of the major attributes of Bling H_2O is the "statement" it makes that the consumer is one of the few who can afford it. But typically a consumer carries around only one bottle of water. And once one bottle of Bling H_2O is purchased, it is easily refillable and can be carried once more with no loss of status. For both reasons, the marginal utility of a second bottle of Bling H_2O is quite low compared to the marginal utility of the first bottle. Ordinary bottled water, however, is purchased more for its hydrating properties than a fashion statement, so its marginal utility falls more slowly because its marginal utility is derived from its hydration.

9 POSSIBILITES, PREFERENCES, AND CHOICES

Answers to the Review Quizzes

Page 204

1. What does a household's budget line show?

    The budget line plots combinations of goods that require all a household's income and describes the limits to its consumption choices.

3. If a household has an income of $40 and buys only bus rides at $2 each and magazines at $4 each, what is the equation of the household's budget line?

    The budget equation states that a household's spending must equal its income. The budget equation is derived for two goods, bus rides and magazines. The amount spent on bus rides is $(P_{bus\ ride}) \times (Q_{bus\ ride})$, the amount spent on magazines is $(P_{magazine}) \times (Q_{magazine})$, and the consumer's income is y. We know that $(P_{magazine}) \times (Q_{magazine}) + (P_{bus\ ride}) \times (Q_{bus\ ride}) = y$. Rearrange this equality by subtracting the amount spent on bus rides from both sides to give $(P_{magazine}) \times (Q_{magazine}) = y - (P_{bus\ ride}) \times (Q_{bus\ ride})$. Finally, divide both sides by the price of magazine to give the budget equation $Q_{magazine} = y/P_{magazine} - (P_{bus\ ride}/P_{magazine}) \times (Q_{bus\ ride})$. Substituting in our values, $y = \$40$, $P_{bus\ ride} = \$2$ and $P_{magazine} = \$4$, gives $Q_{magazine} = \$40/\$4 - (\$2/\$4) \times (Q_{bus\ ride})$ which is equal to $Q_{magazine} = 10 - 0.5\, Q_{bus\ ride}$

5. If a household's money income changes and prices do not change, what happens to the household's real income and budget line?

    A household's real income is the household's income expressed as a quantity of goods the household can afford to buy. For example, the vertical intercept for a budget line measuring soda on the vertical axis is (y/P_{soda}), which is the consumer's real income in terms of sodas. A change in a household's money income changes the household's real income in terms of both goods and causes a parallel shift of the budget line. If a household's money income increases, its budget line shifts rightward and if a household's money income decreases, its budget line shifts leftward.

Page 208

1. What is an indifference curve and how does a preference map show preferences?

    An indifference curve shows those combinations of goods for which a consumer is *indifferent*. The consumer has the same level of satisfaction for any combination on a given indifference curve. The family of indifference curves is the preference map. This map shows the person's preferences because it shows how the person ranks each combination of goods. In particular, the person prefers combinations on higher indifference curves to combinations on lower indifference curves.

3. What do we call the magnitude of the slope of an indifference curve?

    The magnitude of the slope of an indifference curve is called the marginal rate of substitution (*MRS*). The *MRS* measures the rate at which the consumer gives up one good to get more of another good, while remaining on the same indifference curve (keeping the consumer indifferent about the changes). The bowed-in shape of the indifference curve is due to the assumption of diminishing *MRS*.

Page 213

1.   When a consumer chooses the combination of goods and services to buy, what is she or he trying to achieve?

   The consumer is trying to achieve the highest level of well being possible.

3.   If the price of a normal good falls, what happens to the quantity demanded of that good?

   If the price of a normal good falls, the quantity demanded of that good increases because the substitution effect and the income effect both bring an increase in the quantity demanded.

5.   For a normal good, does the income effect reinforce the substitution effect or does it partly offset the substitution effect?

   For a normal good the substitution effect and the income effect reinforce each other, and a decrease (increase) in the price of a good will always result in an increase (decrease) in the quantity of the good demanded.

Answers to the Study Plan Problems and Applications

Use the following information to work Problem 1.

Sara's income is $12 a week. The price of popcorn is $3 a bag, and the price of a smoothie is $3.

1. Calculate Sara's real income in terms of smoothies. Calculate her real income in terms of popcorn. What is the relative price of smoothies in terms of popcorn? What is the opportunity cost of a smoothie?

    Sara's real income is 4 smoothies. Sara's real income in terms of smoothies is equal to her money income divided by the price of a smoothie. Sara's money income is $12, and the price of a smoothie is $3. Sara's real income is $12 divided by $3 a smoothie, which is 4 smoothies.

    Sara's real income is 4 bags of popcorn. Sara's real income in terms of popcorn is equal to her money income divided by the price of a bag of popcorn, which is $12 divided by $3 a bag or 4 bags of popcorn. The relative price of a smoothie is 1 bag of popcorn per smoothie. The relative price of a smoothie is the price of a smoothie divided by the price of a bag of popcorn. The price of a smoothie is $3 and the price of popcorn is $3 a bag, so the relative price of a smoothie is $3 divided by $3 a bag, which equals 1 bag of popcorn per smoothie.

    The opportunity cost of a smoothie is 1 bag of popcorn. The opportunity cost of a smoothie is the quantity of popcorn that must be forgone to get a smoothie. The price of a smoothie is $3 and the price of popcorn is $3 a bag, so to buy one smoothie Sara must forgo 1 bag of popcorn.

Use the following data to work Problem 3.

Sara's income falls from $12 to $9 a week, while the price of popcorn is unchanged at $3 a bag and the price of a smoothie is unchanged at $3.

3. What is the effect of the fall in Sara's income on her real income in terms of (a) smoothies and (b) popcorn?

    a. Sara's real income falls from 4 smoothies to 3 smoothies. Sara's real income in terms of smoothies is equal to her money income divided by the price of a smoothie. Sara's money income is now $9 and the price of a smoothie is $3. Sara's real income is now $9 divided by $3 a smoothie, which is 3 smoothies.

    b. Sara's real income falls from 4 bags of popcorn to 3 bags of popcorn. Sara's real income in terms of popcorn is equal to her money income divided by the price of a bag of popcorn. Sara's money income is now $9 and the price of a bag of popcorn is $3. Sara's real income is now $9 divided by $3 a bag, which is 3 bags of popcorn.

5. Sara's income is $12 a week. The price of popcorn rises from $3 to $6 a bag, and the price of a smoothie is unchanged at $3. Explain how Sara's budget line changes with smoothies on the *x*-axis.

    The budget line rotates inward around the unchanged *x* intercept. The magnitude of the slope of the budget line is equal to the relative price of a smoothie. The relative price of a smoothie is the price of a smoothie divided by the price of a bag of popcorn. The rise in the price of a bag of popcorn lowers the relative price of a smoothie in terms of popcorn. The relative price has fallen so the magnitude of the slope of the budget line has fallen.

7. Discuss the shape of the indifference curve for each of the following pairs of goods. Explain the relationship between the shape of the indifference curve and the marginal rate of substitution as the quantities of the two goods change.

    - Orange juice and smoothies

        Orange juice and smoothies are substitutes. They are not perfect substitutes, so the indifference curves are bowed in toward the origin. The marginal rate of substitution falls moving down along an indifference curve.

    - Baseballs and baseball bats

        These are complements but probably not perfect complements. The indifference curves should be significantly bowed inward. (If a student says these goods are perfect complements, the indifference curves should be right angles, such as those in Figure 9.2A.) If the indifference curves are not right angles, then the marginal rate of substitution falls rapidly moving down along an indifference curve. (If the goods are perfect complements, the marginal rate of substitution does not change moving down along the indifference curve except when moving around the 90 degree point where it goes from infinity to zero.)

- Left running shoe and right running shoe

  These are perfect complements so the indifference curves are right angles, as shown in Figure 9.2A. The marginal rate of substitution does not change moving down along the indifference curve except when moving around the 90 degree point where it goes from infinity to zero.

- Eyeglasses and contact lenses

  The indifference curves should either be linear (for perfect substitutes, as shown in Figure 9.2B) or nearly linear as in Figure 9.2C. If the indifference curves are linear, then the marginal rate of substitution does not change moving down along the indifference curve; if the indifference curves are nearly linear, then the marginal rate of substitution falls slightly moving down along an indifference curve.

Use the following data to work Problem 9.

Pam has made her best affordable choice of cookies and granola bars. She spends all of her weekly income on 30 cookies at $1 each and 5 granola bars at $2 each. Next week, she expects the price of a cookie to fall to 50¢ and the price of a granola bar to rise to $5.

9. a.   If Pam changes how she spends her weekly income, will she buy more or fewer cookies and more or fewer granola bars?

Pam will buy more cookies and fewer granola bars. The new budget line and the old budget line pass through the point at 30 cookies and 5 granola bars. If granola bars are plotted on the *x*-axis, the marginal rate of substitution at this point on Pam's indifference curve is equal to the relative price of a granola bar at the original prices, which is 2. The new relative price of a granola bar is $5/50 cents, which is 10. That is, the budget line is steeper than the indifference curve at 30 cookies and 5 granola bars. Pam will buy more cookies and fewer granola bars.

b.   When the prices change next week, will there be an income effect, a substitution effect, or both at work?

There will be a substitution effect and an income effect. A substitution effect arises when the relative price changes and the consumer moves along the *same* indifference curve to a new point where the marginal rate of substitution equals the new relative price. An income effect arises when the consumer moves from one indifference curve to another, keeping the relative price constant.

Use the following information to work Problem 11.

Boom Time For "Gently Used" Clothes

Most retailers are blaming the economy for their poor sales, but one store chain that sells used name-brand children's clothes, toys, and furniture is boldly declaring that an economic downturn can actually be a boon for its business. Last year, the company took in $20 million in sales, up 5% from the previous year.

Source: CNN, April 17, 2008

11.   Use a graph of a family's indifference curves for used clothing and other goods. Then draw two budget lines to show the effect of a fall in income on the quantity of used clothing purchased.

In Figure 9.3, the fall in income shifts the budget line from BL_1 to BL_2. The quantity of used clothing purchased increases, in the figure from 4 items per month to 5 items per month.

FIGURE **9.3**

Problem 11

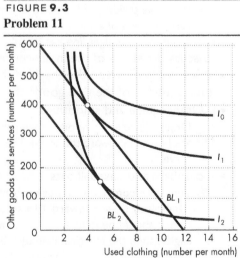

Answers to Additional Problems and Applications

Use the following data to work Problems 13 and 15.
Marc has a budget of $20 a month to spend on root beer and DVDs. The price of root beer is $5 a bottle, and the price of a DVD is $10.

13.   Calculate Marc's real income in terms of root beer. Calculate his real income in terms of DVDs.

   Marc's real income is 4 bottles of root beer. Marc's real income in terms of bottles of root beer is equal to his money income divided by the price of a bottle of root beer. Marc's money income is $20, and the price of root beer is $5 a bottle. Marc's real income is $20 divided by $5 a bottle of root beer, which is 4 bottles of root beer.

   Marc's real income is 2 DVDs. Marc's real income in terms of DVDs is equal to his money income divided by the price of a DVD, which is $20 divided by $10 a DVD or 2 DVDs.

15.   Draw a graph of Marc's budget line with the quantity of DVDs on the x-axis. What is the slope of Marc's budget line? What determines its value?

   The budget line is illustrated in Figure 9.4. The slope of the budget line, when DVDs are plotted on the x-axis is −2. The magnitude of the slope is equal to the relative price of a DVD. The slope of the budget line is "rise over run." If the quantity of DVDs decreases from 2 to 0, the quantity of root beer increases from 0 to 4 bottles. The rise is 4 and the run is −2. So the slope equals 4/−2, which is −2.

Use the following data to work Problems 17 and 19.
Amy has $20 a week to spend on coffee and cake. The price of coffee is $4 a cup, and the price of cake is $2 a slice.

17.   Calculate the equation for Amy's budget line (with cups of coffee on the left side).

   The equation that describes Amy's budget line is $Q_{COFFEE} = 5 - 0.5Q_{CAKE}$. Call the price of a cup of coffee P_{COFFEE} and the quantity of coffee Q_{COFFEE}, the price of a slice of cake P_{CAKE} and the quantity of cake Q_{CAKE}, and income y. Amy's budget equation is $P_{COFFEE}Q_{COFFEE} + P_{CAKE}Q_{CAKE} = y$. If we substitute $4 for the price of a cup of coffee, $2 for the price of a slice of cake and $20 for income, the budget equation becomes $4Q_{COFFEE} + $2Q_{CAKE} = $20. Next, divide both sides by $4 to obtain $Q_{COFFEE} + 0.5Q_{CAKE} = 5$. Finally subtract $0.5Q_{CAKE}$ from both sides to give $Q_{COFFEE} = 5 - 0.5Q_{CAKE}$.

19.   If the price of cake doubles while the price of coffee remains at $4 a cup and Amy's income remains at $20, describe the change in her budget line.

   Amy's budget line rotates inward. If the quantity of cake is plotted on the horizontal axis, the budget line rotates inward around the unchanged vertical intercept (which is the maximum number of cups of coffee Amy can purchase) and becomes steeper.

Use the following news clip to work Problem 21.

Gas Prices Straining Budgets

With gas prices rising, many people say they are staying in and scaling back spending to try to keep within their budget. They are driving as little as possible, cutting back on shopping and eating out, and reducing other discretionary spending.

Source: CNN, February 29, 2008

21. How does a rise in the price of gasoline change the relative price of a restaurant meal? How does a rise in the price of gasoline change real income in terms of restaurant meals?

 The relative price of restaurant meals equals the price of restaurant meals divided by the price of gasoline. The rise in the price of gasoline reduces the relative price of restaurant meals. The rise in the price of gasoline does not change real income in terms of restaurant meals.

Use the following information to work Problem 23.

Rashid buys only books and CDs and Figure 9.7 shows his preference map.

23. Do Rashid's indifference curves display diminishing marginal rate of substitution? Explain why or why not.

 Rashid's indifference curves display diminishing marginal rate of substitution. When moving along either indifference curve the slope becomes smaller as the consumption of CDs increases, which means that Rashid has diminishing marginal rate of substitution of books for CDs.

Use the following information to work Problem 25.

Jim has made his best affordable choice of muffins and coffee. He spends all of his income on 10 muffins at $1 each and 20 cups of coffee at $2 each. Now the price of a muffin rises to $1.50 and the price of coffee falls to $1.75 a cup.

FIGURE **9.7**
Problems 22 and 23

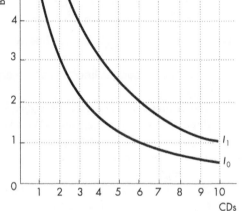

25. a. Will Jim now be able and want to buy 10 muffins and 20 coffees?

 Jim is able to buy 10 muffins and 20 coffees because this combination remains affordable. Jim will not want to buy this combination, however, because the relative price of muffins and coffee has changed. At his consumer equilibrium, Jim's MRS equals the relative price of muffins and coffee and because the relative price has changed, Jim's MRS has changed so Jim will change his consumption point.

 b. Which situation does Jim prefer: muffins at $1 and coffee at $2 a cup or muffins at $1.50 and coffee at $1.75 a cup?

 Jim prefers the $1.50 per muffin/$1.75 per coffee prices because he can attain a higher indifference curve. The new budget line goes through the old budget line at the initial consumption point. But, with coffee measured along the horizontal axis, the new budget line is flatter than the old budget line and lies beyond the initial budget line at all points below the initial consumption point.

Use the following data to work Problems 27 and 29.

Sara's income is $12 a week. The price of popcorn is $3 a bag, and the price of cola is $1.50 a can. Figure 9.9 shows Sara's preference map for popcorn and cola.

27. What quantities of popcorn and cola does Sara buy? What is Sara's marginal rate of substitution at the point at which she consumes?

 Sara buys 6 cans of cola and 1 bag of popcorn. Sara's budget line runs from 8 cans of cola on the x-axis to 4 bags of popcorn on the y-axis and is tangent to indifference curve I_1 at 6 cans of cola and 1 bag of popcorn.

FIGURE **9.9**
Problem 27

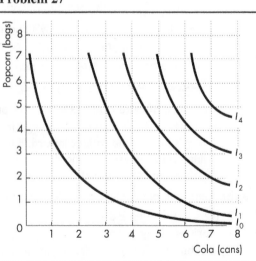

Sara's marginal rate of substitution is ½. The marginal rate of substitution is the magnitude of the slope of the indifference curve at Sara's consumption point, which equals the magnitude of the slope of the budget line. The slope of Sara's budget line is -½ bag of popcorn per can of cola so the marginal rate of substitution is ½ bag of popcorn per can of cola.

29.   Suppose that the price of cola rises to $3.00 a can and the price of popcorn and Sara's income remain the same.

   a.   What is the substitution effect of this price change and what is the income effect of the price change?

      The substitution effect is 1 can of cola. To divide the price effect into a substitution effect and an income effect, take enough income away from Sara and gradually move her new budget line back toward the original indifference curve until it just touches Sara's first indifference curve I_1. The point at which this budget line just touches indifference curve I_1 is 5 cans of cola. The substitution effect is the decrease in the quantity of cola from 6 cans to 5 cans along the indifference curve I_1. The substitution effect is 1 can of cola.

      The income effect is 3 cans of cola. The income effect is the change in the quantity of cola from the price effect minus the change from the substitution effect. The price effect is 4 cans of cola (2 cans minus the initial 6 cans). The substitution effect is a decrease in the quantity of cola from 6 cans to 5 cans. So the income effect is 3 cans of cola.

   b.   Is cola a normal good or an inferior good? Explain.

      Cola is a normal good for Sara because the income effect is positive.

Chapter

10 ORGANIZING PRODUCTION

Answers to the Review Quizzes

Page 226

1. What is a firm's fundamental goal and what happens if the firm doesn't pursue this goal?

A firm's fundamental goal is to maximize its profit. If the firm fails to maximize profit it is either eliminated or bought out by other firms maximizing profit.

3. What are the items that make opportunity cost differ from the accountant's measure of cost?

A firm's opportunity cost includes the cost of using resources bought in the market, owned by the firm and supplied by the firm's owner. Economists and accountants both include the price of resources bought in the market as costs. But accountants omit costs included by economists. For instance, use of a building the owner has already purchased has an opportunity cost that accountants do not include. Additionally the normal profit, interest foregone, and economic depreciation are other opportunity costs not recorded by an accountant.

5. What are the constraints that a firm faces? How does each constraint limit the firm's profit?

The three types of constraints a firm faces are technology constraints, information constraints, and market constraints. *Technology* is any specific method of producing a good or service and it advances over time. Using the available technology, the firm can produce more only if it hires more resources, which will increase its costs and limit the profit of additional output. *Information* is never complete, for the future or the present. A firm is constrained by limited information about the quality and effort of its work force, current and future buying plans of its customers, and the plans of its competitors. The cost of coping with limited information itself limits profit. *Market constraints* mean that what each firm can sell and the price it can obtain are constrained by its customers' willingness to pay and by the prices and marketing efforts of other firms. The resources that a firm can buy and the prices it must pay for them are limited by the willingness of people to work for and invest in the firm. The expenditures a firm incurs to overcome these *market* constraints will limit the profit the firm can make.

Page 228

1. Is a firm technologically efficient if it uses the latest technology? Why or why not?

Technological efficiency occurs when a firm produces a given level of output using the least amount of inputs. Adopting the latest available technology does not necessarily imply that a firm's production process is technologically efficient. As long as the firm is getting the maximum possible output for a given combination of inputs, it is technologically efficient.

3. Explain the key distinction between technological efficiency and economic efficiency.

The difference between technological and economic efficiency is that technological efficiency concerns the *quantity* of inputs used in production for a given level of output, whereas economic efficiency concerns the *value* of the inputs used. Economic efficiency requires technological efficiency, but technological efficiency does not require economic efficiency.

Page 232

1.   **Explain the distinction between a command system and an incentive system.**

   A command system uses a managerial hierarchy, where commands pass downward through the hierarchy and information (feedback) passes upward. These systems are relatively rigid and can have many layers of specialized management. Incentive systems use market-like mechanisms to induce workers to perform in ways that maximize the firm's profit.

3.   **What are the three types of firms? Explain the major advantages and disadvantages of each.**

   The three main ways of organizing a firm have both advantages and disadvantages:

- *Proprietorship.* ADVANTAGES—easy to set up; managerial decision-making is simple and rapid; and profits are taxed only once. DISADVANTAGES—bad decisions on the part of the owner are not subject to review; the owner's entire wealth is at stake because of unlimited liability; the firm dies with the owner; and acquiring capital and labor is expensive.

- *Partnership.* ADVANTAGES—easy to set up; has diversified decision-making so that more than one person's expertise can be utilized; can survive the death or withdrawal of a partner; and profits are taxed only once. DISADVANTAGES—all the owners' wealth is at risk because of unlimited liability; if there are many partners, gaining a consensus about managerial decisions may be difficult; the withdrawal of partner may create capital shortage; labor costs are high compared to corporations; and capital costs can be high.

- *Corporation.* ADVANTAGES—perpetual life; limited liability for its owners; readily available, large-scale, and low-cost capital; can rely on professional managers rather than the talents of the owners; and reduced costs from long-term labor contracts. DISADVANTAGES—potentially complex management structure may lead to slow and expensive decision-making; and profits are taxed twice, once as corporate profit and once as income to the stockholders.

Page 237

1.   **What are the four market types? Explain the distinguishing characteristics of each.**

   Economists identify four market types:

1.   *Perfect competition* is a market with many firms, each selling an identical product. There are many buyers and no restrictions on entry of new firms. Firms and buyers are all well informed of prices and products of all firms in the industry.

2.   *Monopolistic competition* is a market with many firms that produce similar but slightly different goods.

3.   *Oligopoly* is a market in which a small number of firms compete and each firm may produce almost identical or differentiated goods.

4.   *Monopoly* is a market in which only one firm produces the entire output of the industry. There are no close substitutes for the monopolist's product and there are barriers to entry that protect the firm from competition of entering firms.

3.   **Under what conditions do the measures of concentration give a good indication of the degree of competition in a market?**

   Concentration measures give a good indication of the degree of competition in a market if the following characteristics of the industry market are correct:

1. The industry market is national in scope, rather than local or international.
2. There are no concerns about over-stating or under-stating the extent of barriers to entry.
3. Firms are not misclassified with respect to their markets.

Page 239

1. What are the two ways in which economic activity can be coordinated?

    Firms and markets both coordinate resources.

3. What are the main reasons why firms can often coordinate production at a lower cost than markets can?

    Firms can often coordinate production at a lower cost than can markets because firms lower transactions costs and achieve economies of scale, scope, and team production. These opportunities are not present when markets coordinate production.

Answers to the Study Plan Problems and Applications

1. One year ago, Jack and Jill set up a vinegar-bottling firm (called JJVB). Use the following data to calculate JJVB's opportunity cost of production during its first year of operation:
    *   Jack and Jill put $50,000 of their own money into the firm and bought equipment for $30,000.
    *   They hired one worker at $20,000 a year.
    *   Jack quit his old job, which paid $30,000 a year worked full-time for JJVB.
    *   Jill kept her old job, which paid $30 an hour, but gave up 500 hours of leisure a year to work for JJVB.
    *   JJVB bought $10,000 of goods and services.
    *   The market value of the equipment at the end of the year was $28,000.
    *   Jack and Jill have a $100,000 home loan on which they pay interest of 6 percent a year.
        The wages paid, $20,000, and the goods and services bought from other firms, $10,000, are opportunity costs to JJVB. Other opportunity costs include the interest forgone on the $50,000 put into the firm, which could have been used to pay part of the mortgage, so the interest forgone is $3,000; the $30,000 income forgone by Jack not working at his previous job; $15,000, which is the value of 500 hours of Jill's leisure; and the economic depreciation of $2,000 ($30,000 minus $28,000). JJVB's total opportunity cost is the sum of all these opportunity costs and is $80,000.

3. Four ways of laundering 100 shirts are in the table.

Method	Labor (hours)	Capital (machines)
A	1	10
B	5	8
C	20	4
D	50	1

    a. Which methods are technologically efficient?
        All the methods are technologically efficient.

    b. Which method is economically efficient if the hourly wage rate and the implicit rental rate of capital are:
        (i) Wage rate $1, rental rate $100?
             Method D is economically efficient because the total cost is the least. Method D's costs are 50 × $1 + 1 × $100, or $150.
        (ii) Wage rate $5, rental rate $50?
             Method D and Method C are economically efficient because the total cost is the least. Method C's costs are 20 × $5 + 4 × $50, or $300 and Method D's costs are 50 × $5 + 1 × $50, also $300.
        (iii) Wage rate $50, rental rate $5?
             Method A is economically efficient because the total cost is the least. Method A's costs are 1 × $50 + 10 × $5, or $100.

5. Sales of the firms in the tattoo industry are in the table. Calculate the four-firm concentration ratio. What is the structure of the tattoo industry?

Firm	Sales (dollars per year)
Bright Spots	450
Freckles	325
Love Galore	250
Native Birds	200
Other 15 firms	800

    The four-firm concentration ratio is 60.49. The four-firm concentration ratio equals the ratio of the total sales of the largest four firms to the total industry sales expressed as a percentage. The total sales of the largest four firms is $450 + $325 + $250 + $200, which equals $1,225. Total industry sales equal $1,225 + $800, which equals $2,025.
    The four-firm concentration ratio equals ($1,225/$2,025) × 100, which is 60.49 percent.
    This industry is highly concentrated because the four-firm concentration ratio exceeds 60 percent.

7.   FedEx contracts with independent truck operators to pick up and deliver its packages and pays them on the volume of packages carried. Why doesn't FedEx buy more trucks and hire more drivers? What incentive problems might arise from this arrangement?

FedEx does not buy more trucks and hire more drivers because FedEx faces a principal-agent problem. In particular, it is not easy to monitor its drivers and insure that they are working hard to efficiently deliver packages. FedEx overcomes this problem by hiring independent contractors and then paying them based on the amount of packages they deliver. Essentially, FedEx uses a piecework method of payment.

FedEx pays its drivers based on the volume of packages they deliver. This method of payment creates a few incentive potential problems for FedEx. First, FedEx must worry about the quality of its service. In particular, unless FedEx bases part of the payment on quality, its drivers have an incentive to drop the package and race off to the next delivery with no concern for how the packages are handled. Second, FedEx must take care that drivers do not attempt to select only packages that are close to the FedEx location and avoid packages that have a greater than average driving time. Finally, FedEx also must worry that its drivers do not take undue risks while driving in order to deliver as many packages as possible. If FedEx trucks were involved in too many accidents, FedEx would suffer bad publicity and, presumably, would lose some business.

Answers to Additional Problems and Applications

Use the following data to work Problem 9.

Lee is a computer programmer who earned $35,000 in 2011. But on January 1, 2012, Lee opened a body board manufacturing business. At the end of the first year of operation, he submitted the following information to his accountant:

- He stopped renting out his cottage for $3,500 a year and used it as his factory. The market value of the cottage increased from $70,000 to $71,000.
- He spent $50,000 on materials, phone, etc.
- He leased machines for $10,000 a year.
- He paid $15,000 in wages.
- He used $10,000 from his savings account, which earns 5 percent a year interest.
- He borrowed $40,000 at 10 percent a year.
- He sold $160,000 worth of body boards.
- Normal profit is $25,000 a year.

9.   Lee's accountant recorded the depreciation on his cottage during 2012 as $7,000. According to the accountant, what profit did Lee make?

    Lee's accountant will include costs of $50,000 paid for materials, phone, utilities, etc; $15,000 for wages; $10,000 paid for the machine lease; $4,000 paid for interest expense on the loan; and, $7,000 of depreciation expense for a total opportunity cost of $86,000. The total profit according to the accountant will equal total revenue, $160,000, minus total cost, $86,000, for a profit of $74,000.

11.   **The Colvin Interview: Chrysler**

    The key driver of profitability will be that the focus of the company isn't on profitability. Our focus is on the customer. If we can find a way to give customers what they want better than anybody else, then what can stop us?

                                             Source: *Fortune*, April 14, 2008

a.   In spite of what Chrysler's vice chairman and co-president claims, why is Chrysler's focus actually on profitability?

    Chrysler's actual focus is on its profit because if Chrysler continues to incur losses Chrysler eventually will shut down. This statement is correct even in an era of government bailouts because the government will eventually stop offering bailouts if the company does not return to profitability.

b.   What would happen to Chrysler if it didn't focus on maximizing profit, but instead focused their production and pricing decisions to "give customers what they want"?

    In general customers want very elaborate, very costly automobiles sold for an exceptionally low price. In particular, customers want to pay the lowest price possible regardless of the company's profit. If Chrysler focused on only giving customers want they want, Chrysler would continue to incur a loss and ultimately would either close or be purchased by another company.

Use the following data to work Problem 13.

Four methods of completing a tax return and the time taken by each method are: with a PC, 1 hour; with a pocket calculator, 12 hours; with a pocket calculator and paper and pencil, 12 hours; and with a pencil and paper, 16 hours. The PC and its software cost $1,000, the pocket calculator costs $10, and the pencil and paper cost $1.

13.   Which, if any, of the methods is technologically efficient?

    All methods other than "pocket calculator with paper and pencil" are technologically efficient. To use a pocket calculator with paper and pencil to complete the tax return is not a technologically efficient method because it takes the same number of hours as it would with a pocket calculator but it uses more capital.

15. **A Medical Sensation**

Hospitals are buying da Vinci surgical robots. Surgeons, sitting comfortably at a da Vinci console, can use various robotic attachments to perform even the most complex procedures.

Source: *Fortune*, April 28, 2008

a. Assume that performing a surgery with a surgical robot requires fewer surgeons and nurses. Is using the surgical robot technologically efficient?

Using the surgical robot is technologically efficient because the production technique uses less labor (and more capital) than the non-robotic technique.

b. What additional information would you need to be able to say that switching to surgical robots is economically efficient for a hospital?

To determine if the production technique is economically efficient, information about the cost of the robot and the cost of the nurses and doctors and about the number of doctors and nurses each production technique uses is needed.

17. **Where Does Google Go Next?**

Google gives its engineers one day a week to work on whatever project they want. A couple of colleagues did what many of the young geniuses do at Google: They came up with a cool idea. At Google, you often end up with a laissez-faire mess instead of resource allocation.

Source: *Fortune*, May 26, 2008

a. Describe Google's method of organizing production with their software engineers.

In some sense Google is using a command system because Google "orders" its engineers to use one day a week to work on their own projects. But in a larger sense Google is using an incentive system. If one of the engineers comes up with a wildly profitable idea, the engineer will benefit by gaining stature and probably income within Google.

b. What are the potential gains and opportunity costs associated with this method?

The potential gain is that the creative people working for Google will apply their creativity to develop new and better products for Google. The potential drawback is the principal-agent problem. The engineers might use their time for on-the-job leisure rather than for new, cutting edge research.

Use the following information to work Problems 19 and 21.

Two leading design firms, Astro Studios of San Francisco and Hers Experimental Design Laboratory, Inc. of Osaka, Japan, worked with Microsoft to design the Xbox 360 video game console. IBM, ATI, and SiS designed the Xbox 360's hardware. Three firms—Flextronics, Wistron, and Celestica—manufacture the Xbox 360 at their plants in China and Taiwan.

19. Describe the roles of market coordination and coordination by firms in the design, manufacture, and marketing of the Xbox 360.

Microsoft entered the market to hire various firms, Astro Studios and Hers Experimental Design Laboratory to design the Xbox 360 and then entered the market again to hire IBM, ATI, and SiS to design the hardware of the Xbox 360. Finally, Microsoft once again entered the market to hire Flextronics and Wistron, and Celestica to produce the Xbox 360. Once Microsoft had contracted with these firms, the design, manufacture, etc. takes place within the firm.

21. Why do you think the Xbox is designed in the United States and Japan but built in China?

The Xbox is designed in America and Japan because America and Japan have a large number of highly-skilled workers who can successfully design the Xbox. With a large number of technically adept workers, it is less expensive to design the Xbox in these countries. Manufacturing the Xbox, however, takes place in China because China has a large number of lower-skilled workers and so it is less expensive to build the Xbox in China.

Economics in the News

23. **Long Reviled, Merit Pay Gains Among Teachers**

School districts in many states experiment with plans that compensate teachers partly based on classroom performance, rather than their years on the job and coursework completed. Working with mentors to improve their instruction and getting bonuses for raising student achievement encourages efforts to raise teaching quality.

Source: *The New York Times*, June 18, 2007

How does "merit pay" attempt to cope with the principal-agent problem in public education?

The principal-agent problem with teachers in public education is the concern that teachers will not work hard in the classroom. Teachers' efforts are difficult to monitor and so teachers have the incentive to shirk by working less diligently and teaching their students less. Merit pay links the teachers' pay to their students' achievement, presumably performance on standardized exams. With this linkage teachers will be paid more the better their students' performance which gives the teachers the self-interested incentive to work diligently to instruct their students.

Chapter

11 OUTPUT AND COSTS

Answers to the Review Quizzes

Page 248

1. Distinguish between the short run and the long run.

    The short run is a period of time during which the quantity of at least one factor of production is fixed and cannot be changed. The long run is a period of time long enough so that the quantities of *all* factors of production can be varied.

Page 252

1. Explain how the marginal product and average product of labor change as the labor employed increases (a) initially and (b) eventually.

    Initially, as the quantity of labor is increases, the firm experiences *increasing marginal returns*, which means that the marginal product increases as more labor is employed. Increasing marginal returns occur because hiring additional workers allows the workers to specialize and become more productive. Eventually, the firm will experience *diminishing marginal returns* which means that the marginal product decreases as more labor is employed. Decreasing marginal returns occur because eventually the gains from specialization diminish and because more and more workers are working with the same fixed amount of capital. The average product of labor follows the marginal product of labor. Initially, when the marginal product of labor is increasing, the average product also increases. As long as the marginal product of labor exceeds the average product of labor, the average product continues to increase. Eventually when the marginal product is falling it falls enough so that it is less than the average product, at which point the average product of labor decreases.

3. Explain the relationship between marginal product and average product.

    As the quantity of labor initially increases the firm experiences increasing marginal returns and the marginal product of labor increases. The marginal product of labor is greater than the average product over this range of labor, so the average product of labor increases when the quantity of labor increases. Eventually, diminishing marginal returns causes the marginal product of labor to fall. When the marginal product of labor falls below the average product, the average product decreases as the quantity of labor increases.

Page 259

1. What relationships do a firm's short-run cost curves show?

    The marginal cost (*MC*), average total cost (*ATC*) and average variable cost (*AVC*) curves are all related in the short run:

    - When the *MC* curve lies above (lies below) the *AVC* curve, the *AVC* curve rises (falls) with output. This implies that as output increases, the *MC* curve cuts through the *AVC* curve at its lowest point.

- When the *MC* curve lies above (lies below) the *ATC* curve, the *ATC* curve rises (falls) with output. This implies that as output increases, the *MC* curve cuts through the *ATC* curve at its lowest point.

- As output increases, the *ATC* curve becomes vertically closer to the *AVC* curve.

3. What does the law of diminishing returns imply for the shape of the marginal cost curve?

    The law of diminishing returns states: As a firm uses more of a variable factor of production, with a given quantity of the fixed factor of production, the marginal product of the variable factor eventually diminishes. The law of diminishing returns means that each additional worker produces a successively smaller addition to output. So to get an additional unit of output, ever more workers are required. The cost of an additional unit of output—marginal cost—is increasing, so the marginal cost curve eventually slopes upward.

5. What are the shapes of the *AVC* curve and the *ATC* curve and why do they have these shapes?

    The average variable cost (*AVC*), and average total cost (*ATC*) curves are both U-shaped.

    - The marginal cost (*MC*) curve shows how total cost changes when output increases by one unit. If the *MC* curve lies below the *AVC* curve, *AVC* is falling. Diminishing marginal returns means that eventually the *MC* curve slopes upward. At some point the *MC* curve lies above the *AVC* curve, and the *AVC* curve is upward sloping.

    - *ATC* is the sum of average fixed cost (*AFC*) and *AVC*. Initially the *ATC* curve falls as the quantity produced increases because the *AFC* is initially quite large, but drops rapidly as total fixed costs are spread over greater levels of output. However, eventually diminishing returns cause marginal product to fall below average product, and average product decreases. As a result *AVC* increases as the quantity produced increases. If *AVC* rises more quickly than *AFC* falls, then the *ATC* curve is upward sloping.

Page 263

1. What does a firm's production function show and how is it related to a total product curve?

    A firm's production function is the relationship between the maximum output attainable and the quantities of both capital and labor. The total product curve shows the maximum output that a given quantity of labor can produce for a given quantity of capital.

3. What does a firm's *LRAC* curve show? How is it related to the firm's short-run *ATC* curves?

    The long-run average cost curve (*LRAC*) shows the relationship between the lowest attainable *ATC* and output when both plant size and labor are varied. The *LRAC* curve reflects the minimum possible *ATC* the firm can attain for any given level of output. For any level of output the firm might choose to produce, the *LRAC* reflects the lowest possible *ATC* taken from an *ATC* curve that corresponds to a particular plant size. Once the firm has chosen that plant size, it will incur costs corresponding to the *ATC* curve associated with that plant size.

5. What is a firm's minimum efficient scale?

    Minimum efficient scale is the smallest quantity of output at which long-run average cost reaches its lowest level. If the long-run average cost curve has the typical U shape, the minimum point of the *LRAC* identifies the level of output that represents the firm's minimum efficient scale.

Answers to the Study Plan Problems and Applications

1. Which of the following news items involves a short-run decision and which involves a long-run decision? Explain.

   January 31, 2008: Starbucks will open 75 more stores abroad than originally predicted, for a total of 975.

   > This decision is a long-run decision. It increases the quantity of *all* of Starbucks' factors of production, labor and the size of Starbucks' plant.

   February 25, 2008: For three hours on Tuesday, Starbucks will shut down every single one of its 7,100 stores so that baristas can receive a refresher course.

   > This decision is a short-run decision. It involves increasing the quality of Starbucks' labor and so only one factor of production—labor—changes and all the other factors remain fixed.

   June 2, 2008: Starbucks replaces baristas with vending machines.

   > This decision is a short-run decision. It involves changing two of Starbucks' factors of production, labor and one type of capital. But other factors of production, such as Starbucks' land and other capital inputs such as the store itself, remain fixed.

   July 18, 2008: Starbucks is closing 616 stores by the end of March.

   > This decision is a long-run decision. It decreases the quantity of *all* of Starbucks' factors of production, labor and the size of Starbucks' plant.

Use the table to work Problems 3 and 5.

The table sets out Sue's Surfboards' total product schedule.

Labor (workers per week)	Output (surfboards per week)
1	30
2	70
3	120
4	160
5	190
6	210
7	220

3. Calculate the average product of labor and draw the average product curve.

   > The average product of labor is equal to total product divided by the quantity of labor employed. For example, when 3 workers are employed, they produce 120 surfboards a week, so average product is 40 surfboards per worker. As Figure 11.2 (on the next page) shows, the average product curve is upward sloping when up to 3 workers are hired and then is downward sloping when more than 4 workers are hired.

5. a. Over what output range does Sue's Surfboards enjoy the benefits of increased specialization and division of labor?

   > The firm enjoys the benefits of increased specialization and division of labor over the range of output for which the marginal cost decreases. This range of output is the same range over which the marginal product of labor rises. For Sue's Surfboards, the benefits of increased specialization and division of labor occur until 2.5 workers are employed.

FIGURE **11.2**
Problem 3

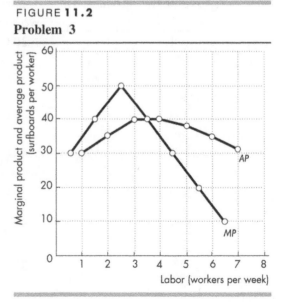

b. Over what output range does the firm experience diminishing marginal product of labor?

  The marginal product of labor decreases after the 3rd worker is employed.

c. Over what output range does the firm experience an increasing average product of labor but a diminishing marginal product of labor?

  The marginal product of labor decreases and the average product of labor increases between 2.5 and 3.5 workers.

Use the following data to work Problems 7, 9 and 11. Sue's Surfboards, hires workers at $500 a week and its total fixed cost is $1,000 a week.

7. Calculate total cost, total variable cost, and total fixed cost of each output in the table. Plot these points and sketch the short-run total cost curves passing through them.

  Total cost is the sum of the costs of all the factors of production that Sue's Surfboards uses. Total variable cost is the total cost of the variable factors. Total fixed cost is the total cost of the fixed factors. For example, the total variable cost of producing 120 surfboards a week is the total cost of the workers employed, which is 3 workers at $500 a week, which equals $1,500. Total fixed cost is $1,000, so the total cost of producing 120 surfboards a week is $2,500. Figure 11.4 (on the previous page) shows these total cost curves.

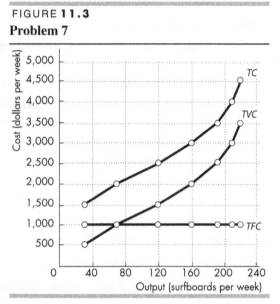

FIGURE **11.3**

Problem 7

9. Illustrate the connection between Sue's AP, MP, AVC, and MC curves in graphs like those in Fig. 11.7.

Labor (workers)	Output (surfboards)	AP (surfboards per worker)	MP (surfboards per worker)	AVC (dollars per surfboard)	MC (dollars per surfboard)
1	30	30.0		16.67	
			40.0		12.50
2	70	35.0		14.29	
			50.0		10.00
3	120	40.0		12.50	
			40.0		12.50
4	160	40.0		12.50	
			30.0		16.67
5	190	38.0		13.16	
			20.0		25.00
6	210	35.0		14.29	
			10.0		50.00
7	220	31.4		15.91	

The table sets out the data used to draw the curves. Figure 11.5 shows the curves and the relationships. When the *AP* curve rises the *AVC* curve falls and vice versa. When the *MP* curve rises the *MC* curve falls and vice versa.

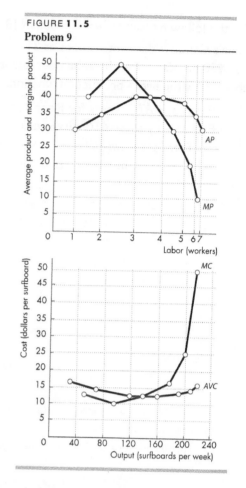

FIGURE **11.5**
Problem 9

11. Workers at Sue's Surfboards negotiate a wage increase of $100 a week per worker. If other things remain the same, explain how Sue's Surfboards' short-run average cost curves and marginal cost curve change.

The increase in the wage rate is a variable cost, so total variable cost increases. The increase in total variable cost increases total cost but total fixed cost does not change. Average variable cost is total variable cost per unit of output. The average variable cost curve shifts upward. Average total cost is total cost per unit of output. The average total cost curve shifts upward. The marginal cost curve shifts upward while the average fixed cost curve does not change.

Labor (workers per day)	Output (rides per day)			
	Plant 1	Plant 2	Plant 3	Plant 4
10	20	40	55	65
20	40	60	75	85
30	65	75	90	100
40	75	85	100	110
Canoes	10	20	30	40

Use the following data to work Problem 13.

Jackie's Canoe Rides rents canoes at $100 per day and pays $50 per day for each canoe operator it hires. The table shows the firm's production function.

13. Graph the *ATC* curves for Plant 3 and Plant 4. Explain why these *ATC* curves differ.

These are drawn in Figure 11.6. The curves differ because the number of plants differs.

FIGURE **11.6**
Problems 12 and 13

Answers to Additional Problems and Applications

15. **A Bakery on the Rise**

Some 500 customers a day line up to buy Avalon's breads, scones, muffins, and coffee. Staffing and management are worries. Avalon now employs 35 and plans to 15 more. Its payroll will climb by 30 percent to 40 percent. The new CEO has executed an ambitious agenda that includes the move to a larger space, which will increase the rent from $3,500 to $10,000 a month.

Source: CNN, March 24, 2008

a. Which of Avalon's decisions described in the news clip is a short-run decision and which is a long-run decision?

Hiring the additional 15 workers is a short-run decision; increasing the size of its space, that is, the size of its plant, is a long-run decision.

b. Why is Avalon's long-run decision riskier than its short-run decision?

Avalon's long-run decision is riskier than its short-run decision because it is more difficult to change the long-run decision. In particular if Avalon decides to reverse its short-run decision to hire more workers, it is straightforward to fire the workers. However to reverse the long-run decision of increasing the size of its plant is more difficult and takes much longer to do.

17. Terri runs a rose farm. One worker produces 1,000 roses a week; hiring a second worker, doubles her total product; hiring a third worker doubles her output again; hiring a fourth worker increased her total product but by only 1,000 roses. Construct Terri's marginal product and average product schedules. Over what range of workers do marginal returns increase?

The easiest way to construct the marginal product and average product schedules is to use the total product schedule, in the table to the left. Then the average product of labor is equal to the output divided by the quantity of labor and the marginal product of labor is equal to the change in output divided by the change in the quantity of labor. Marginal returns increase over the range of 3 workers. After the third worker, the marginal product decreases as more workers are hired.

Labor (workers per week	Output (roses per week)	Average product (roses per week)	Marginal product (roses per week)
1	1,000	1,000	
			1,000
2	2,000	1,000	
			2,000
3	4,000	1,333	
			1,000
4	5,000	1,250	

19. Bill's Bakery has a fire and Bill loses some of his cost data. The bits of paper that he recovers after the fire provide the information in the following table (all the cost numbers are dollars).

Bill asks you to come to his rescue and provide the missing data in the five spaces identified as A, B, C, D, and E.

A is the average fixed cost, AFC, when the output is 20. Average fixed cost equals total fixed cost divided by output, or $AFC = TFC \div Q$. Rearranging gives $TFC = AFC \times Q$. So the total fixed cost for the problem equals 120×10, which is $1,200. A equals $1,200, TFC, divided by 20, Q, which is $60.

B is the average variable cost, AVC, when output is 20. Use the result that $AFC + AVC = ATC$ by rearranging to give $AVC = ATC - AFC$, so average variable cost equals $150 - $60, which is $90.

D is the average total cost, *ATC*, when output, *Q*, equals 40. Average total cost equals total cost divided by output, or $ATC = TC \div Q$. Rearranging gives $TC = ATC \times Q$. So the total cost when 30 units are produced is 130×30, which is $3,900. Marginal cost, *MC*, equals the change in total cost divided by the change in quantity, or $MC = \Delta TC \div \Delta Q$. Rearranging gives $\Delta TC = MC \times \Delta Q$, so the change in total cost between $Q = 30$ and $Q = 40$ is 130×10, or $1,300. Therefore the total cost when *Q* equals 40 is $3,900 + $1,300, or $5,200. The average total cost when *Q* is 40 is $5,200 \div 40$, or $130.

TP	AFC	AVC	ATC	MC
10	120	100	220	
				80
20	A	B	150	
				90
30	40	90	130	
				130
40	30	C	D	
				E
50	24	108	132	

C is the average variable cost, *AVC*, when output, *Q*, equals 40. Use the result that $AFC + AVC = ATC$ by rearranging to give $AVC = ATC - AFC$. As a result, average variable cost equals $130 - $30, or $100.

E is the marginal cost, *MC*, when output increases from 40 units to 50 units. Marginal cost, *MC*, equals the change in total cost divided by the change in quantity, or $MC = \Delta TC \div \Delta Q$. To calculate marginal cost, the total cost when output is 40 and the total cost when output is 50 are needed. Average total cost equals total cost divided by output, or $ATC = TC \div Q$. Rearranging gives $TC = ATC \times Q$. So the total cost when 40 units are produced is 130×40, which is $5,200 and total cost when 50 units are produced is 132×50, which is $6,600. So the marginal cost equals ($6,600 - $5,200) \div 10, which equals $140.

Use the following table to work Problem 21.

ProPainters hires students at $250 a week to paint houses. It leases equipment at $500 a week. The table sets out its total product schedule.

Labor (students)	Output (houses painted per week)
1	2
2	5
3	9
4	12
5	14
6	15

21. Explain why the gap between ProPainters' total cost and total variable cost is the same no matter how many houses are painted.

    The gap between total cost and total variable cost is total fixed cost. Because the fixed cost is the same at all levels of output, the difference between the total cost and total variable cost is constant.

Use the table above and the following information to work Problem 23.

If ProPainters doubles the number of students it hires and doubles the amount of equipment it leases, it experiences diseconomies of scale.

23. Explain how the *ATC* curve with one unit of equipment differs from that when ProPainters uses double the amount of equipment.

    Because ProPainters experiences diseconomies of scale, when ProPainters doubles its inputs the *minimum* average cost is higher than when it uses the lesser quantities of inputs. Even so, at high levels of output the average total cost of producing the large level of output with the greater quantities of inputs is lower than the average total cost of producing this large level of output with the smaller quantities of inputs.

Use the following information to work Problems 25 and 27.

The table shows the production function of Bonnie's Balloon Rides. Bonnie's pays $500 a day for each balloon it rents and $25 a day for each balloon operator it hires.

Labor (workers per day)	Output (rides per day)			
	Plant 1	Plant 2	Plant 3	Plant 4
10	6	10	13	15
20	10	15	18	20
30	13	18	22	24
40	15	20	24	26
50	16	21	25	27
Balloons	1	2	3	4

25. Graph the *ATC* curves for Plant 1 and Plant 2. Explain why these *ATC* curves differ.

To find the average total cost for each plant, at the different levels of output add the variable cost, which is the cost of the workers or $25 per worker, to the fixed cost, which is the cost of the balloons or $500 per balloon. For Plant 1, the total cost for 6 rides is $750; for 10 rides is $1,000; for 13 rides is $1,250; for 15 rides is $1,500; and, for 16 rides is $1,750. The average total cost is calculated by dividing the total cost by the quantity of rides. These average total costs are plotted in Figure 11.8. The curves differ because the number of plants differs.

FIGURE **11.8**
Problems 25 and 26

27. a. On Bonnie's *LRAC* curve, what is the average cost of producing 15 rides and 18 rides a day?

The long-run average total cost curve is illustrated in Figure 11.8 as the darker line. The long-run average cost curve is comprised of the segments of the different short-run average total cost curves that have the minimum average total cost for the different levels of output. For 15 rides a day the average cost is $100 and for 18 rides a day the average cost is $97.22.

b. Explain how Bonnie's uses its long-run average cost curve to decide how many balloons to rent.

Bonnie's will use its long-run average total cost curve by building the size of the plant that minimizes its long-run average cost at the number of balloon rides that Bonnie's expects to produce.

Economics in the News

29. **Starbucks Unit Brews Up Self-Serve Espresso Bars**

Coinstar has installed automated, self-serve espresso kiosks in grocery stores. Kiosks cost just under $40,000 each and Coinstar provides maintenance. The self-serve kiosks remove the labor costs of having a barista serve Starbucks' coffee and store personnel refill the machine.

Source: MSNBC, June 1, 2008

a. What is Coinstar's total fixed cost of operating one self-serve kiosk? What are its variable costs of providing coffee at a self-serve kiosk?

The fixed costs are the cost of the machine itself, $40,000. The variable costs include the cost of the coffee beans and other ingredients and, presuming that the kiosks need more maintenance the heavier their use, the cost of maintaining the kiosks.

b.   Assume that a coffee machine operated by a barista costs less than $40,000. Explain how the fixed costs, variable costs, and total costs of barista-served and self-served coffee differ.

The fixed cost of the Coinstar machine exceeds that of the barista-operated machine. The variable cost of the barista-operated machine exceeds that of the Coinstar machine. The total cost of the Coinstar machine is probably higher than that of the barista-operated machine at lower levels of output and is probably lower at higher level of outputs.

c.   Sketch the marginal cost and average cost curves implied by your answer to part (b).

Figure 11.10 shows the different marginal costs and average total cost curves. The costs with the barista-operated machine are labeled "1" and the costs with the Coinstar are labeled "2". The average total cost of the Coinstar machine is higher than that of the barista-operated machine at low levels of output and is lower than the average total cost of the barista-operated machine at high levels of output. The marginal cost of the Coinstar machine is lower than the marginal cost of the barista-operated machine.

FIGURE 11.10
Problem 29c

Use the following news clip to work Problem 31.

Gap Will Focus on Smaller Scale Stores

Gap has too many stores that are 12,500 square feet. The target store size is 6,000 square feet to 10,000 square feet, so Gap plans to combine previously separate concept stores. Some Gap body, adult, maternity, baby and kids stores will be combined in one store.

Source: CNN, June 10, 2008

31.   How might Gap take advantage of economies of scale by combining concept stores into one store?

At 12,500 square feet Gap's stores were too large and Gap was incurring diseconomies of scale. When Gap combines its separate Gap concept stores into a smaller space, Gap will use fewer resources, particularly less capital and less labor. Gap's costs will be less as a result. Additionally Gap's sales will be less but the proportionate decrease in cost will exceed the decrease in Gap's production. In this case Gap's average costs will decrease so that Gap can reap economies of scale it currently is not enjoying.

12 PERFECT COMPETITION

Answers to the Review Quizzes

Page 273

1. Why is a firm in perfect competition a price taker?

    One firm's output is a perfect substitute for another firm's output and each firm is a small part of the market. These points imply that each firm cannot unilaterally influence the market price at which it can sell its good or service. It must accept, or "take" the market equilibrium price—hence the term, *price taker*.

3. In perfect competition, why is a firm's marginal revenue curve also the demand curve for the firm's output?

    A perfectly competitive firm's demand curve is a horizontal line at the market price. This result means that the price it receives is the same for every unit sold. The marginal revenue received by the firm is the change in total revenue from selling one more unit, which is the constant market price. So a perfectly competitive firm's demand curve is the same as its marginal revenue curve.

Page 277

1. Why does a firm in perfect competition produce the quantity at which marginal cost equals price?

    A firm's total profit is maximized by producing the level of output at which marginal revenue for the last unit produced equals its marginal cost, or $MR = MC$. In a perfectly competitive market, MR is equal to the market price P for all levels of output. These points imply that a perfectly competitive firm will maximize profit by producing the quantity at $P = MC$.

3. What is the relationship between a firm's supply curve, its marginal cost curve, and its average variable cost curve?

    The firm will produce output as long as the price is greater than the minimum AVC. It will choose the level of output where $MC = P$, which means the firm's supply curve is the firm's MC curve above minimum AVC and along the vertical axis, producing zero, below the minimum AVC.

Page 281

1. How do we derive the short-run market supply curve in perfect competition?

    The short-run market supply curve is the horizontal sum of each individual firm's supply curve. That is, the amount supplied by the total market equals the sum of what each firm in the industry supplies at a given price.

3.   In perfect competition, when market demand decreases, explain how the price of the good and the output and profit of each firm changes in the short run.

   When market demand decreases, the market price of the good falls and the market quantity decreases. Because the price equals marginal revenue, the fall in the price means marginal revenue falls. As a result, each firm moves down its marginal cost curve so each firm decreases the quantity it produces. The firm's economic profit falls (or its economic loss increases). If the firm had been making a normal profit before the decrease in demand, after the decrease the firm incurs an economic loss.

Page 283

I.   What triggers entry in a competitive market? Describe the process that ends further entry.

   When firms in a competitive market make an economic profit, the economic profit serves as an inducement to other firms to enter the market. As the other firms enter, the supply increases and the price falls. The fall in the price eventually eliminates the economic profit, at which time entry stops.

Page 287

Describe what happens to output, price, and economic profit in the short run and in the long run in a competitive market following:

I.   An increase in demand.

   An increase in demand increases the market quantity, and the market price rises above *ATC* for each firm. *In the short run*, firms in the market make an economic profit, attracting firms from outside the market to enter the market in the long run. This entry shifts the market supply curve rightward, lowering the price as the market quantity continues to increase. The fall in the price shrinks the firms' economic profit until the price again equals the minimum point on each firm's *ATC* curve. At this point, firms return to zero economic profit and entry stops. *In the long run*, the price returns to the original level, market output is larger than the original amount, the number of firms is larger, and economic profit for each firm returns to zero.

3.   The adoption of a new technology that lowers production costs.

   Technological advances result in lower costs for the firm that adopts them and initially these firms make an economic profit. Two actions occur in the market: i) firms from outside the market enter the market; ii) firms with old technology either exit the market or adopt the new technology. These two actions shift the market supply rightward, decreasing market price and increasing market quantity. In the long run, all firms in the industry will be new technology firms, economic profit for each firm will return to zero, market quantity will increase, and market price will fall to the new minimum *ATC* for each firm.

Page 289

I.   State the conditions that must be met for resources to be allocated efficiently.

   Resource use is efficient when the economy produces the goods and services that people value most highly. This situation requires that consumers are on their demand curves, thereby allocating their budgets to get the most possible value from their income. If the people who consume a good or service are the only ones who benefit from it, then the market demand curve measures the benefit to the entire society and is the marginal social benefit curve. Efficient resource use also requires that firms are on their supply curves, thereby getting the most value out of their resources. If the firms that produce a good or service bear all the costs of producing it, then the market supply curve measures the marginal cost to the entire society and the market supply curve is the marginal social cost curve. And resources are used efficiently when marginal social benefit equals marginal social cost.

3.   Describe the choices that producers make and explain why producers are efficient on the market supply curve.

Competitive firms maximize profit. We derive the firm's supply curve by finding the profit-maximizing quantity at each price, which means that firms are efficient and get the most value out of their resources at all points along their supply curve.

Answers to the Study Plan Problems and Applications

1.   Lin's makes fortune cookies. Anyone can make and sell fortune cookies, so there are dozens of producers. All fortune cookies are the same and buyers and sellers know this fact. In what type of market does Lin's operate? What determines the price of fortune cookies? What determines Lin's marginal revenue?

   Lin is operating in a perfectly competitive market. The equilibrium price is determined at the intersection of the market demand curve and the market supply curve. Lin's marginal revenue equals the market price of a box of cookies.

Use the following table to work Problem 3.
Pat's Pizza Kitchen is a price taker and the table shows its costs of production.

Output (pizzas per hour)	Total cost (dollars per hour)
0	10
1	21
2	30
3	41
4	54
5	69

3.   What is Pat's shutdown point and what is Pat's economic profit if it shuts down temporarily?

   The shutdown point is the price that equals minimum average variable cost. To calculate total variable cost, subtract total fixed cost ($10—when output is zero, total variable cost is $0, so total cost at zero output equals total fixed cost) from total cost. Average variable cost equals total variable cost divided by the quantity produced. The average variable cost of producing 2 pizzas is $10 a pizza. Average variable cost is a minimum when marginal cost equals average variable cost. The marginal cost of producing 2 pizzas is $10. So Pat's shutdown point is a price of $10 a pizza. When Pat shuts down the economic "profit" is actually an economic loss equal to Pat's fixed cost. In particular Pat's economic loss is $10.

5.   The market for paper is perfectly competitive and 1,000 firms produce paper. The first table sets out the market demand schedule for paper. The second table sets out the costs of each producer of paper. Calculate the market price, the market output, the quantity produced by each firm, and the firm's economic profit or loss.

   The market price is $8.40 per box of paper. The market price is the price at which the quantity demanded equals the quantity supplied. The firm's supply curve is the same as its marginal cost curve at prices above minimum average variable cost. Average variable cost is at its minimum when marginal cost equals average variable cost. Marginal cost equals average variable cost at the quantity 250 boxes a week. So the firm's supply curve is the same as the marginal cost curve for the outputs equal to 250 boxes or more. When the

Price (dollars per box)	Quantity demanded (thousands of boxes per week)
3.65	500
5.20	450
6.80	400
8.40	350
10.00	300
11.60	250
13.20	200

Output (boxes per week)	Marginal cost (dollars per additional box)	Average variable cost	Average total cost
		(dollars per box)	
200	6.40	7.80	12.80
250	7.00	7.00	11.00
300	7.65	7.10	10.43
350	8.40	7.20	10.06
400	10.00	7.50	10.00
450	12.40	8.00	10.22
500	20.70	9.00	11.00

price is $8.40 a box, each firm produces 350 boxes and the quantity supplied by the 1,000 firms is 350,000 boxes a week. The quantity demanded at $8.40 is 350,000 a week. The market output is 350,000 boxes a week. Each firm produces 350 boxes a week.

Each firm incurs an economic loss of $581 a week. Each firm produces 350 boxes at an average total cost of $10.06 a box. The firm sells the 350 boxes for $8.40 a box. The firm incurs a loss on each box of $1.66 and incurs a total economic loss of $581 a week.

7.   In Problem 5, in the long run, what is the market price and the quantity of paper produced? What is the number of firms in the market?

In the long run, the price equals the minimum average total cost, $10 a box. The number of firms in the long run is 750. In the long run, as firms exit the industry, the price rises. In the long-run equilibrium the price will equal the minimum average total cost. When output is 400 boxes a week, marginal cost equals average total cost and average total cost is a minimum at $10 a box. In the long run, the price is $10 a box. Each firm remaining in the industry produces 400 boxes a week. The quantity demanded at $10 a box is 300,000 boxes a week. The number of firms is 300,000 boxes divided by 400 boxes per firm, which is 750 firms. In the long run, the 750 firms together produce the equilibrium quantity of 300,000 boxes.

9.   In perfect competition in the long-run equilibrium, can consumer surplus or producer surplus be increased? Explain your answer.

Once at the competitive equilibrium quantity, which is the same as the efficient quantity, the sum of consumer surplus plus producer surplus is as large as possible. If the price is lowered, consumer surplus increases but only at the expense of a larger decrease in producer surplus. And the lower price is not the long-run equilibrium price.

If the price is raised, producer surplus increases but only at the expense of a larger decrease in consumer surplus. And the higher price is not the long-run equilibrium price.

Answers to Additional Problems and Applications

Use the following news clip to work Problem 11.

Money in the Tank

Two gas stations stand on opposite sides of the road: Rutter's Farm Store and Sheetz gas station. Rutter's doesn't even have to look across the highway to know when Sheetz changes its price for a gallon of gas. When Sheetz raises the price, Rutter's pumps are busy. When Sheetz lowers prices, there's not a car in sight. Both gas stations survive but each has no control over the price.

Source: *The Mining Journal*, May 24, 2008

11.   Describe the elasticity of demand that each of these gas stations faces.

Each station's elasticity of demand is very high. When one station raises its price even a bit, it loses a *lot* of customers to its competitors. And when one of the stations lowers its price, it gains a *lot* of customers from its competitor.

13.   Figure 12.1 shows the costs of Quick Copy, one of many copy shops near campus. If the market price of copying is 10¢ a page, calculate Quick Copy's

FIGURE **12.1**

Problem 13

   a.   Profit-maximizing output.

Quick Copy's profit-maximizing quantity is 80 pages an hour. Quick Copy maximizes its profit by producing the quantity at which marginal revenue equals marginal cost. In perfect competition, marginal revenue equals price, which is 10 cents a page. Marginal cost is 10 cents a page when Quick Copy produces 80 pages an hour.

   b.   Economic profit.

Quick Copy's economic profit is $2.40 an hour. Economic profit equals total revenue minus total cost. Total revenue equals $8.00 an hour (10 cents a page multiplied by 80 pages). The average total cost of producing 80 pages is 7 cents a page, so total cost equals $5.60 an hour (7 cents multiplied by 80 pages). So economic profit equals $8.00 minus $5.60, which is $2.40 an hour.

15.   **Chevy Volt Production Temporarily Shut Down**

GM will temporarily lay off 1,300 employees as the company stops production of the electric car, Chevy Volt, for five weeks. GM had hoped to sell 10,000 Volts last year, but ended up selling just 7,671. It plans to maintain inventory levels by adjusting production to match demand.

Source: *Politico*, March 2, 2012

   a.   Explain how the shutdown decision will affect GM Chevy Volt's *TFC*, *TVC*, and *TC*.

The shutdown decision has no effect on GM's *TFC*. It will lower GM's *TVC* and *TC*.

   b.   Under what conditions would this shutdown decision maximize Chevy Volt's economic profit (or minimize its loss)? Explain your answer.

GM will shut down its plant when the price of a Volt is less than its average variable cost, that is, when $P < AVC$. By shutting down, GM incurs an economic loss equal to its total fixed cost, which is the minimum loss that it can incur in this situation.

c. Under what conditions will GM start producing the Chevy Volt again? Explain your answer.

GM will start producing the Chevy Volt again when the price of Volt exceeds its average variable cost, that is, when $P > AVC$. In this case, even if GM is still incurring an economic loss, its loss will be less if it produces than if it shuts down.

17. Do firms enter or exit the market in the long run? What is the market price and the equilibrium quantity in the long run?

The firms are incurring economic losses, so some firms exit the market. As firms exit the market, the market supply decreases so that in the long run the price rises to equal the minimum average total cost, $4.25 per smoothie. When the price is $4.25 for a smoothie, the equilibrium quantity is 550 smoothies per hour.

19. **Exxon Mobil Selling All Its Retail Gas Stations**

Exxon Mobil is not alone among Big Oil exiting the retail gas business, a market where profits have gotten tougher as crude oil prices have risen. Gas station owners say they're struggling to turn a profit because while wholesale gasoline prices have risen sharply, they've been unable to raise pump prices fast enough to keep pace.

Source: *Houston Chronicle*, June 12, 2008

a. Is Exxon Mobil making a shutdown or exit decision in the retail gasoline market?

Exxon Mobil is making an exit decision. It is permanently leaving the market.

b. Under what conditions will this decision maximize Exxon Mobil's economic profit?

This decision maximizes Exxon Mobil's economic profit if Exxon Mobil's retail gasoline operation is incurring an economic loss. In this case by closing its retail gasoline stations, Exxon Mobil increases its economic profit.

c. How might Exxon Mobil's decision affect the economic profit of other gasoline retailers?

Exxon Mobil's exit will decrease the number of retail firms selling gasoline. The decrease in the number of firms decreases the supply and raises the market price of retail gasoline. As a result of the higher market price the surviving firms' profits rise.

21. In a perfectly competitive market, each firm maximizes its profit by choosing only the quantity to produce. Regardless of whether the firm makes an economic profit or incurs an economic loss, the short-run equilibrium is efficient. Is the statement true? Explain why or why not.

The statement is true. A perfectly competitive firm is a price taker and so it has no choice about what price it will charge. If there are no external benefits or external costs, then when a competitive market is in equilibrium, it is efficient. Regardless of the firms' profits, as long as they are producing along their supply curves they are producing efficiently and obtaining the most value for their resources.

Economics in the News

23. **Smartphones: 2.6 Billion and Rising**

Smartphone subscriptions increased by 40 percent in 2013 to reach 2.6 billion. This number is expected to rise to 5.6 billion by 2019. Emerging markets, especially China and India, provide most of the growth as many people buy their first smartphone.

Source: CNET News, November 11, 2013

a. Explain the effects of the increase in global demand for smartphones on the market for smartphones and on an individual smartphone producer in the short run.

In the short run the market demand for smartphones increases. The price of a smartphone rises and the market equilibrium quantity increases. Because the market price rises, individual smartphone producers increase the quantity they produce and make an economic profit.

b. Draw a graph to illustrate your explanation in part (a).

FIGURE **12.5a**
Problem 23b

FIGURE **12.5b**
Problem 23b

Figure 12.5 shows the short-run outcome. Figure 12.5a shows the market equilibrium. In the market, demand increases and the demand curve shifts rightward from D_0 to D_1. In the short run the supply curve remains S_0. As a result of the increase in demand the market price rises to $250 a smartphone and the market quantity increases to 1,200 million. Figure 12.5b shows the situation at a representative firm. The rise in the market price raises the firm's demand and marginal revenue curve from MR_0 to MR_1. The firm responds by increasing the quantity it produces from 200 million smartphones a year to 225 million smartphones a year. It makes an economic profit because the price exceeds the firm's average total cost.

c. Explain the long-run effects of the increase in global demand for smartphones on the market for smartphones.

In the long run the economic profit attracts entry into the market. The market supply increases which drives the price down. The market equilibrium quantity increases. The fall in the price decreases and, in the long run, totally eliminates the firms' economic profit so the firm makes zero economic profit.

Chapter 13 MONOPOLY

Answers to the Review Quizzes

Page 299

1. How does monopoly arise?

   Monopoly arises if a firm is selling a good that has no close substitutes and if the firm is protected from competition by a barrier to entry. As a result, a monopoly is the *only* firm in its market.

3. Distinguish between a price-discriminating monopoly and a single-price monopoly.

   A single-price monopoly charges every consumer the same price for each unit of the good or service the consumer buys. A price-discriminating monopolist might charge different consumers different prices for the same good or service or charge the same consumer different prices for different units of the good or service. When a firm practices price discrimination, it sells different units of a good or service for different prices.

Page 303

1. What is the relationship between marginal cost and marginal revenue when a single-price monopoly maximizes profit?

   A single-price monopoly firm maximizes profit by producing an amount of output so that marginal cost equals marginal revenue ($MR = MC$).

3. What is the relationship between price, marginal revenue, and marginal cost when a single-price monopoly is maximizing profit?

   $MR < P$ for every level of output. A profit-maximizing monopoly firm produces the amount of output that sets $MR = MC$. As a result, MC must be below price: $MC = MR < P$.

Page 307

1. Why does a single-price monopoly produce a smaller output and charge more than the price that would prevail if the market were perfectly competitive?

   The market supply curve for a competitive market is the horizontal sum of the individual firm's marginal cost curves. Equilibrium output in this competitive market is determined where the market supply curve intersects the market demand curve, and at this point price equals marginal cost, that is $P = MC$. Equilibrium output for a single-price monopoly is determined at the intersection of its marginal cost curve and its marginal revenue curve. Marginal revenue is less than price, which means that $MR = MC$ at less output than that for which $P=MC$, so the monopoly produces less than a perfectly completive market. For a monopoly price exceeds marginal revenue which, in turn, equals marginal cost. Therefore for a monopoly, $P > MC$ which means the monopoly price exceeds the price in a perfectly competitive market.

3.   Why is a single-price monopoly inefficient?

In a competitive market, the supply curve is the marginal social cost curve for society, and the demand curve is the marginal social benefit curve to society. The perfectly competitive market is efficient because production occurs where the quantity supplied equals the quantity demanded so that $MSB = MSC$. The monopolist is inefficient because price exceeds marginal cost at the quantity of output the monopoly produces. When the monopoly equates $MC = MR$ to choose the profit-maximizing level of output, it charges a price from the demand curve that is greater than marginal cost, which means $MSB > MSC$. Consumer and producer surplus are not maximized and society suffers a deadweight loss.

Page 311

1.   What is price discrimination and how is it used to increase a monopoly's profit?

Price discrimination is the practice of selling different units of a good or service for different prices. To practice price discrimination, a monopoly must be able to: i) identify and separate different buyer types, and ii) sell a product that cannot be resold. The key idea to price discrimination is to charge different consumers different prices, according to their willingness to pay for the good. This transfers potential consumer surplus under the single-price scenario into producer surplus, raising the monopoly's profit.

3.   Explain how consumer surplus, economic profit, and output change when a monopoly perfectly price discriminates.

Perfect price discrimination occurs when a monopoly charges each consumer the maximum price he or she is willing to pay. The closer the price paid is to the value placed on the good, the smaller is the consumer surplus. This transfers the *entire* consumer surplus to producer surplus. Consumer surplus is eliminated. Producer surplus increases because it gains an amount equal to the lost consumer surplus. Producer surplus also increases because the quantity produced increases to the output at which price equals marginal cost. The monopoly increases its economic profit compared to charging a single-price to all customers. This outcome achieves efficiency by eliminating the deadweight loss.

Page 315

1.   What is the pricing rule that achieves an efficient outcome for a regulated monopoly? What is the problem with this rule?

Regulating the actions of a natural monopoly to achieve an efficient outcome implies setting the level of output at the quantity where $MB = MC$, and the monopoly must set its price equal to marginal cost. This type of regulation is called the marginal cost pricing rule. A marginal cost pricing rule maximizes total surplus. However, when the monopoly price equals marginal cost, average total cost exceeds price and the monopoly incurs an economic loss. A monopoly that is required to use a marginal cost pricing rule will not stay in business because it is not covering its costs. Two possible ways of enabling the firm to cover its costs are by price discrimination and by using a two-part price (called a two-part tariff). The government might also grant the firm a subsidy. But this subsidy must be raised through imposing taxes on other economic activity, which creates deadweight loss and prevents efficient resource allocation in the markets affected by the tax.

3.   What is a price cap? Why might it be a more effective way of regulating monopoly than rate of return regulation?

A price cap is a price ceiling, a regulation that sets the maximum price the regulated firm can charge. This type of regulation might be a more effective method of regulation than rate of return regulation because rate of return regulation gives managers the incentive to inflate their costs. Price cap regulation, however, gives the regulated firm the incentive to operate efficiently and not inflate its costs.

Answers to the Study Plan Problems and Applications

1.   The U.S. Postal Service has a monopoly on non-urgent First Class Mail. Pfizer Inc. makes LIPITOR, a prescription drug that lowers cholesterol. Cox Communications is the sole provider of cable television service in some parts of San Diego. Are any of these firms protected by a barrier to entry? Do any of these firms produce a good or service that has a substitute? Might any of them be able to profit from price discrimination? Explain your answers.

   The U.S. Postal Service and Pfizer are protected by legal barriers to entry. The Postal Service has the legal right given to it by the Private Express Statutes to be the only first class non-urgent mail service and Pfizer has a patent on Lipitor. Cox Communications has a natural barrier to entry because it is a natural monopoly. It also has a legal barrier to entry because it has been given the public franchise to be the only cable provider in its area.

   Substitutes for the U.S. Postal Service include email, fax, and private delivery services, such as FedEx or UPS. Substitutes for Lipitor are generic Lipitor, other statin drugs, such as Zocor, non-statin drugs that also lower cholesterol, and exercise. Substitutes for Cox Communications include satellite television services, Hulu, and other Internet provided television service.

   All three of the firms practice price discrimination. The second ounce in a first class letter is less expensive to mail than the first ounce. Lipitor's price varies according to the insurance policy a customer has. Cox Communications bundles packages of services that have a lower price than each item taken separately so that additional units of service are less expensive than the initial units.

Use the following table to work Problem 3.

Minnie's Mineral Springs is a single-price monopoly. Columns 1 and 2 of the table set out the market demand schedule for Minnie's water and columns 2 and 3 set out Minnie's total cost schedule.

Price (dollars per bottle)	Quantity demanded (bottles per hour)	Total cost (dollars per hour)
10	0	1
8	1	3
6	2	7
4	3	13
2	4	21
0	5	31

3.   At what price is Minnie's total revenue maximized and over what range of prices is the demand for water elastic? Why will Minnie not produce a quantity at which the market demand is inelastic?

   Interpolating along the demand curve, Minnie's total revenue is maximized at a price of $5. At this price she sells 2.5 bottles an hour for total revenue of $12.50.

   The demand for Minnie's Mineral Springs water is elastic between $5 per bottle and $10 per bottle.

   Minnie will not produce a quantity at which the demand for her water is inelastic because producing at such a price does not maximize her profit. If Minnie is producing where her demand is inelastic, she can decrease the quantity she produces and 1) increase her total revenue, and 2) decrease her total cost. Because her total revenue increases and her total cost decreases, Minnie's total profit increases. Anytime Minnie's production is at a quantity at which demand is inelastic, she can always increase her total profit by decreasing her production.

5.   Use the data to work Problem 5.

   a.   Use a graph to illustrate the producer surplus generated from Minnie's Mineral Springs' water production and consumption.

Figure 13.2 shows Minnie's producer surplus. The producer surplus equals the area of the grey polygon on the figure.

FIGURE **13.2**
Problem 5

   b.   Is Minnie's an efficient producer of water? Explain your answer.

Minnie's is not an efficient producer of water. Efficiency requires that the amount of production sets the marginal cost of water equal to its marginal benefit. The marginal benefit is measured by the demand curve, so in Figure 13.2 the efficient quantity of water to produce is the quantity where the marginal cost curve intersects the demand curve, which is 2 1/9 bottles per hour.

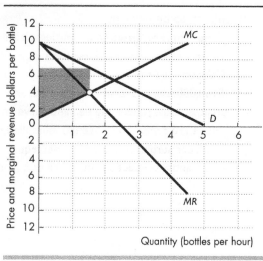

   c.   Suppose that new wells were discovered nearby to Minnie's and Minnie's faced competition from new producers. Explain what would happen to Minnie's output, price, and profit.

Competition would force Minnie's to lower its price. Minnie's output would decrease as would its economic profit.

Use the following figure to work Problems 7 and 9.

The figure shows Calypso, a U.S. natural gas distributor. It is a natural monopoly that cannot price discriminate. What quantity will Calypso produce, what price will it charge, and what will be the total surplus and deadweight loss if Calypso is:

7.   An unregulated profit-maximizing firm?

As shown in Figure 13.5, Calypso will produce 2 million cubic feet a day and sell it for 6 cents a cubic foot. The marginal revenue curve will run from 10 cents on the y-axis to 2.5 cubic feet on the x-axis. The profit-maximizing output is 2 million cubic feet at which marginal revenue equals marginal cost. The price charged is the highest that people will pay for 2 million cubic feet a day, which is 6 cents a cubic foot. The consumer surplus is $40,000, the producer surplus is $80,000, and the deadweight loss is $40,000. The consumer surplus is the triangular area under the demand curve and above the price. The price is 6 cents, so consumer surplus equals (10 cents minus 6 cents) multiplied by 2 million cubic feet/2, which is $40,000. The producer surplus is the rectangular area under the price and above the MC curve. The price is 6 cents, so producer surplus equals (6 cents minus 2 cents)

FIGURE **13.5**
Problems 7

Quantity (millions of cubic feet per day)

multiplied by 2 million cubic feet a day, which is $80,000. The efficient output is 4 cubic feet, at which marginal cost equals price (marginal benefit). The deadweight loss is the triangular area between the demand (or marginal social benefit) curve and the marginal cost curve between the equilibrium quantity and the efficient quantity. So the deadweight loss equals (4 million cubic feet minus 2 million cubic feet) multiplied by (6 cents minus 2 cents)/2, which is $40,000 a day.

9.   Regulated to be efficient?

If the firm is regulated to be efficient, it will produce the quantity at which price (marginal social benefit) equals marginal social cost—at the intersection of the demand curve and the marginal cost curve. Calypso will produce 4 million cubic feet a day and charge 2 cents a cubic foot. The consumer surplus is $160,000, the producer surplus is $0, and the deadweight loss is $0. The consumer surplus is the triangular area under the demand curve and above the price. The price is 2 cents, so consumer surplus equals (10 cents minus 2 cents) multiplied by 4 million cubic feet/2, which is $160,000. There is no producer surplus because the price equals the marginal cost. And there is no deadweight loss because the quantity produced is the efficient quantity.

Answers to Additional Problems and Applications

Use the following list, which gives some information about seven firms, to answer Problem 11.

- Coca-Cola cuts its price below that of Pepsi-Cola in an attempt to increase its market share.
- A single firm, protected by a barrier to entry, produces a personal service that has no close substitutes.
- A barrier to entry exists, but the good has some close substitutes.
- A firm offers discounts to students and seniors.
- A firm can sell any quantity it chooses at the going price.
- The government issues Nike an exclusive license to produce golf balls.
- A firm experiences economies of scale even when it produces the quantity that meets the entire market demand.

11.   Which of the seven cases are natural monopolies and which are legal monopolies? Which can price discriminate, which cannot, and why?

It is not possible to determine if the second case is a legal barrier or natural barrier to entry because we do not know the type of barrier. The sixth case describes a legal barrier to entry because Nike has been given an "exclusive license" by the government. The seventh case is a natural monopoly because it describes the firm as having economies of scale over the entire market demand.

Coca-Cola in the first case cannot price discriminate because there are not separate classes of customers with different willingness to pay. The fifth case, the firm that can sell any quantity it wants at the going price, is a perfect competitor and cannot price discriminate. The fourth case, the firm offering discounts to students, and seniors, *is* price discriminating. The other situations describe firms that *might* be able to price discriminate if there are different classes of customers and if the firm can determine into which class a customer falls.

Use the following information to work Problems 13 and 15.

Hot Air Balloon Rides is a single-price monopoly. Columns 1 and 2 of the table set out the market demand schedule and columns 2 and 3 set out the total cost schedule.

13.   Draw a graph of the market demand curve and Hot Air's marginal revenue curve.

Figure 13.6 illustrates Hot Air's demand curve and marginal revenue curve.

Price (dollars per ride)	Quantity demanded (rides per month)	Total cost (dollars per month)
220	0	80
200	1	160
180	2	260
160	3	380
140	4	520
120	5	680

15. If the government imposes a tax on Hot Air's profit, how do its output and price change?

As a result of the tax, Hot Air's fixed cost changes, but its marginal cost does not. The profit-maximizing level of output is still 2 1/2 rides a month and the price still equals $170. The tax decreases Hot Air's economic profit but does not change its output or price.

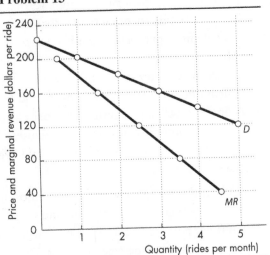

FIGURE 13.6
Problem 13

17. Figure 13.7 illustrates the situation facing the publisher of the only newspaper containing local news in an isolated community.

a. On the graph, mark the profit-maximizing quantity and price and the publisher's total revenue per day.

Profit is maximized when the firm produces the output at which marginal cost equals marginal revenue. As Figure 13.8 shows, the marginal revenue curve runs from 100 on the y-axis to 500 on the x-axis. The marginal revenue curve cuts the marginal cost curve at the quantity 267 newspapers a day. The highest price for which the publisher can sell 267 newspapers a day is read from the demand curve. So the profit-maximizing quantity is 267 newspapers a day and price is 73 cents a paper. The daily total revenue is $194.91 (267 papers at 73 cents each). This amount is equal to the rectangular area C in Figure 13.8.

b. At the price charged, is the demand for this newspaper elastic or inelastic? Why?

Demand is elastic. Along a straight-line demand curve, demand is elastic at all prices above the midpoint of the demand curve. The price at the midpoint is 50 cents. So at 73 cents a paper, demand is elastic.

FIGURE 13.7
Problem 17

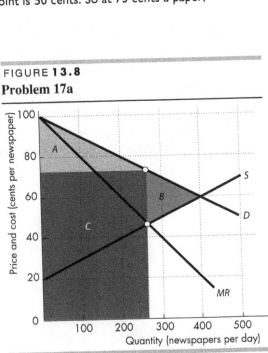

FIGURE 13.8
Problem 17a

19. If the newspaper market in Problem 17 were perfectly competitive, what would be the quantity, price, consumer surplus, and producer surplus? Mark each on the graph.

FIGURE 13.9

The quantity would be 400 newspapers a day and the price would be 60 cents a newspaper. The consumer surplus is the triangular area under the demand curve and above the price, marked as area A in Figure 13.9. The price is 60 cents, so consumer surplus equals (100 cents minus 60 cents) multiplied by 400/2 papers a day, which is $80 a day. The producer surplus is the triangular area under the price and above the supply curve, marked as area B in Figure 13.9. The price is 60 cents, so producer surplus equals (60 cents minus 20 cents) multiplied by 400/2 papers a day, or $80 a day.

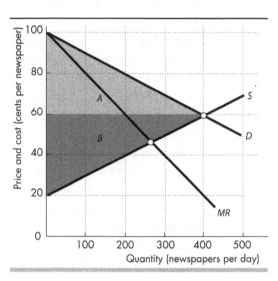

21. **AT&T Moves Away From Unlimited-Data Pricing**

AT&T said it will eliminate its $30 unlimited data plan as the crush of data use from the iPhone has hurt call quality. AT&T is introducing new plans costing $15 a month for 200 megabytes of data traffic or $25 a month for 2 gigabytes. AT&T says those who exceed 2 gigabytes of usage will pay $10 a month for each additional gigabyte. AT&T hopes that these plans will attract more customers.

Source: The Wall Street Journal, June 2, 2010

a. Explain why AT&T's new plans might be price discrimination.

AT&T's new plans are price discrimination because users pay a different price per gigabyte of data depending on the quantity of data they download. AT&T's marginal cost is the same, regardless of how much data is downloaded, so the price difference does not reflect a difference in cost.

b. Draw a graph to illustrate the original plan and the new plans.

FIGURE 13.10a
Problem 21

FIGURE 13.10b

Figures 13.10 can be used to illustrate the original plan and the new plan. Initially AT&T charged everyone a fee of $30 per month regardless of how many or how few gigabytes of data were used. In Figure 13.10a, 13.10b, and 13.10c, with the original plan there are 20 million users, each paying $30 per month. Each figure shows that AT&T has total revenue equal to the area of the rectangle with the light grey upper part and dark grey lower part. With the new plans, Figure 13.10a shows the customers who opt for the $15 per month plan. In the figure there are 35 million users who sign up for this plan. AT&T's total revenue equals the area of the rectangle with the dark grey left side and the light grey right side. Next Figure 13.10b shows the users who opt for the

FIGURE **13.10c**
Problem 21

$25 per month plan. In the figure there are 25 million customers who sign up for this plan and do not use more than 2 gigabytes of data. From these customers AT&T's total revenue equals the area of the rectangle with the dark grey left side and the light grey right side. Finally, Figure 13.10c shows the customers who opt for the $25 per month plan and use more than 2 gigabytes of data. In the figure, there are 40 million of these users. Assuming they use only 1 gigabyte more, AT&T's total revenue from them is $25 multiplied by 40 million plus the area of the rectangle with the dark grey left side and the light grey right side.

Economics in the News

23.   After you have studied *Economics in the News* on pp. 316–317, answer the following questions.

   a.   Why did the European regulators say that Google was misusing its monopoly power? Do you agree? Explain why or why not.

   The European regulators asserted that Google was abusing its power in search to extend its reach to other markets, such as commercial searches for digital cameras or hotels, because Google's search engine highlights links to Google services that search for these (and other) products. The European regulators said that Google gave less prominent space to rivals for these sorts of commercial searches.

   b.   Explain why it would be inefficient to regulate Google to make it charge the same price per keyword click to all advertisers.

   Efficiency requires that Google sell the number of clicks so that the marginal social cost of a click equals the marginal social benefit of a click. The marginal social cost of a click equals the marginal cost and the marginal social benefit equals the price. Only if the price per click equals the marginal cost of a click would Google sell the efficient number of clicks. At any other price Google would sell an inefficient quantity of clicks. So only if the marginal social cost of all clicks is the same and Google is regulated to charge precisely that price would this regulation be efficient.

c. Explain why selling keywords to the highest bidder can lead to an efficient allocation of advertising resources.

Selling keywords to the highest bidder allocates the words to those bidders who value them most highly, which means the words and hence advertising resources, are allocated efficiently. By selling each click at a separate price to the highest bidder, Google is trying to perfectly price discriminate. If Google perfectly price discriminates, then the market achieves the efficient outcome, albeit with no consumer surplus

25. **Antitrust Inquiry Launched into Intel**

Intel, the world's largest chipmaker, holds 80 percent of the microprocessor market. Advanced Micro Devices complains that Intel stifles competition, but Intel says that the 42.4 percent fall in prices between 2000 and 2007 shows that this industry is fiercely competitive.

Source: *The Washington Post*, June 7, 2008

a. Is Intel a monopoly in the chip market?

Intel is not a monopoly because a competitor, Advanced Micro Devices, has a 20 percent market share. If Intel was a monopoly it would have no competitors.

b. Evaluate the argument made by Intel that the fall in prices "shows that this industry is fiercely competitive."

This argument is not sound. Technology has advanced rapidly in the microprocessor market. Technological advances shift the firm's marginal cost curve downward. Even if Intel was a monopoly, such a downward shift in the marginal cost curve would lead the firm to increase its profit-maximizing quantity and lower its profit-maximizing price. So the fall in price is not necessarily evidence that the industry is competitive.

Chapter

14 MONOPOLISTIC COMPETITION

Answers to the Review Quizzes

Page 325

1. What are the distinguishing characteristics of monopolistic competition?

    The distinguishing characteristics of monopolistic competition are: i) a large number of firms, each producing a differentiated product than its competitors, ii) firms compete on quality, price, and marketing, and iii) there are no barriers to entry into the industry.

3. Provide some examples of industries near your school that operate in monopolistic competition (excluding those given on the text page in the figure).

    Hamburger restaurants, coffee shops, and juice bars are examples of firms competing in their own respective industry, each industry being a market described by monopolistic competition.

Page 329

1. How does a firm in monopolistic competition decide how much to produce and at what price to offer its product for sale?

    A firm that has already decided the quality of its product and its marketing program produces the output at which its marginal revenue equals its marginal cost ($MR = MC$) because this output maximizes profit. The price is determined from the *demand curve* for the firm's product and is the highest price the firm can charge for the profit-maximizing quantity.

3. Why do firms in monopolistic competition operate with excess capacity?

    A firm's capacity output is the output at which average total cost is at its minimum. In monopolistic competition in the long run, $MR = MC$ and $P = ATC$. At the long run equilibrium, it is the case that $MC < ATC$, which means that ATC is falling in this range and so production occurs at an output level that is *less* than capacity output.

5. Is monopolistic competition efficient?

    Monopolistic competition is not efficient by the requirement for allocative efficiency $MSB = MSC$. The price equals the consumer's willingness to pay, which is the marginal social benefit and the firm's marginal cost is the marginal social cost. Product differentiation in monopolistic competition means that $P > MR$, which implies that $P > MC$ at the quantity where $MR = MC$. Because $P = MSB$ and $MC = MSC$, the result is that $MSB > MSC$, which signals inefficiency. However, when compared to the perfectly competitive alternative that all goods are identical, the variety offered by monopolistic competition makes monopolistic competition potentially efficient.

Page 333

1. How, other than by adjusting price, do firms in monopolistic competition compete?

   The two main ways firms in monopolistic competition compete other than by adjusting price is through product development and advertising.

3. Explain how selling costs influence a firm's cost curves and its average total cost.

   Selling costs increase a firm's fixed cost, which increase the firm's total cost. This means that an increase in selling costs shifts the average fixed cost (AFC) curve and the average total cost (ATC) curve upward. Variable costs do not change, so the marginal cost (MC) and average variable cost (AVC) curves remain unchanged.

5. Are advertising and brand names efficient?

   Advertising and brand names can increase consumer information about product differences and quality. This information increases consumers' wellbeing and increases efficiency. But advertising and creating a brand name also are costly endeavors. If the MSB from the advertising and brand names is greater than the MSC of the advertising and brand names, then advertising and brand names increase efficiency. But if the MSB from the advertising and brand names is less than the MSC of the advertising and brand names, then advertising and brand names decrease efficiency. Basically, if the additional benefit that consumer's gain from advertising and brand names exceed the costs, then advertising and brand names have a surplus for society and should be increased until their marginal social benefit equals their marginal social cost.

Answers to the Study Plan Problems and Applications

1. Which of the following items are sold by firms in monopolistic competition? Explain your selections.

    *   Cable television service

        The cable television market is not an example of monopolistic competition because at any locale, there are not a lot of firms competing.

    *   Wheat

        The wheat market is not an example of monopolistic competition because the many competing firms each produce an identical product.

    *   Athletic shoes

        The athletic shoe market is an example of monopolistic competition. There are several producers of athletic shoes, with extensive product differentiation and competition on quality, price, and marketing.

    *   Soda

        The soda market is not an example of monopolistic competition because there are only two producers who together have a very large market share.

    *   Toothbrushes

        The toothbrush market is an example of monopolistic competition. There are many producers of toothbrushes, with extensive product differentiation and competition on quality, price, and marketing.

    *   Ready-mix concrete

        The ready-mix concrete market is not an example of monopolistic competition.

Use the following information to work Problem 4.

Sara is a dot.com entrepreneur who has established a Web site at which people can design and buy sweatshirts. Sara pays $1,000 a week for her Web server and Internet connection. The sweatshirts that her customers design are made to order by another firm, and Sara pays this firm $20 a sweatshirt. Sara has no other costs. The table sets out the demand schedule for Sara's sweatshirts.

Price (dollars per sweatshirt)	Quantity demanded (sweatshirts per week)
0	100
20	80
40	60
60	40
80	20
100	0

3. Calculate Sara's profit-maximizing output, price, and economic profit.

    Sara produces the quantity that sets her marginal cost equal to her marginal revenue. Sara's marginal cost is $20. Between the quantity of 20 and 40 sweatshirts, Sara's marginal revenue is $40. Between 40 and 60 sweatshirts, Sara's marginal revenue is $0. So at the quantity of 40 sweatshirts Sara's marginal revenue is $20. To maximize her profit, Sara produces 40 sweatshirts. When Sara produces 40 sweatshirts, the price from the demand schedule is $60 per sweatshirt. Sara's total revenue is $2,400. Her total cost is $1,000 (fixed cost) plus $800 (variable cost), or $1,800. Sara's economic profit equals $2,400 − $1,800 or $600.

Use Figure 14.1, which shows the situation facing Flight Inc., a producer of running shoes, to work Problems 5 and 7.

FIGURE 14.1
Problems 5 to 8

5. What quantity does Flight produce, what price does it charge, and what is its economic profit?

    To maximize profit, Flight produces the quantity at which marginal revenue equals marginal cost, so it produces 100 pairs a week. Flight charges the highest price that enables it to sell the 100 pairs of shoes. As read from the demand curve, Flight charges $80 a pair. Economic profit equals total revenue minus total cost. The price is $80 a pair and the quantity sold is 100 pairs, so total revenue is $8,000. Average total cost is $60 a pair, so total cost equals $6,000. Economic profit equals $8,000 minus $6,000, so Flight makes an economic profit of $2,000 a week.

7. Does Flight have excess capacity in the long run? If it has excess capacity in the long run, why doesn't it decrease its capacity?

    In the long run, monopolistically competitive firms produce less output than the amount which minimizes the average total cost, which means that in the long run they have excess capacity. Flight produces at the average total cost that is the minimum average total cost for the quantity it produces. If Flight decreased its capacity it would shift its average total cost curve upward. This shift would increase its average total cost for its profit-maximizing quantity and Flight would incur an economic loss.

9. Suppose that Tommy Hilfiger's marginal cost of a jacket is a constant $100 and the total fixed cost at one of its stores is $2,000 a day. This store sells 20 jackets a day, which is its profit-maximizing number of jackets. Then the stores nearby start to advertise their jackets. The Tommy Hilfiger store now spends $2,000 a day advertising its jackets, and its profit-maximizing number of jackets sold jumps to 50 a day.

    a. What is this store's average total cost of a jacket sold (i) before the advertising begins and (ii) after the advertising begins?

        Before the advertising begins, the average total cost of a jacket is $200. The average total cost equals the total cost divided by the quantity. The fixed cost is $2,000. Because the marginal cost is $100 per jacket, the total variable cost is $2,000. So the total cost is the $2,000 fixed cost plus the $2,000 variable cost, which is $4,000. So the average total cost is $4,000/20, which is $200.

        After the advertising begins, the average total cost of a jacket is $180. The average total cost equals the total cost divided by the quantity. The fixed cost is $4,000. Because the marginal cost is $100 per jacket, the total variable cost is $5,000. So the total cost is the $4,000 fixed cost plus the $5,000 variable cost, which is $9,000. The average total cost is $9,000/50, which is $180.

    b. Can you say what happens to the price of a Tommy Hilfiger jacket, Tommy's markup, and Tommy's economic profit? Why or why not?

        If the advertising has decreased the demand and made it more elastic, which is likely the case if all firms advertise, then the price will fall. However, if the advertising has increased the demand and made the demand less elastic, then the price will rise.

        If the price falls, then the makeup falls; if the price rises, then the markup rises.

        It is not possible to determine the effect on the profit in the short run. In the long run, however, the economic profit will equal zero as it does for all monopolistically competitive firms in the long run.

Answers to Additional Problems and Applications

11. The HHI for automobiles is 2,350, for sporting goods it is 161, for batteries it is 2,883, and for jewelry it is 81. Which of these markets is an example of monopolistic competition?

    Sporting goods and jewelry are examples of monopolistically competitive markets.

Use the following information to work Problem 13.

Lorie teaches singing. Her fixed costs are $1,000 a month, and it costs her $50 of labor to give one class. The table shows the demand schedule for Lorie's singing lessons.

Price (dollars per lesson)	Quantity demanded (lessons per month)
0	250
50	200
100	150
150	100
200	50
250	0

13. a. Do you expect other firms to enter the singing lesson business and compete with Lorie?

    Lorie is making an economic profit so other firms will enter the singing-lesson industry to compete with Lorie.

   b. What happens to the demand for Lorie's lessons in the long run? What happens to Lorie's economic profit in the long run?

    As new firms enter the singing-lesson industry, the demand for Lorie's lessons will decrease. In the long run Lorie's economic profit is eliminated and Lorie makes zero economic profit—a normal profit.

Use Figure 14.2, which shows the situation facing Mike's Bikes, a producer of mountain bikes, to work Problems 15 to 17. The demand and costs of other mountain bike producers are similar to those of Mike's Bikes.

15. What will happen to the number of firms producing mountain bikes in the long run?

    The firms are incurring an economic loss, so some firms exit the market. In the long run, the number of firms producing mountain bikes decreases.

17. Is there any way for Mike's Bikes to avoid having excess capacity in the long run?

    If Mike's Bikes maximizes its profit, it will have excess capacity. If Mike's Bikes increases its production so that it produces at the minimum of its average total cost, it will incur an economic loss.

FIGURE 14.2
Problems 14 to 18

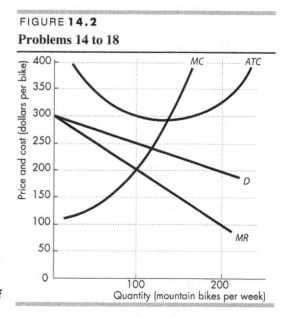

Use the following news clip to work Problem 19.

Groceries for the Gourmet Palate

No food, it seems, is safe from being repackaged to look like an upscale product. Samuel Adams' $120 Utopias, in a ridiculous copper-covered 24-oz. bottle meant to resemble an old-fashioned brew kettle, is barely beer. It's not carbonated like a Bud, but aged in oak barrels like scotch. It has a vintage year, like a Bordeaux, is light, complex, and free of any alcohol sting, despite having six times as much alcohol content as a regular can of brew.

Source: *Time*, April 14, 2008

19. a.   Explain how Samuel Adams has differentiated its Utopias to compete with other beer brands in terms of quality, price, and marketing.

Samuel Adams differentiated Utopias by bottling it in a unique container, ageing it in oak barrels, and giving it a vintage year. Samuel Adams also has brewed the beer to have six times the alcoholic content but not have an alcohol sting.

b.   Predict whether Samuel Adams produces at, above, or below the efficient scale in the short run.

In the short run Samuel Adams might produce at, above, or below its efficient scale; it is not possible to predict which.

Use the following news clip to work Problem 21.

Swinging for Female Golfers
One of the hottest areas of innovation is in clubs for women, who now make up nearly a quarter of the 24 million golfers in the United States. Callaway and Nike, two of the leading golf-equipment manufacturers, recently released new clubs designed for women.

Source: *Time*, April 21, 2008

21. a.   How are Callaway and Nike attempting to maintain economic profit?

Callaway and Nike are innovating by creating golf clubs for women. They expect that the demand for women's clubs will be high and so they will be able to (temporarily) make an economic profit.

b.   Draw a graph to illustrate the cost curves and revenue curves of Callaway or Nike in the market for golf clubs for women.

Figure 14.3 shows the situation at Callaway or Nike. The firm produces 200,000 golf clubs per year and sets a price of $140 per club.

c.   Show on your graph in part (b) the short-run economic profit.

The economic profit equals the area of the darkened rectangle labeled A in Figure 14.3.

FIGURE **14.3**
Problems 21b and 21c

Use the following information to work Problems 23 and 25.

Bianca bakes delicious cookies. Her total fixed cost is $40 a day, and her average variable cost is $1 a bag. Few people know about Bianca's Cookies, and she is maximizing her profit by selling 10 bags a day for $5 a bag. Bianca thinks that if she spends $50 a day on advertising, she can increase her market share and sell 25 bags a day for $5 a bag.

23.   If Bianca's advertising works as she expects, can she increase her economic profit by advertising?

If additional advertising enables sales to increase so that total revenue increases more than total cost, she can increase economic profit. In the case at hand, her total revenue will increase by $75 and her total cost will increase by $50 plus whatever is the increase in her variable cost of producing the cookies. Because her AVC when she produces 10 bags is only $1, it is likely that her variable costs will increase by less than $25, which means that advertising will be profitable.

25. If Bianca advertises, will she continue to sell her cookies for $5 a bag or will she change her price?

> In the short run, presuming that advertising raises her demand, Bianca will raise the price of her cookies. In the long run Bianca's price will equal her average total cost. If her average total cost remains below $5 a bag, in the long run her price will be forced down below $5 a bag.

Use the following news clip to work Problem 27.

A Thirst for More Champagne

Champagne exports have tripled in the past 20 years. That poses a problem for northern France, where the bubbly hails from—not enough grapes. So French authorities have unveiled a plan to extend the official Champagne grape-growing zone to cover 40 new villages. This revision has provoked debate. The change will take several years to become effective. In the meantime the vineyard owners whose land values will jump markedly if the changes are finalized certainly have reason to raise a glass.

Source: *Fortune*, May 12, 2008

27. Assuming that vineyards in these 40 villages are producing the same quality of grapes with or without this plan, why will their land values "jump markedly" if this plan is approved?

> If the vineyards can label their wine as "Champagne," then the demand for their wine is likely to "jump markedly" because consumers value the brand name. Essentially at very low cost the vineyards will be able to convey to consumers the information that their wine is high quality. With this information the demand for their wine will increase, which will increase their economic profit.

Economics in the News

29. After you have studied *Economics in the News* on pp. 334–335, answer the following questions.

a. Why do you think Babolat worked with the firm that helped Nintendo develop the Wii remote?

> Babolat's designers have expertise in designing tennis rackets, not remote sensors. The company that helped develop the Wii remote has expertise in remote sensing and therefore is able to design and produce the remote sensors at lower cost than could Babolat. Consequently Babolat worked with that company so that each company concentrated on its competitive advantage.

b. How would Babolat's cost curves (*MC* and *ATC*) have been different if they had not worked with the Wii developer?

> Babolat's average total cost and marginal cost would have been higher if it had attempted to create the smart racquet by itself. Consequently, its *ATC* and *MC* curves would have been above the *ATC* and *MC* curves when it partners with the other company.

c. How do you think the launch of Babolat's new-technology racquet has influenced the demand for other firms' racquets?

> The creation of the smart racquet decreases the demand for older generation racquets.

d. Explain the effects of the introduction of the new-technology racquet on Prince and other firms in the market for tennis racquets.

> The introduction of the smart racquet decreased the demand for existing racquets made by Prince and other companies. This change lowered the price and quantity of their racquets and decreased the firms' profit.

e. Draw a graph to illustrate your answer to part (c). Explain your answer.

Figure 14.5 shows how the smart racquet affected the demand for other firm's racquets. The demand for existing, say, Prince racquets decreased and the demand curve shifted leftward from D_0 to D_1. The price of a Prince racquet falls (in the figure from $225 per racquet to $100 per racquet) and the quantity decreased (in the figure from 400,000 racquets per year to 200,000 per year). Prince's economic profit decreases. In the figure, after Babolat's introduction of its smart racquet, Prince is incurring an economic loss because Prince's price is less than its average total cost.

FIGURE **14.5**

Problem 29e

f. What do you predict will happen to the markup in the market for smart racquets?

In the long run, there will be entry into the market for smart racquets. As more firms enter, the demand for the incumbent firms' smart racquets decreases. As the demand decreases, the markup between marginal cost and price also decreases.

g. What do you predict will happen to excess capacity in the market for smart racquets? Explain your answer.

In the long run, similar to all firms in monopolistic competition, the producers of smart racquets will have excess capacity. In the short run, however, the firms might not have excess capacity. Indeed, in the short run it is possible for the manufacturers to produce at a point beyond their capacity output.

15 OLIGOPOLY

Answers to the Review Quizzes

Page 343

1. What are the two distinguishing characteristics of oligopoly?

    Oligopoly has two distinguishing characteristics: Natural or legal barriers prevent the entry of new firms, and a small number of firms compete in the industry.

3. Why do firms in oligopoly face a temptation to collude?

    Firms in oligopoly face the temptation to collude because if they can successfully collude, they can boost their economic profit.

Page 351

1. What are the common features of all games?

    All games share four common features: rules, strategies, payoffs, and outcome.

3. Why does a collusive agreement to restrict output and raise price create a game like the prisoners' dilemma?

    Each firm has the possibility of sharing monopoly profits with other members of the cartel if each firm complies with the agreement. But each firm has an incentive to cheat on the collusive agreement in a cartel. If they all cheat, the outcome for each firm is worse than if they had all held to the agreement.

5. What is the equilibrium strategy for each firm in a duopolists' dilemma and why do the firms not succeed in colluding to raise the price and profits?

    Each firm sees that its own profit is higher if it cheats on the agreement, and this strategy is best *regardless* of how any of the other firms act. This motivates *all* firms to cheat, and they all suffer an outcome that is far less profitable than if they all had complied with the agreement.

Page 355

1. If a prisoners' dilemma game is played repeatedly, what punishment strategies might the players employ and how does playing the game repeatedly change the equilibrium?

    Two strategies for motivating compliance in a repeated prisoner's dilemma game are: i) a *tit-for-tat* strategy, where cheating by one firm in the current period is punished by the other firm cheating in the next period, but compliance by one firm in the current period is rewarded by compliance in the next period, ii) a *trigger* strategy, where cheating by one firm in the current period is punished by cheating by the other firm in all subsequent periods. Both strategies may create a cooperative equilibrium where all players share in the maximum possible benefit.

Page 359

1.   What are the two main antitrust laws and when were they enacted?

The two acts of Congress that make up our main antitrust law and the years of their enactment are:

    a. The Sherman Act of 1890

    b. The Clayton Act of 1914

3.   What is an attempt to monopolize an industry?

In theory, attempts to monopolize an industry mean a firm is trying to become a monopoly. In practice, attempts to monopolize an industry are more difficult to define and are a matter of interpretation by the courts. The "rule of reason" seemed to say that size alone doesn't constitute an attempt to monopolize as in the 1920 *U.S. Steel* case. But the "rule of reason" was overturned when size did matter as in the 1945 *Alcoa* case. Even in more recent cases, it is difficult to predict what the court will define as an attempt to monopolize. Decisions continue to be divided in this area of the law.

5.   Under what circumstances is a merger unlikely to be approved?

A merger is likely to be approved by the Justice Department as long as the pre-merger HHI is less than 1,500. If the pre-merger HHI is between 1,500 and 2,500, the merger would be challenged if it raises the HHI by 100 or more points. If the pre-merger HHI is greater than 2,500, the merger generally would be blocked if it raises the HHI index by 200 or more points.

Answers to the Study Plan Problems and Applications

1. Intel and Advanced Micro Devices make most of the chips that power a PC. What makes the market for PC chips a duopoly? Sketch the market demand and cost curves that describe the situation in this market and that prevent other firms from entering.

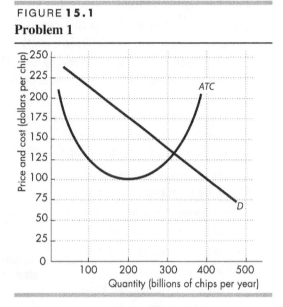

FIGURE **15.1**

Problem 1

The market for PC chips, in particular the processor, is a natural oligopoly, most likely a natural duopoly. There are only two firms in the market, Intel and AMD, and there are no legal barriers to entry which limit the number of firms to two. Because other firms *could* enter the market but do not do so supports the idea that this industry is a natural duopoly. The cost curves and demand curve for this market would be similar to those in Figure 15.1, which shows the situation for a market in which two firms can satisfy the market demand. In this situation if a new firm entered the market it would be at a significant cost disadvantage compared to Intel and AMD and would likely incur an economic loss. Such a prospect deters entry by new competitors.

3. **Oil City**

In the late 1990s, Reliance spent $6 billion to build a world-class oil refinery at Jamnagar, India. Now Reliance's expansion will make it the world's biggest producer of gasoline—1.2 million gallons of gasoline per day, or about 5% of global capacity. Reliance plans to sell the gasoline in the United States and Europe where it's too expensive and politically difficult to build new refineries. The bulked-up Jamnagar will be able to move the market and Singapore traders expect a drop in fuel prices as soon as it's going at full steam.

Source: *Fortune*, April 28, 2008

a. Explain why the news clip implies that the global market for gasoline is not perfectly competitive.

The news clip asserts that there is not free entry into the refining market. In particular, in the United States and Europe political reasons make it extremely costly for new refiners to enter the market. Therefore the few large refiners, such as that at Jamnagar, produce a significant share of the world market and hence one firm—Jamnagar—can influence the market price.

b. What barriers to entry might limit competition and allow Reliance to influence the price?

Political barriers to entry limit entry into the refinery market. The public in the United States and Europe apparently considers refineries as undesirable neighbors because of pollution and, as such, do not want refineries situated nearby. Politicians respond to this pressure by enacting laws and regulations that make new refineries extremely costly to build in the United States and Europe.

5.   Soapy Inc. and Suddies Inc., the only soap-powder producers, collude and agree to share the market equally. If neither firm cheats, each makes $1 million profit. If one firm cheats, it makes $1.5 million, while the complier incurs a loss of $0.5 million. If both cheat, they break even. Neither firm can monitor the other's actions.

a.   What are the strategies in this game? Construct the payoff matrix for this game.

Each firm has two strategies: to comply with the agreement or to cheat on the agreement. The payoff matrix has the following cells: Both comply by the agreement: Soapy makes $1 million profit, and Suddies makes $1 million profit; both cheat: Soapy makes $0 profit, and Suddies makes $0 profit; Soapy cheats and Suddies complies with the agreement: Soapy makes $1.5 million profit, and Suddies incurs a $0.5 million loss; Suddies cheats and Soapy complies with the agreement: Suddies makes $1.5 million profit, and Soapy incurs $0.5 million loss. These payoffs are shown, in millions of dollars, in the matrix to the right.

Soapy's strategies

	Comply	Cheat
Comply	$1 M / $1 M	$1.5 M / −$.5 M
Cheat	−$.5 M / $1.5 M	0 / 0

(Suddie's strategies: Comply, Cheat — rows)

b.   If the game is played only once what is the equilibrium? Is it a dominant-strategy equilibrium? Explain.

The equilibrium is that both firms cheat and each makes normal profit.

The equilibrium is a dominant strategy equilibrium because for each firm, regardless of the opponent's choice, the best strategy is to cheat. If Suddies complies with the agreement, the best strategy for Soapy is to cheat because it would make a profit of $1.5 million rather than $1 million. If Suddies cheats, the best strategy for Soapy is to cheat because it would make a profit of $0 (the competitive outcome) rather than incur a loss of $0.5 million. So Soapy's best strategy is to cheat, no matter what Suddies does. Repeating the exercise for Suddies shows that Suddies's best strategy also is to cheat, no matter what Soapy does.

7.   If Soapy Inc. and Suddies Inc. play the game in Problem 5 repeatedly, on each round of play:

a.   What strategies might each firm might adopt?

Each firm can adopt a tit-for-tat strategy or a trigger strategy, strategies that were not possible in a one-time game.

b.   Can the firms adopt a strategy that gives the game a cooperative equilibrium?

The game has a cooperative equilibrium. If the firms employ a trigger strategy or a tit-for-tat strategy, they can reach the cooperative comply/comply outcome. Take the case of the tit-for-tat strategy. If both firms comply for, say, three periods, both firms make $3 million profit. If a firm cheats in the first period while its opponent complies, the cheater makes a $1.5 million profit. In the second period, the opponent cheats, so if the first firm complies, it losses $0.5 million. In the third period the opponent will comply so the first firm can again cheat and make $1.5 million. However, in these three periods the total profit is only $2.5 million, so the cooperative equilibrium is possible.

c. Would one firm still be tempted to cheat in a cooperative equilibrium? Explain your answer.

If the firms employ a trigger strategy or a tit-for-tat strategy, they can reach the cooperative comply/comply outcome. In these cases, the *long-run* profit from complying with the agreement exceeds that from cheating and so the cooperative equilibrium is likely. But a firm's *short-run* profit would be larger if the firm (and that firm alone) cheated. So each firm still has an incentive to cheat because each firm can temporarily increase its profit.

Answers to Additional Problems and Applications

9. **An Energy Drink with a Monster of a Stock**

    The $5.7 billion energy-drink category, in which Monster holds the No. 2 position behind industry leader Red Bull, has slowed down as copycat brands jostle for shelf space. Over the past five years Red Bull's market share in dollar terms has gone from 91 percent to well under 50 percent and much of that loss has been Monster's gain.

    Source: *Fortune*, December 25, 2006

    a. Describe the structure of the energy-drink market. How has that structure changed over the past few years?

    > The structure of the energy-drink market has changed from a virtual monopoly several years ago, when Red Bull had 91 percent of the market, to a more oligopolistic market, in which Red Bull's market share is well under 50 percent and Monster's market share has grown significantly.

    b. If Monster and Red Bull formed a cartel, how would the price charged for energy drinks and the profits made change?

    > If Red Bull and Monster successfully form a cartel, the price of energy drinks would rise and their profits would increase.

Use the following data to work Problem 11.

Bud and Wise are the only two producers of aniseed beer, a New Age product designed to displace root beer. Bud and Wise are trying to figure out how much of this new beer to produce. They know:

  (i)   If they both produce 10,000 gallons a day, they will make the maximum attainable joint economic profit of $200,000 a day, or $100,000 a day each.

  (ii) If either firm produces 20,000 gallons a day while the other produces 10,000 a day, the one that produces 20,000 gallons will make an economic profit of $150,000 and the other will incur an economic loss of $50,000.

  (iii) If both produce 20,000 gallons a day, each firm will make zero economic profit.

11. Find the Nash equilibrium of the game that Bud and Wise play.

    > The Nash equilibrium is for both Bud and Wise to expand production. From Bud's perspective, if Wise limits production Bud's profit is larger if it expands production. If Wise expands production then Bud's profit is larger if Bud expands production. For Bud "expand production" is a dominant strategy. Wise's situation is similar, so Wise, too, has a dominant strategy of "expand production."

13. Suppose that Mozilla and Microsoft each develop their own versions of an amazing new Web browser that allows advertisers to target consumers with great precision. Also, the new browser is easier and more fun to use than existing browsers. Each firm is trying to decide whether to sell the browser or to give it away. What are the likely benefits from each action? Which action is likely to occur?

    > The more people use a particular browser, the more advertisers are willing to pay. And charging for a browser also generates profit. If the browser is given away and the competitor charges, likely the one given away gains market share and that company makes a large economic profit. The other company incurs an economic loss. If both browsers are given away, both companies probably make a comparable economic profit. And if both browsers are sold, both companies probably make the largest economic profit because they collect from both advertisers and consumers.

A payoff matrix is to the right that reflects this analysis. The numbers in the matrix are the economic profit in millions of dollars. Microsoft's profits are in the grey upper triangles and Mozilla's profits are in the white lower triangles. The fact that for any given situation Microsoft's profits are larger than Mozilla's is realistic but does not affect the analysis. The joint profit is the largest when the browser is sold and is the smallest when the browser is given away. With the profits in the payoff matrix, the Nash equilibrium is to give the browsers away for free.

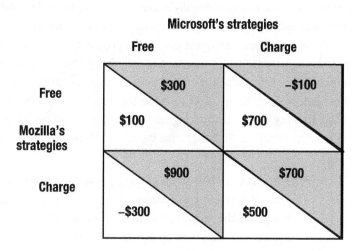

Use the following news clip to work Problems 15.

PS4 vs. Xbox One Battle Means Gamers Win, Sony Says

Microsoft's latest move in the PlayStation 4 vs. Xbox One battle was to lower the price of Xbox One to $399—the same price as the PS4.

Source: *GameSpot*, July 1, 2014

15. a. Thinking about the competition between Sony and Microsoft in the market for game consoles as a game, describe the firms' strategies concerning design, marketing, and price.
    Strategies are all the possible actions of each of the players. The news clip shows that the current strategy in the game between Sony and Microsoft is setting the price, with the possibility of setting a high price or a low price.

   b. What, based on the information provided, turned out to be the equilibrium of the game?
    The equilibrium of the game was the outcome that occurred in the market for game consoles: Both ultimately set a low price as Microsoft lowered its price to equal Sony's price.

17.   If Bud and Wise in Problems 10 and 11 play the game repeatedly, what is the equilibrium of the game?
    If the game is played repeatedly, then Bud and Wise might be able to reach the cooperative equilibrium (both limit production) if they use a tit-for-tat or trigger strategy.

19.   **Oil Trading Probe May Uncover Manipulation**
    Amid soaring oil prices the Commodity Futures Trading Commission (CFTC) is looking into manipulation of the oil market—withholding oil in an attempt to drive prices higher. The CFTC has found such evidence in the past and it's likely it will find evidence again. But it is unlikely that a single player acting alone would be able to run the price up from $90 to $135.

Source: CNN, May 30, 2008

    What type of market does the news clip imply best describes the U.S. oil market?
    The news clip implicitly views the oil market as an oligopoly.

Use the following news clip to work Problem 21.

Gadgets for Sale ... or Not

How come the prices of some gadgets, like the iPod, are the same no matter where you shop? No, the answer isn't that Apple illegally manages prices. In reality, Apple uses an accepted retail strategy called minimum advertised price to discourage resellers from discounting. The minimum advertised price (MAP) is the absolute lowest price of a product that resellers can advertise. Marketing subsidies offered by a manufacturer to its resellers usually keep the price at or above the MAP. Stable prices are important to the company that is both a manufacturer and a retailer. If Apple resellers advertised the iPod below cost, they could squeeze the Apple Stores out of their own markets. The downside to the price stability is that by limiting how low sellers can go, MAP keeps prices artificially high (or at least higher than they might otherwise be with unfettered price competition).

Source: *Slate*, December 22, 2006

21.   Why might the MAP strategy be against the social interest and benefit only the producer?
      The MAP might harm consumers because it keeps the price of iPods higher than would otherwise be the case if the retailers competed more vigorously on price. In this case, the producers benefit but society is made worse off because the high price means that fewer than the allocatively efficient quantity of iPods are sold.

Economics in the News

23.   **Boeing and Airbus Predict Asian Sales Surge**
      Airlines in the Asia-Pacific region are emerging as the biggest customers for aircraft makers Boeing and Airbus. The two firms predict that over the next 20 years, more than 8,000 planes worth up to $1.2 trillion will be sold there.

Source: BBC News, February 3, 2010

a.   In what type of market are big airplanes sold?
     There are only two sellers of big airplanes, so this market is an oligopoly.

b.   Thinking of competition between Boeing and Airbus as a game, what are the strategies and the payoffs?
     Boeing and Airbus are playing the duopolists' game. They can set either low prices or high prices. If both Boeing and Airbus set low prices, then they will both make a smaller profit, perhaps even zero economic profit. If they both set high prices, then both will make a large economic profit. However, if one sets a low price and the other sets a high price, then the one with the low price will make a very large economic profit and the one with the high price will incur an economic loss.

c.   Set out a hypothetical payoff matrix for the game you've described in part (b). What is the equilibrium of the game?
     The payoff matrix is to the right. In it the profits are in millions of dollars. The equilibrium is the prisoners' dilemma equilibrium, that is, both firms set low prices and both make zero economic profit.

d.   Do you think the market for big airplanes is efficient? Explain and illustrate your answer.
     The market for big airplanes is probably not efficient. It is efficient only if Boeing and Airbus compete against each other as if they were in

perfect competition. But this outcome is unlikely. More likely is an outcome in which Boeing and Airbus together operate a monopoly or, if not precisely as a monopoly, then approaching that status. This outcome is especially likely because Boeing and Airbus will be playing a repeated game in which they (potentially) compete with each other for over two decades. In that situation, the repeated game makes it more likely that they will reach the cooperative equilibrium in which they operate together as a monopoly.

Figure 15.3 shows the range of outcomes. If the two firms compete with each other, the equilibrium will be the competitive equilibrium, where they sell a total of 300 planes per year at a price of $15 million per plane. This outcome is the efficient outcome. However if Boeing and Airbus

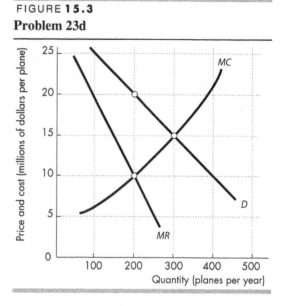

FIGURE **15.3**

Problem 23d

attain the cooperative equilibrium in which they act together to reach the monopoly outcome, then a total of 200 planes per year is sold and the price is $20 million per plane. In this case the outcome is inefficient and a deadweight loss results.

16 PUBLIC CHOICES, PUBLIC GOODS, AND HEALTHCARE

Answers to the Review Quizzes

Page 373

1. List the economic functions of governments.

    Governments exist to establish and maintain property rights, to provide nonmarket ways of allocating resources, and to create methods that redistribute income and wealth.

3. Distinguish among public goods, private goods, common resources, and natural monopoly goods.

    Public goods are nonexcludable and nonrival. As a result, anyone can consume the good whether or not he or she paid for it and one person's use of the good does not decrease the amount available for other people. Private goods are excludable and rival. As a result, only the person who pays for the good can consume it and one person's use decreases the amount available for others. Common resources are nonexcludable and rival. As a result, anyone can consume the good whether or not he or she paid for it and one person's consumption decreases the amount available for other people's consumption. Natural monopoly goods are nonrival and excludable. Potential users of the good can be excluded if they do not pay but once having paid their use of the good is nonrival.

Page 377

1. What is the free-rider problem? Why do free riders make the private provision of a public good inefficient?

    If a firm were to provide a public good, it would suffer from the *free-rider problem*, which arises when non-paying consumers consume the public good without paying, enjoying a "free ride." Public goods are, in part, characterized by inability to exclude nonpaying consumers. A private firm would not receive a sufficient level of revenue to provide the efficient level of the public good.

3. How do rationally ignorant voters and budget maximizing bureaucrats prevent the political marketplace from delivering the efficient quantity of a public good?

    If the marginal benefit to the voter of becoming well informed about a particular policy issue is much smaller than the marginal cost of becoming well informed, the voter is likely to remain *rationally ignorant* about the policy and the level of any related public goods provision. The marginal benefit of providing public goods is very high to both bureaucrats and the contractors who are employed to produce and distribute the public goods. So they have a concentrated interest in lobbying politicians to direct the bureaucrats to provide more than the efficient quantity of the public good, even to where the net benefit to the economy is zero.

Page 383

1.   **What is special about healthcare that makes it a good provided by the government?**

The government provides healthcare services because the marginal social benefit of healthcare exceeds the marginal benefit perceived by its consumers, Consumers underestimate the benefit of healthcare because they underestimate the health risks they face. They also underestimate their future needs for healthcare. And some people cannot afford the healthcare they need. For these reasons the majority of voters want healthcare to be available on need rather than on the ability and willingness to pay

3.   **How do Canada and the United Kingdom deliver healthcare and what is the problem left unresolved?**

Canada and the United Kingdom provide healthcare using a universal coverage, single payer system. Everyone is covered by health insurance and the government pays for all healthcare services. The government's public choice determines the quantity of healthcare services provided. Consumers pay little or nothing for any healthcare service. Consequently the quantity of healthcare services demanded exceeds the quantity provided by the government which creates a problem: There often is a long waiting period until a patient receives services.

5.   **What is the problem that Obamacare seeks to solve and how does the solution work?**

The Patient Protection and Affordable Care Act, or Obamacare, attempts to overcome the problem of too many people who do not have health insurance. It seeks to make quality, affordable, private health-insurance plans available for those currently uninsured and to stop insurance companies from denying coverage of pre-existing conditions, This act created a Health Insurance Market in which subsidized health insurance is provided. On the supply-side of the market are private healthcare insurance companies. On the demand-side are individuals. Many of the consumers qualify for subsidies which lower the cost to them of the healthcare insurance. By reducing the price, the act increases the number of people with healthcare insurance.

Answers to the Study Plan Problems and Applications

1. Classify each of the following items as excludable, nonexcludable, rival, or nonrival. Explain your answer.

    *   A Big Mac

        A Big Mac is excludable and rival. It's excludable because a person must pay for a Big Mac to consume it. It's rival because one person's consumption decreases the quantity available for others to consume.

    *   Brooklyn Bridge

        The Brooklyn Bridge is nonexcludable (because there is no toll for using it) and rival (especially when it is crowded).

    *   A view of the Statue of Liberty

        Viewing the Statue of Liberty is nonexcludable and nonrival. It is nonexcludable because a person cannot be prevented from viewing the statue and it is nonrival because one person's view does not decrease people's views.

    *   A hurricane warning system

        A hurricane warning system is nonexcludable and nonrival. It is nonexcludable because once a warning is sounded, everyone can learn of it and nonrival because one person learning of the warning does not limit other people's use of the warning.

3. For each of the following goods, explain why a free-rider problem arises or how is it avoided.

    *   July 4th fireworks display

        The fireworks display is a public good so there is a potential free-rider problem. Area residents might be taxed to finance the display, but visitors to the area, who don't pay local taxes, are free riders.

    *   Interstate 81 in Virginia

        Interstate 81 potentially has a free rider problem. However if the state of Virginia uses the gas tax revenue it receives from the sale of gasoline near the interstate to pay to maintain the freeway, then users of the Interstate pay for the road. In this case there is no free rider problem.

    *   Wireless Internet access in hotels

        Wireless Internet access in hotels can avoid the free rider problem if the hotel limits access to guests staying at the hotel.

    *   The public library in your city

        The public library has a free rider problem because people can use the library even if they pay no taxes to support it. Potentially the free rider problem can be mitigated if the library charges a fee for its services.

Use the data on a mosquito control program in the table to work Problem 5.

5. What quantity of spraying would a private firm provide? What is the efficient quantity of spraying? In a single-issue election on mosquito spraying, what quantity would the winner provide?

    Mosquito spraying is a public good and subject to free riding. As a result, a private mosquito would supply no spraying. The efficient quantity of spraying is 3 square miles a day, which is the quantity at which marginal social cost equals marginal social benefit. In a single issue election, the outcome will be that each party eventually proposes spraying 3 square miles per day and the election outcome will be the efficient quantity of spraying.

Quantity (square miles sprayed per day)	Marginal social cost	Marginal social benefit
	(thousands of dollars per day)	
1	2	10
2	4	8
3	6	6
4	8	4
5	10	2

Use the following figure, which shows the marginal benefit from health insurance and the willingness and ability to pay for it, to work Problems 7 and 9.

The marginal cost of insurance is a constant $6,000 per family per year. Marginal social benefit from insurance exceeds the willingness and ability to pay by a constant $4,000 per family per year.

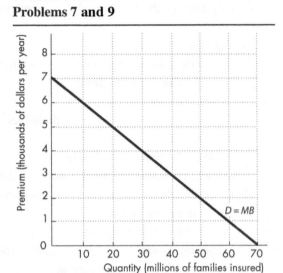

FIGURE **16.2**

Problems 7 and 9

7.   With no public health insurance market, how many families buy insurance, what is the premium, and is the coverage efficient?

With a private and competitive health insurance market, the price of health insurance equals the marginal cost, or $6,000 per year. At this price, 10 million families buy insurance. The coverage is not efficient because the marginal social benefit exceeds the marginal (private) benefit. When 10 million families are insured the marginal social benefit is $10,000, which exceeds the marginal cost of the insurance. Accordingly insurance is underprovided by the private market.

9.   If the government subsidizes private insurers, what subsidy will achieve the efficient coverage?

To insure 50 million families, the insurers' total cost equals $6,000 per family multiplied by 50 million, or $300 billion. With 50 million families covered, the demand curve shows that a family is willing to pay $2,000 per policy. Accordingly families will pay 50 million × $2,000, or $100 billion. Therefore the government must provide a subsidy of $200 billion to private insurers.

Answers to Additional Problems and Applications

11. Classify each of the following items as excludable, nonexcludable, rival, or nonrival.

- Homeland security

  Homeland security is nonrival (the use of homeland security by one person does not decrease the quantity available for someone else) and nonexcludable (it is impossible to prevent anyone from benefiting from it).

- A Starbucks coffee

  A Starbucks coffee is rival and excludable.

- A view of the Liberty Bell

  A view of the Liberty Bell is nonexcludable and nonrival.

- The Appalachian Trail

  The Appalachian Trail is nonexcludable. It is generally nonrival except in areas where is becomes very crowded.

- A google Search

  A google search is nonexcludable because anyone can search for the same item and is nonrival because one person's search does not decrease the searches available to anyone else.

13. Classify each of the following goods as either a private good, a public good, a natural monopoly good, or none of the above.

- Chewing gum

  Chewing gum is excludable and rival so it is a private good.

- Cable TV

  Cable TV is a natural monopoly good. It is excludable because a consumer must pay for access. But once access is granted, use of the cable TV system is nonrival.

- The New York City subway

  The subway is a private good because it is excludable and, when crowded, is rival.

- A skateboard

  A skateboard is a private good.

- The Santa Monica beach

  The beach at Santa Monica is nonexcludable and rival so it is none of the above. (It is a common resource.)

15. What is the principle of diminishing marginal benefit? In Problem 14, does Sam's, Nick's, or the society's marginal benefit diminish faster?

    The principle of declining marginal benefit asserts that as the quantity of the good or service consumed increases, the marginal benefit of an additional unit decreases. Society's marginal benefit decreases more rapidly than does Sam's marginal benefit or Nick's marginal benefit. For every additional street light, Sam's marginal benefit decreases by $2, Nick's marginal benefit decreases by $3, and society's marginal benefit decreases by $5.

Use the following news clip to work Problem 17.

A Bridge Too Far Gone

The gas taxes paid for much of America's post-war freeway system. Now motorists pay about one-third in gas taxes to drive a mile as they did in the 1960s. Yet raising such taxes is politically tricky. This would matter less if private cash was flooding into infrastructure, or if new ways were being found to control demand. Neither is happening, and private companies building toll roads brings howls of outrage.

Source: *The Economist*, August 9, 2007

17. What in this news clip points to a distinction between public *production* of a public good and public *provision*? Give examples of three public goods that are *produced* by private firms but *provided* by government and paid for with taxes.

> The difference between private provision of a public good and public provision hinges around who—the private sector or the public sector—actually produces the public good. For instance, many local governments contract with private agencies to provide street sweeping services, a public good. For another example, some states have contracted with private companies for the day-to-day running of parks. Finally, some states, such as Texas, have allowed private firms to produce toll roads.

19. Obamacare Hits Enrollment Goal

A last-minute enrollment surge enabled the White House to meet its 7 million sign-up target for the Affordable Care Act. President Barack Obama said on Tuesday that 7.1 million people had signed up on federal or state exchanges for coverage under the healthcare law.

Source: *CNN*, April 1, 2014

a. If the White House target was to enroll the efficient quantity of families in Obamacare, how would it have determined that target?

> The target would be the quantity of families that sets the marginal social benefit of healthcare insurance equal to the marginal cost.

b. Draw a graph to illustrate the health insurance market and illustrate how the Obamacare subsidy influences the number of families covered.

> Figure 16.4 shows the market for health insurance. In the absence of any subsidy, the price of a health insurance policy is $4,000 per year and 30 million families buy a policy. The subsidy under Obamacare increases the quantity of families buying health insurance. Presuming that the subsidy brings about the efficient outcome, the figure shows that the subsidy is $4,000 per family. With this subsidy, 50 million families will buy insurance because the price paid for a policy falls to $2,000. In the figure, Obamacare has increased the number of families insured from 30 million to 50 million.

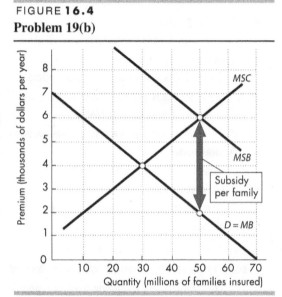

FIGURE **16.4**

Problem 19(b)

c. How would the demand for health insurance change if the penalty for not signing up for Obama care were abolished? Draw a graph to illustrate the outcome

> The penalty increases the demand for health insurance. In Figure 6.5, with the penalty the demand curve for health insurance is $D_{Penalty}$ and the $4,000 subsidy per family leads to the efficient quantity of families insured, 50 million. But if the penalty is abolished, the demand curve for insurance is $D = MB$. In this case, the same $4,000 subsidy leads to only 40 million families being insured. There is a deadweight loss because the quantity of insured families is less than the efficient quantity. To reach the efficient quantity, in the absence of the penalty the subsidy needs to be increased to $6,000 per family.

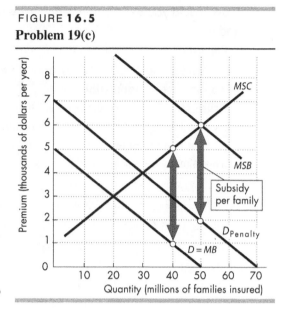

FIGURE **16.5**
Problem 19(c)

The marginal cost of health insurance is a constant $8,000 a year and the figure shows the marginal benefit and willingness and ability to pay curve. Suppose that the marginal social benefit of insurance exceeds the willingness and ability to pay by a constant $2,000 per family per year.

21. If the government decides to provide public health insurance (like Canada), what healthcare fee does it charge to achieve an efficient coverage? How much will taxpayers have to pay?

> If the government provides public health insurance as does Canada, Canada will insure 20 million families. The cost of insuring each family is $8,000. Canada uses a single payer method of health care, which means that the Canadian government pays for all health care expenditures. Therefore Canadian taxpayers must pay for the entire cost of the insurance, $8,000 × 20 million or $160 billion.

Economics in the News

23. After you have studied *Economics in the News* on pp. 386–387, answer the following questions:

a. What is the source of revenue for constructing and maintaining the transportation infrastructure?

> The gasoline tax is the main source of funds for constructing and maintaining the transportation capital.

b. Why has that revenue source not grown fast enough to deliver an efficient scale of infrastructure provision?

> As cars become more fuel efficient, they use less gasoline, thereby generating less gasoline tax revenue. Taxpayers remember scandals over past use of these funds, so there is little support for raising the gasoline tax.

c. What other revenue sources can you suggest that could provide a solution to underprovision?

> General tax revenue could be used to maintain the infrastructure. More tolls could be established for using bridges and freeways, with the funds generated devoted to the infrastructure. Drivers might be taxed for the miles they drive rather than the gasoline they use, which could generate additional funds.

d. How would you expect population growth to influence the marginal social benefit of highways and bridges?

Population growth increases the marginal social benefit of highways and bridges.

e. Illustrate your answer to (d) by drawing a version of the figure on p. 385 that shows the effect of an increase in population.

Figure 16.8 shows how the marginal social benefit curve shifts rightward to MSB_1. As a result, the efficient number of bridges to repair increases from 6,000 per year to 8,000 per year.

FIGURE **16.8**
Problem 23(e)

Answers to the Review Quizzes

Page 392

1.   What are the four types of externality?

Externalities can be: a negative production externality, a positive production externality, a negative consumption externality, or a positive consumption externality.

Page 400

1.   What is the distinction between private cost and social cost?

A private cost of production is the cost of producing a good or service that is borne only by the producer. A social cost of production includes the private costs of production as well as the external costs of production borne by people other than the producer.

3.   How can external costs be eliminated by assigning property rights?

The existence of a negative externality means some group must bear some of the costs of a production or consumption activity for which they are not involved. The Coase theorem implies that assigning a property right to either the group generating the externality or the group bearing the externality costs will eliminate the inefficient allocation of resources. The Coase theorem applies if the number of parties involved is small and if transactions costs are low.

Page 405

1.   What is the tragedy of the commons? Give two examples, including one from your state.

The tragedy of the commons is the absence of incentives to prevent the overuse and depletion of a commonly owned resource. The private market place will not produce the efficient quantity of a common resource. Some examples include the congestion of traffic during rush hour, the congestion near a college football stadium whenever a major game is played, or the free Internet access computer at the local library.

3.   Review three methods that might achieve the efficient use of a common resource and explain the obstacles to efficiency.

There are three different methods that government can use to obtain the efficient allocation of resources in the event of a common resource:

- *Property Rights* are assigned to private property, which is a resource that someone owns and has an incentive to use in a way that maximizes its value. However, assigning property rights to resources is not always feasible, such as with the fish that migrate over the vast depths of the oceans.

- *Production Quotas* can be set for total catch and divided among harvesting consumers so that the marginal social benefit from harvesting equals the marginal social cost of harvesting. However, it is in every harvester's best interest to cheat on the quota, because marginal private benefit from exceeding the quota allotment is greater than the marginal cost of harvesting.

- An *Individual Transferable Quotas (ITQ)* is a production limit that is assigned to an individual harvester who is free to transfer the quota to someone else.

Page 409

1. Why would the market economy produce too little education?

    The markets for education will produce less than the efficient quantity because consumers of education take account of *only* the benefits that accrue to them. They ignore the marginal external benefit that others gain. Therefore the consumers' demand for education is less than the marginal social benefit from education.

3. What are the key differences among public production, private subsidies, and vouchers?

    Public production means that the government is the producer of the product. Private subsidies, however, are given to *private* producers of the product. Both public production and private subsidies affect the supply-side of the market. Vouchers, however, are given to households to help pay for the product. Vouchers therefore affect the demand-side of the market.

Answers to the Study Plan Problems and Applications

1. Describe three consumption activities that create external costs.

   Wearing heavy perfume creates an external cost; littering fast-food containers or soda cans creates an external cost; and, a drunk at a bar creates an external cost.

Use Figure 17.1, which illustrates the market for cotton, to work Problem 3. Suppose that the cotton growers use a chemical to control insects and waste flows into the town's river. The marginal social cost of producing the cotton is double the marginal private cost.

3. If no one owns the river and the town takes no action to control the waste, what is the quantity of cotton and the deadweight loss created?

   400 tons of cotton is produced. In Figure 17.2, the deadweight loss that is created is equal to the area of the grey triangle. So the deadweight loss is equal to ½ × ($75 per ton − $37.50 per ton) × 100 tons, which is $1,875.

Use Figure 17.3 to work Problem 5.

The figure illustrates the market for North Atlantic tuna.

5. a. What is the quantity of tuna that fishers catch and the price of tuna? Is the tuna stock being used efficiently? Explain why or why not.

   When the market is unregulated, the quantity of fish caught and their price is determined by the equilibrium between supply and demand. The demand curve is the same as the MSB curve so Figure 17.3 shows that the equilibrium quantity of tuna is 80 tons and the equilibrium price is $100 per ton. The tuna stock is not being used efficiently, The efficient quantity of tuna is determined by the intersection of the MSC curve and the MSB curve. Figure 17.3 shows that the efficient quantity of tuna is 40 tons. Tuna, a common resource, is overfished.

   b. What would be the price of tuna, if the stock of tuna were used efficiently?

   If tuna were used efficiently, 40 tons per month would be caught and the price would be $150 per ton.

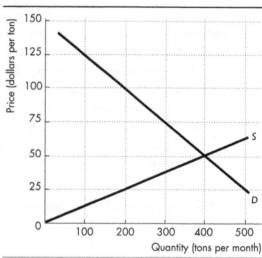

FIGURE **17.1**

Problems 3 and 4

FIGURE **17.3**

Problems 5 and 6

Use Figure 17.4, which shows the demand for college education, to work Problems 7 and 9.

The marginal cost is a constant $6,000 per student per year. The marginal external benefit from a college education is a constant $4,000 per student per year.

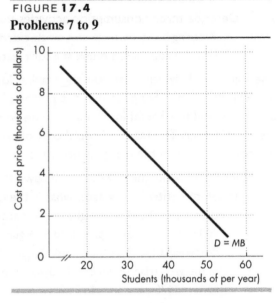

FIGURE **17.4**
Problems 7 to 9

7.   What is the efficient number of students? If all colleges are private, how many people enroll in college and what is the tuition?

The efficient number of students is 50,000 because this quantity is the number of students that sets the marginal *social* benefit equal to the marginal cost. If all colleges are private, then 30,000 students enroll in college because this quantity is the number that sets the marginal benefit equal to the marginal cost.

9.   If the government offers students vouchers, what is the value of the voucher that will achieve the efficient number of students?

The efficient number of students is 50,000. The value of the voucher must be $4,000 a student. The private colleges charge tuition of $6,000 per student and, of this tuition, students pay $2,000 so 50,000 students enroll.

Answers to Additional Problems and Applications

11.   What externalities arise from beautiful and ugly buildings and how do we deal with them?

Beautiful buildings create external benefits from the pleasure that people get from observing them. For ugly buildings, it is the reverse: They create external costs from the displeasure people get from observing them. To try to create more beautiful buildings, some locations require architectural review in which the planned building must pass inspection. Buildings of significant historical value are given heritage designations. People who pile trash around their buildings are fined.

Use the following data and Figure 17.5, which illustrates the market for a pesticide with no government intervention, to work Problems 13 and 15.

When factories produce pesticide, they also create waste, which they dump into a lake on the outskirts of the town. The marginal external cost of the waste is equal to the marginal private cost of producing the pesticide (that is, the marginal social cost of producing the pesticide is double the marginal private cost).

13.   What is the quantity of pesticide produced if no one owns the lake and what is the efficient quantity of pesticide?

If no one owns the lake the equilibrium quantity of pesticide produced is determined at the intersection of the demand curve and supply curve, 30 tons per week. The efficient quantity is

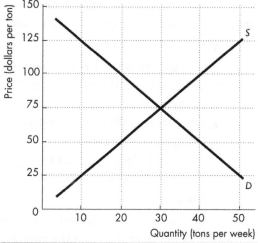

FIGURE **17.5**
Problems 13 to 16

determined at the intersection of the marginal social benefit curve and the marginal social cost curve. The marginal social benefit curve is the same as the demand curve. But the marginal social cost curve differs from the supply curve because of the external cost. The efficient quantity of pesticide is 20 tons per week because at this quantity the marginal social benefit, $100 per ton, equals the marginal *social* cost, also $100 per ton.

15.   If the pesticide factories own the lake, how much pesticide is produced?

Assuming that the transactions costs are low so that the Coase theorem applies, if the pesticide companies own the lake, 20 tons of pesticide is produced. In this case the residents pay the company to limit the dumping of waste.

Use the following table to work Problems 17 and 19.

The first two columns of the table show the demand schedule for electricity from a coal burning utility; the second and third columns show the utility's cost of producing electricity. The marginal external cost of the pollution created equals the marginal cost.

17.   With no government action to control pollution, what is the quantity of electricity produced, the price of electricity, and the marginal external cost of the pollution generated?

With no pollution control, the quantity of

Price (cents per kilowatt)	Quantity demanded (kilowatts per day)	Marginal cost (cents per kilowatt)
4	500	10
8	400	8
12	300	6
16	200	4
20	100	2

electricity produced is 400 kilowatts per day, the price of electricity is 8¢ per kilowatt, and the marginal external cost of the pollution generated is 8¢ per kilowatt.

19.   If the government levies a pollution tax such that the utility produces the efficient quantity, what is the price of electricity, the tax levied, and the government's tax revenue per day?

> The tax will equal the amount of the marginal external cost at the efficient quantity, 6¢ per kilowatt. The quantity of electricity generated is 300 kilowatts per day and the price of electricity is 12¢ per kilowatt. The government collects as revenue 6¢ per kilowatt × 300 kilowatts per day, which is $18 per day.

Use Figure 17.6 to work Problems 21 and 23.

A spring runs under a village. Everyone can sink a well on her or his land and take water from the spring. Figure 17.6 shows the marginal social benefit from and the marginal cost of taking water.

21.   What is the quantity of water taken and what is the private cost of the water taken?

> With no government intervention, the quantity of water taken is 400 gallons per day, determined in the figure by where the marginal social benefit and the marginal *private* cost curves intersect. The marginal private cost of this quantity of water is 20¢ per gallon.

23.   If the village council sets a quota on the total amount of water such that the spring is used efficiently, what would be the quota and the market value of the water taken per day?

> The quota would be set at 200 gallons per day. This quantity of water would sell for a price of 30¢ per gallon, so the market value of this quantity of water is 200 gallons × 30¢ per gallon, which is $60.

FIGURE **17.6**
Problems 21 to 23

Use the following data to work Problems 25 and 27.

The table shows the demand for college education. The marginal cost of educating a student is a constant $4,000 a year and education creates an external benefit of a constant $2,000 per student per year.

Price (dollars per student)	Quantity (students per year)
6,000	10,000
5,000	20,000
4,000	30,000
3,000	40,000
2,000	50,000

25. If all colleges are private and the market for education is competitive, calculate the number of students, the tuition, and the deadweight loss.

The equilibrium number of students will be 30,000 and the tuition will be $4,000. To calculate the deadweight loss, Figure 17.7 is helpful. The efficient quantity of students is 50,000. Therefore deadweight loss is equal to the area of the grey triangle in the figure, which is $20 million.

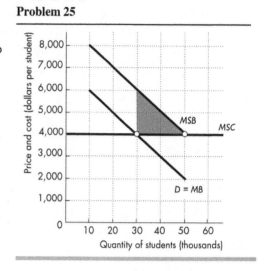

FIGURE **17.7**
Problem 25

27. If the government decides to subsidize private colleges, what subsidy will achieve the efficient number of college students?

The subsidy must equal to the marginal external benefit at the efficient quantity, or $2,000 per student.

Economics in the News

29. After you have studied *Economics in the News* on pp. 410–411, answer the following questions:

a. What are the marginal private costs of and marginal private benefits from using gas rather than coal to generate electricity?

The marginal private cost of using gas is the price paid by the utilities for the gas; the marginal private cost of using fuel made from coal is the price paid for the fuel plus any additional taxes or fees imposed on the fuel. The marginal private benefit from using gas is the same as that using coal, namely the marginal private benefits from electricity.

b. What are the marginal social costs of and marginal social benefits from using gas rather than coa to generate electricity? |

The marginal social cost of using gas is the marginal private cost of the fuel (the price paid by the utilities for the fuel) plus the marginal external cost from the (smaller amount of) carbon dioxide emitted. The marginal social cost of using fuel from coal is the marginal private cost of the fuel (the price paid by the utilities for the fuel) plus the marginal external cost from the (larger amount of) carbon dioxide emitted. The marginal social benefit from using gas is the same as that from using coal, namely the marginal social benefits from electricity.

c. How will the EPA's plan for power utilities to switch from coal to gas change the price that households pay for electricity?

The price of electricity will rise as utilities switch from the lower-cost fuel, coal, to the higher cost fuel, natural gas.

d. How will the EPA's plan for utilities to switch from coal to gas change the efficiency of electricity production?

The efficiency will increase because utilities will use less coal, which generates a larger external cost, and more natural gas, which creates a smaller external cost.

18 MARKETS FOR FACTORS OF PRODUCTION

Answers to the Review Quizzes

Page 420

1. **What are the factors of production and their prices?**

   The factors of production and their prices are: labor, which is paid a wage rate for labor services; capital, which is paid a rental rate for capital services; land, which is paid a rental rate for land services; and entrepreneurship, which receives a profit or bears a loss that results from business decisions.

3. **What is the distinction between the price of capital equipment and the rental rate of capital?**

   The price of a unit of capital is how much must be paid to acquire the piece of capital equipment. The rental rate of capital is the amount that must be paid to use the unit of capital equipment. For instance, the copy machine at the local Quik Print has a price of $10,000 but its services can be rented from the Quik Print for $50 per hour.

Page 423

1. **What is the value of marginal product of labor?**

   The value of marginal product of labor is the value to the firm of hiring one more unit of labor. The value of marginal product of labor, VMP, is the change in total revenue from employing an additional unit of labor.

3. **How is the demand for labor derived from the value of marginal product of labor?**

   The demand for labor is determined by the value of marginal product of labor. To maximize its profit a firm hires the number of workers that sets the wage rate equal to the value of marginal product of labor. When the wage rate changes, the firm changes the quantity of labor it demands so that the (new) wage rate equals the value of marginal product. So when the wage rate changes, the firm moves along its value of marginal product of labor curve to determine the quantity of labor demanded, thereby making its value of marginal product of labor curve its demand for labor curve.

Page 431

1. **What determines the amount of labor that households plan to supply?**

   When households decide how much labor to provide in the labor market, they compare the market wage rate to the value of the lost leisure that supplying labor would entail. If the market wage rate exceeds the individual's reservation wage rate, the individual forgoes leisure and supplies labor to the labor market. The quantity of labor the person supplies depends on the wage rate. At most wage rates the substitution effect dominates the income effect so that a person increases the quantity of labor supplied if the wage rate rises. But at high wage rates the income effect dominates the substitution effect so that a person decreases the quantity of labor supplied if the wage rate increases.

3. **How do labor unions influence wage rates?**

Unions increase their members' wage rates by increasing the demand for their members' labor and decreasing the supply of labor. In particular, to increase the demand for their members' labor, unions: increase the value of marginal product of union members by sponsoring training schemes and apprenticeship programs; encourage import restrictions so that consumers must buy goods and services produced by union members; and, support minimum wage laws to raise the wage of a substitute for their members' labor. Unions also try to restrict the supply of labor, say by supporting immigration restrictions to decrease the supply of low-skilled labor. By decreasing the supply of low-skilled labor, the wage rate paid low-skilled labor rises, which increases the demand for high-skilled union labor.

5. How is the wage rate determined when a union faces a monopsony?

When a monopoly seller, such as union, bargains with a monopsony buyer, such as a large firm, the situation is called bilateral monopoly. The wage rate will be lower than the union's monopoly wage rate and higher than the buyer's monopsony wage rate. Within this range, the actual wage rate depends on the cost that each party can inflict on the other. Everything else the same, the more cost that one party can inflict on the other, the closer the actual wage rate will be to that party's desired wage rate.

Page 435

1. What determines demand and supply in rental markets for capital and land?

The demand for capital depends on the value of marginal product of capital; the demand for land depends on the value of marginal product of land. The higher the marginal product of capital or land, the greater the demand for capital or land. Additionally the demand for capital depends on the rental rate of capital and the demand for land depends on the rental rate of land. The higher the rental rates, the lower the quantities demanded. The supply of capital depends on the rental rate of capital. The higher the rental rate of capital, the greater is the quantity of capital supplied. The supply of land, however, is perfectly inelastic because its quantity is fixed.

3. What determines the supply of a nonrenewable natural resource?

The supply of a nonrenewable natural resource depends on the total known amount, such as the known oil reserves in the market for oil. It also depends on the scale of current production facilities, which determines the marginal cost of producing the resource. For instance, when more oil wells are sunk, the supply of oil increases. The expected future price also affects the supply. The higher the future expected price, the smaller the present supply of the resource.

5. Explain the Hotelling principle.

The Hotelling principle is the result that the price of a nonrenewable natural resource is expected to rise at a rate equal to the interest rate. Only when this situation exists can the market be in equilibrium. For example, if the price is expected to rise more rapidly than the interest rate, supply decreases and demand increases, and the present price rises. Supply will continue to decrease, demand will continue to increase, and the present price will continue to rise until the percentage increase from the present price to the future expected price equals the interest rate. At that point, which is the situation outlined by the Hotelling principle, the market is in equilibrium because supply stops decreasing and demand stops increasing.

Answers to the Study Plan Problems and Applications

1. Tim is opening a new online store. He plans to hire two workers at $10 an hour. Tim is also considering buying or leasing some new computers. The purchase price of a computer is $900 and after three years it is worthless. The annual cost of leasing a computer is $450.

   a. In which factor markets does Tim operate?

   Tim is operating in the labor market when he hires his workers. Tim also is operating in the capital market when he buys or leases his computers. Tim, himself, is an entrepreneur.

   b. What is the price of the capital equipment and the rental rate of capital?

   The price of the capital equipment—Tim's computer—is $900. The rental rate of capital is $450.

Use the following data to work Problems 3 and 5.

Wanda's is a fish store that hires students to pack the fish. Students can pack the amounts of fish shown in the table. The fish market is competitive and the price of fish is 50¢ a pound. The market for packers is competitive and their market wage rate is $7.50 an hour.

Number of students	Quantity of fish (pounds)
1	20
2	50
3	90
4	120
5	145
6	165
7	180
8	190

3. a. Find Wanda's demand for labor curve.

   The demand for labor curve is the same as the value of marginal product curve.

   b. How many students does Wanda employ?

   Wanda hires the number of students that makes the value of marginal product equal to the wage rate of $7.50 an hour. When Wanda increases the number of students from 6 to 7, marginal product is 15 pounds of fish an hour, which Wanda sells for 50¢ a pound. The value of marginal product is $7.50—the same as the wage rate. The value of marginal product is plotted at the mid-point between 6 and 7 students a day, so Wanda hires 6.5 students a day.

Use the following additional information to work Problem 5.

The market price of fish falls to 33.33¢ a pound, but the packers' wage rate remains at $7.50 an hour.

5. How does Wanda's demand for labor change? What happens to the number of students that Wanda employs?

   Wanda's demand for labor decreases because her value of marginal product decreases at each quantity of labor and her demand for labor curve shifts leftward.

   Wanda hires fewer students. At the wage rate of $7.50, the number of students Wanda hires decreases as the demand for labor curve shifts leftward.

Use the following news clip to work Problems 7 and 9.

In Modern Rarity, Workers Form Union at Small Chain

In New York's low-income neighborhoods, labor unions have virtually no presence. But after a year-long struggle, 95 workers at a chain of 10 sneaker stores have formed a union. After months of negotiations, the two sides signed a three-year contract that sets the wage rate at $7.25 an hour.

Source: *The New York Times*, February 5, 2006

7. Why are labor unions scarce in New York's low-income neighborhoods?

   Labor unions probably are scarce because unions find these workers difficult to organize. In particular, most of them are low-skilled workers and the supply of low-skilled workers is probably elastic and difficult for unions to control or influence. In this situation, unions are unlikely to have much success in raising the wage rate.

9. How can this union try to change the demand for labor?

This union can try to change the demand for its members' labor by creating training programs to boost their productivity. In addition, it can support advertising that promotes "buy-American" policies and restrictions of foreign imported sneakers.

Answers to Additional Problems and Applications

11. Venus is opening a tennis school. She plans to hire a marketing graduate to promote and manage the school at $20 an hour. Venus is also considering buying or leasing a new tennis ball machine. The purchase price of the machine is $1,000 and after three years it is worthless. The annual cost of leasing the machine is $500.

   a. In which factor markets does Venus operate?

   Venus is operating in the labor market when she hires her marketing graduate and administrator. If she buys or leases a tennis ball machine, Venus is operating in the capital market. Venus, herself, is an entrepreneur.

   b. What is the price of the capital equipment and the rental rate of capital?

   The price of Venus's capital equipment is $1,000; the rental rate of her capital is $500 per year.

Use the following data to work Problems 13 and 15.

Kaiser's Ice Cream Parlor hires workers to produce milk shakes. The market for milk shakes is perfectly competitive, and the price of a milk shake is $4. The labor market is competitive, and the wage rate is $40 a day. The table shows the workers' total product schedule.

Number of workers	Quantity produced (milk shakes per day)
1	7
2	21
3	33
4	43
5	51
6	55

13. How many workers will Kaiser's hire to maximize its profit and how many milk shakes a day will Kaiser's produce?

   Kaiser's will hire 3.5 workers. The value of marginal product of 3.5 workers is $40 which equals the wage rate.

15. Kaiser's installs a new machine for making milk shakes that increases the productivity of workers by 50 percent. If the price of a milk shake remains at $4 and the wage rises to $48 a day, how many workers does Kaiser's hire?

   Kaiser's hires 4.5 workers because this is the quantity of workers that sets the value of marginal product equal to the wage rate. With the old machine, the marginal product of 4.5 workers was 8 milk shakes. The new machine increases the marginal product by 50 percent to 12 milk shakes. The price of a milk shake is $4. The value of marginal product equals the marginal product multiplied by the price, so the value of marginal product of 4.5 workers is 12 milk shakes × $4 a milk shake, or $48 which equals the wage rate.

Use the following news clip to work Problem 17.

Miner Sacks 17,000 Workers Over Pay Dispute

Impala Platinum has sacked 17,000 South African miners at its Rustenburg mine because they took part in an illegal strike. The miners refused to have their union negotiate in the two-week pay dispute with the world's second largest platinum producer. Mining provides a quarter of all jobs in Rustenburg.

Source: abc.com.au, February 3, 2012

17. How would the wage rate and employment for the Rustenburg miners be determined in a competitive market?

   In a competitive labor market, the wage rate and employment are determined by the supply of labor and the demand for labor. The equilibrium wage rate is the wage rate that sets the quantity of labor demanded equal to the quantity of labor supplied and equilibrium employment is equal to that quantity of labor.

Use the following news clip to work Problems 19 and 21.

The New War over Wal-Mart

Today, Wal-Mart employs more people—1.7 million—than any other private employer in the world. With size comes power: Wal-Mart's prices are lower and United Food and Commercial Workers International Union argues that Wal-Mart's wages are also lower than its competitors. Last year, the workers at a Canadian outlet joined the union and Wal-Mart immediately closed the outlet. But does Wal-Mart behave any worse than its competitors? When it comes to payroll, Wal-Mart's median hourly wage tracks the national median wage for general retail jobs.

Source: *The Atlantic*, June 2006

19. a.   Assuming that Wal-Mart has market power in a labor market, explain how the firm could use that market power in setting wages.

Wal-Mart can use its market power to decrease the wage rate it pays by decreasing the number of workers it hires.

b.   Draw a graph to illustrate how Wal-Mart might use labor market power to set wages.

Figure 18.4 shows Wal-Mart's situation if it is a monopsony in the labor market. Wal-Mart's demand curve is the same as its value of marginal product curve and is labeled $D = VMP$ in the figure. The labor supply curve is upward sloping and is labeled S in the figure. Wal-Mart's marginal cost of labor exceeds the wage rate it pays so the marginal cost of labor curve, labeled MCL, lies above the labor supply curve. Wal-Mart's profit-maximizing quantity of labor is determined at the intersection of the $D = VMP$ curve and the MCL curve and is 1.7 million workers. Wal-Mart determines the wage rate from the labor supply curve as the lowest wage rate it can pay and hire its profit-maximizing quantity of labor. In the figure the wage rate is $9 dollars per hour.

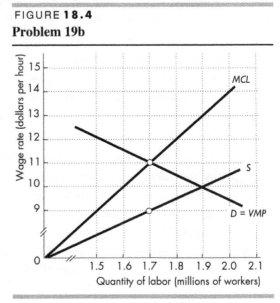

FIGURE **18.4**

Problem 19b

21.   Based upon evidence presented in this article, does Wal-Mart function as a monopsony in labor markets, or is the market for retail labor more competitive? Explain.

The key piece of evidence in the news clip is the point that Wal-Mart's median wage is similar to the national median wage rate. If Wal-Mart had significant monopsony power its wage rate would probably be less than the national median wage rate. Because the wage rates are similar, it appears that Wal-Mart functions in a competitive labor market.

23.   New technology has allowed oil to be pumped from much deeper offshore oil fields than before. For example, 28 deep ocean rigs operate in the deep waters of the Gulf of Mexico.

a.   What effect do you think deep ocean sources have had on the world oil price?

The deep ocean oil fields increased the supply of oil and have kept oil prices from rising higher than they would have otherwise.

b.   Who will benefit from drilling for oil in the Gulf of Mexico? Explain your answer.

The people benefiting from the new technology are the owners of the oil rigs and the firms selling this oil. Consumers also benefit because the price of oil is lower.

25.   **Gas Prices Create Land Rush**

There is a land rush going on across Pennsylvania, but buyers aren't interested in the land itself. Buyers are interested in what lies beneath the earth's surface—mineral rights to natural gas deposits. Record high natural gas prices have already pushed up drilling activity across the state, but drilling companies have discovered a new technology that will enable deep gas-bearing shale to be exploited. Development companies, drilling companies and speculators have been trying to lease mineral rights from landowners. The new drilling techniques might recover about 10 percent of those reserves, and that would ring up at a value of $1 trillion.

Source: *Erie Times-News*, June 15, 2008

a.   Explain why the demand for land in Pennsylvania has increased.

The demand for land increased because the price of natural gas increased. The value of marginal product of the land, which equals the price of natural gas multiplied by the marginal product of the land in producing natural gas, increased so the demand for land increased.

b.   If companies are responding to the higher prices for natural gas by drilling right now wherever they can, what does that imply about their assumptions about the future price of natural gas in relation to current interest rates?

If companies assume that the price of natural gas is expected to rise at a rate that exceeds the interest rate, it is profitable to obtain the natural gas now and hold it in inventory until the price rises.

c.   What could cause the price of natural gas to fall in the future?

Technological change that decreases the demand for natural gas can lead the price to fall in the future. Lower prices for substitutes for natural gas, such as coal or heating oil, will lower the demand for natural gas and lead to a lower price for natural gas. Discoveries of large new reserves of natural gas will lead to a lower price for natural gas.

Economics in the News

27.   Keshia is opening a new bookkeeping service. She is considering buying or leasing some new laptop computers. The purchase price of a laptop is $1,500 and after three years it is worthless. The annual lease rate is $550 per laptop. The value of marginal product of one laptop is $700 a year. The value of marginal product of a second laptop is $625 a year. The value of marginal product of a third laptop is $575 a year. And the value of marginal product of a fourth laptop is $500 a year.

a.   How many laptops will Keshia lease or buy?

Keshia will lease or buy 3 laptops. The fourth laptop's value of marginal product is less than the annual lease rate, so Keisha will never lease the fourth laptop. And the present value of the value of marginal products for the fourth laptop is always less than $1,500 regardless of the interest rate. (The value of marginal products sum to $1,500 when not discounted, so when discounted they must sum to less than $1,500.) Keisha will never rent nor buy the fourth laptop because it is not profitable to do so. For each year the value of marginal product for the third laptop always exceeds the annual lease rate, so leasing that laptop will be profitable. Therefore Keisha will always be willing to lease the third laptop.

b.   If the interest rate is 4 percent a year, will Keshia lease or buy her laptops?

Keshia compares the present value of leasing the laptops to the price of buying the laptops. When the interest rate is 4 percent, the present value of leasing the laptops is

$$\frac{\$550}{1.04} + \frac{\$550}{(1.04)^2} + \frac{\$550}{(1.04)^3} = \$1,526.$$ The present value of leasing the laptops exceeds the price of buying the laptops, so Keisha buys the laptops.

c.   If the interest rate is 6 percent a year, will Keshia lease or buy her laptops?

Keshia again compares the present value of leasing the laptops to the price of buying the laptops. When the interest rate is 6 percent, the present value of leasing the laptops is

$$\frac{\$550}{1.06}+\frac{\$550}{(1.06)^2}+\frac{\$550}{(1.06)^3}=\$1,470.$$ The present value of leasing the laptops is less than the price of buying the laptops, so Keisha leases the laptops.

19 ECONOMIC INEQUALITY

Answers to the Review Quizzes

Page 452

1. Which is distributed more unequally, income or wealth? Why? Which is the better measure?

   The distribution of wealth is more unequally distributed than income. Wealth is distributed more unequally than income because wealth data do not include the value of human capital, while the income data measure income from all wealth, including human capital. That is why income is a better measure for economic inequality than wealth.

3. What are the main characteristics of high-income and low-income households?

   There are four major characteristics that influence the amount of income earned by an individual: i) *Education:* The more education attained by a person the higher the human capital that person has, and the more income that person enjoys; ii) *Type of household:* Married couples earn more, on average, than single people living alone, especially females living alone; iii) *The age of householder:* The oldest and youngest households have lower incomes than middle age households; and iv) *Race:* Individuals living in households headed by an Asian person have the highest incomes, followed by white households, Hispanic households, and then black households.

5. How much mobility has there been through the income quintiles since 2007?

   There is some mobility but not a vast amount, particularly in the lowest and highest quintiles. In both these quintiles, about 70 percent of households remained in the same quintile. In the other three quintiles, somewhere between 45 percent and 50 percent of households remained in the same quintile. But there was some mobility. In the bottom four quintiles, about 25 percent of household moved up a quintile. (It is impossible for a household in the top quintile to move up.) Similarly, in the top four quintiles, about 25 percent of household moved down a quintile. (It is impossible for a household in the bottom quintile to move down.) A few household also moved up and down by more than one quintile.

Page 454

1. In which countries are incomes distributed most unequally and least unequally?

   Brazil and South Africa have the most unequally distributed incomes. Finland and Sweden and some other European nations have the most equally distributed incomes.

3. How can incomes become *more* unequally distributed within countries and *less* unequally distributed across countries?

   Income within nations generally has become distributed less equally. However because the average income within the poorest nations has been rising more rapidly than average income within richer nations, the world distribution of income has become more equally distributed.

Page 458

1.   What role does human capital play in accounting for income inequality?

In general acquiring human capital is a costly endeavor so the supply of workers with a lot of human capital is less than the supply of workers with little human capital. The difference in supply means that the more human capital an individual attains, the more income that individual will likely earn, other things remaining the same. Greater variation in human capital across the population of households increases the degree of income inequality among households. While the level of human capital attained varies across households, this factor alone does not completely explain the observed variation in income across households in the United States

3.   What role might contests among superstars play in accounting for income inequality?

Contests can explain why the super-rich have incomes that have increased greatly over the years. With increased globalization, the pool of "contestants" has increased dramatically. With the larger number of conspiracy, each contestant's probability of winning has shrunk. So contests need to have larger differences in payouts for the winners versus the losers so as to induce larger efforts to win the contest. The result is that the contest winners—be they sports stars, entertainment stars, of CEOs—nowadays have much larger incomes than the vast number of losers.

5.   Does inherited wealth make the distribution of income less equal or more equal?

An inheritance from older to a younger generations can only increase wealth and can never decreases wealth within a family, which helps make the distribution of wealth more unequal over time, all else equal. However if a generation is "lucky" and earns a high income and then passes some of it along as an inheritance to more typical less lucky lower-income generations, then inherited wealth makes the distribution of income more equal.

Page 461

1.   How do governments in the United States redistribute income?

The governments in the U.S. use three main ways to redistribute income and reduce, to some degree, economic inequality: i) *Income taxes:* Taxes on household income are charged by the U.S. federal government and by many state governments,; ii) *Income maintenance programs:* There are three major types of programs that provide direct payments to individuals; and iii) *Subsidized services:* A great deal of income redistribution takes the form of subsidized services, where people other than those who pay for services consume the services provided.

3.   What is one of the major welfare challenges today and how is it being tackled in the United States?

The major welfare challenge is households headed by single mothers The poorest people in the United States are young, minority women who have not completed high school, have one or more dependent children, and live without a spouse. The Temporary Assistance for Needy Families (TANF) program is the current attempt to meet this challenge. TANF is a block grant paid to the states, which administer payments to individuals. It is not open-ended. Adults receiving assistance must work or perform community service. There is a five-year limit for assistance.

Answers to the Study Plan Problems and Applications

1.   What is money income? Describe the distribution of money income in the United States in 2012.

Money income equals market income (wages, interest, rent, and profit earned in factor markets, before paying income taxes) plus cash payments from the government. The distribution of money income in the United States is unequal. While the median household income was $51,017, the poorest 20 percent of household received less than 4 percent of the total income and the richest 20 percent of household received slightly more than 50 percent of the total income.

3.   Incomes in China and India are a small fraction of U.S. income, but incomes in China and India are growing at more than twice the rate of U.S. incomes.

a.   Explain how economic inequality in China and India is changing relative to that in the United States.

Inequality between people in China and India and people in the United States is lessening. Income for the typically poorer people in China and India is increasing more rapidly than income for the typically richer people in the United States, so the fraction of world income going to the people in China and India is growing.

b.   How is the world Lorenz curve and world Gini ratio changing?

The world Lorenz curve is moving closer to the line of equality and the Gini ratio is falling in value.

Use the table to work Problem 5. The table shows the income shares in the United States, Canada, and the United Kingdom in 2009.

Households (percentage)	United States	Canada	United Kingdom
	(percentage of total income)		
Lowest 20	3	7	3
Second 20	8	13	5
Middle 20	15	18	14
Next highest 20	23	25	25
Highest 20	50	37	53

5.   Draw the Lorenz curves for the United States and the United Kingdom. In which country was income less equally distributed in 2009?

To draw the Lorenz curve for Canada, it is necessary to calculate the cumulative percentage of households and cumulative percentage of income. The table to the right has these data.
Figure 19.3, shows the Lorenz curve for the United States and the United Kingdom. Income is distributed less equally in the United Kingdom.

FIGURE **19.3**

Problem 5

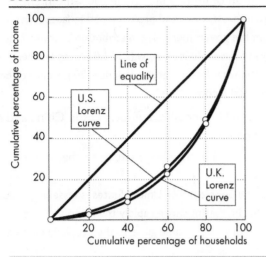

United Kingdom	
Households (quintile)	Cumulative percentage of income
Lowest	3
Second	8
Third	22
Fourth	47
Highest	100

Use the table to work Problem 7.

The table shows three redistribution schemes.

Before-tax income (dollars)	Plan A tax (dollars)	Plan B tax (dollars)	Plan C tax (dollars)
10,000	1,000	1,000	2,000
20,000	2,000	4,000	2,000
30,000	3,000	9,000	2,000

7.   Which scheme has

(i)   a proportional tax?

(ii)   a regressive tax?

(iii)   a progressive tax?

Tax Plan A is a proportional tax. At each level of income, 10 percent of income is paid in taxes.

Tax Plan C is regressive. When income is $10,000, 20 percent of income is paid in taxes; when income is $20,000, 10 percent of income is paid in taxes; and, when income is $30,000, 6.67 percent of income is paid in taxes.

Tax Plan B is progressive. When income is $10,000, 10 percent of income is paid in taxes; when income is $20,000, 20 percent of income is paid in taxes; and, when income is $30,000, 30 percent of income is paid in taxes.

Answers to Additional Problems and Applications

Use the table to work Problem 9. The table shows the distribution of market income in the United States in 2007.

Households (quintile)	Market income (percentage of total)
Lowest	1.1
Second	7.1
Third	13.9
Fourth	22.8
Highest	55.1

9. a. What is the definition of market income?

Market income is the before-tax income earned by factors of production in the marketplace. Labor earns wages, capital earns interest, land earns rent, and entrepreneurship earns profit.

b. Draw the Lorenz curve for the distribution of market income.

Figure 19.5 shows the distribution of market income. To draw this Lorenz curve, plot the cumulative percentage of households on the x-axis and the cumulative percentage of market income on the y-axis. Make the scale on the two axes the same. The Lorenz curve will pass through the following points: 20 percent on the x-axis and 1.1 percent on the y-axis; 40 percent on the x-axis and 8.2 percent on the y-axis; 60 percent on the x-axis and 22.1 percent on the y-axis; 80 percent on the x-axis and 44.9 percent on the y-axis; and 100 percent on the x-axis and 100 percent on the y-axis.

FIGURE **19.5**

Problem 9b

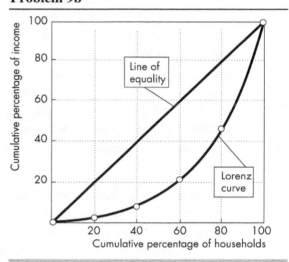

Use the table to work Problems 11 and 13. The table shows shares of income in Australia.

Households (quintile)	Market income (percent of total)
Lowest	7
Second	13
Third	18
Fourth	24
Highest	38

11. Draw the Lorenz curve for the income distribution in Australia and in Brazil and South Africa (use the data in Fig. 19.6 on p. A160). Is income distributed more equally or less equally in Brazil and South Africa than in Australia?

Figure 19.6 shows these Lorenz curves. Income is distributed less equally in Brazil and South Africa.

13.   What are some reasons for the differences in the distribution of income in Australia and in Brazil and South Africa?

> In both Brazil and South Africa there are wealthy citizens descended from European settlers and poorer citizens descended from large indigenous native populations. The income disparity between these two relatively large groups creates an unequal distribution of income in Brazil and South Africa. In Australia the indigenous native population is smaller, so the population is comprised mainly of citizens descended from European settlers. Because there is not a large pool of low-income indigenous natives, the distribution of income is more equal in Australia.

FIGURE **19.6**
Problem 11

15.   **Where Women's Pay Trumps Men's**

Men work more than women on the job, at least in terms of overall hours. That's just one reason why in most fields, men's earnings exceed women's earnings. But Warren Farrell found 39 occupations in which women's median earnings exceeded men's earnings by at least 5 percent and in some cases by as much as 43 percent. In fields like engineering, a company may get one woman and seven men applying for a job. If the company wants to hire the woman, it might have to pay a premium to get her. Also, where women can combine technical expertise with people skills—such as those required in sales and where customers prefer dealing with a woman—that's likely to contribute to a premium in pay.

Source: CNN, March 2, 2006

a.   Draw a graph to illustrate why discrimination could result in female workers getting paid more than male workers for some jobs.

> Figure 19.8 shows a labor market in which men are discriminated against in favor of women. With the discrimination, the value of marginal product of women exceeds that of men. As a result, the value of marginal product curve for females, labeled VMP_F, lies above the value of marginal product curve for males, labeled VMP_M. In the figure the supply of male labor is the same as that of females, so the supply curve is labeled $S_M = S_F$. The figure shows that the wage rate paid women, $40 per hour, exceeds the wage rate paid men, $20 per hour.

b. Explain how market competition could potentially eliminate this wage differential.

Men are paid less than women. If men and women are equally productive and the price paid for their output is the same, then firms which hire men have lower costs and higher profits than firms which hire women. Firms that hire men would increase their sales at the expense of the high-cost and therefore higher-price firms that hire only women. The increase in sales of firms that hire men increases the demand for men, which raises their wage rate. Firms that hire women lose sales and so the demand for women decreases, which lowers their wage rate.

c. If customers "prefer dealing with a woman" in some markets, how might that lead to a persistent wage differential between men and women?

If customers prefer dealing with a woman, then women's value of marginal product remains permanently higher than men's value of marginal product so the wage rate paid women remains permanently higher than the wage rate paid men.

FIGURE **19.8**

Problem 15a

Use the following information to work Problem 17.

In 2010, 828,000 Americans had full-time management jobs that paid an average of $96,450 a year while 4.3 million Americans had full-time retail sales jobs that paid an average of $20,670 a year. Managers require a high school certificate while retail sales people don't but they undergo training.

Source: Bureau of Labor Statistics

17. If the online shopping trend continues, how do you think the market for salespeople will change in coming years?

Shopping on-line decreases the demand for in-person salespeople. If on-line shopping continues to increase in importance, the decrease in demand for salespeople will lower the salary and decrease the quantity of salespeople. If, in response to the lower salary, the supply of salespeople also decreases, then the employment definitely decreases but the effect on the salary becomes ambiguous.

19. Describe the effects of increasing the amount of income redistribution in the United States to the point at which the lowest income group receives 15 percent of total income and the highest income group receives 30 percent of total income.

If the highest income group's share falls from 55.1 to 30 percent of total income, redistribution takes 25.1 percent of income from this group. If the lowest income group's share rises from 1.1 to 15 percent, redistribution raises this group's share by 13.9 percent of total income. The other 11.2 percent (25.1 minus 13.9 percent) would be distributed to other groups.

This redistribution scheme would require a tax on the highest groups of 45.5 percent—(25.1/55.1) × 100 percent. Such a large increase in the tax rate and redistribution might create the big tradeoff effect. The highly taxed people might choose to do less work and if they do, total income decreases.

Use the following news clip to work Problem 21.

The Tax Debate We Should be Having

A shrinking number of Americans are bearing an even bigger share of the nation's income tax burden. In 2005, the bottom 40 percent of Americans by income had an effective tax rate that's negative: Their households received more money through the income tax system than they paid. The top 50% of taxpayers pay 97% of total income tax and the top 10% of taxpayers pay 70%. The top 1% paid almost 40% of all income tax, a proportion that has jumped dramatically since 1986.

Given the U.S. tax system, any tax cut must benefit the rich, but in terms of the change in effective tax rates: The bottom 50% got a much bigger tax cut under the Bush tax cut than the top 1%. Did the dollar value of Bush's tax cuts go mostly to the wealthy? Absolutely.

Source: *Fortune*, April 14, 2008

21. How might the benefits of tax cuts "trickle down" to others whose taxes are not cut?

The benefits of tax cuts can trickle down because tax cuts mean that the wealthy have more income, some of which they might invest in the businesses they run. For instance, a wealthy entrepreneur who is given a tax cut might increase the size of his or her business, which creates more employment and higher wages for less wealthy workers. Additionally the wealthy spend some of their additional funds on goods and services. Some of the firms producing these goods and services expand, once again increasing the employment and wage rate of less wealthy workers.

Economics in the News

23. **The Best and Worst College Degrees by Salary**

Business administration is always a strong contender for honors as the most popular college major. This is no surprise since students think business is the way to making big bucks. But is business administration really as lucrative as students and their parents believe? Nope.

In a new survey by PayScale, Inc. of salaries by college degree, business administration didn't even break into the list of the top 10 or 20 most lucrative college degrees. A variety of engineering majors claim eight of the top 10 salary spots with chemical engineering ($65,700) winning best for starting salaries. Out of 75 undergrad college majors, business administration ($42,900) came in 35th, behind such degrees as occupational therapy ($61,300), information technology ($49,400), and economics ($48,800).

Source: moneywatch.com, July 21, 2009

a. Why do college graduates with different majors have drastically different starting salaries?

The differences in starting salaries are the result of differences in the demand for and supply of the different majors. Different majors require different skill sets and different amounts of human capital. These differences mean that the value of marginal product and therefore the demand for different majors can be substantially different. In addition different numbers of students major in the different subjects because some majors are high-cost majors (in terms of time and/or effort) while other majors are lower cost. This difference means that the supply of the different majors can be substantially different.

b. Draw a graph of the labor markets for economics majors and business administration majors to illustrate your explanation of the differences in the starting salaries of these two groups.

Economics majors likely have more human capital and more marketable skills than do business administration majors, so the demand for economics majors is greater than the demand for business administration majors. There are probably more business administration majors than economics majors, so the supply of business administration majors exceeds the supply of economics majors. Both these differences are illustrated in Figure 19.9. In the figure the demand curve for economics majors is labeled D_E and lies to the right of the demand curve for of business administration majors, labeled D_{BA}. Also in the figure the supply curve of business administration majors, labeled S_{BA}, lies to the right of the supply curve of economics majors, labeled S_E. These different demand and supply curves result in a starting salary for economics majors of $48,800 and for of business administration majors of $42,900.

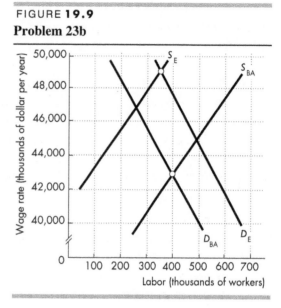

FIGURE **19.9**
Problem 23b

© 2016 Pearson Education, Inc.

Chapter
20 UNCERTAINTY AND INFORMATION

Answers to the Review Quizzes

Page 472

1. What is the distinction between expected wealth and expected utility?

   Expected wealth is the money value of what a person expects to own at a point in time. Expected utility is the utility value of what a person expects to own at a point in time. These concepts both measure the value of what a person expects to own at a point in time but they differ because expected wealth is the money value and expected utility is the utility value.

3. What do people try to achieve when they make a decision under uncertainty?

   When making decisions under uncertainty people maximize their expected utility.

Page 475

1. How does insurance reduce risk?

   Insurance reduces the risk any individual faces because insurance pools risks. Everyone pays into the pool but only the small fraction of people who suffer a loss are paid from the pool. Essentially people reduce the risk of a large adverse financial outcome in exchange for the small, certain payment to the insurance company.

3. How can an insurance company offer people a deal worth taking? Why do both the buyers and the sellers of insurance gain?

   Insurance companies work by pooling risks so that everyone pays into the pool but only the (small) fraction of people who suffer a loss are paid from the pool. Although the likelihood of a bad occurrence is small for each individual, for a large enough group the total number and total amount of losses can be estimated very closely. The insurance company can calculate the size of the pool required to cover losses. From this calculation the company can compute the amount of the premium each person must pay into the pool to cover all the anticipated losses and other costs the company incurs. People buy insurance because they are risk averse; they want to avoid unwanted outcomes. Insurance is worth buying because people are willing to give up a relatively small amount of income all the time to guarantee that they do not face the uncommon occurrence of having to give up a large amount of income since this deal increases their expected utility. An insurance company will always try to take in more in premiums paid than claims paid out to claimants so that their owners receive at minimum a normal profit.

Page 480

1. How does private information create adverse selection and moral hazard?

   Both moral hazard and adverse selection are the result of private information. Moral hazard occurs when, after an agreement has been reached, one of the parties to the agreement has the incentive to gain additional benefits at the expense of the other party. Adverse selection refers to people who accept certain contracts and have private information that allows them to benefit from the contract while harming the other party. Both moral hazard and adverse selection can affect negatively the way in which markets function.

3.   **How do markets for loans use signaling and screening to cope with private information?**
Lenders in the loans market want to separate high-risk borrowers from low-risk borrowers so that they can charge high-risk borrowers a high interest rate and low-risk borrowers a low interest rate. They use signals and screens to help them do so. They screen borrowers by asking for information that helps them assess the riskiness of the loan and the borrower. If the borrower does not reveal the information requested, the lender has screened the borrower into the high-risk category. The information requested will provide signals about the borrower's riskiness. For instance, if a borrower has defaulted on debt in the past this fact signals that the borrower is a high-risk individual.

Page 481

1.   **Thinking about information as a good, what determines the information people are willing to pay for?**
People are willing to pay for information so long as the marginal cost is less than or equal to its marginal benefit. For instance, consumers are willing to purchase information that has a marginal benefit to them that exceeds the price they must pay. Consumers might be willing to purchase information about the price(s) of large-ticket goods and services that are of interest. Workers might well be interested in buying information about salaries paid in occupations that interest them or salaries paid their co-workers. Employers are willing to buy information about the average salary offer given to college graduates with different majors.

3.   **Why are some of the markets that provide information likely to be dominated by monopolies?**
Objective information about, say, the quality of a good or service or the risk associated with a particular activity is costly to obtain. Once it is obtained, however, the marginal cost of disseminating it is low. With the low marginal cost, the firm can enjoy significant economies of scale, so these markets might be close to natural monopolies, that is, a market in which one firm can meet the demand at lower cost than could two or more firms.

Answers to the Study Plan Problems and Applications

1. The figure shows Lee's utility of wealth curve. Lee is offered a job as a salesperson in which there is a 50 percent chance that she will make $4,000 a month and a 50 percent chance that she will make nothing.

    a. What is Lee's expected income from taking this job?

    Lee's expected income is $(0.5 \times \$4,000) + (0.5 \times \$0) = \$2,000$ a month.

    b. What is Lee's expected utility from taking this job?

    When Lee's income is $4,000, her utility is 100. When Lee's income is $0, her utility is 0. So Lee's expected utility is $(0.5 \times 100) + (0.5 \times 0) = 50$.

    c. How much would another firm have to offer Lee with certainty to persuade her not to take the risky sales job?

    Lee would have to be offered about $1,250 a month with certainty to persuade her not to take the risky job. Lee would have to be offered the income that would give her with certainty 50 units of utility. This income, $1,250, is read from the graph at the 50 units on the y-axis.

    d. What is Lee's cost of risk?

    Lee's cost of risk is the difference between Lee's expected income, $2,000, and the certain income that gives her the same total utility, $1,250. Lee's cost of risk is $750.

FIGURE **20.1**

Problem 1

Use the following news clip to work Problem 3.
Larry lives in a neighborhood in which 20 percent of the cars are stolen every year. Larry's car, which he parks on the street overnight, is worth $20,000. (This is Larry's only wealth.) The table shows Larry's utility of wealth schedule.

Wealth (dollars)	Utility (units)
20,000	400
16,000	350
12,000	280
8,000	200
4,000	110
0	0

3. High-Crime Auto Theft, an insurance company, offers to sell Larry insurance at $8,000 a year and promises to provide Larry with a replacement car worth $20,000 if his car is stolen. Is Larry willing to buy this insurance? If not, is he willing to pay $4,000 a year for such insurance?

    If Larry buys the insurance for $8,000 his wealth will be $12,000 with no risk. This amount of wealth gives him utility of 280. This amount of utility is less than what his utility would be if he did not buy insurance, so Larry will not buy the insurance for $8,000.

    If Larry buys the insurance for $4,000 his wealth will be $16,000 with no risk. This amount of wealth gives him utility of 350. This amount of utility is more than what his utility would be if he did not buy insurance, so Larry will buy the insurance for $4,000.

5. You can't buy insurance against the risk of being sold a lemon. Why isn't there such a market? How does the market provide a buyer with some protection against being sold a lemon? What are the main ways in which markets overcome the lemons problem?

    There is not a market for "lemon insurance" for several reasons. Defining a "lemon" is far from clear cut. The definition would need to be specified in the contract. But that leads to a moral hazard problem because a buyer with a car close to meeting the requirements for a lemon will behave in a way that increases the probability that the car will be deemed a lemon. Moral hazard also arises once the insurance is purchased but before the car is bought. Once the customer has the insurance, he or she will no longer search for a "non-lemon," a creampuff. So it is likely that many of the cars purchased by people with the insurance will be lemons. These reasons combine to make it impossible for an insuring company to offer the insurance at a price that customers will pay and that allows the insurance firm to make a profit. Adverse selection also enters because people who are less likely to spend time searching for a high-quality car are more likely to buy the lemon insurance.

Even without insurance, the market does give protection against lemons. Warranties are designed to help cope with the moral hazard and adverse selection problems on cars. Warranties signal that the car is not a lemon because if the car is a lemon servicing the car would be costly. The fact that the seller, who is the person with the private information, is willing to offer a warranty signals that the car is not a lemon.

Answers to Additional Problems and Applications

Use the table, which shows Jimmy's and Zenda's utility of wealth schedules, to work Problems 7 and 9.

Wealth	Jimmy's utility	Zenda's utility
0	0	0
100	200	512
200	300	640
300	350	672
400	375	678
500	387	681
600	393	683
700	396	684

7. What are Jimmy's and Zenda's expected utilities from a bet that gives them a 50 percent chance of having a wealth of $600 and a 50 percent chance of having nothing?

    Jimmy's expected utility is $(0.5 \times 393) + (0.5 \times 0) = 196.5$.
    Zenda's expected utility is $(0.5 \times 683) + (0.5 \times 0) = 341.5$.

9. Suppose that Jimmy and Zenda each have $400 and are offered a business investment opportunity that involves committing the entire $400 to the project. The project could return $600 (a profit of $200) with a probability of 0.85 or $200 (a loss of $200) with a probability of 0.15. Who goes for the project and who hangs on to the initial $400?

Wealth	Jimmy's utility	Jimmy's marginal utility	Zenda's utility	Zenda's marginal utility
0	0		0	
		2.00		5.12
100	200		512	
		1.00		1.28
200	300		640	
		0.50		0.32
300	350		672	
		0.25		0.06
400	375		678	
		0.12		0.03
500	387		681	
		0.06		0.02
600	393		683	
		0.03		0.01
700	396		684	

    Jimmy puts his money into the project, but Zenda does not. Jimmy maximizes his expected utility. If Jimmy puts his money into the project and it makes a profit, his utility is 393; if Jimmy puts his money into the project and it fails, his utility is 300. So Jimmy's expected utility from the project is $(0.85 \times 393) + (0.15 \times 300)$, which equals 379. If Jimmy keeps his $400 and does not join the project, his utility is 375. Jimmy will choose to join the project because joining gives him greater utility. Zenda maximizes her expected utility. If Zenda puts her money into the project and it makes a profit, her utility is 683; if Zenda puts her money into the project and it fails, her utility is 640. So Zenda's expected utility from the project is $(0.85 \times 683) + (0.15 \times 640)$, which equals 677. If Zenda keeps her $400 and does not join the project, her utility is 678. Zenda will choose not to join the project because not joining gives her greater utility.

Use the following information to work Problem 11.

Two students, Jim and Kim, are offered summer jobs managing a student house-painting business.

There is a 50 percent chance that either of them will be successful and end up with $21,000 of wealth to get them through the next school year. But there is also a 50 percent chance that either will end up with only $3,000 of wealth. Each could take a completely safe but back-breaking job picking fruit that would leave them with a guaranteed $9,000 at the end of the summer. The table shows Jim's and Kim's utility of wealth schedules.

Wealth	Jim's utility	Kim's utility
0	0	0
3,000	100	200
6,000	200	350
9,000	298	475
12,000	391	560
15,000	482	620
18,000	572	660
21,000	660	680

11.   What is each student's maximized expected utility? Who has the larger expected wealth? Who ends up with the larger wealth at the end of the summer?

   Jim's expected utility is 380; Kim's expected utility is 475. Jim has higher expected wealth. Jim's expected wealth is $12,000; Kim's expected (and actual) wealth is $9,000. It is not possible to determine who has the actual larger wealth because Jim's wealth is uncertain.

Use the table, which shows Chris's utility of wealth schedule, to work Problem 13.

Chris's wealth is $5,000 and it consists entirely of her share in a risky ice cream business. If the summer is cold, the business will fail, and she will have no wealth. Where Chris lives there is a 50 percent chance each year that the summer will be cold.

Wealth (dollars)	Utility (units)
5,000	150
4,000	140
3,000	120
2,000	90
1,000	50
0	0

13.   If Chris cannot buy cold-summer insurance, what is her expected wealth and what is her expected utility?

   Chris's expected wealth is $5,000 × 0.50 + $0 × 0.50, which is $2,500. Her expected utility is 150 × 0.50 + 0 × 0.50, which is 75.

Use the following information to work Problems 15 and 17.

Larry has a good car that he wants to sell; Harry has a lemon that he wants to sell. Each knows what type of car he is selling. You are looking at used cars and plan to buy one.

15.   If both Larry and Harry are offering their cars for sale at the same price, from whom would you most want to buy, Larry or Harry, and why?

   If you know that Larry's car is a good car and Harry's car is a lemon, you most want to buy from Larry. If you do not know that Larry's car is a good car and Harry's car is a lemon, you are indifferent between the two.

17.   How can Larry signal that he is selling a good car so that you are willing to pay Larry the price that he knows his car is worth, and a higher price than what you are willing to offer Harry?

   Larry can offer a warranty on his car. For instance, Larry might offer to pay any repair bills (aside from accidents!) that come about for the next 6 months.

19. Why do you think it is not possible to buy insurance against having to put up with a low-paying, miserable job? Explain why a market in insurance of this type would be valuable to workers but unprofitable for an insurance provider and so would not work.

> Insurance against a low-paying job is not available because of moral hazard and adverse selection. In particular, the moral hazard exists that once someone purchased this type of insurance, the person could then take a low-paying job that he or she, for some reason, enjoyed. The person could then easily document that the job is low-paying and could also (falsely) assert the job was miserable and thereby collect on the insurance. Adverse selection also makes the insurance unlikely because the people most likely to wind up with low-paying jobs are the most likely to buy the insurance, whereas people who are most likely to wind up with high-paying jobs are least likely to buy the insurance.

Use the following news clip to work Problem 21.

Why We Worry About the Things We Shouldn't ... and Ignore the Things We Should

We pride ourselves on being the only species that understands the concept of risk, yet we have a confounding habit of worrying about mere possibilities while ignoring probabilities, building barricades against perceived dangers while leaving ourselves exposed to real ones: 20% of all adults still smoke; nearly 20% of drivers and more than 30% of backseat passengers don't use seat belts; two thirds of us are overweight or obese. We dash across the street against the light and build our homes in hurricane-prone areas—and when they're demolished by a storm, we rebuild in the same spot.

Source: *Time*, December 4, 2006

21. How can information be used to improve people's decision making?

> Information can improve people's decision making by providing them with data about the potential outcomes of their decisions. With this information readily at hand, the marginal benefit and marginal cost of actions can be more readily determined. Related to the news clip, with more information people might worry less about mere possibilities and pay more attention to probabilities, thereby making better decisions so that society is more efficient.

Economics in the News

23. **Are You Paid What You're Worth?**

How do you know if your pay adequately reflects your contributions to your employer's profits? In many instances, you don't. Your employer has more and better information than you do about how your salary and bonus compare to others in your field, to others in your office, and relative to the company's profits in any given year. You can narrow the information gap a bit if you're willing to buy salary reports from compensation sources. For example, at $200, a quick-call salary report from Economic Research Institute will offer you compensation data for your position based on your years of experience, your industry and the place where your company is located.

Source: CNN, April 3, 2006

a. Explain the role that asymmetric information can play in worker wages.

> Asymmetric information can lead to adverse selection and moral hazard, which both play a role in determining workers' wages. For instance, adverse selection occurs if a firm offers to pay its salespeople a fixed wage. The firm will attract generally lazy workers; more industrious workers will prefer to work for firms that pay them based on their results. Moral hazard results if salespeople are paid a fixed wage because every salesperson—including those who had previously worked hard—now has no incentive to work hard. These sorts of adverse selection and moral hazard issues exist with virtually all workers, not just salespeople.

b.   What adverse selection problem exists if a firm offers lower wages to existing workers?

    If a firm offers lower wages to its existing workers, the most productive workers will leave for a job at another company that pays them more, and the least productive workers will stay.

c.   What will determine how much a worker should actually pay for a detailed salary report?

    The benefits the worker expects to receive from the salary report will determine how much he or she is willing to pay. For instance, if a worker believes that his or her salary is very low compared to similar jobs elsewhere, the worker will be willing to pay more for the salary report than if the worker believes his or salary is in line with salaries elsewhere. The worker's private information also determines how much he or she is willing to pay for a detailed report. If the worker knows that he or she is hard working and quite productive, that worker's marginal benefit from a report detailing how much different companies paid in bonuses based on results would be high, which would increase the amount the worker is willing to pay.

GRAPHS IN ECONOMICS

Answers to the Review Quizzes

Page 28

1. Explain how we "read" the three graphs in Figs. A1.1 and A1.2.

    The points in the graphs relate the quantity of the variable measured on the one axis to the quantity of the variable measured on the other axis. The quantity of the variable measured on the horizontal axis (the x-axis) is measured by the horizontal distance from the origin to the point. Similarly, the quantity of the variable measured on the vertical axis (the y-axis) is measured by the vertical distance from the origin to the point. The point relates these two quantities. For instance, in Figure A1.2a, point A shows that at a price of $1.37 per song, 3.8 million songs are downloaded.

3. Explain how we "read" the three scatter diagrams in Figs. A1.3 and A1.4.

    The scatter diagram in Figure A1.3 shows the relationship between box office ticket sales and DVDs sold for 9 popular movies. The figure shows that higher box office sales are associated with a higher number of DVDs sold. But the figure shows that the relationship is weak.

    The scatter diagram in Figure A1.4a shows the relationship between income, in thousands of dollars per year, and expenditure, also in thousands of dollars per year, for the years 2001 to 2011. The scatter diagram shows that higher income leads to higher expenditure. The figure also shows that the relationship is relatively strong.

    The scatter diagram in Figure A1.4b shows the relationship between the inflation rate and the unemployment rate for the years 2001 to 2011. The figure shows that for most of the years, there was a weak relationship between these variables, with perhaps higher inflation being associated with lower unemployment.

5. Draw a graph to show the relationship between two variables that move in opposite directions.

    A graph that shows the relationship between two variables that move in the opposite directions is shown by a line that slopes downward. Figure A1.2 illustrates such a relationship.

FIGURE **A1.2**
Review problem 5

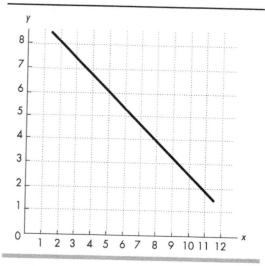

7. Which of the relationships in Question 5 is a positive relationship and which is a negative relationship?

    The relationship in Question 4 between the two variables that move in the same direction is a positive relationship. The relationship in Question 5 between the two variables that move in the opposite directions is a negative relationship.

9. How do we graph a relationship among more than two variables?

    To graph a relationship among more than two variables, hold constant the values of all the variables except two. Then plot the value of one of the variables against the other variable.

11. Explain what change will bring a *shift* of a curve.

    A curve shifts when there is a change in the value of a relevant variable that is not graphed on the axes. In this case the entire curve shifts.

Answers to the Study Plan Problems and Applications

Use the spreadsheet to work Problems 1 and 3. The spreadsheet provides data on the U.S. economy: Column A is the year, column B is the inflation rate, column C is the interest rate, column D is the growth rate, and column E is the unemployment rate.

	A	B	C	D	E
1	2003	1.6	1.0	2.8	6.0
2	2004	2.3	1.4	3.8	5.5
3	2005	2.7	3.2	3.4	5.1
4	2006	3.4	4.9	2.7	4.6
5	2007	3.2	4.5	1.8	4.6
6	2008	2.9	1.4	−0.3	5.8
7	2009	3.8	0.2	−2.8	9.3
8	2010	−0.3	0.1	2.5	9.6
9	2011	1.6	0.1	1.8	8.9
10	2012	3.1	0.1	2.8	8.1
11	2013	2.1	0.1	1.9	7.4

1. Draw a scatter diagram of the inflation rate and the interest rate. Describe the relationship.

    To make a scatter diagram of the inflation rate and the interest rate, plot the inflation rate on the x-axis and the interest rate on the y-axis. The graph will be a set of dots and is shown in Figure A1.4. The pattern made by the dots tells us that as the inflation rate increases, the interest rate usually increases so there is a (weak) positive relationship.

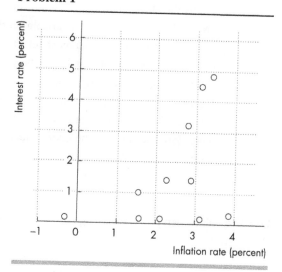

FIGURE **A1.4**

Problem 1

3. Draw a scatter diagram of the interest rate and the unemployment rate. Describe the relationship.

    To make a scatter diagram of the interest rate and the unemployment rate, plot the interest rate on the x-axis and the unemployment rate on the y-axis. The graph will be a set of dots and is shown in Figure A1.6. The pattern made by the dots tells us that when the interest rate increases, the unemployment rate usually decreases so there is a negative relationship.

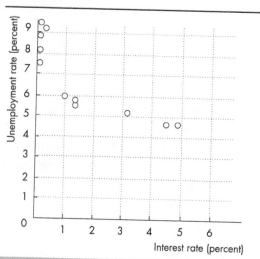

FIGURE **A1.6**

Problem 3

Use the following news clip to work Problem 5.

Lego Shatters More Records:
Source: Boxofficemojo.com,
Data for weekend of February 14–17, 2014

Movie	Theaters (number)	Revenue (dollars per theater)
The LEGO Movie	3,775	$16,551
About Last Night	2,253	$12,356
RoboCop	3,372	$7,432
The Monument Men	3,083	$5,811

5. Calculate the slope of the relationship between 3,775 and 2,253 theaters.

The slope equals the change in revenue per theater divided by the change in the number of theaters. The slope equals ($16,551 − $12,356)/(3,775 − 2,253) which equals $2.76 per theater.

7. Calculate the slope of the relationship shown in Figure A1.8.

The slope is −5/4. The curve is a straight line, so its slope is the same at all points on the curve. Slope equals the change in the variable on the y-axis divided by the change in the variable on the x-axis. To calculate the slope, you must select two points on the line. One point is at 10 on the y-axis and 0 on the x-axis, and another is at 8 on the x-axis and 0 on the y-axis. The change in y from 10 to 0 is associated with the change in x from 0 to 8. Therefore the slope of the curve equals −10/8, which equals −5/4.

FIGURE **A1.8**
Problem 7

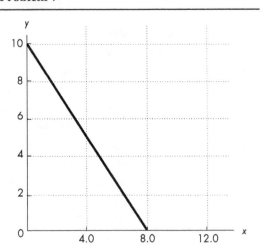

Use the relationship shown in Figure A1.9 to work Problem 9.

Price (dollars per ride)	Balloon rides (number per day)		
	50°F	70°F	90°F
5	32	40	50
10	27	32	40
15	18	27	32

9. Calculate the slope across the arc AB.

The slope across the arc AB is −1.125. The slope across an arc AB equals the change in y, which is 4.5 (6.0 minus 1.5) divided by the change in x, which equals −4 (2 minus 6). The slope across the arc AB equals 4.5/−4, which is −1.125.

FIGURE **A1.9**
Problems 8 and 9

Use the table to work Problem 11. The table gives the price of a balloon ride, the temperature, and the number of rides a day.

11.   What happens in the graph in Problem 10 if the temperature rises to 90°F?

         If the temperature rises to 90°F, the curve shifts rightward. This shift is illustrated in Figure A1.11. In that figure, both the initial curve, which applies when the temperature is 70°F, and the new curve, which applies when the temperature is 90°F, are illustrated. The curve when the temperature is 90°F lies to the right of the curve when the temperature is 70°F indicating that at every price, more balloon rides are taken when the temperature is 90°F rather than 70°F.

FIGURE **A1.11**
Problem 11

Answers to Additional Problems and Applications

Use the spreadsheet to work Problems 13. The spreadsheet provides data on oil and gasoline: Column A is the year, column B is the price of oil (dollars per barrel), column C is the price of gasoline (cents per gallon), column D is U.S. oil production, and column E is the U.S. quantity of gasoline refined (both in millions of barrels per day).

	A	B	C	D	E
1	2003	31	160	5.7	8.9
2	2004	42	190	5.4	9.1
3	2005	57	231	5.2	9.2
4	2006	66	262	5.1	9.3
5	2007	72	284	5.1	9.3
6	2008	100	330	5.0	9.0
7	2009	62	241	5.4	9.0
8	2010	79	284	5.5	9.0
9	2011	95	354	5.7	9.1
10	2012	94	364	6.5	9.0
11	2013	98	353	7.5	9.1

13.   Draw a scatter diagram of the price of gasoline and the quantity of gasoline refined. Describe the relationship.

Figure A1.13 shows the scatter diagram between the price of a gallon of gasoline and the quantity of gasoline refined. It shows a weak positive relationship.

FIGURE **A1.13**
Problem 13

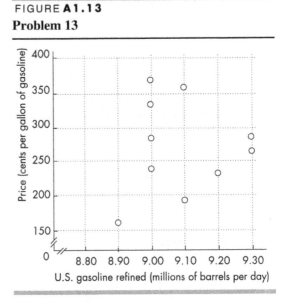

Use the following data to work Problems 15 and 17.

Draw a graph that shows the relationship between the two variables x and y in the table to the right.

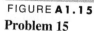

x	0	1	2	3	4	5
y	25	24	22	18	12	0

FIGURE **A1.15**

Problem 15

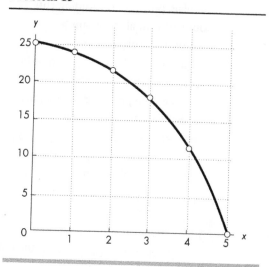

To make a graph that shows the relationship between x and y, plot the x variable on the x-axis and the y variable on the y-axis. Figure A1.15 shows this graph.

15. a. Is the relationship positive or negative?

The relationship is negative because x and y move in opposite directions: As x increases, y decreases.

b. Does the slope of the relationship become steeper or flatter as the value of x increases?

The slope becomes steeper as x increases.

c. Think of some economic relationships that might be similar to this one.

The less expensive a good, the greater is the number of people who buy it. The higher the interest rate, the smaller is the number of people who take out home mortgages. The less expensive gasoline, the greater the miles car owners drive.

17. Calculate the slope of the relationship across the arc as x increases from 4 to 5.

The slope is −12. The slope of the relationship across the arc when x increases from 4 to 5 is equal to the slope of the straight line joining the points on the curve at x equals 4 and x equals 5. When x increases from 4 to 5, y falls from 12 to 0. The slope equals the change in y, 12 (12 minus 0), divided by the change in x, −1 (4 minus 5), so the slope across the arc is −12.0.

Use Figure A1.17 to work Problem 19.

19. Calculate the slope at point A and at point B.

The slope at point A is −4, and the slope at point B is −1. To calculate the slope at a point on a curved line, draw the tangent to the line at the point. Then find a second point on the tangent and calculate the slope of the tangent.

The tangent at point A cuts the x-axis at 2.5. The slope of the tangent equals the change in y divided by the change in x. The change in y equals 6 (6 minus 0) and the change in x equals −1.5 (1 minus 2.5). The slope at point A is 6/−1.5, which equals −4. Similarly, the slope at point B is −1. The tangent at point B cuts the y-axis at 5. The change in y equals 3, and the change in x equals −3. The slope at point B is −1.

FIGURE **A1.17**

Problems 19 and 20

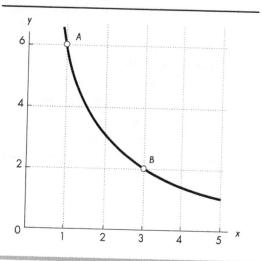

Use the following table to work Problems 21 and 23.
The table gives information about umbrellas: price, the number purchased, and rainfall in inches.

21. Draw a graph to show the relationship between the price and the number of umbrellas purchased, holding the amount of rainfall constant at 1 inch. Describe this relationship.

Price (dollars per umbrella)	Umbrellas (numbers per day)		
	0	1	2
	(inches of rainfall)		
20	4	7	8
30	2	4	7
40	1	2	4

Figure A1.18 shows the relationship. To draw a graph of the relationship between the price and the number of umbrellas when the rainfall equals 1 inch, keep the rainfall at 1 inch and plot the data in that column against the price. This curve is the relationship between price and number of umbrellas when the rainfall is 1 inches. The relationship between the price and the number of umbrellas is an inverse relationship; as the price rises, the number of umbrellas decreases.

FIGURE **A1.18**
Problem 21

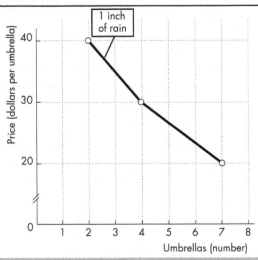

23. What happens in the graph in Problem 21 if the rainfall increases from 1 inch to 2 inches?

As shown in Figure A1.19, the curve shifts rightward. In that figure, both the initial curve, which applies when the rainfall is 1 inch, and the new curve, which applies when the rainfall is 2 inches, are illustrated. The curve when the rainfall is 2 inches lies to the right of the curve when the rainfall is 1 inch indicating that at every price, more umbrellas are purchased when the rainfall is 2 inches than when the rainfall is 1 inch.

FIGURE **A1.19**
Problem 23

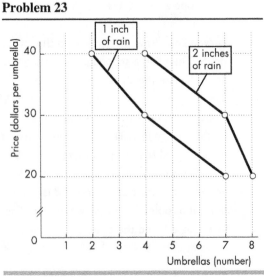

CHAPTER 8 | Firms, the Stock Market, and Corporate Governance

Brief Chapter Summary and Learning Objectives

8.1 Types of Firms (pages 238–241)
Categorize the major types of firms in the United States.

- There are three legal categories of firms: sole proprietorships, partnerships, and corporations.

8.2 The Structure of Corporations and the Principal-Agent Problem (pages 241–242)
Describe the typical management structure of corporations and understand the concepts of separation of ownership from control and the principal-agent problem.

- Corporations have a separation of ownership from control. The conflict between the interests of shareholders and the interests of top management is the principal-agent problem.

8.3 How Firms Raise Funds (pages 242–249)
Explain how firms raise the funds they need to operate and expand.

- Owners of small businesses can obtain funds for expansion by reinvesting profits, taking on partners, or borrowing from relatives, friends, or a bank. Firms can raise external funds by relying on financial intermediaries or through financial markets.

8.4 Using Financial Statements to Evaluate a Corporation (pages 249–251)
Understand the information provided in corporations' financial statements.

- An income statement sums up a firm's revenues, costs, and profit over a period of time. A firm's balance sheet sums up its financial position on a particular day.

8.5 Corporate Governance Policy and the Financial Crisis of 2007–2009 (pages 251–255)
Discuss the role that corporate governance problems may have played in the financial crisis of 2007–2009.

- Between 2007 and 2009 a problem in the market for home mortgages led to the worst financial crisis since the Great Depression. In 2010, Congress overhauled regulation of the financial system with the passage of the Wall Street Reform and Consumer Protection Act.

Appendix: Tools to Analyze Firms' Financial Information (pages 261–267)
Understand the concept of present value and the information contained on a firm's income statement and balance sheet.

Key Terms

Accounting profit, p. 250. A firm's net income, measured as revenue minus operating expenses and taxes paid.

Asset, p. 238. Anything of value owned by a person or a firm.

Balance sheet, p. 251. A financial statement that sums up a firm's financial position on a particular day, usually the end of a quarter or year.

Bond, p. 243. A financial security that represents a promise to repay a fixed amount of funds.

Corporate governance, p. 241. The way in which a corporation is structured and the effect that structure has on the corporation's behavior.

Corporation, p. 238. A legal form of business that provides owners with protection from losing more than their investment should the business fail.

Coupon payment, p. 243. An interest payment on a bond.

Direct finance, p. 243. A flow of funds from savers to firms through financial markets, such as the New York Stock Exchange.

Dividends, p. 245. Payments by a corporation to its shareholders.

Economic profit, p. 251. A firm's revenues minus all of its implicit and explicit costs.

Explicit cost, p. 250. A cost that involves spending money.

Implicit cost, p. 250. A nonmonetary opportunity cost.

Income statement, p. 250. A financial statement that shows a firm's revenues, costs, and profit over a period of time.

Indirect finance, p. 243. A flow of funds from savers to borrowers through financial intermediaries such as banks. Intermediaries raise funds from savers to lend to firms (and other borrowers).

Interest rate, p. 243. The cost of borrowing funds, usually expressed as a percentage of the amount borrowed.

Liability, p. 250. Anything owed by a person or a firm.

Limited liability, p. 238. The legal provision that shields owners of a corporation from losing more than they have invested in the firm.

Opportunity cost, p. 250. The highest-valued alternative that must be given up to engage in an activity.

Partnership, p. 238. A firm owned jointly by two or more persons and not organized as a corporation.

Principal-agent problem, p. 241. A problem caused by an agent pursuing his own interests rather than the interests of the principal who hired him.

Separation of ownership from control, p. 241. A situation in a corporation in which the top management, rather than the shareholders, controls day-to-day operations.

Sole proprietorship, p. 238. A firm owned by a single individual and not organized as a corporation.

Stock, p. 245. A financial security that represents partial ownership of a firm.

Wall Street Reform and Consumer Protection Act (Dodd-Frank Act), p. 253. Legislation passed during 2010 that was intended to reform regulation of the financial system.

Key Terms—Appendix

Present value, p. 261. The value in today's dollars of funds to be paid or received in the future.

Stockholders' equity, p. 267. The difference between the value of a corporation's assets and the value of its liabilities; also known as *net worth*.

Chapter Outline

Facebook Learns the Benefits and Costs of Becoming a Publicly Owned Firm

Nine years after Mark Zuckerberg started Facebook in 2004, the company had more than 1 billion active users. Zuckerberg started Facebook because he believed that people were less interested in meeting new friends online than they were in finding a better way to stay in touch with friends they already had. In the fall of 2011, Facebook needed to raise funds quickly to finance its expansion. Turning Facebook into a public firm and selling stock would raise revenue, but buyers of the stock would have a partial claim on its profits and could question Zuckerberg's leadership. In May 2012, Facebook finally did sell shares of stock to the public. But during the following year, Facebook had difficulty selling advertisements and revenue grew more slowing than expected. In 2013, Facebook's stock finally rose above the initial price, providing gains for investors who bought at that price.

8.1 | Types of Firms (pages 238–241)
Learning Objective: Categorize the major types of firms in the United States.

In the United States, there are three main categories of firms. A **sole proprietorship** is a firm owned by a single individual and not organized as a corporation. A **partnership** is a firm owned jointly by two or more persons and not organized as a corporation. Most law and accounting firms are partnerships. Most large firms are organized as corporations. A **corporation** is a legal form of business that provides owners with protection from losing more than their investment should the business fail.

A. Who Is Liable? Limited and Unlimited Liability
The owners of sole proprietorships and partnerships have unlimited liability, which means that there is no legal distinction between the personal assets of the owners and the assets of the firm. An **asset** is anything of value owned by a person or a firm. Beginning in the early nineteenth century, state legislatures began to pass laws that allowed firms to be organized as corporations. Under the corporate form of business, the owners have limited liability. **Limited liability** is the legal provision that shields owners of a corporation from losing more than they have invested in the firm. The personal assets of the owners of the firm are not affected if the firm fails. Limited liability makes it possible for corporations to raise funds by issuing shares of stock to a large number of investors. Corporate profits are taxed twice—once at the corporate level and again when investors receive a share of corporate profits. Corporations are generally larger than sole proprietorships and partnerships and more difficult to organize and run.

B. Corporations Earn the Majority of Revenue and Profits
Although only 18 percent of all firms are corporations, corporations account for the majority of revenue and profits earned by all firms.

Extra **Solved Problem 8.1**
The Risks of Private Enterprise: The "Names" of Lloyd's of London

The world famous insurance company Lloyd's of London got its start in London in the 1600s. Ship owners would come to Edward Lloyd's coffeehouse to find someone to insure (or "underwrite") their ships and cargo for a fee. Coffeehouse customers—merchants and ship owners themselves—who agreed to insure ships would make payments from their personal funds if a ship was lost at sea. By the late 1700s, each underwriter would recruit investors known as "Names" and use the funds raised to back insurance policies sold to a wide variety of clients.

By the 1980s, 34,000 people around the world had invested in Lloyd's as Names. A series of disasters in the 1980s and 1990s—such as earthquakes and oil spills—resulted in huge payments made on Lloyd's insurance policies. It had become clear that Lloyd's was not a corporation and the Names did not have the limited liability that a corporation's stockholders have. Many Names lost far more than they had invested. Some of those who invested in Lloyd's had the financial resources to absorb their losses, but others did not. Tragically, as many as 30 Names may have committed suicide as a result of their losses. By 2011, only about 700 Names remained invested in Lloyd's. New rules allow insurance companies to underwrite Lloyd's policies for the first time, and Names now provide less than 15 percent of Lloyd's funds.

a. What characteristic of Lloyd's of London's business organization was responsible for the financial losses suffered by the Names who had invested in Lloyd's?

b. In the early 2000s, corporations such as Enron and WorldCom suffered severe losses after it was discovered that executives of the firms had falsified financial statements to deceive investors. How were the losses suffered by Enron and WorldCom stockholders different from the losses suffered by Lloyd's of London's Names?

Solving the Problem

Step 1: **Review the chapter material.** This problem is about firms and corporate governance, so you may want to review the section "Types of Firms," which begins on page 238 in the textbook.

Step 2: **Answer part (a) by explaining what characteristic of Lloyd's of London's business organization was responsible for the financial losses suffered by the Names who had invested in Lloyd's.** Lloyd's of London was a partnership. A disadvantage of partnerships, as well as sole proprietorships, is the unlimited personal liability of the owners of the firm. The liability Lloyd's partners, or Names, incurred went beyond the amount of funds they invested in the company. Therefore, when the insurance company was hit with a series of financial losses some of the Names suffered severe financial losses.

Step 3: **Answer part (b) by explaining how the losses suffered by Enron and WorldCom stockholders were different from the losses suffered by Lloyd's of London's Names.** Enron and WorldCom were corporations, so their stockholders had limited liability. Their losses were limited to the amount they had invested in these firms.

8.2	**The Structure of Corporations and the Principal-Agent Problem (pages 241–242)**

Learning Objective: Describe the typical management structure of corporations and understand the concepts of separation of ownership from control and the principal-agent problem.

Corporate governance is the way in which a corporation is structured and the effect that structure has on the corporation's behavior.

A. Corporate Structure and Corporate Governance

Corporations are legally owned by their shareholders, the owners of the corporation's stock. Shareholders do not manage the firm directly but elect a board of directors to represent their interests. The board of directors appoints a chief executive officer (CEO) to run day-to-day operations and may appoint other top management. Managers may serve on the board of directors; they are referred to as inside directors. Outside directors are directors who do not have a management role in the firm. The top management of a large corporation does not generally own a large share of the firm's stock, so there is a **separation of ownership from control:** A situation in a corporation in which the top management, rather than the shareholders, controls day-to-day operations. The separation of ownership from control is an example of a **principal-agent problem:** A problem caused by an agent pursuing his own interests rather than the interests of the principal who hired him.

Teaching Tips

Although the principal-agent problem is a serious one, managers who pursue their own goals at the expense of the firm's best interests invite the scrutiny of institutional investors such as mutual funds and pension funds. Unlike many shareholders who have modest stock holdings, institutional investors often hold a significant percentage of a firm's outstanding shares. These large investors can demand that a board of directors make strategic and personnel changes if a firm's performance is unsatisfactory and they may cause a drop in share prices by selling some or all of their stock holdings.

Extra Making the Connection	Take Me Out to the Board Room

The Topps Company, famous for selling baseball cards and Bazooka bubblegum, saw its fortunes slump beginning in the mid-1990s as its youngest customers turned to video games and the Internet. Topps management decided to put the company up for sale. In the spring of 2007, Tornante Co., headed by former Walt Disney CEO Michael Eisner, and another firm offered to buy Topps. A majority of Topps' board of directors approved the deal and recommended that its shareholders do so as well. But three of the ten board members dissented, claiming that the price Eisner's group offered was not high enough. In fact, Upper Deck, a rival in the baseball card market, later submitted a bid for Topps that was 10 percent higher than the bid that the Topps board approved. After several months, Upper Deck's management finally withdrew its bid but not before publicly complaining that Topps consistently ignored Upper Deck's requests for "information about the company's operations." The lower bid of the Eisner group was finally accepted in the fall of 2007. But why did Topps not welcome Upper Deck's offer? Some analysts perceived a principal-agent problem because the CEO and other Topps executives may have lost their jobs if the firm were sold to Upper Deck. In announcing his bid, Eisner made it clear that he and his partners were interested only in taking a financial interest in Topps and that management changes would not be made.

Sources: Tennille Tracy, "Topps Throws Spitballs Into Upper Deck," *Wall Street Journal Online*, August 23, 2007. http://blogs.wsj.com/deals/2007/08/23/topps-throws-spitballs-into-upper-deck/; Dana Cimilluca, "At Topps, a Bench Clearing Brawl," *Wall Street Journal Online*, March 14, 2007. http://blogs.wsj.com/deals/2007/03/14/at-topps-co-a-bench-clearing-brawl/

8.3 How Firms Raise Funds (pages 242–249)

Learning Objective: Explain how firms raise the funds they need to operate and expand.

To earn a profit, a firm must raise funds to pay for its operations. If a small business is successful and the owner decides to expand, it can obtain funds in three ways. First, the firm can reinvest its profits, called *retained earnings*. Second, the owner can take on one or more partners who invest in the firm. Third, the owner can borrow funds from relatives, friends, or a bank.

A. Sources of External Funds

Unless firms rely on retained earnings, they must obtain the *external funds* they need from others. The economy's financial system transfers funds from savers to borrowers—directly through financial markets or indirectly through financial intermediaries such as banks. Firms raise external funds in two ways. **Indirect finance** refers to a flow of funds from savers to borrowers through financial intermediaries such as banks. Intermediaries raise funds from savers and lend to firms (and other borrowers). The second way to acquire external funds is through *financial markets*. **Direct finance** refers to a flow of funds from savers to firms through financial markets, such as the New York Stock Exchange. A financial security is a document that states the terms under which funds have passed from the buyer to the borrower. A **bond** is a financial security that represents a promise to repay a fixed amount of funds. The **interest rate** is the cost of borrowing funds, usually expressed as a percentage of the amount borrowed. The interest rate on a bond is equal to the **coupon payment**, which is an interest payment on a bond, divided by the amount borrowed. For example, if the annual interest payment on a $1,000 bond is $40, then the interest rate is:

$$\frac{\$40}{\$1,000} = 0.04, \text{or } 4\%$$

Many bonds that corporations issue have *maturities* of 30 years. The interest rate that a borrower selling a bond has to pay depends on how likely bond buyers think that the bond seller is to default. The higher the *default risk* on a bond, the higher the interest rate.

A **stock** is a financial security that represents partial ownership of a firm. When a corporation sells stock, it is increasing its financial capital by bringing additional owners into the firm. A shareholder is entitled to a share of the corporation's profits. Corporations generally keep some profits—known as retained earnings—to finance expansion. The remaining profits are paid to shareholders. **Dividends** are payments by a corporation to its shareholders. A corporation must make promised payments to bondholders before it can make dividend payments to shareholders.

B. Stock and Bond Markets Provide Capital—and Information

Most buying and selling of stocks and bonds involves investors reselling existing stocks and bonds. There is no single place where stocks and bonds are bought and sold. Some trading takes place in buildings called exchanges, but computer technology has spread the trading of stocks and bonds to dealers outside of exchanges. Changes in the prices of stocks, bonds, and other securities reflect investors' future expectations. A bond that was issued in the past may have its price increase or decrease, depending on whether the coupon payments being offered on newly issued bonds are higher or lower than on existing bonds. The price of a bond will also be affected by changes in default risk, or investors' perceptions of the issuing firm's ability to make coupon payments.

Changes in the value of stocks and bonds offer information for a firm's managers as well as investors. An increase in the stock price means that investors are more optimistic about the firm's profit prospects, and the firm might want to expand as a result. A decrease in the firm's stock price indicates that investors are less optimistic about the firm's profit prospects, so management might want to shrink the firm's operations.

C. Why Do Stock Prices Fluctuate So Much?

Stock market indexes are averages of stock prices with the value of the index set equal to 100 in the *base year*. The three most widely followed U.S. stock indexes are: the Dow Jones Industrial Average, the Standard and Poor's (S&P) 500, and the NASDAQ composite index. All three indexes follow a roughly similar pattern: Increases in stock prices during expansion and declines in stock prices as the U.S. economy is in a recession.

Teaching Tips

The double taxation of corporate profits—once from the corporate profits tax and again from the income tax on shareholders' dividends—gives corporations an incentive to raise funds more through debt (bonds) than equity (stocks). Some economists have criticized the corporate profits tax for the incentive it gives corporations to incur debt solely for the tax consequences of doing so.

Extra Solved Problem 8.2

Does the Principal-Agent Problem Apply to the Relationship between Managers and Employees?

Briefly explain whether you agree with the following argument:

> The principal–agent problem applies not just to the relationship between shareholders and top managers. It also applies to the relationship between managers and workers. Just as shareholders have trouble monitoring whether top managers are earning as much profit as possible, managers have trouble monitoring whether employees are working as hard as possible.

Solving the Problem

Step 1:   **Review the chapter material.** This problem concerns the principal–agent problem, so you may want to review the section "Corporate Structure and Corporate Governance" which begins on page 241.

Step 2:   **Evaluate the argument material.** You should agree with the argument. A corporation's shareholders have difficulty monitoring the activities of top managers. In practice, they attempt to do so indirectly through the corporation's board of directors. But the firm's top managers may influence—or even control—the firm's board of directors. Even if top managers do not control a board of directors, it may be difficult for the board to know whether actions managers take—such as opening a branch office in Paris—will increase the profitability of the firm or just increase the enjoyment of the top managers.

To answer the problem, we must extend this analysis to the relationship between managers and workers: Managers would like employees to work as hard as possible. Employees would often rather not work hard, particularly if they do not see a direct financial reward for doing so. Managers can have trouble monitoring whether employees are working hard or goofing off. (Is that employee in his cubicle diligently staring at a computer screen because he is hard at work on a report or because he is surfing the Web for sports scores or posting to his Facebook page?) So, the principal–agent problem does apply to the relationship between managers and employees.

Extra Credit: Boards of directors try to reduce the principal–agent problem by designing compensation policies for top managers that give them financial incentives to increase profits. Similarly, managers try to reduce the principal–agent problem by designing compensation policies that give workers an incentive to work harder. For example, some manufacturers pay factory workers on the basis of how much they produce rather than on the basis of how many hours they work.

8.4 Using Financial Statements to Evaluate a Corporation (pages 249–251)

Learning Objective: Understand the information provided in corporations' financial statements.

Before a firm can sell new issues of stocks or bonds, it must provide investors with information about its finances. In the United States, the Securities and Exchange Commission (SEC) requires publicly owned firms to report their performance according to *generally accepted accounting principles*. Some private companies (for example, Moody's Investor Service and Standard and Poor's) collect information from businesses and sell it to subscribers. Investors and the managers of firms need information regarding the firm's revenues and costs, as well as information regarding the value of the property and other assets the firm owns and the firm's debts or other liabilities it owes to others. A **liability** is anything owed by a person or a firm. The information investors need to know to decide whether to buy a firm's stocks or bonds is contained in the firm's *financial statements*.

A. The Income Statement

A firm's **income statement** is a financial statement that shows a firm's revenues, costs, and profit over a period of time. **Accounting profit** is a firm's net income, measured as revenue minus operating expenses and taxes paid. **Economic profit** is the firm's revenues minus all of its implicit and explicit costs. Because economic profit takes into account all costs, it provides a better indication than accounting profit of how successful a firm is. Economists always measure cost as opportunity cost. **Opportunity cost** is the highest-valued alternative that must be given up to engage in an activity. An **explicit cost** is a cost that involves spending money. An **implicit cost** is a nonmonetary opportunity cost. The firm's most important implicit cost is the opportunity cost to investors of the funds they have invested in the firm. The minimum amount that investors must earn on the funds they invest, expressed as a percentage of the funds invested, is called a *normal rate of return*. If a firm fails to provide at least a normal rate of return, then it will not remain in business over the long run.

B. The Balance Sheet

A **balance sheet** is a financial statement that sums up a firm's financial position on a particular day, usually the end of a quarter or year. A balance sheet summarizes a firm's assets and liabilities. Subtracting the value of a firm's liabilities from the value of its assets leaves its *new worth*. Net worth is what the firm's owners would be left with if the firm were closed, its assets sold, and its liabilities paid off.

Teaching Tips

Although it is a macroeconomic topic, your students may be interested in the role stock prices play as an admittedly imperfect leading economic indicator. Changes in stock prices reflect firms' expected future performance. A sustained rise or decline in stock prices (as reflected in the Standard and Poor's average of 500 stocks or the Dow-Jones Industrial Average of 30 stocks) over several weeks or months can be an early notice of a turning point in the business cycle from recession to expansion or expansion to recession, respectively.

Extra Making
the | A Bull in China's Financial Shop
Connection

Prospects for Sichuan Changhong Electric Co., manufacturer of plasma televisions and liquid crystal displays, looked excellent in 2008, with rapidly growing output, employment, and profits earned from trade in the world economy. And Changhong was not alone. In the 2000s, the Chinese economy was sizzling. China's output grew by 11.4 percent during 2007, dominated by an astonishing 24 percent growth in investment in plant and equipment. The Chinese economic juggernaut caught the attention of the global business community—and charged onto the U.S. political stage, as China's growth fueled concerns about job losses in the United States.

Yet at the same time, many economists and financial commentators worried that the Chinese expansion—which was fueling rising living standards in a rapidly developing economy with 1.3 billion people—would come to an end. The debate seemed to be over whether China's boom would have a "soft landing" (with gradually declining growth) or a "hard landing" (possibly leading to an economic financial crisis).

Why the debate? Although China's saving rate was estimated to be a very high 40 percent of gross domestic product (GDP)—double or triple the rate in most other countries—the financial system was doing a poor job of allocating capital. Excessive expansion in office construction and factories was fueled less by careful financial analysis than by the directions of national and local government officials trying to encourage growth. With nonperforming loans—where the borrower cannot make promised payments to lenders—at unheard-of levels, China's banks were in financial trouble. Worse still, they continued to lend to weak, politically connected borrowers.

China's prospects for long-term economic growth depend importantly on a better developed financial system to generate information for borrowers and lenders. Many economists have urged Chinese officials to improve accounting transparency and information disclosure so that stock and bond markets can flourish. In the absence of well-functioning financial markets, banks are crucial allocators of capital. There, too, information disclosure and less government direction of lending will help oil the Chinese growth machine in the long run.

Chinese firms, like Changhong, may well play a major role on the world's economic stage. But China's creaky financial system needs repair if Chinese firms are to grow rapidly enough to raise the standard of living for Chinese workers over the long run.

8.5 Corporate Governance Policy and the Financial Crisis of 2007–2009 (pages 251–255)

Learning Objective: Discuss the role that corporate governance problems may have played in the financial crisis of 2007–2009.

Firms disclose financial statements in periodic filings to the federal government and in *annual reports* to stockholders. The management of a firm has two reasons to attract investors and keep the firm's stock price high. First, a higher stock price increases the funds the firm can raise when it sells a given amount of stock. Second, to reduce the principal-agent problem, boards of directors often tie the salaries of top managers to the firm's stock price. However, problems that surfaced during the early 2000s revealed that some managers inflated profits and hid liabilities. At other firms, managers took on more risk than they disclosed to investors.

A. The Accounting Scandals of the Early 2000s

In the early 2000s, top managers at some firms, such as Enron and WorldCom, falsified their firms' financial statements to mislead investors about how profitable they were. The federal government regulates how financial statements are prepared but cannot guarantee the accuracy of the statements. To guard against future scandals, the Sarbanes-Oxley Act of 2002 was enacted, which requires CEOs to personally certify the accuracy of financial statements. Most observers acknowledge that the Sarbanes-Oxley Act increased confidence in the U.S. corporate governance system, though problems during 2007–2009 at financial firms again raised questions of whether corporations were adequately disclosing information to investors.

B. The Financial Crisis of 2007–2009

Beginning in 2007 and lasting into 2009, the U.S. economy suffered the worst financial crisis since the Great Depression. Beginning in the 1970s, financial institutions began securitizing mortgage loans. Mortgage-backed securities are similar to bonds—buyers receive regular interest payments, which in this case come from the payments made on the original mortgage loans. At first, the securitization process was carried out by the Federal National Mortgage Association ("Fannie Mae") and the Federal Home Loan Mortgage Corporation ("Freddie Mac"). Fannie Mae and Freddie Mac would buy mortgages granted to borrowers and bundle them into securities that were sold to investors. In the 1990s, private financial firms began securitizing mortgages. By the early 2000s, many mortgages were granted to "subprime" borrowers, borrowers with flawed credit histories, and "Alt-A" borrowers, who failed to document that their incomes were high enough to afford their mortgages. Housing prices soared but began falling in 2006. By 2007, many borrowers began to default on their mortgages, and many financial institutions suffered heavy losses.

Many investors complained that they weren't aware of how risky some of the assets on the balance sheets of financial firms were. In the fall of 2008, Fannie Mae and Freddie Mac were brought under direct control of the government. The **Wall Street Reform and Consumer Protection Act (Dodd-Frank Act)**, is legislation passed during 2010 that was intended to reform regulation of the financial system. The act created the Consumer Financial Protection Bureau to write rules to protect consumers in their borrowing and investing activities. The act also established the Financial Stability Oversight Council, which is intended to identify and act on risks to the financial system.

C. Did Principal-Agent Problems Help Bring on the Financial Crisis?

Beginning in the 1990s, private investment banks began to securitize mortgages. Investment banks had traditionally concentrated on providing advice to corporations selling stocks and bonds and on *underwriting* the issuance of stocks and bonds. To address the risks of investment banking, Congress passed the Glass-Steagall Act in 1933 to prevent firms from being both commercial banks and investment banks. Congress repealed the Glass-Steagall Act in 1999. Many of the best-known financial firms remained investment banks. Mortgage-backed securities originated by investment banks were sold mostly to investors, but investment banks retained some of the securities as investments. When the prices of the securities declined in 2007, the investment banks suffered heavy losses. Lehman Brothers declared bankruptcy, Merrill Lynch and Bear Stearns were sold to commercial banks, and Goldman Sachs and Morgan Stanley became bank holding companies. The era of the large Wall Street investment bank appeared to have ended.

Traditionally, Wall Street investment banks had been organized as partnerships, but by 2000 all had become publicly traded corporations. With a publicly traded corporation, the principal-agent problem can be severe. Some economists believe that the financial crisis may not have occurred if investment banks had remained partnerships.

Extra Economics in Your Life:
Spreading the Risks of Stock Ownership

Question: Buying shares of stock would be risky even in the absence of principal-agent problems. Shareholders enjoy limited liability, but unlike bonds, stock dividends are not always paid, and shareholders face the possibility that stock prices can fall below the level paid for them. Aside from buying shares of well-known companies, how can people with limited funds minimize the risks involved in investing in stocks?

Answer: Many people choose to purchase stocks through mutual funds, which are professionally managed investments that combine, or pool, the funds of many investors. Mutual fund managers can use these pooled funds to buy a variety of stocks, rather than just one or two, to minimize the risk that a fall in the price of one stock will result in large losses. Mutual funds are sold through many investment firms, and there are funds that specialize in different categories of financial instruments; for example, growth stocks (stocks with high potential for earnings growth, but with a low potential for slow or negative growth), stocks of firms in a particular industry, and stocks of firms headquartered in foreign countries. There are also mutual funds that invest in bonds and short-term assets.

Extra **AN INSIDE LOOK** News Article to Use in Class
Visit www.myeconlab.com for current **An Inside Look** news articles.

Appendix
Tools to Analyze Firms' Financial Information
(pages 261–269)
Learning Objective: Understand the concept of present value and the information contained on a firm's income statement and balance sheet.

Large firms raise funds from outside investors, and outside investors seek information on firms and the assurance that the firms' managers will act in the interests of investors.

Using Present Value to Make Investment Decisions
If you own shares of stock or a bond, you will receive payments in the form of dividends or coupons over a number of years. Most people value funds they already have more highly than funds they will receive in the future. **Present value** is the value in today's dollars of funds to be paid or received in the future. Assume that you are willing to lend $1,000 today if you are paid back $1,100 one year from now. In this case, you are charging 10 percent on the funds you have loaned. Economists would say that $1,000 today is equivalent to the $1,100 to be received one year in the future. $1,100 can be written as $1,000 (1 + 0.10). Or:

$$\$1,000 \times (1 + 0.10) = \$1,100$$

If we divide both sides of this equation by $(1 + 0.10)$, we can rewrite this as:

$$\$1,000 = \frac{\$1,100}{(1+0.10)}$$

This formula states that the present value is equal to the future value to be received in one year divided by one plus the interest rate. Writing the formula more generally:

$$\text{Present Value} = \frac{\text{Future Value}_1}{(1+i)}$$

The present value of funds to be received in one year can be calculated by dividing the amount of those funds to be received by 1 plus the interest rate. The formula can be expanded to calculate the value of funds to be received more than one year in the future. Suppose you are asked to lend $1,000 for two years and are promised 10 percent interest per year. After two years, you will be paid back $1,100 $(1 + 0.10)$ or $1,210. Or:

$$\$1,210 = \$1,000\ (1 + 0.10)(1 + 0.10),$$

or

$$\$1,210 = \$1,000\ (1 + 0.10)^2.$$

This formula can be rewritten as:

$$\$1,000 = \frac{\$1,210}{(1+0.10)^2}$$

We can generalize the concept to say that the present value of funds to be received n years in the future equals the amount of funds to be received divided by the quantity 1 plus the interest rate raised to the nth power. Or, more generally:

$$\text{Present Value} = \frac{\text{Future Value}_n}{(1+i)^n}$$

where Future Value$_n$ represents funds that will be received in n years.

A. Using Present Value to Calculate Bond Prices

The price of a financial asset, such as a bond, should be equal to the present value of the payments to be received from owning that asset. The relevant interest rate used by investors in the bond market to calculate the present value and, therefore, the price of an existing bond is usually the coupon rate on comparable newly issued bonds. The general formula for the price of a bond is:

$$\text{Bond Price} = \frac{\text{Coupon}_1}{(1+i)} + \frac{\text{Coupon}_2}{(1+i)^2} + \ldots + \frac{\text{Coupon}_n}{(1+i)^n} + \frac{\text{Face Value}}{(1+i)^n}$$

where Coupon$_1$ is the coupon payment to be received after one year, Coupon$_2$ is the coupon payment to be received after two years, up to Coupon$_n$, which is the coupon received in the year the bond matures. The ellipsis takes the place of the coupon payments received between the second year and the year the bond matures. Face Value is the face value of the bond, to be received when the bond matures. The interest rate on comparable newly issued bonds is *i*.

B. Using Present Value to Calculate Stock Prices

The price of a share of stock should be equal to the present value of the dividends investors expect to receive as a result of owning the stock.

The general formula for the price of a stock is:

$$\text{Stock Price} = \frac{\text{Dividend}_1}{(1+i)} + \frac{\text{Dividend}_2}{(1+i)^2} + \ldots$$

Unlike a bond, a stock has no maturity date so the stock price is the present value of an infinite number of dividend payments. Another difference between the stock formula and the bond price formula is that you don't know for sure what the dividend payments from owning stock will be.

C. A Simple Formula for Calculating Stock Prices

It is possible to simplify the formula for determining the price of a stock if we assume that dividends grow at a constant rate:

$$\text{Stock Price} = \frac{\text{Dividend}}{(i - \text{Growth Rate})}$$

Dividend is the dividend investors expect to receive one year from now, and Growth Rate is the rate at which dividends are expected to grow.

Going Deeper into Financial Statements

Key sources of information about a corporation's profitability and financial position are its principal financial statements—the income statement and the balance sheet.

A. Analyzing Income Statements

A firm's income statement summarizes its revenues, costs, and profit over a period of time. Listed first are the revenues the firm earned. Listed next are operating expenses, including the cost of revenue, which is commonly known as cost of sales or cost of goods sold. The difference between a firm's revenues and its costs is its profit. A firm's operating income is the difference between its revenue and its operating expenses. Most corporations have investments, such as government and corporate bonds, that generate income. The federal government taxes the profits of corporations. The net income that firms report on their income statements is referred to as their after-tax *accounting profit*.

B. Analyzing Balance Sheets

A firm's balance sheet summarizes its financial position on a particular day, usually the end of a quarter or year. Subtracting the value of a firm's liabilities from the value of its assets leaves its *net worth*. Because a corporation's stockholders are its owners, net worth is often listed as stockholders' equity. **Stockholders' equity** is the difference between the value of a corporation's assets and the value of its liabilities, which is also known as *net worth*. The value of a firm's assets must equal the value of its liabilities plus the value of stockholders' equity. An important accounting rule holds that balance sheets should list assets on the left side and liabilities and net worth, or stockholders' equity, on the right side. Included on the asset side of the balance sheet are current assets, which are assets that the firm can convert into cash quickly, and goodwill, which represents the difference between the purchase price of a company and the market value of its assets. Current liabilities are short-term debts such as accounts payable, which is money owed to suppliers for goods received but not yet paid for, or bank loans that will be paid back in less than one year. Long-term bank loans and the value of outstanding corporate bonds are long-term liabilities.

Solutions to End-of-Chapter Exercises

8.1	**Types of Firms** Learning Objective: Categorize the major types of firms in the United States.

Review Questions

1.1 A sole proprietorship is owned by a single individual and isn't organized as a corporation. A partnership is owned jointly by two or more persons and isn't organized as a corporation. A corporation is a legal form of business that provides the owners with limited liability.

1.3 Because the stockholders of a corporation can never lose more than the amount they invested in the firm, firms can raise more funds from a large number of investors.

Problems and Applications

1.5 With limited liability, corporations will be able raise more funds for investment, including spending on research and development, thereby shifting the country's production possibilities frontier to the right over time.

1.7 Early in the nineteenth century, state legislatures in the United States began passing general incorporation laws, allowing firms to be organized as corporations. These laws gave owners of incorporated firms limited liability, making it possible for firms to raise funds by issuing shares of stock to large numbers of investors. As a result, firms were able to raise enough funds to operate railroads and other large-scale businesses.

1.9 Most entrepreneurs in the United States obtain funds to start new firms by using their own or family funds, by borrowing on credit cards, or by taking out loans against the value of their homes. In developing countries, typically entrepreneurs would have considerably less personal and family funds to use to start new businesses, and less or no access to credit cards, and little or no collateral to use to get loans.

8.2	**The Structure of Corporations and the Principal-Agent Problem** Learning Objective: Describe the typical management structure of corporations and understand the concepts of separation of ownership from control and the principal-agent problem.

Review Questions

2.1 In most large corporations the top management, rather than the shareholders, control day-to-day operations. Typically, top management does not own a significant percentage of the stock a large corporation has issued. So the top management controls the firm, in the sense of making the key decisions about how the firm will be run, while the owners—the stockholders—do not exercise active control of the firm.

2.3   The outside directors are more likely to represent the interests of shareholders, rather than the interests of top management, and so can act as a check on the decisions of top management.

Problems and Applications

2.5   Top managers know more about how the company is run than do the firm's shareholders. The principal–agent problem might be overcome if shareholders had all the information about the company and about the consequences of the actions taken by the firm's managers that the managers themselves possess.

2.7   You should disagree with the argument. Boards of directors, as the shareholders representatives, could easily detect and then remove top managers who work short days, take long vacations, and slack off. The issue isn't top managers slacking off as much as it is top managers pursuing their own personal goals such as short-run profits and maximizing the value of stock options as opposed to the long-run profitability of the firm.

2.9   Private equity firms do reduce problems in corporate governance by helping to establish a market for corporate control, which can reduce principal–agent problems by providing a means to remove top management that is failing to carry out the wishes of shareholders.

8.3 How Firms Raise Funds
Learning Objective: Explain how firms raise the funds they need to operate and expand.

Review Questions

3.1   Direct finance occurs when a firm obtains funds directly from savers through the stock or bond market. Indirect finance occurs when firms obtain funds from savers indirectly through an intermediary such as a bank. Borrowing money from a bank to buy a car is indirect finance, as the bank channels the funds from its depositors to you. Borrowing money from your friend to buy a car would be direct finance.

3.3   Stock and bond markets provide information about what investors expect to happen to the firm. If they are optimistic and think the firm will earn higher profits, then they will bid up the price of its stock. If they are pessimistic, then the price of the stock will fall. If they are pessimistic and fear that the firm might suffer financial losses and default on its bond payments, then investors will be less willing to buy the firm's bonds, and the prices of the bonds will fall. Optimism about the firm will increase the prices of the firm's bonds. So, the successes and failures of the firm will result in rising or falling prices for the firm's stocks and bonds in the stock and bond markets. Changes in investor expectations about the firm's likely future profitability will also affect the prices of the firm's stocks and bonds.

Problems and Applications

3.5   You would be better off if you had bought the stock because it will have increased in value, while the interest the firm pays on the bonds will have remained the same.

3.7 Facebook's initial public offering (IPO) occurred in the primary market because Facebook sold newly issued stocks directly to the public. It was an example of direct finance as Facebook acquired external funds through financial markets, as opposed to going through a financial intermediary.

3.9 **a.** Google's stock price will fall because its expected future revenues and profits will have fallen.

   b. Google's stock price will rise because Google's after-tax profits will rise.

   c. Google's stock price will fall because expected future profits will fall. In these circumstances, the board of directors is not likely to provide independent supervision of top management, which will make the principal-agent problem worse.

   d. Google's stock price will rise because expected revenues and profits will rise.

   e. Google's stock price will fall because profits were lower than expected. The higher expected profits were already reflected in Google's stock price and the lower actual profits will cause Google's stock price to fall.

3.11 The statement is false. These shares were traded in the secondary market (the NASDAQ), so the money went from the new shareholders to the previous shareholders. The money didn't go to Microsoft.

3.13 **a.** Starbucks stock price went up $0.01, as indicated by the net change, from the day before.

   b. Starbucks stock price varied $1.68 (between the high price of $65.09 and the low price of $63.41).

   c. Starbucks stock price varied (over 52 weeks) from $43.04 to $65.09.

   d. 6,794,623 shares, as indicated by the volume, of Starbucks stock were traded on that day.

8.4 Using Financial Statements to Evaluate a Corporation
Learning Objective: Understand the information provided in corporations' financial statements.

Review Questions

4.1 An asset is anything of value that a firm owns (such as a building). A liability is a debt or obligation owed by a firm (such as an unpaid electric bill).

4.3 An explicit cost is a cost that involves spending money; an implicit cost is a nonmonetary opportunity cost. A firm has both explicit costs, such as the rent it pays for a warehouse, and implicit costs, such as the opportunity cost of the services a sole proprietor supplies to her own firm. Accounting profit is a firm's revenue minus its operating expenses and taxes paid (explicit costs); economic profit is a firm's revenue minus all of its implicit and explicit costs.

Problems and Applications

4.5 Paolo has forgotten to take into account the opportunity cost of keeping the money invested. If he were to keep the money invested in bonds, he would earn an interest rate of 10 percent per year.

So, the opportunity cost of selling the bonds and using the funds to start a pizza restaurant is 10 percent per year. Therefore, selling the bonds is a *more* costly way of gaining funds to start his business than is taking out a bank loan with a 7 percent interest rate.

4.7   **a.** Accounting profit = revenues − explicit costs. Explicit costs are those that involve spending money, which include $75,000 paid to assistants and $10,000 for utilities. Accounting profit = $200,000 − $85,000 = $115,000.

      b. Economic profit = revenue − opportunity cost (explicit cost + implicit cost). Implicit cost for Dane includes $200,000 in forgone wages, $20,000 in forgone rent on his duplex, and interest forgone by not selling his $1,000,000 in extraterrestrial gear and investing the funds. His economic profits are negative because his opportunity costs vastly exceed his revenues.

8.5 Corporate Governance Policy and the Financial Crisis of 2007–2009

Learning Objective: Discuss the role that corporate governance problems may have played in the 2007–2009 financial crisis.

Review Questions

5.1   The Sarbanes-Oxley Act of 2002 attempts to strengthen the reliability of corporate financial reports. It was passed in reaction to the accounting fraud at companies like Enron and WorldCom.

Problems and Applications

5.3   Corporate governance is the way in which a corporation is structured and the effect a corporation's structure has on the firm's behavior. Stronger corporate governance laws may reduce the principal–agent problem and increase a corporation's value and profitability for shareholders.

5.5   Though difficult to estimate, it would be possible to put a dollar value on the benefits to the economy of corporations complying with Sarbanes-Oxley. If Sarbanes-Oxley succeeds in reassuring investors, thereby increasing the flow of funds through financial markets, then economic growth should increase, raising living standards, and benefiting society as a whole. The benefits to corporations include the reduction in risk, which may reassure investors, and thereby make it easier for firms to raise funds. Investors benefit to the extent that Sarbanes-Oxley reduces accounting fraud. Identifying the benefits does not necessarily mean that they exceed the costs to corporations of complying with the Sarbanes-Oxley Act.

5.7   **a.** Investors in primary and secondary markets make decisions on which firms to invest in, when to invest, how much to invest, and when to sell based on information about firms. If the information is misleading, investors will invest less or, possibly, stop investing. Capital markets depend on accurate information and can function poorly when information is misleading.

      b. Corporate boards of directors sometimes link top managers' compensation to the corporations' stock price to lessen the principal-agent problem caused by the separation of ownership from control. Linking compensation to stock prices provides managers with an additional incentive to maximize shareholder profits. But tying compensation too closely to stock prices can cause management to maximize short-run profits over long-run profits and to commit corporate fraud ("cook the books") to make the firm appear to be more profitable than it is with the intention of increasing the firm's stock price.

Solutions to Real-Time Data Exercises

8.1 The two graphs on the next page show the S&P 500 stock index from 1957 to 1985 and from 1986 to 2013. Dividing the period into two graphs allows us to see more clearly changes in S&P 500 stock index during the earlier years when the values were much smaller. The table below describes how stock prices moved just before, during, and just after recessions from 1957 to the present. Stock prices have typically declined before recessions. Immediately following the ends of recessions, stock prices have typically fallen, although there are several exceptions. The movement of stock prices during recessions has been quite varied.

Date of Recession	Stock Prices Before Recession	Stock Prices During Recession	Stock Prices After Recession
August 1957 – April 1958	Declined	Declined, then rose	Rose
April 1960 – February 1961	Declined	Rose and Declined, but generally rose	Declined
December 1969 – November 1970	Declined	Declined, then rose	Rose
November 1973 – March 1975	Stable	Declined, then rose	Rose
January 1980 – July 1980	Declined	Rose, Declined, then rose	Rose
July 1981 – November 1982	Stable	Very volatile, but generally rose, declined and then rose	Declined
July 1990 – March 1991	Declined	Declined, then rose	Rose
March 2001 – November 2001	Declined	Declined, rose, declined, then rose	Rose
December 2007 – June 2009	Declined	Declined	Declined

Solutions to Chapter 8 Appendix

Review Questions

8A.1   Money received at some future date is worth less than money received today because if you have the money today, you can use it today to buy goods and services and receive enjoyment from them. In addition, prices are likely to rise, so money received later won't buy as much. Finally, there is some risk that you will not receive the money in the future. Present value = Future value/(1 + interest rate). So, if the interest rate rises, the present value goes down.

8A.3   The present value of bond payments is generally much more certain. The coupon payments and the face value are part of the bond contract, but the future dividends of the firm are not known with certainty. In addition, the bond payments are spread out over a specific number of years, but the stock dividends extend out toward infinity (or the life of the firm). The main similarity is that both sets of future payments are discounted by dividing by (1 + interest rate) raised to the number of years in the future that the payment will be received.

8A.5   An income statement reflects the revenues, costs, and profits of a firm *during one year* (or some other period of time). A balance sheet reflects the assets, liabilities, and equity of a firm *at one moment in time*. Assets are listed on the left side of a balance sheet; liabilities and stockholders' equity are listed on the right side.

Problems and Applications

8A.7   **a.** Hamilton's contract was not worth $125 million in present-value terms because most of the money will be received in future years and is therefore worth less in present-value terms. This statement would be correct only if the interest rate equaled zero.

   b. To find the present value of the contract, you must find the present value of each year's payment and add them together. At an interest rate of 10 percent, the present value of the contract is:

$$\$10,000,000 + \frac{\$15,000,000}{(1+.10)} + \frac{\$15,000,000}{(1+.10)2} + \frac{\$23,000,000}{(1+.10)3} + \frac{\$30,000,000}{(1+.10)4} + \frac{\$30,000,000}{(1+.10)5}$$

$$= \$10,000,000 + \$13,636,364 + \$12,396,694 + \$17,280,240 + \$20,490,404 + \$18,627,640$$

$$= \$92,431,342$$

   c. At an interest rate of 5 percent, the present value of the contract is:

$$\$10,000,000 + \frac{\$15,000,000}{(1+.05)} + \frac{\$15,000,000}{(1+.05)2} + \frac{\$23,000,000}{(1+.05)3} + \frac{\$30,000,000}{(1+.05)4} + \frac{\$30,000,000}{(1+.05)5}$$

$$= \$10,000,000 + \$14,285,714 + \$13,605,442 + \$19,868,265 + \$24,681,074 + \$23,505,785$$

8A.9   The decision of which is more valuable depends on the rate of interest used in calculating the present value. At a 10 percent interest rate, the present value in 2011 of the 25 one-year payments of $1,193,248.20 would equal:

$$\$10,000,000 + \frac{\$15,000,000}{(1+.05)} + \frac{\$15,000,000}{(1+.05)2} + \frac{\$23,000,000}{(1+.05)3} + \frac{\$30,000,000}{(1+.05)4} + \frac{\$30,000,000}{(1+.05)5}$$

$$= \$10,831,162.$$

The present value in 2000 of this $10,831,162 in 2011 would equal:

$$\frac{\$10,831,162}{(1+0.10)^{11}} = \$3,786,256.\text{H}$$

So, at a 10 percent interest rate, Bonilla would have been wise to take the $5.9 million lump sum in 2000.

At a 5 percent interest rate, the present value in 2011 of the 25 one-year payments of $1,193,248.20 would equal $16,817,573.98. The present value in 2000 of this $16,817,573.98 in 2011 would equal $9,832,887. At a 5 percent interest rate, Bonilla would have been wise to take the 25 one-year payments.

8A.11 Interest rates on newly issued bonds are likely to rise as a result of inflation. This will cause the price of your bond to fall.

8A.13 Values are in millions of dollars.

Assets		Liabilities	
Current assets	$4,220	Current liabilities	$2,210
Property and equipment	2,659	Long-term liabilities	895
Goodwill	399	Total liabilities	3,105
Other assets	962	Stockholder's equity	5,135
Total assets	$8,240	Total liabilities and stockholder's equity	$8,240